EDEN
THE LIFE AND TIMES OF ANTHONY EDEN
First Earl of Avon, 1897–1977

EDEN
THE LIFE AND TIMES OF ANTHONY EDEN

First Earl of Avon

1897–1977

===

D. R. THORPE

Chatto & Windus
LONDON

Published by Chatto & Windus 2003

2 4 6 8 10 9 7 5 3 1

Copyright © D. R. Thorpe 2003

First published in Great Britain in 2003 by
Chatto & Windus
Random House, 20 Vauxhall Bridge Road,
London SW1V 2SA

Random House Australia (Pty) Limited
20 Alfred Street, Milsons Point, Sydney,
New South Wales 2061, Australia

Random House New Zealand Limited
18 Poland Road, Glenfield,
Auckland 10, New Zealand

Random House South Africa (Pty) Limited
Endulini, 5A Jubilee Road, Parktown 2193, South Africa

The Random House Group Limited Reg. No. 954009
www.randomhouse.co.uk

A CIP catalogue record for this book
is available from the British Library

ISBN 0 7011 6744 0

Typeset by SX Composing DTP, Rayleigh, Essex
Printed and bound in Great Britain by
Mackays of Chatham Ltd, Chatham, Kent

Contents

List of Illustrations

Pandit Nehra with Walter Monckton.

Hugh Gaitskell with Bulganin.

Norman Brook with General Templer.

Jim Thomas with Harold Macmillan.

Air Chief Marshal Sir Dermot Boyle, Marshal of the RAF Sir William Dickson, First Sea Lord Mountbatten. Eden with his back to the camera.

Winston at Chequers in 1956.

Eden with Sid Holland, the Prime Minister of New Zealand.

Anthony Eden and Selwyn Lloyd at Broadchalke, 30 May 1958.

Nicholas Eden.

The private royal visit to Villa Nova in 1966.

Lord Avon at de Gaulle's funeral, November 1970, with, among others, a top-hatted Harold Macmillan, Harold Wilson, Edward Heath and the Prince of Wales.

Meeting Haile Selassie in Bermuda.

An unexpected late friendship: Eden with Lord Welensky at Alvediston.

Eden with President Johnson at the White House.

Eden with Avon Priam.

The Avons in the garden of the British Embassy in Paris.

Cartoons by Low (5 July 1939 and 29 July 1955) and Vicky (29 October 1951): Associated Newspapers. The author and publishers are grateful to Dr Tim Benson and the Political Cartoon Society.

The author and publishers thank the Countess of Avon for her generosity in supplying most of the photographs, many of which are from private family albums.

For Patrick Croker

A politician's character and position are measured in his day by party standards. When he is dead, all that he achieved in the name of party is at an end. The eulogies and censures of partisans are powerless to affect his ultimate reputation. The scales wherein he was weighed are broken. The years to come bring weights and measures of their own.

Winston Churchill on his father, Lord Randolph Churchill

List of Abbreviations

AC	Austen Chamberlain
ADC	Aide-de-camp
AE	Anthony Eden
ANZUS	Australia, New Zealand and United States
AP	*Avon Papers*
BBC	British Broadcasting Corporation
BEF	British Expeditionary Force
CAB	*Cabinet Papers*
CC	Carlton Club
CENTO	Central Treaty Organisation
CIA	Central Intelligence Agency
CID	Committee of Imperial Defence
CIGS	Chief of the Imperial General Staff
C-in-C	Commander-in-Chief
DBFP	*Documents on British Foreign Policy*
DCL	Doctor of Civil Law
DGFP	*Documents on German Foreign Policy*
DO	Dominions Office
DSO	Companion of the Distinguished Service Order
D(T)C	Defence (Transition) Committee
ECSC	European Coal-Steel Community
EDC	European Defence Community
EEC	European Economic Community
EOKA	Ethniki Organosis Kyprion Agoniston
ERNIE	Electronic Random Number Indicating Equipment
FDR	Franklin Delano Roosevelt
f-n.	Footnote
FO	Foreign Office
FRUS	*Foreign Relations of the United States*
FS	Foreign Secretary
HMG	His/Her Majesty's Government
HMSO	His/Her Majesty's Stationery Office
H of C	House of Commons
IRA	Irish Republican Army
ITV	Independent Television
JIC	Joint Intelligence Committee

KCB	Knight Commander, Order of the Bath
KG	Knight of the Garter
KGB	Komitet Gosudarstvennoi Bezopasnosti
KORR	King's Own Royal Regiment
KRRC	King's Royal Rifle Corps
LCC	London County Council
LDV	Local Defence Volunteers
LG/Ll. G	Lloyd George
MC	Military Cross
MCC	Marylebone Cricket Club
MI5	Directorate of Military Intelligence
MI6	Secret Intelligence Service
MP	Member of Parliament
NATO	North Atlantic Treaty Organisation
NC	Neville Chamberlain
NUR	National Union of Railwaymen
NY	New York
OEEC	Organisation for European Economic Cooperation
PM	Prime Minister
POW	Prisoner of war
PPS	Parliamentary Private Secretary
PRO	Public Record Office
PUS	Permanent Under-Secretary
RA	Royal Archives
RAB	R. A. Butler
RAF	Royal Air Force
RMS	Royal Mail Steamer
RNVR	Royal Naval Volunteer Reserve
RSC	Royal Shakespeare Company
SB	Stanley Baldwin
SC	Stafford Cripps
SCUA	Suez Canal Users' Association
SEAC	South-East Asia Command
SEATO	South-East Asia Treaty Organisation
SELO	*Selwyn Lloyd Papers*
SIS	Secret Intelligence Service
SL	Selwyn Lloyd
S of S	Secretary of State
UK	United Kingdom
UNEF	United Nations Emergency Force
UNO	United Nations Organisation
US	United States

USA	United States of America
VIP	Very Important Person
WEU	Western European Union
WSC	Winston Spencer Churchill
YMCA	Young Men's Christian Association*

---

* Also used as the nickname for a group of young progressive Conservative backbenchers in the 1920s and 1930s who followed the ideas of Noel Skelton on 'the property-owning democracy'.

Author's Preface

The Countess of Avon asked me in 1991 if I would consider writing a new biography of her late husband, Anthony Eden, First Earl of Avon. At the time I was working on the official life of Alec Douglas-Home, whose career dovetailed with Eden's in several crucial respects.

Conventional wisdom has been as unremittingly hostile towards Eden over Suez as towards Neville Chamberlain over Munich. Suez and Munich were the most divisive political crises of the twentieth century, indeed memories of the first conditioned responses to the second. It is not difficult to see why the controversies have endured. Munich has been mythologised by its critics as unprincipled abandonment, based on self-interested expediency; Suez as devious recklessness, anachronistic colonialism masquerading as a police action. One crisis was a prelude to war; the other the clearest indication of Britain's declining post-war position as one of the world's great independent powers. Eden was a central figure in both events. Twenty-five years after his death, and nearly half a century since Suez, a long term view is possible, and this is one aim of the present study, part of an unfinished (and unfinishable) process of assessment of the recent past.

Eden served three periods as Foreign Secretary, a unique twentieth-century record. Other issues central to his career have assumed fresh relevance, not least 'Europe', one of the dominating political issues of the new century. For some commentators, the significant watershed came in 1955 during the Messina Conference, which began in the week Eden became Prime Minister. Britain had 'observer' status, and missed the opportunity to move towards a Common European Market. This, say some Europhiles, was a more important cause of Britain's decline than Suez, which was its symptom. Eden's own views on Messina, published here for the first time, are a compelling addition to the ongoing European debate.

By any standards Eden remains one of the seminal figures of his age. As with Sir Robert Peel, Joseph Chamberlain and Winston Churchill, his response to events helped to shape the course of history. Undertaking a fresh account, built around Eden's career, of political issues between 1920 and 1970, was a prospect of considerable fascination to me, especially in the light of the vast amount of new material in public and private archives, here and abroad, that is now available. There is also scope in less inhibited times for a greater candour about how aspects of Eden's private life impinged upon his public career, and how his increasingly tense post-war relationship with Churchill, in particular over the delayed succession to the Conservative Party leadership, affected both domestic and international events.

I did not, however, wish to commit myself to writing a new biography until I had spoken to Sir Robert Rhodes James, whose 1986 life of Eden, the first to be based on the private papers, and also undertaken at the invitation of the Countess of Avon, will always be a landmark in Eden studies. I am grateful for Sir Robert's generous understanding towards me, in what I know was a delicate situation, as well as for the material advice he gave me. His premature death in May 1999 was a grievous shock to the many historians and biographers who had for so long laboured in neighbouring vineyards.

'I have no doubt', wrote Sir Robert in 1986, 'that more documents not yet available for inspection or publication will be discovered and published about Eden's life and career, and that judgments may have to be amended in the light of these. There will be further, and different, assessments.'[1] The fact that two contrasting studies have appeared since Sir Robert Rhodes James' biography, as well as several television documentaries, shows the fascination that Eden's career still has, and is a testimony to his towering presence in the politics of the twentieth century.*

Towering presence he may have been on the international scene, but often he was a prophet without honour in his own country. French colleagues of the 1940s who have spoken to me were at one in being mystified by the relatively low esteem in which so many of Eden's fellow countrymen hold him. But then after the war Eden was widely regarded as 'the one British statesman for whom France had ever felt any tenderness.'[2] However, at home it is a different story. In his magisterial survey of the post-war Premiership, Professor Peter Hennessy concluded that Anthony Eden 'falls into a catastrophic category of his own.'[3] Yet when a BBC poll at the turn of the century listed Eden last among the nineteen twentieth-century Prime Ministers, an informed debate ensued as to whether this ought actually to be his final placing, especially as the relevance of his views on the Middle East and Europe came to be acknowledged.[4]

---

* Victor Rothwell, *Anthony Eden: A Political Biography 1931–1957*, Manchester University Press, 1992. David Dutton, *Anthony Eden: A Life and Reputation*, Arnold, 1997. The vast cover price of the Rothwell book, an elegant and balanced short study, has militated against its recognition as arguably the best of all introductions to Eden's career. The Dutton book, a thematic study rather than a biography, and following on from his studies of Austen Chamberlain, Eden's first political mentor, and John Simon, one of his first political adversaries, is an essential source. The strangely disconcerting cover derives from the fact that the photograph of Eden is printed the wrong way round. Dr Dutton continues his examination of Eden's career in the 1930s in his *Neville Chamberlain* (2001), a masterly summation.

Whatever opinions may be held on his Premiership, Eden was for several decades a major world figure. He was, like his American colleague Dean Acheson, 'present at the creation'. He was an enduring influence on the shaping of the post-war world, as well as one of the generation who saved freedom for that world by his service from 1940 to 1945. In France, this has always been recognised.

Other voices encouraged me to accept Lady Avon's invitation, and I am particularly grateful to the late Lord Goodman for formalising the arrangements and setting me on my path. It was accepted that I could not for some time devote myself fully to researching Eden's career. However, in the course of the five years before the publication of my Home biography in 1996, much parallel work was possible, particularly interviewing Foreign Office officials who had worked with both Eden and Home. I was also able to discuss Eden's career with Alec Douglas-Home (who referred to the Eden biography as my 'overtime'), one of the dwindling band who had been alongside Eden in the House of Commons in the 1930s, and whose first post of Parliamentary Under-Secretary at the Foreign Office in 1945, was under Eden, whom he regarded as 'a master of the situation and of all the diplomatic arts.'[5]

By one of those chances of circumstance, each of my six biographical subjects over the past three decades – Rab Butler, Austen Chamberlain, Lord Curzon, Alec Douglas-Home, Anthony Eden and Selwyn Lloyd – has served as Foreign Secretary. Indeed from Curzon's appointment as Foreign Secretary on 23 October 1919 to Rab Butler's resignation of the office on 16 October 1964, one or other of these six figures worked at the Foreign Office in some capacity for all but nine of those forty-three years. They span the Foreign Office eras of Sir Eyre Crowe and Sir Thomas Brimelow, from the economic consequences of the Peace Treaty of 1919 to the economic consequences of the Yom Kippur War in October 1973. Eden's career filled the years framed by these chronological bookends. Versailles and Peacemaking provided the back-drop to his work with Austen Chamberlain in the 1920s, and at Geneva in the 1930s; whilst the Arab-Israeli conflict proved to be one of the postludes of the Suez crisis of 1956. Eden, to adapt Bagehot, was the buckle that joined, and the hyphen that fastened, many of the central foreign policy concerns of a troubled century, and was the one figure who had been in Parliament with all these Conservative Foreign Secretaries from Curzon to Butler. Among his first speeches in the House of Commons was a contribution to the debate on 17 March 1924 on the Peace Bill arising from the Lausanne Treaty negotiated by Curzon; his last action as Prime Minister was to signify to the Queen 'that my own debt to Mr Butler while I have been Prime Minister was very real.'[6]

Eden was given his first significant parliamentary promotion by Austen Chamberlain, who proved an important mentor. Writing to Dame Ivy Chamberlain, when Foreign Secretary himself, Eden stated that 'for however long or short a time it may be my destiny to sit at this desk, it will be his standards and his teaching that I shall seek to follow.'[7] Eden first gave the future Prime Minister, Alec Douglas-Home, Cabinet Office in April 1955; and his symbiotic relationship with Selwyn Lloyd, who also first entered the Cabinet under him, and was his Foreign Secretary throughout the Suez crisis, was central to the political scene in the 1950s. In Foreign Office terms, Eden remains a pivotal figure. With Sir Edward Grey (a distant kinsman) and Ernest Bevin (a trusted war-time colleague and friend), he was one of the undisputed triptych of 'great' twentieth century Foreign Secretaries, whose influence, both in institutional reform and policy-making, was extensive and far-reaching.[8]

During Eden's lifetime, only seven politicians served as both Foreign Secretary and Prime Minister – Salisbury and MacDonald (both simultaneously), Balfour (subsequent to his Premiership), Macmillan (prior to his); with Eden, Home (also a post-Premiership Foreign Secretary) and Callaghan as the trio that moved from King Charles Street directly to Downing Street. Eden remains the only Conservative member of the House of Commons in the twentieth century to have gone straight from the Foreign Office to Downing Street, and the only Conservative Foreign Secretary of the modern age never to have held office in a domestic department. Even more unusually, he is the only senior member of any potential governing party whose eventual translation to the highest office was anticipated for nearly two decades. The majority of heirs apparent somehow manage 'to mock the expectation of the world'. Such a period of 'close-lipp'd patience' makes Eden the undisputed 'Crown Prince' of modern British politics, and this theme, with its consequences, is also one that the present study seeks to examine.

The book is not primarily a study of British foreign policy throughout this lengthy period, as such an approach would entail many volumes; I have, rather, concentrated on the portrait of a man on his journey through life.*

Eden's career falls naturally into four phases, and the shape of the book reflects that pattern. Part One ('The Rose of Youth') deals with the

---

* Specialist examinations of all phases of Eden's career are readily available. Apart from Eden's three volumes of memoirs, the five essential studies are A.R. Peters *Anthony Eden at the Foreign Office 1931–1938*, Elizabeth Barker *Churchill and Eden at War*, John W. Young *The Foreign Policy of Churchill's Peacetime Administration 1951–1955*, James Cable *The Geneva Conference of 1954 on Indochina* and Keith Kyle *Suez* (1991), together with its revised edition, *Suez: Britain's End of Empire in the Middle East* (2003). Details of all six books are in the bibliography.

traumatic effect of the Great War, and the subsequent years of promise to the outbreak of the Second World War. The pivotal moment of this phase remains Eden's resignation from the Chamberlain Government in February 1938, a seismic shift in the long ideological battle between the proponents of appeasement and their opponents. Eden's rôle in this crucial debate is by no means as clear-cut as was once thought, nor was his position accurately reflected by Churchill's romantic portrait of him, ten years after the event, as the 'one strong young figure'. Indeed, this book argues that many of Eden's post-war difficulties stem from Churchill's premature indication of the identity of his successor.

Part Two ('The Business of War') deals with the crucial years from Eden's rehabilitation, first as Dominions Secretary, then as War Secretary, before his five year spell as Churchill's war-time Foreign Secretary, arguably the peak of his career. His relationship with the Americans and the Soviets, cultivated over numerous conferences, and his place alongside Churchill at the key moments of the global struggle, were to position him at the heart of the fight for the survival of civilisation, and to shape many of his post-war attitudes.

Part Three ('Crown Prince') deals with the years leading up to the Premiership. Eden's contribution to Conservative renewal in the immediate post-war years, in fields as diverse as finance, philosophy and organisation proved seminal for the Conservative Party, and gave the lie to the myth that he had no interest in, or aptitude for, domestic political concerns. The fact that this revivalist contribution came at a time of great difficulty in his private life, which in a more prurient age almost ended his political career, adds to the poignancy of the almost unparalleled drama of the final phase, with 1954 standing as an *annus mirabilis* of diplomatic achievement. Then, after waiting for the succession for seventeen years, his fate was to be a stop-gap Prime Minister. As Harold Macmillan wrote in his diary on the day that Eden became Prime Minister, 'It is a pretty tough assignment to follow the greatest Englishman of history.' Eden never cast off the shadow of Churchill's massive presence.

Part Four ('Greatness Going Off?') looks at Eden's culminating years, and argues that many of the difficulties that arose during Eden's Premiership, even before Suez, were exacerbated by the intense and covert disloyalties of ambitious subordinates, disloyalties of which he was well aware.

A postlude looks at Eden's fluctuating reputation since his death and the way that mythology and fable, as ill-founded as those pre-war myths from appeasement days, have served as a substitute for historical truth.

Eden's lengthy career inevitably produces a bulky book, but as Virginia

Woolf said when writing the life of Roger Fry, 'You can cut a novel by 250 pages, but how do you cut a life?'

I am most grateful to the following people who have generously given of their time to talk to me about aspects of Anthony Eden's life and career:

The Hon. Alex Allan, Lady Allan of Kilmahew, the late Lord Amery of Lustleigh, the late the Hon. Sir John Astor, Sir Roger Bannister, Correlli Barnett, Mr Peter Beck, the late Sir Martyn Beckett, the late Sir Harold Beeley, Mr Jeremy Bennett, Mr Alan Bell, Dr B. S. Benedikz, Sir Frederick Bishop, Sir Richard Body, Professor Vernon Bogdanor, Sarah Bradford, Dr Piers Brendon, the late Lord Brimelow, Sir Julian Bullard, M. Etienne Burin des Roziers, the late Lord Butler of Saffron Walden, Lady Butler of Saffron Walden, Dr David Butler, Sir Michael Butler, the late Sir James Cable, the late Lord Caccia, Mr and Mrs Neil Cairncross, Lord Callaghan of Cardiff, Dr John Campbell, Lord Carr of Hadley, Sir Bryan Cartledge, the late Lord Charteris of Amisfield, M. Claude Cheysson, the late Mr David Clarke, Professor Richard Clogg, the late Sir John Colville, the late Lord Colyton, Lady Colyton, Mr David Coulson, the late Sir John Coulson, Mr Nevil Coulson, Baroness Martine de Courcel, the late M. Maurice Couve de Murville, Mr Tam Dalyell, the late Sir Robin Day, the late Sir Patrick Dean, Lord Deedes, Mr John Devine, Mr John Dickie, Professor David Dilks, Mr Piers Dixon, Sir Douglas Dodds-Parker, Mr James Douglas, Lord Eden of Winton, Lord Egremont, Mr John Ehrman, Professor Peter Fitzgerald, the late Lord and Lady Fraser of Kilmorack, Lord Gilmour of Craigmillar, the late Lord and Lady Gladwyn, Miss Sylvia Goodfellow, Sir Philip Goodhart, the late Lord Goodman, Sir John Graham, Mr Graham C. Greene, the late Lord Greenhill of Harrow, the late Lord Hailsham of St Marylebone, Dr Jonathan Haslam, Lord Healey, Sir Edward Heath, Mr Simon Heffer, Sir Nicholas Henderson, Professor Peter Hennessy, the late Mrs Kathleen Hill, the late Lord Home of the Hirsel, Mr Alistair Horne, Mr Anthony Howard, the late Sir David Hunt, Lord Hurd of Westwell, the late Lord Inchyra, Professor Douglas Johnson, Dr Saul Kelly, Mr Alistair Kingston, Mr Keith Kyle, Mr Robert Lacey, the late Mr Richard Lamb, Mr Christopher Lee, M. Denis Lefebvre, Mr Frederick Leishman, Sir Donald Logan, Mr Andrew Lownie, Professor W. Roger Louis, Mr Hugh Lunghi, Sir Donald and Lady Maitland, Dr Robert Mallett, Dr Peter Mangold, Mr Iverach McDonald, Sir Guy and Lady Millard, Mr Anthony Moncrieff, Sir Anthony Montague Browne, Lord Morgan, Mr A. J. Nicholls, Professor Joseph Nye, the late Sir Anthony Nutting Bt., Sir John Nutting Bt., Mr Paul Odgers, Sir Michael Palliser, Professor Ben Pimlott, the late M. Christian Pineau, the late Sir David Pitblado, Mr John Prescott, the Hon. Sir Peter Ramsbotham, Mr Brian Rees, the late Sir Patrick Reilly, the late Sir Robert Rhodes James, the late Lord Roberthall, Mr Andrew Roberts, the late Sir

Frank Roberts, Mrs Patricia Roberts, Mr Kenneth Rose, the late Sir Archibald Ross, Dr John Rowett, the late Sir Algernon Rumbold, Professor Keith Sainsbury, the late Lord Sherfield, Professor Avi Shlaim, Mr Anthony Shone, Lady Soames, Mr Nigel Spearing, the late Mr Peregrine Spencer Churchill and Mrs Spencer Churchill, the late Earl of Stockton, Dr Thomas Stuttaford, Mr John Tahourdin, Sir Peter Tapsell, the late Lord Thorneycroft, Lady Trend, Professor Edward Ullendorff, Lord Wakeham, Professor Geoffrey Warner, Lord and Lady Williams of Elvel, Lord Windlesham, the late Sir Philip Woodfield, Sir Denis Wright, Dr Steve Yui-Sang Tsang, and the late Sir Philip de Zulueta.

The following corresponded with me about Anthony Eden:

The Marquess of Anglesey, Mr T. W. Campbell, Sir Peter Hall, Dr Jana Howlett, Sir Peter Hordern, Mme Marie-Clair Mendès France, M. Chantel Morelle, Mr Nigel Nicolson, Sir Henry Rumbold, Professor Bernd Jürgen Wendt, and Mr William Yates.

I am particularly grateful to Professor Peter Hennessy for much help and encouragement over the years and for allowing me to see in advance a typescript copy of his chapter on Eden from his book *The Prime Minister: The Office and its Holders since 1945*. I also acknowledge the help of Dr Saul Kelly in allowing me to see his study of Sir Roger Makins (Lord Sherfield) at the typescript stage, and for many stimulating conversations on the Anglo-American relationship in the 1950s. Dr Robert Mallett kindly let me see the typescript of his forthcoming study *Mussolini and the Origins of the Second World War, 1933–40*. I am grateful to Professor John Young of Leicester University for help and advice over French archival material, and Dr Jonathan Haslam for his help over Russian archives.

I am indebted to many individuals and institutions for their help with the research. The Avon Papers (and those of Neville and Austen Chamberlain) are housed in the Heslop Room at the University of Birmingham Library, and without the dedicated help of Christine Penney, Librarian of the Special Collections, Martin Killeen and the staff at Birmingham over many years, this project would not have been possible.

I would also acknowledge with gratitude the help of:

Sir Robin Janvrin, the Queen's Private Secretary, Mr Oliver Everett, the former Royal Librarian and Assistant Keeper of the Royal Archives, and Lady de Bellaigue, Registrar, for their help with the Royal Archives at Windsor Castle; Michael Simmonds, Director of the Conservative Political Centre; Mr Michael Mates MP and the Executive of the Conservative Party 1922 Committee; Dr Martin Maw and Jill Davidson, successive Conservative Party Archivists at the Bodleian Library, Oxford; Helen Langley of the Bodleian Library; Dr John Jones and Mr Alan Tadiello of Balliol College, Oxford; John E. Davies, County Archivist, Carmarthenshire Record Office, and Mrs Julie Tancill, Senior Archivist; Dr Piers Brendon and the staff at the Churchill Archives Centre, Churchill College, for their unfailing help and advice, in what is the foremost British equivalent of the American Presidential Libraries; Dwight L. Strandberg, Archivist, Dwight D. Eisenhower Library, Abilene, USA; Ms K. V. Bligh, Archivist (Modern Collections), at the House of Lords Record Office; Dr Richard Palmer, Librarian and Archivist, and Miss Melanie Barber, Deputy Librarian and Deputy Archivist, at Lambeth Palace Library; Professor Stanley Wells and Mr William Weston over material connected with Eden's time as President of the Royal Shakespeare Company; Sir Henry Rumbold for help over the papers of his father, Sir Anthony Rumbold; Mr M. J. Hatch, Headmaster of Sandroyd School, and Will Lowis and Charlie Pitt Ford who worked through the archives on Eden's time at the school; Mrs Penelope Hatfield, Archivist at Eton College Library; Jonathan Smith, Manuscript Cataloguer at Trinity College Library, Cambridge; Dr Judith Bogdanor of the Jericho Health Centre, Oxford, who conclusively shows that George Wyndham could not have been, as has so often been surmised, the father of Anthony Eden; Professor John Grenville over research in German archives; at St Antony's College, Oxford, Mrs Amanda Kaye, former Bursar, the Librarian, Ms Rosamund Campbell, Mrs Clare Brown, Archivist of the Middle East Centre, and the Librarian of the Middle East Centre, Mrs Diane Ring; at Christ Church, Oxford, Mrs Judith Curthoys over Eden papers held at the College; at Magdalen College, Oxford, the then Archivist, Dr Robin Darwall-Smith; at Nuffield College, Oxford, the Archivist, Mrs Eleanor Vallis; at the Hartley Library, Southampton University, Dr C. M. Woolgar, for help over the Mountbatten papers; Sir Percy Cradock for help over Joint Intelligence Committee records; at News International plc, Eamon Dyas, Group Records Manager, and Sarah Hepworth, Assistant Archivist at *The Times* Archives and Record Office; at the Warwick and Leamington Conservative Association, Mr Anthony Wood and Mrs Brenda Smith; and at Wolfson College, Oxford, Dr Mark Pottle of the Lady Asquith of Yarnbury Research Project, and Dr Anne Deighton. I am indebted to Lady Soames for supplying me with copies of the letters of her parents, Sir Winston and Lady Churchill, that are relevant to the career of Eden.

As a former Prime Minister, and three times holder of the Foreign Secretaryship, Anthony Eden merited one of the longest notices in the forthcoming *New Dictionary of National Biography*. I am grateful to the late Professor Colin Matthew for commissioning me to undertake this responsibility. His guidance over many issues regarding Eden's career, particularly its proportions, was of inestimable value in the preparation of this biography.

Others who have helped in various valuable ways and to whom I am extremely grateful, include Sir Eric Anderson, Provost of Eton College, and Lady Anderson, Dr John Avison, Mr James Bayliss, Dr Timothy Benson, Professor Richard Cooper, Mr Richard Crawford, Mr John Davies, the late Mr Anthony Day, Mr Hugh Gammell, Sir Martin Gilbert, Marie-Andrée Guyot (Chef du Département des Archives Historiques, Ministère des Affaires étrangères, Quai d'Orsay, Paris), Mr and Mrs Robert Ingram, Mr and Mrs Robert Kellock, Mr Nigel Jaques, Mrs Frances Marshall, Mr Richard McMillan, Mrs F. M. Myles, Mr and Mrs John Peters, Miss Brenda Smith, Mr Brian Souter, Mr David Twiston Davies, Mr George Walker, Mr Frank Wiseman, the Revd John Witheridge, Mr Philip Ziegler and Dr Ernst Zillekens. As during my work on *Alec Douglas-Home*, I am greatly indebted to the staff of Locland Computers of East Kilbride, especially Mr Raymond Mair, for their technical support.

The complete typescript has been read by various people, and for this valued help, I am particularly grateful to Professor Vernon Bogdanor, Mr Graham C. Greene and Professor Geoffrey Warner for their comments, and to Mr Keith Kyle for his observations on the Suez chapters. Responsibility for the final version and the interpretation of events, however, is mine alone.

I thank the Warden and Fellows of St Antony's College, Oxford, and Alistair Horne, for electing me to the Alistair Horne Fellowship at the College from 1997 to 1998 to facilitate my researches, a privilege and most happy memory. I am indebted also to Lord Windlesham, Principal, and the Fellows of Brasenose College for electing me to Senior Membership of Brasenose for the final years of the project. Nobody could have laboured in a happier vineyard.

At Chatto & Windus, I owe much to Penelope Hoare and her staff, who have worked tirelessly to prepare this volume for publication.

My greatest debt, however, remains to the Countess of Avon, for entrusting me with the responsibility of writing a new life of her husband, for her unfailing help in making available new material and for providing introductions to so many people, whilst at no time seeking to influence my interpretation.

I dedicate this book with gratitude to Patrick Croker, Brasenose historian, who first set my steps on the paths of research over forty years ago, and whose former college was the place of its completion.

D. R. THORPE
Oxford, November 2002

PRELUDE

To understand a man, Napoleon once said, one has to know what was happening in the world when he was twenty. For the generation that came to adulthood during the Great War this precept was particularly apt. The timing of Anthony Eden's birth (in June 1897) meant that he achieved the age of twenty in the most desperate year of that bloody conflict, and at one of the defining moments of his military career.

In the second week of June 1917, Anthony Eden was awarded the Military Cross: he had rescued his platoon sergeant, Bert Harrop, from no-man's-land, bringing him back through barbed-wire entrenchments with a stretcher party. On his actual birthday, 12 June, one of glorious sunshine, Eden was dug in by the Ypres–Comines Canal at the start of the Battle of Passchendaele. There was no sign then that the conflict would become what Lloyd George called the battle of the mud, although it was already clear from initial skirmishes that the human losses would be horrendous. In the preceding months Eden had already witnessed the deaths of many young friends in the fierce struggle for Messines and its heavily defended ridge. From the morning of his twentieth birthday, in forty-eight uninterrupted hours of fighting and bombardment in the push for Ravine Wood, 200 men were killed by shells alone and countless more by the strafing of machine-gun fire. Few survivors could have emerged mentally unscathed from such an experience.

At desperate risk to himself during the previous autumn Eden had gone out at dead of night to find the body of his commanding officer, the Earl of Feversham, who had fallen in action; Eden had hoped after the war to return personal effects to Feversham's family. 'Most soldiers, even the least religious, will pray at some time,' he later wrote. 'In battle it was for many of us a prayer of fear.'[1]

Only with the publication of his memoir, *Another World 1897–1917*, in the year before his death did many realise the intensity of these formative experiences for Eden and how they had shaped his attitudes. However, even then, with the reticence bred in him from early childhood, he stressed as an enduring theme, not the horror and anguish of life in the trenches, but the camaraderie in adversity.

For Eden's generation, born at the end of the nineteenth century, when the British Empire was seemingly at the height of its influence and power, war was to prove an inescapable burden. In the 1920s, when he was establishing himself in Parliament, Eden wrote fiction for cathartic relief, and in one short story about the Great War recorded that the company commander had said to the new recruits, who had found things surprisingly quiet, 'War will come to you all right before you're through with it, you've no need to go looking for it.'[2] So it was throughout Eden's own lifetime.

'War makes rattling good history,' observed Thomas Hardy, 'but Peace is poor reading.'[3] The drama of Eden's life is, in part, because it was so bound up with war and the fear of war. His early childhood was lived against the backdrop of the Boer War, the subject of of Kipling's poem, *The Lesson* from which Anthony Nutting was later to take the title of his book on Suez.[4]

One of Kipling's most famous poems, 'Recessional', had actually been written in June 1897, the month of Eden's birth. Often mistaken for a Diamond Jubilee celebration, 'Recessional' was more of a prophetic warning that empires can so easily go the way of Nineveh and Tyre, a premonition that, as far as the British were concerned, was actually to be fulfilled during Eden's lifetime.

Rumours of war accompanied Eden's adolescence. When war was declared in 1914, he volunteered for active service as soon as he was of age. 'I have been to the War Office today to find out about my commission,' he wrote to his mother in October 1915. 'I am to be gazetted in "four days" which will probably mean next Monday, but I may wear my uniform at once and *must* wear it as soon as I am gazetted.'[5]

For those who survived trench warfare ('which I feel sure I shall do,' Eden confided to his mother),[6] a global struggle attended the much-changed days of maturity. In Eden's case, his executive capacities were tested to the full as Foreign Secretary in what proved a sustained campaign to repel a tyranny that threatened the extinction of civilisation itself. 'For some of us the challenge has come a second time in our generation,' Eden said in a broadcast to the Empire on 11 September 1939. 'There must be no second mistake. Out of the welter of suffering to be endured we must fashion a new world that is something better than a stale reflection of the old, bled white.'[7]

Both world wars, which he saw as essentially defensive and reactive struggles to maintain humanitarian values, brought Eden great personal loss. His eldest brother, Jack, was killed in October 1914 in France, and his youngest brother, Nicholas, was killed, just sixteen, while serving as a midshipman at the Battle of Jutland in May 1916. These scars never left Eden, who determined that a future son of his should be called Nicholas in memory of the brother to whom he was particularly close. However, when his first son was born prematurely in 1924, he shrank from such a christening, lest the name bring bad luck, and gave the name instead to his youngest son, born in 1930.[8] He called his eldest son Simon. With tragic irony, it was Simon who was killed in the Second World War, on active service like the uncle he never knew. Only days before the ending of hostilities in the Far East, and a few months short of his twenty-first birthday, Simon Eden was in an RAF plane that crashed into a desolate jungle hill while on a reconnaissance mission in Burma. Among his effects, reflecting the literary tastes of his upbringing, was a copy of Shakespeare's *Henry V*. In his last letter, a few days before the fatal flight, Simon had written to his father:

> Have got the Burma star (I think) and the 1939–45 one as well. I suppose there will be a Jap star and probably a Singapore star so I shall return home looking like a map of the Heavens![9]*

Burma, when Simon Eden died, was a colony on the fringes of the British Empire, both geographically and politically. Three years after the war Burma gained independence, part of the process of decolonisation embracing the subcontinent of India and Ceylon.

Few in June 1897 forecast such a retraction; nor, as a corollary, was there any thought of the emergence of a Commonwealth of Nations in place of the imperial family. After all, a quarter of the world's population was then under British rule and the cartographers were well supplied with red ink. The transformation of Empire into Commonwealth was only one of the many far-reaching political changes during Eden's lifetime that can be traced back to the impact of the Great War.

When Eden entered Parliament after the December 1923 General Election, the Labour Party was replacing the Liberal Party as the main party of opposition to the Conservatives, a process accelerated by political divisions during the Great War. Eden believed in 1922 that 'the next election will be fought with the old party names Conservative and Liberal.'[10] Yet his first experience of Parliament was under a Labour Government.

But for Eden's generation, the most far-reaching change following the

---

* For Eden, who had a Shakespearean quotation to mind for most events, this letter seemed unconsciously to echo Juliet's lines:

> And, when he shall die,
> Take him and cut him out in little stars,
> And he will make the face of heaven so fine
> That all the world will be in love with night,
> And pay no worship to the garish sun.
>
> *Romeo and Juliet*, III.ii. 21–5.

5

Great War was the decline of Empire. For him, 24 May (Queen Victoria's birthday) was always synonymous with Empire Day, just as 11 November signified the Armistice, and a time for pause and remembrance of fallen colleagues, as, even on a weekday, traffic halted and people stood in silence.

If any one event symbolised this imperial focus for the British people it came on 22 June 1897 when the Queen Empress Victoria rode in an open carriage to St Paul's Cathedral for the celebration of her Diamond Jubilee. 'The sun never looked down until yesterday,' enthused the popular press 'upon the embodiment of so much energy and power.' And how the sun shone that day – 'Queen's weather' as her subjects said.[11] For *The Times*, the processions and festivities showed that Britain's was 'the mightiest and most beneficial Empire ever known in the annals of mankind.'[12] Forty-six thousand troops from every realm over which Great Britain had dominion rode behind Field Marshal Lord Roberts, VC, a display of power never before witnessed in the capital city. But appearances were deceptive. Even the Prime Minister, Lord Salisbury, had his private doubts and in his idiosyncratic way observed 'our mistake is having an empire.'[13]

Despite the general rejoicings of Diamond Jubilee Day, the cusp had been passed and the next phase of Empire was to have different political priorities and economic perspectives. For those born into the late-Victorian age, like Eden, to be British was no longer necessarily to have drawn first prize in the lottery of life.

Ten days before Queen Victoria's Diamond Jubilee, Robert Anthony Eden was born into that era of illusory certainties, at Windlestone Hall, County Durham. He was to die in January 1977 at his home in Alvediston, Wiltshire, three weeks before Queen Elizabeth II's Silver Jubilee. His life was thus spent in a period of radical readjustment, spanning eighty of the most tempestuous years in history, with the economic, political and social assumptions of his Edwardian childhood largely unrecognisable by the time of his death.

Eden's was a complex personality, but the experiences of war were to define his attitudes. Towards the end of the 1955 General Election campaign, Eden, as Prime Minister, was heckled in a South London park by a crowd, who chanted 'Warmonger' at him repeatedly. His temper roused, he threw away his prepared notes and spoke from the heart. His response won over a hostile audience, who then cheered him to the echo. Nevertheless, he himself was bitterly upset because he had allowed the taunts of the crowd to pierce the protective emotional carapace that he had so carefully constructed.[14]

At the height of the Suez crisis a year later, Eden broadcast to a national audience:

All my life I have been a man of peace, working for peace, striving for peace, negotiating for peace. I have been a League of Nations man and a United Nations man and I'm still the same man, with the same convictions. I couldn't be other, even if I wished.[15]

Again the sincerity of his remarks shone through, even to his critics.[16]

Yet the dilemma remains – a man of peace, who sent British troops into an 'armed conflict'.[17] The concept was not, for Eden, contradictory. To hold to peace, it is sometimes necessary to fight for peace. This was the view of the majority of Eden's 1955 Cabinet, the last in British history to be dominated by men whose seminal experience had been the Great War. Eden's ultimate attempt to solve – by military means – the economic consequences for a declining power of the nationalisation of the Suez Canal Company in 1956 was to yield a bitter political and personal legacy, but was not at odds with his revulsion in the face of war. His attempt, a reaction against appeasement, was bred of the patriotism that remained a central part of his personality, and whatever he did was because he genuinely believed it was for the good of his country.

'Germans are furious with England for not remaining neutral,' the schoolboy Eden had written in his diary on 5 August 1914, 'but England cannot stand by and see the neutrality of Belgium violated without losing all her prestige as a first-class power.'[18] In this, as in so many things, the child was father of the man. 'Anthony,' wrote one former colleague on Eden's death, 'was the last, for my generation, of those who saved freedom for us all – who led and unified us in the dark days from 1933 to the end.'[19]

The economic and industrial contractions that reduced Britain from the status of 'a first-class power' were brought home vividly to Eden in his last years. As a child at Windlestone, set among 8,000 acres of County Durham, that Palatinate of Prince Bishops and nursery of Labour politicians, he had been warned not to brush against the bushes or vegetation of the gardens and park, because the clinging film of coal dust from the many neighbouring collieries would spoil his clothes. On his final visit to his former home, he saw that 'what had been spacious and elegant was now gaunt and vacantly lonely,'[20] and there was no longer the distant hum of busy activity.

Eden grew up in an age of unprecedented political change, the seismic gratings of which, even before the Great War, were already discernible to the young schoolboy. His letters home from Eton are full of references to contemporary events. In 1915, the year of Gallipoli, he heard about the state of the Navy's ships, and, in the first reference in his papers to the man with whom he was to have such a symbiotic relationship, asked, 'Why can't W. Churchill look after those sort of things instead of making strategical plans about which he knows nothing at all?'[21]

As a young man he had an acute sense of historical perspective and the consequences of wars. 'Do you realise that tomorrow is the centenary of Waterloo?' asked Eden of his mother on 17 June 1915, not a question that many of his contemporaries would have put. 'How very different to what everybody thought it would be like!'[22] And how different the world would be when Eden came home from his Waterloos. 'Men are beginning to see,' said the American President, Woodrow Wilson, at Manchester in December 1918 on his way to the Paris Peace Conference, 'not perhaps the golden age, but an age which at any rate is brightening from decade to decade, and will lead us some time to an elevation from which we can see the things for which the heart of mankind is longing.'[23]

Such were the hopes after the Armistice, hopes that Eden shared, but they were to be cruelly dashed in the inter-war period.[24] As a result of this disenchantment, there was a greater sense of realism in 1945 about the difficulties that lay ahead, a cautiousness that Eden reflected in his speeches at the time. On the eve of VE Day, Eden broadcast to the American people and to the United Kingdom from the San Francisco Conference:

> As the great world conflict draws more nearly to an end we begin to look forward into the future. Here at San Francisco we have been charged with an essential task. Our work, if it is to be successfully concluded, as I believe it will be, cannot by itself alone ensure the peace of the world.[25]

From the Great War through to the Cold War, Eden was drawn to the responsibilities of international diplomacy. His first thought had been to seek a purely diplomatic career, but he feared that this would be a slow track world, 'forever handing round teacups in Teheran'.[26] Yet Eden's political experience of international relations showed how rarely expectations matched achievements, which is why the memory of the 1954 Geneva Conference, when results transcended expectations, was so special for him.*

He believed, with Lord Acton, that so often 'ideals in politics are never realised but the pursuit of them determines history.'[27] That pursuit determined his own political life during three terms as Foreign Secretary, between wars, during war and in one of the tensest phases of the Cold War. Whenever he returned to the institution of the Foreign Office, he felt he was like a man coming home.[28]

During his varied life, Eden was shaped by many differing institutions, but the King's Royal Rifle Corps from his native Durham held the strongest ties for him and was the focus of his deepest affection. He was always 'a rifleman'. For those who had followed the profession of arms,

---

*See Chapter 14 for an analysis of Eden's role at Geneva.

particularly as Great War volunteers, he had the deepest empathy and his service in the 21st Battalion the Yeoman Rifles of that Durham Regiment remained the most searing of his experiences. As a result Eden's subsequent life was to prove a paradigm of Napoleon's dictum. Even when he was the most powerful figure in the country, he did not forget his comrades from the trenches. Visiting Queen Elizabeth II at Balmoral on Prime Ministerial business, Eden still found time to see in nearby Ballater one of the survivors from Ploegsteert Wood and Passchendaele. For Eden, the Great War was the Rome of the twentieth century; all roads led to it, and all roads led from it. As a result, the memory of the world when he was twenty never left him.

PART ONE

The Rose of Youth

He wears the rose
Of youth upon him, from which the world should note
Something particular.

Antony and Cleopatra, III.xiii. 20–22

CHAPTER ONE

The Way They Lived Then

1897–1915

Another fifty years will see the end of life as we knew it.

George Moore to Sybil Eden

Fair seed-time had my soul, and I grew up
Foster'd alike by beauty and by fear.

William Wordsworth, *Prelude*, Book One

The descent of the Edens of County Durham is complex and varied, but it was a topic that intrigued the most famous of the line, Robert Anthony Eden, second Prime Minister of the reign of Queen Elizabeth II.

One of the portraits at Windlestone, the family home at Rushyford, was of Barbara Villiers, Duchess of Cleveland, by whom Charles II had five acknowledged children, including a daughter, Charlotte, who married the Earl of Lichfield. As Eden noted of this daughter, 'Unlike her mother she was a pattern of modesty and wifely virtues.' The Lichfields' own daughter later married Lord Baltimore, and was 'therefore the direct ancestress of the Edens of the eighteenth and nineteenth century'.[1] This connection prompted the economist Maynard Keynes to ask Eden whether he had any Villiers blood. Eden was able to confirm further connections. When he had visited Sweden on Foreign Office business in October 1934, he had been greeted as a descendant of 'a saintly early Swedish king'[2] and given a detailed family tree revealing that the link was Barbara Villiers.

Despite these royal connections, the Eden family into which Anthony was born in 1897 was minor aristocracy. The 8,000 acres surrounding Windlestone did not amount to much in a county of Lambtons and Londonderrys, while in neighbouring Northumberland, and over the Scottish border, several titled families lived on far grander estates, clans that Harold Macmillan called 'right-down regular' peers.[3] In the accustomed manner, however, there was much intermarrying, and one of the right-down regular peers, Alec Douglas-Home was a collateral kinsman.

Titles came relatively late in the Eden family's history, the first creation of the baronetcy of West Auckland (Eden's father being the seventh) dating from the patronage of Charles II in 1672. As Anthony Eden's father was also the fifth baronet of a second creation (of Maryland) from 1776, Timothy Eden, the eldest surviving son and Anthony Eden's brother, was, unusually, a baronet twice over when he succeeded his father on 20 February 1915. None of these dignities came Anthony Eden's way.

Distinction had been added to the Eden line, not just by baronetcies, but also by judicious and profitable marriages to Fairfaxes, Kenes, Sheffields, Widdingtons and Veres.[4] Sir John Moore, buried 'darkly at dead of night'[5] at Corunna, was another ancestor.

Through his mother's line, Eden could claim kinship with Sir Edward Grey, who enjoyed the longest continuous spell at the Foreign Office of the twentieth century. The young Anthony Eden thus had both landowning and political threads among his antecedents, though he was the first modern Conservative statesman of the first rank to come from an area heavily associated with the emerging Labour Party and the Trade Union movement. Nevertheless, his upbringing near the Durham coalfields was to give him an underestimated insight into domestic issues that was to place him firmly in the Tory 'One Nation' tradition and, all his life, he was to retain an affection for the county of Durham and its people, especially those of military stock.

There was a traditional saying in the family that 'There is an Eden in every generation who achieves renown.'[6] Sir William Eden, Anthony's father, had five children – Elfrida Marjorie (known as Marjorie, born 1887), John (Jack, 1888), Timothy Calvert (Tim, 1893), Robert Anthony (Anthony, 1897) and William Nicholas (Nicholas, 1900) – but was in no doubt that his fourth child would be the one to justify that precept. Anthony was a thoughtful and reflective child, not given to horseplay or boyish exuberance, and when his father saw 'little' Anthony going to play soldiers with his older brothers, he noted, 'he is wearing a toy helmet and in one hand carries a toy sword, but under the other arm he carries a book. Ah, a bookworm, a bookworm, a man of note someday.'[7]*

Members of the Eden family had seen political service in territories as far afield as Baltimore in the United States and Auckland (named after one of Eden's ancestors) in New Zealand. Indeed, when Eden was at a low point – in the Coronation summer of 1953 – he seriously contemplated retiring from active front-line politics altogether and entering the House of Lords with the title of Lord Baltimore. When he eventually chose Avon as the title of his hereditary earldom in 1961, it was after the river that flowed through all the towns of his former constituency of Warwick and Leamington, from Coventry to Stratford.

The family's links with the county of Durham had extended over 700

---

*One literary forebear was Emily Eden (1797–1869), author of *The Semi-Attached Couple*, which Anthony Eden much admired. He wrote a foreword for the 1928 reprint of this novel, first published in 1859.

years by the time of Anthony Eden's birth. The earliest recorded male ancestor of the Eden family was born during the reign of Edward III, one Robert Eden, who died in 1413, and possessed significant holdings of land at Preston-on-Tees, lands that remained in the family till 1844. As a result, Preston-on-Tees was known as 'the cradle of the Edens'.[8]

Neighbouring Stockton-on-Tees was to be the first constituency of Harold Macmillan, who took its name for his belated earldom. Unlike Macmillan, Eden had no eye for the intricate niceties of social position, though he annotated in his own hand his copy of the 1907 Pedigree of the Eden family, which ends in bald poignancy with details of the death of his youngest brother Nicholas at the Battle of Jutland in 1916. A very different slant permeates Macmillan's genealogical musings. Of the young Reginald Maudling, Macmillan noted dismissively: 'Maudling – no background.'[9] He privately referred to Selwyn Lloyd, as 'a middle-class lawyer from Liverpool', while Lord Hailsham, once his favoured choice as successor, was dubbed 'a temporary gentleman'.

Just as the Churchills (from the time of Lord Randolph Churchill) were to alternate the Christian names Winston and Randolph, so the head of the Eden family and his heir bore alternately the names of John and Robert for ten generations. Robert was one of Anthony's given names, and the name given to his second son, who died shortly after birth. One of Eden's part namesakes, Sir Robert Eden (1741–84) became the Governor of Maryland in America in 1768, and a baronet of Maryland in his own right, after his marriage to Caroline, the daughter of the 5th Lord Baltimore. A great friend of George Washington, Sir Robert Eden enthusiastically supported America's Declaration of Independence in 1776, and was granted lands in the brave new world. Winston Churchill, proud of his part-American ancestry through the Jerome line of his mother, was always conscious and a little envious of the fact that Anthony Eden's line of transatlantic forebears was actually of far greater standing and distinction than his own.[10]

A strong degree of social concern characterised Sir Frederick Morton Eden, 2nd Baronet of Maryland (1766–1809), whose pioneering study, *The State of the Poor*, a work of considerable importance in the history of economic sociology, greatly influenced Anthony Eden's own thinking on domestic matters. Karl Marx praised the work in *Das Kapital*, and Anthony Eden kept a copy on his shelves throughout his life.

The nineteenth century saw a degree of retrenchment, as Sir Robert Johnson Eden (1774–1844), the 5th Baronet of West Auckland, sold the Preston-on-Tees estate and, having razed the old family home, Windlestone, to the ground, rebuilt it with the proceeds in 1840. On his death, childless, the family estates passed to his cousin Sir William Eden (1803–73), 4th baronet of Maryland and 6th of West Auckland, and Anthony Eden's grandfather.

This Sir William Eden had many characteristics later seen in his grandson. He was an exceptionally well-read man, of cultivated, aesthetic tastes, which he pursued on his many travels. When in Naples he bought Carel Fabritius' painting 'An Instrument Dealer at his Booth in the Open Air', a work later displayed in the National Gallery. He built the large Mausoleum at Windlestone, where he was buried in 1873, and where later six of his eleven children were also buried.[11] Sir William Eden, 7th Baronet of West Auckland and 5th of Maryland (1849–1915), Anthony Eden's father, was the fourth of these children, and renowned for his irascibility. He was so bad-tempered that he was known on the magistrates' bench as 'The Bloody Baronet', or, on polite days, as 'Seven and Six', because of the fine he usually imposed. He was not averse to destroying any barometer that failed to warn of inclement weather, or to hurling a joint of roast lamb out of the window if the menus were repetitive. His irrational dislikes included red flowers and the smell of whisky fumes. In a frank private* memoir his wife Sybil recalled:

> Sir William's impatient temper, which expressed itself in a vast invective, the colour and erudition of which had to be heard to be believed (the miners of Durham used to make long journeys to his shoots and to the local police court on the days when he presided over the local magistrate's bench, just because it might be an opportunity of hearing 'Willy' swear) was mercifully imbued with a sense of humour, devastatingly Puckish though it was.[12]

Although he was a renowned amateur of the arts, whose greatest regret in old age came when he could no longer apply brush to paper, Sir William had rakish, Regency tastes, prize-fighting among them. He had his own trainer, the formidable 'Bat' Mullens, and he liked to spar with the famous 'Bombardier' Billy Wells. 'A fight to the finish is the QED of practical life' was one of his maxims. Once a boxing match was arranged between Sir William and a sporting acquaintance, but it was stopped on the instructions of a mutual friend of both pugilists, who declared, 'They are both impetuous men and neither will give in till one is dead.' As Willie was both impatient and hated smoking, attendance at the typical small-hall boxing tournament, with its lengthy ritual preliminaries and smoke-filled atmosphere, was a tantalising penance for him before the fighting began. So he arranged matches in his London residence, 11 Bruton Street, inviting

---

*Private because her surviving sons suppressed it.

a wide social spectrum of spectators, moving furniture to the side of the room and dispensing with all preliminaries. More often than not, he was 'on the card' himself. There were also bloody boxing matches with his gamekeepers at Windlestone.

Willie's impetuosity was legendary. When on horseback he jumped closed level-crossing gates, 'without thought of the oncoming train'. He engaged in a very public quarrel with Whistler over what he considered an unsatisfactory portrait of Lady Eden. He even temporarily changed the family name by Royal Proclamation to Shafto.[13] Yet his complexities included a tender sensibility, and not only in aesthetic matters. The fate of Oscar Wilde touched him deeply. Willie and his wife, Sybil, had met Oscar Wilde soon after the birth of Wilde's first-born. Wilde did not at that stage have a name for his son, and Sybil Eden suggested 'Oscar'. 'Oh! dear no,' came the reply 'there can only be *one* Oscar Wilde in the world.' Many sad years later, Willie and Sybil saw Wilde in a Paris hotel dining room in his years of disgrace and exile. After their meal, Willie suggested that they cross over to speak to him. 'I think he was pleased,' recorded Sybil.

Sir William's delight in architecture was measured against the standards of Wren. 'Above all,' he would say, 'there is St Paul's.' And the beauty of his wife, 'even until the day of his death, never ceased to throw him into ecstasies.'[14] In old age, he was 'a fierce old baronet overpowering his friends and terrifying his family, finding consolation from life in the genius of his own water-colours, shaking his stick at the Victoria Memorial and falling in love with the washerwoman of Degas'.[15] This enigmatic and distant figure, given to emotional outbursts, was an accomplished painter, exhibiting at the New English Art Club. He was also a noted collector of art. Once, when dining with a neighbour, he identified the painting over the chimneypiece as Velázquez's 'Rokeby Venus'. His aesthetic tastes, as Anthony's later, were well in advance of contemporary thinking. 'You know, something ought to be done about it,' said their neighbour at Wynyard Park, the Tory grandee, the Marquess of Londonderry. 'Willie actually gave good money for these things.'[16] He did so with a purpose, always intending that his art collection would be a financial lifeline for what he called 'his little boys' (which included his daughter Marjorie). Unfortunately, the surviving 'little boys' sold the paintings, which included ones by Corot and Degas, and in 1918 they fetched a fraction of what they would have achieved some years later.

Willie Eden spelled out his philosophy of life to his sons on the outbreak of war in 1914. 'Suppressed emotion is much more noble than enthusiasm, which is often mere hysterical gush. Mafeking! the *hoi polloi gushed*. The nativity! the angels *gushed*. Gushing is feminine and unmanly.' On hearing of the death of his eldest son, John, in action that October, it was recorded: 'Whatever Eden thought, he gave no sign. He gazed into the fire for a moment and then – "A fine death!"'[17] The same reticence accompanied Anthony Eden on receiving the news of the death of his eldest son, Simon, in action in the Second World War.[18]

But Anthony Eden also inherited his father's volatility, the fierce mood swings between charm and rage, stoicism and fury. Winston Churchill's doctor, Lord Moran, who observed Eden closely in the 1940s and 1950s, wondered how far this could be attributed to Eden's upbringing at Windlestone. Moran was familiar with the story of Eden's father in the family history, written by Timothy Eden, *The Tribulations of a Baronet* (1933). 'It makes sad reading,' Moran explained:

> Sir William's uncontrolled rages terrified his children, who were always on tenterhooks, fearing that they might say something that would start an explosion. A barking dog might give rise to a terrible tornado of oaths, screams and gesticulations. Sir William was a gifted egoist without any control, so that at any time there might be a terrible scene of rage and tears. Anthony did not inherit his father's instability, but it must have been a handicap to be brought up in such an atmosphere.[19]

There were, as it happened, persistent rumours in society that Sir William was not Eden's father, and that his real father was George Wyndham, an intimate of Sybil Eden (no 'stainless petal'). Wyndham was a figure of coruscating brilliance in Edwardian society, as well as an eminent politician.[20]

Anthony Eden was later very relaxed about this question mark over his paternity, talking openly of it in retirement with dinner guests. Whether he was George Wyndham's son was not resolved in his lifetime. The possibility, which he never troubled to dispel, gave him an enigmatic aura, though he did not like the logical corollary that his mother had conducted a serious extramarital affair. But he freely discussed the rumours, not least because of the undoubted aesthetic talents of George Wyndham, 'the most elegant man in England' as W. E. Henley described him,[21] and one of the most famous members of 'The Souls', that brilliant turn-of-the-century coterie formed 'as a reaction against the aggressive philistinism of aristocratic society at the time'.[22]

Cynthia Gladwyn records a visit to John Wyndham at Petworth in November 1961:

> In conversation about the Edens, I was surprised to discover that John had never heard the rumour that Anthony was the son of George Wyndham. There certainly is a resemblance, which is particularly striking in the bust of George Wyndham at the Musée Rodin.[23] When we

stayed with the Avons in the spring we somehow began talking about this, and Anthony said he didn't really know the truth of it at all; but that when he went to Australia first, somebody had said to him, 'Your voice is exactly like George Wyndham's.' Clarissa avers that he would much prefer to be his father's son, and it must be said that Anthony could have inherited his violent uncontrolled temper equally from Sir William Eden or George Wyndham.[24]

Eden could also have inherited his aesthetic sensibilities from either man. William Eden was a skilful watercolourist, and George Wyndham wrote verses and produced a scholarly edition of Shakespeare's poems.[25]

One of Wyndham's principal recreations was lawn tennis – as was Anthony Eden's. Wyndham had restless energy, and lacked a feeling of repose, something that was characteristic of Eden too when under pressure. But there were also differences. Eden, who adored the society of female company, would never have believed, with Wyndham, that the best proportion of men to women at a house party was seven to three. Wyndham's grounds were that this left some of the men free to talk to each other, 'and as for general conversation, if clever women take part in it three are enough since they are more impatient in talk than men so that six or seven of them discussing a subject are like a pack of hounds worrying a fox.'[26] Had Wyndham lived thirty years later, he would have been prominent in what disparagingly became known as café society. Anthony Eden was never a man of the 'salon' (one of the causes of his later antipathy towards Duff Cooper). There was always an air of earnestness, particularly in his younger days, and gaining a First at Oxford by dint of sheer hard work was not a Wyndham characteristic.

However, one surprisingly overlooked fact squashes all rumour: Wyndham was in South Africa at the time of Anthony Eden's conception. Having spent most of the summer in the South of France, Wyndham sailed to South Africa on 15 August 1896 for a three-month visit to Cape Town and Johannesburg. 'Just Goodbye and all love to you, till I come back in November,' he wrote to his mother from Southampton.[27] Anthony Eden was born on 12 June 1897. His mother was largely at Windlestone the preceding autumn.[28]

Anthony Eden's birth was registered in the Sub District of Bishop Auckland on 23 July 1897, his parents correctly named on the birth certificate as William Eden, Baronet, and Sybil Frances Eden, formerly Grey. The infant was baptised on 4 September in the Parish of Coundon by the Rev J. J. Richmond.[29]

From his mother, an elegant society beauty, not over-cautious in financial matters, Eden inherited his charm and 'handsome being'. Sybil Eden, who

had many of the characteristics of Lady Randolph Churchill in that she
lived for the present, had a hectic schedule of engagements, travelled
widely and lived beyond her means. Her favourite was the youngest-born,
Nicholas, while Sir William's was the second-eldest boy, Tim. Marjorie
and Anthony felt 'left out', which was why they became so close. The
conventional, fulsome phrases of Eden's prolific correspondence with his
mother disguise the fact that the relationship was actually at one remove.
Nevertheless, as he grew up, the young Anthony was solicitous towards his
mother's sensibilities, and proud, when she visited him at school, of her
undoubted glamour. He had an intuitive sense of what concerned or
disturbed her, as when he wrote to her in June 1913:

> I was afraid George Wyndham's death would be a dreadful shock to you.
> It certainly does seem a great shame. There is a good notice about him in
> the [Eton College] Chronicle which I will send you.[30]

It is not clear when Eden became aware of the rumours that Wyndham
might have been his father, but his later diaries and letters are punctuated
with references to him, even twenty years after Wyndham's death. 'Dined
at Grillions,' he noted in his diary on 23 March 1932, when he sat
next to St John Brodrick, one of the original figures in the coterie of
'The Souls'. 'St John told me a good story of Curzon's record of an
attempt to induce Salisbury to give his – St John's job – Under Sec. at
W[ar] O[ffice] to George Wyndham when Curzon went to India.
Salisbury showed every sign of boredom. When Curzon began to
perorate, Salisbury began to shake ominously & finally the single phrase:
"I don't like poets"!'[31]

Anthony Eden was devoted to his younger brother, Nicholas, and close to
his sister, Marjorie, who, at ten years his senior, proved a protective shield
against the unpredictable whims of his eccentric parents. When she
married Guy Brooke, later the 6th Earl of Warwick, in 1909 it was a
turning point in his childhood.

Eden's childhood proved a strange one, a mixture of comfort and
anxiety. He played childhood games and sports because his brothers did,
rather than from any real liking for them, though he was a keen supporter
of Sunderland FC. He seemed more fond of his favourite pony, Tom Tit,
than of his older brothers. He was a loner, a characteristic of his later life,
and spent hours cultivating his own little garden, which contributed to his
often dishevelled appearance. 'He was certainly not Britain's best-dressed
boy,' his mother wrote. 'He was quite careless of his clothes as a boy. He
always seemed to be tumbling out of them.'[32] This was very much in
contrast to his later days when it was said that haberdashers swooned as

he approached their establishments, and he was regularly acclaimed as Britain's most elegant politician.*

Awakening spiritual feelings came through his pantheistic love of nature, not organised religion. Although his mother was a devout Anglican, his father was self-consciously atheistic, and Eden inclined to the views of his father. Religion was never a powerful element in his life. Its political consequences, not only in Ireland, he always approached with caution, once writing on a memorandum regarding the Vatican during the Second World War, 'These religious ideas are apt to raise many complexities.'³³ He loved the beauty of Windlestone and admired from afar the stream of glamorous and exotic figures who passed through its doors. A vivid description of Windlestone in its social heyday can be found in Violet Asquith's diary. Anthony Eden was eight years old when Violet was in the house party in October 1905:

> This place is very lovely – like an enormous Easton Grey without the river. Built in nice brown stone, pure Italian with Gothic pillars and balustrades à clair and round all a green stretch of park full of elms and beeches. Frosty mornings and cawing rooks and over all a smell of damp ribes and falling leaves ... Sir William gallant and not chary of bad language. Lady Eden a dream of loveliness, arranging everything, patiently worried.³⁴

As a young boy, Eden countless times saw from the staircase elegantly dressed guests processing to dinner. The guest lists contained some of the most famous society figures of the day. Eden liked the outgoing and eccentric figures, people such as the celebrated actress, Mrs Patrick Campbell, who entered the names of her Pekinese in the visitors' book, and whose thespian allure awakened in him a love of theatre. Amateur dramatics became a feature of life at Windlestone. The atmosphere was not unlike that in the Bertram household in Jane Austen's *Mansfield Park*, in which a performance of *Lovers' Vows* gives impromptu possibilities for vicarious and innocent flirtations. As Eden grew older he often took a part, including the role of Jack Worthing in Oscar Wilde's *The Importance of Being Earnest*.

Although Eden was surrounded by beauty at Windlestone, he also experienced childhood fears. In a memorable passage in his unpublished autobiographical jottings, he recollected, not entirely in tranquillity, his apprehensions:

> Most of us have, I suppose, a childhood memory of a haunting fear. In the evenings when we were summoned before the grown ups in the East

---

* It was said that even his pyjamas were well-cut and double-breasted.

Hall after our nursery tea, standing uncertainly on one leg and then the other, I would take refuge hurriedly with my mother, who was generally pouring out tea, or my sister Marjorie, or any other guest I knew well enough. But I dreaded the command to go to bed, not because I preferred life downstairs to the nursery or schoolroom, I had no strong feelings about that, but because of what lay on my way. The main staircase out of the East Hall, a handsome combination of oak treads and mahogany balustrade, branched at the half-way mark, the left-hand flight leading to a landing from which a heavy baize door admitted a small boy to the nursery wing. The journey would have been easy enough, but on the landing, at the head of the stairs, hung a picture which I hated to pass. I was not sure what it represented, but it seemed to be a collection of rich stuffs and plate, game and jewels, dominated by a dimly-lit and glistening ogre's head. As I climbed the stairs, this creepy, grasping centrepiece was ready to seize me in its toils. The spell was broken only by stages. A dead hare, when identified, brought some comfort, but it was a long time before I dared to analyse this sumptuous still-life, for I never passed that way by day. Childhood's fears have a strangely haunting quality, more enduring than any sudden turn of panic in battle.[35]

As the fourth child (and third son) of notably spendthrift parents, the rights of primogeniture ensured that Eden would have to make his own way in the world. He was brought up in a spacious house at the heart of a great park, but 'the heir and the spare' were both already in place. Eden's thoughts about his family home remained surprisingly objective. 'I was very fond of Windlestone,' he later wrote. 'As I knew it would never be mine, my affection was not possessive.'[36]*

Eden was familiar from his earliest years with the need for a career, and his boyish letters to Marjorie are full of references to possible choices. For a long time, the Regular Army and the Diplomatic Service were the two front-runners, until in January 1919, while waiting for demobilisation, he revealed to his sister that his true ambition was to follow a political career and, if possible, to become Foreign Secretary.[37]

Money remained a constant worry in Eden's life. One of the first objects of his romantic feelings was Sybil Fitzroy, daughter of the Earl of Southampton and a frequent guest of his mother at Windlestone, when Eden recorded in his diary that she 'looked very pretty'. Lest he became too attached, his father one day reminded him that he was without prospects. Poignantly, Eden later added in his diary, 'Father told me she would have married me if I were not a younger son!'[38]

---

*As it happened, Windlestone eventually had to be sold. His mother's extravagancies led to the disposal of the estate in 1936, a painful process which he believed could have been averted if his brother Tim had taken more professional advice. (The agent expressed the wish that Anthony Eden had been in charge.)

His status as a younger son was brought home to him when he went away to his preparatory school, Sandroyd, in Cobham, in April 1907. His elder brother Timothy was already at the school, and Anthony was always listed in the Sandroyd divisions as 'Eden, R. A., mi', a process of differentiation repeated at Eton when luggage labels and lists reinforced his subordinate place in the family hierarchy.

Sandroyd School took its name from the home of the Rev. L. H. Wellesley Wesley, who founded it in 1888 as a small coaching establishment for the sons of friends who were planning to go on to Eton. In 1895, on Wesley's marriage, the business was taken over by Mr Wilson and Mr Hornby as joint headmasters and moved to extensive premises at Cobham. Set in forty Surrey acres, the school, unusually for the time, possessed an indoor heated swimming-pool (a place of repeated humiliation for Eden), a nine-hole golf course and two squash courts.[39] The appropriately emboldening school motto was *Niti est nitere* (To strive is to shine) and the tone of the school magazine made it clear that Eton was the expected destination of Sandroydians, who were 'Unionists to a man and almost to a boy.'[40]

Anthony did not see much of Timothy at Sandroyd. They were four years apart in age, and by schoolboy custom that was an unbridgeable gap. Anthony had companions of his own age, but he made no enduring friendships. He suffered from undiagnosed illnesses that caused him to miss much school work. When his mother arrived unexpectedly with news of his sister's engagement to Guy Brooke, she had to seek him out in the school sanatorium, where he was confined with measles. In what must have been mortifying for a ten-year-old schoolboy, Eden Minor was named in the school magazine after his first term as 'one of four boys unable to swim two lengths' in the school pool.[41] He was a studious schoolboy, rather than an athletic one. 'I have taken to chess and I like it very much,' he wrote to his mother in October 1909.[42] The next month, he wrote, 'I am trying hard to get some prizes this term, and I won't give up without a struggle.'[43] Nor did he. The year of 1910 was one of quiet academic triumph, when he won prizes, initially for Latin prose, and then for maths, history and French. Languages were always one of Eden's strong points. Between them the family spoke fourteen languages, and, as Sybil Eden recorded, once on the train travelling north a guard spoke to them at York in a very broad Yorkshire dialect. After he had gone, the young Anthony asked in all seriousness and with a deep sigh, 'Have we got to learn another language?'[44]

By the standards of the time, Lady Eden was a dutiful parent, taking a keen interest in the school. Unlike Sir William, she often visited Sandroyd, especially for the big social events such as the Christmas Supper Night.

Lists of guests, in strict order of social importance, were published in the school's December magazine. In all Anthony's years at Sandroyd, Lady Eden's name was at the head of the list. 'I can still remember the thrill of pride I felt on supper-nights at Sandroyd,' recalled Eden, 'when my mother would sweep in on the arm of one of the headmasters, truly beautiful.'[45]

On his eleventh birthday, his mother wrote:

> My darling Anthony,
> 11 years old!! How time is flying. I can scarcely believe you are growing up so fast & that I shall soon have 3 *big* sons to take care of me. God bless you Darling & help you to grow into a *good* man, always ready to help others. I want all my boys to be loved & respected . . . I am so glad you are having a happy time. I shall think of you on your birthday – I do hope it will be a lovely fine day so that you will have a successful Tea party.[46]

By the age of eleven, the young Eden's interest in politics was already discernible. Travelling north by train, he would look out of the window and tell his mother which constituency they were passing through, the name of the local member and details of the majority.[47] He first attended a parliamentary count in 1910 in the neighbouring Bishop Auckland constituency. The Labour candidate, who came a poor third, declared when the results were announced, 'One day Labour will win.'[48]

Eden's first reference to what was to be his life's work came in a letter of April 1910 (at a time when the House of Lords crisis was dominant in political conversation.) 'I am reading *Politics and Politicians*. It is very interesting.'[49]

Eden left Sandroyd in December 1910. His last term was his happiest, because his beloved younger brother Nicholas had arrived. 'Anthony Eden has taken the Middle IVth at Eton', read his valedictory notice in *The Sandroydian*, 'but he has hardly reached the standard of his brother, T.C., but principally owing to interruptions in his work. Happily, the family will still be represented at Sandroyd after his departure.'[50] It was hardly a ringing endorsement. In later life, Eden had few contacts with the school (he was never a 'professional' old boy) and, significantly, neither of his own sons was educated there. His most enduring Sandroyd memory was that seventy-two of his contemporaries were killed in the Great War, including Nicholas, whose name is engraved on the war memorial that stands today outside the school chapel at Rushmore. Eden's own name is also listed – among the many who served and survived.

Anthony Eden arrived at Eton in January 1911, and was placed in the house of E. L. ('Jelly') Churchill.[51] More than in other boarding schools, the choice of a house at Eton, the compatibility of its ethos and the relations (easy or otherwise) with the housemaster were crucial for a boy's career, and often stamped a pupil for life. Eden was fortunate in that the family tradition led him to 'Jelly' Churchill's house. The only downside was the mixed blessing of being his elder brother's fag. 'Jelly' Churchill was an outstanding figure in the Eton of his day and the first great influence on Anthony Eden's life. Not only did he take immense care, writing perceptive and lengthy letters to Lady Eden about any problems that arose, but he awakened in the young Anthony the feeling that he might be able to achieve something noteworthy in life, despite not being a schoolboy 'star'. 'He was sound old oak throughout,' wrote a later Eton housemaster of 'Jelly' Churchill. 'To be immensely high and even rigid principled, inflexible, and kind hearted ought not to be a rare combination, but somehow it is. No one was ever more respected and indeed loved.'[52]

Although Eden attended Eton in the 'golden era', bounded by Fowler's match[53] and the outbreak of the Great War, he was never one of its golden boys. Less than six years earlier, a notable quartet of Etonians – Gladstone, Salisbury, Rosebery and Balfour (the first three Christ Church men, as Eden was to be) – had come to the end of a twenty-five year span as Prime Minister, bringing to seventeen the number of Etonians to have held the post. Few could have forecast in January 1911 that the rather shy, gangly boy from Rushyford would be the next (and eighteenth) Etonian Prime Minister. That honour would have seemed more likely to have fallen to Eden's contemporary at Eton (and later Christ Church), Victor Cazalet, a future Conservative colleague in the House of Commons. All the glittering prizes fell into Cazalet's lap at Eton (though, ironically, he loathed the place) and he ended his career as President of Pop, the self-electing oligarchy who were the true rulers of Eton. No lesser a personage than Lord Curzon, the former Viceroy of India, wrote to Cazalet to tell him that 'no matter what position you have in life, you'll never hold a prouder position than that'.[54] Eden never came within a mile of being elected to Pop – he was not that kind of Etonian – but, as at Sandroyd, ploughed a solitary and eventually productive furrow that 'Jelly' Churchill respected as one way of establishing integrity and fulfilment. For 'Jelly' Churchill 'pressing on' regardless of setbacks was the key thing. Once, when his Queen was captured in a game of chess, 'Jelly' merely said after a long pause, 'Yes, I'm glad she's gone; she was rather in the way.'[55]

As well as Victor Cazalet, Eden's generation included his future parliamentary colleagues Robert Boothby, Bobbety Cranborne (later Lord Salisbury) and Oliver Lyttelton. Although Cranborne was later to be one of Eden's closest friends in politics, their friendship did not blossom at school. As at Sandroyd, Eden did not make many friendships at Eton. One of the exceptions was in the same house: Henry Segrave, future holder of the world land- and water-speed records. Both boys were in the Middle Fourth; another point of contact was that Segrave had been born in Baltimore, a place of note in the Eden family history. Eden was greatly saddened when Segrave died on Lake Windermere in June 1930 while breaking the world water-speed record.

Eden continued to be fascinated by politics and his boyish essays were forthright. At fifteen he wrote of Charles James Fox, one of his Etonian predecessors as Foreign Secretary: 'Fox was what I call an awful blackguard, he joined North simply to keep in office and to put money into his pocket.'[56]

He also began taking part in house debates, where he proved a persuasive advocate for what might have seemed, in the Eton context of the day, forlorn causes. Eden challenged the orthodoxies of his contemporaries. In one of his early debates he discussed Socialism and, with his knowledge of County Durham (not to mention the 1910 Election at Bishop Auckland), explained why this creed would be a political force in the years to come. On 11 October 1913 the Society met to discuss whether Canada or Australia was the more valuable British possession. 'Mr Eden opened in favour of Canada,' record the minutes. Eden showed a detailed grasp of Canada's geographical benefits, and technical knowledge of the country's infrastructure, as well as the economics of railways, forestry and fishing, which demonstrated careful preparation and research. Not surprisingly, 'An even debate ended in Mr Eden's victory.' Other subjects included the political situation in South Africa and Russia, and in November 1914 the subject was whether native troops should be allowed to fight in Europe. Eden showed real passion and historical knowledge of how Clive and Warren Hastings employed native soldiers. 'It would be folly and incredible ingratitude,' he concluded, 'had our government listened to those canting hypocrites who disdain to fight beside a man because he is not of their own colour.' Again Eden's speech swung the vote his way.[57]

His growing seriousness was also shown by his triumph in the Brinckman Divinity Prize, one of the few events in his schooldays, his mother recorded, that created a great stir in the family, largely because of their astonishment. Sir William was sarcastically dismissive, not regarding a religious award as being of any worth, whereas Anthony had been glad to win a prize of any kind. This maturity was also evident in the summer half of 1912, when there was trouble in 'Jelly' Churchill's house regarding a junior boy who was wrongly suspected of sneaking about 'moral matters'. The boy was subsequently ostracised, especially as his tormentor was expelled. Eden was prominent among those who wanted to set things right, as 'Jelly' Churchill explained to Sybil Eden in July 1912 with Eden's reports:

> I have observed – without saying anything – that one of the first and most persistent in setting this boy [the suspected sneak] at his ease, he being a highly strung, nervous boy in some ways, though with lots of pluck about danger, was Anthony. And this means that he is on the right side himself, and not afraid of showing it, as just at the start boys out of the house got hold of the wrong idea about all the business and had to be told they were fools by some of my bigger Lower Boys. So at present he is a son of whom you may be quite proud.[58]

In his report of July 1913, 'Jelly' Churchill wrote, 'He has quite ceased to be petulant or childish, and is getting much more thoughtful and steady.'[59]

As at Sandroyd, Eden preferred individual sports, and in Eton parlance he became a Wet Bob, spending hours on the Thames, where he became an increasingly accomplished oarsman. In fact he was on the river when he heard news of the assassination of Archduke Ferdinand of Austria at Sarajevo in June 1914. 'Murder of Austrian Archduke has caused rather a sensation,' he recorded in his diary. 'Things looking rather black ... it looks like an European war.' He felt the response, particularly in Chapel, to be inadequate. 'Have forgotten who preached. Some weird Bishop.' And where were the politicians who would resolve the increasingly entangled diplomatic situation? Joseph Chamberlain died four days later. 'He was the last great figure in English politics. There is now no one left deserving the name "great".'[60]

Eton life continued in its unhurried way. In July 1914, 38,000 spectators (Eden and his family among them) thronged Lord's for the two-day Eton–Harrow cricket match. At the start of the Michaelmas Half, the chronicler of 'Jelly' Churchill's *House Book* recorded that 'everything is much the same as ever'.[61]

But then came the first obituaries. Eden's eldest brother, John (Jack), was killed near Ypres on 17 October.

Eden's last year at Eton was spent under the shadow of war; 180 boys, and many members of staff, had left to take up commissions, and Eden was increasingly impatient to join them. More than 1,100 Etonians were to be killed in the next four years on active service, over 20 per cent of those who volunteered. Among Eden's own age group, the figure was nearer 30 per cent.[62]

In March 1915 Eden was on the fringe of controversy. His headmaster was the Revd Edward Lyttelton,[63] a noted cricketer, who once confessed that he could never walk down the nave of a church without wondering whether it would take spin. It was Lyttelton who preached a sermon at St Margaret's, Westminster, which (rather in the manner of Archbishop Runcie's St Paul's sermon after the Falklands War in 1982) was seen by some as too conciliatory towards the enemy. The great difference in 1915 – the year of Gallipoli – was that the war was then at an unresolved and critical stage. Calls were made nationally for Lyttelton (who, it was remembered, had also been pro-Boer during the South African war) to be sacked as Headmaster. Eden was among those Etonians, led by Victor Cazalet, who were outraged that Lyttelton's patriotism should have been called into question, and letters of support were sent.

For his part, Lyttelton did all he could to aid those senior boys who now sought commissions. 'Jelly' Churchill, however, was very much against Eden going to the front at this stage, as he explained to Lady Eden in June 1915:

> The headmaster had an interview with two of the most prominent war office officials on June 1st. They repeated what Lord Kitchener [Secretary of State for War since 5 August 1914] said last October. They do not want the training of subalterns accelerated; they do not want any boys sent to France (except in rare cases of precocious physical and mental development) before they are 19. Anthony is not precocious at all. To send him out to stand a winter campaign at 18 and a half seems to me unfair to him – & useless to the country – nay, worse than useless for it will but add one to the number who need looking after.[64]

But Eden persuaded his mother to let him leave at the end of the summer half. Eton had brought him on, maturing him beyond recognition from his Sandroyd days, and the priorities were now different. The world beyond Windsor beckoned, as 'Jelly' Churchill found out abruptly on one of his house rounds:

> 'You'll stroke our House Four next year,' Churchill announced peremptorily.
> 'But sir, haven't you read a letter from my mother?' asked Eden. 'Because she told me she'd write to you to say that I was leaving.'
> 'Leaving – What are you leaving for?' asked Jelly Churchill.
> 'For the war, sir,' replied Eden.
> 'Oh, you fool, you fool. You won't be any use in the war. You might be some use in the House Four.'[65]

Eden could have stayed at school – but he unhesitatingly chose war.

Postscript: the Great War Generation

Eden was born into a generation that was to leave a marked impression on world history, sometimes malign, sometimes fruitful. Those born within five years of Eden included both titans and tyrants, and there were many who faced the challenges he did, and who were to be among the foremost shapers of the twentieth century. The unifying factor was that all of them were influenced and shaped by the events of the 1914–18 war.

Among Eden's British contemporaries were two future monarchs, Edward VIII (born 1894), and George VI (1895), as well as their cousin, Earl Mountbatten (1900), with whom Eden was to clash over Suez. Among his native political contemporaries were Oliver Lyttelton (1893), Harold Macmillan (1894), Oswald Mosley (1896), Aneurin Bevan (1897) and R. A. Butler (1902).

For Eden, relations with America were to play a complex part in his career. He drew lessons from history by analogy, perhaps too often; but perceptively he once said that the United States and Britain were not dissimilar to Austria and England in 1815, in that the United States had taken the place of England, and England had taken the place of Austria.[66] The Americans of Eden's generation play a massive part in his story.

Although the US Secretary of State, with whom he was to have his most strenuous disagreements, John Foster Dulles (born 1888), was considerably older than Eden, two American Secretaries of State were his near contemporaries – Dean Acheson (1893) and Edward Stettinius, Jr (1900). With the latter, whom he dominated, he forged the United Nations, whose first Secretary-General (a post that could have been Eden's for the asking) was the Norwegian politician, Trygve Lie (1896).

Future national leaders among his contemporaries include General Franco (1892), Haile Selassie (1892), Josip Tito (1892), Sidney Holland (1893), Robert Menzies (1894), Nikita Khrushchev (1894), Nikolai Bulganin (1895), John Diefenbaker (1895), Chou En-lai (1898), Solomon Bandaranaike (1899), his exact contemporary at Christ Church, Georges Bidault (1899), Emperor Hirohito (1901) and Mohammed Neguib (1901). Among other contemporaries are Hermann Goering (1893), Joachim von Ribbentrop (1893), Walter Ulbricht (1893), Krishna Menon (1897), and the diplomat Gladwyn Jebb (1900). Roger Makins (Lord Sherfield) and Harold Caccia, also diplomatic figures of considerable importance in Eden's career (Caccia was also one of his pre-war private secretaries), were of a slightly younger generation, born in 1904 and 1905 respectively. Presidents de Gaulle and Eisenhower, both born in 1890 – although slightly older than Eden – were of the same decade and later two of the figures most dramatically involved in Eden's story. Hitler (1889) was eight years Eden's senior. Of the major figures in Eden's political life, only President Nasser (1918) was of a significantly younger generation.

CHAPTER TWO

In the Ranks of Death

1915–19

We must all do our share.

Anthony Eden, 20 October 1914

I have done one braver thing
Than all the Worthies did,
And yet a braver thence doth spring,
Which is, to keep that hid.

John Donne, *The Undertaking*

Eden was not a particularly religious man. The memory of the institutionalised services in College Chapel at Eton, where he had heard the 'weird Bishop', had long ago dissipated any such interest. 'Usual dull service,' he had written in his diary on 5 February 1913. The pattern was repeated in the holidays. 'Managed with some difficulty to go to Holy Communion,' he wrote on New Year's Day 1914, a reference to his doctrinal reserve, not the earliness of the hour.[1] But his spiritual side remained strong, especially through his love of nature and art, and was brought into sharp focus by the experience of war. He later wrote of the deeper feelings he had experienced on the eve of conflict:

> We each had, I suppose, our form of weakness. Some might try to strike a bargain: (in the form of) if Almighty God you will do this for me, I will promise reform, to obey the Commandments scrupulously, or whatever the offer might be. For me the prayer was always at heart the same: Please God if I am to be hit let me be slightly wounded or killed, but not mutilated. I cannot explain what prompted this dread of the loss of limbs or other mutilation for life. To be killed did not seem all that bad. After Jack and Nicholas [killed in 1914 and 1916 respectively] and so many young friends, perhaps it was that death in battle seemed if not normal at least acceptable . . . but at least many had gone that way before and it did not seem a business to make such a fuss about, especially if it was quick and with little suffering, but to be mutilated for life, with all that this conjured up for me, I just had not the courage to face it.[2]

News of the death of his brother Jack had come to him at Eton. 'M'tutor told me after twelve that Jack had beeen killed in action probably at dawn on Sunday morning. Poor Mummie she will feel it dreadfully.'[3]

He wrote to her at once. 'M'Tutor has just told me. How dreadful for you. I will do what I can and whatever you want of course.' Echoing *Henry V*, he continued, 'we must all do our share and the greater the share the greater the honour if it is nobly borne'. Three days later he wrote again. 'As we all must die some day why not now by the most honourable way possible, the way that opens the gates of Paradise – the soldier's death?'[4] It was an attitude that encapsulated the distinctive mood of the time, and the courage Eden would later show himself.

His sympathies were not only for his mother, but also for Pamela Fitzgerald, whose engagement to Jack had been the cause of a rift between Sir William Eden and his eldest son, largely on financial grounds. At Jack's memorial service at Windlestone, Eden was captivated by Pamela's beauty. He was deeply shocked when his mother said that Anthony and Pamela would now be able to flirt. Although she also died very young (in 1918), Pamela's was a memory and presence that never left him, as the special girl who would have married Jack, had they both lived.

'I pray all my boys will consider all their lives "Duty First",' Lady Eden had written to Anthony after Jack's death.[5] All of them did. Tim had been in Germany when war broke out on 4 August and, as an alien, had been interned in a concentration camp (a term as yet without its later historical resonance) at Ruhleben, near Berlin. He spent the next two years in captivity, before being released in an exchange of prisoners, after which he spent the latter part of the war as a Lieutenant in the Yorkshire Light Infantry. Eden's brother-in-law, Guy Brooke, was serving in the Warwickshire Royal Horse Artillery, and his sister Marjorie became a nurse. Later Lady Eden, widowed on 20 February 1915, was to turn Windlestone into a convalescent hospital. Nicholas, the youngest son, was at the Royal Naval College at Dartmouth and shortly to go to sea. The choice of a regiment was, therefore, for Anthony a matter of prime urgency in his last months at Eton.

His exemplar was his uncle, Robin Grey, a cousin of the Foreign Secretary, Sir Edward Grey, of whom eager, boyish Eden, who had a low opinion of the wartime Cabinet, had written approvingly, 'I hear that Winston Churchill and Sir Edward Grey were the only members of the Cabinet in favour of going to war.'[6] A glamorous and handsome figure of great vivacity, Robin Grey, who served in the fledgling Royal Flying Corps, would not have been out of place in a John Buchan novel, where he would have been a lively companion for Mr Standfast. Eden admired his uncle immensely. When the Liberal MP for Bishop Auckland, Sir Henry Havelock-Allan, announced he was standing down, Eden recorded in his diary, 'Cheers! Good riddance of bad rubbish. Vote for Robin!'[7] In 1916 Robin Grey's plane was shot down. He was captured and imprisoned, and although he escaped, was later recaptured. As a cousin of the British Foreign Secretary, he was placed in closely guarded solitary confinement, and thus he spent the rest of his war.

Marjorie became Anthony's main support in seeking a regiment, suggesting at first Guy Brooke's Warwickshire Royal Horse Artillery. When this did not work out (Eden was diagnosed with weak eyesight), she approached her uncle by marriage, Sidney Greville, in the hope that her brother might be commissioned into the Grenadier Guards. In May 1915, as the Dardanelles operation encountered fresh difficulties, Eden wrote to his mother: 'I think the war looks very bad, and even if the Americans do come in (which I don't for a minute think they will do) I cannot see of what use they can be.' He outlined his continued difficulties in finding a suitable regiment (to the relief of his mother), but still hoped 'to get a commission in some regiment of Guards like the Coldstream, Grenadiers, etc'.[8] The problem again was his poor eyesight; it was not until August 1915 that he could report any progress, and then through an unexpected development.

Kitchener, the Secretary of State for War since August 1914, had achieved spectacular success with his recruiting drive ('If not a great man, at least a very good poster,' commented the Prime Minister's wife, Margot Asquith).[9] He now sought to form a series of Yeomanry Regiments (in some cases reviving existing structures) and encouraged recruitment by guaranteeing that all those from one area would stay together. Although this was well intentioned, the downside came when regiments suffered horrific losses, for then localised communities were bereft of a whole concentrated generation of their young men.

The Earl of Feversham, commanding officer of the Yorkshire Hussars, was appointed to take charge of the Northern Command, and at once set about raising what became the 21st Battalion the Yeoman Rifles, of the King's Royal Rifle Corps (Sixtieth Rifles). For Eden, this was a stroke of luck. Charlie Feversham was married to Guy Brooke's sister, Marjorie ('Queenie') Greville. The two Marjories – Lady Feversham and Eden's sister – had been friends for years, and Eden's cause now had influential advocacy. In August 1915 he received a letter from Charlie Feversham, asking if he would recruit in County Durham for the Yeoman Rifles. As Eden had yet to attain his majority (twenty-one in those days), Charlie Feversham and Queenie Greville came to Windlestone to complete the formalities with Sybil Eden. Shortly afterwards Eden started work in County Durham (his first recruit was from a local farm, Windlestone Grange, and many others came from an agricultural background). He underwent medical tests, and on 30 September 1915 was commissioned as a temporary Lieutenant. So began Eden's lifelong connection with the King's Royal Rifle Corps, after which he was always proud to call himself 'a Rifleman'.[10]

He knew his regiment's history intimately and kept records of its achievements and setbacks, as well as of his own military service. The regiment had been raised in 1755. Its military record spanned the Indian Mutiny, Wellington's campaigns in the Peninsula, and the defence of Ladysmith during the Boer War. Eden always referred to the 'KRRC' as 'our gallant Regiment.'[11]

Training took place at Duncombe Park, the Feversham family home.[12] This had a bucolic air. Feversham decided that the best way to practise an advance in open order across the fields was towards a herd of deer that he wanted to move from the Fallow Deer Park to the Red Deer Park. All went well until the deer counter-attacked and scattered their assailants.[13]

In December, Eden underwent officers' training at Woodside, near Ipswich, a far tougher assignment, which he was relieved to complete successfully. His interest in political life, particularly the emerging Labour movement, continued and he attended meetings whenever he could spare the time. Back at Windlestone, he went with his sister Marjorie to hear the Trade Union Leader Ben Tillett speaking in Bishop Auckland. As one of the founding fathers of the Independent Labour Party in 1893, and of the Labour Party at the turn of the century, Tillett was to prove a pivotal figure in radical politics. He was also, unlike some of his colleagues, a fierce advocate for the war effort. Eden was unequivocal in his admiration for this stance. 'He was quite wonderful, and he spoke very straight.'[14]

In the Yeoman Rifles, Eden much admired the enthusiasm of Reg Park and his friend Norman Carmichael, corporals and later sergeants in Numbers 9 and 10 Platoons respectively, and their interest in current affairs. From them he learned much about the attitudes of working people, not only in Northumberland, and about class divisions in society, sharing with them hopes for a better future when the war was over. Reg Park was to be killed in action, but Norman Carmichael remained a lifelong friend of Eden's, and was one of those who read the typescript of *Another World* in 1975, adding his reminiscences to Eden's own. The portrait of Lord Feversham in *Another World* owed much to Carmichael's memories, as well as Eden's:

> Charlie Feversham was of middle-height, thick-set and with a moustache which today would be called bristling. The general effect could be intimidating, but he was a popular commanding officer with the riflemen, not least because he was essentially a countryman and so were many of them. He was not a professional soldier as was Foljambe, his second-in-command, but he had a good brain and enough experience to adapt himself to his new tasks as an infantryman. Despite which he was happiest on a horse and looked his best there.[15]

Lt-Col. the Hon. Gerald Foljambe was also a countryman, a shrewd judge of character and was trusted implicitly by his subordinates. After Feversham's death in action, he was to assume command of the regiment. He often railed against the inefficiency of military bureaucracy, especially when the safety of his men was compromised, and Eden judged him the most professional of all the senior officers he served.

After Duncombe Park and Woodside, the regiment moved to North Camp, Aldershot, for final training before embarkation. There were long hours and unexpected dangers, the worst of which occurred on 10 December 1915 when a controlled explosion went badly wrong. Eden narrowly missed being hit and two of the men were severely injured. 'We discovered that they had both been hit by different pieces of iron flung down from where the explosion occurred at least 150 yds away,' Eden wrote in a matter-of-fact way to his mother.[16]

'Thank God 1915 is coming to an end at last,' Eden wrote to his mother on New Year's Eve. 'What a ghastly year!'[17] The New Year, though, was to bring a bitter harvest.

'I have just received your letter saying that Nicholas has gone to join his ship,' Eden wrote to his mother on 6 January. 'He will no doubt be very happy and he is very lucky to get his first service during the war.'[18] Admiral Beatty took a personal interest in Nicholas's progress. For the young man, everything was still a great adventure. Nicholas's letters home from HMS *Indefatigable* almost had the ring of a midshipman's life during the Napoleonic Wars. 'During the night watches I have to go around kicking the gun crews awake,' he wrote to his mother. 'Me a boy of fifteen!'[19] He told his sister, 'I hope to get some more leave, about six days, in September or thereabouts. But before that I hope the Germans will have summoned up courage enough to try conclusions with us. It ought to be a good fight, I think.'[20] It was the last letter he wrote.

In March 1916 came news that Anthony's brother Tim was to be freed from his camp in Ruhleben. 'What splendid news about Tim!' Eden wrote to his mother. 'So he is going to be exchanged at last!'[21] Tim now returned to Windlestone as owner of the estates, 8th Baronet of West Auckland and 6th of Maryland. Stewardship was a task for which he had no earlier expectation or preparation, and in any case he was soon serving abroad, his captors having failed to include in his release documents the normal clause excluding repatriated soliders from becoming combatants again for a specified time.

Difficulties on the western front and military stalemate had led to the recall of Sir John French in 1915, and his replacement as Commander-in-Chief of the British forces by Sir Douglas Haig, whose name was to be synonymous with the trench warfare of the next three years. Eden's real war was about to begin. The 21st Battalion of the King's Royal Rifles left Aldershot and entrained at Farnborough Station on 5 May 1916. They sailed from Southampton for France at 7 p.m. on the SS *Marguerite*. Their ultimate destination was the small Belgian village of Ploegsteert, popularly known to the British soldiers as 'Plug Street'. Earlier in the year, Churchill had commanded the 6th Royal Scots Fusiliers in the same zone. Ploegsteert Wood, where Eden first saw action with Number 9 Platoon, was to the east of the village and just south of the Ypres salient, which jutted out into British-held territory. Not unlike the surroundings of Duncombe Park, the countryside reminded many of home. One of Eden's young farmer recruits was asked on sentry duty if he saw anything. 'Aye,' he said 'I see a bloody good field of hay going to waste.'[22]

But military cemeteries were already appearing by the roadside as the battalion dug in for its routine of trench warfare, 'two weeks in the line, one in support and one in reserve and all in the wood.'[23] Eden's first thought when the inevitable casualties came was whether they could be sent to the hospital at Windlestone.

He returned to Windlestone briefly in early 1917:

> Despite the comparative peace of Windlestone and my joy at being home again, on some days everything seemed impregnated with the war even during that first leave. I would sometimes stand at the south fence and look at the elm tree which my father had painted so often, and across to a rolling countryside, and wonder if I could ever again see them free from the memory of those other shell-torn trees and ravaged fields with their torn wire and heaped and silent bodies.[24]

Three weeks after arriving in France, Eden was told that Nicholas was dead. Charlie Feversham gave him the details personally. On 31 May 1916, during the 'Battle of Jutland', the *Indefatigable* had been engaging the German battle-cruiser *von der Tann*, when it was hit at 4.02 p.m. by three eleven-inch shells, which penetrated the upper deck and exploded within the heart of the ship. Immediately the ship began to sink by the stern; as it foundered, the *Indefatigable* was hit again on 'A' turret. Within three minutes the ship had disappeared beneath the waves with the loss of more than 1,000 lives. Nicholas was just two months past his sixteenth birthday. The theme of the memorial service at Windlestone later in the year was 'Many waters cannot quench Love, neither can the floods drown it.'[25]

A desperate month in the fortunes of the war ensued. Six days after Jutland, the SS *Hampshire*, en route to Russia, went down after hitting a mine off Scapa Flow, with the loss of the majority on board, including Kitchener, the War Secretary. The first public hint of the tragedy before the news was officially announced was the sight of the War Office blinds being lowered. Though Margot Asquith, the Prime Minister's wife, thought that Providence must have been on the side of the Allies after all, most of the country was plunged into the deepest mourning for Kitchener. In the Second World War many of the commanders were killed in action, but Kitchener was the only principal figure to meet a violent end in the First World War. His successor was Lloyd George.

Then three weeks later, on 1 July, began the Battle of the Somme, with unimaginable losses on both sides. Edwin Montagu, the Chancellor of the Duchy of Lancaster, had suggested to Prime Minister Asquith that Lloyd George be appointed to the War Office, as he would then be held responsible for the inevitable disaster on the Somme.[26] As a cynical tactic for fending off the ambitious Welshman, it proved unsuccessful. Margot Asquith was more prescient; when she heard that Lloyd George was to be the new War Secretary, she foresaw that soon he would be Prime Minister: 'We are out. It is only a question of time when we shall have to leave Downing Street.'[27]

On 6 June 1916, the day that Kitchener's death was announced, Eden – still in deep shock over the loss of Nicholas – wrote to his sister, 'We are at present in the trenches and I have so much work to do, that I barely have time to think, but when one does have time, one naturally feels very lonely and depressed.'[28] Marjorie was the recipient of his deepest feelings. He told her that he dreaded coming back to England, as he knew that it was at Windlestone that he would miss Nicholas most.

By the autumn, Eden had sufficiently come to terms with his loss to contemplate home, though realistically he knew the battalion was in for a long haul. Reg Park, his sergeant, and one of his trusted friends, had been killed by shellfire. His successor was a regular soldier, Sergeant Bert Harrop, from Sheffield.

On 14 August 1916, Foljambe told Eden that divisional headquarters had decided to have a night attack on the German trench position at Ploegsteert, and that their sector had been chosen as offering the best chance of success. The aim of the raid was to identify the Germans (recent arrivals, it was suspected) and, if possible, capture the sentry, who could be heard on still nights. Eden took a small party with Sergeant Harrop across no-man's-land on a moonless night. As they set off, Major Foljambe said to Harrop, 'At all costs, Sergeant, do not let the enemy capture the young officer who is going over with you. That boy has a wonderful career before him.' In fact, it was Eden who saved Harrop's life. The German trenches were barely a hundred yards away and speed was of the essence.

The plan was to cut through the German wire, bomb the trench and then seize some identification from the sentry, dead or alive. But the Germans were vigilant and, although the progress across no-man's-land was initially swift, they were spotted. Within minutes the unmistakable patter of machine-gun fire bombarded the party. Eden ordered retreat, crawling back through the long grass. But Harrop was hit, and was bleeding profusely. Eden fixed a tourniquet, but knew that unless they could get a stretcher to Harrop before dawn, his sergeant was done for. A volunteer fetched a stretcher. 'Then came the difficult decision,' wrote Eden:

> We had only fifty yards to go, and even though we stooped, we would all four have to stand up to carry Harrop's stretcher. The longer we waited the better the chance of the night growing quieter, but the worse for Harrop and the more extended the risk for us all. I wanted to get it over with, and we did. To this day I do not know whether the enemy saw the stretcher and held his fire, or saw nothing in the flickering Verey lights.[29]

Harrop later recalled Eden's action:

> Everybody liked him and he was popularly known as 'The Boy'. After we had been in any heavy fighting Mr Eden would see that we were well provided for and made reasonably comfortable before he gave any thought to his own comfort . . . I owe my life to Mr Eden, who, as soon as he found I had not returned, at once set off back with two or three of the men and dragged me to safety. He knew just where I would be lying.

Harrop was then in hospital for two years, during which he underwent thirty-three operations. Eden never lost touch with him and even exchanged letters with him in the weeks leading up to his resignation as Foreign Secretary in February 1938, when the pressures on his time were nigh insupportable. For his part, Harrop gave Eden a gold penknife, which he always kept on his desk.[30]

For his act of bravery, Eden was recommended for the Military Cross. A citation followed, but initially nothing more. On 30 August, Eden wrote to his mother, omitting all mention of his heroics. 'Excellent news Rumania coming in. That should shorten this wicked war a bit. I *shall* be glad when it is all over and I am safe back in England . . . But I am afraid it is bound to be a slow business.'[31] So it proved. The next month the battalion was in action in a major new offensive on 15 September at Flers in the ongoing Battle of the Somme.

Charlie Feversham was at the head of the reconnoitring party in the furthest cornfields when he was struck down. 'The Colonel is killed,' wrote Eden to his sister the same day. 'Our company has suffered worst as far as I can make out.' Their losses totalled 127 fatalities, with many more wounded. 'The Colonel was wonderful by all accounts,' wrote Eden, 'and was killed rallying his men.'[32] Foljambe initially took over the command and the immediate consequence for Eden was that he was appointed Adjutant of the 21st Battalion, one of the youngest in the British Army, a post that he held until further promotion in July 1917. Although many of the casualties were recovered, Feversham had been in such an advanced position that his body lay near the German front line. Three weeks later, at the first opportunity, Eden went out with a party to locate and, if possible, bury their commander. He wrote to his sister:

> We have had a pretty hellish time I can tell you and I was never so glad to get away from anywhere. This morning I went out and had a look for Charlie's body, and with the help of a map reference given me by a gunner officer, I managed to find him. I took the ring off his finger and the locket, and I gave them to Foljambe who is sending them to Queenie.'[33]

As the battalion had suffered so many losses, its special Durham character vanished. Replacements were largely Londoners, whom Eden admired for their resilience, a characteristic needed as they all dug in for winter. 'It really is a horrible war,' he wrote to Marjorie in November. 'There goes a burst of shell, ours I think, I shall be glad when I never hear another of their beastly shrieks or see another burst!'[34]

Christmas greetings to Marjorie were muted, as memories of Nicholas and another dreadful year flooded in:

> Christmas Eve! What a way of spending it. It is a perfect day and quite mild. We are in the line and of course it is impossible to do anything except sit still and wish that the war was over. I think that the Bosch must be having a joyful day, as he is giving us quite an unnecessary number of Christmas presents this morning. But of course we are being equally generous ... Next year I hope that we shall all be able to spend Christmas at home. Another present from the Bosch just gone by!! This time last year we were both on leave together at Windlestone, and now ...[35]

At the beginning of 1917, Eden had a short spell of leave, before the next big push in Flanders. He saw his sister and brother-in-law, Guy Brooke, who was recovering from battle wounds. He sought out Charlie Feversham's mother, a poignant meeting. Windlestone had too many painful memories, and the atmosphere of London he found empty and shallow. It was a dispiriting time for a sensitive man who, though still only nineteen, was now old beyond his years.

He returned to find that Foljambe had been promoted, and a new commanding officer, Lt-Col. Talbot Jarvis, in place. In his previous posting Jarvis had shown that he was always determined that his officers and men should receive recognition for their bravery, and he resubmitted the recommendation of an award for Eden. News of Eden's MC came through in the week of his twentieth birthday. Jarvis wrote to Eden's mother on 16 June 1917:

> I just want to tell you what a very great pleasure it has been to work with your son as my Adjutant, he has worked so hard and has the Battalion so very much at heart that all ranks are delighted to hear that he has been given the Military Cross.
>
> I do trust he will come through the War safely and also that he will have a very successful career on the Staff [Eden had been offered an important post at Second Army Headquarters]. I admire him all the more because he could have gone before the attack but he wisely and magnificently refused to go.'[36]

When he was preparing his account of these years, *Another World*, Eden wrote to the Public Record Office in London for help over military records. He was particularly interested in what he called 'the British Army's brilliant victory in the period of trench warfare, the battle of Messines.'[37] For two years, General Sir Herbert Plumer, a commander whom Eden much admired, had been planning to drive the Germans off the Messines ridge, south of the Ypres salient. The strategic importance of the elevated ground meant that the Germans had control of the land in three directions, and until the ridge was seized there was no hope of further advance for the Allies. Plumer had the ridge comprehensively mined, and when the detonation took place at 3.10 a.m. on 7 June, the explosion could be heard by Lloyd George in Downing Street. The third Battle of Ypres had begun.

The King's Royal Rifle Corps was in the initial attack, Eden on the left flank as the mines exploded. For the next five hours he experienced some of the bitterest fighting of the war, as dawn broke on the most beautiful of June days. 'We have been giving the Germans a good doing,' Eden wrote to his sister on 8 June. 'We did very well and hundreds of Germans were killed and taken prisoner . . . The men were splendid.'[38]

The fighting continued for the battalion until 4 August, with another major offensive on 31 July. Such was their success in this operation that they were inspected personally by Field Marshal Sir Douglas Haig. George V sent a message of congratulation to Haig on a decisive victory. Contrary to Eden's earlier expectations, the first contingents of American servicemen were now arriving. The end, it seemed, was in sight. But the third Battle of Ypres still had months to run, and it was not until 7 November that the destroyed village of Passchendaele, which gave its name to the collective struggles, was occupied.

By this time Eden had accepted the promotion offered to him before the battle for Messines ridge, that of a temporary Captain and GSO (3) in the 58th Division, Second Army Headquarters, a post he held from 19 November 1917. He was now able to observe Sir Herbert Plumer's methods at close quarters. He held a higher opinion of Plumer than the politicians at home. 'Lloyd George has made a very stupid speech in the House, I see,' he wrote to his sister on 23 December. 'I wish they would muzzle . . . all those infernal politicians until after the war. My God, they are brutes and murderers, they make me see red at times.'[39]

A break from such frustration came when Eden was in Bruges and took the chance of visiting the Brussels Art Gallery, a foretaste of many such expeditions on the Continent in the early 1920s. Another staff posting under General Cator followed, before, in the spring of 1918, Eden was appointed to the 198th Infantry Brigade, as the youngest Brigade Major in the British Army. This appointment coincided with the last great push of the German Army, General Ludendorff's Offensive of 21 March. It was a desperate time for the Allies, a period later captured in R. C. Sherriff's play *Journey's End*, and one that had political, as well as military, consequences. On 9 April the Germans broke through between La Bassée and Armentières. Ploegsteert was retaken shortly afterwards – all that loss of life for nothing. 'The House of Commons seems to be more out of touch with the war than ever,' wrote Eden on 14 April. The contrast at this time between the men dying in the trenches and the Commons was one that Eden found intolerable. 'They seem to be the last people in the whole country to realise that this is the final struggle and that the fate of their own beastly skins hangs on the result.'[40]

As Ludendorff pushed westwards through territory once occupied by allied troops, questions were asked in the House of Commons about Haig's lack of reinforcements. Suspicions were voiced that Lloyd George had wilfully denied Haig what he wanted, so appalled had he been at the carnage in France. Major-General Sir Frederick Maurice, Director of Military Operations at the War Office, had written to the Press setting out his version of the figures, which differed from those supplied in Parliament by Lloyd George and Bonar Law, the Unionist [Conservative] leader.[41] Voting in the so-called Maurice Debate on 9 May, which was opened by the former Liberal Prime Minister, Herbert Asquith, later proved the benchmark of party allegiance in the 1918 General Election, a division of the ranks that was to have fatal consequences for the Liberal Party.

When the Maurice Debate took place, Eden was encamped by the River Oise, near La Fère, where he saw his last action of the war. When Eden met Hitler in 1935, he mentioned that it was the anniversary of Ludendorff's spring offensive, and 'it emerged that we must have been opposite each other round about La Fère on the River Oise'. After dinner, the French

Ambassador in Berlin, André François-Poncet, asked Eden if it was true that he fought opposite Hitler in the war. 'Et vous l'avez manqué? Vous devriez être fusillé.'[42]

For Eden, the last months of the war lacked the sense of camaraderie that he had first experienced with the Yeoman Rifles. The hours were long, and the logistics of staff work demanding. The end of the war was unexpected. Eden recorded his impressions of Armistice day in November – the eleventh hour of the eleventh day of the eleventh month – in a letter to his sister:

> At 9.0 a.m. we heard that the armistice had been signed. I am ashamed to say that I was still in bed having come out of the line the previous evening after our final battle. We collected all the men we could and at 1.0 we had a service.
>
> All the guns fired as hard as they could during the last half hour [Eden narrowly missed being hit by one of the very last shells] and then there was a sudden quiet.
>
> Our service was very simple. 'O God our help in ages past' followed by the Lord's Prayer, the Marseillaise and God Save the King. The General said a few words before the service began. I think it was the most impressive service I have ever been at.

To his sister's surprise, he ended the letter, 'I have been thinking rather seriously of standing for Parliament at the next General Election.'[43] His motivation was simple. The experience of war, and the close companionship he had forged with all classes of soldiers, had brought home to him, more vividly than life at Windlestone ever could, the true state of what Disraeli had called 'the condition of England', and had developed in him a sense of responsibility for his country's welfare. For the likes of Eden, the experience of the trenches gave him the inspiration to serve his fellow countrymen in the years ahead. Indeed, the genesis of modern 'One Nation' Conservatism, articulated by Disraeli in his Crystal Palace speech of 1872 ('The Tory Party, unless it is a National Party, is nothing'), can be traced back to the experience of figures including Eden and Macmillan during 1914–18. The Great War was to have another profound effect. By and large, the appeasers of the 1930s were to be those who had not led men in battle. Those who had fought knew that there were times when one had to stand up against tyranny, however painful that option would prove.

But the so-called 'Coupon' Election,[44] a paper triumph for Lloyd George, took place within a month of the Armistice on 14 December 1918, and Eden, still in uniform, was not to stand for Parliament until 1922. The 'Coupon' Election was as speedy as the end of the war was sudden, and Eden often wondered why the German collapse had been so quick after the initial successes of the Ludendorff offensive. Some years later he wrote:

41

As long as the German people, in the War of 1914, continued to believe that they were fighting for ideals they stood firm. As soon as they were told that they were fighting only for their daily bread they began to give up the struggle.[45]

After wintering with his brigade in the Ardennes, the landscape as desolate as the weather, Eden longed to return to England and a new life. 'Definite news at last,' he wrote with relief to his mother on 25 May 1919. 'We sail tomorrow to Tilbury leaving Antwerp in the evening.'[46]

Eden's was the classic experience of the upper-class officer of the Great War: selfless, courageous and modest, with the innate reticence of his upbringing (he made no mention of his MC in *Another World*). He came of age, literally and metaphorically, among his companions in the King's Royal Rifle Corps, his discharge from the Army coming on 13 June 1919, the day after his twenty-second birthday. He was then styled Captain Eden, the name by which he was to be known on his early election leaflets. His wartime service had echoes of a particular brand of English heroism, from Sir Philip Sidney to Rupert Brooke and beyond. He took comfort in adversity from the finest range of literature, citing the French dramatist Corneille to sum up what he and his companions believed the struggle had been about:

> Mourir pour le pays n'est pas un triste sort;
> C'est s'immortaliser par une belle mort.[47]

Hundreds of thousands of men lay in the fields over which Eden had tramped and fought, and he always noticed in later years how the village war memorials, the length and breadth of Britain, and especially in his native County Durham, contained far more names from 1914–18 than from 1939–45. In war he had learned about the precarious demands of leadership from men he had admired, figures as disparate as Charlie Feversham, Gerald Foljambe and Herbert Plumer, as well as from his everyday companions, such as Reg Park, Bert Harrop and Norman Carmichael; and he had learned to appreciate that executive responsibility was best fulfilled through practical attention to detail. He mistrusted instant solutions, particularly the panaceas of political leaders. As a survivor of the 'lost generation', he felt it incumbent upon himself to work, in however small a capacity, to create a better world. Idealism, not cynicism, was the legacy Eden drew from his experiences in war, and this unsentimental sense of responsibility for the welfare of others was always to condition his thinking.

CHAPTER THREE

Oxford and Political Apprenticeship

1919–24

> The influences and atmosphere of Oxford are what he needs.
>
> Lady Eden, 24 July 1919

> I feel that if one has a chance of winning one seat for
> Conservatism one should take it.
>
> Anthony Eden to Lady Eden, 3 April 1922

The civilian world to which Anthony Eden returned in 1919 was very different from that of pre-war days. Windlestone was no longer a beloved haven. His father and two of his brothers were dead; his mother was showing increasing signs of financial fecklessness; and there was growing tension in his relationship with his only surviving brother Tim, now Sir Timothy Eden, Bt., and the owner of Windlestone. Eden shared his anxieties and frustrations with Marjorie. 'You will have to watch Dear Mama carefully, because she has the most extraordinary idea of what is legal and what isn't,' he had written from Belgium. When he found out what had happened at Windlestone in his absence, he wrote more bitterly. 'I shouldn't worry about Tim. He isn't worth it . . . He has seized all Jack's things and all Daddie's and I have not had the most trifling article that ever belonged to either of them!'[1] As the war ended, Eden knew that his future, whatever it might be, lay elsewhere.

On a national level, the sense of euphoria was soon evaporating, and after the relief of the Armistice came inevitable disillusionment. 'They may ring their bells now', said Bonar Law, the Conservative leader, echoing Sir Robert Walpole, 'before long they will be wringing their hands.'[2] The return to peace was bedevilled by a multitude of problems, few of which were to be properly resolved. Lloyd George famously declared that he would make Britain a land fit for the returning heroes to live in; by 1922 his opponents were saying that he had succeeded, as one needed to be a hero to live in it.

The problems of reconstruction proved intractable. Debates on the dismantling of wartime controls brought no consensus, only apprehension. For Germany had been weakened as a nation state, but not destroyed, and many – most famously J. M. Keynes in *The Economic Consequences of the Peace* – were apprehensive about long-term European fiscal and political

43

stability. After the United States Senate failed to ratify the Peace Treaty in 1920, France had no guarantee of Anglo-American support in the face of any future German aggression. Hohenzollerns, Hapsburgs and Romanovs had been ejected; their replacements were as yet an unknown quantity.

In Britain, the political atmosphere became increasingly bitter (the call to 'Hang the Kaiser' an early symptom), as the fall in commmodity prices brought a slump after an illusory boom. The pound of 1914 was worth 8s. 8d. in January 1919, and 7s. 9d. by July 1920.[3]

Social unrest in the Labour market was a European phenomenon, over-shadowed and inspired by the Russian Revolution of 1917. The Troubles in Ireland remained unresolved. At Westminster, the burning question was how to assimilate rising working-class political consciousness into the democratic process, with many Asquithian Liberals, sensing electoral oblivion, hoping to repeat, a generation later, the astute accommodations of Gladstone with the forces of radicalism. But it was a new landscape. The Representation of the People Act in 1918 had completed the extension of the male franchise, and women over the age of thirty had voted for the first time in the 'Coupon' Election that December. Throughout 1919, the Labour Party made a series of spectacular by-election gains at the expense of the Coalition across a wide geographical spectrum, culminating in the famous Spen Valley contest that saw the defeat of Sir John Simon, the former Liberal Home Secretary, who was attempting to re-enter the House after losing his Walthamstow seat in December 1918. Labour consolidated their position in County Durham. Many now saw Labour as a possible future governing party.[4]

Eden's letters reflected the sense of turmoil. 'I am afraid that now the war is over and the reaction has set in,' he wrote to his mother, 'we shall find the loss of the old life harder than ever to bear.'[5] He never forgot this growing sense of disillusionment in the wake of the Great War. Twenty-six years later at the San Francisco Conference these memories were still strong and Eden, by then one of the brokers of the return to peace, was determined to avoid the mistakes of 1919, and what he called 'the lost opportunity at the end of the last World War.'[6]

As Eden waited for demobilisation in the harsh winter of the Ardennes, he had ample time to ponder his future. At first he considered a military career, but explained the disadvantages to Marjorie. 'It is quite impossible to get a regular commission at present but I expect that we shall hear something soon about the volunteer Army they are going to raise for Russia next year according to the papers.'[7] Even then he felt that the order of the day would be boredom, hanging around and (with sadly accurate pessimism) waiting for the next war in about twenty years. A month later he was writing to Marjorie (now Lady Warwick, as her husband Guy had succeeded to the Earldom) with further reflections. He had been thinking about the Foreign Office. 'Sounds very interesting and just what I should like. Would like to get abroad. Am quick at languages. The exam sounds rather alarming. Are you sure it is necessary for those entering from the Army?' He told his sister that he had forgotten everything he had learned at Eton. He ruled out some of the alternatives, including the Home Office ('Don't like the idea'), the City and, a surprising option, shipping. On the other hand, he felt that the Colonial Service might offer interesting opportunities. 'African Civil. Worst pay. Best climate and I hear best possibilities. Undoubtedly an advantage to know something of East Africa if I go in for politics.' Gradually that winter, drawing together the lessons he had learned in war, the future shape of his life was coming together in his mind. 'So there we are,' he summed up. 'The choice seems to lie between the Foreign Office and the African Civil.' In a revealing conclusion, he confided to his sister, 'My ultimate aim and object in politics is Secretary for Foreign Affairs or something like that. Rather ambitious!!'[8]

Eden was twenty-one when he wrote this letter. Sixteen years later he was to achieve this ambition.

Sybil Eden may have had little idea of the value of money, but she knew the importance of education. From Sandroyd days, she had kept Anthony's interests at heart, and on his return to England she persuaded him that it would be a mistake to forgo university. Reluctantly ('What, go back to school?') he agreed. The family college was Christ Church, Oxford. Anthony's father and his brother Tim had been there; Anthony's two sons were to follow him. The Lawrence portrait of his ancestor, William Eden, Lord Auckland, hung in Christ Church Hall. Tim had made tentative enquiries on Anthony's behalf in June 1919, an approach followed up in a letter to the Dean of Christ Church in July from Sybil Eden, who showed a shrewd insight into the character of her youngest surviving son:

> Anthony has brains and is very steady & good, too much so! He left Eton to go to the War & after a year in the Trenches got a Staff appointment & became Brigade Major. I am told he did extraordinarily well, but the life of responsibilities & association with Colonels & Generals all much older than himself has deprived him of all *youthful* ideas & thoughts & made him prematurely old & given him a narrow staff-office aspect of Life. He has no Father & I find it difficult to influence him now & feel very strongly that he should be in the Society of men of his own age, see another side of Life & learn to un-bend. I fear, if he does not go to Oxford in October, he will look out for work elsewhere & chuck an

University career. This will be greatly to his detriment in the future . . . I know that the influences & atmosphere of Oxford are what he needs.[10]

Although at first there was some doubt as to whether a place would be available for the Michaelmas Term, owing to the lateness of his application, Anthony Eden was admitted to Christ Church in October 1919 to read oriental languages. He had chosen this school in preference to modern history, in the hope of understanding better what he felt would be the future melting pot of international politics. His flair for languages was considerable and he continued his studies in French on several visits to La Rochelle. His continental travels in the early 1920s were extensive and also ensured his fluency in German. As a result, Eden was later able to converse privately with foreign political counterparts in their own favoured language (including in French with Chou En-lai at the Geneva Conference in 1954), though he deliberately never negotiated in a foreign language, thereby avoiding the difficulties suffered by some twentieth-century Prime Ministers, who had an exaggerated confidence in their linguistic abilities. At the Casablanca Conference in June 1943, Harold Macmillan noted admiringly how Eden, as Foreign Secretary, 'spoke in excellent and idiomatic French'[11] and while in Moscow in October 1944 Eden was able to interrogate some German prisoners of war in their own language.

Those who matriculated with Eden included Victor Cazalet, fresh from his triumphs at Eton; Derick Heathcoat Amory, Minister of Agriculture in Eden's 1955 Cabinet, and later Chancellor of the Exchequer; and Solomon Bandanaraike, a future Prime Minister of Sri Lanka. The next year saw the arrival of Henry ('Chips') Channon, the future MP for Southend and Parliamentary Private Secretary to Rab Butler at the Foreign Office, whose diary reveals his antipathy towards Eden. As Eden's interests were primarily aesthetic, his associates were members of Oxford's literary and artistic world, such as John Rothenstein, future Director of the Tate Gallery; Lord Balneil, a future Trustee of the National Gallery and Conservative MP; Edward Sackville-West, man of letters; and Lord David Cecil, literary polymath, through whom he met a Cecil cousin, Mary ('Molly'), daughter of Lord William Cecil, Bishop of Exeter. Molly was Eden's first love at Oxford and he was deeply disappointed when she later married Francis Manners. Disappointment and sadness seemed never-ending to the young undergraduate, and his private life lacked the stability he craved. Lord David Cecil's twenty-first birthday party, at which Eden was a guest, saw a coming together of Oxford's artistic and political worlds; guests included Robert Boothby and John Strachey, then making their names in university journalism and both future MPs. Gradually Eden mingled in both worlds.

Christ Church inspires a special affection in its alumni, though Eden never became sentimental about its beauties. It is indeed unique among the Oxford colleges. Originally founded by Cardinal Wolsey in 1529 as Cardinal College, and further expanded by Henry VIII in 1532, Christ Church is one of the richest and most extensive of Oxford colleges.[12] Under the shadow of Tom Tower is the largest quad in Oxford, the biggest Gothic Revival range and the grandest eighteenth-century building. The college even has a cathedral in its grounds.[13]

The House, as Christ Church is known, has always had its aristocratic element, and with its air of Eton-by-the-Cherwell was an uninterrupted extension of an accepted pattern of life for many Etonians, although not for Eden. Its size meant that it had many different facets, though essentially there were then two broad divisions: the impecunious undergraduates, frugal scholars, who lived simply, often in the Old Library buildings (where Eden took up residence for part of his time); and then the rich scions of the great aristocratic houses, who set up in Peck Quad, hunted with the Bicester and joined the Bullingdon. But behind this Brideshead atmosphere, Christ Church was a college where serious work was done and its proportion of Firsts was high. Eden, who was not rich by Christ Church standards (in 1921 he received £7,675 from his father's estate and paid his Oxford fees himself), nevertheless came from aristocratic stock; although not a scholar of the college, he was hard-working. In a chameleon-like way, he drew from the best traditions of both sides of Christ Church society, and never narrowed the range of his response to individuals. In this he was helped by the fact that the average age of the undergraduates was older than that of the pre-war entrants, and this encouraged a more serious approach. Many of his contemporaries had also come through the fire and anguish of the trenches and there was a feeling that there was more to life than frivolity. Sybil Eden was correct in saying that her son was old before his time; he was serious and mature, and always remembered that there was a world outside. One of the events he remembered most about his first Michaelmas Term of 1919 was the inaugural Armistice Day on 11 November and the two-minute silence.

As oriental languages was a minority subject, Eden received most of his tuition outside Christ Church. His nominal tutor at the House was at first the Revd A. E. J. Rawlinson, a future Bishop of Derby, but much of his work in Persian studies was done under Professor R. Paget Dewhurst, who saw in Eden a single-mindedness in pursuit of specific goals that he predicted would make him Foreign Secretary before he was forty. Eden studied Arabic at New College under the supervision of the Revd D. S. Margoliouth, Laudian Professor for forty-eight years and the first figure of world renown in his field that Eden had encountered. Not many undergraduates got past the carapace of Margoliouth's formidable scholarship, but Eden was one of those who did. Margoliouth engaged his considerable conversational skills only when addressed in Turkish or Arabic and, as his Arabic was so refined as to be largely beyond contemporary usage, such occasions were rare. His real flair was for linguistic scholarship. He discovered anagrams in the opening lines of the *Iliad* and the *Odyssey* that showed details of Homer's life, but was largely known as the foremost interpreter of Islam to the modern world – heady stuff for a serious-minded undergraduate such as Eden. Gilbert Murray said that no scholar of his generation left so deep and permanent a mark on oriental studies.

Eden immersed himself in the literature of Persia, much admiring Curzon's stupendous energy in compiling his magisterial history *Persia and the Persian Question*, and became President of the Asiatic Society. In a talk on Persian literature to the society on 7 March 1921, he said, 'it seems a curious coincidence that Fitzgerald's one good poem should be a translation of a somewhat minor Persian poet'. What attracted him about Persian literature, he explained, was 'the charm and melody of its verse, with its depth of dreams, richness, its descriptive and varied vocabulary, couched in a language as beautiful as it is expressive.'[14]

For relaxation, Eden devoured the novels of Balzac, Flaubert, Stendhal and Zola, as well as the most challenging contemporary French literature and philosophy. No trip to Paris, one of his favourite cities, was complete without a visit to the second-hand bookstalls along the banks of the Seine. Eden's library, still intact, has as its glories a comprehensive survey of French culture as well as oriental books of great rarity, many given to him by the last Shah of Persia.

Eden had planned to take his first exams in 1921, but political troubles intervened. As the slump worsened in the early months of the year, the Government nevertheless pressed ahead with its plans to de-control the coal industry. The failure of the Miners' Federation to secure a settlement from the National Wages Board led to a strike on 1 April when the old contracts expired. Durham was one of the areas that suffered the greatest reductions when the new scales were published. On 'Black Friday', 15 April 1921, the threat of a general strike was removed when the Triple Alliance of the Miners' Federation, the Transport Workers' Federation and the National Union of Railwaymen collapsed, a day of infamy in Trade Union lore, not forgotten at the General Strike in 1926. The coal strike continued in a forlorn way until June, but left considerable residual bitterness in County Durham, of which Eden was only too well aware. One of the factors that contributed to the failure of the strike was the formation of a national body of Defence Forces, which recruited 75,000 volunteers in ten days. Many of the leaders of these forces were ex-officers, specifically targeted by the Government to help maintain civil order. As Eden was also prominent in his local Territorial Army, he joined the Durham Defence Force and commanded the Spennymoor detachment. On 17 April he wrote to the Censor of Christ Church, Robert Dundas, to say that he had not received special leave to return to Oxford from the military authorities. As a reservist, he was not officially released until June. His brother Tim wrote a letter to J. C. Masterman, by then Eden's tutor, explaining that Eden could not return to Oxford on 22 April for the start of Trinity Term. 'In the south a prolonged coal-strike may not seem so serious,' he wrote, 'but we are well aware of it here.'[15]

On his eventual return to Oxford, Eden began to attend political meetings in the surrounding villages on behalf of the local Conservative Party. He regarded this as a more valuable training than the rather 'precious' air of Union debates, which, like another Foreign Secretary, Edward Grey, he never attended. The coal strike of 1921 concentrated his mind on domestic political issues. He was convinced there must be a better way of tackling mining problems – issues he later addressed in a speech to the House of Commons on 29 January 1946. Rather in the manner of his final weeks at Eton, when he was anxious to enlist, Eden now felt that Oxford was a phase of life that needed to be completed as quickly and efficiently as possible. He worked hard in his last year, though in the vacations he continued to travel, one highlight being a grand tour to Constantinople, taking in many of the art galleries of Europe en route.

Eden sat Final Schools in oriental languages in Trinity Term 1922 and was placed in the first class. Had he read French and German he could have achieved an equally distinguished result. 'Jelly' Churchill, who had always urged the importance of persistence, was among the first to congratulate him. Eden's scholarship was now undoubted, though his contemporaries never considered him an intellectual.

Politics was not the only circumstance that took Eden into the Oxfordshire countryside during his time at Christ Church. Ever since the visits of Mrs Patrick Campbell to Windlestone, Eden had been fascinated by the theatre. He joined the Oxford University Dramatic Society and, surprisingly, for one who had an inherent shyness, took to the boards with gusto. For one who later had a reputation for a certain woodenness in his speeches, Eden proved a skilled mimic. His flair, particularly in romantic comedies, surprised his peers. One of his successes was as the Duke in a rare revival of G. K. Chesterton's first play *Magic*. The Duke, 'a healthy hearty man in tweeds', bore comparison with his father, and many subtle touches in Eden's performance drew on pre-war life at Windlestone. The undergraduate production, unusually for those days, toured to Nettlebed and Henley, where it was warmly received in the local halls. Eden was at last learning to unbend. In the 1970s one of his fellow actors wrote to Eden, recalling the venture. 'I do, indeed, remember Chesterton's "Magic",' Eden replied. 'We had great fun touring the neighbourhood with the play.'[16] Eden's taste for drama continued at Windlestone after he had graduated and married. He made a mark in January 1924 as Algernon Moncrieff (with his wife Beatrice as Cecily Cardew) in his own production of Oscar Wilde's *The Importance of being Earnest* at the village hall in Kirkdale.[17]

When Barbara Castle, the Labour politician, described Eden as being like a character from a Noël Coward play, she was not intending to be complimentary, but the young Eden could certainly have essayed any of Coward's leading roles with aplomb.[18] He could also have declaimed the tragic parts in Corneille and Racine with conviction.

Eden's greatest contribution to life in Oxford, however, lay not in drama, but in the field of art. Often described as his 'hobby' (as though it was akin to woodwork), the study of painting proved his passion and consuming intellectual interest. In November 1920, Eden, together with David Cecil and Robert Gathorne-Hardy, issued an invitation from Christ Church to any who wished to join them:

> It has been suggested [the prospectus ran] that a Society be formed in Oxford, to be called 'The Uffizi Society', to discuss painters and Painting, past and present. Efforts will be made to induce leading critics and painters to address the Society.

Names suggested included Augustus John, George Moore, Roger Fry and Walter Sickert.* Eden became the President and gave the inaugural address on Italian art to the time of Tintoretto. Chips Channon was one of more than thirty people who joined the Society.[19]

When George Moore was unable to accept an invitation to address the Uffizi, Eden nevertheless visited him to discuss the prevailing aesthetic issues of the day and was astonished to hear from Moore that before the war he had advised Eden's father not to invest in Cézanne watercolours. Sir William, who had reserved some Cézannes at one exhibition, was persuaded against such a course by Moore and had released several masterpieces to the market. Eden's main disappointment was artistic, rather than financial, for Cézanne, whom he considered the father of modern art, was already one of his special enthusiasms. 'He was the first,'

---

* It was later one of Eden's regrets that when Sickert offered to paint his portrait in 1931, the logistics proved impossible in the time available.

Eden considered, 'to assert the right of the artist to paint for his own pleasure pictures representing directly the refinement of his own feelings, unfettered by any school and unhampered by any laws or traditions, forms or influences.'[20] Eden's paper on Cézanne for the Uffizi Society, later privately printed, was long remembered for its far-sighted appreciation of the artist's innovations. His conclusion did not lack sharpness:

> Cézanne has died too recently to enable us to make a correct estimate of his influence on the art of the world. In England we have been without art for so long that there has not been any subject for his influence. Mr [John Singer] Sargent would continue to paint like Mr Sargent were there ever so many earthquakes. His impression of the Styx could hardly differ from his impression of the Grand Canal. Such things could hardly affect the brilliant technique of the American painters of Society portraits. Elegantly-booted and spurred cavaliers will no doubt mount and dismount from Mr. Munnings' gaily caparisoned steeds in his Elysian fields.[21]

J. C. Masterman regarded Eden's talk on Cézanne as one of the most brilliant papers ever delivered by an Oxford undergraduate. John Rothenstein, later Director of the Tate Gallery, wrote:

> I played some part in the activities of the Uffizi – a club so exclusive that it withered away because eventually nobody was considered worthy of election. It was at the Uffizi that I heard Anthony Eden deliver his lecture on Cézanne. This lecture caused something of a sensation, for it was regarded as audaciously incongruous, rather as a lecture by a general on Jackson Pollock would be today. Anthony Eden, although only in his middle twenties, was already an august and highly traditional figure, and Cézanne, outside a narrow circle, was still a controversial painter. Anthony Eden was not only august, he was positively regal: he had a fine presence; he was as serious and gifted as he was handsome. Had the Oxford of those days had occasion to elect a President, he would surely have been the overwhelming choice. I never knew him well, but there was a link between us: Whistler had quarrelled with my father, on account of his refusal to break with Eden's father, Sir William, when Whistler quarrelled with him.[22]

Rothenstein mentions Eden's handsome bearing, and he certainly captured many hearts. Eden always loved the company of attractive, lively and intelligent women, and they were usually flattered by the attentions of such a dazzling escort. As he became more powerful, so did his charms. He was also an empyrean figure for those men who appreciated such an exemplar of grace and poise. When Chips Channon was charmed by the Duchess of York at a society ball in the 1930s, he was even more charmed by Eden, her partner on the ballroom floor, noting that 'she danced with Anthony Eden who is really becoming very handsome and important.'[23]

For his part, Eden was suspicious of alluring men of ambiguous taste, noting of the great society news of 1922, 'Miss Edwina Ashley is engaged to Lord Louis Mountbatten. What a waste.'[24] His opponents in the Whips' Office knew how to wound when they dubbed his anti-appeasement followers in 1938 'The Glamour Boys'.

Eden may have taken the lead in romantic comedies, but success in private life still eluded him. Sybil Fitzroy had been the focus of adolescent hankerings, a passing infatuation; Pamela Fitzgerald had been an admired, but unattainable beauty; Mollie Cecil's marriage was a serious disappointment. It has been said of Eden's loves that 'they were all in Debrett's'[25] and the recipients of his letters at this time – Aline, Ann-Marie, Celia, Mary, Serena and Ursula – were certainly high-born. But as his Oxford career came to its end, Eden's enthusiasm for the theatre brought him a potentially more adventurous relationship, which could have had damaging consequences for his fledgling political career, had it come to the notice of a local Conservative Association. In his diary, Eden records his visit to John Gay's *Polly*, the sequel to *The Beggar's Opera*. In 1729 its melodramatic mixture of ungentlemanly amorous advances, cross-dressing and a mixed marriage had been broad even by eighteenth-century standards, and the play was banned from stage performance by the Lord Chamberlain. In the 1920s, it matched the febrile atmosphere of the flapper age and enjoyed a considerable vogue. Eden took up with the leading actress (not a figure in Debrett's), whom he calls 'Polly' in his diary. This was his first passionate love affair. But it brought him no happiness, especially as his sister Marjorie made her displeasure plain. Tim, as a man of the world, was less judgemental. 'A very extravagant day,' Eden wrote in his diary. 'Visited the second hand book shops in Charing Cross Road [en route to the theatre where 'Polly' was appearing]. Fatal! Bought a very beautiful edition of *Manon Lescaut* and one or two other French novels and plays – must not go again for many a long day.' Six days later he wrote, 'Wish I had some more capital!' Tim's wedding day was for Eden 'a critical day', as it brought home his own failure to marry and reinforced his sense of emotional isolation. His diary entries in the month that he ended the relationship with 'Polly' show his despair. 'The future stretches out bleaker and more desolate than ever. My own fireside as unattainable, happiness more than ever distant.'[26]

Eden was always prone to mood swings, often mirroring stock-market fluctuations which were crucial for him, and this was a particularly low time, analogous to the late 1940s. Yet there was much to be thankful for as he now embarked on his life's work. As the economic uncertainties increased, he had the insurance of his outstanding degree, was free of any immediate encumbrances and had a modest capital. His intellectual interests were lively and varied. Eton and Christ Church counted for a lot, and, although he never capitalised on the fact, in the aftermath of the Great War many doors automatically opened for a holder of the Military Cross. From this base he would eventually hold the highest office in the land.

Eden left Oxford with a range of experience few previous generations could replicate (the university class of 1946 would be the next parallel), although modestly he thought he 'knew little except war and schooling.'[27] Of course, he knew far more than that, and, unlike some future political generations, had what was later called a hinterland. His Christ Church contemporary Solomon Bandaranaike had stood on Magdalen Bridge on his last day at Oxford and, contrasting the beauty of the scene with the deprivations and problems he knew awaited him in his homeland, said that Oxford was all the dearer to him because she had taught him to love his country better. Eden also knew the inequalities of his own society. Some years later he poured out these feelings to his friend Robert Bruce-Lockhart, who recorded that Eden 'would like to see the breakdown of this out-dated class system and its replacement by something which would give more equality of chance'. He told Bruce-Lockhart that 'our system gave no chance to late developers [a fair description of Eden himself] unless rich, i.e. to get benefits of supposedly better education poor people's children had to get scholarships at thirteen.'[28] Not many Tories of Eden's generation expressed views such as these.

A hitherto unrecorded footnote illustrates Eden's love–hate relationship with his former college. On leaving Christ Church, he had received the customary certificate of financial discharge, stating that he owed nothing to the college.[29] It was therefore a matter of considerable surprise and annoyance to him when, in October 1930, he received a sudden demand for payment of outstanding battels (the Oxford term for the college account), particularly as the sum was a not inconsiderable one, approximately £500 in present-day values. He politely pointed out that he had discharged all obligations on going down, but Christ Church refused to accept this. Eden was furious and wrote to the Dean (ironically on Warwick Castle writing paper, where he was staying on constituency business, but which suggested a life of privileged hospitality), severing all links with his *alma mater*. 'I know that you will not think that I have ever been, or ever could be, anything but loyal to the House, which makes me not the less regretful to bring my connection with it to an end. I do not see, however, that I have any choice.'[30] He asked for his name to be expunged from all records and declined to receive further mailings from the college. The matter did not show either party in a favourable light. Christ Church should not have ignored Eden's 1922 certificate of discharge. Eden would have been better advised to send the certificate, though this was not immediately to hand. As it was, the issue, even though ultimately he was shown to be in the right, caused him to lose all sense of proportion, and was certainly worthy of his father in his more headstrong moments. For its part, Christ Church drew an unhappy episode to an end, but only after an interval of eleven years, when it offered Eden an Honorary Studentship (Fellowship) in 1941, which he accepted. His portrait, by Sir William Coldstream, now hangs in Christ Church hall.[31]

Eden left Oxford determined to be adopted in the Conservative cause before the General Election, due by December 1923, but expected earlier. The Lloyd George Coalition was drawing, not all that peacefully, to its close. The combination of the Chanak crisis in September 1922 (when Britain was almost plunged into war with Turkey) and the continuing 'Die-Hard' Conservative resentment over the sale of honours (Cardiff was known as 'the city of dreadful knights') led to back-bench demands for the Conservatives to break free from the Coalition, and to fight the next election as an independent political force. Bonar Law retired, on the grounds of ill-health, from the Conservative and Unionist leadership in March 1921. This proved a fatal weakening of Lloyd George's position. Bonar Law's successor, Austen Chamberlain, proved less adept at controlling dissident Conservative back-benchers, of which there were a growing number in 1921. When the Conservatives held their famous meeting at the Carlton Club on 19 October 1922, voting by 186 votes to 85 in favour of Captain Ernest Pretyman's motion that the Conservatives should fight the next election as an independent party, with their own leader and programme, it proved one of the great turning points of modern British political life, drawing a line under the old party system.[32] It was also the first time since Lord North's day that a Prime Minister had been dismissed, not by a defeat in the House of Commons or in a General Election, but in this case by an adverse vote taken by a private meeting of MPs. On hearing the vote, Lloyd George resigned the Premiership and Austen Chamberlain, always playing the game and always losing it, gave up the Conservative leadership. Bonar Law came out of retirement and took the jobs of both men. His first act as Prime Minister was to call a General Election for 15 November. The new age of Conservatism versus Socialism was ushered in.

For Eden this was an unexpectedly early opportunity to make his mark on the hustings. Unfortunately for him, the North-East had never been natural Conservative country, but Eden nevertheless sought adoption in his home county. He could live at Windlestone while campaigning, and the cost of setting up residence elsewhere was a contributory factor in his decision. The whole process proved a testing, but invaluable, exposure to the rough-and-tumble of political life. Eden was assailed by opponents on all sides. In the local pit villages the Durham Miners' Association held political sway, while the nonconformist tradition ensured bastions of fiercely independent Liberalism among many in the professional classes, especially in the rural areas. The Conservatives lacked a coherent political elite willing to undertake the time-consuming, but necessary, work of grass-roots activism. A further complicating factor was the increasingly fraught Irish question, which meant that the Marquess of Londonderry, the titular focus of Conservatism in the county, was often absent from Wynyard Park, the family seat near Stockton, as leader of the Senate of Northern Ireland. He has been aptly described as 'a decorative emblem rather than a source of strength.'[33] It was at Wynyard Park that Eden had first met Winston Churchill, Londonderry's cousin, while on vacation from Oxford, when Churchill asked the young undergraduate if he intended to enter politics.[34]

Londonderry was Eden's principal supporter, but this proved a mixed blessing during the campaign, as Eden's Labour opponent, Joseph Batey, had been a miner since the age of twelve, and Londonderry was a coal owner, albeit one who showed benevolent concern for the welfare of his employees. Eden and Londondery were later ministerial colleagues. When Eden, moving ever upwards, became Minister without Portfolio for League of Nations Affairs in June 1935, Londonderry succeeded him as Lord Privy Seal, his final post, by which time their relative political standings had been almost entirely reversed.

Loyalty to County Durham was not the only factor that led Eden to cut his political teeth in the North-East. A young, untried candidate could not expect a winnable seat to drop into his lap like a ripe plum. That came only with a combination of luck, patronage and money. Eden had none of these. What he did have was a connection with Spennymoor from his recent service with the Durham Defence Force, though this solidified the mining vote against him. Early in 1922, Eden's candidature had been considered by the local Conservative Association. At the time he was taking his final examinations in Oxford, but agreed to let his name go forward. Some local Conservatives thought a scion of Windlestone would be able to underwrite their losses. Their eventual endorsement, despite this initial misunderstanding, was a tribute to the personal impression that Eden later made. A further encouraging factor for the local Conservatives was that, in the volatile state of party allegiances in 1922, the Asquithian Liberals, who had held the seat since 1918, agreed a Conservative–Liberal Pact in the two constituencies of Spennymoor and Bishop Auckland, a tacit acknowledgement of Labour's growing strength. However, there were now two Liberal parties, and this pact did not stop a Lloyd George Liberal from standing, which made it an even tougher assignment for Eden to win the seat, given an inevitable split in the anti-Labour vote.

Eden soon found that the County Conservative Association was 'deeply in debt', and the constituency of Spennymoor overdrawn to the tune of £400, a considerable sum in the early 1920s to expect a local candidate to guarantee. A local grandee eventually obliged, though long-term difficulties were to remain.[35]

Cuthbert Headlam, fighting the neighbouring constituency of Barnard Castle for the Conservatives in 1924, was particularly gloomy in his analysis. 'There are lots of good sound Conservatives everywhere, but they are disunited and disheartened, and no wonder – they have no leaders – and no sort of organisation.'[36] This may have been the downside, but for Eden in 1922 it was also an opportunity. As a local man in a radical stronghold, he could be accused of neither carpet-bagging nor opportunism. It also gave him the chance to experience electioneering at its most demanding and dispiriting. At the beginning of April 1922, he summed up the prospects to his mother:

> *Spennymoor* – I have accepted to stand and I have to attend a meeting in Durham on Wednesday week to be adopted. The position is this – the Coalition as such [Lloyd George's 'Coupon' alliance from December 1918] will not last much longer and the next election will be fought with the old party names Conservative and Liberal. I shall stand for Spennymoor as a Conservative . . . S is a fairly large division and difficult to work . . . There is no money or organisation but they are very enthusiastic. It was explained to the Liberals that I was a strong Conservative, the Chief Liberal man at once got up and said that it did not matter a damn what I was, they would support an Eden. Pretty good.

Eden did not accept that he was fighting a forlorn cause, and gave a remarkably accurate diagnosis of how national politics might unfold during 1922:

> If I can scrape 10,000 votes I should win. It will be a very close thing. I hope that you and Tim will not mind my doing this, but it seemed a good chance and I could not resist it. There will be no need to support L[loyd] G[eorge] as he is going very soon – and even if he does not the Coalition as such is to break up again into Conservative & National Liberals, the former under Austen [Chamberlain] or Bonar Law, the latter under Lloyd George or Winston [Churchill]. There is no doubt that Labour will make a very big fight next election & if they win heaven help us. The

Leicester result was very bad – A Labour victory & a turnover of nearly 10,000. I feel that if one has a chance of winning one seat for Conservatism one should take it.[37]

It is difficult now to recapture the sense of fear felt among non-Socialists at the prospect of a Labour Government in the early 1920s. The Civil Service, the Armed Forces and the City of London were all considered to be 'at risk', with a punitive confiscation of savings to follow. Some even thought 'that under Labour the marriage tie would not be sacred, and that free love would receive official sanction.'[38] For many, the barbarians were at the gates, and Labour was unfairly associated, in the aftermath of the Russian Revolution, with events such as riots in Glasgow in 1919, described as 'a Bolshevist rising.'[39]

Although Eden was a left-of-centre figure ('I shall always be a Jacobin,' he had once written to his mother),[40] his concerns about the unknown factor of a 'Socialist experiment' were also very real. His relationship with Tim was not helped by his brother's increasingly right-wing stance, over which they had fierce arguments. One guest remembers the brothers setting off for a walk, both with walking sticks. When they came back the sticks were snapped, and the guest wondered how the differences had been resolved and feared for the trees and bushes that had been hit.[41]

The 1922 Election was a disaster for Lloyd George, as the Conservatives, winning 345 seats under Bonar Law's leadership, formed their first independent administration for seventeen years. The fledgling Labour Party became the second-largest party, with 142 seats, while the Lloyd George and Asquithian Liberals, with sixty-two and fifty-four seats respectively, finally paid the electoral price of their post-war split. With Austen Chamberlain and his followers in exile after the Carlton Club vote, Bonar Law's Government proved the most aristocratic of the century, containing six peers in addition to the Lord Chancellor, five of them with inherited titles. Churchill dubbed it a government of the second eleven, Lord Birkenhead a government of second-class intellects; Lord Robert Cecil retaliated by saying that the election showed that Britain preferred to be governed by second-class intellects, rather than by second-class characters.

Eden's first election ended in defeat, but it was the only time he failed to be returned to Parliament. He suffered much abusive heckling. When he was accused of being a member of the idle rich, he pulled out both of his trouser pockets to show that they were empty. Although he did not wish to mention his war service, the local Conservatives insisted that his military rank appear on the ballot paper, very much the custom of the time, as it was to be in 1945. Eden was pleased to meet again one of his platoon from Ploegsteert, needless to say a firm supporter, but was unable to get the 10,000 votes for which he had hoped. Joseph Batey, a member of the executive committee of the Miners' Federation, was comfortably elected as the Labour MP. The figures were:

Joseph Batey (Labour)	13,766
Captain R. A. Eden (Conservative)	7,567
Tom Wing (Liberal)	6,046
Labour Majority	6,199

It was a respectable, but not outstanding, performance. The main benefit for Eden was that he had been blooded in the political process and noticed beyond the boundaries of County Durham. Fred Peart, Labour Leader of the Lords at the time of Eden's death, remembered the election from his schooldays. In his tribute to Eden, Lord Peart recalled: 'My school was a polling station and, peeping over the wall, I could not help being impressed by the tall Conservative candidate, with his handsome face, black hair and moustache. He came from an old North County Durham family with a great history of public service. He was linked with the history of my own county; he was part of it.'[42]

After his defeat at Spennymoor, Eden kept his eye open for a winnable seat, tacitly admitting to himself that he would have to look beyond the North-East.* He took a flat in London, began writing for the *Saturday Review* and visiting the galleries. But there was still an emptiness at the core. He had no full-time job and no wife. Before 1923 was out, however, he had both.

After the General Election of November 1922, Eden believed that it might be the best part of five years before he had another opportunity to stand for Parliament. Events, however, were to prove otherwise. The first stage in a process that was to bring further General Elections in both 1923 and 1924 came in May 1923 with the resignation of Bonar Law as Prime Minister. Although he never knew the extent of his illness, Law was terminally ill with throat cancer, and died on 30 October. 'Bonar Law resigned,' Eden recorded in his diary on 21 May. 'Very heavy blow for the present Govt. I wish that Chamberlain could step into his shoes. I mistrust these die-hards, they are an ignorant and unbalanced crew & will ruin the party if once they obtain control.'[43]

---

*Two of the candidatures he considered, nevertheless, were still local ones, Sedgefield and Hartlepool. A sign of a changing political landscape is that by 2000 both were solid Labour seats, Sedgefield represented by the Prime Minister, Tony Blair, and Hartlepool by Peter Mandelson, sometime Cabinet Minister and architect of New Labour.

But Austen Chamberlain and his Conservative Coalitionist followers ('a slice off the top,' as J. C. C. Davidson, Law's Parliamentary Secretary, dubbed them)[44] were still in political exile, and George V faced the difficult choice between Lord Curzon and Stanley Baldwin as the fourth Prime Minister of his reign. In circumstances of considerable poignancy, only partly owing to the fact that he was a member of the House of Lords and the Labour Party was now the official Opposition, the imperious Foreign Secretary, Lord Curzon, was passed over in favour of Stanley Baldwin, Chancellor of the Exchequer, whom he dubbed 'a man of the utmost insignificance.'[45]

Eden was delighted when Queenie Feversham, widow of his commanding officer, remarried. Her second husband was Sir Gervase Beckett, 1st Baronet, a widower with four children from his first marriage. Beckett was a prominent figure in Yorkshire life, MP for Leeds, as his father had been, a leading banker and, most significantly for Eden at this stage, proprietor of the *Yorkshire Post*. Eden was given a platform in the paper for his articles, a valued source of extra income, as well as helping him make his political mark. Beckett's was not an act of charity; he felt the articles were useful for the *Yorkshire Post*, bringing a fresh and more youthful perspective to a wide variety of issues, so there was mutual advantage in the arrangement. Although a Conservative paper, the *Yorkshire Post* frequently took an independent line under its long-serving editor, Arthur Mann, who advocated the break-up of the Coalition in 1922. Later Mann was a consistent and forthright opponent of Chamberlain's appeasement policy at a time when most newspaper editors backed it, as did most prominent politicians except for Churchill and Eden. A clear division between appeasers and anti-appeasers was already apparent.

The paper's influence was felt beyond Yorkshire, notably in December 1936, when Arthur Mann penned his celebrated leader about King Edward VIII, precipitating the Abdication crisis.[46] Eden learned much from Mann, and from journalists on his staff such as Collin Brooks, about the interplay of press and politics, and Beckett's initiative significantly extended Eden's range of experience. However, Eden owed Beckett more than an introduction to the newspaper world.

Eden had known Ger Beckett (as he was called by family and friends) since the end of the war and had stayed on occasion at his home, Nawton, in Kirkdale, North Yorkshire. Ger admired Eden for his war record and for his courage in fighting an unpromising seat such as Spennymoor. A worldly and tolerant figure, who nurtured Eden as a protégé, Ger prided himself on his ability to spot rising talent in the worlds of politics and journalism. He thought Eden could go far in both.

By his marriage to Queenie Feversham, Ger Beckett became Marjorie Brooke's brother-in-law. In Eden he saw the possibility of even closer family links. He was aware of the rumours that Eden was not Sir William's son, but Ger understood that in this world you may never know who your real brothers are, and was unconcerned. Beckett was himself the likeliest natural father of Rupert Hart-Davis, the distinguished publisher, who on attaining his majority was informed by the MCC that he had been put down at birth for membership by a Yorkshire baronet, of whom he had never heard.[47]

So Ger engineered and encouraged the marriage between his rather wayward eighteen-year-old daughter, Beatrice, and this up-and-coming aristocratic Tory with a Military Cross and an Oxford First. Beatrice's whirlwind romance with a Yorkshire hunting squire had strained Ger's tolerance. He had taken his daughter away to South Africa to draw a line under the affair. On their return in the spring of 1923 he was looking for a settled match for his daughter. Eden seemed the answer to his prayers. For his part, Eden was breaking up with 'Polly', who was always more mistress than prospective bride, and wanting to end his loneliness. Events soon had their own momentum. 'I hope that one day I shall marry Beatrice,' he wrote in his diary on 9 July 1923. Later that month he sent her a copy of Shakespeare's poems and sonnets, in the edition by George Wyndham, for her birthday. 'I really am daring to hope,' he wrote on 28 July. Three days later ('the greatest day of my life'), Beatrice, 'the truest and the best woman in the world', accepted his proposal of marriage. 'I have indeed won a treasure,' he wrote on 1 August. 'I have added cubits to my self-respect in the last 24 hours.' Ger gave his future son-in-law 2,000 shares in his bank to mark the engagement. The happy couple began house-hunting in Haworth, Brontë country, and the wedding was arranged for the fashionable St Margaret's, Westminster, 'a beautiful church for a wedding and not expensive' Eden recorded.[48]

Contrary to some later suggestions, Eden's marriage to Beatrice was not one of political convenience. He was genuinely captivated by his bride-to-be, whom he admired with an intimate tenderness, maturing into deep love that survived their eventual separation and divorce, the most painful events of Eden's life.

Underlying doubts were felt in both families. Ger acknowledged that Beatrice was very young and, with hindsight, her family accepted that she had never really been in love with Eden, and would have been happier with a Yorkshire landowner.[49] The age difference was not, however, the problem; it was rather that Beatrice shared none of Eden's interests and was different from him in so many ways. She loved jazz, café society, and was bored by politics, her future husband's vocation.

*

On 19 October 1923, the first anniversary of the Carlton Club meeting, Eden recorded in his diary, 'Heard by wire an invitation to contest by-election of Warwick & Leamington.'[50] By such small measures are careers determined. The constituency was to prove the buttress of his political life for one-third of a century, and the noble English river flowing through its length was to give him the name of his eventual title. The unexpected by-election arose because the sitting MP, Sir Ernest Pollock, became Master of the Rolls, which meant a hasty search by the Warwick and Leamington Conservative Association for a first-class candidate.[51] Local contenders proved unappealing and the approach to Eden was something in the nature of a pre-emptive strike against those already hoping to be in the field.

To the list of those who aided Eden in his life – 'Jelly' Churchill, Professor David Margoliouth, Arthur Mann and Ger Beckett – must now be added the name of Richard Greville Verney, 19th Baron Willoughby de Broke (1869–1923). A former MP for Rugby, and a founding father-figure of the 'Die Hard' Opposition in the House of Lords to the Parliament Act of 1911 in the wake of Lloyd George's 'People's Budget', Lord Willoughby de Broke was like a character from Disraeli's novel *Lothair*. Aware that much of the political power of the aristocracy was inevitably dwindling, he nevertheless believed that its only justification was by maintaining a sense of responsibility towards others, a creed that he practised on his estate at Compton Verney in Warwickshire. It was this Disraelian 'One Nation' philosophy that attracted him to Eden, whose election addresses at Spennymoor had been noticed beyond County Durham. As a firm supporter also of the Territorial Army, speaking progressively in the Lords for improvement in their conditions of service, he appreciated Eden's selfless membership of the Durham Defence Force, which had not been to his political benefit in Spennymoor.[52]

Eden's name was submitted to the association's executive 'as a suitable candidate' by Lord Willoughby de Broke on 18 October after enquiries of Conservatives in London. Eden was considered alongside the 'local' candidate, Sir Henry Fairfax-Lucy, Bt, and also Sir Thomas Platt. At the age of sixty-three, Sir Henry Fairfax-Lucy of Charlecote Park, apart from his position as Chairman of the Warwickshire Army Association, had considerable experience of the political world, as a former private secretary of the Financial Secretary to the Treasury, and to the Solicitor-General for Ireland. In addition, he had recently contested Holland-with-Boston in Lincolnshire in the 1922 General Election. Sir Thomas Platt, who was fifty-eight, had contested Louth a quarter of a century earlier, before serving in various Foreign Office posts, including spells in Athens and Uganda. During the Great War he had been a railway officer and interpreter until he was invalided out in 1916.

But Lord Willoughby de Broke's patronage, Eden's youth and his war record proved decisive. On 24 October, Eden met members of the association at the Salisbury Hotel, Leamington. At this meeting Lord Willoughby de Broke said that Captain Eden – and he emphasised the military rank – had 'a double link with the ancient borough of Warwick' as the brother of Lady Brooke and as the fiancé of Beatrice Beckett, step-daughter of the daughter of the Countess of Warwick. (What he did not know at the time was that the Countess of Warwick was being adopted as Eden's opponent that same day.) More important, though, for Willoughby de Broke was Eden's political outlook. 'Having contested an industrial constituency in the North,' he told the meeting, 'Captain Eden was conversant with the feelings of those intimately connected with the problem of unemployment.' Eden's lengthy address to the association was a tour de force, ranging over the whole area of international and domestic politics. His understanding of 'industrial problems' made him an unusual Conservative candidate in the early 1920s, and it is ironic that his entry into Parliament was aided by his knowledge of domestic affairs, later mistakenly believed to be his Achilles heel. The association's Minute Book records the outcome of the evening:

Captain R. Anthony Eden, having addressed the meeting and answered questions was unanimously, and with great enthusiasm, adopted as the Conservative Candidate for the constituency.[53]

At the same time at Labour headquarters, the Countess of Warwick 'declared herself in favour of recognising the Soviet government in Russia, and admitting Communists into the Labour Party.'[54] Her reward was that her smart Warwick relations campaigned ostentatiously on Eden's behalf.

The election was interrupted by preparations for the Eden wedding, which took place on 5 November, twelve days after his adoption as Conservative candidate. 'Married to Beatrice at 2.15 at St Margaret's Westminster by the Archbishop of York and the Bishop of Wakefield', Eden recorded in his diary.[55]

It proved an unusual day for Cosmo Gordon Lang, the Archbishop of York. That morning he had officiated at the state funeral of Bonar Law in Westminster Abbey, a few yards from St Margaret's; the ashes of the former Prime Minister had been interred in the south nave, to Asquith's waspish epitaph: 'It is fitting that we should have buried the Unknown Prime Minister beside the Unknown Warrior.' That day, Westminster was awash with Premiers, past, present and future. Balfour and Asquith, Baldwin and Ramsay MacDonald were pallbearers at Bonar Law's funeral, and the congregation included the Dominions Prime Ministers who were in London for their conference. The great west door of the abbey was then left open for the rest of the day to enable thousands of mourners, many from the Dominions, to file past Bonar Law's grave. The seemingly endless tide of humanity departed from the abbey by the north door, which gave directly on to St Margaret's Church, where in the afternoon of that cold, dank day onlookers saw Anthony Eden and his wife Beatrice emerging after their wedding. Photographs of the occasion show extensive crowds, and not just the onlookers drawn to any society wedding; but the sombreness of people's apparel gives away the primary reason for their presence in Westminster. Thus was the Unknown Prime Minister buried on the same day as the marriage of the Unlucky Prime Minister-to-be.[56]

Beatrice was married against the political backdrop of a state funeral, and within the month saw her husband elected to Parliament in the 1923 General Election. These twin events gave her a foretaste of her future life with Eden. Sadly, it was to prove a life in which she had little interest. When Leo Amery mooted Eden as a possible Viceroy of India in August 1940, the suggestion fell on stony ground as 'the King was very funny about his difficulties in getting a word out of her [i.e. Mrs Eden]'; Amery also found Beatrice 'hard going' at social functions, recording of her at an official lunch in July 1941, 'poor dear, has nothing to say for herself.'[57] Nevertheless, Beatrice Eden acted as Chair of the Women's Divisional Council of the Warwick, Stratford-upon-Avon and Leamington Constituency Association, presiding at the Annual General Meetings. Her last signature on the minutes was at the meeting of 21 March 1947.

The Edens had a two-day honeymoon in Sussex before returning to Warwick to continue the campaign. At one stage Eden planned to honeymoon at Warwick Castle and campaign simultaneously, but decided against it, seemingly with some reluctance. However, the way things turned out, he could have had a longer honeymoon, for on 13 November, only nine days before the by-election, Stanley Baldwin unexpectedly announced in the House of Commons that he had sought a dissolution of Parliament from the King. Polling Day for what became known as the 'Protection Election' was fixed for Thursday 6 December.[58] The Warwick and Leamington contest was thus subsumed in the larger battle, and by electoral law the slate had to be wiped clean.

Eden's first entry into Parliament thus came about after the longest campaign in British electoral history. This protracted battle was by no means a disadvantage. He had time to become acquainted with a large and scattered constituency.[59] He took nothing for granted, despite the enthusiasm of many of the 19,000 first-time women voters, which gave a distinctive boost to his campaign. A handsome newly-wed candidate was a pollster's dream, and crowds flocked to the meetings. After the unexpected dissolution, Eden had been unanimously re-adopted by his association on 23 November. His second acceptance address to Conservative supporters was described as being 'devoid of promises of the pie-crust character.'* The Liberal candidate was George Nicholls, a former radical MP for North Hampshire. But the candidature that ensured national coverage for what was to prove a bizarre and eventful campaign was the appearance in the Socialist cause of the Countess of Warwick, mother-in-law of Eden's sister, Marjorie, and – so intertwined were the family relationships – the mother of Lady Beckett, the former Queenie Feversham, to whose step-daughter, Beatrice, Eden was now married.

Daisy Warwick, mistress of the Prince of Wales (later King Edward VII), was one of the most colourful characters to cross Eden's path. When Lord Warwick was considering divorce, the list of fourteen co-respondents whom he produced for his lawyers included (in addition to the Prince of Wales) the Duke of Marlborough and Lord Randolph Churchill. Not for nothing was Daisy Warwick known as 'the babbling Brooke'. Renowned for her devotion to charitable good works, she was the only woman of her time, other than Florence Nightingale, to be praised in the House of Commons for her social concern. In 1897 she had appeared as Marie Antoinette at a fancy-dress ball, and paid out of her own pocket for all the guests to eat cake. Normally, the Countess of Warwick campaigned in her forty-horse-power Wolseley car, which had been repainted bright red to make her sympathies plain. But for this campaign, cutting a figure that was a mixture of Dame Clara Butt and Queen Boadicea, she made an even more distinctive display, touring the constituency in a carriage drawn by four milk-white steeds. Unfortunately for her cause, she was mistaken by many voters as an advertisement for *The Garden of Allah* at the Leamington Playhouse.

Election day on 6 December was very foggy, which cut down the number of voters in some of the outlying rural areas. Nevertheless, there was a good overall turnout of 75 per cent. At the age of twenty-six, Eden was elected to the House of Commons in a safe Conservative seat. The figures were:

Captain R. A. Eden (Conservative)	16,337
George Nicholls (Liberal)	11,134
Lady Warwick (Socialist)	4,014
Conservative Majority	5,203

---

*A reference to Jonathan Swift's 'Promises and pie-crust are made to be broken', *Polite Conversation*, Dialogue 1. Details of the speech and meeting are in the Warwick and Leamington Conservative Association Minute Book, 1923. Warwick County Record Office, Warwick. File CR 1392.

On the national level, Baldwin's premature call to the electorate rebounded severely. The Conservatives were reduced to 258 seats and lost their overall majority; the Labour Party increased their number of seats to 191, and the uneasily reunited wings of the Asquithian and Lloyd George Liberal Party came third with 159 seats. For the moment Baldwin remained as Prime Minister, knowing that everything would hinge on which way Asquith and the Liberals voted when Parliament reassembled in January to consider the King's Speech.

Eden's delight in his successful campaign was tempered by the news of Lord Willoughby de Broke's sudden death on 16 December 1923, ten days after Eden was elected to the House of Commons. He was saddened that his mentor never saw him in Parliament (he first attended the House with his father-in-law, Ger Beckett, on 8 January 1924 for the re-election of the Speaker), especially as he was aware how much he owed to Willoughby de Broke. But he made good cause with his son, the 20th Baron, who, like Eden, had a Military Cross. In the New Year, a more personal bereavement came on 15 January 1924, with the death of Marjorie's father-in-law, the 5th Earl of Warwick. Marjorie was now the Countess of Warwick. Sadly, Guy Brooke was 6th Earl for only four years, dying on 31 January 1928.

The King's Speech was presented to Parliament on 15 January. Two days later, the Labour Party moved a motion of no confidence in the Baldwin Government. Baldwin had already been under pressure to resign; Asquith too had received countless messages, imploring him to save the country from the horrors of Socialism. But Asquith had already made his position plain in a speech on 18 December. As the electorate had voted against protection, Labour – the largest anti-protection party – deserved office; with the Liberals holding the balance of power, Asquith claimed, it would be a controlled experiment under the safest conditions. On 21 January, the Liberals voted with Ramsay MacDonald and the Labour Party, and Baldwin's Conservative Government fell by 328 votes to 256. The next day Ramsay MacDonald kissed hands on his appointment as Britain's first Labour Prime Minister. He also became Foreign Secretary. 'Today 23 years ago dear Grandmama died,' wrote the King in his diary that night. 'I wonder what she would have thought of a Labour Government'.[60] Queen Victoria, we can be sure, would not have been amused. Eden, on the other hand, had for some time considered the prospect inevitable. Now his first direct parliamentary experience would be in opposition, facing a minority Labour Government.

CHAPTER FOUR

From Warwick to Geneva

1924–9

Our main object in the immediate future is the destruction of the
Liberal Party and the absorption of as much of the carcass as we
can secure.

Leo Amery diary, 8 December 1923[1]

I have become more hopeful about this election [October 1924].
I think that our people will poll better; that we had more than
our fair share of seats lost by very small majorities last election,
that we shall get more Liberal votes & that 20 or 30 Liberals
will vote steadily with us in every critical division in the new
house, & that Squiff & Co will not again put a Socialist Govt.
into office in a hurry.

Austen Chamberlain to Hilda Chamberlain, 11 October 1924[2]

The majority was a surprise to everyone ... I can only suppose
that many moderate Liberals voted for me.

Anthony Eden diary, 30 October 1924[3]

When the Conservatives took their places on the Opposition benches after
MacDonald's appointment as Prime Minister on 22 January 1924, it
seemed to many of them that the Speaker was sitting in the wrong place.
They were unaccustomed to craning their necks to the right to secure his
eye. The visceral urge for power and dominance, the motivating force that
made the twentieth century largely a Conservative one, was behind their
sustained attempt to reverse this unnatural state of affairs as soon as
possible. Even they were to be surprised by how quickly this was to be
achieved.

The Parliament of January 1924 was unusual in many ways. The two
senior former Prime Ministers, the Liberals Asquith and Lloyd George,
were in the House, but never to hold office again. Baldwin, a former Prime
Minister of only eight months' standing, faced an uncertain future in a
party that included an active former leader in Austen Chamberlain, whom
Baldwin had passed over for office in May 1923. To complete a unique
situation, Ramsay MacDonald, who had never before held any Government post, was both Prime Minister and Foreign Secretary. Such was the
mixture of bruised egos and wary expectations that jostled in uneasy

66

coexistence when Anthony Eden first took his place on the Conservative benches.

For Eden a toe-hold in Westminster, where many of his ancestors had been, was excitement enough at this stage, even though his senior Tory colleagues were profoundly shocked by developments. 'Politically I have risen from the undignified position of an unknown & ignominiously defeated candidate for a little-known constituency,' he wrote, 'to be a member by more than 5000 majority for one of the most historic seats in England.'[4]

Eden was the only future Prime Minister elected in the December 1923 contest (Harold Macmillan did not enter the House until October 1924). The new intake was not a vintage political class. Apart from Eden, the only other front-rank figure to be elected for the first time was Herbert Morrison, Labour MP for South Hackney, a future Home and Foreign Secretary and Deputy Prime Minister. Eden grew to admire Morrison greatly, especially after their joint service in Churchill's wartime Cabinet. Indeed, he was to regard it as a national misfortune that Morrison did not succeed Attlee as Labour leader in 1955.

As MP for Warwick and Leamington, Eden now had his first regular salary (£400 a year), though without Ger Beckett's occasional, and much appreciated, help ('He is an amazingly generous person'),[5] things would have been very difficult financially. Eden kept up the appearances required of a Conservative member in those days, but without the substantial means that many of his contemporaries took for granted. In fact, the unusual combination of two General Elections in his first year (1910 and 1974 were the only other examples in the twentieth century) reduced significantly the days for which he was actually paid, and no parliamentary or secretarial expenses were then covered. The constituency was also a drain on his limited funds. As Eden noted tersely, 'Election expenses are about £140 short which I shall have to find – Damn!'[6]

Ger Beckett's support of his new son-in-law MP was not only financial; he made a point of introducing Eden to the ways of Westminster life in those early weeks of 1924. Eden soon found that the only thing uniting the majority of Conservatives was the feeling that Baldwin, by calling an unnecessary election, was the man responsible for getting them into their unexpected predicament. The jealousies of Westminster were not to Eden's liking, and he eschewed the smoking room and bars, something that was later to prove a parliamentary handicap, making him seem aloof and out of touch.

In the course of 1924 the Conservatives faced key decisions. The first was the question of Baldwin's leadership. Despite the criticisms of the Rothermere press, perhaps indeed because its unbridled ferocity was counter-productive, Baldwin survived at a meeting of the party at the Hotel Cecil on 11 February. 'A large attendance,' Eden wrote in his diary. 'Baldwin spoke better than usual, but not a word or even a hint of resignation'.[7] Baldwin was confirmed in office by the National Union the following day, though until October 1924 his leadership had something of a provisional air. As so often in politics, moves to displace an incumbent leader foundered on the absence of a coherent and credible alternative. But the vultures would circle again.

The second question was that of Protection versus Free Trade, the issue that Herbert Morrison, the new Labour MP, called 'a poisonous red herring drawn across the path of the common people by monopolist profiteers.'[8] Baldwin had chosen Protection, but now that he had seen its electoral disadvantage, he 'unchose' it, making sure (in the days before formal Shadow Cabinets) that he carried his senior colleagues with him. Eden saw the decision as inevitable, his main concern being employment prospects.

Unifying the party was now a priority. Austen Chamberlain and the Coalitionist Conservatives ('the slice off the top') were brought back into the fold after the Carlton Club schism of October 1922, a process sustained by the inclusion of senior figures such as Churchill, Balfour and Birkenhead in the next Conservative Cabinet after October 1924. In the long term, the most material development during the nine months of the minority Labour Government was the squeezing of the Liberal Party, a deliberate policy by the Tories. As Leo Amery noted in his diary, 'One of the three parties has to disappear and the one that is spiritually dead and has been so for thirty years or more is the natural victim.'[9] By putting Labour into office as a controlled experiment, Asquith had effectively sealed the electoral fate of Liberalism. The Liberal demise (the two combined wings of the party won only forty seats in the October 1924 General Election) had two effects: Labour was firmly established as the alternative to the Conservatives, and the assimilation of anti-Socialist Liberals into the Conservative Party tempered the die-hard Toryism that had so appalled Eden in his first attempts to enter Parliament. 'The hard-faced men who look as if they had done very well out of the war'[10] in Baldwin's famous phrase, still held considerable sway, but if the Conservatives were to attract moderate Liberals, even former Labour men, to their cause, then other counsels would have to prevail. Leo Amery wrote that the Labour MP Haden Guest was thinking of such a move on fiscal grounds, and 'while there are some reactionaries in our Party with whom he will find it very difficult to work, he could very happily follow Baldwin and myself and work with younger men of the Eden and Lumley type'.[11] Eden then was regarded as one of the progressive figures of his generation within a few months of arriving at Westminster.

A further sign of Liberalism's decline was the shift in Winston Churchill's party allegiance. Originally a Conservative, Churchill had crossed the floor to join the Liberals in 1904. After the loss of his Dundee seat in November 1922, the convalescent Churchill described himself as being 'without office, without a seat, without a party, and without an appendix'.[12] Defeated as a Liberal Free Trader in Leicester West in December 1923, he then stood as an 'Independent Anti-Socialist' at the by-election for the Abbey Division of Westminster in March 1924, losing by only forty-three votes. Churchill was then seen as the one figure who could deliver discontented Liberals to the Conservative fold, and the penultimate stage in his rehabilitation was his election in October 1924 for Epping as a Constitutionalist. Baldwin's abandonment of Protection provided a fig-leaf of credibility to what Churchill called his 're-ratting'.

Two days after Ramsay MacDonald became Prime Minister, Eden moved with Beatrice into his first London home, 2 North Street (later Lord North Street). As was customary in the 1920s, even among substantial sections of the professional classes, Eden did not buy property, but rented the house, for £250 a year.[13] An interesting commentary on prevailing social conditions is that Eden, who was not well-to-do, could nevertheless install himself in one of the most prestigious streets in the Division Bell district, with indoor servants. His house was next to the one Harold Wilson occupied in his last spell as Prime Minister from 1974 to 1976, and three from that used by Brendan Bracken in the 1930s (and later by Jonathan Aitken in the 1980s) as a celebrated political *salon*.[14]

Unfortunately, Lord North Street was not a success. 'Moved into the new house,' Eden wrote in his diary. 'Very dirty; the cook cried and confusion was general.' The couple later took a house at 1 Mulberry Walk, Chelsea, again a desirable address, though Eden conducted the removal with economy. 'With great energy travelled by tube and carried luggage to Mulberry Walk thereby saving taxi!'[15]

Many Conservatives were socially condescending towards Labour members, but not Eden. The gleeful stories of ministerial *faux pas* passed him by; nor did he gloat over Asquith's decline, for he considered him the most polished and dignified speaker he had ever known, because he could say concisely in twenty minutes what took others in the House at least three-quarters of an hour. *Schadenfreude* was a feeling totally alien to Eden's character. What he long remembered was the advice Baldwin had given new Conservatives that spring about their Labour opponents. 'Though you may have had better educational advantages, do not presume upon that, they know more about unemployment insurance than you.'[16] Eden saw Baldwin as a conciliatory figure, a man whose concern for social harmony mirrored his own, and he was greatly to admire Baldwin's handling of the General Strike. He regarded the recall of Austen Chamberlain and his Carlton Club followers to the front bench as a shrewd political move by Baldwin, which would avoid the kind of fissure that had fatally wounded the Liberals after the 1918 Maurice Debate. In time, he was to serve both Chamberlain and Baldwin, as Parliamentary Private Secretary and Foreign Secretary respectively.

A key moment in any political career is the maiden speech. Eden's was unorthodox in three respects. His decision to speak was taken on the spur of the moment; his tone was controversial; and his subject (air defences), unexpected, as Eden was more noted for his interest in domestic policy and labour relations. 'Dined early & returned to the House in time for the Air Force debate,' wrote Eden in his diary for 19 February 1924. 'Hoare spoke first – the under-secretary for air [William Leach] replied in a sanctimonious and unimpressive manner which drove me to speak ... I was terrified, & did not, I thought, acquit myself with any credit. But the house was very generous & cheered very well when I sat down.'[17]

The debate was on a motion put down by Sir Samuel Hoare, Secretary of State for Air in 1922 in the wake of the Chanak crisis, when Britain's air defences had totalled twenty-four planes. In his short first spell at the Air Ministry, Hoare had quadrupled this figure. The point of the debate was not to bring him personal retrospective credit, but to embarrass the Labour Government, whose declared policy was one of retrenchment. William Leach, the Under-Secretary at the Air Ministry, was a well-known pacifist, and his speech reinforced MacDonald's recent statement on National Defence that his bargaining power as Foreign Secretary in the future would depend on the rationale of his policy, not on military might. The Conservatives regarded this as naive wishful thinking and it confirmed their view that Labour would be 'soft' on defence. It was an issue that plagued Labour for decades. In October 1957 Labour's Shadow Foreign Secretary, Aneurin Bevan, in one of his most explosive speeches, told the party conference in Brighton that a policy of unilateral disarmament would be akin to sending 'the British Foreign Secretary, whoever he was, naked into the Conference Chamber'.[18] This was precisely what Eden felt in February 1924.

Eden was appalled by Leach's speech. Feelings were running high on both sides and the House was restive. When the member for Merthyr, R. C. Wallhead, who had been in the Independent Labour Party delegation to Russia in 1920, called for 'a diminution of arms', Eden decided that he must speak. As a maiden speaker, he could be assured of the Speaker's eye. Such speeches are customarily received in silence, but this was not to be a customary speech. After a few courtesies, Eden changed tack abruptly:

The last speaker made great play of a little geographical tour and he asked us from what quarter we expected an attack from the air. I do not know, but I do not think that is the point we want to discuss. Surely the point is rather that we should prepare to defend ourselves against an attack from any quarter.

Eden stressed the importance of adequate military provision:

In the first place it is not in the nature of things possible to provide hastily and at a moment's notice for air defence; and in the second place, the very heart of our country, the city of London, is especially vulnerable to attack from the air. For these reasons I hope that the government will not be tempted too much by sentiment, and will rather act, as we gather from the speech of the Under-Secretary, not in accordance with his principles but in accordance with the programme he has inherited from other parties, and that the government will, as a matter of insurance, protect this country from the danger of attacks from the air.

The description of Labour's stance as a 'sentiment' was too much for many Labour back-benchers. When Eden went on to declare that 'Attack is the best form of defence', the Chamber erupted with shouts of 'No, no!' from the Labour benches. Eden warmed to his theme:

I expected hon. members opposite would be a little surprised at that doctrine: I was not suggesting that we should drop our bombs on other countries but simply that we should have the means at our disposal to answer any attack by an attack. It is a natural temptation to hon. members opposite, some of whose views on defence were fairly well known during the years of the war, to adopt the attitude of that very useful animal the terrier, and roll on their backs and wave their paws in the air with a pathetic expression. But that is not the line on which we can hope to ensure this country against attack from the air. I believe and hope that the hon. members opposite will carry out the programme which they have inherited and will safeguard these shores, so far as they may, from the greatest peril of modern war.[19]

In one short speech, Eden had prefigured one of the principal political questions of the 1930s. Baldwin, who was later to declare that 'the bomber will always get through',[20] was impressed, but the speech was not an unqualified success. The next speaker, William Wedgwood Benn, ignored the maiden speech completely. This lack of praise was highly unusual in the Commons.

The next day Eden wondered whether he had been right to speak in such forthright terms, a sign of his self-critical sensitivity and lack of assurance. For Conservatives with military associations, however, his reputation as a 'sound' man had been reinforced. He remembered Labour supporters in his platoon in the war, and there was no questioning their patriotism or bravery. He was no longer an anonymous newcomer. First impressions in the House of Commons count for much, and Eden was seen as a patriotic defender of British interests, his identifying quality in the 1930s and beyond.

Eden's reading often mirrored contemporary circumstances. He was reading Shakespeare's history plays, for example, in the weeks before the D-Day landings in 1944. In the week of his maiden speech he was absorbed by Thomas Hardy's novel of the Napoleonic Wars, *The Trumpet Major*, with its underlying theme of the defence of the realm. Fear of foreign domination permeates Hardy's novel, the atmosphere in the Wessex villages having much in common with the feelings Eden experienced when recruiting for the King's Royal Rifle Corps in County Durham. In both instances, rural figures flocked to the colours. But the parallel with the current debate was even more striking and had a subliminal effect on Eden's utterances. An 'Address to all ranks and descriptions of English-man' in *The Trumpet Major* invites men to 'come forward in defence of everything that is dear to you' – the theme of Eden's maiden speech. In 1924, no less than in 1805, as Hardy put it, 'Victory will never belong to those who are slothful and unprepared.'[21]

When Persia was discussed a week later, Eden spoke on the question of consular guards, exhibiting technical knowledge of the country and insight into the workings of the oriental mind. Although again an impromptu speech, the impression was conveyed of someone who really knew his subject. Eden's speeches now followed at regular intervals: domestic matters such as housing policy concerned him; and he returned to the question of national defence, and related issues such as army marriage allowances. He was beginning to be noticed, a process assisted by his regular articles for the *Yorkshire Post*. He recorded in his diary, when he had a minor traffic accident on the way to Euston station, running into a car, 'I don't know whose, but they knew me – great excitement!!'[22]

On 7 March 1924 Eden was invited to a function at Buckingham Palace. 'The King was very affable, sent for me & talked for quite a long time,' wrote Eden in his diary. Although it was their first meeting, George V, to Eden's surprise, obviously knew about his war service and entry into Parliament. The King soon got on to the subject of the Warwick and Leamington constituency. 'He was very severe upon Lady W[arwick],' Eden recorded, though whether for her politics or her reputation within the royal family is not clear.[23]

Eden was now known not only to the Head of State, but also to the Head of the Government. Ten days after his meeting with the King, in a prelude to a major contribution to a foreign-affairs debate, he asked Ramsay MacDonald when there would be an opportunity for the House to discuss the Treaty of Lausanne, one of Lord Curzon's last diplomatic triumphs, which among other things defused the Chanak crisis. 'He [Ramsay MacDonald] answered very carefully & he treated my supplementary in the same way,' noted Eden in his diary.[24]

The ratification of the Treaty of Lausanne was considered during the second reading of the Peace Bill (Turkey) on 1 April, the occasion of Eden's first foreign-affairs speech in Parliament. Many of the earlier contributions were woolly and xenophobic. Eden's speech this time was no impromptu intervention. His survey of the situation since the Armistice in Asia Minor proved something of a tour de force, which impressed politicians on both sides by its range and insights. Here was a young politician with knowledge of his subject, drawing conclusions about the realities of the new nationalism in Turkey under Mustapha Kemal, in a more informed manner than Ramsay MacDonald, and quite on a par with Lloyd George. Eden emphasised that the Treaty of Lausanne (1922–3) was very different from that signed at Versailles in 1919, when we could dictate our terms to the vanquished:

> At Lausanne the tables were turned and the position was reversed. In the eyes of the Turks we were the vanquished, not from the military point of view but because, rightly or wrongly, they looked on this country as having sympathised with aspirations of their enemies. Consequently they claimed that the defeat of the Greeks was a moral defeat of this country also. Further, as we all know, there was very little unity among the Allies at Lausanne. We had to deal not with a vanquished enemy but with the representatives of a nation fresh from a great victory – proud, and justly proud of the achievements of their armies, and knowing full well that they could only obtain the approval of their countrymen by securing terms which would redound to the credit of their country. I suggest that under those conditions – and that is a true précis of the conditions – it is a matter of the greatest congratulation to our representatives that an agreement of any kind was arrived at, and it is a great tribute to the patience, the tact, the zeal, and the understanding of our representatives at Lausanne.

What mattered now was how Kemalist Turkey would develop:

> It is nationalism that rules Turkey to-day. I believe that as time goes on other influences will prevail, and that a spirit of toleration will make itself felt, and then this country on the basis of this Treaty will be able to step in and share in the better relations between the two countries.

MacDonald, in his capacity as Foreign Secretary, associated himself 'profoundly with what was said.'[25] There were none of the cries of dissent that had greeted Eden's maiden speech. Specialist analysis, careful preparation and the succinct brevity that he so admired in Asquith's speeches made for a thoughtful triumph.

Before the Easter recess, Eden asked further questions on India, and took part in a heated debate on Rent Restrictions. 'MacDonald made an obscure situation even more obscure; and Baldwin spoke against him,' Eden wrote. 'Many Liberals ratted at the last moment but even so we carried the division by 9! Great excitement.'[26] The Government was defeated again in a further division later that night. For the first time Eden felt the Conservatives might be in office before the end of the year.

The Edens spent Easter in his constituency, where they saw Guy and Marjorie Warwick. Guy was now in the grip of a debilitating illness and further disturbing news came from Windlestone with more examples of Lady Eden's profligacy.

A less stressful interlude was his first visit with Beatrice to Stratford, a town that was always special to Eden, because of its associations with his beloved Shakespeare. On Easter Monday (21 April), he took Beatrice to see *The Merry Wives of Windsor* ('well done and most enjoyable'), the first of three plays on successive evenings. On Tuesday, they saw *Othello* ('a tremendous play but harrowing'), after which Eden considered how narrowly the characters in *The Merry Wives of Windsor*, especially the jealous Ford, escaped the tragic fate of those in *Othello*. For Eden, an enduring truth about Shakespeare concerned the progress of the characters towards self-knowledge. Those who learned the truth about themselves, in time to profit from that recognition, inhabited the world of the comedies, where all ended well; delayed recognition inevitably led to tragic downfall, as for Othello. On 23 April, Shakespeare's birthday and St George's day – both important landmarks in the calendar of the 1920s, they saw *King Lear*, a play highly rated by the cognoscenti, but about which Eden (despite choosing a phrase from it as the title for the first volume of his memoirs) was always ambivalent. 'I enjoyed it, but was also horrified. Tremendous though it is, I cannot but feel it is at times unnatural, and at others too natural.'[27]

After their Shakespeare-fest, the young couple stopped en route at Oxford, where Eden 'took Beatrice round several of the colleges & showed her hall, my old rooms etc.' It was while visiting Christ Church that Beatrice told Eden that she wished he had become a don.[28]

On the day that the Edens had attended *King Lear* at Stratford, King George V opened the Empire Exhibition at Wembley, transforming a previously anonymous north-west London suburb into a venue famous around the world. It proved the most ambitious such project since the Great Exhibition of 1851 and evoked unparalleled enthusiasm. One of the enduring and unlikely images in the flickering newsreels of the time is that of the formally dressed Queen Mary (King George the fifth and Queen Mary the four-fifths, as the wags put it) taking a journey on the precarious miniature railway. Eden was struck by the educational possibilities of the Wembley exhibition, and when the House met after Easter he made two speeches on education, the first on the finances of maintained secondary schools, and the second on consolidating the benefits of the Wembley exhibition with regular school visits to museums and art galleries for educational purposes. With luck, Eden felt, this might even improve national tastes and prevent any more artistic disasters such as the Albert Memorial!

The main parliamentary excitement after the recess was Philip Snowden's Budget on 29 April. Although the abolition of the protective McKenna duties caused great concern in the growing motor industry in the Midlands, Eden felt that overall 'it might have been much worse.'[29] As his own contribution to saving money, Eden started travelling third-class on train journeys: 'comfortable' and 'very economical', he recorded.[30]

His eclectic reading that month included Scott's *Kenilworth* (useful for constituency background) and *Rob Roy*, Hardy's *The Woodlanders*, Thackeray's *The Newcomes*, and the Shakespeare play that he came to admire the most, *Troilus and Cressida*. He agreed with Goethe, who said, 'would you learn to know Shakespeare's unfettered spirit, read *Troilus and Cressida*'. When speaking at Stratford on the quatercentenary of Shakespeare's birth in 1964, Eden told his audience that 'the speech of Ulysses to the warrior [Achilles] sulking in his tent is one of the finest things in Shakespeare, worthy of the study of any statesman in his upward flight.'[31]

Eden's own upward flight was increasingly evident. Foreign policy was of abiding interest to him. He applauded the improvement in Anglo-French relations and MacDonald's presence in September at the Assembly of the League of Nations in Geneva. Other aspects of Labour's approach left him less easy. In February, MacDonald had recognised the Soviet Government as the ruler of the old imperial territories, and the day before Parliament prorogued for the summer recess on 7 August, he agreed an Anglo-Russian Treaty – in effect two treaties, one on commercial matters of trade and recognition of the rights of British bond-holders, the other a declaration of intent regarding a British loan to the Soviets. Conservative and Liberal anxieties were widespread, and Eden felt that MacDonald was trimming with Bolshevism. From within his own party, MacDonald was subject to a different kind of criticism, one that was later to be levelled at Eden, that he concentrated on foreign affairs at the expense of domestic ones.

As the Liberals shared Conservative anxieties, there was a distinct feeling that the summer recess would be the last before another General Election. Instead of welcoming the prospect of sitting for the first time on the Government benches, Eden was concerned about the additional expenses. It also meant that part of the summer was taken up with electioneering. A visit to Swansea on 9 August was not a success. 'A terrible place,' wrote Eden uninhibitedly. 'I do not like the Welsh. Undersized little humbugs with radical instincts.'[32] Eden could be judgemental in the privacy of his diary. Of Cosmo Gordon Lang, Archbishop of York, who had married the Edens in November 1923, he wrote: 'I am not sure that I really like him, he is a little "smarmy", a view that was to find wider currency after the speech that Lang, then Primate of All England, made at the end of the Abdication crisis in December 1936, about Edward VIII's social circle 'whose standard and way of life are alien to all the best instincts and traditions of his people.'[33]

On 25 July, J. R. Campbell, editor of the *Workers' Weekly*, a Communist newspaper, had published an article urging the military never to take up arms against their fellow workers. The Attorney-General, Sir Patrick Hastings, had indicated that a prosecution would follow under the Incitement to Mutiny Act. By September nothing had happened, and when the matter was raised in Parliament, Hastings admitted that he had decided to drop the prosecution. What escalated the episode into a full-blown crisis, together with a Conservative motion of censure, was MacDonald's statement to the House denying that he had been consulted about the withdrawal of the prosecution, a statement that Maurice Hankey, the Cabinet Secretary, privately described as 'a bloody lie'.[34]

When the Liberals, who wanted a select committee, added an amendment to the Conservative motion, the Cabinet decided on 6 October to treat both motions as a vote of confidence. 'A general election seems more & more imminent though there is just a possibility that the Liberals & the Govt may agree to a judicial committee to enquire into the Campbell case,' wrote Eden in his diary, adding 'I dread the idea of an election,'[35] a reference to his financial anxieties, not his political concerns.

The subsequent Campbell Debate on 8 October was the first great parliamentary event at which Eden was present, one of only two occasions in the twentieth century when a Government was brought down following defeat in a confidence motion.[36] Eden was caught up in the parliamentary drama. 'House in the afternoon & evening. Interesting. Hastings made a very good case, especially from his own point of view – Simon was nasty, but effective – Asquith in his best form.' In Eden's opinion, the most notable Conservative contribution came from the former Chancellor of the Exchequer, Sir Robert Horne, with the legal side well put by the former Conservative Attorney-General, Sir Douglas Hogg. Labour were very much on the defensive:

> Ramsay rather pompous & beating the electioneering drum, but his followers seemed delighted. [J. H] Thomas [Colonial Secretary] made a clever eleventh hour defence . . . We were bound to turn them out if & when we could, but the least convincing aspect of Ramsay's defence – for it was really he & not Hastings who was on trial – was his unwillingness to face an enquiry . . . An election is now almost certain.[37]

So it proved. The Government was defeated by 364 votes to 198 on the Liberal amendment. The next morning MacDonald asked for a dissolution and Polling Day was fixed for 29 October.

The 1924 General Election was dominated by the Soviet issue: the Campbell case, the Russian treaties, and then, with dramatic unexpectedness on the weekend before polling, the Zinoviev letter. On 25 October, the *Daily Mail* declared evidence of 'Civil War Plot by Socialists. Moscow Order to our Reds. Great Plot Disclosed Yesterday'. Whether the letter, from Zinoviev, the President of the Presidium of the Communist International in Moscow, to the Central Committee of the British Communist Party, was genuine or not (the accepted historical view is now that it was a forgery), its impact was considerable in a country where many voters, including educated left-of-centre figures such as Eden, were wary of 'Bolshevism'.

The Conservatives won 419 seats, Labour 152 and the Liberals just forty. Asquith's Commons career was brought to an end. Labour would come to power again (within five years, as it happened), but the real losers were the Liberals. In contested seats, the Conservatives increased the proportion of their vote from 42.6 per cent in 1923 to 51.9 per cent in 1924, mainly at the cost of the Liberals. This was certainly the case in Warwick and Leamington.

In the absence of the Countess of Warwick, Eden had a straight fight against his Liberal opponent. 'Left at 8 a.m. to make a tour of the constituency & very well received everywhere & scenes of great enthusiasm,' he wrote on Polling Day. 'There can be little doubt now but that we are in, though hardly with as big a majority as last year, probably 2000-3000.'[38]

Eden's estimate was unduly pessimistic. As a rural seat, Warwick and Leamington declared the following day, by which time Eden recorded 'The morning papers brought cheering news of sweeping Conservative victories in the towns.' He went with Beatrice to the count at 11.45. 'As soon as the sorting into files began it became evident that we were in, though as the count went on the size of the majority staggered us.' The figures were:

Capt R. Anthony Eden (C)	19,575
G. Nicholls (Lib)	12,966
Conservative Majority	6,609

'The majority was a surprise to everyone because there can be little doubt that Nicholls got many Socialist votes,' wrote Eden. 'I can only suppose that many moderate Liberals voted for me.'[39] Among the personal telegrams of congratulation was one from Baldwin.

Before Parliament reassembled, Eden read *Great Expectations*, 'a very good tale,' he wrote. 'I am inclined to think the best Dickens.'[40]

With the dramatic decline of the Liberal Party – a process accelerated even during his short spell in the House – Eden now believed it was vital for the Conservatives to appeal to progressive-minded non-Socialist voters. In a steadily more polarised political climate, there would be an overwhelming need for imaginative social-welfare policies, especially in employment and housing. During his Election tour Eden had been appalled at the state of some of the slums in his constituency. Already he saw property as the key to a stake in society. Over the next few months these views would be channelled into his most important social contribution to Conservative thinking. With Arthur Mann's encouragement, he addressed these issues in some of his *Yorkshire Post* articles. 'I believe a great many people will pay particular attention to what you may say in relation to domestic problems,' Mann wrote to Eden later, urging the Conservatives not to allow Labour a monopoly in these matters, in the eyes of the electorate.[41]

Stanley Baldwin now formed his second administration. The most significant appointment for Eden's future career came with the rehabilitation of Austen Chamberlain, who was appointed Foreign Secretary. Also important for Eden in the shorter term was the appointment of Sir William Joynson-Hicks ('Jicks') to the Home Office, with Godfrey Locker-Lampson as his Under-Secretary. Birkenhead returned to the fold as Secretary of State for India, and Neville Chamberlain, whom many thought the likeliest Chancellor of the Exchequer, became Minister of Health. Baldwin was to spring his biggest surprise over the tenancy of 11 Downing Street. Eden suspected that Churchill's re-election at Epping would be the prelude to a Government post, but in common with many other Conservatives he was astonished when that post turned out to be the Chancellorship of the Exchequer. (Even Churchill himself initially thought that the offer of the Chancellorship referred to the Duchy of Lancaster.) Eden had been wary of Churchill's mercurial unpredictability since his schooldays. What the economic consequences might now be, he dreaded to think.

Before Parliament reassembled on 2 December, a personal event occupied the Edens. Their first child was born prematurely. 'I do hope it is a son,' wrote Eden on 12 November. A boy was born the next day, after a difficult confinement. 'Beatrice well, but very tired,' wrote Eden. 'The baby quite a fine little chap for his 8 Months.'[42]

After his brother's death at Jutland, Eden had determined that any future son should be called Nicholas in his memory. Now he shrank from such a christening lest the name bring bad luck. The Edens called their son Simon Gascoign.

At the beginning of December, Eden took his place on the Government side of the House of Commons for the first time. During his next thirty-three years in Parliament he was to be on that side for all but two spells, 1929-31 and 1945-51. He was one of only four twentieth-century Prime Ministers never to have been leader of the Opposition, or to have led his party from the Opposition benches.[43] Just as the late Victorian generation was destined to have its formative experience in war, so Conservative politicians of that era would experience a political legacy of largely unbroken office.

Eden did not intend to be a village Hampden in the new Parliament, but soon found that the way to political preferment was punctuated by delays and disappointments. The Conservative landslide meant that there were many other fish swimming in a very large pool, and competition for office proved fierce. Rather in the manner of 1945, however, those Conservatives who had been elected in December 1923, in what proved to be a Labour Parliament, had an advantage over the later intake. Eden, Macmillan and Rab Butler, the dominating Conservative figures of the 1950s, entered Parliament in 1923, 1924 and 1929 respectively, and Eden was the first to receive preferment. Butler followed in 1932, while Macmillan, by far the oldest of the trio, had to wait until 1940. But he made up for it later, at the expense of both Eden and Butler. Most of the Under-Secretaryships in October 1924 were given to middle-aged figures. Baldwin had himself been a late starter in politics, serving a political apprenticeship of nearly ten largely anonymous years before his first post at the age of fifty. In the opinion of one commentator, Baldwin, in filling the second-rank posts in his administration with fifty-year-olds, probably thought he was giving youth its chance.[44]

Eden soon found that patience was a parliamentary virtue; unfortunately, he was never very patient. His restless energy, if not that of a young man in a hurry, was certainly that of one who wanted to be busy. The comparatively gentle demands of Warwick and Leamington did not fulfil these needs.

In December 1924 Eden had an opportunity to join a parliamentary delegation to the Persian oil-fields. It was a welcome break from back-bench life and his first visit to the country that had been at the heart of his intellectual experience at Oxford. Also on this journey, he took in Egypt, 'the most important country' as Napoleon had called it, lying as it did at the confluence of Africa, Asia and Europe. His experience of Egypt brought him up against fierce poverty as well as scenery of haunting appeal. 'I have never seen anything so fascinating and so saddening as the Sphinx by moonlight' he wrote in his diary. 'Quite intoxicating in its beauty.'[45]

On his return, Eden was invited by Godfrey Locker-Lampson, Under-Secretary at the Home Office, to be his Parliamentary Private Secretary. 'Locker-Lampson rang up in the morning and I went round to see him at the Home Office, and to be initiated into my new duties,' Eden recorded in his diary on 17 February.[46] He found the work interesting, though not very demanding, but it gave him his first inside view of a great department of state, and at a time of growing social unrest, when its concerns were at the heart of Government business. Although an unpaid post, and one that limited Eden's freedom of action in speaking in the House, it was not an opportunity to let pass. He was on the ladder, albeit the lowest rung.

After a spell in the Diplomatic Service, Godfrey Locker-Lampson had been in the House since 1910, and was well versed in its ways. An Etonian and a veteran of the trenches, he struck up an immediate rapport with Eden. With his younger brother Oliver, Godfrey Locker-Lampson may not have been widely known to the general public, but nevertheless they both proved conscientious Westminster figures, indispensable for the efficient despatch of parliamentary business. Both brothers had spells working for Austen Chamberlain, and Godfrey Locker-Lampson's recommendation to Chamberlain was eventually to pave the way for Eden's assignment in the Foreign Office, a significant moment in its history. Godfrey was a distinguished minor poet, and a prolific author on a wide range of subjects.[47]

He urged Eden to get into print as soon as possible. As Eden was finding the work for Gervase Beckett's *Yorkshire Post* both interesting and lucrative, he needed no prompting. The problem of finding a suitable subject solved itself when Arthur Mann invited him to be the *Yorkshire Post*'s correspondent at the 1925 Imperial Press Conference in Melbourne. Some have suggested that Eden's haste in accepting a position that would mean a six-month absence from the House showed that, at bottom, he did not care for work at the Home Office and was only wanting to advance his credentials for a post in overseas affairs by becoming an expert in that field. Nothing could be further from the truth. By the standards of the day, Eden was already an expert in foreign matters. Work at the Home Office was of abiding interest to him, both in social and fiscal policy. He was aware that behind the photogenic tourist attractions of his Warwick constituency lay a largely unseen backdrop of mean streets and poor housing. How these slums could be cleared, and social conditions improved, was something he cared about deeply.

One of the figures Eden befriended in his first year at Westminster was Noel Skelton, the Unionist MP for Perth since 1922. An initial point of contact was that both were Christ Church men. Skelton, an Edinburgh advocate, is one of the largely forgotten figures of Conservatism, but had he not died prematurely of cancer in 1935, he could well have been one of the great figures of the party, even a possible future leader. His loss was a blow to progressive Conservatism akin to the deaths of Oliver Stanley in 1950 and Iain Macleod in 1970, but his name lived on in the hearts of many who believed in improving 'the condition of the people'. Skelton's two most prominent admirers, both future Conservative Prime Ministers, were Eden and Alec Dunglass (later Douglas-Home), whose initial attempt to enter Parliament had been endorsed by Skelton. Another Skelton admirer, and friend of Eden, was Walter Elliot, a future Secretary of State for Scotland.[48] Skelton's reputation had been made by a series of articles in 1923 in *The Spectator*, in which he addressed the central question of what the Conservative (or, as he preferred, the Unionist) Party should stand for in the post-war era. These political essays achieved wider currency when published in book form as *Constructive Conservatism* in 1924. Also a writer for the *Yorkshire Post*, Skelton represented the enlightened Conservatism that Eden believed essential for the party to retain its electoral appeal. The famous phrase about 'the property-owning democracy' is most associated with Eden, but it was actually coined by Skelton in one of his *Spectator* articles and became a consistent theme in both men's political thinking. 'Until our educated and politically minded democracy has become a property-owning democracy, neither the national equilibrium nor the balance of the life of the individual will be restored,' Skelton wrote in *Constructive Conservatism*. 'To restore that balance is the master-problem of the era.'[49] To this concept he added the then revolutionary ideas, developed further by Eden in the years of Opposition after 1945, of co-partnership between employers and workforce, share options and greater industrial democracy. Skelton returned to this theme in an article, 'The

Conservative Task: A Property-Owning Democracy', in the *Yorkshire Post* in 1930:

> In urban industrial life the road lies through profit sharing and co-partnership. The basic institution is, today, democracy. It can be stabilised and maintained by being founded on property-owning ... there is, in truth, no other way ... To develop in Britain a property-owning democracy – that, it is submitted, is at once the fundamental task of Conservatism and an objective for the nation consonant with its character and with the natural evolution of its life. That is Conservatism's true answer to Socialism.[50]

No more succinct summary could be found of Eden's beliefs, not only at this time but also throughout his career.

In a bipartisan spirit, Skelton and Eden had endorsed the efforts of the first minority Labour Government, through John Wheatley's Housing Act of 1924, to expand the provision of municipal house-building, a programme continued under successive governments. By 1933 more than half a million houses at affordable rents had been made available. Even as an elder statesman in the Lords, Eden did not forget Skelton's Disraeli-like influence: on the eve of the 1964 General Election, he sent Alec Douglas-Home, then Prime Minister, a message of good wishes, restating Skelton's belief that 'a property-owning democracy is the aim.'[51]

Eden spoke for the first time from the Government benches in a debate on unemployment on 25 March. His description of the Dominions in his overall economic survey was positively Baldwinesque in its tone and pre-echoed much of the thrust of the Ottawa Imperial Preference Conference in 1932. Afterwards Baldwin, greatly impressed, asked him when he was going to speak again. Modestly, Eden said he felt that silence was golden. At this stage of his career he was content to learn by listening, and felt that over-exposure had its dangers. He became an assiduous attender in Parliament, witnessing at first hand on 28 April one of the historic Budgets of the century when Winston Churchill, much influenced by Montagu Norman, the Governor of the Bank of England, announced Britain's return to the Gold Standard at the pre-war parity of $4.86. History, in the shape of J. M. Keynes, has not been kind to Churchill's efforts to restore 'normality', though Eden was not alone in thinking that Keynes's eventual polemic criticising Churchill's strategy should have been called *The Economic Consequences of Mr Norman*. At the time Eden, like many others, was impressed. 'Winston made his Budget statement. Two and a half hours and a masterly performance,' he wrote in his diary. Assessing its impact on his own finances, he added, 'The Budget means about £40 per year more to us next year which is always something.'[52]

82

In fact, Eden's own financial situation was to gain a welcome boost as a result of his world tour, for which the *Yorkshire Post* paid him £500, more than his annual salary as an MP. It meant that Beatrice was able to accompany him, though Simon was too young to travel with his parents.

On his return to England in November, Eden lost no time in joining Godfrey Locker-Lampson and Noel Skelton in print. The book of the political odyssey, notably Curzon's *Persia and the Persian Question*, which Eden had admired so much at Oxford, was a fashionable genre at the time. (Curzon had died on 20 March and the obituaries had praised his youthful literary triumphs.) The imperialist MP Leo Amery was another exponent of the literary *tour d'horizon*. So Eden was in good company when he eventually published an account of his travels.

The Edens sailed for New Zealand, by what was known as 'the all-red route', on 11 July 1925, arriving in Auckland on 16 August. Like many before him, Eden was impressed by the Scottishness of the New Zealand scenery. 'Motored to Mount Eden* from which a magnificent view of the surrounding country & of the harbour,' he wrote in his diary. 'Have never seen a finer anywhere. Very proud of my mountain! We were photographed on top of it.'[53]

In Australia, a stranger came up to Eden after a speech and said that he sounded exactly like George Wyndham. His visit coincided with the Australian Federal Elections. Protectionist policy was one of the burning issues and Eden devoted much of the Australian section of his subsequent book to the question of Imperial Preference. By November he was at Suez, his one journey through the Canal. 'Reached Suez after midnight,' he wrote on 21 November. The next day he was on board early to see the Bitter Lakes. 'All the morning going through the Canal. Attractive experience.' Journey's end was not so attractive. 'Did not like Port Said. The Egyptians cheeky and the town without charm.'[54]

By 30 November he was back at his desk at the Home Office, catching up with the parliamentary news from Godfrey Locker-Lampson. 'Jicks [Joynson-Hicks, the Home Secretary] does not seem to have been too discreet,' Eden recorded, 'otherwise the Govt. stands well, especially the two Chamberlains.'[55] Locker-Lampson told Eden the remarkable story of how Joynson-Hicks was convinced that the Premiership was his for the taking; he had spoken openly about it at dinner parties, had sent a junior secretary into the Smoking Room to canvass support, and had even made tentative offers of posts to Cabinet colleagues, including Philip Cunliffe-Lister,[56] the President of the Board of Trade, in his putative administration.

---

*Leo Amery went one better than Eden, as a mountain in the Canadian Rockies, of which he made the first ascent, was named after him personally.

In the frustrating wait for the succession after the Second World War, Eden did not forget the lesson of this episode, which marked a turning point in Joynson-Hicks's political career.

By contrast with Joynson-Hicks, Neville Chamberlain had successfully piloted the Pensions Bill through Parliament, and Austen Chamberlain was basking in the triumph of his part in the signing of the Locarno Treaty in October and the subsequent award of the Garter and the Nobel Peace Prize. Though the two Chamberlains were eventually to be of supreme importance in the development of Eden's inter-war career, Baldwin was still his most important mentor at this stage. When Eden collected his *Yorkshire Post* articles into book form, Baldwin contributed a foreword, in effect a public vote of confidence. *Places in the Sun*, published in 1926, had a muted reception, and Eden was disappointed by the sales of only 2,000 copies. Although no one would claim it was a Curzonian master-work, *Places in the Sun* is of more than passing interest. When Baldwin described Eden as 'a shrewd observer' of the imperial scene, this was not mere politeness.[57]

In its seventeen chapters, Eden reflects on countries from Canada to Ceylon (a particularly vivid section), combining a Baedeker-like account of the many places he visited with an examination of economic and political issues, such as immigration and Imperial Preference. He derided 'Socialist' enclaves, such as Queensland in Australia, where he claimed the unfortunate results of centralised state control were plain for all to see. The agricultural sections were of special relevance to many of his Warwick constituents. Prophetically, he said that the affairs of strategic landmarks such as Suez and Singapore should engage the Dominions jointly. The book's faults lay in its earnest tone and Eden's tendency to lapse into generalisations when not describing his own personal experiences. Nevertheless, the book brought his name before a wider public and was part of his learning process. The publishers, John Murray, produced an elegant volume with evocative photographs, and in Warwick and Leamington it proved a popular birthday and Christmas present, for uncles and aunts rather than nephews and nieces, but none the worse for that.

If Eden felt that his new status as a first-time author would enhance his chances of promotion, he was disappointed. He was passed over for a vacancy in the Whips' Office, and on 7 December 'heard that Locker-Lampson had been transferred to the Foreign Office.'[58]

Godfrey Locker-Lampson invited Eden to accompany him, but Eden hesitated. It would stop him speaking in the House on foreign affairs, and would not give him enough scope. He decided that it would be better to remain a 'freelance', which Locker-Lampson eventually accepted was for the best. 'He was urgent that I should not stay with him at the F.O., the job being too junior & Muzzling me on Foreign Affairs. He urged the making of speeches.'[59]

Eden was aware that he was not one of the liveliest speakers in the House and set about improving his technique. 'I don't seem to be able to get going at that place, the bored atmosphere makes it difficult especially when the House is nearly empty,' he recorded after a speech on 8 December. 'To make matters worse I found that the Press Gallery found difficulty in hearing, especially when I turned my back so the Press Reports are bad. Must correct this in future.'[60]

His first opportunity came just before Christmas in a debate on Iraq, when Eden argued against Britain abandoning its Mandate responsibilities. His side-swipe at what he saw as the Press barons' ambiguities over Soviet infiltration in the Middle East ('Are we to see Bolsheviks perusing the columns of the *Daily Express* and Noble Lords bustling to Fleet Street in Russian boots?')[61] was not forgotten by Beaverbrook. In later years, Eden traced the origins of Beaverbrook's unremitting hostility towards him to this speech and the impact it made on the Tory rank and file, not to mention on Baldwin, the continuing target of both Beaverbrook and Rothermere.[62]

'Certainly the most successful speech that I have yet made,' Eden noted privately, the verdict also of *The Times*. Sam Hoare told him that 'another such would obtain for me first refusal of the Treasury Bench – he had never heard a better back-bench speech & Francis Curzon [a Junior Lord of the Treasury] said that I had made my reputation that evening, there was no other conversation at the Minister's Table in the dining room'. Eden was pleased with the reception, but not complacent. 'I should have done better', he concluded.[63]

Buoyed by this success and the *Yorkshire Post*'s welcome contribution to his finances, Eden enjoyed the preparations for Christmas ('More successful shopping at Hammonds. If you are a gentleman, shop at gentleman's shops')[64] and his stay over the recess with the Becketts in Yorkshire. Looking back on 1925, he felt that it had been a lucky year. His apprenticeship to Locker-Lampson at the Home Office had given him invaluable insights into a great department of state, and he had eschewed the easy option of tagging along behind Locker-Lampson to the Foreign Office. Now he was using his independent status to speak on a wide range of subjects in the Commons. His world tour had given him first-hand knowledge of imperial matters, and his success on 21 December had established him on the road to a career. 'Thank you very much 1925,' he wrote on New Year's Eve. 'You have been very kind to me. I hate to leave so trusted & loyal a friend. I shall not forget you. And now 1926?'[65]

*

After the initial euphoria that had greeted the signing of the Locarno Treaty, French fears of renewed German ambitions returned. Sir Austen Chamberlain was also disappointed by German attitudes. 'A concession provokes not gratitude,' he wrote, in a striking pre-echo of the problems his half-brother Neville would experience a decade later, 'but some new demand which, but for the concession, they would not have ventured to put forward'.[66] Chamberlain was to be Foreign Secretary for four post-Locarno years, but few of those went by without some tinkering at the margins of the original treaty. With his French and German counterparts, Aristide Briand and Gustav Stresemann, Chamberlain held many Locarno 'reunions'. The outcome of what should have been straightforward ratifications often produced more difficulties than solutions. The question of Germany's eventual admission to membership of the permanent council had been an accepted understanding of the original treaty.

By the time the three Foreign Ministers met in Geneva early in 1926, Poland, Spain and Brazil were also putting forward their claims for inclusion. Sir Austen, a noted Francophile, sided with Aristide Briand's proposal for Poland's simultaneous admission to membership alongside Germany. This was contrary to the spirit of the original agreement, and a clear slight to Gustav Stresemann and German sensibilities. To complicate matters, Chamberlain also favoured Spain's admission – agreed Cabinet policy since 11 November 1925. The League of Nations' Parliamentary Committee expressed its concerns directly to Chamberlain. When Germany was not admitted to membership, Chamberlain faced a censure motion in the Commons in March 1926. It was a striking tribute to Eden's growing reputation in foreign affairs, and the Government's confidence in his abilities, that the Chief Whip, Bolton Eyres-Monsell, invited him to contribute in the debate and help unravel Chamberlain's difficulties.

Eden was briefed on the background issues by Sir William Tyrrell, the Permanent Under-Secretary at the Foreign Office, before speaking on 23 March alongside Sir Austen Chamberlain, Ramsay MacDonald, Lloyd George and Sir John Simon, a formidable and varied company. Hugh Cecil, a firm believer in the potential of the League of Nations, also made a reasoned speech. Eden opened robustly, recalling the tone of his earlier criticisms of Beaverbrook and the Press barons. He now attacked Lloyd George for 'always putting his foot down' and 'always putting his foot in it', very much the attitude of Baldwin, whose main aim in politics since the Carlton Club meeting of October 1922 had been 'to dish the goat'.[67] The optimism of the woolly-headed internationalists of the League of Nations Union also attracted Eden's scorn. Remembering the lessons from his imperial tour, he urged members not to underestimate the importance of the Dominions, and ended by emphasising that the spirit of Locarno, despite current difficulties, was not dead. John Simon, who followed him, said that Eden had 'put a much more reasonable point of view than the view with which the Foreign Secretary concluded.'[68]

Chamberlain survived the censure motion.

The early stirrings of what was to become the General Strike may not have seemed central to the concerns of Warwick and Leamington, but Eden knew the hardships that a prolonged dispute would bring to inter-dependent industries in his constituency. When the Samuel Commission was established in September 1925 to investigate the wages settlement of 1921 and current conditions in the mining industry, coal owners and Trade Unionists began an uneasy truce. The time bought by the appointment of the commission ran out with its report in March 1926, and although there were some welcome recommendations for the welfare of miners, tensions soon rose again. Eden welcomed the commission's proposals for better labour relations through the introduction of profit-sharing schemes, a central part of his own domestic vision, but was concerned about local consequences, if the Triple Alliance of railwaymen, dockers and miners from the 1921 strike was renewed. On 1 May he recorded the rapid developments with growing pessimism:

> On to Stratford when I heard definitely that the Coal Strike had begun. Damn! & that puts it mildly. Everybody seems to have imagined somehow that there would be a settlement at the last moment. The other unions including the Railways threaten to come out on Monday night so we are now in a pretty kettle of fish . . . Caught 5.5 train from Stratford. A wait at Leamington during which I had a long talk with anxious Railwaymen. They don't want to come out.[69]

But come out they had to, and the General Strike began at midnight on 3/4 May 1926. 'A troubled day,' Eden noted. 'To the House after lunch. Statement by the Prime Minister on General Strike & coal position. Not at his best, but allowances must be made for fatigue. All speeches very conciliatory. The Labour men obviously anxious to avoid a dispute. Winston good.'[70]

Eden decided that he must join up as a special constable (an echo of his service in Spennymoor with the defence force in 1921) and was posted to Fulham.

Although the General Strike was called off on 12 May, the event was not a nine-day wonder. Secondary strikes began the next day and the miners, increasingly isolated, did not return fully to work until October. The General Strike polarised class attitudes. Organised labour never forgot 1926, and sought revenge in 1945, and years later in 1974. 'Its cost in goodwill,' C. L. Mowat wrote, 'was soon forgotten by the middle classes, who had tasted only the excitement of the strike and none of its bitterness.'[71] But Eden was not among their number. The General Strike convinced him that a better way had to be found, not only in settling the inevitable disputes that arose in a market economy during a period of recession, but in addressing the underlying attitudes of many in his party (though not his leader) about labour relations and 'the condition of England'. He believed that the delicate situation needed careful handling, and was relieved that Baldwin's speeches were quiet in tone and generous. 'We should have been in Queer St without him.'[72]

Eden had always believed in chance. So far fate had been kind to him. Now it was to bring him another decisive break. He had been disappointed when Roger Lumley became Austen Chamberlain's Parliamentary Private Secretary, the one job he had really wanted at that time. However, in the summer of 1926 Lumley, in a move that heralded a shift towards a diplomatic career, announced that he was to go to Australia for six months. Eden was now offered Lumley's job by Sir Austen Chamberlain. 'After much thought & discussion decided to accept Austen's invitation & to act as his P.P.S.,' Eden wrote on 14 July. 'The offer is really due to Locker-Lampson's good offices in the matter.' Although Eden was initially concerned that he would be unable to speak in the House, an activity for which he was now showing increasing aptitude, he decided to grasp 'opportunities to learn which hereafter may be useful.'[73]

On 20 July he entered the Foreign Office for the first time in an official capacity and was shown round by Roger Lumley. It was a low-key beginning for one whose career had taken what proved to be its decisive step. Although Sir Austen Chamberlain was at the height of his fame when Eden joined him, the lustre had been tarnished by recent events in Geneva over membership of the League of Nations. In truth, Chamberlain's career had reached its peak with Locarno the previous year and the attendant celebrations. In the Foreign Office, the renaming of the Locarno Room,* where the final treaties had been signed, was a physical reminder of Chamberlain's triumph.

Eden, like many MPs, knew Chamberlain by reputation, but not by personal association. The Chamberlains were one of the most famous of political dynasties. Joseph Chamberlain, Austen's father, had made the political weather in his day, splitting both of the two great parties of state, over Irish Home Rule and Imperial Preference. The pictures of Joe that

---

*When a bust of Eden was unveiled at the foot of the great staircase of the Foreign Office by the Countess of Avon on 20 June 1994, guests were afterwards entertained to luncheon in the Victorian splendour of the Locarno Room.

survive show an alert, almost bird-like face, keenly responsive and eager.' In photographs of Austen one can sense the line of the old features, but the vigour under the surface is replaced by calmness; the firm, set stare has been smoothed and refined; only the monocle is the same.

Joseph Chamberlain planned that his eldest son should one day hold the highest political office; Neville, the younger one, would reinforce the family fortunes by growing sisal in the West Indies. Joe's scheme did not go according to plan. Although both sons (half-brothers, as Austen's mother had died in childbirth) were to lead the Conservative Party, Austen never succeeded to the Premiership, and the failure of the sisal project brought Neville back to local government in Birmingham. Westminster followed. Neville became a notable Minister of Health, his favourite post, before taking on the Chancellorship of the Exchequer and the Premiership in May 1937, two months after Austen's death.[74]

Austen held six Cabinet posts in his forty-five years in Parliament, including two spells as Chancellor of the Exchequer and five years in the Foreign Office. Uniquely, he sat in Cabinet first with his father and afterwards with his half-brother. It was said of Austen that he always played the game, and always lost it.[75] People appreciated his fine qualities, and respected his integrity; his point of view was understood and his intelligence admired; but somehow he was never really loved, and he lacked political charm. With stiff correctness, he played with undue relish his favourite role of Aristides – 'the one just man', but the one whom the Athenians exiled because they were tired of hearing him called just.

On a personal level, as Eden soon discovered, Austen Chamberlain was far warmer and more approachable than his public persona suggested. He had an intuitive sense of what worried his subordinates, and soon set at rest Eden's concerns about not being able to speak in Parliament. Eden found other unexpected freedoms in his new post:

> The fact that Sir Austen, like all his predecessors and successors, was more than fully occupied at the Foreign Office, and his somewhat remote attitude to members of Parliament, few of whom he knew personally, gave me exceptional opportunities. All papers and telegrams except the most secret ones were open to me and it was a good training to act as a buffer between the Foreign Secretary and the House of Commons.[76]

Eden's first such opportunity came on 2 August 1926 when, almost belatedly, the House of Commons realised that Chamberlain had made an agreement the previous December with Benito Mussolini, the Italian dictator, over Abyssinia – the very issue that was to propel Eden into the Foreign Secretaryship in December 1935. Mussolini and Austen Chamberlain were unlikely confidants and certainly not political bedfellows.

Yet Mussolini held a strange attraction for Chamberlain, which blossomed into real trust and friendship. Austen and his wife, Ivy, were welcome guests on Mussolini's yacht in the Mediterranean. After Austen Chamberlain's death in March 1937, Dame Ivy's unofficial talks with Mussolini (as the then Prime Minister's sister-in-law, Ivy was accorded semi-official status by the Italians) were to be one of the contributory factors to Eden's growing disillusionment with Neville Chamberlain's influence over foreign policy, and to his eventual resignation.[77]

Both Italy and Britain had Abyssinian projects (railways and a barrage at Lake T'ana respectively) that stood a better chance of success through mutual agreement. Accordingly, on 20 December 1925, Mussolini confirmed that, in return for Italian support over the Lake T'ana undertaking, the British Government 'will recognise the exclusive character of the Italian economic influence in the West of Abyssinia'.[78] Chamberlain's agreement with Mussolini aroused mistrust in France, and his statement in the Commons that Italy would have no special economic influence over Abyssinia was an unconvincing defence. In the corridors of Westminster, Eden held many hurried conversations with worried backbenchers, many of whom remembered Bonar Law's remark when Mussolini had come to power in 1922: 'Look at that man's eyes, you will hear more of him later.'[79] The parallels with the later crisis at the time of the Hoare-Laval Pact are uncanny, the only difference being that Chamberlain was never under any serious pressure to resign. The episode proved an important moment in confirming Eden's disquiet about the true intentions of the Italian dictator, feelings that were to be fully justified by events. It was a testing baptism in his new job.

Another issue that was to be a pre-echo of Eden's later career came over Egypt. The British Protectorate in Egypt had been ended by the British Government in 1922, though with four reservations, including imperial communications through the Suez Canal. With Cabinet backing, Chamberlain hoped to negotiate a new Anglo-Egyptian Treaty. 'We must be content to work the 1922 declaration loyally,' he wrote, 'and to give the Egyptians in the largest measure possible the independence which we promised them.'[80] But Chamberlain was not the first British politician to find Egypt an intractable problem. The importance for Eden lay in the fact that he had access to all the background material ('I don't much like the smell of the Egyptian business')[81] and followed at first hand the fraught negotiations with the Egyptian Prime Minister, Pasha Sarwat, a learning process that stood him in good stead when, as Foreign Secretary, he completed a new Anglo-Egyptian agreement in 1936.

Eden's eventful three years with Chamberlain introduced him to a wide range of international issues. He soon realised that British overseas commitments were not backed by appropriate military and economic strength. The civil war in China had important implications for Britain, not least over bases in Hong Kong, after the attack on the British concession in Hankow in January 1927. Baldwin took to having informal talks with Eden about his views. 'The PM came into my room,' he wrote on 7 December, 'and we had a long talk about China & Russia.' Subconsciously identifying what was to be his own Achilles heel, Eden added, 'I do envy him his serenity – I suppose an essential for a Prime Minister in these days.'[82]

Concerns about communism were not confined to Russia. Evidence came to light of Russian intelligence activities under cover of the Soviet Trade Delegation and the All Russian Co-operative Society (ARCOS), which led to Baldwin, Chamberlain and Joynson-Hicks sanctioning the ARCOS raid on 12 May 1927, and to the recall of the British mission in Moscow. Further problems for Chamberlain followed disagreements with the Americans at the Three Power Naval Disarmament Conference in Geneva in June–August 1927, which ended with the resignation of Lord Robert Cecil, Britain's representative at the League of Nations. It was a period of high hopes that were to end in disappointment. The event that most symbolised this process was the agreement brokered between Aristide Briand and the American Secretary of State, Frank Kellogg, to which Britain was a signatory. The Kellogg-Briand Pact renounced war as an instrument of national policy, an altruistic hope negated by the growth of political nationalism in the next decade.

Eden regarded the most valuable part of his time with Austen Chamberlain as the vicarious opportunity for witnessing the conduct of personal diplomacy. The first time Chamberlain invited Eden to accompany him to Geneva for one of his frequent 'salons' with Briand and Stresemann, Eden declined, but without admitting that the true reason was that he could ill afford the expense. The 'political freebie' was then an unknown concept. The following year he accepted.

The Foreign Secretary's journey to Geneva in those expansive days was like a royal progress. As Eden later recalled: 'The top-hatted stationmaster and the Foreign Office representatives at Victoria, the harbourmaster at Dover bowing us on to the ship, the *préfet* and the mayor at Calais, then a drive across Paris and dinner at the Embassy, the night train at the Gare de Lyon . . .'[83] Eden viewed these Curzonian displays with some distaste and when he became Foreign Secretary cut back on some of the more inconsiderate excesses, such as the customary morning welcome from the entire British delegation at Geneva station at 7.30.

Once Eden had spoken about Briand and Stresemann in his speeches; now he was able to meet them face-to-face in Geneva and hear at first hand the world view of the makers of a hoped-for international peace. Eden always believed that an interesting insight into the ways of human nature could be ascertained by a person's conduct at mealtimes. (When he got to know Mussolini, he felt that the dictator's abominable table manners were part of a pattern.) First impressions of Stresemann were not of his bonhomie, or sharp intelligence, but of his formidable appetite. For Eden, Stresemann's premature death in 1929 removed from the scene a man whose ambitions for Germany would have been revealed only covertly. His demise was also the death-knell for the Weimar Republic and paved the way for Hitler's rise. Stresemann had provided the cement to hold together the coalition of serious opposition to the Nazis in the 1920s. Had he lived, history could have been different. Some saw him as a Prussian Mephistopheles; Eden believed him to be the greatest German since Bismarck.

As befitted a man who was, if anything, even more of a Francophile than Austen Chamberlain, Eden much admired Aristide Briand, for seven years Foreign Minister of his country, and the embodiment of the spirit of the League of Nations. The remarkable aspect of Briand's personality for Eden was how his presence brought out the best in both Chamberlain and Stresemann. The three Foreign Ministers in concert were more than the sum of their individual parts. Briand had a sharp wit, which eased tensions at just the right moment. One deadlocked day, when the oppressive humidity was insufferable in the Council Chamber, one delegate wrapped his overcoat ever more closely about him. 'Look at our friend,' said Briand. 'As they push the coffin into the furnace, you will hear his voice crying, "For God's sake, shut that door. There's an awful draught!" '[84] Briand's greatest influence on Eden was to remove his initial scepticism about what the League of Nations could achieve, though he was never wholly optimistic about the longer term.

In 1928 Austen Chamberlain fell seriously ill and was absent from the Foreign Office for two months. Although Lord Cushendun, the Chancellor of the Duchy of Lancaster, took temporary charge of the Foreign Office, inevitably Eden's workload increased, especially as he was available in the Commons, speaking on the controversial Anglo-French naval agreement that Chamberlain had negotiated before his illness. Eden believed, as did Chamberlain, that the best way to maintain peace in Europe was by being on good terms with France, while moving towards an understanding with Germany, something which critics felt had been compromised by the exclusive naval agreement. When Eden attended the annual meeting of the Council of the League at Geneva that August in an official capacity for the first time, with Cushendun and Godfrey Locker-Lampson, the controversy still rumbled on and Eden was struck by the fissiparous and transient nature of the negotiations in the absence of Chamberlain, one of the triple pillars of the European diplomatic scene.

Personal life did not match the upward sweep of Eden's career. Relations with his brother Tim over the problems of his mother's finances worsened. An exploratory visit to his old home only increased Eden's sense of unease. 'Windlestone as beautiful as it is melancholy,' he wrote on 2 September. 'Impossible to explain sense of sorrow that hangs over everything.'[85] His brother-in-law, Guy Warwick, had died prematurely and relations within the Warwick family, especially between Marjorie and her son, Fulke, the new Earl of Warwick, were not easy. To complete a wretched autumn there came, quite unexpectedly, one of the saddest moments in Eden's life, the poignancy of which never left him. His second child died.

Most published books speak of Beatrice and Anthony Eden having two sons: in fact, they had three. Their second son was born on 15 October 1928, after a decision to operate. The child did not survive. 'Operation successful but little boy only lived a quarter of an hour. The sweetest little baby, quite lovely. Heartrending.'[86] They called him Robert. Three days later Eden was at his lowest ebb. 'I think the most wretched day I have ever been through. The funeral of Robert in the morning. Quietly & well done, poor little chap. There can be little doubt now that the cold was the cause.'[87]

Ger Beckett undertook all the financial arrangements for Beatrice to have the best of care, and convalescence in the West Indies. But the pain and blame and emotional strains of the family tragedy were to prove a turning point in the marriage, especially as her return from the Caribbean coincided with the 1929 General Election, when Eden was heavily committed.

Eden threw himself anew into his work for the *Yorkshire Post*. As well as his political articles for Arthur Mann, in 1928 he submitted a series of substantial articles on artistic matters to another commissioning editor, Collin Brooks, a journalist who later moved to London to join the parliamentary lobby, where his right-wing dissident Conservatism led him into many conflicts with the party establishment, and eventually with Eden.

Few British elections are decided by foreign affairs, and that of 1929 was to prove no exception. Unemployment, which had risen to nearly 1.5 million in January, was the dominating issue. *We Can Conquer Unemployment*, born in March 1929 of the famous Keynesian 'Yellow Books', advocating industrial regeneration through capital expenditure, was the central Liberal plank. Lloyd George promised a return to 'normal' levels within a year, a very different Return to Normality from that which he had forecast at the end of the Great War. Labour's main offering (G. D. H. Cole's *How to Conquer Unemployment: Labour's reply to Lloyd George*) was reactive, rather than original. As Lloyd George said, 'The Labour Party could not make up its mind whether to treat the Liberal plan as a freak or to claim its paternity'.[88] In the midst of this economic debate, the Conservative Party was increasingly sidelined. Baldwin's slogan of 'Safety First' (echoing a current Ministry of Transport poster) was not calculated to set the pulses racing among an electorate that now totalled thirty million voters, including, for the first time, newly enfranchised women over the age of twenty-one. When the Conservatives had extended the franchise with Disraeli's 'leap in the dark' in 1867 they did not reap the benefit in 1868; the same pattern was to be repeated after the Representation of the People Act in 1928. The leap in the dark this time was that female voters outnumbered male by two million, eventually a source of great strength for the Conservatives. When the votes were counted after the General Election that May, the political wags said that 'Safety First' was an ill-advised slogan; the electorate obviously preferred 'Labour first'.

The electoral battle in 1929 proved to be not between capitalism and Socialism, though Tories and Socialists tended to see it in those terms, but between economic orthodoxy and economic unorthodoxy, a battle that went beyond party boundaries. If orthodox thinking was dominated by Montagu Norman and the economic establishment, the followers of J. M. Keynes were a diverse band, incorporating at various times such figures as Ernest Bevin, General Secretary of the Transport and General Workers' Union since 1922; the mercurial figure of Oswald Mosley, soon to be Chancellor of the Duchy of Lancaster in the new Labour Government; the Liberal leader Lloyd George (Asquith had died in 1928); and leftish Tories, such as Robert Boothby and Harold Macmillan. It was with this last group that Eden was to be increasingly associated.

Parliament was dissolved on 10 May and polling set for 30 May. Eden concentrated his efforts in Warwick and Leamington, where he faced a three-cornered contest for the first time since 1923. Austen Chamberlain made several visits to speak on Eden's behalf. 'A great meeting for Austen at Leamington,' Eden recorded on 24 May, 'relayed to Warwick.' On the Sunday before polling, after another visit, Austen reminisced with Eden about how he had twice missed the Premiership:

> Austen spoke very warmly in praise of the PM & conduct in the latter days of the Coalition. He obviously bore no resentment though thus twice deprived of the 'legitimate ambition'. I know no more selfless man in politics than A. C. All the same I suspect that he resented Curzon's

motive in those hours; & rightly, the Marquess was ever thirsty for the fruits of office.[89]

Election night proved 'a grim evening listening to disastrous results.'[90] When all the votes had been counted, Labour was the largest single party for the first time in its history, with 288 seats. The Conservatives won 260 seats, and Lloyd George's Liberals only fifty-nine. Although they once more held the balance of power, it was the end of the road for the old Liberal Party as a potential governing party, as Leo Amery had hoped and predicted in December 1923.

For the first (and only) time in his career, Eden failed to win an absolute majority of votes in Warwick and Leamington. But he did better than Austen Chamberlain, who was returned in West Birmingham by only forty-three votes, after an anxious recount. Eden's figures were:

Anthony Eden (Conservative)	23,045
W. L. Dingley (Liberal)	17,585
C. G. Garton (Labour)	7,741
Conservative Majority	5,460

Baldwin retired to Chequers to consider his position. After five days' reflection, he decided that it would be 'unsporting' to wait for the verdict of Parliament (as in December 1923). He went to the Palace on 4 June and tendered his resignation to the King. Ramsay MacDonald was invited for the second time to form an administration. Among the outgoing Cabinet an end-of-term feeling prevailed. 'We all parted very happily, voting ourselves the best government there has ever been, and full of genuine affection for S. B.', Leo Amery recorded in his diary. 'If we can add to this mutual goodwill some real fighting spirit, generated in opposition, all may yet be well.'[91]

For Eden too, it was time for a recharging of the batteries, especially after the sadnesses and anxieties in his private life. But he could look back on a rewarding six years in public life. This good fortune, of course, came at a price in the green-eyed jungle of Westminster. Many were envious of his swift ascent. The old adage that people will forgive you anything but success was particularly true of Eden. Something about him grated with his critics. Everything had seemed too easy; he was mistaken for an amateur dilettante, a latter-day Beau Brummel, a society ornament, attractive to ladies and café society, whereas the reality was long hours of professionalism and much burning of the midnight oil. As he got to know Duff Cooper in the late 1920s, Eden was appalled, not by the expense, but by what he felt was the sheer waste of time of flamboyant social activity. There was a streak in Eden that shunned hedonism, a paradox, as in many respects he did not conform to conventional standards, and he was certainly not puritanical.

Contemporaries believed Eden was wealthy: all Conservatives were rich; as Eden was a Conservative *and* so immaculately turned out, he must – so it was argued – be very rich, an entirely false syllogism. What Eden earned he spent, and more. Appearances were the non-deductible, but essential, expenses of political life. Eden, with his film-star looks, was already the glass of fashion and the mould of form, cutting a dashing figure in his elegant suits and Homburg, soon known as the Eden hat.* Few penetrated behind the carapace of this ambitious, complex personality; equally, many had little doubt that more would be heard of him when the Conservatives next returned to power. However, the Treasury benches are littered with the bones of future Prime Ministers.

---

*The Duke of Wellington, with his boots, was the only other British Prime Minister to have given his name to an article of clothing or footwear.

CHAPTER FIVE

'A Potential Foreign Secretary'

1929–35

Now why doesn't the PM promote someone young? That nice
Captain Eden who I see has made a good speech.
Clementine Churchill to Winston Churchill, 14 November 1928[1]

Ce jeune homme terrible qui aime tellement la paix.
A French journalist's description of Eden after a League of
Nations Press Conference

For Leo Amery, the 1930s were the 'unforgiving' years; for Sam Hoare, the
'troubled' years, while for Churchill the period was the 'Dark Valley'.[2]
What C. L. Mowat called 'a devil's decade'[3] fell into two distinct periods.
The first half saw a worldwide depression, nearly as traumatic for the
unemployed as the experience of the trenches had been for an earlier
generation; the second half was dominated by wars and rumours of wars.

The priorities of Eden's career reflected these changing concerns. His
early political reputation had been made on issues of social and economic
policy; as he moved up the ladder of preferment, the focus altered to the
broader perspective of international relations. He was one of the very few
British public figures whose career was enhanced, even defined, by his
performance in the 1930s.

Initially in May 1929, together with other Conservatives, Eden faced the
problem of how best to make a positive contribution to political life in
opposition. He achieved this both inside and outside Parliament, by
speeches, by membership of committees and by cultivating cross-party
friendships. An assiduous attender in the Commons, he became a frequent
contributor to a wide range of debates.*

---

*Particularly, as in 1924, those involving Philip Snowden, Labour's Chancellor of the
Exchequer, and Arthur Henderson, Labour's new Foreign Secretary. Later Eden was to work
closely with both men. After the formation of the National Government in August 1931, he
often sat with Snowden on the front bench, where he admired his resolute courage in the face
of physical disability and personal abuse, while being taken aback by Snowden's bitterness
towards his former colleagues for their failure to face up to economic reality. 'Uncle' Arthur
Henderson, whom Eden saw as the Labour equivalent of Stanley Baldwin, with an intuitive
understanding of his party's grass-roots, was to be an even closer colleague when Eden served
from March 1931 as a member of the all-party committee on disarmament. Later they were
drawn together, during Henderson's Chairmanship of the World Disarmament Conference in
Geneva, after Henderson's brief leadership of the Labour Party in Opposition in 1931–2.

The Beaverbrook and Rothermere Press, campaigning for a protective tariff and 'Empire Free Trade', did their best to dislodge Baldwin. This was no whispering campaign: criticisms were bruited from the rooftops and the campaign did not run out of steam until Duff Cooper's victory against an independent 'Empire Free Trade' Conservative at the St George's by-election in March 1931, when Baldwin famously declared, 'What the proprietorship of these papers is aiming at is power, and power without responsibility, the prerogative of the harlot* throughout the ages.'[4]

For his part, Eden recorded that during this leadership crisis Beaverbrook was 'the foulest influence in British public life today.'[5] Eden was steadfast in his support for Baldwin ('He is the only statesman we possess'),[6] and in his loathing of Beaverbrook's capacity for mischief. 'So long as Mr Baldwin leads the Conservative Party,' he wrote to *The Times*, 'so long will its "right" wing be unable to dominate the party's counsels and narrow its purposes.'[7]

Eden was not dogmatic on the Tariffs issue; the key question was whether unemployment could be reduced. 'The only useful test which can be applied in these fiscal controversies,' he said in the Commons, 'is the result which is actually achieved.'[8] Political activity was not for Eden a confrontational, destructive activity; he believed it should be directed towards productive outcomes, and his character lacked that malevolent edge found among the Beaverbrooks of the political jungle. Alliances and associations in Opposition can often be a focus for dissidence. But Eden was never an habitué of the political Cave of Adullam,† where the discontented dwell.

Instead, early in 1930, Eden became one of the principal members of a left-of-centre Conservative group. Its guiding spirit was Noel Skelton, with his call for 'a property-owning democracy'. The other regulars were Walter Elliot, W. S. ('Shakes') Morrison, William ('Billy') Ormsby-Gore and Oliver Stanley. Apart from Skelton, who died prematurely, all were future Cabinet ministers. Had the prophets looked for a future Conservative Premier among this group in 1929, the choice would probably have fallen, not on Eden, but on Oliver Stanley. Had he not died in 1950, this could well have happened, though Eden thought Stanley's mind 'a shade too destructive for leadership,'[9] an interesting comment, considering some felt that the gentlemanly Eden was not destructive enough.

---

*The famous phrase about the harlot was suggested to Baldwin by his cousin, Rudyard Kipling. At the climactic moment of the speech, the Duke of Devonshire turned to his son-in-law, Harold Macmillan, and said, 'Now Stanley's lost us the tarts' vote.' Harold Macmillan to the author, 23 April 1975.

†The Adullamites was the name given by John Bright to former members of the Reform Party who opposed the Franchise Bill in 1866. The biblical origin of the name can be found in 1 Samuel. xxii.1–2.

Destructiveness, however, was not their aim. If anything, these MPs were seen, even by some on their own side, as self-regarding, even sermonising. As a result, Skelton's progressive followers were not to the liking of some harder-nosed Conservatives, who dubbed them the 'YMCA' (Young Men's Christian Association). When Eden had his differences with Neville Chamberlain at the end of the 1930s, the successors of the 'YMCA' – by then dismissively dubbed 'the Glamour Boys' – backed Eden to the hilt.

When Labour took office in May 1929, the King's Speech promised improvements in transport, revival of the depressed export market, the economic development of the Overseas Dependencies, and positive measures for agriculture and fisheries.[10] For a while, there were hopes that many of these objectives could be achieved, but in October came the Wall Street Crash. The subsequent collapse in world commodity prices and spiralling unemployment cast their shadow over Europe and the global economy. The crisis of the capitalist system was at hand, and the fear of inflation, no less than the fear of hunger which was its potent offspring, was to have decisive economic and political consequences.

The first schism in the Labour Cabinet's ranks came in May 1930 with the rejection of Oswald Mosley's Keynesian Memorandum on Unemployment. Mosley departed to lead the New Party, and, after being annihilated at the 1931 General Election, the British Union of Fascists. On the Continent the collapse of Austria's Credit Anstalt Bank in May 1931 contributed to the growth of a poisonous anti-Semitism, and indirectly contributed to Hitler's rise to power. As hyper-inflation ravaged Germany, Ramsay MacDonald was to appear on the cinema newsreels, a medium of growing importance, brandishing million-mark bank notes as a warning of the need for financial probity.

The world economic crisis spawned a National Government in Britain, and eventually a managed economy. In 1933 Roosevelt's twelve-year Presidency of the United States began, and Hitler became Chancellor of Germany. Roosevelt was soon forging the first New Deal programme. Hitler too embraced public works, of which the new autobahns were the most visible expression; and the Italian dictator Mussolini embarked on similar economic regeneration, including the draining of the Pontine marshes, a task that defeated Julius Caesar. In Russia, Stalin was undertaking his second Five Year Plan, a prelude for the Russian leadership to the inevitable conflict between Marxist-Leninism and the capitalist system. In China, the Long March, which established Mao Tse-tung's rule, began in October 1934. Of all these world figures, Eden regarded Mussolini as the most ominous, even without knowledge of

Mussolini's 1931 exhortation to his generals to be ready for war within four years.[11]

Parliament met on 25 June 1929. Ten days later Eden questioned Arthur Henderson in the Debate on the Address. His concern was over the Government's relations with the Soviet Union, arguing that there should be no further negotiations about restoring the relations broken in May 1927, unless the Third International (the Comintern) ceased their propaganda against Britain. 'I hope the country will take wide note of the gulf which differentiates the professions and speeches for political purposes of the party opposite and the actions and the speeches of the Foreign Secretary.'[12] His persuasiveness won the day. Eden never viewed the Soviet Union through the rose-tinted spectacles some adopted in the 1930s and when he became the first Western statesman to meet Stalin in Moscow in 1935, he did not forget that 'the short, thick-set man with hair *en brosse*'[13] smiling before him was a tyrant.

Reform of the Conservative domestic agenda was for Eden the quickest way to regain power. At the end of November 1929 he spoke to Conservative workers in London about the need for the party 'to set its own house in order'. He emphasised that the Conservative objective 'must be to spread the ownership of property as widely as possible' – in short, 'to enable every worker to become a capitalist',[14] issues to which he returned after 1945. His constituency speeches were predominantly on 'the condition of England'.*

On 29 June 1931, in a speech that showed a growing experience since the time of his maiden speech on air defences, Eden outlined the situation in which Britain could now be a stabilising European influence:

> The seeds of war psychology still exist in Europe. I even doubt whether during the last two years what is usually called the spirit of the League has grown in strength in Europe. On the contrary, the probability is that it has weakened. I do not wish to be alarmist, but I do not think that anyone who studies the European situation today can be otherwise than anxious about it. It seems to me that we can divide Europe for this purpose into two groups of nations. There is the group which is, if not dominated, at least influenced by fear, and the group which is dominated or influenced by impatience.[15]

Much of the minority Labour Government's pragmatic approach he approved of: Ramsay MacDonald's personal diplomacy on Anglo-

---

*Although he spoke in the Commons on housing policy, most of Eden's interventions there were on foreign affairs – India, the League of Nations, the Singapore Naval Bases, and the difficulties for Britain as the mandatory power in Palestine. A presence in India and Singapore remained essential for him if Britain was to fulfil her imperial responsibilities, and his faith in the potential of the League remained absolute.

American relations, the need for international arbitration to settle unresolved disputes, and partial acceptance of the rise of Chinese and Egyptian nationalism.

In the light of Eden's later experiences in the 1950s, his views on Labour's Egyptian policy in the debate on 23 December, opened by Sir Austen Chamberlain, have been surprisingly neglected. Earlier ministerial negotiations with the Egyptian Prime Minister, Sarwat Pasha, had proved fruitless; the High Commissioner, Lord Lloyd, had been ignominiously recalled from Egypt by Arthur Henderson in July, and feelings were running high in the House. 'Winston speaks early to catch the press,' wrote Hugh Dalton, Eden's predecessor as Under-Secretary at the Foreign Office, 'and rants wildly'.[16] Eden's authoritative contribution was on a different plane altogether. Not only was he well informed about Middle Eastern matters, but he showed that he was not a Tory die-hard. On his return from his recent imperial travels he had come through the Suez Canal, and now spoke at first hand of its geographical importance. Egypt and Suez occupied the first part of his speech; future relations with the Egyptian people the second. He warned against the alarmism of Churchill, stressing that the importance of the canal lay 'as a link in our chain of Imperial Defence'. But its significance was greater than that. 'Its importance is no less to our Dominions, and to Australia and New Zealand in particular. If the Suez Canal is our back door to the East, it is the front door to Europe of Australia, New Zealand and India.' In a striking metaphor Eden described the Suez Canal as 'the swing door of the British Empire, which has got to keep continually revolving, if our communications are to be what they should'. Its importance was equally clear in 1956 as in 1929. 'None of us should be content,' Eden continued, 'to leave the protection of a vital artery, the jugular vein of the British Empire, to the good will of the people of Egypt'. Yet the inevitable corollary of the 1954 Suez Canal Base treaty, which led to the withdrawal of British troops, was what proved an unsuccessful dependence on a goodwill that never materialised.

In 1929 Eden saw more clearly the difficulties that might arise after a period of transition, and wanted to know what British responsibilities would be if the Egyptian Government was unable to keep civil order. 'When the ocean has delivered the pearl,' he asked, quoting the Persian poet Hafiz, 'what further concern have we with the ocean?' He made it clear that Britain should have every concern. Henderson seemed to be abrogating any further responsibilities 'for Egypt's internal affairs'. That was not an attitude, Eden concluded, that inspired confidence.[17]

Eden feared an increasing compartmentalisation of Labour foreign policy. Ramsay MacDonald was in charge of Anglo-American relations, Colonies and Dominions had their individual Cabinet ministers, as did

India, while Arthur Henderson dealt with the rest. Eden believed in maintaining an overview of the whole area of policy. He was as willing to speak on Egypt as Singapore, on Naval Treaties or the League. One of his political admirers was Asquith's widow, Margot, who urged him 'to go out with courage' on his own and not be dependent on newspaper support.[18]

His views on France were still clearly in tune with Austen Chamberlain's. Difficulties with Louis Barthou and Pierre Laval had not yet dented his youthful optimism. Eden was convinced that Anglo-French understanding was the most hopeful way of maintaining political stability in Europe. Austen Chamberlain's Francophile leanings had been influenced by aesthetic considerations; for Eden, memories of the trenches, and fear of another war, motivated his strategic thinking. Diplomatic progress in Europe was 'rather like a 1917 campaign in Flanders', he later wrote to Baldwin, 'and, as in Flanders, the pill-boxes are occupied by Germans!'[19] When progress was achieved, as at the Nyon Conference in September 1937, it showed that 'co-operation between Britain and France can be effective' and that 'the two Western democracies can still play a decisive role in European affairs.'[20]

His world tour had confirmed him as an imperialist, not in a narrow jingoistic sense, but as one who believed in a mutual dependency that would not only support the mother country's interests, but also provide a valuable economic cartel. His hopes for Protectionism were not rigidly doctrinal; its real value, he thought, was not as a fiscal policy *per se*, but as a contribution to political unity in the larger framework of the imperial family. Whenever he crossed into America from Canada, he was conscious that he was no longer in the fiefdom of that family; like Harold Macmillan later, he always believed that the big mistake in dealing with the Americans was to think of them as Anglo-Saxons.

American, Russian and Japanese concerns were to come later in Eden's career. His field of interest and expertise in the early 1930s was the European and Middle Eastern theatre. Eden may have followed Austen Chamberlain in his Francophilia, but there was no such fellow feeling over Italy. Memories of Locarno had given Chamberlain an exaggerated respect for Mussolini, but there was never any question of Eden donning a sailor's cap and taking holidays in the Mediterranean on the Italian dictator's yacht. For Eden, Mussolini was 'the complete gangster and his pledged word means nothing.'[21] Consequently Italy was, in his view, even after Hitler's rise to power, the real threat to European peace.

Although Eden was increasingly seen as a 'foreign' expert, his membership of the Skelton dining group and his work in the constituency on social policy, proved him no narrow specialist. After his participation in the Egypt Debate, his next big contribution in Parliament was in the Debate on

Tariffs on 16 April 1930, two days after Philip Snowden's first Budget of the Parliament, described by Snowden's biographer as 'like the charge of the Light Brigade translated into fiscal terms.'[22]

Snowden's Budget was attacked by the Independent Labour Party on the one side (for seemingly closing the door on any future redistributive taxation), and by young Tories such as Oliver Stanley and Eden on the other (for its caution). Eden felt that Snowden's Gladstonian orthodoxy had done little to tackle unemployment, the burning question of the hour. As in 1924, Snowden proved a willing follower of Montagu Norman's cherished doctrines of Free Trade, debt repayment, maintaining the Gold Standard and presenting a balanced Budget. Whether this was the right policy when 10 per cent of the working population was unemployed was another matter. 'I think the Chancellor of the Exchequer has a medieval mind,' said Eden during the debate. 'He would have made an admirable Minister, for instance, for the Medici.' He felt that Snowden dealt in 'fiscal bigotry'. The Liberals too came in for censure. 'One of the reasons why the Liberal Party is slowly but steadily fading away, is that its attitude on these matters is as medieval as the attitude of the Chancellor of the Exchequer.' But the main thrust of Eden's argument concerned the longer term. 'Are we satisfied with the present relation of our financial and fiscal policy to our industrial need?', he asked. The Labour left, including Jimmy Maxton, dissented from Snowden's measures because the confiscatory nature of its taxation was limited, and fixed for the rest of the Parliament. Eden dissented because of its timidity. 'I regret this Budget because it is so wholly unimaginative, and because it has no relation to the pressing industrial needs of our people.'[23] Shortly afterwards Eden made a tour of northern towns, including Huddersfield, to speak at Conservative meetings and to see conditions at first hand.

On 1 September 1930 the Edens moved to a new home at 17 Lower Berkeley Street, a family property of the Becketts, Mulberry Walk having proved too expensive. Beatrice was expecting their third child, and, after the tragedy of Robert's short life, it was with some horror that they found that Simon, now nearly six, had come out with scarlet fever just a fortnight before the confinement. 'An anxious day,' Eden wrote in his diary on 3 October. 'Went for a walk in the afternoon. When I called at home at 6 p.m. did not have long to wait before news of arrival of lusty son. Beatrice wonderful considering & the son a splendid specimen. Both of us pleased that it should be a boy.'[24]

It was a long time since Jutland, and the son was christened Nicholas in memory of Eden's younger brother. For a time the birth of Nicholas brought Beatrice and Anthony Eden closer. Their marriage was far from orthodox. It was tacitly understood from an early stage that both partners were free agents. This led to many extramarital affairs on both sides. Beatrice was bored with political life and had endured long spells of loneliness. Infidelities followed, and, although Beatrice did not advertise these, neither was she disingenuous about them with her husband. At the time of Beatrice's pregnancy, Eden had an intense relationship with 'Ursula', about whom he wrote in Arabic in his diary, and occasionally *en clair*. 'She is charming and lively as ever,' he had written on 10 May 1930.[25]

While a blind eye was turned in 'society' to such affairs, as long as they remained discreet, public scandal could have a devastating effect on a professional career. To an extent not easily appreciated in a different era, Eden was walking with danger, and underneath his outward insouciance was a nervousness that not even circumspection could entirely dispel. He was only too well aware that his career could be ruined if he was betrayed.

For divorce was still the great taboo, as King Edward VIII was to discover in 1936. The lessons of Sir Charles Dilke and Charles Stewart Parnell were always there in the background.[26] The Conservative Party did not accept divorcees as candidates until after the Second World War, and even then at first only in exceptional circumstances. The BBC, under the inter-war leadership of Sir John Reith, was particularly censorious. As Lord High Commissioner of the General Assembly of the Church of Scotland, Reith also had influence over invitations to royal garden parties in Scotland. When one (excluded) dignitary pointed out to Reith that he was the innocent party in his recent divorce, Reith declared, 'That may get you into the Kingdom of Heaven, but it'll no get you into the Palace of Holyrood House.'[27]

The Duke of Norfolk's attitude in 1953 was similarly unbending, as Chips Channon recorded in his diary:

> One peer, who had been divorced, suggested to the Earl Marshal that he feared he would be ineligible for a place in the Abbey: the reply is said to have been 'Of course you will; this is the Coronation, not Ascot'.[28]

Even as late as 1959, Hugh Carleton Greene believed that his divorced status would disqualify him from consideration for Lord Reith's former post of Director-General of the BBC.[29]

Parliament reassembled four weeks after Nicholas's birth. The economic situation was sombre. By the time of the Debate on the Address in November 1930, unemployment (two million in the summer) had increased by a further 200,000; as was pointed out, this was twice the number of a capacity crowd at the new Wembley Stadium. The question of tariffs was again to the fore. At the Imperial Conference in London, Richard Bennett, the Canadian Prime Minister, had advocated a 10 per cent imperial preference tariff, and some announcement was expected in the King's Speech. But none was forthcoming.

Eden addressed the question in his speech in the Debate on the Address on 3 November. After a tribute to the integrity of the late H. H. Asquith, whom he described as 'a perfect example of the intellectual Free Trader', he suggested that present-day Liberals fell far short of their former leader. For Eden, the Liberals were an increasing irrelevance, an escape clause for the guilt-ridden middle classes, and one of the reasons he opposed the Alternative Vote was because it would artificially prolong the life of an ailing political force, and prevent firm government. For Eden, even greater issues than fiscal ones were at stake, and he argued that the Government should 'make a close and careful study of the causes of the collapse of Parliamentary government in Europe since the War. It has not always, or even usually, been because these countries are temperamentally unfitted to work the Parliamentary machine. It has been for a far simpler reason, because Parliament has failed.' With reference to Italy, he felt that democracy had failed there 'because it could not adapt industry or agriculture to post-war conditions'.

He believed it not too melodramatic to claim that Britain also faced a watershed. Democracy at a time of dramatically rising unemployment could prove a fragile flower. He then moved on to the Protective Tariff, the vexed question of the hour. 'It is not the end of all,' he said. 'It is simply a means to an end, and if you choose to ignore that means and incur the responsibility of failure, I am certain that in the course of time, probably within the next five years, this country will see the introduction of Protection by one government or another.' In a side-swipe at Beaverbrook, he drew comparisons with Canada, approving of Richard Bennett's response to the slump. By contrast, he felt that Herbert Samuel and Philip Snowden were living in a past era, embracing outdated orthodoxies. Eden was withering in his scorn for Samuel, deputy leader of Liberalism's diminished band:*

> He expressed with remarkable courage the very true doctrine of the Victorian era. He should have been sitting beside the Chancellor of the Exchequer, the two of them together crinkling their crinolines, and we should like to have seen them drive away tonight in a growler escorted by gentlemen in mutton-chop whiskers mounted on tricycles.'[30]

---

*After the 1931 General Election, Liberalism fractured even more. Herbert Samuel led the Liberal Party, and Lloyd George led a smaller group of Independent Liberals, family members imbued with the spirit of Criccieth, while Sir John Simon led what became known as the National Liberals. It was at this time that Lloyd George said, 'When they circumcised Sir Herbert Samuel, they threw away the wrong bit.'

At the end of 1930, Eden noted in his diary, 'Have only made a few speeches in this Parliament, but they seem to have been fairly successful.'[31] This was an unduly modest assessment. What stood out was the range of subjects he chose to address (his forthright denunciation of the Alternative Vote had gone down particularly well with the Tories), his ability to vary the tone and even, on occasions, his touches of wry humour. He avoided rambling monologues, knowing that the House soon got bored, stood tall in his place and made his points clearly. Nobody could say, as was being said of Leo Amery, that had he been half a head taller and his speeches half an hour shorter, he might well have become Prime Minister.

The year of 1931 was to be one of the most dramatic of political years. For Eden it began quietly. His agent in Warwick and Leamington had retired and Eden decided to advertise for a successor. 'We should be able to find an absolutely first-class man – which we need to keep so vast an electorate alive.'[32] He never made the mistake of neglecting his grass-roots supporters, which was important in 1931, as he was at odds with his 'Die-Hard' executive committee over Baldwin's continued leadership and over the party's Indian policy. For the Conservative Die-Hards, India was a convenient stick with which to beat Baldwin. The first Round Table Conference to consider India's future constitutional position had led to Churchill's resignation from the Conservative inner 'Business Committee' of the Shadow Cabinet and marked the beginning of his wilderness years. The effect on Eden was to separate him from Churchill just at the time when their political friendship could have had mutual benefits. Assailed by Empire Free Traders on one side, and by an unleashed Churchill on the other, totally opposed to an All-India Federal Government, Baldwin was at a low ebb. It was only the support of younger figures such as Eden that made him feel it was worth while continuing as leader. 'S.B. asks me to come to his room,' Eden wrote in his diary on 4 March 1931. 'He is depressed and worried. We go through drafts of his speech for Friday on India. It is on this subject that I cannot disagree with him that the party is more die-hard than he or I.'[33]

The next day the terms of the pact between the Viceroy, Lord Irwin (later Lord Halifax), and Mahatma Gandhi, of the Indian nationalist Congress Party, were made known and paved the way for an end to civil disobedience and a second Round Table Conference. The Gandhi–Irwin Pact also proved a turning point in Baldwin's campaign to retain the party leadership. Eden did not disguise his delight. 'Our die-hards are very angry. Bracken's face as red as his hair, Jix taking defeat as the ill-bred do, but the party as a whole assessing the position pretty soundly.'[34] A week later, on 12 March, Baldwin rewarded Eden's loyalty by asking him to serve as one of the Conservative delegates on the all-party committee preparing for the World Disarmament Conference later in the year in Geneva. The other Conservative representatives – the past and the future so to speak – were Austen Chamberlain and Sam Hoare. So began Eden's central work in the 1930s, a period of which Roy Jenkins later wrote, 'From the start of the Abyssinian conflict and the Spanish Civil War to the beginning of appeasement under Chamberlain he was almost consistently right.'[35]

Eden's first speech on the subject came as early as 26 March, and his contribution was widely noticed. Surprisingly, an even more substantial analysis in the Disarmament debate on 29 June received less attention. In his speech (which fills ten columns of *Hansard*) Eden drew attention to many of the anomalies that existed, especially over the state of Russia's military preparedness. He pointed out that Russia had the 'largest standing Army in Europe' and emphasised the onus that this placed on Britain to be the durable force in a volatile European situation. It followed that 'certainly the nation which is to be the stabilising nation of Europe should not be too weak'. And in an observation that foreshadowed his attitude to 'European' questions in the 1950s Eden added, 'We shall be the better Europeans the closer the attention, in the immediate future at least, we pay to our responsibility to this nation.' Military strength in modern warfare, though, was not merely a question of troop numbers. 'I fear there is a real danger that in future wars it will not be personnel that will play the dominating part.' Then, in a rare public reference to his military service, Eden recalled the reality of war in 1918:

> Those particularly who saw the last months or the last weeks of the last War had a vision of what the next War might be expected to be. I remember an evening in the very last weeks of the War, in the last stages of our advance, when we had stopped for the night at brigade head-quarters in some farmhouse. The night was quiet, and there was no shell fire, as was usual at the end of the War, but quite suddenly it began literally to rain bombs for anything from 10 minutes to a quarter of an hour. I do not know how many bombs fell in that time, but something between 30 & 40, I suppose. It seemed to us to be hundreds.[36]

Earlier in 1931, Eden had been the recipient of many of Baldwin's private inner doubts; now, in the summer, he found, to his surprise, that Ramsay MacDonald increasingly sounded him out, in the Commons newspaper room and in the lobbies. Eden's impression was of a short-tempered man, fearful that he was losing his control over events, who had some psychological need to use sympathetic MPs as a sounding board to try out his ideas, a sign of his growing isolation within his own party. 'Why he should come to me remains a mystery,' wrote Eden after one such talk.[37]

As the time neared for the report of Sir George May's independent Committee on National Expenditure, appointed by Philip Snowden, MacDonald sought out Eden again. 'Somewhat to my surprise, he engaged me in conversation – All of course about himself', Eden wrote in his diary. 'Ramsay creates this impression in conversation that, not only do all the cares of the world rest upon his head, but that nobody can ever have been Prime Minister of England before.'[38]

The intractable problem of unemployment* was the particular care that exercised MacDonald. To add to his woes, the publication on 31 July of the May Report, with its starkly pessimistic account of Britain's economic state, provoked a further run on the pound. By the end of the first week of August, Sir Ernest Harvey, Deputy Governor of the Bank of England, told Philip Snowden that in one month £60 million of gold reserves and foreign exchange had been lost. The cupboard was almost bare. The Labour Government split on the scale of the economies needed. In circumstances that still provoke controversy, King George V brokered a deal whereby on 24 August Ramsay MacDonald became Prime Minister of a National Government that included Stanley Baldwin, Sir John Simon's National Liberals and Herbert Samuel's Liberals. For reasons of health, unacceptability and political exile, the maverick trio – of David Lloyd George, Oswald Mosley and Winston Churchill – were excluded from consideration. MacDonald declared that the National Government was a temporary expedient to see through the current crisis. In fact, the National Government, in its various guises, was to last until 23 May 1945, and to oversee even more critical events. Apart from one brief interval from 20 February 1938 (when he resigned the Foreign Secretaryship) until 3 September 1939, when Neville Chamberlain appointed him to the Dominions Office, Eden was to be a member throughout its history. No other figure exceeded his length of service during that time.

For Eden, the formation of the National Government was one of those unforeseen circumstances that completely transformed the political landscape, as well as his own prospects. Of MacDonald's senior colleagues, only Philip Snowden, Sankey (the Lord Chancellor), Earl De La Warr and J. H. Thomas, renowned for his earthy humour and lack of aspirates, stayed with him, and the vacuum left by the departing Labour ministers provided the opportunity to resurrect many a fading career, as well as to blood fresh talent. The younger Conservatives did well and, of

*The total continued to rise inexorably throughout the summer, reaching 2,880,000 by September, and peaking at 2,955,000 in January 1932.

Eden's progressive dining group, only Shakes Morrison and William Ormsby-Gore did not receive immediate preferment.[39]

As in the earlier crisis of December 1916, when Lloyd George formed his Coalition Government, there was an undignified scramble for office. 'That is indeed putting a pistol at my head,' Balfour had said then, when offered the Foreign Office, 'but I at once say yes.'[40] Unfortunately, there are never enough pistols to go round. Political expediency ensured that in the division of the spoils the Liberals were awarded two of the 'great' offices of state, more than their parliamentary strength strictly warranted. On 25 August Sir Herbert Samuel became Home Secretary, and Lord Reading Foreign Secretary. The appointment that most appalled the Conservatives was that of Lord Crewe, already past his best in Asquith's day. When the rumour spread that Crewe might return, Brendan Bracken bet £1 that he was dead. However, when Crewe's appointment as War Secretary was announced, some said Bracken should be excused payment, as Crewe *was* dead, and had been appointed only as a measure of economy.[41]

On 27 August Eden lunched with Austen Chamberlain, who told him that, with Baldwin's approval, he had put Eden's name forward to Reading. 'The F.O. in a National Govt. with the S. of S. in the Upper House is higher than I hoped for and I do not expect that I shall get it,' Eden wrote in his diary. The next day Stanley Baldwin confirmed to Eden that this was the likely outcome, the only obstacle being MacDonald's wish to put his son Malcolm in the post. But Baldwin was hopeful that all would be well in the end. 'He told me that he wanted me to go to the F.O. where he had intended to send me for a spell himself if our party had been returned, and added that he regarded me as "a potential Foreign Secretary" in about ten years' time and that was why he wanted me to have the experience as soon as possible.'[42]

On the recommendation of Sir Austen Chamberlain, and with Baldwin's approval, Reading invited Eden to serve as his Under-Secretary and representative of the Foreign Office in the Commons. He too believed that Eden would one day be Foreign Secretary, an expectation fulfilled four years later in the last week of Reading's life.[43]

When Parliament met on 8 September, the benches were crowded and there was an air of bruised hostility among MacDonald's former colleagues. MacDonald's opening speech was greeted with wrath by Arthur Henderson's followers, as was Snowden's emergency Budget on 10 September. By chance, it fell to Eden that day to answer the first oral question put to a member of the National Government, as Private Notice Questions to the Foreign Office opened the proceedings. With Reading in the House of Lords, it was the first of many such appearances on the front bench for Eden, but few occurred in such a hostile and febrile atmosphere.

The topic was China and British attitudes to Chiang Kai-shek, which he had been researching for a week, following another attack on the British concession at Hankow on 4 August.[44]

The formation of the National Government did not 'solve' the financial crisis; it moved it on to the next phase, which culminated in the great psychological watershed of 21 September 1931, when Britain went off the Gold Standard, finally abandoning the Ark of the Covenant that had seemed the essential buttress of the international capitalist system. Montagu Norman, recuperating on a foreign cruise from stress-related illness, received a coded telegram from the Deputy Governor, Sir Ernest Harvey, about the state of the Old Lady of Threadneedle Street – 'Old Lady goes off on Monday'. Unfortunately, Norman did not decipher its cryptic message, thinking it referred to his ageing mother's holiday plans, and when he disembarked at Liverpool docks that fateful morning he was greeted with newspaper headlines proclaiming the fall of the pound from $4.86 to $3.80. (It eventually settled at $3.40.) To one who had devoted his life to the Treasury orthodoxies of a balanced budget, it seemed like the end of the known world. The American President, Herbert Hoover, thought Britain was like a defaulting bank, unable to turn its assets into cash, closing its doors to its customers. But the end of the Gold Standard was not another Credit Anstalt failure. It was the beginning of the era of the managed economy and eventually of the Keynesian revolution.

In the midst of his new responsibilities at the Foreign Office, Eden was desperately worried about his own finances. It had been an expensive year, with a new house and a new baby, and he noted that his capital had shrunk to £805 (approximately £24,000 in present-day values).[45] Also, by accepting Government office, he had had to sever his few City connections and this was a further anxiety. The one consolation was that work at the Foreign Office was of absorbing interest. 'Nothing could have suited me better,' he noted, 'and everybody there very friendly.'[46]

Eden's short spell at the Foreign Office under Reading was to prove more congenial than that under his later chiefs, Simon and Hoare, and this stemmed not only from the autonomy he enjoyed in the Commons, but from the trust and confidence Reading showed to him. Reading was one of the few Foreign Secretaries for whom the job was, in essence, a 'retirement' one. He had nothing more to prove and had no long-term ambitions. He made only two foreign trips – to Paris in the wake of the abandonment of the Gold Standard for talks with Pierre Laval, and to Geneva at the time of the outbreak of the Manchurian crisis. Reading knew that the future would be with Eden's generation. For his part Eden, who was a shrewd listener, was able to draw on Reading's lifetime of experience. 'I shall always remember your many kindnesses to me when it was my privilege to serve under you at the FO,' he wrote later, 'and I am quite sure that I shall never again enjoy a political experience as much as I did those few months.'[47]

Reading's brief tenure of the Foreign Office (two months and eleven days) ended after the General Election of 27 October. In dissolving Parliament, MacDonald had sought a 'Doctor's Mandate', to diagnose and cure the nation's ills. The contest was the most atypical of the century. If the 1929 Election had been a battle between financial orthodoxy and unorthodoxy, the 1931 campaign was seen in terms of a 'patriotic' and 'unpatriotic' divide. The National Government won 554 seats (473 of them Conservative ones), with 14.5 million votes. The Labour Party, briefly under the leadership of Arthur Henderson (he lost his seat at the election, but continued as leader till 1932), were reduced to fifty-two seats, their position a quarter of a century earlier. In Warwick and Leamington, Eden, like many National candidates, had his biggest-ever majority. The threat of a Beaverbrook-inspired Empire Free Trade candidate had vanished, and, as the Liberal candidate had withdrawn to back the National Government, Eden faced a straight fight with C. G. Garton, his Labour (now Independent Labour) opponent from 1929. Garton made a direct pitch for the former Liberal vote by advocating a programme of Free Trade, but to no avail. The figures were:

Anthony Eden (Conservative)	38,584
C. G. Garton (Independent Labour)	9,261
Conservative Majority	29,323

MacDonald had ushered in an era in which the Conservatives were to have an inflated numerical advantage that they could never have won by themselves in 'normal' conditions. The disadvantages of this artificial situation may not have been immediately apparent, but eventually the Conservatives, associated in the public consciousness with the 'locust years', were to reap a bitter electoral harvest in 1945.

On 5 November, Sir John Simon succeeded Reading at the Foreign Office, an appointment dictated by the compromises of coalition. Austen Chamberlain told Eden that had he known Simon was in the running, he would have sought to return to the office himself. History has not been kind to John Simon, the epitome of the cold, calculating lawyer, of whom it was said, 'There'll be no moaning at the Bar, when he puts out to sea.' His smile was said to shine like the brass plate on a coffin, while for Lloyd George, 'Sir John Simon has sat on the fence so long that the iron has entered his soul.'[48] The fruitful relationship Eden had enjoyed with Reading was replaced by one of cautious reserve. Having lost his autonomy in the Commons, Eden now found himself cabined, cribbed and confined. Simon's supposed lack of social graces did not concern Eden, nor his comfortable, but essentially bourgeois, lifestyle.[49] More germane for Eden was Simon's ignorance of diplomatic technicalities, and his unwillingness to put in the hours. Eden did much of the work, virtually taking up permanent residence in Geneva. 'John Simon arrives tomorrow,' he wrote to Beatrice, 'but when he finds amount of work awaiting him and its complexity, I don't suppose that he will stay long.'[50]

In an uncanny way, Eden seemed an 'old hand' when Simon, twenty-four years his senior, arrived at the Foreign Office in November 1931. Eden was already settled in his office down the corridor from the Secretary of State's great room overlooking St James's Park, and was well briefed on the latest developments in Manchuria and the preparations for the World Disarmament Conference in 1932. Later there were to be the intricate details of Mussolini's proposed Four-Power Pact to avoid the danger of a split in Western Europe. Eden immersed himself in the finer points of these complex matters, unlike his political master. When Simon's assistant private secretary, Henry Hopkinson, asked the Secretary of State for his decision on Mussolini's proposals, Simon replied, 'You know if there is one thing that bores me more than Disarmament it is the Four-Power Pact.'[51]

Nor did Eden have a fruitful relationship with the Permanent Under-Secretary, Sir Robert Vansittart, a wealthy, insouciant grandee, who looked with a patronising air on subordinate figures, among whom he certainly numbered Eden. Unlike Vansittart, Eden never accounted the sacrifice of Abyssinia a price worth paying for Italian friendship, and when Mussolini's forces later became involved in Spain, he cautioned Vansittart, 'By all means let us show ourselves ready to talk, but in no scrambling hurry to offer incense on a dictator's altar.'[52] Vansittart and Eden were ill-suited temperamentally. 'I fear that he is not balanced,' Eden wrote in his diary, 'and is in such a continual state of nerves that he will end by making would-be aggressors think the more of us as a possible victim!'[53] Later, Vansittart, for his part, told Hugh Dalton 'that he thought of Eden as a man with whom he had often had to go out tiger shooting and who, at the end, had shot him in the back.'[54] Looking back in tranquillity, Eden felt the roots of the eventual disenchantment lay in Vansittart's relentless, even ruthless, interpretation of his role. 'The truth is that Vansittart was seldom an official giving cool and disinterested advice based on study and experience,' Eden wrote. 'He was himself a sincere, almost fanatical crusader and much more a Secretary of State in mentality than a permanent official.'[55]

Another distinguished diplomat, Alex Cadogan, had admired Eden's work under Austen Chamberlain, and had been optimistic in the early 1930s that Eden's fresh look at the framework of British policy would lead to a fruitful renewal of the disarmament process. 'I don't think any Secretary of State I served,' Cadogan later wrote of Eden, 'excelled him in finesse, or as a negotiator, or in knowledge of foreign affairs.'[56] Henry Hopkinson (later Lord Colyton) was well aware that Eden, even at this early stage, had his critics, who thought him vain and temperamental. Although Eden could be capricious, Hopkinson thought 'he was temperamental on issues', and 'his vain qualities were on his appearance, not on status.'[57]

One of the greatest temptations for the historian is to judge the values of one age by later standards. Photographs of Eden in the 1930s make him seem like a character from a Noël Coward play, with his pristine waistcoats and snowy-white spats. But this was the uniform of the day, even though few matched the rigour of Eden's adherence to such outward forms. Lord Robert Cecil, President of the League of Nations Union, whose standards of dress were notoriously lax, was excused only on grounds of aristocratic eccentricity, although Archbishop Cosmo Gordon Lang, one of Eden's *bêtes noires*, upbraided Cecil, 'If you cannot dress like a gentleman, I think you ought at least to try and dress like a Conservative.'[58]

Life in the Foreign Office in 1931 still retained echoes of Curzonian expansiveness. Pinstriped trousers were *de rigueur*. For country house weekends Eden had a pinstriped green tweed suit. In the Foreign Office frockcoated servants bore in the scarlet-and-gold despatch boxes, foreign dignitaries were received from the neighbouring Ambassador's Waiting Room with quasi-regal formality, and banquets of legendary splendour (what a later Foreign Secretary, Selwyn Lloyd, regretfully observed had declined to 'a two sardine barbecue')[59] were held in the sumptuous Locarno Room. Eden was comfortable in such a world, but he never mistook these shadows for the substance. In fact, unlike the Vansittarts of the diplomatic world, he found the expenses involved in his work embarrassingly heavy. There were no free houses or chauffeured cars, as in later days, and the cost of day-to-day entertaining (other than official banquets) was the responsibility of the minister.

Like Lord Curzon, Eden burned the midnight oil, though without leaving silver chocolate wrappings by his desk, a sign to the secretaries that his Lordship had been working late. Diplomatic reality for Eden became a combination of unsocial hours, interminable telegrams and intricate negotiations, during which, as Henry Hopkinson put it, 'he was very good with the foreigners.'[60] Such were the nuances of a now-vanished age.

Over Christmas, Eden read the fourth volume of Lady Gwendolen Cecil's life of Lord Salisbury, the great Victorian Prime Minister and Foreign

Secretary. 'Not as well done as I had hoped,' he wrote, after his recent foray into books on Bismarck and German diplomacy. Political biography was now assuming increasing prominence in Eden's extensive reading, though he had still found time for Anthony Trollope's *Framley Parsonage*. Reading the life of Salisbury allowed Eden instructive comparisons between the Victorian and contemporary methods. 'His methods at the Foreign Office are interesting in their independence,' noted Eden of Salisbury, 'in contrast to the subservience to routine of the present day.'[61]

Eden soon settled into the routine of the long-awaited World Disarmament Conference which began in Geneva on 2 February 1932, under the chairmanship of Arthur Henderson. Before long Henderson was complaining of Simon's absences, 'running away back to England' as he put it.[62] So, in a roundabout way, Eden eventually regained some of the autonomy he had enjoyed under Lord Reading. He made the most of this to bring new purpose and urgency to British initiatives. The paper Simon presented to Cabinet in September 1932, for instance, on Germany's withdrawal from the conference, was largely Eden's.

Simon failed to punch his weight in Cabinet. Partly this was owing to his position as a National Liberal in a Cabinet dominated by Conservatives, three of whom were service ministers, Viscount Hailsham (War), Sir Bolton Eyres-Monsell (Admiralty) and the Marquess of Londonderry (Air), unwilling to commit themselves to extensive disarmament. Lady Londonderry scathingly referred to Simon at her celebrated soirées as a 'silk worm'. 'He will not fight for his own policy,' Eden recorded with exasperation in the summer of 1932. 'He expects the Cabinet to find his policy for him. That they will never do. They want to be told. The only result of present procedure is F.O. pushed into the background, which is not good either.'[63]

The British delegation set up their Geneva headquarters at the Beau-Rivage Hotel, a place Eden was eventually to regard as something of a second home. Most days Eden could be seen lunching with Alec Cadogan or Henry Hopkinson at a small restaurant, La Perle du Lac, before scurrying back to the offices that had been set up in Rooms 60 and 61. Until Cadogan was posted to Peking at the beginning of January 1934, Eden and he were the driving forces behind new British initiatives, and the journalists regarded the omnipresent Eden as the leading British spokesman, closely followed by Lord Robert Cecil. Indeed, Major-General A. C. Temperley, who was the chief military adviser to the British delegation, later wrote that 'Lord Cecil and Mr Eden seemed to me to be the only Ministers who ever knew the subject thoroughly.'[64]

The first World Disarmament Conference, the culmination of five years' preparation among the League of Nation's various committees, was widely seen as the most important international gathering since Versailles. Much of its work inevitably addressed issues from 1919. However, the failure of the member states to establish an agreed policy on the global reduction of arms was to prove a foretaste of the League's declining influence in the 1930s. In 1933, Germany left the League, and, although Russia was accepted into the League in 1934, bringing vigorous proposals for disarmament, there was a lack of collective will. And the League proved politically impotent. It was unable to halt Japanese action against China, Italy's invasion of Ethiopia, or Germany's disavowal of the original Treaty of Versailles and Hitler's pursuit of *Lebensraum* in Europe. This lack of solidarity, if not political will, in the face of international aggression was to bring a ferocious and destructive legacy.

The conference began with a Service of Dedication in Geneva Cathedral at which the preacher was William Temple, Archbishop of York following Cosmo Gordon Lang's translation to Canterbury in 1928. For Eden this was not a promising start. He had suspicion of the involvement of the higher clergy in matters political, and the fact that William Temple had publicly announced his allegiance to the Labour Party in 1918 made him even more wary. Towards the end of his sermon in Geneva Cathedral before the assembled dignitaries, Temple referred scathingly to the War Guilt clause in the Versailles Treaty, 'which affixes to one group of belligerents in the Great War the whole guilt for its occurrence' – one of the first-recorded instances of the 1960s liberal mantra that 'we are all guilty'. Jim Thomas, Dominions Secretary, turned to Alec Cadogan in the cathedral, and asked loudly, 'Oo wrote that bloody muck? Bob Cecil, I suppose.'[65] Like many former servicemen, Eden was appalled, but held his peace, unlike Austen Chamberlain, who said that it was 'a denial of Christian morals, to say that all nations were equally guilty'. Two years later Temple was to tell Neville Chamberlain what his economic priorities should be in the forthcoming Budget; as his half-brother had done, Neville Chamberlain let the Archbishop know what he thought of priestly interference.[66]

Eden soon found that the League of Nations aroused contradictory emotions. There were those, such as Robert Cecil, whose whole political purpose was identified with the internationalism of Geneva; others were more cautious. Initially Eden was in the latter camp. Manchuria was the issue that altered his perception, as his ideas on foreign policy matured. When Japan invaded Manchuria in September 1931 Eden, representing British interests on the League's Committee of Twelve, accepted that the League had moral authority on its side, but knew that without American support there was little Britain and France could do militarily to address

Chinese grievances, even had they been prepared to involve troops in the Far East. Tacitly, this was an acceptance that words pay no debts without deeds. But when Japanese aggression extended beyond the Shanghai district, where the British had invested heavily, Eden saw the League as the best – perhaps only – way out of the morass. Two factors complicated the issue. The Americans were not members of the League of Nations and, at a time when financial considerations were assuming even greater importance in policy making, Britain also had extensive Japanese trading interests, and was in no position to act unilaterally, or with France. It was a delicate balance, where financial (rather than ethical) considerations were uppermost, one of Eden's first experiences of *realpolitik*. In February, the month delegates assembled in Geneva for the Disarmament Conference, Japan proclaimed Manchuria as the new state of Manchukuo. The crisis had escalated because the League had shown earlier impotence. It was a striking pre-echo of the events of 1956, especially as Eden found himself at odds, not for the last time, with an American Secretary of State.

Henry Stimson, Secretary of State throughout Hoover's Presidency, was the author of the so-called Stimson Doctrine (7 January 1932), which refused to recognise territories seized by aggression, specifically Japan's establishment of the puppet state of Manchukuo. However, isolationalist pressure being what it was in America, neither Stimson nor Hoover was prepared to add military pressure to the moral. The Japanese were not driven from Chinese territory; but they did in time depart from Geneva.

Stimson made it clear he wanted formal backing from Britain for his doctrine, but in London the Cabinet adopted an approach based on working within the framework of the League, though Eden was not in favour of recognising Manchukuo. 'Long talk with Simon & Van as to future action,' Eden wrote in his diary on 18 February. 'The Lausanne Conference [on reparations settlement] another anxious problem with which we must make headway in the next few months & then of course this Shanghai trouble over all leaves us with a heavy burden of work to divide up.'[67]

Further initiatives from Stimson, and what the Americans interpreted as 'a plain rebuff'[68] from the British Government followed. Eventually Eden, a member of the Cabinet Committee on the Far East, set out the British position in a speech in the Commons on 29 February 1932, when he said, 'It would be wholly improper for the Government of this country, which is a member of the League of Nations, to express by action on its own account independent of the League its judgement upon a matter which is now under investigation.'[69] Collective action by the League was the preferred option. In his memoirs Stimson laid the blame for what he saw as a fundamental breakdown in Anglo-American cooperation firmly at Eden's door, though Simon did not escape censure.

Eden was too lowly a player at this stage to deserve such obloquy, and later the two definitive histories of the crisis, by Reginald Bassett and Christopher Thorne, both absolved him.[70] He was not a delegate to the conference, nor a member of the Cabinet.

What the episode did show was Eden's awareness of how foreign policy imperatives should be conditioned by Britain's long-term interests, and his growing belief that it was through the League that those interests could be best protected. 'The Manchurian affair,' A. J. P. Taylor has written, 'far from weakening the coercive powers of the League, actually brought them into existence.'[71]

Whatever the rights and wrongs, the sense of grievance rumbled on in America for some time. Baldwin summed up what many in Britain felt when he said, 'You will get nothing out of Washington but words. Big words, but only words.'[72]*

Eden may not have gained the trust of Stimson, but he had impressed Ramsay MacDonald by his diligence, although in private the feelings were not reciprocated. 'No small part of the difficulty is Ramsay himself who seems incapable of taking a decision & abiding by it,' Eden observed tartly, after one of the endless meetings about Geneva. 'His late Cabinet did not call him MacShuffle for nothing.'[73]

At the end of 1932, MacDonald suggested to Simon that Eden be made a delegate to the conference, and with added status as Lord Privy Seal. As this could have been interpreted as a slight on his own abilities and commitment, Simon only partially accepted the proposal, which stemmed from his frequent complaints that he was overworked. Eden, no deadbeat, was signed up for front-line service, being promoted in 1933 to lead the British delegation. In practice, this meant that Simon could spend more time in London (and on Tadmarton Heath), while Eden and Cadogan conducted business in Geneva. Even Vansittart, no admirer of Eden, admitted, 'it was all dreary, all ingenious, its vain details deserve no chronicle, but helped Eden to make a name'.[74]

MacDonald was more at ease with the Conservatives in the National Government than with the various Liberal factions. In fact Eden, whose political bogey among the Liberal ranks was the fading figure of Lloyd

---

*In 1956, Eden was to recall the truth of this prophetic statement. Reality for America was to obtrude sooner than that. As one of her leading historians has observed, 'On the wind-scoured plains of Manchuria, Japan thus set the match in 1931 to that long fuse that would detonate the attack on Pearl Harbour just ten years later.' David M. Kennedy, *Freedom from Fear: The American People in Depression and War, 1929–1945*, Oxford University Press, Oxford, 1999, p.94.

THE ROSE OF YOUTH

George, was sometimes used by MacDonald as a stick with which to threaten troublesome Liberals within his ranks. 'A meeting in the afternoon in P.M.'s room,' Eden noted in his dairy:

> Van, Hankey [the Cabinet Secretary], P.M. & self to discuss roster for Geneva – Samuel anxious to go to establish himself with his own people. Date I suggested to him found to clash with Budget week & when he was summoned said this would never do as he would have to be here.
> P.M. 'You won't start making trouble over that I hope.'
> Samuel. 'Oh no, but I should like to be here to restrain my people.'
> P.M. 'Well, don't you stir them up anyway or I'll turn Anthony Eden on to you.'[75]

Even if such a role was hardly a natural one for the gentlemanly Eden, it was one indication of the confidence MacDonald had in him that he was even considered for it.

Eden's own finances continued to decline. Apart from London expenses, Simon's preparatory school (Cothill) had to be paid for, and the Edens took an active part in all the social activities in the Warwick and Leamington constituency. Eden liked to quote the line 'In Warwickshire I have true hearted friends' from Shakespeare's *Henry VI*.[76] Performances of Shakespeare vied in his diary with agricultural shows at Stoneleigh and summer fêtes at Warwick Castle. In April 1932 came the opening at Stratford-upon-Avon of the new Shakespeare Memorial Theatre by the Prince of Wales on St George's Day. Fulke Warwick had a house party at Warwick Castle, where Stanley and Lucy Baldwin, and Anthony and Beatrice Eden were the principal guests. As the local MP, Eden was involved in all the ceremonial. It seemed that the whole of Warwickshire was *en fête*; 100,000 people thronged Stratford to see the dignitaries arrive for the gala matinée performance of *Henry IV Part One*. Eden's only disappointment was with the production itself, which was over-elaborate and under-rehearsed. But the national coverage brought his constituency to the forefront and the new theatre, a controversial modernist building, was the focus for an expanding tourist industry that transformed the local economy.[77]

Eden wished that his finances could be transformed likewise. He noted sombrely in July 1932 that his capital had shrunk to £570 (just under £18,000 in today's currency). In August there was a family summit at Windlestone, which may have seemed a change from Geneva, but which also proved fraught and tortuous. 'At Windlestone for a week where much talk with Tim about his financial difficulties. He cannot make up his mind to sell or no. Meanwhile we spend our time searching for undiscovered masterpieces which is entertaining &, in two instances, may be fruitful.'[78] By the Christmas recess Eden was more gloomy still. 'I should not be so anxious about our own financial position if I were not fearful of Tim crashing & my having to do rescue work here – all together out of my depth.'[79]

On Christmas Day 1932, George V gave his inaugural radio broadcast to the people of the Mother Country and the British Dominions and Colonies. Eden, in common with the majority of the population, listened and was struck by the possibilities that such technology opened up, quite apart from its symbolic significance. Ironically, Eden was never to prove a fluent broadcaster himself.

Across the Atlantic, one of the great communicators was about to take office. Elected President of the United States in November 1932, Franklin D. Roosevelt was inaugurated in Washington on 4 March 1933. Eight days later he gave the first of his Fireside Chats, appropriately on the Great Depression.

Hitler became Chancellor on 30 January 1933. On 27 February the Reichstag was set on fire in Berlin, and on 1 May Dr Josef Goebbels claimed that Germany was now marching into the new age. What this might entail was made clearer the next day when leading Trade Unionists were arrested. With Stalin coming to the end of the first Five Year Plan in Russia, and Mussolini consolidating his power in Italy, four of the central players of the forthcoming world conflagration were now in place – the great American Democrat and the three European dictators.

When Eden, with his enhanced responsibilities, returned to Geneva on 17 January, a new era had begun there also. The Germans had returned to the conference, but the whole negotiating process was grinding to a halt. Eden was convinced that some new dramatic initiative was necessary. Amid a growing sense of pessimism, Japan had quit the League, and the French Government of Edouard Herriot had fallen, to be replaced by the first of Edouard Daladier's three administrations. Eden's initial point of association with Daladier was their joint military service during the Great War. Stimson had also departed the scene and Cordell Hull was the new Secretary of State, a post he was to hold until 27 November 1944. An internationalist, like his President, Hull was one of those figures who, by dint of overlapping longevity, was often to figure in Eden's story. 'He possessed an agreeable personality and a high order of intelligence,' Hull was to write of Eden, noting that he 'was always on the alert when any matter pertaining to Great Britain or peace was involved'. Having suffered from the chances and changes of political life himself, Hull was perceptive.

'I considered Eden a person of unusual promise in the political field, barring the changes of fortune implicit in politics,' he wrote in his memoirs.[80]

The change of fortune that had in effect made Eden Britain's leading representative in Geneva had not been replicated by any similar progress in the conference hall. It was a case of 'strong mutually antagonistic governments everywhere', as Evelyn Waugh was to describe it in *Scoop*.[81] With Cadogan, Eden drafted Britain's proposed disarmament convention. His exasperation with Simon continued. 'Simon has been trying to get me back to attend a Cabinet to help clear matters up at that end,' he wrote home to Beatrice. 'I really cannot leave in the middle of the week, & he really must act as Foreign Secretary at least in London if I have to do the real work here.'[82]

On 2 March, Eden returned to London with his plan. He lunched with MacDonald and Simon at the Athenaeum and warned that the conference was on the verge of collapse. The Cabinet's Disarmament Committee was not due to meet, but Eden pressed for a meeting that very night, which he addressed about the deteriorating position in Geneva. His main warning was that failure in the conference hall would lead to general rearmament by Germany. It was incumbent upon Britain to put forward concrete proposals. Eden's document was so formidable in its range – with technical details on troop numbers, aerial bombardment, naval policy, future consultative arrangements and future long-term strategy – that Hailsham, the War Secretary, stalled for time, claiming that it would take his department at least three days to assess all its implications.[83]

Eden persuaded MacDonald to come out to Geneva, where he addressed the conference on 16 March. The contrast between Eden, a man the Press now openly 'acknowledged on all hands to have been the outstanding success at Geneva,'[84] and MacDonald, 'a tired and failing old man, straining for rhetorical effects which he could no longer achieve, and in places unable to hold the thread of what he was trying to say,'[85] was palpable and painful.

16 March 1933 was the moment when Eden made a decisive step towards international recognition. Thenceforth he needed no identifying name-tag on his jacket lapel in the contemporary political cartoons. Cuthbert Headlam, Conservative MP for Barnard Castle, echoed the view of many when he wrote in his diary, 'He is now the blue-eyed boy of the National Govt. and is said to have done splendidly at Geneva. He is a charming young man and an excellent speaker.'[86] Austen Chamberlain was also in no doubt. Writing to his sister Hilda 'on the P.M.'s recent performance', he noted, 'I did not like his speech at Geneva – it made me feel uncomfortable as one is made uncomfortable by someone who strikes

just the wrong note in a Society.' By contrast, 'for all that part of the Govt. policy Eden made a really admirable & conclusive defence'.[87] Four months later, Simon was so exhausted that he was being urged 'to take a long sea voyage'. Austen Chamberlain thought a bold step was in order. 'I wish he [Simon] were a better man for the job. It was the wrong place to put him. I swear Anthony Eden would do better.'[88] Without any prompting from Chamberlain, *The Times* and the *Daily Mail* both pursued the same line, much to Simon's chagrin.

Although in practice Eden's proposal for a draft convention was never likely to get off the ground, the persistence and skill with which he presented the British case brought him wide recognition. In private, he was realistic. 'We are not doing well here. The Germans are proving extremely unhelpful,' he wrote to John Simon. 'A strange conjunction of chances is combining to make us look as though we had produced a Convention for our own Convenience.'[89] The truth was that the Germans were playing out a charade. Their delegates in Geneva were discussing limitations on arms; in Germany their service chiefs were pushing ahead with vigorous rearmament. During a long, hot summer there seemed no way out of the approaching impasse. On 14 October, the Germans withdrew from the conference; the same day Hitler announced that they were also leaving the League of Nations. It was the end of the Locarno phase of post-First World War. Ironically, it was also the day that Simon arrived for his autumn appearance in Geneva, and the German withdrawal had been timed to coincide with his speech. Eden's diary is caustic in its dismissiveness. 'It is very difficult to feel anything but contempt for the man at these times. It is not only "nerves" at the speech which we might all suffer or excuse but I truly believe an utter lack of moral courage.' Britain had proved powerless and an unsuccessful broker. 'In the afternoon news of German departure. The conference was becoming a sham so that it is perhaps just as well now. All the same I should not like Simon's conscience about the earlier part of last year when Brüning [Federal Chancellor 1930–2] was still in power. We missed the bus then & could never overtake it.'[90]

'Geneva' may have been a failure; the League of Nations may have been revealed as a well-meaning and impotent force; but 1933 was the year that made Eden's name. He was even being noticed in America, where a newspaper poll declared him 'the 4th best-dressed man in Europe'.[91]

The end of the year was bound up with recriminations and post-mortems. On 7 November 1933 Eden spoke in the big Disarmament Debate in the Commons. He spoke of how historians were already considering the origins of the Great War and in a telling anecdotal aside (a veiled reply to Archbishop Temple), told of the two distinguished statesmen, one French and one German, who discussed this very issue:

The German said to the Frenchman, 'After all, when the history of the War comes to be written it will be difficult to decide where the greater measure of blame lies', and the Frenchman replied, 'Well my friend, the one thing that history will not say is that Belgium invaded Germany.'

With the example of Roosevelt and Cordell Hull to hand, Eden was encouraged to feel that 'a policy of isolation has scarcely any friend'. Interestingly, he drew a distinction between the electorate's attitudes to the big contemporary issues of unemployment and disarmament. 'There is also this deep distinction between foreign and domestic policy. On the main issues of domestic policy the electorate is conscious of its ability to decide for itself, but in foreign affairs it necessarily relies, and is conscious of relying, on public men of all parties to guide them.'[92]

The year of 1933 had been a troublesome one of infinite complexities, but it was to end with partial reward for Eden. On 19 December MacDonald sent for him to explain his thinking on a forthcoming reshuffle. 'After careful consideration this was the offer he would make to me,' Eden recorded in his diary. 'He was determined not to have two F.O. Ministers in Cabinet. Previous experience had proved to him that it did not work, he argued. He would however like me to accept the office of Lord Privy Seal without a seat in Cabinet.' The offer, though welcome, especially on the financial side, was not quite the decisive promotion some had hoped for. Eden was not given a place in the Cabinet, or, as yet, a Privy Councillorship. He consulted Baldwin, who knew all the background, and told Eden that he had proposed him for a KCB, as 'he thought Sir Anthony would sound well!' Eden replied, 'if the idea was Geneva status I was quite happy as I was & nobody troubled about status there.'[93]

Eden may not have worried about status, but his new job was certainly seen as conferring it. Chips Channon wrote, 'Of our Oxford set, Anthony Eden has made the most progress, Lord Privy Seal at 35.'[94] The office of Lord Privy Seal is one of those non-departmental posts that varies in importance depending on the Prime Minister's allocation of responsibility. At the time it was no sinecure. In 1929, as Lord Privy Seal, J. H. Thomas had been charged with resolving unemployment; in 1938, while holding the post, Sir John Anderson was to be put in charge of air-raid preparations. MacDonald told King George V of his thinking behind Eden's promotion:

The Prime Minister now proposes to increase the team at the Foreign Office. He proposes to appoint Captain Eden Lord Privy Seal with the intention that he shall continue his duties at the Foreign Office under the Secretary of State, devoting special attention to work in connection with the League of Nations.[95]

The appointment was announced on New Year's Day and received a chorus of approval in the national Press. Cuthbert Headlam felt the promotion was in large part owing to Eden's decisiveness compared to Simon. 'Anthony Eden, they tell me, can make up his mind (probably the F.O. point of view) and give advice clearly – hence his success and advancement. He also possesses a pleasant manner, is nice looking, and does the right things in the right way – what more is required?'[96] The classically educated, with knowledge of the reversals of Greek tragedy, would probably have added – continued luck and good health. In the end, Eden was to be afforded neither of these.

The Edens were bidden to Sandringham for the first weekend of 1934 to meet the royal family, and for Eden to receive his seals of office as Lord Privy Seal from King George V. Although such invitations were the custom for new ministers, Eden was anxious about the niceties and requirements of protocol and asked the King's secretary, Sir Clive Wigram, for guidance. He was told that things were much more informal at court nowadays, and that white tie and tails would be quite acceptable for dinner on the Saturday night. 'For the evening – tail coat, white waistcoat and decorations, but not knee breeches.' Although relieved that he would not have to purchase buckled shoes, Eden thought the list of informal requirements – including a silk top hat for church on Sunday morning – was formidable.[97] For weekend reading he took a copy of Disraeli's *Coningsby*.

The Edens arrived at the little station of Wolferton on the afternoon of 6 January. The first person they met was the Archbishop of Canterbury, Cosmo Gordon Lang, who in the strict formality of the Order of Precedence* now only narrowly outranked Eden. 'We find an Archbishop, pregnant with sermon on the station platform,' Eden noted with some apprehension in his diary. 'We are bowed through a booking office, panelled, flowered & carpeted.' The weekend unfurled like some magic carpet of the past. The King and Queen greeted their guests personally in the front hall at Sandringham. The atmosphere initially was stilted. 'We hover round belated tea, rapidly exhausting gambits of conversation,' Eden wrote. He was relieved when he was summoned to the King's study to be sworn in as Lord Privy Seal. 'Contrive to kneel on right knee holding testament in right hand – gymnastic difficulty – Equerry attempts to read oath but loses spectacles and becomes incoherent.' A second attempt

---

*The first seven places in the Order of Precedence, and an indication of how far Eden had climbed so early, are: the Archbishop of Canterbury, the Lord High Chancellor, the Archbishop of York, the Prime Minister, the Lord President of the Council, the Speaker of the House of Commons, the Lord Privy Seal. Uniquely, Eden at this stage was not a Privy Councillor as Lord Privy Seal.

proved little better. 'What should I do?' Eden wondered. 'Out of practice in Norfolk atmosphere, so I bungle.'[98]

With some relief, the ceremony was eventually completed, and the King and his new minister were left alone. To Eden's surprise, the King then discoursed for an hour on foreign policy. It was the first of many such encounters. Unlike the awkwardness of the small talk at tea, there was no stopping the King when he was talking 'business'. Far from keeping the conversation going, Eden found himself hard-pressed to get a word in edgeways. Later that summer at Buckingham Palace he was received, unusually, in the north-east corner room, as the private apartments were undergoing repairs. The disadvantage was the proximity of the bandstand below in the forecourt. 'It is all right, however,' the King reassured him, 'I have told the band not to play till I give the word.' The King then embarked on a comprehensive outline of all the topics Eden would be facing later that week in Geneva. As the audience drew to its conclusion, Eden attempted to make one or two points of his own. 'Just one second,' said the King, summoning a page, 'Tell the bandmaster that he can start playing now . . . You were saying . . .?'[99]

Dinner at Sandringham in January 1934 reverted to stiff formality. It was not a gathering of the *jeunesse dorée*. 'We are clocked off beforehand. Boys one side (average age 80) girls the other (average age Aunt Blanche).' Eden omitted to say in his diary entry that his Aunt Blanche had in fact died in 1865. 'I stray into wrong pen, by accident (not lechery). Confusion. Equerries rush. I am rescued from temptation. Everybody very kind, but I fear Charles II should have been our King. We are very sleepy but where are our sweet Nells & spoilt Monmouths?'[100]

The next day came the Archbishop of Canterbury's sermon in the tiny Sandringham Church of St Mary Magdalene. 'Paraded for Church at 11 a.m.,' wrote Eden of the precise organisation. Afterwards the King again sought out Eden for a talk. News had arrived of a speech the previous day by Sir Stafford Cripps, Labour MP for Bristol East and the former Solicitor-General. Answering questions after an address on 'War and Fascism', Cripps had declared that the next Labour Government would 'have to overcome opposition from Buckingham Palace'. Under further questioning, he said he was referring to 'Court circles and officials and other people who surround the King.'[101] According to Eden's diary, it was the second remark that most angered George V:

> He launched out into a tirade against Cripps' speech which broke out again at intervals throughout the day. The excuse only made it worse. 'What does he mean by saying that Buckingham Palace is not me? Who else is there, I should like to know? Does he mean the footmen? D'you see the fellow says there is going to be a General Election in August? Who

is he to decide that? D——d cheek I call it. I have seen moreover in one of his earlier speeches he says that if Labour gets back with a clear majority then a Trade Union Congress is to tell *me* who is going to be Prime Minister. I'll see them d——d first. That is my business and I'll send for whom I like', etc.

There was more in the same vein, with Eden also forceful against Cripps. 'You'll have to answer him,' declared the King. After straying into these delicate constitutional waters, the formalities of luncheon came as something of a relief. During the afternoon the Queen and the seven-year-old Princess Elizabeth took the Edens round the Sandringham stud. Despite all the kindnesses the Edens were shown during their eventful stay, Eden found it as exhausting as some of the sessions at Geneva. 'I should never make a court flunkey,' he wrote.[102]

On his return to London, one of his first responsibilities as the new Lord Privy Seal was to receive Joachim von Ribbentrop, the former champagne salesman, now Hitler's foreign-affairs adviser, and soon to be the German Ambassador in London.

Ten years earlier Eden had taken his first step on the ladder of preferment as Parliamentary Private Secretary to Godfrey Locker-Lampson. His choice now of Viscount Cranborne (1893–1972) as his own Parliamentary Private Secretary was the beginning of the most important and enduring political partnership of his career. 'Bobbety', as he was known, was the elder brother of Eden's Oxford friend Lord David Cecil, and, like Eden, a veteran of the western front. MP for South Dorset since 1929, Cranborne represented continuity in politics. Grandson of one Prime Minister, the great Victorian Lord Salisbury, cousin of another, A. J. Balfour, and son of James, the 4th Marquess of Salisbury, holder in his time of five separate Cabinet posts, Cranborne could trace his descent from Elizabeth I's Lord High Treasurer, William Cecil, Lord Burghley, the possible model for Shakespeare's Polonius. Also 'a man faithful and honourable,'[103] Cranborne had an independence of spirit that contributed to a stiffening of the sometimes urbane orthodoxies of Eden's despatch-box manner. He could be icily ferocious when crossed, and cared not a jot for conventional opinion, speaking his mind without fear or favour. His most famous (or infamous) speech came in March 1961, when he denounced the then Colonial Secretary, Iain Macleod, as being 'too clever by half'. But in the build-up to his peroration, he gave a sketch of Macleod's character that could very well have been a self-portrait: 'He is, as we all know, a man of most unusual intellectual brilliance; and he is, moreover, both brave and resolute. Those are valuable and not too common attributes in politics.'[104]

They were attributes that were valued by Eden. The two were together from the days of Geneva and Abyssinia, through Munich and the Second World War, to the post-war settlements of the 1945 San Francisco Conference, the years of renewal in opposition and the Conservative Governments of the 1950s. Salisbury, as he became in 1947 on the death of the 4th Marquess, was Eden's preferred choice for Foreign Secretary in April 1955, and, after the dramas of Harold Macmillan's brief tenure, Eden always regretted that he had not followed his first instinct.[105] After Suez and Eden's resignation in January 1957, it was Bobbety Salisbury, with that aristocratic difficulty in pronouncing the letter 'r', who was to put to the Cabinet that all-important question about the identity of Eden's successor, 'Wab or Hawold?'[106]

Unlike Churchill, with his coterie of confidants and followers, Eden never surrounded himself with like-minded figures and lacked a power base in the House of Commons, a severe handicap when the going got rough. The YMCA and the Glamour Boys were labels, rather than a following. To a surprising degree among political figures of the front rank, Eden was a loner. His gregariousness was a social, rather than a parliamentary one. Bobbety Cranborne was both a social friend and a political colleague. So was J. P. L. ('Jim') Thomas, later Viscount Cilcennin, who was to join Eden's Foreign Office team as Parliamentary Private Secretary in 1937, with Cranborne as Under-Secretary, the apogee of their time as a political equivalent of the Three Musketeers. Like Cranborne, Thomas was to resign with Eden in February 1938, returning with his master to the Dominions Office on the outbreak of war. But the Royal Navy was his great love – his expertise in this field was a valuable link for Eden – and he twice served in the Admiralty, during the war as Financial Secretary, and in the 1950s as its political head, when with characteristic self-effacement he said that the only test of a First Lord was, 'Will he look well in a yachting cap when visiting the fleet?'[107] His dependable, down-to-earth qualities proved a buttress for Eden during many dark days.[108]

On 6 February 1934, in the course of an important foreign-affairs debate, it was announced that Eden would be visiting Paris, Berlin and Rome with the terms of the new British Memorandum of 29 January on disarmament. Eden's responsibilities as broker were his most arduous to date; he regarded the document as a compromise, but one with an outside chance of bringing Germany back to the conference. Hitler wanted 'equality' of treatment, which he interpreted as a land army of 300,000; British proposals were for 200,000, with limitations on tanks and 155mm guns, and naval details to be resolved at a later date. Everything would hinge on French and Italian reactions.

Eden set off from Victoria Station on 16 February, embarrassed by the fuss, with Sir John Simon at his most oleaginous, and the French, German and Italian ambassadors all in attendance. Nevile Butler, the Prime Minister's private secretary, represented MacDonald and Baldwin. Eden's principal advisers were William Strang, a future Permanent Under-Secretary; Bobbety Cranborne, who kept a diary of their journeyings; and his new private secretary, Robin (Robert) Hankey, eldest son of the Cabinet Secretary, and a future ambassador. Eden had set out the Government's position in the Foreign Office debate ten days earlier. If the memorandum was accepted, 'There would be no race in armaments; Nations would know their own commitments, their own programmes and those of their neighbours, for ten years to come.'[109] It was to prove wishful thinking.

The mission got off to a dispiriting start, as Bobbety Cranborne recorded. 'First there was a fog in the Channel, which held us up, & then when we did get to Calais, we ran into the pier.' Calais was torn by riots as they landed, a consequence of the Stavisky financial scandal that had broken the Government of Camille Chautemps, and there were fears of physical violence against the train. 'In any case, no one interfered with the Golden Arrow, & we started off at full speed through an impenetrable fog.' Impenetrable fog was an apt metaphor for the next three weeks, which proved an unpropitious time to be engaging in complex nego-tiations, as the new French Government had not had time to assimilate details of the British proposals. But what they could not offer by way of understanding, they made up for with ceremony, as Cranborne noted. 'At the Gare du Nord to his great surprise he [Anthony] had an almost royal reception.'[110]

Before the talks, Eden met Sir William Tyrrell, the British Ambassador, who told him with great prescience what of the memorandum the French would and would not accept. As a man who had taken to his bed for three days on the appointment of Sir John Simon, Tyrrell was not hopeful. 'The trouble with the Foreign Secretary,' he said, 'is that you can load him but he doesn't fire.'[111]

Eden was concerned at the frequency with which the French changed their leadership. 'Dominating impression is France's unhappy internal political state. I fear much trouble ahead. This govt. cannot last long. There is the rot of corruption in her whole parliamentary system.'[112] Eden was now meeting a new Prime Minister, Gaston Doumergue, with Louis Barthou as the latest Foreign Minister. But there was to be no long-term stability. On 9 October Barthou was receiving King Alexander of Yugoslavia at Marseilles, when both were gunned down with what Eden called 'the first shots of the second world war.'[113]

The French team soon made clear their unease at the British proposals. Memories of the opening of the Great War were still strong. Eden was not impressed. 'Politically poor France is in an unhappy state and her troubles are by no means over,' he reported to Simon. 'This is not a national government in our sense of the word, but a collection of old gentlemen forced to come together by mobs of exasperated, and mostly middle-class Parisians.'[114] Although he did not greatly care for Barthou's manner, Eden felt Barthou had the best understanding of the political realities. Alone among the French delegation Barthou knew that failure was not an option. As Eden wrote later, 'Having learned that Anglo-French co-operation had to be, he had vigour enough to make such co-operation real.'[115]

On his last night in Paris, Eden relaxed at the theatre. The play was *Les Temps Difficiles*.

Three days later, on 19 February, the British party was in Aachen *en route* to Berlin. From the train Eden had noticed the stillness of the Ruhr and the lack of smoking chimneys in Essen. But there were other signs of smouldering activity. 'There were three Nazi storm troopers on the platform at Aachen, the most military figures that can be imagined, goose-stepping up & down in khaki uniform, and wearing Sam Browne belts on military greatcoats,' as Cranborne noted. 'We got to Berlin at midnight to find the station thronged with press photographers & eminent Nazis in fur coats. We drove straight to the Adlon, where we found the most palatial suite of rooms & Herr Adlon bowing in the hall. Evidently they are pleased that a British minister should have come.'

Both Eden and Cranborne were conscious of the restrictive nature of the society in which, as prominent guests, they found themselves. 'One soon becomes conscious,' recorded Cranborne, 'that one is in a country where liberty of thought no longer exists. The mildest criticism of the Government invites, & gets, the severest punishment.' This made 'a painful impression on the visitor'. The military atmosphere permeated everywhere, but this had an unexpected benefit for their mission, because of Eden's war record.

'The other thing that strikes one is the intense natural militarism of the inhabitants,' wrote Cranborne. Ernst Roehm, the head of the Nazi para-military organisation, the SA (Sturm Abteilungen), which Hitler was to liquidate in the 'Night of the Long Knives' on 30 June, was clearly too prominent a potential rival to survive long. 'Roehm, the head of the SA, told someone that he would rather speak to an enemy soldier than to a German civilian, & the fact that Anthony had fought in the trenches was undoubtedly of the greatest assistance to him in his negotiations with Hitler.' Cranborne thought that 'in these circumstances, it is indeed remarkable that the Government should be willing to negotiate on Disarmament at all. They have left Geneva. They are free to do what they like.'[116]

Eden was briefed by the British Ambassador, Sir Eric Phipps, who had served for two spells in the Paris Embassy, and who was to return to France as Ambassador in 1937. With his degree from Paris University, and education also in Dresden and Vienna, Phipps had a deep understanding of all things French and an intuitive feel for the European perspective. His up-to-date experience of both France and Germany was invaluable to Eden.[117] Although Phipps mistakenly thought Hitler would not risk a war for another ten years, he gave Eden a worrying picture of Germany's clandestine air rearmament.

The next day (20 February) was long remembered by Eden. 'In the afternoon,' he wrote in his diary, 'went with Phipps to see Chancellor who received in vast room of cinema palace proportions. We approached this through many passages, guards etc' – a technique of subtle intimidation that he also found employed by Mussolini:

> Chancellor himself was friendly & talked at considerable length. I am told that he was quieter than usual. Certainly he listened to what I had to say. The man is clearly much more than a demagogue. He knew however what he was speaking about & seemed to me more sincere than I had expected. He has even a suspicion of humour, & at close quarters resembles the average Austrian much more closely than appears from his posters.[118]

Eden made more headway on the paramilitary organisations, the SS (Schutzstaffel) and the SA, than on German re-entry to the League, which Hitler refused to link with the rearmament question. Cranborne was surprised how helpful Hitler appeared to be:

> He gave every evidence of wanting to get an agreement. Anthony had two interviews with him. The first, on Tuesday, was at his office, & lasted nearly three hours. At this meeting, at which Neurath [German Foreign Minister from 1932 to February 1938, when Hitler replaced him with Ribbentrop] & Eric Phipps were also present, the Chancellor dealt entirely with our White Paper, & explained what he could not accept & why. His tone was friendly, & his intention obviously rather to persuade than to threaten ... Anthony pointed out our anxiety with regard to para-military forces.
>
> At the second meeting, the Chancellor put forward some suggestions for dealing with the various points which had been raised the previous day. They have been put before the Government at home, & it is to be hoped that they will be given fair consideration ...
>
> I was not present at the conversations, but had one opportunity of seeing the Chancellor, at lunch at the Embassy. It was something of an

occasion, as it was the first time that he had been inside any Foreign Embassy, & great precautions had been taken to prevent the fact being known ... He is much less dominating than one would have expected from his photographs. Indeed, one certainly would not notice him if one passed him in the street ... his appearance is essentially ordinary ... In that way he is not unlike Baldwin, whom indeed he resembles more than any statesman I have seen ... To see him in fact gives one some clue to the personality of Joan of Arc. Both are examples of inspired peasants.[119]

The luncheon at the British Embassy was convivial and agreeable. 'Hitler thawed materially,' wrote Eden, 'especially when we discussed the war which he likes to recall like most Germans. We discussed the various sectors where we had each been on. I took the chance to rub in that ex-soldiers should be the last even to wish for another war. He assented heartily.' Eden was struck by Hitler's dislike of the atmosphere of Berlin (which Eden could well understand, even after twenty-four hours in the city) and his nostalgia for the countryside:

We also spoke of Bavaria & he begged me to come & stay with him in his cottage on the Austrian frontier. He warmed up as he described its scenery. It is clear that he does not like Berlin & the rumour that he thinks of moving his capital to Munich may not lack foundation. A talk with Goebbels [the Nazi Propaganda Minister from 1933] after luncheon. He seemed principally delighted at the visit of so young a Minister & harped on that theme, as also my war experiences. They are my two chief assets here![120]

Eden was not alone in thinking well of Hitler after a first meeting. Lloyd George was positively fulsome after his visit to Berchtesgaden in September 1936, comparing *Mein Kampf* to Magna Carta. For him, Hitler was the George Washington of Germany. 'Unquestionably a great leader,' he declared, adding, 'great leaders are not being thrown up by the European democracies.'[121] In October 1937 the Duke of Windsor, the former King Edward VIII, made a visit to the Berghof, and was later reported as saying of the 'miracle' of German social conditions, 'one can only begin to understand it when one realises that behind it is one man and one will.'[122]

It should perhaps be remembered that this meeting between Eden and Hitler took place before the Night of the Long Knives, before the murder of the Austrian Chancellor Dolfuss (25 July 1934) and before the remilitarisation of the Rhineland. Possibly Eden, then, was seeing through a glass darkly; but long before *Kristallnacht* and the *Anschluss*, he was seeing face-to-face. In February 1934, however, he reported positively back to London – 'I find it very hard to believe that the man himself wants war' – with details of Hitler's proposals,[123] especially on paramilitary organisations such as the Green Police, which Hitler was prepared to reduce from 140,000 to 90,000, and supervision of the SS and SA.

Hitler knew how to turn on the charm when needed, and he played all the cards with Eden, a tacit acknowledgement that Eden would be an important witness back home in Britain. Their joint bond as survivors of the western front proved a powerful emotion, and Eden confessed in a letter to Beatrice that he had rather liked Hitler.

On his last day in Berlin, Eden called on the eighty-six-year-old President Hindenburg. For the former Captain from the King's Royal Rifle Corps, this meeting with the former German Field Marshal and Chief of the Greater German General Staff was an unforgettable moment. 'Fine simple courtly old man – Interested, like all those Germans, only in soldiering. He asked me if I had been in British cavalry charge at Cambrai in 1917 – One of the finest episodes of the war, he said,' Eden wrote, admitting in the privacy of his diary, 'I had never heard of it.'[124] When Churchill gave Eden an inscribed copy of his book *Great Contemporaries* in 1937, the first essay to which Eden turned was that on Hindenburg.

Eden thought his talks with Hitler would remain confidential, but found on arrival in Italy that Mussolini was fully apprised of them, except for the detail about the Green Police. His despatch to Simon had not been well received, as telegrams between London and Sir Eric Phipps revealed. Both these pieces of unwelcome news became clear to Eden when he arrived at the British Embassy in Rome on the next stage of his tour during the afternoon of 24 February. 'Found some profoundly irritating telegrams at the Embassy showing Simon & Van's manifest mistrust in all I am doing. It is really hopeless to attempt to work for such a man. He is not only a national but an international calamity.'[125]

The sunshine and Italian scenes that Eden so loved were in sharp contrast to his mood and the harsh and intimidating atmosphere in the streets. Cranborne noted that 'the discipline is still more than the British public would stand. I noticed that if anyone got in Anthony's way, he was unceremoniously kicked out of it. But they do not seem to mind this.' The contrast with the comforts of diplomatic life were marked. Eden's party was welcomed to the Embassy by Sir Eric Drummond (later the Earl of Perth), the first Secretary-General of the League of Nations, a figure Eden knew well and on whose judgement he would rely during the next few difficult days. 'In the evening a big dinner at the Embassy,' recorded Cranborne:

> After dinner Anthony sat on a sofa at the end of the drawing room, in a niche between two pillars, with the French Ambassador on 1 side & the German on the other. He looked just like Alice between the Red & the White Queen.[126]

On Sunday 25 February the *Observer* published a damaging account of Eden's mission, containing criticisms such as 'He is not competent either to negotiate or to prepare for negotiation.'[127] Although the words were not Vansittart's, the article was inspired by him, and Eden was understandably furious. Simon had no viable alternative policy in London, and Eden, without the authority of Cabinet membership or a Privy Councillorship, was undertaking an exploratory tour on behalf of the Government. The article caused much offence in London among those in the know, and Baldwin received a passionately worded complaint from William Ormsby-Gore. Phipps and Drummond both independently defended Eden in their despatches to Simon from Berlin and Rome. Eden never had confidence in Simon; from this moment he looked forward to the time when he would be free of such an unhelpful chief. Surprisingly, he did not feel the same personal antagonism towards Vansittart and met him socially, playing tennis at Vansittart's country home at Denham.[128]

The combination of the German leak and the *Observer* article did not put Eden in the best of moods for his meeting with Mussolini. With the perspective of history, Mussolini may be a subordinate figure compared to Hitler, but this was not how matters appeared in the early 1930s. Mussolini was the towering figure, renowned for his industriousness and a proven force for economic regeneration. At the time of his meeting with Eden, international opinion was becoming more wary of Italian threats to collective security, a feeling that hardened with the Abyssinia Crisis. Within the year, Count Grandi, the Italian Ambassador in London, was branding Eden as public enemy number one, an oblique tribute to his understanding of the true aims of Fascist expansionism. Eden was never confident that Italy would form an understanding with France or Britain; Mussolini's rapprochement, he rightly feared, would be with Germany. 'Recent research in Italian military and diplomatic archives,' one of the leading historians of this period has written, 'indicates that Eden's assessment of Mussolini's character, aims, and objectives had frequently been accurate.'[129]

Before Eden met Mussolini for the first time on 26 February, he was granted an audience with Pope Pius XI. 'An impressive approach through room after room, each occupied by its own type of guards. Beautiful & variegated uniforms. All presented arms, though most of them with but moderate efficiency, so that even if the Vatican is the most heavily armed state we need not greatly fear!' Eden spoke for half an hour with the Pontiff, who greeted him as 'l'apôtre de la paix'. On the way out, Eden made sure he had time to see the Sistine Chapel and the other artistic treasures of the Vatican.[130]

Eden's appointment with Mussolini at the Palazzo Venezia was scheduled for 5 p.m. He was led to the presence through a myriad of corridors. His first impression was of Mussolini's journalist's instinct for news. He clearly liked to have a good gossip. He was well informed on British matters, and even knew of the recent Wavertree by-election in Liverpool on 6 February, where the intervention of Randolph Churchill, Winston Churchill's son, as an Independent Conservative had split the National Government vote and led to a Labour victory. Mussolini had never met Hitler and was full of questions about the Führer. The substantive part of the talks centred on French attitudes to German rearmament. Mussolini accepted German demands for 'equality', but held out hopes that thereafter Italy would stand firm with Britain and France on further German demands, and call for Germany's return to the League. 'Mussolini was most accommodating,' recorded Cranborne. 'He will accept our memorandum, if we can persuade the French, with pleasure.' Although in the long run this was to prove a vain hope, at the time the signs were not unfavourable. Cranborne was struck by Mussolini's fascination with all things German. 'He asked a great deal about Hitler & Berlin. What did they talk about there? Anthony said, the last war. He roared with laughter & said they had forgotten* all about it in Rome.'[131] Mussolini's comment after their stormy meeting on Abyssinia the following year was less urbane. The Duce said then, 'I never saw a better-dressed fool.'[132]

On Tuesday 27 February copies of the British weekend papers arrived, including the offending *Observer*. 'Alarms & excursions.' recorded Cranborne:

> The *Observer* arrived containing very offensive & disparaging references to Anthony & also a mischievous & misleading account of the situation, apparently inspired. Anthony was, not unnaturally, furious. He rang up the P.M. in London, found he was out, & gave a piece of his mind to Nevile Butler. After that, he felt better.[133]

By 1 March the British party was back at the Quai d'Orsay. Eden had hoped to tie up the loose ends of his Berlin and Rome meetings with the French, but was to be disappointed. French internal concerns had prevented the Cabinet from even considering the British memorandum. *Coriolanus* was being staged at the Comédie-Française, but so inflammatory was Shakespeare's most political play considered to be in a period of domestic instability that the authorities had banned it, a striking pre-echo of the events in East Berlin in June 1953 when performances provoked a workers' uprising.[134] Fresh from his talks with the imperious

---

*Eden was not so sure and remembered Augustine Birrell's comment that 'It is better to read about a world figure than to live under his rule.'

and bragging Mussolini, Eden was in doubt that he had met the man who could have played the role of Shakespeare's Roman leader to perfection; indeed, Mussolini's eventual fate in April 1945 was to have striking parallels with that of Coriolanus, parallels emphasised by Laurence Olivier in his celebrated 1959 performance at Stratford.

Eden noted the contrast between the democracies and the dictatorships with sadness. 'In Berlin and Rome, the men I met were completely in command of their subject, familiar with its every detail and ready to take decisions.'[135] The French had not even done their homework. In retrospect, the whole episode was for Eden a missed opportunity. Internationally accepted ground-rules were not established, and the consequences were to be grievous. As Cranborne recorded:

> They [the French] couldn't even keep to the point. They kept shooting off at a tangent, & making long & passionate speeches. Every now and then, A. would try to bring them back to the point by asking them if they had any comments on our memorandum ... It was obviously no good staying any longer in Paris, so Anthony decided to leave by the 4'o clock train for London.'[136]

Mussolini's intentions were never going to be deflected by the visit of a junior minister, but some Italian commentators considered that Eden's appearance in Rome had exacerbated an already difficult situation.[137] If this was the case, the fault lay with Mussolini. Similarly in Berlin Eden's function was an exploratory, not an executive, one. Only in France, where the countries were ostensibly singing from the same hymn sheet, was there real disappointment, as the French were still embroiled in the fall-out from the Stavisky scandal.

Eden reported to the Cabinet and, rather dispiritedly, to the House of Commons on 14 March, where he had a tetchy exchange with John Wilmot, Labour victor at the famous East Fulham by-election in October 1933.[138]

To all intents and purposes, the memorandum was dead. The next month the French announced that their security was more important than disarmament, and in May the Geneva Conference met for what proved to be the last time. Reflecting this change of emphasis, Eden made important speeches in Kenilworth (28 June) and Stoke (5 July) on Britain's defensive needs.

On 30 July 1934 the RAF estimates provided for forty-one new squadrons, and Baldwin warned that in 'the defence of England you no longer think of the chalk cliffs of Dover, you think of the Rhine. That is where our frontier lies.'[139] The Labour Party voted against these estimates

(*Above*) Anthony Eden's mother, Sybil. 'My father paid the bills but my mother did the work.'

(*Below left*) 'A resemblance, which is particularly striking in the bust of George Wyndham at the Musée Rodin.' It was whispered that Sybil's admirer, George Wyndham, was Anthony Eden's natural father, but the rumours were mistaken. (*Below right*) Anthony Eden, aged three.

(*Above*) Windlestone Hall in 1918.
'As I knew it would never be mine, my affection was not possessive.'

(*Below*) Timothy, Marjorie, Nicholas (seated between his parents), Jack, Anthony: the Eden family at Windlestone, a photograph to commemorate the silver wedding of Sir William and Lady Eden and Jack's coming of age. Both Jack and Nicholas died in the First World War; Nicholas was killed at Jutland aged just sixteen.

(*Above*) Anthony Eden, seated second left, with members of the King's Royal Rifle Corps in 1916.

(*Below*) The Brigade Major, on his favourite horse, The Cat. 1918.

Anthony Eden with his brother Tim, at Windlestone after the Great War.

Captain Eden in his Warwick and Leamington Constituency. 1928.

The wedding of Anthony Eden and Beatrice Beckett at St Margaret's, Westminster, 5 November 1923. They were married by the Archbishop of York, Cosmo Gordon Lang, who, earlier the same day, had officiated at the funeral of the former Prime Minister, Bonar Law, in neighbouring Westminster Abbey.

Eden about to set foot on Russian soil in 1935. It seemed to some as if Tolstoy's Count Vronksy were alighting at the platform.

(*Above*) Austen Chamberlain with Gustav Stresemann and Aristide Briand in Geneva, 1927. 'Whatever the official performance, it was their private conversations which mattered.'

(*Below*) Anthony Eden's first visit to Moscow in 1935. 'More like the annual dinner of some branch in the Society of Oddfellows.' Bobbety Cranborne on left.

(*Above*) 'The Triumvirate', not always marching in step: Sir Samuel Hoare, Anthony Eden and Sir Robert Vansittart.

(*Below*) Simon and Eden. 'John Simon arrives tomorrow, but when he finds the amount of work awaiting him, I don't suppose he will stay long.'

in the Commons, a fact later conveniently forgotten in the *Guilty Men** interpretation of the 1930s.

Soon other problems pushed their way on to the front pages – the Saar, the Balkans and, most ominously in Eden's view, Abyssinia.

On 23 May Eden 'received a letter from P.M. that I am to be made a Privy Councillor in the birthday honours'. He was the only Lord Privy Seal not to have been a Privy Councillor on appointment, so he 'hardly expected to get it a few months later.'[140] He was sworn of the Privy Council on 29 June, the day after an important speech at Kenilworth, in which he warned his constituents:

> We have in no sense solved the main difficulties of the European situation. These consist in the present relations of the chief powers of Continental Europe. Unless they can be improved there will be no disarmament agreement, no political *détente*, and in consequence no extension of international trade recovery in Europe.[141]

His Privy Councillorship sealed two important years for Eden. Though little had been gained in absolute terms on disarmament, he had built a store of experience on which he was able to draw in the years ahead, and his reputation for diplomacy, particularly abroad, had been firmly established. An overdue holiday that summer in France with Beatrice was a welcome restorative. For the second year the Edens had gone to a quiet corner of Brittany, 'still a land of poor cottages scarcely more than mud huts', a marked contrast with the 'churches scarcely less than cathedrals'.[142]

When Eden returned to Geneva in the autumn, the first major event was the admission of Russia to the League of Nations delegation. 'The entry of the Soviet passed off without acclamation,' Eden reported to Simon. 'The atmosphere might better be described as one of overheated depression.'[143] Eden played his part in overcoming the opposition of Holland, Portugal and Switzerland. A more consequential event three weeks later was the assassination in Marseilles, by a Croat refugee with Hungarian links, of King Alexander and the French Foreign Minister Barthou.† Eden was 'particularly sorry about the latter on personal grounds. He may have been foxy, & something of a scamp, but he had courage, perhaps the most essential quality in a Foreign Secretary at this time.' A gloom descended on Geneva as the implications of the assassination became clearer.[144]

---

*By selective quotation from the speeches of Conservative leaders, notably Baldwin, the polemic *Guilty Men* by 'Cato' (Gollancz, 1940) successfully established a partial interpretation of the complexities of 1930s defence policy in the public mind. The authors were Michael Foot, Peter Howard and Frank Owen.
†His successor was Pierre Laval.

For many it seemed that a European war was now both inevitable and imminent. Eden accepted the position of *rapporteur* at Geneva, a figure acceptable to all parties from the so-called Little Entente of Czechoslovakia, Romania and Yugoslavia, in the escalating confrontation with Hungary. In a remarkable parallel with the events following the assassination of Archduke Ferdinand in June 1914, the major powers began to square up behind the respective alliances, Italy warning Britain 'that Mussolini would feel it necessary to take up the cudgels in defence of Hungary.'[145]

It was almost certainly owing to Eden's personal diplomacy that the conflict did not begin there and then. Few of those involved take much credit from an entangled and inflammatory political situation. Neither Italy nor Hungary was blameless, and Eden certainly turned a blind eye to some of the underlying realities, when holding the ring between Italy and France. It was a case of expediency winning over absolute morality. For Eden, political choice in this instance lay not between the desirable and the undesirable, but between the unpalatable and the disastrous.

'I think he was regarded at first as just a debonair young politician who talked excellent French and could be trusted to keep things going without friction,' wrote Major-General Temperley, who was with Eden throughout the negotiations. 'As time went on he became one of the biggest figures in the Conference and his reputation had spread all over Europe.' Of the Yugoslav settlement in particular, Temperley considered that 'too much praise cannot be given to Mr Eden for what he accomplished; & every statesman at Geneva was well aware that there was no other man in Europe who could have done it'. As for the Abyssinian crisis, Temperley believed that 'The failure of the policy cannot be laid at his door. The evil genius was M. Laval.'[146]

The remarkable thing about the resolution of the Balkans dispute was that simultaneously Eden was heavily involved in the question of a plebiscite on the Saar coalfields. 'Continual worries & interruptions over Saar arrangements which prevented concentration I wished to give to Yugoslav–Hungarian dispute which is now more important.'[147]

Pierre Laval had told Eden that there was no question of French forces intervening as international peace-keepers. Against the wishes of Sir John Simon, an increasingly marginalised figure, and Lord Hailsham, the War Secretary, Eden persuaded Baldwin that British forces would have to be committed to this peace-keeping role, which was eventually accepted by the League on 8 December 1934. Italy, Holland and Sweden joined British forces to ensure a peaceful conclusion to the plebiscite. Eden was particularly pleased that he had persuaded the Swedes to join the force, as earlier in the autumn he had made an extensive tour of Scandinavia to explain League policy.

The success of this tour was widely reported, and on his return Eden was summoned by both King George V and the Prince of Wales for private audiences. While at Buckingham Palace, Eden was told by Sir Clive Wigram that the King hoped that Baldwin and the older men would soon make way for Eden, Oliver Stanley 'and the younger men.'[148] As Eden laconically noted in his memoirs, it was a refrain he was to become accustomed to hearing in the next twenty-one years.[149]

Another younger man who was showing increasing impatience was the Prince of Wales, who summoned Eden for a talk on 7 November. 'A whisky & soda & a talk about Scandinavia & other matters,' Eden recorded in his diary. Although the two had met before, this was their first extensive *tour d'horizon*. They had much in common, stemming from their formative experiences during the Great War. Both had a restless energy, reflected in a fierce competitiveness at golf and tennis respectively. (Eden was often seen on the tennis courts in Geneva at 7 a.m. before the day's work began.) Other shared characteristics were a complicated private life, social concern for the 'condition of England', and impatience with royal protocol, while still believing in the values of the imperial family, especially in Canada and Australia. Defence of the Empire was, for Eden, one of the imperatives of British foreign policy. Where they differed was on the dictators, and Edward VIII (as he was to become in 1936) was privately very critical of Eden as Foreign Secretary. This lay in the future. But towards the end of George V's reign, the two handsome, charismatic figures, born within three years of each other, were seen as the hope of a new generation. 'South America was his favourite topic,' Eden noted, '& as to domestic politics he regretted absence of Morrison from Nat. Govt. I agreed. He shows a shrewd appreciation of men & matters & is probably more receptive than the King.'[150]

Eden was exhausted at the end of 1934, and his health had not been good. He was overworked, and he was looking forward to Christmas. Simon was now ten, flourishing at Cothill, where he was proving an adept actor, the love of theatre inherited from his father. Nicholas was four, the apple of Beatrice's eye.

The Privy Councillorship was one form of recognition; another that meant a great deal in a different sphere was Eden's appointment in the New Year as a Trustee of the National Gallery. He took over from Ramsay MacDonald and was to serve two full terms until 1949. With Kenneth Clark as Director, the National Gallery was entering a famous phase in its history and it was one of the public appointments Eden most enjoyed. Clark was an old friend; they had gone nightclubbing together in their younger days, and Eden was keen on Clark's wife, Elizabeth, a feeling that was reciprocated.

Eden's reputation for level-headedness was well established. The Balkans crisis and the issue of the Saar plebiscite had shown him at his pragmatic best. In later crises, he was not known for his patience, but at Geneva he was Job-like. Herr Nadolny, a German delegate of antagonistic unhelpfulness, could be relied upon to turn many meetings into a shouting match. Eden proved to be one of the few who could deal with him, as Major-General Temperley witnessed. 'I admired Mr Eden very much during these difficult discussions,' he wrote. 'Although the rough-and-tumble methods of Herr Nadolny must have been extremely distasteful to him, he never lost his head or his temper.'[151]

In the wider perspective, Eden cleverly balanced the British public's desire and expectation for disarmament (especially aerial disarmament) with an understanding of strategic defence needs. As the emphasis changed, Eden was a reassuring figure; he had a good political bedside manner and, as broadsheet newspapers often gave verbatim reports, used constituency speeches like a latter-day Robert Peel, making 'Tamworth'* pronouncements addresses for a countrywide audience.

In a National Government that was showing disturbing incoherence, he was one of the few younger figures (thirty-seven at the time) who looked to the wider perspective. 'Coalition always needs a man or theme to hold it together' he wrote in his diary. 'We have neither.'[152]

Henry Stimson's view encapsulated Eden's own feelings. 'A Foreign Minister,' Stimson wrote, 'must never permit his vision of the future permanent welfare of his country to become obscured by the pressure of immediate interests.'[153] In the New Year, Eden wrote to Cadogan, 'The country is perhaps a bit bored with us, with some of us in particular.' He did not need to spell out his continued reservations about Simon. 'If, however, we face this fact and reorder our ranks accordingly, we should, I believe, be able to secure a decent majority when the election comes. Much depends, however, upon the thoroughness of our own overhaul.'[154]

MacDonald's retirement from the Premiership after George V's Silver Jubilee would bring Baldwin to 10 Downing Street for the third time, but the limited reshuffle was to disappoint Eden, and not only on personal grounds. Britain, however, had political stability, unlike the French. Eden never quite knew who his opposite number from the Quai d'Orsay might be at any given moment. Shortly he was to begin one of his most fruitful alliances with the emerging Léon Blum. His difficulties with Barthou and Laval were born of his unrealistic belief that the French would accept limitations on their defence needs, while at the same time recognising the

---

*Sir Robert Peel's declaration to his constituents in Tamworth in 1834 was a manifesto aimed at a national political audience.

right of Germany to expect a removal of some of the more severe provisions of the Versailles settlement. Events proved his optimism in Britain's ability to constrain Italian expansionism to be excessive; and by focusing on Mussolini's ambitions he underestimated the speed with which the Germans would outstrip the Italians as a strategic threat.

Nevertheless, Eden was rightly regarded as a forward-looking 'internationalist' figure. The most significant example of the trust he inspired among senior figures in the National Government was their readiness to employ him as Britain's itinerant ambassador to the European powers, a role that was to be significantly expanded in 1935. Already known to figures as diverse as Hitler and Mussolini, Ribbentrop, Stimson and Grandi, Eden was to become the first Western minister to visit Russia since the Revolution. A by-product of this forthcoming tour was that visits to Berlin and Moscow would permit a call in Warsaw. He would accompany Simon to Berlin, but travel on alone. Such an arrangement could have produced difficulties of protocol. Would a 'reduced' delegation cause offence in Poland? Eden recorded the outcome in his diary:

> Rex Leeper [Head of the Foreign Office News Department] told me of an interesting conversation with Raczynski (Polish Ambassador here).
> Rex. Would you be hurt if two ministers went to Berlin & only one to Warsaw?
> R. No, not if the one who went on was Eden.[155]

Eden's appeal was a cross-party one. Respected at home for his progressive social outlook, he commended himself to Labour figures such as Harold Laski, not known for their approval of Conservative figures within the National Government. Of course, this was balanced by jealousies and brickbats. Randolph Churchill was already beginning his youthful journalistic onslaughts on the man who had taken Baldwin's side against his father, and whom he saw as denying Duff Cooper his place in the sun. Simple antagonisms were to become increasingly complex in the years ahead, when Eden in essence displaced Randolph Churchill as Winston Churchill's political son.

On 8 January 1935 Eden spoke in Edinburgh of how Britain was 'now going through a period of transition'. Almost imperceptibly a change was taking place and a new order in the world was being evolved.[156] In Britain, Eden was dramatically to become an ever more central part of that process. One event was to prove the catalyst. Abyssinia lay between the Italian colonies of Eritrea and Somalia. By the end of November Italian troops had occupied the south-eastern grazing lands of Ogaden, a fact discovered almost by accident by an Anglo-Ethiopian Boundary Commission. On 5 December hostilities broke out. Superior Italian numbers inflicted heavy casualties. Abyssinia referred the dispute to the League of Nations, seeking arbitration under the terms of the Italo-Abyssinian Treaty of 1928. It was to prove the League's greatest test, and a crisis that was to alter Eden's political life for ever.

CHAPTER SIX

Burdens of Office

1935-7

News of Eden's triumph at Geneva in settling the Abyssinian difficulty. It looks certain now that he will become Foreign Secretary. How angry all the young Tories will be.

Harold Nicolson diary, 26 May 1935[1]

Just as the British public had grown tired of Curzon and Austen Chamberlain in the ten years after the First World War, so in the spring of 1935 there was a widespread outcry for a new Foreign Secretary. The choice seemed gradually to be narrowed down to Eden and myself.

Sir Samuel Hoare on his appointment as Foreign Secretary, 7 June 1935[2]

At the beginning of 1935 the National Government had been in existence for more than three years. The temporary expedient was becoming part of the political furniture. But it was National only in name and Conservative domination was to be reinforced further when MacDonald left Downing Street. MacDonald's last months in office were not his happiest. An increasingly gaunt and fading figure, vilified by his former Labour colleagues, his loss of spirit was palpable. It seemed only a matter of time before he handed over to Baldwin, or even Neville Chamberlain.

Meanwhile Eden's career was approaching its first climacteric. The next three years were to bring into sharp focus the divisions over appeasement. Ever since the end of the Great War, the question that had dominated foreign policy was how best to avoid another conflict between the great European powers. This divide crossed party lines and transcended normal political debate. In the conflict of mighty opposites that this division necessarily entailed, it was Eden's fate to be the principal figure within government ranged against Neville Chamberlain.

The underlying advocacy of appeasement was born of guilt. This emotion was particularly strong among those who had not fought in battle, a characteristic that linked MacDonald, Baldwin, R. A. Butler, Chamberlain, Hoare and Simon. They were determined that the new generation should be spared the horrors of Flanders, a feeling fervently held by Neville Chamberlain, whose cousin Norman had been killed in

France in 1917. Those who had seen military action – figures such as Churchill, Eden, Macmillan and Duff Cooper – felt no such guilt, and Eden's attitude to appeasement was another example of how his experience of war conditioned his response. This did not mean that the anti-appeasers were warmongers. As Churchill was to say in 1950 at the time of the Korean War:

> Appeasement in itself may be good or bad according to the circumstances. Appeasement from weakness and fear is alike futile and fatal. Appeasement from strength is magnanimous and noble, and might be the surest and perhaps the only path to world peace.[3]

For Eden – 'ce jeune homme terrible qui aime tellement la paix' – there were times when winning that peace meant fighting for it also.

The basic difference, however, between Baldwin and Chamberlain on the one hand, and Eden on the other, lay in their attitude to Europe. Baldwin and Chamberlain believed that, in the last resort, what happened on the Continent did not necessarily affect Britain. Chamberlain, in particular, was an imperialist and wanted to knit the Empire more closely together as his father had done. In this context, the frontier problems of Central Europe were bound to appear rather small beer. Eden (and Churchill), by contrast, believed that Britain was inextricably affected by what happened across the Channel, and that it was crucial to Britain's role as a great power that a balance of power be preserved on the Continent. The judgement of history on who was right in this great debate, as we shall see, was to go through many stages, and the shadow of the 1930s was to lie heavily over the rest of Eden's career.

The year of 1935 began with the supervised plebiscite on 13 January. The Saar voted for reunion with Germany. 'Germany is now well on the way to rearmament,' Eden noted. 'She is no longer afraid of a "preventive war" against her and in a few years – four I am told is the popular figure in Berlin – she will be strong enough to ask, in a tone which will not brook refusal, for her desiderata.'[4]

The Saar plebiscite concentrated British and French minds on fresh negotiations aimed at persuading Germany to rejoin the League. At the same time, Ivan Maisky, the Russian Ambassador in London, pressed for a British visit to Moscow. On 4 March it was decided that Simon and Eden would visit Berlin, and that Eden would then undertake a further tour of Moscow, Warsaw and Prague. Although Eden was surprised that Simon, as Foreign Secretary, showed no wish to go on to Moscow, a new arena of diplomatic activity, he was not unhappy at the opportunity to meet Stalin face to face.

Just before the British party's planned departure, Goering announced details of the *Luftwaffe*, and a week later Hitler introduced German conscription, military actions that were a clear breach of the Versailles Treaty. The future of the mission was in serious doubt and Eden was despatched to Paris to address French concerns. A compromise was reached. Eden never really trusted Laval and one curious episode convinced him that the French Foreign Minister could embroider any tale. 'Laval remarked to me at luncheon that S. B. had told him in London I was to be Secretary of State', Eden recorded in his diary. Laval asked him why he was not already Foreign Secretary, a question that Eden, who did not believe Baldwin would have spoken in this way, was hard pressed to answer with the appropriate degree of humility.[5]

After concluding his consultations with the French, Eden set off with the faithful Cranborne, flying over the battlefields of Béthune and Ypres, with all their painful memories, before linking up with John Simon in Amsterdam. The party then flew on to Berlin where they were met, in Eden's words, by 'very warlike guard of S.S., the leader of whom saluted a startled J. S. with a naked sabre worthy of John the Baptist's executioner.'[6]

Cranborne summed up this visit to Germany as 'both depressing & alarming'. Both Cranborne and Eden were struck by the change in atmosphere. 'It seems much more prosperous than when we were here last year' wrote Cranborne on 24 March. 'Then, in the Ruhr, no chimneys were smoking. Now about ½ of them seemed in full blast. Does this mean munitions?' In the streets, the British party were watched by expectant, yet apprehensive, Berliners. 'On both sides of the avenue [the Unter den Linden], right up to the Brandenburg Gate, & down the Wilhelmstrasse to the British Embassy, the pavements were lined with huge crowds, 6 or 8 deep, waiting silently & patiently in the rain for the arrival of Simon & Anthony,' wrote Cranborne. 'It was like the arrival of an Emperor.'[7]

Before the two meetings on 25 and 26 March, Simon and Eden were briefed by the embassy staff on the current German situation. Unfortunately, there was little agreement on either diagnosis or prognosis. Sir Eric Phipps, the Ambassador, was the most pessimistic about chances of an agreement.

The meetings with Hitler were very different from last time. 'Seven hours of talk,' Eden recorded of the first day, with Hitler 'more sure of himself than a year ago'. No concessions were forthcoming. 'Results bad,' noted Eden. 'Whole tone and temper very different to a year ago, rearmed and rearming with the old Prussian spirit very much in evidence.' Only at dinner did the Germans unbend, when 'Hitler & I discovered by chance that we were opposite each other at La Fère, March 1918. Eden reminded

Hitler that the Germans had outnumbered them by ten to one. 'Together we drew a map on the back of a dinner card, which I still possess, signed by both of us, Hitler marking in some places and I others,' Eden later wrote. 'The corporal on the German side had as clear a recollection of place names and dispositions as the young staff officer, as I had then just become, on the British.'[8]

The next day, largely a survey of armaments since Locarno, brought no measurable progress. Disagreements came on air defences and on military training of the young. In fact, Eden was virtually accused of duplicity when he denied that Eton was a paramilitary organisation analogous to the German models. Hitler said that the pupils trained with rifles, and therefore the real purpose of an Eton education was clear. Eden said this was a grave misapprehension. Most Etonians regarded military field days as the opportunity for a clandestine cigarette. Such truthful levity did not soften Hitler's stubbornness. 'Mr Eden stressed Britain's faith in the League of Nations,' reported the official German record. 'The alternative was a return to the old alliances which had led to the World War.' The one point of contact was military service. 'He fully shared the feelings of a soldier which the Chancellor had expressed.'[9]

Before leaving with Cranborne on the long train journey to Russia that night, Eden compared notes with Simon. 'Total results of visit for European settlement very disappointing,' he wrote. He thought Simon completely out of his depth, and was appalled that 'Simon toys with idea of letting G[ermany] expand eastward'. In a pre-echo of the unfolding events of the late 1930s, he wrote, 'I am strongly against it – Apart from its dishonesty, it would be our turn next.'[10] But Simon believed that Hitler's ambitions lay away from France and, ultimately, Britain. Hitler, he thought, was like 'an Austrian Joan of Arc with a moustache'.[11] With such reassurance, Eden set off for Moscow.

Eden's train journey to Russia took a laborious thirty-six hours. Maisky was in attendance. The train pulled its way slowly through the Polish countryside that was to be the scene of war within four years. So unappealing was the landscape that Eden was reminded of Shakespeare's description of Poland as 'a little patch of ground/ That hath in it no profit but the name'.[12] Eden took the opportunity of the long train journey to send a pessimistic report to the Cabinet on the German visit. 'The essential question seems to be does a basis now exist for a general European settlement? A year ago I believe there was such a basis, but it is exceedingly difficult to maintain that it exists now.'[13]

Towards dusk on 27 March, the train slowed down to pass a frontier and Maisky inclined his head towards Eden. 'Let me welcome you to

Russia' he said. When Eden set foot on Russian soil on the morning of 28 March, he was the first Western Minister to do so for eighteen years and the first since the Revolution.[14]

The British party was met at Moscow station by Maxim Litvinov, Stalin's Commissar for Foreign Affairs since January 1931, already known to Eden through their work in Geneva. Litvinov was well disposed towards Eden for his welcome to the Soviets on their return to the League. For his part, Eden found Litvinov, who had lived and worked in the West and had an understanding of European thinking and a desire for cooperation, more sophisticated than many in the Kremlin. Like Eden, Litvinov was an 'internationalist', with an overview of competing issues and controversies. At the League of Nations he was to argue for action against the Axis of Nazi Germany and Fascist Italy, which sealed his eventual fate at home, for he was dismissed on the eve of the signing of the Soviet-Nazi non-aggression pact in August 1939. Vyacheslav Molotov, his successor, and already in evidence at the forthcoming talks, as Chair of the Council of People's Commissars, was a different proposition altogether, unrelenting, grim and inscrutable.

Both Eden and Cranborne were sensitive to the nuances of the various countries they visited. 'Apart from the Kremlin', wrote Cranborne in his diary, 'the thing which strikes one most is the pall of horror & suspicion which hangs over the city. One feels it at once.' They were taken, inevitably, to Lenin's tomb, but found it 'a little too like a very luxurious public lavatory'. The contrast between the political reality of oppression and the beaming hosts with their prolific supplies of vodka and caviar, was incongruous. 'One had to remind oneself that they were all murderers,' wrote Cranborne, 'they didn't look like it, more like the annual dinner of some branch of the Society of Oddfellows.' At a time when many of his domestic political opponents had a rose-tinted view of Russia, Eden never forgot that he was dealing with a tyrannical state, especially as the visit coincided with the murder of Sergei Kirov, a once-trusted intimate of Stalin, and with an extensive purge of alleged traitors.

Eden's first talks were with Litvinov, accompanied by the two ambassadors, Maisky and Britain's Viscount Chilston, for whom Litvinov had a high regard. Chilston's skill in re-establishing Anglo-Soviet relations after a difficult period had done much to bring about the visit. Eden brought Litvinov up-to-date with the latest German demands. With prophetic realism, Litvinov claimed that, whatever Hitler said, the reoccupation of the Rhineland would be one of his first objectives.

For a while it seemed that Eden's meeting with Stalin, the central purpose of the visit, would founder on Chilston's exclusion. Chilston spoke Russian fluently and Eden felt it vital to have his record of what transpired. Eventually the Russians relented.

Eden's meeting with Stalin on 29 March completed a remarkable triptych of face-to-face meetings with the three central dictators of the twentieth century. For a relatively junior figure on the international stage, it was an unprecedented opportunity. Eden had no doubt that Stalin was the most impressive of the three, intellectually and temperamentally. Hitler was stubborn, physically anonymous when not surrounded by fawning lieutenants, and *au fond* strangely insecure. Mussolini was brutish and vulgar, a bullying egoist, who lived for the adrenalin of the moment. Stalin, on the other hand, conducted himself with an inner strength, never raising his voice, always in control of the arguments. This first impression was confirmed during all their later wartime conferences.

Stalin asked Eden whether the current European situation was as alarming as that in 1913, or more so. Eden felt that 'anxious' was a more apt description than 'alarming'; because of the existence of the League of Nations, structures were in place to contain aggression. Stalin disagreed. 'In 1913,' he said, 'there was only one potential aggressor, Germany. Today there are two, Germany and Japan.' To Eden's surprise, Italy was not on Stalin's list. Walking over to a map of the world on the wall, Stalin pointed to Britain and said that on so small an island, with its power and influence in the world, would rest so many hopes for collective security. Throughout a long meeting, Stalin's comprehensive survey of the international scene revealed to Eden a man in command of his subject. This was something he never forgot in his dealings with the Soviets.

'After tea,' Cranborne recorded:

A. came back & dictated a telegram on his visit to Stalin. He had evidently been impressed by his ability. He knew all about the European situation & expressed himself with force, point & humour. But both A. & the Amb were struck by the intense cruelty of his face. They said that he was not in the least like an enlightened European ruler but an Oriental potentate of the type which Russia has had so many examples in the past.

At the Bolshoi that night, Eden was the centre of attention. 'When he appeared at the front of the imperial box he was given a rousing reception. The orchestra played God Save the King with terrific vim, as if it were a revolutionary hymn, the conductor whirling his arms round his head to get most passion into it, & the whole house clapped & applauded while we stood rather smugly to attention.' Cranborne noticed that the audience 'never took their eyes off A. whenever the lights were up'.

It was the same during their visit next day to the House of the Red Army, full of photographs of the Revolution and the shooting of Tsarist officers, where, to their embarrassment, Eden and Cranborne were filmed being toasted by Red Army officers. 'It all had the effect of a rather disreputable carouse, not at all the thing, we felt, for Weymouth or Leamington Spa.'

More to Eden's taste, and a visit that was specially arranged for him, was a private viewing of the Russian collection of great French Impressionist paintings, though the Russians were put out that Eden wanted to see such specimens of Western decadence. Nevertheless, his hosts were solicitous throughout. A lavish lunch at Litvinov's country estate even had pats of butter imprinted with the words 'Peace is indivisible' in both languages. This meant guests were reluctant to cut the butter, for fear it would bring bad luck.

Back in the capital, the seemingly endless round of talks resumed. Overall, Eden and Cranborne found Moscow 'a grim place', with 'an indescribable feeling of horror & squalor'. An interesting observation about Russia was made towards the end of the visit, when 'Litvinov confessed to A, & it is obvious even to the most superficial observer, that she is far behind other Western nations, & that it will take her at least 50 years to catch them up.' Ironically, this realism was accompanied with a formality that reminded them of Versailles. 'There is no country in the world,' wrote Cranborne, 'where more attention is paid to precedence.'[15]

The blandness of the final communiqué, with its references to 'a full and frank exchange of views', disguised disagreements, especially over Stalin's wish for an Eastern Pact. Nevertheless, Eden's visit had laid the basis for later Anglo-Soviet cooperation, disturbing though this was for many Conservatives at home, who regarded any pact with Communism as akin, in Eden's words, to 'supping with the devil.'[16] The pace of events had prevented Eden from fully informing London of the details of his talks and he was uncertain how Simon would react. 'I fear that J. S. is timorous and uncertain which way to turn,' he wrote. 'Van drives him but J. S. is reluctant to travel. Yet he clings to the F. O. It is an unhappy situation for us all.'[17]

As in Germany, Eden was under no illusions that he had changed anything, but he felt more hopeful of some form of rapprochement with the Soviets. After a tour of the Moscow underground system, his name was to be given to one of the stations, an unsolicited and unusual mark of favour. (Later a street in Addis Ababa was also named after him, in honour of his work for the beleaguered Abyssinian people.[18])

At one dinner, a commissar's wife sympathised with Eden for living in Britain, as the women there were so ugly. Eden explained, with gentlemanly patience, that she was much mistaken. This cut no ice, so he pointed out that the elegant Lady Chilston, across the table, disproved his dinner companion's theory. 'Yes, Lady Chilston is all right,' she admitted, 'but we know that is part of your propaganda.'[19]

Eden left Russia as he had entered it, in the imperial train with all its crockery and decorations from Tsarist times. Litvinov's parting words to him were, 'I wish you success. Your success will be our success – now.'[20]

After another lengthy journey through the Polish countryside, Eden's party eventually reached Warsaw on 1 April, where they were met by Colonel Beck, the Polish Foreign Minister. Eden told Beck that 'he doubted whether Russia was in a position to take an offensive',[21] but Beck remained suspicious of Eden's dealings with Germany and Russia, especially when reports emerged in *Pravda* and *Izvestia* of Russian satisfaction over the recent visit. Beck had no wish for an Eastern Pact, preferring to deal with Russia and Germany separately.

Eden's talks with Marshal Pilsudski, conducted in French, were unproductive. Pilsudski confused Eden with Lloyd George, and thought he was interfering in questions of Poland's national identity. The aged President Moscicki dispensed extensive hospitality (a banquet of twelve courses, lubricated by Polish mead saved from Napoleon's occupation of Warsaw in 1806) before showing Eden the paintings of the Zemek Palace. As Eden wrote, the eventual communiqué 'said little and meant it.'[22]

Eden was now on the last leg of his extensive tour, and full of home thoughts from abroad. His final call was in Prague, where he had talks with Eduard Beneš, the Czech Foreign Minister, well known to Eden from Geneva, and Jan Masaryk, the future wartime Foreign Minister, and a close friend of Eden until his death in 1948 in mysterious circumstances. Beneš was hopeful that the forthcoming Stresa Conference, where Eden was expected to represent Britain, would address the question of what he called the 'Eastern Locarno' and bring home to Hitler the need for European peace. Eden told Beneš that intelligence from the British Embassy in Berlin suggested that Hitler would not be ready for war for another five to eight years. Driving Eden to the airport, Beneš stressed the need to stand firm.

Eden could be an anxious traveller. At Prague airport, gales were blowing and the skies had darkened. But he needed to get back to report to the Cabinet. He had already drafted a report in which he stressed that if Britain appeared irresolute 'then we shall encourage Germany's demands and, no less serious, encourage the weaker powers to take refuge with her in the belief that the collective peace system can never be effective because England will never play her part in its support.'[23] Against his better judgement he boarded the plane, the only one in the area that took to the skies that day, and flew from Prague to Leipzig. On the second part of the flight he met with the roughest weather imaginable. 'Leipzig to Cologne violent snow flurries seized & shook the plane like a terrier shakes a rat.

Felt utterly wretched.' In fact, Eden had suffered a heart spasm.

'At Cologne weather & my heart would not allow us to go on,' he wrote. 'Pulse 45. Heart "sehr slecht" said German doctor.' Hitler heard of Eden's misfortune and at once offered a private plane to return him to London. But medical opinion forbade him to fly. Instead he was confined to bed in the Dom Hotel in Cologne, which he had known from his period in Germany at the end of the war. The next day, he was allowed to travel by train and boat, via Ostend and Dover. He was met at Victoria station by an anxious Beatrice and Sir John Simon. Condolences came from the King, who requested that Eden see the royal heart specialist, Sir Maurice Cassidy.

Cassidy was adamant. Eden had to rest for six weeks. MacDonald put out a statement from 10 Downing Street, expressing his concern and distress. Shortly afterwards he visited Eden at his home and said that in the circumstances he had decided to attend the Stresa Conference himself.

Eden was doubly depressed. MacDonald was on the verge of retirement from the Premiership, and a reluctant delegate. In a submission to Cabinet before the Stresa Conference, Eden wrote:

> The greatest care should be taken to avoid any suggestion that Germany's proposed non-aggression pacts are enough, since they are less in fact than the obligations all members of the League undertook towards each other and no less than the undertakings which we have undertaken under Locarno.[24]

Eden was not confident of Simon's tenacity when it came to addressing the central question of Germany's expansionist aims, and, even more worryingly in his view, Mussolini's ambitions towards Emperor Haile Selassie's Abyssinia, together with his desire to make the Mediterranean an Italian lake. As Mussolini had tacit French support at the time of Stresa, it was going to need a more determined British delegation than MacDonald and Simon, if the question of Abyssinia was ever going to be addressed in any meaningful way.

The outcome of the conference sadly fulfilled Eden's doubts, even though Simon, visiting Eden on his sick bed, assured him that he was taking a Foreign Office expert from the Abyssinian Department, Geoffrey Thompson. But Thompson's expertise was never used, and Abyssinia not even discussed. MacDonald told the press afterwards that the question was 'irrelevant'.[25] The French delegates, Premier Pierre-Etienne Flandin and Foreign Minister Pierre Laval, were more concerned with continued German violation of the Versailles Treaty's arms limitation. Mussolini skilfully drove a path between these two agendas. The subsequent Stresa front of Britain, France and Italy against Germany was a sham. In return for a nominal agreement in Europe, Mussolini interpreted silence on

Abyssinia and French North Africa as acquiescence for his plans beyond Europe. Thomas Jones, the former Deputy Cabinet Secretary, was later to trace many European difficulties to this botched Stresa meeting. 'Looking back at the wretched story,' he wrote, 'you have the original blunder at Stresa when MacDonald and Simon funked talking straight out to Mussolini because they wanted his support in Europe.'[26]

Eden watched from the sidelines during his convalescence, part of which took place with Sir Philip Sassoon, Chairman of Trustees of the National Gallery, at his country home, Trent Park, New Barnet. Here Eden was able to play some tennis and indulge his love of paintings and *objets d'art* amid Sassoon's celebrated collections. He read a newly published history of the Battle of Jutland, which awakened poignant memories. 'Poor Nicholas', he wrote in his diary. 'What a nightmare the seventeen minutes in action of the *Indefatigable* must have been.'[27]

As Sassoon, MP for Hythe, was Under-Secretary of Air, Eden also discussed the expected reshuffle of the Government, and the call, in April, by seventy Conservative MPs for the removal of Simon. Sassoon was one of many who felt that Eden not only deserved the reversion to the Foreign Secretaryship, but that he would in fact be appointed. 'I am sure you will get it,' he wrote encouragingly after one of Eden's weekend visits.[28] Billy Ormsby-Gore and Roger Lumley also pressed Eden's claims and a head of steam built up in the newspapers for a bold approach and a younger man. Eden was counting no chickens. He knew that politics was a stern taskmaster and that it could dispense bitter disappointments. He was content to let events unfold.

Gradually Eden returned to the domestic political fray. One of his first commitments was a wide-ranging speech on 17 May at Fulham Town Hall on the dangers posed by a rearming Germany. His main point was unequivocally anti-isolationist. 'We shall always be found arrayed on the side of the collective system against any government or people who seek by a return to power politics to break up the peace which by that system we are seeking to create.'[29] A sign of the impact the speech made is that it was condemned in Germany. Vansittart, whose anti-German credentials were never in doubt, wrote to congratulate him.

More congratulations were in order after Eden's return to Geneva on 19 May. The worsening situation regarding Abyssinia seemed likely to prove more intractable than the Saar. Once again Eden was granted considerable autonomy from London in bringing the matter before the League. Eden had talks with Pierre Laval and René Massigli, the main French diplomatic adviser, before meeting the Italian diplomat, Baron Aloisi, who had been present at Eden's two meetings with Mussolini. Aloisi bluntly told Eden that Italy would not brook interference by Britain or the League of Nations over its imperial commitments in Africa, a message that he received 'through clenched teeth', as Aloisi reported to the Duce.[30]

By invoking the 1928 Treaty under which Italy had guaranteed not to use force against Abyssinia, and with the firm backing of Massigli, Eden impressed upon Simon back in London that Britain and France were standing firm on this issue of principle, a point Simon communicated to Count Grandi. For whatever reason, but no doubt influenced by Anglo-French unity, Mussolini appeared to agree. The Abyssinian delegation was satisfied and a unanimous council vote at 2.30 a.m. on 25 May seemed to have established a *modus vivendi*. The 'Italian delegation,' Eden telegraphed to the Foreign Office, 'have been compelled to acknowledge the right of the council to keep in touch with arbitration and to intervene should it be necessary.'[31]

Eden's persuasive powers had brokered a solution, even if only in the short term. 'News of Eden's triumph at Geneva,' Harold Nicolson wrote in his diary. 'It looks certain now that he will become Foreign Secretary. How angry all the young Tories will be.'[32]

Not only the young Tories. Count Grandi now orchestrated a campaign against Eden in the Italian Press, where snide comments began to appear about his sartorial taste, and he was dubbed public enemy number one.

Eden himself was not optimistic, despite receiving a personal message from the Emperor Haile Selassie, thanking him for 'furthering friendly solution of dispute with Italy.'[33] Eden cautiously told Miles Lampson, the High Commissioner in Egypt, 'we have done little more than make it harder for Mussolini, in the eyes of the world at least, to proceed to take extreme measures against Abyssinia.'[34] However, Eden and René Massigli had forged a bond of trust and understanding that endured a lifetime. Thirty years later Eden still remembered their work in Geneva together, and the Massiglis were welcome guests of Eden in retirement. 'I have still some Latour 1934,' Eden wrote enticingly before one visit, 'the vintage a nostalgic reminder of the days when the world was young and hopes of peace lay before them.'[35]

The Baldwins and the Edens were fellow guests at Cliveden the weekend before MacDonald's retirement. Speculation about the Cabinet changes was quite open, with Baldwin asking advice from J. L. Garvin, Editor of the *Observer*, a situation of some delicacy for Eden. Thomas Jones thought Eden very level-headed. 'Success has not yet damaged him at all', he wrote.[36]

In Eden's travels around the country at this time, he saw hopeful signs of domestic revival. Since Britain left the Gold Standard in 1931, economic activity, especially in the South of England, was making discernible headway. When Eden journeyed by train, he saw the unfolding scenery from a political perspective, as on the long journey through Poland in March. Now he saw clear signs of the house-building boom, with ribbon development by the railways, especially 'Metroland', north-west of London, and along the arterial roads. Housing Acts in 1933 and 1935 had led to a massive increase in council-house provision in London and the big Midlands conurbations. Mortgage rates had fallen to 4.5 per cent by April 1935, and average terms of repayment increased from sixteen to twenty-five years.[37] Many in the upper and middle classes, often living comfortably in substantial older properties, resented this encroachment, which scarred the greenery of rural England and eroded a nostalgic idyll. But for Eden the growth in house-building, which outstripped other industries, was not only a welcome boost to employment prospects, but also a practical move towards Noel Skelton's dream of the property-owning democracy.

On 6 May 1935 King George V celebrated his Silver Jubilee, an event orchestrated by the National Government. According to the cynics this was a device to boost the government's popularity. The outpouring from all sides of affection towards the King, however, showed a spontaneity beyond the powers of orchestration. Eden was present in Westminster Hall when both Houses of Parliament gave homage. When George V had come to the throne in 1910, Eden was still a nervous Sandroyd schoolboy, hoping to pass his swimming test. Now he was on the verge of one of the great offices of state.[38]

The aftermath of the Jubilee saw the long-awaited Government reshuffle. MacDonald had been visibly fading for months. The handover, when it came, was a relief. Even then MacDonald did not make a clean break: when Baldwin took office as Prime Minister for the third time on 7 June, MacDonald became Lord President of the Council. Simon's departure from the Foreign Office was taken for granted. To the surprise of many, he returned to the Home Office, a post he had held during the Great War. 'The fact is the House detests him,' Neville Chamberlain wrote to his sister, 'he hasn't even a friend in his own party.'[39]

In a talk with Baldwin on 16 May, Eden had said he was unhappy about continued separation of Foreign Office responsibilities between two ministers. Tacitly, this was tantamount to saying that he would not serve at the Foreign Office *except* as Secretary of State, a bold and possibly reckless position for a non-Cabinet minister to adopt, though actually he still hankered for the Admiralty to broaden his experience with a service department.

Baldwin consulted widely over what was to prove the trickiest of this appointments to the new Cabinet. He received conflicting advice and in the event had to choose between Hoare and Eden. Sam Hoare had risen to prominence with his work, in the teeth of fierce opposition from Churchill, on the complex India Bill. When Baldwin met Hoare on 2 June he asked him whether he would prefer to be Viceroy of India or Foreign Secretary. Although Hoare indicated India, Baldwin was still undecided. Geoffrey Dawson, Editor of *The Times*, was for Hoare, as was Neville Chamberlain, who felt that Hoare deserved his chance after the India Bill, and that Eden would be better with wider experience before becoming Foreign Secretary. It was the older men who wanted youth, both MacDonald and Lloyd George advising Eden. On 4 June Baldwin decided on Hoare, offered him the post and was accepted.

Rumours that Eden was to become Foreign Secretary had spread, with Maurice Hankey, Cabinet Secretary, even telling Eden on 5 June that he had heard this from MacDonald. Baldwin saw Eden in the afternoon on 5 June. 'Sam is to go to the Foreign Office,' he said, 'and I want you to stay on and help him there.'

Eden was bitterly disappointed. One uncongenial chief in Simon had been bad enough; now he feared a repetition with Hoare, whom he had once described in his diary as 'slippery Sam'.[40] F. E. Smith had been even more dismissive, once referring to Hoare as 'the last in a long line of maiden aunts'.[41]

Eden reminded Baldwin of their earlier talk, but to no avail. Equally frankly, Eden explained his reservations to Hoare. Eventually it was agreed, by both Baldwin and Hoare, that the arrangement would be temporary.

There were two compensations. Cranborne was appointed Parliamentary Under-Secretary for League of Nations Affairs, and Eden at last entered the Cabinet, five days before his thirty-eighth birthday. But even then there was a hitch. Baldwin had given Eden the cumbersome title of 'Minister without Portfolio for League of Nations Affairs'. However, the Attorney-General, Sir Thomas Inskip, with a lawyer's attention to detail, pointed out that the name was technically invalid, so Eden was given the even more unwieldy title of 'Minister for League of Nations Affairs (without portfolio)'. Such were the semantics of high office in the summer of 1935.

Eden remained convinced that the appointments were a mistake. He felt that Baldwin should have gone for boldness, not only in his own area, but in others.[42]

The most powerful figure in the new Cabinet was Neville Chamberlain, Chancellor of the Exchequer since 1931 and Baldwin's obvious successor.

There was no room for Churchill, still in political limbo over India, nor for Lloyd George, who harboured ambitions of a recall, and even of the Foreign Secretaryship.[43]

National Labour representation was now minimal. Apart from Ramsay MacDonald, only Jimmy Thomas (at the Dominions Office) remained, though MacDonald's son Malcolm, at thirty-four, became Colonial Secretary, pipping Eden as the youngest of the Cabinet Ministers. Members of Eden's old dining club did well. Walter Elliot (Agriculture), Oliver Stanley (the Board of Education), Shakes Morrison (Food) and William Ormsby-Gore (Ministry of Works) were all in the Cabinet. Only Noel Skelton stayed as an Under-Secretary (at the Scottish Office), but in his case there was a tragic reason. He was now gripped by cancer, and made his last appearance in the Commons in July, answering parliamentary questions. He was to decline swiftly over the summer. Eden was greatly saddened when Skelton died on 22 November 1935. He never forgot his first mentor and his commitment to social welfare, and it was largely through Eden that Skelton's political memory was kept alive after the Second World War.

Summer 1935 was again dominated by foreign concerns. Although strictly a junior Cabinet minister in a subordinate position, Eden was nevertheless at the centre of the main agenda, as the problems over Hitler's ambitions and Mussolini's attack on Abyssinia multiplied. Three possible courses were open in 1935. The utopian one of disarmament, putting moral pressure on the dictators to do likewise, and then the establishment of some kind of international military force, was that favoured by the Labour Party under George Lansbury. The system of collective security under the aegis of the League of Nations, backed when necessary by sanctions, was another option, shortly to face its severest test over Abyssinia. Thirdly, there was rearmament and, when necessary, negotiations, freely entered into with the dictators, as a form of expedient demarcation. By and large, Baldwin's National Government followed an amalgam of the last two options, the emphasis changing according to the individual crisis. Eventually, this led to what became known as 'appeasement', a policy backed by *The Times* under the editorship of Geoffrey Dawson, a firm supporter of Sam Hoare.*

Eden was firmly for rearmament, but pragmatically he also favoured keeping the doors ajar for negotiation. 'It is vital to hasten and complete our own rearmament,' Eden urged in a memorandum submitted to Cabinet

---

*When the *History of The Times, Volume IV, Part II 1921–1948*, The Times, 1952, was published, Dawson's policy was heavily criticised. Harold Macmillan commented, 'The Times is always wrong, and every twenty years publishes a history to prove the fact.' Private information.

in January 1936 on 'The German Danger'. 'In view of what is so openly proceeding in Germany, we must be ready for all eventualities.'[44] Although circumstances suggested otherwise, he still clung to the hope that the League could be a force for good in a troubled world. 'To the average League supporter,' *The Spectator* commented on Eden, 'he symbolises not merely British policy but the ideal League policy.'[45]

Indeed, within a fortnight of entering the Cabinet he was on his way to Rome for a second meeting with Mussolini. Recently released Italian Naval Archives show that Mussolini's covert intentions were far from hidden from his own Chiefs of Staff, and that Eden's intuition about Mussolini's ultimate agenda was correct. As Robert Mallett has written, 'Mussolini did indeed have a pre-determined programme for war against the Western Powers alongside Germany, a war whose ultimate objective was to wrest control of the Mediterranean from Anglo-French hands.'[46]

Some commentators claim that Eden was as much an 'appeaser' as Hoare or, later, Neville Chamberlain, and by no means as firm an opponent of Mussolini as he later claimed in his memoirs, *Facing the Dictators*.[47] A. J. P. Taylor's comment on those memoirs – 'Eden did not face the dictators; he pulled faces at them'[48] – played to a particular gallery. Taylor was one of the first to question Eden's anti-appeasement credentials, on the grounds that he did not resist the militarisation of the Rhineland, and that he was impressed when he first met Hitler, and was more an opponent of Mussolini.[49]

Unlike Chamberlain, however, Eden was an empirical statesman, and when he saw that Hitler and Mussolini broke agreements, he was wary of signing new agreements with them. There was, of course, to be a distinct similarity here in 1956. Nasser, too, had broken an agreement that he had freely signed – the 1954 Anglo-Egyptian Treaty – by nationalising the Suez Canal Company soon after the last British troops had left.

More serious was the charge of Richard Lamb that 'the image of Eden as the knight in shining armour is founded on hypocrisy'.[50] Under the conditions of 1935, Eden was an 'appeaser' in that he was prepared to negotiate; by 1938 the word had acquired quite different pejorative overtones, and Eden had resigned from the Cabinet. As Eden later wrote:

> I had by this time [January 1936] occasionally used the word 'appeasement' in a speech or minute for the Foreign Office in the sense of the first meaning given in the *Oxford English Dictionary*, 'to bring to peace, settle (strife, etc.)'. It was not until some years later, when the results of the foreign policy pursued by Mr Chamberlain became apparent, that the word was more strongly associated with the last meaning given in the dictionary, 'to pacify, by satisfying demands.'[51]

Of course, Churchill and Eden both used their memoirs to establish their positions for posterity, something that premature death denied Chamberlain, alone among the major figures of the period. (Sam Hoare's *Nine Troubled Years* is an ingenious and well-documented defence of appeasement.) Eden made a point of quoting from the memoirs of Dr Paul Schmidt, Hitler's interpreter, which unfailingly showed him in a favourable light, especially over the labyrinthine issue of imposing oil sanctions on Italy. Churchill's celebrated description of Eden as the 'one strong young figure standing up against long, dismal, drawling tides of drift and surrender'[52] was written ten years after the event, and blurred some of the ambiguities of a multi-layered diplomatic crisis.

Historical revisionism, especially in the 1990s, has shown the great appeasement debate in a new perspective. In the light of archival evidence, Chamberlain's reputation has been reassessed more favourably, a process that has in turn led to a post-revisionist attempt to re-establish him as the 'guilty man'. Assessments of Eden have inevitably fluctuated as the Churchillian version has been subjected to harsher scrutiny. Questions over Eden as the 'one strong young figure' even pre-dated research into primary material. As Oliver Harvey, Eden's private secretary for much of this period, wrote in his diary on 8 November 1941, when diplomatic records of the late 1930s were on the verge of early release:

> A. E. is anxious about the effect on his own reputation and fears he may look like an appeaser too. I've today read all the documents through which concern him and he really has nothing to fear. The truth is everybody was an 'appeaser' of Germany at one time or another.[53]

Churchill's view of Eden at the time was also by no means as romanticised as it later became.

Eden's first Cabinets were dominated by preparations for the London Naval Conference to be held in the autumn, and the consequences of the Anglo-German Naval Treaty hastily agreed in Simon's last days at the Foreign Office. Ribbentrop, leading the German delegation, agreed that the German Navy should not exceed 35 per cent of the British strength, but on submarines negotiated a worrying figure of 60 per cent. Eden took no part in the negotiations, but expressed reservations about what such a policy, in direct contradiction of the Stresa front, and conducted in isolation, would do to Britain's relations with France. One of Eden's first missions in his new post was to Paris to soothe ruffled feathers.

Modernisation of the British Navy* was a key priority in the summer of

---

*This was one of the reasons why Eden had been attracted by the idea of moving to the Admiralty, had a top job at the Foreign Office not been offered to him.

1935. As Britain's representative in Geneva, Eden was in an anomalous position. On the one hand he was committed to diplomatic activity to avert war, a policy overwhelmingly endorsed by the Peace Ballot on 27 June; yet he also knew how resistance to Mussolini's Abyssinian adventures necessitated a strong Britain equipped for self-defence against any German expansion westwards. The Peace Ballot, organised by the National Declaration Committee under the chairmanship of Lord Robert Cecil, was a private referendum that put five questions to the electorate; 11.5 million responded. The final question was the crucial one:

Do you consider that, if a nation insists on attacking another, the other nation should combine to compel it to stop by
(a) Economic and non-military measures?
(b) If necessary, military measures?

The questions permitted only a 'Yes' or 'No' answer and, as Eden observed, 'were too complex to admit of simple answers.'[54] The results, which were hailed by the League of Nations Union as an endorsement of pacifism, were not so simple either. Ten million voted in the affirmative to question 5 (a), with only 635,000 against; yet for 5 (b), 6,784,368 were for military sanctions, and 2,351,981 against. As Eden observed, it was not possible to separate the two forms of sanction, as economic sanctions always carried the possibility of escalation into military action. The tactics of Baldwin and Hoare at this time were unconvincing. Believing that collective security was impracticable, they wanted this to be demonstrated clearly to the British people, using the Abyssinian crisis for the purpose. Their assumption that, with the League shown to be a sham, the public would then realise the need for rearmament was too clever by half and inevitably involved delay.

The results of the Peace Ballot coincided with Mussolini's increasing threats against Abyssinia, also a member of the League. Though this was not the intention, the 'pacifist' lessons drawn – none too accurately – from the data may actually have contributed to a heightening of the crisis.

In his first days in office, Hoare had extensive talks with Eden and Vansittart about a new approach to Mussolini. He deferred to the experience of both men, particularly Vansittart. In modern parlance, Hoare did not 'hit the ground running'. On 16 June all three were staying with Philip Sassoon at Trent Park, where Vansittart outlined a strategy for Eden, endorsed by the Cabinet, to present personally to Mussolini. The plan was to grant Abyssinia the port of Zeila in British Somaliland and a corridor to the sea, as compensation for Abyssinian cession of territory to Italy in the Ogaden region. The Ogaden-Zeila proposal was ingenious *realpolitik*, with the intention of saving Abyssinia from Italian invasion, but prospects depended on Mussolini's whim. With Eric Drummond's encouragement from Rome, Eden decided it was worth visiting Mussolini. He was uneasy, however, that territorial concessions might prove a slippery slope. Had he known that a spy in the British Embassy had forewarned Rome,[55] he would have been even more uneasy. Eden later explained the Government's thinking to the German Ambassador in London, Leopold von Hoesch, who reported to Berlin:

> Eden emphasised that the British Government had decided to make this 'offer' in order to make quite clear that their attitude to the Italy-Abyssinian conflict was not dictated by selfish motives, and especially in order to deprive Italy of any pretext for further suspicion of Britain.[56]

The mission began in unpropitious circumstances. Leaks in the weekend press after the tripartite Trent Park meeting led to adverse public reaction against any cession of territory whatsoever to Mussolini, even though the ultimate aim was to prevent the extinction of Abyssinia.

Eden's second meeting with Mussolini proved a defining moment in establishing hostile Italian attitudes towards him. Personality plays its part in political life, no less than policy. Austen Chamberlain achieved far more than expected through close friendship with Briand and Stresemann. By contrast, Eden's successes in Italian diplomacy were always limited by the active, and reciprocated, dislike that Mussolini felt towards the 'best-dressed fool' that Britain had sent as its emissary.

Much controversy surrounds the personal circumstances of their second meeting. The pressure on Eden to deliver was considerable.* Mussolini, too, had followers to impress. In 1935 this was an uneven contest. The talks were conducted at the Palazzo Venezia and they communicated in French. 'We were able to record no progress,' Eden reported to London of his two meetings on 24 and 25 June. 'In the event of war the name of Abyssinia would be wiped off the map.'[57]

Eden's appeal to Mussolini to consider the Covenant of the League provoked the response that, if necessary, Italy would leave the League: Mussolini intended to invade Abyssinia; indeed, seizing the territory by force would have the added benefit of expunging the shameful memory of Italian defeats in the region in 1896.

Rumours soon circulated that Eden and the Duce had quarrelled. Eden denied this in his memoirs in 1962. In a contemporary minute he had written, 'Mussolini was definitely cordial throughout – our final interview was of course gloomy – it had to be – but sad rather than bad, and there

---

*Especially with an autumn Election hanging over the Conservatives.

was no personal feeling whatever.'[58] This is confirmed by the Italian historian, Mario Toscano, who concluded that 'the entire conversation was a far from stormy one and had the normal character of a courteous meeting between persons of differing views'.[59]

What was certain was that the Italian Press, orchestrated by Mussolini through Count Grandi, now took against Eden with a vengeance. 'For the Fascists,' Toscano has written, 'Eden represented from that moment forward the symbol of blind opposition to Italy's legitimate right to win her "place in the sun" in Africa; the Italian public thought of him as Enemy Number One.'[60]

Another matter of contention and rumour concerned Eden's supposed discourtesy towards the Duce by being late for his second meeting on 25 June, owing to a lengthy luncheon at Ostia with Count Ciano and his wife. In fact the meeting took place in the evening. Had Mussolini scheduled an afternoon meeting, he, too, would have been absent, for during the Ostia luncheon, the guests had looked out to sea, and, as Eden recalled, 'there was Mussolini dashing over the waves in a speedboat, standing in its stern with his chin thrust out. I thought for a moment that he was going to dive in and join us for luncheon. The Italians in our party seemed deeply impressed.'[61]

Eden was impressed in a different way. His meetings with Mussolini, in 1934 and 1935, left a permanent mark on his psyche. Where the Italians saw charisma and salvation, he saw the bullying arrogance of the gangster mentality and an absence of social graces. Mussolini's behaviour towards ladies at mealtimes, pushing ahead and eating first, were alien to Eden. Over Abyssinia, Eden saw what a strong, popular political figure could do to incite national feeling, and he never forgot the lesson.

In the wake of Eden's mission in June 1935, Count Grandi reported to Mussolini on reactions in London. 'The beating that you gave that ambitious young upstart Eden during the meetings in Rome has already provoked much serious reflection here', he began. Grandi went on to claim that the British Press were treating Eden's visit with a certain 'irony'. Eden had, Grandi continued, stirred up a major debate in British political circles. Traditional British 'imperialists' viewed any cession to Italy of Abyssinian territory in East Africa with alarm. This would, Grandi noted, give them cause for concern as regards the strengthening of Fascist Italy's position as a regional power. On the other hand, Eden had also stirred up 'socialists and pacifists', who were by nature opposed to all imperialism. Either way, Grandi believed, Eden had generated considerable difficulties for Mussolini's expansionist policies, and propaganda must continue to be directed against him from Rome.[62]

The furore marked the end of British attempts at personal diplomacy as a means of solving the Abyssinian quandary. Thereafter, the British worked within the machinery of the League, or directly with the French.

Any political career needs its modicum of luck. Eden used up one of his lives in the summer of 1935. True, the Ogaden-Zeila plan was Vansittart's, not Eden's and, true, Eden was the agent of higher executive authority. But it was a close-run thing and he could have been forced from office.

Abyssinia continued to occupy Baldwin's Cabinet throughout the summer. During a wide-ranging meeting on 22 July it was decided that sanctions against Italy in the event of military intervention should be used only as a last resort.[63] What the Government should do, apart from contributing to collective action by a far from united League, was not so clear. At the end of July, Hoare and Eden canvassed views from a wide variety of leading political figures, including George Lansbury (who was to be driven from the Labour leadership in October at the time of Mussolini's invasion of Abyssinia), and Attlee (who was elected to replace him as Labour leader). Others consulted included Churchill, Lloyd George, Herbert Samuel, Austen Chamberlain and Robert Cecil. The consensus was against any unilateral action on the British part. The overwhelming view was for Anglo-French cooperation. Drummond's view from the embassy in Rome was the same, as Vansittart reported to Eden when tensions rose over sanctions. 'The mentality of Mussolini is now such that he would probably regard the refusal to take Italian imports on the part of ourselves and the smaller Powers as a *casus belli*. He does not, however, anticipate that Mussolini would take this course if the French were also in it.'[64]

On 2 October, Mussolini finally invaded Abyssinia. Under Article XVI of the Covenant, limited sanctions (excluding iron, oil and steel) were imposed upon Italy by the League, though non-members remained free to trade with Italy. Eden was in Paris when the Abyssinian war started and was disturbed by Laval's timid response to this aggression. Returning to Geneva, where he was at one remove from the immediacy of Cabinet decision making, Eden argued for a ban on Italian imports and the lifting of an Abyssinian arms embargo.

A worried Grandi at once warned Mussolini that Eden formed part of an axis that also comprised Baldwin and Vansittart. This axis, Grandi believed, wanted war against Italy. First, he prophesied, they would apply progressive economic sanctions by military means and duly provoke an Anglo-Italian incident, thus resulting in war. This was, Grandi concluded, little to do with the League, but rather more to do with the defence of British imperial interests from Fascism. In any case, Eden needed careful watching.[65]

Nor was Eden's political chief forthright in his opposition to Italy.

Hoare wrote to Eden on 16 October urging 'caution' until there was clarification of the French position. 'I feel myself,' wrote Hoare, 'that it is essential that we should go slow.'[66] Earlier, Eden had been the one advising restraint. Hoare had been the one advocating grandiose commitments. When Abyssinia was eventually invaded, their respective positions were largely reversed, so that it could be argued that consistency was the first casualty of the Abyssinian crisis.

The unpalatable truth was that the crisis had uncomfortable electoral implications. In the wake of the Peace Ballot, Baldwin feared a public backlash, so in the run-up to the General Election, he took every opportunity of stressing Britain's commitment to the League and its policy of collective action. Eden reinforced this message in a series of wireless broadcasts from 14 August until the eve of polling, and his speeches, holding up the League as the one way out of the morass, were reprinted in *The Listener*. Although newsreels were to play their part, the 1935 General Election, which Baldwin called for 14 November, was above all the 'Wireless Election', and Eden one of the principal broadcasters. Eden faced a straight fight in Warwick and Leamington against a new Labour opponent. As if to emphasise that he was 'part of the furniture', he was granted the freedom of Leamington at the outset of the campaign, an unsolicited boost.[67] The result of the contest was never in doubt, and, although Eden made the appropriate and dutiful tours of the constituency, he was also able to a greater extent than before to appear on the national stage, especially in the North of England. His electoral message was improving 'the condition of the people' and maintaining a European peace, the two issues that were to come back to haunt the Conservatives in 1945. When the poll was declared, the figures in Warwick and Leamington were:

Anthony Eden (Conservative)	35,746
J. Perry (Labour)	10,930
Conservative Majority	24,816

Although the Government was still nominally a 'national' one, it was increasingly dominated by the Conservatives. The election results confirmed this trend. Ramsay MacDonald was comprehensively beaten at Seaham by Emanuel Shinwell, and Malcolm MacDonald lost Bassetlaw. The death of Noel Skelton a week later meant a by-election for the Scottish Universities, and Ramsay MacDonald re-entered the Commons for that constituency in February, keeping his post as Lord President in the interim. Overall, Baldwin won a majority of 247. The Conservatives and their supporters won 53.7 per cent of the vote and 432 MPs. Labour, now under the 'temporary' leadership of Clement Attlee, won 154 seats.[68] The Liberals, in their disparate alliances, were the principal losers. Lloyd George was returned for Carnarvon Boroughs, but not Sir Herbert Samuel at Darwen. John Simon only just survived at Spen Valley by 642 votes.

The Parliament elected in November 1935 was to last for nearly ten years, though Baldwin's triumph contained the seeds of the Labour landslide victory of July 1945. So comprehensive was the Conservative ascendancy that when the voters came to vote against the legacy of the 1930s – unemployment and the Great Depression, the failure of the League to withstand aggression, and, above all, appeasement – the obloquy was theirs. The historian of the campaign, Tom Stannage, has written:

> Perhaps most importantly, the result of the 1935 General Election disguised the growth of class politics. The 1929 General Election had shown the unacceptability of the Conservative Party in areas where working-class Toryism had long been a fact of political life. The elections of 1931 and 1935 cut through this development by making it possible for electors to vote for a National Government rather than a Conservative one.[69]

The return to two-party politics in 1945, a development underlined by the virtual collapse of the Liberals as a serious political force, meant a belated, but decisive, retribution on the Conservatives for the locust years.

Baldwin made few changes in the composition of the Government, apart from those brought about at Under-Secretary level by Noel Skelton's death. In Cabinet, however, he replaced Londonderry as Leader of the Lords and Lord Privy Seal with Halifax,* a significant promotion. Again Press speculation centred on the possible return of Churchill. With the forthcoming London Naval Conference, it was rumoured that he might become First Lord of the Admiralty, but Baldwin took advice, particularly from Neville Chamberlain, his kingmaker, and opted for safety first. The overwhelming victory at the polls actually limited his freedom of choice, for the result was seen as a vote of confidence in the whole administration, so Baldwin considered widespread changes inappropriate. But within a month circumstances were to force his hand.

The fateful meeting between British Foreign Secretary Hoare and Laval, now French Prime Minister as well as Foreign Minister, came about more by accident than design at the beginning of December. Laval wanted to settle the vexed question of oil sanctions and to coordinate an agreed line with the British. Mussolini, with whom Laval kept in close contact on a private telephone line, had indeed made it clear that he would regard such

---

*Nicknamed the Holy Fox.

a sanction as an act of war. Laval was prepared to come to London, but Hoare, on the advice of his doctors and with Baldwin's prompting, was planning a skating holiday in Switzerland. So it was agreed that Hoare would break his journey in Paris en route. Eden became acting Foreign Secretary during Hoare's absence from the country.

Laval and Hoare felt one meeting would suffice. Circumstances dictated otherwise. On the morning of 7 December impenetrable fog prevented Hoare's planned flight, and his belated arrival at the Quai d'Orsay, after a difficult journey by boat train, was not the best preparation for complex and unfinished negotiations. He agreed to stay on in Paris for a further day and a second series of talks began at the Quai d'Orsay at 10.30 a.m. on Sunday 8 December. Exploratory talks soon gave way to firm proposals.

On the Sunday morning Eden, concerned by the tone of the initial reports, telephoned the embassy in Paris for details, but without success. 'All I could get was a secretary,' he scrawled on a minute.[70] Baldwin, returning from Chequers for the first plenary session of the London Naval Conference on 9 December, also had no idea what was happening, beyond a telegram from Hoare stating, 'I greatly hope that you will have a Cabinet at once to confirm what I propose.'[71]

Gradually details emerged, but it was not until the early morning of Monday 9 December that Eden received at his home a four-page summary of the Hoare–Laval Pact, brought over on the night ferry by Maurice Peterson, head of the newly formed Abyssinian Department at the Foreign Office. The stark reality of the additional concessions to appease Mussolini baffled Eden, as Hoare had told him before leaving, 'I shall not commit you to anything. It wouldn't be fair on my way through to my holiday.' Eden showed the draft to Baldwin as soon as he could extricate him from the London Naval Conference, and a hurried study of a large map in Eden's room revealed the extent of Mussolini's gains under the proposals. Abyssinia was to retain sovereignty over most of her territory but Italy was to have ill-defined 'economic rights' and considerable territory, around Adowa and Adigrat in the north, as well as land in the east and south-east bordering Italian Somaliland – what was termed euphemistically 'rectification of frontiers'. In return, Abyssinia would be granted the choice of either Assab or Zeila as a port, initially without railway access through Italian-held territory. The Hoare–Laval proposals were produced under the auspices of the League, and were intended to be put to the League for approval.

Eden told Baldwin he was 'astonished' by these terms, and that his position as regards Hoare was now extremely delicate. In October he had been out of London and Hoare had made the running; now the positions were reversed, but Eden was outranked. His choice seemed to be resignation or endorsement.

An emergency Cabinet was summoned. Baldwin's view was that, what-ever had been decided, the Cabinet as yet had none of the detailed reasoning behind it. The first imperative was for Emperor Haile Selassie, who was not included in the timetable at all, to be told of the proposals at the same time as Mussolini was told. However, French papers hostile to Laval had appeared in Paris with detailed criticisms. A bandwagon was already rolling. Monday's evening papers picked up the story in London and feelings were clear. The next morning's national dailies would prove crucial to Hoare's chances of survival. The Cabinet first tried to persuade Hoare to renounce his proposals, and Eden had the sensitive task of telephoning the Foreign Secretary to persuade him that this would be for the best.

The government wanted to keep Hoare, and it was even suggested that if he went, he would be back soon; but he alone remained willing to defend the proposals. On 10 December, amid growing Press outrage in Britain, Baldwin spoke in the House of Commons, stating enigmatically, 'My lips are not yet unsealed', which J. C. C. Davidson, Chancellor of the Duchy of Lancaster, later confirmed was a reference to Mussolini's secret payment to Laval for his part in the partition of Abyssinia.[72]

Eden did his best to defend the absent Foreign Secretary from his detractors in the Commons, by stressing that the Committee of Eighteen in Geneva had approved Anglo-French attempts to find a settlement. But it was not a convincing performance.

To add to Hoare's discomfort, physical as well as political, on the same day as Baldwin's statement, he suffered a fainting fit on the ice rink in Zuoz, fell and broke his nose in two places, which delayed any possible return to London until 15 December. Meanwhile, Eden was shuttling between London and Geneva.

On 12 December Eden reported from Geneva on the League's reaction to the pact. 'Impression which Paris proposals have made upon opinion here is even worse than I had anticipated,' he telegrammed, telling of the 'devastating effect which the proposals had here.'[73]*

Baldwin, Neville Chamberlain and Eden visited Hoare, confined to his home in Cadogan Gardens, on 17 December. The meeting was tense, as Eden had been authorised at the Cabinet meeting that morning to inform the League later in the day that Britain would no longer endorse the Hoare-Laval proposals, if they did not meet with the tripartite agreement of

---

*With hindsight, some may interpret this as a pitch for Hoare's job, but Eden no longer wanted such a poisoned chalice, and in any reshuffle following Hoare's likely departure still hankered after the Admiralty. British naval weaknesses underlay Hoare's response to Laval, a problem which the First Lord would need to address and rectify. Stephen Roskill, *Hankey: Man of Secrets, Volume III 1931–1963*, Collins, 1974, p.190.

Abyssinia, Italy and the League, a vain hope. Hoare's acceptance of this formula was sought; the political reality was that Hoare had no option, and Eden left after a few moments to catch the boat train.

The Cabinet met on 18 December. Halifax took the lead in calling for Hoare's resignation, as the issue affected 'the whole moral position of the Government before the world.'[74] J. H. Thomas, William Ormsby-Gore and Walter Elliot also found their lips unsealed by the Holy Fox's arguments. The minutes of the meeting make uncomfortable reading even after seven decades, as erstwhile colleagues lined up to contribute to Hoare's political assassination. When Eden heard what had happened, it seemed to him like a scene from *Julius Caesar*:

> Let's kill him boldly, but not wrathfully;
> Let's carve him as a dish fit for the gods,
> Not hew him as a carcass fit for hounds.[75]

This was one Cabinet meeting Eden was glad to miss.

Hoare bowed to the inevitable. In a striking parallel with the fate of the Earl of Bute after the hostile reception accorded the Peace of Paris in 1763 during the Seven Years War, Hoare resigned as Foreign Secretary on the evening of 18 December. Still bearing the scars of his recent accident, he made his personal statement from the back-benches the next day. He ended by wishing his unknown successor 'better luck than I have had in the last two weeks.'[76]

After the war, when Churchill was writing his history of the Second World War, he sent Eden drafts for his comments. When Eden read the proposed account of the Hoare-Laval Pact, he wrote to Churchill:

> It is quite true that I was much upset by the Hoare-Laval proposals & by the way they were negotiated & sent back to us. But once they had been agreed in Paris I did try to do my best for Sam Hoare & for them. The whole story is a complicated one from my angle & from that of anybody who had anything to do with it! One day I may weary you with it. Meanwhile, since I did put up a defence of the proposals in the House which is on record, but which you didn't hear because you were away, I would be grateful if you would leave out a comment after my name on Page 14 line 10: 'who had been opposed to the Hoare-Laval agreement.'[77]

The Hoare-Laval Pact was indeed a watershed, internationally and for Eden personally, encapsulating the dilemma of the appeasement period. If collective security was a sham, if only Britain was willing to act, and if the oil sanction meant war, then the Hoare-Laval proposals were better than what eventually happened, the loss of the whole of Abyssinia. On the other hand, had Mussolini been resisted, this might have deterred Hitler in the Rhineland.

The history of the Hoare-Laval Pact is more properly part of Hoare's story than Eden's.[78] The consequences of the crisis, however, were to propel Eden into the front rank of international politics, a position that he held for the next twenty-two years. 'The political beneficiary was Eden,' R. A. C. Parker has written. 'He won immense and durable prestige from this crisis simply through not being Hoare, through not having been at the meeting with Laval in December, through association with Geneva rather than Paris.'[79]

Eden returned from Geneva with Stanley Bruce, the Australian representative at the League. Both agreed that Austen Chamberlain, despite the fact that he was in favour of the appeasement of Mussolini (though not of Hitler), would be the right figure to replace Hoare. He was a respected elder statesman, a Nobel Laureate, a League man through and through, and had been vocal in his criticism of the Pact, though he would hardly have been a convincing exponent of sanctions against Italy. Though too old to entertain a lengthy second spell at the Foreign Office, Chamberlain was, in their opinion, undoubtedly the man to steady the ship in the short term. Eden made it patently clear to Bruce that he did not seek the post himself. But circumstances dictated otherwise.

On arrival in London, Eden was at once summoned to meet Stanley Baldwin at 10 Downing Street.[80] The subsequent interview, in the small library, was one of the strangest of Eden's career. Baldwin was extremely nervous and gave the impression he had no idea whom to appoint as Hoare's successor. Essentially, he wanted to use Eden as a sounding board, and find the solution by a process of elimination. Whom did Eden think should be appointed? When Eden suggested Austen Chamberlain, Baldwin ruled him out at once. 'Too old,' he said. 'Anyway I saw him yesterday and told him so.' The next day Chamberlain told Eden that Baldwin had been blunter – 'he told me I was ga-ga' – and that the interview had been a painful one. Any other suggestions, asked Baldwin? Tentatively Eden put forward Halifax's name. Baldwin rebuffed this suggestion also, on the grounds of Halifax's contentious record as Viceroy in India, and his membership of the House of Lords.* The list of possibilities was now seemingly exhausted and silence fell over the interview. With an air of resignation, Baldwin concluded, 'It looks as if it will have to be you.'

---

*Two years later, Lord Halifax was to become Foreign Secretary, but in April 1955 Eden remembered Baldwin's reservations when, against his better judgement, he decided not to appoint Cranborne, then Marquess of Salisbury, to the post of Foreign Secretary in his own administration, a decision he always regretted. See Chapter 16 for an account of Eden's Cabinet making.

In such a dispiriting manner did Eden, at the age of thirty-eight, become the youngest Foreign Secretary since Lord Granville in December 1851. It was not a propitious time to take on such responsibilities. Mussolini was in the process of 'swallowing' Abyssinia, and Hitler was on the verge of marching into the Rhineland. The Spanish Civil War in 1936 would be widely seen as a dress rehearsal for a larger conflict, and the Middle East seemed in perpetual ferment.

On 23 December Eden travelled to Sandringham to receive his Seals of Office. It was the last time he met George V, for within the month the old King was dead. 'A Sandringham day – cold & foggy,' he wrote in his diary (the first entry for several months, such had been the pressure of work). 'King friendly, Queen more so. Had an audience before ceremony. H.M. very down on plan of Paris.'[81] When Hoare had surrendered the Seals, the King had bluntly told him that the pact was a mistake. 'I said to your predecessor: "You know what they're all saying, no more coals to Newcastle, no more Hoares to Paris." The fellow didn't even laugh.'[82]*

'I expect the greatness of his office will find him out,' Churchill wrote to his wife Clementine after Eden's appointment on 26 December. 'Austen wd have been far better; & I wonder why he was overlooked. Poor man he always plays the game & never wins it!'[83]

From Rome Sir Eric Drummond sent Eden Italian views. 'The withdrawal of the proposals came as a double shock. In the first place, it removed the possibility of any early settlement. In the second place, it seemed to imply an acceleration of British hostility to Italy. Such an implication, it must regretfully be admitted, is felt to have been strengthened by your nomination to the Foreign Office.'[84] The wires of the European chancelleries rang with the news. The French Ambassador in London reported that the appointment had been well received by 'les jeunes conservateurs et dans les milieux de gauche', and that Baldwin's position was considered to be 'très fortifiée par cette nomination'. The message from the French Embassy in Berlin to the Quai d'Orsay was that Eden's appointment 'a fait en Allemagne la plus profonde impression', and that it was 'une date décisive dans les annales de l'Europe.'[85] The German Ambassador in Italy, Ulrich von Hassell, reported to Berlin that 'Hoare's

---

*In his biography of King George V, Kenneth Rose casts doubt on the accuracy of Eden's recollections. 'It is inconceivable he [King George V] should have thrown so cruel a jest in Hoare's face at the nadir of his political fortunes, then mocked him for his supposed lack of humour.' Kenneth Rose, *King George V*, Weidenfeld & Nicolson, 1983, p.400. Although the story improved with the telling in his memoirs, it had been noted by Eden in his diary on the actual day, 23 December 1935, 'No more coals to Newcastle, no more (w)hores to Paris!' So it can be assumed that the episode did occur, as Eden's day-to-day diary is notably accurate.

resignation was tantamount to a victory for Eden, who increasingly cast himself in the role of the younger Pitt *vis-à-vis* Napoleon.'[86] The Russians, too, took note of Eden's sudden rise. Vladimir Potemkin, Soviet Ambassador in Paris, telegrammed to Moscow on 19 December. 'It is apparent to everyone that he is exultant at the collapse of the Laval–Hoare Plan.'[87] On this main issue, 'it was almost worth going through the experience to produce the present firm reaction,' the Governor-General of Australia wrote to the King. 'Mr Eden is splendid & deserves his laurels. He bids fair "out of the nettle danger to pluck the flower safely." '[88]

Eden's appointment undoubtedly ruffled many feathers, as Harold Nicolson had predicted. Senior colleagues, even Austen Chamberlain, saw themselves displaced by the onward march of youth. Human nature being what it is – Eden always believed in the maxim that people will forgive you anything but success – his rapid rise was the source of much envy. George Lloyd, a figure on the imperialist wing of the Conservative Party, was particularly resentful. 'I sometimes wish I were Foreign Secretary,' he wrote to his wife, unimpressed by Eden's stance towards Mussolini. 'I think I could do something more than these minnows can.'[89]

Eden's immaculate appearance – together with his growing reputation as the Beau Brummel of British politics*, his glamour spawning articles in glossy magazines such as the *Tatler* – got up people's noses, and led many commentators mistakenly to think of him as a lightweight. Collin Brooks, a figure from his *Yorkshire Post* days, wrote in his diary, 'It seems a long time ago, although it is only seven years, since he did art notes for me for the *Yorkshire Post*. The appointment fills me with forebodings.' The dismissive phrase 'art notes' speaks volumes. Brooks was later to write 'an arraignment so "savage"' of Eden that his putative publisher 'says he dare not publish it.'[90] Unfortunately for Brooks, he submitted the manuscript in the week of Eden's resignation in February 1938 when his stock, especially with non-Conservative voters, was very high. But Brooks's attitude, from a right-wing perspective, showed clearly how, even in pre-war days, Eden was not the golden boy for everyone. Indeed, even among his admirers there was a sense of foreboding, as Cuthbert Headlam, MP for Barnard Castle, noted in his diary, 'He has had a meteoric career, but I should not be surprised to see him fall just as quickly as he has risen – I hope I may be wrong for he is a very good fellow.'[91]

Eden became Foreign Secretary at a critical time in international relations. Japan, Germany and Italy were all three potential enemies of Great Britain and, although Eden did not regard Europe and the Far East as separate

---

*Eden later lived in Beau Brummel's house in Chesterfield Street.

problems, he was more hopeful of Anglo-American cooperation against Japan's advances into China than in conflicts nearer to home.

Eden's concerns on taking office lay not only in the international arena. Sir Warren Fisher, head of the Civil Service, made it clear (on doubtful authority) that he wished ambassadorial appointments to be submitted through him to the Prime Minister. Eden flatly refused to comply, stating that his constitutional duties in this matter were to serve the monarch, not a civil servant. In the subsequent battle of wills, Eden eventually prevailed, but not without the avoidable expense for a man of his temperament of much emotional energy. He was also conscious initially of the scrutiny of his predecessors, five of whom remained in Parliament in December 1935.*

Eden's first full day of work was on Christmas Eve. He went early to the Foreign Office, was greeted by Vansittart on the Great Staircase under the gilded dome and taken to the Secretary of State's room on the first floor, overlooking St James's Park. Here his kinsman, Sir Edward Grey, had stood by the middle window on the eve of the Great War to watch the lamps going out all over Europe, as he famously said. 'Telegrams about Egypt prepared & despatched,'[92] Eden wrote, of preparations for the Anglo-Egyptian Treaty, which was to secure the Suez Canal for twenty years. His first official meeting was with the Dominion High Commissioners. In a Cabinet minute earlier in the month, Eden had argued for oil sanctions against Italy. Recent events had clouded the picture and he told the High Commissioners that 'for the moment at any rate, it was desirable to pause and take stock.'[93] Although Eden returned to the question in Cabinet on 26 February, the pause entailed a loss of momentum in the months before Hitler's reoccupation of the Rhineland in March. 'More work at F.O. in p.m.,' Eden concluded in his diary of this first day, 'mostly replies to telegrams & letters which have really been legion.'[94]

Christmas Day proved a short respite, before detailed work with Vansittart on German intentions, and a short break in Yorkshire with the Becketts.

Ministerial office at this level brought commensurate rewards. Eden now drew a Secretary of State's salary of £5,000 a year (approximately £166,000 in present-day values), at a time when nearly 75 per cent of the working population received the average industrial wage of approximately £4 a week. A 'good' middle-class income at the time was £8–10 a week; £1,000 a year was considered riches indeed, though many professional

---

*In order of seniority, the five former Foreign Secretaries were Ramsay MacDonald, Austen Chamberlain, Lord Reading, Sir John Simon and Sir Samuel Hoare. Reading died a week after Eden's appointment. Arthur Henderson, another predecessor, had died on 20 October 1935.

people deferred marriage till they had attained that sum. For the first time in his life, Eden had no immediate short-term financial worry, though even here there was a canker in the apple. Two of his three predecessors (Reading and Hoare) had lasted only a few months in the post. 'I am bothered about money,' he wrote to Beatrice. 'There is no security in politics, and I feel that for boys' sake and my own old age I ought to take something that will last a few years.'[95] In a more formal society, much was expected of a Secretary of State (and his wife) in a representational role, and this involved heavy additional expenditure. To put it simply, Eden was now earning approximately twenty-five times the average wage, but was unable to build up his capital.

Eden's style was soon established in King Charles Street. He arrived early, worked long hours and left late. He expected others to be equally dedicated and was a fierce, but fair, taskmaster. A small flat was created on the upper floors of the building, where Eden stayed when the obligations and burdens of office became unpredictable. Beatrice used the flat from time to time, which was to cause some difficulty and embarrassment during the war when the marriage was under increasing pressure. Eden's ministerial team was predominantly from the Upper House. He could always rely on Halifax (like Grey, another of his distant kinsmen) as Leader of the Lords to represent his position there, and could also call on Lord Stanhope (and later Lord Plymouth) as Under-Secretary. Pre-war politics remained a close-knit world. Before the year was out, Beatrice's step-brother, Lord Feversham, son of Eden's commanding officer in the war, was to marry Halifax's daughter, Anne.

The hub of the team remained Eden and Bobbety Cranborne, the bond of trust going back a long way. Newcomers included Oliver Harvey, as the Principal Private Secretary, with Harold Caccia as his Assistant Private Secretary.

Eden struck up an immediate rapport with Harvey, who had a distinguished war service. Harvey served Eden from January 1936 to February 1938 in the first instance, and then from June 1941 – when Eden, during his second spell at the Foreign Office, reinstated him as his Principal Private Secretary, a post that Harvey filled with an almost partisan loyalty – until his promotion to Assistant Under-Secretary in December 1943. In the two volumes of his published diaries, Harvey left an unrivalled account of the day-to-day concerns of the Secretary of State, as the world moved closer to war, and then of the turmoils that followed. By contrast, Harvey's final posting to the Paris Embassy was almost an anti-climax.

Harold Caccia had entered the diplomatic service in 1929, serving first in Peking. His appointment as Assistant Private Secretary (till 1939) preceded a dangerous mission in Athens, though he was to come to prominence on Harold Macmillan's staff in Algiers in 1943. As Chief Clerk at the Foreign Office after the war, his task was to implement the administrative reforms Eden had outlined for the service in 1943. Unlike Harvey, Caccia's final posting was the culmination of a distinguished career, as he became Ambassador in Washington during the Suez crisis and its aftermath. Caccia became very much part of the Eden family, a close friend of Simon Eden and of Martyn Beckett, Eden's brother-in-law. The Edens invited the Caccias to accompany them on holiday and, in hitherto unseen private papers, following one such working trip after the Spanish Civil War and the Abdication, Caccia left one of the most perceptive accounts of Eden's personality in middle life and how it impinged on his pre-war public responsibilities:

> He could not have been nicer, more thoughtful or more forthcoming to Nancy and myself. He treated himself far more as our host than as my taskmaster – in that his reputation for charm is a good & correct repute ... Beatrice E was equally good to us after her manner, which is rather reserved & quiet. She obviously wanted to be Mrs E & not the wife of the Foreign Secretary, and I think she enjoyed giggling with Nancy. She is clearly very fond of him & he of her: though I shd. say he was not ever much entertained by her reflections on things or politics. At the same time she is passably well read on the subjects that interest him, modern artists & pictures for instance, & she knows something about good food & drink of which subject he is a master.
>
> As a man rather than a pleasant holiday companion he struck me as very quick on the uptake, sensitive & with all the points & some of the failings of a thoroughbred. Sometimes his nervousness wd get the better of him & one bad course wd. be enough to spoil a whole dinner. Applied to Foreign Affairs these characteristics have given him through the years that he has now been connected with the FO a wide knowledge of his subject and a feel for it which is usually the property only of the trained diplomat. At the same time his first reaction to any question is always the politician's – how will such & such a course go down in the House of Commons or with country. And he is a politician by family & connection as well as by profession; in the tradition of a Grey or a Balfour rather than a Baldwin or even a Chamberlain ...
>
> He was complaining of the little support that he got from the P.M. [Stanley Baldwin], who for instance asked him to call at the end of his three months holiday last autumn [1936] & never once in an hour's talk ever raised any foreign issue or even appeared ready to listen to external affairs, this at a time when the Spanish Civil War was perhaps still at its most dangerous stage for Europe. Mrs. Simpson was all that he wanted to talk of: nothing else mattered.

Caccia was very struck by Eden's negative feelings about Italy:

> His first reaction to seeing Italians, hearing Italian spoken & noticing an Italian ship is one of strong antipathy, almost physical repulsion.

On the other hand, he could put such personal prejudices aside when it came to political business. Eden's account of his talk with Mussolini in June 1935 was, to Caccia:

> ... very balanced & unprejudiced – in fact he often repeated that he thought that it wd. be a good thing if he cd have a talk to him, for he believed he could do business with him.

But above all Caccia, who had been too young to serve in the Great War, was struck by:

> ... the interest which he takes in army matters & his regiment, the 60th. He often talked of the K.O.R.R. – & the war. When in Berlin he had even found that the Führer had been in a section of the line opposite to him in 1917.
>
> And to sum up this man – in many ways a traditional English gentleman, the son of a sixth Bart, Eton, the 60th. How say anything but good of this attractive character with his natural & unaffected kindness & generosity, with his quickness & brightness, with his sense for art & his knowledge of it as well as his aesthetic satisfaction in all things well done – Surely this is a superior man – a thoroughbred.

Then came the sting in the tail:

> And yet admitting and admiring his qualities I cannot help the suspicion that some essential things are lacking: greatness, firmness, fixity of purpose, the quiet confidence that in these perilous years 'I know I can save England and no-one else can'. These things may come with time.[96]

Eden's immediate concern on becoming Foreign Secretary remained Abyssinia, and the vexed question of oil sanctions against Italy, soon complicated by continued concerns over Anglo-German relations, the Spanish Civil War, and the aftermath of the Franco-Soviet Pact of 1935. Francophobia in Britain at this time, an inevitable consequence of the Hoare-Laval Pact, was equalled only by the open hostility towards all things Soviet, especially among Tory back-benchers, as well as among the party leadership. 'I told Eden yesterday,' Baldwin said to Tom Jones, 'that on no account, French or other, must he bring us in to fight on the side of the Russians.'[97]

At times Eden felt that Baldwin's idea of foreign policy was not unlike that of one of his Eton schoolmasters, 'Tuppy' Headlam, who once observed, 'I am told on good authority that there will shortly be an internecine struggle between the white races, the black races and the yellow races. My prayer is that we shall draw a bye in the first round.'[98] His talks with Baldwin usually comprised nebulous expressions of goodwill, but rarely concrete suggestions or practical advice. 'Talk with S. B. in evening,' he wrote after one frustrating meeting. 'He wants better relations with Hitler than with Musso – we must get nearer to Germany. "How?" I asked. "I have no idea, that is your job." '[99]

Eden felt the Foreign Office lacked organisational discipline and consequently failed to identify talent early enough.[100] He had been put off a diplomatic career, sensing that it would be a slow-track career over teacups in Teheran. Now he wanted the brightest and best to rise quickly – throughout the service. In the long term, Vansittart would have to be replaced as Permanent Under-Secretary, and with this in mind, Eden brought Alec Cadogan back from China as Deputy Under-Secretary, an appointment announced on 20 February 1936. Cadogan's knowledge of the Far Eastern situation, where he had worked closely with the American diplomatic team, was to be invaluable. Eden utilised Cadogan's experience to offset Foreign Office stubborn incomprehension of Japanese policy and to underline the importance of American support for Britain's position in the Far East.

One organisational change of great import, especially in the long term, was the formation in July 1936 during Eden's first year as Secretary of State of the Joint Intelligence Committeee (JIC), which then coordinated the work of the three services in this vital field. The Secret Intelligence Service (SIS), known as MI6, had been formed in 1909, and was the conduit for Eden at the Foreign Office on security matters. The Government Code and Cypher School also answered to Eden, and when necessary he knew of developments in the field of counter-espionage conducted by the Security Service (MI5).[101] What he did not know of initially was the work done behind his back by Sir Joseph Ball, a former MI5 officer, for Chamberlain in establishing unofficial contacts with Italy.

Almost inevitably, Eden's first overseas visit as Foreign Secretary was to Geneva on 19 January 1936, where he found the new French Foreign Minister, Pierre Flandin, opposed to oil sanctions and unresponsive to the need to influence American opinion. In fact, Von Neurath's view of Mussolini's economic and political difficulties proved as inaccurate as his assertion that Germany had no plans to reoccupy the Rhineland. Suddenly the Rhineland seemed to be the question on all lips, especially French ones. Flandin disagreed with Von Neurath's analysis, his concerns exacerbated by the seeming complacency of the French General Staff. The Russian view of developments was uncompromising. Lunching with Eden, Maxim

Litvinov told him that Germany 'must be made to understand that a close understanding exists among the peaceful nations', among which Eden counted Russia for her part in helping to maintain Anglo-French security. Eden agreed with Litvinov that such states 'must be strong', as 'Germany only understands force.'[102]

Proceedings in Geneva were interrupted by the news of the sudden death of King George V at Sandringham on 20 January. Eden returned for the funeral, using the occasion for further talks with Foreign Ministers who had not been in Geneva. He was struck by the ominous warnings of M. Paul Van Zeeland, the Belgian Prime Minister, for whose judgement he had particular respect, about German threats to his country's borders. After the funeral, Eden was received by the visiting royals, King Carol of Romania, King Boris of Bulgaria and Prince Paul of Yugoslavia, the last such gathering of the European monarchs, many of whom were to be swept away in the maelstroms of the next decade.

The old order was passing. On his first appearance in London, the new King, Edward VIII, had arrived 'hatless from the air'.[103] Many were shocked to hear that Lloyd George had been commissioned by the newspapers to write an account of the funeral; those near him in St George's Chapel, Windsor, were even more shocked to see him taking notes on his service sheet.[104]

Following his earlier meetings with the Prince of Wales, Eden had been impressed by his progressive views and openness. Now, as Edward VIII, he seemed a monarch for the new age, sweeping away the stuffiness of outmoded protocol. In common with many others, Eden's optimism soon faded. He heard from an exasperated Baldwin of the King's dilatoriness and unpredictability. Conscious of his responsibilities for the security services, Eden unprecedentedly restricted the sensitive Foreign Office material that went in the red boxes to the King's weekend retreat at Fort Belvedere; he had heard how papers often lay about unattended, stained by the rings of his guests' abandoned cocktail glasses.[105]

Despite the unresolved question of oil sanctions against Italy, Eden and Vansittart regarded Anglo-German relations as the major priority in these early months. On 17 January, Eden had presented the Cabinet with a series of reports from the British Embassy in Berlin, together with his own summary on 'The German Danger', in which he warned of Germany's desire to re-establish herself as 'the dominating power in Europe'. He drew two conclusions from this situation. The first was that 'it is vital to hasten and complete our own re-armament'; secondly, 'it will be well to consider whether it is still possible to come to some *modus vivendi* – to put it no higher – with Hitler's Germany which would be both honourable and safe for this country.'[106] Throughout his first Foreign Secretaryship these remained his twin goals.

In Cabinet on 29 January, Eden argued for one supreme effort to reach accommodation with Hitler, though he warned that any such agreement would 'not easily be realised.'[107] Cranborne began exploratory talks with the German Counsellor in London. 'I am in favour of making some attempt to come to terms with Germany, but upon indispensable condition,' Eden told the Cabinet, 'that we offer no sops to Germany. There must be no concession merely to keep Germany quiet, for that process only stimulates the appetite it is intended to satisfy.'[108]

Critics, such as Lloyd George, suspected that Eden's concentration on Anglo-German relations had led him to neglect the Italian question. As a result, Eden found himself under attack in the Commons on 25 February over Britain's failure to impose oil sanctions, so his maiden speech as Foreign Secretary adopted an essentially defensive note, partly to spare French sensibilities at an awkward juncture. In the Distinguished Strangers' Gallery, Count Grandi, the Italian Ambassador, heard Eden declare that 'Oil is a sanction like any other, and must be judged by the same criterion, whether its imposition will stop the war.'[109] In Cabinet – on 15 and 26 February – Eden urged oil sanctions, but the impression that Grandi received from the debate, where Eden made a halting figure, was that Mussolini had little to fear.

Flandin, meanwhile, was instrumental in deciding on 27 February 'that in the event of a German violation of the Rhineland Zone they would act not alone but only in concert with the co-signatories of Locarno,'[110] a decision communicated to Eden just forty-eight hours before Hitler struck.

On 5 March, the same day that he received Flandin's message, Eden outlined details in Cabinet of a proposed Air Pact with Germany – on arms limitation and mutual assistance – proposals that he put to the German Ambassador, Leopold von Hoesch, the next day. The following day Hitler violated both the Versailles Treaty and the Locarno Pact, when German troops reoccupied land that had symbolic significance for both Weimar and Nazi consciousness. In Churchill's later catalogue of 'long, dismal, drawling tides of drift and surrender', Hitler's demilitarisation of the Rhineland was to prove a seminal moment. Yet the British and French had been negotiating an end of the demilitarised zone with Germany, so could hardly go to war. Hitler was not taking as much of a gamble as is usually thought, and it was only in hindsight that many people regarded it as a watershed. Eden, however, was clear from the start about the long-term consequences, and in Cabinet on 11 March, warned that 'if Germany was allowed to remain unmolested in military occupation of the Rhineland, war in two years time was a certainty and would be fought under very unfavourable conditions.'[111] But it was a minority view at the time. On 13 March, Joachim von Ribbentrop met Eden for talks on 'reconstruction', after which Eden told Flandin through the Paris Embassy that 'British public opinion was not prepared to go to war in order that the Germans should be compelled to go out of the Rhineland one week and be allowed to come into it the next.'[112] Three days later, Hitler reintroduced conscription in Germany. The Air Pact was dead, and Hitler had established a vital breakthrough in his push for *Lebensraum*. An additional benefit from the German perspective was the subsequent rift between Eden and Flandin on Anglo-French policy. At a meeting at the Quai d'Orsay on 10 March, Flandin argued for the imposition of economic, financial and military sanctions against Germany; Eden's fear was that Britain, France and Belgium would be isolated, no support would be forthcoming from the League, and certainly not from the nominal Locarno ally, Italy, and that Europe could stumble into war on the lines of August 1914.

Eden laid much store on a comment from his taxi-driver, 'I suppose Jerry can do what he likes in his own back-garden, can't he?', which, in days when opinion polling was in its infancy, he felt sure 'represented the majority opinion in Britain.'[113] His colleagues agreed. 'It seems to me futile to take any action against Germany', Leo Amery wrote in his diary, 'and the whole thing is likely to fizzle out in talk,'[114] a prognosis confirmed by events in Geneva, where the League soon became bogged down in talks about international forces on the frontier. With one strike Hitler had matched – even superseded – Mussolini, in his audacious disregard for international diplomacy.

Under the shadow of Hitler's occupation of the Rhineland, Eden's opening speech in the Foreign Affairs Debate on 26 March, outlining the British position, appeared one of his trickiest assignments, and yet, despite repeated sniping from Lloyd George, he carried the day. 'Anthony made the speech of his life,' Neville Chamberlain wrote, 'and it was not only a good speech, it showed both courage and statesmanship and more than anything else it brought the House to see the situation in a truer perspective.'[115] But the die had been cast, and the situation that now faced Germany's neighbours, and, ultimately, the whole of Europe, was to have the profoundest consequences.

The question remains whether things could have been handled differently; indeed, whether Eden as British Foreign Secretary should have taken a stronger lead. In retrospect, he acknowledged this himself. 'I think I should also admit that I should have been more responsive to what the French appeared to want to do and stiffer to Hitler.'[116] Short of direct military action, there was little that could have been done differently. Flandin may have been keen for joint military action, but the French

General Staff were unconvinced, an admission of the lack of military preparedness, rather than political will. Public opinion in Britain, whether in the guise of Eden's taxi driver, or the correspondence columns of the Press, was at best ambiguous. What was more significant was the attitude in Parliament. Leo Amery was not a lone voice. At a dinner in London on 8 March, Duff Cooper, War Secretary no less, told the German Ambassador, Leopold von Hoesch, that 'though the British people were prepared to fight for France in the event of a German incursion into French territory, they would not resort to arms on account of the recent occupation of the Rhineland ... they did not care two hoots about the Germans re-occupying their own territory.'[117]

In such an atmosphere, Eden's freedom of action was severely limited. It is easy to be wise after the event, but nevertheless the occupation of the Rhineland was a decisive turning point, from which, it could be argued, all later events stemmed, and Eden and Flandin did not escape obloquy. Indeed, one of Eden's closest friends and admirers, Alec Cadogan, recognised this five years later, just before the Japanese attack on Pearl Harbor, when he confided to the privacy of his diary:

Monday, 1 December [1941]

... P.M. also decided *not*, at present to publish documents on the origin of war. I think he is right again. A. [Anthony Eden] wants to publish them, but I think this is 'ideological'. Why rake up controversy now? Have them ready by all means. Does A. realise that *he* is responsible for the great and tragic 'appeasement' – not reacting to German occupation of the Rhineland? How lucky he is – no one has ever mentioned *that*! and *that* was the turning point.[118]

Few saw things in such a light until the historical revisionism of recent years.[119]

The moment passed, and as if to underline the comprehensive nature of his new responsibilities, and how events move on, the day before his speech in the Foreign Affairs Debate in the House, Eden had been one of the signatories of the treaty signed at the end of the London Naval Conference, before beginning an extended five months work on the new Egyptian Treaty regarding the future security of the Suez Canal. 'A somewhat tiresome C.I.D. about Egypt,' Eden wrote typically, in his diary on 27 April. 'Difficult to make all understand consequences of being in Egypt *without* a Treaty & with a triumphant Italian neighbour.'[120] He outlined for the Cabinet the necessity for the British 'to take such measures as are necessary for the protection of the Canal' and that 'in time of war Egypt has to place her ports and communications at the disposal of His Majesty's Government'. He was hoping for an agreement of twenty years, but

emphasised that 'after this period they may be replaced by other provisions, but that these provisions must provide for the position of His
Britannic Majesty's imperial communications

In a clear tribute to his first mentor, Eden arranged that the signing of
the Egyptian Treaty on 26 August should be held in the Locarno Room.
The agreement had the double benefit of securing British routes to the Far
East by playing on Egyptian fears of further Italian expansion, whilst at the
same time allowing British troops in Alexandria and Cairo to be
redeployed to deal with growing unrest in Palestine. 'The Treaty terminates
the military occupation of Egypt by British forces (article 1) and establishes
an alliance between the two countries (article 4). It continues for a period
of twenty years, after which, if either party so request, both parties will
negotiate with a view to revising its terms by agreement in the light of the
then existing circumstances.' It was accepted that the future security of
rights of passage through the Suez Canal was central. The memorandum
by John Somers-Cocks of 20 August 1936 read: 'Whilst the Suez Canal is
an integral part of Egypt, it is stated by the parties to be a universal means
of communication and an essential means of communication between the
different parts of the British Empire.'[122]*

The Egyptian delegation was treated to 'much junketing and many heavy
meals'[123] when they arrived on 23 August for the signing, including a tour
of Warwick Castle. Eden received effusive congratulations. 'A very bright
star you have suddenly put into a grim & dirty sky,' wrote one ambassador.
Eden was more cautious, writing to the Chairman of the Conservative
Foreign Affairs Committee, 'I believe that it is a reasonable compromise.'[124]
But the mills of history, though they grind slowly, grind surely, and what
may have seemed an agreement in perpetuity in 1936, proved far from that
two decades later. Eden anticipated such problems. 'I am clear that we must
go some way to meet Egypt in situation after 20 years,' he wrote, 'for that
will, in last resort, depend on our strength then.'[125]

As Mussolini tightened his grip over Addis Ababa, the Emperor Haile
Selassie went into exile. 'The news of the Emperor's flight from Abyssinia
is in the Sunday paper,' wrote Thomas Jones on 3 May. 'Eden has played
his hand out. It has been magnificently consistent but was it diplomacy?
Did he fail to foresee the debacle or did he prefer to be consistent?'[126]

With Haile Selassie's fall, the League suffered a rebuff, one of many in

---

*John Somers-Cocks's memoranda were legendary in the Foreign Office for their
thoroughness, but also for their expansiveness. After the war, a vast file was placed before
Ernest Bevin with a shrug of the shoulders and the apologetic explanation 'Somers-Cocks'.
'Some 'as, and some 'asn't,' replied the Foreign Secretary, 'but it's all the same to 'arold
Nicolson.' Private information.

1936, from which it never recovered. It was the end of an era in Eden's own life. He had invested much emotional and political capital in the Covenant of the League, an extended episode of disappointed expectations, later replicated in the responses of the United Nations to post-war crises. His personal help in finding the exiled Emperor appropriate accommodation near Bath had its element of expiation. The League of Nations was by no means an ignoble experiment, but Halifax's biographer told the unpalatable truth:

> Overall, the League of Nations tended to do Britain more harm than good. Not only did it harm relations with Italy, but it fostered the belief that 'world opinion' mattered. It gave the dictators a forum in which to look strong without giving lustre to the Allies' essential decency.[127]

The French changed their leadership again in the summer of 1936 after elections in May made the Socialists, for the first time, the largest group in the Chamber. Léon Blum, who was to become a close friend of Eden, formally became Prime Minister of the Popular Front Government on 18 June 1936. Eden's first meeting with Blum was on 15 May for talks on Abyssinia, an occasion marked by optimism and goodwill on both sides. Eden found a civilised and humane figure on the verge of power, and as he got to know Blum better he regretted that such a figure, with his resolute intellectual force, had not held the reins in France earlier. The chemistry between the two was at once apparent, helped by Blum's literary sensibilities and civilised aura. Eden later became a frequent guest in Blum's house on the Île-St-Louis in Paris, where he could browse in one of the finest private libraries in France. They exchanged treasures and gifts from their respective literary heritages. An Anatole France first edition, inscribed by the author to Blum, and then from Blum to Eden, matched a rare edition of Henry Fielding from Eden.[128]

A month after Blum became Prime Minister, the Civil War in Spain, which was to leave its tragic scars for many decades, broke out between the followers of the constitutional Republican Government and insurgent nationalists under the military leadership of General Franco. Blum was in London for a meeting with Eden on 22 July, about Locarno, inevitably subordinated to the developments in Spain. The Spanish Government had asked Blum for arms. Eden's warning, in Blum's words, was 'It's your business, but I beg you to be careful,'[129] the genesis of what became the Non-Intervention Committee of twenty-six nations, which met in London on 9 September. It was clear to Eden that the French Government wanted non-intervention, for otherwise the Popular Front government would collapse, since the Radicals could not countenance intervention. Yet had the powers kept to non-intervention, the Republic might well have won.

Eden agreed with the great Duke of Wellington that there was no European country in which foreigners could interfere with so little advantage as Spain, and his main aim, outlined in October 1936 at the Conservative Party conference at Llandudno, was one of non-intervention, but not indifference. His main concerns were to keep Italian intervention at bay and to maintain British freedom of commerce in the Mediterranean, a policy accepted by Blum, who became the architect of a wider non-intervention agreement, with Anglo-French solidarity at its core.

A Labour delegation, led by Arthur Greenwood, came to see Eden on 26 August to convey its misgivings. He told them that 'M. Blum's attitude had been the correct one and, indeed, a brave one in view of the situation in France. There was the European as well as the Spanish situation to consider. The last thing we wanted, more particularly just before entering upon a five-Power Conference, was the division of Europe into *blocs*.[130] Eden described his policy in the House of Commons on 29 October as 'an improvised safety curtain'[131] and the best means of limiting the escalation of the Spanish war, in which the Soviets, Germans and Italians were now actively participating, in various guises and with conflicting motives. But Eden's policy came at the cost of reconstruction of the Stresa front, an unrealistic concept by that stage, and any check on Germany's expansionist goals.

Not that Eden was under any illusions about Hitler's long-term aims. German and Italian archives show that on 3 September 1936, Count Grandi came into possession of thirty-seven documents Eden had prepared for the British Cabinet, collectively entitled 'The German Peril', which emphasised Eden's view that 'Hitler's foreign policy might be synthesised as the destruction of the order established by the peace treaties and the restoration of Germany to her dominant position in Europe'. As a result, Eden felt it was vital to complete British rearmament, whilst seeking a *modus vivendi* with Germany. Alerted by Grandi to the existence of these papers, Mussolini told Hitler of Eden's views, hoping that Ribbentrop could now be enlightened 'on what could be the result of his mission [to London]: England intends to *ménager* Germany only in order to gain time to complete her rearmament.'[132] At this stage, it was a moot point whether Eden was more loathed in Rome or Berlin.

November 1936 saw the establishment of the Rome-Berlin Axis, and the Anti-Comintern Pact between Germany and Japan to oppose international communism. Not all agreed with Eden that this posed the greatest threat to Russia. But when Italy joined the Anti-Comintern Pact the following year and left the League of Nations, Count Ciano, the Italian Foreign Minister and Mussolini's son-in-law, confided to his diary that the pact was 'unmistakably anti-British.'[133]

In this bitter-sweet year, Eden had two major diplomatic successes. One of these was the Egyptian Treaty, which had established the international character of the Suez Canal, recognised the Egyptian demands for independence, whilst at the same time guaranteeing British forces a presence in the Suez Canal Zone. Even more important was Eden's contribution at the Montreux Convention on 20 July over the delicate question of the passage of warships through the Dardanelles, a matter settled in a manner acceptable to Turkey, thus improving relations between the two countries, which brought substantial benefits for the Allies during the early years of the Second World War. One of Eden's severest critics has acknowledged that the convention 'constituted one of the most enduring and valuable, if generally underrated, of his achievements.'[134]

On a personal level, 1936 was also a bitter-sweet year for Eden. Memories of his childhood enthusiasm returned when Sunderland, for the first time in their history, won the FA Cup at Wembley Stadium, a feat they were to repeat unexpectedly as a Second Division team in 1973 in the last years of Eden's life. In the summer of 1936 Eden's thirty-ninth birthday coincided with the first of his honorary degrees, a DCL from Oxford, at the instigation of Lord Halifax, Oxford University's Chancellor.[135] At the Encaenia at the Sheldonian Theatre for the award, Eden was honoured alongside another future Prime Minister, Harold Wilson, who read from his winning undergraduate essay for the Gladstone Memorial Prize.[136]

Such pleasant interludes were more than counter-balanced by the protracted family row over the sale of Windlestone. His brother Tim had finally accepted the inevitable, but at the cost of acrimonious relations with their mother.

Simon, now twelve, was on the verge of going to Eton, where at first he was very unsettled. As Eden and his wife spent more time apart, Simon was the one who became closer to his father. Nicholas, nearly six, was more often in the company of his mother.

The year ended with the dramatic event that occupied Baldwin's waking thoughts to the exclusion of most other considerations, the Abdication of King Edward VIII to marry Mrs Simpson, a twice-divorced American. The importance of this episode in Eden's career lay in the deleterious effect it had on his relations with Churchill, who took the King's side. Eden, who had an essential reticence that set him apart from 'maverick' MPs (he was always wary of 'colourful backbenchers'), felt that Churchill had acted intemperately. Passions ran high and across party lines. Eden recorded Baldwin's feelings in Cabinet on 5 December. 'S. B. admitted to a "bloomer" in having agreed that Winston should see H[is] M[ajesty]', a meeting that led to Churchill's call for the King to be allowed more time. 'My chief concern,' wrote Eden, 'is that our position should be frankly &

clearly stated to the Empire in our H. of C. There is still considerable public misunderstanding, & this is dangerous.'[137]

Churchill intervened in Parliament on 7 December and 'was completely staggered,' noted Leo Amery, 'by the unanimous hostility of the House, as well as being called to order by the Speaker.'[138] Eden could well understand the personal dilemma the King faced, but his view was essentially that of Queen Mary, who articulated the feelings of many when she later wrote to her son in exile, 'It seemed inconceivable to those who had made such sacrifices during the war that you, as their King, refused a lesser sacrifice.'[139]

The King signed the Instrument of Abdication on 10 December, broadcast to the nation (his most memorable phrase about 'the woman I love' coming from Churchill) and then sailed into exile.

Eden had his first audience with the new King, George VI, on 17 December, after a discreet briefing from the King's private secretary, Sir Alexander Hardinge. 'I am sure that he is a trier,' he wrote afterwards, 'very like his father even in his writing & he may do very well given time to gain confidence. He was a little shy, so that on Alec's advice I prattled away. He was frank & not a little touching about his brother. "I have always been to him about everything, even more than to my father when he was alive."' After the audience, Eden had a long talk with Alec Hardinge, a sign of how he was now becoming something of a fixture in court circles.[140] Among Cabinet ministers, the Foreign Secretary has a special place in dealings with the Monarch and contact can be a sustained experience even beyond that built up by the Prime Minister in weekly audiences. Eden was determined that his relations with the new King should be fruitful ones. Whereas some may have thought Eden, with his charisma and dashing good looks, was more akin to Edward VIII, actually he shared distinct characteristics with George VI – both were somewhat reserved in public, called to high responsibility suddenly, but not entirely unexpectedly, and had a deep concern to do what was good for the country's well-being.

The cruise on the *Nahlin* in the summer of 1936 had seen the first disagreement between King Edward VIII and his Foreign Secretary, as the original itinerary involved a journey calling at various ports in Italy. Eden personally explained why this was undesirable, and it rankled. 'I was not quite sure which he feared most,' the Duke of Windsor wrote fifteen years later, 'that I might be jeered at by the Italians, because my Government had imposed sanctions, which would be bad for British prestige, or that I might be cheered by the same people as a friend of Italy, which would have offended the faithful supporters of the League of Nations.'[141]

Eden felt that the transition from one brother to the next, though painful, was ultimately providential. He came to admire greatly George

VI's spirit and bravery, particularly in overcoming his marked stammer, and his earlier attempts at fostering understanding between different classes through the Duke of York's camps at Southwold, a social experiment that appealed to the Skeltonian side of Eden's nature. For his part, George VI reciprocated and a sense of trust grew up between them. Queen Elizabeth was resistant, suspecting that Eden had too much of the 'film star' about him, but eventually his natural courtesy and gentlemanly reticence were to win the day.[142]

The activities of the Duke of Windsor (as Edward VIII became) were to cause the Foreign Office endless difficulties. As he passed through various European countries, ambassadors telegrammed home for advice, not least when he proposed a visit to Hitler in October 1937. As Foreign Secretary Eden had to lay down the ground-rules for the new situation. After consultations with the Palace, it was established that 'as a general line Eden feels that our representatives should treat the Duke of Windsor and his wife rather as they would a member of the Royal family on a holiday; but that if anything were contemplated which might give to the visit a more serious aspect, our representatives must necessarily refer home.'[143] Subsequent despatches were not without their revealing details, as in the report on the Duke's meeting with Hitler, when Eden was told that great offence had been taken that 'no tips were given at the Kaiserhof where he stayed.'[144]

Parliament met for the first time in the new reign on 14 December, George VI's forty-first birthday. The opening business of the reign was a parliamentary answer from Eden on the situation in Japan.*

The turn of the year saw Eden focusing on important ambassadorships. 'It is vital that our personnel in the F.O. & diplomatic service should be posted to best advantage, & Van's place in that scheme of things is Paris', he wrote to Baldwin over Christmas. 'The difficulty will come if he cannot be persuaded to see his duty as we see it.'[145]†

---

*By chance, Eden was also to bring down the parliamentary curtain on the King's sixteen-year reign, speaking on 5 February 1952, in a two-day Foreign Affairs Debate, the last parliamentary business during George VI's lifetime, which came to an unexpected end in the early hours of the next morning.

†Eden always took great care over this responsibility (as he did with bishoprics when Prime Minister), both in appointing British envoys and accrediting foreign ones. Edward VIII had not been helpful over the new Spanish Ambassador the previous April, because the proposed appointee was divorced (ironic in the light of subsequent developments). Eden hoped that 'despite the difficulty in regard to the divorce', the Spanish submission, already announced in Madrid, would be acceptable. The Palace pointed out that 'the other day we had made a rather similar request in respect of a Siamese and if this went on there would soon be no knowing whom we had here as foreign representatives'. The record continues: 'The Palace were most anxious to avoid doing anything which might give grounds for people to say that the moral standards observed in this reign were a great deal less strict than they had been in the time of the late king.' The name was eventually accepted with reluctance. FO 954/vol. 27, fol. 10-11.

Eden was anxious to have Cadogan as Permanent Under-Secretary; but Vansittart saw Paris as a demotion.[146] 'A talk with S. B. in the morning,' Eden noted with some exasperation. 'Said he had seen & spoken to Van & told him straight that it was his duty to go to Paris. I thought so, so did he. None the less he was not sanguine; nor did he think him in good trim. "I doubt if he feels he can do Paris". "Then clearly he cannot do the harder job of London."' Sir Eric Phipps went to Paris instead.*

Conversation also turned to Sam Hoare, who had unexpectedly returned to high office as First Lord of the Admiralty in a limited reshuffle on 5 June 1936. Eden complained about Hoare's manoeuvrings behind his back. 'He was a born intriguer & wanted to be P.M.', he told Baldwin. '"Well he must be mad,"' replied Baldwin, assuring Eden there was no such possibility.[147]

Phipps's move to Paris in place of the reluctant Vansittart left a vacancy in Berlin. The question of his replacement was clearly crucial. For the only time in his career, Eden appointed an Ambassador whom he had never met personally. The view of the service was that Sir Nevile Henderson, Ambassador in Buenos Aires, was the best candidate, largely because of his success in dealing with King Alexander when Ambassador in Yugoslavia. Vansittart was strongly in favour. The other candidates considered were Sir Miles Lampson, formerly High Commissioner, and now the first Ambassador in Egypt, and Sir Percy Loraine, Ambassador in Turkey. Following the Egyptian Treaty, Eden did not think it right to ask Lampson to move so soon. In an unguarded moment, Sir Percy Loraine had let it be known that he regarded Ankara as a 'godforsaken hole'; his translation might imply official sanction of his opinion. So, relying on reports from within the service, Eden appointed Henderson in January 1937. Henderson's own reaction, when he decoded the telegram from London, was 'a sense of my own inadequacy for what was obviously the most difficult and most important post in the whole of the diplomatic service',[148] a sense not dispelled by later events. In retrospect, Eden considered this appointment, and its manner, the biggest mistake of his pre-war Foreign Secretaryship.

One of his best appointments, in December 1937, was that of the radical diplomat, Archibald Clark Kerr, to China, a sensitive and important post, to which he rightly thought Clark Kerr would bring special qualities.[149]

*

---

*At a farewell tea with the Goerings, Sir Eric Phipps and his wife were entertained by 'the little children of our amiable host and hostess executing dances to the strains of an old-world musical box'. Sir Eric Phipps to Anthony Eden, 13 April 1937. Despatch No. 241 [C 2840/78/18].

At a meeting of Ministers on 8 January, Eden presented a memorandum on the Spanish Civil War, warning that it had ceased to be an internal Spanish issue and had become an international battleground for Nazi adventures. 'It is to be remembered that in the language of the Nazi party any adventure is a minor adventure.' With prescience, he continued, 'they spoke thus of the Rhineland last year, they are speaking thus of Spain today, they will speak thus of Memel, Danzig or Czechoslovakia tomorrow.'[150]

As the situation worsened with the bombing of Guernica on 26 April, with the loss of 1,645 lives, Eden was appalled by how much of his time was taken up with ticklish problems of protocol, some deriving from the Duke of Windsor's excursions through Europe, others from the invitations to his brother's coronation on 12 May. The Italians had raised objections to the Emperor of Abyssinia being invited. Eden pointed out to Sir Eric Drummond in Rome that 'there is no question of the Emperor himself attending Coronation, any more than any other crowned head . . . to have made special exception to rule by not sending invitation to Emperor would have been a definite initiative on part of His Majesty's Government towards *de jure* recognition of the annexation of Abyssinia and would have been regarded in this country as such.'[151]

Invitations to Buckingham Palace in coronation week were also fraught with diplomatic difficulties, especially over the Italian Prince of Piedmont. Eden warned the Palace of the Italians' hidden agenda in sending the Prince. 'What in truth the Italians are asking us to do is to take a step in the *de jure* recognition of Italy's conquest of Abyssinia in advance of all other members of the League.'[152]

Coronation week saw Eden and his wife hosting several functions; the service itself in Westminster Abbey, a respite from these representational duties, was conducted by Cosmo Gordon Lang, who had married the Edens in 1923 in neighbouring St Margaret's.* A fortnight later Neville Chamberlain succeeded Baldwin as Prime Minister.

Neville Chamberlain's dominance in Cabinet in the early months of 1937, together with his spell as acting Premier during Baldwin's illness the previous year, meant that he was the only possible successor to Baldwin. Chamberlain was fortunate in the timing, if not ultimately the agenda, of his inheritance. He had been the likeliest heir apparent since the time of the Ottawa Conference of 1932, and the changeover was relatively smooth. The most poignant aspect was that Austen Chamberlain did not live to see

---

*Uniquely, Eden was Foreign Secretary at two Coronations, that of King George VI on 12 May 1937, and that of Queen Elizabeth II on 2 June 1953, though post-operative convalescence prevented him from attending the service in 1953.

his half-brother in 10 Downing Street. He had died suddenly at his home in London on 16 March. Eden wrote to Austen Chamberlain's widow, Ivy, from the Foreign Office. 'For however long or short a time it may be my destiny to sit at this desk, it will be his standards and his teaching that I shall seek to follow.'[153]*

As Lord Salisbury had done in 1902, Baldwin retired full of years and honours in a coronation summer. The long-expected handover came on 28 May. Had anything befallen Neville Chamberlain during Baldwin's last months, Eden would almost certainly have been chosen as Prime Minister – a tantalising 'What if?' of modern political history. When Robert Menzies, the Australian Attorney-General (and later Prime Minister), was visiting London, Baldwin had spoken to him about the longer-term leadership of the Conservative Party, asserting that there were 'only two in it' – Eden and, somewhat surprisingly, W. S. 'Shakes' Morrison. Baldwin's one doubt was, as Eden wrote, 'whether I wanted it (I had told him I had not).'[154] However, the fact that the matter had been discussed at all showed that Eden was considered *papabile* by the Conservative hierarchy.

Baldwin's retirement marked the end of the initial phase of Eden's first spell as Foreign Secretary. With Baldwin he was an appointed protégé, 'Baldwin's curly-headed boy' as one observer described him;[155] under Neville Chamberlain, he was an inherited fixture. The distinction was to prove increasingly important. Where Baldwin was relaxed and easy-going, albeit at times frustrating in his detachment from foreign-policy concerns, Chamberlain (aided and abetted by his *éminence grise*, Sir Horace Wilson) wished to strengthen Downing Street's involvement in Eden's sphere of activity. Not surprisingly Eden resented this incursion into his bailiwick. Although he admired Chamberlain's contributions, particularly as Minister of Health, to the field of domestic social improvement – his own Skeltonian agenda – he did not feel that Chamberlain, after six years at the Treasury, had enough knowledge of the diplomatic issues, though he understood Chamberlain's wish for tighter political control after the relaxations of Baldwin's last phase.

The period from May 1937 to February 1938 was to prove the making of Eden's reputation. Under Baldwin, Eden had been finding his feet in the international arena and by and large proved a reactive figure, often continuing the policy initiatives of Hoare, particularly over Abyssinia. By the time of Chamberlain's premiership, Eden was more proactive.

Churchill famously said that Chamberlain would come badly out of history, because he (Churchill) would be writing the history. As a result,

---

*Ironically, before the year was out, the unofficial diplomacy of Dame Ivy Chamberlain in Italy was to prove one of the contributory factors to Eden's premature departure from the Foreign Office.

The Gathering Storm (1948) underlined the public perception of Eden as the leading anti-appeasement figure of the inter-war period, after, inevitably, Churchill himself. But even here there was a blurring of the grey edges of historical truth. It is not generally appreciated that, after Eden's resignation in February 1938, Churchill signed a round-robin letter, supporting Chamberlain's stance, and reassured the Chief Whip, David Margesson, that 'he felt sure that the Prime Minister's point of view on the present foreign situation and his own were not divergent.'[156]

Chamberlain's Cabinet changes were minimal. He needed a new Chancellor and other consequential changes sufficed. To the satisfaction of the National Liberals, if few others, John Simon completed the then unique triptych of the 'great' offices of state on his appointment to the Treasury. Sam Hoare had advised Chamberlain to have a Cabinet as unlike the previous one as possible – advice obviously ignored in his case, for when he moved from the Admiralty to the Home Office, the old guard were still very much in place. Duff Cooper took Hoare's place at the Admiralty, the post that Eden had so long coveted, but which he had now overleaped. Ramsay MacDonald, who was to die in November, took his final leave, and was replaced as Lord President of the Council by Halifax, an increasingly important figure. Had Chamberlain been bolder, this would have been the time to promote figures such as Cranborne. Harold Macmillan, who came to prominence later, had resigned the whip when sanctions had been removed from Italy the previous year and was also opposed to the National Government's domestic policy, so he stayed on the back-benches. As a result, Eden remained the undoubted leader of the younger ministerial generation, though never an acknowledged deputy in the way Chamberlain had been for Baldwin from 1935 to 1937. Eden was a focus also for the hopes of those outside Cabinet, who, like him, strongly supported collective security and resistance to dictators. Nevertheless, Eden's relative lack of seniority for a great office of state meant that many colleagues felt they had a better claim to the post. At such times Eden remembered Baldwin's reassurance that whereas there were twenty potential Foreign Secretaries in Cabinet, only one aspired to be Minister of Labour.[157] It was something he had to live with. Even so, Eden could not have expected to have his two predecessors – John Simon and Sam Hoare – sitting alongside him in Cabinet.

At first, Eden welcomed Chamberlain's robustness and his decisiveness in managing the Cabinet agenda. Baldwin had been a fading figure, with much of the responsibility devolving upon Chamberlain in 11 Downing Street, and initially there seemed a greater purpose and direction to Government business. On 26 March, a few weeks before Chamberlain's accession to 10 Downing Street, Eden had visited him, confined to his bed at the time, for a long talk about the new dispositions. Eden reported favourably on the meeting to Oliver Harvey, who noted in his diary:

> He found him in very good spirits and looking forward to becoming Prime Minister. He told A. E. he intended to give him much more support at F.O. than he had had hitherto. He had also been impressed by memo A. E. had sent him on necessity of relaxing our Ottawa obligations somewhat in order to facilitate foreign economic relations. Chancellor agreed as to necessity of some relaxation, although he believed trade ties did help to keep the Dominions with us ... A. E. thought Neville Chamberlain had makings of a really great Prime Minister if only his health held out. I said 'if he isn't too grim': but A. E. thought this need not necessarily matter: he had a grip of affairs which Stanley Baldwin had never had.[158]

With such high hopes, Eden embarked on service under his third Prime Minister. These hopes were soon to be disappointed.

CHAPTER SEVEN

The Path to Resignation
1937–8

> I fear the difference between Anthony and me is more
> fundamental than he realises. At bottom he is really dead against
> making terms with the dictators.
> Neville Chamberlain to Hilda Chamberlain, 15 October 1938[1]

> I fear that fundamentally the difficulty is that N. believes that he
> is a man with a mission to come to terms with the Dictators.
> Anthony Eden diary, 17 January 1938[2]

Neville Chamberlain and Anthony Eden were regarded, by colleagues and opponents alike, as the twin assets of the new administration. Measures to assist economic renewal, culminating in the Special Areas Act of 1937, had contributed to Chamberlain's high standing after six years at the Treasury. By September 1937, unemployment was at its lowest level for eight years. In foreign affairs, Eden was in a position of strength following Sam Hoare's demise, and was one of only six ministers to retain his portfolio. He remained the most prominent protagonist of collective security through the League of Nations, and the focus of many hopes. Where reassurance was needed, Chamberlain and Eden proved a comforting duo.

The year of 1937 seemed to promise better times. Renewal took different forms, from Butlin's first holiday camp at Skegness to Lord Nuffield's £1 million donation to fund a postgraduate college in Oxford. Unemployment fell, even in the distressed areas, though often through workers settling elsewhere.* Apart from the continuing conflict in Spain, Europe appeared unnaturally quiescent, and there were signs of cautious relief that foreign dangers had not reignited dramatically. Eden did not share such optimism.

Among traditionalists, there was relief that the monarchy had stabilised under a new king, George VI, with his two young daughters, who embodied family virtues. The Coronation Naval Review at Spithead on 20 May seemed a nostalgic echo of a glorious past, though many of the ships were ageing hulks from the Great War that revealed to keen foreign eyes the ill-equipped nature of the British Fleet. The contrasting presence of the

---

*18,000 unemployed workers received special assistance in 1937, and a further 13,000 moved 'unofficially'.

German pocket battleship *Graf Spee*, far from appearing a portentous threat, added to the glamour of the occasion and appeared to be a sign of greater Anglo-German rapport. 'The fleet's lit up,' reported the BBC commentator with memorable enthusiasm, adding, which was certainly true in his own case, 'we're all lit up'.[3] Sober truth was in time to bring a harsher reality.

In no area was this disillusionment swifter than over the League of Nations. 'The long and short of it,' Cuthbert Headlam had already forecast, 'is that collective security is only another name for an alliance on the continent sufficiently strong to preserve the balance of power, and that the League of Nations is a sham and a delusion so long as some of the Great Powers are outside it'. He doubted whether even Eden paid more than lip service to the two concepts – 'he is wise enough to see at last that neither of these things mean anything at all'.[4]

Chamberlain increasingly came to favour personal contact, as a means of bypassing the intricate structures of Geneva, a preference that culminated in his three visits to Hitler.

Chamberlain and Eden had much in common. Thorough and conscientious in their methods of working, and with long apprenticeship in their chosen fields, they shared a genuine sense of social concern. The Jarrow Crusade the previous year had struck a deep chord with both men, particularly Eden with his North-East links. Their constituencies were in the heart of middle England, geographically and politically, which gave them a non-metropolitan perspective. Health and housing were important issues to both. As young men, both had experience of remote lands, from Andros to Australia. Outside political life, they were exceptionally knowledgeable about Shakespeare, and sensitive to the wisdom to be found in books. Both were accused of vanity by their opponents, though nowhere in Eden's papers does one find a remark such as Chamberlain made to his sister Ida in August 1937, 'I have only to raise a finger and the whole face of Europe is changed!'[5]

But there were important differences. Although both wanted to keep Britain out of a European war, especially one involving Germany, they could not agree on the best means of achieving this. As an isolationist, Chamberlain believed that England could survive even if the balance of power on the Continent was irredeemably destroyed, and his defence policy underpinned isolation. Eden, like Churchill, favoured a balance of power in Europe.

Temperamentally, too, Chamberlain and Eden were poles apart. Chamberlain was sixty-eight when he became Prime Minister; Eden was nearing forty, a vast generational divide and one that meant Eden had direct experience of war and no residual feelings of guilt, because he had personally faced the terror and carnage, and fought for his country.

Chamberlain had a fixity of purpose that brooked no interference. Sir Horace Wilson, initially an industrial adviser in Baldwin's day, but now Chamberlain's right-hand man on foreign affairs, felt this vein of obstinacy was one of his strengths. 'The Prime Minister,' he wrote, 'was always ready to consider carefully views and arguments put before him and he took time before making up his mind what course to follow.' However, as Eden was soon to find out, 'when that course was settled he did not wonder whether it was right and whether it would have been better to decide to try something else.'[6]

Eden was less unwavering, more willing to travel the long road, the diplomat rather than the autocrat. His natural courtesy and charm could smooth over differences, but whereas Chamberlain rarely seemed ruffled, Eden could be volatile when standards fell short of the perfectionism he so prized. His flash of anger after the Press coverage of his Berlin visit fulfilled a therapeutic need – he had 'felt better' after sounding off – though he rarely let the sun go down on his wrath. And he was the opposite of Chamberlain in other ways. Chamberlain's background was in the science and engineering of Mason College, Birmingham, not the urbanities of Peck Quad.

A man of sixty-eight cannot change his character overnight. Chamberlain expected political agreement to be like business practice, where your word was your bond. He had met many dubious figures in his business life, but a contract, even a verbal one, was inviolable. 'In God we trust,' quipped the more hard-bitten, 'the rest pay cash.' Chamberlain, for instance, believed that if some Italian 'volunteers' withdrew from Spain, this might go some way to legitimising Italy's presence in Abyssinia; Eden realistically knew this would never happen until Mussolini knew that Franco had triumphed. To his surprise, Eden soon missed Baldwin's avuncular presence. 'He did much to kill class hatred and unite the country,' he wrote later. 'He did not understand the storms that raged without, nor did he make Neville's mistake of believing that he did.'[7]

More important than differences in temperament, were those in outlook. It could never be said of Eden, as Lloyd George and Attlee had said respectively of Chamberlain, that 'he saw foreign policy through the wrong end of a municipal drainpipe', and that he was like a wireless permanently 'tuned to Midland Regional.'[8]

Eden, who still believed that Mussolini was an aggressor, had Italy reclassified as a potential enemy. Chamberlain felt that some accommodation with Italy was both possible and desirable, and became increasingly irritated by what he saw as the obstructiveness of the Foreign Office.* 'I believe the double policy of rearmament and better relations with Germany and Italy will carry us safely through the danger period,' he wrote, 'if only the F.O. will play up.'[9] Eden doubted such certainties, as he reckoned Mussolini's word meant nothing.

Eden's rapid rise over his contemporaries had left Roger Lumley, whom Eden had succeeded eleven years earlier as PPS to Austen Chamberlain, becalmed at the same level. Lumley's move to the governorship of Bombay was, in essence, a form of extra-parliamentary compensation. Jim (J.P.L.) Thomas's appointment as Eden's PPS stemmed from Baldwin's last month, and the Chamberlain team had ulterior motives for welcoming it. Warren Fisher, with whom Eden had already clashed over ambassadorships, and Horace Wilson saw Thomas as their possible eyes and ears in the Foreign Office. They soon summoned him to a private meeting. Thomas has left a record of his reactions:

> I had known Horace Wilson for some years and he had been particularly helpful to me during the period when my former Chief, J. H. Thomas, was involved in the inquiry about a leakage of Budget secrets. I had no idea as to why Warren Fisher wanted to speak to me but it was soon made clear during tea that both he and Sir Horace Wilson were thoroughly dissatisfied with the working of the Foreign Office and especially with Robert Vansittart. They pointed out that Van was an alarmist; that he delayed all attempts which the Government wished to make to get in friendly contact with the Dictator States, and that his influence upon Anthony Eden was very great.
>
> They told me that they had strongly backed the suggestion that I should become P.P.S. at the F.O. because I was known to Horace Wilson and at 10 Downing Street, and that Horace Wilson and I would be in a position to build a bridge between the two departments to make a better understanding between them and try to minimise the damage done by the present attitude of Van and the Foreign Office in general.
>
> I replied that this was placing me in a most awkward position, for although I did not even know Van and held no particular brief for him, it seemed to me that I was expected to work behind the back of my own chief. Whereupon Warren Fisher and H. W. toned down their suggestions and said that all they wanted to know was my personal opinion of the capabilities of some of the leading officials in the Foreign Office and again asked for my help in creating good will between the F.O. and No. 10.[10]

*In the long history of mistrust between 10 Downing Street and the Foreign Office, the Chamberlain/Eden period has its special place, alongside such troubled alliances as Lloyd George and Curzon, Churchill and Halifax, Harold Wilson and George Brown, Margaret Thatcher and both Geoffrey Howe and Francis Pym, and, of course, Eden himself and Macmillan in 1955. See Chapter 16 for an analysis of the intricacies of the Eden/Macmillan relationship.

The transparency of Wilson's approach was what offended Thomas most. It was not a propitious start and did not bode well for improvement of relations between Number 10 and the Foreign Office, ostensibly the motive for the meeting. The next day Wilson backtracked and said that, owing to Warren Fisher's impulsiveness, he did not think Thomas had obtained a clear view of what was wanted. Thomas replied that, on the contrary, the view was only too clear.

Initial differences of approach between Chamberlain and Eden could be seen during the Imperial Conference, held in London from 14 May to 15 June, when leading Dominion figures were in London for the coronation. Eden believed that everything should be done to secure American co-operation, even if only for its psychological effect upon the dictators, whereas Chamberlain felt such support to be superfluous. At the opening session of the conference, Eden emphasised that 'the United States were ready to help so far as they possibly could'[11] – not Chamberlain's view at all, or, as later emerged, America's either. But Eden talked it up, as though it were an accomplished fact, in speeches at the conference and in Aberdeen. One American historian has even claimed that Eden at this stage 'made Anglo-American co-operation the supreme goal of British policy'.[12]

Eden was determined that differences should not arise over Japan, a potentially dangerous question, and was to ask the British Ambassador in Washington, Sir Ronald Lindsay, to provide him with a comprehensive account of how the Roosevelt administration's policies were developing, how it might react to future events and any pitfalls of which he should be aware.[13] Chamberlain was not so sure this was the right approach, at least until the Japanese attack on American and British shipping in December in the Yangtze, but by that time the Brussels Conference (over which Eden had consulted the American Ambassador in London in advance, about Roosevelt's views) had been and gone, and an opportunity missed.[14]

Anglo-American relations were not the only source of disagreement between Chamberlain and Eden. Central to their eventual break was the divergence of opinion on Italy, as Mussolini continued to press for *de jure* recognition of his Abyssinian conquest, which was anathema to Eden, who had seen clandestine Italian moves in this direction already during the coronation festivities. British imperial defence policy was not, in Eden's view, going to be helped by such recognition. However, Chamberlain laid great stress on his personal approaches to Mussolini, and, as is now clear, this only increased Mussolini's contempt for Britain, as was also to be the case with Chamberlain's overtures to Hitler. When Chamberlain visited Rome in January 1939, Mussolini concluded that these men were not the conquistadors of the age of Raleigh. 'People who carry an umbrella,' he said, 'can never found an empire.'[15]

As Chamberlain continued to woo Mussolini, initially through Grandi and Ciano, Eden was now focusing far more on Anglo-German relations, belatedly as his critics in Cabinet considered. Chamberlain had a vain hope that Italy could be detached from Germany and he thought that by this means he could have saved Austria. This was never a realistic proposition. Increasingly Chamberlain and Eden were like ships that passed in the night, trawling the familiar lanes, recognising each other's lights through the gloom and avoiding collison, but essentially under different flags. In Cabinet on 2 June Eden had pressed for an invitation to von Neurath, the German Foreign Minister, for talks in London on the Spanish Civil War and 'a general review of the international situation.'[16] After initial acceptance, Berlin prevaricated, and the visit was postponed. The British Government's case on Spain, to maintain the peace of Europe by confining the war to Spain, 'extremely well put by [Ernest] Bevin at an International Socialists Rally', as Eden recorded in his diary,[17] was certainly a contributory factor. But what worried Chamberlain was how Eden's approach to Berlin had caused unease in Rome, hampering efforts at a rapprochement with Mussolini.

When Chamberlain, rather than Eden, spoke in the Commons on the matter on 25 June, Berlin made sure this was interpreted as a sign of a rift between Chamberlain and Eden. Nevile Henderson, now installed in the embassy in Berlin, told Eden that 'certain circles' in Germany were using the situation 'to set up the Prime Minister as against yourself'.[18] Although this was exaggerated, Chamberlain was against Eden's approval of Australian proposals for a Pacific Pact on the island territories in the Far East, which he (rightly) thought would have little impact on Japan, the third potential aggressor against British worldwide interests. 'We are having a frightful time at the Imperial Conference', Maurice Hankey wrote to his son Robin, who as a former Secretary had first-hand knowledge of Eden's methods. 'A. E. chucked a spanner into a most critical situation today, and wrecked the P.M.'s most promising efforts at a solution. The P.M. is very annoyed with him.'[19]

Annoyance was also felt in 'official' England with the Duke of Windsor's choice of date for his wedding to Mrs Simpson at the Château Candé in France, as 3 June would have been the late King's seventy-second birthday. Eden hoped that a line would now be drawn under any controversy relating to the Duke of Windsor, but that particular loose cannon was to trouble him till the end of the war.

The genesis of the final break between Chamberlain and Eden can be traced back to this Imperial Conference and their divergences over Germany, Italy and Japan. Though Eden, in Hankey's opinion, had 'great charm and parliamentary gifts of a high order', he felt that he was 'much too subservient to France and the minor nations', and proved an important 'doubter' in the Chamberlain circle.[20]

One thing Chamberlain and Eden did agree on was Vansittart, but from opposite vantage points. Eden had long resented Vansittart's condescension, and differed fundamentally with him over possible Italian aggression. Chamberlain feared Vansittart's rabid anti-Germanism might sabotage his attempts at personal diplomacy, and was mistrustful of Van's influence over Eden. As a result Chamberlain began to bypass Eden, whose principles were a hindrance in Chamberlain's push for Anglo-Italian rapprochement, and through Sir Joseph Ball, Director of the Conservative Research Department, arranged a series of private meetings with Count Grandi, the Italian Ambassador in London. After his own personal meeting with Grandi on 27 July, Chamberlain sent a letter to Mussolini, which ended, 'I wish to assure you that this Government is actuated by the most friendly feelings towards Italy and will be ready at any time to enter upon conversations with a view to clarifying the whole situation and removing all causes of suspicion or misunderstanding.'[21]

Chamberlain later admitted, 'I did not show my letter to the Foreign Secretary, for I had the feeling that he would object to it.'[22]

No political relationship could long survive such subterfuge. What further complicated the matter was that Dame Ivy Chamberlain, Sir Austen's widow, now embarked on a programme of 'unofficial diplomacy' with the Duce in Rome, with the knowledge and encouragement of her brother-in-law. The combination of Horace Wilson's influence and the non-specialist intrusions of Ivy Chamberlain was to undermine Eden's position fatally.

August can be the cruellest political month and so it proved for Eden in 1937. He had taken 'Stanswood', a house near Southampton Water, for the family holiday. There was tennis and swimming with the boys, and walks among the pine trees by the sea, just the kind of relaxation he needed. In Eden's absence, Chamberlain pressed on with his Italian overtures and put Halifax, the Lord Privy Seal, in charge of day-to-day Foreign Office business. Eden was soon disturbed by the tenor of routine telegrams that pursued him, even on holiday. 'We should decline to be rushed into conversations,' he wrote to Halifax, inviting him down to Stanswood to talk things over. 'I am very reluctant to recognise "de jure" conquest.'[23] Halifax was now cast in the role of reluctant go-between. At Cabinet on 8 September Eden insisted that any *de jure* settlement could only come as part of a general settlement with Italy, an unlikely conclusion following Italy's unprovoked attacks on oil tankers in the Mediterranean.[24] For once, Chamberlain and Eden were in accord. The situation worsened after the sinking of the British tanker SS *Woodford* on 2 September with loss of life.

The Nyon Conference, which convened near Geneva on 10 September, was a response to the widespread anger and anxiety felt throughout Europe over this urgent need to protect Mediterranean shipping routes against piracy. Its proceedings were dominated by Eden and his French opposite number, Yvon Delbos. Although Italy and Germany were absent, ten nations (including Russia, victims of much of the piracy), attended. Mussolini ensured personally that Ciano would not meet Eden or Delbos. 'It is possible that the Russians desired to prevent the Germans and Italians from attending the Conference,' Eden explained in one of his regular despatches to King George VI. 'If this were their objective they have now realised it.'[25]

The outcome of the Nyon Conference was a considerable personal triumph for Eden, and notably even-handed. It showed what might have been achieved in the long term, if Eden's approach had been persevered with. The Italians were even granted an area to patrol. The downside for Eden personally was that the determined Anglo-French accord in the face of Italian aggression flew in the face of Chamberlain's earlier assurances to Grandi and Mussolini. 'The really important political fact,' Eden wrote to Churchill four days later, so swiftly was agreement reached at Nyon, 'is that we have emphasised that co-operation between Britain and France can be so effective and that the two Western democracies can still play a decisive part in European affairs.'[26]

Nyon therefore had a singular effect, on the one hand enhancing Eden's popularity in the country, whilst simultaneously undermining his position with Chamberlain. Churchill's praise of Eden's handling of the Nyon conference at the Conservative Party Conference in Scarborough on 7 October thus proved to be counter-productive.

Six days later there was a new development that in the long term was to widen the rift between Prime Minister and Foreign Secretary even further. On 13 October Halifax received an invitation to visit Germany, in his personal capacity as Master of the Middleton Foxhounds, for a hunting exhibition in Berlin arranged by Hermann Goering as Game Warden of the Reich. Halifax sought Eden's agreement to accept the invitation on 14 October. Indeed, after the war Halifax emphasised that both Chamberlain and Eden had urged him to go.[27] The rebuff over the Von Neurath initiative, far from discouraging Chamberlain from further personal contact with German leaders, led him to welcome this invitation as an opportunity for exploratory talks.

Goering did nothing by halves, and the hunting festivities, with excursions to the Black Forest in pursuit of wild boar, were no exception.

His taste for excess was the subject of much discreet humour in Berlin at the time. The motorist who supposedly ran into Goering's car on a dark night was acquitted, on the grounds that the Field Marshal had 'forgotten to dim his decorations'. Another story going the rounds was that 'The English have so many aeroplanes that the sky is black with them, and the French ones are so numerous that you can't see the sun for them; but when Hermann Gœring presses the button, the birds themselves have got to walk.'[28]

When a further invitation came for Halifax to visit Hitler at the Berghof at Berchtesgaden, alarm bells began to ring in the Foreign Office. So concerned were senior officials that a private meeting was held at Eden's house on 7 November to discuss the implications. Chamberlain had conveniently portrayed calling on Hitler as a mere courtesy following the hunting schedule, but that was not the Foreign Office view. 'None of us liked the idea of the Halifax visit', recorded Oliver Harvey.[29]

Vansittart also (he had not been at the private meeting) was bitterly opposed to the initiative, a welcome underlining for Eden's group of the view that to be seen to woo the Führer would give entirely the wrong signals. Writing from Brussels, where he was attending the Nine Power Conference on the Far East, Eden had emphasised to Chamberlain 'that we have got to meet the challenges of the dictators and that to do so we have to be strong in armaments.'[30] Few foresaw the pace of the inevitable conclusion, but as his biographer has written, 'Halifax became the involuntary catalyst for the eventual break up between Prime Minister and Foreign Secretary.'[31]

Eden saw Chamberlain the next morning, a meeting which, he told Oliver Harvey, 'went very badly'. Chamberlain had ended by suggesting that Eden go home and take an aspirin. After a heated correspondence, Chamberlain, with great insensitivity, pressed Eden, who had only recently returned from Stanswood, to take a holiday.

Jim Thomas was so concerned that he saw Horace Wilson privately. It was made clear to Thomas that Chamberlain was going to press ahead with attempts to meet the dictators personally, and that far from being jealous of the Foreign Office, he was saving Eden from himself.[32] 'The majority of the Cabinet are against A. E.', wrote Harvey of his master's increasing isolation from Chamberlain's inner counsels. 'His supporters in the Cabinet are flabby or unassertive, i.e. Stanley, MacDonald, Elliot, De La Warr; his opponents, Simon, Sam Hoare, Kingsley Wood, Swinton, Hailsham, are important and effective.'[33]

Halifax went, nonetheless, to the Berghof. Stepping from his car on arrival, the tall, patrician Halifax was on the verge of handing his coat to a small, unimposing figure he assumed to be a retainer, when von Neurath whispered anxiously, 'Der Führer, der Führer.'[34]

Eden had told Halifax to 'confine himself to warning comments on Austria and Czechoslovakia', but when Halifax gave the Foreign Secretary a written record of the meeting on his return to London on 22 November, Eden was aghast to see a reference to 'possible alterations in the European order which might be destined to come about with the passage of time. Amongst these questions were Danzig, Austria and Czechoslovakia.'[35]

The officials who had met at Eden's house on 7 November had been correct in their foreboding, and in retrospect Eden accepted that his own position had been weakened and that it had been a major mistake to have agreed to a disastrous visit that did much damage through Halifax's ill-advised comments to Hitler.

The speedy agreement at Nyon was not replicated when the Nine Power Conference on the Far East convened at Brussels from 3 to 24 November. Eden believed that only Anglo-American cooperation could satisfactorily address Japanese expansionism, and he welcomed American participation in the conference. But the exact American position was unclear. On 5 October, Roosevelt had delivered the so-called 'quarantine' speech in Chicago. 'The epidemic of world lawlessness is spreading,' the President said. 'When an epidemic of physical disease starts to spread, the community approves and joins in a quarantine of the patients in order to protect the health of the community against the spread of the disease.'[36] Eden asked Norman Davis, the United States representative in Brussels, for clarification, but the reply only seemed to confirm Chamberlain's earlier view that one could count on the Americans only for words. The 'quarantine' speech had raised a storm of protest among American isolationists, and Cordell Hull, the American Secretary of State, was prominent among those who dampened down any expectation that this indicated American willingness to take hostile action against aggressor nations. 'The truth is that here again there is a divergence between A. E. and P.M.,' wrote Oliver Harvey, 'as latter is strongly opposed to any sort of economic boycott in the Far East even with U.S.A. A. E., on the other hand, would welcome joint action with U.S.A.'[37] Indeed, in a statement in the Commons two days before he travelled to Brussels, Eden had written, 'To get the full co-operation on an equal basis of the United States Government in an international Conference, I would travel, not only from Geneva to Brussels, but from Melbourne to Alaska.'[38]

Not surprisingly the Japanese Government was deaf to Hull's polite diplomatic appeals and, not for the last time in his career, Eden was to be disappointed by the response of an American Secretary of State. As the Rhineland had been one kind of Rubicon, so the Brussels Conference was another, failing to halt the Sino-Japanese conflict through international pressure. After the Japanese sank the American ship *Panay* in the Yangtze on 12 December, Chamberlain began to see the force of Eden's wish for Anglo-American cooperation (or at any rate American cooperation) when he admitted in a letter to his sister, 'It is always best and safest to count on *nothing* from the Americans except words but at this moment they are nearer to "doing something" than I have ever known them and I can't altogether repress hopes.'[39]

As a result, Chamberlain intensified his personal involvement in the conduct of foreign affairs. The problem for Eden was that, whilst he had been toiling officially at Nyon and Brussels, Chamberlain had been toiling equally fervently in unofficial ways, with the assistance of Sir Joseph Ball and his sister-in-law, since the time of the Grandi conversations in July, which, in the opinion of one historian, 'not only started Chamberlain on his quest for an understanding with Italy, but they established the secret channel as part of his diplomatic options'. Continuing for the rest of his Premiership, this channel 'operated almost as a parallel foreign office' and 'all the participants were born intriguers'.[40] When Eden protested at Dame Ivy Chamberlain's interventions, which came to a head with a meeting with Mussolini in the Palazzo Venezia in Rome in February 1938, followed by 'talks' with Count Ciano, the Italian Foreign Minister, Chamberlain apologised and promised to curb his sister-in-law's activities. Privately, Chamberlain was delighted that friendly contacts were being made with Mussolini and Ciano.

At the outset of his Premiership, Chamberlain had promised Eden that the Foreign Office would have more support than in Baldwin's day; in practice this meant more interference. 'Really that F.O.,' Chamberlain had written to his sister in October, 'I am only waiting my opportunity to stir it up with a long pole.'[41] That opportunity had now come. By removing Vansittart to the euphemistically titled position of Chief Diplomatic Adviser (on 1 January 1938), Chamberlain was subtly undermining Eden's position, even though Eden also wanted Vansittart removed, so that Cadogan could be Permanent Under-Secretary. Eden failed to see the dangers to his position when Chamberlain wanted Sir Findlater Stewart, Permanent Secretary at the India Office, instead of Cadogan. 'This is a first step toward undermining or sidetracking you'[42], Vansittart had warned Eden on 9 December, and he prophesied that 'If I go, you won't last long.'[43]

Sir Horace Rumbold, the former Ambassador to Berlin, wrote to his son Anthony (later Eden's Principal Private Secretary from 1954) about Vansittart's 'demotion':

Nobody seems to know exactly what Van's new post amounts to or why it was created. Some say that it was a polite way of getting rid of him but he is not the sort of man to be easily got rid of. Moreover he is apparently going to keep his room at the F.O. I am told that the foreign representatives will, in future, consider that Cadogan is the man they must go and see. So *when* and how often is Van going to advise?[44]

These were pertinent questions about the potential ambiguities in the command structures at the Foreign Office in the opening days of 1938.

Underneath the outward sense of unity, there were growing fissures over the National Government's often confused and contradictory foreign policy. The Conservative Party has often spawned factions and the late 1930s was a golden time for such covert dissent. Forty MPs, led by Sir Edward Spears, had formed a 'December' Club in February 1936, named after the month of the Hoare-Laval Pact, urging vigilance in foreign relations and a clear policy of rearmament. There was the 'Focus for the Defence of Freedom and Peace', and another critical association, 'The Group', formed in 1938, when discontented Tory MPs, led by Sidney Herbert (Baldwin's former PPS) and Patrick Donner, met each Thursday to coordinate awkward defence questions in the House.

At the end of 1937, Eden prepared his first résumé of the international situation for King George VI. By and large, he kept off Italian difficulties, but his knowledge of the state of affairs in other troubled countries showed a comprehensive grasp of his brief:

> Egyptian events are troublesome but not unexpected. King Farouk & Nahas Pasha [leader of the Wafd party] have become wholly incompatible ... It remains to be seen whether the new Government will be equally loyal. So far there is nothing to complain of in their public declarations, but it is difficult to avoid the suspicion that Rome may be pleased at the change ... the boy King could hardly have begun more rashly. Events in Roumania are also difficult to follow. It appears that King Carol, in his anxiety to avoid a government by the Iron Guard, has called in a minority party which clearly has inadequate backing in the country. Since the personalities at the head of this party have had Swastikas on their badges for a long time, it is natural to feel some anxiety at the foreign policy which Roumania may now follow.[45]

Modestly, Eden did not mention his very real personal achievement at the Nyon Conference, or his disappointment at the aftermath of Roosevelt's quarantine speech. He wrote to Chamberlain on 31 December stressing that in the New Year the aim must be to 'do everything we can privately to encourage the Americans'.[46]

After Christmas 1937, the Edens took a long overdue holiday at the Hotel Park Palace at Grasse on the French Riviera. Eden looked forward to a break from the red boxes and to opportunities for tennis and swimming, his two principal recreations. But even on the French Riviera, politics intruded. Churchill and Lloyd George, also on holiday in the area, lunched with him on 5 January. 'Both strongly opposed to any recognition of the Italian conquest of Abyssinia,' Eden recorded in his diary. 'I told them something of our efforts to ensure co-operation with the U.S. Both seemed impressed with the progress that had been made.'[47]

But it was a false dawn. Within days, a protracted correspondence between the Prime Minister and his Foreign Secretary, on the question of *de jure* recognition of Italy's Abyssinian conquest, underlined the extent of their disparity. Letters and telegrams flowed between Downing Street and Grasse. After one acrimonious difference of opinion, Eden wrote on 9 January, 'Mussolini is, I fear, the complete gangster and his pledged word means nothing.' He declared, 'It would be most unfortunate to take any action at this time which gave Mussolini the appearance of a diplomatic triumph. There is no doubt that such a triumph is just what he needs to rally his disgruntled fellow-countrymen, and maybe, to reconcile them to a further expedition to Spain.' Chamberlain disagreed. 'The one way,' he replied, 'in which we can maintain our moral position is to make recognition part of a general scheme for appeasement in the Mediterranean & the Red Sea.'[48]

Eden thought this was expediency, not morality.

'Astonished to receive on Friday morning by telephone an urgent request to return to London at once,' Eden wrote on 14 January. 'No details could be given by telephone.'

He was met by Alec Cadogan, now Permanent Under-Secretary, and Oliver Harvey at Folkestone after a stormy crossing. 'Alec gave me the messages from Washington which showed that Roosevelt was planning some form of initiative as a result of which he hopes to put forward plans for the betterment of international conditions.' The message had been received in London on 12 January, with a deadline of 17 January, if the proposal was to be put into action. 'I really do not feel that this initiative of President Roosevelt need necessarily injure the attempts which we are making to improve relations with Germany,' Eden wrote to Chamberlain, 'nor even have any repercussions on the conversations which I know you are so anxious to start with Italy.'[49]

The Foreign Office was only too aware that a march had been stolen on them. As time was now running short, they needed to retrieve the situation at once. Some of the details of Roosevelt's plan Eden thought vague, but he applauded the general spirit. 'The P.M., however, did not like it.'[50]

So began their final rift.

Many myths have become established about Eden's motives for resigning the Foreign Secretaryship. The person closest to him during those dark days was Jim Thomas, and after the dust had settled, he set down his impressions. 'The full story of Anthony's resignation has never yet been told,' he began:

> It has been suggested that he resigned suddenly, in a moment of pique, on a matter of detail. This is a view which was at the time expressed publicly by more than one of his former colleagues in the Cabinet. Presumably they were saying what they believed to be true, though it is a little difficult for anyone who had been in touch with the events of preceding months and had witnessed the growing tension between the Foreign Office and Downing Street to understand this. Actually, it was no sudden storm. It had been blowing up for months.

After a survey of the previous six months, including the part played by Count Grandi, Thomas came on to the Roosevelt initiative:

> One day, quite unexpectedly, a telegram arrived from Washington containing a message from President Roosevelt to the British Government. It stated that the President was becoming increasingly concerned about the deterioration of the situation in Europe, and that he was himself prepared to take an initiative with a view to facilitating a solution of the issues that divided European nations.

Roosevelt's proposals involved an approach to some of the smaller and more vulnerable nations in Europe, as a preliminary to calling a conference. 'The object it would seek to achieve would be the negotiation of a new and comprehensive European settlement, based on the fundamental principles of international law.'[51]

Without consulting his Foreign Secretary, or Cabinet, Chamberlain applied what Sumner Welles, the American Under-Secretary of State, later called 'a douche of cold water'[52] to the proposals, as he was still hoping to lure Mussolini away from Hitler by *de jure* recognition:

> Anthony, informed privately of these developments, rushed back to England [Eden added here in his own hand on Thomas's manuscript, 'was summoned back to England by Cadogan'], in the hope that he might be able to persuade the Prime Minister not to send his reply to Washington until the matter had been more fully considered. He was not so much concerned with the details of the President's plan. That might or might not be a good one. But he felt it was madness to discourage any tendency on the part of the United States to take a more active part in international affairs. For some months now, the President and his advisers had been moving in the right direction. They had sent warships to Singapore. They had sent a representative to the Brussels Conference. They had, within the last few weeks, sent, privately, an officer [Captain

R. E. Ingersoll] from the Navy Department for unofficial staff talks in London. Was this the moment to snub them? But he was too late. The answer had already gone.'[53]

Eden was not the only person discomfited by these developments, as he did his best to retrieve the situation, but he was two days behind the game. Sir Ronald Lindsay had recommended a quick acceptance of Roosevelt's offer, but Chamberlain would not commit the Government. 'After some discussion with Alec,' Eden wrote of his meeting on the evening of 15 January with his advisers, 'we sent a telegram to Lindsay explaining that I had been away and expressing hope that no final decision would be taken on one reply.'[54]

In a furious confrontation with Chamberlain at Chequers on Sunday 16 January, Eden pointed out that the choice lay between Anglo-American cooperation and a dubious piecemeal settlement with an untrustworthy Mussolini over *de jure* recognition. He told Chamberlain that 'the less strong Mussolini was the less he appealed to Hitler'. If Britain recognised his imperial conquest, it would 'increase his authority, and, therefore, make him more attractive to Hitler.'[55] It was an argument that cut no ice with Chamberlain, who was already planning more approaches through Dame Ivy Chamberlain. As in the earlier struggle with Warren Fisher, Eden eventually prevailed and lines to America were not severed immediately, but it proved a temporary and hollow victory.*

The next day (17 January) Roosevelt's reply came, 'specially strong against recognition of Abyssinia', as Eden noted hopefully. 'I agree with every word of it, and as somebody remarked, might indeed have drafted it myself. We all agreed at the office that in view of these telegrams we must at once accord full support to Roosevelt's initiative.' At 5 p.m. Eden saw Chamberlain, who insisted that he would ask Roosevelt to withdraw his initiative. 'I fear that fundamentally the difficulty is that N. believes that he is a man with a mission to come to terms with the Dictators. Indeed one of his chief objections to Roosevelt's Initiative was that with its strong reference to International Law it would greatly irritate Dictator Powers.'[56]

At Eden's request, the Cabinet was summoned, even though most were still on holiday. Jim Thomas's narrative picks up the story:

---

*After Eden had left the Government, Roosevelt's initiative, like the American offer of funding for Nasser's Aswan High Dam in 1956, 'withered on the vine', prompting speculation in some quarters that the President's hidden agenda all along had been support for Chamberlain in his difficulties with Eden, and a covert way of removing an articulate opponent of America's isolationism. Private information. It is a view examined, and not dismissed, in R. A. C. Parker, *Chamberlain and Appeasement: British Policy and the Coming of the Second World War*, Macmillan, 1993, p.118.

At the meeting of the Cabinet, the Prime Minister told the story up to date and Anthony pressed strongly his view that to turn down the proposals, whatever their intrinsic merits, was unwise in the extreme. Ultimately, after lengthy discussions, it was decided, as a concession to Anthony's views, to appoint a sub-committee of the Cabinet to draft a further telegram to Washington, toning down the Prime Minister's original answer. Very reluctantly, Anthony accepted this compromise. He would like to have resigned, but it did not seem to be a possible course.

The problem was that 'the national interest, and the extreme delicacy of some of the issues involved, inevitably debarred him from giving a full description of the events.'[57]

To complicate the issue, Grandi now returned from leave and called on Eden at the Foreign Office on the afternoon of 19 January. *De jure* recognition was still the price for any further conversations with Italy. At a special meeting of the Foreign Affairs Committee that evening, Chamberlain revealed for the first time the extent of his sister-in-law's activities in Rome. If that were not enough to raise Eden's temperature, the chance sighting of Sir Thomas Inskip's notes as Minister for Co-Ordination of Defence, confirmed only too clearly his isolation within Cabinet. 'Eden's policy to line up the U.S.A., Great Britain and France, result war.'[58] The meeting broke up without any agreement. Later that evening, Cadogan, Cranborne, Thomas and Harvey joined Eden at his house to consider the next move. Cadogan knew that no full explanation was possible and agreed to draft a further telegram.

Eden saw Chamberlain just after noon on 20 January. Overnight Chamberlain had moved to a position of accepting a parallel approach, the Roosevelt initative *and* British conversations with Mussolini. Eden thought this was unrealistic, because of Roosevelt's attitude on the *de jure* question, which Eden recognised was the most hopeful of all the developments since he had returned from France. At the Foreign Affairs Committee that afternoon, Eden was given authority to draft three new telegrams, the net effect of which was to keep options open. But he felt (rightly) that this would be only a temporary pause in Chamberlain's strategy.

That evening a further meeting of his supporters took place at his house. Oliver Harvey wrote of this meeting, 'A. E. would be better outside the government as the "old gang" will watch to trip him again. Anyway, he can afford to be as firm as he likes as now they realise he would resign on it they are afraid of him. Next time he may not have such a good wicket. We know that the P.M. hates American co-operation and wants to make peace with the dictators.'[59]

A further meeting of the Foreign Affairs Committee on 21 January considered Eden's telegrams. It was the fourth long meeting at which Eden had argued his case against an increasingly sceptical section of the Cabinet, who backed Chamberlain. But his persuasiveness did lead to a partial compromise, and four telegrams were sent to the Washington Embassy, including one from Chamberlain for Roosevelt, and Eden did persuade the Committee that the *de jure* question should be 'reconsidered in the light of R.'s appeal.'[60]

At this critical stage in the crisis, Eden had to return to Geneva for League of Nations business and was absent from London as the situation unfolded. Such was the position at the end of January.

February opened badly with the sinking of two British ships in the Mediterranean, which led to a renewal of the 'Nyon' patrols. On his return to London, Eden was told by Chamberlain that Grandi wished to have what were termed 'preliminary' talks. At the same time he heard from the British Embassy in Rome of Dame Ivy Chamberlain's latest visits to Mussolini and Ciano. Eden was furious both at the secrecy and at the undermining of his position. Meanwhile, Sir Joseph Ball was stepping up his contacts with Grandi, all of which had the effect of downgrading Eden in the eyes of Rome. On 8 February, Eden heard more of Ivy's activities. 'Without wishing to be unduly punctilious', he wrote to Chamberlain at once, 'I am sure you will understand that this kind of unofficial diplomacy does place me in a most difficult position.' Chamberlain apologised for his sister-in-law's 'unorthodox procedure', but added, 'I don't really think however that she has done any harm.'[61]

That was an opinion not shared by Eden. The conclusion in Rome from their political intelligence was that Eden was not long for the Foreign Office, which contributed to his lack of real progress with Grandi in talks on 10 February.

By chance, Eden was booked to speak to the Junior Imperial League of the Western Midlands area on Saturday 12 February in Birmingham Town Hall, an historic venue that had seen much political drama in its days. In a speech of great commitment that underlined his anti-defeatist, anti-dictator credentials, Eden aroused the young audience to whole-hearted enthusiasm, especially with his ringing peroration, a striking precursor of a later more infamous moment, 'we want peace not only in our time but in your time.'[62]

By this time the Press were concentrating on supposed differences between Eden and the Prime Minister, rather than on the details of Eden's speech. Because of the timing of his speech on a Saturday evening, it was thirty-six hours before written reports reached a wider audience.

A busy week then saw Chamberlain and Eden concentrating on meetings with the Chiefs of Staff about their Locarno commitments and Hitler's first ominous moves against the Austrian Chancellor, Kurt von Schuschnigg. 'A. E. feels more and more the difference between colleagues and himself,'[63] Oliver Harvey noted, especially over the forthcoming Italian talks.

Grandi had been imposing conditions both on venue and agenda. In one of their last joint actions, Neville Chamberlain and Anthony Eden summoned Grandi on the morning of 18 February to discuss this vexed question of whether conversations with Italy were going to start. After Grandi had left (to report to Rome that Chamberlain and Eden were 'two enemies confronting each other, like two cocks in true fighting posture),[64] Chamberlain told Eden he was all for accepting that the meetings should take place in Rome and for announcing the decision publicly that afternoon. Eden said he could not agree, as it would 'look like capitulation to blackmail or panic.'[65]

After consulting Cranborne, Cadogan, Jim Thomas and Harvey, Eden decided to insist on a Cabinet. Chamberlain reluctantly agreed that ministers should meet on Saturday afternoon, 19 February – a sign of the urgency of the crisis, as such an inconvenient timing was virtually unknown in peacetime. Before the Cabinet, at which the issue would finally be resolved, Eden had to fit in an overnight visit to Leamington, but he returned the next morning to the Foreign Office, where his regular team of advisers was joined by Rex Leeper and Harold Caccia. Malcolm MacDonald also came in later and proved a stolid buttress during this critical period.

After lunch, Eden walked over to Downing Street in sombre mood with Oliver Harvey. The crowds cheered as he went in. It was more than three hours before he re-emerged.

The majority of the Cabinet present had no idea why they had been summoned. 'So little was I aware of what was going on,' Lord Halifax later wrote, 'that I passed a note to Sam Hoare, who sits next me, to ask what was the purpose of this rather boring lecture on history.' Only when Eden replied to Chamberlain did things, in one sense, become clearer. 'Anthony followed,' Halifax's account continued, 'with an explanation, very reasonably given, of why he differed: Italians untrustworthy; their present economic embarrassment; desirability of further preparation; impossible complications of Spain etc.' The Cabinet soon divided into two camps. Chamberlain, Simon, Hoare, Hailsham and Swinton were Eden's principal opponents. MacDonald and Elliot were two of the few who sympathised with Eden. Halifax was for compromise, with nothing substantive to be agreed until the issue of Spain, and withdrawal of Italian troops, had been clarified. Eden announced that in the light of this discussion he had no option but to tender his resignation.

At this, panic seemed to set in. Chamberlain told his ministers that another Cabinet must be held at 3 p.m. on the Sunday afternoon. (It was not a good weekend for Simon's golf at Tadmarton Heath.)

After the Saturday Cabinet, Halifax, together with Oliver Stanley, went over to seek out Eden in the Foreign Office. Halifax wrote:

> I felt at once that the atmosphere, emanating mainly from Bobbety, was very much pro-resignations. It produced on me somewhat of the effect I should have expected from the corner of a boxing ring when the 2nds received back the pugilist & restored his vitality by congratulations & encouragement. I could almost hear them saying, I thought, 'You have done very well. You have won the 1st round. Hold firm & all will be well!' We talked for some time in a rather restless atmosphere of whiskies & sodas, & cigarettes, but without, I felt, making any impression, & when we came away Oliver Stanley said to me, 'He has been through Hell to make up his mind, & he's d—— well not going to unmake it.'[66]

At Sunday lunchtime Chamberlain sent for Eden before the Cabinet 'and asked me whether I had qualified my view of the night before'. Eden replied that he had not. 'In the conversation that ensued he made it quite plain that with infinite reluctance he had come to the conclusion that it was in the national interest that we should part, adding as qualification, "You will have a lot of persuasion from some of the colleagues though, when you meet this afternoon." '[67]

The Cabinet at 3 p.m., 'a strenuous but ineffectual meeting', as Eden described it,[68] was not quite the last act in an extended crisis. No progress was made and at 4.45 the Cabinet adjourned, so that a smaller group – consisting of Chamberlain, Eden, Malcolm MacDonald, Inskip, Stanley and Shakes Morrison – could try to resolve the issue. The others dispersed for a protracted tea, after which Kingsley Wood tried to persuade Eden that Neville Chamberlain had learned his lesson and that things would be different in the future. Eden disagreed. A brief meeting followed at 6.10 p.m., during which Eden withdrew to the Foreign Office to consult his advisers. Shortly afterwards, the Cabinet resumed its deliberations and at 7.35 p.m Eden formally resigned.

A somewhat chastened and subdued Cabinet meeting began at 7.40 p.m., without Eden, to consider the changed situation. Finally, at 10 p.m. Chamberlain convened the final Cabinet of a long day.[69]

Yet it was not until 25 February that Chamberlain settled, controversially, on Halifax as Eden's replacement, with Rab Butler as his Under-Secretary – for Bobbety Cranborne and Jim Thomas had departed with Eden, in one of the most dramatic Government upheavals since Lord Randolph Churchill's resignation as Chancellor of the Exchequer in 1886.

Jim Thomas was as firm for resignation as Eden and Cranborne, but all three were disappointed that Oliver Stanley stayed in the Government. Lady Cranborne observed acidly, 'the Stanleys have been trimmers ever since Bosworth field.'*

'The events of the last few days have made plain a difference between us on a decision of great importance in itself and far-reaching in its consequences. I cannot recommend to Parliament a policy with which I am not in agreement,' Eden wrote formally to the Prime Minister on tendering his resignation. 'It cannot be in the country's interest that those who are called upon to direct its affairs should work in an uneasy partnership, fully conscious of differences in outlook yet hoping they will not recur.'[70] So much for Kingsley Wood's attempt at conciliation.

In the end it was Spain, not Italy, that tilted the balance. The issue of Mussolini's 4,000 'volunteers' in the Spanish Civil War, and Ciano's insistence through Grandi that the British should go to Rome for talks, was the final straw that drove Eden to resignation on 20 February. 'Why should we go to Rome?' Thomas wrote. 'We were not debtors in this affair. We were the creditors. It was not we who had broken our word and damaged our reputation. It was Italy. If she wanted good relations with us, let her come to London.'[71]

Halifax, who was to be the short-term beneficiary of Eden's decision, was also one of the most perceptive and understanding of his motives.

> My impressions are still somewhat blurred as to the way things worked in Anthony's mind. I cannot help thinking that the difference on the actual time table of conversations was not, & never has been the principal difference. I suspect it has been the cumulative result of a good many different things: partly sub-conscious irritation at Neville's closer control of foreign policy; partly irritation at his amateur excursions into the field through Lady Chamberlain, Horace Wilson, & his own letter to Mussolini; partly Anthony's natural revulsion from dictators, which I have always told him was too strong in as much as you have got to live with the devils whether you like them, or not; & partly, as I have also often told him, his excessive sensitiveness to the criticism of the left.'[72]

Halifax tried, not unnaturally, to minimise the significance of Eden's resignation, but his memorandum overlooked the fact that on all the key foreign policy issues of the previous year, Eden's judgement had been sound and perspicacious, whereas Chamberlain's had been muddled and naive. Eden did not resign on a whim, or because of personal irritation, or because he was highly strung, but as a result of a deep-seated divergence of

---

*A remark to Harold Caccia, cited by Andrew Roberts, *The Holy Fox: A Biography of Lord Halifax*, Weidenfeld & Nicolson, 1991, p.85. 'What says Lord Stanley? Will he bring his power?' asked Shakespeare's Richard III. 'My lord, he doth deny to come.' *King Richard III*, V.iii. 343–4.

view on foreign policy, illustrated by Chamberlain's response to Roosevelt and his dealings with Grandi and Mussolini. In fact, Grandi ensured that Eden's position with Chamberlain became insupportable, as it was in Italy's interests to see him replaced at the Foreign Office by a more malleable personality.

Eden's resignation was also immensely brave, a fact minimised by those who attributed his departure to personal motives. He was just forty and perhaps throwing away for ever succession to the Premiership. Other ministers who agreed with Eden did not resign, and most of the Cabinet elders tried to persuade him to stay.

News of the resignation reached Sir Horace Rumbold at Luxor whilst on a Nile cruise. He was soon penning his thoughts to his son:

> I wonder what you feel about Eden's resignation? I am a whole-hearted adherent of his and think he was quite right to resign. In fact I wrote to tell him so immediately we heard the news emphasising the fact that I was writing as an average Englishman. In that capacity I resent the appearance we have of licking the boots of that snarling blackguard Mussolini who is already in some respects on his beam ends.
>
> I don't think Chamberlain knows the technique of dealing with dictators, who are necessarily bullies. The more you truckle to them the more arrogant they become. Why should we help Mussolini out of his difficulties? By an act of international piracy he has created a bargaining counter and Eden was quite right in holding that Mussolini should give an earnest of his good faith by clearing out of Spain before we began conversations with him. If Chamberlain doesn't pull off an agreement with the Italians he will lose so much face as to be useless and may well dish his party as well.[73]

In fact, with Eden gone, there was now no longer any barrier to the blunders that Chamberlain and Halifax were about to commit, for other ministers were too feeble to oppose them.

Eden's resignation made an international impact. For many it was the moment when the seriousness of the situation finally became apparent, even for well-informed observers. 'I shared the enthusiasm of my father (and other people I admired) for what the League of Nations stood for; but for years I failed ignominiously to spot the need for national rearmament if Hitler and Mussolini were to be stopped', John Redcliffe-Maud wrote in his memoirs. 'It was only when Eden resigned as Foreign Secretary in February 1938 that the truth dawned.'[74]

So swiftly had events moved in the last two days that King George VI, much to his annoyance, had been forced to rely upon the *Sunday Express* for his political intelligence. It came as a considerable surprise to the King on the morning of 20 February to read that Eden was on the verge of resignation. He promptly rang Alec Hardinge, who tried unsuccessfully to contact Hankey, to find out the latest. Eventually Hardinge located Oliver Stanley. They discussed 'whether a private letter from the King to Eden expressing his great concern, and his earnest hope that, in view of the effect on the international situation, he would hesitate before leaving the Government at this juncture, would be likely to secure any useful purpose'. Stanley felt Halifax would be better placed to answer that question. At 1.30, having failed to get Halifax, Hardinge spoke to Horace Wilson. 'He said that Eden had only just left the P.M., that the former had taken the stand that no compromise was possible, as the disagreement was a fundamental one, that he therefore intended to resign at the Cabinet meeting at 3.00 p.m. In these circumstances he felt that a letter from the King on those lines could only cause Eden embarrassment and distress.' Hardinge reported all this to the King at 2 p.m., who thus had the shortest possible notice of what was about to unfold.[75]

The definite news broke, owing to the first scoop in the career of the young journalist Hugh Cudlipp, then with the *Daily Mirror*. Sensing that something was in the air, he rang Eden at his home at midnight on 20 February and asked directly whether he had resigned or planned to do so. 'Putting the correct interpretation on the latter's monosyllabic "Oh!"', Cudlipp published and was not damned.[76]

The news made global headlines and was the end of Eden's apprenticeship of promise. After this, he would be more hardened; he had been bruised too often in the battles of wills, and he grew to be more guarded. Many felt his act of particular courage would prove an irrevocable burning of his political bridges. It was a path that sympathisers, such as Walter Elliot and Duff Cooper, did not follow, though Cooper was to resign later over the Munich agreement. Eden's resignation divided opinion. His friends saw him as the knight in shining armour; his opponents dismissed him as a pernickety annoyance, with too pronounced a high moral tone. Churchill retrospectively described the night of 20 February in one of his most celebrated passages of prose:

> On the night of February 20, 1938, and on this occasion only, sleep deserted me. From midnight till dawn I lay in my bed consumed by emotions of sorrow and fear. There seemed one strong young figure standing up against long, dismal, drawling tides of drift and surrender, of wrong measures and feeble impulses. My conduct of affairs would have been different from his in many ways; but he seemed to me at this moment the life-hope of the British nation, the grand old British race that had done so much for men, and had yet some more to give. Now he was gone.[77]

Eden received letters from all over the world. 'As I see the situation', Sir Horace Rumbold wrote to him, 'there is a race between the gangster or aggressive states and the big democracies in the sense that the former are trying and will try to get away with as much as they can before the democracies are strong enough to call a halt.'[78] But such words were scant consolation for Eden, who believed that war would eventually prove inevitable. As he looked at the seeming ruin of his life's work, there was no guarantee that he would ever again return to Government. Nor did it seem that he wanted to. After his resignation, he sought solace with the Becketts in the Yorkshire Dales and, following a generous letter of consolation from Halifax, confessed, 'The moors in this glorious weather do not exactly encourage me to contemplate a return to political life, ever.'[79]

PART TWO

The Business of War

All the business of war, and indeed all the business of life, is to endeavour to find out what you don't know by what you do; that's what I called 'guessing what was at the other side of the hill'.

The Duke of Wellington

STILL ON THE DOORSTEP

CHAPTER EIGHT

A New and Sharper Sword

1938–9

The callous and irresponsible betrayal
Of the Czech Republic has brought not peace
But a new and sharper sword.

Hugh MacDiarmid[1]

Nothing dampened the ardor for Anthony Eden. Even when the
word began to spread, as such words do in huge crowds, that
Eden was coming over only to get us into war, nobody was quite
willing to give up a main-floor seat. The explanation is that
people want to *see* AE. It does not matter what he says or does –
they want to see him. He is knighthood in flower.

American newspaper report, December 1938[2]

Count Talleyrand, that shrewd and cynical observer of statecraft, was once
at a diplomatic gathering when a worldly-wise colleague suddenly
collapsed and died. 'Now, I wonder what he can have meant by that?'
asked Talleyrand. Reactions to Eden's sudden resignation in February
1938 were not dissimilar.

A sense of puzzlement, tempered by ignorance of the details between the
lines, made many suspect that there was more to it than met the eye. But
one thing was certain. Eden's resignation made headlines around the
world, not all of them complimentary. Chamberlain's team made sure of
that, by squaring the Press barons in advance. Clear backing for Eden in
the national Press came only from the *Daily Herald* and the *News
Chronicle*, reflecting Labour and Liberal support. The *Manchester
Guardian*, independently Liberal, also backed Eden.* The most whole-
hearted champion of Eden's action, however, was Arthur Mann's
Yorkshire Post. Eden never forgot the support of the *Manchester Guardian*
and the *Yorkshire Post*, which he called 'two honourable exceptions to the
appeasement-minded Press'.[3] *The Times*, not an honourable exception,
wrote that Eden's resignation would bring no fundamental change to
British aims, and welcomed the appointment of Lord Halifax as Foreign
Secretary, largely on the grounds that he was a kinsman of Sir Edward

---

*Over Suez in 1956 the paper was to be among his principal critics.

Grey. *The Times* felt this a sure sign that the new man would be more than an 'ingenious diplomatist', a phrase implying that Eden was too clever by half. What annoyed Eden, however, was the use of the Grey lineage as vicarious praise for his successor, when both Halifax and he himself shared equal ties of descent from the Liberal statesman.[4]

The Chancelleries of Europe reverberated with the news. The French Ambassador in Berlin reported to the Quai d'Orsay of Hitler's delight and forecast one less target for 'les flèches acérées' that the Führer 'a lancées à plusieurs reprises contre l'Angleterre, l'opinion anglaise, la presse et le Parlement Britanniques, et M. Eden en particulier'. A month later the French Ambassador in London related Eden's pessimistic view regarding the prospects for an enduring peace: 'Il est de ceux qui croient personellement le conflit inévitable et il juge également inévitable que l'Angleterre soit obligée d'y participer.'[5]

Despite the orchestrated criticisms of the Press lords, popular opinion in Britain remained firmly behind Eden: 71 per cent thought he was right to resign.[6] In America, there were demands that Eden should visit. Meanwhile, the object of all this adulation remained apart, a latter-day Cincinnatus.*

After the customary statement in the House, the Edens went to the Beckett home in Yorkshire to avoid the limelight. Sir Gervase Beckett had died in August 1937, much mourned by Eden, but Beatrice's roots still remained in Kirkdale and it was where they could avoid the metropolitan crowds.[7] Later they went to the South of France for the best part of two months, much to the disappointment of Eden's supporters, who had expected him to lead a move against Chamberlain in Parliament, a fundamental misreading of his character. For a while the Edens were fellow guests of Sir Sidney Herbert on the Riviera, with Stanley and Lucy Baldwin. Political talk dominated into the small hours. Baldwin told Eden that, if Chamberlain fell, he would recommend that the King call upon Eden to form a new administration, and even suggested names for his Cabinet. Baldwin also hoped that Eden would not play second fiddle to Churchill in the months ahead. Neither of these hopes was realised. Eden's had been a polite resignation, and it remained a polite aftermath.

Eden's formal letter of resignation to Chamberlain had been low-key, with the result that some outsiders wondered what all the fuss was about.†
On 21 February, there was an air of expectation in the House before Eden's resignation speech.[8] It was an expectation largely disappointed. The

---

*Lucius Quinctius Cincinnatus was called from his farm in 458 BC to save Rome.
†Just as Eden later voluntarily refrained from saying anything about Royal-Family attitudes to Suez in the wake of misinformation from Lord Mountbatten (see Chapter 20), so now he eschewed any mention of Roosevelt's secret plan.

combination of Eden's gentlemanly reserve and the extreme secrecy of the Roosevelt initiative meant that he could talk only in bland tones. Those who knew about the American terms were nevertheless disappointed that he did not speak about Italy and *de jure* recognition. There was none of the drama of Oswald Mosley's resignation speech on 28 May 1930, when, in the words of his biographer, 'for those minutes he was the undisputed leader of his generation.'[9]

Nevertheless, Eden indisputably became the focus of hope for those in despair at the drift of British policy towards the dictators, and his resignation defined him as the vigorous symbol of expectation and resistance, an image that was never dimmed in darker days. Eden's quintessential English decency and forthright stand, however much colleagues close to him may have felt it to have been compromised, remained one of the ineffaceable memories of the 1930s, and Eden in his Homburg hat was as potent a symbol of the age as Jarrow and the Abdication, pebble-dash housing and the poetry of pylons, 'Monopoly', hiking or the music of Ivor Novello.

Eden did not seek personal advancement (in the short term his finances were seriously diminished); he did not seek to bring down the incumbent Prime Minister, nor did he dream of a Centre Party or a break from the institutions of parliamentary democracy. As Harold Caccia had observed after a fortnight at close quarters *en famille* in 1937, Eden never had, nor attempted to communicate, the feeling that he was the one man who could save England. He was a realist, not a man of destiny. His resignation speech was heard respectfully, but did not fire his audience. Never a natural orator, though always a sincere one, he was understandably nervous, especially at the burden of expectation. 'No man would willingly sever the links which bind him with colleagues and friends,' Eden said. However, he continued, 'there are occasions when strong political convictions must override all other considerations. On such occasions only the individual himself can be the judge; no man can be the keeper of another man's conscience.'[10]

Leo Amery described Eden's as 'a speech full of sincerity and high purpose.'[11] Harold Nicolson, one of Eden's supporters, was privately more critical. 'He could either have taken the aggressive style and appealed to the country or else have made a perfectly calm statement without recrimination,' he wrote. 'As it was, there was just sufficient note of recrimination to spoil the dignified effect and not enought to constitute an appeal.'[12] Nevertheless, Nicolson wrote to his wife, 'Don't be worried, my darling. I am not going to be one of the Winston brigade. My leaders are Anthony and Malcolm [MacDonald].'[13]

THE BUSINESS OF WAR

Chamberlain, however, had no difficulty in securing the broad sympathy of the House, though Attlee, the Labour leader, made a potent point when he said, 'it looks rather curious to us that when a colleague is being attacked by people overseas, by foreign countries, when, week after week, he is abused in every possible way, his colleagues do not stand by him.'[14] The vote of censure proposed by Labour's Arthur Greenwood was defeated the next day by 330 votes to 156.

Some of the Cabinet were apprehensive about what Eden might say to his constituents in a speech at Leamington Spa on 25 February. They need not have worried. As Chips Channon noted in his diary, Eden would not show bitterness, 'firstly because he is a gentleman, and secondly because he is too shrewd a statesman to burn his boats irretrievably. Already there is talk of him coming back, like Sam Hoare, in the autumn.'[15] Eden, anxious to avoid the charge of sour grapes, even had his speech vetted in advance by Hankey, the Cabinet Secretary – not the move of a rebel who was out to cause trouble.*

Hiring the biggest hall available (the Leamington Public Baths), Eden appealed to his constituents for a vote of confidence, given with overwhelming vocal approval, no formal count being deemed necessary. Eden always considered this speech in Leamington, to non-Conservatives as well as his own party supporters, the surest hand he played in February 1938.†

Although Eden had no ambitions to displace Chamberlain, his actions after 20 February very much left the door open for an eventual return to the Cabinet, as Churchill and many others wanted. The lesson of

---

*Hankey's attitude to Eden's resignation depended on the audience. To Sir Eric Phipps he wrote on 21 February, 'The Foreign Secretary was always chopping and changing, blowing hot one day and cold the next' (Sir Maurice Hankey to Sir Eric Phipps, 21 February 1938. Phipps papers, Churchill College, Cambridge, PHPP 3/3, f.81), and he looked for greater consistency under Halifax. However, the same day Hankey wrote to Eden, 'Almost a professional peace-maker myself, this time I thought the peacemakers were wrong. I have never admired you more than the way you stuck to your guns against all appeals, cajoleries, blandishments', adding with no sense of conscious irony, 'I didn't live at the heart of the LLG-Curzon controversy for nothing!' (Sir Maurice Hankey to Anthony Eden, 21 February 1938. AP 8/2/10A.) Churchill was scathing of Hankey's missive, which Eden gave him in 1947 as background material for his memoirs. 'Considering that you were giving up everything and going out into the wilderness,' Churchill wrote, 'and Chamberlain, who was wrong, on the merits, was gaining complete control of the Foreign Office, I can only describe his [Hankey's] letter as the caress of a worm.' (Winston Churchill to Anthony Eden, 18 February 1938. AP 19/4/9.)
†When Selwyn Lloyd was sacked as Chancellor of the Exchequer in the Night of the Long Knives in July 1962, Eden advised his former Foreign Secretary to seek a vote of confidence from his local constituency party in the Wirral as soon as possible. Not only would the vote be a foregone conclusion, but it would put him in a much stronger position with regards to his eventual political rehabilitation. (D. R. Thorpe, Selwyn Lloyd, Jonathan Cape, 1989, p.350.) In practice, the tactic bore fruit on both occasions. Eden returned to office within nineteen months of his resignation; Selwyn Lloyd within fifteen months of his dismissal.

Churchill's extended exclusion from office in the 1930s was something few young politicians forgot at that time. Later generations know how Churchill's story was to continue; MPs in 1938 could only conjecture, and the omens for Churchill were not good. Eden's former colleagues, fearing indiscretions based on privileged information, breathed a sigh of relief after the Leamington speech which was widely reported in the national and international Press. Neville Chamberlain even wrote to Eden from Chequers, thanking him. 'Whatever the temptations you have resisted them, and the dignity and restraint of your speech must add further to your reputation,'[16] – not the kind of letter Mrs Thatcher would have sent to Geoffrey Howe in November 1990 after his destabilising resignation and destructive parting speech.[17]*

Eden's resignation in 1938 was that rare, if not unique, occurrence – a "civilised" resignation that was not soon forgotten.

The episode revealed Eden's nature, however much this may have disheartened his followers who wanted him to wield the knife. But Eden's undemonstrativeness was not at home with the vulgarian aspect of politics. Unlike his near-contemporary, Harold Macmillan, Eden eschewed the rough house tactics that many felt the times warranted, but his attitude was akin to that of Henrik Ibsen's Judge Brack, 'One doesn't *do* that kind of thing.'† If that was a political failing, so be it. 'Simply the thing I am shall make me live.'‡

On the other hand, Churchill warned Eden not to be too diffident. 'It seems to me vital that you shd not allow yr personal feelings of friendship to yr late colleagues to hamper you in doing full justice to yr case, & above all you shd not say anything that fetters yr action in the future. You owe this not only to yrself – which you no doubt feel the least part of the event – but to your cause which is also the cause of England.'[18] The cause of England was to owe much to both men in the next seven years.

Eden may have behaved in a gentlemanly manner, but his opponents within the Conservative Party hierarchy did not. Sir Joseph Ball squared the Conservative Press, which accounted for the lack of Fleet Street backing;[19] Sir John Simon began a whispering campaign about Eden's

---

* 'If one feels sufficiently strongly to resign from a government one ought to press the issue on which one resigns, especially when . . . it affects in so fundamental a way our relations with other countries', Vernon Bogdanor wrote to Geoffrey Howe on that occasion, adding, 'There is no point in a "civilised" resignation which is soon forgotten.' Vernon Bogdanor to Sir Geoffrey Howe, 5 November 1990. Geoffrey Howe, *Conflict of Loyalty*, Macmillan, 1994, p.661.
†*Hedda Gabler*, final line of Act Four.
‡Parolles in *All's Well That Ends Well*, IV.iii. 322-3.

instability owing to ill health, and the Whips dubbed Eden's followers 'The Glamour Boys'. There was even talk that Eden was suffering from some kind of mental breakdown. To disprove the rumours about his health, Eden made a point of attending the debate in the House on 22 February and even made a brief contribution on the withdrawal of Italian volunteers from Spain, which he said would have made no difference to his decision to resign, had he known of it in advance.[20]

The combination of concern at what he might do, and Machiavellian intrigue to destabilise his position, was one form of compliment. So was the reaction among the dictators. 'In London the crisis is on,' Ciano wrote in his diary. 'The Duce has been telephoning from Terminello [a winter sports centre in the Abruzzi] for information every half hour.' Ciano's intelligence was comprehensive.

> Eden was cheered by the crowd when he left, surly and alone, with shouts of 'Eden Prime Minister.' Labour, Liberals and left-wing Conservatives have already tabled a motion in favour of Eden. The crisis is perhaps one of the most important which has ever taken place. It may mean peace or war. I have authorised Grandi to take any step which may add an arrow to Chamberlain's quiver. An Eden Cabinet would have as its aim the fight against the dictatorships – Mussolini's first.'[21]

From Germany, Nevile Henderson, who owed so much to Eden, was positively gleeful. 'Of course everybody here is at heart profoundly relieved at Eden's departure,' he wrote to Halifax on 27 February. 'Eden and Hitler could never have agreed. I cannot therefore, since I regard an understanding with Germany as indispensable if we are not slowly or even rapidly to drift into war again, regard either Eden's resignation or your own appointment with anything but the utmost relief.'[22]

Although Eden received supportive letters from Robert Menzies in Australia, Norman Davis (the United States representative at the Brussels Conference) and the British Ambassadors in Belgrade and Cairo, official approval was far patchier than the popular reaction. In the next few weeks Eden received more than 6,000 letters from the wider public. As with the Suez Crisis in 1956, their tone was almost uniformly favourable, sometimes fervently so. Personal correspondents ranged from 'Jelly' Churchill, now retired from Eton, to the Archbishop of Canterbury, Cosmo Gordon Lang. The first letter gratified him, as 'Jelly' Churchill had forecast great things for Eden; the second surprised him, as the Anglican Church's political stance, through Geneva and the Abdication, had struck him as singularly ill-judged. Eden had all the letters acknowledged and wrote himself to trusted friends. Foremost was Bobbety Cranborne. 'It could not have been otherwise,' Eden wrote on 2 March. 'The further we recede from the actual issue the more glad I am that we acted as we did. The survivors are embarked on increasingly hazardous courses; of that I am certain. We could not have pretended to believe that we thought them well chosen.'[23]

In a further letter of 21 June, Eden wrote to Cranborne:

> Chief risks of war lie in two miscalculations, which are, I believe, at present being made.
> (1) First risk lies in our underestimating here forces – hurricane forces – which are loose in the world.
> (2) Second lies in the underestimate in certain other lands of the strength & resolution of the British people. And by strength & resolution I do not refer to armaments but to character.[24]

Cranborne wished Eden had expressed these views in Parliament, rather than in private correspondence. Then a proper debate could have unfolded. Eden had based his view of international strategy on two priorities – minimal involvement in Europe and, within practical limits, a defence of British overseas assets. The events of 1938 dealt a savage blow to these twin designs, not only with the rise of the European dictators, but also with political upheaval in the Middle East, India and the Far East. Japan loomed ever larger as an unpredictable rival. In Cranborne's opinion, Parliament needed to consider these questions. Eden's belief, fostered by the experience of his 1920s tour, in the protective role of the Dominions was growing. For five years he had worked on the intractable details of disarmament, the Saar plebiscite, Mussolini's invasion of Abyssinia, the Spanish Civil War, Anglo-Soviet relations and the German reoccupation of the Rhineland. It was clear to him that Britain now needed to call on all its global resources, especially as events in Europe gave a clear indication of greater troubles to come.

The *Anschluss*, the enforced union of Austria with Germany on 12 March 1938, shocked many out of their complacency. Hitler's putsch entailed the removal of the Austrian Chancellor, storm troopers over the border, anti-Jewish edicts and the Führer's triumphant appearance in Vienna on 13 March. Neville Chamberlain heard the news of the *Anschluss* whilst lunching with Ribbentrop and Churchill at 10 Downing Street. Eden was in the South of France with Marjorie, his sister, at Cap Ferrat, keeping in touch on a crackly radio. He had regarded the *Anschluss* in some form as inevitable. On a personal level, his absence from the Foreign Office at this time proved something of a blessing in disguise, as, short of military action – an unrealistic proposition in early 1938 – there was little Britain could do, with or without French support, to reverse Hitler's audacious coup. Eden knew war would come sooner or later. What he had not anticipated was the speed with which Chamberlain concluded an Anglo-Italian agreement that entailed *de jure* recognition of Mussolini's Abyssinian conquest.

'The most anxious feature of the international situation, as I see it', wrote Eden to Churchill on 22 April, 'is that temporary relaxation of tension may be taken as a pretext for the further relaxation of national effort, which is already inadequate to the gravity of the time.'[25]

Despite their joint concerns, Eden and Churchill had a complex and far from easy relationship at this time (and indeed later). Tacitly, they were rivals for the eventual vacancy at 10 Downing Street, and, before May 1940, Eden was considered by many Conservatives as the likelier heir. For Churchill, nearly twenty-three years older than Eden, this was an unpalatable situation, and there were lingering resentments and imagined condescensions that affected Churchill's treatment of Eden later when the positions were reversed. In the aftermath of the *Anschluss*, Hugh Dalton thought a duumvirate more likely, with Churchill as Prime Minister and Eden as Foreign Secretary, heading a Government of national unity. 'This breakaway plus Labour plus Liberal would command a majority in the House of Commons.'[26]

However, there were too many imponderables, especially as Eden's resignation had seemingly strengthened Chamberlain's hold on power. Many Tories, even those sympathetic to Eden, were unsure who their next leader might be. Churchill, with his controversial record, aroused great antagonisms, and Eden's low profile since his resignation had dampened his prospects. He seemed a manager rather than a leader. Typical was Harry Crookshank's reaction. Secretary for Mines since 1935, Crookshank was no lover of Chamberlain's foreign policy, but he remained wary of Churchill, whom he saw as a turncoat Liberal. Crookshank might have seemed a natural Eden supporter. His background was strikingly similar – Eton contemporary, decorated war hero, diplomat, Baldwin protégé, northern MP. Yet he had his doubts. 'Dined with Anthony Eden for a good gossip,' he recorded in his diary on 19 July. 'S. B. has marked him out to lead the party. I wonder.'[27] So did many others, as Eden's self-imposed exile from mainstream political life continued.

After Austria, Czechoslovakia was next on Hitler's list. Twenty-four foreign affairs debates occupied the House during the summer months, and Czechoslovakia was central to most of them. In the autumn Chamberlain and Halifax invited Walter Runciman, the former Liberal minister, to undertake what became known as the Prague Mission, as an 'independent negotiator' between the Czechoslovakian Government and the Sudeten Germans. The mission was misbegotten and doomed, as Chamberlain's

Parliamentary Private Secretary, Alec Dunglass, recognised, in that the French were the allies of Czechoslovakia, and were unlikely to go along with any accommodation of Hitler's Sudetenland claims. By the time Runciman returned from Prague, the European crisis had worsened appreciably and Chamberlain had already made his first visit to Hitler.

On the sidelines during this time, Eden had undertaken an extensive survey of social conditions, especially in the depressed areas, and on 19 August had written to Baldwin to tell him of his findings:

> I spent two days earlier this week on a tour of Tyneside similar to that I made in Durham in July. Their problems are different, but scarcely less serious or intractable. For the moment armaments provide a means of employment, but there is too little else. Export coal continues to fall sharply, being cut out by Polish & German competition. Except for one big electrical manufacturer concern employing 6000 men (Reynolds), there is no important expanding new industry on the Tyne ... I saw a large number of people. Coal owners, shipping, including Runciman's son,[28] Gateshead trading estate, Trade Union leaders, Social Service leaders & so forth. The remedies prescribed were varied, but all were united in uncertainty & grave anxiety for the future. They feel that insufficient thinking ahead is being done by the Govt, & they were at a loss to provide guidance for themselves.
>
> I have now promised to pay a visit to South Wales, & may make another to Lancashire before the House meets. I confess that I found the problems absorbingly interesting, & my present anomalous position is easier in that all kinds & conditions can & do express themselves without hesitation.[29]

Eden also visited Glasgow, where he studied industrial problems at first hand, particularly in shipbuilding. His visit to Wales was a comprehensive tour and offered a valuable insight into the state of the nation on the eve of war. Such tours give the lie to those who see Eden as a figure devoid of domestic experience. A phrase such as 'absorbingly interesting' underlines a telling truth, as does his record in Opposition after the war.[30]

Five years earlier, J. B. Priestley had made a similar journey, after which he had posed the rhetorical question, 'How many Members of Parliament could give even the roughest description of the organisation and working of a coal-mine?'[31] The Member for Warwick and Leamington was one. 'The condition of England', in the Disraelian sense, was central to Eden's political vision, and his visits to the humdrum streets of the industrial heartlands, with their moribund factories and despairing workforces, was always a potent reminder to him that 'It is those we are fighting for, foremost of all.'[32]

Despite his vigorous programme of social enquiry during the summer months of 1938, Eden felt underused, especially after his intense activity of the previous decade. With the loss of his ministerial salary, the lure of writing assumed a higher priority. However, Eden wanted to move on from journalism, even the hardback journalism of *Places in the Sun*, to an altogether higher level. Recent, rather tetchy, correspondence with Harold Macmillan (as publisher, not politician) about American literary rights had disillusioned him. The rewards of syndication for smaller pieces were not worth the candle. He now considered a substantial book, and was taken with the idea of writing a major biography. Churchill's activities in this field – he was working on the final volume of his life of Marlborough during that summer – and the recent publication in 1937 of *Great Contemporaries* (an inscribed copy of which he had sent to Eden) had inspired Eden to try his hand in this field. Just as he was considering what subject might be appropriate, literary agents approached him on 8 August with a firm proposal that he should write Stanley Baldwin's life.[33] It was an enticing prospect. Baldwin's official life, with access to the papers, would be a major project and, in the light of his own involvement in some of the recent events, the opportunity for a serious contribution to the historical record. The project never got off the ground, as Munich brought him back to front-line political activity. When G. M. Young was appointed Baldwin's biographer in 1944, Eden helped over interviews, but was not alone in thinking the book, finally published in 1952, unsympathetic and a grave disappointment. Eden's *Baldwin* remained a tantalising might-have-been.

During the latter part of August, the Edens took a holiday in Ireland, but he returned for two meetings on 9 and 11 September with Halifax on Britain's stance towards Czechoslovakia's proposed negotiations with the Sudetens. On 12 September *The Times* published a letter from Eden, warning that 'it is a dangerous illusion to assume that once a conflict had broken out in Central Europe it could be localised.'[34] Two days after Eden's letter, the Cabinet considered, and approved, Chamberlain's plan to visit Hitler at Berchtesgaden. On 16 September Chamberlain made the first of three flights to Germany.*

The second meeting (at Godesberg on 22 September) led to a memorandum that Hitler demanded the Czechs accept by 2 p.m. on 28 September. Jan Masaryk came to see Eden on 24 September after hearing reports of the humiliating Godesberg terms, an indication of Eden's standing with the beleaguered Czechs. 'He was in a state of great distress and reiterated several times that his Government could not accept them,'

---

*After the final one, his critics (though not Eden) quipped, 'If at first you don't concede, fly, fly, fly again.'

Eden wrote in his diary. 'He thought it incredible that the Prime Minister of Great Britain could forward such a document to a friendly power.'[35]

After Godesberg, Duff Cooper, First Lord of the Admiralty, ordered the mobilisation of the fleet, and steps to protect the Suez Canal, 'one of the most vital and vulnerable points in the Empire.'[36] War seemed very close.

At 10.30 p.m. on 27 September in Downing Street, Chamberlain received a message from Hitler, signifying that he was prepared to look again at the ultimatum. For his part, Chamberlain was prepared, if necessary, for a third flight to Germany. At 11.30 a.m. on 28 September, the Foreign Office despatched messages to Hitler, expressing Chamberlain's willingness to attend a four-power conference in Germany, with the French and the Italians, and one to Mussolini urging him to persuade Hitler to agree. The Chief Whip issued a three-line whip for 2.45 p.m., when the Prime Minister would make a statement on the international situation.

Rarely can the House of Commons have sat in more tense circumstances. As MPs gathered for the statement, those walking down Whitehall noticed knots of people quietly placing flowers on the steps of the Cenotaph. Eden remembered an initial sense of melancholy resignation in the Chamber of the House. Chamberlain's statement, a chronological résumé of the events of August and September, was heard with rapt attention and, such was the demand, relayed to listeners in the Lords library, the first time in parliamentary history that such a transmission had been authorised. Shortly after 3.30 p.m. Sir Horace Wilson beckoned to Alec Dunglass from behind the Speaker's chair. He was holding a piece of paper that was handed with some difficulty to Dunglass, who gave it to Sir John Simon. It was, as Simon recorded, 'a telegram from Hitler, inviting Chamberlain to fly to Munich the next morning, when Mussolini would be there. Daladier had also been invited.' At an appropriate break, Simon handed the historic telegram to Chamberlain, who announced the news to an exultant House.

As the cheering echoed and re-echoed round the Chamber, Eden remained firmly in his place. So did Leo Amery, Winston Churchill and Harold Nicolson. Their silent reserve did not go unnoticed. 'Liddall, behind me, hissed out "Stand up you brute",' Nicolson recorded in his diary; whilst Chips Channon, with some satisfaction, noted in his, 'How foolish the anti-Italians now looked, and Anthony Eden's face – I watched it – twitched, and he seemed discomforted.' Simon had no doubt that the scene 'was incomparably the greatest piece of real drama that the House of Commons has ever witnessed.'[37]

The subsequent days have often been described, together with the terms of the agreement reached at Munich, an agreement which betrayed the Czechs and which transferred the German-speaking fortified Sudetenland frontier region to Hitler. 'A pretty ignoble result,' Leo Amery wrote in his diary, adding, 'had a word with Eden, who is pretty gloomy about it all.'[38] Eden rang Halifax to express his dismay, especially at the demand that the Czech Government agree immediately to the terms.

The ramifications of Munich, its rights and wrongs, resonate still, and attitudes to it became a defining benchmark in many a career. The next forty years were to be heavily influenced by memories of Munich. Had the agreement stood, or had Hitler been replaced by a more accommodating regime, then three future Conservative Prime Ministers – Churchill, Eden and Macmillan, all of whom abstained during the Munich Debate – might have sunk without trace, or at least not achieved their later prominence.

Eden's stance, both at his resignation and during the Munich period, illustrated his deep belief in the sanctity of diplomatic agreements as a means of underpinning international stability. He showed himself to be an optimistic idealist in these matters, one of the reasons why the liberal-left looked favourably upon him, but not on Churchill, whose maverick pessimism was distasteful to them, quite apart from the baggage of his past career. Eden's belief in upholding a regulated structure in the conduct of foreign relations was to underpin his actions in the post-war era also, particularly at Geneva in 1954, but also in his detailed work on the Western European Union and the European Defence Community. Even Nasser, who eventually broke the 1954 Suez Base Treaty, was a man with whom Eden at first negotiated in good faith.[39] One Swedish envoy, who saw Eden at close quarters over many years, declared that he 'could change the atmosphere of a conference from deep pessimism and general mistrust to mild optimism and willingness to co-operate.'[40] These were instincts Eden never set aside.

Munich made Eden, just as surely as it unmade Chamberlain. Kingsley Wood's prophecy – 'Well, one result of this business is that we shall hear no more of Anthony Eden'[41] was spectacularly inaccurate. For Eden, Munich was always 'a collapse before the foe', and, like Churchill, he believed that 'in time all the men of Munich would be driven out'.[42]

After Munich, all the loose pieces of Eden's resignation fitted into place, even the timing, which had puzzled many. His spell in the wilderness had spared him much obloquy. He was not associated with the tame responses to the *Anschluss*, and he had not paid emotional tribute on the runway at Heston Airport or in the triumphalist scenes in Downing Street. Duff Cooper's resignation from the Admiralty on 1 October was a damp squib by comparison ('Good riddance of bad rubbish,' Cadogan wrote.[43]) Such are the strange workings of politics that Duff Cooper was not rewarded with the fruits of major office, after Chamberlain's fall. When Eden once more became Foreign Secretary,

Cooper, with hindsight the real hero of Munich, was still languishing in the Ministry of Information.

The events surrounding the Munich Agreement should have brought Eden and Churchill closer together as natural allies in 'the cause of England'. But their response was different, in both degree and tone, and there was a good deal of recrimination among the various anti-Munichois. Eden was not a natural rebel, and was uncomfortable at the prospect of being at odds with the Conservative Party machine, whatever his isolation from Chamberlain. The 'Eden Group', which now met weekly at Ronald Tree's Queen Anne's Gate house, was far more disruptive than its eponymous hub. As a result, it was not long before Sir Joseph Ball had arranged to have Tree's telephone bugged. Almost as a *quid pro quo*, Vansittart, isolated as Chief Diplomatic Adviser, fed Eden's group details of what was unfolding, so that the elements of intrigue and double-dealing escalated rapidly. The same techniques were to be used against Eden, from within, during the Suez Crisis. Some participants even had experience of breach of trust in both crises and from several standpoints.[44]

Other dissenting groups vied for Eden's patronage, but with little success. Eden was retrospectively blamed by Violet Bonham Carter for not signing a telegram from the anti-appeasement 'Focus Group' to Chamberlain on 29 September, a refusal that left Churchill in tears.[45]* Feelings ran high on all sides. Though the public mood was celebratory, many had their doubts. The Scottish poet Hugh MacDiarmid penned a bitter response:

> The callous and irresponsible betrayal
> Of the Czech Republic has brought not peace
> But a new and sharper sword.[46]

The Prime Minister returned to England amidst relief that war might be averted and that it might be 'peace in our time'. One cinema proprietor advertised the newsreel, with a poster declaring, 'Chamberlain the Peacemaker: for one week only.'[47]

Eden broke his parliamentary silence on 3 October 1938 at the opening of the three-day Munich Debate. 'During the last three months,' he said, 'it has been my privilege to listen in silence to many Debates upon Foreign

---

*Violet Bonham Carter's account was written nearly twenty years after the event, and in the wake of Eden's resignation from the Premiership. Eden then denied that he had been rung up and asked to sign, though Harold Nicolson's contemporary diary account of 29 September records that both Eden and Attlee refused to sign, Eden on the grounds that it would appear as a personal vendetta against Chamberlain. In any case, Eden had made his views abundantly clear in speeches in Leamington during the last half of September.

affairs.' Now it was time to speak again. Unfortunately, in comparison with Churchill's forthright denunciation of Munich – 'we have sustained a total and unmitigated defeat'[48] – Eden's speech, though unambiguous, did not have the same impact. 'Successive surrenders bring only successive humiliation', he said, 'and they, in their turn, more humiliating demands.'[49] But this was not the ringing call anticipated by his followers, 'who, whatever the House of Commons may have thought,' Oliver Harvey wrote, 'were disappointed, not to say shocked.'[50]

Among the younger generation, Bonar Law's son, Richard, made the most compelling speech, as Eden was to acknowledge in his memoirs. When the House divided, the figures were 369 for the Government and 150 against, but the headlines were made by the thirty Conservatives who abstained, thirteen remaining in their places as the division took place. Churchill, Richard Law and Harold Nicolson were among those who stayed in the Chamber; Amery, Duff Cooper, Eden and Macmillan were leading figures among the other seventeen. A Rubicon had been crossed. In retrospect, the orchestrated abstention was a vital staging post in Chamberlain's decline; it also saw Churchill assume the leadership of the anti-appeasers from Eden's tenuous grasp. From this moment, until the outbreak of war, Churchill was the principal inspiration for the discontented of all parties.

Different groupings still existed, as Harold Nicolson recorded in his diary on 9 November of 'a hush-hush meeting with Anthony Eden'. Others present included Amery and Macmillan. 'All good Tories and sensible men,' recorded Nicolson, adding, 'This group is distinct from the Churchill group.' All were 'deeply disturbed by the fact that Chamberlain does not seem to understand the gravity of the situation.' They agreed to meet on a regular basis. In the early hours of the next morning, Hitler ordered an attack on Jewish homes and synagogues. It was known as *Kristallnacht* (The Night of the Broken Glass). Eden's condemnation of what he called this 'unspeakable tyranny'[51] was seen by Nicolson as a sensation, not least because of the puzzled reaction in the country as to his motives. 'I know what he is doing,' wrote Nicolson to his wife. 'He is trying to wake up the country to real energies and sacrifice.'[52]

Although he had broken all links with Chamberlain, Eden still kept in touch with Halifax, who poured out his troubled feelings. 'Had an hour's conversation with Edward this afternoon', Eden recorded on 11 October. 'He said that he was very unhappy and counting the hours to the time when he should leave the office. I told him that in my own view the proper solution was a National Government in the broadest sense to include Labour and Liberals. We could not go much faster in armaments without some form of mobilisation of industry. Mobilisation of industry would require the co-operation of Labour, even if Labour was to refuse, N's position would be much stronger.'[53]

Events in Europe since Munich now exercised the concerns of many Americans, including former isolationists. 'In the United States, observers are beginning to say that we are giving ground, not because we couldn't stand firm if we wished, but because our nerve has gone – Nothing could be more dangerous than such an impression as that,' Eden wrote privately after Munich, adding 'We have not lost our old spirit. We are not effete. But how dangerous to let such an impression get abroad.'[54] He now determined to do all he could to correct these misunderstandings.

Joseph Kennedy, the newly arrived American Ambassador in London, invited Eden to lunch with him in late November. Kennedy had heard that Eden had previously declined an invitation to speak in America to the annual conference of the National Association of Manufacturers. He begged him to reconsider, so that Americans could hear British 'attitudes' at first hand. Tacitly, this was understood to be 'anti-Chamberlain attitudes'. Eden's first concern was that he should not be seen as criticising his own country abroad – in his book the ultimate taboo – but on reflection, and after further pressure from Kennedy, he accepted. The decision was to consolidate his international position and make him, in American eyes, the acknowledged leader of his generation.

So swiftly had events moved on that the travel arrangements proved hectic. Eventually, Eden and Beatrice secured passages on the *Aquitania*, but the liner was delayed by heavy weather, and there was doubt as to whether he would be in time to fulfil his principal engagement. As the liner came within sight of land, the time for Eden's speech neared, and he was taken by special cutter from Battery Point and rushed to the Waldorf Astoria with a police escort and screaming sirens, a dramatic entry to New York. The strains of 'Land of Hope and Glory' greeted Eden as he entered the main dining hall, where more than 4,000 people were waiting expectantly. As Eden was seated, a note was handed to him from Noël Coward, on a neighbouring table, telling him not to mind the photographers, welcome advice in this strange new world.

The keynote of Eden's speech, broadcast live on three networks, was 'the gathering storm', which was to provide Churchill with the title for the first volume of his war memoirs. So great was the impact that, at the suggestion of Nevada Senator Key Pittman, the speech was printed in the Congressional Record. Pittman, Chairman of the Senate Foreign Relations Committee, later told Eden that no unofficial visitor to America had ever been accorded such a welcome.

Eden continued with a hectic programme. On 13 December he met

Sumner Welles, the Under-Secretary of State, who took him on to the White House for private talks with President Roosevelt, an exceptional privilege for a foreign back-bencher. Protocol was observed on both sides and Chamberlain was not on the agenda. The conversation ranged widely, over the importance of air defences and Roosevelt's own commitment to rearmament, as well as developments in the Middle and Far East. Later Eden and his wife were invited to tea with Mrs Roosevelt. Beatrice's empathy for all things American also contributed to the success of the tour, which included visits to the Metropolitan Museum and to the Eden family mansion in Baltimore. Eden was described as Britain's Prime Minister-in-waiting, and the adulation in the Press, even by American standards of hyperbole, was remarkable. The *New York Herald Tribune* led the way:

> He is Prince Charming. He is St George fighting the dragons. He resigned for principle. He isn't a trimmer. He can stand up till the last round and come back after a knockout. He is an Englishman.[55]

On his return to London, Eden was invited to address the American Chamber of Commerce. 'No visit I have ever paid to any land,' he said at the luncheon in his honour, 'has given me so much interest and so much pleasure as that brief week in the United States of America.'[56] Official responses to his tour, sent to Halifax from Victor Mallet, Counsellor at the British Embassy, confirmed the impact Eden had made:

> Mr Anthony Eden's visit to the United States has been the major sensation of the week. I am told on all sides that not for many years has any visitor from abroad excited such interest and enthusiasm. The American public seemed to have decided to make Mr Eden its hero on account of his championship of democracy and his well-known antipathy to dictators.[57]

Returning to Britain, Eden wrote to Stanley Baldwin from the *Queen Mary*. Underneath all the razzmatazz, he identified worrying trends in American opinion. 'I was horrified at the atmosphere I found. Poor Nancy & her Cliveden set has done much damage, & 90% of the US is firmly persuaded that you & I are the only 2 Tories who are not Fascists in disguise. Certainly HMG has continued to lose Americans sympathy utterly.' Roosevelt may have steered clear of Chamberlain, but Eden's other hosts were not so punctilious:

> Most of my time was spent in asserting that Neville was not a Fascist, nor John Simon always a 'double crosser'. You see how American I became. I hope that I have not perjured myself too often on J. S.'s behalf. They (US) were wonderfully kind. The whole reception can only be compared to electioneering at home. There was no official welcome, so that it was

all spontaneous. If one was perhaps stuck in a traffic block near Wall St at the luncheon hour & recognised, they would begin to clap & cheer. Al Smith [the prominent Democrat] said, 'You could run for President here & take it in your stride.' With all allowance for American exaggeration it really was an amazing welcome.

Eden took the opportunity of reminding Baldwin how much he owed him:

> If I have been able to help my country, or even the govt at all, it is down to you, so that I am very happy not to have to repeat a flop. But [Joseph] Kennedy was right to be worried, & I am still. This govt is too far to the right to regain these people, & Nancy should be compelled to shut Cliveden.[58]

Eden's reaction to the 'Cliveden set', a supposed gathering of like-minded appeasers invited by Nancy Astor to her country house by the banks of the Thames, was uncharacteristically fervent, reflecting his frustration at the reputation of the National Government abroad. But not all who accepted the Astor hospitality were appeasers. Cliveden was an arena, not an agenda. The Edens had even been principal guests at a house party there in October 1937, when they were described by Thomas Jones as 'the highest lights'. That weekend had proved one of Eden's rare chances for lengthy talks with Nevile Henderson. 'Politics all day and all night,' Jones wrote. 'Eden has aged since I saw him six months ago and is dog-tired at the start of the Session. I sat between him and Henderson after the ladies left last night and found they differed widely in policy.'[59]

Appeasement divided communities (from Cliveden to All Souls), professions and families, and stances were often remembered for years to come, with striking consequences. Eden prospered, but Duff Cooper dwindled; the reputation of Rab Butler, Halifax's Under-Secretary, was permanently tarnished, whilst Alec Dunglass, Chamberlain's PPS, suffered no serious rebuff. For anti-appeasers, the Cliveden set, in the words of one commentator, 'had become an accepted myth not only in Great Britain but abroad', and as such, proved 'a convenient target.'[60] With his comments to Baldwin, Eden showed that he was not averse to aiming such barbs.

One of the urgent political questions of early 1939 was whether Churchill and Eden might return to the Government. Jim Thomas reported to Cranborne on 8 March that David Margesson, the Chief Whip, had told him 'that he and some of the Cabinet were very anxious that Anthony should return as soon as possible'. But there were still complications before this could be achieved:

> Alec Dunglass spoke to me a day or two later about Anthony & I was

very careful to give him the impression that Anthony was by no means tumbling over himself to return. Alec said he did not know what was in the P.M.'s mind: he, himself, felt that the majority of the House of Commons would like to see the P.M.'s foreign policy succeed beyond all doubt before Anthony's return as his inclusion in the Cabinet might send the dictators off the deep end once more!'[61]

Mention of Eden's name, especially since his visit to America, tended to have this effect on Hitler. In his speech at the Kroll Opera House in Berlin on 30 January, the sixth anniversary of his rise to power, the German Chancellor singled out Eden (together with Churchill and Duff Cooper among the British) as one of the 'agitators', who threatened the peace of Europe. By chance, two of these 'agitators', Eden and Churchill, were together in the lobby of the House of Commons on 15 March when news came that Nazi troops had moved into Prague. Six days later the Lithuanian territory of Memel was surrendered to the Reich. By the end of the month, the Spanish Civil War had concluded with Franco's defeat of the Republicans. Not to be outdone among the genuine agitators, Mussolini sent troops into Albania on 7 April, driving King Zog into exile, and the two kingdoms of Italy and Albania were 'united' under King Victor Emmanuel III.

For Eden and Churchill, the need for continued rearmament became even more urgent. As Eden never believed that Hitler would back down, he accepted that war was necessary. On 4 April Eden was visited by Colonel Joseph Beck, the Polish Foreign Minister, immediately after his meeting with Chamberlain, a sign of the talismanic role Eden filled for so many. They discussed British guarantees to Poland, and Beck made it clear 'that Poland would in no circumstances submit to German rule, nor be included within the German sphere of influence,'[62] confirming Eden in his view that Poland would prove the final exigence. He sent Halifax an account of his talks, and spoke to Chamberlain about the possibility of forestalling any subsequent Nazi-Soviet Pact by seeking some form of understanding with Russia over securing peace in the eastern Mediterranean, a theme to which he returned in a speech in the Commons on 19 May.

Eden even offered to help with such a mission himself, even though Maxim Litvinov had by now been replaced as Russian Commissar for Foreign Affairs by the largely unknown Vyacheslav Molotov. Halifax was in favour,* but Chamberlain, doubting the long-term consequences, had no wish to see Eden in the corridors of Geneva again.

*

---

*Ideological Tory objections to any alliance with the Soviets, without which guarantees to Poland could be worthless, had largely dissipated. The main reservation was now over Russian military capability. Meanwhile reports from Berlin confirmed that Hitler had been seeking some kind of agreement with Stalin, ostensibly over trade. *New York Times*, 9 May 1939.

After his offer had been spurned, in the summer of 1939 Eden holidayed with his family at the Spithead Hotel, Bembridge, on the Isle of Wight. There was something unreal about the atmosphere as war drew ever closer, and for once tennis and swimming did not lighten his mood. He was now forty-two, beyond the age specified in April's Conscription Bill; nevertheless, without office, he felt it his duty to prepare for active service. So he joined the London Rangers, as second-in-command of a Motor Battalion of his beloved King's Royal Rifle Corps. As he once more organised military manoeuvres (with Toby Low, a future Brigadier and Tory MP), it was as though the intervening quarter of a century had never been. Comparisons with 1914 were inevitable. Among his men Eden found no less an enthusiasm to serve, but greater physical fitness and intelligence. News of the Soviet-German Pact on 22 August, signed by Ribbentrop and Molotov, reached him in his tent early one morning when he was in camp at Beaulieu. A junior officer asked Eden what this meant. 'I had to say that it meant war.'[63]

On 29 August, Churchill and Eden were photographed walking to the House of Commons for the recall of Parliament, amid demands for their return to high office. 'If we are to have an inner War Cabinet,' ran the caption, 'it is difficult to see how either of them can be left out of it.'[64] That night Eden broadcast to America, affirming that Britain would honour all obligations to Poland. The last days of peace were at hand.

On 1 September the Territorials were placed on active service and Eden's battalion was put in charge of defending London's bridges. Before the day was out, news came of Hitler's invasion of Poland.

Eden was genuinely undecided: should he serve in the Armed Forces, or accept Government office, if offered? He heard Chamberlain's declaration of war with his Group at Ronald Tree's house on Sunday 3 September. 'It seemed the lament of a man deploring his own failure,' he felt, 'rather than the call of a nation to arms.'[65]

Eden walked to the House with Duff Cooper, to the sound of air-raid sirens. In the Chamber he heard the Prime Minister formally affirm that Britain was now at war. In the afternoon Chamberlain summoned Eden to Downing Street and offered him the Dominions Office, a subordinate post for a former Foreign Secretary, though one for which he proved well suited. Eden was disappointed – he would have preferred a service ministry – but he regarded it as his duty to serve. Churchill became First Lord of the Admiralty, the post he had held on the outbreak of war in 1914. Kingsley Wood and Hore-Belisha retained their posts at the Air Ministry and the War Office.

On his return from Downing Street, Eden wrote first to Cranborne:

This is to confess that I am back in the govt. I have accepted Dominions with many doubts and regrets, especially about my Rangers. I am not officially in War Cabinet, but in fact I am because I can attend & take part in discussions whenever I wish, on the analogy of Balfour in War Cabinet when For. Sec in first war.[66]

CHAPTER NINE

Uphill All the Way

1939-41

Watched the bombing of French ports after dinner; the firing
was certainly heavy & some good flashes lit up the sky which we
hoped were bombs among the barges. Behind us we could also
hear the rumble of the guns & the explosion of bombs in more
distant London.

Anthony Eden diary, 21 September 1940[1]

Dined with Winston & Clemmie alone . . . He was pleased I was
at FO & asked me to confess I was also! I did so! Yes said W it
is like moving up from fourth form to the sixth!

Anthony Eden diary, 20 January 1941[2]

Morale here continues amazingly good. We are going through a
sharp, cold spell, which is not too agreeable for those with
broken windows, but the spirit of the nation seems able to rise
above almost any discomfort.

Anthony Eden to Sir Samuel Hoare, 3 January 1941[3]

For the second time in a quarter of a century Eden's actions were now
determined by war. As he returned to Fitzhardinge Street on the evening of
3 September an uncertain prospect stretched ahead. He knew better than
many how military preparations were at best barely acceptable. To offset
this, a few days earlier in camp at Beaulieu he had been cheered by the
spirit of determination among the soldiers under his command. The
immediate task was to match this patriotic will with proper logistical
support. As Secretary of State for the Dominions, Eden was to play an
extensive part in establishing and coordinating this process on a wider
canvas, a strategy he had advocated from the back-benches as essential to
any future war effort.

Eden's war can be divided into three phases, not dissimilar to the overall
pattern of the wider global struggle. The first was from 3 September 1939
to June 1941, when Hitler invaded Russia and the pattern of the war
changed decisively. The second, a period of alliances and conferences, was
from June 1941 to Christmas 1944, and was marked by America's entry
into the war after Pearl Harbor and Eden's enhanced role in Government

as plenipotentiary extraordinary and Leader of the House of Commons, an almost insurmountable burden. The final phase, in the first seven months of 1945, saw the historic gatherings at Yalta, San Francisco and Potsdam, where Eden's hopes were that the victors would avoid the mistakes of Versailles. The Potsdam Conference coincided with the Conservative defeat at the General Election of July 1945, and Eden's first spell in Opposition for fourteen years. The final negotiations at Potsdam were no longer his responsibility, though he kept in close touch with his successor as Foreign Secretary, Ernest Bevin.

'War,' General Wolfe of Quebec had said, 'is an option of difficulties.' Eden became well aware of the truth of this aphorism, quoting it in the Commons in May 1941. Britain was the one nation continuously ranged against Germany, and Eden one of only five* men to serve in Government without a break from 3 September 1939 to 27 July 1945.

In political terms, Eden's sustained contribution to overall victory during these six years, years he described as 'the hardest and proudest of my life,'[4] was second only to Churchill's.

The Dominions Office, where Eden began his war, had been created in July 1925 to deal with business in connection with the self-governing countries, such as the Irish Free State (later Eire), Southern Rhodesia and the South African territories, and with matters relating to the Imperial Conferences. Important in peacetime, the office became of vital significance in war. Eden's six predecessors as Secretary of State had included Leo Amery and Malcolm MacDonald, whom he much admired, but none had faced his amount of work. In June 1939 the office had received 223 telegrams and despatched 194; in September 1939 those figures rose to 779 and 783 respectively, and the totals continued to mount. Eden's main job was to coordinate the work of five departments, of which the most important was the one dealing with the political and constitutional questions of war, foreign affairs and publicity. His remit also included Naval, Military, Air and Civil Aviation questions, together with any necessary censorship. Financial matters included Exchange Control, Trade, Supply, and Migration. Liaison with the League of Nations was also his responsibility. The main function of the important 'Department E' was 'contact with forces', the duty from which Eden derived most personal satisfaction. As Secretary of State, he attended all meetings of the War Cabinet, though he

---

*Apart from Churchill and Eden, the others were Sir John Anderson, R. A. Butler and Sir John (later Viscount) Simon. From 1942, Eden and Anderson, in that order, were Churchill's nominated successors in the event of Churchill's death. Alone of the quartet, Eden was primarily involved in advising Churchill on military strategy and coordinating international relations.

could not contribute to non-Dominions matters, and his main task was to advise on the probable reaction of Dominions Governments to any particular proposal.[5]

Although the Dominions Office was a lowly post for a former Foreign Secretary, and even insulting according to some of Eden's friends, since the offer came without formal membership of the War Cabinet, Chamberlain had in fact given Eden the opportunity for important service. The downside was less immediately obvious. By accepting re-entry into Government at this level, Eden was ruling himself out of the immediate succession if Chamberlain fell, just as a mountaineer at too lowly a camp cannot make a single-handed push for the summit even if the weather clears. In March 1939, an opinion poll had revealed that 38 per cent of the public favoured Eden as the next Prime Minister, whereas the two who were candidates in May 1940 – Halifax and Churchill – had the backing in 1939 of only 7 per cent respectively. At the Foreign Office, or outside the Government altogether, Eden would have been *papabile* in May 1940.

In the short term, the Dominions Office proved a place of significant responsibility. Eden's military background and his personal knowledge of Dominions from Canada to New Zealand, together with his recent work at the League of Nations, made him well qualified to coordinate the contribution of the protectorates. The Dominions Office gave Eden an overview of the executive responsibilities of war that he would not easily have gained elsewhere, granted that Chamberlain was not going to reinstate him in the Foreign Office.

Eden's Permanent Secretary at the Dominions Office was Sir Edward Harding, a stalwart of the 1912 Royal Commission on the Dominions, and head of the department since 1930. No civil servant had worked harder for Commonwealth unity in the face of the coming war, and Harding had prepared the path for the incoming Secretary of State with both foresight and precision. Eden's Under-Secretary at the Dominions Office was the Duke of Devonshire,[6] though much of his day-to-day work was with his private secretary, Norman Archer. The faithful Jim Thomas, as Archer noted, was installed as Parliamentary Private Secretary in a 'wretched little passage room which was all that an overcrowded D.O. could give him close enough to you'.

On 4 September Eden was sworn in as Secretary of State at Buckingham Palace, after which he went straight to the office, where his first action was to institute daily meetings (soon dubbed 'the junior War Cabinet') with the four Dominion High Commissioners from Australia, Canada, New Zealand and South Africa. Norman Archer's later recollection was that Eden 'developed these High Commissioner meetings into a new method of keeping the Dominions in the closest possible touch with everything that was going on', as a result of which there was 'a remarkable atmosphere of reciprocal frankness and common purpose, which was reflected in the whole field of relations between the UK and Dominion Governments.'[7] Eden's routine also included a Cabinet meeting at least once a day.

Eden's first concern was barely disguised resentment at Eire's neutrality ('a country still in name a part of the British Commonwealth')[8] and the consequent lack of south-western Irish ports, access to which would have reduced allied shipping losses considerably. Eden was determined that there should be British representation in Dublin, where Germany, Italy and Japan had a diplomatic presence, and after negotiation with Éamon de Valéra, a former colleague at Geneva, Eden brought Sir John Maffey,[9] a former Permanent Under-Secretary at the Colonial Office, out of retirement as British 'Representative'. This proved an appointment of the utmost importance.

Mindful also of building on his good name in America by emphasising Britain's determination to fight for eventual victory, Eden broadcast coast-to-coast on 10 September, reminding his recent hosts that, whatever hardships might be endured, 'our new civilisation will be built just the same, for some forces are bigger than men, and in that new civilisation will be found liberty and opportunity and hope for all.'[10] Even though Eden was a Secretary of State, on 26 September he applied to be put on the reserve of the 2nd Rangers.[11]

With Vincent Massey, the Canadian High Commissioner, and General Henry Crerar, Eden had greeted two Canadian contingents on their arrival in Greenock on 18 and 30 December, later inspecting the 1st Canadian Division in training at Aldershot, which evoked memories of his own period in the garrison town before embarkation for France in 1916. There was intense security, and, as Norman Archer recalled, 'some absurd Censor stopped the publication of all the photographs on the ground that the sprinkling of snow visible in them would have revealed valuable meteorological information to the enemy.'[12]

Eden's first overseas trip as Dominions Secretary was to Egypt in February 1940 to welcome Dominions troops from Australia and New Zealand. It proved a deeply moving moment, seeing these young men, many facing the threat of death within weeks, rallying to the call, as he and his contemporaries had done a quarter of a century earlier. 'These men,' he said on his return to England, 'who might very well have been excused had they failed to appreciate the extent of the peril that pressed in the first instance upon us, saw clearly from the first.'[13] Eden also used the visit to take stock of the military situation, meeting General Wavell and other allied commanders, including Admiral Cunningham. Eden was deeply impressed by Wavell's quiet integrity and inner calm, as well as his shrewd and frank assessments of strategic needs, which he unfolded to Eden as they travelled together to the Suez Canal on 12 February to inspect defences. 'The keeping open of the Suez Canal must be regarded as a prime task,' Churchill later insisted.[14] The keeping of Wavell was not to prove such an urgent priority for Churchill, and although Eden championed Wavell's cause against what he felt were Churchill's partial onslaughts, in the end it was to no avail. 'The truth was that Churchill never understood Wavell,' Eden believed, 'and Wavell never seemed to encourage Churchill to do so.'[15]

Whilst in Egypt, Eden also had an audience with the young King Farouk, whom he had met in England in the 1930s when he was at Woolwich. The contrast with Wavell's dignity and mature wisdom was very marked, and Eden feared for the political stability of the region. 'Unhappily,' he concluded, 'there is no Egyptian Melbourne to guide and warn.'[16]

After his audience with King Farouk, Eden met again the signatories to the 1936 Anglo-Egyptian Treaty at the British Embassy, an occasion of warmth and goodwill. 'The visit was a colossal success from every point of view. Its unexpectedness gave dramatic interest and caught the public mind,' Sir Miles Lampson, formerly British High Commissioner, and since the 1936 Treaty the first Ambassador to Egypt, reported to Sir Horace Wilson. 'He [Eden] himself was quite indefatigable and I marvelled how he stood the physical fatigue and strain. It was a very full and tiring programme, but he didn't jib at a single item, & never wilted once however long the programme or the number of people with whom he talked.'[17]

During his return to England, the perilous nature of wartime air travel was vividly brought home to Eden, as his plane only just succeeded in reaching Gibraltar from Malta on the second leg of the homeward journey. Beatrice Eden was very apprehensive about these air journeys (as Eden's second wife, Clarissa, was to be over the use of helicopters at Chequers in 1955) and hoped, in vain, that their son Simon would not become keen on flying. For Beatrice, as for so many wartime wives, this was a lonely time. The Edens had taken a house in Frensham against the time when London would be bombed. Ironically, Frensham became a risky area because of the visibility of its many lakes from the air, lakes that eventually had to be drained for the duration. Inevitably Eden was away for long stretches, and Beatrice did not find the depths of Surrey congenial. Simon was finishing at Eton and then in the RAF, and Nicholas had begun to board at Ludgrove School. The roots of eventual separation and divorce were already in place.

Eden's appointment as Dominions Secretary had removed the eponymous focus of his 'Group', but not its motivation. What Harold Nicolson had called 'his inner nucleus'[18] still met, and Leo Amery presided at a dinner on 27 September of 'the ex-Eden group'. The following week Eden dined with the group. 'It was pretty clear,' Amery recorded, 'that he thought Hore-Belisha [Secretary of State for War] was not on top of his job, and that there was a lack of real control and drive in many directions.'[19]

That very morning in Cabinet, Eden had supported the proposal (originally from Hankey) that Amery be given a job in Government. 'I had passed it up on a slip of paper,' he wrote in his diary, 'and Neville pushed it away with an irritated snort.' Eden felt Chamberlain lacked magnanimity, and that Churchill and he himself were only there under sufferance because of public pressure. As there were no such backing for Amery, Chamberlain could vent his true feelings. 'It was a revealing little explosion,' Eden wrote, of Chamberlain's scorn.[20] Even in the last weeks of his life in October 1940, when, as Lord President of the Council, Chamberlain swore in Cranborne as Dominions Secretary, he did so without a single acknowledgement or polite word.

Eden was favourably surprised by the variety and importance of the work at Dominions. 'This place is more interesting than I had expected,' he wrote to Baldwin after three days.[21] Nevertheless, his sights were ultimately fixed on Hore-Belisha's job at the War Office, because he genuinely believed that he could contribute better to the formation of strategy, and to the morale of military personnel at all levels. Charles Mott-Radclyffe, a future colleague of Eden in the House, who was to advise him on the Suez Canal Base in 1954, often hosted ministerial visits during his wartime service in Greece and the Middle East. In Mott-Radclyffe's recollection, there was never any VIP 'who displayed to the same degree the unerring touch that Eden had with troops'. He found Eden 'completely relaxed and in his element', talking to 'every man in the front and rear rank of my Company', and even having his hair cut in the Corporals' Mess. 'His subsequent address to the troops, assembled in a semi-circle in the sand, was a masterpiece.'[22]

By the end of the year, Eden's rehabilitation was well under way. He had made a favourable impression on the Dominion representatives when hosting a big gathering in London in late October, which included a visit of inspection in France and talks with the French Prime Minister, Édouard Daladier. Eden was disturbed by the under-equipped front-line defences. He feared that the next months would prove a critical time.

'A. E. is lying pretty,' was Oliver Harvey's summary of 1939, 'but might well get the War Office *vice* Belisha and he would certainly adore to get it.'[23] At the same time, Eden's future Foreign Secretary, Selwyn Lloyd, then on the Staff Course at Camberley, was articulating many of Eden's own feelings regarding Hore-Belisha. 'Our M.P.s from here went up to heckle

Hore-Belisha,' he wrote. 'They all hate him like poison – and he never tells the truth publicly about the Army or the state of its equipment.'[24] A tacit element of anti-Semitism contributed to the opposition to Hore-Belisha. There was a general sense of relief among the military experts when he lost his job in January 1940. Hore-Belisha's nemesis came in the form of Lord Gort, his appointee for Chief of the Imperial General Staff, who prevailed in a battle of wills, by winning the ear of Neville Chamberlain. Hore-Belisha's meeting with Chamberlain on 4 January proved a painful one on both sides. Initially, it seemed that Hore-Belisha might be moved to the Ministry of Information, or even the Board of Trade. 'I think I am entitled to know what is the prejudice of which you spoke and which you feel disinclined to resist,' Hore-Belisha asked Chamberlain, who 'replied that it was prejudice in the Command in France', a coded way of saying that Hore-Belisha was rude to superiors in front of inferiors, and was too vociferous in his criticism of Gort's strategy.[25] Churchill pressed Chamberlain to promote Eden in Hore-Belisha's place, but his request fell on deaf ears.

Chamberlain chose to appoint Oliver Stanley, who became War Secretary on 5 January 1940. Eden, surprisingly, was not unduly disappointed, as he believed that his time would come. Jim Thomas wrote to Baldwin, who liked to keep in touch with news of his protégés:

> Some of the colleagues wanted AE; I know the War Office and the BEF staff did, & there is much disappointment, but he himself is glad he was not chosen at this particular moment. A few months hence it might have been different but he feels that the Dominions wd. have resented his leaving them after only 4 months & there are still important jobs to be done in laying the foundations of the Empire effort.
>
> A little later it wd. have been ideal; a premier real administrative job in a service which has his heart more than any other. But he is happier at the DO now than at any other time since he went there & is lying fairly pretty. Even the Beaverbrook press told our new public relations officer that 'it was now not worth their while attacking him as he was doing too well & his following in the country was too great.'[26]
>
> Oliver Harvey reassured Eden 'how well placed' he was at the Dominions Office, ' "in, but not of, the Cabinet", seeing all that goes on but not being responsible for the conduct of the war and so becoming discredited, having very useful and important work keeping the Dominions straight on foreign policy and representing their point of view in Cabinet'.[27]

Sometimes Eden was an unhappy messenger, as in November 1939, when New Zealand, the country he loved most outside Britain, put forward a proposal for a negotiated peace.[28] A more congenial assignment was his work in setting up the Empire Air Training Scheme. The scheme proved an outstanding success of what the British High Commissioner in Ottawa called 'intra-Imperial relations', producing 125,000 airmen from Canada alone, and large numbers from the other Dominions.

Eden's move to the War Office was not long delayed. Political promotions often entail equivalent demotions or retirements. Eden's way to the Dominions Office was paved by Chamberlain's removal of Inskip, albeit to the comforts of the Woolsack. Chamberlain's own fall in May 1940, and Oliver Stanley's return to active service, occasioned Eden's subsequent move to the War Office.

Although Eden was at the Dominions Office for only a relatively short time, he laid important foundations for what proved a historic and sustained programme of world-wide support for the allied effort. Part of this achievement came from his appreciation that the Dominions were independent entities and that any attempt to mould a 'Dominion point of view' would be resisted, as each country would inevitably look at things in its own individual manner,[29] as seen in New Zealand's unwelcome initiative the previous November. Common purpose would not be enhanced by an imposed conformity, as he pointed out in a later Foreign Office despatch to all British representatives overseas.[30] Field Marshal Smuts of South Africa acknowledged this at a meeting of Dominions Prime Ministers just before D-Day, when he said to the War Cabinet that the manner in which 'the British Commonwealth, with its comparatively slender resources, had fought Germany and Italy at a time when Russia was bound by treaty to the enemy, and when Europe was overrun, would stand out in history as one of the most remarkable achievements ever known.'[31] Eden's skill in coordinating the early stages of this process was not the least of his many contributions to overall victory.

One of the ironies of history is that both Lloyd George and Churchill came to the Premiership during the two world wars after disasters that were formally the responsibility of their respective departments. In December 1916, the stalemate of the first five months of the Battle of the Somme, led to the War Secretary supplanting Asquith; in May 1940, the failure of the Norwegian naval campaign brought the First Lord of the Admiralty to Downing Street.

The Germans had invaded Norway on 9 April, thus bringing to an end the so-called 'Phoney War'. Eden's part in the events leading to Chamberlain's fall after the Norwegian debate in the House, when ninety-three Conservatives withheld their support, was minimal. As the extent of the Norwegian reversal became clearer, it was still uncertain whether Halifax or Churchill would become Prime Minister. Eden lunched with Norman Archer in Fitzhardinge Street one day and the next dined with

Churchill, who 'told me he thought it plain N.C. would advise King to send for him,' Eden recorded in his diary. 'Edward [Halifax] did not wish to succeed. Parliamentary position too difficult.' Churchill outlined his intentions. 'W would be Minister of Defence as well as P.M. W quiet and calm. He wishes me to take War. I told him I would obey orders and serve or not and where he thought I could best help.' Eden was in no doubt as to the potential difficulties. 'Position will be very difficult one for state of army is inglorious, and it will not be easy to maintain harmony with W.'[32]

The next day, 10 May, one of the most significant in British history, events unfolded as Churchill had prophesied: Churchill became Prime Minister and Eden got the War Office. Eden, though still not in the War Cabinet, was in Churchill's first list of ministers, which still included Neville Chamberlain, as Lord President; the Labour leader Clement Attlee, as Lord Privy Seal; Labour's Arthur Greenwood, as Minister without Portfolio; and the Liberal, Archibald Sinclair, as Secretary of State for Air. When Labour's A. V. Alexander was appointed to the Admiralty, the three service ministries were held by representatives of each of the political parties, in a Government that was National not only in name, but in reality, something Eden had long advocated during the late 1930s.

As Secretary of State for War, Eden was following in the steps of many famous predecessors, including Kitchener, Lloyd George and Churchill himself. He assumed his responsibilities on the afternoon of Whit Sunday, 12 May, believing 'there was no more important work to be done anywhere else.'[33]

His first meeting was with the Chief of the Imperial General Staff, General Ironside, an urgent review of the military situation on the Continent, particularly in Belgium. The next day Liège capitulated, as the German push westwards increased in pace.

Eden knew that his key relationship in his new post at this parlous time would be with the Service Chiefs. Ironside had succeeded Gort as CIGS, but was temperamentally unsuited to the work, though he recognised in Eden his strength of character for the War Office and wrote well of him in his diaries. After Churchill became Prime Minister, Ironside's days as CIGS were numbered. On 27 May, he was replaced by Field Marshal Sir John Dill, and became C-in-C Home Forces. Churchill did not appreciate Dill's qualities either – he dubbed him 'Dilly-Dally' and put him on a par with 'wavering' Wavell, two spectacular misjudgements – and more moves took place before the fateful summer months were out. On 19 July Eden summoned General Alan Brooke at short notice and told him that he was to succeed Ironside as C-in-C Home Forces. The Dill-Brooke team was to be central to the conduct of the war (in December 1941 Brooke was to succeed Dill as CIGS and principal military adviser to the War Cabinet, whilst Dill became Head of the Joint Staff Mission in Washington) and Eden had his part in setting this team on its historic course. As early as 3 June Eden had minuted to Churchill, 'Brooke has done brilliantly';[34] the same could be said of Eden, whose record in picking key personnel arguably exhibited a surer touch than the Prime Minister's.

Another key figure, but one whom Eden inherited, was the Permanent Under-Secretary at the War Office, Sir James Grigg (universally known as P. J.).* Eden's Joint Parliamentary Under-Secretaries were Sir Henry Page Croft and Sir Edward ('Ned') Grigg, both experienced and loyal figures. From August he had Captain Charles Cobb, DSO, a veteran of the Great War, as his PPS. Before he became MP for Preston in 1936, Cobb had served for some years on the LCC and had headed its Education Committee. Eden drew on Cobb's experience, unusual for a Conservative MP, to increase his knowledge in this field. Meanwhile, the ubiquitous Jim Thomas, promoted to the team of Government Whips, continued to act as Eden's eyes and ears in the Westminster jungle.

On 13 May, Eden faced his first question as War Secretary from the MP for East Fife, James Henderson-Stewart, on whether he would 'consider the immediate formation of a voluntary corps composed of older, responsible men to be armed with rifles and Bren guns and trained for instant action in their own localities in case of raids.'[35] The plans were already in hand and the next day Eden made his famous broadcast appeal for able-bodied men to join a proposed body of Local Defence Volunteers, an initiative that became part of the folk memory of the war, through Robb Wilton's contemporary radio sketch, 'The day I joined the Home Guard', to the inclusion of a recording of Eden's broadcast at the outset of the film version of the 1960s television comedy series *Dad's Army*.

By 21 May, Eden was reporting to the House that 'the response has been most satisfactory', and outlined details of how 'the force will be supplied with arms, ammunition and uniform.'[36] One response, however, was critical. 'I don't think much of the name LOCAL DEFENCE VOLUNTEERS for your very large new force,' Churchill minuted Eden, with the famous red sticker ACTION THIS DAY. 'The word 'local' is uninspiring. Mr. Herbert Morrison suggested to me today the title "Civic Guard", but I think "Home Guard" would be better.' Eden initially resisted this suggestion, on the grounds that 600,000 armlets had already been manufactured and

---

*In an unprecedented move, Grigg was to become War Secretary himself in February 1942. 'Despite the undesirable precedent of promoting civil servant to be political chief of his own Department, there is much to be said for it,' Eden wrote in his diary. Anthony Eden diary, 20 February 1942. AP 20/1/22.

distributed, but Churchill persisted. Duff Cooper, Minister of Information, backed Eden. 'The alternative of H.G. would suggest the association of the Horse Guards or with Mr Wells.'[37] Eventually, Churchill's wishes prevailed and the Home Guard it became, one of the benefits being the phasing out of the alternative meaning of the acronym LDV, which some cynics dubbed the 'Look, Duck and Vanish Brigade'. The episode – minor in the context of the overall situation following the retreat from Dunkirk and the fall of France – nevertheless gave Eden an early indication of the stubbornness with which Churchill would fight his corner on any matter, and how any submission to the Prime Minister had to be backed by rigorous argument and convincing explanations.

The retreat from Dunkirk was an episode that brought home to Eden in sharp focus the dilemmas of war, as one of the first difficult options he faced was over the evacuation of the BEF. On 25 May he overruled Ironside, who wished to withdraw the British brigade from the defence of Calais. As a result of this decision, which Eden described as one of his most painful of the war, especially as it involved the fate of a battalion of the King's Royal Rifle Corps, two German divisions were unable to close in on Dunkirk and ships continued to avoid the sandbanks by using the route off Calais.

Churchill's minutes to Eden, often several a day, form one of the unique records of the conduct of war policy in Britain from 1940 to 1945.[38] The first of this historic series, on 17 May – direct, like so many, and pragmatic in intention – read simply, 'Are you proposing to arm the men of the balloon barrages? I understand they have no weapons. Surely they should be included?' Many minutes were suggestions based on Churchill's experience of Government during the Great War, as on 10 July when he advised Eden to avoid minor business in the House, by using his two Under-Secretaries as shock absorbers and Members' friends. For his part, Eden's minutes gave Churchill a vivid eye-witness account of national defences, particularly in Kent, West Sussex and Surrey, which he visited during the third week of June. 'While we were in the Isle of Thanet Area there were two air raid warnings,' Eden reported on 23 June. 'No bombs were dropped. The Germans were no doubt taking photographs of the progress of our defences in preparation for the work of their dive bombers.'[39]

Eden continued to consult Baldwin a great deal at this time. And Douglas Fairbanks Jr, whom he had befriended aboard the *Aquitania* in 1938, kept him in touch with American opinion, especially the standing of isolationists. Eden was ever more convinced that Paul Reynaud's chances of survival as French Prime Minister (he had succeeded Daladier in March

1940) and of France staying in the war, were to a large extent dependent on the attitude of the United States. 'If Roosevelt could go a step further and break off relations with Germany, even without declaring war, if such an action be possible,' he wrote to Churchill, 'he would perhaps give our hard-pressed French friends just that spice of encouragement they need.'[40] Such a letter shows the increasing part Eden played in Churchill's inner group of advisers, though not among his cronies, such as Beaverbrook and Bracken, who were a separate group, arousing the suspicion even of Mrs Churchill.[41]

Eden believed his prime task was to put contrary, and even unpalatable, views. It was no use being a 'yes' man. Although this led to inevitable ructions, it was psychologically the correct approach. On 14 August, Eden had a late-evening talk with Churchill on Wavell's future. He found himself defending Wavell's continued employment. 'Winston maintains that he is a good average Colonel, & would make a good chairman of a Tory association. But he was always anti-appeasement & is a Winchester scholar, which hardly seems to fit. Personally, I feel sure that he has ability.' A week later, Eden dined à deux with Churchill. 'W worried about govt. Feels he gets little help from colleagues – very generous about my efforts,' Eden wrote, recording Churchill's opinion that 'He & I & Max [Beaverbrook, Minister of Aircraft Production] had to carry the govt.'[42]

The combination of Churchill's penchant for late-night parleys and ferocious diet worried Eden, who sensibly took the conscious decision that he must build up his stamina by a rigorous programme of fitness. That August, when in Surrey, he took to early-morning runs, one typical entry in his diary reading, 'Simon and I went for a run at 6 a.m. I left him to rest halfway. Not bad for 43!'[43] Eden had always been an enthusiastic tennis player and thought nothing of playing for hours at the weekend ('I played five sets which did me much good'),[44] so that guests became accustomed to acting in relays as opponents.

On 31 August there was an aerial dogfight over his house and a Messerschmitt was brought down in the neighbouring woods, a sign of the next phase of the battle for domination. Journeying up to the capital, he saw the devastation of the Blitz. 'As we approached London,' he wrote on 8 September, 'one big fire & several smaller ones were burning in Thames Estuary.' Later he added in pencil, when consulting his diaries for his memoirs, 'This was Goering's mistake: switching to towns.' By 21 September, the damage was widespread and in certain areas not a window remained. 'South London is certainly heavily scarred, & the loss of glass will be serious if we have a hard winter,' he recorded.

On Sunday 22 September, at the beginning of the crucial week of the

Battle of Britain, Churchill rang Eden, then at a rented house in Dover, after receiving (mistaken) American intelligence reports that the Germans would be invading at 3 p.m. Eden walked to a hilltop overlooking the Channel and reported back to London that the only reward for any Germans taking to the boats that afternoon would be seasickness.

The next day the disastrous Dakar expedition (Operation MENACE) was launched by Free French forces against the strategically important West African port held by Vichy forces, one of the lowest moments of the war for Charles de Gaulle, leader of the Free French movement in Britain. Not for the last time in the war, Eden found himself a mediator between Churchill and de Gaulle, whose easily bruised ego and indomitable sense of national pride made him a difficult presence in his Carlton Gardens headquarters. After de Gaulle had given an anti-British interview to a US journalist at Brazzaville in French Equatorial Africa in August 1941, Churchill's wrath knew no bounds. 'He has clearly gone off his head,' he wrote to Eden, who replied in a conciliatory manner, 'He has a real and deep respect for you which he does not extend to any of our military commanders. If we cannot come to terms with de Gaulle, the chief loss to ourselves will be in increased confusion in the minds of the French people.'[45]

Eden found this period difficult, as Churchill was tetchy and resentful of any criticism, however well intentioned (as was Vansittart, who had finally resigned his post as Chief Diplomatic Adviser). 'We talked till after 1 a.m.,' Eden noted of an evening with Churchill on 24 September. 'He told me that I ought not to be so violent with him for he was only trying to help me.' A reconstruction was in the offing and Churchill wanted Eden closer to the executive centre. 'He spoke of govt's future. Neville was ill, cancer of lower bowel & would have to give up soon. When he did he must bring another Tory into War Cabinet, & I was only one country would accept.' A week later Churchill went further. 'He reiterated that he was now an old man, that he would not make Ll G's mistake of carrying on after the war, that the succession must be mine.' When they discussed possible changes, Eden urged Cranborne, then Paymaster-General, for the Dominions Office. But still there seemed no answer to the log-jam at the Foreign Office, as Churchill had no other job for Halifax. 'He lamented that he could not give me F.O. & thus bring me into War Cabinet & seemed distressed at this. "It is not what I want," he repeated many times. He thought at F.O. I could help much with USA. I begged him not to worry about all this. Said with truth that I was happier where I was. He said "we shall win this war together."'[46] One of the best ways to set this on the right course, replied Eden, was to send reinforcements to the Middle East, something the Cabinet and its Defence committee accepted before the month was out.

When Chamberlain finally resigned at the beginning of October, Churchill moved Sir John Anderson to the Lord Presidency of the Council from the Home Office. Herbert Morrison became Home Secretary, a promotion Eden felt of great potential for the domestic war effort. Morrison and he were to work well together. 'From my point of view at the War Office', he later told Morrison's biographers, 'Herbert delivered the goods.'[47]

As to his own position, Eden made it clear that he would take any office that would lighten Churchill's burden, but that if the matter was left to his personal choice, he would prefer to stay at the War Office, reiterating, 'there was no more important work to be done anywhere else.'[48] Eden's wish was fulfilled, as was his wish to see Cranborne at the Dominions Office. Gradually Churchill was turning an inherited administration into his preferred shape. 'In time,' he told Eden, 'all the Munich men will be driven out.'[49]

In the last weeks of his life Chamberlain contacted most of his former colleagues. 'You know my personal friendship for you has never wavered,' he wrote to Eden in a wavering hand on 11 October, the day of his final broadcast to the nation.[50] On 9 November, Churchill and Eden were guests of Ronald Tree at Ditchley, discussing yet again Wavell's position, when the news reached them that Chamberlain had just died. Despite their bitter differences over policy, Eden was saddened by the swift demise of a man Churchill was to describe in his tribute as 'an English worthy,'[51] and he wrote in kindly terms to Anne Chamberlain.

Yet in the history of Conservative leadership, both Chamberlain and Eden were to be remembered for one closing crisis, not for their lengthy and fruitful careers. 'Men's evil manners live in brass,' wrote their beloved Shakespeare, 'their virtues we write in water.'* For too long, this was to be the coterminous fate of both Chamberlain and Eden. There are kinder parallels – although Eden's contemporary allies would not have chosen to bracket him with the man they dubbed 'The Coroner'. Both Chamberlain and Eden had a deep patriotism, and an instinctive determination to enhance the welfare of their fellow citizens. Both found their happiest fulfilment in departments outside the 'great offices' of state, the Ministry of Health and the War Office respectively. Admiration for the one has too often implied an automatic belittling of the other.[52] 'The only guide to a man is his conscience,' said Churchill of Chamberlain. 'The only shield to his memory is the rectitude and sincerity of his actions.'[53] The words are equally applicable to Eden.

*

---

*Henry VIII, IV.ii. 45–6.

Beatrice Eden became interested in many new friendships and was often absent at this time. Eden, meanwhile, found much consolation in the company of his elder son, as Simon approached the end of his schooldays and the beginning of military service with the RAF. They were like an older and younger brother. Eden was one of those fathers more at home with his offspring when they were young adults rather than young children, a consequence of his driven nature and interminable schedules.

Simon was not Eden's only consolation at this time. On 23 May 1940, the Earl of Erne, a close friend from Eden's many Irish holidays in County Fermanagh, had been killed in action in France at the age of thirty-two. Circumstances drew Davina Erne, the widowed Countess, and Eden together, and her presence was to be a constant factor over the next five years, until in 1945, despairing of ever gaining Eden's hand in marriage, she married Monty Woodhouse (later Lord Terrington), whom she had first met as a fellow weekend guest at Eden's home. Davina Erne always had a special place in Eden's heart. Younger daughter of the 2nd Earl of Lytton, Davina's vivacious intelligence and beauty left its mark on all who met her. Eden's diary entries about her often had a gentle humour that testified to the ease and happiness of their growing relationship. 'Found Davina broken down (her car I mean!) outside a garage on the road.' She soon became a regular fixture in the country. 'Davina & I went for a long walk to Farthingpole farm, & then back to the windmill.' As a result, his life was to become increasingly complicated, moving between Fitzhardinge Street, Frensham and a small Government flat in the War Office. 'Gave Beatrice luncheon,' he wrote in his diary on 25 April 1941 of one London visit, before adding, 'Motored Davina to Frensham in evening.'[54]

The small Government flat was badly damaged when the War Office received direct hits from German bombers on 12 October. Fortunately for Eden, he had left London the day before for a second visit to Cairo. On 14 October the party reached Egypt, where they were met by Sir Miles Lampson and General Wavell, whose continued command very much depended on Churchill's interpretation of Eden's despatches.

Eden had extensive talks with Wavell, Lieutenant-General Sir Henry 'Jumbo' Wilson and Admiral Cunningham. As always, Eden felt most at home when able to talk to the troops on the ground. On 15 October, he dined with Cunningham, who was so absorbed by Eden's table talk that he did not notice that everyone else had left. 'He's a nice man,' recorded Cunningham, 'perhaps a little full of Anthony Eden but he has the right ideas about winning the war.' By the autumn of 1940 Eden felt the main Middle East problems for the next six months would be the defence of Egypt, the liquidation of Italian East Africa, and the support of Turkey and Greece in their struggles. Cunningham took Eden on to the Fleet Club. 'He was mobbed going out and his back thumped. Being a politician, he loved it.'[55]

On 19 October Eden was again inspecting defences at the Geneifa Camp by the Suez Canal. Before returning to Cairo the following night, he walked down to the Indian monument at the end of the Suez Canal in the cool of the evening, alone with Miles Lampson, 'where [as Lampson recorded] we sat and discussed affairs of the world at large.'[56]

The next day he visited the Western desert with General 'Jumbo' Wilson. Whilst Eden was in the desert, news came of the Italian invasion of Greece. This development led to one of Eden's first differences with Churchill, who wanted reinforcements sent from the Middle East. In telegrams to London, Eden warned that diverting forces to Greece would endanger the position in Egypt, and would not guarantee the situation in the Balkans. Churchill returned to Wavell's lack of offensive zeal. What Eden could not tell Churchill, until he returned to London on 8 November, was that, in great secrecy, he had advance knowledge of such an offensive, codenamed COMPASS, which Jumbo Wilson launched on 9 December.

Despite their differences over Greece, Churchill remained apologetic that he could not give Eden the Foreign Office. However, an unexpected opportunity presented itself with the sudden death of Lord Lothian, British Ambassador in Washington, on 12 December. A Christian Scientist, Lothian had refused medical attention for a minor internal problem ('he could easily have been saved by a stomach pump or even a purgative,' noted Chips Channon)[57] and with his death three names, with varying degrees of enthusiasm, were seen as possible successors – Eden, Cranborne, and Halifax. Leo Amery came closest to prophesying the eventual outcome, when he wrote, 'The right way out would probably be Halifax, transferring Eden from the War Office to the FO. An alternative might be Lloyd George, but whether he would be quite reliable or trusted by Winston is another matter.'[58]

Far from not being trusted, the former Prime Minister was in fact Churchill's first choice as Ambassador. Lloyd George consulted his doctors, but the outcome was inevitable. 'Winston told me that LG would not have Washington,' Eden wrote in his diary. 'Horder [Sir Thomas Horder, the celebrated physician] had ruled him out, but he had been flattered at invitation.'[59]

Lloyd George's refusal led to an elaborate and at times labyrinthine episode of pass-the-parcel. Halifax came to see Eden on 17 December. 'He said we must first rule out two best, himself and myself.' Eden pressed for Cranborne, which Halifax saw as one way out. At midnight Churchill sent for Eden for a lengthy rumination, in the course of which, Eden recorded, 'his preference was for Edward & self to FO'. But things were not to run smoothly. On 18 December Churchill formally offered Halifax the post of Ambassador to Washington, which he refused. 'I asked if E had suggested anybody else,' recorded Eden. 'No except that as a result of my talk with E, I might like to go.'

Eden went round to Downing Street. He found Churchill tired, but cheerful, more prone to reminiscence than grasping the Washington nettle. 'We spoke of the dark days of the summer. I told him that Portal & I had confessed to each other that in our hearts we had both despaired at the time. Winston said "Yes. Normally I woke up buoyant to face the new day. Then I awoke with dread in my heart."'

Things were left unsettled, but the next day Churchill told Halifax it was his duty to go to Washington. With reluctance, Halifax accepted the inevitable. He was very reproachful towards Eden when they lunched together. 'He said "I am afraid you have let me down" with a smile & I replied "What do you mean? I only told Winston that I was not keen to go, which you told him I was." Edward retorted, "I only said that I thought you might hate it a little less than myself."'[60] So Edward Halifax became the second 'man of Munich' to be moved to an Ambassadorship. The first was Sam Hoare, who became Ambassador in Madrid.*

Eden's return to the Foreign Office was in circumstances very different from 1935, not least in the organisation of Government. The War Cabinet had a primacy and an enhanced position for its various committees. Eden inevitably was a coordinator, rather than a formulator of policy. As the Government was now truly National, he also had a great deal to do with the Labour representatives, especially Attlee and Morrison, who became for him the equivalent of his colleagues in the trenches from the Great War. On 31 December, Eden lunched with Attlee. 'We talked of F.O. personalities there and past errors of policy. He paid generous tribute to Winston,' Eden wrote. 'Back to F.O. 1.15 (a.m.) – Lights out 2.30 a.m. New Year!' So ended one of the most anxious and critical years in Britain's long history.

Churchill had now shaped the Government in the form he had long wanted, though it had taken the deaths of Chamberlain and Lothian to give him the necessary openings. His conduct of business led to a dual system of war control that circumscribed Eden's autonomy. On the one

---

*When Eden returned to the Foreign Office on 22 December for his second spell as Secretary of State, one of his first letters was from Hoare. 'When I compare the moment when you became S of S for the 1st time with the present,' Hoare wrote, 'I think in each case of Mussolini & Italy. May your second term of office see Mussolini's destruction & the defeat of Fascist Italy.' Sir Samuel Hoare to Anthony Eden, 24 December 1940. Templewood papers, Cambridge University Library. XIII File 21, fol. 3.

hand, there were the logistical planners, largely Labour ministers – Attlee, Bevin and Morrison – who directed the preparations and supplies of war, the control of factories, the personnel, the weapons, providing the administrative clarity vital to the smooth running of a massive machine. Although Labour's was a less glamorous contribution than that of Churchill and Eden, with less of the high public profile, it was an essential underbedding of the whole war effort, and Eden never forgot this. As Foreign Secretary, and the clear heir apparent if anything happened to Churchill, Eden was confirmed as an international figure of the front rank, a process leading on from the favourable press he had received after his resignation in 1938. There was, however, an unregarded downside. The real direction of policy lay with Churchill and the Chiefs of Staff. Alan Brooke was more than Eden's equal, a position unthinkable in peacetime conditions. Despite all his achievements in the next five years, Eden's Foreign Secretaryship was conducted against the background of abnormal circumstances. Churchill's control, and the strength of the Cabinet Committee system, confined Eden, who had to act, almost inevitably, on a more limited canvas than the public realised.

With his return to the Foreign Office, for what proved his longest continuous spell as Secretary of State, Eden was reunited with Alec Cadogan, the Permanent Under-Secretary. In 1938 they had been together at the head of the diplomatic service for barely nine weeks before Eden's resignation. Henry Hopkinson was Cadogan's private secretary in the PUS's great downstairs room, a further renewal of Geneva days. Compared to 1937, Cadogan found Eden more edgy, but resolute on the things that mattered. At an early discussion about Russia, Cadogan recorded that he was 'glad to find A. not ideological and quite alive to uselessness of expecting anything from these cynical, blood-stained murderers.'[61]

When Oliver Harvey heard of Eden's return to the Foreign Office, he commented, 'What a signal justification of his previous period there. He now succeeds his own successor who leaves with a very dusty reputation.'[62] Eden inherited Ralph Stevenson (who in 1956 was to be the British Ambassador in Egypt during Suez) as Principal Private Secretary, but as Stevenson's two-year spell of duty was due to end in 1941, in January Eden asked Harvey, languishing in the Ministry of Information after evacuation from the Paris Embassy, if he would rejoin him as Principal Private Secretary. Although technically a demotion, Harvey agreed at once, and Eden began negotiations with Duff Cooper at the Ministry of Information for Harvey's transfer, which was finally effected on 27 June. The previous weekend Eden had brought Harvey up-to-date with the customs of the new regime. 'He told me how difficult the P.M. was,' Harvey wrote in his diary.

'In spite of splendid qualities as popular leader, he had a devastating effect on planning.'[63]

Eden believed the big mistake had been for Churchill to combine the Premiership with the Ministry of Defence, which may have seemed appealing on psychological grounds, but proved undesirable on logistical ones. Harvey was one of the key figures, even more so to Eden than his Parliamentary Private Secretary, Charles Ponsonby, a 'most bone-headed and elderly' figure, according to Hugh Dalton.[64] Ponsonby, MP for Sevenoaks since 1935, was to serve in the post a full five years, but is hardly mentioned in accounts of the time, meriting only one brief reference in Eden's memoirs. Yet he was intensely loyal, his standard comment on his master being that he was 'developing', and would one day lead the party.[65]

Eden had three Under-Secretaries during the next five years. From Halifax he had inherited Rab Butler, who served till 20 July 1941, when he began his great work as President of the Board of Education. Eden's relations with Butler – a potential rival for the centrist leadership after the war – were courteous, but not close. There was too much baggage on both sides, not least the presence of the Chamberlainite 'Chips' Channon as Rab Butler's PPS. Eden was now carefully cultivating his image as an anti-Munichois second only to Churchill, and there was always an element of reserve when dealing with Municheers. For his part, Butler had told Halifax that he was not keen to serve under Eden 'if I can help it.'[66] In fact, Eden eventually found Rab Butler very helpful over House of Commons business and thought he would be difficult to replace. At first he hoped a Labour Under-Secretary would be the solution, but no name immediately came to mind. So in July 1941 Richard Law, Bonar Law's son, was moved from a junior post at the War Office to succeed Butler, which had the added advantage for Oliver Harvey of removing 'Chips' Channon from the scene. 'Dick' Law enjoyed a great bond of trust with Eden and shared his innermost thoughts and doubts. 'Dick and I dined together at Carlton Grill and had some political talk afterwards,' Eden had written earlier in the year. 'He talked much of the Tory party & my duty to lead it. I told him that I had little sympathy with it or men who composed it.'[67]

On 25 September 1943, George Hall, an old Labour stalwart from the Admiralty team, succeeded Law, though Eden had by then hoped that Jim Thomas, who took Hall's place at the Admiralty, might rejoin his team. As Oliver Harvey noted, this disappointed Thomas, who 'even said to me he would prefer to resign from the Whips' Office and become A. E.'s PPS again sooner than bury himself in the Admiralty', but the upside was that Hall 'will have a value as carrying an insight into the F.O. into the Labour Party.'[68] Eden considered this important, as he was well aware of the class feelings the Foreign Office provoked, one of the key considerations of his 1943 reforms in the service.[69]

When Neville Chamberlain went to Berchtesgaden to meet Hitler in 1938 it was his first flight; at the end of the war, when Ernest Bevin flew to the Potsdam Conference, it was likewise his first time in an aeroplane. As Cadogan returned to London in June 1945 from the San Francisco Conference he calculated that he had flown 87,500 miles on his diplomatic travels during the war, and Eden even more.[70]

Not only the means of transport indicated that British diplomatic policy was entering a new era. As the autonomy of resident ambassadors declined in wartime conditions, peripatetic Foreign Secretaries such as Eden became ambassadors-at-large in their own right, settling business in an expeditious manner, or ascertaining at first hand the obstacles to such settlement. For Eden, the trouble arose when heads of government, often without specialist background knowledge, brought their own personal diplomacy to bear, one of the reasons he considered Roosevelt meandering and feckless. When combined with high-handedness, the recipe could be catastrophic.*

Such tensions were already clear in the wake of Eden's two-month tour to the Middle East in the spring of 1941, his first extended mission in his new role, and one of his most controversial. As the threat of German invasion of Britain itself had receded after the Battle of Britain, priorities changed, and Eden felt 'it looks like being a race whether we can cause complete defeat of Italians in Libya before Germans loose their attack on Greeks as I feel sure they mean to do.'[71] In Cairo, Sir Miles Lampson felt the same. 'I suspect myself,' he wrote on New Year's Day, 'that the struggle

---

*At the Teheran Conference in November 1943, as Cadogan recorded, 'without any previous Anglo-American consultation, President [Roosevelt], in his amateurish way, had said a lot of indiscreet and awkward things'. At Yalta in February 1945, when the need for an international security organisation (the United Nations) was under consideration, Churchill, a 'silly old man' in Cadogan's words, 'without a word of warning to Anthony or me, plunged into a long harangue about the World Organisation, knowing nothing whatever of what he was talking about and making complete nonsense of the whole thing'. In Cadogan's experience, Potsdam in July 1945, after Roosevelt's death, was even worse, as Churchill refused to do the necessary background work. 'If he knows nothing about the subject under discussion, he should keep quiet, or ask that his Foreign Secretary be heard,' wrote Cadogan with exasperation. 'Instead of that, he butts in on every occasion and talks the most irrelevant rubbish, and risks giving away our case at every point.' On the other hand, Harry S. Truman, who had succeeded Roosevelt as President on 12 April 1945, had not succumbed to such hauteur. 'Truman is most quick and businesslike,' wrote Cadogan approvingly. However, 'every mention of a topic started Winston off on a wild rampage from which the combined efforts of Truman and Anthony with difficulty restrained him.' Sir Alexander Cadogan diary, 27 November 1943, 8 February and 18 July 1945. Cadogan Papers, Churchill College, Cambridge. ACAD 1/12, ACAD 1/15.

will shift during the course of the year very much to the Eastern end of the Mediterranean.'[72]

Germany's ambitions were only too clear. 'A mass of information has come to us over the last few days,' Eden wrote to Churchill on 6 January, 'all of which tends to show that Germany is pressing forward her preparations in the Balkans with a view to an ultimate descent upon Greece.'[73] Mussolini had attacked Greece in October 1940, but without decisive advantage, and it was clear from ULTRA decrypts from Bletchley Park that the Greeks would be the next target of German forces, though advance intelligence could not compensate for vastly superior enemy forces, which was to prove the case in the Balkans. By the terms of the Balkan Pact, signed in 1934 by Greece, Romania, Turkey and Yugoslavia, defence of the whole region depended on a form of collective security, which did not prevent Romania falling to Germany in January 1941. Eden hoped to save the remainder of the Balkan region from Axis control by co-ordinating the response of the surviving members of the pact. It was to prove a complex and intractable problem, arguably made worse by British involvement. Greece was interested in British support only if it could be guaranteed on two fronts, against Mussolini from Albania and the new threat of German advances through Bulgaria, but only Salonika seemed on the agenda. As Yugoslav ambitions included Salonika, Greece was warned that if British troops became established there, Yugoslavia could allow German troops free passage through their territory. Meanwhile, the Turks feared that any British military aid to their traditional rivals would merely bring German reprisals closer, which proved the final complication to Eden's mission to prevent Axis infiltration in the Balkans.

After Wavell's forces had driven the Italians back to Benghazi, Eden had to resolve whether allied forces could be diverted to the aid of Greece, and how best Turkey and Yugoslavia could then be harnessed to the allied cause. Conflicting military and political priorities made a tidy solution impossible. As at the Montreux Conference in 1936, Eden believed that Turkey was the key. His unresolved hope was to see Turkey in a triple alliance with Greece and Yugoslavia. In a reversal of his earlier position, Eden now wanted a British military presence in Greece to stiffen Turkish and Yugoslav resistance to German expansion in the Balkans, even though this would mean a weakening of Wavell's resources. As a member of the Cabinet Defence Committee – on which he had insisted, fearing that otherwise he would be marginalised – Eden was party to the initial decision in London on 10 February to send troops and materials to Greece. His actions in the next two months were conditioned by this overriding factor. Eden saw it as his job to enforce a Cabinet decision, but as circumstances changed, so did the viability of the original strategy.

On 12 February, together with a team that included Sir John Dill, Ralph Stevenson and Pierson (Bob) Dixon[74] of the Foreign Office's Southern Department, Eden embarked on what proved another perilous journey (aeronautically as well as politically) via Gibraltar to the Middle East. The long delay in reaching Cairo (the journey took the best part of a week) had its knock-on effect as events unfolded, as did the decision to visit Athens before Ankara during the negotiations for a united front.[75]

Churchill had given Eden plenipotentiary powers, and all the apparatus of sealed envelopes, to decide on the best course of action. Churchill wanted Yugoslav and Turkish help in resisting any German assault on Greece. Eden saw it as his job to persuade these two countries that alliance with Britain could prevent German advances in the southern Balkans, and, eventually, occupation of the Turkish straits.

With great thoughtfulness, Churchill invited Beatrice Eden, whose personality he much admired, to Chequers as a weekend guest from time to time during Eden's long absence from Britain. At the same time, Eden met Winston Churchill's son, Randolph (like Eden, a product of Sandroyd, Eton and Christ Church), at the Cairo Embassy in the spring of 1941. Ironically, in the light of Randolph Churchill's later long-standing feud with Eden in the post-war years, his first impressions of the Foreign Secretary at work were highly favourable. 'Although he has been very busy since his arrival I have seen quite a lot of him, & have been very much impressed,' Randolph Churchill wrote to his father on 6 April. 'I think he is gaining in self confidence & stature daily. And I think the military people here find it a great comfort to have him by their side at this time.'[76] For his part, Eden sent accounts of Randolph's doings to Churchill. 'He is looking fit and well and has the light of battle in his eyes' was one message. Unfortunately, in the transcript, this was decoded as 'the light of bottle.'[77]*

Events in the Balkans unfolded badly. Eden was rebuffed by Prince Paul, Regent of Yugoslavia, who repeatedly refused to meet him in southern Serbia, for fear of German reprisals. Hitler wanted to enrol Yugoslavia in his tripartite pact, not that he needed Yugoslav assistance for his planned invasion of Greece – only access through Bulgaria and isolation of the British. In Athens on 22 February, with Dill, Wavell and Francis de Guingand, Wavell's Chief of Staff, Eden met the Greek Commander-in-Chief, General Alexander Papagos. He was greeted with tremendous enthusiasm in the streets, but less warmly by Papagos, who was suspicious

---

*It was on this visit to Cairo that Randolph Churchill tried to pull rank, abruptly asking one airport official, 'Do you know who I am?', to which the reply was, 'Yes, you're Vic Oliver's brother-in-law.'

of British intentions. The Greeks made it clear they were willing to resist Germany alone. Eden told Papagos that Britain would send troops, if the Greeks abandoned Thrace and established a new defensive position on the Aliakmon river line between Edessa, near the Yugoslav frontier, and Veroia. This military plan was agreed on the evening of 22 February. A visit to Ankara four days later failed to woo the Turks to this strategy. Eden warned Churchill that the Turkish leaders thought their turn would come next, and that if they became involved in a war with Germany they would be vulnerable to Russian attack. 'The common cause would be better served,' Eden wrote to Churchill, 'by Turkey remaining out of the war until her deficiencies had been remedied.'[78]

The one benefit from the Ankara visit was the bond of friendship and understanding Eden was able to forge with Sir Stafford Cripps, the British Ambassador in Moscow. 'We are back in an atmosphere of possibility and not of impossibility,' Cripps wrote in his diary after his talks in Turkey with the new Foreign Secretary.[79] He was encouraged by Eden's open-mindedness regarding Russia's perils, and by his progressive attitude to the eventual post-war settlement. 'Their developing relationship,' Cripps's biographer has written, 'was to be important in the politics of the next eighteen months.'[80]

On his return to Athens on 2 March Eden found that Papagos had failed to organise the agreed defensive position on the Aliakmon line, believing it conditional on Yugoslavian support, which Prince Paul (whose antipathy to Eden went back to Oxford days) was in no mood to grant. Nevertheless, on the evening of 5 March, after intense discussion, it was agreed to stick to the original plan and hold the Aliakmon line, albeit with a smaller number of Greek divisions.

Events in Yugoslavia soon upset this precarious position. On 25 March Prince Paul finally signed a pact with Germany, but two days later was overthrown by a *coup d'état* organised by anti-German factions. On 28 March, Eden telegrammed to Churchill suggesting urgent four-power talks with the Balkan Pact countries 'to form a common front to aggression.'[81] So hurriedly arranged was Eden's return journey to Athens to set these talks in motion that the pilot of his plane unwittingly flew over what was the Battle of Cape Matapan raging beneath.

Axis advances were not long delayed, both in North Africa and the Balkans. When the news of the fall of Benghazi came on 4 April, Alan Brooke wrote in his diary, 'It looks as if we have reinforced Greece at the expense of the Tripoli front to a dangerous degree.'[82] After bitter fighting, Belgrade fell on 12 April. The German invasion of Greece, begun on 6 April, led to the evacuation of the Greek Government to Crete two weeks later. Crete fell in May after heavy losses on both sides. It was small comfort at the time that, following such losses, the Germans never attempted such an airborne operation again during the war. Meanwhile, Rommel's Afrika Korps made rapid counter-offensives, overrunning Cyrenaica and opening the gateway to Egypt once more. Twenty-two days after the fall of Crete, Germany invaded Russia. The parallels with May 1940 were as uncomfortable as they were unexpected. Eden's discomfiture, when defending the decision to help Greece in a speech in the House of Commons on 6 May, gave private satisfaction to Chamberlain's dwindling band of supporters in Parliament, though in the larger context, the time and energy expended by Hitler in invading Yugoslavia and Greece diverted and stretched his resources in the next crucial stage of the global conflict. The only positive was that Turkey remained neutral. In the context of his second spell at the Foreign Office, the Balkan mission remained a reversal for Eden – the equivalent, some felt, of a Narvik (harsher critics thought the Dardanelles a better parallel) or a Dieppe.[83] However, as with Churchill and Mountbatten, the failed mission did not prove an insurmountable blow to Eden's political position, largely owing to Churchill's unwavering support. If there was any one time when Churchill 'kept Eden in the game', it was in May 1941. The real loser, unfairly, was Wavell, over whom Churchill had never enthused. Plaudits for Wavell after Benghazi were to prove short-lived, and in June he was replaced as Commander-in-Chief Middle East Command by General Auchinleck, after Rommel's blistering series of counter-attacks. In time, Auchinleck was to suffer the same fate.

As the man on the ground, Sir Miles Lampson closely observed Eden at this early crisis in the management of the war. 'A E could not have striven harder than he has to get things on the right rails,' he wrote of Eden's efforts over Greece and Serbia.[84] Eden was not so sanguine. 'After dinner A. E. & I sat in the small drawing room & he rather let himself go on what he regards as the failure of his mission,' Lampson recorded on the eve of Eden's return to London. 'A. E. takes it all very philosophically but naturally is greatly disappointed at not going home with Serbia in the bag.'[85] Looking ahead to the post-war situation, Eden feared Soviet expansion into the area, which nothing short of a strong military presence would long delay, a correct analysis.

The best contemporary analysis of Eden's mission came from one of his own erstwhile supporters, Oliver Stanley. In conversation with Hugh Dalton on 28 April, Stanley attacked 'the terrible error, as he judged it, of sending anything beyond a small token force to Greece'. The blame, Stanley felt, was primarily Churchill's, compounded by Eden as he got caught up in events.

The decision had been taken against all military and naval advice. It should have been seen from the start that the adventure was quite hopeless. The only real way to help Greece was to win the war. Instead of that we might now lose both Greece and Egypt. We had thrown away a most valuable Air Force in Greece. At least four squadrons of fighters and three squadrons of bombers had been destroyed. It was quite wrong for Eden to have gone to the Middle East and worst of all to go to Athens. There he had been cheered in the streets and smothered in roses. How in such surroundings could he keep his judgment clear? A Foreign Secretary should stay always in the Foreign Office protected by distance and his officials from such local impressions.[86]

Eden returned to the worst press yet of his career. There was an undisguised sense of *Schadenfreude*, not only among the Chamberlainites. Even Oliver Stanley exhibited 'a not unhappy smile' to Dalton when he confirmed 'that many people were gunning after Eden now.'[87]

Eden's speech in the debate on 6 May was not a success. Yet Dalton felt there were mitigating circumstances. 'Eden makes a poor speech in difficult conditions, since clearly in public session there are many things, e.g., about Turks, which he cannot say.'[88] Eden seemed dazed by the setback. On the way home, Anthony Quayle, then serving as an ADC in Gibraltar, met Eden for the first time, and, as Bob Dixon recorded in his diary, 'remarked that he seemed like an actor playing the part of A. E. – an interesting remark from a professional actor'.[89]

This Middle East mission remained a sensitive issue for Eden. After the war, he asked Churchill to make changes in his original draft on the episode for his war memoirs, and took legal action in 1947 to curb Francis de Guingand's criticisms in his book *Operation Victory*. Francis de Guingand, whose job had been to assess the possibility of military success, became an implacable opponent of Eden thereafter, and at the height of the Suez crisis sought a meeting with Hugh Gaitskell, leader of the Opposition, to feed him long-forgotten details of the Greek campaign, an interesting insight into what he considered acceptable use of secret military details, derived from his time serving as a commissioned officer. Gaitskell recorded details of their conversation in his diary:

All the military evidence according to de Guingand was absolutely against the campaign. It was clearly going to be a disaster from the start. But Eden had obviously made up his mind that we had got to do it, and according to de Guingand he was quite unscrupulous and tried to make him fudge the figures, counting rifles as guns, and things like that. He said that in fact the campaign had not been more of a disaster only because of very good luck and some extremely good generalship. He also objected to the fact that Eden had claimed that the Germans had delayed their attack on Russia because of our rearguard action in Greece. De Guingand thought there was nothing in this at all, and in fact he quoted other authorities, German ones, to the effect that the attack on Russia had been delayed entirely on account of the weather.[90]

Yet de Guingand's analysis is not accurate in every respect. The basic decision on Greece was taken by Churchill in London. Eden, together with Attlee, should have stressed the potential difficulties at an earlier stage during the War Cabinet discussions, though this would have required exceptional perspicacity, not to mention courage in the face of Churchill's intransigence. In fact, the Dardanelles proved a more apt parallel than many of Eden's critics perhaps realised, as the episode was another example of Churchill resisting military advice, changing his stance (in January 1941) and even bullying his advisers, particularly Wavell. 'Destruction of Greece would eclipse victories you have gained in Libya,' he told Wavell. 'You must therefore conform your plans to larger interests at stake. We expect and require prompt and active compliance with our decisions.'[91]

Nevertheless, Eden's reputation had been seen to have suffered in the circumstances of war, and such a perception by itself can often have fatal political consequences. After the Balkan mission, his empirical side taught him the dangers of being out of touch with political colleagues at home, as the complexities of a situation unfolded overseas, problems that had faced Foreign Secretaries before, and would again, notably Selwyn Lloyd in America in the autumn of 1956.[92]

Three factors can be set in the record in mitigation of Eden. By a 1939 agreement, Britain was committed to defend Greece, and for Eden this was a matter of honour; secondly, military leaders had assured Eden (mistakenly in the event) that the situation in North Africa was now contained; and, above all, the Cabinet Defence Committee had taken its decision on 10 February, confirmed by a meeting of the War Cabinet on 24 February, after which Churchill had telegrammed to Eden, 'Full Steam Ahead'.[93] Eden's impossible job had been to implement that decision in the face of conflicting political and military advice on the ground, and against the backdrop of the differing agendas of three separate Balkan states. The decisions were not taken without considerable agonising. 'A. E. questioned me as to what I really felt about this Greek venture,' Sir Miles Lampson recorded in his diary on 6 March. Both felt 'it would be excessively difficult to give any appearance of abandoning Greece provided it was clear that Greece was determined to continue the struggle & to fight Germany if invaded. A. E. told me that he had really no doubt in his own mind that this was the right line but he admitted that it had been a very big decision to take & one which had worried him considerably.'[94]

The whole episode brought home to Eden how fragile political success was, and how reputations, built up over time, could be so easily blighted by one unexpected reversal. 'In the reproof of chance,' as Shakespeare's Nestor had put it, 'lies the true proof of men.*

The reversals of the Greek campaign were but one setback in a dramatic spring. On 23 May, HMS *Hood*, the pride of the Royal Navy, was sunk by the *Bismarck* with the loss of all but three of its crew. Four days later ('a day which had its compensations' as Eden wrote,[95]) the *Bismarck*, leaking fuel from its first encounter, was tracked and sunk, but the psychological blow of the sinking of the *Hood* was long remembered.[96] Whilst this news was being assimilated, Eden was dealing with what he called 'one of the strangest personal dramas of the war,'[97] Rudolf Hess's flight to the Duke of Hamilton's estate in Scotland on 10 May 1941. Hess hoped that the Duke would be able to arrange a meeting with King George VI to discuss peace terms. After Hess had parachuted on to the moors near Eaglesham, he was taken to Giffnock police station, south of Glasgow. In great secrecy, Eden arranged that Hess should be interviewed by John Simon, the Lord Chancellor, in Aldershot. 'I agree that you must say that you have come with the Govt's approval', Eden told Simon, 'though I hope that it would not be necessary to emphasise this much since the man dreams of a change of govt!' He made it clear that the Government were 'not prepared to enter into negotiations for peace either with Hess or any other representative of Hitler. Our policy remains as publicly stated on many occasions.'[98]

Eden had long hankered after a country house of his own. Frensham had been only an interim, and not altogether successful, option. In June 1941 he investigated the lease, from the Goodwood estate, of Binderton House, one mile north of Lavant in Sussex. On 14 June, Beatrice and he travelled to Sussex to view the property. 'Liked it very much,' Eden wrote in his diary. 'William and Mary with Adam changes. Good rooms which will take our furniture & above all, lovely country. Even on so dull a day we were fascinated by it.' The house, which features in Nikolaus Pevsner's guide to Sussex, had been built originally in 1677 'in the form of a half-H with exceptionally long wings.'[99] A central porch was added in the late eighteenth century. The glory of the interior was a late seventeenth-century staircase, which reminded Eden of long-ago Windlestone. The house afforded easy access to Chichester and the coast, and was much loved by Simon and Nicholas. No house, however, is perfect, and Binderton's

---

* *Troilus and Cressida*, I.iii. 35–6.

disadvantage was its proximity to the main road. For the next eleven years, however, Binderton was the focus of Eden's non-professional life, and a place where the duty secretaries could easily stay for the weekends. The house fulfilled many functions. In a Conservative Party that still laid store by the outward forms, it conferred status, as a kind of latter-day Hughenden. Unlike Disraeli, however, Eden had had to pay for his property himself. Although he could now metaphorically hold his head up alongside Macmillan and Butler, each of whom had inherited substantial country properties, Binderton and its staffing were a constant drain on his resources. Meanwhile, at Binderton he could indulge his passion for gardening, countryside walks and, above all, tennis. All his secretaries, from Nicholas Henderson, who joined the team in 1944, to Robert Carr, in the early 1950s, remember the tennis parties. Beatrice and Eden furnished the interior with exquisite taste, but, despite their joint pride in their new home, Binderton did not save their marriage.

In the summer of 1941 Eden found himself much in the company of Churchill's cronies – Frederick Lindemann (the Prof), Brendan Bracken and the ubiquitous Max Beaverbrook. He was well aware that he was not in this circle of proximity to the Prime Minister, but as membership of the court entailed keeping Churchill company half the night, this was an exclusion he could well bear. Nevertheless, Eden did hear much table talk that kept him in touch with inner dealings, and he became an alternative sounding board for Churchill's schemes, worries and elations. On one occasion Eden's young son Nicholas was present, as Churchill poured out his feelings à trois, an unforgettable childhood memory for the Ludgrove schoolboy. On 12 July Churchill rehearsed his proposed Cabinet changes for Eden's approval. 'They include a move up for R. A. B. [to the Board of Education] which I agreed was due.' (The next day at Ditchley, in partnership with Beatrice, he defeated Ronnie Tree and David Niven 6–0 at tennis.) On 14 July Churchill confided more, 'all this talk on what he calls a father confessor basis.'

Unlike Churchill, Eden was already thinking ahead to the peacetime settlement. In the first week of September he told Churchill that he 'felt no desire to work with Tory Party as now constituted after war, & unless we could re-people it, I saw little future for it.' Eden added that he 'felt so little enthusiasm for party politics I would rather finish up my time by helping in some non-party capacity, e.g. India, if that were thought useful.' It was a mild suggestion on which Churchill was to act sooner than Eden expected.[100]

At a dinner with Churchill and Beaverbrook that week, the table talk both fascinated and repelled Eden. 'Winston at top of his form,' Eden recalled:

Talk much of past events, some long past. Winston said that he would like best to have F. E. [F. E. Smith, 1st Earl of Birkenhead] back to help him. Not F. E. of last sadder years, but F. E. about '14 or '15. Next he would like A. J. B. [the former Prime Minister, Arthur Balfour]. Max told Winston that if he had played his cards well when he was at Admiralty early in last war, especially with Tory Party, he could have been PM instead of [Lloyd] George. Winston agreed.

Beaverbrook then played the same game with Eden's career:

He (Max) said that had I played my hand strongly I must have succeeded Neville. Winston said I was right to take D.O. My own feeling about it all was that I do not truly believe my own contribution at any time to be so overwhelmingly good as to be prepared to drive it à outrance. A fault in a politician no doubt. I thought as I listened to Max & Winston revelling at every move in these old games and even Winston, for all his greatness, so regarding it all, that I truly hate the 'game' of politics not because I am better than these, God forbid, but because I lack the spunk.

Later Beaverbrook urged Churchill to put it in writing that Eden was his nominated successor, 'lest he did meet a bomb'. Eden urged Churchill not to, as being unlucky. 'He retorted I need not worry that it would do me harm.'[101]

Eden's view of domestic political life was not conditioned by thoughts of the succession (though it was to be after 1945), but by the needs of Warwick and Leamington, and even in the busiest days of the war he found time to write to bereaved constituents and, in happier circumstances, to celebrants of golden weddings and the like.[102]

A few days after the dinner with Churchill and Beaverbrook, Eden went with Jim Thomas to talk to a meeting of Trade Unionists, with Ben Tillett in the chair. 'I enjoyed myself, spoke without a note & "off the record",' Eden wrote of the evening. 'It is no doubt unfortunate for a Tory M.P. but I am infinitely happier among these folk than in the Carlton Club, & they like me better than does the C.C. I am in the wrong party it seems.' Ironically, he had to lunch the next day at the Carlton Club, 'which I always abominate.'[103] In the afternoon, the Edens moved into Binderton.

CHAPTER TEN
Alliances and Conferences
1941–4

CORDELL HULL: My, Mr Eden, I had no idea you were such a politician.
ANTHONY EDEN (quoting Lloyd George): 'A statesman is a politician with whom one happens to agree.'

Conversation at Quebec, 21 August 1943[1]

ULTRA decrypts from Bletchley Park were now a vital weapon in the conduct of the war. Admiral Cunningham had relied heavily on such information in the run-up to the successful naval action off Cape Matapan, and Eden, who was privy to the secret information, knew on 12 June 1941, through a decrypted telegram from the Japanese Embassy in Berlin, ten days before the event, that an invasion of Russia by the Nazis was imminent. William Cavendish-Bentinck, Chairman of the Joint Intelligence Committee from 1939 to 1945, was instructed by Eden to tell Ivan Maisky, the Soviet representative in London, of these developments, and Cavendish-Bentinck even forecast accurately the day of the actual invasion to an incredulous Maisky.[2] 'During the past week or so,' Miles Lampson wrote in his diary, 'Anthony Eden has been warning the Russian Ambassador in London of an impending attack.'[3]

When the news was confirmed on 22 June, Eden was staying at Chequers and fully backed Churchill's unilateral decision to treat the Russians as equal partners in the struggle against Hitler. Eden assured the Russians of Britain's continued determination to resist Hitler, and on 12 July concluded an Anglo-Soviet agreement on mutual support. Privately, he believed the invasion of Russia would prove a tactical error, second only to Hitler's targeting of towns rather than airfields in September 1940.

Sir Stafford Cripps, Britain's Ambassador and Special Envoy to the Soviet Union since June 1940, had first suggested that Eden visit the Soviet Union in February 1941, when he had travelled to Ankara to consult Eden on his Balkan talks. Churchill had brushed this suggestion aside, ostensibly on security grounds. 'Best way of gaining Russians is a good throw in the Balkans', he had telegrammed to Eden on 23 February. 'A mere visit would do no good. They might simply trade it off to Germany. I would hardly trust them for your personal safety or liberty [not a consideration that had worried Churchill at the time of Chamberlain's flights to Germany]. Of course, if they thought we would win, all would be well, but then your visit would be unnecessary and they would come to us.'[4]

The Russian Pact of friendship with Yugoslavia, signed on 5 April, just before the German attack on Belgrade, was evidence that the Soviets could give succour to countries under Nazi threat. Eden's priority was now clear. Whatever the personal risks, another meeting with Stalin should take place as soon as practicable.

In mid-June, Eden assured Ivan Maisky, Soviet Ambassador in London, that 'in the event of hostilities, we should be ready to send a mission representing all three services to Russia, not because we pretended to any superiority in the art of war over Russian commanders, but because it would be composed of officers who had the most recent experience in actual conflict with the German forces.'[5]

The day after BARBAROSSA (as Hitler's invasion of Russia was codenamed) Eden renewed his offer to Maisky, which set one part of the record straight, as in Moscow the former Russian Foreign Minister, Maxim Litvinov (shortly to become Soviet Ambassador in America), had initially thought Hitler's invasion part of some arrangement concocted after Hess's flight to Scotland, and was reassured by British support.[6] For Russia, however, 'real' support meant the establishment of a 'Second Front' in western Europe – however welcome, on a smaller scale, Cripps's military mission in June and the Anglo-American supply mission in September might have been. Eden had been the driving force behind the Anglo-Soviet invasion of Persia on 25 August that secured oil supplies, warm-water ports for Soviet supply routes, and pre-empted any Nazi control in Teheran. Without him, Harvey noted in his diary, 'the P.M. and the Chiefs of Staff would never have moved.'[7]

Later a grateful Maisky told Harold Nicolson that 'of all our statesmen Anthony Eden was the one he trusted most. He said, "He understands. Churchill does not wholly understand."'[8] Recently declassified Soviet documents, however, show that Maisky enjoyed the trust and friendship of senior British politicians such as Churchill and Eden to an unprecedented extent, and was eventually recalled to Moscow in June 1943 because of Stalin's suspicions that he was becoming too much of an Anglophile.[9]

At dawn on 7 December, Eden set out from Binderton for London, where his delegation to Russia had gathered. From the Foreign Office he took Alec Cadogan, the Permanent Under-Secretary; the ubiquitous Oliver Harvey; and that 'titan' of diplomatic affairs, Frank Roberts, then at the Central Department, whose special responsibility was to advise on the delicate question of Polish-Soviet relations.[10] His military team was headed by Lieutenant-General Sir Archibald Nye, newly promoted Vice-Chief of the Imperial General Staff. Ivan Maisky, the Soviet Ambassador to London, joined Eden's group, unknown to many of his staff, travelling alone by Underground train from the Russian Embassy to avoid recognition. The group departed in conditions of secrecy in a special train from a siding at Euston station, bound for Invergordon in the eastern Highlands of Scotland.

At 5 p.m. Eden hosted a meeting over tea in his private carriage. Both Eden and Maisky had noticed scenes of strange excitement, even agitation, at the small stations through which they passed. Eden now asked for the train to be stopped at the next station, which it did at 6 p.m. Here he was told the news of Pearl Harbor from the crowd gathered on the platform of a small halt.

At 2 a.m. the train was stopped again and Oliver Harvey was handed a telegram from Churchill. When the team arrived at Invergordon at 8 a.m., Eden, who was already suffering from the symptoms of the gastric influenza that would hinder him throughout the mission, spoke to Churchill from the Naval Commander's Office at the Naval Base.[11] As so often in moments of crisis, Churchill was exuberant and told Eden excitedly of his plans to go to America to see Roosevelt 'next Thursday'. Eden was horrified. This was no time for both the Prime Minister and the Foreign Secretary to be out of the country simultaneously, but there was no holding Churchill back from his American journey, even though Eden sought Attlee's help, which was also to no avail.[12] 'The Cabinet are a poor lot for stopping anything,' wrote Oliver Harvey in his diary.[13]

Eden's team sailed from Scapa Flow at 11.30 a.m. to join the cruiser HMS *Kent*. For the next four and a half days Eden, debilitated by his gastric influenza, and by continued worries about Churchill's safety, endured an uncomfortable and perilous voyage to Murmansk in the bitter wintry weather. The captain of HMS *Kent* advised his passengers to put on lifebelts as they were sailing through an active war zone, but the crew thought differently. So terrible were these Arctic waters, they told Eden's party, that it was better to sink at once.[14]

Further difficulties awaited the party as they reached Murmansk. Thick fog precluded the planned connecting flight to Moscow and the only alternative was a lengthy train journey. Before they set off, Eden went with Maisky on a drive round Murmansk, in the grip of a harsh winter. On a hillock, Eden looked over the city. 'Nature is severe here,' he said to Maisky, 'but it has its beauty.' At the station, he saw Soviet and British flags, standing out as patches of colour against the snowy background. 'That is a symbol,' he said to Maisky. 'In it lies the hope of final victory over Hitler.' Then in the night sky came the sight of the Aurora Borealis.[15]

*

The overriding question in the latter part of 1941 had been when, and on what pretext, America would formally join the war. Eden's secretary, Oliver Harvey, had heard from Charles Peake, Counsellor in the British Embassy at Washington, of the general sense of gloom there 'about prospects of F. D. R. bringing America in soon', despite the historic meeting in August with Churchill in Placienta Bay, off Newfoundland. 'He even doubts his being very keen to bring her in at all,' Harvey had written in his diary of his talk with Peake. 'F. D. R. not a leader. Hitler, on the other hand, will never help us by provoking America or sinking a U.S. warship. A sort of impasse.'[16]

The *casus belli* when it came had been from an unexpected quarter. In the early hours of 7 December, the Japanese had launched an unprovoked attack on the American fleet at Pearl Harbor. When Churchill heard the news at Chequers, in the company of John Winant, the American Ambassador, and Averell Harriman, Roosevelt's Special Envoy, he observed, 'So we had won after all!'[17]

Any remaining doubts on that score were removed when, on 11 December, Hitler, together with Mussolini, declared war on the United States, the second crucial (and to some, inexplicable) decision of 1941 that was to lead to his ultimate defeat.

The issue of Japan now threatened to overshadow Eden's visit to Moscow. On 30 September, Eden had submitted a memorandum to the Cabinet in which he stated 'that a display of firmness is more likely to deter Japan from war than to provoke her to it,'[18] and on 17 October had urged naval reinforcements to the Far East at a meeting of the Defence Committee. Pearl Harbor ensured that this advice was now followed, ending any immediate hope for Stalin of the British units he wanted to help in the defence of Russia, as reinforcements were now needed in the Far East for the defence of Malaya. Heated disagreements had taken place at the War Cabinet on 4 December, about what Eden could, or could not, offer Stalin.[19] However, Stalin's fear that the Japanese might now also strike northwards led to a sharp increase in the exchange of Anglo-Soviet intelligence material, which marked a new era in relations between the two countries.[20]

Late on 15 December Eden and his delegation arrived in Moscow, in the grip of fifty-eight degrees Fahrenheit of frost. As the German forces were only nineteen miles from the Russian capital, a strict blackout was in force, though in honour of Eden's arrival, the terminus was lit up for fifteen minutes. The atmosphere awaiting them was one of 'alcoholic cordiality',[21] where any refused toast (and at the final seven-hour meal there were thirty-six) was seen as a grievous solecism. This could have posed problems for

Archie Nye, a teetotaller, but he overcame them by arranging with the waiters to be served 'vodka' (in fact, still water); this endeared him to Stalin above all the British delegation, as he so clearly possessed stamina and a preference for Russia's national drink above the finest of wines.[22]

Despite the outward conviviality, Stalin was in no mood for compromise. He wanted recognition of Russia's 1941 frontiers, in effect acceptance of his gains in Poland, and other territories under the Molotov-Ribbentrop Pact. Eden's insistence that he had no authority to deal with such matters, and that the Allies should concentrate first on winning the war, was not well received. For his part, Eden wanted a Russian declaration of war on Japan. Stalin retorted by mentioning his own need for allied help (though demands for a Second Front were not pressed), and a formal agreement on the post-war territories. 'A declaration I regard as algebra', Stalin told Eden, 'but an agreement as practical arithmetic. I do not wish to decry algebra, but I prefer practical arithmetic.'[23] Under the terms of the Atlantic Charter in August 1941, such a division of the spoils was forbidden without a popular plebiscite, and Eden made it clear that 'it was quite impossible for His Majesty's Government to commit themselves at this stage to any post-war frontiers in Europe.'[24] The War Cabinet later sent a telegram backing Eden's non-committal stance on this question, though Stalin returned to it with vigour at the final meeting, successfully manoeuvring Eden into accepting that the question might be considered further in London.

At the conclusion of the subsequent 'thirty-six toast' dinner in the early hours of 21 December (Stalin's sixty-second birthday), a wrestling match was staged for the dinner guests between the British champion, a Junior Secretary at the Embassy, and Stalin's champion. There was no victor, but pyrotechnics on both sides.[25] It was an apt metaphor for the three days of talks.

Eden had visited Moscow at a perilous moment of the war, and despite the lack of concrete agreement – the communiqué omitted all references to the post-war frontiers – felt the mission had served its purpose. Coinciding with Churchill's American visit, the Soviet visit gave out all the right signals as to the importance Britain attached to Anglo-Soviet solidarity, something that Churchill, deeply mistrusted by the Soviets, would never have been able to achieve. Fears of a Hess 'conspiracy' were long forgotten. Eden's decision to take a Trade Union delegation back to London with him was specially well received, and overall there was greater understanding, if not agreement, on the issues that divided the two countries. Cripps, coming to the end of his eighteen-month stint in Moscow, had attended the final discussions and helped draft the statement pledging the ultimate defeat of Germany. Molotov, Eden's opposite number, 'showed himself friendly and reasonable throughout', Eden later reported to the King's secretary, '& it does not seem too much to hope that we have laid the foundations for really useful constructive work here in the years ahead.'[26]

To replace Cripps, Eden nominated as Ambassador Sir Archibald Clark-Kerr, whose ability to work with Stalin and calm his impatient demands for a premature Second Front by the Western Allies was a notable contribution to the success of his mission.

Eden's main memory of the visit was of the contrasts, especially between the poverty and shortages in the Moscow streets and the sumptuous lifestyle inside the Kremlin. On 19 December, Eden had visited the war-torn Klin district, liberated only four days earlier, winning the undying gratitude of Marshal Georgi Zhukov, defender of Moscow against the German invaders, both for his visit and for his later rousing comments in England, on the BBC and in Parliament.[27] With Maisky, he had also toured Tchaikovsky's ransacked house, where the invading Germans had scattered torn manuscripts like confetti, the fate that he felt would have befallen British artistic treasures if the Nazis had ever invaded British shores. At Klin he saw six young German prisoners of war, timid, cold and frightened, their only protection against the Russian winter being the meanest of ragged cardigans. The interpreters could get no sense from them, and it fell to Eden to talk to them in idiomatic German and find that they came from the Sudetenland, Mannheim and Dresden. The contrast between Hitler's claims of Nazi invincibility and the all-too-certain fate of these vulnerable youths (roughly the same age as his son Simon) was specially poignant to Eden. That same night he attended the ballet in Moscow, only a few hours after seeing the torn Tchaikovsky scores. Their sophisticated realisation at the Bolshoi was another contrast long remembered, and for Eden one hopeful sign that the spirit of civilisation would ultimately endure.

On his return to London on 30 December, Eden penned a report for the King, which he incorporated in his customary End of Year Report from the Foreign Office:

> There were certainly some uncertain moments and some difficult ones but in the end Mr Eden believed that some at least of the Russian suspicions were allayed. The future of our relations with this country will depend upon how far it proves possible to follow up the work of the mission in the political and military spheres.[28]

Back in Cabinet on 1 January 1942, Eden argued, correctly, albeit unsuccessfully, that Stalin should be accommodated regarding the 1941 frontiers, apart from Poland. Had the Cabinet accepted this view, the outcome for Poland at Yalta could have been very different.

Stalin was weaker in 1942 than he was at Yalta. Eden's attitude to America was equivocal: the common language should not delude the British into believing that the Americans also had common interests. He was wary of the price the Americans might eventually exact from Britain for their support, views he shared with Halifax in the Washington Embassy, to whom he reported his opinion that Stalin was 'a political descendant of Peter the Great rather than of Lenin.'[29]

Of the 'Big Three' (Stalin, Roosevelt, Churchill), Stalin was a permanent fixture, having removed all rivals and with no need for any electoral* mandate. Roosevelt was impregnable after his 1940 Election victory; Churchill was vulnerable. At the beginning of 1942, the 'unthinkable' was actually being thought by a growing number of people. Many of the 'old' Tories had never forgiven Churchill for his political peregrinations, whilst the growing progressive element in the House of Commons saw him as an anachronism. Inner members of his circle, Eden included, were exasperated by his methods of working, and his symbolic retention of the post of Defence Minister. After the 'postponement' of Hitler's invasion plans, even the stirring speeches did not seem to carry the same sense of urgency. In the nature of political coups, success demanded a replacement candidate on whom all the conspirators were agreed. There were three possibilities: Beaverbrook, Cripps and Eden.

Beaverbrook, sensing the way the wind blew, and infuriated that he had not been made overlord of all war production, left the Cabinet in March 1942. Although Churchill may not have been fully aware of it, Cripps was a far more potent threat. Cripps's pre-war career had made him the leader of the Labour left, but his new scepticism towards the Soviet Union, fostered during his ambassadorship, had broadened his appeal, and he had a growing reputation overseas. Stanley Bruce, Australian High Commissioner in London and the Australian representative in the War Cabinet, believed that Cripps would be a better war Premier than Churchill, and tried to persuade Attlee and Eden likewise. Failing that, Robert Menzies was a possibility.[30]

As for Eden, it was never in his character that he should wield the knife himself. As the Australian historian David Day has written, 'Eden was never quite ready to take the plunge, was isolated in the Conservative Party for his progressive views and was hypnotised by his appointment as Churchill's heir apparent.'[31] Eden, however, shared Bruce's frustrations. On 3 April he unburdened himself to Cranborne (elevated since January

---

*On being told by Ernest Bevin at the Potsdam Conference in late July 1945 that Churchill was no longer Prime Minister after that week's British General Election result, Stalin replied through his interpreter, 'We do things very differently in Russia.' The late Sir Frank Roberts to the author, 1 July 1992.

1941 to the Lords by writ of summons of the sovereign, as Baron Cecil of Essendon, one of his father's subsidiary titles, to enable him to speak on foreign affairs in the Upper Chamber):

> Truth is I am much troubled about present methods of conducting the war, and am in some doubt what I should do. There is no real improvement, no greater order other than charge. Winston continues to keep the military side entirely in his hands in contact with Chiefs of Staff. One would not boggle at that, if the results were good, but they're not! Brilliant improvisation is no substitute for carefully planned dispositions made in time. I am particularly unhappy about the Air Ministry, which seems the least far seeing of a short sighted lot ... What troubles me is that I, and I suppose other members of War Cabinet, are regarded by public as those running the war, & we don't one little bit. Even the Defence Cte doesn't. It only meets once a week anyway; Wednesday after dinner. It is true that I now see all important operational telegrams – since the last ten days – but I am pretty sure that I am the only member of the Defence Cte who does, except, of course, Winston, & seeing these documents has not decreased my anxieties. I still believe that the right way to run this is by a small Cabinet of four or five that meets daily, but I don't believe Winston will ever accept that. Altogether I am most unhappy.[32]

This letter reveals much about Eden's desire to act patriotically, and his frustration at being hamstrung. It also shows how thoughts of replacing Churchill did not enter into the equation, even though there was a growing progressive atmosphere throughout the country. Eden's appeal as a centrist figure was strong, especially among servicemen. Part of this appeal lay in his clear concern for the eventual peacetime settlement, typified by his nationwide broadcast on 4 January about his visit to Russia, when he stressed the importance he attached 'to the discussions which we had upon the organisation of peace and security after the war.'[33]

James Stuart, Chief Whip, warned Churchill of the cross-party feelings of dissent about his leadership. When Churchill came to realise the threat to his position, which included a vote of confidence in the Commons at the end of January, he shrewdly brought Cripps into the Cabinet as Lord Privy Seal and Leader of the House on 19 February, in a minor reshuffle that nevertheless managed to offend both Attlee, who did not want Cripps in the Government, and Eden, who believed that he himself had earlier been offered the post of Leader of the House. Eden, who would have been willing to serve as Minister of Defence (the post he really wanted) in a Cripps Government in February 1942,[34] was an alternative Prime Minister, but he was never a Brutus, and in the next few weeks Churchill moved to formalise Eden's position as his nominated successor, a tactic he was to employ on and off for the next thirteen years.

The catalyst for the nomination was Churchill's visit to America on 17 June to discuss with Roosevelt, among other things, the timing of the Second Front. The day before his departure Churchill wrote to the King, marking the envelope 'For His Majesty alone'. At their weekly lunch a few days earlier, the King and Churchill had discussed the procedures to be followed in the event of the Prime Minister's death and Churchill had recommended then that Eden should be invited to form a Government. However, the King wished this arrangement to be put in writing, hence Churchill's constitutionally unique letter:

> In case of my death on this journey I am about to take, I avail myself of Yr Majesty's gracious permission, to advise that He shd entrust the formation of a new Government to Mr. Anthony Eden, the Secretary of State for Foreign Affairs, who is in my view the outstanding Minister in the largest political party in the House of Commons and in the National Government over which I have the honour to preside, and who I am sure will be found capable of conducting Yr. Majesty's Affairs with the resolution, experience & capacity which these grievous times require.

On 28 January 1945, the day before his departure for the Yalta Conference together with his Foreign Secretary, Churchill supplemented this original letter to the King with a second one that took the process a stage further by nominating Sir John Anderson, the Chancellor of the Exchequer, as the 'heir presumptive' in the event of Eden's death at the same time as his own.[35]

These letters, drafted in wartime conditions, were to resonate in Eden's life throughout the remaining years of Churchill's leadership of the Conservative Party, a post Churchill only relinquished on 6 April 1955, at the age of eighty. Circumstances change, advice alters, yet once the intention had been set down as one of the tablets of the faith, it was extremely difficult, as long as Eden remained in front-line politics, for the intention to be revoked, a situation that was to cause all manner of difficulties for both Eden's friends and his rivals.

Yet the King's caution was understandable. Several high-profile figures died in air crashes during the war, and Eden himself had some narrow escapes. On 12 April 1943, Leslie Howard, the film actor, sought Eden's special permission to visit Spain and Portugal with the British Council. His plane was shot down on 1 June, as he returned to England. Four weeks later, Victor Cazalet, Eden's exact Eton contemporary, was killed at Gibraltar with General Sikorski. General 'Strafer' Gott's plane was shot down *en route* to Cairo, where he was due to take up his appointment as Commander of the Eighth Army. Eden regarded Gott, a fellow Rifleman, very highly and had been party to the decision that he should replace Auchinleck. On the eve of the vital engagement at El Alamein, a new commander was needed. The tide in the affairs of men produced the name of Bernard Montgomery, and the rest was history. Eighteen days after Gott's death, the King's younger brother, the Duke of Kent, died in an accident in the north of Scotland, when his Sunderland flying boat crashed into rising ground above Brora. The accident remains one of the mysteries of the war. One theory even claims that among those killed on the flight was Rudolf Hess, a double later taking his place in Spandau prison. For Eden, who knew the Kents, it was a personal tragedy. The fact that the Sunderland boat had set off on its fatal flight from the Invergordon Naval Base, from where Eden had embarked for Russia a few months earlier, added to the immediacy of the disaster. On 4 July, American Independence Day, Princess Marina had given birth to her third child, Prince Michael, and President Roosevelt was among the godparents. On hearing the news of the crash, Eden at once sent a personal telegram to the King on behalf of the diplomatic service and the overseas territories. 'The sudden death of His Royal Highness on active service has come as a grievous shock to the allied peoples everywhere.' In time, after his divorce from Beatrice in 1950, Eden's name would be mentioned, incorrectly, as a possible suitor for the hand of the widowed Princess Marina.

The political threat to Churchill's war leadership, conveniently omitted from many accounts of the period, was no less a danger than the logistical ones. The key period of unpopularity came at the beginning of 1942 and continued for some months, fuelled by a continued tide of reversals, including the break-out of the German battle-cruisers *Scharnhorst* and *Gneisenau* through the Channel on 12 February; the fall of Singapore on 15 February; Rommel's successful offensive against Auchinleck in the Western Desert, culminating in the fall of Tobruk in June; and later the costly failures of the Dieppe raid in August. A second vote of confidence on Churchill's conduct of the war was held after a debate on 1–2 July 1942, when twenty-five MPs voted against Churchill and forty abstained, an uncomfortable echo of the weakening of Chamberlain's position in May 1940. Cripps was not alone in believing that Eden should now succeed Churchill as Prime Minister.[36]

Salvation for Churchill came from an unexpected quarter, when on the first day of the debate, the Conservative MP Sir John Wardlaw-Milne, who had been demonstrating with some cogency the failings of Churchill's strategy, suggested that the command of the British Army should be entrusted to the Duke of Gloucester. This proposition was greeted with laughter, and Wardlaw-Milne lost his audience.

The next night, after the vote, Eden dined with Churchill and his brother Jack.[37] 'Much discussion of war situation,' Eden wrote in his diary.

'Winston said repeatedly that we had not done as well as we should. "I am ashamed," etc.'[38]

Eden knew that political survival had been a close call, and that one more big military reversal could well provoke a fresh crisis of confidence. The momentum was now with Stafford Cripps, riding a wave of popularity on his return from Russia, but as Burma was invaded, Cripps went to India, seeking the support of the subcontinent for the war effort, in return for self-government afterwards. During the 'Cripps Mission', Eden became acting Leader of the House of Commons on 11 March, a post to which he would be appointed permanently on 22 November, and would keep to the end of the war. His team had been strengthened by the arrival as assistant private secretary of Guy Millard, who was later to be a key figure during Suez, but the demands on his time became almost insurmountable, especially after the arrangement became permanent. 'My first question as Leader of the House,' he noted on 12 March. 'Cannot say I enjoyed the role much.'[39] In fact, the job was one for which he proved eminently suitable, good on the representational side, open-minded in steering through parliamentary business with the minimum of fuss, and with an appeal to non-Conservative members that few of his colleagues could match. The Leader of the House has to represent the House to the Government, and the Government to the House. Eden's consensual, non-partisan approach was tailor-made for these requirements.

Eden's main concerns included Britain's relations with America and Russia, with de Gaulle's Free French, and with the wider imperial family. In each case, he was to have disagreements with Churchill.

Unlike Churchill, Eden never believed that America would prove the panacea for all Britain's difficulties; nor was he reluctant to negotiate over Soviet frontiers, believing that 'the failure of the British Empire and Russia to agree their policies in advance had made possible three great conflicts, the Napoleonic war and the two world wars.'[40] He thought that Churchill's attitude to India, regarding Gandhi as Britain's 'bitter enemy', represented the worst of the old Tory imperialism, and he recognised Churchill's undermining of the Cripps mission by going behind his Cabinet colleague's back to the Viceroy, Linlithgow, as a means of bolstering himself against any threat Cripps might offer to his own position.[41] Eden's disagreements with Churchill over America and Russia were policy-based. Over India, he found himself personally hostile to Churchill's old cavalry subaltern's attitude and his antagonism towards the 'half-naked fakir'.[42] Disagreements over the Free French also hinged on questions of personality, and the often uncomfortable presence of Charles de Gaulle in Carlton Gardens. Eden had recognised de Gaulle's National Committee of

Free France in September 1941 and was noticeably more sympathetic to the Frenchman than either Roosevelt or Churchill, who once said that the biggest cross he had to bear was the Cross of Lorraine. In fact, Eden's role in regard to de Gaulle was akin to that of Walter Monckton with Stanley Baldwin and Edward VIII at the time of the Abdication, a conciliatory go-between, keeping open channels of communication. He warned Churchill that de Gaulle saw himself 'in the role of Joan of Arc liberating his country from Vichy; his war is a private war against Vichy.'[43]

For his part, Churchill warned Eden that he must not 'allow our relations with the United States to be spoiled through our supposed patronage of this man ... whose accession to power in France would be a British disaster of the first magnitude'.[44] Not that Eden found de Gaulle easy to deal with, either. One of the worst crises arose with Operation IRONCLAD, the invasion of Vichy-occupied Madagascar, in April 1942, over which de Gaulle was neither consulted nor informed, to his under-standable fury.* 'A stiff meeting with de Gaulle about Madagascar,' Eden recorded on 11 May. 'He is a most difficult creature to handle & I had no easy task to keep my temper. But I am sorry for any exile, so I just did!'[45]

In this respect, Eden did better than Clementine Churchill, who had a row with de Gaulle about the Vichyite French Admiral, François Darlan. 'In argument she often waxed passionate and partisan,' her daughter has written of Clementine Churchill, 'and when the talk took a tone or direction of which she disapproved, she would after a time suddenly "erupt", and could maul most savagely those of whose views or characters she either temporarily or habitually disapproved.'[46] So it was on 28 November with de Gaulle. That evening Eden was speaking with Churchill when the argument (in the absence of de Gaulle) erupted again. 'At a moment of the shouting match W[inston] said "Well D[arlan] is not as bad as de Gaulle anyway. That man hates us & would give anything to fight with Germans against us." This nonsense is due to Clemmie having had a row with de Gaulle at luncheon.' Churchill's mind was now stubbornly set. 'I fear that W who has of course accepted C's account of this interview will be passionately anti D-G in consequence,' commented Eden,[47] who always remembered the hardening of attitudes on both sides caused by Clementine's quarrel. In January 1963 de Gaulle vetoed Britain's appli-cation to join the Common Market and Eden believed his mind-set had been fixed since November 1942.[48]

Also at this time, Eden witnessed a drunken Randolph Churchill rowing

---

*Fears were that the occupying Vichy forces could allow Japanese occupation of this strategic island, a consummation that would threaten allied routes to the Far East.

with his father, which he thought inexcusable. 'It was a revelation to me,' he wrote sadly, 'that R. was so stupid.' Rows in his own family had recently centred on his mother's continued financial profligacy, and after a difficult conference with Tim and Marjorie in the summer, Eden had contributed £2,000 he could ill afford to a rescue package for his mother. At least this financial crisis coincided with Simon's last bills on leaving Eton, and his entry into the Empire Air Training scheme, but it was still a heavy, unexpected burden.[49]

Marjorie, always his favourite sibling, was in the grip of the cancer that was to kill her, and when she died on 10 February 1943, it was another break with the Windlestone past. 'Poor Marjorie,' he wrote. 'As B[eatrice] said she was the one member of my family who was consistently kind to me from my childhood onwards thro' the years. She has played a part in every phase, marriage, constituency, & against mother.' He thought the funeral service grim. 'But then how to avoid that? Funerals always strike me as barbaric.'[50] Relations with his surviving brother were never easy, though Marjorie's death brought the two to a closer understanding. 'Don't, in future, have any more "complexes" about me, and I will not about you,' his brother Tim wrote after Marjorie's funeral. 'Your patience with me yesterday has quite triumphed over my hasty temper & sour spirit – all the more admirable, in that I know that you, too, have the Eden temper.'[51]

More agreeable was Eden's regular series of luncheons with the King. After Churchill had formally nominated Eden as his successor on 16 June, Eden's relationship with the King – always amiable, though a little stilted and awkward owing to George VI's inherent shyness and stammer – subtly altered. The King initiated a regular series of luncheons, sometimes à deux, sometimes with intimates such as Bobbety Cecil, which were almost advance weekly audiences against the time when Eden might suddenly be propelled into the highest office. George VI asked to be brought up to date with what was really going on, and to discuss how things might unfold after the war, a topic to which he frequently returned. He found Eden's views on the post-war settlement of abiding interest, especially his views on worker cooperation, share options and profit-sharing, all of which were symptomatic of the mood change that he, as Duke of York, had been trying to achieve in the 1930s at a younger age level with his camps at Southwold for boys from many different social classes. Eden's table talk gave a different perspective from Churchill's, and from Attlee's, the one often over-exuberant, the other taciturn to the point of terseness. 'Lunched alone with the King,' Eden wrote on 5 August, the day he announced in the Commons that the Munich Agreement was formally rescinded, a piece of historical tidying that much pleased him. 'He was very friendly. Some discussion of the future. He was correct, but the hints were pretty obvious. On the whole the most human talk I have yet had with him.'[52]

The King found Eden an atypical Tory – in a way, not a Tory at all. There was none of the condescension of some of his colleagues, and Eden had this ability to get on with people from different backgrounds, parties and countries, again not a characteristic associated with the descendants of Stanley Baldwin's 'hardfaced men', who had done well out of the Great War. Two days after his luncheon with the King, Eden was at a formal dinner. 'Two young 60th officers there,' he wrote. 'Invited them over to a drink & had a good regimental gossip.' As acting Leader of the House, he found most of his evenings were taken up with formalities. On 9 August he revealed his feelings in the privacy of his diary. 'A terrible woman called Lady Chetwynd there, a distant cousin of our lot and a terrible woman I thought. Just the type I abominate, incredible airs & stomach-turning snobbery, e.g. "people like us with handles to their names."' Constituency business demanded his attention also, and on 14 August Eden found himself in a late and overcrowded train on the return journey, with nowhere to sit. 'Gossiped to some soldiers standing in the corridor,' he wrote. 'That was best part of the day.'[53]

Despite his indispensable position in the Government, Eden genuinely wondered whether he had backed the right horse in taking up a political career:

> I do not really feel confidence in myself as No 1 at home, and it looks as if, *faute de mieux*, I might drift that way! Beatrice saw the force of all this but argued that I had gone too far to turn back now. Tho' she admitted India [the Viceregalship] was only possibility. Truth is I feel too tired to tackle these post-war problems. I am desperately in need of a change and I do not know enough of economics.[54]

India would be one solution, although no Viceroy, despite Curzon's lifelong ambition, had ever returned from the subcontinent to assume the Premiership. Linlithgow was coming to the end of his term of office and the question of his successor was one that was already vexing Churchill, who had twice extended his tenure. Meanwhile, the Cripps mission to India had been a failure. Far from uniting the Congress Party behind the British, it had intensified the 'Quit India' campaign. Cripps's popularity withered as fast as it had blossomed. Jokes about his ascetic lifestyle and moral superiority – 'there but for the grace of God, goes God' was one Churchill circulated – reflected a new public perception. Cripps was still openly critical of Churchill's conduct of the war, but Churchill's position was made stronger by the transformation of the military situation. The Anglo-American landings (Operation TORCH) in North Africa on 8

November represented the beginning of a new phase that was to culminate in the surrender of German and Italian forces in Tunisia in May 1943. More immediate in its impact was Montgomery's victory over Rommel's Afrika Korps at El Alamein between 23 October and 4 November. 'Now this is not the end,' said Churchill in one of his most memorable wartime addresses. 'It is not even the beginning of the end. But it is, perhaps, the end of the beginning.'[55] Churchill ordered the church bells to be rung in national celebration. Eden knew that the element of relief in this decision was strong, and one of the best examples of Churchill's eternally optimistic belief: *Alle Zoll Recht Kommen.*

The year 1942 ended with more difficulties over Admiral Darlan, the cause of the original row between de Gaulle and Clementine Churchill, that did so much to turn Churchill against de Gaulle and the Free French. When the TORCH landings took place in North Africa, Darlan, who had supported France's armistice with the Germans in 1940, took command of the Vichy forces opposing the Allies. After the ceasefire on 10 November, in a remarkable *volte face*, he undertook to work for the Allies and was appointed the French High Commissioner in North Africa. Brendan Bracken, Minister of Information, warned Eden in advance of this 'fantastic suggestion hatched in Washington'[56] and British official opinion was frankly incredulous. 'How can we work with Darlan who is a traitor?' asked Harvey, a rhetorical question that required no answer.[57]

Eden was appalled, but the ineffectiveness of his protests showed how much Churchill was now prepared to accommodate the Americans, who had brokered the Darlan deal. On 26 November Eden wrote his last despairing letter on the matter to Churchill. 'In Europe as a whole the "filthy race of quislings", as you once so aptly called them, will take heart since they now have reason to think that if only they happen to be in authority when the forces of the United Nations arrive, they will be treated as being the government of the country.'[58] He assured de Gaulle, who was deeply moved by Eden's obvious personal distress, of his opposition to the American initiative. De Gaulle declared that he would be prepared to work with General Giraud, an escaped POW, who was given the command in North Africa after the Casablanca Conference, as he was anti-Vichy, but Darlan was quite beyond the pale.

The situation suddenly clarified, because Darlan was assassinated on 24 December. 'I had not been home long when Winston rang thro' & told me that Darlan had been murdered,' wrote Eden that Christmas Eve. 'We agreed that the event could be turned to profit. I have not felt so relieved by any event for years.'[59]

*

As 1942 drew to its close, Jan Karski, emissary between the Polish Government-in-exile in London and the Polish Socialist Party, who had admired Eden when a student in Geneva in the 1930s, had given the Foreign Office details of the Nazi extermination of the Jews, information he also handed to Roosevelt. Despite Karski's photographic memory and attention to detail of the horrors in the Warsaw ghetto and the Belzec extermination camp, disbelief was the first response of many in the West.

On 7 December Eden told Halifax in Washington that the evidence was incontrovertible. After a meeting of the War Cabinet on 14 December, during which Eden gave his colleagues details of what Karski had told him personally, a Joint Anglo-American Allied Declaration was issued, denouncing Jewish persecution by the Nazis. The same day (17 December) Eden read this declaration in the House of Commons to a sombre gathering, condemning 'in the strongest possible terms this bestial policy of cold-blooded extermination'. Eden's speech, after which the House stood to observe a one-minute silence, made a considerable impact, both on those for whom such news came as a shock and on those who knew of the atrocities, such as James de Rothschild, MP for the Isle of Ely, who afterwards wrote to thank Eden on behalf of all British Jewry.

Many later felt that the Allies had not done enough and that sympathy was not the same as action. Eden did not escape his share of obloquy.[60] Despite Karski's urgings, the priority of the Allies was the defeat of the Third Reich. Eden knew that his statement was not enough, but in the conditions of 1942, it was the best he could do. 'It had a far greater dramatic effect than I had expected,' Eden wrote in his diary. 'Ll. G said to me later "You were very impressive this morning. I cannot recall a scene like that in all my years in Parliament." '[61]

Karski is not mentioned in Eden's memoirs; but neither is the Zionist leader Chaim Weizmann, whose meeting with Eden in the early part of 1944 about the extermination of Hungarian Jews led to decisive action over the bombing of railway lines to the death-camps. Eden sought neither praise nor blame for his part in the central humanitarian tragedy of the war. But, after the passage of time had enabled him to recollect in tranquillity, and after the appalling facts of the Holocaust were fully and undeniably known, he felt both shame and regret that he had not done more. It is easy to be wise after the event, but there is no denying that in the complex *realpolitik* obtaining in wartime, Eden's decisions came at a fearful moral price.

The main theme of 1943 was to be one of alliances and conferences. Roosevelt and Churchill met at Casablanca from 14 to 24 January to discuss future strategy. The policy of unconditional surrender was announced and the decision taken on the Combined Bomber Offensive against Germany. Eden was in favour of the first, and convinced of the expedience of the second. The daylight raids on Berlin began on 30 January, appropriately the tenth anniversary of Hitler's rise to power. Though Eden did not attend the Casablanca Conference (somewhat to his relief), he played the decisive part in persuading de Gaulle that he should attend, despite the presence of General Giraud, which led (despite some bruised egos) to the formation of the French National Committee for Liberation.

Although Eden knew that the road to ultimate victory would be long and arduous, he increasingly turned his mind to the post-war settlement. War was a means to an end, not an end in itself. 'A. E.'s interest in post-war planning questions is increasing steadily,' Oliver Harvey noted in his diary on 15 October 1942. 'The chief obstacle remains the P.M.'[62] Churchill's main belief was in a post-war Anglo-American hegemony. Eden had the foresight to see that Russia and China would also have to be central figures in any United Nations of the peace, though he was not alone in failing to anticipate how swiftly Britain would fall in the hierarchy of nations in this 'Four-Power Plan'.[63]

Post-war admission to the diplomatic service had exercised Eden since 1941. In January 1943 he published his ideas in a White Paper, *Proposals for the Reform of the Foreign Service*, which proved the blueprint for the most radical overhaul of the service for nearly 200 years.[64] As the majority of these ideas were to be implemented after the war, they became known as the Eden-Bevin reforms, after the author and his successor. Bevin influenced the White Paper, as he had published a memorandum on the need for reform when joining the War Cabinet in 1940, which Eden discussed with him before formulating proposals that were widely welcomed among progressive elements in the service.[65] In the White Paper, Eden directly addressed the public perception of the Foreign Office as a socially exclusive, antediluvian institution:

> Among criticisms which have been brought against the Diplomatic Service the view has been expressed that it is recruited from too small a circle, that it tends to represent the interests of certain sections of the nation rather than those of the country as a whole, that its members lead too sheltered a life, that they have insufficient understanding of economic and social questions, that the extent of their experience is too small to enable them properly to understand many of the problems with which they ought to deal, and that the range of their contacts is too limited to allow them to acquire more than a relatively narrow acquaintance with the foreign people amongst whom they live.[66]

To tackle these problems, Eden proposed a liberalisation of recruitment policy, greater opportunities for female entrants, and increasing parity of

Consuls and Commercial Officers with political specialists in overseas Chancelleries. The proposals were very much in tune with the mood of the time, preceded as they were by William Beveridge's proposals for the welfare state and followed by Rab Butler's educational reforms.

On 4 February 1943, the Edens and Bobbety Cecil met William Beveridge, basking in acclamation for his recently published report on Social Insurance and Allied Services. Although the agenda Beveridge embraced had echoes of Noel Skelton, which Eden welcomed, he was unimpressed by Beveridge himself, finding him vain and curiously uninformed. 'Bobbety, B[eatrice] & I all had the same impression,' he wrote, 'that the old man didn't seem to know much about his report.'[67]

Yet Eden saw the proposals as vital for the future stability and prosperity of the nation in the post-war era. Unlike many sceptical Tories, he wanted to see the Beveridge Report implemented as soon as possible, and not postponed. 'We at home have to do better,' he had said on 29 March 1942. 'There can be no return to what was bad in the old days.'[68] Eden's enthusiasm for reconstruction clearly pre-dated both military success at El Alamein and social reform with the publication of the Beveridge Report at the end of 1942, and his stance was well ahead of the majority of his party, which suffered when this issue of timing became a crucial dividing line between the two main parties, leading eventually to Labour overtaking the Conservatives in the polls.

As Leader of the House, Eden had to preside over a rare parliamentary event, the arrangements following the death in office of the Speaker, Captain Edward Fitzroy, an uncle of Sybil Fitzroy, whose beauty had captivated Eden in far-off Windlestone days. He supervised the election of Clifton Brown on 9 March 1943, though his own preferred candidate was Gwilym Lloyd George.

Two days later, Eden took a night-time flight from Prestwick Airport in Scotland with a party that included William Strang (one of the first beneficiaries of the Eden-Bevin reforms, when, from outside the charmed world of public school and Oxbridge, he rose to become Permanent Under-Secretary), Gladwyn Jebb and Oliver Harvey. As Friday 12 March dawned, Eden was high above the busy Atlantic convoy routes, before landing after fifteen hours at Gander aerodrome in Canada, *en route* to Washington.*

---

*Increasingly this was to be the pattern of Eden's war now: lengthy and uncertain flights, a select group of trusted advisers in attendance, and major decisions to be taken with the leaders of the alliance, often on his own initiative. In the next two years he would attend the first Quebec Conference (August 1943), the first Cairo Conference (November 1943), Teheran (November 1943), the second Cairo Conference (December 1943), the second Quebec Conference (September 1944), Yalta (February 1945), San Francisco (May–June 1945), and finally Potsdam (July 1945).

Although the circumstances were now very different from his previous visit to America in 1938, he was received with equal enthusiasm.

Eden was in America for eighteen days, and had talks with President Roosevelt; Henry Wallace, the Vice-President; Cordell Hull, the Secretary of State; Sumner Welles, Under-Secretary of State; Harry Hopkins, Roosevelt's special envoy during the war; General Marshall, to be one of the key makers of the post-war order; and John Winant, the American Ambassador in London, who had returned to America specially for the visit. In the American manner, Eden found that most of these talks were held in separate offices à deux, and he was never quite sure how well co-ordinated all the debriefing was, confessing to Oliver Harvey that 'he felt more at home in the Kremlin', as 'there at least they meant business.'[69] But he succumbed to the charm of Roosevelt, who pulled out all the stops to welcome his guest, making no difficulties over contentious issues such as Poland, and inviting Eden as a personal guest to the White House for the last three days of the visit, a signal honour. It was at Roosevelt's suggestion that Eden made one of his keynote speeches to the American people at the State Legislature of Maryland in Annapolis, where he spoke in front of the portrait of his great-great-grandfather, Sir Robert Eden, who was the last Governor before the War of Independence, which made the Americans feel that their guest was 'an Annapolis boy who had made good.'[70]

Eden was in no doubt about the predominant part Roosevelt foresaw America taking in world affairs after the war. Not all was sweetness and light. Eden was concerned about Roosevelt's attitude to France, which to his mind underestimated the proud defiance of the Free French and denied them appropriate standing when the peace came, which sat strangely with Roosevelt's sympathy towards Indian independence. They also differed on policy towards Yugoslavia, and Roosevelt's bizarre plan to create a new post-war state of Wallonia from areas of Belgium, France and Luxembourg. But objectively Eden realised that the visit had done much good, and although he was not to know it, had markedly raised his standing among some of the doubters in Roosevelt's entourage, such as Harry Hopkins, who now revised his earlier, dismissive attitude towards Eden, after his ultra-secret meeting with him on what was known as 'Tube Alloys', the development of the atomic bomb.

Halifax's report to London confirmed the success of Eden's visit. 'From the first,' Halifax wrote, 'he clicked with everyone from the President downwards, both in private and in public. He has never put a foot wrong.'[71]

On the way home, via Canada, for three days of further talks with the Canadian Prime Minister, Mackenzie King, Eden visited the Air Training scheme, an initiative of even greater interest to him now that

Simon was training under its auspices. But the Earl of Athlone, Governor-General of Canada, thought Eden an exhausted man, writing to Queen Mary after the visit, 'what these poor tired-out men are expected to do is really appalling.'[72] Eden arrived back in London on 3 April after a flight of more than eleven hours. Churchill at once invited him to Chequers. 'A pity!' recorded Oliver Harvey. 'No rest for him and a late night.'[73]

Nine days after Eden's return from Washington, Polish-Soviet relations, on which Eden had expended so much time and energy, were dealt a blow with the terrible news (from Germany) of the discovery at the Katyn Forest near Smolensk of the bodies of up to 10,000 Polish officers in mass graves. Initially, some (though not Eden) dismissed these reports as Nazi propaganda. It was even thought that the Nazis, and not the Russians, had perpetrated the murders. 'Alas, the German revelations are probably true', Churchill admitted. 'The Bolsheviks can be very cruel.'[74]

Eden stuck to his guns. He did not allow this atrocity to damage the warm relations between the British and the Russians, which he had been at such pains to build up. His critics have judged him harshly about 'the guilt of Katyn' and his 'betrayal' of the Poles. But, at the time, and under the pressure of war, he had to choose between two 'options of difficulties'. On the one hand, Poland stood as the oppressed country, on whose behalf Britain had mobilised in 1939; on the other hand, since 1941 Russia had been one of the main panels of the triptych on which ultimate victory depended. For Eden, the priority was to maintain the Anglo-Soviet alliance, though the consequence was, at best, morally ambiguous. Noel Newsome, Director of the BBC's European Service, met Eden on 7 May, after which he noted that the Foreign Secretary was entirely on the Soviet side, though thinking that the Russians probably did kill the Polish officers. History indeed shows that Eden's sympathetic attitude to the Soviets was mistaken, at least in the light of the Cold War that was to follow. It is difficult to escape from the conclusion that he was over-influenced by his fears and frustrations lest his hard diplomatic work should be jeopardised – and that there was not enough principled agonising. Stalin did not hesitate to use 'Katyn' as a catalyst, thereby ruthlessly driving a wedge between the Polish resistance and their compatriots in exile. 'That Katyn should have been remembered long after other atrocities were forgotten was less a Nazi achievement than a Soviet choice,' Michael Stenton has written. 'Stalin's decision to use Katyn against the Poles made it the defining instance of his policy; the British response was the harbinger of theirs.'[75]

*

Shortly after his return from his successful American visit, Eden almost became Viceroy of India, succeeding the long-serving Marquess of Linlithgow. Oliver Harvey was appalled: 'I hope no one will take this seriously,' he wrote. 'For A. E. to go would be to lose all he has now gained – to miss the P.M.-ship, to miss the vital peace-making years, to confound his friends and confirm his critics.'[76] The trouble was that many people took it very seriously indeed. What complicated matters was that one part of Eden was attracted to the idea, whereas cold reason told him it would be a mistake. Gossip in London had been rife for some time, and names canvassed had included Bobbety Cecil, Miles Lampson and Archibald Sinclair. The Nizam of Hyderabad, who had obviously not heard of the reception accorded to Sir John Wardlaw-Milne's speech in the Commons regarding the command of the British Army, favoured the Duke of Gloucester.

On 15 February Leo Amery, Secretary of State for India and Burma, who wanted to send the best available candidate, discussed the vacancy with Eden. Initially, becoming Viceroy had its attractions – an end to his disagreements with Churchill, a degree of autonomy, and possession of what Curzon had once called the holy guardianship of one-fifth of the entire human race. On the other hand, the powers were circumscribed, especially in 1943 in the context of global war.* Eden had accepted the Dominions Office with grace and patriotism in 1939; he was now prepared to go where his Prime Minister thought he could best contribute – Curzon had said that India was duty writ with five letters rather than four – and, as Amery noted in his diary, 'He is quite willing to consider going there himself, realising the greatness of the task and prepared to take his chance over his future political position here. That shows a fine spirit and I am not sure that he is not by nature a much better Viceroy than a leader of the Conservative Party.'[77]

Eden consulted Baldwin and Halifax, both of whom pointed out that he was heir apparent to the Premiership. Nor was George VI in favour. 'Opinion had been final and against it,' Harvey recorded. 'So that bogey is allayed! Anyway A. E. thinks much good will have come of it being brought up in this way as it will show the P.M. that he is not so eager to succeed him as he may think.'[78]

But Churchill still had not given up on the idea of an Eden Vice-regalship and he wrote to the King on 23 April, pressing again the arguments in favour. On 28 April, King George VI sent the Prime

*It sounds grand to be Viceroy over 180 millions of men,' Lord Kimberley had declared, when declining the post in 1872, 'but it is in truth a much greater thing to be a member of the governing committee of the whole Empire, India included.' Cited in John P. Mackintosh, *The British Cabinet*, Stevens & Sons, 3rd edition, 1981, p.257.

Minister a lengthy reply, which showed how strongly he felt on the matter:

> There are, in my opinion, several strong arguments against his appointment at the present time. From the point of view of the general conduct of the war he is, I know, very much in your confidence. He is, so to speak, your second-in-command in many respects, and, while I appreciate your readiness to let him go, I cannot help feeling that you might well find the loss of his assistance and support too great an addition to the heavy burden which you already have to bear. As regards Foreign Affairs, he has won for himself a unique position among the United Nations. He enjoys, in an exceptional degree, the confidence both of the United States and of our Soviet Allies. If he were to go away to India now, the benefit which the country derives from his very special position would be, to a large extent, lost to it, just at a time when the delicate international problems of the post-war settlement are coming more and more to the front. I think, too, that it might be rather disturbing to the country to feel that his part in the general conduct of the war against Germany was thus being brought to a close, and while I argue that we ought in principle to send overseas the best man that we can spare, the conduct of the war from the United Kingdom must, I feel, take precedence over everything else.[79]

Even then, Churchill did not give up. So the problem remained unresolved, with new names such as Sir John Anderson and Oliver Lyttelton being mooted. Anderson was disqualified when it was considered, in the manner of those days, that his wife was not of Vicereine quality, no such objection being raised against Beatrice Eden, who was willing to go if Eden had considered it his duty. Had Beatrice become Vicereine, the slow drifting apart that was to occur in the Eden marriage in the last two years of the war might well have been delayed, even if not avoided altogether in the longer term.

Finally, on 7 May, Amery told Linlithgow that the idea of Eden was being dropped, on the King's insistence. But there was still no acceptable alternative and two days later Amery wrote to Eden asking him to reconsider. Presciently, Amery realised that the Conservatives might not be returned at the Election after the war, in which case, he argued, Eden might be very glad to be in India:

> From one point of view you might hate to be away at a moment when your personal influence might help to swing things one way or another. From another point of view, of course, you could be better occupied keeping India going than on the Opposition Front bench![80]

Had Eden accepted the post, the history of post-war Britain could have been very different. It was one of those watershed moments that come in so many careers. Eden followed the principle that 'when in doubt between two duties, it is wise to choose the most unpleasant.'[81] In 1943, being in Churchill's shadow was less attractive than New Delhi, but Eden chose the shadow, not because he wanted to guarantee his future Premiership, but because he genuinely believed – and was encouraged so to believe by the King – that it was in Cabinet as a counter-balance to Churchill's wilder excesses, that he could make the most valuable contribution to the war effort.

The issue remained unresolved until 8 June, when Eden finally resisted Churchill's pressure. By lunchtime that day they were discussing a shortlist of six names, from which emerged the unexpected choice of Field Marshal Wavell. A week earlier, an elderly member of Pratt's Club, oblivious to Wavell's presence at the table, had inadvertently brought a discussion on the subject to an abrupt halt with his intervention, 'Why not send old Wavell?'[82] Churchill agreed, with relief. Why not?

Wavell was as surprised as anyone. 'I wish you had been able to take it,' he wrote to Eden on 17 June. 'I went to the theatre the other night where an announcement was made that the leading lady was unable to play and that an understudy had to take up the part at very short notice. I recall the groans of disappointment of the audience.'[83]

Eden always considered that he had made the right decision over India, which had originally attracted him as a 'real' job. 'B and I motored home,' he wrote after the decision had been taken. 'It looked & smelt lovely as usual. We are glad not to be giving it up for a splendid palace at Delhi.'[84] But his responsibilities as wartime Foreign Secretary and his position as Prime Minister-in-waiting were, in the Platonic phrase, 'the really real' job.* Eden's work at the San Francisco Conference in 1945 was, in the longer term, to be of greater world importance.

Two further considerations weighed with Eden. De Gaulle's position as Leader of the Free French could have been fatally weakened in his absence; and in all probability, Beaverbrook would have entered the War Cabinet – a consummation, in Eden's view, devoutly to be avoided. Modestly, what he did not consider was the likelihood that Churchill would have made more mistakes had Eden been absent, certainly the tacit concern of the King. Also Eden would never have been free of the Prime Ministerial

---

*Linlithgow was the last of the old-style Viceroys; both his successors, Wavell and then Mountbatten, were on short-term special contracts. Wavell, the soldier-scholar, had to ensure that India's contribution to the war effort did not falter, with the combination of calls to the British to 'Quit India' and the rapid Japanese advance to the eastern borders of the subcontinent. Mountbatten, the well-connected regal showman with his flair for publicity, had the job of winding up the long history of the Raj. Eden, with his diplomatic skills, would have been more suited to the second of these two tasks, but that was not on the immediate agenda when Linlithgow finally retired in autumn 1943.

influence, even in New Delhi, as Churchill held strong views on India ('I hate Indians,' he had told Amery, 'they are a beastly people with a beastly religion.')[85]

The long road of the 8th Army through North Africa ended with the surrender of the Germans at Cape Bon at the tip of Tunisia on 9 May. Eden saw a great deal at this time of Harold Macmillan, newly installed as Resident Minister of State in North-West Africa. At this stage Macmillan admired Eden's flair and versatility, particularly his fluency in languages, shown on a visit to Algiers with Churchill to meet the French Committee for National Liberation, which effected a partial reconciliation between Giraud and de Gaulle, whom Eden saw as latter-day equivalents of Octavius Caesar and Mark Antony. At a luncheon at Admiral Cunningham's house to celebrate this rapprochement, in the presence also of Jean Monnet and René Massigli (one of Eden's close French contacts from 1930s' Geneva onwards), Eden summed up the philosophy that should motivate their countries. 'The Foreign Secretary spoke in excellent and very idiomatic French,' Macmillan recorded in his diary. 'A short and very well-phrased speech, referring to the necessity of England and France holding together after the war for the reconstruction of the things in which they mutually believed – freedom, tolerance and the rights of the people to enjoy their own lives at their fullest development.' However, unlike some other politicians, Eden did not negotiate in foreign languages, though his French and German were the equal of any.[86]*

Back in London on 12 July, as reports of the allied successes in Sicily came in, Eden spoke with Churchill on the need to coordinate Anglo-American-Soviet collaboration, the genesis of the Teheran Conference in November, writing to Churchill afterwards, 'You have often met President Roosevelt, and we have both met Stalin, but there have as yet been no triangular meetings, and there is no machinery for quick and effective exchange of ideas. There has been a tendency for us to agree matters with the Americans first and to present the results to the Russians, and there are signs that the Russians resent this procedure.'[87]

Along with Sir Orme ('Moley') Sargent, Deputy Under-Secretary at the Foreign Office, and Sir Ronald Campbell, now Ambassador in Lisbon, he discussed many post-war options at this time, including the future containment of Germany by an Anglo-French alliance, and the future of

---

*Eden's French was in a different class from Macmillan's or Blair's. Both these two got into trouble trying to discuss affairs of state with their counterparts. On one occasion Blair misunderstood a word that sounded the same, but had a different meaning in English; and Macmillan exasperated de Gaulle by trying to talk to him in French about NATO.

Italy after unconditional surrender. He submitted a paper to Churchill on the need to avoid the mistakes of 1919–39, which, according to Eden, necessitated on all possible occasions discussing plans and views with the Soviets as a matter of course, despite Roosevelt's reservations, expressed to him in Washington in March, of Communist expansion.[88]

Italy was now the soft underbelly of the Axis, following the allied victories in Tunisia and Sicily, and after the invasion on 10 July its transient state was underlined by Mussolini's fall. 'Winston rang up about 11.30 p.m. to announce the great news that Musso had resigned,' Eden wrote in his diary on 25 July 1943. 'It is terrific news for me. Eight years since all my troubles with Musso began.' The news caused him to speculate again on how things might have been handled differently. 'Looking back the thought comes again. Should we not have shown more determination in pressing thro' with sanctions in 1935 and if we had could we not have called Musso's bluff & at least postponed the war. The answer I am sure is Yes. We built Musso into a great power.'[89]

The long build-up to the Teheran Conference now began in earnest. Eden was present at QUADRANT, the first conference at Quebec, a venue suggested by Roosevelt, from 17 to 24 August. Whilst agreement was made on the Italian campaign and OVERLORD, the D-Day landings, Eden had less success in talks with Cordell Hull, now an ageing figure not in the best of health, on recognition of the French Committee of National Liberation. 'We both got quite heated at one time,' wrote Eden, 'when I told him we had to live twenty miles from France and I wanted to rebuild her so far as I could.'[90] The tortured question of post-war relations with Russia also occupied Hull and Eden, whose fears were that any meeting in Moscow that failed to promise a Second Front in 1943, or concede Russia's claims on the 1941 frontiers, would be doomed to failure. 'My, Mr Eden, I had no idea you were such a politician,' said Hull, implying that he was himself a statesman. Eden's riposte was well chosen. He asked Hull if he knew Lloyd George's definition of a statesman – 'A statesman is a politician with whom one happens to agree.'[91]

The subsequent Foreign Ministers' meeting of Eden, Hull and Molotov began in Moscow on 18 October, after the surrender of Italy. Eden's initial fears were that any agreements would be valid politically only in the short term; to his surprise, the progress proved more statesmanlike, considering that the main participants brought different agendas to the table. Eden's position was essentially defensive. He wanted to avoid questions about the date of the Second Front and the vexed frontier question, whilst establishing a rapport for post-war cooperation. Meanwhile, Hull had been instructed to push Roosevelt's plan for a Four-Power declaration on the interim peace, whilst Molotov wanted an end to the war as soon as humanly possible.

In fact, the war was clearly entering its final phase and the Foreign Ministers' meeting, despite its unpromising background, proved one of the most productive Eden attended in an executive capacity. He persuaded Stalin that OVERLORD could not be launched before 1944. Other topics on which agreement was forthcoming included the question of Arctic convoys, the Soviet mission to Tito's Yugoslavia, plans for the division of Germany into zones of occupation, and the genesis of arrangements for the United Nations, through a Four-Power declaration, including China at America's insistence. Eden had gone to Moscow with Churchill demanding summary justice for war criminals. When this issue arose, Eden tempered matters by cautioning that all legal forms should be observed.[92]

In Eden's party was General Hastings Ismay, one of Churchill's inner circle as Chief of Staff to the Minister of Defence. Not previously an admirer of Eden, who had, he felt, 'gained the palm without the dust', he now revised his opinion, realising that without Eden's combination of personal diplomatic skills and capacity for work, the positive results would never have been achieved. 'His hours of work were phenomenal, and he was extremely thorough,' Ismay later wrote. 'Nothing was too much trouble and he never went to a meeting without making sure that he had every aspect of the problem at his finger tips. He could be tough when necessary, but he could also give way gracefully if the situation demanded it.'[93]

Some of this was achieved by tacit avoidance of areas such as Soviet-Polish relations, on which there would inevitably have been disagreements, and the Czech-Soviet Treaty of Alliance of July 1941, which had granted Czechoslovakia the status of an allied fighting power and advantageous funding arrangements. Eden accepted that to some extent *realpolitik*, especially the conceding of some autonomy for Molotov, would be the order of the day, but this expediency advanced arrangements for the meeting of the Big Three at Teheran in November, Eden's personal contribution being a vital ingredient. 'So far as I can judge the mood of these incalculable people,' Eden wrote to Churchill from Moscow, 'they are now in the current to move with us in all matters, provided that they can be made to feel that they are in all things our equals & that we are holding nothing back.'[94]

Before Teheran, Roosevelt, Churchill and General Chiang Kai-shek met at Cairo for the Allied Conference (SEXTANT) from 23 to 26 November. 'I was much impressed by Chiang,' Eden wrote. 'He would be difficult to place in any category and does not look a warrior. He has a constant smile, but his eyes don't smile so readily and they fix you with a penetrating unswerving look, in marked contrast to Uncle Joe's habit of looking at one's navel. His strength is that of the steel blade.'[95] Roosevelt was at his most emollient and unbusiness-like. For once Eden was impressed with Churchill's patience. Miles Lampson was appreciative of Eden's contribution too. 'One thing is quite certain,' he wrote. 'Anthony has a tremendous position with Winston: in fact between them I gather they are practically running the government of Great Britain.'[96]

Eden wrote after the war:

When all the work was done some telegrams came in to the Embassy which I thought W should see before I answered. It was by this time late in the night, but that did not affect W and I was tough in those days – so I drove out to his house. I found a noisy scene. R[andolph] drunk & shouting furiously, W shouting protestingly, Sarah [Churchill's daughter] in floods of tears. My arrival broke up the party & my business with Winston was soon done – As he walked with me towards the door he stopped, looked at me & with tears in his eyes said: 'I hope that your Simon will never cause you the pain Randolph has caused me.'

I would gladly have shot Randolph at that moment, like a mad dog. We had just been through our most difficult conference & Winston's handling of it had been masterly. Teheran was to follow & I thought it a crime that Randolph should debauch himself & distress his father at such a moment. I have no doubt that R guessed what I thought.[97]

The Allied Teheran Conference from 28 November to 1 December (EUREKA) has its place in history for several reasons, not least as it was the first occasion on which the Big Three had met together. The moods of all these wartime conferences differed. Teheran was full of hope, exhilarating and exciting. The war had reached a turning point and the end was in sight. Churchill was in buoyant mood, teasing Eden about his supposed love of puns. 'They don't come over in translation,' he warned, 'so no more about polls apart.' When others lapsed into this conceit, Churchill smiled and gave Eden a knowing look over the table.[98] Acronyms also led to some genial banter. South-East Asia Command (SEAC) had been established the previous month at the first Quebec Conference. The American military dubbed this 'Save England's Asian Colonies'.

At Teheran, Eden was practical and forthright (Churchill had told him beforehand not to smooth things over in the Foreign Office manner), especially in his discussions with Molotov, whom Stalin had a habit of denigrating in front of foreign visitors, saying to Eden at one stage that Molotov was responsible for Chamberlain's actions during the Munich crisis, adding, with a wry smile, 'although not 100 per cent.'[99] The traditional British diplomats could never quite fathom the enigmatic Russian leadership. 'It's too sad that Stalin and Molotov were not at Eton & Harrow,' read one Moscow Embassy telegram, 'but what can we do about it?'[100]

At lunch at the British Legation in Teheran, Molotov began making substantive points. Eden turned to his interpreter, Hugh Lunghi, who was attached to the military mission in Moscow, and said, 'I hope you're taking all this down.' With no paper to hand, Lunghi began transcribing the main points as best he could at the end of his 1943 diary. As only four weeks remained of the year, there was not much room for detail. Yet Eden was able to refer to the hasty notes later to check Molotov's points. Molotov was especially concerned with establishing post-war bases for security against enemy states, especially Germany and Japan. 'Marshal Stalin would like to see Bizerta and Dakar under control of the USA and Great Britain,' said Molotov firmly at one stage. 'One of them should be placed under British control to serve as a strategic point to ensure US control in the Atlantic.' When Eden said Britain did not want to acquire more territory, Molotov said that they should then pass to the U.S., adding, 'France needs to be punished for giving in so feebly to the Germans and turning into collaborators.' Eden replied, 'I do not think we should apply that term to the whole French nation.' The talk continued with awkward details on Poland, Turkey and the date of OVERLORD, the whole episode being an example of how even on ostensibly social occasions Eden always had to be on his guard about what might be thrust forward in the guise of negotiation.[101]

Though Eden was concerned with the wider strategic implications, he was also capable of personal kindness towards individuals, arranging for the release of two naval personnel whom others had forgotten about.[102] And earlier in the year he had lent a young rifleman, who had lost a leg at Tobruk, a cottage at Binderton for his mother.[103]

'When I was at Teheran,' Churchill admitted in 1944, 'I realised for the 1st time what a very *small* country this is. On the one hand the big Russian bear with its paws outstretched – on the other the great American elephant – & between them the poor little British donkey – who is the only one that knows the right way home.'[104] The little British donkey was certainly poor. And the terrain was now to be dominated by larger and more dangerous creatures. Roosevelt's priority was to avoid American involvement in the Balkans and to concentrate on talks with Stalin. As a result, Churchill resented the way in which the British were sidelined from certain meetings. Eden's frustration was the lack of equivalent preparation by the Americans on detail, whilst Cadogan was 'appalled at the haphazard, amateurish surroundings of the President.'[105] Britain had stood alone in 1940;

increasingly, by the end of 1943, she had to stand aside. It was not so much the 'Big Three' as the 'Big Two and a half'.

Eden found this particularly galling with the question of Poland, over which he now had great worries, and little help from Harry Hopkins. 'The Americans are terrified of the subject,' he noted, 'which Harry called "political dynamite" for their election.'[106]*

The Russians drove into Poland on 6 January 1944 and the dispositions for OVERLORD saw General Eisenhower appointed Supreme Commander, much to the chagrin of many in the British military establishment. The fate of Poland continued to exercise Eden. One of his advisers put the options in stark form, pre-echoing one of the central issues at Yalta. 'The real choice before us seems to me, to put it brutally, to be between on the one hand selling the corpse of Poland to Russia and finding an alibi to be used in evidence when we are indicted for abetting a murder, or putting the points of principle to Stalin in the clearest possible way.'[107] Eden was very disappointed with the lack of progress that had been made after Moscow, believing this was entirely due to the American attitude. By contrast, he told Lord Robert Cecil, he felt that Russia had been most helpful, and was exceedingly anxious to work in with the Western powers or, at least, to be regarded as respectable.[108]

Preparations for the Second Front occupied much of Eden's time in the New Year. 'Staff meeting in p.m.', he recorded on 19 January. 'W & myself & Chiefs of Staff about "Overlord" & other plans.'[109]

Eden was exhausted at the beginning of April. Before taking a month's sick leave at Churchill's insistence, he imposed restrictions on all diplomatic traffic to prevent any premature news of D-Day. Even the King, who continued to seek out news from Eden in his regular meetings, did not know all the details:

> Lunched with King and Queen alone [Eden wrote after one such meeting]. Much rather wearisome discussion about affairs of Balkan Kings. I do find them insufferably tedious. Of them all I like little King Peter [of Yugoslavia] the best. He is at least lively and not to blame for his troubles. Luncheon seemed really to be Royalty Trade Union expressing its anxieties which is not much different from any other, Admirals, politicians, lawyers doing the same. Managed to bring in Far Eastern strategy problems towards the end as W[inston] had invited me to do, and tried to explain issues there. All very friendly.[110]

---

*It was not the last time that an American Presidential Election was to have its effect on Eden's preferred policy. Teheran was the beginning of a long process that was to reach a climax with Suez in 1956.

After the war, Eden said that his greatest regret was the way Britain had abandoned its support of the Chetnik guerilla leader in Yugoslavia, General Mihailovic, whom he felt would prove the main buttress against 'anarchy and communist chaos' in a volatile area.[111]

In May, with D-Day only a few weeks away, Eden returned to his duties and hosted the Dominion Prime Ministers' Conference, an important preliminary to the Dumbarton Oaks Conference in the autumn. The mood was one of optimism, but Eden did not entirely share the view of the representatives, many of whom he had known since his Dominions Office days. His despondency centred on the moribund state of the Tory Party, which he sensed was in danger of missing the mood of the times. With Churchill he had attended a screening of the The Life and Death of Colonel Blimp – 'poor film, with much confused thought', he wrote[112] – and though he did not go as far as Churchill in wanting to see its circulation restricted, or even banned, he felt the political agenda was leaving the Conservatives marginalised. 'This is a stale Parliament,' he had written in his diary on 18 January, '& Tory party as a whole is discredited.'[113]

Rumours reached him that the Chiefs of Staff would like Sir John Anderson to become Prime Minister, as a 'safe pair of hands' after Churchill's waywardness. To intimates who urged him to be more forceful about his own claims, Eden 'made it plain I was not bursting myself to go to No 10 & would never move a little finger to get there.'[114]

On 24 January Eden had dined with Jim Thomas and Bobbety Cranborne. 'We discussed party's future, and ours! Bobbety was firm that bad as Tory party was there was no better "'ole". There had always been reactionary right wing, even in his grandfather's day, but they could be ignored, they had nowhere else to go.'[115]

On Tuesday 6 June, Eden received early reports of the long-awaited Normandy landings. 'News good in morning except for one American beach,' he wrote. By the evening de Gaulle's fury at having been kept in the dark about the date was awesome. At midnight Churchill and Eden had a furious row about the General. 'I didn't lose my temper & I think that I gave as good as I got,' Eden noted, fearing the 'American hate of de Gaulle, & perhaps all Frenchmen'. Eden was despatched to Carlton Gardens to soothe ruffled feathers. 'Rather like a visit to the Führer,' he noted. 'Guard of honour drawn up outside, officers at intervals up the stairs & eventually shown in to great man's salon.'[116]

Shortly after D-Day, the war on the domestic front took a more sinister turn, as flying bombs began to rain down on London and the southern counties. On 18 June, the day one landed on the Guards Chapel at Wellington Barracks, a stray flying bomb petered out over Binderton and crashed in the gardens. Many of the windows were blown out, but Eden was relieved that the framework of the house had survived the blast.[117] He had heard the engine cutting out as the flying bomb came in from the coast over Chichester and knew what to expect. 'I had plenty of time to think & wasn't particularly worried,' he wrote in his diary. 'I thought it was the end but was not particularly perturbed. Surprised & impressed that house stood up. Yet an approaching shell always terrified me in last war.'[118]

Three days later Macmillan came to see Eden on his return to London from Naples. He found the Foreign Secretary much changed since their last meeting. 'Poor Anthony – he has a difficult life,' he recorded in his diary. 'He has the leadership of the House of Commons, the Foreign Secretary-ship (with P.M., Moyne,[119] and myself, as well as Hull, the President, the American and British Chiefs of Staff all acting as rival Foreign Secretaries) and, of course, the interminable talks and late hours which the P.M. delights in. No wonder he seems a little jaded.'[120]

Cordell Hull was more than jaded. He collapsed in October and was replaced as Secretary of State by Edward Stettinius, who was both junior to Eden and less experienced.

Beatrice was abroad much of the time, latterly on military service in Paris, and at the end of July 1944 Eden invited C. M. Woodhouse,* a colonel at twenty-six, and already a veteran of the Allied Military Mission to occupied Greece, to Binderton for the weekend for a wide-ranging talk on the Balkans. Woodhouse later wrote:

> Eden sent a car for me on Saturday morning, 29 July. The driver explained that he had to pick up another guest, the Countess of Erne. It filled me with foreboding: I foresaw a social weekend making polite conversation to a political dowager instead of talking seriously with Eden. We drove to the address I had been given, off Belgrave Square. I rang the bell, & the door was opened by a girl, whose image is still with me.
>
> I assumed this was the Countess's lady's maid, for she was surrounded by luggage. I helped to put it in the car, and looked around for the Countess. But no, no one else came. Amazing: this *was* the Countess! We got into the car and drove off. Her name was Davina. My opinion of Eden went up sharply.[121]

Monty Woodhouse married Davina Erne in 1945. Eden's refusal to

---

*C. M. (Monty) Woodhouse, 5th Lord Terrington (1917–2001) was a legendary Byronic figure, described in 1944 as 'the most famous man in Greece'. Grandson of the Liberal MP for Huddersfield, he was Conservative MP for Oxford from 1959 to 1966 and from 1970 to October 1974, an appropriate constituency for a scholar who was a double first and Gaisford Prizeman. After the war, he said he felt like Matthew Arnold 'wandering between two worlds, one dead, the other powerless to be born.' (Arnold, *The Grande Chartreuse*).

Shuttle diplomacy in the 1930s. Eden with Halifax at Le Bourget, 11 March 1936 (*above*); and Neville Chamberlain returns from his second visit to Germany, 16 September 1938 (*below*).

(*Left*) The Beau Brummel of British politics, 1935. Later, Eden lived for a time in Beau Brummel's house in Chesterfield Street.

(*Above*) Eden with Chips Channon.

(*Right*) Eden greets the Belgian Prime Minister, Paul van Zeeland, in the week of the funeral of King George V, 1936. Eden was among the first to turn formal visits of heads of state and foreign colleagues into opportunities for friendly diplomacy.

(*Above left*) July 1937: Eden and his son Simon walk through St James's Park towards the Foreign Office. (*Above right*) 25 February 1938: on his way to his Warwick and Leamington constituency after his resignation as Foreign Secretary.

(*Below*) Out of office: the backbencher in the south of France, with his wife Beatrice and Lucy and Stanley Baldwin. 1938.

(*Above*) In Camp at Beaulieu, August 1939. A few days later, Eden was recalled to the Government as Dominions Secretary

(*Below*) Middle East Headquarters. Eden with the Chief of the Imperial General Staff, Sir John Dill (on his right) and Pierson Dixon (on his left) at a conference in 1941.

(*Right*) In the Western
Desert in 1941:
Randolph Churchill
'with the light of
battle in his eyes'.

(*Below*) In Egypt in 1941. Christopher Smart, Terence Shone, Nahas Pasha with whom Eden
had signed the Anglo–Egyptian Treaty in 1936, Amin Osman Pasha, Oliver Harvey, Eden.

The War Cabinet in October 1941.

Standing: Arthur Greenwood, Ernest Bevin, Lord Beaverbrook, Kingsley Wood.
Seated: John Anderson, Winston Churchill, Clement Attlee, Anthony Eden.

(*Above*) Moscow, 1943: Eden with Molotov and Maisky.
'He never went to a meeting without making sure that he had every aspect of the problem at his finger tips,' wrote General Ismay of Eden that week.

(*Below*) With troops in Egypt, 1943.

(*Above left*) With troops in Italy, 1944. (*Above right*) Beatrice in Paris, 1945.

(*Below*) Mary Churchill and Anthony Eden surrounded by Russian and British servicemen. In Berlin, outside the Reichstag, 1945.

divorce Beatrice had caused a long-standing friendship to come to an end. Eden always held a special place in his heart for Davina Erne – even Woodhouse said she would have been a wonderful wife for Eden – and he accepted their inevitable break with resignation, but no sense of jealousy for her new husband's good fortune. He wished her well; his regret was that he lacked the freedom to make a new start himself.*

Meanwhile, in the summer of 1944, with Simon an RAF sergeant-pilot in Burma and Beatrice abroad much of the time, Eden took on all the responsibilities for the welfare of his younger son Nicholas, now approaching his fourteenth birthday and his first half at Eton. In the school holidays, this meant tennis, swimming, long country walks and evening readings of Shakespeare, this last not the most exciting pastime for a teenage boy, though Eden drew many contemporary parallels, especially with the famous lines from the end of *King John*:

> This England never did, nor never shall,
> Lie at the proud foot of a conqueror.[122]

Nicholas Eden's brush with history was not only vicarious. On 4 August, on the eve of his visit to Eisenhower and Montgomery on the Normandy beaches, Churchill, by himself in Downing Street, heard that the Foreign Secretary and his son were similarly placed, and asked Eden to bring Nicholas to dinner. The three of them dined alone. A month earlier, Churchill had been testy and argumentative. Now he was charm itself on a memorable evening:

> I have never seen W in greater form [wrote Eden in his diary] – He, of course, completely fascinated Nicholas who listened & looked all ears & eyes. Stories of his young days at Harrow, how he was for two terms (or two years, I forget) bottom of the whole school, how his father was famous then, & when the school filed by, as it frequently did, spectators used to point at him and say 'Look there he is, the very last of all.' How he hated Harrow & implored his mother not to send him back, even for his last half. Long quotations from *Henry VI* & advice to 'read only Shakespeare' etc etc. All this to the accompaniment of a good dinner & the best possible bottle of champagne. Finally when I got into the car I found Nicholas bubbling with excitement & he confessed that £2 had been thrust into his hand with injunctions not to tell 'him'![123]

Shortly afterwards, Churchill went to Italy and Eden became acting

---

*In her address at the Joint Memorial service for Monty and Davina Terrington at New College Chapel, Oxford, on 13 October 2001, the late Baroness Young of Farnworth mentioned Eden's part in introducing the two. Eden's discretion had been such, however, that it was clear that Baroness Young had no idea of the full story.

Prime Minister for the first time. He took the opportunity to visit the battlefields of France – and flooding back came all those memories of the 'shell-torn trees, twisted wire and heaped and silent bodies.'[124] With Eden committed to the home front, Cadogan represented him at the Dumbarton Oaks Conference in late August, but from 12 to 16 September, Eden and Churchill were at the second Quebec Conference (OCTAGON) which secured Lend-Lease whilst the war with Japan continued, and American acceptance of the French Committee for National Liberation, first as the civil authority and, by October, as the provisional government. The conference, however, was remembered more for Eden's public disagreement with Churchill over the merits of the Morgenthau Plan* for the de-industrialisation of Germany, which Eden thought analogous to turning the Black Country into Devonshire.

Many unanswerable moral questions were now finding their way to Eden's desk, the historian Meier Sompolinsky even commenting that 'ministerial responsibility for the "Jewish Subject" was put solely on the shoulders of a very strong Cabinet personality, Foreign Secretary Anthony Eden.'[125] Although Eden had made a powerful condemnation in the House of Commons on 17 December 1942 of the persecution of the Jews, he was not considered a 'natural' supporter of the Zionist cause. Some Jewish leaders considered it unfortunate that Eden was in charge of the subject, as the Foreign Office had a pro-Arab reputation. Oliver Harvey certainly thought this the case with Eden, of whom he wrote, 'The Arab myth clouds his mind.'[126] On 26 July, however, Eden had managed to assuage some of these concerns when he met a Jewish group at the Foreign Office. As Sompolinsky put it, 'the delegation left the meeting encouraged by Eden's promise to grant a haven for all [Jews from Hungary].'[127] Eden's commitment to RAF action on railway lines to concentration camps was also well received, as an indication of practical resolve and support.

Although Eden's reputation never sustained attacks on the scale faced retrospectively by Harold Macmillan,[128]† Eden's opponents have found much to criticise in the moral minefield of the latter months of the war. Following the D-Day landings the Allies realised that many of their prisoners of war were Soviet citizens, who now sought political asylum. As many had been forcibly enlisted to fight for the Axis forces, it was clear

---

*A scheme by the US Treasury Secretary, Henry Morgenthau Jr, for the pastoralisation of large tracts of Germany, which won the support of Roosevelt and Churchill, but not their advisers. It was superseded by arrangements at Potsdam in July 1945.

†Britain was accused of being involved in sending 'Cossacks' and 'White' Russians back to the Soviet Union, to face possible torture and death at the hands of the 'Reds'. Macmillan was accused of being implicated in sending anti-Communist Yugoslavs (who had fought alongside the Germans) back to Yugoslavia, where Tito's partisans gunned them down into graves ready dug for them.

what their fate would be if forcibly repatriated. Yet Stalin was adamant. Any granting of political asylum to these Soviet citizens, many in German uniforms, would be an affront. On 17 July 1944 the War Cabinet acceded to Stalin's demands, a decision confirmed on 4 September after concerns had been raised by some junior ministers. By November it was clear that the Americans would do likewise. The British Cabinet's decision, in the situation then obtaining, may have saved Greece from being devoured in the Communist maw, but it was hardly an example of ethical foreign policy, and in the end upwards of two million citizens were repatriated.

Other matters also had their share of moral ambiguity. The famous 'percentage agreement' meeting in Moscow from 9 to 19 October (TOLSTOY) ordained the degree of influence Russia and Britain should have over the Balkan States, with 90 per cent of Greece coming under the United Kingdom in accord with America. In complex negotiations with his Russian opposite number, Molotov, Eden haggled over the percentages for Bulgaria and Hungary. But Churchill's view, expressed to his doctor, Lord Moran, was that 'the Foreign Secretary could be obstinate, he must be told that there is only one course open to us – to make friends with Stalin.'[129]

In a manner reminiscent of Mark Antony and Octavius Caesar before the Battle of Philippi, the soon-to-be victorious powers decided, disposed and divided. Throughout 1944 Eden had faced the dilemma of the fate of German nationals abroad, many of whom had fled the Nazi regime years earlier. On 30 March, Eden had sent a circular letter to all Foreign missions, on this matter:

1. One of the conditions under contemplation to be imposed upon Germany after her collapse is that she should comply with any directions issued by the United Nations for the recall of German nationals resident abroad.
2. There are no doubt German subjects resident in the country to which you are accredited whom through their association with the enemy's espionage, sabotage or similar activities it might be desirable to recall to Germany under the above-mentioned condition.
3. I shall be glad if you will prepare and transmit to me a list of such persons, keeping it up to date by periodical revisions.

This was followed up by a second letter on 10 November, which read:

There is a class of Germans not covered by the instructions in my despatch under reference whom through their association with the enemy's espionage, sabotage or similar activities it might be desirable to recall to Germany.

One area where these matters were of particular sensitivity was in Latin America, especially Uruguay, because of Cordell Hull's earlier plan (details of which were sent to Eden by Lord Halifax on 1 July 1944) to allow Germans living in Latin America to return to Germany in exchange for Jews holding passports for Latin America, who were then in Nazi concentration camps. It was an audacious and humanitarian plan that foundered for two reasons – the inability of the authorities in Uruguay to determine which list of Germans ('obnoxious Germans' as they were deemed) would be of no value to the Reich in its final struggles, and Eden's flat rejection of the plan because of his belief that the Jews would enter Palestine and cause trouble for Britain. Eden was at this stage of his career sympathetic to the Arab world. His whole training from the Oxford schools to his service in the Foreign Office made this an almost inevitable consequence which later circumstances were only partially to alter. In addition, there were joint fears that returning able-bodied Germans with technical skills (the lists of Germans included the many skilled professions represented) would be of invaluable help to Hitler in a crucial stage of the war. On 15 November, Eden wrote to Gordon Vereker, the British Ambassador in Uruguay:

> These Latin American passports were for the most part issued on the understanding that they are utilisable for journeys anywhere but to the countries of the issuing authority. Most of the holders of these documents are of Jewish race who have been accepted as immigrants to Palestine, and the passports are good for a journey thither, provided the holders succeed in leaving the enemy or enemy-occupied territory.
>
> In these circumstances it appears doubtful that it will ever be possible to carry out the exchange envisaged by the United States Government. On the other hand, the mere fact that it is under discussion, that the Germans are aware that certain persons in their power hold travel documents and that in certain circumstances these persons might be the means of seeing the return of a number of German nationals, provides at least ground for hope that the German Government will abstain from exterminating these unfortunate people and will keep them in camps open to outside inspection.[130]

History records that the 'ground for hope' expressed in the final sentence was misplaced. These were circumstances of war, and it is easy to be censorious after the event, to judge one generation's action by the hindsight of a later one. When these letters were released under the Government's Open Government initiative on 20 July 1999, newspaper editorials were uniformly critical of Eden whose hopes could be seen as naive. US PLAN TO HELP JEWS WAS BLOCKED BY EDEN ran one such headline.[131]

Belsen was liberated on 15 April 1945. Thereafter, of course, the scale of the human tragedy was only too apparent, and Eden's 'ground for hope' may be seen as dangerous, obtuse and naive. Since 1942 he had known about the Warsaw ghetto and the Belzec extermination camp; and from 1944 about the need to bomb the railways. He did not need the liberation of Belsen to tell him 'who' was incarcerated in the camp or what its purpose was.

However, there was no guarantee that Hull's proposal was one that the Germans would be ready to accept. 'This story,' one historian has commented, 'appears to be one more which blames the British for crimes committed by Nazi Germany.'[132]

The day after this second letter – the date was the emotively resonant 11 November – Eden was one of those, together with an emotional Churchill and the new British Ambassador to France, Duff Cooper, who marched down the Champs Élysées in Paris with de Gaulle in a symbolic re-entry into the French capital. In the aftermath of this historic event, Eden wrote to Churchill on 29 November, outlining his views about the latter stages of the war and the priorities for the return to peace:

I entirely agree with you that it would be both absurd and highly dangerous for us to enter into any commitment for the defence of Norway, Denmark, Belgium or Holland except in conjunction with the French and as a part of some general plan for containing Germany evolved under the aegis of a World Organisation. On these two points the Foreign Office has never had any doubts and I have repeatedly made them clear myself.

I further agree with you that the Western European countries behaved very foolishly between the two wars and were grossly unprepared to meet the blow when it fell. But our own record in this period was not entirely praiseworthy and we only escaped their fate by the skin of our teeth and thanks to the Channel. It has always seemed to me that the lesson of the disasters of 1940 is precisely the need to build up a common defence association in Western Europe, which would prevent another Hitler, whencesoever he may come, pursuing what you have so aptly called the policy of 'one by one'. The best way of creating such an association would obviously be to build up France and we can only hope that during the period of the occupation of Germany such a build up will be possible. It is, in fact, only when we evacuate Germany that the desirability of any regional defence organisation of Western Europe arises in a concrete form.

Nevertheless, there seems every reason to start thinking about it now, since if our Western European allies and more especially the French have the impression that we are not going in future to accept any commitments on the Continent it may well be (as you suggest) that they will come to the conclusion that their only hope lies in making defence arrangements, not with us, but with the Russians. And surely the development of long range missiles proves that somehow or other, if we are to retain our independence, we must obtain some kind of 'defence in depth'?

As I see it, then, a properly organised Western Europe can provide us with depth for defence and large resources of manpower which would greatly ease our burden and enable us to avoid a huge standing army which would cripple our economy.[133]

Herein can be traced, not only the genesis of the European Defence Community of the 1950s, but also the idea of a federal Europe itself. Eden's other major concern at the end of 1944 was how to prevent Greece falling to the Communists, like Hungary and Yugoslavia, and he had many difficult meetings with King George II of Greece. 'I like him and am really trying to help,' Eden noted on 17 November, 'but he is curiously obtuse.'[134] Eden's plan to install Archbishop Damaskinos as Regent was not one that found favour with Churchill. 'W. has his knife into the Archbishop', Eden noted, 'and is convinced that he is both a quisling and a Communist.'[135] Eden did not take this outburst seriously. In a way he was relieved. It showed that Churchill no longer had de Gaulle as his *bête noire*, and the Archbishop was a convenient substitute.

As the situation deteriorated and civil war loomed in Greece, Churchill decided on the spur of the moment on Christmas Eve to fly to Athens, despite the considerable physical risks. Eden's plans for a quiet family Christmas were abandoned and he joined Churchill on the flight, a personal sacrifice of considerable poignancy (he even offered to go instead of Churchill), as it was Simon's last Christmas at home before joining the RAF in Burma.

Eden was not best pleased when much of their first day was taken up by events unrelated to the political situation, and he realised that they could quite well have come on Boxing Day. The Christmas Day service at the embassy was conducted by a vicar under armed protection, who referred in his lengthy sermon to the angels as 'God's airborne division.'[136]

To Eden's relief, Churchill was charmed by the Archbishop when he met him, and the plan that the Foreign Office had been urging for weeks – that the Archbishop should be appointed Regent with powers to form a new Government – was accepted. The Greek situation was by no means resolved, but Eden felt that 'at the least the Greek people would now have a chance to choose their destiny without fear.'[137]

Churchill and Eden returned to London on 29 December. It was not long before another Prime Ministerial missive reached Eden at Binderton. '"Hands off the British Empire" is our maxim, and it must not be weakened or smirched to please sob-stuff merchants at home or foreigners of any hue.'[138]

Churchill's tone, belligerent and forceful, betrayed an underlying sense of the impermanence of the imperial ideal, a hidden doubt well justified by the turn of subsequent events. 1944 had not been an easy year, but 1945, as the war came to its end, far from being the apotheosis of Eden's life was to prove, professionally and personally, the saddest of all his years.

CHAPTER ELEVEN
Avoiding Versailles
1945

A talk with Alec C[adogan] about a meeting of the three great
men. I am much worried that the whole business will be chaotic
& nothing worth while settled, Stalin being the only one of the
three who has a clear view of what he wants & is a tough
negotiator. P.M.'s all emotion in these matters, F. D. R. vague &
jealous of others.

Anthony Eden diary, 4 January 1945[1]

Well, the war is over in Europe. You are back from San
Francisco – which sounded rather enjoyable except the hard
work. It is a place that I have wanted to visit. I see that Party
politics have reared their ugly head, forcing Churchill to resign.
Whom do you think will win the General Election?

One of Simon Eden's last letters to his father, May 1945[2]

Two assumptions were widely held at the beginning of 1945, namely that
Germany was on the verge of military defeat, and that the Conservatives
were poised to form the first peace-time government after the allied victory.
These assumptions were not shared by Anthony Eden. Despite his
privileged knowledge of the development of atomic weapons (so secret that
it was always referred to by the codename Tube Alloys), Eden believed that
the last stages of the conflict would prove messy. The outcome of the first
General Election since 1935 also seemed to him to be an unknown quantity.
Even its date proved difficult to decide upon. Should it be held after the
defeat of Germany, whenever that might be, or should voting be delayed
until after the final defeat of Japan at some later date? When Churchill
asked his Foreign Secretary for a preference between June and October, the
two likeliest dates, Eden urged Churchill to take the earlier option, even
though a part of him wanted the Coalition Government to continue until
after the defeat of Japan. For Churchill, the date (like the Brighton line for
Lady Bracknell) was immaterial. The Conservatives were going to win
anyway. On 28 January, Churchill told the King that 'it is very likely that
there will be a substantial Conservative majority in the new Parliament.'[3]
Eden was not so sanguine. 'Cannot help an unworthy hope that we may lose
– or rather have lost – this election', he wrote on 17 July 1945. 'If it were
not for the European situation I am sure that it would be better thus.'[4]

Eden's year began with uneasy talks with King George II of Greece. On
12 January he attended a 'terrible Cabinet'. 'Whole thing lasted 4½ hours.
Really quite intolerable . . . W rambles so that everything takes many times
longer to decide than is necessary.'⁵

The build-up to the Yalta Conference brought into sharp focus the
differences between Churchill and Eden on France and de Gaulle. Eden
argued strongly for the inclusion of the French at Yalta. 'We have reached
the stage now when we must plan for the future, and I find it difficult to
contemplate a future in which France will not be a factor of considerable
importance,' he wrote to Churchill on 16 January. With considerable
prescience he concluded, 'she must be interested in almost every European
question. If we do not have her cooperation, she will be able – not at once
perhaps – to make difficult the application of any solution which does not
suit her.'⁶ But Roosevelt had scotched any suggestion of French involvement and Churchill was not prepared to reopen the question. 'The whole
character of our discussions would be destroyed if de Gaulle were present,'
he told Eden.⁷

Of all the wartime conferences, Yalta (ARGONAUT), held at Vorontzov
from 4 to 11 February 1945, remains the most controversial. No less than
Munich, Yalta became a symbol of appeasement and abandonment.
Ironically, some of its fiercest critics were to be erstwhile Municheers. Yet
it began as a beacon of hope to the beleaguered peoples of Europe, weary
of the long years of war and ignorant of Stalin's deep suspicion of the
capitalist Allies. Russia had torn the guts out of the Nazi forces, in
Churchill's vivid phrase, whilst many in the West believed that Soviet
Communism would lead to a better and fairer society. Their hopes were
misplaced – but nevertheless continued for many years, in some cases even
after the days of Mikhail Gorbachev.

Eden was not among their number. 'I take the gloomiest view of Russian
behaviour everywhere,' he wrote shortly after Yalta, later warning
Churchill, 'I am deeply concerned at the pattern of Russian policy, which
becomes clearer as they become more brazen every day.'*

To the Yalta Conference came the representatives of the Soviet Union led
by Stalin, of America led by Roosevelt, and of Britain led by Churchill;
these leaders were supported respectively by Molotov, Stettinius and Eden.
Yalta is often taken as the start of the Cold War. In reality, the Cold War
began much earlier with Stalin's premature demands for a Second Front.

---

*When Churchill was later praised, particularly in America, for his supposed perception
about Russia's expansionist philosophy, Eden minuted, 'This is almost all untrue and quite
nauseating.' Anthony Eden diary, 23 March 1945. AP 20/1/25. Anthony Eden to Winston
Churchill, 17 July 1945. AP 20/13/231. Eden Minute, 22 November 1954. AP 11/10/230B.

By the time of Yalta, the Soviet Army was in the ascendant after its powerful January offensive, and Stalin was not in the giving vein. Eden had feared such an outcome as early as January when he had written in his diary, 'I am much worried that the whole business will be chaotic & nothing worthwhile settled, Stalin being the only one of the three who has a clear view of what he wants & is a tough negotiator. PM's all emotion in these matters. F. D. R. vague & jealous of others.'[8]

The British and American delegations foregathered at Malta, before going on to the Crimea to meet the Russians. One of the British planes crashed off the island of Lampedusa; Eden's doctor and one of his detectives were killed, as was Peter Loxley, a promising young official in the Diplomatic Service.

On 1 February Eden had extensive talks with Edward Stettinius, the new American Secretary of State, on the intractable question of Poland; they hoped for a new government combining the 'free' Poles in London and the provisional Communist-backed Lublin Government. Meanwhile President Roosevelt and Prime Minister Churchill also met in Malta, but Roosevelt refused to talk about tactics or strategy for the forthcoming conference.

Eden was exasperated by the lack of Anglo-American coordination. 'George III has a lot to answer for,' he wrote. 'He still bedevils Anglo-American relations!'[9] He protested to Harry Hopkins, Roosevelt's long-standing adviser, that possibly the most decisive conference of the war was about to begin without any agreement on an agenda. To make matters worse, it was clear to all those who saw him at close quarters that Roosevelt was seriously ill. When he disembarked from his aircraft at Saki airfield, the first impression was of his sunken, yellowy cheeks; during the conference he often sat for long minutes, mouth open, staring ahead.[10] Ten weeks later he was dead.

Churchill was depressed by the evident waning of Roosevelt's powers. The gate was open for Stalin to enter at will. Before Teheran, Stalin had obtained Churchill's agreement to the 1920 Curzon frontier line as the border between Russia and Poland, thus keeping the Polish territory acquired under the Molotov-Ribbentrop Pact in August 1939; at Teheran, Roosevelt also acquiesced. The pattern continued at Yalta.

At Yalta, Eden, Molotov and Stettinius met in the morning sessions, each hosting the meeting in turn at their respective headquarters, before the Heads of Government foregathered in the afternoon. The British delegation kept the War Cabinet in London informed on a daily basis of the major developments, many of which had been the subject of three Cabinet meetings the previous autumn. One such vexed issue was repatriation. Earlier talks had been held in Moscow between Eden and Molotov and at that time (October 1944) Eden had been hopeful of Anglo-Soviet cooperation. According to Bob Dixon, Eden's secretary, the subject came up casually on the last day of the Yalta Conference.*

At Yalta, a reciprocal arrangement on war prisoners was formalised as the Yalta Repatriation Agreement of 11 February. British and Russian subjects liberated by Russian and British forces respectively were to be handed over. Eden's action in signing this agreement has provided fuel for his fiercest critics. Cadogan noted in his diary at the time that an essential part of the process was 'an important agreement with the Russians about the treatment of our prisoners whom they liberate',[11] a substantive issue as the Russians pushed relentlessly westwards. Once again, the pressures and confusions of war, and the need to protect one's nationals, had led to painful compromises.

What could not be foreseen at Yalta was the fate of 40,000 'White' Russian troops with Nazi connections, and in some cases German uniforms, who surrendered to General Charles Keightley (later Allied Forces Commander at Suez) in Austria in May 1945, were sent back to the 'Red' Soviet Union and were butchered. Although the main obloquy was retrospectively directed at Harold Macmillan and Brigadier Toby Low, Eden did not escape censure. Three factors explain, even if they will never excuse, the decisions taken by the full War Cabinet. Eden was always hopeful of future Anglo-Soviet cooperation, though Yalta dulled his optimism; secondly, he was concerned that any retrospective reneging on the earlier Moscow discussions would have serious consequences for liberated British prisoners of war; and thirdly, the moral dilemma posed by the fate of those who surrendered to Keightley had not yet arisen in its sharpest form. Nevertheless, the repatriation issue was one to which Eden returned in old age, when reminiscing with former political colleagues and Foreign Office officials.†‡

---

*A few weeks later, reflecting on the *realpolitik* that then obtained, Dixon wrote in his diary, 'For five years we have had to condone acts represented as necessary for political reasons, and have been regarded as Cassandras when we foretold political disadvantages.'

†After one such talk, Sir Patrick Dean wrote to Eden on 19 December 1974, 'It was not a nice decision to have to make.' AP 20/52/388.

‡In 1973 Bob Dixon's son, Piers Dixon (then MP for Truro), was instrumental in getting the secret files on Yalta released by the Public Record Office, not a move welcomed by Harold Macmillan, who feared – rightly as it turned out – that the files would stir up controversy over his role at the time. The combination of Bob Dixon's private diary and the Yalta files convinced Piers Dixon that Eden and Toby Low (later Lord Aldington, who became a target for abuse) were completely exonerated by the record – not something that was so clear in the case of Macmillan and Fitzroy Maclean, Commander of the British Military Mission to the Yugoslav partisans. Pierson Dixon diary, 14 May 1945 (in the possession of Piers Dixon). Piers Dixon letter of 15 December 2000.

There was a fourth reason, also. At the time the main controversy was not repatriation but the 'elastic' agreement over Poland.* Poland was on the agenda at seven out of eight plenary sessions. Yet the question of the post-war Polish Government (whether it should consist of 'free' Poles from London, the Lublin puppets or a mixture of both) was not resolved, nor was the definition of the Oder–Neisse line (the German-Polish post-war border). The subsequent Polish Government of National Unity, recognised by the Allies on 5 July, and headed by a former Comintern agent, proved a sham and satisfied nobody, least of all critics in the House of Commons. The complex frontier question was to drag on till Potsdam. For Stalin, whether the Poles had any territory was 'a quarrel in a straw'; for the British, ever since 3 September 1939, it was 'honour at the stake.'† Stalin's preferred solution was to give the Poles territory in the west, at Germany's expense. Just as Eden wanted a 'strong' France, so Stalin wanted a 'strong' Poland firmly under Soviet control, to prevent its use as a corridor for advancing forces against the Soviet Union.‡

Another issue was the continued presence of Soviet troops in Iran. Britain was prepared to withdraw her troops after the cessation of hostilities, but wanted reciprocal action from the Soviets. Although Stettinius gave Eden his support, agreeing to full American withdrawal, Molotov was intractable. Eden eventually bypassed Molotov and spoke directly to Stalin on the issue. Later that summer, British and American troops began their withdrawal from Teheran. Russian troops proved harder to dislodge from Azerbaijan, though eventually Eden's personal initiative bore fruit.

On the question of Germany, Eden argued against Soviet plans for its complete dismemberment, and was prominent in establishing the Allied Control Commission, with the subsequent system of zones of occupation. He fought to ensure that France, in its rehabilitation to major-power status, was one of the occupying powers, part of his long-standing wish to see a reinvigorated 'buffer' country on Germany's western border.

---

*On 10 April, for instance, Eden was to receive a Liberal Party delegation, which included William Beveridge and Lady Violet Bonham Carter, to hear their concerns about the Yalta formula. Lady Violet Bonham Carter told him directly that Yalta was 'appeasement enshrined in an international character'. He shared their concerns. 'Anthony did not seek to defend the formula in any way whatever,' Lady Violet Bonham Carter wrote in her diary. 'He simply said the Russians wldn't look at anything less – & they had had great difficulty in screwing them up to this point. He said they were being very difficult to deal with at this moment.' Lady Violet Bonham Carter diary, 10 April 1945. Mark Pottle (ed.), *Champion Redoubtable: The Diaries and Letters of Violet Bonham Carter 1914–1945*, Weidenfeld & Nicolson, 1998, p.336.
†A question debated by Hamlet after the Norwegian captain had told him of Fortinbras's plans to invade Poland. *Hamlet*, IV.iii, 55–6.
‡Poland had already been twice used as a corridor for invasion.

On a positive note, arrangements were set in hand for a conference at San Francisco (Stettinius' choice of venue) that would eventually establish the United Nations, a major step towards avoiding the mistakes of Versailles, and a partial counterweight to Russia's continued demands for reparations from Germany, which to Eden's mind was too uneasy an echo of 1919.

When Eden returned to London on 19 February, the plane was diverted to Lyneham in Wiltshire, rather than the scheduled Northolt. In a hasty arrangement, Eden motored back to London with Jock Colville, whilst subordinate staff took to a Green Line bus. Poland was still on Eden's mind, and Colville recorded the Foreign Secretary's somewhat defensive feelings in his diary:

> Eden said that he thought the Tories had no right to complain about Poland. The P.M. had not sold the pass. On the contrary the Curzon line was a boundary proposed as fair by H.M.G. after the last war; we had not committed ourselves to accepting any specific western frontier for Poland; and finally we had only undertaken to recognise a new Polish Government in Poland if and when we were satisfied with its composition.[12]

But complain the Tories did. Privately, Eden was mortified by the way Churchill treated the Poles at Yalta. Nor did he share Churchill's confidence – expressed to the War Cabinet on 19 and 21 February – that Stalin 'meant well to the world and to Poland' and 'that the Russians would honour the declaration [on Liberated Europe] that had been made.'[13]

The two-day debate on Yalta began on 27 February and had embarrassing echoes of the Norway Debate nearly five years before. Twenty-one Conservatives put down an amendment regretting that 'the territory of an Ally' should be transferred 'to another power'. Although this amendment was defeated by 398 votes to twenty-five, many Conservatives abstained and many more voted only with a heavy heart. Lord Dunglass, Chamberlain's former PPS and a future Prime Minister (as Alec Douglas-Home), was one of those who spoke critically in the debate.*

Comparisons with the aftermath of Munich were inevitable. Yalta

---

*At the time of Churchill's centenary on 30 November 1974, when Alec Home paid tribute to Churchill's memory, he did not skirt the question of Yalta. 'In a tense debate on it I criticised our government's capitulation,' he said in his broadcast address. 'In it Churchill had used a phrase which I could not let go by. He had seemed to accept a Russian occupation following victory as "an act of justice" – to use his words. I could recognise it as a fact of power but repudiated any suggestion of an act of justice.' Manuscript of broadcast of 30 November 1974. Earl of Home papers, the Hirsel, Coldstream.

committed the signatories to a democratic Poland, at least on paper. The actual agreement had its undoubted compromises, both morally and politically, but the fact that Stalin never regarded those terms as sacrosanct was to be its real weakness, and not the terms themselves. Eden was not the only one to be wary of Stalin's true aims. By July 1945, Lieutenant-General J. A. H. Gammell, Head of 30 Mission (the British Military Mission in Moscow), was warning the Foreign Office of an 'iron curtain now drawn across Eastern Europe'[14]* and was forecasting that Russia would be one of the major post-war problems for the West. It was not a message Eden would ever forget.

A footnote to Yalta came at a glamorous wedding reception in January 1946 attended by Chips Channon and Lady Cunard. It was as if the war had never intruded. As the champagne flowed, Chips Channon indicated the luxurious scene approvingly to Emerald Cunard and said, 'After all, this is what we have been fighting for', to which she replied, 'What, are they all Poles?'[15]

On his return to London, Eden began his preparations for the penultimate great wartime conference, that at San Francisco from 25 April. He wanted first to resolve the question of French involvement in the development of the atom bomb. 'The French have made it clear,' he wrote to Churchill, 'that, if we and the Americans do not in due course admit them to participation, they will have to turn to Russia.' Five days later Churchill vetoed any involvement of the French in the project, or the dissemination of any information about it, an episode still remembered by de Gaulle in 1963 when he was the one doing the vetoing.[16]†

On 12 April Roosevelt died of a cerebral haemorrhage at his retreat in Warm Springs, Georgia. Four hours later Harry S. Truman was sworn in as the thirty-third President of the United States. Churchill's initial reaction was to fly at once to America for the funeral, but in the end it was decided that Eden would represent Britain. So many ministers were abroad that Churchill felt his duty to be at home, which led to some criticism in America.‡

Eden arrived in Washington on 14 April. The Countess of Athlone, wife

---

*General Gammell's use of the phrase 'iron curtain' pre-dated Churchill's famous Fulton speech by eight months. He was in doubt about the nature of Soviet society. 'In best Monty style, he used to go for a run every morning before breakfast, and was invariably followed by a sweating secret policeman, who was clearly deeply suspicious of what he was up to.' Hugh Gammell to the author, 24 March 2002.
†De Gaulle vetoed Britain's application to join the Common Market on 29 January 1963.
‡President Lyndon B. Johnson did not attend Churchill's funeral in London in January 1965. Some said this was because Churchill's supposed slight to Roosevelt's memory in April 1945 had not been forgotten in America.

of the Governor-General of Canada, described the funeral to her sister-in-law Queen Mary:

> The service at the White House was at 4. It was in the ball-room (no larger than the Chesterfield House one) & just Alge [the Earl of Athlone], Eden – Pres: of the Phillipines & Feisal were on one side with Mrs FDR & family on the other & behind the ambassadors & his own aid[e]-de-camps. The service was short, then Mrs FDR walked out followed by the family & Alge returned to his Embassy – No word of greeting or thanks from anyone – when one thinks Eden had flown the Atlantic to be present & show the sympathy of the British Gov: & Alge that of the King of England.[17]

The next day Eden did see Mrs Roosevelt, who 'said how touched she was that our country had sent a special representative and added that as the immediate responsibilities we had all to share were so heavy, she thought that I should meet her husband's successor at once'. A few moments later Eden was introduced to the new President and Mrs Truman. Of the three American Presidents (Roosevelt, Truman and Eisenhower) with whom Eden had dealings, he thought most highly of Truman, whom he regarded as a fighter for the causes in which he believed, and a pragmatist. Initially these feelings were not reciprocated by Truman, who thought Eden 'much over-rated'.[18]

One of the first consequences of Roosevelt's death was Stalin's decision to send Molotov to the San Francisco Conference, instead of Andrei Gromyko, which meant that the three Foreign Secretaries – Molotov, Eden and Stettinius – would meet again. After Roosevelt's funeral, Eden told Stettinius that 'it would do the Russians no harm to know how deep was our concern at the failure of the Moscow Commission thus far to make progress on the basis of the Yalta decisions.'[19] At this stage Eden was in favour of postponing the San Francisco Conference until there was some clear resolution of Russia's stance over Poland, but this was never a viable option.[20] In the event, James Byrnes became the new American Secretary of State, and Stettinius attended the San Francisco Conference as the first American Ambassador to the United Nations.

Before the end of April, Mussolini and Hitler were also dead, leaving Churchill, Stalin and Prince Fumimaro Konoye of Japan as the senior figures of the great conflict. By the end of the year Stalin stood alone. Churchill was defeated at the polls in July, and Prince Konoye committed suicide in December rather than face trial as a war criminal. When VE Day was celebrated on 8 May, Eden was in San Francisco. 'All my thoughts are with you on this day which is so essentially your day,' Eden wrote at once to Churchill. 'It is you who have led, uplifted and inspired us through the worst days. Without you this day could not have been. I hate not to be with you.'[21]

The San Francisco Conference began formally on 25 April, a fortnight after Roosevelt's death, and continued until 26 June, by which time Britain was on the verge of its first General Election for ten years, with Eden back in London. The conference was attended by representatives of fifty nations. Eden headed the British delegation, which included Clement Attlee, Bobbety Cecil and Lord Halifax. One notable absentee was Poland, as America did not recognise the Lublin Committee as an independent government. The agenda continued much of the works of the Dumbarton Oaks Conference in establishing a United Nations Security Charter, and provided for the use of a veto among the Permanent Membership of the Security Council, comprising China, France, Britain, America and Russia. Britain was to use the veto for the first time on 31 October 1956 during the Suez Crisis.[22]

VE Day was treated cautiously in San Francisco, the main fear still being what surprises an undefeated Japan might yet spring, a point picked up by attending journalists, who included John F. Kennedy (the future American President), and, from Britain, Michael Foot. One of the American delegates, Arthur Vandenberg, had many private talks with Eden, whom he rated 'a great guy'. 'Everything will depend on whether Stalin *really* wants this League to succeed,' Vandenberg wrote. 'Eden quite frankly said that the League is *not* being organised along the lines he would prefer; but that it is all worth while in order to see if we *can* live with Russia in the post-war world.'[23] Judging by Molotov's performance at San Francisco, the signs were not hopeful. Eden's daily letters to Churchill are punctuated by details of Molotov's uncompromising attitude. 'It proved impossible to move Mr Molotov on any point,' was one typical report on 23 April. 'He was completely stubborn & unaccommodating.' Attlee also reported to Churchill, praising Eden's efforts. 'Anthony had a very fine reception at the Conference. His speech was excellent & really captured the Conference,' he reported on 28 April. 'Difficulty over the Chairmanship of the Conference was smoothed out today, but speeches at Plenary threaten to waste much time. We are trying to accelerate business.'[24]

Doubts about the date of the General Election also increased the sense of urgency. 'As far as I can judge,' Eden wrote on 9 May when asked for his advice, 'all signs point to greater difficulties in October than today. An election in that month is likely to be even more harmful in relation to the international situation than an election in June.'[25] By 14 May, Churchill had settled on 5 July as a possible Polling Day if Labour would not continue in the Coalition until the defeat of Japan, and he pressed for

Eden's return. The same day Eden met President Truman. 'I was struck by the President's air of quiet confidence in himself,' he wrote to Churchill. 'He said at one point in our talk, "I am here to make decisions, & whether they prove right or wrong I am going to take them".'[26] With the conference still in session, Eden reluctantly returned to Britain on 17 May, leaving Bobbety Cecil as the chief British delegate, though Eden could take credit for the blueprint that was to establish the United Nations Charter.

On 23 May, Churchill resigned as Prime Minister of the National Government, and began choosing his list of ministers for the Caretaker Government, which was to hold the reins until the July General Election. Eden was reappointed Foreign Secretary on 25 May.* William Mabane became Minister of State and Eden's two Under-Secretaries were Lord Dunglass, despite (or, some felt, because of) his criticism of Yalta, and Lord Lovat. On 28 May, Churchill bade farewell to all the ministers and Under-Secretaries of the National Government at a party at Downing Street. In a moving speech he told them, 'The light of history will shine on all your helmets.'[27]

For Eden, the interim period before the Election was to prove the most distressing of his life, despite the plaudits that were now coming his way, including Bobbety Cecil's report on San Francisco to the King:

> The main credit goes to Anthony Eden and to Edward Halifax, who after his departure handled the affairs of the Delegation with the greatest ability and with a patience which was beyond all praise. My part was a very subsidiary one. On the whole, I think that the result was not unsatisfactory. We had of course to make numbers of compromises, and the Charter that eventually emerged was not all that we might have hoped when we left England. But at any rate the main purpose, which was to create an organisation acceptable both to the United States and Russia, was achieved – In that respect, the new organisation is a very much better and more hopeful one than the League of Nations, and there are in the charter a good many other improvements on the Covenant. If the member states really mean to work it, it should be a considerable contribution to future peace.[28]

The unremitting pace of his wartime service finally caught up with Eden, and he now retired to Binderton with a duodenal ulcer. Any canvassing in the forthcoming Election was ruled out. Beatrice, who had never enjoyed electioneering, had to return from Paris, where she had been running a Forces canteen (and living with C. D. Jackson, publisher of *Fortune*

---

*Although Eden is generally accounted to have had three spells as Foreign Secretary, technically speaking he served in four separate administrations, the Caretaker Government from 25 May to 27 July 1945 being the third of the four.

magazine, and one of Eisenhower's wartime representatives in Europe)[29] and take over Eden's duties in Warwick and Leamington. It was a watershed in the marriage. Eden's affair with Davina Erne was over, and Beatrice hankered after life in the New World. They reached an accommodation. If Eden remained in politics and there was a prospect of the Premiership, she would stay with him and there would be no divorce. But if he became Secretary-General of the new United Nations Organisation – a distinct possibility – then they would separate. Her preference was for the United Nations job to materialise. 'We had some good talks,' Eden wrote, 'and I hope that all will be well. She is very restless, which is a change for her & due to war.'[30]

Meanwhile Beatrice had been under surveillance by the security forces,[31] and Eden's own position – as the possible victim of blackmail over his private life – was not entirely risk-free.[32]

On 10 June, Sybil Eden, drifting in and out of consciousness during her final illness, wrote a last pencilled letter to her now-famous son. 'All blessing for your 49th year. How time passes. You in your *49th* & I in my *79th* year – I would like a few more years on this planet for life will be so interesting but I fear very uncomfortable!!'[33] Five days later she suffered a fatal stroke. She died on 19 June. Eden was unable to make the long journey north for the funeral.

The same week, he received two messages from his elder son, who was in the Far East. 'Have got the Burma Star (I think) and the 1939–45 one as well,' Simon wrote excitedly. 'I suppose there will be a Jap star and probably a Singapore star, so I shall return home looking like a map of the Heavens!' He wrote again on 6 June. 'Many happy returns of the day. This is timed to reach you by the 12th, but I am afraid it may be a day or two late. I will write again soon. All love, Simon.'[34]

Whilst convalescing at Binderton, Eden was cheered by a visit from Norman Carmichael, Sergeant of Number 10 platoon in far-off Flanders days. Eden was preparing for a major election broadcast on the radio (or wireless, as his generation knew it), and from his American experience knew that the secret was not to imagine an audience of hundreds of thousands, but one listener to whom the broadcaster was speaking face-to-face (a skill Baldwin had also quickly learned in the inter-war period). As much of the talk with Carmichael had been of Plugstreet days, Eden decided to imagine he was talking to Sergeant Harrop. The broadcast went out on 27 June and was an outstanding success, unlike Churchill's ill-advised broadcast of 4 June, when he raised the spectre of the Labour Party – if elected – establishing 'some form of Gestapo'.[35] In his address, Eden evoked the spirit of Noel Skelton and looked to the domestic future. 'I will give you the only pledge I propose to give tonight,' he said. 'We will do everything in human power to get the maximum number of houses in the shortest possible time.'[36] The Conservative campaign, by turns complacent, patronising and offensive received much criticism. Patrick Reilly, then a young official at the Paris Embassy (and later Ambassador in both Moscow and Paris) wrote to his father in India, 'From Churchill's first broadcast it hit the wrong note, and only Eden got it right', a view shared by many at the time.[37]

During Carmichael's visit, Simon Eden, on the other side of the world, was preparing to set out in a Dakota aircraft on a routine air-supply sortie from Akyab to various destinations in Burma.

On 27 June, Bob Dixon was the duty secretary at Binderton. He came down from London, and he brought with him a fateful telegram. Bob had to choose his moment carefully, as Eden was still frail and was only allowed up for short periods each day. That night, Eden wrote in his diary, 'B & I went for a walk round garden when he showed me telegram saying that Simon was missing since 23rd. It was from [Air Chief Marshal Sir Keith] Park. There is nothing one can write. Did some weeding as best thought destroyer.'[38]

The next morning Eden received a telegram from Churchill, sympathising profoundly with his anxiety. At lunchtime a telegram arrived from Mountbatten, who told him that Simon's commanding officer had spoken well of him and had recommended him for a commission. 'Poor Beatrice,' Eden wrote in his diary. 'It is hell for her tackling constituency in all this. It is not much better lying here.'[39]*

For more than three weeks, there was no news about Simon and his fellow airmen. Eden received anguished letters from parents of other members of the crew, who hoped that, as Foreign Secretary, he might have had special or advance knowledge of the fate of the Dakota. But, like them, he waited in torment, and could give no hope, for he had none himself. He kept the situation confined to his immediate circle. Only Jim Thomas was made privy to the secret. 'I have bad news' Eden wrote on 28 June:

> We got a telegram yesterday morning from Park – Air Marshal in Far East – that Simon's aircraft has been missing since 23rd. Monsoon weather makes search difficult – Dickie [Mountbatten] wires later that crews often do turn up after several weeks in jungle. There it is – one can only be sure that they will do all they can to find the crew. Please don't tell anyone – I haven't – But wanted you to know.[40]

Eden's main motive in not wanting the news to come out before the election was that people should never say, even privately, that he was

---

*The only grain of comfort was their joint pride in the news of the M.C. awarded to Martyn Beckett, Beatrice's half-brother, for his bravery in a tank engagement at Wesel.

trying to gain sympathy and make political capital out of his son's misfortune.

Gradually snippets of information leaked out. 'Bad telegram from Group Commander including phrase "little hope",' Eden wrote on 2 July. 'Later message from Park shows he fears they have run into "nasty range of hills". It is all horribly grim and hard to bear.' The next day the father of the wireless operator of the crew rang him up. 'I could give him no comfort.' On 4 July, Robert Bruce Lockhart called to see Eden. 'He showed me the various telegrams about the missing bomber,' Bruce Lockhart wrote in his diary. 'To my mind they held out no hope, but I did not wish to say so.'[41]

On Polling Day, 5 July, Eden was at his lowest ebb. 'Am beginning seriously to doubt whether I can take on FO work again. It is not work itself which I could not handle, but racket with Winston at all hours! He has to be headed off so many follies.'[42]

July 1945 was the month of the long wait – for news of Simon, for the start of the Potsdam Conference, and for the counting of the General Election ballot papers, delayed for three weeks to allow arrival of the forces' postal votes from all parts of the world. In the interim, Eden, in 'thought destroyer' mode, diverted himself by reading biographies of Canning and Castlereagh. 'I am not so conceited as to suggest that I am like C[anning],' he wrote on 6 July. 'He had brilliant classical scholarship, exceptional oratorical gifts, all the things I have not.'[43] But thoughts of Simon were never far away. 'Spend much of afternoon replying to Simon's Group Captain & Squadron leader which I found pretty heart-rending.'[44]

On 17 July, Eden arrived at Potsdam, west of Berlin, for the final conference of the war (TERMINAL), together with Alec Cadogan. The next day Beatrice joined him, with encouraging news of the campaign in Warwick and Leamington, but Eden's constituency was not typical of the country as a whole. Now there was work to take his mind off the deadening weight.

TERMINAL, which lasted until 2 August, was to prove the longest of all the meetings in which the leaders of the Grand Alliance took part, marking a consummation no less than the Congress of Vienna in 1815, or the Treaty of Versailles in 1919. But there were several unusual factors. First, the overall conflict was not yet at an end, and the problem of Japan was high on the agenda. Secondly, there were new faces, such as that of Truman, the new American President. Thirdly, the British politicians were under an electoral sword of Damocles, and would all go home for three days in the middle of the conference, for their election results on 25 July.

With Germany defeated, the main concerns were the Japanese surrender and the boundaries of post-war Europe, including the seemingly interminable question of Poland and the Oder–Neisse line. War crimes, press freedoms in Eastern Europe, and questions regarding Italy, Yugoslavia, Turkey and Persia were also high on the agenda. Eden warned Churchill that Russia's demands on Constantinople should be resisted, because once a toehold was established by the Soviets at the eastern end of the Mediterranean, there was no telling what the infiltration might foretell, a poignant reminder of the Dardanelles in 1915, and a pre-echo of the broader strategic questions that would arise at Suez eleven years later.

'The Conference was difficult both morning and afternoon,' Eden recorded on 20 July:

> Molotov produced a monstrous paper about the Balkans to which I had to react violently & there were differences on other issues . . . Afternoon meeting rather worse . . . Back to my villa & was working in garden when Bob (Dixon) brought the letter from Peter Portal which he warned me was bad news of Simon. They have found his aircraft & him. Told poor B. Life seems desperately empty.[45]

The conference was only in its third day. The Edens had been bidden to dine with Churchill that evening. Churchill heard the news just before dinner and told his daughter Mary with tears streaming down his cheeks. To his astonishment, Eden came, insisted the news be kept from the other guests and went through the function with an undimmed gaiety that gave no sign of inner turmoil. One of the fellow diners was Lord Moran, Churchill's doctor, who had been privately warned. He had unbounded admiration for the conduct of both Beatrice and Eden, doubting that he could have matched their stoicism if he had just heard that his son had been killed in action.[46]

Eden wrote to the other bereaved parents. Simon's burnt-out plane had been found by a Gurkha patrol on a mountainside near Sumsen village on 16 July, together with the remains of the crew. Among Simon's personal effects was a copy of *Henry V*. On his return from Potsdam, Eden received the parents at the Foreign Office. Beatrice saw privately those mothers who could not brave this meeting, and the mother of Simon's girlfriend, Sheila Smith, whom he had planned to marry after the war.[47] Eden set up a memorial fund 'providing bursaries to assist the education of children of men who have lost their lives on R.A.F. service'.[48]

Letters came from all over the world, two of the first being from Queen Mary and Eden's Labour opponent in Warwick and Leamington. Simon's name was eventually placed on the 1939–45 war memorial in the cloister leading to Christ Church Cathedral, above the inscription: *All these were honoured in their generations and were the glory of their time.*

*

Meanwhile, work on the overlap between war and the peace ahead had to continue at Potsdam. The eleven plenary sessions were held in the Cecilienhof, 'a stockbroker's idea of paradise.'[49]*

Inevitably the focus was on Truman, Stalin and Churchill. As Eden was not confident that Churchill would have command of all the technical detail, he had already set out a summary of the likely course of events:

> 1. As you know the Foreign Office have been considering, with a view to discussions at Terminal, what cards we hold for a general negotiation with the Russians, in the shape of things which the Russians want from us and which it is in our power to give or to withhold. The following is the best list we have been able to make.
> 2. *Credits*. The Russians would not be interested in any credits from us of a size that we could afford to give. But they have approached the Americans for very large credits. The Americans have told the Russians that such a proposal would require special legislation and that this is at the moment out of the question.
> 3. *Germany*. Here again we hold a certain number of assets which the Russians require such as the merchant navy and a substantial part of the industry and industrial sources of Germany. For instance, 70% of German steel making capacity is situated in the British zone. Physical control of these assets gives us an advantage which we could turn to account in securing acceptable reparation and other settlements.
> 4. We and the Americans hold jointly the greater part, possibly the whole, of the German diplomatic archives. The Russians are pressing us for access to them. Our intention had been to grant this on a basis of reciprocity, though this would be largely a formality as we doubt if the Russians hold anything of importance to us. In view however of recent Russian behaviour to us I would not give access to these documents until we are met on other issues.
> 5. The Russians may also want information from us about German secret devices. This, however, is a card we would not wish to play.
> 6. Finally, there is the German fleet, the major part of which is in our control. The Admiralty are submitting a Cabinet paper about this, which seems to be a good card in our hand. The Russians want badly their share of the ships and we hold all that are seaworthy. We ought not to meet their demands without getting a settlement of our requirements on other outstanding issues.[50]

After he had seen this memorandum, Lord Dunglass, the Under-

---

*A visit by the author to the Cecilienhof and its facilities in 1993 revealed quite clearly the inferior accommodation and facilities accorded the British delegation. Truman and Stalin were the undoubted Big Two; and Britain (not only metaphorically) was adapting to diplomatic realities in an annexe to the main participants.

Secretary, returned, as he had done in the debate over Yalta, to the Polish
question, in a submission to Eden:

> I see that the subject of 'Poland' has been taken off the version of the
> agenda for 'Terminal' which was sent to the Russians and I hope this will
> not prevent you from raising the question of the organisation of Free
> Elections in Poland.
>
> I cannot see the House of Commons being ready to accept a pledge by
> this Provisional Government as sufficient and we do not want to start off
> the new Parliament with our own side making a very critical attack,
> which in the light of the Yalta debate, would be difficult to meet.
>
> Could you have a shot at getting the Russians and Americans to join
> with us in a request to the Provisional Government that, when the time
> comes, they will consult with the three Governments as to the adequacy
> of the machinery prepared for carrying out the Yalta decisions? It is
> possible that the Russians (doubtless with many mental reservations)
> might agree to such a request at this stage. I am sure that we should not
> be content with the present position and that we should press some such
> addition to the pledge with great force and good reason.[51]

Eden outlined these concerns to Churchill, and the further problems he
foresaw over troop withdrawals from Persia:

> The Russian grip on Persia is becoming tighter. The remedy is to secure
> a complete withdrawal of Russian forces as soon as possible. We can
> only do this if we are prepared to offer a complete withdrawal of our own
> forces. I want to get this settled at Terminal. I should like to offer
> complete joint withdrawal in three stages:– (1) Both Allies to withdraw
> their forces completely from Tehran at once. (2) The next stage would be
> withdrawal from the whole of Persia except the Abadan and southern
> oilfield area, in return for the Russians withdrawing from the whole of
> Persia except for a zone in either the North-East or the North-West.
>
> ... In my view the supremely important thing is to get the Russians
> out of Persia and there will be much more risk to the oil fields if we fail
> in this than in leaving their protection to the Persians, as in years gone
> by.

With ironic prescience, he concluded, in a postscript to Bob Dixon on 13
July, 'We are likely to have trouble with Egypt later on.'[52]

At Eden's first meeting with Molotov at 30 Kaiserstrasse, near Potsdam, he
was accompanied by Cadogan, and Molotov by Andrei Vyshinsky, Stalin's
former state prosecutor. Molotov was keen to add to the agenda the
subject of what he called Territorial Trusteeship. It was agreed that 'it
would be desirable to follow the Yalta precedent and arrange for meetings
of the Foreign Secretaries in the morning and the Big Three in the

afternoons'. It was hoped they might finish their work by 25 July, when the British had to return for the Election result.[53]

On the war-crimes issue, Eden had expressed his reservations to Molotov, and to James Byrnes, Truman's new Secretary of State. He summed these up to Churchill on 17 July:

> I have personally some doubts about Keitel and would like to know more of the reasons for his inclusion. It also seems rather rough to drag Hess out after all these years to face a trial but Russians will include him anyway and if we leave him out we shall increase their suspicions that we favour him for some sinister reason.[54]*

On 19 July there was some fierce sparring between Eden and Molotov after the Russians had submitted a memorandum on the Yalta Declaration of liberated Europe, which Eden had to deal with on the day of the news of Simon's death:

> After studying this [the official report read], Mr Eden said that he must point out at once that the description which it contained of the situation in Greece was a complete travesty of the facts. The Soviet Government had no official representative in Greece nor, as far as he knew, any source of information save a correspondent of the Tass Agency. The Soviet Government were, therefore, not in a position to know what the true situation was. There were, on the other hand, British troops in Greece; and their commander, Field-Marshal Alexander, was here in Berlin and would be able to assure M. Molotov that there was in fact no 'Terrorism' in Greece. The Press of the world were free to go to Greece and see for themselves what conditions were like and they were free to telegraph full and uncensored reports of what was going on. The same could not be said of Roumania and Bulgaria.[55]

By 21 July it became clear that the proposed zones of occupation in Berlin would make Britain and France appear inferior to the Russians and the Americans. On Sunday 22 July, as time was running out for the British delegation before the enforced interlude, Eden accompanied Churchill to the negotiating table at the Plenary Session, submitting the report from the meeting of Foreign Secretaries that morning. The western frontier of Poland continued to prove one of the most disputatious issues.

By 23 July it was clear that the conference could well last until the end of the first week in August. That afternoon Eden sent a lengthy minute to

---

*Keitel was the German Field Marshal who had signed Germany's unconditional surrender. But he was also responsible for the decree 'bei Nacht and Nebel' (the Night and Fog decree) of December 1941, which encouraged underground activity and sanctioned the lynching of allied airmen by German civilians. Eden was cautious about branding him a war criminal because Keitel had been a brave soldier in the Great War. Keitel was, nevertheless, tried at Nuremberg and subsequently hanged.

Attlee on the security regime for the Baltic and other sea passages, about which Attlee had enquired. One passage, in the light of subsequent events, is of particular interest. 'You express the fear,' wrote Eden, 'that we may run ourselves into an intolerable burden of defence expenditure by seeking to maintain our special interest in places like Gibraltar and the Suez Canal area. It does not seem to me, on the showing of this war which has proved them vital to our national existence, it is unrealistic to hold that we should continue to maintain our special position in these two areas.'[56] The security of Suez was also brought up by Stalin at the Seventh Plenary Meeting that afternoon at 5 p.m., towards the end of which it was agreed to hold a Plenary Meeting during the morning of 25 July and another in the late afternoon of 27 July. Whilst Eden was away for the British Election results, Sir Alexander Cadogan would represent the British Foreign Secretary at the Foreign Secretaries' meetings.

The 8th Plenary Session, attended by Churchill and Eden, was held at the Cecilienhof at 5 p.m. on Tuesday 24 July. The next day the British politicans returned home to learn their fate. Eden's plane landed at Down Ampney airport, near Swindon, the nearest to Ditchley, where he was to spend the night before travelling to his constituency for the count. At Ditchley he was reunited with Nicholas, a tense occasion, as it was their first meeting since Simon's death, and Eden had not yet decided on the best way of breaking the news.

The melancholy tone continued throughout the next historic day, as fifteen-year-old Nicholas accompanied his father through pouring rain to the constituency. By 1 p.m. it was clear from radio reports that Labour were on course for a landslide victory. Eden's own majority, one of the largest in the country, was however assured. The figures were:

Anthony Eden (Conservative)	37,110
Donald Chesworth (Labour)	19,476
W. Dingley (Liberal)	3,908
Conservative majority	17,634

After hearing the result, Eden drove to Stratford – 'a fervent demonstration, where I told damp but cheering supporters that the heart of England had been wiser than the limbs'.[57] He then went on to London, where he found Churchill in a surprisingly belligerent mood, talking of meeting Parliament (as Baldwin had done in January 1924) and challenging Attlee to defeat the Conservatives and their allies in a vote. Eden had wiser counsels, advising Churchill to do nothing precipitately, but wait for the picture to clarify. By 7 p.m. Churchill had accepted the inevitable and tendered his resignation to the King. The final totals gave

Labour 393 seats, the Conservatives 213 and the Liberals twelve, the first ever overall majority for a Labour Government. Among the twenty-two other results was two Communist members.

Eden continued to work at the Foreign Office on 26 and 27 July, clearing outstanding business, until Ernest Bevin succeeded him as Foreign Secretary, and Herbert Morrison as Leader of the House. Churchill's final Cabinet meeting of the Caretaker Government took place on 27 July. Eden wrote in his diary:

> It was a pretty grim affair. After it was over I was on my way to the front door when W called me back and we had half an hour alone. He was pretty wretched, poor old boy. Said he didn't feel any more reconciled this morning, on the contrary, it hurt more, like a wound which becomes more painful after first shock. He couldn't help feeling his treatment had been scurvy. 'Thirty years of my life have been passed in this room. I shall never sit in it again. You will, but I shall not', with more to the same effect.
>
> I replied as best I could that his place in history could have gained nothing by anything he might have achieved in this room in the post-war years. That place was secure anyway. This he accepted and at length we parted.[58]

Eden's final telegram as wartime Foreign Secretary – to Cadogan, who was holding the fort at Potsdam – was despatched at 2.40 a.m. on 28 July.[59] Later that day he surrendered his seals of office to King George VI. On 4 August, Eden wrote again to Cadogan, thanking him for all his support during the years they had been together. 'I won't pretend to you that I am not very sad to leave the Foreign Office. I loved the work, and after the first sense of relief & spell of holiday, I know that I shall miss it', adding, 'I am very glad that Bevin is my successor. He is the best man they have, and will hearken to you & the experience you bring.'[60]

Churchill now proposed that he should recommend Eden for the Garter in the Dissolution Honours. Eden was in no doubt that he should refuse, as he explained to Sir Alan Lascelles, the King's secretary, when he went to the Palace to surrender his seals of office. Churchill was not taking the Garter, and in any case the highest order of chivalry was in the personal gift of the monarch. On 30 July, Lascelles saw Churchill about the Dissolution Honours List. 'He read to me a letter from A. Eden in which he said that he did not wish to accept the Garter. I said I did not think Eden could be expected to take any other line. Mr Churchill, after a moment's reflection, said that perhaps it was better so.' A public announcement was made that Churchill had declined the Garter, but at Eden's insistence, no mention was made of the 'offer' to himself. Lascelles wrote admiringly of

Eden, 'I've always thought of him as the legitimate successor to Edward Grey and Lansdowne.'[61]

Thus it was that Churchill and Eden never returned to Potsdam. Attlee and Ernest Bevin took their places. Molotov and Vyshinsky gave a luncheon party on 31 July for Bevin, together with Archibald Clark Kerr and Alec Cadogan. At first Molotov did not know how to adjust to the vastly different presence of the new Foreign Secretary. Truman mistakenly thought Bevin a British version of the maverick American Union leader, John L. Lewis.[62] Bevin moved swiftly to dispel any misapprehensions. 'The Secretary of State confirmed that the result of the General Election had been quite unexpected. He had thought that Mr Churchill's popularity would have assured him of a majority of 50', ran the official record. 'Talking of Mr. Eden and his great ability as a Foreign Secretary, M. Molotov received from the Secretary of State an assurance that the continuity of the British foreign policy would be preserved.'[63]

On 1 August, Attlee wrote to Eden to assure that this was in fact the case:

My dear Eden,
The Conference ended tonight in a good atmosphere. I would like to let you know the broad results before the communiqué is issued.
We have, of course, been building on the work you did and there has been no change of policy. It was clear that without agreement on Poland and reparations we should get nowhere. We had wanted to stand on the Eastern Neisse but the Americans rather suddenly gave way. We therefore agreed to the Western Neisse after having had long meetings with the Poles from whom we extracted very specific pledges on elections, Press facilities and the repatriation of the Polish forces ... Bevin picked up all the points very quickly and showed his skill as a negotiator. If you would care to come and see me to hear more details, I should be delighted. Yours ever, C.R.A.[64]

Eden replied from Binderton:

My dear Clem,
Thank you for your letter & for telling me the broad results in this way. It will be interesting to read the full communiqué tomorrow. I agree with you in a strong preference for curtailing these excessive Polish demands to the West. I cannot believe that it is to Poland's own interest to obtain territories to the Western Neisse. Thank you also for your action in proposing thanks in a message to me from the Berlin Conference. As I mentioned in the House I am grateful that you should have thought of this. I hope to spend all next week here but if after that

either you or Ernest Bevin want to see me on any point I am, of course, available. I hope, though, that you will both get a few days off. It must have been hard going to conclude the conference and form a govt. in the same week. Yours ever, Anthony.[65]

VJ followed on 15 August, a date with poignant associations for Eden, as Simon had been lost in the theatre of war in the Far East.

Famously, Clementine Churchill thought the results of the 1945 General Election a blessing in disguise, and privately hoped that her husband would now retire.[66] But things did not work out like that. Whilst Churchill busied himself with his own interests – travel, war memoirs, painting, global utterance – on Eden devolved the acting leadership of the Opposition and the hard graft of policy revision. If the Conservatives were ever to regain power, much of the preparation and responsibility in the next years would be Eden's.

With Attlee, Eden had been the key figure in Churchill's historic wartime Government, a fact recognised by Attlee many years later, when he wrote, 'I think that it was Balfour who said that what Winston needed was a strong-minded woman secretary to say every now and then "Don't be a bloody fool." We performed that useful function.'[67]

In 1970, the historian Robert Blake wrote of the Conservative defeat of 1945: 'The mass of the electorate was voting in defence of full employment and against a reversion to the economic depression of the 1930s. To this was added the impetus of Socialist utopianism inspired by the anti-capitalist writings of a whole intellectual generation.'[68] Eden agreed. The political 'intellectual', epitomised by Hugh Gaitskell, had always struck a raw nerve with him. He understood that wartime conditions had had a deeply important social impact, and he never forgot that the Armed Forces, who voted by post, had overwhelmingly supported Labour – which led some to say that the Army Bureau of Current Affairs' most notable campaign medal was that for the 1945 General Election. Nor was Eden under any illusions that he would have done any better had he been Conservative leader. 'If Winston had resigned in 1945 as he told me in 1941 that he intended to do,' Eden wrote later, 'I would have lost that General Election as he did – and all would have said: if only Winston had been there the Tories would have won. Two things lost it. Distrust of Tories after Chamberlain, Hoare etc. W not the man they wanted for the peace.'[69]

In addition, one largely unconsidered aspect of the 1945 Election concerns 'the Election that never was' in 1940. The elderly generation that would have voted in 1940 (many of them for the last time), came to political consciousness when the Conservatives and the Liberals were the two principal parties; the twenty-one-year-old generation voting for the first time in July 1945 grew up in the inter-war period when the Labour Party became the only viable alternative Government. Anti-Conservative feelings therefore overwhelmingly benefited Labour, marking a new beginning in the electoral system.

Eden's main sympathy was for Churchill in his hour of despair. 'It is a staggering change of fortune from a week ago when at his nod came running secretaries to Chiefs of Staff & behind this was real power,'* wrote Eden in his diary on 1 August. 'Of course he feels the blow heavily & his pride is hurt. But maybe it is best for his reputation in history. For he would not have been happy in his handling of these tangled peace questions, especially at home. History will dub the British people ungrateful, whereas perhaps they were really only wise.'[70]

Eden, too, now faced 'a staggering change of fortune'. In the course of two months he had lost his mother, his son, Simon, to all intents and purposes, his wife, as the death of Simon was the final blow that caused the eventual parting; and his office as Foreign Secretary. He later said that one never recovered from the death of one's child: Simon was the second of his sons (after the infant Robert) to predecease him. The circumstances would have broken the will of a lesser man. Facing an uncertain and lengthy period in Opposition, where his own policy input would be crucial, and with the party leadership by no means assured, Eden's life and career were now at the crossroads.

---

*With his intimate knowledge of Shakespeare, Eden was thinking of Mark Antony's great cry of despair:

> Authority melts from me: of late, when I cried 'Ho!'
> Like boys unto a muss, kings would start forth,
> And cry, 'Your will?'
> *Antony and Cleopatra*, III.xi. 90–2.

INTERLUDE

Peacocks and Lilies

You were made for enjoyment, and the world was filled with things which you will enjoy, unless you are too proud to be pleased by them ... Remember that the most beautiful things in the world are the most useless; peacocks and lilies for instance.

John Ruskin, *The Stones of Venice*, vol. 1, ch. 2, 17

'I have a great shock for you,' wrote the young Anthony Eden to his mother from Munich in 1921, when on vacation from Christ Church. 'No I am not engaged to be married, but I have bought a Constable! A little beauty & thanks to the exchange rate quite cheap, £200.'[1]

Eden's papers are full of such snippets about his collecting triumphs. His enthusiasms and excitements come across undiminished, as they did in his own lifetime. From his impecunious undergraduate days to more expansive times, his eye for fine art remained as keen as ever. When he bought his Constable, he was travelling across Europe to Constantinople with Lord David Cecil and Eardley Knowles, another fellow member of Oxford's Uffizi Club. Their progress was not the usual youthful escapade, breaking free from the restraints of family, school or college. War had already hastened this process, and the songs they sang now were ones of experience, not innocence; the theme was seriousness, not frivolity. In the towns and cities they visited, Eden sought out the museums and art galleries, the great houses and public buildings, theatres, concert halls and bookshops. All played their part in his aesthetic education.

The visual arts were always special to him. As he had been brought up in a house containing works by Degas, Corot and Murillo, his taste was ahead of that of his contemporaries, even the *cognoscenti*. Representational painting was never his favourite medium; he preferred Maratta (another of his small purchases on the Constantinople odyssey), Braque and, later, Picasso, whose blue period was to Eden among the most notable in the history of art – by no means then the conventional contemporary view. Such 'advanced' tastes followed those of his father, so long the despair of Charlie Londonderry.

His rich contemporaries – Chips Channon, in particular – were great collectors of art; with Eden the aesthetic took precedence over the monetary. He bought for pleasure, not for later profit. The first painting he ever bought was a watercolour by Dunoyer de Segonzac, 'Le Canotier', reflecting his love of all things French, literature as well as art. In his late years he took a great interest in the Lombardy school. Ironically, when taste 'caught up' with his dabblings, the investment value far outweighed anything he could have gained in the markets. Similarly, Eden judged a house not by its financial potential, but how it would serve as a backdrop for art. Even when living in Government properties, he leavened the taste of officialdom with a sprinkling of his own treasures in the private rooms. Upstairs in 10 Downing Street, he drew solace from Derain and what his father called 'my own immaculate Degas'.[2]

André Derain drawings were a special pleasure and for many years he visited Zwemmers in Charing Cross Road to assess the latest offerings as they became available. He picked up an 1880 Monet in Dieppe. One of his shrewdest purchases was a Picasso pencil sketch of 1905, 'Le Gamin'. He bought a 1939 Braque 'Nature morte avec huîtres', and when Prime Minister was given an etching by Dunoyer de Segonzac, inscribed by the artist on the back 'Pour Sir Anthony Eden, ami de la France et ami des arts. En hommage.' The division of the spoils after Beatrice's departure to America was the cause of some anomalies. A Corot oil painting, a Beckett possession, was left behind, but the '£200 Constable' went to America.

With Timothy, Eden visited the Biennale in Venice in 1920, wondering afresh at the genius of his beloved Cézanne. During the 1930s, political tours to Germany, Russia and Italy were never complete without visits to the treasures of the Pergamon, the Hermitage or the Vatican. His diary comments on art could be as astute and uninhibited as those on political matters. On 16 January 1926, Eden went to the prestigious John Singer Sargent retrospective exhibition at the Royal Academy. Sargent had once painted his mother, but this did not prevent some sharp observations:

> My opinion of Sargent is not in any way changed – Brilliant painting, no
> subtlety, little sense of colour. Direct to bluntness. No sensibility. Hence
> the harshness and sometimes the ugliness of his water colours. It is never
> "I must have that picture, I cannot live without it – but, how brilliant,
> how damnably clever." Nevertheless an interesting exhibition if only for
> the technical brilliance of the work.[3]

When Christ Church commissioned his portrait after his Premiership, Eden hoped it would be painted by Oskar Kokoschka. At this suggestion, the college authorities were distinctly uneasy.* Had not Kokoschka been exhibited in the Exhibition of Degenerate Art (*Entartete Kunst*) in Munich in July 1937? The memories of Graham Sutherland's 1954 portrait of Churchill – 'this remarkable example of modern art', as its subject had declared – were then still fresh, and there was no telling what

---

*Except for Roy Harrod, in whose fiefdom such responsibilities lay.

modernistic and unsuitable splash of primary colours might ensue as a backdrop to the festal light in Christ Church Hall. Nevertheless, Eden pressed for Kokoschka to be considered. Enquiries established that, although Kokoschka did not normally travel to England for commissions, he would be prepared to do so for Eden, whom he greatly admired. The fee would be £6,000, which proved a relief and an excuse for Christ Church, as it was far beyond the available budget.[4]

So Sir William Coldstream, who shared Eden's enthusiasm for Braque, Cézanne and Picasso, was commissioned, but the resulting portrait, despite its technical assurance, was never for Eden a substitute for what might have been.[5]

Eden envied Churchill his facility for painting and regretted that he himself had never taken to it seriously. 'An amateur of the arts, who if circumstances had been different, might have been a painter' was the considered opinion of one expert.[6]

Literature was, after the visual arts, the discipline that most engaged Eden in his leisure hours. From earliest days, his diaries were full of comments about his literary explorations, with pithy and often unconventional assessments. Of Spenser's *Faerie Queen*, he noted: 'This is a considerable work to embark upon, especially by one who is apt to be more bored than moved by poetry. Still, I enjoyed this first book though one feels that Spenser has not as yet quite written himself in.'

As Eden (and Spenser) got into his stride, a greater symbiosis was evident: 'The IXth is immeasurably the best canto in the book,' Eden commented. 'The speech of Despair is superb, surprisingly modern in places and saturated throughout with that mysticism which defies the hand of time.'

In the same month, Eden also read Laurence Sterne's *A Sentimental Journey*, which he much admired, and, for relaxation, G. K. Chesterton's *The Man Who Knew Too Much*. Eden was one of those voracious readers who kept three or four contrasting books 'on the go', to suit his changing moods. The picaresque English novelists of the eighteenth century were much to his taste, and after a re-reading of *Roderick Random*, Eden declared, 'I am one of those who consider Smollett a great novelist.'[7]

For Eden, the greatest of English novelists remained Dickens. He read and re-read the whole canon, even *Pickwick Papers*, which he regarded as atypical and not on the same level as *Great Expectations* or the great works of Dickens's maturity, *Little Dorrit, Bleak House* and *Our Mutual Friend*. Other favourites he revisited included Walter Scott – the excitement of *The Heart of Midlothian* – Stevenson and Trollope. He had his antipathies and blind spots. Byron's *Childe Harold* he felt overrated, and Kilvert's diary, which achieved cult status when published in 1938, was not his thing at all. 'Some interest,' he noted of Gosse's *Father and Son*, 'despite a precious vein that dates it.'[8] Its account of 'a struggle between two temperaments' was not unlike Eden's own childhood, though without the backdrop of religious fanaticism.

Among English writers Eden accorded the palm to Shakespeare, though not uncritically. He preferred his Shakespeare in the theatre to the study, and when the theatre was not available, in family readings with Beatrice and his sons. 'Finished reading *As You Like It* with family after dinner,' he wrote in September 1943. 'Rather disappointed. There are of course some lovely, & famous passages, but too much of it is in prose.'

He never travelled without a Dent pocket-edition Shakespeare play, marking favourite passages in pencil, particularly in *Troilus and Cressida*, from which he drew parallels, both on a personal and political level. For Eden, no other Shakespearean speech approached that of Ulysses on the calumniating effects of Time, for its insights into the impermanence of human nature, the fickleness of political fortune and the need for endeavour and perseverance.[9]

Eden encouraged both Simon and Nicholas in their acting, and Nicholas even built a miniature theatre at Binderton, in which he would entertain the family, and any visitors not sharp enough to be otherwise occupied, with lengthy monologues from *Macbeth*, 'tho' I think he had but the faintest notion of what it was all about', his father noted.[10]

Eden had many theatrical friends, including Anthony Quayle and Noël Coward. 'Noël sang us some of his new songs after dinner,' he wrote during the war, ' "London Pride" & a ballad which were delightful.'[11] Cinema too became a great interest. 'Special performance of *William Pitt* put on for us at Fox Film Studios,' he wrote in wartime. 'Enjoyed it very much & even tho' Pitt is a completely different type to the real figure, the story was so good that I did not feel historically outraged.'[12]

After his second marriage, to Clarissa Churchill in 1952, the circle and range of artistic friends increased immeasurably, to include, for example, Cyril Connolly, Lucian Freud and Greta Garbo. Anthony and Clarissa Eden were a glamorous couple in a unglamorous decade, bestriding the world of politics and letters. In her novel *The Towers of Trebizond* (1956), Rose Macaulay based one of the characters on Clarissa Eden. Diarists such as Naomi Mitchison and Frances Partridge, and letter writers such as George Lyttelton and Rupert Hart-Davis, included the Edens in their copy.

Eden was an assiduous reader of political biographies, his pencilled marginalia and underlinings giving insights into his own beliefs. In his copy of Buckle's life of Disraeli, he noted approvingly the subject's 'high and inspired patriotism', and 'that imaginative quality in him which fired the imagination of others' in his great series of political novels, as well as in his public actions. Presidents and Prime Ministers sent Eden inscribed copies of their memoirs. Parcels of books, with admiring inscriptions, came from many other sources. Dale Carnegie's *How to Win Friends and Influence People* was inscribed 'to Anthony', who 'doesn't need to read this book. He *lives* it.'[13]

French was like a first language for Eden, and over the years much of his money was spent in bookshops on the Left Bank. Not many of his political contemporaries read and re-read Proust in the original. His tastes were catholic – the great novelists, Zola, Stendhal, Balzac (*Père Goriot* a particular favourite, with its echoes of *King Lear*), Victor Hugo; the short stories of Maupassant; the philosophy of Montaigne; the dramas of Racine, Corneille (he quoted from *Le Cid* in *Another World*)[14] and Molière. He greatly admired Anatole France and the humane tolerance of Sainte-Beuve. 'I have been reading Sainte-Beuve,' he wrote to Bobbety Salisbury in the first months of retirement. 'Very lucid and soothing for the modern world I thought.'[15] Each year in retirement Eden visited de Gaulle in Paris and took the opportunity to buy the latest French novels. His library, still extant, contains more than 250 French books, all of them read and most with pencilled comments.

Arabic and Persian literature he also devoured in the original, which led him to look critically at Edward Fitzgerald's translation of the *Rubáiyát of Omar Khayyám*, and regret that he had not chosen better poems to bring to an English audience, a kind of benevolent elitism that would have been incomprehensible to a later political generation. For Eden, literature gave an insight into national character; one could learn more from *War and Peace* than from any number of pronouncements from the Politburo; more from Thomas Mann than from *Mein Kampf*. Eden was more widely read and cultivated than many university dons, yet this was hidden from the public – quite a contrast with Harold Macmillan, who took every opportunity in his memoirs to boast of his erudite and learned reading.

Eden, in short, was one of the most cultivated Prime Ministers to occupy Downing Street in the twentieth century, not so much an 'intellectual', with all its pejorative associations, but rather an aesthetic figure. In what later became a fashionable term, he had a 'hinterland'. Latterly, there may not have been much competition from that quarter for unforced and natural sophistication, but in palmier times, Asquith had his classical literature; Balfour, his philosophy; Chamberlain, his Shakespeare; Churchill his art, especially as a practitioner; Heath, his music; even Bonar Law had his chess, and to international standard. The special characteristic of Eden, as Dr Johnson wrote of *Hamlet*, was that he could be accorded 'the praise of variety'. He came from that rounded and civilised English generation, for whom allusion was not pretension, quotation not display, but the civilisation of learning the very fabric of spiritual maturity.

In a short story, Hugh Walpole quipped of one of his characters, 'He was at Eton, and therefore had no education.'[16] The syllogism is a false one. Like Osbert Sitwell, who famously declared in his *Who's Who* entry that he was educated 'in the holidays from Eton', Eden's aesthetic education was a lifelong process. His fluent French and German were not the product of formal teaching, but came through his own aptitude, interest and flair. His knowledge of literature and architecture was self-taught. His love of architecture, particularly the William-and-Mary style of his beloved Binderton, was deeply felt and knowledgeably expressed. Eden had the magpie instinct of the born collector, drew solace from different traditions, but had the urbanity to see things whole. What he could have achieved with the resources of a William Burrell is unimaginable.

In the crises of his life, and in the long years of retirement, such aesthetic passions sustained Eden, becoming a defining part of his character and a true solace in time of trouble. As such, the peacocks and lilies of his life – seemingly the useless beautiful things – remain an essential clue to what made him the man he was.

PART THREE

Crown Prince

For twenty years he waited for the succession, first as Heir
Apparent and then as the established Crown Prince.

James Margach, *The Abuse of Power*, 1978

Dined with Winston, Brendan only other present. W talked of
future and suddenly said that if anything happened to him I
should have to take over.

Anthony Eden diary, 11 November 1941

In June 1942 Mr Churchill gave more authority to his decision
about me in a formal submission to the King, at His Majesty's
request. The long era as crown prince was established, a position
not necessarily enviable in politics.

Anthony Eden, *Full Circle*, 1960

ANTHONY AND CLEOPATRA

CHAPTER TWELVE

Towards the Property-Owning Democracy
1945–51

Winston is becoming rather a pathetic spectacle. The barber's shop downstairs at the House was all through the war decorated with pictures of Churchill in every possible pose. When the new Parliament assembled all this had been taken down and, the day after my Budget Statement, the old boy went in to get his hair cut. The barber, so I am informed by one who was present, said to him, 'Sir, why don't you go right away? That would be much better than hanging about this place like you're doing.'

Hugh Dalton diary, 7 December 1945[1]

You have been thinking in terms of a property-owning democracy. I have been thinking in terms of a spreading of capitalism. Yours is perhaps the more tactful phrase. But we mean the same thing . . . All this is, of course, the very antithesis of socialism, and, I believe, would have a very good chance of capturing the imagination of an electorate exasperated by practical experience of what socialism really means.

Bobbety Cecil to Anthony Eden, 9 August 1946[2]

Only three former Conservative members of the War Cabinet survived the defeat of the Conservatives in 1945 – Churchill, Eden, and Oliver Lyttelton – together with Sir John Anderson, an Independent member for the Scottish Universities, who was regarded by the Labour Party, with some bitterness, as a Conservative. Twenty-nine ministers from the 'Caretaker Government' were defeated, including Leo Amery and Brendan Bracken. Another high-profile casualty was Harold Macmillan, defeated at Stockton, though he soon returned in a by-election.

Had Churchill won the 1945 General Election, even by a small majority, the odds are that he would have stepped down in mid-Parliament in favour of Eden, not least because of the historical (and financial) imperative of setting down his record of the war years, something he could not have done whilst still in Downing Street. Churchill was conscious that, like Neville Chamberlain (and Balfour from an earlier era), he had never been *elected* as Prime Minister, and now, to exorcise that particular demon, he had to remain and fight on. He also wanted to avenge his defeat. Meanwhile, he was able to get on with the war memoirs, draw breath, and then come back refreshed to fight and eventually win his mandate.*

Churchill's promise to Eden, that he would not make Lloyd George's mistake of staying on after the war, soon had a very hollow ring. This was doubly unfortunate for Eden. Not only did he have to wait – and wait – to become Prime Minister; but also on him devolved the daily grind of Opposition leadership during the years of austerity, whilst Churchill wrote his books, relaxed with his painting and made global utterances. Eden found the famous Iron Curtain speech at Fulton (1946) inflammatory and unhelpful, and the question of 'Europeanism' that Churchill spoke of in Strasbourg (1949) too ambiguous. Meanwhile, the more successfully the ground was laid for Conservative revival by Eden, Butler and their lieutenants, the more certain it was that Churchill would delay his eventual retirement.

Eden was exhausted, dispirited, not very well and without the stability of a secure family life. Further illnesses were to take their toll in the years ahead, which conspired to give Churchill the excuse to stay on even longer. It was to prove a bitter cycle.

For Eden, the years of Opposition were to be ones in which he returned to the field of domestic concerns – housing, industrial policy, share-ownership, workers' participation and the expansion of educational opportunity. 'The standard of life of too large a part of our people is still too low, the housing leaves much to be desired,' he wrote privately, echoing Disraeli's concerns. 'How can physical conditions improve unless living conditions in respect of nutrition & light & air improve also?'[3]

In addition to his speech on 'the property-owning democracy' at the 1946 Party Conference in October, that year saw four other major pronouncements on the home front, as well as several parliamentary speeches on Labour's domestic legislative programme. In the international field, Eden established an immediate rapport with Ernest Bevin and laid the foundations of a bi-partisan approach that was to last throughout the six years of Labour Government. In a foreign-affairs debate on Greece in 1947, he stated, without rebuff from his successor, that he and Bevin had no policy differences.

The Conservatives remained in a state of shock for most of 1945. No autumn conference was held that year, as a mood of stunned disbelief seemed to have settled on the party after the consequences of a defeat comparable to those of 1832 and 1906 became increasingly apparent.

---

*Churchill lost two (1945 and 1950) and won one (1951) of his three General Election campaigns. Only four twentieth-century Conservative leaders avoided defeat at the polls. As with Bonar Law (1922) and Harold Macmillan (1959), Eden won his one General Election campaign (1955). Mrs Thatcher's three consecutive victories came after his lifetime.

However, organisational changes soon followed. To Eden's delight, Jim Thomas became Vice-Chairman of the party, responsible for the candidates list. Different honours came Eden's way with the Freedom of Durham in October 1945 and, on 16 November 1945, his installation as Chancellor of Birmingham University, a post he was to hold conscientiously until 1973. His two predecessors had been Joseph Chamberlain and Lord Robert Cecil. Eventually Eden's papers were to be placed as a gift for the nation in the University Library at Birmingham alongside Joseph Chamberlain's, where the Eden Room adjoins that holding the Austen and Neville Chamberlain archives.

On 19 November 1945, three days after the ceremonies at Birmingham, Herbert Morrison announced the Government's intention to nationalise electricity, transport and gas before the next election. Parliamentary war was now engaged in earnest, spurred on by an angry mood at the 1922 Committee about the low profile that Churchill and Eden were said to be adopting in the Commons – true in Churchill's case, but not in Eden's. Only Oliver Stanley and Oliver Lyttelton had been on the front bench when Morrison made his statement, and the subsequent discontent led to the promise to back-benchers that in future either Churchill or Eden would be on the front bench for major debates or statements. In practice, this meant Eden.

On 29 January 1946, for instance, Eden led for the Conservatives in the two-day debate on coal nationalisation. Overall his speech, according to one Labour historian, 'offered little more than token criticism'.[4] The debates between February and April 1946 on the repeal of Baldwin's 1927 Trades Disputes Act, forever regarded by Labour stalwarts as a vicious piece of anti-working-class legislation, sparked some of the bitterest exchanges of the whole Parliament, but not from Eden, whose knowledge of social conditions in pre-war Durham ran too deep for such a partisan approach. As acting leader of the Opposition during Churchill's prolonged absence from the House, Eden bore the brunt of the all-night sittings, which became a debilitating part of Westminster life, as on 1-2 April, when no fewer than one hundred Conservatives remained in the Chamber throughout.

To compensate for the loss of his Cabinet minister's salary (Churchill was paid an official salary as Leader of the Opposition, though Eden was in effect doing all the work), Eden took on his first commercial directorships since the 1920s – with the Westminster Bank, which had taken over the Beckett family bank, and the Board of the Phoenix Assurance company. But emotionally it was a difficult time. Oliver Lyttelton, who knew Eden well, once made a sharp observation to Violet Bonham Carter about what he called the 'common deficiencies' of Eden and Rab Butler,

'They have neither of them ever been inside White's Club – or ever got drunk in their lives.' To which Violet Bonham Carter added, 'The only difference between them is – women.'[5]

Women fascinated Eden, and women were fascinated by him. When Clarissa Churchill first met him, she noticed at once that he was more like a continental figure than an Englishman; he had little time for the carapace of upper-class English male life – the leather armchair in the London club, the camaraderie of the tribal Conservatives, the drink with cronies in the smoking room late at night. When relaxing at dinner, weekend parties, theatres and art galleries, his eyes shone in female company, and women likewise responded to his charm and courtesy. 'And the older the woman, the deeper the swoon', as one of his friends remembered it.[5] The Binderton visitors' book shows there was hardly a weekend when the house was not full of guests. Rarely did his male friends come alone.

The marriage with Beatrice did not survive the blow of Simon's death. In December 1946, Eden, together with Beatrice and Nicholas, sailed for America on the *Queen Elizabeth*. They did not return as a trio. Beatrice had now decided finally to make a new life in America. Marriage with C. D. Jackson did not materialise, but she later hoped to marry an eminent American surgeon. There were other dalliances, but none of them led to that elusive second marriage. The separation in December 1946 meant that after three years Eden would be able to sue for divorce and, of crucial importance for his Westminster career, as the innocent party. There was no shortage of ladies who would have liked to become the second Mrs Eden. The widowed Duchess of Kent was an admirer, as were a number of married women such as Fulke Warwick's wife, Rose, Jane Clark (wife of Kenneth Clark, surveyor of the King's Pictures), and Lady Caroline Paget, eldest daughter of the 6th Marquess of Anglesey, on whom it has been claimed Eden fathered a son.[7]

Eden, at this time, was of course free to have affairs, but not free to marry again. Sometimes infatuation led to desperate measures. The memory of one dreadful day in late 1949 never left him. Calling on a friend in her London flat, he found that she had taken an overdose in a forlorn attempt at suicide. He could have panicked, but remembered that Jim Thomas lived nearby. He telephoned and Thomas came at once. In one of the most selfless actions he ever undertook on Eden's behalf, Thomas assumed control. As a bachelor, his reputation was not at stake in any press reportage, so he told Eden to leave the scene immediately, before summoning a doctor and an ambulance. Though Eden, deeply affected, felt this would be dishonourable, Thomas kept a cool head and insisted. In fact, the story never made the papers, but had it done so, with the Shadow Foreign Secretary's name blazed across the headlines, it would almost certainly, in the social conditions of the time, have marked the end of Eden's political career.[8]

Not all Eden's women friends were enamoured by the thought of taking on the high-profile part of a prominent politician's wife, in essence the canker in the apple of his first marriage. Beatrice hated public life, to the incomprehension of Violet Bonham Carter, for whom politics was the very fabric of being. 'Talked to Beatrice Eden,' wrote Violet Bonham Carter in her diary on 11 October 1943. 'Anthony is in Russia. She says he hates going abroad & she feels claustrophobia in England. I couldn't bear to be out of it.'[9]

Eden had attempted a rapprochement during 1946 at Binderton. They spent a wonderful weekend, during which Eden worked hard to reconcile their differences. After dinner, he couldn't resist telling Beatrice about his big speech the next week at Bradford. 'It's no good,' she said, 'it won't work.'[10] In Eden's most private papers, there is an envelope marked 'From B from New York', and a further note 'C[larissa] to open & decide re. biographer'. The envelope – sent for his fiftieth birthday – contained a precious letter, which he had carefully kept:

> June 10th [1947]. I find that I'm still very happy in this fantastic country. I think there must be some pioneer (or buccaneering) blood in these elderly veins. I'm afraid I won't change my mind now – but I do really hope you'll find happiness, peace & contentment – I'm sure you will before too long – Anyway many many much happier returns of the Day & all possible blessings to you always. B.[11]

Just as Eden had been in two minds about whether to accept the Viceregalship of India in 1943, so at the beginning of 1946 he was drawn by the idea of becoming the first Secretary-General of the United Nations Organisation, whilst remaining fully aware of the drawbacks, and not only domestically. In the international field, the Russians, as Permanent Members of the Security Council, would always have regarded him with suspicion.[12] Eden wrote to Bobbety Cecil:

> I think I should confess to you that I may be under pretty heavy pressure about UNO in the next days – maybe not. No definitive move yet, but I gathered from Bevin whom I saw yesterday on other business (his Moscow travels) that I may be approached. If I am, I shall be tempted to accept. First because I should really care about the work, & though obviously leaving British politics for three or five years is in some ways a wrench, and leaving one's friends still more so, I feel that I can do, perhaps, some good in UNO; none, I think, here – Winston is very keen I should take it. No doubt he has many reasons and friendship among them. But I also think that, though he may not know this himself – or

own it to himself – he would be relieved to see me settled elsewhere & then he would feel easier in his mind about keeping on the leadership of the Tory party as he clearly wants to do. It would be a different matter if W contemplated giving up the party, in the near future. Then we should have to remodel & fashion it. But as it is there is no likelihood of this & men like James Stuart [Chief Whip] & [Ralph] Assheton [Chairman of the Party] will do their best to persuade him to stay on – They are unhappily reconciled to me, but want to put off the evil day for as long as they can. Meanwhile I am to be in charge, rather like a governess on approval, with the Beaver growling away as almost my only stimulant.[13]

This letter showed a perceptive awareness of Churchill's psyche, and a knowingness about Eden's own unpopularity among certain influential members of the party. After two months 'standing in' for Churchill, Eden confessed to Bobbety Cecil, 'I am not sure that I really feel fit enough to undertake the leadership for any long period.'[14] From Binderton in May he reported that 'things with Winston are no easier.'[15]

In the autumn, thoughts of the United Nations post long gone, Eden turned his attention to the necessary remoulding of the Conservative Party. On 7 August 1946 he outlined his thoughts to Bobbety Cecil again:

As we approach the Party Conference I become increasingly concerned at our failure to work out anything in the nature of an industrial policy.[16] Yet it is surely this that we most need. It is not possible to get much in the way of constructive help from Oliver Lyttelton, whose ideas on this business are not mine anyway.

As I see it the struggle in these days is between a Socialist state and a property owning democracy . . . If this be true then we must take every step in our power to help the man engaged in industry to become a partner in that industry – The means have then to be considered. They may be by some form of profit sharing, by ownership of shares, by production Councils, or by a score of ways . . . Then what about the Trade Unions? . . . I have a strong feeling that on our understanding of them & handling of them depends the contribution we can make to our national future . . . I can strike no spark from Winston on this. He is now deeply interested in the party's name & wants to raise the issue at the party conference. No doubt this is important, but what we put in the bottle surely matters more than the label.[17]

Of Churchill's possible retirement there was no sign. 'I rather feel that his present inclination is to go on with everything for as long as he can.'[18]

By July 1946 a major reorganisation of the party machinery was well under way. Eden became President of the Conservatives' Young Conservatives Committee, with Anthony Nutting as Chairman, the first occasion on which the two were to work closely together. He saw in

Nutting – whom a cartoonist later portrayed as 'Eden's Eden' – much of his own youthful promise, and indeed glamour.[19] It was the beginning of a relationship of increasing importance over the next ten years, but one that was to end in great bitterness.

Another figure he now met for the first time at Westminster was his future Foreign Secretary, Selwyn Lloyd. The first point of contact was the fact that Brigadier Lloyd, one of many 'Honourable and Gallant' members in the new House of Commons, had undertaken distinguished wartime service with the Second Army, including assisting with the logistical planning of OVERLORD and the subsequent invasion of Normandy. Politically, he was on the progressive domestic wing of the 1945 Tory intake and, as a former Liberal, very much a Skeltonian social reformer. When the Conservatives returned to office in October 1951, Eden asked for, and got, Selwyn Lloyd as his Minister of State at the Foreign Office. Lloyd often dined out on the story of his appointment at Chartwell. When Churchill mentioned the Foreign Office, Lloyd said, 'I've never been to a foreign country, I don't speak any foreign languages, I don't like foreigners', to which Churchill replied, 'Young man, these all seem to me to be positive advantages.'[20] Eden was never keen on this anecdote receiving wide currency. 'You mentioned that you were going to describe your shortcomings for the F.O. as you put them to Winston,' he later wrote when Lloyd was preparing his memoirs. 'I see no objection to that, but please do not overdo it to the point of making me seem half-witted in having chosen you for the job, because I was not, you know.'[21]

The 1945 Parliament was a wonderful opportunity for the new articulate and ambitious Tory back-benchers. The party leaders were not tucked away in Government, as had happened in Eden's first years in Parliament in the 1920s, but accessible and anxious for the newcomers to take their part in attacking the Labour Government, and on all subjects. It meant that Eden, together with Rab Butler (who also wanted Selwyn Lloyd's services in Government in October 1951), saw at first hand the talents of the 1945 intake, which included (in addition to Selwyn Lloyd and Anthony Nutting) future ministers such as Derick Heathcoat Amory, John Boyd-Carpenter, Freddie Erroll, Ernest Marples and Derek Walker-Smith, all of whom he encouraged to speak up and to speak out.

Eden took a prominent part himself in speaking on behalf of the Conservatives, travelling the length and breadth of the country. On 1 March 1946, for instance, he spoke at Kingston-upon-Hull on the party's new industrial thinking, never falling into the trap of buoying up hopes excessively. 'Let me say at once that anyone who expects the Conservative Party to produce an industrial policy that can be summed up in one word or even one phrase will be disappointed.'[22] He was more combative in a rare appearance at the Oxford Union on 21 November that year, as one of the principal speakers opposing the motion that the Conservative Party offered no constructive alternative – a motion lost by 615 votes to 397, a then unprecedented majority for the Conservative cause. Arguably Eden's most famous speech was delivered at the Conservative Party Conference at Blackpool on 3 October, when he called for a Nationwide Property-Owning Democracy, the apotheosis of Skelton's social thinking of the 1920s.[23] 'The ownership of property,' Eden maintained, 'is not a crime or a sin, but a reward, a right and a responsibility that must be shared as equitably as possible among all our citizens.'[24]*

Eden remained a welcome guest at Ditchley Park, Ronnie Tree's beautiful home near Enstone. One weekend, he was sitting alone in a window seat before dinner in the vast library, with its double fireplaces. Looking up from his book, he noticed a fellow guest coming into the room. Eden went over and introduced himself. The woman who had caught his eye was Ronnie Tree's sister-in-law, Dorothy. She was the wife of David Beatty, a Tory peer, son of Admiral Earl Beatty, who had commanded the fleet at the Battle of Jutland, where Eden's younger brother Nicholas had been killed in 1916. There was an immediate rapport between them, and Eden soon became a regular guest at the Beattys' nearby country house, Astrop Park. Eden and Dorothy Beatty took holidays together in Bognor Regis and discovered a joint love of Shakespeare, especially the poetry of *Antony and Cleopatra*, which they recited to each other:

---

*Ironically, Harold Macmillan's later success in implementing this vision – as Housing Minister from 1951 to 1954 – was to put him in the position from which he was able to overleap Butler in the Conservative hierarchy and replace Eden as Prime Minister after Suez. Butler was always, to Eden's mind (and to others such as Henry Hopkinson), too keen to claim overall paternity of the Conservative reforms after 1945, a view shared by Professor John Ramsden. (John Ramsden, *A History of the Conservative Party: The Age of Churchill and Eden, 1940–1957*, Longman, 1995, p.145.) Eden could be very sharp when newspapers downgraded his own part in the post-war revival, as on the occasion in April 1972 when he read the following extract in a Sunday newspaper: 'Lord Butler, when he was an aspiring Tory Chancellor, once envisaged a Britain of the future as a "property-owning democracy", which at the very least was a brilliant political slogan. But it also stuck, as an expression of the hopes and aims of nearly all, whatever their political persuasion.' (*Sunday Telegraph*, 9 April 1972.) Eden sent the cutting to Robert Carr, his Parliamentary Private Secretary from 1951 to 1955, and a founder member of the One Nation group of young Tory MPs: 'I thought it might amuse you to see this if you had not already read it in the newspaper. Rab of course had about as much to do with that quotation as he had with the Battle of Agincourt. As you may remember it was Noel Skelton who gave birth to it some time in the Twenties. All I did was to revive it, I think at our first post-war Party Conference at Blackpool.' (The Earl of Avon to Robert Carr, 11 April 1972. AP 33/6.) This underestimates the impact that the speech had. By the 1950s, the phrase was being printed in capitals in the official Party Conference handbook, 'an honour otherwise reserved in Party publications for such Disraelian *obiter dicta* as "the elevation of the condition of the people"'. (John Ramsden, *op. cit.*, p.141.)

Eternity was in our lips and eyes,
Bliss in our brows bent.[25]

They were soon lovers. Far from being outraged at his wife's behaviour, the 2nd Earl Beatty saw her affair with Eden as an opportunity to further his own political ambitions, which had become becalmed by the combination of the war and his elevation to the Lords on the death of his father in 1936. Beatty hoped that Eden would deliver him a place in the Shadow Cabinet. When it became clear that Eden neither wanted, nor was able, to fulfil this aim, Beatty's mood changed dramatically. Dorothy moved out (to Pelham Place in Kensington) and private detectives were hired to spy on her and Eden, as David Beatty prepared the ground for divorce proceedings.

Eden had narrowly avoided being cited in the divorce courts by Fulke Warwick, but now he saw no alternative to public exposure. He went direct from Pelham Place to tell Churchill at his nearby London home, 28 Hyde Park Gate. 'I must see you at once,' he said to a startled Churchill, in front of a secretary. 'We will talk privately,' said Churchill, ushering Eden into his study. When Eden, in some agitation, outlined the unfolding situation, Churchill took charge. All Eden's solicitors' correspondence was dealt with at 28 Hyde Park Gate, and a special table was set up where mounting paperwork piled up. Eventually an officer in the Coldstream Guards, who was very much in love with Dorothy Beatty himself, agreed to sit in the house at Pelham Place till 2 a.m. on a night when Beatty's hired detectives were in attendance outside, and he was duly cited in the divorce proceedings.[26]

As Eden left Hyde Park Gate when the crisis had passed, Churchill turned to one of his secretaries and said, 'Anthony must be more careful in future.'[27] Eden's love affair with Dorothy lasted four years. It had drained him emotionally, and his nervous energy was exhausted. The main consequence, however, was subtle. Eden had twice avoided being cited as co-respondent. He had managed to keep his private life secret. This was no mean achievement in the prurient world of 1940s press intrusion, particularly as the broadsheets sneakily covered celebrity divorce cases by quoting extensive transcripts from the courts. His narrow escapes gave him an exaggerated sense of his ability to maintain a 'charmed' life.

Eden was finally granted a decree nisi on 8 June 1950 by Mr Justice Hodson, on the grounds that Beatrice had refused to return with him after their joint visit to the United States in 1946. He was the only witness at the hearing. Despite this ultimate break, Eden always held a place in his heart for Beatrice and was to visit her in New York. Their occasional letters were civilised and showed touches of the old affection.

Eden understood that prolonged periods of office can be as dis-advantageous to a party's inner vitality as lengthy spells in Opposition. For the Conservatives, the opportunity for considered reflection and fresh policies was long overdue. In that sense, Clementine Churchill was right in thinking the defeat a blessing in disguise. Either by themselves or in Coalition, the Conservatives had been in Government for all but three years since 1916. Now they had the chance to look afresh at the three key areas of finance, philosophy and organisation.[28]

Jim Thomas was disappointed not to get the job of Party Chairman, when Churchill appointed the avuncular Lord Woolton, the wartime Minister of Food, to this vital job. Rab Butler took over the Chairmanship of the Conservative Research Department in November 1945, and gathered around him a talented team that included future stars of the 1950 intake, such as Iain Macleod, Reginald Maudling and Enoch Powell, with Michael Fraser in the Secretariat, under David Clarke's vigorous director-ship. Of these newcomers, Eden worked most closely with Reginald Maudling, a keen intellect, who helped him on the financial side of his speeches, including the famous conference utterance on the property-owning democracy. Sir David Maxwell Fyfe (later, as Secretary of State for Wales, dubbed Dai Banana in the principality) revolutionised the party's financial position by completely revamping the rules on contributions, directly involving far more ordinary members. It was a golden period, analogous to the reshaping of the party under Sir Robert Peel after the calamitous 1832 defeat. The Shadow Cabinet – properly speaking, the Party's Consultative Committee – had regular meetings (and gigantic lunches at the Savoy Hotel paid for by Churchill). The inner council were Churchill, Eden, Butler, Harry Crookshank, Oliver Lyttelton, Oliver Stanley, Bobbety Salisbury (who succeeded to his father's Marquessate in April 1947) and Lord Woolton. Eden did not host Savoy lunches, but he chaired endless committees, including the Shadow Cabinet's one on policy review, which accepted the extensive programme of Charters on 24 April 1947.

Although Eden was always the favourite to succeed Churchill (an attempt coordinated by James Stuart to get Churchill to retire in 1947 came to nothing), there was a feeling in the upper reaches of the party even then that he might not last long when he did get his chance. As a result, when the difficulties of the Labour Government increased, there was a certain amount of jostling for position, although Oliver Stanley was very much – albeit informally – the Number Three in the hierarchy. Stanley's premature death in 1950 set off a fresh wave of speculation about the new order, and it was generally accepted that, if anything happened to Eden, Butler would be the heir presumptive.

The most substantial product of the policy overhaul came with the publication of *The Industrial Charter* on 11 May 1947. Eden introduced its themes at a mass meeting at Cardiff Castle before an audience of 17,000 Welsh Tories the following week.[29] For traditional Tories, especially Sir Waldron Smithers and Sir Herbert Williams, this programme, which accepted the mixed economy, a commitment to full employment and central planning, seemed little better than 'pink Socialism'. Nevertheless, at the Brighton Conference that autumn, discreet backroom work by Eden, Butler and Macmillan ensured that only four people voted against the amendment welcoming *The Industrial Charter*. On 3 October, Eden and Oliver Stanley had also talked with Churchill into the small hours, trying to persuade him that a statement of Conservative principles was an essential ingredient of his leader's speech. This Churchill accepted only reluctantly, as he preferred the broad brush stroke in Opposition, so as not to leave any later hostages to fortune. A more enlightened view came from Cuthbert Headlam, MP for Newcastle North, who wrote in his diary:

> The Party Conference appears to be going well – it has adopted the 'Industrial Charter' almost unanimously, only poor old Waldron Smithers seems to have spoken against it. He considers it to be milk and water Socialism which perhaps it is – but, so far as I have studied it – and that is not a great deal – it seems to lay down as an 'industrial policy' the practices that exist today between employers and employees in the best managed firms – there does not seem to me much harm in this.[30]

In August 1947, Eden invited Cuthbert Headlam, whom he saw as a kindred spirit, to stay at Binderton. Their Durham links went back to the inter-war period, when Headlam had been Chairman of the Durham County Conservative Association and Chairman of the Northern Counties Area. His pre-war constituency, Barnard Castle, bordered on Eden's own birthplace and the site of his first parliamentary contest, Spennymoor. Headlam was later MP for Newcastle North from 1940 to 1951 and a close observer of Eden throughout the war and the years of Opposition. Eden found him both congenial and sensible, and liked to use him as a sounding board. Headlam wrote vividly of Eden's home life:

> Friday 1 August (at Binderton House, Chichester). This is a charming house but too close to the main road – still one has a pleasing view towards the Downs – Goodwood in sight. No one here except Anthony and his son – a very tall youth of 16 at Eton. There are some charming pictures, some quite good furniture and the internal decoration of the house is pleasing – a fine staircase of the Charles II period and a finely moulded ceiling. A gave me a good welcome and I was well lodged for

the weekend. We have discussed men and things this evening. A was very communicative and friendly. He has great charm and one realises that he has ability – but one wonders whether he has the patience and forbearance which are required in a party leader, and whether he is a good judge of men.

The next day Eden unburdened himself to Headlam, who recorded their talk in his diary:

Saturday 2 August. It has been hot and sultry all day . . . Anthony and his boy played some lawn tennis and gathered early apples. A has been very friendly and forthcoming telling me all about his difficulties both domestic and political – his wife and Winston seem both to be worrying him. The former appears to have gone potty about some American who has now left her and gone back to his own wife – the latter is always being tiresome about one thing and another, and shows no sign of retiring from the active leadership of the party. A appears to be resigned to his wife's behaviour and is waiting for her to return to him – she is at present in Bermuda. He is restive about Winston – talks about giving up politics etc. My advice to him was to stick to the job – to abide in patience – not to retire when the ball was at his feet.[31]

Opposition gave Eden an opportunity to travel once more, rather in the manner of his early days in Parliament in the 1920s. Places he visited included Barbados, Trinidad, Rio de Janeiro, Persia, Bahrain and Saudi Arabia. Nor did he neglect the opportunity to address non-parliamentary audiences at home. In Warwick and Leamington he welcomed enthusiastically the 1948 Agricultural Charter, with its potential for rural revival,[32] and on 30 April he spoke at Guildhall on the European situation. Violet Bonham Carter wrote of the occasion:

I had some talk with Anthony about the prospects of war. He is one of the few people who had dealt with Stalin so his comments are interesting. He said he thought Stalin wld see further ahead than to believe that just to reach the Channel Ports wld do him much good in the long-run. I asked whether he still had power & this he cldn't say. He was critical of the F.O. as he said it seemed to have given up any attempts to keep in any sort of touch with the Russians. He agreed the Berlin situation was very ticklish & the worst danger-point. We cldn't move out – but the Russians might force us to seem to take the offensive.[33]

Eight days later, at the Congress of Europe meeting at The Hague, Violet Bonham Carter had a further talk with Eden about European integration. 'He is very definitely *not* a Federalist' she recorded.[34] Eden's lukewarm attitude to Europe was already well known. Pro-Europeans in all parties liked to claim Churchill, with his 'United Europe Movement', as one of their number after his Zurich speech of 19 September 1946, in which he spoke of 'a kind of United States of Europe'. Although Churchill was later to speak of 'a merger of national sovereignty,'[35] like Eden, he saw Britain's future world position as being primarily at the centre of three circles: the Empire, Europe and the Atlantic Alliance. (The North Atlantic Treaty Organisation – NATO – was established on 4 April 1949, as a vital defensive safeguard against Russian expansion in Europe.) 'Nothing could have been further from his thoughts,' one historian has commented, 'than the emergence of a European super-state presenting exactly those pretensions to executive authority which Churchill regarded as the prerogative of the nation-state.'[36] Neither Churchill nor Eden foresaw how the European issue was to become so divisive for all parties.

In early 1948, Eden had a complicated appendicitis operation. During his convalescence in the London Clinic, and later at Binderton, he began to read pre-publication presentation copies of the first two volumes of Churchill's war memoirs. He was far from happy with some of the emphasis, as he explained to Bobbety Salisbury:

> Winston has left me with his first two volumes, of which I had only seen up to the present the chapter on my resignation, of which you know. On a hasty glance I have the impression that we shall not like the Italian part very much, for he seems to have accepted the entire Van thesis on this – No doubt Van has been talking to him on these lines. I don't suppose it matters much, but I shall probably be driven to put pen to paper one day. It really is the greatest nonsense that Mussolini would have been on the side of law and order if only he had been allowed to gas the Abyssinians.[37]

In fact, Eden had already put in hand plans to write a book on his two spells as Foreign Secretary, engaging F. H. Hinsley of St John's College, Cambridge, who had served in the Foreign Office during the war, to help and advise on research. Eventually the work done at this stage became the core of *The Reckoning*, the third – and some would say the best – of his three volumes of memoirs, published in 1965. Eden's taste for renewed literary activity had been stimulated by reading Churchill's proofs, and the need to make money was once again a powerful impulse.

The King and Queen sent messages of encouragement to Eden after his operation, and Eden replied to Sir Alan Lascelles in a letter that revealed his feelings on the parliamentary situation:

> I have been gaining strength rapidly ever since I have been down here with the help of this wonderful weather. I hope to be quite fit in three weeks.

Meanwhile it is very agreeable neither to have to study the newspapers nor to attend the House of Commons. Watching the spring flowers bloom is a more congenial occupation than listening to Mr. Gallacher, or even Sir Waldron Smithers,* and even distance lends no enchantment to the parliamentary scene![38]

Eden's wry comments about William Gallacher, the Communist member for Fife West, and Sir Waldron Smithers, MP for Orpington and the epitome of the reactionary Conservative, showed his distaste for extremism at either end of the political spectrum, and his disenchantment with the increasingly confrontational nature of life in the House of Commons during the first Attlee Government. He kept Lascelles informed from time to time of things the Palace would not otherwise hear in formal submissions. In one letter Eden told Lascelles that he was 'fully occupied with a restless Tory Party whilst Lord Beaverbrook skirmishes on the flank. Couldn't you make him Governor of the Falkland Islands or something?!'[39]

It was not only the Tory Party that was restless. After the high hopes of July 1945, problems began to mount for the Labour Government in the austere post-war years of rationing and controls, the age of 'Fish and Cripps', as Macmillan dubbed it, after Dalton's resignation as Chancellor of the Exchequer in November 1947 following a Budget leak. Even the fish was likely to be that strange tinned variety from South Africa called 'snoek', beside which the ubiquitous wartime 'Woolton Pie' appeared appetising. The bitter winter of 1947 was the nadir, with fuel and food shortages, which led to the Tory slogan of 'Shiver with Shinwell and Starve with Strachey'.

In the international field, Bevin faced difficulties in Palestine, where the British Mandate ended in May 1948. Nationalism was becoming a potent force in Africa and Asia. India was partitioned with dreadful loss of life in sectarian violence, and in August 1947 gained independence.

---

*Sir Waldron Smithers (1880–1954) was, even in a strong field, one of the most antediluvian figures of the post-war Tory Party, and could have graced the pages of an Evelyn Waugh novel. Unlike Sir Herbert Williams, with whom he was often associated, and behind whose bluff exterior lay a keen brain, Smithers was regarded as an eccentric figure. He fulminated in the Westminster bars against the modernisers – 'bloody rubbish' – and when four votes were recorded at the 1947 Party Conference against Rab Butler's *Industrial Charter*, the wags said it was Waldron and a friend putting up both hands – an observation made before Smithers badly damaged his wrist by punching a wall in frustration at the direction the party was taking. After the *Charter* had been adopted, Sir Waldron, organist of his local village church in Kent, published a paper, 'Save England', liberally spattered with biblical quotations. 'Then considered to be on the lunatic fringe of the right,' Ian Gilmour has memorably observed, Smithers 'would now probably be thought a moderate Thatcherite'. Ian Gilmour, *Whatever Happened to the Tories: The Conservatives since 1945*, Fourth Estate, 1997, p.33.

Financial problems also multiplied after the convertibility crisis of July 1947, culminating in Cripps's devaluation of the pound in September 1949. In a speech at Harvard on 5 June, General Marshall had outlined his plan for economic aid for Europe. Eden was consulted by Bevin on how he should respond. His predecessor's enthusiasm for Marshall's vision – which Eden was later to describe as bringing 'new hope to Europe and the world'[40] – confirmed Bevin in his course of action, which Eden did all he could to support from the Opposition benches. Without Marshall Aid in June 1947 the prospect, not only for Britain, but for Europe as a whole, would have been very bleak. Eden also gave every encouragement to Bevin over the Brussels Treaty of 1948, which proved an important forerunner of NATO. Eden and Bevin had an influence at this time together that transcended their nominal positions. Attlee, like Churchill, faced a threat to his leadership in 1947, and it was not inconceivable that Bevin and Eden could have found themselves leading their respective parties.

Labour's myriad difficulties convinced many Conservatives that they had a genuine chance of recapturing power at the next election, despite the scale of the 1945 defeat, and the popular implementation of the main planks of the welfare state. Eden was not so sanguine. He always believed that the parliamentary mathematics would mean two contests before a return to office. Even so, he did not anticipate how greatly Labour's majority would be eroded. Many Conservatives believed that the party would have a better chance of recapturing the initiative under Eden's leadership, but Churchill showed no signs of retiring. As a result, Eden had the worst of both worlds, dealing with the day-to-day responsibilities, but lacking executive authority to shape strategy. The frustrations were increasingly clear to his colleagues, and in July 1948 Cuthbert Headlam noted in his diary, 'waiting to step into a dead man's shoes is always a tiring business, but when the "dead" man persists in remaining alive it is worse than ever.'[41]

The Conservative Party Conference took place, unusually, at Earls Court in London from 12 to 14 October 1949, and not at one of the regular seaside venues.[42] As several younger members wanted Churchill to step down, a circular letter was sent privately to all candidates, stating that the party's best hope for victory in 1950 was under Eden's leadership, and asking for support to that end.[43] The failure to win the South Hammersmith by-election in February 1949 had led to severe criticism of Churchill's leadership, disenchantment that had lasted throughout the year, with opinion polls now indicating that the Conservatives would do better under Eden's leadership. 'But the people love me,' Churchill said to the young psephologist David Butler. 'Why, when I came into my house the other day, there was a workman in the street with tears in his eyes as he greeted me.'*

Preparations for the 1950 Election were coordinated under Eden's Chairmanship of a sub-committee of the Shadow Cabinet that included Rab Butler, with David Clarke and Henry Hopkinson as the secretariat. The manifesto, *The Right Road for Britain*, sought to move the agenda from 'controls' to 'freedom'. Introduced by Eden on the BBC, it struck a chord with that section of the electorate disillusioned by the idea that 'the gentleman in Whitehall really does know best'.[44]

One of the dangers for a prominent national politician is neglect of his constituency. Eden never made that mistake. In 1949, as the Election approached, he made thirty extended visits to the constituency, now universally known as the Garden of Eden. A highlight of the year was the mass rally held at Stoneleigh Abbey in July to celebrate Eden's twenty-fifth anniversary as the local MP.[45] Since the spring of 1948 a new, young agent, John Devine, had held the fort for Eden in Warwickshire, following the sudden death of A. J. Gibbs, agent since 1931. Previously agent for Wednesbury, a Labour stronghold, Devine, who took office in the week of Eden's appendix operation at the London Clinic, had been interviewed and approved by him. For the next nine years Devine was to be a crucial part of Eden's electoral team. In London, Eden maintained day-to-day links with Warwickshire through Chloe Otto, an unflappable private secretary for many years, who was smitten by him and may even have harboured illusory, but unreciprocated, hopes.[46]

The first problem Eden and Devine addressed during his convalescence was the Boundary Commission's proposals, first mooted in October 1946, for widespread changes to the Warwick and Leamington constituency. Over the years it had grown to the unmanageable level of an electorate of 86,431, largely owing to the influx of workers in light industry, and to the merging with Stratford District after the First World War. Under the new proposals, the electorate would be reduced to 57,983, by the hiving-off of Stratford, Alcester, Shipston-on-Stour and Southam. In pre-war days, Warwick and Leamington had relied heavily on local figures of substantial means – businessmen, solicitors, landowners – not merely for financial support, but also, taking their lead from Lord Willoughby de Broke (and

---

*Butler had been summoned to Chartwell in February 1950 to explain the Cube Law of Elections which he had mentioned in an article in the *Economist* on 3 January. He was to be summoned again on 20 October 1951 to Hyde Park Gate. As they parted, Churchill asked Butler directly if he was a handicap to his party. After some hesitation, Butler replied to this infinitely embarrassing question, 'I don't think you are the asset you once were, Sir.' Dr David Butler to the author, 16 November 2001.

later Lord Leigh and Sir Fordham Flower), for paternalistic help for those less prosperous members of society. Although this element was still important and valued in the 1940s, its influence was inevitably diminished, a development Eden regretted, for it was the social and political tradition that he himself most admired. Yet Eden always felt that, despite its size of several hundred parishes, Warwick was, unlike an urban seat, one where it was still possible to know a vast number of constituents personally.

The proposed boundary changes posed a dilemma for Eden, and there was considerable speculation in the local Press as to which constituency he would choose to represent at the next General Election. The West Midlands, comprising six counties, was a volatile electoral district, often a significant pointer to the national mood and outcome, where nothing could be taken for granted.

Eden asked Devine to provide a study of how the two new constituencies – Warwick and Leamington, and Stratford and South Warwickshire – would fare after the changes. Devine took a comprehensive study to Eden at the House of Commons. His forecast – accurate, as it transpired – was that the 'old' seat, with the complete loss of the residential voters in Stratford Rural District Council and the dubious 'gain' (in electoral terms) of Kenilworth, would be much more difficult to hold, with a putative Conservative majority of 2,000–3,000 in an average year (discounting the advantageous factor of Eden's own personal vote). Stratford and South Warwickshire, on the other hand, predominantly rural and residential, should return a Conservative member with a more comfortable majority of 8,000–9,000. Eden's response to this information was selfless, and he opted to remain in Warwick and Leamington, insisting that a newcomer could not fairly be expected to take the responsibility of fighting the more difficult of the two seats.[47] He also recommended that the revamped local organisation should be known as the Warwick, Leamington and Kenilworth Conservative Association, and made Kenilworth one of his priorities when on constituency business. On 28 July 1948, Eden wrote to Sir Fordham Flower, Chairman of the Warwick, Stratford-on-Avon and Leamington Association, to say that he had decided to contest the new Warwick and Leamington seat ('A division that has lost its rural character,' according to the local Press),[48] and in January 1949 the new Warwick, Leamington and Kenilworth Conservative Association was formed.

Attlee called the Election, injudiciously for Labour as it transpired, for 23 February 1950. The campaign was fought on an old register, in bad weather, and entailed the cancellation of a planned Jubilee Conference that month to mark the Labour Party's half-century. Eden was adopted at the Nelson Hall, Warwick, on 30 January. When John Profumo was adopted as Conservative candidate for Stratford-upon-Avon for the 1950 Election,

Eden did everything he could to help. At one meeting outside the Stratford theatre, when Eden was speaking for Profumo, a heckler cried out, 'How can we have a man called Profumo in the home of Shakespeare?' Eden replied, 'Would you like us to change his name to Prospero?'[49]

Eden's routine on constituency visits had been long established, and merely went into overdrive at election times. The normal pattern was for him to 'come down' to Warwick on Friday afternoons, sometimes for a factory visit, but usually for an early evening function at the Conservative Association, perhaps drinks followed by a series of speaking engagements in village halls, or a dinner and speech in Leamington. Unusually for a Tory grandee of those days, Eden held Saturday morning surgeries, from ten till one, though in practice they often went on until two, or even later, which meant a rush before an afternoon fête or similar function at a local school. Henley-in-Arden was particularly favoured as a venue for the latter.[50]*

Saturday evening usually saw the big dinner of the weekend, or a dance at the Nelson Hall in Warwick, the sports and social club. When in the constituency, Eden tended to stay at Warwick Castle for three reasons – family connections, security (detectives always accompanied him) and privacy. Once a year a large function would be hosted at Warwick Castle, but Eden was aware that if the Conservative Association were using the facilities, they would be denied to other organisations who paid a commercial rate, and he took care not to abuse the hidden subsidy given to the Conservatives by the Greville family's hospitality.

Eden was a man of humility and humanity who possessed the gift of making those to whom he was speaking have his full attention, not as a form of political calculation, but because he was genuinely interested in their achievements and problems. Nigel Spearing, Labour candidate at Warwick and Leamington, found that this respect long survived Eden's time, even among Labour voters.† In October 1964 Spearing was canvassing in a small house in Leamington. As he left, the lady, who was a Labour voter, said to him, 'Before you go, I think you ought to know that Sir Anthony Eden has been in this room.'[51]

Eden was not overly optimistic about the Conservatives' national prospects in February 1950. At a local level, the keenest interest was in

---

*When Eden became Prime Minister, the local Labour Party felt they could make political capital out of a claim that Eden neglected his constituents' interests. When the Conservative Association got wind of this political tactic, they arranged for every ward to find two parishioners to write a letter outlining practical ways in which Eden had helped them in his years as MP. The flood of letters, way beyond what was asked for, or expected, meant that Labour quietly dropped their scheme – a good example of how sensitive political antennae among local party officers defused potential difficulties with the national Press.

†The local Labour Party even considered in 1955 whether putting up a candidate against Eden, the Prime Minister, might not be construed as being 'unpatriotic'.

how the majorities would work out in the newly divided seats. Both Eden and Profumo were comfortably returned. The figures announced were:

Anthony Eden (Conservative)	26,326
Howel Bithell (Labour)	17,512
Conservative majority	8,814

In fact, the Warwick and Leamington result, declared by the acting returning officer, Edgar Stephens, was one of the rarest of electoral phenomena, a result incorrectly announced and later amended by special declaration. At first glance in the rush of Election night, John Devine felt there was something wrong with the original figures, but as there was no question of a recount, the result was accepted. Next day a detailed check showed that the number of votes polled did not tally with the declared final totals. Devine rang Eden to point out that the complications of electoral law might delay his return to the Commons, or even require a second contest. So the returning officer was consulted, and when the error was discovered and conceded by Edgar Stephens, he sent the following letter to Eden and his opponent and released its contents to the Press:

My attention has been drawn to the fact that the total number of votes cast in the recent General Election for each of the two candidates in the Warwick and Leamington constituency, as officially announced after the count, does not correspond with the total number of votes actually polled in the division and recorded at the count.

An examination of the lists, from which the figures included in the announcement were taken, reveals that a line setting out the number of ballot papers counted at one of the tables was omitted, thus creating the deficiency in the total of the number of votes polled for each candidate. The correct figures are:

Eden	27,353
Bithell	18,400
Majority	8,953

I very much regret the mistake which was made. I may add that I have explained the facts to the agents of both parties who are satisfied as to the correctness of the amended figures.[52]

Nationally, the result was far closer. Labour won 315 seats, the Conservatives 298 and the Liberals nine, with three others. The cushion of the 1945 landslide had now been removed and the Tory cry was for 'One more heave'. In retrospect, the most significant development for Eden was Hugh Gaitskell's promotion to the Ministry of Economic Affairs. As

Cripps was a dying man, Gaitskell was in effect acting Chancellor, a vital staging post on his route to the Labour leadership during Eden's Premiership. Eden believed that an early attempt to drive Labour from office in the wake of the Election would be premature and counter-productive. In the Debate on the Speech from the Throne in early March, Eden promised no factious or fractious opposition, and the continuation of a bipartisan approach to foreign affairs. He was deeply suspicious of Harold Macmillan's attempts to persuade Churchill to press for a Government defeat within three weeks. 'I find it hard to forgive Harold M., who is less than 75, & has less excuse for this rapaciousness for high office,' Eden wrote to Bobbety Salisbury on 3 March, adding with uncharacteristic bitterness, 'Macmillan lives to toady.'[53]

Buckingham Palace continued to be anxious over the political uncertainty. On 20 April, Sir Alan Lascelles asked Eden how he felt things would unfold. Eden told him that he believed the Government would survive on a crucial division (on petrol supplies), adding that 'the majority of the Conservative front bench (*not* including its Leader) would not welcome the government's fall just yet'. But the Government's narrow majority meant that its survival was far from certain. After his talk with Eden, Lascelles recorded that 'it does not seem probable that the Government will be faced with resignation during the next few weeks, but even if this should happen the only difficult position which The King might be called on to solve is the decision to grant or to withhold a dissolution; in present circumstances the arguments in favour of granting it seem to outweigh those against it'.[54]

Among the intake of ninety-three Conservative MPs at the 1950 General Election, forty-one were destined for ministerial careers, and even Aneurin Bevan described it as the most notable Tory vintage in history. Eden was keen to identify the stars of future. He soon picked out Robert Carr, MP for Mitcham, after hearing him speak in progressive terms on industrial matters, of which he had extensive experience. Carr not only accompanied Eden on two important visits to Canada and America in 1950 and 1951, but then became Eden's PPS for four years after the Conservatives returned to power in October 1951, both at the Foreign Office and in Downing Street, before his first ministerial post at the Ministry of Labour.[55]

The summer of 1950 saw the last act of Eden's first marriage. On 8 June, just before his fifty-third birthday, Eden was granted his *decree nisi*. He made no comment on leaving the court and went straight back to work. In June 1950, the People's Democratic Republic in North Korea, with Soviet support, invaded South Korea, which was backed by the Americans. The South Korean capital, Seoul, fell on 28 June and the most serious threat to global peace since the end of the Second World War was under way. Eden gave Bevin every support over this conflict, an important factor since the Government's majority was so small, since February, and endorsed Truman's action in sending troops to Korea to repel the invasion. Fifteen nations, including Britain, contributed to a United Nations task-force. For Eden there were many parallels with the 1930s. The Soviets had a massive presence by way of divisions in Eastern Europe, and he was in no doubt that over Korea, Stalin was testing the temperature to see if there would be a vigorous, united response from the Free World. In a speech in the Commons on 5 July, Eden recalled his meeting with Stalin in December 1941, and how Stalin had said to him then that Hitler's great mistake was in not knowing when to stop:

> I suppose I smiled. At any rate Marshal Stalin turned to me and observed, 'You are smiling, and I know why you are smiling. You think that if we are victorious, I shall not know when to stop. You are wrong. I shall know.' Tonight I am wondering whether the time has not come when it would be well to stop.[56]

Nine months later the heroic defensive battle of Imjin River against Chinese-North Korean forces stirred Eden to make one of his few public references to his own military service:

> By the merest chance I happened to read this morning in an American newspaper an account of the recent fighting of the 29th Brigade in Korea, and in particular of the achievements of the Gloucester Regiment [Eden said in Parliament on 1 May 1951]. It is a column-and-a-half of the most magnificent writing & the most generous tribute. As one who has taken some part in these things, I could follow and live through every moment of this action.
>
> It is the warmest and most generous tribute to a British battalion one could imagine. I should like everyone to hear it on the wireless. I think it would do them good.[57]

On 30 January 1951, Eden wrote to his son Nicholas, now at Christ Church after National Service with his father's old regiment, about the political situation. 'Jim [Thomas] & James Stuart both believe the Govt. to be in a bad way, & a General Election likely soon.' Eden himself was not so sure. 'They may be right, but condemned govts can live long.'[58] Nevertheless, he was not happy with the drift of Churchill's tactics. 'Politically things are going well for us in the country, but I think we made a mistake to divide the House on defence this week,' he wrote on 17 February. 'I tried to persuade W of this before the event, but in vain. As a result we suffered our worst defeat, & gave Bevin an opportunity he used very well.'[59]

*

In January 1951 Eden heard that George VI was planning a visit to Warwickshire in the spring. He got in touch with Buckingham Palace, as he was keen that the King should visit his constituency during Festival of Britain year. 'I think the programme admirable,' he wrote to Sir Alan Lascelles on 17 February. 'I have only one small point I would like to offer, which is, that there are two routes from Warwick to Leamington Station; one is largely through fields and the other is through streets, including some poor ones. I do hope the latter, though less picturesque, will be chosen.'[60]*

The impending visit of the King caused John Devine to question whether Eden's constituency car, a second-hand pre-war Flying Standard, bought from a local farmer, would be the right vehicle in which to accompany the royal progress. Its provenance was only too obvious, with dents and ingrained mud, and its reliability uncertain – excuse enough to accept the loan of a chauffeur-driven Armstrong Siddeley from a local garage for the day. Eden casually asked his agent, John Devine, if he would like to meet the King and Queen, a thoughtful gesture, which in days of more relaxed security did not greatly disturb the arrangements, but was long remembered.[61]

Eden was well aware of how much Warwick and Leamington had changed since the days when the Countess of Warwick toured the streets with her milk-white steed. 'The constituency becomes steadily more industrial', he wrote to Nicholas at the time of the royal visit, 'with an influx of workers from Liverpool & South Wales.'[62]†

Eden remained very proud of local associations, delighting particularly in the fame of Sir Frank Whittle, inventor of the jet engine, who was a former pupil of Leamington College. In the spring of 1951, a very different Leamington world-beater came in the person of the middleweight boxer Randolph Turpin, who won the world title from Sugar Ray Robinson in a highly charged night of national pride at Earls Court. The achievements of Warwickshire County Cricket club that year also brought vicarious fame to the constituency, and in the summer of 1951, after he had been named as Parliamentarian of the Year, Eden wrote to his son Nicholas, 'What do you think of Warwickshire these days? The best boxer, the best cricket side and the best M.P.?!'[63]

Eden saw much of George VI in what was to be the last year of the King's life. The King felt (mistakenly, as it happened) that the Churchill era in domestic British politics was drawing to a close, and as Attlee's

---

*The latter was chosen, to the delight of the constituents whose homes were on the route.
†In the BBC2 *Reputations* programme on Eden (broadcast on 6 June 2000), Barbara Castle claimed that Eden had no understanding of 'ordinary' people, as he represented an archetypal leafy, affluent middle-class constituency. Both assertions are inaccurate.

Government continued to experience considerable difficulties, it was not impossible that Eden might become Prime Minister before the end of the year. As a result, the King made every effort to re-establish their wartime links, which, after a cautious start, had developed into feelings of real warmth. When it became clear that Churchill had no intention of fading from the scene, Eden was the recipient of many of the King's private thoughts. At the Diplomatic Party at Buckingham Palace in February, the King confided his anxieties to Eden. 'The King came up & I had a full twenty minutes, I should think', Eden wrote to his son. 'He was very frank about many things, including the Govt & Mr C! . . . The length of our talk was, of course, observed & commented on, but I don't think that matters. We are not in the days of Charles II & the poor man can't make me his first minister tomorrow, even if he wanted to!'[64]

Eden's finances continued to give him concern. 'Things are pretty grim in this poor country,' he wrote to Nicholas. 'Coal & travelling both up in price. Cost of living will continue to soar . . . I am very "broke".'[65] His interest in Gaitskell's first (and only) Budget, due on 10 April, was not merely political. 'We all expect further horrible taxes in next month's Budget,' he wrote to Nicholas on 3 March. 'I am trying with another directorship, which will not bring in much, but is not heavy work, & will help to keep a roof over our heads.'[66]

On 9 April, in his weekly letter to Nicholas, he wrote, 'The bills continue to go up – even though I put more ice in the cocktails – & the budget tomorrow is sure to contain more unpleasantness.'[67]

Whether the roof over their heads would continue to be Binderton ('Old Binders', as Eden affectionately called his Sussex house) was increasingly in doubt:

> It is impossible to tell how long this govt. will go on. Might be six months or longer or less. But the whole tone becomes daily more bitter – I cannot pretend that I enjoy it at all. I find I need my city activities more than ever to keep me sane, if not solvent. Also dear Binderton . . . Altogether I am weary of the endless publicity of political life too – & feel I'd love to escape to a combination of the City & Binderton. But I suppose that there is no life in which one is more a prisoner than politics.[68]

As Churchill showed no signs of retiring, Eden seriously considered going to the Lords and taking the title of Lord Baltimore. 'We are not having a very easy time with Mr C,' he wrote to Nicholas, 'who becomes very deaf & not a little impatient.'[69]

John Devine was invited to stay at Binderton in March. When it became clear that Easter Day would involve morning service at the local church, Devine was horrified to find that he had no small change and felt obliged to put his only pound note (a not insubstantial sum in 1951 from a lowly paid agent's salary) into the open collection plate. This left him without enough money for his return journey to Warwick, and with some embarrassment he asked Eden if he could borrow thirty shillings. Eden lent Devine the money before he departed, ten shillings of which Devine then used to tip Eden's butler, as he did not wish to commit any solecism on this his first visit to the country-house world. It later transpired at their next meeting in Warwick, when Devine returned the loan, that Eden himself had been short of ready money that weekend, and had actually borrowed the thirty shillings from his butler, later refunded with interest at Binderton. Both Eden and his agent were amused to find that, in this triangular instance of the Keynesian multiplier, it was the butler who had profited from deficit financing.[70]

When Bevin, a dying man, was made Lord Privy Seal in March 1951 and replaced as Foreign Secretary (on his seventieth birthday) by Herbert Morrison, Eden's criticisms of the Government's tepid response to Dr Mussadeq's nationalisation of the Anglo-Iranian Oil Company's refineries at Abadan that April were uninhibited. Eden's stance was motivated by concern for Britain's economic interests through maintenance of Middle Eastern oil supplies (this was before the days of North Sea oil). Unlike some Conservatives, he did not see the crisis primarily as an opportunity to show personal vindictiveness towards Morrison, with whom he felt a sense of camaraderie dating back to their joint membership of the wartime Coalition. He always regarded Morrison as Attlee's natural successor, and was disappointed when Gaitskell was elected Labour leader in December 1955.

On 14 April, Bevin died in harness, the key of a red box in his hand in the Lord Privy Seal's Office. Eden's feelings were profoundly stirred. He had admired Bevin as the best of Labour's men ever since the days they had worked together in the War Cabinet. He had an intuitive feeling for Trade Unionists and what would today be called 'Old Labour' figures. Bevin was the towering example of both traditions and a patriot through and through. The corollary was Eden's instinctive mistrust of the Labour 'intellectual', epitomised by Hugh Gaitskell, with whom he had little rapport. Adlai Stevenson, shortly to be the Democratic Party's candidate for the American Presidency, was another cerebral figure with whom Eden could never quite empathise.

Bevin's death came in the week of Hugh Gaitskell's controversial Budget, introducing charges on false teeth and spectacles. 'The govt. seems in pretty poor shape', Eden wrote to Nicholas on 16 April. 'Bevin's death is a loss to them, sick tho' he was – They may hold on until the autumn, but one can no longer exclude an election this summer.'[71]

Attlee again timed the Election badly. Although the Government was finding its small majority irksome, he could have soldiered on past the autumn of 1951. The minority Callaghan Government in the mid-1970s lasted for three years in far more parlous circumstances. But the King was due to be away on a tour of Australia and New Zealand in the New Year and Attlee felt that polling should not take place in his absence. In the event, the King was too ill to travel and his place was taken by Princess Elizabeth and the Duke of Edinburgh, only for them to return to Britain within a week when the King died on 6 February 1952.

During the 1951 recess Eden went to America again with Robert Carr. His reception was akin to that he was accorded in December 1938. Americans clamoured for $100 tickets for dinner in Chicago on 20 August after Eden's address (broadcast coast-to-coast on American radio) in the Concert Hall. He was widely seen as the British Prime Minister-in-waiting. Despite his gruelling schedule, which included a visit to Los Angeles, Eden made time to fly to New York for a day to see Beatrice, a sign of the ties that were never truly broken for him. Shortly after his return, Parliament was dissolved on 5 October and Polling Day set for 25 October.

The electorate in Warwick and Leamington was now a more manageable 56,766 and, despite his national commitments, Eden canvassed widely in the constituency on the party's keynote slogan of 'Set the People Free'. One of the sponsors on Eden's nomination form was Dick Turpin, the brother of Randolph Turpin, who in controversial circumstances had recently been denied membership of the local Conservative Association; this was a sign of solidarity from the Turpin family to show that they did not attribute any blame to Eden for Randolph's exclusion.[72]

In the course of the campaign, Eden made political and broadcasting history by appearing in the first televised Election broadcast in Britain, a carefully scripted exercise by a deferential Leslie Mitchell ('Well now, Mr Eden with your very considerable experience of foreign affairs'), who guided Eden through a pre-rehearsed sequence of questions, though 'the second half was an effective address straight to camera by Eden.'[73]* After the broadcast Mitchell dined with Eden at his new London home at 4 Chesterfield Street. It was a far cry from the confrontational broadcasting pattern of later years.

Eden's majority in Warwick and Leamington, in a straight fight against a new Labour opponent, saw a slight improvement on February 1950. The figures, with no mistakes in the accounting this time, were:

---

*Interestingly, Eden drew attention to the difficult domestic issues that the new Government would have to face, leading some to believe, particularly with hindsight, that it might have been a shrewd move for Eden, at least initially, to have taken a home department in Churchill's third and final administration.

Anthony Eden (Conservative)	28,282
William Wilson (Labour)	18,479
Conservative majority	9,803

In neighbouring Stratford, John Profumo had a majority of 10,795.*

Nationally, the Conservatives won an overall majority of seventeen seats on a slighter lower poll than that achieved by Labour.† In a contest that divided between domestic issues such as housing (on which Eden spoke widely) and international affairs, with both Churchill and Eden being accused by their opponents of being warmongers,[74] the push for Liberal votes had proved crucial, as the Conservatives won 321 seats, Labour 295 and the Liberals only six.

Churchill went to Buckingham Palace at 5.45 p.m. on 26 October to kiss hands on his appointment as Prime Minister. His first act on returning was to reappoint Eden to the Foreign Office. It was the fourth time in less than sixteen years that Eden had received such a commission, and during this term he passed even Sir Edward Grey's record length of service as Foreign Secretary.‡ It was like a man coming home. 'His return to office seemed to be everywhere greeted with delight and relief, as if a popular cricket captain had returned to the field', recorded his new private secretary, Evelyn Shuckburgh. 'I shall never forget walking with him into the Assembly on his first appearance at the United Nations in Paris in November 1951: Foreign Ministers and diplomats crowding up to welcome him on every side and everyone – including Eden himself – feeling that a new era had begun in Europe and for the cause of peace.'[75]

---

*Although Eden was not to know it, the 1951 Election was to be the penultimate contest of his parliamentary career, during which he lost once and was returned nine times.
†The position was to be reversed in another close election, that of February 1974.
‡Though Grey's eleven-year term – from 10 December 1905 to 10 December 1916 – was continuous.

CHAPTER THIRTEEN
Coming Home
1951-3

On 22 August 1951 Churchill was journeying to Venice by train.
At one point he escaped death by seconds when his detective
pulled him back from the train window seconds before a
concrete pillar almost grazed the train. 'Anthony Eden nearly got
a new job then, didn't he?' joked Churchill.
Norman McGowan, *My Years with Churchill*, 1958, p.101

If you drive a nation to adopt procedures which run counter to
its instincts, you may weaken and may destroy the motive force
of its action . . . You will realise that I am speaking of the
frequent suggestion that the United Kingdom should join a
federation on the continent of Europe. This is something which
we know, in our bones, we cannot do.
Anthony Eden speech, Columbia University, 11 January 1952

We are the transitional generation, who have climbed to the
watershed and will soon look down the other side, on a new
world. It will be wiser neither to think nor to speak too much of
the past.
Sir John Colville diary, 15 June 1952[1]

I feel like an aeroplane at the end of its flight, in the dusk, with
the petrol running out, in search of a safe landing.
Winston Churchill to R. A. Butler, 11 March 1954[2]

Peace is not just something that happens.
Anthony Eden, *Full Circle*, 1960, ch. VIII

Anthony Eden succeeded Herbert Morrison as Foreign Secretary on the afternoon of 27 October 1951, two days after the General Election. 'A great and signal improvement,' wrote Dean Acheson, 'except on Iran', where the American Secretary of State felt Eden was too dependent on advice from 'the bureaucracy of the Anglo-Iranian Oil Company, the Ministry of Fuel and Power, and the Treasury'.[3] Privately, Acheson was even more scathing, saying that over Iran, the British 'were behaving like a bunch of rug merchants'. When Eden got wind of Acheson's bluntness, 'his feelings were so badly hurt that Dean Acheson had to tread easy for a few days'.[4]

More than feelings were to be hurt in the next few years. The Abadan oil crisis that had so bedevilled Morrison's unhappy few months in office was not the only aspect that made Eden's return to the Foreign Office less smooth than it seemed on the surface. The confidence of the security services was at a low ebb in the wake of the defection to Moscow in June of the idealistic Communists Guy Burgess and Donald Maclean, who worked in the Foreign Office on specialist atomic-energy questions and who had attended the Anglo-American conferences on the subject. Eden did not want any retrospective blame attached to Morrison over a débâcle that could not have been predicted. In those days, the Foreign Office was a much smaller body, more like a family, and when it was found out that there were two black sheep, it went beyond mere professional abhorrence.[5]

Guy Burgess, at the time of his defection a Second Secretary at the Washington Embassy, had been Eden's chauffeur for his 1950 American visit, and despite his tendency to lose the car keys at crucial moments, they had got on well. Burgess's hostility to German rearmament, outlined on frequent journeys together round the American capital, had seemed to Eden more sensible than Churchill's. Burgess had also been instrumental in effecting a reunion between Eden and the ageing Cordell Hull.[6]

Eden had come back from Washington convinced that the question of German rearmament would be a central consideration for some years. Britain's participation (or otherwise) in the new European Defence Community (EDC), proposed on 25 October 1950 by the French Defence Minister, René Pleven, would also be high on the agenda if ever he became Foreign Secretary again. So it was to prove. And there was no shortage of other problems. The Cold War was at its peak, a seemingly irreconcilable conflict of ideology. With no sign of an armistice in Korea, this Cold War conflict was to drag on for nearly two more years, whilst the Abadan crisis was all too clear an indication of the political volatility and instability in the Middle East. The rise of Arab nationalism in Egypt, especially since Britain's withdrawal from Palestine in May 1948, was leading to demands that Britain abandon its Suez base, and for the abrogation of the Anglo-Egyptian Treaty that Eden had negotiated in 1936. In the Far East there were differences of opinion with Australia over whether Britain should join the Australian-New Zealand-United States (ANZUS) Pact, and fears of being drawn into France's colonial disputes in Indo-China. Britain's own colonial difficulties in Malaya and Kenya were to be an intractable problem for many years to come. For Eden, with his experience of the various crises of the 1930s and 1940s, 'coming home' might thus seem to be a case of *déjà vu*. But the situation was now markedly different.

From 1951 to 1955 the central theme of Eden's Foreign Secretaryship was that of maintaining Britain as a front-rank world power in the face of superpower competition and economic difficulty. Three key moments had seemed to cast doubt on Britain's worldwide role – the voluntary retreat from India in 1947; the abandonment in 1948 of the mandate in Palestine; and the loss of the oil refineries in Abadan in 1951. In a memorandum of June 1952 on Britain's overseas obligations, Eden recognised the country's fundamental dilemma:

> The essence of a sound foreign policy is to ensure that a country's strength is equal to its obligations. If this is not the case, then either the obligations must be reduced to the level at which resources are available to support them, or a greater share of the country's resources must be devoted to their support.[7]

Britain's inherited world responsibilities were of long standing, as Eden acknowledged in his memorandum, and yet, in the absence of a world security system, the country always faced the possibility of external threat, because it was highly vulnerable, not being a self-sufficient economic unit. This was, in essence, to be the problem of Suez. These financial difficulties were exacerbated by unrealistic expectations, particularly in the field of social welfare and military expenditure. 'We were all agreed when we took office that the defence programme we inherited was beyond the nation's means,' Rab Butler was to warn the Cabinet in October 1952. 'It was based on assumptions about American aid and the strength of our economy which have since been proved false', and he added starkly, 'we are attempting to do too much.'[8]

In the 1930s, Eden was a rising star, whose reputation towered over his far-from-sparkling predecessors. During the war, he was the acknowledged and admired lieutenant, whose work alongside Churchill was of vital importance to the war effort. Times had now moved on. In the autumn of 1951, Ernest Bevin's tenure of the Foreign Office was remembered with affectionate nostalgia by the diplomatic community. Bevin's flaws were considered venial. When he mispronounced foreign names, it was a question of 'Good old Ernie, heart of gold, knows what he's talking about', but when Herbert Morrison infamously pronounced Euphrates (in a foreign-affairs debate on 30 July 1951) as two syllables, with the emphasis on the first, there was no holding back the snobbish abuse.* After Bevin, Eden, with his pin-striped trousers and impeccable accent, was seen as a slightly anachronistic figure – ironically in part because of the impact of his own internal office reforms of 1943.

Eden had been out of office for six years and his main concerns in

---

*'Ernie Bevin didn't know how to pronounce the names of the places either,' was one such comment, 'but at least he knew where they were.' Private information.

Opposition had been with domestic reform and internal party reorganisation. Though Bevin and he had seen a great deal of each other, it was not
the same as directing policy himself. Inwardly, Eden was preparing himself
for the long-promised succession to the top job itself. It was to prove a
frustrating wait. Had Eden known in October 1951 that he would not
become Prime Minister until 6 April 1955, he would probably have retired
from politics that autumn.[9]

The main problem was Churchill's unwillingness to indicate his plans.
His Cabinet-making gave a fairly clear indication that he intended to
prepare for the long haul. Initially, Churchill retained the post of Minister
of Defence, a nostalgic exercise tacitly admitted to be a mistake when Earl
Alexander of Tunis was recalled from the Governor-Generalship of
Canada to take on the post in March 1952, only to be succeeded in turn
by a buoyant and ambitious Harold Macmillan, fresh from his triumphs at
Housing, in 1954. Rab Butler became Chancellor of the Exchequer;
Bobbety Salisbury,* Leader of the Lords and Lord Privy Seal; and Lord
Woolton, Lord President. Churchill's wartime allies, Lord Ismay and Lord
Cherwell, became Commonwealth Secretary and Paymaster-General
respectively. It was an elderly administration.

When Eden dined alone with Churchill on the night of the Conservatives' victory on 26 October, the Prime Minister broached the idea of
Eden combining, as in wartime, the two roles of Foreign Secretary and
Leader of the House. As Eden had previously found this double harness
nigh unsustainable, he refused to take on the Leadership of the House,
which was just as well, since in his first five weeks at the Foreign Office he
spent just eight days in London. The Leadership of the House passed to
Harry Crookshank, in addition to his responsibilities as Minister of
Health. Eden may not have relished the responsibilities of Leader of the
House, but he very much wanted the reassurance that he was recognised
formally as Deputy Prime Minister. Rab Butler was already being spoken
of in some quarters as the next leader 'if, for any unhappy reason, Mr Eden
fell out,'[10] and there was always the possibility that the Tories might skip
a generation altogether. To reassure Eden, Churchill agreed to a title that
had no constitutional validity. The difficulty came when the Cabinet list
was presented to the King. With his keen eye for precedence, the King
insisted that the appendage of Deputy Prime Minister be removed from
alongside Eden's name. Alan Lascelles had advised that such an arrangement might weaken the royal prerogative. The net result of the episode was
that Eden's probable succession, which he had wanted guaranteed, was
now shown to be only one possible option, depending on circumstances.

---

*'The People's Bobbety', as Lord Altrincham (John Grigg) ironically dubbed him.

From his point of view, Eden was now actually in a worse position, even though in practice he acted unofficially as Deputy Prime Minister.*

As Leader of the House, Harry Crookshank soon became disenchanted with Churchill's meanderings. At the interminable Cabinet meetings, he began to ask in not too disguised a stage whisper, as the clock moved inexorably towards 2 p.m., when the port was going to be passed round, especially as Churchill kept a large cigar box by his side from which he offered Eden alone the pickings.[11]†

On 16 June 1952, Harry Crookshank met with Bobbety Salisbury, James Stuart, the Scottish Secretary, and Patrick Buchan-Hepburn, the new Chief Whip, to see how best they could get Churchill to set a retirement date.[12] As in 1947, Eden was not involved. Again, the Chief Whip was despatched to Number 10, where he received cold comfort for his pains.

Two circles gathered at the heart of Government in 1951. The Churchillians in Number 10 included Lord Cherwell ('the Prof.'); Lord Ismay (soon to be joined from the warriors by Field Marshal Alexander); Jock Colville, recalled as private secretary, despite the fact that David Pitblado was already *in situ*; and trusted advisers, such as Lord Leathers and Lord Woolton. Nostalgia was the order of the day.

Across the road was Eden's team, at times feeling as isolated as Eden had done in the days of Neville Chamberlain and Horace Wilson. (Number 10 secretaries were generically dubbed 'Sir Horace' by Eden's team.)[13] Selwyn Lloyd was Minister of State, with Lord Reading (son of one of Eden's 1930s predecessors as Foreign Secretary) and Anthony Nutting as Under-Secretaries. Robert Carr began his important stint as Eden's Parliamentary Private Secretary, unusually following his master to Number 10 in 1955. 'He picked me out principally because I was lucky enough for him to hear my Maiden Speech in the House of Commons which was on the subject of industrial relations,' Carr later wrote, 'and I had no idea until he saw me afterwards, of the importance he attached to this and closely related subjects, and how much he wished to increase his information about them.'[14] It was a younger team, more interested in the future than the past, as shown by the fact that Eden was often seen socially, and in the House,

---

*Eden was more crestfallen than he need have been, for since the war the compensatory title of Deputy Prime Minister has proved something of a poisoned chalice, and in the long line from Herbert Morrison to John Prescott, only Eden has actually succeeded to the Premiership itself. *Vide* John Wheeler-Bennett, *King George VI: His Life and Reign*, Macmillan, 1958, p.797, and Vernon Bogdanor, *The Monarchy and the Constitution*, Clarendon Press, Oxford, 1995, pp.87–9. The list of Deputy Prime Ministers includes such 'nearly men' as Rab Butler, Reginald Maudling, George Brown, Willie Whitelaw, Geoffrey Howe and Michael Heseltine.
†Churchill was a Victorian, for whom luncheon was a meal taken after two. He never came to terms with the changed circumstances of the 1950s, when colleagues had speaking engagements an hour earlier and were therefore looking to leave the Cabinet room by 12.45 p.m.

in the company of forward-thinking Bow Group supporters.* Peter Tapsell, his personal assistant at the time of the 1955 General Election, was to come from its ranks.

Among the officials, the days of Vansittart, Cadogan and Moley Sargent were over. Sir William Strang was Permanent Under-Secretary – in some respects, with the lack of a public-school and Oxbridge background, the first major beneficiary of the Eden-Bevin reforms – and with him a formidable team of Deputy Under-Secretaries, including Roger Makins, Ashley Clarke, Bob Dixon and Frank Roberts. The key ambassadors included Oliver Harvey, Eden's former private secretary, in Paris; Ivone Kirkpatrick, a future Permanent Under-Secretary, as British High Commissioner in Germany; Oliver Franks in Washington; and Gladwyn Jebb as second holder of the new post of Ambassador to the United Nations. The private office was headed by Evelyn Shuckburgh. It was a variegated team and Eden was in his element as its coordinator.

His return to the Foreign Office brought a sense of stability, not least in the House of Commons. Although Eden was never considered a sparkling orator, he did bring a sense of gravitas to his exposition of the themes of the hour, which impressed people on opposite sides of the political spectrum. 'He held the House of Commons,' Jo Grimond, later Liberal Party leader, has written of these times. 'He made Foreign Affairs appear important and British foreign policy as explained by him seemed of weight and significance. No one else could do it as well.'[15]

Before speeches Eden would immerse himself in the details of his brief, sometimes for three weeks, and this paid dividends. For Julian Amery, one of the right-wing Suez Group from 1954, who opposed withdrawal from the Canal Bases, Eden was then the consummate professional. Winding up foreign affairs debates is a notoriously boring, and difficult, parliamentary responsibility. Yet Eden accomplished the task brilliantly, making people understand even the most wearisome detail, going back on points if necessary to avoid confusion – in short, he was an elegant practitioner of the diplomatic arts.[16]

The early 1950s were lived under the shadow of nuclear war. 'The election has had a real result on both parties,' Richard Crossman, Labour MP for Coventry, wrote in his back-bench diary. 'It has made them realise that the people of this country really do want peace and I fancy Winston and Eden have a better chance than Attlee and Morrison. The latter had to lean over

*The Bow Group was founded in 1950 by Peter Emery and Denis Walters. It took its name from the Bow and Bromley Conservative Club, its first meeting place. From 1957, its magazine *Crossbow* was essential reading for progressive Conservatives. In essence, the Bow Group was the post-war equivalent of Eden's YMCA.

backwards in being pro-American for fear of being accused of appeasing Communism. Winston and Eden have to lean over backwards trying to get peace with Stalin, in order to rebut the charge of warmongering.'[17] Even here, détente with Russia was to complicate the relationship between Churchill and Eden. If a summit was to be held with Stalin, then clearly Churchill would be the man to lead the British delegation, as at Yalta and Potsdam. However, the longer that summit was delayed, the longer Churchill could justify staying on as Premier. When Stalin eventually died in March 1953, Churchill could claim that he must get to know the new · regime, so that Eden was frustrated again.

The European question also had its complications, though William Strang with typical forthrightness believed that the best and simplest policy was to keep America in and Russia out.[18] British integration in Western Europe was for Eden another matter altogether. In a manner that has attracted both praise and obloquy, he made it clear that Britain had no place in a European federation. The French had surprisingly launched the initiative of the Schuman Plan in May 1950, a proposal for a central authority to take over control and production of all steel and coal in Western Europe. This was followed in October by the Pleven Plan for an integrated European Army. Eden made it clear in a Press Conference at the end of the four-day NATO meeting in Rome on 28 November 1951 that no British military formations would be made available, disappointing the EDC countries, which interpreted Eden's assurance of close relations as a fig-leaf for less than full-hearted European commitment.

In fact, Eden wanted 'a united Europe because the security and prosperity of Europe can only be achieved by united efforts'. It was only when 'plans for uniting Europe take a federal form that we cannot ourselves take part, because we cannot subordinate ourselves or the control of British policy to federal authorities.'[19] He wrote to Churchill on 15 December 1951, 'We want a united Europe. There is no doubt about that, or our sincerity',[20] and in the Commons on 5 February 1952 Eden reiterated:

> It is also our intention to associate ourselves as closely as possible with the EDC in all stages of its political and military development . . . There is one thing I must make plain . . . Let it be clearly understood that we on this island are resolved to maintain armed forces on the continent of Europe for as long as is necessary.[21]

In January 1952 Eden accompanied Churchill on a nine-day visit to Washington for talks with Truman and Acheson, the first substantial opportunity to discuss issues on which Britain and America had differed during the latter months of Attlee's administration. Before the visit, Churchill and Eden had exchanged views with the French Government at the Hôtel Matignon, Paris, on 17 December 1951. Eden's fear was that the downside of the EDC might be a lessening of the American commitment in Europe. In Washington, Dean Acheson reassured him that this was not the case. Eden's position remained that he would support the EDC, as the 'safe' way to see German rearmament within a supranational structure. But Britain would not join it. If the EDC failed, then he would propose a new structure.

Churchill was in an expansive and nostalgic mood during much of the Washington trip, asking the Prof. (Lord Cherwell) – who was in the party along with Pug Ismay and Oliver Franks – to calculate how high a tide the combined total of alcoholic beverages he had consumed in his lifetime would make, if poured into the wardroom of the *Williamsburg*, Truman's presidential yacht. Eden confined himself to discussing American attitudes on the Soviet Union, Korea, European integration and the EDC, and the rising nationalism in Iran and Egypt.[22]

Whilst in America, Eden was given an honorary degree at Columbia University. In his speech on 11 January, he addressed the 'European question' directly:

> The American and British peoples should each understand the strong points in the other's national character. If you drive a nation to adopt procedures which run counter to its instincts, you weaken and may destroy the motive force of its action.
>
> This is something you would not wish to do – or any of us would wish to do – to an ally on whose effective co-operation we depend.
>
> You will realise that I am speaking of the frequent suggestions that the United Kingdom should join a federation on the continent of Europe. This is something which we know, in our bones, we cannot do.

What Violet Bonham Carter had already discerned privately, regarding Eden and European federation, was now made clear publicly in one of his most significant speeches. But Eden denied that it meant he was 'anti-Europe':

> Is this to abandon Europe?
>
> We have played a leading part in the reconstruction of the economy of Europe. We have promised our full support to all European efforts to achieve greater unity. Our position on all this is well understood by our European friends. When the Prime Minister and I were in Paris, shortly before we came to you, we had talks with the French Government on these matters, and the statement which we issued jointly then showed how thoroughly we are agreed. I do not think there should be any more misunderstandings.[23]

But misunderstandings remained. The French thought Britain was moving towards an isolationist stance, whereas the Americans were suspicious of Britain's continued pretensions to a leading world status, as some kind of honest broker between the superpowers.*

Eden's phrase 'which we know, in our bones, we cannot do' became as famous retrospectively as that about the 'property-owning democracy', and was cited by critics as a sign of his supposed inflexibility and hostility towards Europe, when in fact it was defining his response towards 'federation'.

The contemporary political situation in Europe must not be overlooked. France and Italy were unstable, and Germany was an uncertain new democracy. Many in Britain, with memories of Britain's relatively recent wartime place at the world's top diplomatic tables, wondered whether it was really worth joining a federation with these, or other smaller and less important countries, though in his speech on the Schuman Plan in the Commons in June 1950, Churchill had said, 'We must find our path to world unity through the United Nations Organisation, which I hope will be re-founded one day upon three or four regional groups, of which a united Europe should certainly be one.'[24]

Such general aspirations, however, did not concern themselves with the small print. Even membership of related organisations such as the European Defence Community was unappealing to many. 'Nobody at that time thought that we could have joined it [the EDC] and to have attempted to substitute a non-federal plan,' Eden wrote to Robert Carr in July 1969, 'would have created confusion and resentment.' For Eden, 'the only course was to help the EDC from without as the previous government had proposed.'[25] At the time (in June 1952) he told the Cabinet that he saw Britain's policy as one of 'encouraging the movement towards federation in Europe and associating the United Kingdom as closely as possible with it short of a merger.'[26]

Eden's overall attitude was in fact very similar to Churchill's often over-looked conclusion to his Zurich speech when he had stressed that Britain would be partners of, not participants in, the European unity. As Churchill was to write to his constituency Chairman, Mrs Moss, in Woodford in August 1961 after Britain had applied to join the EEC, there was one role Britain could never abdicate and that was leadership of the Common-wealth, though that of course was not incompatible with joining the EEC.[27]

*

---

*The concept of 'Great Britain's position in the world as some kind of honest broker' was mercilessly satirised in 1962 during Macmillan's Premiership and Kennedy's Presidency in the revue *Beyond the Fringe* – 'I agreed with him, when he said that no nation could be more honest; and he agreed with me, when I chaffed him and said that no nation could be broker.' Roger Wilmut (ed.), *The Complete Beyond the Fringe*, Methuen paperback, 1987, p.54.

One unfortunate by-product of the Washington meeting concerned John Foster Dulles, Truman's special representative in negotiating the Japanese Peace Treaty. When Dulles released the 'Yoshida letter' (from the Japanese Prime Minister) recognising the Nationalists in Formosa as the Chinese Government, without informing the British in advance, Eden felt betrayed and compromised. As a result, in the words of Dean Acheson's biographer, 'a residue of suspicion remained on Eden's part, especially against Dulles for what he considered a devious trick'.[28] Churchill was more forthright, regarding Dulles as the only bull he knew that carried around his own china shop.[29] These things were not to be forgotten later at Geneva and Suez.

On his return from Washington, Eden went straight to Paris to report to Maurice Schumann on the American talks, but despite his best endeavours could not satisfy French demands over mutual aid in the event of military aggression. Nevertheless, he agreed to alter the emphasis in his forthcoming statement to the Commons on military integration of air forces, to meet at least some of Schumann's concerns.

On the afternoon of 5 February, Eden opened a two-day foreign-affairs debate, in the wake of a deterioration of the position in Egypt.[30] Fighting had broken out near Ismailia and British troops had been in action against Egyptian insurgents. Shepheard's Hotel in Cairo had been looted, and Nahas Pasha, the Prime Minister, and his ministers dismissed by King Farouk on 27 January. Eden had instructed Ralph Stevenson, the British Ambassador, to resume negotiations with the Egyptians, and his statement in the House – 'admirable and calm,' wrote Dean Acheson – was notable for its restraint.[31]

In the early hours of 6 February 1952, George VI died at Sandringham.

Eden had been a recent guest and the unexpectedness of the news shocked him. The King had been gravely ill, but he seemed to have turned the corner. Eden was deeply saddened by this death, as he had got to know George VI well during the war, and then in the years of Opposition when the Attlee Government was in difficulties and it seemed that Eden might soon be the new Premier. Also there was the unspoken link that the King had seen action as a midshipman at Jutland, like Eden's long-lost younger brother, Nicholas. Eden's personal tribute to the King's devotion to duty – in which he quoted Henry V's lines, 'What infinite heart's ease Must Kings neglect that private men enjoy!' – was printed and circulated widely, especially among his constituents in Warwick and Leamington. Eden was the first Cabinet minister to address the House at the beginning of George VI's reign, and, on 5 February 1952, the last.[32]

On 7 February Eden went with Churchill and Attlee to Heathrow to meet the new Queen on her return to Britain from Kenya, and the photograph of the grave counsellors of state greeting the young sovereign was to be an unforgettable image of the new reign. Eden had now served four monarchs. For the second time he was Foreign Secretary and, at the beginning of a new reign, as in January 1936 on the death of King George V, he liaised with the overseas dominions and the telegrams were soon winging their way across the world.

The large attendance of foreign politicians at the King's funeral on 15 February meant that Eden had the opportunity for extensive talks with Dean Acheson over Korea, Egypt and Iran, and with Acheson, Maurice Schumann and Konrad Adenauer, the West German Chancellor, over unresolved EDC matters, ahead of the forthcoming Lisbon Council of NATO. Anglo-American agreement was reached on guaranteeing the EDC against either external or internal challenges and did much to pave the way for the successful Lisbon meetings later in the month. 'Working funerals' were later to become an accepted concept in international relations, but Eden was one of the first to realise their potential. At the meetings, Adenauer made it clear that German participation in the EDC – what he called full integration into Western Europe – was an essential pre-requisite to his country's reunification, but as this came with stringent conditions, the French National Assembly was to reject Schumann's advocacy of German inclusion, even though Acheson considered that 'the choice was between the European Defence Community and a national German army, general staff and all the rest.'[33]

The arguments continued over the weekend of 16/17 February, with Acheson still advocating Germany's inclusion in a grand defensive alliance. Eden was able to assure Schumann, who feared the consequences of any later German secession from the EDC, of Britain's solid support and continued military presence on mainland Europe. As the topics under consideration included the Saar, Eden could be forgiven for thinking he was back in the 1930s. His patience and diplomatic skill meant that the Foreign Ministers headed for Lisbon, after a convivial dinner at 1 Carlton Gardens, with a better understanding of each other's feelings. Adenauer, in expansive mood, promised to be kind to the French in his memoirs, and the French responded likewise. Acheson told Eden this was a bad deal, as Adenauer's age meant he was more likely to die first.[34]

Before leaving for the NATO Council meeting in Lisbon, Eden submitted a memorandum to Cabinet on the current state of European unity:

> The movement for unity in Europe, which led to the creation of the Council of Europe, is now flowing along two main streams: the Atlantic Community, a wide association of states which, without formal surrender of sovereignty, is achieving increasing unity of purpose and action

through the machinery of the North Atlantic Treaty Organisation; the European Community, a small group of states which are moving towards political federation by the progressive establishment of organisations exercising supranational powers in limited fields.[35]

Like Churchill Eden believed that Britain's position was at the hub of the various interlocking circles, of which Europe was but one, together with the United States and the Commonwealth. (He was to make this concept the centrepiece of his speech at the Conservative Party Conference in Margate in October 1953.) He considered the Council of Europe, founded at The Hague in 1949, to be stranded between the two streams identified in his memorandum. It needed, in Eden's view, a more concrete, less nebulous purpose, but without elaborate superstructure.[36] With the advent of the European Coal and Steel Community, he proposed that the Council of Europe's most effective function would be to serve that new body directly, together with the EDC, and any other new bodies that might be formed. To his gratification, 'the Eden Plan', as it became known, received wide publicity and was adopted unanimously by the Council's Committee of Ministers in May. Much of the background work had been done by Anthony Nutting, who was clearly Eden's protégé. The political links with Europe were now close and fruitful, but remained, as Eden wished, well short of federation.

Eden was not an anti-European. 'Anthony Eden has been something of a hate figure for British enthusiasts for membership of the European Community', the official historian of the links between Britain and the European Community has written. 'Relentlessly criticised as being either indifferent or antagonistic to continental federalist aspirations, Eden was neither. He did not believe such aspirations were for Britain. Nor did he believe that there was anything Britain should or could do to divert them. He was not in the least antagonistic to them; other members of the government, who played a much more assertive role in the Council of Europe, and often found it approved by 'pro-Europeans', were.[37] Eden's views were in fact much more balanced and consistent than he has been given credit for, and he proved observant of the implications of his colleagues' varied proposals and observations. 'What Macmillan's paper [on the Eden Plan] seems to me to ignore', he wrote to Churchill on 17 March 1952, 'is that so much of Europe wants to federate.'[38]

On 19 February, Eden flew to Lisbon for the NATO Council meeting. He was accompanied by Sir Edwin Plowden, Chief Planning Officer in the Treasury, who earlier that day had first heard, with some dismay, of the economic plan called 'Operation Robot'. To Plowden's relief, the plan, which had serious ramifications for Britain's foreign relations, could not go ahead without Eden being consulted. Plowden explained his reservations to Eden and, as a result, the Council meeting in Lisbon was to be remembered not for continued discussions over the EDC, or for the increase in the number of NATO divisions in Europe over the next two years – central though these were to its agenda – but for Eden's decisive intrusion into the field of economic policy.

Over the winter, as the economic position had worsened, a group of Treasury mandarins – Sir Leslie Rowan, George Bolton and Otto Clarke – had persuaded Rab Butler to advocate a scheme, acronymically named ROBOT after its progenitors, which envisaged the immediate convertibility of sterling, linked with a floating exchange rate (currently set at $2.80 after the Cripps devaluation of 1949), together with a blocking of the sterling balances. The package would inevitably entail painful deflationary policies. Lord Woolton was the first Cabinet minister to insist that Eden must be consulted, as the scheme affected Britain's relations with Foreign and Commonwealth Governments, not to mention the EDC. Without this intervention, ROBOT could have been nodded through and been included in the Budget, then planned for 4 March, with severe consequences for unemployment, whatever its other benefits.

When Eden received details of ROBOT in Lisbon, he urged that no decision be taken until his return to London. His letter to Churchill, written in consultation with Edwin Plowden, cast crucial doubts over the viability of the proposals, arguing that ROBOT should only be contemplated as a last resort, because of its profound implications for employment and Britain's foreign relations.[39] His letter brought a pause for reflection. The fact that his view prevailed showed Eden's standing in the party and his concern for what Disraeli had called 'the condition of the people'. His fears were threefold: convertibility would threaten the dollar reserves, as in the 1947 financial crisis (he was not convinced by so-called safeguards against such an eventuality); secondly, deflation would adversely affect the property-owning democracy; and finally the Trade Unions, responsive to Walter Monckton's emollient approach as Minister of Labour, would be unnecessarily antagonised. Eden was unconvinced that the price mechanism would successfully regulate an economy that was in essence put on automatic pilot, and felt that the plan was being rushed and would have unforeseen consequences. It was the triumph of common sense over the dismal science. Eden later wrote:

> While I was in Lisbon [Sir Eric] Berthoud [Assistant Under-Secretary at the Foreign Office] came out with a senior Treasury man [Herbert Brittain], sent by Winston, with an outline of Budget intentions. I did not like them at all. They seemed to me ill thought out & I was by no means convinced that they would work. In such conditions I couldn't endorse proposals that would strike a grievous blow at some of our

Commonwealth friends, throw Europe into disarray & impose increased unemployment (so I judged) on our own people ... Next day saw [Sir Edwin] Plowden, who I found took much the same view. Wrote to W urging no commitment. He was not enthusiastic himself.

When Eden returned to London, he dined alone with Churchill and told him of his concerns over ROBOT:

At Cabinet in due course expressed my views which I found were shared by Leathers, Prof (more violent) & later Bobbety ... I was much troubled about all this. Later Roger Makins arrived back from Mid East & I was greatly relieved when he told me that I had been 100% right. The Treasury was much divided. Some parts of it inclined to be rather hysterical. Not impressive.[40]*

A decisive meeting took place on 25 February between Churchill, Eden and Butler. After Eden had declared that ROBOT would undermine all that he was trying to achieve in Europe, Churchill turned against the plan, and when C. F. ('Kim') Cobbold, Governor of the Bank of England, joined the group, it was clear to him that the scheme was doomed.[41] Further opposition at the Cabinet meetings on 28 and 29 February meant that, to Butler's chagrin, the Budget had to be put back a week to 11 March, to take account of changed circumstances.

Plowden was in no doubt as to the importance of this intervention, writing later that 'Eden stepped in at a critical moment to arrest the momentum which the plan had developed and gave its opponents more time to organise.'[42] As these opponents included Cherwell, Crookshank, Salisbury and Macmillan (and other Cabinet ministers as the disadvantages were rehearsed), together with economic advisers such as Plowden, Robert Hall and Donald MacDougall, it was one of Eden's most important interventions in economic policy and Butler never really forgave him for it.[43]

An interesting footnote to Eden's part in ROBOT is recorded in Gaitskell's diary on 9 November 1954. Political advantage had not been among Eden's considerations in moving to stop the plan, but Labour's former Chancellor, and shortly to be its Leader, was in no doubt that ROBOT would have been disastrous for the Conservatives' electoral prospects, even berating Plowden for having given his opponents such sensible advice:

---

*The lengthy diary entry begins on '14 February' in a ruled 1952 office diary, but was clearly written later, as the first meeting with Plowden was over the weekend of 22–3 February, the meeting in London with Churchill and Butler was on 25 February, and the two Cabinet meetings that scuppered the plan were on 28 and 29 February. In all probability, Eden wrote up his account on the evening of 29 February, and, as a single day's space would not suffice, turned back a few pages into an earlier part of the month and then wrote without restriction.

'I wish you had not advised him that way. If they had been so foolish as to go for convertibility, we might now be back in power, or at least have a much better prospect of getting there.'

'That', said Edwin, 'is exactly what I told the Foreign Secretary. "If you want to stay in power,", I said, "do for heaven's sake reject his proposal." '[44]

Eden was relieved that the Foreign Office did not replicate the internal divisions at the Treasury. He attributed this to working with people he knew, or with newcomers whom he implicitly trusted. In the first category he counted Pierson Dixon, Harold Caccia and Anthony Nutting, all of whom had had previous spells as his private or parliamentary secretary. Among the newcomers, Robert Carr was proving an outstanding success as Eden's Parliamentary Private Secretary, particularly on the domestic side. 'He is one of the few back benchers on our side who knows industrial problems and transport problems from the inside,' Eden was to write to Churchill, '& his ability is, I consider, first rate.'[45] Younger blood was being encouraged on all sides, but there was still no sign that the elderly occupant at Number 10 would move over.

On 26 June, Acheson addressed both Houses of Parliament and in the course of private conversations gave details of the Yalu River bombings in Korea, of which Britain did not have advance notice. Eden found this another tiresome example of Acheson's imperiousness. Relations between the two were not easy. At an audience with the Queen in February, at the time of the King's funeral, Acheson had breached diplomatic conventions by rehearsing all his points of disagreement with Eden. There were sharp words between Eden and Acheson in Lisbon at the NATO conference.[46]

Now Eden felt that he was being further compromised on Korea. *Newsweek* soon picked up on their lack of personal chemistry, pointing out that matters were not improved by Acheson's oft-repeated view that Bevin was the greatest of British Foreign Secretaries, whilst Eden regarded Cordell Hull as nonpareil on the American side.[47]

On 1 July Churchill spoke in the Commons on the Yalu bombings and faced heavy criticism from the Labour benches. 'Rarely has he been more devastating,' wrote Chips Channon in his diary, 'perhaps he is aware of the growing Tory discontent.' Not only was Churchill aware of these rumblings, he was prepared even to joke about the succession, and within Eden's hearing. At a lunch for Acheson at Downing Street, Churchill had deliberately teased Eden by taking Acheson to the window and explaining that the poplars along the garden wall would have to come down because they obscured his view of the annual Trooping the Colour. As this ceremony had already taken place that year, the implication was obvious, and Eden, taking the bait, left his conversation with Maurice Schumann to protest. Acheson recorded the outcome:

'Why not?' demanded the Prime Minister. 'I live here, don't I?'

Eden agreed, but added reasonably enough that living there did not mean owning the place. Then the trap was sprung.

'Ah!' Churchill said sadly. 'I see what you mean. I'm only the life tenant. You're the remainder man.' To my relief Schumann got the point without translation or explanation.[48]*

In the summer of 1952 Eden married Clarissa Churchill, only daughter of Winston Churchill's younger brother, Major John Spencer-Churchill and Lady Gwendeline Bertie, daughter of the 7th Earl of Abingdon. Like her cousins, Randolph and Mary Churchill, she is a granddaughter of Lord Randolph Churchill.

Clarissa Churchill had hesitated before accepting Eden. Not only was there an age difference of twenty-three years, but her interests were not at that time political, and she took advice from her friend Woodrow Wyatt, Labour MP for Birmingham Aston, about the duties expected in those days of a constituency wife, and the inevitable appearances on the international stage. She had studied art in Paris in 1937, and philosophy in Oxford, where her wide circle of friends included Isaiah Berlin, Maurice Bowra and Lord David Cecil (of Eden's Oxford Uffizi Society). She was exceptionally well read, especially in French literature, and had a discerning taste in art and letters, counting among her friends Cecil Beaton, Cyril Connolly, Anthony Powell, Lucian Freud and Peter Brook. Travel was an enthusiasm; she had been in Romania in August 1939, when the question of her safety in the event of war had greatly exercised Winston Churchill.

Unlike many of her aristocratic contemporaries, who toiled not, nor span, from the start Clarissa Churchill had made her own way, an experience that made her equally at home in the worlds of Hatfield and Fitzrovia. During the war, together with Anthony Nutting, she had decoded ciphers in the Communications Department at the Foreign Office, where she had greatly impressed Jock Colville with her independence and efficiency. After the war she worked for *Vogue*, reviewing cultural matters; then for Sir Alexander Korda, in the publicity department of London Films, a golden era for British cinema; then for the publisher George Weidenfeld on his new venture *Contact*, which she edited.

Although she had first met Anthony Eden in 1936 as a fellow guest at Cranborne, when her main memory was of his tweed pinstripe trousers

---

*Churchill was to be in Downing Street for two further ceremonies of Trooping the Colour.

with matching bottle-green tweed jacket, it was only in the late 1940s that she became part of his life, going to house parties at Binderton and sharing visits to London's galleries and theatres. They decided in January 1952 that they would get married, but Eden wanted to keep it secret until August, 'the silly season', to avoid too much publicity. Eden wrote first to his son, Nicholas, who was now serving in Ottawa as aide-de-camp to Vincent Massey, the first native-born Governor-General of Canada: '*an utter secret* . . . it will be as quietly as we can contrive & probably next month.'[49] At the same time, Clarissa wrote a touching letter to 'Aunt Clemmie', who was travelling on the Continent:

> Anthony Eden & I want to get married as soon as possible now. I do so hope you will be pleased about this & give us your blessing. We have known each other for some time, & we decided a few months ago that we would like to be together for always. I am terribly happy about it, & only wonder & hope that I will prove capable of being some comfort & help to him in his life.
>
> I have wanted you to be the first to know our news. I have not seen Uncle Winston, though I hope he will be able to see me for a moment in the course of the next few days.
>
> We plan to make an announcement in the papers, giving no date, & then be married a day or so later. I do hope you will be back in England soon. We both want you to be there.[50]

Clarissa Churchill's hopes were to be fulfilled. It was the beginning of a serene marriage of great happiness that lasted a quarter of a century. Without her 'comfort & help', Eden would certainly not have survived for twenty years of fulfilled retirement. Eden's private life had not been uneventful in the past, but such adventures were now over for good. He had found harbour after the storm, calm and peace, and was the most loyal and solicitous of husbands.

The Churchills gave the marriage the best possible send-off. 'Aunt Clemmie' returned from the Continent, hastily and with some difficulty, changing her plans so as to make all the arrangements for a Downing Street wedding. As Clarissa's mother had died in 1941, and her father in 1947, Winston Churchill took on the paternal duties and gave his niece away at the ceremony.

The announcement of the Edens' engagement was made on 12 August and the marriage took place two days later. They had hoped for the minimum of publicity, but August is traditionally a quiet month for news, and in the drab aftermath of the King's death, good news was seized upon by the media as manna from heaven. Against their wishes, the Edens' wedding – 'The Romance of the Year', as the cinema newsreels proclaimed it – became a quasi-royal event that made headlines around the world, as

Clarissa Churchill joined Violet Bonham Carter and Olwen Carey Evans (daughters of Asquith and Lloyd George respectively) as one of only three brides to have been married from Downing Street in the twentieth century.

As Eden was a divorced man, the actual marriage took place at Caxton Hall, a venue suggested by the Archbishop of Canterbury, Dr Geoffrey Fisher, who swiftly dismissed any question of a church ceremony.[51]

In a notorious leading article, the *Church Times* was not slow to criticise, drawing comparisons with the Abdication and declaring how far public standards had fallen since 1936. In a robust response, the *Manchester Guardian* said that the remarks 'will rather make most of us glad that we do belong to "a pagan generation" if the alternative is the rule of an intolerant clericism'.[52]

It is difficult for later generations to understand the standards by which Eden's divorce and remarriage were judged in some quarters. Questions continued to be about whether Eden would be able to fulfil his duties over ecclesiastical preferment, if ever he became Prime Minister. At Lambeth Palace, Dr Fisher was in receipt of many letters of protest from church-goers around the country. A typical reply from the Archbishop* contained the following observations:

> It is a distressing thing that Anthony Eden should marry again after divorce. As to the divorce itself I am sure that there was no moral error on Anthony Eden's part: it was a flat refusal by his wife to be married to a politician any longer or in the end to live in England. Thus the stigma which attaches to Anthony Eden is not, so to speak, in the ordinary sense a moral stigma but, if one may put it like that, an ecclesiastical stigma of departure from a true understanding of what the Church Law requires. Even so, as I say, it is very distressing in the case of one in his position.[53]

Eden was never keen on clerics. Had he known of this letter, Fisher might have come even lower in his estimation than he did anyway.

The adverse reaction to Eden's remarriage, reflecting the mores and conventions of a different age, fluttered the Central Office dovecotes, and soundings were taken as to grass-roots feeling. Although there was an element of 'filtering' in the reactions reported, Eden was told by Mark Chapman-Walker, Director of Publicity at Conservative Central Office, that he had nothing to worry about. One letter that came as balm (Eden was a sensitive man and the criticisms had upset him) was from Jim Thomas, who told him of the reaction of the saintly Dr Cyril Garbett, Archbishop of York:

---

*Fisher's reputation as an upholder of moral rectitude suffered grave damage through the 1984 claims of Roald Dahl, a pupil under Fisher at Repton, in an autobiographical memoir, of his headmaster's sadistic delight in the caning of teenage boys.

I am back from the constituency & I thought you wd. both like to know how very well your wedding has gone down & the great wrath at the *Church Times* article even among the clergy. Incidentally our old friend the Arch. of York tells me how much he wd like you to have his good wishes although he would not bother you with a letter. He has more guts than Cantuar![54]

Many commentators have believed that marrying Clarissa gave Eden political advantages. Churchill's heir apparent had underlined his claims now that he was Churchill's nephew-by-marriage. Things were not so simple. Becoming 'family' had added a further layer to Eden's already complex relationship with Churchill, who was now not only his political chief, but also 'Uncle Winston'. Business and family do not always mix, and Eden felt a degree of reserve over the extent to which he could press his claims to the succession (which his Cabinet supporters, especially Harry Crookshank, urged him to do). Nor did Eden feel now that he could threaten to retire from politics altogether. The Secretaryship-General of NATO had been his for the asking earlier in the year, and he had been sorely tempted.

Being 'family' also brought him into even more conflict with Churchill's son, Randolph, always a loose cannon. As Clarissa Churchill had been brought up as a Catholic, Evelyn Waugh criticised her marriage to a divorcee, which made Randolph briskly tell Waugh that Clarissa's marriage was no business of his, as he was neither a Cardinal Archbishop nor the Editor of the *Tablet*. But Randolph told Clarissa: 'I'll give you two years to knock him into shape.' Randolph dubbed Eden 'Jerk Eden' and had often attacked him in vindictive journalism. After Randolph's agreement with Clarissa, the flow of nasty articles dried up. But, true to his word, on their second wedding anniversary – 14 August 1954 – Randolph published a particularly offensive article about Eden, and continued thereafter with increasing venom. Descending the steps of his London club, White's, on 6 April 1955, the day that Eden became Prime Minister, he saw a policeman placing a parking ticket on his car outside, and observed: 'The Eden terror has begun.'[55]

Clarissa's marriage increased Randolph Churchill's antagonism towards Eden. Not only had Eden, to his mind, displaced him as his father's political son, but now Eden was a surrogate 'son-in-law', as well as a pretender to his father's crown. Randolph was not allowed to spoil the actual wedding day, an event the staff at Downing Street look back on as one of the legendary moments of Churchill's Indian summer.[56] After the ceremony at Caxton Hall, a wedding breakfast was held in Downing Street, before the Edens left for their honeymoon in Portugal. *En route* they telegrammed to the Churchills, 'We are still so overcome by your overwhelming kindness which has made this the most perfect day for us. Thank you & bless you both. Clarissa and Anthony.'[57]

On his return from honeymoon, Eden decided that his share-holdings in the Anglo-Iranian Oil Company were incompatible with his position as Foreign Secretary. Financially, this was a ruinous decision, as the shares were then at an all-time low, and the immediate consequence was the disposal of his beloved Binderton in September. The Foreign Secretary's residence, 1 Carlton Gardens, became his main home

In the autumn of 1952 Eden undertook a tour of European capitals, a tour that included a bold initiative in flying to Belgrade for talks with Marshal Tito of Yugoslavia on the vexed and long-standing problem of Trieste, which Churchill had described in March 1946 in his Fulton speech as one of the limits of the Iron Curtain, extending to the Adriatic from Stettin in the Baltic. Eden was the first Western statesman to visit this Communist regime since Tito had broken with the Soviets in 1948. 'It is by drawing Tito into our councils and camp,' Sir Ivo Mallett, British Ambassador in Belgrade had advised, 'that we shall best advance the liberalisation of the regime.'[58] Eden agreed and despite the fact that, in a difficult period of the Cold War, his visit was not received with universal acclaim in the Conservative Party, he felt that in the long term it would be justified by events. He disarmed criticism by laying the foundations for the resolution (in October 1954) of the Italian-Yugoslav dispute over Trieste, under Anglo-American military occupation since the end of the war, which led to Dean Acheson (not always the easiest or most admiring of allies) telling Eden, 'If there was one thing you could have done better it has escaped me.'[59]

As Tito was a widower, Eden had decided against taking his wife with him on this first mission, much to their joint disappointment, but when he arrived in Belgrade, the invitation lists for the reception at the White Palace revealed that the sixty-year-old leader had recently married a twenty-eight-year-old major in the Yugoslav Army. ('He might have told me before I left!', wrote Eden.) It was not the only surprise of the visit. When Eden politely suggested that Tito might care to visit Britain, the Communist leader not only accepted, but fixed a date there and then for early 1953. Eden wrote to his wife, 'Trieste is very tough. I believe I shall yet screw an offer out of them, tho' I doubt if it will be enough for Italians. The friendliness has been remarkable from the Marshal to the crowds in the street.'[60]

Although the negotiations on Trieste were indeed tough, Eden laid the foundations for an eventual settlement that ended the military occupation and brought peace to the divided Adriatic. It ranks as one of his foremost achievements in what was to prove a sustained period of peace-making.

Churchill's only question on Eden's return from his tour was what he had done to get the Duke of Windsor invited to the Paris Embassy. Meanwhile attacks on Eden continued in the Beaverbrook Press, which Evelyn Shuckburgh suspected might have been tacitly condoned, or even instigated, by Churchill himself, as a means of extending his time in Downing Street.[61] 'I gather that W is prolonging his stay at Max's villa while Max prolongs his attacks on W's Foreign Secretary,' Eden wrote to his wife from Vienna. 'I am told I had a whole leader to myself the other day. "Manure", as Carson once said in similar circumstances, but strange goings on even for this govt.'[62]*

On 7 November, Eden flew to New York to attend the seventh session of the United Nations General Assembly. The American Presidential Election two days earlier had seen the return of a Republican administration (the first since Herbert Hoover's had ended in 1933) headed by General Dwight D. Eisenhower. John Foster Dulles sought 'talks' with Eden, but Eden was embarrassed as Dulles had not yet replaced Dean Acheson as Secretary of State. 'A. thinks he is trying to make himself Secretary of State and is stalling,' wrote Shuckburgh.[63] Reluctantly Eden saw Dulles on 13 November. Eisenhower later recorded that Eden made his reservations over the prospect of Dulles as Secretary of State personally known to him and expressed the hope that he would appoint someone else.[64]†

Eden's main speech to the Assembly, appropriately on Armistice Day, 11 November, played its part in ending the war in Korea, by simultaneously satisfying the Americans, the French and the Indians, a task previously thought to be impossible. Much abrasive behaviour on Acheson's part towards Eden and Selwyn Lloyd, Minister of State, was overlooked.[65]

Churchill and Eden both had their apprehensions over the advent of Eisenhower. Churchill feared that the new American President might be too bellicose, whilst Eden was wary of the prospect of a rerun of the Roosevelt-Churchill partnership. Ironically, these fears were shared by Eisenhower, who wrote in his diary:

> Winston is trying to relive the days of World War II. In those days he had the enjoyable feeling that he and our President were sitting on some rather Olympian platform with respect to the rest of the world, and directing world affairs from that point of vantage.

---

*Sir Edward Carson (1854–1935) was leader of the Ulster Unionist Party at the time of the Home Rule crisis before the First World War.
†Eden denied that this was the case.

In the present situation, Eisenhower wrote, 'such a relationship is completely fatuous', and he hoped that Churchill would soon hand over leadership to 'younger men.'[66]

For Eden, Eisenhower was always the rather prickly four-star general, who had come to prominence nearly a decade earlier, for quasi-political rather than military reasons, when there were better British candidates for the post of Supreme Commander. As Eden's memories of Eisenhower were conditioned by the experience of war, when Eisenhower had been below him in the hierarchy, Eden tended still to think in those terms, rather than acknowledging that things had moved on: Eisenhower was now the head of the Western alliance and nominally the most powerful man in the world. Eden failed to appreciate that Eisenhower was no longer eager to achieve agreement with Britain. Indeed, until his retirement, Eden found it difficult to adjust to the fact that Britain would inevitably have to play a secondary role alongside America.*

Eden had seen Roosevelt as a scion of upper-class lineage who, like himself, was a benevolent paternalist with the good of the people as his aim. Truman he had admired from a different vantage point, an American Bevin or Morrison, the hard-working pragmatist from the wrong side of the tracks, who never lapsed into languorous indecisiveness, but got on with the job and took tough decisions promptly. 'Ike' fitted into neither of these categories. He was certainly not 'a gentleman', nor did he seem hard headed. The British upper class tended, to their disadvantage, to patronise him. Churchill soon felt Ike was 'both weak and stupid', whilst Jock Colville thought him 'a trifle naive',[67] judgments from which Eden did not dissent. Eisenhower's failure to take Berlin or Prague at the end of the war, and the consequent ease with which the Iron Curtain had descended, weighed heavily against him, in Eden's view.

Eden's attitude to John Foster Dulles was even more complex. Montgomery had once described one of his generals[68] as 'a good plain cook', and that was Eden's view of this puritanical Presbyterian New York lawyer, a kind of American version of John Simon. Eden was not prone to ratiocination. He was intuitive. Dulles, who had a streak of the *prima donna*, reacted badly to this, as did Eden to Dulles's long rambling monologues. Temperamentally they were poles apart: Dulles suspicious of Eden's old-fashioned good manners, and Eden averse to the steering hand

---

*It is interesting to compare Selwyn Lloyd's reverse reaction, with respect to Field Marshal Montgomery. As a Brigadier in the Second Army, working on the logistical planning for D-Day, Lloyd had been in awe of Montgomery; as Eden's Defence Secretary in 1955, he could never quite believe that the Commander of the allied NATO forces in Europe was now the one seeking his ear, and offering his help. D. R. Thorpe, *Selwyn Lloyd*, Jonathan Cape, 1989, p.186.

on the elbow and the tactile over-familiarity. Dulles was actually less prone to such perceived effusiveness than some, as Eden was repelled by Dulles's fierce halitosis and tended to keep his distance.[69]

Their first extended meeting in London in February 1953 was a cautious affair, as if two big beasts of the jungle were warily tracing the other's spoor. Dulles did not find Eden at his best. The Conservative Party, from Churchill downwards, was rent with divisions over Eden's Egyptian policy, which entailed a negotiated withdrawal from the Canal Base before the former Anglo-Egyptian Treaty expired in 1956. Against Churchill's wishes, Eden had also accepted the need for Sudanese independence, not least as a buffer against Egyptian aspirations, and was perfectly prepared to come to terms with colonial nationalism. With his memories of the Sudan going back to the Battle of Omdurman in 1898, Churchill proved less biddable. 'I'm not sure I'm on our side,' Churchill said to Selwyn Lloyd, when asked if he would be speaking on the topic.[70] Later, in a cruel personal jibe that Eden found deeply offensive, Churchill told his Foreign Secretary that he had not known before that Munich was situated on the Nile.[71]

Whilst in Washington at the beginning of March for further talks with Eisenhower and Dulles on these Egyptian negotiations, Eden heard that Stalin had had a stroke and was not expected to live. 'General discussion of everything especially Egypt (Russia scarcely mentioned),' Eden wrote in his diary on 4 March. 'Ike was very friendly but still rather vague in ideas & finds Winston's messages tiresome. "Here comes trouble" he said he had told someone when first one arrived.'[72] Stalin's death the next day heralded a new era in the Soviet Union, with Nikita Khrushchev eventually emerging as leader of the Communist Party. Churchill now had cause to seek rapprochement with the new Soviet regime and renewed reason to delay further his own departure.

Before the end of March the eighty-five-year-old Queen Mary had also died. Eden had last seen this formidable matriarch, a link with the world of Gladstone, at Sandringham in January. 'A stimulating talk to Queen Mary,' he had written then. 'She is a wonderful old lady with a mind as alert as a woman thirty years younger & more knowledgeable than most. She would make an admirable Foreign Secretary.'[73]

Press criticism of Eden's Egyptian 'scuttle' continued, fuelled by Marshal Tito's five-day visit to London on 16 March, regarded with suspicion by the Tories' imperialist wing. On this occasion it was not only the Beaverbrook Press that was in full cry. What Eden's critics failed to appreciate was that by treating Tito as the acceptable face of Communism, a clear message was being sent to the rest of the world – and especially Stalin's successors in Russia – that Yugoslavia's geographical and political position behind the Iron Curtain was not going to prevent understanding, and even dialogue, with the West. Two other factors showed Eden's subtlety of purpose. By separating Tito from his Communist masters, Eden won the grudging admiration of one element in the Tory Party, and by dipping his foot in the waters of détente he was showing that Churchill was not indispensable for that process.

Napoleon had always wanted his generals to be lucky, and Eden had been blessed with his fair share of luck, especially before the war. But at this point, whilst London was preparing for the coronation of Queen Elizabeth II on 2 June – a possible moment for Churchill to depart the scene, as Lord Salisbury had done in 1902 and Stanley Baldwin in 1937 – Eden's luck ran out.

He had not felt well in Washington and on his return things were no better. A routine examination on 2 April by his doctor, Dr Rossdale, revealed 'apparent gall bladder trouble'. The next day Eden was examined by Sir Horace Evans, probably the most famous general physician of the day. On 4 April, he was seen again by Horace Evans, who brought with him Basil Hume, a senior general surgeon from St Bartholomew's Hospital. The diagnosis was that there might be gallstones in the bile duct, and after tests their prognosis was gloomy. 'Immediate operation,' Eden wrote starkly that evening. 'So there we are.'[74]

The subsequent operation at the London Clinic on 12 April (not 'immediate', as Eden wrote in his diary) was to change the course of post-war history. Ann Fleming, one of Clarissa Eden's closest friends, recorded the horrors of that day. 'Anthony was over three hours on the operating table, I went to the clinic to be with Clarissa, a grim day for her – sixteen doctors and Winston tampering with all the bulletins.'[75] It was not only the bulletins with which Churchill tampered. The story that senior medical figures have told the author has never before been told.[76]

Churchill, fired by the adrenalin of the crisis, took up ACTION THIS DAY stations after hearing of the original diagnosis by Evans and Hume. Consultations followed with Lord Moran, who assured Churchill that Eden would be safe in British hands, and indeed that any thought of sending him abroad at this stage (for example to the world famous specialist, Dr Richard Cattell, in Boston) would be regarded as a slight on the reputation of Britain's medical profession. To make the assurance doubly sure, Churchill let it be known to Hume, who was to undertake what in essence was a routine operation, that it was vitally important that nothing should be allowed to go wrong. No surgeon likes to be inhibited by others, and under this unexpected and unwelcome pressure, Hume was experiencing considerable concern about the forthcoming ordeal.

At the time of the D-Day landings in 1944, only the King had been able to dissuade Churchill from crossing the Channel on a destroyer. Sadly, nobody gave similar advice in April 1953 about the need for Churchill to step back and let the professionals get on with it. Horace Evans was drawn into Churchill's web and became, as it were, Downing Street's representative in the hospital, reiterating the Prime Minister's concerns to an anxious Hume, who was now being asked for regular updates. Even as Eden went under the anaesthetic in the operating theatre, a message came to underline the eminence of the patient. By this time Hume was in such a state of agitation that, even though Eden was now unconscious, the operation had to be put on hold for nearly an hour to allow the surgeon to compose his nerves. When the operation eventually began, those present could not remember so much loss of blood in a patient. It was turning into a nightmare. A difference of opinion then ensued about whether the gall bladder was actually the cause of the trouble. The consequence had an air of inevitability. Further probing, in the tensest of atmospheres, led to the bile duct being severed. The problem now was not gallstones, but saving Eden's life. Hume was unable to continue, and Guy Blackburn, his main assistant, took over. The situation was saved, but only on a temporary basis.

A second operation, which Hume felt he could not attempt, was then scheduled, with Blackburn in charge from the start. In retrospect, it is easy to say that this team should never have been entrusted with the task. Yet they had been present on 12 April, and could not otherwise have taken over at such short notice for the second operation. This operation, which took place on 29 April, proved even more tense than the first, and Eden was within a whisker of death at several stages of the lengthy and traumatic process. Afterwards he was not guaranteed to be free of cholangitis – all part of a piece with the inflammation, obstructions, fever and jaundice from which he was now suffering intermittently. Further salvaging operations would still be needed, but whether they would be any more successful than the first two was far from certain.

By chance, Dr Richard Cattell, the world's greatest expert in patching up gall bladders, was in London addressing a medical conference. He was approached by the London Clinic and at once offered to operate on Eden, but insisted that for the highest chance of success, the operation should be done at the New England Baptist Hospital in Boston, where Cattell's own specialist team would be to hand. Churchill's initial reaction was that this would reflect badly on Britain, and he objected strongly. There was much talk of how he had had his appendix out 'on the kitchen table'.

There were two problems. Eden was not strong enough yet to cross the

Atlantic and the financial cost would be quite beyond his means. The expenses of Eden's medical treatment and convalescence in the United States exercised Churchill greatly. But, together with Lord Woolton, Chairman of the Party, Churchill made it clear to Eden before his departure that the Conservative Party would make funds available to cover all these expenses.[77] He also put Chequers at Eden's disposal, so that he was able to convalesce in all comfort to gather his strength before the ordeal. At such moments Churchill's humanity shone through. Indeed, even the anxieties he had communicated to Hume before the operation derived from the best of motives, however disastrous their effect.

Churchill was not the only one who rallied round at this desperate time. During Eden's illness Robert Carr stood in as a locum in the constituency, in addition to discharging his own responsibilities in Mitcham. He also spent long hours reading to Eden at the London Clinic and cheered him with his comforting presence and concern. In any list of those who stood by Eden in dark days, the name of Robert Carr stands high.

Even during his convalescence, when messages of goodwill poured in from all sides of the House (he was especially touched by all the messages from Labour members, from Attlee downwards), Eden followed political developments with keen interest, and not always approvingly. In the post-Stalinist era, Churchill publicly proclaimed his belief that détente could be placed on the political agenda. In his speech on foreign affairs in the Commons on 11 May, about which neither the Cabinet nor Eisenhower had any advance warning, Churchill declared 'that in spite of all the uncertainties and confusion in which world affairs are plunged, I believe that a conference at the highest level should take place within leading Powers without long delay'.[78] It struck a populist chord, but not with many of the older hands in the Foreign Office, who remembered Chamberlain's belief that he could cut through professional diplomacy by personal 'summits' with Hitler and Mussolini, which then resulted only in British concessions. Eden was not the only one appalled by this flagrant defiance of the official Foreign Office line in his absence, and he only just persuaded Bobbety Salisbury not to resign. Eden was in no doubt that Churchill's pronouncement was a major miscalculation. 'It must be long in history since any one speech did so much damage to its own side.'[79]

Eden was unable to attend the coronation on 2 June, as he had done in 1937. Clarissa had to go by herself. Thanking the Queen for her message of good wishes, Eden replied, 'My greatest regret is to have missed the historic ceremonies of this week.'[80] The Edens flew to Boston after the coronation, Churchill taking temporary charge of the Foreign Office, and Selwyn Lloyd, as Minister of State, attending Cabinet. Before departing for America, Eden's final words to Selwyn Lloyd, who was not so averse to

Churchill's initiative as his master, were 'Don't appease that Russian bear too much in my absence.'[81]

In America, the British Ambassador, Sir Roger Makins, who had been on Eden's staff at Geneva in the 1930s, was responsible for many of the arrangements at the Boston end. Cattell told Makins there was a 50:50 chance that Eden would die during the operation, a 20 per cent chance that he might regain some of his earlier health, but only 10 per cent that there would be a full recovery.[82] Eden's subsequent eight-hour operation in Boston was so complex that even the skill of Cattell's team was uniquely stretched. He was told afterwards that the operation was in essence a holding one, and that further treatment would be necessary at intervals for a considerable part of his life.* So pessimistic were the rumours in Britain about Eden's health that David Astor asked Bobbety Salisbury for delivery of an immediate obituary notice on Eden for the *Observer*.[83]

Before departing for the United States on 5 June, Eden had left instructions with Evelyn Shuckburgh that his firm opposition to sponsored television should be made known when the issue resurfaced. It was the one big domestic issue on which he differed from his Minister of State, Selwyn Lloyd, whose minority report as a member of the Beveridge Committee on Broadcasting in 1949 had made him in many eyes 'the father of commercial television'.[84] On 22 June, Eden wrote further to Shuckburgh from the New England Baptist Hospital on the television issue, which exercised him greatly.[85] The advocates of commercial broadcasting, such as Selwyn Lloyd, believed that it would raise standards, as the BBC 'would have to compete by excellence of its programmes.'[86] Eden was not so sanguine. Competition is for popularity, in relation to which conventional notions of excellence appear rather remote.

Meanwhile Churchill pressed on with his plans for the Western summit in Bermuda, hopefully as a prelude to a Four-Power meeting in the autumn, involving Khrushchev. Ironically, the belief that peace could only be achieved if the leaders met personally was a throwback to the vain hopes that had motivated Neville Chamberlain at Munich. But events were to put all these matters on hold.

On 23 June, Churchill was entertaining the Italian Prime Minister Alcide de Gasperi to dinner at Downing Street when he was taken ill. It was clear to his staff that he had suffered a stroke. Eden and Clarissa were staying at Moorland Lodge, Newport, Rhode Island, for Eden's continued convalescence, when the first worrying news reached them. A telegram, with

---

*Eden was to return to Boston for a major operation in 1957 after his retirement, the first of many such visits for surgery every few years for the rest of his life.

the 'official' details, was sent by Sir William Strang on 27 June. This posed more questions than it answered and was kept deliberately vague. The Edens were understandably anxious to know what was actually happening between the lines of the Press releases.

On 26 June, Jock Colville wrote from Chartwell, where Churchill had been taken in conditions of great secrecy. His letter was to Clarissa. Although it was clearly intended that the contents of the letter should be given to Eden, it is an indication of how Churchill's entourage were viewing Eden's illness that it was felt better to inform his wife first.

> My dear Clarissa,
> Last Tuesday the P.M. gave a dinner party for De Gasperi (one of those dreary Government hospitality affairs, at which for once the food was surprisingly good!). He made a little speech at the end in his very best style and humour, and left the dining room in perfect health & vigour. Then suddenly, due as we now know to an arterial clot, he lost control of his legs and his articulation became slurred and indistinct. We got rid of the guests as fast as we could and more or less helped him to bed, by which time he spoke more clearly & felt better. However next day paralysis set in in his left arm and he could walk only with difficulty. He nevertheless presided at the Cabinet, apparently without anybody seeing that something was seriously wrong. The doctors, for their part, think it quite possible that the whole thing will clear up, as it did once before; but they at present rate it as a so-so chance. He has shown, and is showing, remarkable courage and philosophy. Moreover his brain is still absolutely clear and, although he quickly tires, he can do a certain amount of work. Lady Churchill is acting magnificently.[87]

The news came as a bombshell to Eden. He was not even reassured by a kindly letter from Rab Butler the following day:

> I want you and Clarissa to know one thing, how brightly his [Churchill's] loyalty to you burns & how we are holding the post for your return. Nor need we rush you out of yr. well earned convalescence. We'll get the House up somehow, then the summer pause comes to our aid.[88]

On 1 July 1953, Eden wrote to Jock Colville at Chartwell:

> My dear Jock,
> Clarissa has asked me to write to thank you for your letter as she is writing to Clemmie this morning. We were both very grateful to you for writing as fully as you did. We were not hearkening to rumour, but were naturally deeply distressed & trying to conjecture what lay behind the official words, about Winston's health.
> Forgive the writing of this but I have only just begun to put pen to paper again.

You, and others, may like some details of dates as my Dr in Boston has sent them to Horace Evans at the latter's request.

If all goes normally with convalescence, as so far it has, I should be fit, completely so, in October. That is the surgeon's view. We can only see how the human performance compares! & what the physician Horace Evans has to say after he has seen me in early August.

I am so sad that all this should have happened in this way & at this time, and I feel a horrible guilt that FO work must have, of course, added to PM's burdens these months. It is when something like this happens that one realises how wide the Atlantic is. We feel very far away.[89]

In the meantime, Eden had received a reassuring letter from Jim Thomas, in which Thomas reiterated that Churchill 'says you are his spiritual son'.[90] In his intermittent periods of consciousness, Churchill made it clear that he did not wish 'Dear Anthony' to be denied the Premiership. But there were matters that even Churchill did not know.

The situation was deemed to be so grave that all contingencies had to be catered for. In the event of Churchill's death, the advice to the Palace was that Lord Salisbury should be appointed as caretaker Head of Government. When he heard of this development, Eden feared that such an expedient, even if intended to be temporary, might be difficult to reverse constitutionally. In addition, any consequent reshuffle following Salisbury's appointment (and many scenarios were discussed at Chartwell among the inner circle) could prejudice the future of any of the great offices of state involved if Eden became Prime Minister in due course.

However, to the astonishment of Lord Moran, Churchill rallied over the weekend and was even able to reply to the Queen's letter of good wishes for his full recovery. 'He told Her Majesty,' Lord Moran wrote in his diary, 'that he was not without hope that he might soon be about and able to discharge his duties until the autumn, when he thought that Anthony would be able to take over.'[91] So the moment passed and Salisbury did not become 'the People's Bobbety'.

Evelyn Shuckburgh also kept Eden informed about Churchill's plans. His letter of 23 July made gloomy reading for Eden, as Shuckburgh stressed that Churchill had gone from strength to strength 'and is talking of plans which lead well beyond October'. He concluded:

> I feel it only right to warn you – in case you should be under a contrary impression as to how things stand – that it may still want some careful handling. This will, I fear, be exasperating for you, and may mean some impatient times ahead. But of one thing there seems to be no sign of any argument – that you are the only candidate.[92]

Salisbury also kept Eden, by now on a convalescent cruise in Greece, informed of Churchill's changing intentions. The message on 14 August was, from Eden's point of view, the gloomiest yet:

> He is now thinking of putting it off till the Queen gets back from Australia, that is, well into next year. His idea apparently is that you should become Lord President, lead the Commons and speak for the Govt on Foreign Affairs, & that he should appoint another Foreign Secretary (name unknown) on the grounds that, if you go on at the F.O. you will in fact lose your reversion of the Prime Ministership. The plan, I think, is from the point of view of the Party, a thoroughly bad one. You will be neither Prime Minister, nor Foreign Secretary, which will lead to impair your position with your supporters, while he will remain in the background and only emerge to make pronouncements like that of 11th May [on détente with Russia], on which his colleagues may or may not be consulted.[93]

Meanwhile, Churchill had been speaking at Chartwell with Lady Violet Bonham Carter about the succession. 'It is Anthony's turn – he's been at it longer,' Violet Bonham Carter recorded Churchill as saying, 'Rab is younger & can wait. The 1922 Committee are divided between them, but if you asked the rank & file in the country which cld win a General Election they wld say Anthony unhesitatingly.' Violet Bonham Carter was very much in favour of Churchill staying, because of the medical progress he had made, and 'begged him not to take a hurried decision.'[94]

Garbled messages continued to arrive at various ports. On 29 August, Robert Carr warned Eden that Walter Monckton was being mentioned as a possible Foreign Secretary.[95] 'Many letters about politics on arrival at Athens,' Eden wrote in his diary. Salisbury and Macmillan both urged him to return to London to protect his kingdom. Eden's reaction was a revealing one. 'Troublesome. I don't want to. I cannot feel it to be really necessary, though this may be due to my lack of enthusiasm for politics which remains constant.'[96] His main concern in his reply to Salisbury related to what might happen if Churchill had to resign suddenly whilst the Queen was in Australia. 'A new PM would have presumably to fly out to the Antipodes! – a new variant of Asquith's journey to Biarritz to see Edward VII after Campbell-Bannerman's demise or resignation.'[97]

Eden stayed on in Greece throughout September, visiting temples and art galleries, sailing round small islands and stopping at quiet inlets for picnics and swimming. One of the few people he saw was Alexander Papagos, for the first time since their dramatic meeting in 1941. Eden's loyal lieutenants in London continued to keep him abreast of developments, though he was not told of one of Churchill's mischievous asides in a Cabinet on the foot-and-mouth outbreak, when he had said to Thomas Dugdale, the Minister of Agriculture, 'I'm very worried about this myxomatosis. You don't think there's any chance of Anthony catching it?'[98]

Robert Carr's assessment of the situation was shrewdly realistic. 'My first assumption is that the PM is determined to try and carry on. This may be bad and I can well imagine, alarming to those who have to work with him. But I do not see what can be done about it. This 2nd assumption is that the PM will be compelled to give up after a short time – perhaps a few months or perhaps only a few weeks after the House meets.'[99] In fact, as Shuckburgh pointed out, everything turned 'on one's estimate of the PM's staying powers.'[100] Nobody in the Eden camp, even at their most pessimistic moments, could have foreseen that the Churchill Premiership was to run for another nineteen months.

The crucial hurdle – for both Churchill and Eden – was going to be the Conservative Party's Annual Conference at Margate, due to begin on 8 October. Both would return to a defining test of their stamina, as much as their political acumen.

If Churchill had retired at the time of his stroke, and Eden after his Boston operation, the way would have been left open for Rab Butler to become Prime Minister. There is a moment in every political career when the peak has been passed, and that was certainly not the case with Butler in the summer of 1953, when he was acting Prime Minister, as well as Chancellor of the Exchequer, and coordinator of Government strategy. It was an unfair burden, even for a short time. Despite his earlier setback over ROBOT, Butler was a strikingly successful Chancellor.

With hindsight Butler himself considered that July 1953 had been his best chance of becoming Prime Minister. The Churchillians, though, were not going to let their man go without a struggle. Jock Colville and Christopher Soames, Churchill's PPS and son-in-law, kept the show on the road; but had Butler stood out and said that he would not continue as a pliant factotum, the succession would surely have been his.[101] This was Butler's view. It is not certain, however, that this would have been the outcome. He was too unpopular with backbenchers, who remembered appeasement, even fifteen years after Munich, and he was perceived as indecisive. Also, the defeat of ROBOT had not established him as a mover and shaker in Cabinet circles. Nevertheless, Salisbury, sensing the danger to Eden's chances, persuaded Butler out of any such pre-emptive move during July.[102]

If Rab Butler had become Prime Minister in 1953, British politics would have moved in a new direction. In the nature of political life, problems would undoubtedly have arisen ('events, dear boy, events', as Macmillan often remarked), but Butler's succession would have resolved many of the immediate questions within the upper reaches of the Conservative Party. It only needed Jock Colville and Christopher Soames ('the Prime Minister who never was') to have acted differently, or the Press barons to have broken their silence on the nature of Churchill's illness, for Churchill's long career to have ended. The fact that Churchill survived says much about the loyalty he inspired among those closest to him.

And, as long as Churchill survived, Eden's chances of the succession survived with him. Just as Butler's chances were never higher, so, in the summer of 1953, Eden's were never so perilous. A politically sensitive medical man would have read such runes. Had the well-connected establishment figure of Sir Horace Evans made it clear to sympathetic Conservatives (Jim Thomas would have been the perfect intermediary) that on the grounds of health there were many advantages in Eden retiring to the Lords, Eden could well have taken this path, towards which his inner thoughts were already tending. Even his own desire for the top job was understandably low that summer. 'Clarissa is right,' he told Evelyn Shuckburgh, even before his illness. 'I should go at the coronation.'[103] Eden's political friends could have argued the case for a changed emphasis in his public life as an hereditary peer (with consequent advantages for Nicholas, whose interests were taking him into the field of diplomatic administration), where he could have kept in contact with great events, taken on the role of the Conservative Party's beloved elder statesman, and influenced the progressive trend of domestic policy with regular speeches on the major international issues of the day. It would have been a fulfilled conclusion to a nigh-unblemished career.

CHAPTER FOURTEEN
Waging Peace
1953–4

'The trouble with you, Foster, is that you want World War
Three.'
Anthony Eden to John Foster Dulles, on the steps of the Hôtel
du Rhône, Geneva, 3 May 1954

On 1 October 1953, his first day back at work since his illness, Eden had
an awkward meeting with Churchill at Downing Street. Their policy
differences, over the Suez Canal Base and the possible visit to Malenkov,
were one source of tension, but Churchill's repeated refusal to give any
indication of when he might retire frustrated Eden even more. 'Made it
clear to W that I was ready to serve in any capacity,' he wrote in his diary,
'but he made it evident he wanted me to stay on at F.O. Asked him about
plans & he wanted to try himself out, first in Margate & then in the House
– Have some doubts as to how that will go physically.'[1]

Eden's burdens on returning to the Foreign Office were so substantial
that he had contemplated becoming Leader of the House as something of
a 'breather' before assuming greater responsibilities as Prime Minister,
whenever that might be. The immediate FO schedule was bound to be
demanding. However, as Churchill wanted him to continue as Foreign
Secretary, Eden had no option, short of resignation, but to comply and see
how things unfolded after the House had met on 17 October.

On his return to Carlton Gardens at 12.30, on his first day back at work,
Eden began a series of meetings with Bobbety Salisbury, Rab Butler and
Walter Monckton to discuss the situation in the light of Churchill's
intention to make the leader's speech at the forthcoming Margate
Conference and then to meet Parliament. If Churchill came through these
twin ordeals, there was no telling when he might retire. Salisbury offered
to resign on grounds of age (he was sixty) to set Churchill (who was just
short of his seventy-ninth birthday) an example, but Eden knew it would
be a futile gesture. During the afternoon, he began preparing his keynote
conference speech on foreign affairs.

That same night, on the eve of the first Cabinet meeting of the autumn,
Eden dined at Number 10 with Churchill. Butler and Salisbury were fellow
guests. The conversation soon became strained when Churchill (as Eden
recorded in his diary) 'maintained that in the war it was only the Stalin

Roosevelt Churchill meetings that had made our Foreign Secretaries' work possible'. Eden denied that this was the case. He added:

> Nor was it true that to meet without agenda was the best method with Russians. I believed they like to have an agenda which they could chew over well in advance. Our most productive meeting with them had been with Hull at Moscow in 1943 before Teheran when we had used just these methods about Second Front, creation of UNO, Austria etc. This had led to Teheran meeting. Anyway the important question was 'what next?' On this W appeared to have no ideas.[2]

The Margate Conference from 8 to 10 October was a critical challenge for both Churchill and Eden. Their performances would indicate whether they had overcome their respective illnesses, particularly in Eden's case, as his medical difficulties were more widely known. If Eden had any doubts about how he was regarded by the rank and file, these were soon dispelled by the rapturous welcome he received when he rose to speak. Although Evelyn Shuckburgh thought the draft speech full of platitudes ('We must not by any of our actions injure the unity of N.A.T.O. No N.A.T.O., no security'), Eden judiciously mixed broad-based generalisation with detailed observations. Of particular importance was his statement of the 'three circles' concept, with Britain at the heart of an interlinking alliance of the United States, Commonwealth and Europe, which Edward Heath later described as 'an imaginative and morale-raising prediction.'[3]

Churchill's fifty-minute speech on 10 October was also accounted a success, though it was achieved only through diligent use of large-print prompt cards, which Churchill at one stage muddled, but skilfully disguised. His generous references to Eden were enthusiastically received, but Churchill went on to reiterate the principles behind his 11 May call for a Four-Power summit. The party faithful, as well as the inner circle, now knew that Churchill would not be standing down in the immediate future. The Queen was about to embark on her Australian tour, and if Churchill was still in harness when the Queen departed, he could hardly retire while she was abroad. Eden had been outmanoeuvred again.

During the summer Sir William Strang had retired from the Foreign Office as Permanent Under-Secretary. For his replacement, Eden had chosen Sir Ivone Kirkpatrick, British High Commissioner in Germany since 1950, and a stalwart of King Charles Street, whose association with Eden went back to 1935. Unusually among the senior figures at the Foreign Office, Kirkpatrick had not received a university education, though he had been accepted for a place at Balliol. A voluble figure, who, strangely for one in his position, did not like meetings, he left people to get on with their work.

As a veteran of the First World War, his fierce antipathy to the Nazis, fostered by his time as Chief of Staff to Nevile Henderson in Berlin, had made him, within the confines of his pre-war responsibilities, Eden's kindred spirit over appeasement. He had seen at first hand the European dictatorships during his early career, felt guilty that his generation had not prevented war and was convinced that appeasement only brought bigger problems in its wake, an attitude that was to be significant during the Suez crisis when his loyalty to Eden was unchallengeable.

Preparations continued for the much-postponed Bermuda Conference, with Dulles and the French Foreign Minister, Georges Bidault, visiting Eden in London in October. Eden had hoped for broad American support for some form of international defence system in the Middle East after Britain's negotatiated withdrawal from the Suez Canal Base, to be finalised in 1954, but in the event such a plan was not forthcoming. Eden's difficulties with Bidault over the ratification of EDC were not easily resolved either, and were complicated by the protracted timetable for possible Russian talks. In the run-up to Bermuda, Churchill and Eden had clashed behind the scenes on Russia, which Eden argued was little changed since the Stalin era, a view shared by Sir William Hayter in the Moscow Embassy. Much of the time at Bermuda was occupied with seemingly endless talks on how to respond to Moscow's proposal of 26 November for a Four-Power meeting of the Foreign Ministers. Dulles's pessimistic view was that the Russians hoped to delay any Western plans for enhanced security through ratification of EDC, and warned that the Americans might have to 'reappraise' their European policy unless progress was made. Eden firmly believed that 'the Russians are making very great efforts by all sorts of means to drive wedges between us and the Americans.'[4] Like Eisenhower, Eden remained sceptical of the value of a summit with the Russians, despite the fact that the country was supposedly changing after Stalin's death. What those changes might be were as yet unpredictable. However, for Eden one thing was certain. 'The permanent challenge of communism transcends personalities, however powerful.'[5]

The Bermuda Conference was bedevilled throughout by small problems, which contributed to the edgy atmosphere. The lights fused on the first night and the first plenary session by candlelight was reminiscent of the meetings in Athens on Christmas Day in 1944. Joseph Laniel, the new French Prime Minister, was taken ill with a fever, and there was much traffic between his sickbed in the hotel and the conference room, which was not good for Eden, who was decidedly below par himself. As a result the French, who became preoccupied by internal rows, were largely sidelined, which did not help over EDC matters. Churchill had caused great offence on his arrival by paying more attention to the regimental goat of the Royal Welsh Fusiliers than to the welcoming Joseph Laniel. The diplomatic correspondents were reduced to sitting around and twiddling their thumbs. Eden told Iverach McDonald, Foreign Editor of *The Times*, after one fruitless midnight meeting, 'Never, never again.'[6]

Eden was upset that nothing had been properly discussed at either Prime Ministerial or Foreign Secretary level, and was apprehensive about Eisenhower's perceived willingness to impose American wishes by selective use of nuclear strikes in the Far East. Churchill stayed in bed most days reading C. S. Forester's *Death to the French*, and when he did stir was not *au fait* with the latest developments. To Eden's relief, Eisenhower and Dulles shared his view of Russia as a leopard that had not changed its spots, though Eisenhower's metaphors were more earthy. (His barrack-room language shocked the British delegation.)[7]

Eden vowed that if he was ever in charge of a similar timetable he would hold 'broad-brush' Heads of Government meetings first, with the details being decided later at a separate gathering of the Foreign Ministers, a procedure followed in the autumn of 1955.

The absence of an agreed agenda in Bermuda led to considerable time-wasting. Churchill was frequently late for meetings, which exasperated Eisenhower, who formed a very critical view of British leadership as a result, conditioning his later attitudes.[8] Even the weather initially failed to deliver. 'This room should be lovely in fine weather but it is now pure Wuthering Heights,' Eden wrote home to his wife. 'W has just been in as I was writing this. Amiable but completely vague. We are to dine together tonight alone. I expect it will end up with *Oklahoma*.'[9]*

Dulles and Eden found themselves thrown into each other's company, and as the weather improved they started the day with early-morning swims, during which the snorkels of the circling security men seemed like the fins of watchful sharks closing in on their prey. Much of the future detail was agreed between the two of them, beginning with proposals for the Four-Power Foreign Ministers' meeting in Berlin in January. 'They lay amicably together on the beach,' observed one British official, 'Eden soaking up the sun and Dulles displaying some gaudy shorts that belied his reputation for puritan austerity.'[10] Only their joint persistence ensured a final communiqué.

Eden was dispirited by the Bermuda Conference. At a meeting of the North

---

*Churchill's fondness for late-night films was well known. He reputedly saw *That Hamilton Woman* (1941), a patriotic melodrama set in the Napoleonic Wars, eighty-three times (*The Times*, 3 October 2001), partly because he was enamoured of Vivien Leigh, who played Emma Hamilton. (The Countess of Avon to the author, 12 February 2002.)

Atlantic Council in Paris on his return, he discussed with Adenauer how the Russians could best be assured that Germany's association with EDC was in essence a defensive measure. (Adenauer was a good friend to Eden over the years. When Eden had been in the London Clinic for his operations, Adenauer paid a special courtesy call to Clarissa at Carlton Gardens to express his hopes for a successful outcome.) Dulles meanwhile reiterated to Eden at the Council that if the French did not ratify EDC, then the Americans would have to 'reappraise' policy towards Europe. As Eden feared that the inherent volatility of French politics (echoing the 1930s) made ratification doubtful, he was concerned about any parting of the ways with America that such a failure might bring, and argued with Dulles for an enhanced NATO role in controlling Germany.

Eden spent Christmas in Wiltshire at his wife's cottage, Rosebower, at Broadchalke near Salisbury. As the cottage was remote, the Post Office had not earlier felt it economic to erect a telegraph pole and run wires for half a mile from the village. Now that Eden was occasionally in residence, arrangements had to be made, and a hut for the police was also erected close by.

One of the few things on which Eden and Churchill agreed was their opposition to a European Army. At Cabinet on 29 December, a fierce disagreement arose over financial arrangements with Egypt, but for once Churchill had to give way to the combined opposition of Eden and Rab Butler. On the vexed question of the Suez Canal Base agreement, Eden warned that this was a prerequisite to any withdrawal, otherwise 'we should have lost the right of return and might have weakened our influence with other Arab states'.[11] What 'the right of return' meant in practice was not adequately considered, either by Eden or by the Cabinet. If one was unable to hold the base while troops were there, the prospects were hardly propitious after their withdrawal. But whether Cyprus would prove an adequate replacement was an open question that exercised many in the Conservative Party, from Churchill downwards.

The year of 1954 promised to be critical. Early in January Eden discussed with his Minister of State, Selwyn Lloyd, how the year might unfold, but it was not long before the talk turned to Churchill's retirement, as Lloyd noted in his diary:

> Eden discussed personal problems. There have lately been rumours that WSC wanted at last to go. He said something to that effect just before Christmas. He was very disappointed with Bermuda and quite ill there. The family are reputed to have urged him to go ... Anthony said to me that he had ceased to worry about the future, and events could develop without his interference.[12]

*

On 22 January, Eden travelled to Berlin for the Foreign Ministers' Conference. Molotov's agenda, which was accepted by the Western Foreign Ministers, covered the forthcoming Five-Power Conference in Geneva, the German question and Austria, and aimed at finding the best methods of reducing international tension. As such, it was not a great success, and rifts soon developed. Even within the Western alliance there were differences, notably over the Soviet proposals for the Austrian Peace Treaty. 'There is little other life here but conference which takes most of the day with its preparations & sessions,' Eden wrote to his wife from Berlin. 'Americans are showing signs of being touchy, including Dulles who pays too much heed to outside advisers of the C. D. Jackson type & too little to his State Dept officials. The result is amateurish.'[13]*

To add to Eden's many concerns at this time, Clarissa was expecting a child and it seemed there might be complications. The subsequent miscarriage in March was to be the one great sadness of their marriage.

Eden, whose experience of Russian leaders went back to the mid-1930s, had a lengthy meeting with Molotov over dinner on 27 January. It was an uncomfortable encounter. Molotov at once made it clear that his attitude towards Churchill, following the 'very harsh things' he had said about the Soviet Union in his war memoirs, 'was in no way cordial',[14] an opening gambit that called on all Eden's powers of tactful rescue. During the week Molotov emphasised his antagonism towards NATO and EDC, which he would not accept as defensive organisations. One of the few positive things to emerge from Berlin was the agreement to hold a Five-Power Conference at Geneva on Korea and Indo-China, though to the undisguised apprehension of Dulles, this was to include a Chinese delegation, led by Chou En-lai. Back in Washington, Red China was the devil incarnate.

Eden had already considered during his convalescence how peace could best be restored to South-East Asia. As he wrote to Churchill on 14 February, he sought a settlement 'that will meet the bear without parting us from the eagle.'[15] Now he was about to test these ideas in an international forum. Geneva was going to be his show, and there was a mood of 'I was right in the Thirties; I can deal with these problems'.

He did not want Dulles muscling in and ruining the prospects with his fervent anti-Communism. Both Eden and Molotov had implicitly accepted in Berlin that a favourable – if not ideal – outcome in Geneva was better than going for broke and failing.

The Berlin Conference continued until 19 February with social engagements, meetings and dinners. Eden found that Bidault, the French Foreign Minister, was keen to meet the Chinese because of a growing peace lobby

---

*C. D. Jackson was the American for whom Beatrice Eden had left her husband.

in the French Parliament, which threatened to destabilise Laniel's centre-right Government. The hotel lobbies were thronged with foreign correspondents, all eager for the latest story. Eden's happiest memory of the social side was as guest of honour at an inter-services boxing tournament, when he received a 'spontanous demonstration such as I have never known', as he wrote to Clarissa, adding, 'Really pleased because it was from ordinary soldiers.'[16]

Back in London, there was speculation that Churchill was about to resign. Robert Carr kept Eden in touch with developments. A poll in the *News Chronicle* showed that 54 per cent thought Churchill should go, and 52 per cent of all voters (not just Conservatives) thought Eden should succeed him.[17] On 3 February *Punch* published a hostile cartoon of an aged Churchill – 'Man goeth forth unto his work and to his labour until the evening' – which caused considerable offence. By contrast, Eden was being hailed as 'the arbitrator between nations'.[18]

On his return to England, Eden reported to the Cabinet on the Berlin Conference and 'the extreme rigidity of the Soviet attitude towards European problems', together with their alarm at 'the development of United States bases throughout the world and by the large programme of aircraft construction in Western Europe'.[19] Nevertheless, he felt that 'it was even possible that Mr Molotov had recognised that the EDC was itself an insurance against future German aggression.'[20] Ratification of the EDC was for Eden the most urgent question of the hour.

Russian fears of American aggression were another matter. On 1 March the Americans tested their second hydrogen bomb at Bikini Atoll in the Pacific, the same day as riots broke out in Khartoum when the new Egyptian nationalist leader, General Neguib, arrived in Egypt for talks with Selwyn Lloyd over Sudanese independence. Both events were to be a backdrop to Eden's work at Geneva. Churchill considered sending British troops to Khartoum, and on 5 April made his long-awaited speech in the House on America's testing of the hydrogen bomb. Its failure capped a disastrous week for the Prime Minister, with the Press, both national and international, drawing critical comparisons between the Churchill of 1940 and the present situation. The *Daily Mirror* published a leader on 'The Twilight of a Giant', while the *New York Times* thought Churchill 'unsure of himself and tired' – a contrast 'all the more marked when Foreign Secretary Anthony Eden rose from his seat beside Sir Winston to answer a question and divert some of the pressure from the Prime Minister. Mr Eden was precise, confident and clear.'[21]

The Labour benches were very hostile. On 5 April Bessie Braddock,

MP for Liverpool Exchange, shouted repetitive vulgar abuse, while others called openly for the Prime Minister's resignation, a situation unparalleled since the House had turned against Churchill during the Abdication crisis.

In retrospect, this was the moment when Eden could tacitly have acquiesced in a move to secure the Premiership. Two ministers met him privately and urged him *not* to rescue Churchill.[22] The situation was uncannily reminiscent of the time in 1940, when Churchill had been called upon to bolster Neville Chamberlain's position. But it was not in Eden's nature, as Churchill so shrewdly understood, to wield the knife, or even indirectly cause it to be wielded, and he 'sustained the Old Man, but managed at the same time to soothe the House and reduce everyone to calm', even though privately he believed Churchill to be gaga and unable to finish his sentences.[23] Had Macmillan been the recognised heir apparent instead of Eden at this moment, Churchill might not have lasted the week.[24]

From the scene of one of Churchill's most embarrassing disasters, Eden moved to the arena of one of his own greatest triumphs: the 1954 Geneva Conference on Korea and Indo-China. To an extent rare, even in the darkest days of the war, Eden now faced simultaneously a whole raft of problems, and this is one of the reasons why his memoirs of this period unfold thematically, rather than chronologically. In August, Eden summed up for Bobbety Salisbury how he had attempted to deal with these problems, acknowledging that only occasionally do circumstances combine to make resolution possible:

> In peace or war action is determined by events rather than by fixed ideas. One is fortunate when one has the power to decide in accordance with the factual circumstances of the day or even of the hour. I always reserve to myself as much of this advantage as I can get. Not only does one thing affect many others, but their proportions alter in an ever-changing scene.[25]

In the ever-changing scene of 1954, many such opportunities occurred and Eden made the most of them. The list of achievements of that year still makes astonishing reading. Following the fall of Dr Mussadeq on 19 August 1953, the Iranian oil dispute entered its last phase, and after detailed negotiations the oil was flowing again by 1954; the long-running Trieste dispute was finally settled, and the occupying forces evacuated; progress was made towards the eventual signing (in May 1955) of the Austrian State Treaty, which was to end military occupation there also; Britain's association with the European Coal and Steel Community was formalised under a Treaty of 11 December 1954; a collective defence organisation for South-East Asia (SEATO) was established through the Manila Treaty on 8 September 1954. Eden's own personal initiative in establishing the Western European Union (WEU) after the French Assembly had failed to ratify the EDC on 31 August capped a remarkable year, which his assistant private secretary Andrew Stark defined as an *annus mirabilis*.

At the heart of this period lay the Geneva Conference, which convened from April to July, and which tested Eden's experience and diplomatic skills to the limit. Here, he waged peace with such power that it was not long before hostile cartoonists were replacing his famous Homburg hat with the Chamberlain umbrella. The Geneva Conference was, in the words of its historian, 'the last example of an independendent British policy exercising significant influence in the resolution of a major international crisis.'[26]

The subject of Indo-China, and France's increasingly precarious colonial foothold in the region, was first discussed in Cabinet on 17 March, when Eden had circulated a paper saying that Indo-China had become 'top priority' for the Americans, a phrase originating from Robert Scott, British Minister in Washington.[27] The reason was the deteriorating French military position in Indo-China. The Communist Vietminh forces, which were helped by Chinese advisers, had launched their first assault on the improvised fortress of Dien Ben Phu on 13 March, with a view to strengthening their position at the upcoming Geneva Conference.

Preliminary meetings with Dulles in Paris and London in the early part of 1954 had not dispelled Eden's fears over the nature of Anglo-American cooperation. On 29 March Dulles had publicly launched a call for 'united action' against the Communists in Indo-China.[28] Since both Eden and the British Chiefs of Staff had approved a Foreign Office briefing paper for the Geneva Conference, which called among other things for the partition of Vietnam, the British Government was unhappy about Dulles's implied threat of direct action against China. The Cabinet discussed the matter on 7 April (together with Eisenhower's communication to Churchill three days earlier, which seemed to assume some kind of British military involvement in any such action) and agreed with Eden that any attempt to compel China to desist from helping the Vietminh, which she was already doing, was unlikely to succeed and, because of the Sino-Soviet Treaty of 1950, could even provoke a general war.[29]

When Dulles came to London on 11 April in an attempt to sell 'united action', Eden was careful to distinguish between the two aspects of the American proposal. The first was the question of forming a lasting collective security system for South-East Asia, which the British

Government supported, and which led eventually to the establishment of SEATO. The second was immediate action of some kind in Indo-China, to which Eden refused to commit the British Government until after the negotiations at Geneva had been given an opportunity to succeed. A major misunderstanding between Eden and Dulles then occurred. Dulles thought he had gained Eden's agreement to begin preliminary negotiations with interested powers, with a view to reaching a South-East Asia collective security agreement. Eden flatly denied that he had agreed to anything of the sort and it was this disagreement – rather than the Geneva Conference itself – which marked the breach between Dulles and Eden, and which so marred their subsequent relationship. In a despatch on 17 April to Roger Makins in Washington, Eden revealed his sense of frustration when he stated that the 'Americans may think the time past when they need consider the feelings or difficulties of their allies'.[30]

Tension was added to an already fraught situation after Eden had warned the British Chiefs of Staff in Paris on 22 April that the French were likely to be defeated in the decisive battle for Dien Bien Phu. At the outset Eden had told the British Cabinet that 'above all Western unity must survive the Conference unimpaired.'[31] Thanks to Dulles, it was to prove a close-run thing.

Geneva was the last of the old-style conferences, and for Eden there was an element of Proustian recall in visiting once more the scene of so many meetings of the 1930s.* Even the little restaurant by the lake, where Eden had lunched in those far-off days, was still there, and on arrival, as he wrote, 'we drove to the hotel which the British Foreign Secretary has always used.'[32]

On the first night, Paul-Henri Spaak, the Belgian Foreign Minister, came to dinner with the Britons at the Hotel Beau Rivage, which was so lacking in basic security requirements that they were reduced to banging the table at the same time as speaking to provide covering noise, because the Chinese, with a direct view from across the lake, were thought to be eavesdropping by some bugging device. As a result, Eden established himself on 29 April at the spacious Le Reposoir villa on the outskirts of Geneva with his secretariat, including Harold Caccia, Denis Allen, Evelyn Shuckburgh (later Anthony Rumbold took over from Shuckburgh as Principal Private Secretary) and Andrew Stark. Because of Eden's uncertain

*Much of the detail in the following account comes from comments in Eden's own handwriting in Sir John Wheeler-Bennett's personal copy of Robert F. Randle, *Geneva 1954: The Settlement of the Indochinese War* (Princeton University Press, Princeton, New Jersey, 1969), discovered by the author on an open shelf in the Wheeler-Bennett Library Bequest at St Antony's College, Oxford, and now in the Special Collections there. Sir John Wheeler-Bennett was the prospective official biographer of Eden, but predeceased him. The comments were clearly intended for use by Wheeler-Bennett in his task.

health, Churchill had arranged that Clarissa should accompany her husband, an unusual privilege in those days, and she now took over arrangements for the running of the house.[33]

Lord Reading, the second Minister of State at the Foreign Office, kept a British presence in the Hotel Beau Rivage and acted as Eden's eyes and ears, especially on the occasions when Eden had to return to London for consultations and Cabinets, and in June when Churchill and Eden went to Washington. Lord Reading was the loyal lieutenant, who underpinned much of Eden's conference work, moving effortlessly from his labours in the old India Office room in London (once occupied by his father) to Geneva. Unlike some of those jostling for position in the aftermath of Churchill's expected retirement, Reading was above such manoeuvres.

The Geneva Conference was to last nearly four months and fell into three phases. Initially, there were many procedural problems over delegations, with Eden negotiating mundane, yet divisive issues such as *placement*, and the precise distance between the delegations, so that those who did not want to sup with their respective devils could claim that, Rattigan-like, they truly were at separate tables. The middle section of the conference moved on to the hard negotiations, not only on the partitions proposed for Vietnam, but on subsidiary issues such as Korea. Meanwhile Britain had the simultaneous business of the Egyptian and Sudanese negotiations, and it seemed to many delegates that it was hardly possible for any one man to keep as many balls in the air simultaneously as Eden did.[34]

The conference opened formally on 26 April, in accordance with the arrangements settled at the meeting of Foreign Ministers in Berlin in February. Its main aims were to discuss the post-war future of Korea, after the 1953 July armistice, and to solve the problem of the eight-year war in Indo-China between France and the Communists, led by the Vietminh resistance movement, a one-time colonial war that now threatened to become a global Cold War conflict. The inclusion at Geneva of the People's Republic of China ended their diplomatic isolation since 1949. The arrival of two hundred Chinese delegates caused a tremendous stir, as they had not been seen in the West before. At first there was a hesitancy and little interdelegation hospitality (one effect of which was that Russian typists had to feast on supplies of left-over caviar).

It was the Russians who had wanted to broaden the agenda and include China. This was acceptable to Britain and France, where Joseph Laniel's coalition Government was on the verge of collapse, but not to an America only just recovering from the McCarthyite era. The hawks in Washington, such as Admiral Radford, Chairman of the United States Joint Chiefs of Staff, knew exactly how they would prefer to deal with intransigent

Communists, and the essential dilemma for Eden was whether Britain should go along with Dulles's interventionist wishes (involving aerial bombardment of Vietminh positions around Dien Bien Phu, thus risking a Third World War), or refuse to go along and thus end, or damage, the special relationship.[35]

In the first fractious phase of the conference, Eden did much to get the ball rolling, and was then, as one of the three rotating Chairmen, highly expeditious. He had too many memories of the frustrations caused by Churchill's meandering Cabinets to go into a meeting without a clear agenda. In a long talk with Dulles on 27 April, as he noted, 'I agreed that it must be our purpose to help the French by the strongest possible joint moral support & I hoped he did not think we were in any way luke-warm in our desire to induce the French to carry on the fight even if Dien Bien Phu should fall. That was why we were so anxious to get to grips with the negotiation here & to get some kind of settlement which we would subsequently guarantee.'[36]

From the start, the conference was seen as a crucial, if not final, opportunity to prevent the outbreak of a third world war. *The Times* declared this to be the most dangerous crisis facing the world since 1945,[37] especially as all the delegations came with different agendas. For the French, Indo-China was the colonial possession which should have restored France to power and prestige after the humiliations of the Second World War; they did not relish failure or retreat from Indo-China. For the Americans, Indo-China was the line in the sand to prevent further Communist expansionism. For the British, French power in Indo-China had meant greater security for Singapore and Malaya. For the Chinese, Geneva marked their emergence from diplomatic isolation. For the Russians, Geneva was an opportunity to test Western resolve, as an essentially bilateral dispute threatened to escalate into an international one. Dulles's declared position of wanting to roll back Communism caused considerable apprehension in the West, and Eden's determination to rein back the American hawks and avoid nuclear armageddon was absolutely crucial, helped by the calm, 'rather civil servantish' atmosphere he sought to instil into the proceedings.[38]

Such calm soon proved illusory. The pattern of each day in the main hall initially followed a fixed routine. The plenary session began with each delegation delivering a prepared paper and then answering questions on the paper. The Russians at first gave their *ex cathedra* pronouncements and then walked out, refusing to answer questions. This happened time and time again and tested the patience of the delegates, as the Russians, headed by Molotov, swept down the corridors and the minor functionaries pressed back against the walls to let them pass.

Eden always made a point of calling in each morning for a word with the British secretaries in their office, all of whom were bowled over by his charm – 'a dear' as they called him privately. During a lull one day, while waiting for the work to arrive, one secretary was whiling away the time by doing some knitting, which she put away hastily when Eden entered and he affected not to notice. But the next day when the typewriters were going like little Nibelungen anvils he said, with a twinkle in his eye, 'How's the knitting today?' At the end of the conference the Edens gave a great party at their villa, and Eden made a point of going round and speaking to everyone.

The 1954 Geneva Conference took place in the last age before intercontinental ballistic missiles. This, in the atmosphere of the Cold War, put Great Britain and Europe in a far more vulnerable position than America. Whatever Eisenhower and Dulles may have claimed, there was for Americans none of the urgency that faced the British and the French, who would be the first targets, bearing the initial brunt of any Third World War. Since nuclear war was not unleashed, it is hard now to re-create the tremendous apprehension felt in East Anglia, for instance, especially around Mildenhall, where the United States had an air base. Eden's belief that he had saved the world from global conflict at Geneva was in essence true, but it was never appreciated by the Americans. Only when longer-range missiles drew the Americans into the net during the Cuban crisis of 1962 did their tune change dramatically.

Eden and Dulles had got on well at Bermuda, but this was to prove the one happy interlude in their relationship. Eden's determination now to give the lie to the fact that Britain was the junior partner in the special relationship was something Dulles resented. As a result, the initial week at Geneva confirmed Dulles's feelings about Eden following their April disagreements, and he stored up his resentments to disastrous effect for Britain in 1956. Only after Dulles, unable to stomach the presence of the Chinese delegation, among other things, had flounced out of the conference after a week, to be replaced by General Walter Bedell Smith, Eisenhower's wartime Chief of Staff and now Deputy Secretary of State, was a fruitful relationship established between the leading allied Foreign Ministers. Eden seized the opportunity. The chemistry between Bedell Smith and himself worked from the start. Bedell Smith understood the British, having worked with them during the war; for his part, Eden admired and liked Bedell Smith, not least because of his military record. Bedell Smith's conciliatory desire to help the diplomatic process knew no bounds. Had he been appointed Secretary of State in 1953, instead of Dulles, the history of Anglo-American relations in the 1950s – and indeed, that of the whole decade – would have been markedly different. This was apparent in the brief 'overlap' period at the beginning of May when both Dulles and Bedell Smith were present.

On 1 May 1954 the three men – Foster Dulles, Bedell Smith and Anthony Eden – dined together with their advisers. The evening proved a fraught occasion, as Eden recorded the next morning:

> I dined last night with Mr Dulles, Lord Reading accompanied me and General Bedell-Smith, Mr Merchant and Mr Robertson of the State Department were also present. After some discussion as to the reason for the present mutual hostility between the United States and China, in spite of the close relations which had existed between them in the past, the conversation turned to the situation in Indo-China and we were subjected to a prolonged, and at moments somewhat heated, onslaught upon our attitude. Only General Bedell-Smith seemed to have any real comprehension of the reasons which had led us to take up our present position. Mr Dulles began by saying that the situation was very disturbing. In the past we had always been in accord on our policy of conferences; now we were in complete disarray. I said that we were not in any disarray as regards Korea but as regards Indo-China. I simply did not know what it was that we were being asked to do. If it were that we should intervene with armed forces, I could only say that I had already explained fully the reasons why such action was impossible and that anyhow I was unable to discover what steps we were being asked to take and what result was expected to follow.

Eden was disappointed with Dulles's demands for British military involvement, a blank cheque that he was not prepared to deliver. His note continues:

> It was a highly disturbing conversation, for it became apparent that the Americans were deeply aggrieved by our refusal to support them in such military measures as they may think advisable and that except for General Bedell-Smith, they could not or would not understand why we were holding aloof. At the same time they evidently had no definite plans of their own of any kind but were searching about for some expedient which would serve to restore or at least to hold the situation. There is clearly a danger that, being baffled in their attempts to find a solution of the problem, they may be ready to attribute the blame for their failure to us.

In a second note, Eden considered the wider implications of this meeting. He was pessimistic about the consequences:

> I am conscious of the effect of our differences over this question upon Anglo-American relations. But I am sure our only wise course is to follow a consistent line. This means we must refuse, pending the outcome of negotiations here, not only to allow ourselves to be drawn into the Indo-

China war but also to promise our moral support for measures of which we do not yet know the full scope.[39]

To Eden's relief, Dulles was only in Geneva for another forty-eight hours, and his departure relieved the pressure. 'I went to see Foster off. It was meant as a gesture but I don't think it did much good. Americans are sore, mainly I suspect because they know they have made a mess of this conference,' Eden wrote in his diary on 3 May. 'Bedell came to dinner. We surveyed the ground at length . . . I think that we made progress.'[40]

What Eden did not confide to his diary was that as Dulles and he waited on the steps of the Hôtel du Rhône for the car to take Dulles to the airport, he turned to the American Secretary of State and said, 'The trouble with you, Foster, is that you want World War Three.'*

The Geneva Conference was to show Eden at his most persuasive and informal. He liked conducting business on the margins of the conference, in the corridors and at the dinner table; he employed the quick conversation, the steering arm, the consoling word, as he found these more productive on many occasions than the formal setting of a plenary session, where too many egos jostled. He proved masterly at soothing ruffled feathers, of which there were plenty.

Despite his quickly established friendship with Bedell Smith, Eden's relationship with Molotov, one of the co-Chairmen, was the truly productive alliance of the conference, even though there were difficulties on the way, which Eden resolved with the exercise of all his diplomatic experience. Molotov recognised this, saying to Eden on 8 May, 'I think you are the man who has all the difficulties at this conference.'[41] Both implicitly understood that war over issues that were of essentially secondary importance to the British and Soviet agenda would be in nobody's interests. Molotov, whose name meant Hammer, certainly lived up to his billing, yet had the look of a tetchy schoolmaster or bewildered professor who had mislaid his lecture notes, belying the fact that he was one of the great survivors of twentieth-century politics. He had begun his first spell in Siberia at the time Eden was starting his first term at Eton. Their relationship went back to the 1930s, when Molotov was President of the Council of Commissars. Eden, whose sense of history was keen, never forgot that Molotov had been present at one of the historic turning-points of the twentieth century, the signing with Ribbentrop of the German-Soviet Non-Aggression Pact in August 1939. Eden was determined that Geneva in 1954 should also be an important turning-point, but on this occasion for

---

*John Tahourdin, who was present at the conversation, to the author, 5 December 1997. I am grateful to John Tahourdin for his help over the intricacies of the Geneva Conference, at which he was one of the British officials.

the general good of humanity. Molotov and Eden both feared that everything was going to the brink, and they had no desire to go down that path. It was different for Dulles – 'one more brink and he'll be brunk,' said the wags[42] – and progress was swift once he had departed the scene.

Eden always believed that China was a more revolutionary state than Russia and his first impressions were that Chou En-lai (almost his exact contemporary, having been born in 1898, but with a background and experience so different as to seem from another planet) was a harsh, unyielding anti-capitalist figure. In time, this view of Eden's was to soften. As Prime Minister and Minister for Foreign Affairs since 1949, Chou En-lai proved a figure of great experience and decisiveness, whose business-like approach to intractable problems greatly appealed to Eden, as did his unfolding view that Anglo-Chinese relations should be put on a more formal basis. As with Molotov, Eden's methods of personal diplomacy were to reap their reward. He invited Chou En-lai and his senior delegates to dine at Le Reposoir, as a prelude to presenting his scheme for giving Cambodia and Laos a measure of independence free of Communist control. 'Called on Chou-en-lai at 10.30,' Eden wrote in his diary on 27 May. 'He was in a much easier mood than in our earlier conversations. Think our talk about Laos and Cambodia may have been useful.'[43]

The Chinese reciprocated Eden's hospitality. Their villa was even more splendid than Le Reposoir, and Eden's many visits there in the course of the next few months revealed an aesthetic side to the Chinese character (they delighted in their specially imported porcelain) that formed a genuine point of contact. In Eden's opinion such rapprochement contributed on 16 June to one of the crucial break-throughs when, in a private conversation, Chou En-lai agreed that Laos and Cambodia should be treated separately from Vietnam.

Georges Bidault, the French Foreign Minister, was the other principal figure with whom Eden had extended dealings. By this stage of his career, Bidault was tired and in many ways a disappointed man. When others took a tea break, Bidault always went for a whisky break. Eden discovered that Bidault had been the private recipient of Dulles's forthright criticisms of him at Bermuda, disturbing evidence because Eden had previously believed that he and Dulles had been in agreement on many things. Now Eden received, involuntarily, Bidault's equally harsh criticisms of Dulles. But there was a volatility about the French political scene and arguably the French had most to lose at Geneva. They wanted to establish themselves once more as a front-rank power to be taken seriously in international circles after the humiliations of the dark years of the Second World War. Geneva had for them the air of a last desperate throw, which added to the tensions within their own delegations – tensions that Eden worked Job-like to pacify.

During the second phase of the conference, after Dulles had gone and before Mendès France had replaced Laniel as Prime Minister of France, Eden found that Britain was having to take all the initiatives ('Here I am struggling with the world's ills'[44]). This was the period when he kept the show on the road. On 10 June, so slow was the progress that he warned that the conference might have to be abandoned. Three days later the Laniel Government resigned after losing a vote of confidence in the National Assembly in Paris. Although this was the low point, it concentrated minds. Mendès France then became Foreign Minister (as well as Prime Minister) and a new urgency and purpose began a process of renewal, initially through Eden's talks with Chou En-lai, after which Eden was more hopeful, noting, 'It really looks as if the Chinese may want a settlement in Laos and Cambodia.'[45]

In addition to this, there was further pressure in June when Churchill and Eden travelled to Washington for talks with Eisenhower and Dulles. Much of the drama of the conference was concentrated in July, after the self-imposed deadline of 20 July set by Mendès France, putting his own career on the line if there was no settlement. If he failed, he made it clear that honour would compel him to resign, another imperative for Eden to reach a successful conclusion.

In the third phase – the time of the Mendès France deadline – the initiative inevitably passed to the French and Eden deliberately adopted a more responsive, secondary role. The result was what mattered, not who should take the credit.

Bidault's fears, which Eden understood, had been that the conference would mark the end of France's historic mission in Indo-China. For the French losing Indo-China replicated the pain that the British had experienced when India, the Jewel in the Crown, became independent and was partitioned. As long as Bidault was Foreign Minister it was difficult to get an agreement, especially as the Russians, sensing a weakness in the French executive, slyly raised questions over procedure. Eden was at his best in resolving these. Jean Chauvel, Ambassador to Berne, and the most senior of the French diplomats, much admired Eden's outstanding table manner at the conference during this phase, when for the French the proceedings had much of the aura of a Munich in reverse.[46]

The conference could not have achieved what it did without Eden as the hub of a great interlinking network of different agendas. His influence was seen in many ways. His informal approach even reduced the need for security men. The initial arrival of the various delegations in their bullet-proof cars, surrounded by burly men who had clearly not been invited aboard for their diplomatic skills, was reminiscent of something out of Al Capone's Chicago. By contrast, Eden travelled to the Palais des Nations with a lady driver and a single detective, and gradually the paraphernalia were scaled down. In any case, the Swiss crowds wanted to see Eden, and were not so exercised by the others once the novelty of the 200 Chinese delegates had faded.

Geneva marked the apogee of Eden's Foreign Secretaryship. Eden as Foreign Secretary during the war had been deferential towards Churchill's views, and he had refused to commit himself to ratifying agreements such as the Oder-Neisse Line without clearance first from Downing Street. In contrast, Geneva showed Eden Mark Two. Here, it was a question of how he could keep Churchill out of things, and limit interference on issues about which the Prime Minister knew nothing. 'I have lived seventy-eight years without hearing of bloody places like Cambodia,' Churchill had told Lord Moran,[47] and Eden did not want any of that in Geneva. (At one stage during the negotiations he rushed to Paris for a NATO meeting to prevent Churchill going instead.) His memoranda for Churchill were selective, rather than comprehensive, broad-brush rather than technical. In these he used the traditional colonial names, so that Churchill would understand and take notice, especially when he stressed the positive aspect, for example that Malaya was a dollar earner for the sterling balances. Had Eden written in detail about the Vietminh, there was no telling what reaction there might have been from London. He also showed the Americans that British policy would be made in the Foreign Office, not in Washington, with the tacit understanding that when he became Prime Minister he would aim to improve relations between the Communist and non-Communist world. He used Geneva as a future building-block.

His experience reshaped his attitudes towards the French and the Chinese. Eden felt that the French had lost their will, and feared that the danger of outside interference by China or the United States in Indo-China would lead to future global war. He never forgot that China (in the form of Chiang Kai-shek's Kuomintang regime of Taiwan) had a veto in the Security Council of the United Nations, which made the parallels with the League of Nations, emphasised by many, somewhat inexact. War as ever for Eden being the option of difficulties, he aimed to follow the least disadvantageous course overall, that of restraining the Americans without discouraging the South Vietnamese. Eden understood that politics was not the art of the possible, but the choice between the unpalatable and the disastrous, never wavering later from his belief that Suez fell into the first category.

He was aided by the fact that the French very much wanted to emerge from their political chaos and welcomed his help in finding a way through the jungle. In the difficult times at Geneva Eden showed exceptional patience, refusing to throw in the towel as lesser men would have done, even during the crisis of 10 June, keeping his waspish comments to the margins of the memos – at forty-five degrees in red ink. Fortunate in that Dulles was not at Geneva too long, Eden knew exactly when to call on Molotov. Delegates felt that he had stood up to the Russians, soothed the Chinese, won over the Americans (or Bedell Smith, which was not the same thing) and squared the French. Few could have matched this range of achievements.

At the end two issues dominated – where the demarcation line should be established between North and South Vietnam, and when the elections in South Vietnam should be held. The Communist view on elections was the sooner the better, 'next Thursday' preferably. Eden and Molotov persuaded them that it would be unrealistic to hold them for two years, which would give time to sort out the political dimension. The final settlement let the French off the hook – as a defeated power they got more concessions than they deserved – and gave the South Vietnamese a defensible partition line. Eden was in his element tying up all these loose ends.

The final days were intensely dramatic. On 15 July 1954 Pierre Mendès France arrived in Geneva, 'accompanied by the very friendly and comforting Eden'.[48] On the evening of 16 July, Eden and Mendès France met Molotov to seek clarification on the demarcation line. The next day Eden wrote to Bobbety Salisbury:

> The position here is extremely complicated & becoming tense as well. It is anybody's guess how it will work out, but I could not put the chances of success above 50:50 – they are probably less . . . If we have failed here we shall be faced with position of utmost gravity in France as well as in Indo-China. I fear Communists would soon mop up all latter, including Laos & Cambodia.[49]

On Sunday 18 July the delegations met at the Palais des Nations for a plenary session called at the request of Molotov. Two days of intense bargaining followed. On the morning of 20 July the end seemed in sight. The Vietminh demand was for the demarcation line to be on the thirteenth parallel. For Mendès France, the 'eighteenth' parallel remained the ideal solution, but one on which the French were willing to compromise. At the French villa at 5 p.m. on 20 July the main players assembled: Chou En-lai, Eden, Mendès France, Molotov and Pham Van Dong, the Vietminh delegate. At 5 p.m. Molotov said, 'Let us agree on the seventeenth parallel.' For Eden and Mendès France, this was not an unreasonable compromise. According to the Anglo-American memorandum of 29 June, which had been agreed in Paris on 14 July as the Western solution, the seventeenth parallel was only fifteen miles from the line accepted. The date of the Vietnamese elections remained the only stumbling block. Molotov suggested two years hence. Eden accepted this suggestion and by 5.20 the main differences had been resolved. But there was a final hitch. The Cambodians refused to sign and the assembled journalists in the Palais des Nations had to wait until past midnight, the French deadline, for delegates to appear. Someone had the fortuitous idea of stopping the clocks at the midnight hour. It was 3.20 a.m. before the delegates sat at the horseshoe table to sign the agreement. At dawn on 21 July the clocks were started again. Nearly eight years of war were, for the moment, at an end.

Despite the agreements reached at Geneva, the forebodings in Eden's letter to Salisbury were to be sadly justified by later events. Geneva had its downsides. It cemented an enduring mistrust between Eden and John Foster Dulles.* After Geneva, Eden could 'walk on water', and critics thought this gave him an exaggerated belief in his own abilities.

Perhaps Eden was doing it all with mirrors in 1954, perhaps it was a case of the Emperor's clothes, but it worked and in diplomacy this counts for a lot. Critics have said that Eden's achievement at Geneva was overrated,[50] as it was essentially a holding operation that did not prevent the agonies to follow. What Geneva did do, however, was to arrest a process that showed every sign of spiralling completely out of control. The spectre of world war was genuine and Eden made his contribution to preventing it. Benjamin Britten once said that it was the duty of a composer 'to be useful – and to the living'.[51] At Geneva Eden ensured that he too was useful to the living. The consequences may not have been harmonious in the longer term, but as J. M. Keynes said in a different context, in the long term we are all dead.

The North Vietnamese started to undermine the Geneva settlement almost before the ink was dry on the paper, and the United States gradually became embroiled in the quagmire of the Vietnam War, the most painful thing that happened to America in the twentieth century. Saigon and the helicopters were the pit that those at the Geneva Conference never foresaw.

Eden was to cling to the Geneva Conference as his undisputed claim to a place in history. It was, as James Cable has written, 'Britain's swan song as a Great Power.'[52] Eden's belief in what had been achieved was summed up by Robert Randle. 'The merits of the settlements should not be ignored or denigrated. Peace had been restored to Indochina, at least temporarily. Procedures for the regroupment and withdrawal of the hostile forces had been established. Independence from colonial rule for Cambodia, Laos and divided Vietnam had been formally and collectively recognised.'[53]

*

---

*To his credit, Eden was aware of this, which makes his later willingness to take Dulles at face value during Suez the more inexplicable.

Had Eden retired from the diplomatic world at that moment, he would have had few retrospective regrets, apart perhaps from the failure of the League of Nations to resist Hitler's pre-war reoccupation of the Rhineland. Even so it was not his Nunc Dimittis. Before 1954 was out, there were two more diplomatic triumphs to add to the record – Trieste and the Western European Union.

'Full agreement on policy to replace E.D.C.,' Eden wrote in his diary on 14 September, adding the next day, 'Trieste troubles me. We must get that settled.'[54] And settled it was.

Italy's dispute with Yugoslavia over Trieste had occupied Eden earlier in his 1952 talks with Tito, but now the problem flared up again. Compared to some of the other issues in 1954, Trieste was resolved comparatively quickly after Eden's personal initiative in brokering an agreement between Italy and Yugoslavia on their disputed zones. Eden was experienced in dealing with zones from the 1930s and 1940s. As a result, his talks with the Italian Prime Minister, Signor Scelba, and once more with Tito – together with judicious economic aid, partly underwritten by the Americans – proved the key. An agreement was signed in London on 5 October and three weeks later the allied military government ended. Eden was to devote a lengthy chapter to Trieste in his memoirs, and although the details may seem arcane half a century later, at the time it was, as he claimed, 'a classic example of the true functions of diplomacy, an open agreement secretly arrived at'.[55]

The EDC was an even longer-running issue, and in some essentials its ramifications still haunt European politics today. When the French Assembly failed to ratify EDC on 30 August, Eden's subsequent tour of European capitals, Brussels (for the three Benelux powers), Bonn, Rome and Paris, was crucial. His replacement 'non-federal' plan, which entailed bringing Adenauer's Germany into NATO, ending the allied occupation of West Germany and establishing a Western European Union as a second security tier alongside the wider Atlantic alliance was audacious in concept, and bold in its timing. Dulles's intervention, which involved him scurrying around the European capitals in Eden's wake, was less so. Nevertheless, within five weeks the crisis was over, and the long saga of German rearmament, first urged in September 1950 by the Americans as the best means of countering Soviet expansion in Europe, was for the time satisfactorily concluded.

Eden had been present at all stages of the odyssey. Until May 1952 he had been concerned to see an EDC treaty actually signed; for the next two years, he had worked for its ratification; and then in the last desperate weeks, following its collapse, potentially NATO's greatest crisis to date, he expounded his alternative scheme for Western European Union, which against all the odds proved acceptable both in Europe and America. Despite the scepticism of Churchill, who saw any European army as a 'sludgy amalgam',[56] and whose speech of 11 May 1953 in Eden's opinion 'probably cost us E.D.C. in France',[57] the new scheme ensured that any disarray in Europe could not be laid at Britain's door. Eden skilfully presented his revisionist plan to the Cabinet on 28 September, when Salisbury's support was crucial, on the day that the quickly convened Nine-Power London Conference, of the six EDC nations, plus the United Kingdom, America and Canada, opened. The next week Eden explained the details to the Conservative Party Conference at Blackpool on 6 October, in his capacity as President of the National Association.

Eden's motives were manifold, but hinged on the overwhelming need for British security. By bolstering Adenauer's domestic position in West Germany, thus putting a check on any Soviet aims to drive a wedge through the Atlantic Alliance, Eden also prevented any 're-appraisal' by Dulles of the American commitment to a European presence. He agreed with Ivone Kirkpatrick that if the Germans avoided the expense and burdens of rearmamament, then British markets would be threatened.[58]

The key to Eden's success was the six-capital tour, as he persuaded disparate countries to set aside their fears over sovereignty. When the conference opened in London, 'Eden's chairmanship', according to Adenauer's biographer, 'showed him at his most elegant and persuasive. Instead of getting submerged in the technicalities, Eden steered the conference to a resolution of the fundamental issues.'[59] Eden publicly committed Britain to a continued military presence of four divisions (together with air support) on the Continent. Coming from a politician who was seen as sceptical over wider European integration, the proposal had extraordinary broad appeal and credibility. As Ben Pimlott has commented, 'what Mr Eden saw as the great advantage of his W.E.U. system was that it offered the inclusion of Germany in the Western alliance and a more united Europe without the unwieldy political superstructure of the federal implications which made British participation in E.D.C. unacceptable to British opinion.'[60] It was a brilliant political balancing act, which according to the Belgian Foreign Minister, Paul-Henri Spaak, saved the Atlantic alliance. And to his senior Foreign Office adviser, Frank Roberts, this was the high spot of Eden's career, surpassing even Geneva.[61]

The shape of a great career, like the extended supporting ridges of great Himalayan peaks that yield additional noble summits, is not always distinct, but time adds its own perspective. In the many vicissitudes of his career, one moment stands out for Lloyd George as the identifiable main peak. On the afternoon of 29 June 1919, King George V greeted his returning Prime Minister at Victoria Station after the signing of the Versailles Treaty and drove with him to Buckingham Palace, as London poured out her citizens in best sort to fetch their conquering hero in. A laurel wreath was thrown into the carriage and the King handed it to the peacemaker, saying, 'This is for you.'[62]

Eden's identifiable moment, though not with such attendant public drama, came on 20 October 1954 when he was awarded the Order of the Garter by Queen Elizabeth II. The honour that he had declined in 1945, on the grounds that he could not have what Churchill did not then take, he now gratefully accepted, as Churchill had received the Garter in April 1953. To Britain and the world, Eden was now for ever 'Sir Anthony'. Like Edward Grey, his kinsman, in 1912, and Austen Chamberlain, his first mentor, after Locarno, he was, unusually, accorded this signal honour while still serving as Foreign Secretary. Before the year was out he had also been awarded the Wateler Peace Prize for his part in 'sorting out the world's ills', which came with £2,100 from the Carnegie Foundation, and even the *Daily Mirror*, normally the bane of Conservatives, had made Eden their 'Politician of the Year'. But 20 October 1954 remained his Everest.

From such peaks there is only one way: down. 'I cannot go on like this with this old man,' Eden wrote to Clarissa, 'I must escape somehow.'[63] He might have solved the world's ills in Geneva, but the problems closer to home, with an elderly Prime Minister refusing to leave Downing Street, were not to prove so tractable.

CHAPTER FIFTEEN

Waiting for Winston

1954–5

He [Winston Churchill] is confiding in no one, but he means to
carry on if he is able, and the question whether he will be able is
hardly ever out of his head. This is his secret battle. There are
moments when he does not want to do anything, when a
dreadful apathy settles on him and he nearly loses heart. But he
always sets his jaw and hangs on.

Lord Moran diary, 6 July 1953

It will be a testing time for colleagues. Their faces were wilting at
Margate; what they will be at Blackpool this month defies even
my Celtic blood to prophesy – But this is safe to forecast – they
all wish to remain in office and to do this the next election must
be won – If they feel that this is in jeopardy, they will roar like
lions!

J. P. L. Thomas to Anthony Eden, 25 August 1954[1]

The timing of retirement is one of the most difficult feats to accomplish, as
Dame Nellie Melba demonstrated on several occasions. There is always
one more farewell performance. As Churchill's eightieth birthday
approached in 1954, the matter was becoming urgent. Yet the method
necessary to get him to step down eluded some of the most determined
minds of the age. Churchill's final victory was won over his own
colleagues.

There were at least seven occasions on which Churchill's resignation was
anticipated, before it actually occurred, yet each time 'the old man' – as he
was affectionately known by some, and not so affectionately by others –
continued in office.* The first possibility was in the wake of the 1945
Election defeat. The war was over and a new world order was coming into
being. Clementine Churchill was foremost among those hoping that 'blest
retirement, friend to life's decline'[2] might now await the man whom
Harold Macmillan called the greatest Englishman in history. The
advantages were clear to many others, apart from Clementine Churchill.

---

*The previous octogenarian Prime Minister, Gladstone, was known as the G.O.M. (the
Grand Old Man), though for the Cecils the initials stood for 'God's only mistake'. Kenneth
Rose, *The Later Cecils*, Weidenfeld & Nicolson, 1975, p.34.

Peace would not enhance the wartime saviour's fame; indeed the hero was likely to be out of tune with its weak, piping times. But such arguments cut no ice with the Great Man, for there was one omission in the record that Churchill was determined to correct before his departure. He had never been *elected* as Prime Minister in his own right and had no wish to be bracketed with Arthur Balfour and Neville Chamberlain,* as a leader the people had never chosen. So one more contest (at least) was essential for this purpose. The problem was that such a contest, after Labour's 1945 landslide majority, was not going to take place for some time, and even then outright victory would be very difficult to accomplish in one campaign.

The subsequent narrowness of Labour's majority in the February 1950 Election gave Churchill his second excuse to carry on, even though, as has been seen, many Conservatives MPs, and even candidates, wanted a palace revolution at the time of the 1949 Party Conference. 'One more push' was a potent slogan employed by Churchill during Attlee's second brief administration, and in October 1951 he was returned to Downing Street.[3] At last, he received the endorsement he so craved, and so partly overcame the demons of his defeat in July 1945.

Not surprisingly, the 1951 election victory did not mark the beginning of the end for Churchill. He set about the reorganisation of the Cabinet system with enthusiasm, introducing a structure of 'Overlords', which did not prove a great success. Then, in February 1952 came the unexpected news of King George VI's death. Churchill now felt, with some justification, that he needed to oversee the transition to the new reign and help, as only he could, an inexperienced twenty-five-year-old monarch. For the third time, circumstances had given him the excuse to continue. Then there was the new Eisenhower administration from January 1953, and the uncertainties of the Cold War, leading to Churchill's speech of 11 May on summitry. Of all the reasons to continue, this indomitable belief that he was the man to establish détente with the Russians, especially after the death of Stalin, was the most powerful, and the one to which he clung most assiduously. Indeed, Anthony Seldon, in his pioneering study of Churchill's peacetime administration, considers that the overriding reason he finally retired was 'the eventual realisation that his proposal for a summit meeting would simply come to nothing.'[4]

Then came the coronation summer of 1953. For advocates of a dignified and orderly handover, this fifth opportunity, with its historical precedents of the retirements of Lord Salisbury (in 1902) and Stanley Baldwin (in

---

*Sir Alec Douglas-Home in 1963 and James Callaghan in 1976 completed the quartet of 'unelected' twentieth-century Prime Ministers.

1937), seemed the most propitious. Eden would then have ample time to set the agenda for the next election and establish a new administration. Again events overtook the option. Within three weeks of the coronation, Churchill suffered his stroke, while Eden was out of action in Boston for his third operation. As Clive Ponting has rightly pointed out, 'If Eden had been fit, there is little doubt that Churchill would have had to resign.'[5] But as Churchill recovered from his stroke, he could claim that he was keeping the place open for Eden by staying on – a magnanimous, not a selfish, decision.

In the autumn of 1954, however, many senior Conservatives were now determined that the seventh opportunity afforded by Churchill's eightieth birthday on 30 November should not pass without the issue being resolved once and for all. Eden had already had a fraught, private meeting with Churchill on 27 August. 'If I was not fit to stand on my own feet now & choose an administration now, I should probably be less so a year from now', he had told Churchill:

> The govt. was not functioning well & this was putting a heavy strain on all the senior ministers. There were able men but there was no co-ordination. Of course he didn't like this & said he had never missed a day since his illness. I said that wasn't the point. There was no co-ordination on home front & Cabinets dragged on far too long. There was much argument about all this which got us nowhere. I said that I would have been glad of the chance to take over a year ago, but it meant less to me now, & would mean much less still next year, if I were still there.

Churchill's response was to outline the alternative, that Eden might, if he wished, lead a rebellion of five or six ministers against him. This was merely turning the knife in the wound, for as Eden wrote, 'he knew perfectly well that I was the last person to want to do this after our many years of work together.'[6]

One minister who was capable of taking such measures into his own hands was Harold Macmillan, who sent Eden a reasoned memorandum arguing the case for the handover and offering to see Churchill personally. This he did on 1 October, following it up with a letter to Churchill the next day, warning that Eden might quit politics altogether. 'Don't you think it worth having another shot at getting him to go on the 80th birthday?' Macmillan wrote to Eden. 'It gives him a fine end – and only a few months less tenure of power than the May Election which he had seemingly considered.' A late autumn break with the past had one other incontrovertible benefit for Macmillan. 'The new Govt wd. start with the new Session', he wrote.[7] But it was not to be. With a tenacity that surprised and even shocked his colleagues,[8] Churchill fended off all suggestions that he might step down, swiftly deflecting any conversations on the subject. At Chartwell in August, faced by a delegation whose purpose he well anticipated, he had shaken his head solemnly over the recent death of Selwyn Lloyd's father, before saying, 'Quite young too, only 90.'[9]

To Eden directly, Churchill employed historical analogy. 'Fag-end administrations have not usually been triumphant. I can remember Rosebery after Gladstone and AJB after Salisbury. Both were brushed aside in spite of their ability, experience and charm.'[10]*

Churchill's disingenous argument about fag-end Governments raised many questions. If he intended to fight the next election, retirement immediately after victory would amount almost to deception of the electorate. If he intended to step down just *before* an election (and one was due by the autumn of 1956), then Eden would have no time to establish his own programme. The clear implication for many Conservatives, not all of them by this time supporters of an Eden succession, was that a second Churchill victory in 1955-6 would merely start the whole circus all over again.

The position of Butler and Macmillan in the equation was crucial. Both had expectations of, and ambitions for, the Premiership. It was in Butler's interests for Churchill to stay on, one of the reasons being that Churchill increasingly confided in him at this time, sensing a kindred spirit, for under that scenario the torch might conceivably be passed to Butler directly, bypassing the long-standing heir apparent. On the other hand, it was in Macmillan's interests for Eden to take over as soon as possible, as this would prevent the even younger Butler closing Macmillan out of the reckoning for ever. Even though Macmillan (born in 1894) was older than both Eden and Butler, he had not yet held one of the 'great' offices of state, and needed time to overtake Butler in the hierarchy, during (or so he hoped) an Eden Premiership that would be very short.

When the celebrations of Churchill's eightieth birthday were over (Graham Sutherland's infamous portrait being uncomfortably close to reality for many), it became increasingly clear that he would retire only at a moment of his own choosing, and that precious little parliamentary time would remain before the next General Election. It was not much comfort when he assured Eden that if he stepped down as Prime Minister before the General Election (though there was no guarantee of this), he would still stand at the polls, 'probably as a Conservative.'[11]

*

---

*Prime Ministers cannot choose their predecessors and Eden, no less than Rosebery or Balfour, was particularly unfortunate in his. In time, his was to become the most blighted fag-end Government of them all, shorter than James Callaghan's from 1976 to 1979, or John Major's seven-year period from 1990, between a Thatcherite and a neo-Thatcherite administration.

The timing of the handover was not the only point of contention between Eden and Churchill that autumn. Their attitudes to détente were radically different. There was a continuing wrangle over the Suez Canal Base Treaty. After meeting Nasser in Cairo in 1953, Dulles believed that Egypt would not join any Western anti-Russian alliance until the British had withdrawn from the Canal Base, so that at their June 1954 Washington talks (in the midst of the Geneva Conference) Churchill and Eden had been given a tacit understanding that American economic aid to Egypt would provide adequate incentive for the Egyptians to keep both the letter and the spirit of any agreement that the British negotiated. Yet for Churchill, it all smacked of 'scuttle'. 'What security have we got that the Egyptians, now breaking your treaty of 1936,' Churchill wrote to Eden, 'will keep any agreement that you will make with them?'[12]

To this strong point, there was no satisfactory answer. The ensuing Suez Base Agreement prepared the way for a phased withdrawal of British troops by 18 June 1956, and led to a considerable schism in the Conservative Party between those who believed that the nuclear age would make the base redundant, and the Suez Group ('the bastards' of the day, to employ John Major's later description of internal troublemakers) – led by Captain Charles Waterhouse, with strong support from Julian Amery, Macmillan's son-in-law – who thought it a dangerous sell-out. It was clear where Churchill's true sympathies lay. When asked by the Chief Whip, Patrick Buchan-Hepburn, to speak at a back-benchers' 1922 Committee meeting that promised to be particularly critical of Eden's policy, he replied, as he had once said to Selwyn Lloyd, 'I'm not sure I'm on our side.'[13] When Churchill paid tribute to Eden's achievements at the Blackpool Conference, he pointedly left Egypt off the list.

Selwyn Lloyd was a close observer of the fractious and deteriorating relationship between Churchill and Eden:

> When Anthony was about, he and Winston had continual arguments. I heard something of this from both sides. Egypt was the first bone of contention, in the end Winston gave way. On Summitry, Winston got his way, in the sense of floating the idea. On Europe, I did not follow the argument closely enough – I do not think Winston liked E.D.C. although much more favourable to Strasbourg than Anthony. The most painful incident between them to which I was a party was when Anthony was in Geneva for the Indo-China conference. W & he had been in agreement about holding off the US & Dulles from intervention to try to save Dien Pien Phu. Then at one stage, Winston wanted to make a statement in the House in answer to a question, I think. I told him that I thought A. would prefer him not to. He said he did not care and would make it. I sent a copy to A. I then had A on the phone from Geneva furious. I must stop the old man ruining everything. I told W. He was furious. I could ring up

and tell A he was PM and would make the statement. I got A on the line, the line nearly fused. I then said to A, I can do no more. I am connecting you to No 10 where W is, you must speak to him yourself. I went over to see W later. He was in the little drawing room upstairs – furious – he gave me a glass of brandy – and then stalked up and down the room saying that A was the most selfish man he had ever known, thought only of himself, had to do everything himself, was a prima donna, and quite impossible to work with, etc., etc. As the storm blew itself out, it transpired that W had truncated his statement to please Anthony.[14]

Such episodes, and they were not uncommon, as Evelyn Shuckburgh's diaries make clear, made a sad coda to a close comradeship that had been one of the central political relationships in twentieth-century British history.

Eden's response to Churchill's limpet-like qualities fell into four phases. Until 1951 he had reluctantly come to terms with the fact that Churchill would seek re-election; what he had most resented was that all the bread-and-butter work had devolved, largely unrecognised, upon him and then, whenever 'big' moments came along, Churchill had re-emerged from Chartwell or Marrakesh to steal his thunder. From 1951 until his illness in the summer of 1953, Eden had become increasingly frustrated with the situation, and, if truth be told, with his own inability, and even unwilling-ness, to force the issue. In these years, he had become not so much the reluctant deputy, as the reticent one.

For the latter part of 1953, Eden – though anxious lest the Conservatives 'skip a generation' (as many were now urging) – was grateful that Churchill did in fact stay, even if this was made possible only by the Prime Minister's circle disguising from the public the true state of Churchill's own health. Nevertheless, Eden was bitterly disappointed with the hand that fate had dealt him. Finally, after his convalescence and return, he began to wonder whether the game was worth the candle, and lost much of his appetite for the challenge. If chance would crown him, it would be without his stir.[15]

Historical opinion is divided as to Churchill's motives in staying on. Some believe that he genuinely wanted to allow Eden time to recover fully his former strength and have his rightful inheritance; others that by 1954-5 he had lost confidence in Eden and was determined that the Conservative leadership should go to a younger man.* Neither explanation bears much scrutiny. Eden's illness came relatively late in the process (in Churchill's

---

*Rather as Attlee's long-delayed retirement in December 1955 was to deal a grievous blow to Herbert Morrison's hopes of succeeding him as Labour leader.

thirteenth year as leader), and his range of achievements in 1954, the disagreement over Egypt notwithstanding, had shown that his health was not an obstacle to him holding his own on the international stage. His stamina impressed all his staff. An Eden succession in October–November 1954 for the new session would have been a natural transition, with plaudits for the octogenarian and the peacemaker in equal measure.*

The truth is that, as an old trouper, Churchill just could not bring himself to abandon five decades of parliamentary experience and write *finis* to his career. He genuinely believed that he was the only one who could be the focus for peace and summitry. October 1951 gave him a new lease of life, with the red boxes, the secretaries, the despatches, the crises. The adrenalin was a better restorative than any medicine. Whether Eden, or anyone else, was the Crown Prince was irrelevant. Churchill could not temperamentally leave the excitements of office and enter 'deserts of vast eternity'. Part of him wanted to die in harness, as Lord Palmerston and Sir Henry Campbell-Bannerman had done.†

As if to illustrate his continuing powers of patronage, Churchill embarked on a major reshuffle of his administration, announced on 18 October. In their August meeting, he had already brought up the old chestnut of Eden leading the House of Commons, but Eden was not won over, even though he knew Churchill's true motives for reconstruction. 'The reshuffle was mainly a device to enable him to carry on longer while doing even less', he wrote. 'He would then do nothing except interfere with the F.O.'[16] To Salisbury he had written:

> He has changed his mind & wants to stay until the General Election. So now we know what you always suspected. Worse still, to enable him to do this, he wants me to leave FO, become Deputy PM & lead the House & look after home front. I have said I cannot see how this can work & that I should prefer to follow Oliver Lyttelton [who had become Chairman of Associated Electrical Industries in 1954] & leave the Govt.[17]

Even beyond the Conservative Party, many felt that Eden was being unfairly put upon. 'Mr Eden's gifts as an emissary are an international asset we are apt to take too much for granted' was the comment in *The Spectator*.[18] So disenchanted was Eden he even began to consider seriously

---

*Nor did Churchill 'do an Attlee', for, under this analogy, who was the Gaitskell to Eden's Morrison? Certainly not Butler, with his Munich past and supposed advocacy of a negotiated peace in 1940. (When Churchill was asked for his opinion in 1957 as to Eden's successor, he recommended Macmillan, not Butler.)

†Though not in the same manner. Palmerston died in far from salubrious circumstances at Brocket Hall. Campbell-Bannerman resigned, and too ill to move out, died shortly afterwards in 10 Downing Street. By comparison, Neville Chamberlain's enforced departure in 1940, which first admitted Churchill to supreme power, had a decorous air.

the title he might take in political retirement, his choice finally settling on Lord Baltimore, after one of his ancestors who had been Governor there. He wrote again to Salisbury on 4 September, 'I am utterly weary of the whole business, including Foreign Affairs where of course one is not one's own master . . . Politics means very little to me now except for working with one's friends. I could not carry on without them; & that's you! We go to Stratford on Monday to see *Troilus and Cressida*.'[19]* The play's portrayal of the quarrels of warring factions matched the mood of the time.

After the Blackpool Conference, where Churchill in his speech had confused 1850 with 1950, Macmillan was summoned to Chartwell on 10 October and offered the key promotion in the reshuffle, taking over from Lord Alexander at the Ministry of Defence, always an important post psychologically for the Conservatives. Duncan Sandys, Churchill's son-in-law, replaced Macmillan at Housing and Local Government, and Selwyn Lloyd became Minister of Supply in place of Sandys. Anthony Nutting was promoted to Minister of State. David Maxwell Fyfe was elevated to the peerage as Viscount Kilmuir on his appointment as Lord Chancellor.

The reshuffle did not make many headlines, largely because the news of Eden's Garter award the same week grabbed public attention. It even rated a mention in the diary of the young Labour MP, Anthony Wedgwood Benn. The honour was widely welcomed. When Eden was installed as a Garter Knight at Windsor in June 1955, however, fundamentalist correspondents took up their pens again and, for example, Archbishop Fisher was in receipt of the following protest: 'By the aid of every kind of pageantry the Church is to do him honour, and his banner is to hang with honour in a Christian church. Not one word of protest at this scandal has, as far as my knowledge goes, been made by those in Authority in the Church.'[20] The past truly is a foreign country.

Earlier in the year Robert Carr had told Eden of Conservative reservations over the Canal Base withdrawal. 'Feeling about Egypt is smouldering,' he had written, as an honest PPS should. 'It is not so violent and obvious as far as the rebels are concerned although there are regular attempts at Question Time. But general unhappiness is, I think, more widespread both inside and outside the House. Even the *Economist* took us to task for not being tough or active enough about Egyptian interference with shipping in the Canal.'[21]

Eden was already acutely conscious that the proof of the Canal Base Treaty would only be in the eating. But he had taken risks before, and they

---

*Talking backstage on his Stratford visit to Laurence Harvey, who played Troilus, Eden remarked that he had, as always when seeing or reading this play, been impressed by Ulysses' speech on degree. 'What?' asked Laurence Harvey, whose knowledge of the play was confined to his own scenes. 'Does he have a big speech too?'

had come off. On balance he felt, as Churchill had written to him in February 1938, that *Alle Zoll Recht Kommen*! He had been greatly influenced by a (previously unpublished) memorandum by Charles Mott-Radclyffe, MP for Windsor, who had visited the Canal Zone in his capacity as Chairman of the Conservatives' Foreign Affairs Committee, and talked to the principal figures, including the new nationalist leader of Egypt, Colonel Nasser, and General Festing, Commanding Officer of the British troops, as well as several officers and men. His report questioned the continued validity of the British presence. 'To sit in a sand-bagged post, illuminated at night by arc lamps, with a village 100 yards away from which shots are fired every night & quite often during the day, without the slightest prospect of being able effectively to return the fire, is quite an ordeal for the old Sweat, let alone for the National Serviceman.' The soldiers were deeply sceptical about the value of their dangerous mission. 'They see the base disintegrating daily before their eyes. They know that at any time the Egyptians could sabotage the Canal if they wished to do so. In short, 20,000 troops are neither guarding the Base nor the Canal. They are merely guarding each other.' To add to their difficulty, the Canal Zone Base was the biggest in the world, 'spread-eagled over an area of 120 by 30 miles'. The logistics were impossible. 'All the senior officers to whom I talked agreed that the Canal Zone is a very convenient location for a base, since it is astride the back door (the Red Sea) and the front door (the Mediterranean) *provided that the population is reasonably friendly & can be relied upon to supply local labour as required.* Without this proviso, all equally agree that the base is a useless white elephant.'[22]

Such considerations did not impress themselves upon Churchill, who at the height of the battle for Egypt in November 1942 had said that he had 'not become the King's First Minister in order to preside over the liquidation of the British Empire'.[23] He tended to the broad view of history, whereas he felt that Eden could not differentiate between the big and the small points. On their joint visit to Washington during the summer, arguments over the Communist revolution in Guatemala, and the admission of China into the United Nations, had arisen out of a cloudless sky and led to angry scenes.[24] The Canal Base Agreement was all part of a pattern for Churchill. Ironically, in the fifteen years between Churchill's assumption of power and his final retirement, the British Empire was well on its way to liquidation.

The final phases of the Western European Union crisis had prevented Eden from contributing directly to the Manila Treaty, establishing SEATO in September 1954, but he was determined to attend the inaugural Council meeting in February, combining it with what he hoped would be his last *tour d'horizon* before entering Downing Street. In December, he attended with the new Defence Secretary a NATO Council meeting in Paris, where Macmillan's unflappable insouciance was much in evidence at the moment when Britain was committing herself to the development of an independent nuclear deterrent.

As Eden was preparing to bow out of the Foreign Office, one diplomatic era was giving way to another. A revealing episode on Eden's return showed that Churchill had not lost his acuity. 'He asked me how I had got on with Harold (Mac) in Paris,' Eden wrote in his diary. 'I said "Very well, Why?" He replied, "Oh, he is very ambitious." I laughed.'[25] Later, Macmillan was often to say that, as an older man, he posed no threat to Eden's position; at such moments Eden's friends thought it time to start counting the spoons.[26]

That same week threats of a national rail strike loomed, a foretaste of the industrial troubles that were to blight Eden's first weeks as Prime Minister. During the discussions in Cabinet, Eden aligned himself with the conciliatory wing, epitomised by Walter Monckton, the Minister of Labour. His main question was always, 'How can we solve this?', and not 'Should we be confrontational?'[27]

The year 1954 had indeed been a remarkable one in Eden's career. Looking back on it, he wrote in his diary:

> It is a strange thing about this year that though many people have written about the problems which we have, we hope, solved: Western European Union, Egypt, Indo-China, Arabia (Buraimi), very few have given much credit to Iran, which was, I believe the toughest of all.[28]

On 6 January 1955, the Edens lunched *à quatre* with Winston and Clementine Churchill. Arguments on the NUR and the proposed strikes soon disturbed the even tenor of what was primarily a social occasion. 'He said I was a Tory,' Eden wrote, 'that my city experience had done me no good & had imbued me too much with rights of private property. I said I had been brought up to believe this was a Liberal principle. Clemmie agreed.'[29]

On 1 February, before leaving for Bangkok, Eden tried to tie Churchill down to a definite date for the transfer of power. 'At my suggestion he sent for calendar. He admitted he could not carry on & after discussion said I could base my plans on his departure during last week of session before Easter [10 April in 1955].'[30]

Churchill became increasingly wary of Eden in these last months of his premiership. He had a distinct foreboding that things would change. In essence, Churchill had been a Coalition man, whereas Eden was more distinctively 'Conservative', although his Conservatism was of a progressive stance.[31]

Eden and his wife left London on 19 February for Bangkok. The tour was to take in Rome, Cairo, New Delhi, Pakistan and Iraq, and was set against the backdrop of the mutual defence pact signed by Turkey and Iraq in February, which Britain was to join on 4 April, Churchill's last full day in office. This 'Northern Tier' of the Baghdad Pact had as its aim a defensive shield against Russian expansionism in the Middle East, and the object of Eden's one, celebrated meeting with Nasser at the British Embassy in Cairo on 20 February was to persuade the Egyptian leader that it would also be in his interests to become actively involved in the Baghdad Pact.

Eden's meeting with Nasser has acquired mythological status. As with many myths, the melodramatic qualities have received greater attention than the more mundane truth. Much has been made of the venue – Sir Miles Lampson's former British Embassy, with its unhappy associations for Arab nationalists. Sir Ralph Stevenson, the British Ambassador and host for the evening, was a professional diplomat in a very different tradition, to whom Nasser gave the impression that he wanted to establish a new era of friendship and understanding now that the British military presence was being withdrawn,[32] an impression seen as a sham within days of the final departure of the last British troops.

When Nasser entered the salon that February evening, Eden greeted him in Arabic and, as they talked together on the sofa, explained that he had studied oriental languages while at Oxford. They talked of the Koran, which Eden had read in the original, and exchanged Arab proverbs, which Eden said contained real wisdom. As the butler hovered to replenish Eden's glass, he observed, *'El agla min esh-shaitan'* ('Haste is of the devil'). Although this was essentially the diplomatic small talk at which Eden was so experienced, Nasser indicated that intentions were friendly, even though there were substantive disagreements on the Baghdad Pact. Eden told Nasser that he had signed the original 1936 Anglo-Egyptian Treaty, which is why he had wanted to present to him a signed copy of the new Canal Base Agreement.

At dinner, Eden and Field Marshal Sir John Harding, Chief of the Imperial General Staff, moved on to the issue of the hour, nuclear weapons, and Nasser expressed his fear that any non-nuclear war would soon escalate into a full-blown nuclear one. Over coffee in the salon, Eden produced more Arab proverbs. He was well aware that the new Egyptian national leaders were 'revolutionaries who owed nothing to his country or government, single-minded in their aims and confident in their abilities to implement them'.[33]*

---

*Mohammed Heikal's description of the Eden-Nasser meeting in this chapter is invaluable for its Egyptian perspective, and not entirely unfavourable to Eden as are some Western accounts.

As he left, Nasser was said to have contemplated the difference between the two worlds. ' "What elegance!" he exclaimed. "It was made to look as if we were beggars and they were princes!" But he felt the occasion had been a useful one and that Eden was the sort of person with whom it might be possible to do business.'[34]* On 31 March, Nasser indicated that he would like to visit Britain in the autumn.[35] It was a visit that never took place.

From Egypt, Eden went on to Pakistan, before arriving in Bangkok on 23 February, where he had not entirely successful talks with Foster Dulles on making SEATO a permanent entity, a Far Eastern equivalent of NATO. Anthony Rumbold, who coordinated Eden's speeches on the tour, went on the principle of 'get peace into your last sentence and you're home and dry'.[36] Unfortunately, this did not always ensure Dulles's compliance.

The Edens began their long journey home with a visit to Simon Eden's grave in Burma, a poignant and emotional moment.†

At Nehru's invitation, Eden addressed the Indian Parliament in Delhi, before visiting the Iraqi leader, Nuri es-Said, in Baghdad, where he sought to reassure him about Nasser's nationalist ambitions. On 8 March he reported to the House of Commons on his tour. It was widely regarded as his last such diplomatic mission.

In his absence, however, Churchill had been rethinking his commitment to an Easter retirement, and Robert Carr had sent worrying details to Eden in the Far East. Churchill now employed a 'count-down' document to guide him, not dissimilar in spirit to the chart he had used as Home Secretary before the Great War, indicating the days left before the execution of a condemned prisoner.[37] At all stages the document stated 'my successor', not 'Anthony Eden'.[38]

The issue of Churchill's retirement came to a head at a dramatic Cabinet on 14 March, the tension increased by the fact that the inner circle of senior ministers, such as Eden, Butler, Macmillan, Salisbury and Crookshank, knew perfectly well what the circuitous discussion was all about, whereas the outer circles were largely in the dark about all the niceties, which suddenly exploded in naked anger on both sides. Harold Macmillan has left a vivid account:

> It looked as if the meeting wd. end without the real issue being dealt with.
> As so often with our countrymen, it was too awkward & painful for
> anyone to say anything about it. Then a dramatic moment came when

---

*Nasser's attitude to Eden was a pre-echo of Mrs Thatcher's feelings about Mikhail Gorbachev.
†The grave was at the time in a temporary location with fine views. Later it was relocated, with other war graves, to the outskirts of Rangoon.

Eden said, slowly & without evident emotion "Does that mean, Prime Minister, that the arrangements you have made with me are at an end?"

Churchill, clearly rattled, muttered about the national interest coming first. Macmillan's account continues:

Eden then blurted out 'I have been Foreign Secretary for 10 years. Am I not to be trusted?' Churchill replied 'All this is very unusual. These matters are not, in my experience, discussed in Cabinets.' There was a long & difficult silence. Salisbury then said 'It is clear that certain plans are known to some members of the Cabinet; would it not be better if they were known to all?' Churchill said 'I cannot assent to such a discussion. I know my duty & will perform it. If any member of the Cabinet dissents his way is open.' After another pause, Butler made a useful intervention saying 'It's not a question of loyalty to you or your leadership, Prime Minister. It's a question of whether an election may become necessary. You have always said that you wd. not lead the party at another election. We must consider all these dates simply from the national interest. In my view another Labour Government now wd. be a disaster from which the country might never recover.'

To this Churchill had no immediate reply and the meeting broke up without any firm decision, but everyone knew that the death-knell of Churchill's Premiership had sounded. Harold Macmillan concluded that it was 'the most dramatic, but harrowing discussion at which I have ever been present'.[39]

Eden had one last visit planned (to Yugoslavia), and it seemed that this duty would finally prove his Nunc Dimittis as Foreign Secretary. But on 29 March, Churchill, clinging to the straw of Bulganin's seeming acceptance of the need for Four-Power talks, sent for Butler (significantly he did not see Eden face-to-face) to warn that things might have to be put on hold. Eden wrote despairingly to Salisbury that evening, 'Position is still not settled tonight, & W talked to RAB of no dates having been fixed. I fear Cabinet may be difficult tomorrow. W is lashing about, according to RAB.'[40]

The next morning Churchill seemed in a more tranquil mood, and in Cabinet concentrated on the date of the Election. But all his colleagues, and tacitly Churchill himself, knew that this would be a matter on which his successor would advise the monarch. At 5.15 Eden held a meeting in the Foreign Secretary's room with Butler, Macmillan, Woolton, Crookshank and Monckton. They talked about the Election date, closely balanced between May and October. Macmillan favoured May, and at the end of the meeting, Eden took him aside to tell him that Churchill had finally confirmed that the following Tuesday, 5 April, would be his farewell Cabinet.

*

Churchill's last days in office were suitably marked. A farewell dinner on 4 April in Downing Street for the Queen and the Duke of Edinburgh made a fitting culmination to his public life. Only Churchill's closest associates were invited – there was no place for Harry Crookshank, James Stuart or Lord Woolton – alongside the extended family. The Edens were there in both capacities. With great thoughtfulness, Churchill had invited Annie Chamberlain, Neville's widow, a reminder of those far-off days when Churchill had taken office at Britain's moment of greatest peril.

Almost inevitably, Randolph Churchill proved a severe embarrassment on what should have been a night of unfettered pleasure and pride for his parents. Before long he was drunk and making gauche advances to some of the female company. When the Edens arrived, he soon confronted Clarissa. 'You ought to know that I am against the new regime,' he declared, adding that he had just written an article for *Punch* setting this on the record.

The next morning, in the midst of all the tasks necessary for the move to Downing Street, Clarissa Eden penned a letter to Randolph Churchill, which was delivered by hand:

> As I believe you do not remember our conversation of last night, here is what I said.
>
> I am sad that you should value our friendship below the pleasure you get from your cheap and futile campaign against Anthony in clubs and, no doubt, in print.
>
> I cannot see what advantage it can possibly be to yourself, Winston or the Conservatives. That it has material advantage for you I can well believe, and I am hurt that you should sell our friendship in this way.

Even Randolph Churchill, not normally sensitive to the feelings of others, was taken aback by this rebuke from his cousin, and tried, in vain, to effect some partial reconciliation, though he went about it in an odd manner, describing Clarissa's original letter in his reply as 'so silly and misguided'. Another letter was soon on its way to Randolph. 'I am genuinely amused and curious of all that the press write on A. but sustained attacks from *friends* I find impossible to take,' Clarissa wrote. 'You must understand that surely and appreciate my dilemma.'[41] Randolph's behaviour during the Eden Premiership, and afterwards, showed little sign that he had understood.

While this correspondence between his son and niece was unfolding, Churchill was holding his final Cabinet, formally announcing that he would be having an audience with the Queen that afternoon to tender his resignation. Anthony Eden then spoke on behalf of the Cabinet, paying tribute to Churchill's long years of service to the nation. 'If in a succeeding Government they met with success,' the Cabinet minutes recorded, 'this would be largely due to the example which he had shown them: if they did less well, it would be because they had failed to learn from his experience and skill as a statesman.'[42]

It was all very polite and English, but the atmosphere positively crackled with tension. There were too many memories for it to be otherwise. Many breathed a sigh of relief when the Cabinet ended, wondering how long the half-truths would suffice.[43]

Churchill's pessimism had been communicated to Jock Colville the night before, after the farewell dinner at Downing Street. Sitting on his bed, berobed and bedecked with the honours of his plenitude, Churchill said to Colville with some passion, 'I don't believe Anthony can do it.'[44]

It was an ungracious end. No Prime Minister in modern times had made it so awkward for his successor to take up the burdens of office in a smooth and trouble-free transition.

Churchill's complex dealings with Eden proved a stain on the record of his peacetime administration, unfortunately obscuring the fact that these were years of full employment, stable prices and relatively placid labour relations. The price for this economic equilibrium would have to be paid later, but in retrospect the years do have about them an aura of golden innocence; 1955 proved the last tranquil year of the old ways before society's assumptions were changed for ever – what Paul Addison has called 'an interlude between two periods of social change: the state-led social reconstruction of the 1940s, and the consumer-driven discontents of the 1960s'.[45] In the broader context, Eden was part of this *ancien régime*, an age when childen still 'Listened with Mother',[46] and deference was part of the hierarchical pattern of both employment and leisure. Eden's misfortune was to take office at the very moment that such deference was beginning to break down. It was not only the young men who were to prove angry in the next phase.

'The trouble with Anthony Eden,' Macmillan said later, 'was that he was trained to win the Derby in 1938; unfortunately, he was not let out of the starting stalls until 1955.'[47] Macmillan did not intend his own political destiny to be blighted in like manner. Eden soon realised the truth of Lloyd George's maxim, that there can be no friendship between the top five men in a Cabinet. It was a lesson that Macmillan already knew well. In 1952, he had written in his diary, 'I like both Butler & Eden. They both have great charm. But it has been cruelly said that in politics there are no friends at the top. I fear it is so.'[48]

PART FOUR

Greatness Going Off?

The soul and body rive not more in parting
Than greatness going off.

Antony and Cleopatra, IV.xi. 5–6

TURNING A NEW PAGE ?

CHAPTER SIXTEEN
'A Pretty Tough Assignment'
1955–6

Glories, like glow-worms, afar off shine bright,
But looked to near, have neither heat nor light.
John Webster, *The Duchess of Malfi*, IV.ii. 148–9

Anthony has no friends except his smooth young men in the
Foreign Office, whereas Butler has acquired a regular following
and Macmillan is also more popular than Eden. Anthony will be
inclined to work closer with Salisbury in the aristocratic Mayfair
tradition. He is a diplomat but Prime Ministers have to give
orders.
Walter Elliot, 1 April 1955[1]

At noon on 6 April 1955, Anthony Eden was summoned to Buckingham
Palace where he kissed hands on his appointment as Prime Minister, the
second of Elizabeth II's reign. Surprisingly, he was the first Foreign Secretary
of the twentieth century to succeed to the Premiership. 'It is a pretty tough
assignment to follow the greatest Englishman of history', Harold Macmillan
wrote in his diary, 'but I feel sure Eden will make a good job of it.'[2]

Others were less sure. The main worries were Eden's health, the
debilitating effect on his temperament of the prolonged wait for the
inheritance, and his relative lack of direct experience of domestic affairs.
Lord Swinton told Churchill bluntly that Eden would prove 'the worst
Prime Minister since Lord North', and thought it a great mistake that he
had been chosen as Churchill's successor ten years earlier. Churchill agreed
with the second proposition, and did not demur from the first.[3]

Hugh Dalton thought Eden in better shape than either Butler or
Macmillan. 'Physically, Eden, though he was three times cut up, has made
a wonderful recovery', he wrote. 'He can still play tennis, and his move-
ments at the box are much freer than either of the others.' Nevertheless, he
also recorded in his diary Robert Boothby's opinion that Eden would not
last eighteen months.[4]

As there was a national newspaper strike, contemporary expectations
were restricted to the provincial Press and political journals. The *Yorkshire
Post* dismissed any fears that Eden would be unable to deal with domestic
issues, and *The Spectator* noted that Conservatism now existed again and

that Eden had succeeded to the leadership of his party 'with as much goodwill as any new Prime Minister can ever have had in time of peace'.[5] The impact of the changeover made itself felt in other, less expected areas. For, 'Il est très distingué', a contemporary French–English phrase book now offered the translation, 'A regular Anthony Eden'.[6]

The House of Commons was at its best for Eden's first appearance as Prime Minister that afternoon. Attlee made a gracious tribute to Churchill, and struck just the right note in welcoming Eden in his place. 'Eden's reply', Macmillan observed, 'was excellent, in time, temper, matter & manner. A very good start. Our boys gave him no end of a cheer.'[7] After question time, Eden consulted in his room at the Commons with Butler, Macmillan, James Stuart and the Chief Whip, Patrick Buchan-Hepburn, on the final shape of the new Cabinet.

Before taking over, Eden had already held several meetings on the two urgent questions of the day – his successor at the Foreign Office and the date of the General Election. Reshuffles inevitably occupy much of a Prime Minister's thinking, but, if successful, the time is well spent, as so much depends on that strange blend of personal chemistry. Eden reshaped his Cabinet twice, first on taking office, and then in December 1955. Neither reshuffle was entirely successful, for different reasons. Eden's freedom of movement at the outset was complicated by the timing of Churchill's retirement, as Rab Butler, then Chancellor of the Exchequer, was about to bring in his fourth Budget on 19 April, less than two weeks away. As a result, the Cabinet reshuffle did not include an overdue change at the Treasury, though Eden promoted Macmillan to the Foreign Office.

Through understandable sympathy for Rab Butler's lonely position (his wife had died the previous December after a harrowing illness), Eden was to shrink from shifting him after the May Election. He conceded this might be a mistake. 'I can't move Rab from the Treasury,' he told Robert Carr, 'even if in the end it proves the destruction of my Government.'[8]

His kindness did no long-term favours to Butler, who in the next few months was severely to damage his reputation for competent fiscal management. Eden's appointment of Macmillan to the Foreign Office was also to backfire. He had wanted to appoint Bobbety Salisbury, but he flinched from the choice. Five peers had held the post in the twentieth century – from Salisbury's own grandfather, through Lansdowne, Curzon and Reading to Halifax – but the last occasion was fifteen years before, and Eden felt that he could not break with the accepted convention that a Foreign Secretary must be in the Commons.[9]*

---

*Not a consideration that was to inhibit Macmillan himself five years later, when he appointed Lord Home to the post, or Mrs Thatcher in 1979, with the appointment of Lord Carrington.

So close was Eden's empathy with Salisbury, and so long their political symbiosis, that Bobbety's appointment to the Foreign Office would have led to a much more fruitful and understanding working relationship than that with Macmillan. Reluctantly passing over Salisbury (who remained Lord President of the Council and Leader of the Lords) was a decision that Eden later regretted.

Arguably he should have embarked on a more radical reconstruction immediately (including changes in the Treasury team) to avoid any accusations that his Government was merely a continuation of Churchill's. Many junior figures were greatly disappointed, and this unease was to be significant later.

The Salisburys were Eden's first guests at Chequers. Characteristically, Bobbety Salisbury was not concerned about his own position, but he did discuss the House of Lords at some length with Eden, stressing that in his view, 'There *must* be a strengthening of the Govt in the Lords after the Election.'[10]

Macmillan's promotion left a vacancy at Defence. 'When I came to form a government early in 1955,' Eden wrote, 'I wanted to select one or two men to bring into the Cabinet who had, as I thought, proved themselves in subordinate offices and might be looked upon to play leading parts in government and party in the future. The two I selected were Mr Selwyn Lloyd in the House of Commons, and Lord Home in the House of Lords.'[11]*

By appointing Selwyn Lloyd to the Ministry of Defence, Eden was not only keeping his promise, but acknowledging that the member for the Wirral had proved a dependable and versatile lieutenant.† Lloyd's post at Supply went to Eden's Research Department assistant of the late 1940s, Reginald Maudling – like Lloyd, a future Chancellor of the Exchequer.

Eden did not prove a good butcher in April 1955. Too much old blood remained. Woolton was prepared to step down, but was persuaded to stay on as Chancellor of the Duchy of Lancaster and Party Chairman to help with electoral strategy, a sensible short-term move, though after the Election he urged Eden to give his post to a younger man. The Earl of Selkirk eventually replaced Woolton in the December reshuffle. One of the few outright casualties in April was Lord Swinton, the Commonwealth Secretary and a veteran of the Baldwin and Chamberlain Cabinets. His acerbic views of Eden were not caused by this sacking (he was acerbic

---

*In time, Home was to provide the higher profile for the Upper House that Salisbury wished, though few could have foreseen this in 1955.
†In this central relationship of the next two years, Lloyd's war record counted for a great deal with Eden. Defence was on the fringe of the 'great' offices of state and would be a stepping stone to the Foreign Secretaryship for Lloyd within eight months.

about most people), but Eden's circle had little time for him, 'a very second-rate politician' in Oliver Harvey's view.[12] Much to Swinton's discomfiture he had to make way for Lord Home. Buck de la Warr was replaced as Postmaster-General by Dr Charles Hill, Nye Bevan's old adversary from his British Medical Association days. For Macmillan the Foreign Office was to prove something of a poisoned chalice; Lloyd and Home, therefore, were to be the two winners of Eden's reconstruction. Entering the Cabinet for the first time, they both rewarded Eden with unfailing loyalty through the darkest of the days that followed, not something that was to be true of all of his colleagues.

Eden's first Cabinet meeting took place at 3 p.m. on 7 April. Only Lord Home, who was in Helensburgh on Scottish Office business, was absent. To general relief, the agenda-less meanderings of Churchill's last years were now replaced by crisp, business-like consideration of three items – the continuing newspaper stoppage, on which Walter Monckton had a discouraging statement; a joint paper by the 'Secretary of State for Foreign Affairs and the Minister of Defence' (Eden and Macmillan), which led to some jocular banter; and a general discussion on the Election date. The overwhelming preference, with Rab Butler the strongest advocate, was for an early contest, lest economic difficulties in the autumn should later take the gloss off the new administration. The only dissent came from Osbert Peake, Minister of Pensions.

'As you know I have been tempted to try to show that we can be a good Administration for at least six months before appealing to the Country,' Eden wrote to Churchill the next day, 'but I am increasingly compelled to take account of these distasteful economic factors.'[13] Churchill was pleased that the decision had been taken so quickly; less so when he found himself largely written out of the script and confined to the margins.

The decision seemed a speedy one. In fact, Eden had been agonising over it for some time, to Woolton's exasperation. Too much was at stake. It would have been the ultimate irony if Eden's government had been voted out within a few weeks. Central Office was concerned lest Clarissa Eden's suspected preference for a later date might influence Eden against capitalising on the moment, and Oliver Poole, the Party Chairman, made discreet (albeit unnecessary) representations through Fulke Warwick.[14]

Nevertheless, the decision by Eden to call an Election was one of considerable bravery, for although the electorate was not as volatile as later, there was no guarantee of victory. In April 1955, the Gallup Poll put the Conservatives on 41 per cent, only one point ahead of Labour, with a predicted final lead of 1.7 per cent. (In a predominantly two-party contest, the eventual margin of victory was 3.3 per cent, more than the overall Liberal vote of 2.7 per cent.) By opting for May, Eden was also subtly capitalising on the British sense of fair play that he 'deserved his turn', a view not limited to Conservative supporters.

Two other factors tipped the balance for an early poll. The workers in the Lancashire cotton towns would be on their 'wakes weeks' around Whitsuntide (a point Butler spotted), and in the days before postal votes were available for holiday-makers, this could deliver some vital North-West seats to the Conservatives. Their overall majority in 1951 had been only seventeen and every seat mattered. More significantly, the Labour Party was in the midst of one its perennial bouts of in-fighting, this time the long-running feud between Gaitskellites and Bevanites, which was to continue even after the deaths of Bevan and Gaitskell in 1960 and 1963 respectively.

By comparison with Labour, the Conservatives had relative youth and glamour on their side. Attlee had been Labour leader for more than twenty years and was now seventy-two. Despite the special circumstances of the 1945 triumph, Attlee's electoral record was not in fact all that good, and May 1955 was to be his third failure in five attempts to deliver victory for his party. Only Edward Heath in modern times was to have a worse record, with three defeats out of four. Delay could mean a new and younger Labour leader, probably Gaitskell, to challenge Eden's hegemony. It was another imponderable to set alongside the economic outlook and confirm a springtime Election.

As a result of all these factors, dissolution was planned for 6 May, with polling on 26 May. 'I really must go to the country,' Eden told his agent, John Devine, 'so that the people can have their say.'[15]*

The 1955 General Election, only ten years on from the Labour landslide that had seemed to change the parliamentary map for ever, was one of the dullest in living memory. Hugh Dalton thought it 'the most tedious, apathetic, uninteresting' of the ten in which he had been involved.[16] In psephological terms it was the classic example of the outcome being influenced, not by current canvassing, but by the memory of the previous campaign.[17]

In 1951, Labour had campaigned predominantly on three issues: unemployment, they claimed, would return to its pre-war levels under the Tories; the welfare state would be dismantled; and (with Churchill's 'finger on the trigger') warmongering would prevail. By 1955, unemployment was

---

*It would be the first May contest since 1929, not a propitious precedent, as Baldwin had then lost a commanding Conservative majority. More encouragingly, the two previous incoming Prime Ministers to seek an early mandate from the electorate – Campbell-Bannerman in January 1906, and Bonar Law in November 1922 – had been successful in their quest.

down on a year-by-year basis; the social services had not been dismantled, indeed there had been an increase in real terms in social expenditure, especially since 1953 in housing provision; and the Korean and Indo-China conflicts had been ended. Eden was popularly seen to have contributed to all these positive factors, and he wisely made the property-owning democracy and progressive Conservatism the theme of his campaign.

Events now followed a brisk timetable. The new ministers went to Windsor on 12 April to be sworn in, and Rab Butler's Budget followed a week later. Eden was confirmed as the new leader of the Conservative and Unionist Party Parliament at a meeting at Church House, Westminster, and Parliament was dissolved on 6 May. Butler's fourth Budget, destined to be his most controversial, was the big political news, containing as it did £135 million of tax relief, including sixpence off the standard rate of income tax, abolition of purchase tax on textiles (a boost for the Lancashire mills in the face of increasing overseas competition) and increased personal allowances. Such an expansionist package, at a time of economic boom, may have been electorally attractive, but many commentators felt that Butler had been badly advised.*

When the General Election was announced, the high command had felt, even hoped, that Churchill would not wish to take any major part in the campaign. Belatedly it became clear that Churchill did wish to take part, and some tact was needed to dissuade him from taking on one of the broadcasts. The situation was one of delicacy for Eden, whose whole *raison d'être* for calling the Election was to make a fresh start in his own image. At a late stage George Christ, one of the senior figures in the Research Department, who had been due to accompany Eden on the hustings, was allocated instead to Churchill, with the job of confining the former Prime Minister to his Woodford constituency for a few ceremonial photo-calls with cigar and Victory sign. What rankled even more with Churchill was Eden's new-found enthusiasm for the Four-Power summit, now scheduled for Geneva in July. 'He made one sly dig at Anthony,' wrote Macmillan in his diary of a visit to Chartwell. ' "How much more attractive a top line meeting seems when one has reached the top!" '[18]

Eden was now without a personal assistant, as all the other senior Research Department figures had already been assigned to Cabinet members. Lord Woolton, the Conservative Party Chairman, who set about finding a replacement at the last minute, was reminded that his speech at the Conservative Party Conference in Blackpool in October 1954 had been

---

*Sam Brittan considered the package 'a serious blunder' that contributed to Butler's failure to win the Premiership in both 1957 and 1963. Sam Brittan, *Steering the Economy*, Penguin Books, Harmondsworth, 1971 revised edition, pp.201, 203.

Simon Eden, a few weeks before his death on active service with the RAF in Burma, June 1945. 'Have got the Burma Star and the 1939-1945 one as well,' Simon wrote in one of his last letters. 'There will be a Jap star and probably a Singapore star, so I shall return home looking like a map of the Heavens!'

(*Left*) April 1945: Alec Cadogan and Eden leave the Capitol in Washington after the first part of Roosevelt's funeral. 'No word of greeting or thanks from anyone – when one thinks Eden had flown the Atlantic to be present & show the sympathy of the British Government.' (*Above*) Robert Carr. 'He has first hand knowledge of industry so if anyone can make sense of our tangled industrial relations he should.' Photographed in New York, August 1951. (*Below*) Clarissa and Anthony Eden outside 10 Downing Street on the day of their wedding, 14 August 1952.

Anthony Eden at the height of his powers: with Pierson Dixon in Rome, 1952.

The Geneva Conference, May–June 1954: Walter Bedell-Smith, American Under-Secretary of State; Georges Bidault, French Foreign Minister; Eden.

Eden with an interpreter and Chou-en Lai.

(*Above left*) Waiting for Winston. Eden and Churchill return from Washington in July 1954, with Churchill still refusing to set a firm date for handing over the leadership to his heir apparent.(*Above right*) Harold Macmillan and Anthony Eden at Le Reposoir, Geneva.

(*Below*) The only meeting. Nasser with Eden and the British Ambassador, Ralph Stevenson, at the British Embassy, Cairo, 20 February 1955.

The 1955 General Election.
(*Left*) Constituency headquarters, Leamington. (*Below*) When the going was good: canvassing with Clarissa. (*Bottom*) 'The older the lady, the deeper the swoon.' Conservative Women's garden party at 10 Downing Street.

(*Above*) Balmoral, 1955: The Queen and the Duke of Edinburgh with Clarissa and Anthony Eden.

(*Below left*) Broadlands, 1955: Anthony Eden with Dickie and Edwina Mountbatten.
(*Below right*) The Prime Minister at the Cabinet Room window.

Sir Anthony Eden and Sir Winston Churchill with their wives at the Garter ceremony at St George's Chapel, Windsor, in 1955.

drafted by a young Conservative Research Department worker, Peter Tapsell.*

As Woolton had used the successful speech virtually word-for-word, it was reckoned that Tapsell should be given his opportunity. All depended on whether Eden 'took' to the late replacement. Shortly after Woolton had spoken to Tapsell, Eden interviewed the nervous young man who faced him alone across the Cabinet table. He was at his most charming, setting Tapsell at his ease and, after a few moments, asking if he would care to accompany him around the country for the next few weeks.

The 1955 Election was the last of its kind, in that the party leaders and senior figures from the Cabinet and Shadow Cabinets travelled the country, largely without security, mixing freely with ordinary voters. Unlike 1959, it was not dominated by television. Big evening meetings were open to the public on a first-come, first-served basis and were not the carefully screened, all-ticket events of later years.[19]

In addition Eden, who was accompanied throughout by Lady Eden, with Tapsell in the front seat by the driver taking notes for the next speech, was keen on stopping the car in lay-bys or at street corners, where people had gathered. He then got out to speak informally, never patronising or 'talking down' to the crowds. One day in Warwickshire, he shared his lunchtime picnic with some road-workers. If the crowd was above a manageable number, then he employed (as John Major was to do in the 1992 campaign) a soap-box, so that he could be seen and heard from the back. When Central Office heard of these unscheduled stops, security was stepped up following anonymous threats, much to Eden's disappointment. 'If I cannot travel in my own country without an armed guard,' he said, 'I would rather retire from politics.' After a detective joined the party, things became more inefficient, as Tapsell followed in a second car and could not work on speeches at the same time as Eden produced ideas, but had to hurry things on in the hotel room before an evening meeting, when Chloe Otto typed up latest drafts. On one occasion Chloe Otto produced the last sheets of a revised speech from a side-room while Eden was being introduced on the platform. Eden took nothing for granted. The Labour Party had a wealth of experience, as well as new talent, such as Harold Wilson ('Nye's dog').

Eden toured the length and breadth of the country, drawing large

---

*Sir Peter Tapsell contested the first post-Suez by-election at Wednesbury in February 1957. He first entered the Commons at the General Election of 1959 as MP for Nottingham West. Subsequently he has represented Horncastle in Lincolnshire from 1966 to 1983, and East Lindsey (Lincs.) from 1983. I am grateful to Sir Peter Tapsell for his account of Eden's 1955 campaign. Unattributed details in this section come from Sir Peter Tapsell and others involved in the 1955 Election.

crowds, even in the poorer parts of the big cities, such as the Gorbals in Glasgow. Of the seventy-one seats in Scotland, the Conservatives were to win an absolute majority of thirty-six. (In 1997 they failed to win a single seat north of the border.) Apart from big set speeches, Eden spoke for candidates in marginal seats, such as Charles Curran in Uxbridge and Sir Keith Joseph in Fulham. One day he found that he was scheduled to speak in Sussex for a candidate whose father had supported Chamberlain in 1938. 'The damage that family has done to this country' was his first reaction, though in the end he went, and was charm itself. Appeasement still cast a long shadow.

On 18 May, Eden, Butler, Macmillan and Iain Macleod appeared on television to be cross-examined by newspaper editors, a most successful initiative, not least because of Eden's courteous charm. To an unexpected extent, foreign affairs became a dominant theme, to Eden's benefit after the signing of the Austrian Peace Treaty on 15 May, and Eisenhower's acceptance of a Four-Power summit in Geneva.

In the Midlands, car firms were keen for Eden's entourage to appear in their products, and Central Office thought this could win votes. After one very comfortable ride in a Black Humber, Eden vetoed further use of such hospitality. 'Attlee is driven everywhere by his wife, Violet, in a Standard Eight,' he said. 'It doesn't look good to be in a boss's car.' Coordination with Central Office on how to prevent clashes was amateurish. Eden was advised that it might be better to speak on foreign affairs, when Rab Butler was discussing agricultural policy in Saffron Walden; if Butler was talking about Treasury matters, then Eden might avoid speeches on the economy. 'I can't arrange my speeches around what Rab is saying,' said Eden. 'I'll speak on what I want to speak about, I'm the Prime Minister.' In any case, to his surprise, crowds always wanted to hear about foreign affairs. National Service was also of particular concern.

When Eden went by train, women came to the windows at the stations to hand in bunches of flowers. As it was springtime, these were mainly daffodils, which soon filled the luggage racks and spilled out into the corridors. 'It's just like a wedding,' said Peter Tapsell. 'Let us hope it doesn't turn into a funeral', replied Eden, always warning against complacency.

Eden gave the final Conservative television broadcast on 21 May, five days before polling. 'By common consent the greatest *tour-de-force* among the television broadcasts was the final one by Sir Anthony Eden,' wrote David Butler in his book on the 1955 Election. 'Without any tricks or visual devices he talked directly to the viewers for a quarter of an hour, speaking in a genuinely extempore fashion, summarising the issues of the election, not attacking his opponents, but presenting the Conservative case with a confident, quiet reasonableness.'[20] In fact, courteousness towards his opponents was characteristic of Eden in those innocent days. He referred to Attlee and his senior colleagues as 'our Socialist friends', and he rejected Central Office advice to make a particular target of Mannie Shinwell, former War Secretary, whose concern for the Army while in office he had much admired. Another thing Eden had in common with Shinwell, though for different reasons, was a low opinion of Gaitskell. The former Chancellor, Hugh Gaitskell, became Labour leader in December 1955. For Eden, he represented everything he detested about the intellectual Winchester tradition. The Wykehamists he liked were the 'doers', who were at home in uniform, Wavell and Monty Woodhouse, not the Hampstead intelligentsia, epitomised by Gaitskell, and figures such as Richard Crossman and Douglas Jay, who thought that the man in Whitehall knew best. At this stage Gaitskell was not widely revered within his own party, many of the Trade Unionist figures disapproving of the way in which Ann Fleming, wife of Ian Fleming, 'showed him the pleasures of upper-class frivolity'.[21]

When the results were announced, Eden's approach was vindicated, and his Government was the first to be returned with an increased majority for nearly a hundred years. On Polling Day he toured the constituency with Clarissa. 'Everybody seemed in good heart,' he wrote in his diary. When he arrived at his own count shortly before midnight he found it almost finished. 'Our majority staggered us. Nearly 4,000 up. I had never thought it possible.'[22] The figures, in a straight fight against his opponent from 1951, were:

Sir Anthony Eden (Conservative)	29,979
W. Wilson (Labour)	16,513
Conservative majority	13,466

Nationally, the Conservatives won 344 seats, Labour 295 and the Liberals six. The Conservative majority was up from seventeen to sixty, with an overall vote of 49.7 per cent, the highest percentage total attained by any party in the post-war age. On 27 May, Eden recorded in his diary, 'It all looks good: better than I had dared hope. But on arrival was plunged into strike troubles with Walter [Monckton].'[23]

The newspaper strike had finally been settled on 21 April, but a dock strike had started on 23 May, three days before the Election, which had not helped Labour's cause; and a rail strike, threatened from 1 May, finally began on 28 May, which did not help Eden's. The Home Secretary, Gwilym Lloyd George, was appointed by Eden to head a Ministerial

Committee on the crisis, a state of emergency being declared on 31 May. When both strikes were ended relatively quickly, without inflationary wage settlements, by the emollient Walter Monckton, who had stayed in his office at the Ministry of Labour during the election, Eden's supporters could point to another triumph. In addition to foreign problems, he also seemed to have the touch to settle domestic ones.

To guard against any further outbreak of trouble, Eden appointed an Industrial Affairs Committee of the Cabinet 'to consider what action should be taken to check strikes and improve industrial relations.'[24] As things were relatively quiescent on the international front, partly owing to Eden's own endeavours, the tone of his administration was initially established by the manner in which it approached domestic problems: moderate, conciliatory, inclusive and with no desire to find scapegoats. Eden invited Trade Unionists, as well as employers, to Downing Street for talks, and was disappointed when the Industrial Affairs Committee, largely owing to Butler's reservations, did not recommend a profit-sharing scheme for employees. Hopes in some quarters of legislation to make secret ballots compulsory before strike action – urged on Eden by Lord Nuffield at a meeting on 28 July – were also not realised, though Eden established the concept of a twenty-one-day 'cooling off' period. As Trade Union leaders were then largely moderate figures, such a conciliatory, rather than a more prescriptive, approach had much to commend it in the atmosphere of the time. Yet, in retrospect, Eden's Government failed, as did later administrations, to grasp the particular nettle of fundamental Trade Union reform, backed if necessary by legislation, that was to be such a central part of the Thatcherite agenda in the 1980s. What Eden did have in common with Thatcher was a desire to win the support of 'the better skilled industrial worker, who could be expected to benefit most from the kind of society we wanted to create'.[25] But he believed that legal sanctions would have alienated the Trade Union leaders, who were mainly moderates.

To help in creating that society, Eden drew on the help of a vintage generation of mandarins. The Head of the Home Civil Service and Permanent Secretary at the Treasury was Sir Edward Bridges; the Cabinet Secretary, Norman Brook, 'the best of the poetry of the Civil Service', it was said in the Cabinet Office, and 'the best of the prose'.[26] Eden trusted Brook, who succeeded Bridges in 1956. Brook continued as Cabinet Secretary, while taking on the Joint Permanent Secretaryship of the Treasury, an unparalleled triptych of responsibility, which was to place him at the heart of the Suez crisis. Macmillan, whom he was to serve in a similar capacity, thought Brook had 'pure inborn judgement', though as a product of Wolverhampton Grammar School, 'he had no background', not a consideration that would have occurred to Eden.[27]

In Downing Street, Eden inherited David Pitblado as Principal Private Secretary (Jock Colville, never an admirer of Eden, had retired with Churchill). Freddie Bishop (who was to succeed Pitblado in 1956) was Private Secretary for Overseas Affairs, a post Philip de Zulueta took over in 1956 on Bishop's promotion. Guy Millard and Neil Cairncross completed the secretariat. Robert Carr was coming to the end of his time as Parliamentary Private Secretary. In December he joined the Government as a Parliamentary Secretary at the Ministry of Labour, and was succeeded by Robert (Bobbie) Allan.* Allan's main function was to keep the lobby happy, and to keep his master reassured.[28] As with so many of Eden's team at this time, Allan was an exceptionally nice man, but he failed to relay to his master gossip from the tea-rooms about plots and back-bencher unease (not a mistake Macmillan made when he appointed John Wyndham as his 'eyes and ears').

The key post, however, was that of Press Secretary, and, in this personal appointment, Eden's instinct failed him. When it came to 'the media', a world in which Eden was an *ingénue*, he went along with Tony Rumbold's suggestion that he sound out William Clark, diplomatic correspondent of the *Observer*, who also had experience of the Commonwealth and had won a place in broadcasting history as the first man to interview a Cabinet Minister on television. Clark was invited to dine at Chequers ('I was reminded of the old saying that AE is the best hostess in London,' he wrote in his diary afterwards)[29] and all seemed well.

Although he was more aware than was Eden of their political incompatibility, Clark accepted the post of Press and Public Relations Adviser. He loved the world of the powerful and influential, and saw his appointment as an entrée. As a schoolboy, he had admired Eden's work at the League of Nations and his stand over appeasement in 1938, and was now in sympathy with Eden's wish to improve industrial relations and eradicate class differences in Britain. 'What strikes me about No 10 is its informality,' he wrote approvingly after a few weeks.[30] But it was not long before Eden became disenchanted. He consulted Clark about how best to present his reshuffles (Eden was worrying about where to place Rab Butler after the autumn Budget), and Clark interpreted this as *carte blanche* to offer his opinions freely on all manner of subjects, from the effect of inflation on the middle classes to Princess Margaret's prospective marriage to Group Captain Peter Townsend. He was particularly free in giving policy advice on America and the Commonwealth, both of which he knew

---

*Allan's son Alex was to be private secretary to both John Major and Tony Blair in the 1990s.

well. Eden thought this was not Clark's function; in essence, he regarded him as a dubious, albeit necessary, part of the public relations industry.

Alec Home, then Commonwealth Secretary, warned Eden about Clark 'getting above himself.'[31]* Coming from a man known for his generosity of spirit, the warning had added edge. Harold Nicolson was more forthright. 'William Clark, whom I remember as a modest little man, has swollen out of his boots since being appointed adviser to the Prime Minister on Public Relations', he wrote in his diary. 'He shows off something chronic. I am saddened a bit since I do not like to witness human vanity on the rampage.'[32]

William Clark proved a calamitous choice as Press Secretary, yet it took time for both sides to see the unworkability of the arrangement. It was not just that Clark represented the left-leaning *Observer* intellectual class (though this did not help). Clark was vain and had an exaggerated view of his importance in the scheme of things. Like Eden, he could be something of a *prima donna*. Some felt his homosexuality played a part in his deteriorating relationship with Eden.[33]† There was a complex mock-modesty about William Clark. He told stories against himself, yet in the end they were essentially self-admiring ones, as when he was accused of being a name-dropper, to which he had ready his witty riposte: 'It's strange that you should think that, as the Queen Mother was saying the same thing to me only yesterday.'[34]

In the age before spin-doctors, Eden was not very *political* in the sense of knowing how to lead and manipulate public opinion. Yet he was very concerned that Government policy should be presented positively, and relied on Clark to arrange matters for him. When their agendas diverged, Clark proved counter-productive. Eden foresaw this and tried to proselytise on his own behalf. He came from that class and generation which believed *The Times* to be the principal newspaper of record. In this, he was at one with Attlee, though Attlee took the paper largely for its cricket coverage. For Eden, *The Times* was a respectable version of *Pravda*, and was often regarded abroad as such.[35]

Eden decided that he should speak to the Editor of *The Times* on a private basis at Number 10, and regular meetings with Sir William Haley began shortly after Churchill's retirement. Haley's accounts of these meetings give a fascinating insight into the pressures faced by a modern Prime Minister. On 4 July 1955, after one particularly frank meeting, Sir William Haley recorded:

---

*In extensive talks with Lord Home over five years, the author heard him speak critically of only two people, apart from Hitler. One of them was William Clark.
†Several figures remarked to the author that many homosexuals were initially attracted by the aura and glamour surrounding Eden, but that few remained lasting friends or admirers.

Lunched with Eden alone at No 10. He was well and confident, is not going to reconstruct his government till after Geneva ('there is no time'); then Monckton wants to go, Eden favours Watkinson in his place. He agreed Crookshank should not go on leading the House. Once again he regretted Winston's last crop of new under-secretaries, which landed him with a number of people he did not want. About Geneva he put German unity as the first objective, then security for all from any dangers it held. He was ready to contemplate a demilitarised Eastern zone, but not for the British and Americans to come back west of the Rhine. He is toying with the idea of an all-party parliamentary committee on Malta.[36]

Expectation and reality rarely tally in politics. Far from departing, Monckton became Minister of Defence in December 1955, hardly the job to give someone who was thinking of bowing out of front-line politics. Monckton was to be one of the key Suez doubters. Crookshank did give up the Leadership of the House in December and was succeeded by Rab Butler. Churchill's October 1954 reshuffle had conspicuously failed to identify new talent. None of the Under-Secretaries appointed then proved to be a future Cabinet minister, and of the Parliamentary Secretaries only Ernest Marples and William Deedes advanced to Cabinet rank.

The major foreign affairs event of 1955 was the Four-Power summit in Geneva in July. Following the disappointments of the Bermuda Conference in 1953, Eden was convinced that Foreign Ministers' meetings should follow those of Heads of Government, and this timetable was arranged for 1955. Eden returned to Le Reposoir, the villa he had occupied a year earlier. Edgar Faure was the new French Prime Minister, and Eden had initial talks with him and Eisenhower on the first day. The Russian delegation was led by Marshal Bulganin and Nikita Khrushchev, who expressed a wish to visit Britain. The groundwork was laid for a trip the following April. Eden hoped they would find time to see the Britain beyond London, mentioning the attractions of Oxford and Edinburgh.

Much of the work was done, as Eden favoured, in private meetings, and the dinner he gave on 22 July for 'B and K', as the British Press now dubbed the Russian leaders,* was a notable success. 'Eden conducted the whole affair brilliantly,' Macmillan observed. 'He exuded all his charm, both at & after dinner.' Eden sensed, as did Macmillan, that the Russians wanted to be loved. The imponderable was Khrushchev. 'How can this fat, vulgar man,' wondered Macmillan, 'with his pig eyes & his ceaseless flow of talk, really be the head – the aspirant Tsar – of all those millions of people & their vast country.'[37]

---

*The British public nicknamed the ponderous Russian leaders in their badly cut suits 'Bulge and Krush'.

Less successful was Eden's suggestion for a demilitarised zone in Germany, which the German observers in Geneva denounced as 'the bad Eden plan'. Problems over the Formosa Straits also remained unresolved in long talks with Eisenhower. Compared with the Indo-China Conference of 1954, there were few tangible results, but the mood was best summed up by Macmillan who, with his instinct for showmanship, declared, 'There ain't gonna be no war.'[38]

On his return to London, Eden read the newly published diaries of Maxim Litvinov, Stalin's Commissar for Foreign Affairs in the 1930s. 'There is a sentence with which I agree completely,' he wrote, 'to the effect that Russia is safer with a Weimar Republic allied with the West than with a Germany whose military are intriguing with the Russian ones. Still truer today. Bulganin might understand this, but Khrushchev never.'[39]

The ramifications of the Burgess and Maclean defection still rumbled on and Eden spent much time being briefed by MI5 and the Joint Intelligence Committee on security matters. Following the disclosure under parliamentary privilege that Kim Philby was the 'Third Man', a debate was held in early November, over which Eden liaised with Attlee, one of the Labour leader's last public duties. For some time one of the stories circulating in the Foreign Office had been that the uncertainties of current Soviet policy had been due to a struggle for power that was going on in the Kremlin between Burgess and Maclean![40]

At the end of September, Haley recorded another of their regular meetings.

> The P.M. wants to have a talk with the Archbishop [Fisher of Canterbury] about the new bishops to be appointed but he has been advised that any meeting between the two of them will at once be ascribed by the Press to the Princess Margaret business. So they are writing letters to each other.[41]

An unusually large number of sees – York, London, Durham and Peterborough – became vacant during Eden's first months in office. With Anthony Bevir, his patronage secretary, Eden took this responsibility seriously, especially so since he personally had little time for organised religion or 'weird bishops'. Cyril Garbett, the Archbishop of York, who died in harness at the age of eighty, was the exception. 'I liked him best of the clerics,' Eden wrote. With Garbett's death, York and London, the second and third posts in the Anglican hierarchy, had to be filled simultaneously. Fisher's recommendation for York was George Bell, Bishop of Chichester. However, Bell was seventy-two and had been passed over to succeed William Temple at Canterbury in 1944 by Churchill, reputedly because of his condemnation of allied bombing policy. Eden too remembered Bell's wartime criticisms of Bomber Command, but more important after this interval was the knowledge that the diocese of York wanted the scholarly Michael Ramsey, Bishop of Durham, to succeed Garbett. However, Fisher wanted Ramsey for London, a prospect that appalled Ramsey, who felt his innate shyness unequal to the administrative demands of that vast and difficult burden. Eden overruled Fisher. 'It is now settled that Durham is to go to York, & I am sure that is right,' Eden wrote in his diary. 'Cantuar wanted Chichester there which would have been most unsuitable – But we had quite a struggle.'[42] This struggle was to colour his future relations with Fisher, which were to reach a crisis point over Suez the next year.

Meanwhile, Princess Margaret was hoping to marry the innocent party in a wartime divorce, Group Captain Peter Townsend. Eden found himself in a position of personal, as well as constitutional, delicacy.* Public opinion was sharply divided, and many parallels were drawn with the Abdication crisis. Those who wished 'true love to follow its course' unfairly demonised Eden as a latter-day Stanley Baldwin. The reaction to the 'Margaret affair' was symptomatic of the repressive atmosphere of the 1950s, and divided opinion across the generations. It was also one of the few episodes over which Bobbety Salisbury took a profoundly different view from Eden. As a divorcé, Eden could empathise with the Princess in her dilemma.

Princess Margaret always blamed Alan Lascelles, the Queen's private secretary, for the outcome, but Lord Salisbury – ironically a personal friend of the Princess – was actually a more significant influence. During the Bournemouth Conference in October, Salisbury rang Eden to tell him that he was lunching with the Queen and that Princess Margaret wanted to see him for a talk afterwards. 'I said this was very dangerous – He would almost certainly be seen,' Eden wrote in his diary. 'Cabinet had not even been told of the matter, & if it were published that he, of all of us, had seen her every kind of extravagant construction would be put upon it.'[43]

When the Cabinet did discuss the matter the next week, Salisbury outlined the constitutional difficulties over continued payment of the Princess's Civil List allowance, if the marriage went ahead against the advice of the Government. Regarding his High Anglican principles as paramount, he said he would resign in that event. There were echoes not only of the Abdication, but also of the events of February 1938, when Salisbury had resigned with Eden on a matter of principle, putting it above personal considerations.

The Edens were at Balmoral at the beginning of October. 'Saw Queen

---

*To this day, Eden remains the only divorced British Prime Minister.

after dinner,' Eden wrote in his diary, 'many topics, but Margaret's problems the chief.'[44]

After a lengthy Cabinet discussion on 18 October and a further audience at Buckingham Palace, the Government's position was made clear. The decision would be Princess Margaret's, but if she married Townsend, it would entail loss of her rights of succession and Civil List allowance. In the climate of the time, a Government of either persuasion would almost certainly have tendered the same advice. An unequivocal editorial on the same lines by William Haley in *The Times* on 26 October then effectively settled the matter.

On 31 October, Princess Margaret announced that she had decided not to marry Townsend. The fourth estate had a Roman holiday, as Macmillan predicted. 'No doubt the gutter press; the Beaverbrook press; and a lot of the sentimentalists will be very angry,' Macmillan wrote in his diary. 'Eden (who has not in fact interfered at all) will be blamed.'[45] Once the 'Margaret business' had died down, many of the papers then turned their attention to demolishing Eden. The age of deference was swiftly drawing to a close.

Haley's account of his September meeting with Eden continues:

> Had a long private talk with Eden after lunch. He looked well and confident. He said he had put off any Cabinet changes till towards the end of the year. He was more and more convinced his key appointment must be the Leadership of the House. He wanted someone as Attlee had had Morrison. He had thought of Butler and, to his surprise, Butler was not against it. But it would be necessary to put the economic measures through first. There might have to be an autumn budget. [The so-called 'Pots and Pans Budget' on 26 October.] On defence they were thinking of cutting the call up to 21 months, or delaying it – he wanted that flexibility. But one way or the other our forces would drop 100,000 men. This would also be useful as a disarmament move to match Russia's.
>
> If Butler took the Leadership [of the House], Macmillan might go to the Treasury. Eden had asked him before he left for New York to think over whether he would prefer that or to stay at the F.O. If he moved, Selwyn Lloyd was a good candidate for Foreign Secretary. But if Macmillan wanted to stay at the F.O. Eden would let him.

Having used Haley as a sounding-board on his thoughts on the reshuffle, Eden then turned to consideration of the Middle East and Nasser. Haley recorded:

> He was not angry at Egypt buying Russian arms. France had been very naughty in selling up to date aeroplanes to Israel, so Nasser had to do something to preserve the balance. He agreed with us that Russia had supplied the arms to get a political finger in the Middle East pie. When

Macmillan had raised the matter at the Foreign Ministers' Meeting in New York Molotov had at once said 'Would you like us all to talk it over together?' To Eden's dismay Dulles had replied it was none of Russia's business. He, Eden, had cabled to Macmillan urging him to bring Dulles around and to get the Russians interested in a Middle East settlement. He did not think the Foreign Ministers' meeting in Geneva would yield much. [Eden was right.] The great thing was to keep the atmosphere friendly. On German unity Khrushchev had said to him at Geneva privately that if Bulganin and he went back to Moscow with a united Germany, the Russian people would say "Stalin would never have agreed that" – and that would be the end of them.

Eisenhower's illness was a major worry. To take only one case, it made any movement in the disarmament talks even more difficult. Nasser kept maddeningly repeating the Eisenhower formula like a gramophone record – and only Eisenhower could change the record.[46]

Haley was not the only person to whom Eden unburdened his thoughts on the reshuffle. 'We have, I think, a good team,' he wrote to Salisbury from Chequers on 18 September, 'but it includes both inexperienced and erratic elements. No harm in that, provided there are wise hands to guide and restrain.'[47] The experienced elements could be erratic in Eden's experience too, especially Rab Butler in the build-up to his October Budget. Eden refrained from saying 'I told you so', but was exasperated that all Butler's reassurances the previous year that the economy was in a healthy state were now proving to be excessively optimistic. 'In the midst of this economic turmoil it is fair to recall that I did sound a note of warning last December [1954],' Eden wrote in his diary. 'He [Rab Butler] was firm in his denial of any faltering in our economy & even rather contemptuous of the suggestion.'[48]

As a result, Eden took a much closer interest in the details of the autumn Budget than he had done in May, writing to Rab Butler on 3 September:

I am sure there should be something in the nature of a capital gains tax. This may not be a good tax technically and it might not bring in much revenue if Stock Exchange prices become steadier. But that would not matter in itself. The tax would show our intention to be politically just, & would be a form of insurance that all sections of the community would have to play their part.[49]

In the privacy of his diary, Eden had been even more forthright:

Cabinet in P.M. Talk on economic situation went well, but was disappointed to find how little R.A.B. was able to suggest in the way of action in respect of capital gains or dividends to balance the demands he is making on others. I have no sympathy for C. Clore & his ilk & would

449

like to hit them hard. We must not appear like the hard faced men of 1918.[50]*

Rab Butler's 'Pots and Pans' Budget on 26 October was to prove a turning point for the Eden Government, quite apart from its deleterious effect on Butler's own career. Butler announced savings of £112 million in public expenditure, including a one-fifth increase in purchase tax, and the inclusion of previously exempt goods such as kitchenware – from which the Budget got its dismissive name – together with increases in telephone charges and a reduction in the housing subsidy, effectively wiping out the concessions from April. Unknown to Butler, his job had already been offered to Macmillan, who was 'considering his position'. In his response, Gaitskell, the Shadow Chancellor, launched a savage attack on Butler's honour. 'He has persistently and wilfully misled the public about the economic situation and he has done it for electoral gain', he said, going on to describe the April Budget as 'a masterpiece of deception' and 'a bribe.'[51] Though the Tories did not like being lectured by a man some saw as a sanctimonious Wykehamist, many privately conceded that the points had struck home.

Eden was determined in future to know much earlier how plans were unfolding, minuting the Cabinet Secretary, 'I should like to be kept in touch with main economic questions.'[52]

The Premiership was Eden's first non-departmental office since that of Lord Privy Seal in 1934, but as that post had carried direct responsibility for League of Nations Affairs, it was in effect his first-ever general coordinating role. However long the expectation of supreme power, the actual experience is unlike any other, and adjustment takes time.[53] Eden liked to know what was going on and found it difficult to delegate, though he remains the one post-war Prime Minister not to have updated *Questions of Procedure for Ministers*, the template for ministerial conduct in public life.[54]

Living 'over the shop' also had its disadvantages, and the goldfish-bowl routine became irksome. Although the Edens still had Clarissa's cottage at Broadchalke, this could not accommodate detectives and secretaries. 'Private' weekends, away from Chequers, thus entailed taking over rooms in the local inn and their presence soon became known. Several Cabinet ministers – including Butler and Macmillan – had substantial country estates for real privacy.

Eden had never been an *habitué* of the smoking room, and this made

---

*Charles Clore (1904–79) was a well-known financier and industrialist of the time.

him seem aloof. Although his 'door was always open', in practice it was not always possible to adjust the timetable.[55] Access to Eden was not easy, especially for middle-ranking ministers. Weary of Churchill's interminable Cabinets, he sought to impose greater order on the agenda. Any minister who wanted to discuss a matter further could see him later, but pressures of parliamentary life meant that few took advantage of this way of doing business. He did not have a good ear for parliamentary gossip, despite the endeavours to keep him in touch of Bobbety Salisbury and Jim Thomas, who was now coming to the end of his ministerial career. And unlike some Prime Ministers, Eden was notably short of cronies.

Received opinion emphasises Eden's fearsome temper, especially on the telephone. During what Randolph Churchill called 'the Eden terror', Downing Street was supposedly a Forsterian world of telegrams and anger. William Clark often dined out on a story of flying inkwells.[56] Both Randolph Churchill and William Clark, as unsympathetic witneses, loved to exaggerate to score points off Eden.

Macmillan's famous motto for the Private Office and Cabinet Room when he became Prime Minister – 'Quiet, calm deliberation disentangles every knot' – was a particular way of distancing himself from Eden; yet Macmillan, under the insouciant appearance of unflappability, was actually far more tense at times of crisis, and often physically sick even before routine speeches. By contrast, Eden was remarkably relaxed, in full command and not at all on edge, even in the House of Commons the day after Nasser had nationalised the Suez Canal.[57]

Many performers, artistic as well as political, need cathartic release. Though Eden could lose his temper alarmingly – Selwyn Lloyd describes a monumental row with Churchill – he did not let the sun go down on his wrath, and his public performances had a quiet dignity. There was a stillness about him in the darkest days when he had taken his decisions, and could do no other.

The 'Pots and Pans' Budget occasioned much criticism, but a longer shadow was cast by the Government's indifference to the Messina Conference, called in Sicily in June 1955 by the Assembly of the European Steel and Coal Community to discuss the prospects for a 'Common Market'. Many politicians and officials in the six ECSC countries wanted Britain to become the seventh. One of the most persistent charges levelled against Eden is that he failed to take the opportunity of getting Britain in 'on the ground floor of Europe', by cold-shouldering this initiative and despatching a minor official, Russell Bretherton, to the post-Messina negotiations.

Eden was what would later be called a European agnostic. For one of his generation, the old Empire, now rapidly becoming the New Commonwealth, and the Atlantic alliance were what mattered. His famous speech at Columbia University in 1952 remains a defining moment. Evelyn Shuckburgh recalled that Eden 'used to say to me that if you were to open the personal mail arriving from overseas in any post office in England you would find that 90 per cent of it came from beyond Europe, from Australia, Canada, India, Africa, anywhere indeed, where British soldiers and administrators had served or British families settled. How could we ignore all that? That was what he meant by "feeling it in his bones." '[58] In his final spell as Foreign Secretary, Eden was instinctively concerned not only with the places he cited to Shuckburgh, but with crises in countries beyond Europe – Persia, Egypt, Cyprus, Kenya and Indo-China. Seen from this perspective, Messina was a place where, in Rab Butler's dismissive 1955 phrase, 'some archaeological excavations' had taken place.[59] Europhiles find Messina a convenient stick with which to beat the Eden Government retrospectively, but there was little dissent at the time.

The Foreign Office conducted an extensive post-mortem on Messina and the subsequent Spaak Committee that sprang from it. On 1 November 1955, Lord Reading, Minister of State, had a meeting with J. W. Beyen, the Dutch Foreign Minister, to discuss the developments over Messina since the initial meeting of the six countries in June. Reading recorded:

> M. Beyen told me that he thought that the recent meetings between the Messina countries had been very useful and he was especially grateful to Her Majesty's Government for having sent a representative. The meetings had proceeded on a gratifyingly informal basis and he was glad that our representative had not been merely an observer but had been enabled to take a valuable part in the discussions.

Beyen was guilty of talking up the prospects of British enthusiasm and involvement. The next day he met Rab Butler at the Treasury. The official record was distinctly more non-committal:

> The political and economic implications for the United Kingdom of a European Common Market had been gone into in the most painstaking manner by our experts; and Mr Butler assured Monsieur Beyen that the approach to it of Her Majesty's Government was anything but petty. [The original typescript reads 'anything but pretty'; painstakingly the 'r' in the third word is deleted in all copies in ink!] But he felt bound to point out that, although Her Majesty's Government had not taken a final attitude, a decision to join the Common Market would call for such major adjustments in United Kingdom policy as to rule it out as a short term possibility.[60]

In this document can be perceived the seeds of forty years of British political division. At the time of the Messina Conference, Sir Ashley Clarke, the British Ambassador in Italy, had sent a report to the Foreign Office. 'The Messina conference did not arouse much enthusiasm in the Italian Press,' he wrote on 11 June 1955, 'which was fully occupied with the Sicilian election campaign. According to my Dutch colleague it was not intended to achieve anything, but all the Foreign Ministers enjoyed their holiday at Taormina.'[61] Even 'the father of Europe', Jean Monnet, regarded Messina as 'an important but somewhat timid step, towards the making of Europe.'[62] Eden was even more wary of European integration. At a meeting at the Treasury on 19 November, it was recorded that 'The Prime Minister agreed that the right policy was to lean towards supporting O.E.E.C. [Organisation for European Economic Cooperation] and to try to keep out of the more far-reaching schemes of the Brussels Powers.'[63]

In December, Roger Makins, Ambassador in Washington, told Harold Caccia of American feelings about Britain's attitude towards European integration: 'The Americans fear that the Messina Powers still suspect that our main aim is to obstruct their initiative, and that we had not made it sufficiently clear that we were prepared to view each particular project on its own merits.'[64]

It is easy to view Messina from the perspective of hindsight. Yet in 1955, many in Britain felt themselves to be on a different level from the principal continental countries. Eden was a man of these times, and he could not be expected to consider federation and loss of sovereignty as a serious option.* For Britain to subjugate her sovereignty in a formal alignment with France (a notoriously unstable political entity) and assume parity with Italy (regarded by many as a volatile country of excitable and unreliable factions) was unthinkable in 1955. Germany's future, too, was an unknown quantity, despite Adenauer's endeavours as the father of the modern nation, which Eden much respected. As for the Benelux countries, they were mere pawns in the game. When Eden spoke about the concept of the 'three circles', everyone knew which one came third, and they knew about it on both sides of the House of Commons.

'It has been suggested in recent years that Britain missed a golden opportunity to enter the Common Market at its inception by refusing to participate in E.D.C.,' Ben Pimlott wrote in 1969. 'Quite apart from other reasons for dismissing it, this view entirely fails to take account of the climate of British political opinion at the time. In 1963 many voices in both

---

*Gaitskell's views on entering a European federation seven years later were that 'it means the end of a thousand years of history.' Speech at the Labour Party Conference on 3 October 1962.

major parties were raised against the Government's decision to try to take Britain into the Common Market; in the mid-fifties the political consensus wholly precluded such a venture.'[65]

In November 1956, a few weeks before becoming Prime Minister, Macmillan said in an adjournment debate on European trade policy:

> I do not believe that this House would ever agree to our entering arrangements which, as a matter of principle, would prevent our treating the great range of imports from the Commonwealth at least as favourably as those from the European countries.[66]

There was no demur from either side of the House. Even if Britain was wrong in her attitude (and it remains a big 'if') then others, apart from Eden, stand in the dock of history. What Isaiah Berlin called the 'hoofbeat of history' was unheard by many in the mid-1950s.

During the Election, immigration had not been a major issue, despite the efforts of a right-wing Tory MP, Cyril Osborne, to introduce a bill to curb 'coloured immigration', with speeches that, if repeated outside the House, would in a later era have seen Osborne himself before the courts. Immigration was inextricably linked with housing and employment policy, and raised awkward questions about the justification for differential treatment between the Old and New Commonwealth. Salisbury was urging that some curbs should be made on Jamaicans. Lord Home, who was about to embark on a Commonwealth tour, prepared a memorandum for the Cabinet that envisaged preferential treatment for India, Pakistan and Ceylon. A draft Bill was prepared in the autumn of 1955, but on 3 November Eden indicated in Cabinet that, in the time-honoured phrase, 'further thought' should be given to the problem before any attempt at legislation.[67]

At the time capital punishment raised more passions than immigration. A series of controversial cases, culminating in the execution on 13 July of Ruth Ellis, the last woman to be hanged in Britain, gave rise to a move, spearheaded by the Labour MP, Sydney Silverman, to review the law. In Cabinet on 18 October, Eden spoke in favour of retention.* At least three members of the Cabinet, however, were in favour of a change in the law – Selwyn Lloyd, Iain Macleod and Derick Heathcoat Amory – but Conservative activists were against any change, and for abolitionists progress was painfully slow. But on 23 October 1956, Eden announced that a Bill would be introduced to curtail capital punishment.

---

*In July 1942, he had argued for the summary execution of Hitler and his lieutenants, as their heinous crimes were beyond the scope of any judicial process – a view endorsed by Churchill who wanted a list drawn up of leading Nazi figures who would be shot within six hours of capture. It was owing to Stalin that the Nuremberg trials took place after the war.

The subject of education also raised fierce passions on both sides of the political divide. Conservative policy was to retain the grammar schools; Labour wanted to abolish the eleven-plus. Gaitskell also wanted radical reform on private education. The Education Minister, Sir David Eccles (once described by Harold Macmillan as possibly the only old Wykehamist who could be mistaken for an old Harrovian), wanted to create new vocational courses in secondary-modern schools, to increase their appeal to parents whose children had failed the eleven-plus. 'Parity of esteem' was not so easily achieved, although the first large comprehensive school, Kidbrooke in Blackheath, opened in 1954.

Macmillan brought a bolder scheme to the table. He believed the property-owning democracy could be significantly expanded, through a system of tax relief on school fees. Despite the fact that contemporary Labour leaders, such as Attlee and Gaitskell, did not feel the need to be defensive at that time about using fee-paying schools for their own children,[68] Eden knew the idea was a political non-starter, and concentrated instead on an expansion of technical education. 'If we are to produce all the trained craftsmen and technicians and technologists that are needed,' stated the draft Cabinet paper of November 1955, 'the pyramid of technical education must have a broader base of school-leavers than it has now.'[69] The aim was to attract 50 per cent of school-leavers into daytime attendance at technical colleges. The White Paper on Technical Education in February 1956 warned that Britain was in danger of being left behind by its overseas competitors, and established a blueprint for colleges of advanced technology and the new polytechnics.[70] 'In home policy,' Richard Lamb has written with justification, 'this was the greatest achievement of Eden's premiership.'[71]

On 7 December 1955, Attlee announced his retirement as Labour leader. For Eden, it was indeed the end of an era. Together they had been through the war as Churchill's principal lieutenants and the camaraderie between them was strong. Three candidates stood for election by the Parliamentary Labour Party as Attlee's successor – Aneurin Bevan, Hugh Gaitskell and Herbert Morrison. 'The final result gave Mr Gaitskell the first place & Mr Morrison the last,' wrote Eden. 'I had no doubt this was a national misfortune.' For Eden, 'Morrison had the sense of politics & was human.' The rapport was never there with Gaitskell, as Eden himself acknowledged. 'I was never able to establish with Mr G the political & personal relations I had enjoyed with all his predecessors, back to MacDonald & Lansbury. We did not seem to speak the same language. It was no doubt my fault, but I was entirely out of sympathy with him.'[72] It was ironic that the retirement of the two great wartime party leaders –

Churchill and Attlee – should have brought such a contrasting legacy for their respective successors. Churchill's timing had not helped Eden at all; Attlee's departure in December 1955 had virtually guaranteed Gaitskell's triumph over more senior colleagues, and Gaitskell became the first Party leader to have been born in the twentieth century (in 1906).

The pressure on the Conservatives to find younger faces was now imperative, and in the wake of Attlee's retirement, Eden's long-awaited reshuffle took place on 20 December. Rab Butler became Lord Privy Seal and Leader of the House of Commons. Four days earlier his predecessor, Harry Crookshank, 'went to see Rab about rumoured changes & as candid friend said that he would be committing political suicide if he left without doing another Budget'.[73]

Macmillan, with a reluctance that had contributed to the delay, moved to the Treasury, having secured from Eden, with doubtful constitutional correctness, an assurance that Butler would not be Deputy Prime Minister. He set strict parameters as to what his responsibilities and powers should be, and Eden confirmed these in a letter of 7 December, stating that 'in addition to control over financial policy', the Chancellor of the Exchequer would have 'full responsibility for co-ordinating all aspects of economic policy, both internal and external'.[74] It was tacitly accepted that the move to 11 Downing Street had political as well as geographical implications.

Yet Macmillan was not Eden's preferred choice, either at the Foreign Office, or now at the Treasury. When Eden had lunched with Oliver Lyttelton in October, he had written subsequently in his diary, 'I wish he were with us & free to go to Treasury now.'[75]

To save Rab Butler's sensibilities, a compromise was arranged, whereby he would preside over the Cabinet in Eden's absence. Few doubted that the pecking order had subtly changed, and not to Rab's benefit. Macmillan, if not the clear Crown Prince, was now *papabile* in a way few would have foreseen only fourteen months earlier when he was still at Housing and Local Government.

Eden's relationship with Macmillan was puzzling to outsiders. For Macmillan, the King's Scholar at Eton, Eden was always a junior Town House Oppidan. For Eden, Macmillan was self-advertising and immodest. The constant harking back to Passchendaele and the Durham miners made Eden cringe. It was not the way a gentleman behaved. Eden's attitude to the Great War was that one was in a certain place at a certain time and did one's duty. If a Military Cross was awarded, it was a private thing, a reward for doing what one should have done anyway. As a result, Eden considered Macmillan a vulgarian* and at heart untrustworthy, as had

---

*One could never imagine Eden inventing Premium Bonds.

Churchill. Yet politics is a vulgar business. Macmillan had an intuitive feeling for what appealed to the electorate, and for the way in which power operated. He understood the machinery of Government and knew how to crank it into action. He was combative and knew that in politics one had to be a salesman; it was not a gentlemanly profession. Despite their shared desire to improve the lot of ordinary people, Eden and Macmillan inhabited different worlds.

To replace Macmillan at the Foreign Office, Eden chose the ever-faithful Selwyn Lloyd.*

> It was not a change which I wholeheartedly welcomed [Lloyd wrote later]. True it was promotion on the grand scale. But I had only been in the Cabinet for eight months, and I believe that the Foreign Secretary ought to be one of the three or four senior members of the party and in the Cabinet. Edward Grey, Curzon, Austen Chamberlain, Halifax are obvious examples and Douglas-Home and Callaghan more recently. However Eden did not agree, perhaps because he himself was appointed Foreign Secretary in 1935 after only five months in the Cabinet and when he was comparatively junior in the ministerial hierarchy.[76]

Macmillan saw the Foreign Secretaryship as being a sun among the planets. Selwyn Lloyd, on the other hand, thought the Foreign Secretary was but one of the planets that revolve around the sun, and never the sun itself. This suited Eden well. 'What matters really,' Lloyd wrote, 'is whether the Prime Minister and the Foreign Minister have complete confidence in one another, whether they trust one another and they know that nothing will be done behind the other's back.'[77] He was convinced that the Chamberlain/Eden difficulties of 1938, and the Eden/Macmillan ones of 1955, would not be repeated. Despite the traumas that were to unfold over the next year, this belief was largely fulfilled.

Walter Monckton, who earlier in the year had been talking of retirement, now became Minister of Defence, insisting on promotion for Harold Watkinson, his loyal Parliamentary Secretary at the Ministry of Labour. Monckton's was a puzzling appointment, which did not work out for the best, complicated by Monckton's real desire to remain in the frame to succeed Lord Goddard as Lord Chief Justice or, failing that, to become (as actually occurred) Chairman of the Midland Bank. (Divorce is generally reckoned to have cost him the first post.) 'He dared not', Monckton's biographer has written, 'at his age and in his financial circumstances, fall between two stools.'[78]

---

*When this had first been suggested to Macmillan, in the event of his move to the Treasury, he had asked Buchan-Hepburn 'if the Prime Minister's purpose was really to get back control of the Foreign Office' (Harold Macmillan, *Tides of Fortune 1945–1955*, Macmillan, 1969, p.688), exactly Selwyn Lloyd's own reaction.

Watkinson's promotion meant that Eden, to his great delight, was able to find a place for his former PPS Robert Carr at the Ministry of Labour, a department he knew would be most appropriate. Christopher Soames was also promoted to a junior post in the Air Ministry. Surprisingly the Press, who usually found something critical to say about Eden at this time, did not pick up on the fact that Soames was Clarissa Eden's cousin by marriage, as the husband of Churchill's daughter, Mary. Nor did they spot the significance of the promotion, after only five years in the Commons, of Edward Heath to the position of Chief Whip.

Inevitably, the casualties in the reshuffle were not best pleased. Viscount de L'Isle, who was replaced at the Air Ministry by Nigel Birch, let it be known that he thought it ironic Eden should commemorate the centenary of the Victoria Cross by dismissing the only two members of his Government (himself and Sir John Smyth) who possessed it.[79] The reshuffle was not well received in the Press, either, being seen as cautious and dull. Suddenly the sparkle seemed to have gone out of the Government. In such circumstances, it is extremely difficult to reverse the trend.

Another recent appointment was that of Lord Mountbatten to First Sea Lord, the fulfilment of a lifetime's ambition after his father's dismissal from the same post during the Great War. This promotion had been approved, after much misgiving, by Churchill the previous October. For a while Mountbatten drew the sting of Randolph Churchill's bile away from Eden. Now that his father had left Downing Street, Randolph Churchill was even more uninhibited, delighting in his ability to cause mischief. Shortly after Mountbatten's appointment, Jim Thomas, First Lord of the Admiralty, took Admiral Eccles, Commander-in-Chief of the Home Fleet, to White's. Propped up against the bar, rather the worse for wear, was Randolph Churchill, who lurched over to buttonhole them with the question, 'What is it like to have a First Sea Lord who is a Communist spy?'[80]

Initially, the relationship between Eden and Mountbatten was productive and marked by amiability. The Edens stayed at Broadlands in February 1955, the only other guests being Nehru and Mrs Pandit, but the visit was not a great success. 'Edwina is so very left & so full of prejudice,' Eden recorded in his diary, 'e.g. against Pakistan that conversation is difficult.'[81]

Mountbatten's vanity* was legendary and he played his royal connections for all they were worth. At the Palace where his influence was considered to be malign, he was known to courtiers as 'the wicked uncle'.[82]

---

*Jim Thomas had once said that the only qualification for his own job of First Lord of the Admiralty was to look well in a yachting cap when visiting the fleet. *Dictionary of National Biography 1951–1960*, edited by E.T. Williams and Helen M. Palmer, Oxford University Press, Oxford, 1971, p. 967.

Press criticism of Eden reached a crescendo at the turn of the year. There were those who thought of him disparagingly as an upmarket haber-dasher's model. Slim and handsome, he in fact just happened to look well dressed, whatever he was wearing. Martine de Courcel, wife of the distinguished French statesman Baron Geoffrey de Courcel, thought Eden, with his unforced charisma and grace the most *naturally* elegant man she had ever met.[83] Other peripheral matters also provided ammunition.

Maud Butt, who lived with her family in a farmworker's cottage on the Chequers estate only 400 yards from the main house, hung her washing on the line in her back garden – and sometimes even in Lime Walk – where it was clearly visible to visiting dignitaries. Clarissa Eden enquired of the administrator of the Chequers estate whether the washing could not be hung on a line in the front garden. Maud Butt dug in her heels. Traffic fumes from the road would spoil the washing (the location is one of rural tranquillity) and she let it be known that she had no intention of changing her domestic arrangements to suit the Prime Minister's wife. To emphasise the point, Mrs Butt then rang the *Daily Mirror*, which published the story, sensing at once its potential as ammunition in the class war. Eden was so angered that he consulted Sir Hartley Shawcross with a view to taking legal proceedings against the paper, as Churchill had done after the 1951 General Election. Shawcross advised against fuelling the flames and Eden let the matter drop, though the episode did disproportionate damage to his image and that of his wife.

The *Daily Telegraph* joined in the chorus. In an article on 3 January 1956 Donald McLachlan wrote, 'There is a favourite gesture with the Prime Minister. To emphasise a point he will clash one fist to smash the open palm of the other hand but the smash is seldom heard.'[84] McClachan claimed that people were waiting in vain for the 'smack of firm government'. 'The article really hurt him [Eden], it really hit him right between the eyes,' Anthony Nutting later recalled. 'I don't think I've ever seen him quite so stricken by a newspaper criticism as he was by that. He went off to Bradford; he insisted upon taking this up and replying to it.'[85]

Eden's references to the matter in his speech at Bradford, initially arranged so that he could speak on the expansion of technical education, were, as he soon realised, a mistake, as his message on the new Colleges of Advanced Technology was thus diluted. He would have been better advised to let the matter drop, like Maud Butt's washing line. Another error of judgement followed. 'Clark rings up to say *People* are to carry story that I am to resign in June', Eden wrote in his diary, '& begging for denial which I reluctantly gave.'[86] 'Never complain and never explain' was Disraeli's sound maxim, and Eden should have done the same. The denial was his worst mistake to date as Prime Minister, though he was bounced into it by Clark, thus provoking hostile speculation.

'Torrents of abuse continue these days in the Press,' Eden wrote in his diary. 'D[aily] T[elegraph] has of course encouraged Tory discontent, because nobody knows the personal vendetta that lies behind it.' The vendetta to which Eden referred concerned Lady Pamela Berry, daughter of F. E. Smith, and wife of Michael Berry, the Chairman and Editor-in-Chief of the *Daily Telegraph*, whose puzzling antagonism towards Eden and his wife knew no bounds. As Pamela Berry was a political hostess of renown, whose invitations were much prized, the potential for damage was very great. When Clarissa Eden tried, with Michael Berry's encouragement, to bury the hatchet, at a dinner at the Italian Embassy during Suez, Pamela Berry cut her dead.[87]

Interviewed by the Press Association at London Airport on 8 January, Butler said, of the current flurry of Press criticism, 'My determination is to support the Prime Minister in all his difficulties.' It was hardly a ringing endorsement from a man who had just enjoyed the Prime Minister's Christmas hospitality at Chequers with his two younger children. Butler was then famously asked whether Eden was 'the best Prime Minister we have'. He assented hurriedly to the proposition. As Butler's biographer has written, 'Such was the origin of, or at least the occasion for, Rab's most famous equivocal remark ever.'[88] Eden never forgot it.*

The Times had contributed to the criticism of Eden, with a leading article on 2 January, regretting the Government's lack of 'high purpose'.[89] On the same day that Rab was interviewed at Heathrow Airport, William Haley noted in his diary:

> The papers (including *Sunday Times* and *Observer*) all say an Eden-must-go government is growing. But who would take his place? Butler is temporarily spreadeagled; his confidence has gone. Macmillan is still coming on but hasn't shone at Defence or the Foreign Office. It is the team that is at present flabby, not just one man: and the Civil Service machine behind the team. I believe the disastrous last year of Churchill's reign, with nothing domestic getting itself settled is now having a delayed action effect.[90]

Nine months earlier *The Times* (when it appeared after the strike) had

---

*When Eden was about to enter the House of Lords as Earl of Avon in July 1961, Beaverbrook warned him not to expect too much of the assembly. 'You are no doubt right about that assembly', he replied. 'On the other hand, to parody the inimitable Rab Butler: "It is the best assembly I have."' Sir Anthony Eden to Lord Beaverbrook, 11 July 1961. Beaverbrook papers, House of Lords Record Office. File C/18.

unreservedly welcomed the arrival of Eden in Downing Street. In the first week of January 1956, Gaitskell had a long talk with Attlee about the current political situation.

I was saying how extraordinary it was that the Government had gone down so much in the last nine months, and added, 'After all, the only important change is the disappearance of Winston. Who would have supposed that he would make so much difference?' Clem said, 'Yep. It's the heavy roller, you know doesn't let the grass grow under it' – which I thought was (a) shrewd, and (b) typical, being a cricketing analogy. It is indeed a possible explanation. Clem also talked about Anthony. 'He has never had any experience of running a team.'[91]

The year of 1955 had not been a good year, despite the sure touch Eden had shown with Bulganin and Khrushchev in Geneva, and the important development of technical education at home. Yet, as so often in politics, perceptions – once established – are difficult to alter. If the feeling grew that Eden could not run a team, then 1956 would prove an even more challenging year.

CHAPTER SEVENTEEN

The Sparks Fly Upwards

JANUARY–JULY, 1956

And as the smart ship grew
In stature, grace, and hue,
In shadowy silent distance grew the Iceberg too.
          Thomas Hardy, 'The Convergence of the Twain'

The Suez Canal was a very great and splendid undertaking. It gave us our direct route to India. It had imperial value. It was necessary that we should have control.
          Oscar Wilde, *An Ideal Husband*

One cannot carry two water melons in one hand.
          Old Arab proverb

The year of 1956 was one of the most dramatic of the twentieth century, fit to be mentioned alongside 1914, 1929, 1939 or 1945.

In February, at the Twentieth Congress of the Communist Party of the Soviet Union in Moscow, Khrushchev denounced the crimes of Stalinism, historical revisionism on the grandest scale. Yet an anti-Communist rising in Hungary in October led to a swift and brutal invasion by Soviet troops. The indomitable spirit of the Hungarians in the face of the eventual crushing of their revolution was nevertheless to be an inspiration for one-third of a century for those struggling for independence from Soviet domination in Central Europe. The fall of the Berlin Wall in 1989, and all the portents stemming from that dramatic event, had their origins in the tank-strewn streets of Budapest in 1956.

The old colonial powers, especially Britain and France, were faced with nationalist demands from Aden and Cyprus (where the Greek Cypriots were calling for *enosis*, union with Greece) to Algeria and Morocco, in the aftermath of the sovereignty granted to India, Pakistan, Burma, Ceylon, Palestine and the Sudan. France recognised Morocco's independence at the beginning of March. Britain's solution to Cypriot demands was not so easily accomplished. By 1956 the march towards decolonisation was becoming an unstoppable process for democracies and dictatorships alike. In the Middle East the Tripartite Declaration of 1950 by America, Britain and France had not guaranteed the hoped-for stable frontiers. Above all,

1956 remains indelibly linked with the problems of what Napoleon called 'the most important country', as Egypt – at the crossroads of Asia, Africa and Europe – became the catalyst for the most divisive political event since Munich. As a result Eden, associated for ever with 1956 (no less than King Harold with 1066 or Charles I with 1649), was to be for a certain spell that rarest of political phenomena – the central figure in the world. To say that Eden has had a bad press over the Suez crisis, which erupted suddenly, and yet to many not entirely unexpectedly, on 26 July, would be to redefine understatement.

In the Far East a measure of equilibrium between the Soviets and the Western powers had been achieved, but in the Middle East the signs were more ominous, especially for Israel as Egypt stockpiled Soviet armaments. To counter the threat of Russian bombers, the British and French, with American support, had supplied Israel with Meteor and Mystère fighters respectively. Ironically, in the light of later events, Israel remained profoundly suspicious of Eden, seeing him as more Arabist than the Arabs, especially after his misjudged Prime Ministerial speech at the Guildhall on 9 November 1955, when he had spoken of the need for Israel to give up territory it had regarded as its own since 1949, and had advocated financial help to Nasser for the building of the Aswan High Dam. Yet the British politician of the time who was most obsessively pro-Arab remained Anthony Nutting, the Minister of State at the Foreign Office.*

In January 1956 Eden visited Eisenhower in Washington. They were to talk about Russian ambitions in the Middle East, fuelled by Nasser's Egyptian-Czechoslovakian arms deal the previous autumn, which intelligence sources had revealed as largely Soviet in origin. (In the wake of the Burgess and Maclean affair, Eden was punctilious about keeping abreast of MI5 material and the work of the Joint Intelligence Committee.) The meeting of Foreign Secretaries in Geneva in November 1955 had been widely perceived as a failure, despite what some had seen as 'the Geneva spirit', and this added to the urgency of the situation.

With Butler presiding over the Cabinet in his absence, Eden set off with Selwyn Lloyd on the 25th, hoping to strengthen the Tripartite Declaration. Eden, for the first time, now saw himself as the co-equal of Eisenhower, with Lloyd (to Eden's relief) taking the brunt of Dulles's idiosyncrasies at Foreign Minister level. There was much speculation on which way Nasser would jump. He had recently attacked Nuri es-Said, the Prime Minister of Iraq, co-founder of the Baghdad Pact, and General Glubb (Glubb Pasha),

---

*When one Private Office secretary told Nutting of his forthcoming marriage, instead of offering a wedding present, Nutting asked if the happy couple would instead like to commemorate the event by contributing to a cow in Jordan. Private information.

Commander of the Arab Legion in Jordan. Yet his continued talks with the World Bank about funding for the Aswan Dam* showed that part of him at least wanted to keep in with the West. Egyptian negotiations with Eugene Black of the World Bank were close to breakdown and, for the first time, Eden and Lloyd appreciated that the financial aid to Egypt, to which they were tied on the coat-tails of the Americans, might indeed never be forthcoming. The British and the Americans were already at odds over Egypt. For Eden, the constant barrage of anti-British propaganda through the radio station, the Voice of the Arabs, was a paramount concern; for Eisenhower, and particularly Dulles, the economic instability of Egypt had deeper resonance, but was not as central to their interests as the Panama Canal.

Yet the atmosphere was friendly – too cosy in many ways for Lloyd, who felt the Americans never fully understood, despite Eden's economic paper outlining the situation, how important the maintenance of Middle Eastern oil supplies was for Britain, now down to her last three months of gold and dollar reserves. At the end of his visit, Eden was granted the signal honour of addressing Congress. He stressed the importance of the Baghdad Pact as a stabilising force in the Middle East, especially in the light of Russian military aid to Nasser's Egypt with all the unknown implications for arms control. 'Brought to a halt in Europe,' he warned, 'Soviet expansion finds its way south and probes in other lands. There is nothing particularly new in this. You can read it all in Russian imperialist history. But the emphasis has changed, and the symbol and method too.'[1]

Next month the Taunton by-election on 14 February saw a majority of 5,542 reduced to one of just 657, an unimaginable swing in those less electorally volatile days. Arguments over bread subsidies also cost Eden much time and emotional energy in talks with Macmillan. Then on 29 February, Eden had a poignant meeting with Churchill at Number 10 over lunch. Afterwards the two 'talked quietly together for half an hour or more – of Russia, the world, guided missiles & our govt,' Eden recorded in his diary. 'I walked with him to the lift. He kept me there a few moments & told me how glad he was he had handed over. How confident he felt that I could do the job, that now he realised how far his strength had fallen, below what was needed. I was moved & sad.'[2] Even if there was an element of guilt in Churchill's endorsement of his successor, it marked a reconciliation that was long overdue.

*

*The equivalent for 1950s Egypt of the Windmill in George Orwell's *Animal Farm*, from which all future benefits would spring.

Selwyn Lloyd embarked on a fateful Middle East tour on 1 March. He was met in Cairo by his Egyptian opposite number, Dr Fawzi, with whom he was to spend many hours before the year was over. The centrepiece of the Egyptian visit was the dinner Nasser gave for the British party that evening. As talks on Anglo-Egyptian problems had been postponed till after dinner, Lloyd wondered how best to avoid endless small talk during the meal. 'Perhaps you can tell us,' he asked Nasser, 'how you rose from being an Egyptian army major to being ruler of your fatherland?' Nasser needed no second prompting, and with a terrible fluidity of self-revelation, proceeded from the soup course through to the dessert and beyond, outlining his complete life story to the British party, who felt it to be the macabre equivalent of hearing Hitler dilate upon *Mein Kampf* without omitting any of the embarrassing footnotes. First of all, Nasser explained, one gets rid of the King (a necessary prelude to getting rid of the British); then one puts in a front man, Neguib; which in its turn is only a prelude to his eventual removal. Finally, all that remains is to get rid of the front man, assume power and cover one's flanks.[3] At the very moment Nasser was explaining his philosophy to Lloyd, King Hussein had summarily dismissed Glubb Pasha from his command of the Arab Legion in Jordan. This was widely interpreted as a sign that Britain should quit the Middle East altogether.

The next morning, Nasser congratulated a still shell-shocked Foreign Secretary on having arranged the dismissal of Glubb as a way of improving Anglo-Egyptian relations. Lloyd did not know whether this was a bad joke, or a way of finding out if the British knew of Glubb's fate before it happened. Lloyd felt that Nasser must have been implicated, but events proved otherwise.

In a metaphor that would have pleased Attlee, Lloyd told Eden that Glubb's sacking was like 'a body-line ball in the middle of the innings'. He felt Nasser was 'fatter and more self-confident than when I last saw him in 1953'.[4] Eden's first reaction was to suggest to Lloyd that he should break his Middle East itinerary and go to Jordan to reason with Hussein. Lloyd felt this ill-advised, as Glubb would probably no longer be in Jordan by the time he arrived, so peremptory had been his sacking, and so a visit would lead only to further humiliation.

Later that day Selwyn Lloyd's party was stoned by anti-British protestors in Bahrain. The mission, which had started with high hopes of improving Anglo-Egyptian relations, was ending in inglorious disarray. One by-product was that its failure increased Nasser's sense of self-esteem. An expert on Arabian matters heard Nasser speak at this time at a Friday mosque. His speech was manipulative, powerful and extraordinarily seductive. If this was the effect on a non-Arab, he felt, what would be the effect on the native population?[5] Nasser was increasing his power not only over his people, but in Syria and Iraq. 'Many important developments stemmed from the tragedy of Selwyn Lloyd's mission,' Mohamed Heikal wrote later, 'but probably the most important was that he personally but in all innocence started the chain of events which led to Nasser's decision to nationalise the Suez Canal.'[6]

Back in Britain, a wave of anti-Eden feeling, with Randolph Churchill to the fore, broke out at the twin humiliations of Glubb's dismissal and the stoning of the Foreign Secretary in Bahrain. Gaitskell, pressing home the attack, called for a Commons debate. This took place on 7 March and was for Eden an abject failure. In his memoirs, Eden admits that the speech 'was regarded as one of the worst in my career'. Clarissa Eden wrote in her diary, 'The events in Jordan have shattered A. He is fighting very bad fatigue which is sapping his powers of thought. Tonight's winding up of the debate was a shambles.' Gaitskell, who had only needed to set the ball rolling, to let mischief take what course it would, wrote of Eden in his account, 'he looked thin and tired and ill and one could not help feeling rather sorry for him, because of all the attacks which he has had to put up with'. The fact that the failure was so rare an occurrence added to its impact. 'Eden never makes a really remarkable speech, since he never says anything memorable,' Macmillan had written at the time of the Party Conference in 1955. 'But he never makes a bad speech.'[7] The 7 March debate proved the exception. The smart money was already on Macmillan as Eden's eventual successor.

Eden wrote to Eisenhower, as he was to do throughout 1956, despite Eisenhower's later public denials to the contrary, keeping him in touch with developments from the British perspective:

> There is no doubt that the Russians are resolved to liquidate the Baghdad Pact. In this undertaking Nasser is supporting them and I suspect that his relations with the Soviets are much closer than he admits to us. Recent events in Jordan are part of this pattern.'[8]

Within two days of the Commons debate, Cyprus was once more to the fore. Indeed, the perceived embarrassment of the debate may have had its knock-on effect on Eden's response to events on that troubled island. Ever since the failure of the London Conference in 1955 on the island's future, the internecine warfare of Turkish and Greek Cypriots, and acts of EOKA-inspired terrorism, had continued unabated. Eden had appointed Field Marshal Sir John Harding, Chief of the Imperial General Staff, as Governor, hoping that his experience in Malaya and Kenya would help in bringing about an orderly solution. When Harding's five months of talks with Archbishop Makarios, the Greek Cypriot leader, foundered, Alan Lennox-Boyd went to Cyprus. Eden had been willing to travel, but his past history with Papagos was not considered conducive to any settlement. Lennox-Boyd was appalled by the Archbishop's intransigent demands in Cyprus and abandoned the talks after only two hours. Harding asked Eden for action. He got it.

In a move that delighted the rank and file of the Conservative Party, and despite the reservations of Lennox-Boyd, Eden had Archbishop Makarios arrested and deported to the Seychelles. For the Tory heartlands, this was the 'smack of firm government' that the *Daily Telegraph* had demanded, and Eden's popularity soared among his core supporters. 'I think it was really from that moment onwards,' Nigel Nicolson, MP for Bournemouth East and Christchurch, later recalled, 'that he felt his role to be that of the strong man who was going to speak up for England and for the Empire, for this is what the Tory Party in the country really wanted, and in a sense he was perfectly right, they did want it.'[9] But it was not gesture politics. Disraeli had called Cyprus 'the key to Asia', and for Eden it was the crucial military base in the Mediterranean, following the Canal Base Treaty of 1954. With Makarios out of the way, talks could, or so he hoped, proceed with more moderate Cypriots and some kind of settlement could be hammered out. But things did not work out as planned. Makarios now assumed the status of martyr – even the Archbishop of Canterbury spoke in the House of Lords about the unease Christians felt at his treatment – and EOKA terrorism reached new heights.

The swift juxtaposition of Egypt and Cyprus revealed a characteristic of Eden's Premiership that many observers noticed. As Foreign Secretary Eden had proved himself adept at dealing with a problem on which he could concentrate, if not exclusively, then certainly for a lengthy period, the 1954 Geneva Conference being the foremost recent example. What did not prove so easy was the quick shift needed between the several different problems that inevitably arose during the evolving schedule of a Prime Minister's day. In the spring of 1956, such demands happened to an unusually frenetic extent, with Egypt, Glubb Pasha, Cyprus, IRA attacks on army depots, bread subsidies and by-election disappointments all jostling for his attention.[10]

As the great crisis of his life approached, Eden had the misfortune to find himself temporarily at odds with his two closest friends, Jim Thomas and Bobbety Salisbury. He had never formed wide or deep friendships in the smoking-room or the Pall Mall clubs. The Tory heartlands of White's, where Randolph Churchill boomed forth, and the Carlton, almost an alternative party headquarters, were alien worlds to him, not least because of their masculine atmosphere.*

Within weeks of Eden becoming Prime Minister, Salisbury, as has been seen, was pressing for a strengthening of the House of Lords in Government. Now he returned to the charge. Embarrassingly for Eden, Salisbury's sights were fixed on Jim Thomas, who had been at the Admiralty since the Conservatives had returned to office in October 1951, a lengthy spell in one post by any standards. Eden did not want to lose Thomas, but, because he wished to honour Thomas's long service, he recommended his name to the Queen for a viscountcy in December 1955. Thomas did not particularly want a peerage. He had been a personally generous host as First Lord, and now, at a time of financial difficulty, was unsure what expenses might be involved in the Upper House. With some reluctance he became Viscount Cilcennin, taking the name from the river flowing through his Carmarthenshire estate. At the closely fought by-election in his former constituency of Hereford in February 1956, the Liberals surprisingly took 36.4 per cent of the vote. Central Office took the Hereford result as a sign of 'the present loss of confidence in the Government and our very bad press'.[11] Eden felt it was a self-inflicted reversal, for if Thomas had not gone to join Salisbury in the Lords, there would have been no by-election.

No sooner was Cilcennin on the red benches, than Salisbury pressed again for a change at the Admiralty, so that the post could be given to a peer not of the first creation, preferably the 6th Baron Carrington or the 2nd Viscount Hailsham. When Cilcennin got wind of this in the New Year, he was understandably furious, especially as Eden felt a change could be beneficial in a complex transitional period of defence cuts. In a difficult meeting with Eden, Cilcennin insisted on remaining, at least until the Naval Estimates of March 1956.[12]

As Jim Thomas, Cilcennin had occupied a special place in Eden's life, and not surprisingly Eden never achieved the same rapport or understanding with his successor, Lord Hailsham, nor did he find the customary calmness and unperturbed routine of former days replicated at the Admiralty in the fraught months that lay ahead. Eden believed he had been badly advised to succumb to Salisbury's pressures in the first place, especially as two of his oldest friends were involved. But his disappointments with Salisbury were not yet over. On a tour of Asia just before their projected visit to Britain, Bulganin and Khrushchev had made some

---

*A more naturally gregarious figure such as Harold Macmillan, who as Prime Minister belonged to five clubs (the Carlton, the Turf, Pratts, the Beefsteak and Bucks), not exclusively Tory in character, and used them all regularly. Anthony Sampson, *The Anatomy of Britain*, Hodder & Stoughton, 1962, p.67.

stridently anti-capitalist speeches, for the consumption of the local audiences, rather than Hatfield House. Nevertheless, as Eden knew from political history, the Cecils have resigning minds, and on 9 April Salisbury wrote to Eden to say that he intended to leave the Government, in protest at the forthcoming Russian visit. 'It seemed to me,' Salisbury wrote, 'that there were passages in those speeches which could only be regarded as hostile to Britain and all Britain stood for.' Despite Eden's pleas, Salisbury insisted on resigning ('I have no option, any more than you had in 1938'), and it was only after protracted persuasion by Alec Home that he agreed to stay on.[13] Reluctantly, Eden now believed that he had after all been correct in not making Salisbury Foreign Secretary in April 1955. It was never again a 'glad confident morning'.[14]

Before the long-awaited arrival in London of Bulganin and Khrushchev, Macmillan delivered his only Budget. After the difficulties of Rab Butler's latter months at the Treasury, Macmillan wanted to make a fresh start and continually tried out new ideas on his civil servants. His sparkling memoranda challenged orthodox thinking – the most famous, *Thoughts from a Treasury Window*, being privately known in the office as *What the Butler never saw*.[15]

For his Budget, on 17 April, Macmillan had planned both defence cuts (especially for the RAF, in the new age of rocketry) and tax increases, but Eden blocked both. In his opening remarks to the House, Macmillan gave a broad, almost insubordinate, hint about his disappointment at no longer being at the Foreign Office. After saying that Churchill had been surprised to find himself at the Treasury in 1924, he added, 'but not half so surprised as I was, thirty-one years later.'[16] Beaverbrook had recently written of Macmillan, 'he will do strange things and he will live to perpetrate a great deal of mischief.'[17] The opening of the 1956 Budget was an illustration, and a hint of things to come.

Eden may have steered Macmillan away from defence cuts and a general tax hike, but he did not dissuade his Chancellor from the one initiative with which his time at the Treasury would always be associated. In a bold move, inevitably criticised by church leaders, especially the Noncomformists, Macmillan introduced Premium Bonds. Privately, Eden thought it vulgar populism, while many churchmen believed combining saving with gambling to be the start of a candy-floss society fostered by Macmillan. The initiative was a vivid illustration of Macmillan's flair for publicity. For the public, National Savings were never again so good, and ERNIE (Electronic Random Number Indicating Equipment) became the best gift to the cartoonists since 'Mr Cube' from Tate & Lyle's anti-nationalisation campaign in 1950.

The cartoonists were also to have a field day after Bulganin and Khrushchev arrived on the cruiser *Ordjonikidze* at Portsmouth on 18 April. Despite the outward smiles, their nine-day visit was fraught with difficulties, and ended with a major espionage row, a sad coda to Cilcennin's last months at the Admiralty. Eden had been determined to establish good relations with the Soviet Union. He realised that the royal part of the visit could have delicate undertones because of the events of 1917, with the murder by the Bolsheviks of George V's relatives, Tsar Nicholas II and his family, but these difficulties were successfully surmounted when the Queen presented the Russian leaders with Tsar Nicholas I's 1849 gift to Queen Victoria of several paintings of St Petersburg. Bulganin and Khrushchev reciprocated handsomely, bringing Russian animals for the royals: horses for the Duke of Edinburgh and Prince Charles, and a bear cub called Nikki for Princess Anne (obviously not knowing of the Queen Mother's dictum never to accept a present that eats) together with sumptuous gifts for the politicians.* After much consideration, a tea was held at Windsor Castle, rather than the traditional state banquet, and things were kept deliberately low-key.

Eden had wanted his Russian guests to see as much of Britain as they could during their visit, but there were many misunderstandings on the way. The Russians could not understand why the crowds did not cheer them in the streets. Indeed, in Oxford they faced rumbustious demonstrations, and a woman spat at Khrushchev. ('Why did she do that?' asked Khrushchev. 'I have done her no harm.') At Chequers, Russian security guards took up overnight positions outside the bedroom doors, until it was quietly pointed out that things did not operate like that in an English country house. When the Russians had lunch in the Painted Hall at Greenwich, Bulganin supposed it to be Cilcennin's private residence, while Holyrood house in Edinburgh was thought by Khrushchev to be some Siberian outpost where the peasants (in actual fact senior members of the General Assembly of the Church of Scotland) were being well cared for in their dotage.[18]

Potentially the most embarrassing episode came at the luncheon for Bulganin and Khrushchev at 1 Carlton Gardens on 25 April. Selwyn Lloyd was extraordinarily nervous lest anything should go wrong with the function and upset Eden's carefully orchestrated arrangements.†

As the regular interpreter had fallen ill, a last minute replacement, unknown to any one in the Private Office, had been drafted in. He looked from his ruddy complexion as though he had already spent some time, as

---

*In due course Eden scrupulously surrendered to the Treasury the marble desk set and paintings given to him.
†The author's account is based on information from people present at the lunch.

he himself might have put it at the nineteenth hole of a local golf course. Over pre-lunch drinks, Selwyn Lloyd introduced Lord Lambton, his Parliamentary Private Secretary, as a 'shooting' Lord. Khrushchev was much moved, and shook hands solemnly with Lambton, believing (as it later transpired) that he was under sentence of death, and shortly to be executed.

By the end of the lunch the interpreter had clearly enjoyed a good many more shots at the nineteenth hole before taking up his position between Khrushchev and Lloyd. In his speech Selwyn Lloyd made it perfectly plain to the Russians that Britain was prepared to defend Middle East oil supplies by force if necessary, the line Eden had emphasised in his talks earlier that morning. How this went down with the two Russian leaders was unclear, as their expressions never changed, and the main bulk of the translation was conducted by the interpreter whom the Russians had brought along.

When Khrushchev began his reply, however, it was time for the red-faced British representative to come into his own. He made the most of his moment in the sun. His first translation began, 'He says he is pleased to be here, but if we are pleased to have him is another matter.' Silence fell and Selwyn Lloyd's expression froze. Khrushchev, unaware of anything untoward, pressed on with his speech. To the Russian leader's comment about Britain and Russia having much in common, the interpreter added his own gloss, 'Don't you believe it, *we* haven't got eight million prisoners in Siberia!' More followed in like vein, before the interpeter was quietly ushered from the room, while Lloyd tried to repair the damage through the Russians' own interpreter. There was no need. When Khrushchev cottoned on to what had happened, he burst into roars of laughter, clearly enjoying the episode far more than Lloyd's speech. Strict instructions were given to those officials present that Eden should never hear of what had happened.

In fact, Anglo-Soviet relations had already been dealt a worse blow by the furious row two days earlier at the Labour Party dinner for Bulganin and Khrushchev, when George Brown, Shadow Defence Spokesman and a future Foreign Secretary, had attacked the Russian guests over the 1939 Molotov-Ribbentrop Pact. In the general slanging match that followed (with 'many frank words in our respective languages', as the 1961 revue *Beyond the Fringe* had Macmillan saying of a bilateral meeting[19]), Khrushchev declared that if he lived in Britain he would vote Conservative. This was manna from heaven for the beleaguered Government and the story, unlike that of the Lloyd luncheon, soon entered political mythology. Khrushchev did not forget it, either. When Lloyd visited Moscow in 1959 with Macmillan, he asked Khrushchev if he would still vote Conservative.

'Of course,' replied Khrushchev, 'it was Bulganin who was Labour and look where he is now!'*

Unknown to Eden, and against his express instructions, MI5 and the Secret Intelligence Service (SIS) had prepared a series of covert surveillance operations for the Russian visit.[20] One of the riskiest of these concerned an examination of the hull and propeller of the ageing Russian cruiser *Ordjonikidze*. A retired RNVR officer, Commander Lionel Crabb, volunteered to undertake the mission. Crabb's first dive was on 17 April. According to some reports he was spotted when he surfaced briefly between the cruiser and a nearby destroyer. He then dived for a second time, but was never seen again. MI5 and SIS moved swiftly to cover all traces, though rumours soon began to spread that something was amiss. The Admiralty made a non-committal and nebulous statement about Crabb's disappearance, which was brought to Eden's attention on 3 May. Downing Street that day 'was full of gold braid',[21] reflecting the seriousness of the situation.

Not surprisingly, Eden was furious that such an episode, 'typical of the slapdash, buccaneering style of SIS at the time', as Percy Cradock has described it,[22] might undo all his diplomatic efforts. The inevitable implication was that Eden did not control, or even have full knowledge of, the actions of the intelligence services. In addition, the damage done to Britain internationally by such a bungled operation raised all manner of related doubts. On advice from Norman Brook, Eden appointed Dick White, head of MI5 (the domestic intelligence service), to head SIS (the foreign equivalent). Such a move was unprecedented and caused tremendous apprehension in the tightly knit security world, not least because Dick White was only just beginning what promised to be a successful overhaul of MI5's practices. Eden acted swiftly to defuse a potentially ugly parliamentary situation. On 4 May he told the Commons that 'what was done was done without the authority or knowledge of Her Majesty's ministers'.[23]†

It is interesting to note how Eden and Gaitskell, though relatively new

---

*Bulganin had been ousted as Prime Minister by Khrushchev in 1958.

†Ironically, the Labour leader, Gaitskell, was to be damaged far more. As the Conservatives had made capital out of the George Brown-Khrushchev row at the Labour Party dinner, so Gaitskell sought to exploit the controversies over the Crabb affair, and called for a debate, making it clear to colleagues that he meant to retaliate in kind. Wiser counsels warned him that such an attack might appear unpatriotic. However, expectations had been raised among the rabble-rousers in his party, so that Gaitskell's actual comments, balanced and perceptive to the outsider, had more than a disappointing whiff of the Grand Old Duke of York for the parliamentary foot soldiers, and his intervention fell between two stools. Gaitskell's sympathetic biographer considered his handling of the episode unwise and the end of his honeymoon as Labour leader. Philip M. Williams, *Hugh Gaitskell*, Jonathan Cape, 1979, pp.414–15.

to their jobs after the long hegemony of Churchill and Attlee, felt they had much to prove to their own followers, who increasingly saw both as being on trial in a new age of polarised and often bitter political differences.

Patriotism was to be a word often heard in 1956. Gaitskell, albeit unfairly, was to find himself disadvantaged. On comparisons, Dogberry has had the last word ('Comparisons are odorous'),[24] but alongside Eden Gaitskell did not always appear the shining knight. None doubted Eden's patriotism throughout his whole career. Nor could those who knew Gaitskell well doubt his. But that was not the general perception, and in politics perception can be more important than reality. The fact that Gaitskell had not been in uniform, unlike Major Attlee and Captain Eden, MC, undoubtedly contributed to this feeling.

Eden's patriotism had often inspired his followers to fulsome, and sometimes unsolicited, praise. 'We all listened-in last night (the family and I) to your broadcast,' Sir Waldron Smithers, MP for Orpington, had written in 1953, 'and when you had finished, I played The National Anthem on the piano! It was a dignified & statesmanlike speech & such a relief to have a gentleman as Foreign Secretary after that dreadful Herbert Morrison.'[25]

Eden had to call on all his reserves of dignity and statesmanship in the face of Nasser's continued vilification of Britain. 'The Voice of Egypt continues unchecked and pours out its propaganda into the area of our oil fields,' he wrote to Selwyn Lloyd on 4 May. 'We have simply got to take action as quickly as possible to establish a broadcasting station of our own to compete with the Egyptians.' It was not until November that this was achieved.[26]

On 7 May, John Peyton, a future Tory Cabinet minister and leadership contender, asked a Foreign Office question about the future regulation of the Suez Canal. Returning to the subject in an adjournment debate on 15 May, Peyton said that Nasser's anti-British stridency meant that nobody should have any confidence in him 'as custodian of an international waterway'.[27] Coming so soon after the Crabb debate, this raised the temperature uncomfortably for the Government. Under the terms of the 1954 Suez Canal Base Agreement, British troops were preparing to leave Egypt, and the Tories of Captain Waterhouse's 'Suez Group' were not the only ones apprehensive about what might then ensue.

The last British troops left Port Said at 12.15 a.m. on 13 June. Ten days later Nasser became President of Egypt after national elections in which he was the sole candidate. Even before the Suez Canal Base Agreement, Eden had accepted that an element of trust was necessary if progress was to be made. On 1 April 1953, Eden, then Foreign Secretary, had written to Eisenhower, only recently installed in the White House:

> We are being asked to give up something of real value; it is something which we have created as a result of the experience which we gained in the last war at the cost of so many lives & so much expenditure of effort, time & money. We are being asked to substitute for this, which we now hold, an agreement which must be in part an act of faith in Egypt. And on this agreement will rest an essential element in the defence of the free world against aggression. That is why your help is so necessary.[28]

Eden had 'sold' the agreement to the Tory Party against the instinct of Churchill, who felt that trusting Nasser had too many echoes of Chamberlain's pre-war attitude to Hitler. Churchill's instinct was correct. Nasser, who had extended the Suez Canal Company's concession until 1968, only six weeks before nationalisation, broke that voluntary undertaking within days of the departure of the last British troops. Eden had believed that Nasser would keep his word. He still believed that the Americans would help Britain. It was his tragedy that in 1956 these twin beliefs both proved to be chimeras.

Eden's visit to Washington in January with Lloyd had shown for the first time that the American offer of financial aid to Nasser for the Aswan High Dam (so called not because of its height, but its position on the Nile near the Sudan border) was not set in stone. The political domino effect of such a withdrawal would be incalculable. Yet, after Nasser's recognition of Communist China in May, and the presence of the Russian Foreign Minister Shepilov in Cairo at a time of ostentatious Egyptian celebration of the British withdrawal from the Canal Zone, such a change of policy was now more likely.

The original understanding had been that the United States, Britain and the World Bank would provide $270 million of the expected $1,300 million cost (Britain's contribution being $14 million) of what was then the largest civil engineering project in the world. But the loans were dependent on Egypt's ability to raise a further $900 million through a properly managed economy. The reality was that if the Western offer 'withered on the vine' (the phrase Dulles eventually used to the British Ambassador in Washington, Sir Roger Makins), then the Egyptians would turn to the Russians, who would be only too ready to gain a foothold in the Middle East by providing alternative finance.

At Cabinet on 17 July, Selwyn Lloyd warned of the impending American withdrawal of finance for the Aswan High Dam. Locked into the tripartite arrangements, Britain had no option but to follow suit, which she duly did on 20 July, the excuse being that the financing of the dam, even with the funding proposed, would be beyond Egypt's resources. Casting doubts on his country's economic competence was guaranteed to inflame Nasser into some dramatic response, and this duly followed on 26 July, the anniversary of King Farouk's abdication.

Nasser's passionate speech in Manshiya Square in Alexandria that evening was one of the great moments in Arab nationalist history, as seventy-four years of colonial domination were denounced in the vernacular language of the street, which increased its populist impact. 'In the past we were kept waiting in the offices of the British High Commissioner and the British Ambassador,' he declared to the ecstatic crowd, 'but now they take us into account.'[29]

The speech was broadcast throughout the Arab world and at the prearranged signal – the use of the name Ferdinand de Lesseps, the French engineer who had built the waterway in 1869 – forces under the command of Colonel Mahmoud Younes, who was to run the nationalised enterprise, took over the operative positions on the Suez Canal. Nasser's speech continued with fourteen more mentions of de Lesseps's name, lest Younes had missed the original signal. There was no need. The offices of the Canal Company and its main installations were already in native hands.

At Downing Street on the evening of 26 July, Eden was hosting a formal dinner in honour of King Faisal of Iraq and his Prime Minister, Nuri es-Said. By chance, many of the key participants in the events of the next four months were present at this function – Selwyn Lloyd, Salisbury, Home and Kilmuir, the Lord Chancellor, from the Cabinet; the Leader of the Opposition, Hugh Gaitskell, and Sir Dermot Boyle, Chief of the Air Staff. Just after 10.15, Philip de Zulueta, the duty secretary, gave Eden the news that Nasser had nationalised the Suez Canal Company. Although details were sketchy, the main gist was clear. Nasser had seized the key installations already and was going to press ahead with the Aswan High Dam project, replacing the original American and British finance by dues collected from the ships using the Suez Canal. In their first considered response, the Joint Intelligence Committee later argued that financial salvation was not Nasser's primary motive:

> There have been a number of indications that he himself has recently had doubts whether the High Dam is the best way of solving his power and irrigation problems, and he must have realised that the net annual profit likely to be derived from the Canal is only a fraction of the Dam's cost.
>
> The building of the Dam had, however, come to be seen in the popular mind as the cure for all Egypt's ills and Nasser's own position and prestige were staked upon its accomplishment. When the Western offer of financial aid was withdrawn, therefore, he urgently needed to distract public attention and at the same time find a new method to arouse their

enthusiasm and to repair any damage his stock might have suffered in other Arab countries. As a means to this end his nationalisation of the Canal has been a triumph; it has also served the subsidiary purpose of retaliation against the West for the withdrawal of the High Dam offer.[30]

'A triumph.' But for whom? Certainly not the West. The events of 26 July showed Nasser's impeccable sense of timing. From the moment the news broke, he had the Western allies on the defensive, and never truly lost the initiative. He struck in such a way that his opponents were flat-footed, and proved in the next months that he had the ability to sell himself to both East and West. Sitting in a darkened hotel room in New York during one of his long spells at the United Nations, and watching a passionate speech by Nasser on television, Selwyn Lloyd said to one of his aides, 'And this is the man we could not match.'[31]*

However, the first general reaction that evening at Number 10, and one from which Eden never wavered, was that the crisis was not about Nasser and Arab nationalism. Its ultimate importance lay in the threat posed to Western *economic* interests. Already there was clear agreement, as Macmilan said, that Nasser had his hand on Britain's windpipe, and that he was going to have to remove it. What was not so easily agreed was the means by which this would be effected.

The dinner broke up, but not before Nuri es-Said had given Eden pivotal advice that was to have long-term consequences. If Nasser was now going to finance the Aswan High Dam, partly through revenues from canal traffic, Nuri es-Said insisted, it only needed Britain and France to refuse to pay. Then Nasser would be forced into a position of transparent illegality by blocking the canal. As the Constantinople Convention of 1888 had clearly guaranteed international freedom of passage ('The Suez Maritime Canal shall always be free and open in time of war as in time of peace to every vessel of commerce without distinction of flag),[32] the West would then have a cast-iron *casus belli* for military intervention. Moreover, Nuri es-Said insisted, Nasser's position in Egypt was by no means as strong as it appeared on the surface, and his internal opponents would only be too willing to rally behind any move to topple him. Ironically, in the light of later events, he concluded that the key ingredient for assured success in this venture was to keep the Israelis out of any invasion of Egypt.[33]

Eden then sought out Gaitskell, who was in the White Drawing Room with Lord Kilmuir, the Lord Chancellor. Gaitskell's initial reaction was

---

*Suez information, even after nearly half a century, remains sensitive. Much of the material in this and the next two chapters was afforded to the author over many years on a confidential basis. To prevent a proliferation of footnotes citing such private information, it should be taken that any comment or fact not directly attributed falls into this category and has been independently corroborated.

very supportive. 'I said that I thought they ought to act quickly, whatever they did', he wrote in his account of that evening, 'and that as far as Great Britain was concerned, public opinion would almost certainly be behind them.'[34]

Alfred Robens, the Shadow Foreign Secretary, was a Trade Union apparatchik with little experience in foreign affairs. He had demonstrated this by his maverick performance in the Foreign Affairs Debate on 27 February, after which Gaitskell had kept a close watch on him, even drafting parts of his statement for the more recent debate on 23 and 24 July to protect the Opposition's stance on Germany and nuclear policy.[35] Eden mistakenly interpreted Gaitskell's positive response as a tacit sign there would be bipartisan support. He did not expect a blank cheque, but on the other hand he did not foresee the bitterness and animosity that would unfold as British troops went into action.

After talking to Gaitskell, Eden then withdrew to the Cabinet Room with four Cabinet ministers – Lloyd, Salisbury, Kilmuir and Home – while waiting for a second batch of invitees, including two of the Chiefs of Staff, to appear. Sir William Dickson, Marshal of the Royal Air Force and Chairman of the Chiefs of Staff, was not available, but Lord Mountbatten, First Sea Lord, who had been dining at the Savoy Hotel, and Sir Gerald Templer, Chief of the Imperial General Staff, soon arrived. The French Ambassador, Jean Chauvel, and the United States Chargé d'Affaires, Andrew Foster, were also invited, as Eden wanted to establish at the outset the international nature of the crisis. Harold Caccia, shortly to move from his position as Deputy Under-Secretary of State to that of British Ambassador in Washington, was present. William Clark and other secretaries were also in attendance.

The group now gathered round the Cabinet table proved a heterogeneous and variously attired body, in black tie, white tie and even, in one instance, no tie. When the conversations became ever more sensitive on the desirability or otherwise of military action, Philip de Zulueta anxiously pointed out to Eden by means of hastily scribbled notes that not all present were Privy Councillors.[36] The unexpectedness of the meeting meant that, almost inevitably, it was ill organised. Eden liked a clear agenda for Cabinet, but after his opening remarks that night there was an element of free-for-all, with the meeting dragging on till nearly 4 a.m. Elizabeth Home, anxiously waiting in her London flat, thought Alec must have met with some kind of accident.[37]

It was not the best time for such a lengthy gathering. As Ibsen's Halvard Solness said, 'After a good dinner, one doesn't count the shillings and pence',[38] and many later problems could be traced to decisions reached in the heat of the moment that evening. Of all the Suez meetings, this hastily

477

convened one in the Cabinet Room was to prove one of the most fateful. The presence of American and French representatives subtly influenced the course of the discussion, and as a result positions were adopted in these crucial few hours from which it was difficult to step back later. In his opening remarks Eden made it clear that Nasser could not be allowed to prevail. He drew no parallels at this stage with the 1930s, though this was to come later – a point his critics have continually harped on ever since, yet the first such parallels were drawn by the *Daily Mirror* and Gaitskell.[39]

In a letter in retirement to Harold Caccia, Eden later wrote:

> I noticed that the *Washington Post* commented that I had learnt too well the lesson of Munich. I feel quite sure that if anyone had attempted to scotch Hitler & Mussolini early in their careers, there would have been plenty to proclaim that they did not deserve it. It would have been better for the world if the attempt had been made all the same.[40]

At this early stage, Eden was very concerned about the legal implications of any British action. Kilmuir, the Lord Chancellor, stressed that 'it was wrong in international law to endanger the international control of an international waterway and that the company had been treated as an international entity'.[41] Things were not quite so clear-cut and the next day (27 July), at the first Suez Cabinet, Eden conceded that Britain would be on weak ground to base its resistance solely on the grounds of alleged illegality. The Cabinet minutes recorded of Eden's views:

> The Suez Canal Company was registered as an Egyptian company under Egyptian law, and Colonel Nasser had indicated that he intended to compensate the shareholders [of which Britain's holding was the biggest at 44 per cent] at ruling market prices. From a narrow legal point of view, his action amounted to no more than a decision to buy out the shareholders. Our case must be presented on wider international grounds. Our argument must be that the Canal was an important international asset and facility and that Egypt could not be allowed to exploit it for a purely internal purpose.[42]

In the next few months there were to be as many opinions as lawyers, and Eden tended to be selective in those whom he heeded. Nasser had after all broken the 1954 Treaty, which had reaffirmed the arrangements for the Suez Canal Company. The Cassandra-like warnings of Sir Gerald Fitzmaurice, the Senior Legal Adviser at the Foreign Office, were given lower priority in Eden's calculations than the more 'helpful' judgements of Professor Arthur Goodhart, former Professor of Jurisprudence at Oxford and Master of University College, who stated in an influential letter to *The Times*:

It has been said that under modern international law force must never be used except to repel a direct territorial attack. This view cannot be accepted, as the use of force is not so limited; thus, for example, a State may take all necessary steps to protect the lives of its citizens abroad. Similarly it may use force to protect a vital national interest which has been imperilled. In such a case it is the State that has altered the Status Quo by the use of force which is guilty of aggression.[43]

Yet the fact that Eden did not accept Kilmuir's judgement on the night of 26 July as the final word showed his determination at that stage to be seen as the plaintiff at the bar of world opinion.

Turning next to Mountbatten in the Cabinet Room discussion, Eden asked what could be done by way of an immediate military response. By chance, a large detachment of ships was in Malta awaiting inspection and on the Friday morning there was to have been a meeting of the Defence Committee of the Cabinet to discuss why so many expensive ships were deployed in the Mediterranean. When the news of Nasser's nationalisation arrived, the meeting was cancelled, but the presence of the ships afforded an opportunity, which Mountbatten now outlined. By sailing to Cyprus these vessels could pick up 1,200 Marine commandos and reach Port Said within a couple of days. There were warships in the region of the northern end of the canal, and a naval presence in the Gulf of Suez. Later the Sea Lords emphasised that the canal could have been blocked there and then, if that was what Eden wanted politically. The problem was Mountbatten's pessimistic assessment of the consequences of having only part of the canal under British control. Templer, too, felt the risks unacceptable, as Egyptian tanks could easily overcome lightly armed commandos. In fact, from the point of view of a swift response, Templer's scenario was decidedly more bleak than Mountbatten's, warning that the plans for a full invasion could not be completed for nearly two months. This caused Eden real consternation. For the RAF, Dermot Boyle set a timetable of approximately one month.

The conflicting advice Eden was receiving from Mountbatten, Templer and Boyle essentially ended any prospect of immediate action. Paradoxically, in view of his outright hostility to military action, Mountbatten was the one adviser who showed that immediate action – albeit limited in the overall context of what Eden required – could in fact have been taken. Mountbatten had a lot to say on Suez, then and later. The fact that the Queen was staying at Broadlands was not without significance, either. Mountbatten was not present at the first important meetings on the Sunday (29 July) with Cilcennin and the Vice-Chief of the Naval Staff, Vice-Admiral Sir William Davis, and during the weekend he had the first opportunity to let the Queen know what was unfolding, and of his own views, which were, as he later declared, 'violently against.'[44] This aspect of the Suez crisis was to prove to be one of great bitterness between Eden and Mountbatten.

With reluctance, and yet inevitably, Eden decided against the 'Commando option', as this would not deliver the whole length of the canal into British hands and would expose the invading force to unacceptable risk. In 1936 when some were calling for sanctions against Italy, with punitive action in the Canal Zone, Eden had warned in the Commons, 'If hon. Gentlemen wish to take military action I must warn them that you cannot close the Canal with paperboats.'[45] Twenty years later, this was even more true. The meeting broke up shortly before 4 a.m. with two clear decisions: Nasser would have to disgorge, and the Chiefs of Staff should begin immediate preparations for the retaking of the canal.

Owing to the seriousness of the crisis, Cilcennin was to stay at the Admiralty all weekend, having meetings with the Sea Lords, though only intermittently with Mountbatten, who was mainly at Broadlands. Although he had not been at the post-dinner meeting at Number 10, Cilcennin always felt that Eden should have 'gone it alone' there and then, trusting to his instinct, without waiting for the unreliable Americans. They were too concerned with their forthcoming Presidential Election – what William Clark memorably called 'the quadrennial winter of the Western World,'[46] – ever to come aboard fully. More detached now from Eden after his *contretemps* over his tenure of the Admiralty, Cilcennin felt the essential problem was that Eden, for all his vast experience elsewhere, had never worked in America and did not fully understand how the American mind worked.[47]

Cilcennin was right in his assessment of the situation, especially Eden's unrealistic belief that American help would be forthcoming. Eden, far from being a proponent of gunboat diplomacy, was an internationalist, with experience of diplomacy going back to the days of the League of Nations, and he believed that freely negotiated agreements were the best way of achieving a stable world order. To maintain this world order, the United States was needed – in 1938, clearly – and now, even more obviously, in 1956. That is why Eden did not 'go it alone', as Churchill – or Bevin, if he had been Prime Minister – would probably have done. But Eden did not realise that the United States' interests were now different. The US would have taken a different line if freedom of passage through the Panama Canal had been involved. But Suez was essentially a 'European' problem.

Over the weekend a clear division of opinion was apparent. The Chiefs of Staff repeatedly stressed that as immediate military action was not to be taken, every effort should be made to encourage Nasser to put himself further in the wrong, so that when action did inevitably follow there would be international backing. Others, particularly in the Conservative Party's Suez Group, felt that a surprise pre-emptive attack could have been launched much earlier from either Libya or Cyprus, and many parallels were drawn with Sir Garnet Wolseley's swift and successful operation over the same terrain ('All Sir Garnet', as the cry went up) in September 1882, which secured Britain's position in the region for a generation and immeasurably enhanced her prestige, while the more timid French stood shivering on the brink. No minister was more clearly in this second camp than Cilcennin, who always believed that if force was to be used, it should have been in July, and not later in the autumn, by which time Nasser had covered many of his tracks.

The Press, which had been obsessed with the Wimbledon tennis championships all week, now turned its attention to Nasser. The headlines were largely unequivocal, the one exception to the otherwise universal condemnation of nationalisation in Egypt coming from the *Manchester Guardian*. The Labour-supporting *Daily Mirror* even dubbed the Egyptian leader 'Grabber Nasser', and on 30 July was to build a sustained comparison with the dictators of the Second World War. 'Remember Benito Mussolini? Mussolini ended up hanging upside down by his feet in a square in Milan,' the paper reminded its readers. 'Remember Adolf Hitler? He ended up burning in a petrol soaked blanket outside his bunker in the heart of devastated Berlin.'[48]

At the Cabinet meeting on the morning of 27 July, Eden brought ministers up to date with what had happened the previous evening. He stressed the economic consequences of failing to regain control over the canal. The first priority must be to reach a common understanding with the French, who were Britain's partners in the Suez Canal enterprise, and with the Americans. Two-thirds of Western European oil supplies came through the canal. The legal ambiguities, which in the cold light of day seemed infinitely more complex than as presented by Kilmuir in the early hours, meant that the approach would have to be an international one. After a consideration of the military options, Eden said that 'against this background the Cabinet must decide what our policy must be'. General agreement was reached on the proposition that British interests 'must, if necessary, be safeguarded by military action and that the preparations to this end must be made.'[49] The most important decision then was for the formation of an *ad hoc* Cabinet Committee – to be known as the 'Egypt Committee' – chaired by Eden and including as regular members Salisbury, Macmillan, Lloyd, Home and Monckton. Rab Butler, ostensibly Number

2 in the Government, was absent through illness, but would not have been included had he been present.[50]*

The Egypt Committee met for the first time at 7 p.m. on 27 July and was to meet on forty-one subsequent occasions, the last time on 9 November. Although there had been such War Committees before (in 1855 during the Crimean War) and were to be again (during the Falklands conflict of 1982), the Egypt Committee of 1956 was of special constitutional significance, and was where the executive power was concentrated. 'The detailed negotiations of the next few months lay with this group, though on key matters of arrangement with the French and through them with the Israelis, the Prime Minister acted with the Foreign Secretary or on his own,' wrote the historian of the Cabinet, J. P. Mackintosh.[51] The four aims were soon established as securing the Suez Canal, ensuring the continuity of oil supplies, the removal of Nasser and keeping the Russians out of the Middle East.

After the Cabinet had met, Eden sent President Eisenhower his assessment of the state of affairs that first weekend:

> The immediate threat is to the oil supplies to Western Europe, a great part of which flows through the Canal. We have reserves in the United Kingdom which would last us for six weeks; and the countries in Western Europe have stocks, rather smaller as we believe, on which they could draw for a time. We are, however, at once considering means of limiting current consumption so as to conserve our supplies; and if the Canal were closed we should have to ask you to help us by reducing the amount which you draw from the pipelines in the Eastern Mediterranean and possibly by sending us supplementary supplies for some time from your side of the world.

Lest Eisenhower interpret Eden's concern as narrow self-interest, he continued:

> It is, however, the outlook for the longer term which is more threatening. The Canal is an international asset and facility, which is vital to the free world.

As such, Eden emphasised, extreme measures would be taken if necessary:

> We ought in the first instance to bring maximum political pressure to bear on Egypt. For this, apart from our own action, we should invoke the support of all interested powers. My colleagues and I are convinced that we must be ready, in the last resort, to use force to bring Nasser to his senses. For our part we are prepared to do so.[52]

---

*Though he was never formally a member of the Egypt Committee, Butler did later take to turning up uninvited, and even on occasion chairing it in Eden's absence.

The importance of this letter lay in the combination of its comradely tone; its avoidance of too much legal jargon, a tacit admission that such considerations were not yet established as conclusive; and, finally, the categorical statement that force would be used, if necessary alone. What Eden sought was American understanding of the issues, together with backing for the British response in the face of Nasser's action. This was to prove an optimistic hope. Britain and France had a different agenda from the Americans. Their prestige had been weakened by Nasser's action, which went beyond the purely commercial and seemed to threaten their other interests in the Middle East. American interests were not threatened in the same way at all; also their attitude towards Middle East nationalism was far more accommodating. Britain, on the other hand, wanted to solve two problems simultaneously – first, guaranteeing its rights of passage through the canal, and, second, making Nasser, or his successor, accept some form of future international control. As the Americans were to point out, these two objectives had a tendency to be mutually destructive. Or, as the old Arab proverb had it, 'One cannot carry two water melons in one hand.'

'The United States was not consulted in any way about any phase of these actions, nor were we informed of them in advance,' Eisenhower declared on coast-to-coast television on 5 November, as the Americans prepared to go to the polls. 'We believe these actions to have been taken in error, for we do not accept the use of force as a wise or proper instrument for the settlement of international disputes.'[53] The first statement was simply untrue, aimed at the domestic political audience; the second, a staggering piece of disingenuousness from a political leader who had seriously considered using nuclear weapons in Indo-China two years earlier. At that moment Republican votes counted for more than the Special Relationship. The truth is that Eden kept the Americans in touch throughout the crisis.

French interests were also subtly different from Britain's. Although the French had even closer historical links with the Suez Canal project, and regarded its seizure as a matter of grave import, their main concern in 1956 was to prevent any Egyptian incursion into North Africa, threatening their traditional colonial territories. The news had thus been received in French political circles with dismay. The main aim of Guy Mollet's recently elected Socialist Government was therefore to see the end of Nasser's regime, a priority that eventually led them into an alliance with Israel and to the adoption of measures to ensure that Eden clandestinely followed suit, despite the warnings from Nuri es-Said. The Chief of the French Naval Staff, Admiral Nomy, was soon on his way to England to bolster up any doubters, and the French Foreign Minister, Christian Pineau, followed on

28 July for meetings with Selwyn Lloyd and the US Deputy Under-Secretary of State in the State Department, Robert Murphy.

Unlike 1917, or 1941, some cynics said, the Yanks arrived early this time, but to caution, not to encourage. It was Geneva 1954 in reverse. Compared to the Americans, the initial French reaction was uncomplicated, so much so that Mountbatten, alerted of developments, briefly left the Queen and the Duke of Edinburgh at Broadlands on Sunday 29 July to come to London.

Essentially, there were three options facing the British that weekend. Firstly, they could take military action aimed at the appropriation and control of the canal, probably with the support of the French; American involvement was by no means guaranteed. This course was fraught with risks and imponderables, especially after the experience of British troops in the Canal Zone in recent years. The second option was to refer the whole matter to the United Nations in the hope of concerted international agreement and action. The uncertainties here surrounded the time-scale and the probable use of a Soviet or Chinese veto in the Security Council, with the matter then dragging on for months, leaving the West seriously short of oil supplies as winter set in. The third option, which some Labour politicians favoured (though not Gaitskell, Bevan, Morrison or Shinwell), was to swallow their pride, accept that Nasser had bought out the shareholders at current market prices in a compulsory purchase, and see how the native Egyptians managed the technicalities of administering the canal.* The advantage of this course was that if the Egyptians could not manage the logistics of maritime passage, then option two would, under the terms of the Convention of Constantinople, have an urgency that might bring a quick international response. In the atmosphere of 1956, when Britain had shown herself at the Geneva Conference of 1954 to be a world player in international disputes, and with memories of appeasement and war still potent in the nation's consciousness, such a utopian approach was unthinkable for any Conservative Prime Minister. It was also an unlikely course for the current Labour leadership, whatever they might have said in the safety of Opposition. The Abadan crisis had caused the previous Labour Government endless trouble and Morrison had favoured force then. Nasser, romanticised by many radicals in Britain as a charismatic Arab nationalist leader, actually had more than a pre-echo of Saddam Hussein. Nasser sought control of Sudan, Syria, the Yemen (where he was to use poison gas) and Jordan – and the destruction of Israel. No stable world order could survive that destabilisation.

The unpalatable truth for Eden was that he was simply on the wrong

---

*To the surprise of many, they proved equal to the task.

square of the political chessboard at a turning point in the growing movement of imperialist aspirations. Whoever had been on that square would have found the problem beyond simple resolution, as Gladstone and Asquith had found to their cost over Ireland, and as the Americans were to find over Vietnam. One side of Eden wanted to act immediately (as Mrs Thatcher was to do over the Falklands in 1982), but his internationalist character, quite apart from the pessimism of the Chiefs of Staff about a speedy logistical solution, led him to adopt a different approach, and this was to cause his downfall. In the wider context, Suez – though melo-dramatically interpreted as the 'end of empire' and 'the lion's last roar' – was actually on a far more limited scale than the Irish troubles and Vietnam. Life went on.

Had circumstances been slightly different, three other politicians could have faced Eden's dilemma during that summer of 1956: Churchill, Attlee, and Gaitskell. The 'what ifs?' of history may ultimately be fruitless, but in this case, the question is germane. How would these three political leaders have reacted, had they been in Number 10? It is inconceivable in the circumstances of the time that they would have acted very differently, or taken the third option. Famously, Churchill told John Colville, 'I would never have dared, and if I had dared, I would never have dared stop.'[54] This can be taken with a pinch of salt. He would not have waited. To Lord Moran, Churchill was more forthright, describing Nasser as 'that malicious swine sitting across our communications' and adding, 'We don't need the Americans for this.'[55]

Attlee would have been more likely to have put his initial trust in the second option.* But what if this had failed to produce the required outcome? During his Premiership, Attlee never shrank from the big decisions, whether on Indian independence or British nuclear capability; had British interests or lives been threatened, force would in all probability have become by default the inevitable solution, though not with the French, whom Attlee described in a speech in the Lords as 'still held throughout Asia to stand for the old colonialism.'[56] Like Churchill, Attlee felt the operation, once started, should have been completed. 'If you've broken the eggs', he said, 'you should make the omelette.'[57]

Although Gaitskell was to change his tune as the crisis developed, he had initially been among the most supportive of Eden's actions. 'It is all very familiar,' he said in the Commons on 2 August. 'It is exactly the same that we encountered from Mussolini and Hitler in those years before the war.'[58]

---

*In response to Iran's nationalisation of the Anglo-Iranian Oil Company in 1951, Attlee stood out against Herbert Morrison's wish to use force, and referred the matter to the United Nations.

If he had found it necessary to 'jump' on the evening of 26 July, it would surely have been in only one direction, whatever the restless backbenchers might later have said.

Whether Churchill, Attlee or Gaitskell had been in Downing Street when the news of Nasser's action reached London, there would have been immense pressure to demonstrate that Britain was not going to be pushed around. The pressures on Eden were even stronger. His career had been built on his forthright defence of British interests, his loathing of Chamberlain's approach in the face of aggression, and a perceptive realisation, long before any other major British politician, of the dangers represented by Mussolini's covert ambitions. In July 1935, Count Grandi had informed Mussolini that Eden was the one British politician who was warning that any cession to Italy of Abyssinian territory in East Africa would be unacceptable.[59] Over two decades later, Nasser's actions were equally unacceptable.

Retrospectively, Eden felt an element of guilt about the earlier warnings, which had been proved correct, and he subtly changed his stance towards Captain Charles Waterhouse and his die-hard back-bench followers in the Suez Group. He needed to prove to them that the British response would set all that earlier history to rights. The Egyptians had reneged on their agreement and would have to face the consequences. 'Nasser is apparently at present in a difficult mood,' Sir Ralph Stevenson, British Ambassador in Cairo, had warned London the previous year. 'He has been listening, it seems, to a number of rumours while he was in Bandung [at a 1955 conference of thirty new independent African and Asian states organised by Nehru and Chou En-lai] about the attitude of the United States & United Kingdom, more particularly the former. He hears that our joint intention is to weaken Egypt & isolate her.'[60]* The withdrawal of the offer of finance for the Dam merely confirmed this suspicion. The game was now afoot.

Suez was to prove a crisis with four constituent parts. In the cauldron of the Middle East there was already a latent conflict between the revolutionary Arabs, with Nasser the talisman, and the conservative Arabs, for whom Nuri es-Said was a key spokesman. Then there was the unresolved question of Israel's borders and her Arab neighbours. Next came the central dilemma of the relationship of the Western Powers with Egypt in the light of Nasser's suspicions since 1955, and the recent withdrawal of

---

*After the publication of *Full Circle* in 1960, one eagle-eyed member of the Carlton Club wrote to Eden to say he had been surprised to find in the index that Sir Ralph Richardson was our Ambassador in Cairo, 'where I presume he must have been "acting" for Sir Ralph Stevenson!' AP 7/18/118A. The mistake is on p. 611 of the first edition.

finance for the Dam. And then finally, to add to the volatile mix, simmering alongside a rapidly diminishing 'Geneva spirit', was the mutual Cold War suspicion between America and the Soviet Union. All four of these factors were to combine with deadly effect in the next few months and destroy any chance of the British Cabinet's four main aims being achieved. How deadly was to become clear very quickly. Sir Garnet Wolseley had called his campaign against the Khedive Ismail in 1882 the 'tidiest war in British history'.[61] The campaign against Nasser in the second half of 1956 was about to prove one of the untidiest.

CHAPTER EIGHTEEN

Into the Maze

July–October 1956

Let us now leave the cloaked collusion that remayned in France,
and return to the open dissimulation which now appeared in
England.

Richard Grafton, *Chronicles of England*, 1562

An ill-disposed Egyptian Government might at any time restrict
traffic going through the Suez Canal either by direct obstruction
or by applying pressure on the Suez Canal Company.

Anthony Eden, Cabinet Memorandum, 28 July 1952[1]

Ah, Enoch, dear Enoch! He once said something to me I never
understood. He said, 'You know, I've told you all I know about
housing, and you can make your speech accordingly. Can I talk
to you about something that you know all about and I know
nothing? I want to tell you that in the Middle East our great
enemies are the Americans.' You know, I had no idea what he
meant . . . I do now.

Anthony Eden, in retirement, recalling a 1940s' conversation
with Enoch Powell[2]

Sayest thou our good lord is fulfilled of all nobleness? – Amen,
and so be it – he has the more need to have those about him who
are unscrupulous in his service, and who, because they know
that his fall will overwhelm and crush them, must wager both
blood and brain, soul and body, in order to keep him aloft.

Sir Walter Scott, *Kenilworth*, chapter V

The Suez crisis was for the generation of the 1950s what Munich had been
for that of the 1930s, dividing families and crossing party lines. Conventional wisdom has it that there was a 'right' and a 'wrong' side in both
crises, and that Eden was in the former category in the 1930s and the latter
in the 1950s, but this is an over-simplified view of political and economic
situations of overwhelming intractability. Historical perspectives change.
Chamberlain's place in history, despite the best efforts of Churchill, is no
longer that of the bumbling *ingénue*, completely out of his depth in the
world of international diplomacy, but increasingly that of the 'misunderstood and under-rated' statesman.[3]

However, Eden still attracts almost universal obloquy for his part in Suez, yet his aim, like Chamberlain's at Munich, was to serve the best interests of his country. His actions are often described as 'imperialist' (a judgement routinely proffered during the Kosovo crisis in 1999, a later example of nations invading a sovereign state without formal – i.e. United Nations – approval), whereas for Eden the two imperatives were *economic* and *diplomatic*. He wanted to defend trade routes through the canal, and protect the safety of oil supplies from the Middle East. In 1938 Western Europe had derived 19 per cent of these supplies from that source; by 1955 the proportion had risen to 80 per cent. In the wider international perspective, Eden wanted to demonstrate that those who broke agreements should not succeed or be rewarded.

Eden's basic premiss was thus sound on economic grounds; the difficulties were, of course, to arise politically. His view of the importance of the Middle East had not changed since his memorandum to the War Cabinet in March 1945, in which he had emphasised that the defence of the area was 'a matter of life and death for the British Empire'.[4]

When Eden became Prime Minister in April 1955 he had been briefed on the scenarios of possible nuclear conflict, after which Norman Brook had written that 'War planning is in itself an exercise in choosing between various risks.'[5] By comparison with atomic warfare, Suez was obviously less cataclysmic, but that did not mean the risks were negligible if military action was launched. The way things turned out were to haunt Eden for the rest of his life and, as Sidney Aster has observed, 'It is a cruel fate, even by the harsh standards of politics to be remembered by one failure and not by numerous achievements.'[6] In this, at least, Chamberlain and Eden were at one.

The Suez crisis was to operate on many levels – political, economic, military – and would involve figures from four continents. It marked the coming together of many strands, dating back to the 1888 Convention, and all the important subsequent staging posts, such as the 1936 Anglo-Egyptian Treaty, the ending of the British Mandate in Palestine in 1948, the nationalisation of the Anglo-Iranian Oil Company in 1951, the overthrow of King Farouk the following year, and the British withdrawal from the Suez Canal Base in 1954. Before the days of North Sea oil, Suez was a crisis waiting to happen.

Although Nasser's aim in 1956 had been to secure funding for the Aswan High Dam, he was also concerned with his own personal prestige. Eden's response was a mirror-image. Eden wanted to maintain oil supplies first and foremost but, rebuffed by a man whom he saw as an upstart, he also wished to bring down Nasser, which would have proved a welcome fillip at a time of domestic political difficulty.*

In January 1951, a Foreign Office minute, during the last months of Bevin's tenure of the Foreign Office, had outlined what were to be two of the key elements during the crisis:

> Suez remains of vast importance as the back door to Egypt and will no doubt be of great importance in the next war in servicing the vital Australian and New Zealand, and also South African, contributions to Middle East Defence.
>
> In a word, Egypt still remains the essential central point from which to defend the Middle East and all that the Middle East entails.
>
> The Americans are just as emphatic as we about the vital importance of defending the Middle East, but regard it as a responsibility which should be borne primarily by the Commonwealth.[7]

Even though the political leaders on both sides of the Atlantic, and the British Chiefs of Staff, were different in 1956, the analysis was still pertinent and the Chiefs of Staff were unflinching in their advice: 'Every effort should be made to encourage Nasser to put himself further in the wrong. At the same time public opinion in this country and the world should be prepared to support any action we might eventually take.'[8]

Public opinion, initially at least, was firmly in favour of action, and the Press mirrored these feelings. 'It is a clear affront and threat to Western interests,' *The Times* declared in its leading article, 'besides being a breach of undertakings which Egypt has freely given and renewed in recent years.'[9] Newspapers not normally supportive of the Conservatives also agreed. 'No more Adolf Hitlers,' declared the *Daily Herald*. 'There is no room for appeasement.' The *News Chronicle* assured its readers that 'The British Government will be fully justified in taking retaliatory action.'[10] The question soon became how far the British could rely on America for more than tacit support, if military intervention proved necessary as a final resort. In 1938 Eden had also sought to bring America in.

Eden's relations with America over the Middle East had initially been constructive and marked by common purpose. Before he became Prime Minister, Eden had set in train with Dulles, then his opposite number, the so-called Alpha Plan, a resourceful and intricate scheme, redolent of his pre-war diplomacy on issues such as the Saar plebiscite, to settle Egyptian-Israeli border disputes by providing a land-link between Egypt and Jordan,

---

*George Kennedy Young, deputy director of MI6, with specific Middle East responsibilities, even considered how best to mount an internal coup against the Egyptian leader, though Eden never sanctioned moves, as some have claimed, to assassinate Nasser.

with compensatory benefits for Israel. Dr Fawzi, the Egyptian Foreign Minister, had proved a helpful conduit to Nasser.[11]*

Nasser's Czech arms deal in September 1955 effectively ended any chance of Alpha's implementation, despite Eden's continued advocacy. The course of Alpha was to have many uncanny similarities with Suez – initial cooperation by Dulles, ambiguous responses from Macmillan, helpful diplomacy on the part of Dr Fawzi, dramatic unilateral action, and then ultimately disenchantment. America's longer-term stance, however, can best be contrasted with the Falklands crisis of 1982, when President Reagan sided with the British Prime Minister, Margaret Thatcher, though after the publication in 2002 of the memoirs of John Nott, Thatcher's Defence Secretary during the war, it can now be seen that this support was perhaps not so unequivocal as was once thought.[12]

Eden was not to have even tacit support from Eisenhower in 1956, and he failed to appreciate how much foreign policy was run by the White House in an Election year. Eisenhower was that distinctive political type (William Whitelaw proved a more recent example in Britain), a mover and shifter behind the scenes, who took the big decisions and stuck by them, yet was mistakenly underestimated as a mere golfing bumbler by unenlightened outsiders. The American State Department was to prove as ambivalent as the White House, undermining the British Government's publicity and denying the Foreign Office the support it needed.[13]

When the crisis broke, Eden said scornfully, 'Dulles, as usual, is away in Peru or somewhere,'[14] whereas Churchill was more colourful in his exasperation, declaring at one stage that Dulles was 'the only bull he knew who carried around his own china shop'.[15] Anglo-American relations were to be conducted very differently during the Falklands conflict, when General Al Haig, the American Secretary of State, repeatedly assured the British Ambassador, Sir Nicholas Henderson, 'Don't worry, we're not going to do a Suez on you.'[16]

A year after he became Prime Minister, and some six weeks before Suez erupted, Eden had presented proposals to the Policy Review Committee of the Cabinet about Britain's overall future defence strategy. One of the country's key objectives, Eden stated, must be 'to protect our vital interests overseas, particularly access to oil'. Priorities had changed as the risk of major war had declined. 'The main threat to our position and influence in the world is now political and economic rather than military.'[17] Suez was to prove a vivid demonstration of this, and ultimately of Britain's economic

---

*Yet Macmillan characteristically wondered whether the project, which the Israelis would never have accepted in any case, was 'Alpha or Omega'. Cabinet Minute, 22 May 1955. PRO. CAB 128/30.

vulnerability in the face of financial sanctions from an erstwhile ally.

Oil supplies were not a recent concern of Eden's. In 1948 he had written a prescient article for the *Sunday Chronicle* on this very issue:

> The demand for petroleum products has been rising for several years until it is now hard to meet. This demand will undoubtedly continue to rise. The needs of the United States are now so large, and expanding so rapidly, that the country which is the world's greatest producer of oil has now become an importer. The requirements of Western Europe were to some extent met from production in Eastern Europe before 1939, but these sources are not now open to us. It is therefore obvious that if the Western economy is to produce the goods which the Middle Eastern lands need, it must have oil from the Middle East.[18]

Difficulties with the Americans were one aspect of Suez, but relations with Mollet's Government in Paris were not to be straightforward either, largely owing to different attitudes towards Israel, highlighted by Eden's Guildhall speech in November 1955, when he was still hoping to salvage Alpha. The mutual suspicions of the Egyptians and the Israelis, heightened after the failure of Alpha, were to prove a constant factor in the Suez crisis, with Mollet's Government even more determined to arm Israel, and to safeguard France's primary interests in their North African colony Algeria, where, with some cause, they suspected Nasser of encouraging rebels taking part in a bitter war for independence.

Even more single-minded than Eden at this early stage, the French nevertheless approached the 'problem' of Nasser from a different perspective, following parallel, but contingent, paths. From 31 July onwards Mollet began an extensive correspondence with Eisenhower, which Eden did not see.[19] Similarly, details of all the developments in London were not always communicated to the French, who eventually were to confide most closely in the Israelis. The French felt they had been spurned by the British at Messina in 1955. A year later, despite their common purpose, the French remained uneasy about being bedfellows with the British, even after the Americans had, in effect, declared them joint pariahs.

Despite the shortness of the night, Eden awoke early on 27 July, the first full day of the crisis. There was much to do, and initially he was sustained by the adrenalin of the moment. 'He has clearly risen to the occasion with exhilaration', William Clark observed. 'He is the only member of the Cabinet who has held a position of comparable responsibility at a comparable period of crisis & it makes him feel his superiority.'[20]

Eden knew from past experience how power operated in the British system. It was not so much that he was an autonomous 'command premier' (in Peter Hennessy's phrase), rather that he used the concept of collective Cabinet responsibility to 'bind in' the doubters. He used Cabinet Committees, especially the new *ad hoc* Egypt Committee (formed on 27 July), to thrash out issues before bringing them to full Cabinet.*

'There are three classes which need sanctuary more than any others,' Stanley Baldwin once remarked, 'birds, wild flowers, and Prime Ministers.'[21] Sanctuary was just what Eden was not to be afforded in the 167 days that remained to him as Prime Minister. Nor, largely owing to his reserved nature, often mistaken for aloofness, and his consequent unclubbability, was there anyone able to play effectively the Sancho Panza to his Don Quixote, as he and Attlee had jointly done for Churchill in the tensest days of the Second World War. All Prime Ministers inevitably experience various degrees of loneliness and isolation while at the top of the greasy pole. In Eden's case, this was to be exacerbated by his character, the nature of his past career, and the unfortunate coincidence of a temporary cooling in his relations with Salisbury and Cilcennin. In his heart, he suspected that Salisbury was not fully behind him as events unfolded, and even wondered if there was a diplomatic element to Salisbury's frequent illnesses in the months ahead.

The full Cabinet met at 11.10 a.m. on 27 July. Nuri es-Said's advice to Eden in Downing Street the previous evening about Nasser had been 'hit him hard, hit him soon, & hit him by yourself'.[22] Nuri es-Said was not, of course, a dispassionate witness, but Eden did genuinely believe that if the Suez Canal was taken Nasser's prestige would collapse. The strong military presence at this first Cabinet was required to address this issue as a matter of urgency, as Mountbatten recorded in his Suez papers:

> We [the Chiefs of Staff] attended a full meeting of the Cabinet at 1110 [a.m.] at which it was clear that practically all the ministers present took a very serious view of what was occurring & wished the Chiefs of Staff to push on with an immediate operation for the seizure of the Canal and the overthrow of Nasser.[23]

Eden's relationship with the military over the next few months was to be central to the developing crisis. Despite their deep differences over policy, Eden actually admired Mountbatten's Prussian thoroughness, regarding

---

*It was how Attlee dealt with sensitive and complex issues during his Premiership (he had 148 standing committees and 313 *ad hoc* ones), but he never received the opprobrium that Eden attracted, while a later Labour Prime Minister, Tony Blair, would largely dispense with Cabinet altogether as an executive decision-making body. See Peter Hennessy on Attlee's use of committees, and the 'demise of anything approaching a genuine system of Cabinet' under Blair, in *The Prime Minister: The Office and Its Holders since 1945*, Allen Lane, The Penguin Press, Harmondsworth, 2000, pp.164, 516.

him as an outstanding administrator, albeit a man of impulsive judgement, especially when he implored Eden to call off the military operation on 2 November, *after* the flotilla had set sail from Malta. He felt that Mountbatten presumed too much on their pre-war acquaintanceship, was prone to expecting special treatment and sidestepped conventions, notably in respect of the military's duty to submit to political control. As events unfolded, Eden found General Sir Charles Keightley, Allied Commander-in-Chief, reliable and unwavering in the despatch of business. He likewise admired the resolve of Marshal of the Royal Air Force, Sir William Dickson, Chairman of the Chiefs of Staff. For his part, Dickson felt Eden 'played an absolutely determining role', dominating those around him 'to a greater extent even than Churchill in time of war, and he had taken on the detailed direction of every move in the game.'[24]

This quasi-Presidential approach, in the context of the British Cabinet system, was to lead to difficulties later, appealing more to the military mindset (apart from Mountbatten's) than the consensual political way of thinking. Eden, befitting his Great War background, got on well with the service leaders, though he made little allowance for the hierarchy, at one stage reproving Air Chief Marshal Sir Dermot Boyle, Chief of the Air Staff, as a junior underling.[25] Eden found Lieutenant-General Sir Hugh Stockwell, Land Task Force Commander, a bluff soldier of the old school, exasperating at times and very difficult on the ground. Stockwell's Chief of Staff for the original timetable for military action (Operation MUSKETEER), Brigadier (later General Sir) Kenneth Darling, he found less excitable, and a tower of strength in his underground War Office bunker, and later in Egypt, dealing expertly with what Darling summed up as 'a most ghastly administrative problem.'[26] The lynchpin, though, remained General Sir Gerald Templer, Chief of the Imperial General Staff, whose understanding of the psychological imperatives of warfare far exceeded that of his political masters.[27]

Apart from the military commanders and advisers, the people with whom Eden dealt most closely in the next five months fell into four broad categories: the Civil Service officials; the media, both in the Press and the BBC; the political figures, at home and abroad; and, finally, the confidants. Most of the categories contained figures who were hostile to his intentions, 'violently' so in Mountbatten's case.[28]

At the head of the professional category of officials were the towering figures of Sir Norman Brook, Cabinet Secretary, and Sir Ivone Kirkpatrick, Permanent Under-Secretary of the Foreign Office. Eden had surprisingly few direct dealings with Sir Edward Bridges, Permanent Secretary to the Treasury and Head of the Home Civil Service during the crisis, though they had been close during the time of Churchill's wartime administration, which makes it unlikely that Eden could have said to Bridges during the Commander Crabb affair, as William Clark claimed, 'Well, Edward, I suppose I've got to try to save this country while you traitors try to break it down in every way you can.'[29]*

Brook, Bridges's successor as Cabinet Secretary, was a vital presence. Despite his private reservations, he proved a dependable and pragmatic secretary of the Egypt Committee, preparing on 14 August, just before the First London Conference, a detailed schedule for the diplomatic, military and political responses, the kind of administrative grist that was absolutely essential if the goals were to be achieved. When Eden's impatience got the better of him – on 26 July he had wanted a military response by 'next Monday' – Brook's explanations of the impossibilities were accepted as the honest truth, however unpalatable the message. As Secretary of the standing Defence (Transition) Committee [D(T)C], Brook was also well versed in the procedures for moving Britain to a war footing, and consequently was kept more fully in the picture about Government policy, even in the final days, than any other civil servant.

Ivone Kirkpatrick's political chief was the Foreign Secretary, Selwyn Lloyd; in practice he came into Eden's orbit far more, a sign of the subordinate position of Selwyn Lloyd. For Eden tended to deal directly with Kirkpatrick at this stage, though later he was to rely more on Patrick Dean. Kirkpatrick was *plus royal que le roi*, as he had been in his fervent opposition to pre-war appeasement. More than any other Whitehall official, he stressed that 1956 was the twentieth anniversary of Hitler's advance into the Rhineland. He was a key figure in advising Eden to discount the (largely unfavourable) legal prognosis of Sir Gerald Fitzmaurice and base his approach on other counsels, notably those of Professor Arthur Goodhart. Eden also used Kirkpatrick to draft his letters to Eisenhower. Judgements such as 'We cannot possibly risk letting Nasser get away with it', and 'we shall have no alternative but to have recourse to force' came from Kirkpatrick's pen.[30] His loyalty was unchallengeable. When Evelyn Shuckburgh, by then Chief Civilian Instructor at the Imperial Defence College, his nerves shot through by exposure to the Middle East, ventured a criticism of Eden's strategy, Kirkpatrick told him firmly that:

---

*It would have been better had they met more often, for Bridges regretted the way that Macmillan was never fully open about the direct warnings he was given over the economy. On 7 September Bridges stressed to Macmillan 'the vital necessity from the point of view of our currency and our economy of ensuring that we do not go it alone and that we have the maximum United States support.' (Sir Edward Bridges to Harold Macmillan, 7 September 1956. PRO. T236/4188.) Only after troops had invaded Egypt did Macmillan speak out about the consequences for sterling. Later Bridges was to say privately that had he still been Cabinet Secretary, a post he relinquished in 1947, then Suez would never have happened. (Private information.)

the PM was the only man in England who wanted the nation to survive; that all the rest of us have lost the will to live; that in two years' time Nasser will have deprived us of our oil, the sterling area fallen apart, no European defence possible, unemployment and unrest in the UK and our standard of living reduced to that of the Yugoslavians or Egyptians.[31]

After Brook and Kirkpatrick, the most important officials for Eden, not all of whom by any means supported his stance, were the relevant Ambassadors. As chance would have it, the post in Washington changed hands at the most inopportune moment in the crisis, when Sir Roger Makins, summoned home to become Permanent Secretary of the Treasury for Macmillan, was succeeded by Sir Harold Caccia, one of Eden's pre-war private secretaries. The timing of the handover was not fortuitous either, as Caccia's journey by sea meant there was a hiatus at a vital moment. Some commentators detected a covert reason for the means of transport. 'Caccia, the successor to Makins, was purposely sent by sea & would not arrive until November 8,' Hugh Thomas wrote in the serialised extract of his influential book, *The Suez Affair*, ten years later. Although the final text was amended to read, 'Makins had left on 11 October and Caccia conveniently did not arrive till 8 November, by sea', the inference remained that Eden had overruled an air journey for political expediency. This was the exact opposite of what actually happened. When *The Suez Affair* appeared, Eden went through it with a fine toothcomb. He did not regard it, as some have, as a work of 'considerable accuracy.'[32] The point about Caccia particularly annoyed him. 'I wanted him to fly, but he wanted a rest & asked to be allowed to go by sea,' Eden wrote in his detailed notes in September 1966, adding, 'I regretted this.'[33] Had he known that Hugh Thomas's version would become one of the first influential accounts from the British side, Eden would have regretted it even more.[34] Fortunately, he did not hear that Eisenhower made Caccia present his credentials at 7 a.m., which was seen by the British Embassy staff as a studied insult.[35]

Timing apart, Eden did not, however, entirely regret the departure from Washington of Makins, whom he felt had gone 'native' after four years' exposure to Eastern-seaboard liberal internationalism. He had the highest regard for Caccia from the 1930s and this was largely reciprocated.[36]

Another former aide, Sir Pierson Dixon, as Ambassador to the United Nations, was an important presence in the crisis as, for different reasons, was Sir Gladwyn Jebb, Ambassador in Paris, who never forgave Eden for excluding him from the summit with the French on 16 October. Had he known that Selwyn Lloyd's private response to his protest was 'You're a deb, Sir Gladwyn Jebb,'[37] he would no doubt have been even more unforgiving.

When it came to the media, surprisingly, one of the first names from the past that came to Eden's mind was that of Sir Horace Wilson, Chamberlain's Industrial Adviser, who had gained the reputation as Downing Street's pre-war *éminence grise*. Eden remembered only too well how Chamberlain had benefited, until his policy collapsed, from favourable Press comment, sustained to a large extent through Wilson's intermediacy. His own problem in 1956 was that he had diminishing confidence in William Clark's ability to fulfil that role, and so decided on 27 July that he must foster such support through his own regular personal initiative, especially as he knew he would never have the support of Hugh Massingham in the *Observer*, Ian Trethowan in the *News Chronicle* or Francis Boyd in the *Manchester Guardian*, whom William Clark called 'the Holy Trinity of the Lobby.'[38]

As a result, Eden was determined to find somebody, apart from Clark, to proselytise on the Government's behalf in influential circles. His choice fell on Iverach McDonald, Foreign Editor of *The Times*, whom he saw for ninety minutes on the afternoon of 27 July, shortly afterwards briefing Arthur Christiansen, the exuberant Editor of the *Daily Express*. 'He seemed calm and resolute,' Christiansen wrote to his proprietor, Lord Beaverbrook, in the South of France, that night, 'and I went away impressed with his firmness of purpose.[39] But McDonald was Eden's main regular contact for the next few months with the turbulent world of Fleet Street, and the first leaders on the crisis in *The Times*, written by McDonald in the absence of the Editor, Sir William Haley, were sympathetic and supportive.

Eden continued to see McDonald, and later William Haley, regularly during the summer; indeed, they had so much secret information on Eden's views about the economic and political threats that faced the whole of Western Europe that it inhibited their dealings with their own leader writers. At his meeting with McDonald on 13 September, Eden poured out his sense of despair. 'Poor country,' he said, 'how can we do anything when the divisions are so deep.'[40] As Eden increasingly felt he had some irresolute colleagues, and far from dependable allies, he used McDonald as the prism through which his views could be disseminated. The Labour Government had backed away from confrontation over Mussadeq's nationalisation of the Anglo-Iranian Oil Company in 1951, and his own Government likewise after the dismissal of Glubb in March. Those times, Eden made clear to McDonald, were now past.

Eden's relationship with the BBC during Suez was uncomfortable at best, despite the fact that the Chairman of its Governors was his former colleague, Sir Alexander Cadogan. As Cadogan was also one of the Government Directors of the Suez Canal Company and Chairman of the Commonwealth-American Current Affairs Unit, the potential for a damaging conflict of interest was very real. Only Cadogan walked a narrower tightrope than Eden in these months, although he was generally sympathetic towards Eden.

Nevertheless, Eden's first major broadcast to the nation on 8 August was a dispiriting event, not helped by the humid August weather and the cramped and crowded conditions in which he had to speak, after climbing several flights of stairs. 'The pattern is familiar to many of us,' Eden said of Nasser's action. 'We all know how this is how fascist governments behave, as we all remember, only too well, what the cost can be in giving in to Fascism.'[41] Harold Nicolson wrote of the broadcast, 'It boils down to the fact that we cannot leave the control of this waterway in the sole hands of a man as unreliable as Nasser.'[42] Grace Wyndham Goldie, a senior television producer, later said she was ashamed 'that the BBC had not been able to provide a Prime Minister with more suitable surroundings in which to make so momentous a broadcast'.[43]

Eden wanted future broadcasts to be from the more congenial and statesmanlike surroundings of Downing Street, and partly blamed William Clark for not having checked the arrangements in advance, which did not help their relationship, already deteriorating since the January episode of the denial of resignation. Philip de Zulueta for one never trusted Clark, and told Eden how he had found him peering at other people's papers in Number 10, and even, on one occasion, in de Zulueta's own house. When it became clear that military forces would be in action, de Zulueta teasingly asked Clark what he would be doing to serve Queen and country, receiving the equally teasing ironic reply, 'I've already run up the white feather.'[44]

For a time, Eden was drawn to the idea of replacing Clark with Christopher Chataway, but Chataway was preparing for the Melbourne Olympic Games that year. In practice, Robert Allan became the *de facto* replacement for Clark. Eden used de Zulueta and Freddie Bishop of the Number 10 staff as his eyes and ears, often privately asking for their opinions while waiting for the lift, in the spot where Churchill had admitted that he had stayed too long as Premier.

Further differences arose between Eden and what he called 'those Communists at the BBC', notably over a proposed broadcast by Menzies putting the Commonwealth view, and over Gaitskell's demands for right of reply at key moments, particularly at the time of the actual invasion. When one of the original Egyptian Free Officers, Salah Salem, the 'dancing Major' (so called because of his escapades in the Sudan), made a contribution to a radio broadcast, 'Special Survey of the Suez Crisis', on the Light Programme on 15 August, Eden told Cadogan it gave 'a deplorably misleading picture of British opinion as uncertain and hesitant'.

His letter continued, 'Many people will judge the strength & determination of Britain by what they hear on the BBC ... This is not a Prime Minister's representation but a personal connection which I thought you should have about this programme last night.'[45]

Eden still remembered Churchill's use of the Ministry of Information as a means of wartime control, and William Clark told Harman Grisewood* that Eden contemplated taking over the BBC and making it an instrument of war at the end of October. This was not true but it complicated and exacerbated the brittle relationship between the BBC and Number 10 as the climacteric approached.

One positive thing to emerge from Eden's broadcasts was the productive and friendly relationship that he struck up with David Attenborough, then a young BBC producer, who became his 'minder'. Eden learned a lot from Attenborough about broadcasting techniques and admired his professionalism.† Despite this, Eden had no real feel for projecting himself. Compared with later Downing Street practice, he ran what was a rather amateurish operation. Many of the people around him lacked the necessary toughness to see things through. A few personal talks with Iverach McDonald and Arthur Christiansen was not the same thing as the tightly controlled professional operations run later by the likes of Bernard Ingham for Mrs Thatcher, or Alastair Campbell for Tony Blair, both of whom had a better feel for the American connection. Throughout Suez the United States undermined the British Government's propaganda, with the State Department's publicity machine notable for its disinformation, which the Foreign Office, not unnaturally, found obstructive and unhelpful. To bind the multifarious links together, Eden found it useful practice to liaise through Patrick Dean, Chairman of the Joint Intelligence Committee, so that he could keep abreast of all that was happening in the Egypt Committee, the Permanent Under-Secretary's Department and MI6.

No Prime Minister can long survive the loss of confidence of his Cabinet, as the fates of figures as disparate as Asquith and Margaret Thatcher demonstrate. Eden came perilously close to losing that support on several occasions after July 1956. His Cabinet can loosely be divided into three categories: the openly loyal, including Selwyn Lloyd and Alec Home, with fervent support from Antony Head and Alan Lennox-Boyd; the covert

---

*Chief Assistant to the Director General of the BBC, Sir Ian Jacob, who was in Australia at the time.
†Eden kept in touch with David Attenborough about his multifarious travels in pursuit of the wildlife of the world, travels that Eden rather envied, especially when they involved trips to Persia.

doubters, including Rab Butler, Walter Monckton and Heathcoat Amory;* and Harold Macmillan, who was a category all by himself. Macmillan shifted and vacillated, behaving as the leading figure, at different times, of both loyalists and doubters. World statesmen mirrored these divisions: Robert Menzies, the loyallest of the loyal throughout, with support from New Zealand Premier, Sid Holland; increasingly vociferous doubters, such as India's Pandit Nehru and Canada's Foreign Minister, Lester Pearson; and – in a Macmillan-like category all of his own – the brooding and ambiguous figure of John Foster Dulles, flitting from the background to the foreground, and alternately blowing hot and cold.

Two figures are often neglected in any analysis of Suez: Clarissa Eden and Queen Elizabeth II. These women were the only two people with whom Eden could speak regularly in an uninhibited manner, knowing that his concerns and fears would go no further.

Clarissa Eden was to deliver the most famous quotation of the crisis, when she said that 'during the past few weeks I have felt sometimes that the Suez Canal was flowing through my drawing room'.[46] There were, inevitably, those who saw her as the Lady Macbeth of Suez. 'Is it really a case of "Infirm of purpose, give me the dagger[s]?"' Cynthia Gladwyn wondered in her diary, referring to 'Clarissa's war.'[47] But this was a misreading of the Edens' relationship during these months, even though William Clark's diary is splattered with spiteful remarks about Clarissa Eden's supposed influence. Her primary concern was for her husband's welfare. She was not a political figure but, like Clementine Churchill, wanted her husband to know what people were saying. Sometimes this could be unintentionally counter-productive.

Evening newspapers were a regular feature then of a London afternoon, with successive editions of the three titles coming out at frequent intervals. Much of their content was speculative, but the headlines were for a competitive commercial agenda, not a considered one. The evening papers, rather than the Suez Canal, flowed through the drawing room that autumn, and as they tended to induce in Eden the frustrations he had experienced over Donald McLachan's article in January, especially as Randolph Churchill was a regular contributor to the *Evening Standard*, the staff at Number 10 felt it would have been better had he been shielded from their criticisms.

Eden refused to reveal the Queen's opinions on Suez. He took the correct constitutional view that the Prime Minister's audiences were a private matter between the sovereign and himself. Although the regular Tuesday-

---

*Although a relatively junior figure at Agriculture and Fisheries, Amory moved up a distinct notch in public awareness during Suez, and less than eighteen months later was to be Chancellor of the Exchequer.

evening audiences became more fitful in their regularity as the crisis deepened, they lasted longer. The Queen was just thirty, her Prime Minister almost twice her age. Within four years of acceding to the throne, the sovereign's knowledge of political events was already extensive from regular conversations with Churchill and Eden, not to mention her more informal talks with Salisbury, a personal friend. Suez gave the Queen experience of a major crisis, together with an understanding of how the machinery of Government operated, far beyond anything that was taught her theoretically by Sir Henry Marten, her constitutional mentor.[48] Churchill has often, and rightly, been regarded as the Queen's educator in politics. But Eden was the first of her Prime Ministers to attend her during a major world event involving Britain. A file in the Public Record Office shows how the Queen was kept informed of allied operations and intelligence briefings continuously from 1 to 22 November.[49] Eden did not keep the Queen in the dark.

The subsequent chronology of the Suez crisis has about it the inexorable momentum of an ancient tragedy, going through through many stages, in a kind of political progress from *Das Rheingold* to *Götterdämmerung*, with the final part of the tetralogy unforeseeable in those late July days as the canal waters were disturbed for the first time. Nasser's timing of his surprise *fait accompli* had been impeccable, and he never lost the initiative. The French, the British and the Americans were all working to different timetables and agendas.

The French wanted immediate military action, as did Eden initially, though the Chiefs of Staff soon persuaded him of its logistical impossibility. The British then settled for two months of diplomatic negotiation, followed by military intervention if that failed, while the Americans always favoured the stratagem of destabilising Nasser's authority without recourse to arms. Eden sensed from the beginning that his Government was going to be in for the long haul, and knew that any firm action would be interpreted as that of a man who was afraid of appearing to be weak, especially after the 1954 Suez Canal base withdrawal. Yet potentially, with the recent 1955 election victory, his was the strongest position politically among the three allies. Indeed, the political stability of Britain since the war – with only three Prime Ministers and one change of Government – was in sharp contrast to the political volatility of the Fourth Republic, where governments seemed to come and go with the changing seasons.*

---

*Yet, ironically, Mollet was not to fall after Suez, and before the year was out Eisenhower was established even more powerfully for a second term, which increased his penchant for moral aloofness.

Nasser's strike left his opponents flat-footed and confused. After setting up the Egypt Committee on 27 July and looking at the planning for military action, Eden had the important responsibility of interpreting and influencing contradictory Commonwealth opinions, which were not divided simply on a basis of the 'Old' and 'New' Commonwealth. India, Ceylon and Pakistan were particularly critical.[50] 'Britain could count on New Zealand standing by her through thick and thin,' Sidney Holland, New Zealand Prime Minister, told Eden, 'Where Britain stands, we stand; where she goes, we go; in good times and bad.'[51] Canada, particularly through the influence of Lester Pearson, External Affairs Minister, under-went a shift in attitudes, and on 24 August Alec Home had to warn Eden that Canada was now 'wobbly', which led on 2 November to Lester Pearson proposing that a United Nations Emergency Force (UNEF) police the canal.[52]

As Commonwealth Secretary, and a member of the Egypt Committee, Home played a pivotal role in keeping Eden in tune with Commonwealth views, especially the malevolent influence of Krishna Menon, the Indian Minister without Portfolio. Menon, who had ambitions to replace Nehru as Foreign Minister, had the distinction of being mistrusted by both sides. Nasser did not have a high opinion of him, mainly because of his habit of behaving as if he was authorised to speak on Nasser's behalf.

Home also queried Eden's instinctive feeling that Eisenhower would con-tinue in the spirit of the wartime relationship, not foreseeing the obstacles that the Americans would put in the way of the use of force. Home thought Eden should have gone to Washington at an early stage to see Eisenhower face-to-face, as this would have given him an insight into the strength of American feeling. By November it was too late. Eisenhower had become very choosy about whom he would see, as Macmillan, who pulled every string, found to his annoyance. Eden much valued Home's 'firmness and discretion' throughout the crisis.[53] As some members of the Cabinet became 'wobbly', Home was the conduit of their specific concerns. And as the going got tough, and negotiations got murky, Home fulfilled another function, of which Eden was well aware. Home was known to be decent and honour-able, and as long as he was 'on side' – which he was from the Downing Street dinner on 26 July 1956 to the dockside at Tilbury on 18 January 1957, when the Edens sailed for New Zealand – many sections of the Conservative Party, concerned about the moral implications of the Govern-ment's response, felt the operation could not be wholly discreditable.[54]

An area in which the Egypt Committee had important responsibilities was that of monitoring the shifting moods of parliamentary and public opinion. Gaitskell's initial response – 'It is all very familiar. It is exactly the same that we encountered from Mussolini and Hitler in those years before the war' –

did not mirror his party's feelings and was not sustained. Eden, in fact, eschewed the Hitler parallel; for him, the analogy always lay with Mussolini's actions in Ethiopia. Herbert Morrison, briefly Eden's predecessor as Foreign Secretary in 1951, drew a parallel with Mussadeq and the Anglo-Persian crisis of that year. Public opinion, contrary to myth, was generally in favour of Eden. Downing Street was flooded with messages of support from all over the country, and in November 1956, at the height of the crisis, Eden's approval rating as Prime Minister among all voters stood at 52 per cent, while that of Gaitskell, the Opposition leader, stood at 44 per cent. By December, when he was fighting for his political life at Westminster, Eden's standing with the public was even higher at 56 per cent.[55]

Keith Kyle rightly demonstrates that 'reflective British people' were deeply concerned about the Government's handling of the unfolding crisis. The Oxford Union voted against the Suez operation by 352 to 206. Of all the consequences of the Suez crisis, the loss of the 'intellectual vote' for the Conservatives was to have the most profound long-term effect. But the view from the Clapham omnibus was very different.

The most important responsibility of the Egypt Committee was in coordinating the first phase of diplomatic activity, including the two London Conferences involving more than eighteen nations, the Menzies mission to Nasser, and the move by the respective Foreign Ministers, Selwyn Lloyd and Dr Fawzi, towards a negotiated settlement based on the so-called Six Principles at the United Nations.

Eden's speech to the House of Commons, for instance, on 30 July had been drawn up, and approved, in consultation with the Egypt Committee. 'No arrangements for the future of this great international waterway could be acceptable to Her Majesty's Government,' Eden said, 'which would leave it in the unfettered control of a single Power, which could, as recent events have shown, exploit it purely for purposes of national policy.'[56]

It was not long before world figures began arriving in London. Christian Pineau, Foreign Minister of France, was one of the first to put in an appearance, and Robert Murphy, America's Deputy Secretary of State, was the harbinger of many American visitors, of whom the most important was Dulles, fresh from Peru, late on 31 July. Murphy believed that Eden 'was labouring under the impression that a common identity of interests existed among the allies'. He gave no succour to that belief. 'The Prime Minister had not adjusted his thoughts to the altered world status of Great Britain, and he never did.'[57] On the other hand, Eden was encouraged by Dulles's declaration that 'a way had to be found to make Nasser *disgorge* what he was attempting to swallow', and by his belief that Britain's best hope lay in a bipartisan approach.[58] On 19 August, Dulles told Eisenhower:

The attitude of the Labor Party is a hard blow for the government at this juncture when bi-partisan unity would give Britain the best chance of retrieving its position without actually having to use force. I have no doubt that Nasser is fully aware of the situation and may calculate that if he stands firm the result will not be solid strength against him but perhaps a Labor government which would be softer.[59]

Dulles was disappointed by what he saw as Gaitskell's equivocation, but for many in the Government, if this was the case, then Gaitskell was in the end only keeping Dulles company.

In a manner that later went out of fashion, Eden was punctilious at this stage about keeping the Commons informed of developments. 'The freedom and security of transit through the Canal, without discrimination, can be effectively ensured only by an international authority,' he said on 2 August. 'It is upon this that we must insist. It is for this that we are working in negotiation at this moment with other Powers deeply concerned. Nothing less than this can be acceptable to us.'[60]

Eisenhower was the regular recipient of a lengthy correspondence with Eden. He had warned Eden on 31 July against the use of force. Eden explained his position more fully in a telegram on 5 August:

> I do not think we disagree about the primary objective; to undo what Nasser has done and to set up an international régime for the Canal. The purpose of this régime will be to ensure the freedom and security of transit through the Canal, without discrimination, and the efficiency and economy of its operation . . .
>
> I have never thought Nasser a Hitler, he has no warlike people behind him. But the parallel with Mussolini is close. Neither of us can forget the lives and treasures he cost us before he was finally dealt with.
>
> The removal of Nasser and the installation in Egypt of a régime less hostile to the West must therefore also rank high among our objectives.[61]

The main outcome of the tripartite talks on 1 August was the first London Conference of twenty-two countries from 16 to 23 August. Of the twenty-four nations invited, only Egypt and Greece declined to attend. Eden's mistake at this stage was to believe that the Americans would maintain a stance of benevolent neutrality, a point David Ben-Gurion, Prime Minister of Israel, noted in his diary on 3 August. 'The issue confronting Eden is how to get the U.S. involved so that should action be taken, it will not be done with only the authority of France and England.'[62]*

---

*Ben-Gurion could not have imagined at that stage his own future part in the joint venture, when the disappointment of these hopes led France and Britain into murkier waters. Machiavelli once said that there was always a tension between politics and morality. If Munich was the failure of an idealistic view of foreign policy, then Suez, it could be argued, was the opposite, where national interests had a greater priority than fulfilling a wider moral purpose. Unfortunately, pragmatism was no greater guarantee of a speedy success than wishful thinking.

William Clark noted from his vantage point in Downing Street, 'For this afternoon's Cabinet (or rather Egypt Committee) Harold Mac. solemnly walked out of No 11 & acknowledged cheers, walked briefly to F.O. & then back to No 10 to acknowledge cheers. He is clearly cutting himself a big swathe at the moment, in the expectation that he might – just might – succeed Eden.'[63] Dulles recorded an extraordinary conversation with Macmillan on 21 August. 'He said that he was thinking of perhaps going back to take over the Foreign Office in the reasonably near future.'[64] Unfortunately for Macmillan, Eden was not thinking along the same lines, either in the near future or at any other time.

On 5 August, Macmillan paid the first of many visits to Churchill. His outline at Chartwell of possible strategies prompted Churchill to motor to Chequers on the Bank Holiday Monday (6 August) with advice for Eden. Churchill wanted Press censorship, a prompt response lest Egyptian defences be reinforced by Russian help, and the use of Cyprus as an air base.[65] Although Eden was exasperated by both the press and the BBC, he knew that what might have been acceptable in 1940 was not viable in 1956. Also, Cyprus was in the grip of unrest and only Nicosia in the north was operational as an air base at that time. The main outcome of the Chequers meeting was a series of detailed letters from Eden to Churchill, keeping the old man up to date.

On 14 August, following earlier correspondence, Eden and Salisbury met Gaitskell in what was planned to be a regular series of briefings with the Opposition parties. The meeting did not go well. Salisbury told Gaitskell that Eden and he did actually have joint experience of dealing with world statesmen together from before the war, and could do without lectures from someone with no such experience. 'Bobbety found his [Gaitskell's] preaching irritating,' Eden wrote in his diary, 'and flashed out.'[66]

Eden soon found that where his policy on Suez most offended was among the liberal upper-middle-class *bien-pensants*, the political class he had always loathed. Suez certainly lost the Conservatives the intellectual vote, always more significant than its numerical strength. Tacit Anglican endorsement was also lost, so that the Church of England could never again be regarded as the Tory Party at prayer. Gaitskell, in Eden's eyes, was the epitome of the self-righteous tendency, and Harold Macmillan described him as 'a sanctimonious Wykehamist with gestures like an Armenian shopkeeper'.[67]

Gaitskell's physical presence as leader of the Opposition tended to bring out the worst in Eden, such was the lack of chemistry between the two men. For Eden, high-minded internationalism went a long way in such intellectual circles, but only *until* the political consequences impinged on their own material self-interest. As one veteran of those distant days said privately to the author, 'Suez was an economic crisis first and foremost, whereas for the *Manchester Guardian* intellectuals it represented all the worst excesses of the old colonialism. Yet when the going got tough, these drawing-room liberals were the first to whinge, as petrol shortages made it less easy for them to visit Hugo and Fiona at their rural boarding schools.'[68] The sense of deep bitterness on both sides cannot be underestimated.

From the first London Conference emerged a formula (the Eighteen Nations Proposals) for a new convention that gave Egypt a place on the board of a mixed operating company for the canal and increased revenues. Eden was more encouraged at this stage by Dulles's seeming acceptance of the eventual need for action. 'F[oster] seemed quite as firm as before & ready to table joint resolution himself,' he noted in his diary. 'He also seemed not to exclude possibility of force.'[69]

On 17 August, Eden wrote to Churchill, thanking him for his good wishes for the success of the London Conference:

> We are only at the beginning but there are some encouraging elements. Most important of all, the Americans seem very firmly lined up with us on internationalisation. Secondly, there are signs that the Middle Eastern States who are also oil producers, e.g. Iraq, Persia and Saudi-Arabia, are in varying degrees opposed to Nasser's plans. In other Arab States demagogy howls in support of Nasser.

Eden had already told Churchill details of the military planning at Chequers on 6 August. Now he brought him further up to date:

> Preparations about which I spoke to you are going forward with some modifications, which should lead to simplification of our plan should the need arise. I am sure that you will think this all to the good.
>
> It is difficult to judge about public opinion. The left-wing intellectuals and some liberals are all out against us. The B.B.C. is exasperating me by leaning over backwards to be what they call neutral and to present both sides of the case, by which I suppose our country's and the Dancing Major's. I am, however, seeing Jacob this afternoon. He and nearly all the seniors have been away on leave. I hope we can improve on past performances.
>
> Bob Menzies has been very helpful and it would help me if you would tell him so when you see him. I will keep you posted.[70]

Robert Menzies, the Australian Prime Minister, was the leader of the so-called Mission to Nasser in Cairo, which attempted to negotiate the acceptance of the Eighteen-Power plan for the future administration of the canal. By the beginning of September this attempt at a diplomatic solution had failed in ignominious circumstances. On his return to London, Menzies gave Eden a dispiriting account of the mission, which he always blamed on Eisenhower, whose ill-advised words (at the very moment Menzies was in Cairo) were 'For ourselves, we are determined to exhaust every possible, every feasible method of peaceful settlement. We are committed to a peaceful settlement of this dispute, *nothing else.*'[71]

After that, thought Menzies, Nasser had *carte blanche*, an opportunity he did not fail to exploit. 'Egypt is not only a dictatorship,' Menzies wrote, 'but it has all the earmarks of a Police State. The tapping of telephone lines, the installation of microphones, the creation of a vast body of security police – all these things are accepted as commonplace.' Menzies did not know whether to laugh or despair at some of the arguments put to him. 'Nasser said to me that he understood that the British Government itself had nationalised the Manchester Ship Canal without regard to contracts.'[72] As Selwyn Lloyd noted of Nasser, 'He certainly possessed a propaganda machine which even Doctor Goebbels would have envied.'[73]

On 24 August, Walter Monckton, a Churchill placeman with no political base of his own, had an outburst at the Egypt Committee, which Salisbury described as 'both painful and rather disturbing'. As a result, Salisbury advised that 'the case for force will clearly need to be closely and cogently argued by those of us who agree with it'.[74]

Meanwhile, Alec Home had written privately to Eden on 22 August warning:

> I sense that Rab is very unhappy. I know your time is full but if you could see him alone it would be well worth while. He is not against the use of force, but he fears that we have got ourselves into a position where we shall press the button before we have a moral basis for action which will carry conviction in this country, the free world and the Conservative Party.

On the day of the Monckton outburst, Home added:

> The anxieties of some, Rab for instance, might be removed if we didn't have to go on thinking in terms of button pushing & dates & had plenty of time for diplomatic manoeuvre. All this is disturbing. For myself I have no doubts that if we cannot make anything of the Security Council, and that largely depends on Dulles, we have no option but to go through with it. I need not say more but I am convinced that we are finished if the Middle East goes & Russia & India & China rule from Africa to the Pacific.[75]

Three days later, Clarissa Eden noted in her diary, 'Alec is warning that

Rab is wobbling to the point of lobbying, as a result of which he has found seven members of the Cabinet who agree with him.'[76]

After the failure of the Menzies Mission, Dulles's suggestions for an alternative basis for negotiation led to the second London Conference from 19 to 21 September, and the idea of a Suez Canal Users' Association (SCUA). The French were wary of 'a SCUA without a point'; and Eden later considered that agreeing to SCUA was his worst tactical mistake.[77]*

By the end of the second London Conference, Eden was impatient for military action and preparations to that end were difficult to hold in check. The original operational plan of the Chiefs of Staff – MUSKETEER – had envisaged an attack upon Alexandria, with a D-Day of 15 September, followed by an advance to Suez through Cairo, and had been accepted by the Egypt Committee on 10 August. In mid-September, with no hope of adhering to the original proposal, this plan was recast by Keightley as MUSKETEER REVISE, operational till the end of October, and with a shorter time-span of eight days between 'button-pushing' and execution, with a direct attack on Port Said as its primary aim. The problem, as winter approached, was that military forces (including reservists, who had been called up on 2 August) could not be kept on hold indefinitely.

'I am not very happy at the way things are developing here,' Eden admitted to Churchill in a further letter on 17 September, 'but we are struggling hard to keep a firm and united front in these critical weeks, firm is even more important than united. Foster assures me that U.S. is as determined to deal with Nasser as we are – but I fear he has a mental caveat about November 6th [the date of the Presidential Election]. We cannot accept that.'[78]

Nasser's imperative to maintain the impetus of his revolutionary movement had grave implications for the Western powers, especially those largely dependent on the Suez Canal for maintenance of their oil supplies in the days before North Sea oil. What is often neglected is that Britain was undergoing a kind of reverse revolution at the same time as Nasser's expansionist nationalism, that of the abdication of her overseas responsibilities in a parallel move towards decolonisation. Any nation finds it very difficult to adjust to a much lower status in the world, and Britain felt this with particular acuteness, both at Suez and later. The United States could afford to be more insouciant over Nasser, not being dependent on

---

*In fact, much time was spent at Lancaster House trying to find an acronym that did not offend some nation's sensibilities. The first suggestion, the Co-operative Association of Suez Canal Users (CASU), proved to be a Portuguese vulgarity. 'Various other combinations were tried,' recorded Selwyn Lloyd wryly. 'Almost all of them meant something revolting, usually in Turkish.' Selwyn Lloyd, *Suez 1956: A Personal Account*, Jonathan Cape, 1978, p.145.

Middle East oil. Britain did not have the luxury of being able to separate the question of free maritime passage through an international waterway from that of the overall management of the Suez Canal Company. She wanted pressure on Egypt.

The most immediate means of pressure on Egypt, short of military intervention, was withdrawal of dues that would deprive Nasser of the wherewithal to continue with the High Dam Project. Eden had discussed this with Dulles on 19 August, but with little progress, as Dulles was concerned about the implications for America over similar developments in the Panama Canal. However, Dulles did let the Russians know that if Britain and France took action, America would not stand aside, which Eden interpreted as tacit, if reluctant, backing.

On 28 August, William Haley dined with Eden, their first extended meeting since March. Haley recorded Eden's concerns:

> He was not quite as relaxed as last time; obviously getting worried over the timing of the Suez business. If Nasser is skilful enough to drag the talks out into the winter, neither we nor the French could take action if they failed.
>
> I told Eden I thought it was essential the public should clearly see that the 18 governments had exhausted every peaceful possibility before they took action. The idea that our national life depended on the canal being in international hands had sunk in; if there was no other way to ensure this then the West would have to do so by force. But the public and the rest of Europe (and America) would want to have seen by events that there was no other way.
>
> Eden asked me if I thought Britain should herself take the matter to the Security Council; a majority of the Cabinet were in favour of it. I said Yes. Nasser or Russia might themselves take the matter there on our action. We should forestall them by indicting Nasser's action. It would also show public opinion we had no desire to by-pass the United Nations if they would be effective.

Such advice confirmed Eden's thinking at the time. Haley's account continues:

> Eden said America would not discountenance the use of force if all else failed but would keep out themselves. Eden thought this would be best as Russia would not then consider herself directly challenged. The two colossi would stand on one side.[79]

Whatever Eden may have gleaned by way of comfort between the lines of Dulles's opaque statements was rudely shattered by Eisenhower's further warning against the use of force on 3 September, an ironic anniversary for such caution. 'Of course there should be no thought of military action before the influences of the United Nations are fully explored,' Eisenhower wrote. 'If the diplomatic front is united and backed by the overwhelming sentiment of our several peoples the chances should be greater that Nasser will give way.'[80]

Meanwhile, Selwyn Lloyd urged Eden first to exhaust whatever possibilities might exist of a solution through the United Nations. While in New York in September preparing for a meeting of the Security Council, Lloyd met his Egyptian and French opposite numbers, Dr Fawzi and Christian Pineau. With great tenacity Lloyd developed the formula of the first London Conference into a statement of Six Principles on which a solution might be negotiated – what Lloyd called 'a good natured preamble to a missing treaty'.[81]

Parliament was recalled on 12 September for a two-day debate on the situation in the Middle East. A fortnight later a similar debate was scheduled for the Security Council. Before this took place, Macmillan finally saw Eisenhower and Dulles in Washington, writing to Eden on 26 September:

> Ike is really determined, somehow or another, to bring Nasser down. I explained to him our economic difficulties in playing the hand long, and he seemed to understand. I also made it clear that we *must* win, or the whole structure of our economy would collapse. He accepted this.[82]

As well as revealing a rather patronising attitude towards Eisenhower ('he seemed to understand'), Macmillan's interpretation of the President's attitude was, even then, seriously misleading, implying that in the end the Americans would stand by the British. Yet Eisenhower had already warned Eden that 'a serious misunderstanding between our two countries'[83] would be the consequence of any attempt to use force against Nasser, an attitude that made Mollet and Eden now want to break free from the stranglehold of American caution and solve the problem on their own initiatives. On the day he received Macmillan's letter, Eden flew to Paris with Lloyd to meet Mollet and Pineau. Eden found the French in a difficult mood because of the lack of progress.

It was not only the French who were disenchanted. The British Ambassador in Paris, Sir Gladwyn Jebb, was furious to be excluded, and let his feelings be known. 'It is, I believe, a novel arrangement for diplomatic business of the highest importance to be conducted by the Principals without any official being present, even to take a note,' he protested to Selwyn Lloyd, who anxiously consulted Eden on how he should reply.

'By arrangement with the French there is nothing we can say. We are very sorry,' Eden wrote to Lloyd when told of Jebb's concerns. 'In fact in the war it often happened that we had talks with no officials present in Washington, London and Moscow.'[84]

Having been told this, Jebb wrote directly to Ivone Kirkpatrick, the Permanent Under-Secretary, asking for some indication of what was happening to be sent to him in code. In language prefiguring some of the more bizarre secret messages of the 1980s television comedy series 'Allo 'Allo, about the activities of the French resistance, Jebb set out the secret language:

(a) In the event of our finally deciding on calling the whole thing off & relying on negotiations:-
  'I am happy to tell you that the bird has flown.'
(b) In the event of our deciding on some course which is likely to involve the use of British & French armed forces:-
  'You will no doubt like to hear that Caroline survived the operation.'
Should you add to this 'but she is still very weak', I should understand that the balloon is likely to go up within a fortnight.
Should you say 'but the doctor says she will be out of action for some time', I shall understand that it will be more likely to be three weeks.[85]

In the event, 'Caroline survived the operation.'

At a news conference on 2 October, Dulles stated, 'There is talk about the "teeth" being pulled out of it [SCUA]. There were never "teeth" in it, if that means the use of force.'[86] For Eden this was the last straw. He continued to warn Selwyn Lloyd in New York to be on his guard regarding Dulles. On 5 October he wrote, 'We must never forget that Dulles' purpose is different from ours. The Canal is in no sense vital to the United States and his game is to string us along at least until polling day.'

The pressures were beginning to tell. The same day Eden was visiting his wife at University College Hospital, London, when he himself was taken ill with a fever. The duty private secretary, who had been forgotten in the drama, after waiting for an interminable time asked one of the staff how Lady Eden was, only to be told he could go home, as Eden was being detained overnight for observation. Although Eden was only out of action for less than a day, it was a sign of things to come.

On 8 October Eden reiterated his warnings to Lloyd in a further letter, 'We have been misled so often by Dulles' ideas that we cannot afford to risk another misunderstanding.'[87] At this stage Eden clearly believed that any progress Lloyd might make with Fawzi on the Six Principles could still retrieve the situation. But there remained one complicating factor. By the terms of the Anglo-Jordanian Treaty of 1948, Britain guaranteed support for Jordan against any aggresssor, and on the night of 10–11 October the worst possible scenario seemed likely, following Israeli air attacks on Jordan, and King Hussein's request for British air support.[88] For a time there was a very real possibility that Britain could be involved in war against Israel, maybe even in concert with Egypt, while the Suez question remained unresolved. Such was the background to the Challe/Gazier visit to Chequers on 14 October, with a French proposal for tripartite action with Israel. A motivating force behind the French proposal concerned Israel's restlessness about her borders. If Israel was going to attack anybody – and clearly the raid against Jordan was not an isolated, or final, adventure – then the French were sure that it would be better for themselves and Britain if their target was Egypt.

The Conservative Party Conference in Llandudno beginning on 11 October showed a striking display of unanimity, with attacks of equal virulence on both Nasser and Gaitskell. Captain Waterhouse and Julian Amery were persuaded to put an amendment commending the Eighteen Nation Proposals, and Anthony Nutting, deputising for Lord Salisbury who was ill, delivered a notably belligerent speech. The speech was Salisbury's, and Nutting was given the opportunity in advance to have the speech attributed to Salisbury, if he wished. He declined, saying, 'Make no mistake. This is to be Nutting's day.'[89] Eden's keynote speech on Saturday 13 October ('We have refused to say that in no circumstances would we ever use force. No responsible Government could ever give such a pledge')[90] brought the conference to a close amid scenes of great enthusiasm.

Eden returned to Chequers that evening. But if he had expected a quiet weekend, he was to be disappointed. Nutting came down to Chequers on the morning of Sunday 14 October with the news that Russia had exercised her veto in the Security Council. The two men despatched a significant telegram at 1.30 p.m. to Lloyd, who was in New York having talks with Dr Fawzi. A negotiated settlement was still on Eden's agenda:

> Should not we and the French now approach the Egyptians and ask them whether they are prepared to meet and discuss in confidence with us on the basis of the second half of the resolution which the Russians vetoed? If they say yes, then it is for consideration whether we and the French meet them somewhere, e.g. Geneva. If they say no, then they will be in defiance of the view of nine members of the Security Council and a new situation will arise.[91]

But by 4 p.m. everything had changed. The next phase was not to be at Geneva but at Sèvres on the outskirts of Paris.

*

There were three decisive moments during the Suez crisis, influencing irrevocably the course of its history. The first was on the evening of 26 July at the Downing Street dinner, when news of Nasser's nationalisation of the canal arrived, and positions were adopted from which it was later difficult to retract. The second, and most important of all, was the surprise French plan put before Eden and Nutting at Chequers between 3 and 4 p.m. on Sunday 14 October. The third was Eden's despatch of Selwyn Lloyd to France, where he met the French and Israeli Prime Ministers at a villa at Sèvres on 22 October.

The *casus belli* for which Eden had been waiting was presented to him at Chequers on 14 October by Major-General Maurice Challe, Deputy to the French Chief of the General Staff, and Albert Gazier, the French Minister for Social Affairs. Eden heard the details in the presence of Anthony Nutting and Guy Millard, the duty private secretary. As the audacious scheme, which the French had been planning with the Israelis for over a fortnight, was revealed, Guy Millard prepared to keep a record of what unfolded. 'There's no need to take notes, Guy,' said Eden. At that moment, Nutting, who could hardly believe what he was hearing, knew in his heart that he had come to a parting of the ways, and that if Eden went along with the French suggestion, he would have to resign.[92]

The Challe/Gazier scenario was deceptively simple. Israel would invade the Suez Canal Zone, then the British and French would intervene as peace-makers, to 'separate the combatants' and thus secure the canal as an international waterway. If only it had been as simple in execution. The question remains why Eden so readily accepted 'The Plan' and even more so, how he believed that its details could be kept secret in perpetuity, or that a short-term occupation of Egypt could in fact be speedily reversed. Temporary expedients have an inconvenient habit of becoming quasi-permanent. As Eden well knew, the occupation of Egypt after Sir Garnet Wolseley's punitive expedition in 1882 had lasted for more than seventy years. But 'The Plan' did seem to offer, at a late stage, and before winter set in, one last chance of ending the impasse. Eden embraced it with enthusiasm.

The first task was to summon Lloyd back from New York. He arrived at Heathrow at 11.15 a.m. British time on Tuesday 16 October and was immediately driven to Downing Street, where, buoyant despite his jet-lag, he told Nutting that a settlement on the basis of the Six Principles was now possible. Lloyd was chastened to hear from Nutting that such a solution was no longer on the agenda. Before he could learn more, he was whisked into a Cabinet meeting (where Nutting as Minister of State had no access to him). After the Cabinet, Eden asked Lloyd to stay behind, and over lunch outlined Challe's scenario. Although Lloyd was initially hostile to 'The Plan' and argued against it, Eden brought all his persuasiveness to bear. Short of resignation, Lloyd had no option but to comply. Eden and Lloyd were to go to Paris that very afternoon to see Mollet and Pineau.

Before their flight took off from Heathrow at 4 p.m., Nutting spoke to Lloyd on the telephone with one last plea. It was too late. 'Eden had clearly used the lunch to devastating effect,' Nutting later wrote, 'for Lloyd not only seemed prepared to acquiesce in the French plan, but now took the line that his agreement with Fawzi would never hold.'[93] This had been the clinching argument that Eden had employed. The Egyptians could not be trusted. They had broken their word over the 1954 Suez Canal Base Agreement; what was to prevent them doing the same over the Six Principles?

Eden and Lloyd were met in Paris by Gladwyn Jebb, who was still smarting from his earlier exclusion from the Anglo-French talks. Eden had no comfort for him. 'It must be *à quatre* – those are our instructions.' As the talks went on into the evening, Mollet and Pineau both expressed trenchant views on how Dulles had double-crossed them over SCUA, which they had seen as a means of pressurising Nasser. Now it seemed that Dulles's real intention had been merely to forestall any Anglo-French appeal to the Security Council. As far as Dulles was concerned, this function had now been fulfilled, and he was no longer interested in SCUA. Lloyd, who had started his day in New York, was also surprisingly combative, considering his journeyings and the number of meetings he had already attended.

The agenda then moved on to the proposed attack by Israel on Egypt. Mollet said that the Egyptians had made repeated threats to exterminate the State of Israel, so if the Israelis got in a pre-emptive strike, there was a case to be made that it was in self-defence. For Eden, the great fear – the nightmare scenario, in fact – was Israel attacking Jordan first. Had this happened, then, by the terms of the 1948 Anglo-Jordanian Treaty, Britain would be obliged to go to Jordan's aid. For the French, the deeper fear was that, having got the British so close to the water, they would be unable to make them drink. Mollet asked Eden bluntly if, in the event of hostilities as outlined, Britain would intervene. Although still expressing his concerns about an attack first by Israel on Jordan, Eden confirmed that she would. Lloyd was now locked into 'The Plan'.[94]

Eden and Lloyd returned to London on 17 October. Lloyd told the Egypt Committee, unnecessarily as events were to show, about his talks with Fawzi in New York. The next day, the Cabinet discussed the ramifications of an attack by Israel on Egypt.

One of the clearest things to emerge from the release of the Suez papers in 1987* is that Cabinet members discussed, at various times, the Challe scenario of initiating an Israeli attack with the object of making Anglo-French intervention possible. On 18 October, Eden reported what he had learnt in Paris of Israeli intentions, also taking advantage of a Prime Minister's privileged access to intelligence to convey information. At this stage an Israeli attack seemed probable. By the time of the Cabinet on 23 October, it appeared improbable; but on 25 October, likely once more. On that day, Anglo-French intervention before the Israeli attacks began was discussed as a contingency. Cabinet might have gone along with Eden's agenda with varying degrees of reluctance – but no one would claim that Cabinet had not been fully informed and consulted.

Although Lloyd was lobbied by both Butler and Monckton, he had crossed his Rubicon and had no intention of returning. He was now the key figure in Eden's efforts to hold the Cabinet together. He did not fail his master and was later to write (accurately) that Monckton 'was privy to all the early decisions, including the decision to use force, and did not oppose them.'[95] On 18 October, Monckton was moved to the post of Paymaster-General, and Antony Head took his place as Minister of Defence.

Intended as the most secret of political meetings, the tripartite conversations at Sèvres on 22 and 24 October between the French, the Israelis and the British have since become some of the most closely examined negotiations in modern history.[96]

One of the rarely asked questions about this episode is why Eden did not himself attend. After all, Ben-Gurion, the Prime Minister of Israel, managed to be present. Herein, of course, lay the rub. If Israel attacked Jordan, which was by no means an impossible scenario, then Britain's obligation was clear. Any knowledge that Eden had supped with Ben-Gurion would have had disastrous consequences. To that extent Selwyn Lloyd was a sacrificial lamb, expendable no doubt if things turned nasty. Also the meeting was a deadly secret, and it was easier to explain a Foreign Secretary's absence than a Prime Minister's, though Lloyd's supposed ill-health was not the cleverest of excuses. As Lloyd was seen in London on his return from the first Sèvres meeting, he could hardly disappear two days later back to Sèvres under the same cover.

Eden did not foresee Lloyd's coldly sceptical attitude at Sèvres. Eden's

---

*Two expectations about the release of the Suez papers at the Public Record Office on 2 January 1987 (the paucity of the material and the inevitable throng to see them) were confounded. The material released on that unforgettable day was extensive and the numbers at Kew no more than average – but one saw some old friends.

legendary charm had won Lloyd over. But it was temporary. His Foreign Secretary's fundamental distaste for the original Challe plan was in the event to make him reluctant to undertake a second journey. For Lloyd, one visit to Sèvres was more than enough. Selwyn Lloyd had an old-fashioned idea of loyalty to his superiors (a trait from his Second Army days onwards), but it did not mean that privately he agreed with all orders from above.

Accompanied by his assistant private secretary, Donald Logan, Lloyd flew from Hendon airfield in conditions of great secrecy* to Villacoublay military airfield on the outskirts of Paris. On the way to the villa at Sèvres the British delegation narrowly missed being involved in a serious car accident, which could have altered the course of history. They arrived at the villa, a wartime resistance base, at 4 p.m. French time. Waiting for them were Guy Mollet, Maurice Bourgès-Maunoury, the French Defence Minister, David Ben-Gurion, the Israeli Prime Minister, General Moshe Dayan, Israeli Chief of Staff, and Shimon Peres, Director-General of the Israeli Ministry of Defence. Other officials, including Abel Thomas of the French Ministry of Defence, and Mordechai Bar-On, Secretary to the Israeli delegation, were on the fringe. The overwhelming impression was that the gathering, feasting on an enormous fish, had been in session for some time. Lloyd's instructions from Eden were to make clear that any British involvement in the Challe scenario must not be regarded as a response to a request from Israel. Little was established at the subsequent meeting, apart from Lloyd's coolness towards the Challe plan, and his reluctance to commit the British without further Cabinet consultation. This was not acceptable to Ben-Gurion, who wanted a definite commitment from Britain over the use of its RAF Canberra bombers from Cyprus against Egyptian airfields before Israeli troops moved. Lloyd's optimistic comments about his recent negotiations with Fawzi in New York were considered particularly irrelevant. It was with some relief on his return to London that Lloyd's conscience was eased by Eden's determination to handle the response himself.

On 23 October at 10 a.m., Lloyd told a small group of senior ministers what had transpired, and then the full Cabinet at 11 a.m. Under Item 6 in the minutes of this Cabinet, Eden recalled that, when the Cabinet had last discussed the Suez situation on 18 October, it was believed that Israel might be contemplating military action against Egypt. The full Cabinet was now told that 'from secret conversations which had been held in Paris with representatives of the Israeli Government, it now appeared that the Israelis would not alone launch a full-scale attack against Egypt'.* It is clear that the British did not encourage the Israelis to make a pre-emptive strike. That was going to happen anyway. The question was whether it could be turned to Britain's advantage.

Meanwhile, the French and the Israelis, who continued in conference at Sèvres during 23 October, were determined to make assurance doubly sure, as they did not trust perfidious Albion to deliver, which is why they went to such an extent to get things down on paper. To this end, they wanted further written confirmation from London, Ben-Gurion being the key figure pressing Mollet to achieve this.[97]

So, following the first meeting at Sèvres, Lloyd confirmed to his French counterparts the understanding that had been reached, though with such bland obliqueness that non-initiates would have little idea what was being discussed. On 23 October, Lloyd wrote the following letter to Pineau:

> I discussed with the Prime Minister and other colleagues this morning our conversations of yesterday.
>
> I feel that I must make it clear, in view of something that was said yesterday, that the U.K. Government have not asked the Israeli Government to take any particular action.
>
> We were asked what our reactions would be if certain things were to happen, and we stated the position of the U.K. Government in the 2 documents given to Monsieur Mollet by the P.M. in Paris last week, the second of which was superseded by the redraft handed by me to you for Monsieur Mollet yesterday.
>
> We stand by what is contained in these documents.[98]

Further talks at Sèvres were inevitable, as Pineau made clear on a lightning visit to London on the evening of 23 October; but Lloyd was determined he would never return to that villa. In any case he was due to make a broadcast for United Nations Day (24 October) and to answer parliamentary questions during the afternoon. Patrick Dean, Deputy Under-Secretary at the Foreign Office, was therefore told by Kirkpatrick that it was his duty to accompany Logan to Sèvres for the final meeting of the conference.

On the morning of 24 October, Eden briefed Dean, making it clear that the British would intervene only if there was a threat to the canal and if the Israelis had advanced beyond their territories towards the canal. Eden was

---

*Professor Peter Hennessy has called this 'a smoking minute', as it reveals, once and for all, that the Cabinet had not, as was previously supposed, been kept in ignorance. (Cabinet Minutes, 23 October 1956. PRO. CAB 128/30. Peter Hennessy, op. cit., p. 222.) The late Sir Robert Rhodes James told the author in 1992 that this was the single most important fact he had discovered in his researches into Eden's career.

adamant that the British were not asking the Israelis to intervene. Dean was told that if the French and Israelis did not accept this stance, then the British would not accept the proposed military plan. The letter Dean took with him to Sèvres confirmed this.[99]

At a full Cabinet later that morning, as Dean and Logan travelled to France, Eden brought ministers up to date with details of Pineau's visit the previous evening. Pineau had stressed that the French wanted any military action against Egypt to be based on grounds that concerned the United Kingdom as well as France.[100]

The second Sèvres meeting had many similarities with the first. It began at 4 p.m., and had already been going on for some time when Dean and Logan arrived. The atmosphere was formal, rather than friendly, and there was an undercurrent of truculence, particularly from David Ben-Gurion. Dean handed over the British letter, and sketch maps were then made, showing the proposed area of Israeli military action near the Mitla Pass. The Israelis were not best pleased by the way the British Government, through its representative, still seemed to be distancing itself from the plans.

At this moment the French produced three copies of a document,* which it wanted those present to sign on behalf of their respective Governments. Dean was taken aback and consulted privately with Logan. Finally Dean agreed to sign, making it clear that he only did so *ad referendum*.

After Dean and Logan had left, the French and the Israelis opened a bottle of champagne to celebrate. Ben-Gurion was happy. Collusion within collusion had worked and the agreement was on paper.

When Dean returned to London late that night, Eden was horrified to hear that a written record existed. The British copy was destroyed, and Dean was despatched back to Paris the next morning to ensure a similar fate for the French and Israeli copies. It was too late. Ben-Gurion had returned to Israel, his guarantee against British perfidy safely in his waistcoat pocket, and the whereabouts of the French copy were not disclosed.†

In retrospect, it can be seen that Eden's attempt to destroy written evidence was foredoomed to failure, as was his belief that the agreement could remain secret for ever. Trying to draw a veil over what had transpired only gave fuel to his critics. A wiser course would have been to follow the dictum, 'They say, what say they, let them say.'

After the signing of the Protocol of Sèvres on 24 October, its essentials were presented to the Cabinet. Reactions were mixed. The doubters

---

*Later known as The Protocol of Sèvres. Reproduced in Appendix III.
†A French copy of the Protocol is today in the Guy Mollet Archives, and the original Israeli copy resides in the Ben-Gurion Archives at Sede-Boker.

included relatively junior figures, such as Derick Heathcoat Amory, who carried little weight. After discussion, the full Cabinet 'agreed in principle that, in the event of an Israeli attack on Egypt, the Government should join with the French Government in calling on the two belligerents to stop hostilities and withdraw their forces to a distance of ten miles from the Canal; and should warn belligerents that, if either or both of them failed to undertake within twelve hours to comply with these requirements, British and French forces would intervene to enforce compliance.'[101]

After the second Sèvres meeting, notwithstanding Eden's dismay at Patrick Dean's signature on the Protocol, Eden wrote to Mollet, on what was St Crispin's Day and the anniversary of a somewhat different Anglo-French encounter: 'Her Majesty's Government have been informed of the course of the conversations held at Sèvres on October 22–24. They confirm that in the situation there envisaged they will take the action described.'

After further messages from Mollet, Eden wrote a second letter on 28 October from Chequers: 'My dear Friend, Thank you so much for your letter. I will certainly at once go with your suggestion, & will let you know what we can do. Yours very sincerely, Anthony Eden.'[102]

The British were on board.

At this moment came one of the more curious episodes of Suez. Eden sent for Anthony Montague Browne, Churchill's loyal secretary. He outlined what was about to happen, and asked Montague Browne if he thought Churchill would accept a post in the Cabinet as Minister without Portfolio. Having Churchill, now almost eighty-two, aboard at this juncture was a prospect as full of imponderables as the Protocol of Sèvres itself, and Montague Browne replied, 'I do not believe that he would like the opposite of the harlot's prerogative.'* The idea was dropped, though Churchill later joked with his secretary about how Montague Browne had taken it upon himself to decline a Cabinet post on Churchill's behalf, without even asking for his opinion.[103]

On Tuesday 30 October, William Haley, with an acute sense already of the background negotiations, wrote in his diary, 'The event one feared has come to pass. Israel has invaded Egypt, and just before the Presidential Election. It will be interesting to see how Eden handles this in the House today in view of the background. If things do not go well for Israel will

---

*In a speech at Queen's Hall, Westminster, on 18 March 1931, during the Westminster St George's by-election, Stanley Baldwin had said, 'What the proprietorship of these papers is aiming at is power, and power without responsibility, the prerogative of the harlot throughout the ages.'

Ben-Gurion keep quiet about the communication that was made to him?'[104]

Before going to the House, Eden telegrammed Eisenhower at 1.28 p.m. on 30 October, 'We feel that decisive action should be taken at once to stop hostilities.'[105] This was the first of two lengthy communications, separated by Eden's statement in the House at 4.30 p.m. – what he later deemed 'an error in timing',[106] as the United States, the Commonwealth and the Opposition had not had time to reflect fully on the letters he had sent them. The United Nations, meanwhile, was calling for an immediate ceasefire. Despite Eisenhower's later public declaration, with one eye firmly on the impending Presidential Election, that the United States had not been informed in advance, he had in fact heard unofficially on 24 October that Britain would shortly be attacking Egypt – information, as one commentator has put it, 'helpfully leaked to the American Ambassador in London by that arch-appeaser and all-purpose cringer in the face of trouble, Walter Monckton'.[107] He had also received regular updates through the official channels from Eden, messages that were handed to him personally by John Coulson, the British Chargé d'Affaires in Washington.[108]

'Both Selwyn & the PM seem curiously euphoric today,' William Clark wrote on 30 October. 'The big decisions are over & they seem calm and detached.' But if Eden had hoped to keep news of the agreements at Sèvres secret, he was to be disappointed, and sooner than he could have anticipated. The CIA had come to only one conclusion, after noting the enormous increase in cipher traffic between Paris and Tel Aviv. As William Clark on the verge of resignation, noted, 'Stories about collusion with Israel are beginning to appear in the American Press.'[109]

As if one cataclysm was not enough at this critical stage of world history, while Israeli forces were preparing to go into action against Egypt, the Politburo in Moscow took the decision to crush the Hungarian revolt, marked by huge student protests on 23 October and the temporary installation of Imre Nagy as Prime Minister. From Eden's perspective, the presence of Russian troops in Hungary – other than as a corridor for occupation forces in Austria – was not a sign of the weakness of the Yalta Agreements, but of Russia's disregard for the treaty, as also evinced by her prevention of internal Hungarian elections.[110] As the tanks rumbled into Budapest, Nagy was overthrown and later executed. Although this Soviet invasion resonated round the world, contributing to some of the most anxious days of the whole Cold War period, British Cabinet records show how little it impinged on Government thinking or policy. The overriding priorities were Egypt and the review of social services investment and military expenditure before the 1957 Defence White Paper (it must not be forgotten that other Cabinet business continued during Suez).

At 5 p.m., Egyptian time, on 31 October, as more Israeli planes crossed over Sinai and paratroopers landed at the Mitla Pass, allied air action against Egypt began. For the moment, the talking was over. Elizabeth Home recorded in her diary, 'The wireless gave news of the Anglo-French offensive by bomber aircraft against military targets in Egypt.' It was actually the calm before the greater storm. 'Much impressed by how well the PM & everyone in the Govt look,' she noted, '& can't understand it.'[111]

CHAPTER NINETEEN

Last Months in Office

NOVEMBER 1956–JANUARY 1957

One should count on *nothing* from the Americans except words.
Neville Chamberlain to Hilda Chamberlain, 17 December 1937[1]

A country which cannot withstand the strain of a run on its
currency or economic privation can ill afford to risk incurring
international wrath.
J. T. Emmerson, *The Rhineland Crisis*, 1977[2]

There is only one motto worse than 'my country right or wrong'
and that is 'The United Nations right or wrong'.
Aneurin Bevan to Richard Crossman

November 1956 was to prove the most painful month of Eden's political
life. Yet, contrary to the myths, as it began, there was a serenity and
composure about him. 'There is a curious peace now at No 10,'[3] William
Clark wrote in his diary, in his last days as Press Secretary. The tranquillity
was noted by others close to Eden at this determining moment, Freddie
Bishop recalling that he was 'remarkably calm and steady',[4] and Selwyn
Lloyd noting that 'when important decisions had to be taken, he was
calm'.[5]

Following the Anglo-Egyptian air attacks against Egyptian military
targets, the General Assembly of the United Nations began its emergency
debate on the Suez crisis on 1 November, one of the most dramatic days of
the whole affair on both sides of the Atlantic. During the course of the
lengthy deliberations in New York, John Foster Dulles said that no delegate could have spoken with a heavier heart than he was doing that night.
Several Commonwealth countries denounced Britain, and the motion for
an immediate ceasefire was passed overwhelmingly by the Assembly, sixty-
four nations voting in favour, with Britain, France, Australia, Israel and
New Zealand voting against.[6]

At this stage Lester Pearson, Canada's Foreign Minister, proposed the
formation of UNEF (United Nations Emergency Force), a suggestion that
eventually won for him the Nobel Peace Prize, an award that at one time,
especially after the Geneva Conference of 1954, seemed destined for Eden.

Events at Westminster proved even more charged and impassioned. 'Mr

Gaitskell Divides Nation in Crisis' ran the morning's headline in the *Scotsman* of the scheduled debate in the Commons.[7] The House of Lords, too, was to have its share of drama, as Kilmuir, the Lord Chancellor, outlined the legal basis for British action, only to be challenged repeatedly by the Archbishop of Canterbury. 'Are we doing the right thing, by the highest and wisest standard that we, as a nation know?' asked Archbishop Fisher in one of his many interventions. 'The point to which the Christian conscience must acutely address itself is whether or not we are standing to the spirit of the United Nations Charter.'*

The debate in the Commons, witnessed in the Distinguished Strangers' Gallery by Clarissa Eden and Gaitskell's wife, Dora, sitting side by side, was for Iverach McDonald one of the most purely shattering experiences he had ever witnessed, terrible in its demonstration of raw anger on both sides.[8] In response to Gaitskell's persistent questioning, Eden had to admit that Britain was not formally at war, but in 'a state of armed conflict'[9] Whether the Geneva Convention applied was thus unclear, though such ambiguities were not to trouble the United States in 2002 over the al-Qaeda prisoners in Cuba during the struggle against the Taleban.

For Eden, with his lifelong memories of military action, it was unforgivable that Gaitskell – 'the Wykehamist who had never worn uniform', as some Tory backbenchers dubbed him[10] – was not supportive when British troops were committed to active service. The wrath of the Tories was now directed personally against Gaitskell, who for them, in addition to betraying his class, was seen in some sections of the party as also betraying his country. Feelings ran high among Conservatives beyond Westminster also. When Gaitskell spoke to the Political Society at Winchester College at the height of the Suez crisis that November, he 'was asked at immense length by a choleric retired housemaster to explain why he had behaved as a traitor.'[11] And on bonfire night at Fettes (Selwyn Lloyd's old school), the traditional effigy of Guy Fawkes was replaced, at the instigation of a senior housemaster, by a particularly unflattering one of Gaitskell, set alight to general acclamation.[12]

But other Conservatives had misgivings. During the acrimonious debate, the Conservative MP for the Wrekin, William Yates, declared that Britain had been engaged in an 'international conspiracy'. On 31 October, Gaitskell had said 'that the whole business was a matter of collusion

---

*Surprisingly, Aneurin Bevan, who wound up for the Opposition in the Commons, was one of the Labour figures less than impressed by Fisher's point. In 1961, Richard Crossman was to report that Bevan had told him at this moment, 'What makes the Labour party go wrong in foreign affairs is that it takes its policies from middle-class intellectuals, devoid of antennae and with a dreadful habit of falling down and worshipping abstractions. In fact, there is only one motto worse than "my country right or wrong" and that is "The United Nations right or wrong."' *Manchester Guardian Weekly*, 28 December 1961.

between the British and French Governments and the Government of Israel', and Alfred Robens, the Shadow Foreign Secretary, also referred to 'collusion' in the House on 13 November.[13] As passions rose, the Speaker suspended the sitting for the first time since 1924 to allow tempers to cool.[14]

'Can you stand it?' Clarissa Eden asked Dora Gaitskell. The Labour leader's wife replied, 'What I can't stand is the mounted police charging the crowds outside.'[15]

The Cabinet meetings that day were equally fraught, as Macmillan outlined details of Britain's precarious financial situation, details that have since been shown to be inaccurate. Macmillan told the Cabinet that gold and currency reserves had fallen by £100 million, when the real figure was £31.7 million.[16]*

News of the vote in the United Nations at 2.30 a.m. came through as dawn broke in London on 2 November. Simultaneously, more Russian troops were pouring into Hungary, ensuring that the two crises would together vie for world attention. Two Cabinet meetings were held on Friday 2 November, neither of which found time for consideration of the Hungarian situation, so cocooned were the British in their own affairs. Yet arguably the Hungarian invasion was to be a portent of longer-lasting significance than the cul-de-sac of Suez. (When a similar invasion of Czechoslovakia took place in 1968, it was the occasion of one of Eden's few major interventions, as Earl of Avon, in a debate in the House of Lords.)[17]

At the Cabinet at 4.30 p.m., Selwyn Lloyd stated that 'we could not hope to avoid serious difficulties with the Arab states for more than a very short time longer, certainly not for as long as it would take us to complete an opposed occupation of Egypt.' As momentum gathered in New York behind Lester Pearson's UNEF scheme, Eden outlined, at the second Cabinet at 9.30 p.m., the conditions that would need to be satisfied before a United Nations force became the peace-keeping body between the various combatants, not all of whom were yet on Egyptian soil. 'It was agreed that, until the UN force was constituted, detachments of Anglo-French troops should be stationed on Egyptian territory between the two combatants.'[18]

Meanwhile, William Clark had given information to Archbishop Fisher. Clark was in possession of such information solely because of his position

---

*Treasury records show total sterling assets on 30 September to be £3,706 million. By 31 December they were £3,622 million, a total fall during the whole period of the crisis of £84 million. Diana M. Kunz, historian of the financial aspects of Suez, concludes, 'it seems obvious that Macmillan knew that he was misleading the Cabinet', as there was little chance of his misstatements being discovered. Diana M. Kunz, *The Economic Diplomacy of the Suez Crisis*, University of North Carolina Press, Chapel Hill and London, 1991, pp. 132, 205.

in Downing Street, though his access to inner secrets had been seriously curtailed after Eden had heard, via Peter Fleming, how much Clark loved telling anecdotes and revelling in gossip. Nevertheless, there were some plums known to William Clark that could profitably be distributed in circles hostile to Eden. Fisher, who exhibited increasing signs as the crisis unfolded of wanting to become a latter-day Cardinal Wolsey, learned of the doubts that had haunted Walter Monckton throughout the crisis, doubts that Monckton had discussed with Clark. Fisher was told about Sir William Hayter's warnings from the Russian Embassy, ten days before Israel's attack, and about Russia's intentions towards Hungary. Fisher was also informed of Sir Ivone Kirkpatrick's fears that Britain might be forced to resign from the United Nations.

After his speech in the House of Lords on 1 November, Archbishop Fisher was attacked in many quarters for his anti-Suez stance, most strongly in a lengthy private correspondence with Lord Hailsham, the First Lord of the Admiralty. 'I should have thought it was entirely right that I should bring to the notice of the Government and of the nation,' Fisher replied to Hailsham at one stage, in a series of letters that became increasingly heated on Hailsham's side, 'the undoubted fact that there was among Christian people a deep division and in a great number of them deep uneasiness and unhappiness.'[19]*

Fisher also wrote several times to Eden, who arranged for Lord Kilmuir to see the Archbishop to discuss his concerns. 'I am sorry that I have not been able to answer your letters before,' Eden wrote to Fisher during a brief lull on 10 November, 'but I know that the Lord Chancellor saw you on my behalf.'[20]

The American Presidential Election remained the constant backdrop to the Suez crisis. On 2 November, the Vice-President, Richard Nixon, declared in a campaign speech, 'For the first time in history we have shown independence of Anglo-French policies towards Asia and Africa.'[21] Whether this was a benefit was not made clear at this stage, but Nixon later regretted how things had turned out. 'It [the Suez Crisis] couldn't have come at a worse time,' he admitted to Julian Amery of the Tory 'Suez Group' in 1987:

Eisenhower was running for re-election on a platform of peace and prosperity. Just a few days before, the United States had joined other countries in condemning Khrushchev for his ruthless suppression of the

---

*Hailsham was outraged many years later when he found that copies of his correspondence with Fisher were effectively in the public domain. Researchers were allowed to consult the bound volume 171 in the Fisher papers on the understanding that no mention should be made of this correspondence during Hailsham's lifetime.

Hungarian freedom fighters. We forced the British and French to abandon their efforts to punish Nasser for his expropriation of the Suez Canal. In our public statements we virtually put the British and French in the same category as the Soviets in unjustifiably resorting to force to achieve their foreign policy objectives. Years later, after he had left office, I talked with Eisenhower about Suez. He told me that it was his major foreign policy mistake.'[22]

Another stormy scene unfolded in the Commons on Saturday 3 November, the very day of the sitting (a pre-echo of the 1982 Falklands crisis), indicating the seriousness of the situation. If anything, passions ran even higher than they had when the sitting had been suspended two days earlier. Selwyn Lloyd was shouted down, and chants of 'Murderer' were hurled at Eden from the Labour benches. This was only a foretaste of what was to happen over the next few weeks. One dispassionate observer of the scene, William Haley, later wrote to Violent Bonham Carter:

Above all, I am disturbed by the behaviour of the House as a whole. There is a mean spirit behind the rowdiness on both sides. I know there were rows and uproars in your father's day, but I am sure they were spurred by nobler passions and on altogether another plane. But a spirit of meanness and almost furtiveness is now infecting almost all our political life.[23]

That night Eden spoke to the nation in a broadcast. Gaitskell demanded that the BBC grant him the right of reply, a move Eden vigorously resisted. The flickering black-and-white television pictures of Eden, addressing the nation at a key moment in its history, are one of the indelible memories of Suez. 'Every time I see his prime ministerial broadcast of 3 November,' Professor Peter Hennessy has written, 'I am struck by the sincerity of Eden's exhausted self belief.'[24] The words were arguably the most famous Eden ever uttered before the British people:

All my life I have been a man of peace, working for peace, striving for peace, negotiating for peace. I have been a League of Nations Man and a United Nations Man, and I am still the same man, with the same convictions, the same devotion to peace. I could not be other, even if I wished, but I am utterly convinced that the action we have taken is right.[25]

Sir Alexander Cadogan, Chairman of the Governors of the BBC, reluctantly acceded to Gaitskell's request to put the Opposition view. 'In the event', as one commentator on the the media during Suez has noted, 'Gaitskell's time on the air probably did him more harm than good. His appeal to Tory waverers backfired and implicit condemnation of the British forces only hours away from battle struck many people as treacherous.' Cadogan thought the speech 'disgraceful', adding, 'but I don't mind, we have given him enough rope'.[26] An interesting footnote is that Eden's speech was broadcast to all the troops *en route* to Egypt, while Gaitskell's reply was confined by the officers in charge to the wardrooms.[27]

In the Warwick and Leamington Conservative Association the response to Eden's Suez policy was overwhelmingly favourable, with some 95 per cent of the membership actively supporting the Prime Minister. This was largely owing to Eden's redoubtable reputation in foreign affairs. Among Labour and Liberal supporters in the constituency the situation was more complex. Many of these voters had great misgivings about the policy, but largely kept their reservations to themselves, lest they be thought unpatriotic. However, after Gaitskell's broadcast this minority became more confident and vocal in its criticisms.[28]

When the Seaborne Assault Force had sailed from Malta for the Canal Area at midnight on 30 October in ships of the Amphibious Warfare Squadron, it had been calculated they would take six days to reach Egypt.[29] The imminent arrival of this flotilla coincided with the news – for Eden, very unwelcome news – that Israel, her military objectives achieved, was willing to accept a ceasefire, subject to forthcoming details about any UNEF force, and if this was reciprocated by the Egyptians. The *casus belli* would thus disappear at the very moment that seaborne landings and parachute drops were due.

As the flotilla neared Port Said on 4 November, any subsequent action depended on further political instructions to the Chiefs of Staff, and then from London to the naval commanders, one of the reasons why Sunday 4 November proved such a crucial day in the unfolding drama, with two Cabinet meetings and two Egypt Committees.

Ministers were telephoned at 11.30 a.m. for an emergency Cabinet, with the inner circle subsequently holding the first Egypt Committee meeting at 12.30 p.m., not breaking for lunch until 2 p.m.[30]

In Trafalgar Square, the Labour Party had organised a vast protest rally against Eden's policies on the theme of 'Law not War', Aneurin Bevan flamboyantly playing to the gallery by shouting, to loud cheers, that 'if Sir Anthony is sincere in what he says – and he may be – then he is too *stupid* to be Prime Minister'.[31] Hailed at the time as a scintillating example of Bevan's oratorical wit, the taunt did not reflect his considered thoughts on the emergency. In May 1957, Bevan famously declared of Nasser's action that 'if the sending of one's police and soldiers into the darkness of the night to seize somebody else's property is nationalisation, Ali Baba used the wrong terminology'.[32] But, in the febrile atmosphere of November

1956, abuse fitted the need. The noise of the agitated crowd as they responded to Bevan's speech could be heard filtering down Whitehall during the second Egypt Committee at 3.30 p.m. in the Cabinet Room. Clarissa Eden went up to Trafalgar Square to witness the demonstration incognito. Some people on the fringe of the demonstration, onlookers rather than participants, recognised the Prime Minister's wife and gathered round to express their support. As this group grew in number, it was noticed by some of the main body of the crowd, who began to investigate what was going on. Fearing an outbreak of violence, Clarissa Eden quietly returned to Downing Street, for other people's safety, as much as for her own.[33]

At the second Cabinet at 6.30 p.m., Eden put three courses of action before the eighteen members assembled, and went round the table to seek individual opinions. The options were: to proceed with the initial phase of occupation, while accepting that the long-term solution would involve UNEF, of which Anglo-French detachments must be a part; to suspend the parachute landings for twenty-four hours (the codeword in this case to the French being NOPE),[34] to allow Egypt and Israel to decide whether to accept UNEF; or to defer military action indefinitely.

Clarissa Eden has left a memorable account, told to her in the heat of the crisis by her husband, of the outcome of the crucial Cabinet on 4 November:

> Anthony called a Cabinet. In the middle he adjourned them and kept Bobbety, who had risen from his sick bed for the occasion, Harold and Rab behind and told them if they wouldn't go on he would have to resign. Rab said if he did resign no-one else could form a government. A Cabinet then reassembled and each was asked in turn what they felt about going on. Selwyn, Alec Home, Harold, Alan [Lennox-Boyd], Antony Head, Peter [Thorneycroft], Eccles, Duncan [Sandys], James Stuart, Gwilym [Lloyd George], and Hailsham were for going on. Kilmuir, Heathcoat Amory, Macleod, Bobbety, Patrick Buchan-Hepburn were for doing what ever Anthony wanted and Lord Selkirk [Chancellor of the Duchy of Lancaster] was unintelligible.[35]

Eden's own preference was clear, and the constitutional convention of Cabinet collective responsibility worked in his favour, as none of the Cabinet (not even Monckton or Heathcoat Amory, the most reluctant buccaneer at all) were prepared to take their doubts to the point of resignation. Eden also knew that such a 'vote' would lock Butler into the action, which is why, in his own later summary, he 'wrestled for hours with Cabinet not to halt us from getting ashore when there was first report of ceasefire between parties.'[36]

*

The British parachute drop took place at first light on 5 November, Keightley having told Eden that the momentum of the operation could not be halted after 11 p.m. British time. At midnight on 4/5 November Eden received a letter from the Russian Premier, Bulganin, threatening to 'crush the aggressors and restore peace in the East through the use of force.'[37]

While the military operations achieved their initial objectives on 6 November – Port Said was soon captured and British forces advanced twenty-three miles down the canal to El Cap – the diplomatic situation was more complex. At 8.30 a.m. on 6 November, Eden rang Sir Pierson Dixon at the United Nations. Dixon recorded the conversation in his diary:

> The P.M. asked me how things were going in N.Y. I said that we had just finished an emergency Session of the Security Council called at an hour's notice by the Russians. The Russian proposal amounted to Russian–U.S. action against France and Britain. The proposal had not even been adopted on the agenda, but I thought the Russians must have seen that something like this would happen and that their object must therefore have been to get themselves in a position where they could say they had tried the U.N. and having failed, now had their hands free for some independent action.[38]

Dixon then told Eden of the concerted efforts, involving the Americans, to draft a United Nations Security Council resolution that would impose economic sanctions on the British and the French if they did not agree to an immediate ceasefire. Eden brought Dixon up to date with the initial successes of the military operation, assuring him that the British forces would shortly have control of the canal. 'This early morning conversation establishes one point', wrote Dixon's biographer (and son), 'Eden at this the greatest crisis of his life was not frightened by the Russians.'[39]

Following the telephone call to Dixon, Eden summoned a Cabinet at 9.45 a.m. at his room in the House of Commons. He gave them the grim news from New York, explaining that he was convinced that some such American resolution involving sanctions would be agreed and put to the vote later that day. All Eden's pleas to Eisenhower the evening before had come to naught. In the most humiliating circumstances, there was no alternative but to call off the operation, within twenty-four hours of its launch. A ceasefire was subsequently announced for 5 p.m. British time.* Eden's telegram of 5 November to the American President had begun:

> It is no mere form of words to say that we would be happy to hand over to an international organisation as soon as we possibly can. As you can

---

*As during the financial crisis of 1931, a British Cabinet's ability to decide on its own course of executive action had been denied by the pressure of an outside agency.

imagine no-one feels more strongly about this than Harold who has to provide the money. We do not want occupation of Egypt, we could not afford it, and that is one of the many reasons why we got out of Suez two years ago.

This forlorn attempt at conciliation skated over some uncomfortable truths, but was the first indication of Macmillan's change of tune in the face of changing realities – 'first in, first out', as Harold Wilson scathingly declared. No real consideration had been given to what would happen in Egypt once (or if) the canal had been taken and Nasser toppled. Eden's essential appeal was for Eisenhower's understanding of the dilemmas they had faced. His message drew parallels with the 1930s:

> I know that Foster thought we could have played this longer. But I am convinced that, if we had allowed things to drift, everything would have gone from bad to worse. Nasser would have become a kind of Moslem Mussolini and our friends in Iraq, Jordan, Saudi Arabia and even Iran would gradually have been brought down. His efforts would have spread westwards, and Libya and all North Africa would have been brought under his control.

Aggrieved by what he regarded as United Nations 'selectivity', Eden drew a further parallel:

> I know how strongly you feel, as I do, the objections to the use of force, but this is not a situation which can be mended by words or resolution; it is indeed ironical that at this very moment, when we are being pilloried as aggressors, Russia is brutally re-occupying Hungary and threatening the whole of Eastern Europe, and no voice is raised in the United Nations in favour of intervention there.

Eden's heartfelt message ended:

> I believe as firmly as ever that the future of all of us depends on the closest Anglo-American co-operation. It has of course been a great grief to me to have had to make a temporary breach into it which I cannot disguise, but I know that you are a man of big enough heart and vision to take up things again on the basis of fact. If you cannot approve, I would like you at least to understand the terrible decisions we have had to make. I remember nothing like them since the day when we were comrades together in the war. History alone can judge whether we have made the right decision, but I do want to assure you that we have made it from a genuine sense of responsibility, not only to our country, but to all the world.[40]

As the United Nations moved towards its resolution, Eisenhower was anxiously awaiting news of the Presidential Election. He had no need for concern, as he was re-elected with a popular majority of over 9.5 million votes, his Democratic opponent Adlai Stevenson winning just seven states. But the result was still not known when he spoke to Eden at 12.55 p.m. (British time) on the rather primitive transatlantic telephone link:

> *The President* First of all, I can't tell you how pleased we are that you found it possible to accept the cease-fire, having landed.
> *Eden* We have taken a certain risk, but I think it is justified.
> *The President* Anthony, this is the way I feel about it. I have not ruminated over this particular situation at length. I am talking off the top of my head. You have got what you said you were going to get in that you have landed. It seems to me that from that – with regard to the cease-fire, and without going to any negotiations, I would go ahead with the cease-fire, not putting any conditions into the acceptance of the resolution and after cease-fire talking about the clearance of the Canal and so on.
> *Eden* We are going to cease firing tonight.
> *The President* Could you not tell Hammarskjöld [the UN Secretary-General] that as far as the cease-fire arrangement is concerned, that that goes without condition.
> *Eden* We cease firing tonight at midnight [Egyptian time] provided we are not attacked.
> *The President* I see.
> *Eden* What you may call the long cease-fire, the cessation of hostilities, that is more complicated.[41]

And so it proved. In their deliberations on 7 November the Security Council excluded Britain and France from any participation in the UNEF force. The British and French forces in Port Said (not treated by the United Nations at all separately from each other) were not ordered to go, pending the arrival of UNEF; on the other hand, they were not encouraged to stay. By 8 November it was clear from messages from Sir Harold Caccia, the new British Ambassador in Washington, that 'there is at present no possibility of aid, which in any event would not be available until after further Congressional action and I think we must take it that there is at present no possibility of an Exim Bank loan'.[42]

At this critical moment, the simmering discontent from within certain sections of the British executive machine boiled over. Mountbatten had already written to Eden on 2 November, begging him to call off the military operations, adding, in his customary green ink, 'I feel so desperate about what is happening'. The next day Mountbatten had told Hailsham, the First Lord, of his concerns, and in effect offered his resignation by asking to be told whether 'to stay or go'. Hailsham took the vigorous line that Asquith had taken with Admiral Jackie Fisher during the Great War, and ordered Mountbatten to remain at his post, writing to Eden, 'I think it would be disastrous to relieve him now, which is the only other possible course.'[43]

Anthony Nutting had known in his heart from the moment that Eden had said to Guy Millard at the Challe/Gazier meeting at Chequers on 14 October 'there's no need to take notes' that their ways were going to have to part.[44] He resigned on 31 October, but agreed that the announcement should be delayed until after the military operations. News soon spread within the rumour mill of Westminster, where his critics were saying that Nutting wanted out because of marital difficulties. His resignation was made public on 5 November, when, turning the knife, he quoted Eden's own words from 1938. Nutting also resigned his seat. Possibly he recoiled from being tarred with the Suez brush. But Eden always felt that the man who, Scroop-like, possessed the key to all his counsels, had betrayed him at the worst possible moment. The fallout from the Nutting resignation was extremely ugly. What would later be called the Government's spin-doctors (without Eden's involvement, or even knowledge) began a whispering campaign to suggest that the real reason Nutting had resigned was because of constituency trouble over an unsavoury and imminent divorce, for which he was using Suez as a means of leaving Parliament. William Clark, who also resigned (on 6 November) – having written in his diary on 3 November, 'Eden must go! But me first!' – was unsuccessfully lobbied to take part in these activities.[45]

Meanwhile on 5 November Ivone Kirkpatrick had met senior staff in the Foreign Office to address their concerns, particularly those of Paul Gore-Booth, a future Permanent Under-Secretary.[46] Within a day the ceasefire had been announced and the most incident-packed twenty-four hours of the crisis were over.

Nutting was not the only minister to resign, though his departure, owing to his almost symbiotic relationship with Eden, was potentially the most damaging. Edward Boyle, Economic Secretary to the Treasury, resigned on 8 November, 'the first really of the fairly sensible people to do so', Elizabeth Home wrote in her diary.[47] 'It is interesting that when Nutting and Boyle resigned', Robert Rhodes James, then a Clerk in the House of Commons, wrote to the author, 'there was great admiration for Boyle's resignation, and none whatever for Nutting's.'[48] There were two reasons for this – the censorious attitude of many in the Tory Party towards Nutting's impending divorce, and the fact that he had been kept on at the Foreign Office by Eden in the face of (pre-Suez) back-bench pressure that he should go. As a result his action seemed a poor reward for Eden's loyalty towards him.

Boyle was soon telling Patrick Gordon Walker, the former Labour Commonwealth Secretary, what had happened:

> I met Boyle in New Palace Yard after the debate on Suez about a week ago. He told me that the reasons for the abandonment of the operation were:
> 1 Macmillan's realisation of the run on gold.
> 2 Selwyn Lloyd's realisation that the Baghdad Pact was breaking up. *These two changed sides together.*
> 3 A united Cabinet (with Heathcoat Amory & Monckton) had only been achieved by accepting the operation alone to restore the peace. The Israeli acceptance of the cease-fire – & thus the achievement of the ostensible object of separating the combatants – made it impossible to go on with a united Cabinet.[49]

A confidence motion was held on 8 November. There was much advance speculation as to what effect Gaitskell's appeal to dissident Tories on 4 November would have on the vote. To Labour disappointment, it solidified the support for Eden, even among those Tories who had their doubts. Only eight Conservatives abstained – Robert Boothby, Anthony Nutting, Edward Boyle, J. J. ('Jakie') Astor, Sir Frank Medlicott, Nigel Nicolson, Col. C. Banks and William Yates – but their names were not forgotten.[50] Four days later, Eden wrote a 'retrospective' letter to Guy Mollet in Paris:

> I have no doubt at all that history will prove that we acted rightly. It becomes increasingly evident to me if only from Moscow's anger that we have uncovered preparations which would have exploded in due course at the time selected by the Russians, through Nasser as their instrument. Indeed, the big issue that seems to me to emerge is that if we had not acted, before very long Nasser would have been the ruler of the whole Arab world on Moscow's behalf.[51]

Mollet understood this. Eden's regret was that he could not persuade Nutting, the great Arabist, of what he saw as this self-evident truth. The means, distasteful, as Eden knew, were nevertheless in his opinion justified by the motives.

Eden took Nutting's resignation personally. Here was the man whose career he had made, a second golden boy, 'Eden's Eden' as the cartoonists drew him. Inevitable comparisons were drawn with Eden's own resignation in February 1938, when he had said 'there are occasions when strong political convictions must over-ride all other considerations'.[52] Eden's last words to Nutting (they never spoke again after November 1956) were '*Tout casse sauf l'amitie*'.[53]

For his part, Nutting miscalculated how difficult it would be to get back into mainstream politics. He was only thirty-six when he resigned, and because his Melton Mowbray constituency wanted him to make a statement, he decided to break with them also, rather than divulge intelligence secrets. Also he felt that he would be vindicated by history and that people would come round to his view. Two prominent party officials, the Duke of Rutland and Donald Byford, offered to hire the de Montfort Hall in Leicester for a full-dress apologia and explanation, but Nutting at that stage kept his counsel.

After Eden, Nutting was the great loser of the Suez crisis. He became *persona non grata* with a considerable section of the Conservative Party and when he died in March 1999 some of the national broadsheet newspapers found it difficult to persuade any senior Conservative of his era to write an obituary.[54] But he also had his admirers. When Rab Butler was offered the Mastership of Trinity by Harold Wilson in December 1964, he favoured Nutting as his successor as MP for Saffron Walden, in itself a retrospective indication of his true feelings about Suez. Nutting was interviewed and was poised to secure the nomination, when he failed to assure the association that, if chosen, he would live in the constituency. All he had to do was to say he would take a cottage or flat, but instead, in a rather wooden-headed manner, he said that he had three houses already, and a fourth would be inconvenient. Also his divorce still resonated in Essex circles. Peter Kirk was chosen instead.[55]

With the collapse of the invasion, it became open season for Eden's critics. At the Lord Mayor's Banquet, his speech was received with applause, but the BBC engineers, forewarned that the largely Establishment audience would be sympathetic, cut the link as soon as he had completed the advance text, so that it appeared to the radio audience that his message had been received in stony silence. Eden's appearance at the Cenotaph for the Remembrance Day Service, a cold day of flurried wind, was the occasion for comments on the 'fear in his eyes'. He was rumoured, incorrectly, to be dependent on Benzedrine.[56]

Eden was indeed ill, and also exhausted. He had recorded in his diary as early as 21 August that the doctors had been wanting him to take a break on health grounds.[57] On 19 November it was announced that the Prime Minister was cancelling all his engagements. Rab Butler took charge of the Government from 23 November until 14 December. In retrospect, this was the moment when Eden, who was to resign on medical grounds only fifty-one days later, could have accepted the inevitable and brought down the curtain on his political career. Had he done so, there would have been a fair measure of sympathetic understanding, and he would have been spared much further anguish and controversy. He did not do so for two reasons. Firstly, he genuinely believed that convalescence in the warmth of Jamaica would prove a turning point. Secondly, he felt the responsibility of unravelling the situation to be his, and believed he would have a better chance of achieving this than a new Prime Minister, either Butler or Macmillan. Any premature departure would also inevitably be interpreted as an admission of failure. So Eden determined to soldier on.

Eden's decision to convalesce at Goldeneye, the remote holiday home of Ian Fleming at Oracabessa, led to a storm of criticism. Not surprisingly, Randolph Churchill was soon in the fray, drawing an offensive parallel between Suez and the Battle of Stalingrad and saying that not even Hitler had wintered in Jamaica. The *Daily Mirror* ran a competition on how best to solve the Suez crisis, with the first prize being a three-week holiday for two in Jamaica.[58] Even Ann Fleming, a close friend of Clarissa Eden, through whose good offices Goldeneye had been made available, had her misgivings. 'The plumbing is not good at the moment, after plugs are pulled noises of hunting horns are heard for at least twenty minutes,' she wrote. 'I think Torquay and a sun-ray lamp would have been more peaceful and patriotic.'[59] Also in Torquay they would not have had to share the premises with an Alsatian watchdog which was called Max, like Beaverbrook. Ann Fleming told the Press that 'the Edens will have to rough it', which was not an attempt to soften the image of Eden enjoying a hedonistic Caribbean holiday while those left behind faced a British winter of petrol rationing, but the literal truth.[60]

The Edens were greeted at Kingston airport by a calypso band singing 'Jamaica the Garden of Eden welcomes Britain's Sir Anthony Eden.'[61] Two detectives stayed in the house, and the gardens were patrolled by policemen and local gardeners drafted in to keep strangers at bay. Privacy and rest were essential, so not even Noël Coward, bearing gifts of caviar and Earl Grey tea, was allowed to visit.[62] After a few days, Clarissa Eden wrote to Ann Fleming, 'We haven't been outside the gates so far.'[63]

When the Flemings took possession of the house again in January 1957 they found that many of the trees in the garden had been engraved by the temporary security men with the words 'God bless Sir Anthony'.[64] The Edens had left behind a crop of detective novels which was appreciated by subsequent visitors to Goldeneye.[65] They also left behind something less tangible, though more permanent: Goldeneye became a permanent footnote to one of the saddest episodes in twentieth-century history.

More damaging to Eden's position than the criticisms of Randolph Churchill and the *Daily Mirror* was the manner in which his absence opened a window of opportunity for his would-be successors. The Tory Party was soon awash with speculation. Fortune did not favour Rab

Butler, the nominal favourite. In this decisive period, he was too engrossed in his responsibilities as acting Head of Government, one of the thirteen occasions on which he was to undertake this task,[66] to look to his personal position. Harold Macmillan, on the other hand, now had free rein to make his dispositions. He did not miss the opportunities presented. 'Macmillan quickly exploited Eden's absence from the Cabinet,' wrote W. Scott Lucas in one of the most scholarly recent accounts of the whole crisis, adding, 'Eden was oblivious to Macmillan's intrigues.'[67]

This latter point is not entirely true. Eden had good intelligence before he flew from Heathrow on 23 November of Macmillan's first private meetings with Winthrop Aldrich, the American Ambassador, at his Regent's Park residence, through Bobbety Salisbury, who had been visited at Hatfield House by Aldrich. What Eden did not know was the extent of the activities of some of the other players in the unfolding drama, notably Butler, the Archbishop of Canterbury and his former Press Secretary, William Clark.

Although Goldeneye was remote and the couriers slow, Eden was kept in touch to a remarkable extent with what was unfolding in London during his absence, both on an official and unofficial basis. Robert Allan kept him abreast of parliamentary developments. Inevitably, there was much talk of Eden's impending resignation, which made him even more determined to ride out the storm. Yet if he returned prematurely to Westminster, it would be interpreted as a panic measure to bolster his position; if he stayed in Jamaica, the belief that he had abandoned ship at a crucial moment would gain currency. Either way, he could not win. The *Spectator* commented, 'Unquestionably Jamaica has done more damage than Suez to Sir Anthony's standing in his party at Westminster.'[68]

The question of Eden's succession was already a live issue, even before he departed to Goldeneye. The Press was full of speculation, and Butler was considered the favourite, though he lifted no finger to aid his cause. Macmillan, on the other hand, continued to tell Winthrop Aldrich that he was 'Eden's deputy', despite the fact that Butler was acting Prime Minister. Shrewdly, Macmillan realised that Eden's successor was going to have to be acceptable to Washington.[69]*

Eden's status with the Americans had been reduced during the Suez crisis. On the morning of 7 November, shortly after his re-election as President, Eisenhower had had a meeting with Foster Dulles, now in the Walter Reed Hospital where the cancer that was to kill him was diagnosed. One of the items on the agenda was the wish of Eden and Mollet to come to

---

*A factor that was eventually to disqualify Lord Hailsham, one of the candidates to succeed Macmillan himself, in October 1963.

Washington for a summit on Suez. The minutes of the Eisenhower's talk with Dulles reveal his scepticism about Eden's motives:

> The President indicated that one of the reasons Eden wanted to come to Washington was that he needs to associate himself with some spectacular act at this time. The President referred to a British opinion poll which Mr. Hoover [Under-Secretary of State] had mentioned to him. This showed British public opinion running strongly against the actions of the British Government in the Middle East.[70]*

The implications of this meeting were clear. As far as Eisenhower was concerned, Eden was in the last phase of his Premiership. New dispositions would be needed.

Macmillan was Eisenhower's preferred successor in Number 10. Their working relationship in North Africa during the war had been of profound importance, and Eisenhower admired what he saw as Macmillan's decisive political touch. Butler was more of an unknown quantity to him – and not a character one could easily imagine drinking bourbons with Ike into the small hours after a leisurely game of golf.

Macmillan now played this wartime link for all it was worth. His main aim was that an Anglo-American meeting, with or without the French, should in fact take place, preferably while Eden was still in Jamaica, and with himself representing Britain. As Chancellor of the Exchequer, he was now a pivotal figure because of the need for American support over sterling. Whether Britain got that support or not, either way made Macmillan's gain, even if his stance had to change, as it did, with events. George Humphrey, US Treasury Secretary, had bluntly told Macmillan (from a telephone in the security of his meat safe in Georgia), 'You'll not get a dime from the US Government until you've gotten out of Suez.'[71]

An even more bizarre exchange took place on 18 November when Selwyn Lloyd, in America in an attempt to mend fences, visited Dulles at the Walter Reed Hospital. 'Selwyn, why did you stop?' said Dulles. 'Why didn't you go through with it and get Nasser down?' Since Lloyd had always regarded the Challe/Gazier initiative as 'The Plan for which I did not care', this was almost too much for him to bear. 'If you had so much as winked at us we might have gone on,' said Lloyd, who always believed that Dulles's hospitalisation at such a crucial moment was an under-estimated contribution to the final outcome.[72]

---

*The opinion polls were in fact very volatile. On 2 November 1956 (before the Anglo-French invasion) the *News Chronicle* showed that 40 per cent agreed with Eden's actions, 46 per cent disagreed and 14 per cent were undecided. By 14 November the figures were 53 per cent in favour, 32 per cent against and 15 per cent undecided. On 11 November, the *Observer* reported that 866 correspondents were against its anti-Suez editorial of 4 November, and 302 in favour.

Macmillan spent ninety minutes with Aldrich at the US Embassy on 19 November, his third meeting with Aldrich in as many days.[73] 'It is interesting to note that in his talk with me last Friday [November 16],' recorded Aldrich, 'Macmillan said to me that perhaps he, Macmillan, could go to Washington as "Eden's deputy" as Eden himself "might not be well enough to come".' Aldrich's conclusion was clear. 'I cannot help wondering whether this might not be a hint that some sort of movement is on foot in the Cabinet to replace Eden.' During Macmillan's private visit to the Ambassador's residence on 18 November, he seemed, according to Aldrich, 'only too willing to outline Eden's planned vacation to recoup his health.' At this meeting, Macmillan began to barter with Aldrich about the effect that United States aid over sterling and oil supplies would have on Tory Party opinion. He promised Aldrich 'a sufficient number of Conservative backbenchers to insure a majority for the government in favour of withdrawal from Egypt.'[74] Aldrich later telephoned Herbert Hoover to say that if such assurances were forthcoming 'the Cabinet is to be completely reshuffled'.[75]

After their third meeting on 19 November, Aldrich sent the following telegram to the State Department:

> Macmillan is desperately anxious to see the President at earliest possible opportunity & apparently consideration being given to appointment of Macmillan as Deputy Prime Minister during Eden's absence in order that such meeting might take place at once after withdrawal British troops!

Such a scenario was a complete fabrication by Macmillan. At midnight on 18 November, only a few hours earlier, a communiqué had been issued to the Press about Eden's condition, and the Lobby had been told that Butler would be in charge during Eden's absence.

Reflecting the barrage of pressure to which he was being subjected, Aldrich reiterated that Macmillan was 'terribly anxious to see the President', and, reflecting Macmillan's assurances to him, told Washington that if he became Prime Minister, America would find him more amenable to their views than the present incumbent of Number 10.[76] 'Macmillan,' Aldrich later despatched, 'faced with London's precarious economic situation, asked "if you can give us a fig leaf to cover our nakedness", he would arrange the withdrawal of British troops from Egypt and the replacement of Eden.'[77] Aldrich then telegrammed the White House, convinced that Eden was on his way out, a move that belied his reputation as a 'social' ambassador, chosen as a reward for his donations to Republican Party funds. Hearing this, Eisenhower encouraged Aldrich to have further meetings with Macmillan. 'To some observers,' one American academic has concluded, 'it appeared that Eisenhower, and certainly Macmillan, were attempting to ease Eden from power.'[78]

The threat of American sanctions, first discussed at the second Cabinet meeting on 4 November, was to be one of the few successful examples of such action, largely because they were imposed by one democracy upon another. Sanctions against dictatorships come in a different category altogether, as the regime can always hide the extent of the difficulties and place the blame elsewhere, a factor that Mussolini had exploited skilfully during the Abyssinian crisis. In November 1956 there was no such hiding place for Britain, a fact that Macmillan turned to his advantage, even at the moment he was saying, 'Oil sanctions! That finishes it!'[79]

Further meetings between Aldrich, Macmillan and Butler took place at the American Embassy in the days ahead, none with Eden's knowledge. On 21 November, Aldrich met Macmillan and Butler at noon, an indication that Eisenhower wanted his Ambassador to be even-handed between the potential successors, and that Aldrich was not taking at face value Macmillan's repeated claim to be Eden's acknowledged deputy.[80] However, the next day Macmillan visited alone again, after which Aldrich telegrammed the State Department, 'Macmillan indicated British Cabinet changes which he has previously forecast will take place within the next few days.'[81]

Two days later, President Eisenhower met three senior advisers (George Humphrey, Herbert Hoover and Brigadier-General Andrew J. Goodpester, the President's Defense Liaison Officer) to consider who might emerge to replace Eden. The Treasury Secretary, George Humphrey, favoured Butler, but Eisenhower stressed the advantages of Macmillan, whom he described as 'a straight, fine man, and, so far as he is concerned, the outstanding one of the British he served with during the war.'[82]

When Eden was 'safely' in Jamaica, Macmillan became even more active in his pursuit of the American link, as well as having further meetings with Churchill at Chartwell. 'Macmillan is telling journalists that he intends to retire from politics and go to the morgue [the House of Lords]', Brendan Bracken wrote to Beaverbrook on 7 December. 'He declares that he will never serve under Butler. His real intentions are to push his boss out of No 10 and he has a fair following in the Tory Party.'[83]

When Butler and Macmillan addressed the Conservative Party's back-bench 1922 Committee, a fractious body at the best of times, on the evening of 22 November, it was Macmillan who made the greatest impact with his famous simile of Britain and America as the Greeks and the Romans, the one with the ideas and the other with the power. After this Macmillan was the favoured choice of the majority of Tory back-benchers, as well as of the President of the United States. It was to prove an unbeatable combination, though the extent of Eisenhower's involvement in the succession is still a matter of dispute. 'A major controversy, which emerged during the period,' one American academic has written, 'is whether the Eisenhower administration, in alliance with Harold Macmillan, arranged the removal of Anthony Eden from office. Although the documentation is not clear-cut, there is sufficient evidence to suggest that Washington was heavily involved behind the scenes.'[84] Macavity, the mystery cat, of course never leaves paw marks.

Few Westminster observers doubted that Eden's days were numbered. On 5 December, Harold Nicolson, who kept his ear close to the ground, wrote in his diary, 'The elder statesmen are convinced that Anthony will have to go.'[85] Two days later, James Stuart, Secretary of State for Scotland, wrote to Rab Butler, fixing up a meeting to discuss Eden's future.[86] It was not the only such meeting Butler attended in December.

On 13 December, the night before Eden returned from Jamaica to England, Archbishop Fisher was invited by Butler to his home at 3 Smith Square at 7 p.m. The Archbishop, as we have seen, was already extremely well informed on what was going on from his talks with William Clark, who had urged him on 13 November to tell Sir William Haley about collusion, in the hope that this would alter *The Times*' stance on Suez. The Fisher and Haley papers confirm how these two key establishment figures – the Archbishop of Canterbury and the editor of *The Times* – had inside contacts at this time. In fact, Butler felt that Fisher knew more than he did.

Theirs was a remarkable conversation that evening in Smith Square, the culmination of many private talks Rab Butler had had with Fisher during the crisis, in all of which he had communicated his doubts. 'He [Rab] took my account in silence and more than once said, "I did not know everything, the matter was kept very tight." If the PM's second in command can say that, things were indeed in jeopardy.' Butler then said to Fisher, 'You seem to have very good information.' Without mentioning Clark as his source, Fisher assured him that he had. Fisher's main feeling was for Butler, whom he saw as being 'in an impossible position – to speak up is to break his party or else to seem to be grasping for the Premiership. He deeply feels the falsity, I am sure.'

Fisher felt the falsity too. For him, the moral implications of collusion overrode all other considerations and justified his actions. The same was true of Clark, though in the overall scheme of things he was inevitably a less important player.[87]*

As regards collusion, Fisher told Rab Butler that 'it was right that the

---

*Butler's assertion of his ignorance of key points is at odds with Eden's 1968 memorandum on how he had been informed and involved throughout. See Chapter 20.

Government should know that I knew.' For his part, Butler 'never attempted to deny some kind of connivance ... he said that the PM had openly said that he kept USA in the dark but that it was unavoidable.' Fisher summed it up: 'It was a confession.' His feeling was that the despondent Butler was not the personality to unify the dispirited Tory back-benchers.

On one level what the head of the Church thought of the crisis had no real impact on its development; on another, it revealed understandable popular concerns, especially over collusion, on which Fisher was particularly exercised. How exactly Eden had been expected to proceed without undertaking confidential negotiations is not clear, yet 'collusion' – once described by Sir Brian Barder, a former Ambassador to Warsaw, as 'the intentional creation of a situation in which we would claim the right to intervene to stop what we had conspired to start'[88] – has become one of the main charges against Eden.

The concept and execution of the Suez military operation has been attacked by many, but the secrecy that attended it was inevitable and a lesser issue – and one that would not have troubled Eisenhower had the boot been on the other foot. Those who regretted that the clandestine meeting at Sèvres took place at all overlook the fact that military action necessitates secret planning, much of it unpalatable. Wartime analogies, however, can be pushed too far. Although Nasser could no more be given the opportunity to anticipate the nature of the action against him than the Germans could have been allowed foreknowledge of where the D-Day landings were going to take place, the parallel is not exact. In 1944 Britain had been at war with Germany for several years, whereas the British were not at *war* with Egypt in October 1956, and never were. Sèvres was an episode into which Eden was drawn, in the hope of resolving the impasse, by two nations seeking to implement and consolidate their plans through British involvement. Inevitably, this brought contradictions. Since January 1956 the Chiefs of Staff had had a contingency plan – codenamed CORDAGE – for neutralising the Israeli Air Force, yet now the Israelis were to be covert allies.

Nevertheless, in one sense Eden was more colluded against, than colluding. His belief that details could remain secret in perpetuity was unrealistic. This was the error of judgement, not the negotiations themselves.

Before Eden returned from Jamaica, the inquest had already begun on 'the lessons of Suez'. In the last week of his Premiership, Churchill had emphasised to his old friend and confidante Violet Bonham Carter, 'We must *never* get out of step with the Americans – *never*.' In August, Churchill was saying to Moran, 'It serves Anthony right. He has inherited what he left me in for.'[89]

The first lesson many drew was that Britain could no longer 'go it alone'. This view was best articulated by General Sir Charles Keightley:

> The one overriding lesson of the Suez operations is that world opinion is now an absolute principle of war and must be treated as such. However successful the pure military operations may be they will fail in their object unless national, Commonwealth & Western world opinion is sufficiently on our side.[90]

Professor D. C. Watt drew a different lesson. 'The result, besides the personal disaster which overtook Lord Avon's career, was largely to discredit the conduct of foreign policy by the light of historical analogy in Britain.'[91]

Yet parallels have arisen since. In 1999, NATO forces attacked Yugoslav targets during the Kosovo crisis, without UN authority, thus interfering with the internal matters of another state. Why did this episode not attract the obloquy accorded to Suez? Supporters of the NATO action in 1999 would of course point to the humanitarian aspect; the action was launched because of the treatment of Albanians in Kosovo. Contemporary judgement thus tended to applaud American intervention as a 'white knight' mission. But this was not the real difference with Suez. In 1956, the United States was against the use of force and used every means to discredit and undermine the operation; in 1999, it was the initiator and used public relations on a global scale to build up the moral authority of its actions.

Suez divided domestic opinion as no issue since Munich. Eden was shielded to some extent from animosity, as the mail that poured into Downing Street was overwhelmingly favourable. To his surprise, as he found when he was in America in May 1957 for further surgery, a different constituency there was also largely in his favour. 'Opinion in this country is far more understanding of the Suez problem than I could have believed possible,' he wrote to Robert Allan. 'Most heartening of all is the support of liberal and academic opinion here. Quite different from at home. This is in part due to the antipathy of most of them to the present administration, but it is not only Democrats who think this way.'[92]

France was furious about the swiftness of the British ceasefire and this had another consequence. After 1956 the French turned increasingly to Germany as a future partner. Indeed, Chancellor Adenauer said to Mollet at the time, 'Europe will be your revenge.'[93] With de Gaulle's return to power in 1958, French disenchantment was eventually to prove a deadly cocktail, culminating in the rejection of Britain's application under the Macmillan Government in 1961 to join the Common

Market.* For the Europhiles in British politics, the sins of Messina and Suez were all of a pattern, and Eden bore a heavy blame for both.

Eden was always defensive about the issue of Europe, writing to Lord Beaverbrook in 1964 after the publication of Lord Kilmuir's memoirs:

> I confess that I was rather surprised to find myself cast as an anti-European ogre defying a combination of Winston, Harold [Macmillan] and Kilmuir. I am not sure that you would recognise me in that role either. All the same, I think that what I did to bring Germany into NATO, and her re-armament under its auspices was a marked improvement on the European Army conception of those days, over which I can shed no tears.'[94]

Suez brought out the worst in nearly all who were involved in it, either as participants or commentators. Eden's reputation has suffered from the fact that among those who were opponents of Suez were articulate members of what might be called the Brains Trust constituency – the Professor Joads and Violet Bonham Carters – while many of his vociferous supporters were precursors of what was later termed 'Essex man'.†

For such patriotic working-class voters, free of all guilt about their xenophobic feelings, Eden had given 'Johnny Foreigner' just the kind of rebuff he had long deserved. It was time Britain stood up for her own interests and ceased being kicked around, an attitude shared by many who had served in the 8th Army and had never liked Egyptians. Jingoistic racism, which Eden deplored, was a decided element in the support he received from this quarter. In the longer historical perspective such attitudes were unconvincing and offensive, and they were never ones with which Eden empathised.

However, Eden's support was not confined to working-class voters. Nigel Nicolson and William Yates were soon in difficulty in their middle-class constituencies in Bournemouth and the Wrekin, and Conservative voters in Norfolk were forthright in their criticism of wavering MPs. Divisions transcended not only party political boundaries, but also demographic ones, and even family members adopted contrasting positions. As the dust settled on the crisis, the supporters tended to draw a line, but the criticisms of the intelligentsia persisted, often in published form.

*

---

*De Gaulle had always remained personally close to Eden. Each time Eden paid his annual visit to Paris to buy pictures and books, de Gaulle had a private talk with him and, not fully realising the medical imperatives, repeatedly urged a return to politics.

†A generic term coined to describe the aspiring working-class voter ('fully prejudiced against all other nations') who helped Mrs Thatcher to three General Election victories. Essex was described by Julian Critchley as a county 'so right-wing that even the newsagents are white'. 'Mrs Thatcher's bruiser', *Sunday Telegraph*, 7 October 1990.

'Returned to find everyone looking at us with thoughtful eyes', wrote Clarissa Eden in her diary on 14 December.[95] It was a desperate time for Eden. Many inaccurate statements were made, then and later, about his medicines and the 'uppers' and 'downers' he supposedly swallowed. 'During the Suez crisis he was continually taking benzedrine,' Cynthia Gladwyn wrote in her diary, 'and by the time it became necessary for him to depart for Goldeneye, he was in such a bad way that he didn't make sense.'[96] This is untrue, as is made clear in Eden's medical records at Birmingham University, not yet generally available for research. Eden's two doctors, Horace Evans and Ralph Southwood, provided Sparine sleeping tablets for Jamaica, but Eden made no use of them. Sir Ralph Southwood's son, Dr Nigel Southwood, confirmed to Lady Avon in 1996 that his father did not care to prescribe stimulants at all for his patients. In the last fortnight of Eden's Premiership, by which time the policy initiatives had in effect passed to Macmillan and Butler, he occasionally took small quantities of benzedrine, but never before he went to Jamaica.[97]

The extent of Britain's economic dependence on America was made clear to Eden by Macmillan at their first meeting. Awaiting Eden was a letter from Butler, which was in essence a directive on how to conduct the next phase. 'People throughout the country are looking forward rather than back', Butler wrote. 'In particular there is a growing wish to end the breach with the United States. It is important that your first pronouncement should be in tune with this.'[98] In Eden's absence, events had been determined by others, and the caravan was inevitably moving on. Salisbury ('et tu, Bobbety?') and Butler even told Eden privately that if his health was not fully restored by Easter then changes would be necessary at the head of Government.[99]

Eden faced the House of Commons on 17 December. Contrary to some reports, he did not face a hostile reaction. 'The press today all report that he had a chilly reception but I must admit,' wrote Richard Crossman in his diary, 'that the reception had been just about right, with the Opposition silent and the Tories careful not to be too enthusiastic, for fear of producing an Opposition demonstration.'[100] Tenseness was all. Further appearances in the Commons were muted affairs.

Then, on 20 December, Eden denied collusion, stating in reply to Gaitskell's questioning:

> I want to say this on the question of foreknowledge, and to say it quite bluntly to the House, that there was not foreknowledge that Israel would attack Egypt – there was not. But there was something else. There was – we knew it perfectly well – a risk of it, and, in the event of the risk of it, certain discussions and conversations took place as, I think, was absolutely right, and as, I think, anybody would do.[101]

This was a nadir for Eden, and a desperate end to the series of speeches he had made in the Chamber since his first, on air policy, on 9 February 1924.

Even more damaging to his own reputation had been the impression he had left on influential members of the back-bench 1922 Committee on 18 December, when he said that, faced with the same problems again, he would deal with them in exactly the same way. 'As long as I live, I shall never apologise for what we did,' he said. 'One of the main charges against us is that we have constantly changed our ground. Of course we have; as events unfolded, new statements had to be made.'[102]*

The final days of Eden's Premiership were soon at hand. He was visited at Chequers over Christmas by six senior ministers, including Butler, Salisbury and Kilmuir, who later recorded in his memoirs, 'I came away with the feeling that he was consumed with grave apprehensions about his personal position.'[103]†

Douglas Dodds-Parker was dismayed at the sense of *Schadenfreude* and the conspiracy theories, current in the rumour-mill of Westminster. 'There is a school of thought,' he recorded, 'that, whereas "Suez" as a method of removing Nasser was always a non-starter, as a way of removing Eden it was brilliant: the threat of resignation in certain quarters (Harold Macmillan) if the attack was NOT soon launched, followed by the same quarters' refusal to see the operation through.'[104]

On 3 January 1957, after presiding at his penultimate Cabinet, Eden had a private meeting with Macmillan about reserve fuel stocks, authorising access, if necessary, to Admiralty reserves at Trincomalee.[105]

Macmillan's subseqent memorandum to Eden the next day began, 'The Suez operation has been a tactical defeat. It is our task to ensure that, like the retreats from Mons and Dunkirk, it should prove the prelude to a strategic victory.' A more wounding parallel for Eden would have been hard to find, and he disputed Macmillan's premiss. His last executive action as Prime Minister for Cabinet on 7 January was to present a paper which began defiantly, 'I do not think that the events of Suez can be reckoned as a tactical defeat. It is much too early to pronounce on an operation of this kind.'[106] In his diary, he wrote, 'Diplomacy is a continuing process. The consequences travel on. You cannot just close a

*Even at this low point, courtesy motivated Eden's actions. When one of his critics, the MP for Bournemouth South East, Nigel Nicolson, was making adverse points and receiving a hostile reception for his pains, Eden intervened to allow him to be heard.
†Kilmuir's memoirs ruffled many feathers when they appeared, the cynics saying that even the title (*Political Adventure*) was inaccurate as the author had omitted the letter 'r' from the end of the second word. (Private information.) At one stage Eden sought counsel's opinion.

chapter if you want to and leave it at that saying this has failed, let's forget it. It may not have failed: no one can tell that at once.'[107]

But a chapter was closing all the same. At 9.45 a.m. on 5 January, after receiving medical advice that allowed no other choice, Eden told Bobbety Salisbury, who had just returned from three days' shooting at Sandringham, that he was resigning as Prime Minister. 'He was obviously sad but quite calm,' recorded Salisbury in a note of the events. 'Better to make the change now. That was the advice he had already been given by Norman Brook.' It was nearly nineteen years since they had both resigned from the Chamberlain Government. Then, as now, Salisbury was Eden's closest confidant.

The Edens went to Sandringham on 8 January, staying overnight. Eden told the Queen of the inevitable, and suggested to Sir Michael Adeane, the Queen's private secretary, that the Cabinet should be canvassed for their views and that Salisbury was the right person to undertake this task. The next morning, Eden returned to London. 'I am too sad for words,' he wrote in a note for Salisbury. 'Your friendship and your help will always be the outstanding memory of my political life.'[108]

Salisbury was waiting for the Edens when they returned to Downing Street. 'We spent upwards of an hour drafting the communiqué, a very melancholy proceeding,' recorded Salisbury, who spoke with Clarissa Eden before leaving Downing Street. 'She looked very white, but did not dissent from the decision, for which indeed I believe she had been pressing.'

Salisbury was to be a key figure in the drama surrounding the succession:

> On Wednesday, after lunch, I got back to my Office to find Michael Adeane, who had come on the chance of catching me, waiting. He told me that the Queen would probably want to ask me for my advice about the leadership. He also asked whether I thought that she should seek advice from Sir WSC, who had let her know that he would be available for this purpose. I replied that I thought she most certainly should. The British people would expect that he should be consulted.

Of the subsequent Cabinet, when Eden announced his decision to a thoughtful and silent gathering, Salisbury noted, 'It was a very short and painful meeting. There was no agenda. A., very bravely and without emotion, informed his colleagues of the Dr's report and of his decision to resign, as he felt that he was no longer in a fit state of health to carry out his duties.'

After the Cabinet, Salisbury conducted his famous count of Cabinet preferences in the presence of Kilmuir, the Lord Chancellor. 'I had already arranged with N[orman].B[rook]. that all the members, with the exception of the 2 aspirants to the PMship, H[arold] & Rab, should come to my room in the Privy Council Office to discuss plans.'

Almost all of those summoned by Bobbety to be asked whether it should be 'Wab or Hawold?' said that it was like a visit to the headmaster's study. In fact, so noisily did the Cabinet ministers chat in Salisbury's anteroom, while waiting, that they had to be restrained. Salisbury recorded, 'All of them voted for Harold with the exception of P[atrick] B[uchan]-H[epburn], who was for Rab & S[elwyn] L[loyd], who, to our gt astonishment, refused to come down 1 way or the other. The L[ord]. Chan[cellor] was greatly shocked by this, which was indeed very surprising in a senior member of the Cabinet.'

Salisbury then saw Edward Heath, the Chief Whip, and Oliver Poole. Heath told him that 'the Suez Group would refuse to follow Rab, who they regarded as having been weak-kneed throughout, while the Left Wing of the Party, though they would have preferred Rab would accept Harold.' In the second interview, Poole told Salisbury that Tories saw Rab as the scapegoat. Although this was manifestly unfair, Poole added, 'he would therefore, at the moment, be a very unpopular choice with the rank and file of the Party in the country.' Salisbury summed up all his findings by noting, 'I now had all the necessary info. to enable me to give advice to the Queen, and I went home to dinner.'

Next morning, at 11.15, before going to the Palace, Salisbury had a word with Alec Home, the Deputy Leader of the House of Lords, 'who fully confirmed the views which I had formed from my other conversations'. Salisbury was part of an ongoing process whereby advice was sought, directly and indirectly, from four separate quarters. The outgoing Prime Minister gave the Queen his views, the Cabinet were formally consulted, backbenchers were systematically canvassed, and the party's grandees, headed by Salisbury and Churchill, went to the Palace, to give the Queen their opinions, and, in Salisbury's case, the results of the formal consultations. On both counts Salisbury recommended Macmillan unequivocally. Michael Adeane later told Salisbury that Churchill had also recommended Macmillan.[109]

On the morning of 9 January Eden had written a dispirited letter to Churchill, giving him advance notice of his resignation, which would be announced at 6.30 p.m.:

> I have heavy news about health. The benefit of Jamaica is not significant. More troubling is that over Christmas & the New Year I have had a return of internal pain, which, apart from its fatiguing effect, worries the doctors in relation to my past operation.
>
> In short they say firmly (and I have refused to accept one opinion & this is the outcome of 3 apart from my own doctor) that I am endangering my life and shortening it by going on. This in itself, as you

will know, would not influence me. What is troublesome is that the immediate result is a gradually increasing fatigue: in short I shall be less & less able physically to do my job as weeks go by.

This seems to me an impossible position, the more so since they give me little hope that I can continue as I am doing without collapse until Easter, & virtually no hope, if I attempt to go on, until the end of summer.

Bobbety & Norman Brook both agree that it will be of no use for me to drag on for such a short period of time.

I am very sad but I did not want you to know by any hand but mine.*[110]

Back-bench Conservative M.Ps. and peers were not slow to make their preferences known. Cyril Osborne and Dudley Williams collected names showing support for Macmillan. Maurice Macmillan was very active on behalf of his father. Sir Robert Boothby was rung up in Strasbourg. Lord Scarborough went personally to the Palace.[111]

Had Eden gone on, Macmillan would have been disqualified by age. Macmillan's only chance of the top job therefore (and he had seen this before 6 April 1955) was if Eden went relatively quickly. Eden's health and the Suez operation provided Macmillan with his opportunity.†

The question of Eden's influence over the succession has been a matter of some dispute. Kilmuir and Macmillan both gave the impression in their memoirs that Eden 'had neither been asked for his advice nor had volunteered it'.[112] The reality is more complex. 'It is untrue, though often alleged, that the Queen did not consult him about his successor,' wrote Robert Blake in his notice of Eden's life in the *Dictionary of National Biography*. 'He never revealed his choice, nor was it necessarily decisive, but there is good evidence that he did not recommend Butler.'[113]

Taking the question of the consultation first, there is ample evidence in Eden's papers to show that the Queen discussed the succession with him.‡ The discussion took place in two stages, informally at Sandringham on 8 January, then in a more structured manner at his resignation audience at Buckingham Palace the next day. As Eden recorded in a memorandum:

Her Majesty received me in Audience on the evening of January 9 when I told her that the doctors' report which The Queen had seen left me in

---

*The letter is on Sandringham writing paper; Eden had stayed there overnight on 8/9 January.
†It was the Attlee/Morrison situation in reverse. Attlee went on as Labour leader and it stopped Morrison; Eden did not go on and it stopped Butler.
‡In a letter to Lord Lambton on 12 June 1967, Eden confirmed that 'normal constitutional procedures were followed' and that he 'was *the first* [author's italics] to be asked to give his advice'. Earl of Avon to Lord Lambton, 12 June 1967. AP 23/43/90A.

my judgment no choice but to ask to be relieved of the duties of Her First Minister. I did this with the greatest possible regret. Her Majesty was good enough to signify that she shared this regret and understood how painful the decision must have been. She also expressed the wish that I would accept an Earldom, not necessarily now if I did not wish to, but perhaps a little later.

Her Majesty spoke of the future and of the difficult choice that lay before her. I agreed that it was certainly difficult. The Queen made no formal request for my advice but enabled me to signify that my own debt to Mr Butler while I have been Prime Minister was very real and that I thought he had discharged his difficult task during the three weeks while I was away in Jamaica very well. Before I left I thanked Her Majesty for her kindness and for the gracious words she used towards me.[114]

Twenty-three years later, however, on 27 November 1970, Lord Avon (as he then was) wrote to Sir Michael Adeane so that a record could be placed in the Royal Archives of what he had told Sir John Wheeler-Bennett (at that time his official biographer) about the resignation audience in 1957:

> I notice that Mr Macmillan's memoirs recently serialised [*Riding the Storm*] repeat the statement first made in Lord Kilmuir's memoirs, that the Queen did not ask my advice about my successor. Mr Macmillan adds that neither did I volunteer such advice. These statements are incorrect. Her Majesty followed the constitutional procedure and asked me my advice as to her choice of my successor. As I consider that all communications between the Sovereign and her Prime Minister are confidential, I do not propose to state here what that advice was, except to say that the course subsequently followed was consistent with that advice.[115]

At first sight, this seems a letter of considerable opaqueness, which contradicts the first memorandum. If the 'course subsequently followed was consistent with that advice', then surely Eden had recommended not Butler, but Macmillan?

As Vernon Bogdanor has written of this second memorandum, 'the word "advice" is perhaps inappropriate here.'[116]* Knowing that Macmillan was almost certain to receive the Queen's commission, perhaps

---

*The closest parallel is with the events of May 1923, when Bonar Law declined to give formal 'advice' to King George V (though this did not prevent others from representing to the King's private secretary, Lord Stamfordham, what that advice might have been), believing – and perhaps fearing – that Curzon was already the inevitable choice. Similarly, in January 1957, Eden knew which way the wind was blowing, and that whatever he said was not going to alter the outcome.

Eden took the opportunity, not to 'recommend' Rab Butler as such, but to praise him to the Queen. The purpose of his 1970 letter to Adeane therefore was to record for posterity that the Queen had not acted unconstitutionally at the time of his resignation. Six years later, in dealings with Sir Martin Charteris, Adeane's successor, he established that the same was true about the Queen's supposed hostility to Suez.[117]

On the night that Macmillan became Prime Minister, Butler received (in the words of his official biographer) 'a very touching letter from Clarissa Eden which, without being explicit, managed to convey the impression that the choice made by the Palace owed nothing to any recommendation offered by the outgoing Prime Minister'.[118] The letter read:

> Dear Rab,
>   Just a line to say what a beastly profession I think politics are – and how greatly I admire your dignity and good humour.
>   Yours ever,
>   Clarissa.[119]

One outstanding piece of business needed tidying up, namely the constituency. On 10 January, Eden invited Lord Leigh, President of the local association, Eric Claridge, Chairman, and his agent, John Devine, down to Chequers, where Nehru, putting personal friendship over and above political differences, had already come down on a visit. The Warwick delegation met Eden in the Long Gallery on the first floor of the house, the windows of which contain the stained-glass heraldic coats of arms of former Prime Ministers. Eden raised the question of whether he should continue as MP for Warwick and Leamington. (The impression that the three visitors had was that he had already decided to step down, but wanted to involve his party association with the 'decision'.) He said that his health would make this very difficult. Initially, the suggestion from John Devine was that he should have a break from the responsibilities and have an MP from a neighbouring constituency as a *locum tenens*, along the lines adopted when Robert Carr stood in during the summer of 1953. Eden ruled out this suggestion at once, as he said that it would be unfair to his constituents to be left in limbo. Sadly, but inevitably, it was agreed that he would sever his connections at once, and Eden drafted a letter for Eric Claridge there and then, in the course of which he wrote, 'I clearly have not the present health.'[120] His intention to stand down as MP for Warwick and Leamington after thirty-three years was anounced on 11 January.

As Eden wanted his constituents to have a representative in Parliament as soon as possible, he was glad that a by-election swiftly followed. The wheel had indeed come full circle, as it was at a by-election in 1923 that

Eden had begun his association with Warwick and Leamington. Oliver Poole, the Party Chairman, was informed at once of the impending vacancy and more than 250 candidates applied for it. Two names tipped locally were Randolph Churchill, which would have been the final insult to Eden, and Valerie Profumo, wife of the Stratford MP. The local association, however, found none of the 250 to their liking and 're-advertised'. This process still failed to produce an acceptable nomination, so the association asked Smith-Ryland, the Lord Lieutenant, if he wished to stand. When he declined, a new shortlist was drawn up, consisting of Philip Goodhart, Victor Goodhew and John Hobson. Each candidate was asked his opinion of Suez. Whichever of the four possible responses (for/against/regret at the aborted invasion/acceptance of its inevitability) the candidate chose, *somebody* on the selection committee was bound to be alienated. Recognising this, Philip Goodhart, who had been in Cairo reporting on the Suez campaign for the *Sunday Times*, spoke of conditions in Egypt, and after that the committee moved on to other subjects. He failed by only two votes to be selected. The winner was John Hobson, after what the local Press called a 'polite, prosaic campaign'.[121] He was duly elected at the by-election on 7 March 1957, but with a vastly reduced majority of 2,157. Eden sent a goodwill message to John Hobson from New Zealand.

The verdicts on 1956 began almost at once. Anthony Nutting believed it was 'no end of a lesson'. 'It has been a commonplace,' Max Beloff wrote, 'to speak of the Suez Crisis as a turning point, but to do so is to raise two kinds of question: what exactly was it that turned, and did it turn because of what happened in the Suez Crisis, or was the crisis simply a "moment of truth", the sign of changes which were taking place, not for one reason but for many?'[122]

Such were the questions Eden himself considered. Buried in a musty file at the Public Record Office is a memorandum he drew up in December 1956, even before the final dust had settled. In this he drew unpalatable conclusions with frankness, 'We must review our world position and our domestic capacity more searchingly in the light of the Suez experience, which has not so much changed our fortunes as revealed realities.'[123] Nearly half a century later, this process is still unfinished.

On 18 January 1957 the Edens sailed aboard the RMS *Rangitata* from Tilbury docks en route to New Zealand and a new life. Many Cabinet ministers and colleagues were there to see them off. Brendan Bracken was unaccountably delayed and missed the casting off. Undeterred, he set off down the quayside, avoiding ropes and capstans, in an attempt (eventually successful) to hand over to one of the crew a gift of cigars for the voyage. A more precious gift was the letter Beaverbrook sent to wish Eden God speed. It read simply, 'Fear nothing for the future. Time will vindicate you.'[124]

The route to New Zealand was to be longer than Eden's journey in the 1920s. 'The ship, of course had to go round by the Panama Canal,' Nigel Nicolson observed, 'because the Suez Canal was closed for reasons that he knew all too well.'[125]

CHAPTER TWENTY

'The Past Gone, Seize Today'

1957–77

Since life fleets, all is change; the Past gone, seize today!
Robert Browning, *Rabbi Ben Ezra*, xxvi

'Former Prime Ministers,' as Gladstone said of Peel, 'are like untethered rafts drifting around harbours – a menace to shipping.'[1] As the RMS *Rangitata* left England behind on a foggy January afternoon in 1957, Eden faced an uncertain future. Any return to active politics was unlikely, apart from considerations about health. Yet Eden was of an age (fifty-nine) when Churchill had not even become Prime Minister for the first time.

After his stay in New Zealand, at the end of which Eden had to fly in an adapted Sunderland aircraft via Vancouver for another operation in Boston, his first priority was his finances. He had given up his Warwick and Leamington seat, and 1957 occurred before the age of generous Westminster pension provision and parliamentary severance pay. With the help and advice of friends, notably Brendan Bracken and Viscount Chandos (the former Oliver Lyttelton), Eden's memoirs were contracted to *The Times* for £160,000, which, paid in a tax-efficient manner, and with spectacular sales, eventually brought in a sum equivalent to nearly £3 million in present-day terms.[2]

Such matters still lay in the future, as the Edens settled to life on board ship. A passenger on the next table in the dining room looked exactly like Attlee, and some members of the crew thought two ex-Premiers were travelling to New Zealand. The Edens' steward was John Prescott, a future Deputy Prime Minister. Eden, who was ill all the way, spent much time reading and writing letters in his cabin. As a result the Captain never fully understood the nature of his celebrated passengers, and was astonished when the ship docked in Auckland to find that Sid Holland, the New Zealand Premier, and the New Zealand Cabinet, with bands, a guard of honour and huge cheering crowds were on the quayside to greet them.

'It is a strange feeling on this ship – completely cut off after so many years', Eden wrote to Salisbury. Reflecting on the past two years, he added, 'I think we were a good Cabinet with little intrigue and many honest men.' Later in the year, Eden was saddened by Salisbury's resignation (over Cyprus) and, remembering 1938, wrote, 'By a strange trick of fate we are both out again together with our party in power.' In July, he let Salisbury know of his misgivings about the American administration. 'Ike is certainly the Neville Chamberlain of the fifties,' he wrote. 'Winston was very critical of U.S. over Suez. His comment about us was that he wished we had let the Israelis go on to Cairo.' He added, 'Winston was also unhappy about the Queen going to the U.S. at this time.'[3]

This latter point was a reference to the Queen's proposed visit to North America in October. Conscious of how this might be interpreted as a tacit criticism of her former Prime Minister, the Queen was to write understandingly to Eden, with whom she now corresponded regularly:

> I do hope our visit will be of value between the two countries. There does seem to be a much closer feeling between the U.S. and ourselves, especially since the Russian satellite has come to shake everyone about their views on Russian scientific progress! Ever since receiving your letter, the Russians appear to be hectoring America again, & one always wonders where that may end.[4]

On her return from America, the Queen wrote to Eden again with her impressions. 'It is extraordinary how much the Americans need the feeling they are liked (even the President spoke sadly about how much his country was disliked in the world) – an illusion which doesn't seem to bother us much!'[5]

Eden revealed more of his true feelings in letters to Selwyn Lloyd, who had retained his post as Foreign Secretary under Macmillan. Thanking Lloyd for all his kindnesses 'in these last and very melancholy days', Eden wrote in his own hand on an airmail letter from the *Rangitata*:

> As you can imagine I have thought much about them here, & though I wish more & more that some other course had been possible, on all personal & political grounds (selfishly of course), I just cannot pretend to myself that I think it was ... I have only one prayer, that you will support the Israelis in their demand for freedom of passage for all commerce in the gulf of Aqaba ... Meanwhile this incredible US administration seems to think the only 2 powers in the world worth courting are Nasser & Ibn Saud [King of Saudi Arabia]. I cannot help thinking the American people will have had enough of this before long. Provided always we stand by what we have done & maintain that it was right. I feel far more strongly about this than I did in 1938. It was just [the word 'just' was added as an afterthought by Eden in the letter] an open question then, I thought, whether appeasement might succeed. Now it cannot possibly ... Sorry for all this lecture, but when I heard after sailing that Boyle was back still proclaiming that he was right to resign, I did not like it. Forgive & keep to yourself please.

Clarissa & I had a small bet anonymously on a horse in one of our ship's games. I couldn't resist it. 'No policy' by Eisenhower out of Dulles, & it won! I swear I had nothing to do with the christening – or anything else.[6]

The ship's games were not confined to horses. Most afternoons a boxing tournament was held on deck – popular with elderly lady pensioners – and the Edens were prevailed upon to be at the ringside from time to time. Eden even stepped into the ring to present prizes in the form of bottled beer to the victors, who usually included his own cabin steward, John Prescott. Indeed, so often was Prescott on the winning side that Eden believed he deserved greater recognition for his efforts, and took to presenting him with bottles of wine, in the privacy of his cabin, so as not to raise expectations elsewhere among the ship's pugilists.[7]

On their return in the summer, the Edens were uncertain about the reception they would get. 'Perhaps we are returning to England too soon?' Clarissa Eden wrote to Beaverbrook. 'But I don't think we could go wandering around any longer, and we must sooner or later see how the land lies at home.'[8] Of all the unlikely figures who rallied round, Max Beaverbrook proved one of the most stalwart. After Churchill's resignation, Brendan Bracken had organised a dinner at his home in Lord North Street for Eden and Beaverbrook to meet, and afterwards Beaverbrook told Bracken that he would now support Eden. He was true to his word. As his biographer has noted:

> Beaverbrook had often criticised Eden in earlier days, particularly at the time of the League of Nations. He became a loyal friend as soon as Eden was in trouble. Thereafter Beaverbrook's flat in Arlington House was always available for Lord and Lady Avon when they passed through London, and his car was always waiting for them at the door. He lent them his house in Jamaica until they found one of their own and accompanied every such offer with a letter of warm affection.[9]

Beaverbrook also lent the Edens his house in the West Country while the Edens began the lengthy process of house-hunting in England, as the cottage at Broadchalke proved too small for permanent residence. Eventually they settled at Fyfield Manor in the Vale of Pewsey in 1959, before moving nine years later to the Manor House at Alvediston. In Barbados they acquired the lease of a nineteenth-century Regency-style plantation house, Villa Nova, on the secluded east coast, where guests over the years included the Queen and the Duke of Edinburgh (who planted two portlandia trees during their visit on 15 February 1966), Noël Coward and, most frequently, Dean and Alice Acheson, who reciprocated hospitality at Mill Reef in Antigua each year.[10]

Meanwhile, Eden began the detailed planning of his memoirs, originally to be in two volumes. As Churchill had done, he engaged a talented group of researchers, including Robert Blake, Bryan Cartledge, David Dilks (who went on to work for Harold Macmillan in a similar capacity) and Alan Hodge (one of Churchill's pre-war team). As Eden had special dispensation on grounds of health, these historians were allowed to fetch sensitive papers from London. They also devilled for him in various other archives, amassing and marshalling the voluminous evidence, with the younger researchers, especially David Dilks, living *en famille* as the work progressed. 'I found David Dilks quite invaluable,' wrote Eden to Harold Macmillan, by way of recommendation. 'He combines a memory I could never fault with the questing qualities of a bloodhound.'[11]*

Eden broke new ground as the first Prime Minister to write full-dress *political* memoirs. Lloyd George and Churchill had written their war-time memoirs, in Churchill's case of both the First and Second World Wars, as well as of the Boer War. Towards the end of his life Asquith had added a small volume (*Memoirs and Reflections 1852–1927*, Cassell, 1928) to other jottings, and Attlee had published a short autobiography (*As It Happened*, Heinemann, 1954), of which even he did not think much. Eden's three volumes, published between 1960 and 1965, were of a totally different order, and he established a trend, followed by every subsequent Prime Minister, of recording from a personal perspective the events in which he had been involved. By doing this, he broke the unspoken taboo that it was *infra dig* to reveal (even if selectively or by paraphrase) details of Cabinet meetings and official political documents, and at a time when a Fifty-Year Rule applied.†

Eden's main purpose in writing a full autobiography was to vindicate his actions over Suez and to demonstrate that his career was all of a unity, as he told Pierson Dixon on several occasions. 'He was sure that it was right to have intervened,' Dixon recorded of their talk at Government House in Ottawa in May 1957. 'The trouble was that one could never prove that the situation would have been worse if action had not been taken,' Eden said, adding, 'had we moved against Hitler over the Rhineland there would have been much criticism but it would have been the right thing to do and many millions of lives would have been saved.'[12]

---

*When Eden heard that Nutting was proposing to write his life, he discouraged the idea by saying that all his papers were with David Dilks, 'a responsible historian'. (Private information.) Nutting turned instead to Nasser as a biographical subject.

†The Thirty-Year Rule, which did more to alter approaches to contemporary history than any other recent development, was introduced by the Wilson Government in 1967. Coincidentally, this was also the year of the Six Day War, which retrospectively did more for Eden's reputation over his Middle East policy than anything he was able to set out in *Full Circle*, his first volume of memoirs.

Eden returned to this theme the next year when the Suez volume was largely written. 'Mostly we talked about his book,' Dixon wrote in a private memorandum afterwards. 'A. E. said that the book was not an autobiography & did not deal with his early life; it started in 1935 when he first held responsible office, and would display his policy as a consistent whole. It was in fact a justification for Suez.' He gave Dixon new insights into how the Americans had behaved, while conceding his own feelings:

A.E. admitted that he had miscalculated on the U.S. attitude. But who could have accepted that they would have actively opposed us? He had anticipated grumbles & irritation, but when they had got over that he reckoned on at least tepid neutrality. Even after the intervention started he had some reason to expect that attitude from telephone conversations with the President, who had been very understanding. He had certainly been assured by the President, after the cease-fire, that we should not be hurried out but allowed to stay on improving our bargaining position.[13]

If Eden did not entirely succeed in justifying his ways in his memoirs, it was not because he drew false historical analogies, or because his original premiss was necessarily wrong, but because of the insistence of *The Times* as paymaster that he should publish out of chronological sequence. As a result, *Full Circle*, the volume on the years from 1951 to 1957, was written too close to the events to be open about matters that were still pertinent to the unstable situation in the Middle East, omitting, for example, mention of the crucial five days between 18 October and 23 October. The absence of any reference to Sèvres inevitably detracts from the historical value. By the time Eden was publishing his third volume, the bibliography on Suez had become more expansive and his earlier circumscribed account was inevitably superseded by fuller accounts.

One of the disadvantages for Eden of the sequence of his publications was that it contributed to a tendency from the 1960s onwards to assess his career *backwards*, rather than beginning with the appeasement era. Eden foresaw this, and was initially keen to do the volumes sequentially. In July 1958 he wrote to Francis Mathew, General Manager of *The Times*, who was in charge of the project, to outline his concerns:

I still believe that from every point of view, particularly quality, I can make a better book if the 2nd volume is not published until after the first. I give 2 examples. 1. It is impossible to know how to treat personalities in the 2nd volume until I have dealt with them in the 1st. 2. The book has a theme, the experiences of the 'thirties & the experience of today. I ought to deal with these in their proper sequence. One concerns the other.[14]

It was little consolation that these points were exactly the ones made, even by sympathetic critics, when *Full Circle* appeared in 1962, quite apart from those who correctly pointed out that over Suez Eden had been, in a later phrase, 'economical with the *actualité*'. *The Times* was insistent, however, on having its Suez pound of flesh first (there was no telling how long Eden would survive).

By the summer of 1959 Eden was sufficiently reconciled to doing the 'difficult bit' first to be able to tell Churchill about progress:

> I have been at work on the book and I have virtually decided to publish first, as a separate volume, the years 1951–57. The chief reason for this is that I wrote these first as being fresh in my memory. If I had gone back to the early 1930s I fear that I would have forgotten a great deal of the 1950s by the time I reached them. Also, I have been influenced by the importance of getting our own story out for these years before others do so.[15]

This contained more than an element of special pleading. Randolph Churchill's 1959 account, largely discounted by most people as petulant and vindictive, had been published before full details of collusion had emerged (though the suspicions had). Eden therefore could avoid facing the issue in his first volume. Had Eden published after Anthony Nutting's account, *No End of a Lesson*, in 1967, he would have had to address collusion.[16]

One of the fortuitous consequences of *The Times*'s demands was that, by the time Eden came to complete his second and third volumes, he had gained immeasurably in the experience of writing and organising his materials. His volume on the 1930s – for which preliminary work was done by F.H. Hinsley – is a major contribution to the political and diplomatic history of the pre-war years, with uniquely personal accounts of epoch-making events and world figures. Equally, his volume on the Second World War provides not only a comprehensive account of international relations, but the details, based on primary sources, of the Churchill-Eden relationship at the heart of the Government.*

Eden's memoirs† did not please everyone. A. J. P. Taylor‡, who resented

---

*Subsequently, Eden considered preparing an edition of their wartime telegrams and memoranda, a pre-echo of the 'Companion Volumes' that Martin Gilbert published alongside the main volumes of the official Churchill biography.
†*The Eden Memoirs: Full Circle* (1960); *Facing the Dictators* (1962); *The Reckoning* (1965).
‡Initially, Eden had supported A. J. P. Taylor for the Regius Professorship of History at Oxford, but after Taylor's publication of his *The Origins of the Second World War* in 1961, he became one of Eden's *bêtes noires*, and the hostility was reciprocated by Taylor. Of the Roosevelt proposal for an international conference in January 1938, Taylor wrote, 'Eden supposed, perhaps sincerely, that such a meeting would draw the United States on to the side of the Western powers.' (A. J. P. Taylor, *The Origins of the Second World War*, Penguin Books, Harmondsworth, 1964, p.183.) Whatever people thought of his policies, Eden was not going to accept a slur on the sincerity of his motives, either over 1938 or 1956.

the fact that Eden had been allowed access to Government records for his period in office, dismissed *Facing the Dictators* cheaply. 'Eden did not face the dictators,' he commented, 'he pulled faces at them'; and of *The Reckoning* he sarcastically wrote, 'its handsome pages provide a great deal of uninteresting information.'[17] Whether the pages were handsome or not (to most readers they were just pages), many others instead echoed Attlee, who wrote admiringly to Eden, adding, 'I find that everyone thinks that your third volume is the best.'[18] Even David Carlton, Eden's fiercest critic, acknowledged that the two later volumes had 'a solidity and a sombre spaciousness worthy of a politician of the first rank'.[19]

The tone of Eden's memoirs made few concessions to the general reader, resembling the style of official diplomatic memoranda, and lacking colour, variety and personal details. 'Goodness the boredom of the Eden memoirs', wrote Evelyn Waugh to Nancy Mitford.[20] As the memoirs appeared, bookshops in Warwick and Leamington had prominent window-displays for each new volume. They proved popular as Christmas and birthday presents, so that many Warwickshire Tories had several copies, given and received simultaneously on festive occasions.[21] Although the memoirs were commercially very successful (by 14 October 1960, *Full Circle* had sold 77,000 copies)[22] they were books for the shelf rather than the bedside. Many a house in Middle England, apart from those in Warwick and Leamington, displayed the three distinctive white volumes, often next to Churchill's six volumes on the Second World War, behind glass doors in 'the front room'.

Eden, however, was not essentially addressing this audience, eager purchasers though its members proved to be. The memoirs are a serious, diplomatic history aimed at a specialist audience, with few concessions to popular taste, a fact also true of his Chatham House publication, *Towards Peace in Indochina* in 1966. When Eden came to write *Another World*, his memoir of the Great War, a decade later, the young Ben Pimlott was preparing for Eden an account of the EDC, in answer to Kilmuir's memoirs. Pimlott was able while working for Eden to read some of the early drafts of *Another World*, and he made various helpful suggestions, successfully encouraging Eden to draw more fully on his personal memories. The book was generally accounted Eden's most readable and individual.* *Another World* was his most personal book in another way: a substantial proportion of the royalties was divided equally between the Rifleman's Aid Society and the RAF Benevolent Fund.

Eden's health remained a matter of concern. In total he had nine major

---

*Neverthless, Eden found it difficult initially to interest a publisher in *Another World*, though when Allen Lane took it on they had a commercial success.

internal operations. The last time Richard Cattell operated on him was in 1961; shortly afterwards he was taken gravely ill himself, and later died of leukaemia. When Dr Braasch, Cattell's assistant, operated in March 1970, it took two hours to make the incision because of the dreadful scarring from all the previous operations. Braasch has left a touching tribute to the stoicism of his patient over his many tribulations, recording that he 'was an extraordinary person with high personal and national ideals and a drive for perfection in the discharge of his duties', adding that 'he was a model of cooperation and possessed an even humor at times of stress.'[23] Many fellow sufferers wrote in for help during these years, and Eden always gave what advice he could in thoughtful letters in his own hand.[24]

Eden never lost his zest for public affairs. He paid avid attention to the radio and television news bulletins and the serious broadsheet newspapers, though the *Observer* never crossed his threshold. In the summer of 1957 he received a letter from the Mahdi:

> This was very friendly in tone [Eden wrote] and told me that a Sudanese judge was to visit England shortly, I think for some conference. He would get in touch with me and would I please see him as he had a further message from the Mahdi . . .
>
> The judge duly arrived, an impressive figure over six feet tall in C's small cottage garden. He told me that the Mahdi had asked him to see me to tell me that the Mahdi and the Sudanese were grateful for the action Britain had taken against Nasser the year before. I thanked him and asked why. He continued that, until the events of the previous autumn, the Sudanese had been uncertain whether they could reject Nasser's demands when made to them, as they were sure they would be before long. Now the limitations of Nasser's military power had been made clear to them and the Sudanese were determined to resist. All they wanted were a few arms of which they would give details.*

Eden was in demand by historians for his recollections, and was visited by former colleagues and world statesman for two decades. 'I have still some Latour 1934,' he wrote welcomingly to René Massigli and his wife before one visit in 1964.[25] He wrote to A. J. Barker, author of *Suez: The Seven-Day War* (1964):

> The Suez action seemed to many an attempt to prevent the wrecking of international order. The failure to do this has resulted in a multiplicity of small but arrogant dictatorships, some of whom pretend to non-

---

*The accuracy of the Mahdi's forecast was confirmed by Nasser's demands upon Wadi Halfa, which followed soon after and were rejected by Khartoum, who got away with their refusal. Typed copy (2 September 1976) of 1957 original manuscript in brown leather tooled book kept in a Government safe. Countess of Avon papers.

alignment, but most of whom plot international blackmail. The fact that Nasser, however battered militarily, got away with it politically, was bad for the future of the world.[26]

Eden also saw Sir Roy Welensky, who had retired to nearby Blandford Forum, and through him kept in touch with the deepening crisis in Rhodesia. 'You have been quite a lot in my thoughts lately,' Welensky wrote after the Six Day War in 1967. 'Few men can have lived to see their actions vindicated to the extent that you have seen yours over Suez!'[27]

When a sixteen-year-old schoolboy at neighbouring Marlborough College sent a letter saying that he had read *Full Circle*, which had been a great help to him for a history project, he invited him over for tea and a talk, which ranged over many topics, including the forthcoming 1960 American Presidential Election, when Eden made it plain he favoured Kennedy over Nixon.[28]

After Nasser's funeral on 1 October 1970, a group of British dignitaries, headed by Sir Alec Douglas-Home, the Foreign Secretary, were sitting on the terrace of the British Embassy as the sun went down after a fraught day of high emotion, during which Nasser's coffin had been lowered on to its final island resting place in the middle of the Nile by a Russian helicopter. Suddenly a death's-head moth splattered itself into oblivion on the windows of the Embassy. 'Will the spirit of Nasser forever haunt the British?' asked the Ambassador.[29] It certainly haunted Eden. From the moment he embarked on the *Rangitata* to the moment on 28 September 1970 when his gardener at Alvediston told him the breaking news that Nasser was no more, and thereafter, Eden never forgot the man he had met but once. 'Eden took me swimming in the gentle rollers,' Anthony Montague Browne, Churchill's private secretary, wrote of one Caribbean visit in 1961. 'I had resolved to guard my too-ready tongue and in no circumstances to mention Suez, but as soon as we were afloat he took up the sad tale. For some twenty minutes he talked of that disaster, now from the trough of a wave, now from the peak. It was obsessive, but also eloquent and touching.'[30]

Eden's frequent letters to Churchill nearly always came back to the same subject. 'Why in the world do we have to join with Dulles to send arms to Tunisia?' he wrote at the beginning of 1958. 'This seems an abrupt denial of our Suez plans. As I see it, the French are fighting for life, all our lives, in Algeria. The oil is there & if the French have it & can control it, the dependence on the Canal will be less & we can be firm at last with Nasser.'[31]

In 1962 Eden met the young Tam Dalyell, an Old Etonian recently elected as Labour MP for West Lothian. He told Dalyell that he was interested in deviant Etonians, hastily adding, 'politically deviant that is!' He asked Dalyell directly why he had become a member of the Labour Party. Dalyell swiftly reckoned that honesty was the best policy. The first reason, he told the former Prime Minister, was unemployment in Scotland, and his belief that the Tories would never grasp it. The second, of course, was simple – in one word, Suez. Eden put his hand on Dalyell's shoulder. 'I can understand that,' he said, 'and I can also respect it.'[32]

As more and more historians and broadcasters approached Eden for Suez information, and as he found that most were duplicating their requests to Selwyn Lloyd, he felt it was time for the two of them to coordinate their response. The first of these meetings took place at Broadchalke on 30 May 1958, records of which found their way into the Government archives at the Public Record Office (Lloyd was Foreign Secretary still). Somehow a reporter on the *Daily Express* got wind of the meeting and took a photograph of Eden in casual clothes and Selwyn Lloyd in one of his customary stiff suits striding down a Wiltshire lane after lunch. During their talk, Eden told Lloyd he believed that the British case was largely going by default, something that he intended to address in his first volume of memoirs. Both agreed that they would thereafter coordinate their response to historians – collusion about collusion as it were – on a discreet and anonymous basis. Eden promised to show Lloyd *Full Circle* when it was written, and to give him full credit for his efforts to prevent Eden agreeing to the Suez Canal Users' Association, an error he admitted to deeply regretting.[33]

One of the historians to receive information from Lloyd under the Broadchalke agreement was Hugh Thomas (though he did not know Eden was aware he had consulted Lloyd),[34] then (1966) researching a series of articles for the *Sunday Times*.* Lloyd was surprisingly frank, even ebullient in his talks with Hugh Thomas, giving a portrait of Eden under stress that showed he was not the autocratic figure during the crisis that outsiders believed:

> He did a great deal of consulting, certainly of his senior colleagues [Lloyd wrote to Thomas after reading an early draft of one of the proposed articles]. If, for example, Butler disagreed at any phase, he had plenty of chance of saying so. In the second place, I don't think you bring out sufficiently that our primary objective throughout was a peaceful settlement, admittedly one under which Nasser would have had to give up a good deal but he would have kept the canal nationalised and

---

*These articles became the basis of *The Suez Affair*, published in 1967, the same year as Anthony Nutting's *No End of a Lesson* (over which Eden and Lloyd were certainly not consulted!).

received the revenues on terms no more onerous than those on which he afterwards got loans from the World Bank. I get the impression from your article that from the 26th of July we were all longing to have a physical smack at Nasser. That really is not true. Eden, Head and I had too much trouble over the Suez base to want to go back to a physical presence in Egypt other than that agreed under the 1954 agreement.[35] This applied to the August Conference, the acceptance of SCUA, and to the final reference of the Security Council. If a peaceful settlement was not possible, then the use of force would be justified.[36]

Sadly, Eden never wrote a frank book on Suez. There are some tantalising hints among his papers and one such is a memorandum he prepared on 9 September 1968:

Normanbrook [the elided name that Norman Brook took for the title of his peerage] remarked to me when I saw him in his house in London today, as he had done before, that it was a calamity that we had had to adapt our views over the Suez business to allay the qualms of the weaker brethren of whom Rab mattered the most. They were not prepared to face direct action against Egypt by the time that our military preparations were ready. On the other hand they were prepared to go along with more devious arrangements which obscured this. Yet Rab was the one member of the Cabinet who since then had spoken in half truths and criticism of all that happened. In other words, those for whom we had bent our tactics proved the least loyal. This is true because I remember how surprised I was that Rab rallied so readily, even enthusiastically to our twisted plans when I explained them to him in detail, as he admitted that they were explained to him in his BBC T.V. interview a few nights ago.

Rab was kept closely informed by me of every development in the Suez business from the beginning to the end. He missed no important Cabinet and when, as sometimes happened, he arrived late, we waited for him. Normanbrook told me that Rab had also attended a number of the meetings of our Cabinet Committee on Suez, on one occasion he had presided over it. At no time, either at a meeting or in private conversation with me throughout those months did Rab ever express criticism of what we were doing or trying to do.

Normanbrook told me that he had looked up the composition of our Cabinet Committee. Usually these committees were left by the Cabinet for the P.M. to select the membership, the decision to set up a committee having once been taken. On this occasion, however, the committee was at my decision set up and its members chosen by the Cabinet itself in session.

I mentioned to Normanbrook the tale which I understood was to appear in the *Sunday Times* that the Queen, as a result of the promptings of Mountbatten, had telephoned her concern to me during the Suez crisis.

There was of course not a word of truth in this. Normanbrook told me that he was sure that there was not.[37]

This memorandum is at direct odds with the account Butler gave to Archbishop Fisher at Smith Square on 13 December 1956. Eden remained ambivalent about Butler, despite his kind words to the Queen at his resignation audience. 'I would only set down that I wish Butler were a man I could respect,' Eden wrote to Beaverbrook at the time of the 1963 Tory leadership contest. 'L.G. once called him "the artful dodger", but if this is important in politics, it is also not enough.'[38]

A later Cabinet Secretary, Sir Burke Trend, had to deal with the repercussions of the publication in 1967 of Anthony Nutting's No End of a Lesson. When it became clear that Nutting intended to go ahead, come what may, the Cabinet Office became involved. Trend met Nutting as early as 19 January 1966 to discuss potential difficulties, and Eden was kept fully informed. 'On this present case I am not hopeful that Nutting will prove to be a gentleman', Harold Wilson wrote to Trend on 10 April 1967.* 'He has gone too far and the cost to the publisher – and probably to himself – would now be very great. But being realistic my guess is he will go ahead whatever we do or threaten to do.' The anxiety was that Nutting's publication would open the floodgates and set a precedent. Of course, there were those who watched these developments with a wry satisfaction. Had not Eden himself set a precedent by his privileged access to material under embargo to others? It is strange that Eden seemed not to recognise that it was inevitable that the floodgates would be opened. He saw Harold Wilson privately at Number 10 on 12 April 1967, by which date the forthcoming Nutting book was in proof. Trend recorded details of the discussions:

> He [Eden] was not complaining about the way in which it [the book] treated him, indeed from this point of view the more outrageous it was, the better. But it was certainly very inaccurate – e.g. it said at one point that, after despatching an official telegram to President Eisenhower, he followed it up with a purely private message; this was quite untrue.

Six days later, Macmillan came to Downing Street to discuss the matter. Trend suggested that his guest might care to come in through the garden gate or via the Cabinet Office's Whitehall entrance. Not so, replied Macmillan, 'he would be quite happy to come through the front door'. On

---

*An ironic worry in the light of his speech at the Labour Party Conference at Scarborough in October 1963 about how, when even the MCC had abolished the distinction between amateurs and professionals, 'we are content to remain a nation of Gentlemen in a world of Players'. Harold Wilson speech, 1 October 1963.

27 June Edward Heath called on Trend and told him 'that Mr Nutting and his friends are putting it about that the book was "cleared"; and he asked me (mainly, I think, at Lord Avon's prompting) how this could best be denied.'[39]

The importance of Nutting's book lay in the fact that it was the first inside British account to confirm details of the secret meetings at Sèvres. This was potentially very damaging to Eden, who had denied collusion to the House and had omitted mention of Sèvres in his own memoirs. From Nutting's point of view, however, the timing of publication was unfortunate. Michael Foot had recently called in Parliament for a inquiry into Suez on the lines of the Dardanelles Commission in the Great War, which had come to naught, and the coincidence of the Six Day War between Egypt and Israel had led many observers, previously uncommitted to Eden's cause, to conclude that he might have been right about Nasser all along. Lord Normanbrook certainly saw it that way. 'Anthony Eden is coming to have a talk with me tomorrow,' he wrote in June 1967. 'The news from the Middle East really is most extraordinary and I expect he will have a good deal to say about it. I think things have turned out well from his point of view and certainly Nutting has not gained any advantages.'[40]

Nevertheless many feathers were ruffled, and Nutting, always something of an independent spirit in the Tory Party, completed the crossing of the Rubicon first entered by his resignation in November 1956.* Although Selwyn Lloyd insouciantly said that No End of a Lesson was all a case of 'Much Ado about Nutting,'[41] Eden regarded it as a betrayal. He had not spoken to Nutting after he resigned, and he never did so again. Lloyd did not think that the book had been written out of resentment; on the contrary, it raised 'a number of important issues'. The most important of these centred on collusion and the extent to which a Prime Minister, Foreign Secretary or any important Cabinet minister should be expected to make a full disclosure to Parliament of all that was happening or that had been agreed behind the scenes. It was a constitutional and ethical issue of fundamental importance.†

The Foreign Secretary of the day is the minister, Lloyd wrote:

> to whom the Secret Service reports. He discusses these matters only with the Prime Minister of the day. He also has to consider the effect of what

---

*In various talks and correspondence with the author over many years, the late Sir Anthony Nutting admitted how acute were the dilemmas faced by participants on all sides of the Suez argument.

†Although Lloyd did not draw the parallel in the notes in his Suez file, Sir Stafford Cripps's repeated denial that the pound was to be devalued in September 1949 – 'His Majesty's Government have not the slightest intention of devaluing the pound,' he told the House of Commons at one stage – was the most recent important example of what might be called justifiably disingenuous.

he says upon British lives and interests overseas. Of course this raises difficulties for the Foreign Secretary of the day – he cannot approve or deny allegation. Mr Nutting has not accused me of telling an untruth to the House of Commons – but of deceiving it by suppressing the full story. Whatever I said to the House was not said in a personal capacity – it was said as an act of State, with the authority of the Prime Minister of the day. I would not have had the slightest hesitation in concealing the truth from the House of Commons if I thought it was in the national interest.'[42]

So it was with Eden, whose last statement in the House after thirty-three years of continuous membership – a denial of collusion – was the most painful he ever had to make.

Douglas Jay is one former Labour Cabinet minister who felt that the denials of Eden and Lloyd were understandable, a case of 'confusion' rather than 'collusion'.[43] The fullest defence was given by Robert Blake:

There must have been a great deal of *suppressio veri* – principally of course in connection with the charge of 'collusion'. No one of sense will regard such falsehoods in a particularly serious light. The motive was the honourable one of averting further trouble in the Middle East, and this was a serious consideration for many years after the event. The conferment in 1971 upon Selwyn Lloyd of the Speakership, the greatest honour which the House of Commons can give, showed that politicians on both sides recognised the dilemma in which he found himself, and did not in retrospect count his conduct against him.[44]

Absolution comes in many forms, but Robert Blake properly relegated 'collusion', whatever might have been felt of other issues, to its proper place on a secondary level in the Suez story. Had Eden addressed it frankly in *Full Circle*, the process might not have taken so long.

To Salisbury, the blip in their friendship now long forgotten, Eden wrote, 'As I worked over the papers', [for his autobiography], 'I came to the conclusion that the Americans behaved much worse after the cease-fire than before, & that it was in their obstinate failure to co-operate then that the missed opportunities were most conspicuous.'[45]

With the publication of *Full Circle* in January 1960, the question of Suez, as Eden had anticipated, scratched like a poor itch, became a scab once more. As the American reviews began to appear, Eden wrote to Harold Caccia at the Washington Embassy:

I noticed that the *Washington Post* commented that I had learnt too well the lesson of Munich. I feel quite sure that if anyone had attempted to scotch Hitler & Mussolini early in their careers, there would have been plenty to proclaim that they did not deserve it. It would have been better for the world if the attempt had been made all the same.

Remembering Eden's customary phrase from his pre-war days as private secretary – 'I know this may shock the Department, but I want to know' – Harold Caccia sent a detailed report from the Washington Embassy on American responses to the book:

> The reaction in the US has not by and large been one of resentment at your criticisms nor bitterness. Of course, there are those who were involved in the State Dept., and elsewhere, who profess to feel hotly and may well have been stung. The most common comment by the so far uncommitted has been: well there were probably faults on both sides and we must learn from that. Seeing that it would be scarcely human for an American to admit to me that all the fault was on their side, I don't think this is too bad or indeed that you yourself would expect it to be![46]

There had been faults on both sides also in Eden's first marriage, but nevertheless he was deeply saddened by the news of Beatrice's death on 29 June 1957 after a long struggle against cancer, never having found the true happiness she had sought in America. For Nicholas, who had always been close to his mother, it was a painful break with the past. Beatrice's funeral was held at the Anglo-Saxon St Gregory's Minster, Kirkdale, near Nawton in Yorkshire, where her ashes were buried in the Beckett family plot.

On a public level, the end of Eden's Premiership in 1957 accompanied the onset of an introspective mood of national self-examination, epitomised by John Osborne's contemporary play *The Entertainer*, which portrayed the *angst* that many, especially among the young, felt after Suez. Osborne's powerful metaphor of Britain as a decaying music hall, living on the memoirs of past glories, soon found political expression with one cartoonist portraying Macmillan as a Westminster version of Archie Rice, its anti-hero, inhabiting a world of nostalgic illusion. The cultural magazine *Encounter* (founded in 1953) contributed to the process with several seminal issues around the theme of 'Whither Britain?' Adrian Mitchell's poem 'Remember Suez?' perfectly captures the mood of that time:

> England, unlike junior nations,
> Wears officers' long combinations.
> So no embarrassment was felt
> By the Church, the Government or the Crown.
> But I saw the Thames like a grubby old belt
> And England's trousers falling down.[47]

In the summer of 1958 Anthony Eden, who had already been a Governor, was invited to become President of the Shakespeare Memorial Theatre in

Stratford-upon-Avon.[48] It was a feather in the company's cap to have a former Prime Minister as their titular head. However, Eden's eight-year involvement with one of Britain's leading arts organisations was of more than symbolic importance. In what was to be a crucial transitional period for the arts, Eden's contacts at the highest level were to prove invaluable in providing Stratford with the wherewithal and freedom to develop its own individual style of theatrical productions. Until the redistribution of boundaries at the 1950 General Election, Stratford had been an important part of Eden's Warwick and Leamington constituency, and from the early 1920s he had been a regular attender at the annual Shakespeare Festivals. Among his political contemporaries only Neville Chamberlain was a knowledgeable Shakespearean on anything approaching the same level.[49] Eden had regularly been joined by his wife and sons in evening family readings of entire plays, and most of the major roles were 'performed' by Eden over the years. In addition, he made time for extensive re-reading of the plays and poetry each year. Nor was his enthusiasm only for the 'plums'. He was, for instance, fascinated by the political aspect of the *Henry VI* trilogy and by the lesser-known plays in general. 'I look forward to *Timon of Athens*,' he wrote to the Chairman, Sir Fordham Flower, in 1965 when that rarity was scheduled.[50]

Eden could recite by heart vast tracts of the Bard's works, and perceptive Shakespearean parallels crop up time and again in his private correspondence. The first volume of his memoirs, on which he was working in the late 1950s, was eventually to bear the Shakespearean title *Full Circle*.[51] One of Eden's favourite Shakespeare plays was the then under-regarded *Troilus and Cressida*, containing the great speech by Ulysses on degree, which Eden perceptively observed to be not primarily about degree, but about confusion, the consequences of the removal of order:

> Take but degree away, untune that string,
> And, hark! what discord follows.[52]

At times during his eight years at the helm of the Stratford theatre, these lines seemed to him particularly apt. For just as Alec Douglas-Home had agreed to take on the Presidency of the Marylebone Cricket Club in 1966, as long as he was not embroiled in any controversy (only then to find himself at the hub of the storm about Basil d'Oliveira and the cancelled South African cricket tour),[53] so Eden took on what he thought would be largely an honorary post, although the next eight eventful years were crammed with artistic, political and financial storms of all kinds.

He revelled in the involvement and gave the Royal Shakespeare Company (as it became in 1961, early in his term) distinguished and active service, until he stepped down voluntarily in the summer of 1966 after the death of Sir Fordham Flower, 'in view of the fact that he now spends several months away from England and when here has a great distance to come for not only the meetings but the various productions in Stratford and London', as the minutes recorded.[54] But Eden remained a Governor for the rest of his life. 'Everyone was delighted at your continued interest in our affairs', he was told on his seventieth birthday.[55]

Eden had been a close personal friend of Glen Byam Shaw, the Artistic Director of the Stratford Memorial Theatre Company in the 1950s, and of Sir Fordham Flower, of the local brewing family that had founded the Stratford Festivals in the mid-nineteenth century, who was also Chairman of his local constituency organisation. On 15 November 1958, the week that Eden took up the reins of the Presidency, it was announced that Peter Hall, the rising young star of British theatre, would succeed Glen Byam Shaw as Director for the 1960 season.

From the start Eden was resolved on two matters. He would not interfere in the day-to-day running of the theatre, and he would attend as many productions as possible. (He was always punctilious about paying for his own tickets, even at special invitation galas.) On 7 November 1958, in his first letter on Stratford business, he wrote to E. R. Bosley, Secretary to the Governors, saying, 'though the last thing I want to do is to intrude in the Theatre's affairs, I would like to know what is going on.'[56]

Clarissa Eden was, of course, an ardent theatre-goer, and a personal friend of Peter Brook. The Edens, together with the Stratford MP, John Profumo, and his wife Valerie (the actress Valerie Hobson), became familiar figures at the Royal Shakespeare Theatre on both official and private occasions.

Eden assumed office at a seminal moment in the development of British theatrical fashion. The traditional star-studded, representational productions, in which the actors wore tights and Verona was Verona, were giving way to minimalist ensemble concepts, staged in a bare white 'box' setting, in modern dress, and even in some cases no dress at all.[57]

The one-hundredth season in 1959 was Byam Shaw's swansong. Laurence Olivier appeared as Coriolanus, Charles Laughton as King Lear, and Paul Robeson as Othello – but Peter Hall showed his hand with a production of *A Midsummer Night's Dream*, which, apart from Laughton as Bottom, was cast with a group of younger ensemble actors. The only concession to traditionalism, and this was not entirely under Hall's control, came in the form of beautifully realised Elizabethan sets, quite unlike those of the celebrated Peter Brook production ten years later, a production that became the apogee of the 'new' style with its brightly lit white-walled box. Although privately Eden said that 'things were never quite the same when the two Peters came in', he recognised the power of Hall's *Dream*, and later of Brook's 1970 production, defending both in correspondence with critical members of the public.

Hall's first full season in 1960–1, a thematic tracing of the development of Shakespearean comedy, coincided with the adoption of the 'Royal' name (why therefore, asked large numbers of correspondents of Eden, is the National Anthem no longer played before performances?) and with the jettisoning of the unfortunate museum associations of the old 'Memorial' tag. Most of the productions in 1960 (*Twelfth Night* was one of spectacular visual beauty) were not dissimilar to what older play-goers had been accustomed to seeing under Glen Byam Shaw. Only the *Troilus and Cressida*, directed by Peter Hall and John Barton, staged in a shallow box full of white sand against the backdrop of a blood-drenched cyclorama, broke new ground. Eden felt this famous 'sandpit' production illuminated one of his long-time favourites in a way quite outside his previous experience. For a compartmentalised play with several different groups of actors, this *Troilus* was above all a triumph of teamwork, unlike the previous Stratford production in 1954. When Eden and his wife had gone backstage after that performance, Eden had congratulated the Troilus (Laurence Harvey), saying he had most enjoyed Troilus's speech 'distasted with the salt of broken tears', and Ulysses's one to the Greek commanders on 'degree'. 'What? Does Ulysses have a big speech too?' was Harvey's puzzled reply.[58]

To the surprise and pleasure of many of the Young Turks at the theatre, for whom Eden might have seemed a likely apologist for the established ways, the new President, despite some of his private reservations, proved a defender of the modern innovative productions,* just as, in the 1920s, his artistic tastes as a collector had been well in advance of conventional opinion. Nevertheless, he cleared his diary in November 1961 to see Sir John Gielgud in Franco Zeffirelli's *Othello*, a four-and-a-half-hour marathon, owing to the multiple changes of sumptuous operatic scenery, and a production whose legendary longueurs discredited the 'traditional' way of tackling Shakespeare at Stratford.

Eden's tastes were eclectic and he respected different approaches to Shakespeare's plays, which he always believed to be capable of with-standing varied interpretations, as long as the concepts were coherent and

---

*Unlike the venerable Dame Edith Evans, cast as old Queen Margaret in the 1961 production of *Richard III*, who was dismayed to find that the early rehearsals, at which she was accustomed to being given 'blocking' instructions, were dominated by discussions of evils such as the Holocaust by an intense group of actors huddled in a ring of canvas chairs. Wandering up to the Dress Circle during a lull in the proceedings, of which there were several, she called out in her best Lady Bracknell tones to the director, 'Do tell me when you're going to begin, as I haven't got long to live.' (Private information.)

intelligent. The next 'starry' production he saw, Paul Scofield as King Lear (in 1962), was built on teamwork and an unobtrusive design that allowed the action to flow, and Eden was fascinated by the radical developments implicit in Peter Brook's influential work. When Nevil Coghill, the Shakespeare scholar, produced a memorandum on lessons to be learned from Brook's production, Eden wrote for a copy.[59]

Peter Hall's ambitions for the Royal Shakespeare Company were not confined to Stratford. He wanted a second base in London (a lease had been signed on the Aldwych Theatre for 1961), where modern plays could be presented alongside Shakespeare. Eden, like some of the other Governors, was concerned that the company might be overstretching itself financially, but he came to realise the advantages of presenting the company's best work in the capital, at a time when Stratford, before motorway links to the Midlands, was not the easiest of destinations for theatre-goers.

Competition between the Royal Shakespeare Company and the embryonic National Theatre for Arts Council funding was intense. The National Theatre's Chairman, Lord Chandos (Eden's former political colleague and friend, Oliver Lyttelton), saw the Stratford company as a potential threat, especially when it moved to London. There was even talk of the amalgamation of the two bodies, as some governors believed that Government funding would not be forthcoming for two 'national' companies. In an atmosphere of mutual suspicion, angry letters were exchanged in October 1962 between Sir Fordham Flower and Sir Laurence Olivier, Director-Designate of the National Theatre, and were copied by both men to Eden as President. At this moment of potential crisis for Stratford, Eden performed one of his greatest services for the Royal Shakespeare Company. He wrote to Harold Macmillan on 11 October 1962 from Fyfield Manor:

Dear Harold,
    Thank you very much for our luncheon.
    So much time did we take up on this troubled world scene, that I entirely forgot to mention to you the Stratford theatre of which I am the President. Briefly, we are in an increasingly difficult position because, though we have been unofficially informed that we would get some financial help, we do not know when this will be forthcoming nor how much it will be. The company is really doing fine work and this uncertainty is making it impossible to plan ahead. I do not ask you to do anything except to ask Reg Maudling [the Chancellor of the Exchequer] if he could please look into the business, and let us know as soon as he can what help he can properly give us.
    Yours ever,
    Anthony.[60]

Eden's letter prompted swift action from the Treasury. Not only did Macmillan find it difficult to refuse Eden, but Maudling felt he had obligations to be helpful, as one of his first jobs in the post-war Conservative Research Department had been working with Eden on his speeches on financial and domestic policy.* Accordingly, on 31 October the Arts Council of Great Britain informed Sir Fordham Flower, some two to three months in advance, that they could expect a grant of £47,000 for the coming season. 'After Lord Avon's appeal to Macmillan,' wrote Sally Beauman, historian of the Royal Shakespeare Company, 'both the Treasury and the Arts Council suddenly found their minds so wondrously concentrated that they could give Stratford the news it wanted, and in advance of normal schedules.'[61]

The Aldwych operation not only raised financial questions, but implied a change of priorities. One of Eden's correspondents believed that the concentration on modern plays at the Aldwych had contributed to Stratford's 'appalling 1963 programme'. Eden did not agree and used all his urbane diplomacy and charm:

> You certainly owe me no apology for writing as you did. I share to the full your admiration for the work of Glen Byam Shaw, who is also a close friend of mine. We are now working with a younger generation, but I must say I enjoyed the production of 'A Midsummer Night's Dream' [a revival of Hall's 1960 Stratford production] at the Aldwych very much. I have not yet seen 'Henry VI' or 'Edward IV' [part of the celebrated Wars of the Roses cycle], but by all accounts they must be remarkable . . . Personally, I too have high hopes for 1964.[62]

In fact, 1964 was to be an even trickier year, with the so-called 'dirty plays' controversy, which ended with one Governor in litigation against the BBC. Towards the end of the London season, which had examined the fashionable concept of 'The Theatre of Cruelty', a group of City Governors, led by Sir Denys Lowson, wrote to Eden, 'alarmed at the choice of plays (far away from Stratford standards)'.[63] This was a thinly veiled reference to Peter Brook's production of Peter Weiss' play, the Marat/Sade,[64] a re-creation of the Marquis de Sade's direction of the murder of Jean Paul Marat by Charlotte Corday in the bathhouse of the Charenton asylum during the French Revolution. One lengthy diatribe from a long-standing Stratford patron ended: 'Fortunately – for the country – I don't think many people from the provinces saw it – the people who thronged

---

*A sign of the admiring friendship between the two men was that when Eden published a volume of speeches in 1947 he entitled it Freedom and Order, the theme of Maudling's first political article for The Spectator in 1943. Reginald Maudling, Memoirs, Sidgwick & Jackson, 1978, pp. 43–4.

the booking office must have been the dark-garbed seekers after sensation, ready to wallow in perversion.'[65]

Eden's reply gives an insight into how he approached his job and into his willingness to explore, before condemning, works that may at the time have been ahead of the public mood: 'I have not seen nor as yet read the "Marat" though I expect to read it in the course of the next few days. I shall, of course, carefully consider what you have written to me as the outcome of your own experience and of your exceptional knowledge of the theatre.'[66]

The 'dirty plays' brought Eden the heaviest postbag of his eight-year Presidency. By the time of Peter Brook's 1966 production of a play on the Vietnam War, US, Eden, who had considerable sympathies with President Johnson over the legacy he had been bequeathed by former President John F. Kennedy in Indo-China, was glad that he was not in the metaphorical firing line. US, which opened in the autumn of 1966, shortly after Eden had stepped down as President, again provoked fierce controversy, this time clearly in his field of expertise. Peter Hall had recognised this when he had written on 17 August 1966: 'Whatever happens, the show will not open before the middle of October, so I don't think there is any possibility of your finding it a source of embarrassment to you.'[67]

In fact, Eden had increasingly regretted the 'politicisation' of the Royal Shakespeare Theatre's work. Fashions move on and he was no longer in tune with the Zeitgeist. 'I am sure that the Executive Council is right to determine to cut our coat according to our cloth,' he wrote in a routine 'financial' letter to Sir Fordham Flower on 4 August 1965, at a time when cutbacks meant the loss of productions, including one of a Bertolt Brecht play. Then he added, 'Do not worry about the Brecht, the thought of it only made me gloomy for it seems to be such dreary left wing propaganda, and now I see we are to have a play about the General Strike.'[68]

Eventually, ill health – and work on his final book, *Another World* – restricted his appearances at Stratford. But Eden always retained a special affection for the small Warwickshire town he had known from early manhood, as well as for the great Englishman whose distinctive genius it celebrated, and his long involvement in its affairs was much more than a dutiful interlude.

A decade after VE Day, the self-confidence of the nation was at a low ebb, and Eden seemed an exemplar of the old guard whose time had passed. Nevertheless, many honours came his way in retirement. He had honorary degrees from thirteen universities, in addition to the honorary Studentship (Fellowship) to which he had been elected at Christ Church in 1941, a happy conclusion to the 'battels controversy'. His portrait by Sir William

Coldstream was hung in Christ Church Hall alongside that of Edward Halifax.*

His main university involvement, however, came at Birmingham, where he had been Chancellor since 1945 (he was to hold the post until 1973), but now Eden was able to fulfil an unusually large number of activities on the university's behalf. In acknowledgement of this link, his extensive private archive now resides in the Avon Room (formally opened by Sir Edward Heath) at the University Library. With an irony he would have appreciated, the voluminous Chamberlain papers of Joseph, Austen and Neville rest cheek-by-jowl in the neighbouring room.[69]

Eden was an honorary bencher of the Middle Temple (1952); an honorary member of the Salters' Company (1946) and of the Fishmongers' Company (1955); an elder of Trinity House (1953); an honorary Fellow of the Royal Institute of British Architects (1955); an honorary Colonel of the Queen's Westminster King's Royal Rifle Corps (1952–60), and of the Queen's Royal Rifles (1960–2). To all of these duties, especially the last two, he was now able to devote time and energy.

Correspondence also occupied much of Eden's time, and letters to and from the great men of the world crossed the thresholds of Fyfield and Alvediston.[70] 'I observe that the Americans are now offering to release some of his money to Nasser,' he wrote to Churchill on 29 April 1958. 'I suppose this is intended to make him feel good towards the West when he flies to Moscow. I am sure that it will have just the opposite effect & make him more attractive to Moscow.'[71]

To Guy Mollet in Paris, he wrote that same spring, 'Many suppose that Nasser's next victim will be Jordan. I am not so sure. In any event I do not believe that his immediate objective is Israel. The scalded cat fears the fire. I think it more likely that he has his eye on King Saud [of Saudi Arabia] and his oil. The Yemen is a useful precedent for including a crowned head in his orbit.'[72]

With the next General Election in mind, Eden asked Harold Macmillan briskly, 'How can one talk of a property-owning democracy and a seven per cent bank rate?'[73] Eden was unduly pessimistic about the Conservatives' prospects in 1959, writing to Patrick Buchan-Hepburn, now Lord Hailes, 'I fear that the General Election is not going very well here [in Wiltshire]. We do not seem to have a theme like "property-owning democracy" last time. There is much complacency over past record & too little about what we can do for the future.' Eden was proved wrong. The Conservatives won 49.4 per cent of the vote (only slightly less than they had achieved under Eden's leadership in 1955) and an overall majority of

---

*Though both were covered up during the shooting of scenes for the first *Harry Potter* film (2001).

100. 'A most encouraging factor was the increased majority of the Suez protagonists,' Eden wrote to Hailes after the Election, '& the strength of those areas where big profit sharing schemes were at work, e.g., Cleveland, Rugby & my own constituency. I wish we could do something to encourage those ideas. They have not been prominent since I went.'[74]

Although Eden was relieved that the Conservatives had won the 1959 General Election (he shed no crocodile tears over Gaitskell's greatest disappointment in public life), privately he feared that Macmillan was now in such a strong position that there would be nobody to keep him in check. Writing to Alan Lennox-Boyd after the election, in a phrase of almost Butlerite ambiguity, he said that 'to take the short and easy way seems the national failing of the day in too many external problems.'[75]

He was dismayed at the news that autumn that Randolph Churchill had been appointed to write the official life of Sir Winston Churchill and determined to make none of his papers available to him, which he would have done had the appointee been someone like Sir John Wheeler-Bennett, whom he now asked to undertake the task of writing his own authorised life.[76]

With America caught up in the throes of its quadrennial Presidential Election, Eden's correspondence at this time is full of references to the forthcoming contest between Nixon and Kennedy. 'Ike has indeed been a disastrous President, poor creature,' he wrote to Salisbury in May, and after the television debate between Nixon and Kennedy in October, he asked, 'I wonder whether you saw Kennedy & Nixon debate Foreign Affairs – I thought the experience profoundly depressing. Not one of them mentioned the word "ally" from first to last, neither seemed conscious that the US has any.'[77]

In May 1961, Eden came to terms with the fact that he would never return to the House of Commons. A recent speaking tour of Yorkshire had debilitated him for some days. 'At the time of my resignation,' he wrote to Macmillan on 29 May 1961, 'Her Majesty kindly suggested that, though I might not feel able to take an Earldom then, she hoped I would feel differently later.'[78] To his request, Macmillan replied that he would be happy to recommend Eden for a Viscountcy. Whether this was a genuine mistake, or a none too subtle rebuff, was never clear, but the wires were uncrossed, and Eden received his Earldom, as was then customary for former Prime Ministers.*

---

*Of the twentieth-century Prime Ministers, Balfour, Asquith, Lloyd George, Baldwin and Attlee all received Earldoms, but Macmillan, who took the title of Earl of Stockton on his ninetieth birthday in 1984, was the last former Premier to receive such a hereditary title. Alec Home, by contrast, had to give up an earldom to become Prime Minister.

Clarissa Eden had foreseen this step for some time. 'I am delighted you think Anthony should be an Earl,' she wrote to Beaverbrook in May 1961. 'He feels it will be the irrevocable step – because he always thinks in the back of his mind that the miracle will happen and he will be able to go back to politics – which, of course, he won't.'[79]

On 26 July, the fifth anniversary of Nasser's nationalisation of the Suez Canal, Eden took his seat in the House of Lords as the first Earl of Avon. On his elevation he pressed for a debate on NATO. He was not interested in an Earldom *per se*, but he did want to be able to speak in the House of Lords.

As Eden and his team began work on *Facing the Dictators*, he was very concerned to hear that Iain Macleod, Chairman of the Conservative Party and Leader of the House of Commons since October 1961, was planning to write a full-scale defence of Neville Chamberlain and Munich in a forthcoming biography. It was not the defence that worried him. Eden rather looked forward to countering any arguments in *Facing the Dictators*. 'A few days ago I received from Macleod a draft copy of his life of Chamberlain,' he wrote on 17 August. 'I have not read it in detail but it is clearly one hundred per cent defence of Munich and appeasement. This will make our book much more important than it might otherwise have seemed.'[80]

What concerned Eden more was the possibility that the book might in some circles be seen as an 'official' party publication by a serving Cabinet Minister with privileged access to Government records. He planned to use *Facing the Dictators* partly as a riposte to Macleod's book. 'I shall do my best to defend our position against all comers', he wrote to Salisbury in a series of letters about Munich and appeasement, 'and I think it can be done.' In one letter he threw in the aside, 'Rab is a pretty feeble appeaser at heart', remembering Rab Butler's much circulated *bon mot* about himself, 'half-mad baronet, half beautiful woman'.[81]

On 18 October 1961, Eden met Norman Brook in the Cabinet Office to express his concerns about Macleod's project. He let Brook know how angry he was that 'this *apologia* for Chamberlain's policy should be published by a minister in office', and he returned to the question of how it would 'cause a good many people to think that the book had some sort of official authority'. With the recent building of the Berlin Wall, he felt that 'the timing of publication, in the midst of the Berlin crisis, was particularly unfortunate.'[82] To Lord Ismay he wrote, 'It is hard to think of a worse time in Europe to champion Munich.'[83] He felt Macleod was being 'too clever by half', and references to Macleod in his papers now became noticeably cool. His old friend from *Yorkshire Post* days, Arthur Mann, thought it had been a bad mistake to make Macleod Chairman of the party. 'I agree with you entirely about Macleod,' he replied frankly. 'In fact I can murmur to you that I am not at all sure about Scotsmen in the Conservative Party anywhere!'[84]

Eden had already mentioned his concern about Macleod's dual roles informally at a luncheon with Philip de Zulueta, one of his former Number 10 secretaries, now serving Macmillan in a similar capacity. Ever dutiful, de Zulueta informed Macmillan of Eden's views:

> He felt that in principle it was a mistake to have the leadership of the House combined with the Chairmanship of the Party. He understood the historical reasons for this, but felt that, particularly with an election coming up, the 2 jobs ought not to be combined as the interests were not quite the same. He felt that the Chairman of the Party should either be a good salesman (a sort of Lord Woolton) or else an orator with an inspiring personality. He said, I think as a joke, that if he got better he would willingly take this job on.[85]

On 1 September 1961, Eden wrote to Churchill about the Macleod book:

> A few days ago there arrived for me to read a copy from Macleod of his MSS. of a life of Neville Chamberlain. This is an astonishing document, being a 100% defence of Munich and appeasement. The main argument is that Chamberlain gained a year by Munich and that his critics were therefore wrong. These chapters cheerfully ignore the fact that Chamberlain believed in the word of the dictators, whereas his colleagues like Duff and myself did not, which is why we had to part. It also glosses over such statements as "Peace in our time" on the grounds that Chamberlain was over-excited after his drive from the airport. As you can imagine, I find the whole reading an exasperating exercise.[86]

Beaverbrook, who liked a book to tell a dramatic story dramatically, was even more scathing. 'Macleod has made a tremendous mess of Neville Chamberlain,' he wrote to Eden. 'He could have told a wonderful story, but he is incapable of it.'[87]

Eden was asked to review Macleod's book by the *Times Literary Supplement*. He was forthright and blunt:

> It is not perhaps a very happy time to bring out a defence of appeasement as it was practised by Mr Chamberlain, because, whatever the opinions in this country about it, Europe has condemned that kind of appeasement, and in the present international situation it is certainly not a policy the West can pursue if it intends to survive.[88]

As events unfolded in 1962 it seemed that the Macmillan government might not survive long either. Macmillan, in a desperate measure to shore up his political popularity, a manoeuvre that spectacularly rebounded, sacked Selwyn Lloyd from the Treasury, and six other Cabinet ministers, on Friday 13 July, in what became known as the Night of the Long Knives. Eden rang up Lloyd to ask 'what on earth had happened' and told Lloyd that he was due to speak to the Young Conservatives at Leamington Spa the following week. He told Lloyd that when he had resigned as Foreign Secretary in February 1938, the first thing he had done was to seek a vote of confidence from his local constituency party. Not only would the result be a foregone conclusion, but it would put Lloyd in a much stronger position for his eventual rehabilitation.

Eden thought Lloyd had been unfairly made the scapegoat for wider failings of strategy, and although it broke convention (in 1962, anyway), he decided to speak out in criticism of his successor in Number 10. His comments – 'I feel that Mr Selwyn Lloyd has been harshly treated' – received wide coverage in the weekend Press. In August, Eden invited Lloyd to Fyfield Manor, where they had a long talk. 'He was full of sympathy and listened to my account of events,' Lloyd recorded. Eden said that he had heard of Rab Butler's activities, adding, 'He does not seem to realise that the antis and the pros sometimes meet.' Eden told Lloyd he was now convinced that Butler would never succeed Macmillan as Prime Minister when the time came. Lloyd's account of the meeting ended, 'Eden said that he did not trust Macmillan and gave me one or two examples to show why, particularly at the time of Suez, Harold had gone behind his back to Winston to complain of military plans.'[89]

Eden's own references to Macmillan in his papers now became much more barbed. Memories of Macmillan's manoeuvres with Winthrop Aldrich while he was in Jamaica were not forgotten. Europe was an issue on which Eden was increasingly sensitive, as Macmillan's attempts to take Britain into the Common Market were vetoed by de Gaulle in January 1963. Eden foresaw that, as Suez faded from the foreground, attention would turn far more to Messina in 1955.

In September 1967 he wrote to Macmillan after one such attack:

> I noticed that the *Times* leader last Saturday made an onslaught upon me, mainly it seems on account of Her Majesty's Government's attitude towards the Messina negotiation. This is a nonsense, for we have no guilt that I know of in this connection. The O.E.E.C., of which you were then Chairman, did some useful work at its July [1955] meeting in Paris and you told the House towards the end of that month that the position of her Majesty's Government was completely open and you welcomed the O.E.E.C. studies for collaboration with the Brussels powers.[90]

The last year of Macmillan's Premiership, from the Cuban Missile crisis

to his own illness and resignation in October 1963, was one of unprecedented upheaval and catastrophe, internationally as well as in Britain.
Eden felt the Americans had brought the Cuban crisis on themselves by
their dilatoriness in 1956, as he explained to Beaverbrook:

> The Cuban situation will develop disastrously. The United States has
> been the prisoner of its own past. If it had given us firm support in the
> first weeks after Nasser seized the Suez Canal, he could have been called
> to order and international authority restored over the Canal. However,
> the United States would not help & Nasser was allowed to get away with
> it. This encouraged the other petty dictators – first Sukarno, then Castro.
> Now the United States has a life-size decision upon its hands. We cannot
> envy them.[91]

When Macmillan resigned in October 1963 (in oddly similar circumstances of ill health, combined with political decline, to Eden in 1957),
Eden was canvassed for his views on the succession by Lord St Aldwyn,
Government Chief Whip in the Lords, as part of the 'customary processes
of consultation' that Macmillan had established. His preferences, in order,
were for Lord Hailsham, Lord Home and Reginald Maudling.[92] Although
he admired 'Quintin for courage and robustness', he had to admit 'to some
shortcomings'. Home he admired, not least for his consistency, and for the
fact that he had never tried with hindsight to abandon his deep sense of
loyalty to Neville Chamberlain, a striking example of Eden's sense of fair
dealing. 'The third possibility is Maudling, who has brains and ability
& kept his balance amidst the Common Market euphoria last autumn –
he could make a sagacious Prime Minister.'[93] Although Eden was surprised that Home eventually 'emerged', an immediate telegram was
despatched: WARMEST CONGRATULATIONS AND EVERY GOOD WISH. WE ARE
DELIGHTED. ANTHONY AND CLARISSA.

In 1964, an American academic, Herman Finer, published *Dulles over
Suez*, a work for which Eden had provided information and help. 'I have
read the first hundred pages of Finer's book *Dulles over Suez* to which
Max [Beaverbrook] refers in the *Daily Express* today,' Eden wrote
enthusiastically to Lord Lambton. 'So far it is a brilliant and penetrating
document. Inevitably there are here and there errors about us and the
French, but the analysis of Dulles & his doings is right on the mark and I
find it quite a comfort to read a verdict of this kind from across the
Atlantic.'[94]

What pleased Eden even more was a generous letter from Eisenhower,
denying one of the points Finer had made:

> His description of one of our telephonic conversations is completely
> false, saying that I used 'less official and rougher, army-life, tongue-

579

lashing language.' I have never spoken to one of my colleagues in such terms, much less to a friend! In fact, my notes show that all of our conversations were carried on in an informal fashion and an examination of all the letters & telegrams I sent to and received from you show no trace of anything of this kind.

My notes on the November sixth conversation, while not elaborate, at least show no other conversations between us that day.

Moreover, the implication that, at any time, I tried to lay down an ultimatum to my British friends is simply ridiculous.'[95]

Not for nothing had Eden once observed, 'Modern communications corrupt good manners.'[96]

As the 1964 General Election approached, Eden wrote to Alec Home, 'A property-owning-democracy is the aim.'[97] Although the contest was lost by four seats, the overall proportion of the vote (43.4 per cent), boosted by the weak showing of the minor parties, was greater than that achieved later by Margaret Thatcher and Tony Blair in their respective landslide victories.

The year of 1965 marked a break with the past, with the death of Churchill on 24 January, the seventieth anniversary of the death of his father, Lord Randolph Churchill. The Edens were at Villa Nova when Churchill had his stroke, and came back to London some days before he died. They called at Hyde Park Gate, where Eden went into the bedroom to see his former chief for the last time.

'Sir Winston's service was to mankind,' Eden said in his tribute in the House of Lords, 'and for this his place will always be among the few immortals.' He proposed a 'Churchill Day', to mark the achievements of 'the greatest of all Parliamentarians whom we shall know.'[98]

Eden was asked by the Earl Marshal, the Duke of Norfolk, to be one of the pall-bearers at the state funeral at St Paul's Cathedral. It was a bitter January day. On the windswept steps of the cathedral (next to a seated, frail Attlee) Eden looked haggard and gaunt. 'My chief memory is of the pall-bearers, in particular poor Anthony Eden, literally ashen grey, looking as old as Clement Attlee', Richard Crossman wrote in his diary. 'It felt like the end of an epoch, possibly even the end of a nation.'[99]

The next week, Eden wrote with gratitude to Clementine Churchill, 'For me there is the indelible memory of the many thousand acts of kindness I have received from him and from you and of what our friendship has meant, culminating in Clarissa's love which has transformed for me these last years of failing health.'[100] In the face of death, all the frustrations of the past were forgotten.

Not all Churchill's comments on Eden, however, were to be forgotten.

Lord Moran's controversial book on Churchill, *Winston Churchill: The Struggle for Survival 1940–1965*, contained many disparaging references to Eden. When Robert Blake, who had helped Moran at an early stage, saw the proofs, his enthusiasm for the book cooled and he asked not to be acknowledged in its preface, an example of the loyalty that Eden inspired in so many who worked for him.[101] As a result Moran removed some of the offending passages from the published version.[102]

One of the notable absentees from Churchill's funeral was the American President, Lyndon B. Johnson – some said because of the long memories of Churchill failing to attend Roosevelt's funeral in April 1945. Eden never felt this to be the case. He had only too vivid memories of the pressures of the last month of the European war. Also, in the very week of Churchill's death, Johnson had been inaugurated for the first time as an elected President. The tragic embroilment of American troops in the Vietnam War also stirred Eden's feelings. Had Geneva 1954 really come to this?

> I feel much sympathy for Johnson over Vietnam [he wrote on 10 June 1965 to an American commentator]. As you know, I think that mistakes were made in that part of the world in the period '54 to '57, but that had nothing to do with Johnson, who has inherited a sorry mess. It seems to me that he is pursuing the only possible course and that the critics, as so often happens, will not face up to the alternatives. For you to abandon your position in Vietnam after all that has happened, would undermine, and perhaps destroy, either spontaneous or planned resistance to communism throughout South East Asia. Thailand would be hard pressed, and Malaya is beset already. Nor are the poor Indians tough; Nehru was forever talking optimistically of the Chinese Communists, and they rewarded him by taking Tibet and nibbling at India. Without the knowledge of American and allied presence in support, India could do little & if the United States were to abandon Vietnam, who could believe that such support would be forthcoming. Reluctantly, therefore, as it seems to me, the United States has now no choice, whatever the alternatives may have been ten or eleven years ago, but to continue to defend South Vietnam. Admittedly this is only the lesser of two evils but, as you know, so it often has to be in foreign affairs.[103]

Alec Home had been succeeded as Conservative leader in July 1965 by Edward Heath. Over the next decade, Eden was consistently supportive of, and encouraging towards, his former Chief Whip. 'I thought that you fought a very gallant fight,' he wrote after the Conservative defeat in the March 1966 Election, 'but Wilson's lead, based on the propaganda which he had directed for so long, could not be overtaken.'[104]

In the closing stages of the 1970 campaign, many again wrote off the chances of the Conservatives. Enoch Powell, who had been sacked from the Shadow Cabinet after his controversial speech in April 1968 about immigration and 'the river Tiber foaming with much blood', issued his own manifesto and made a series of speeches about 'a hidden enemy within' and the dangers facing Britain. Powell, who owed his first Government post to Eden, blew hot and cold about his former leader. In his 1959 Election address he praised Eden, 'whom I believe the nation will remember with gratitude in years to come, as a gallant and upright Englishman who served them well'. Later and less charitably, he said that Eden was merely 'an arrangement of coloured lights'.[105]

'Enoch has done us no good,' Eden wrote two days before polling. 'There is always some sense in what he says but it is salted with too much extravagance. I still find it impossible to believe that Labour will win with a large margin and if it is small it could be better that they should have it than we.'[106]

Heath's victory on 18 June, against all the odds, took Eden by surprise, but when the result was known he sent a telegram to Number 10: WARMEST CONGRATULATIONS ON A SUPERB VICTORY AND A PERSONAL TRIUMPH.[107]

What pleased Eden most about the new Government was the promotion of Robert Carr, his trusted former private secretary, to the Cabinet. 'Heath will have a difficult time,' Eden wrote to Dean Acheson, 'but he has gathered what should prove a competent young team around him. Robert Carr, who is Minister of Labour, has the hardest task in a Conservative administration ... He has first hand knowledge of industry from the factory floor so that if anybody can make sense of our sadly tangled industrial relations he should be able to do so.'[108]

Eden's seventieth birthday in June 1967 had coincided with the Israeli victory over Egypt in the Six Day War. 'There was quite an extraordinary atmosphere of joy and celebration in the pretty Georgian house at Alvediston that Clarissa and Anthony have recently bought,' Cecil Beaton wrote in his diary. 'Despite his plastic duct and continuous fever, Anthony had reached seventy. It was his birthday and the events of last week were a wonderful present. They have meant that, in principle, Anthony's much criticised policy on Suez, and his distrust of Nasser, were correct.'[109]

It was not only Beaton who acknowledged this. Eden heard a poignant tale from General Heaton in America – 'I was Head of the Walter Reid Hospital when Dulles died there [in 1959] – indeed he died in my arms and one of the last things he said to me was that he reckoned that he had been wrong over Suez.'[110]

Eden rarely let the opportunity pass in letters to his friends to draw comparisons with the events of 1956. In October 1968, he wrote to Guy Mollet:

> The developments in the Mediterranean and in the Red Sea are unhappily very much as you and I had anticipated 12 years ago. It is a strange irony that the country which is now most eager for the Suez Canal to be opened, Russia, is the one which opposed most strongly our measures to keep the Canal international. If we had succeeded it would still be open and many other matters in the world would be in much better shape.[111]

Writing to Salisbury, he described Richard Nixon, in the week of his inauguration as America's thirty-seventh President, as 'a horse out of Foster's stable'.[112]

Other events brought forth comparison with the 1930s. The Russian invasion of Czechoslovakia in 1968 and the putting down of the so-called 'Prague Spring' was a case in point. Eden did not attend the Lords often, but in this case he made special arrangements to come to London to speak in the debate. On earlier occasions, like many senior politicians accustomed to the reassuring prop of the Commons despatch box, he had found it difficult to adjust to the back-benches of the Upper House, where no such support was available. For the debate on Czechoslovakia in the House of Lords on 26 August 1968, the Shadow Leader of the House, Lord Carrington, had made arrangements, exceptionally, for Eden to speak from the front bench, even though he was not a member of the Shadow Cabinet.

In opening the debate, Lord Shackleton, the Lord Privy Seal and Leader of the House of Lords, said, 'We particularly welcome the noble Earl, the Lord Avon, to whom this must be a sad occasion with a historical repetitive quality about it.' Eden rose at 4 p.m. to make his speech. Tracing the historical parallels, he paused to refer to the death – 'as I shall always believe the murder' – of Masaryk. His speech was a notable *tour d'horizon*, vividly remembered by some of the younger peers new to the House, not least for the old assurance that returned as Eden spoke, turning first one way, then another, bringing in his whole audience. Many old passions were aroused in the course of the debate. At one stage Eden, flushed and angry, intervened to correct Lord Boothby, who had said:

> At Yalta it looked – it was not intended but it looked – as if sovereign nations were handed round like plums: as if, over the caviar, vodka and cigars they said, "All right, old boy, you can have Bulgaria and Romania so long as you give us Greece."

Eden rose to say, 'There really is not a word of truth in that statement.'[113] The 1968 speech on Czechoslovakia was one of the most substantial of his retirement, like a latter day Cincinnatus returning to public notice.*

Eden took to the rural life, and in his Wiltshire valley became a skilled breeder of Hereford bulls, one, 'Avon Priam', winning first prize at the Royal Highland Show. As he had an 'eye' for a 'good' painting, so he had an intuition at market about the best animals. When ill health forced the dispersal of the herd, Richard Lamb, a neighbouring farmer whom Eden had promoted in 1950 as Conservative candidate for Stockton-on-Tees, bought up much of the stock.[114]

'The sale of the pedigree Hereford herd went better than I had dared hope,' Eden wrote to Sir Roy Welensky. 'Eighty-seven lots fetched over £17,000, which was 50% above the auctioneer's estimate. That will help my farm overdraft, but I will miss the herd very much.' As so often in his letters to Welensky, he then added a political footnote. 'It remains to be seen what difference, if any, Nasser's death will make to the Russian hold upon Egypt. I fear that by now their talons will be deeply dug in, but they have not much experience in handling client states, except by ruling them on the model of the poor Czechs.' Welensky told Eden a story he had heard about Nasser:

> I believe that the end of the British Empire was really signalled by that miserable old Persian Mussadeq, when he thumbed his nose at the British over the oil refinery at Abadan. A friend of mine who spoke to Nasser said that Nasser said to him: 'You British from that moment no longer retained any respect. If Mussadeq could do that to you, why couldn't the rest of us?' and how right he proved.[115]

Apart from ill health, Eden made sure his retirement was fulfilling and varied, a fine example of a man seizing the day. In this context he was delighted when Selwyn Lloyd was elected Speaker of the House of Commons in 1971, not least because he saw it as tacit acceptance by Lloyd's contemporaries that his disingenuousness about collusion had not been held against him or, by implication, against Eden himself.

Even the restrictions of illness in Eden's retirement were accommodated by established routines, and Clarissa's unfailing attentions. Sometimes her intuitive understanding of Anthony's needs at any given moment surprised visitors, as Ann Fleming recorded. 'She is a devoted wife but ministers

---

*Richard Crossman had drawn this parallel the year before, describing one of the speeches of the avuncular James Callaghan as putting party aside. 'He gave an informal chat followed by a kind of appeal from a retiring Cincinnatus. It was a deliberate consensus speech, modelled very much on the style of Anthony Eden.' Richard Crossman diary. Anthony Howard (ed.), *The Crossman Diaries*, Magnum paperback condensed version, 1979, p.414.

roughly, when she thinks his feet should be up she violently kicks foot-stools towards him – it must be a habit to which he is accustomed for he fields them neatly, if he did not the gesture might defeat the object and inflict a serious injury on him or the guests.'[116] In 1974 there was an unfortunate episode when the doctors in Boston saw a shadow on one lung, and immediately operated, removing three ribs. There was nothing there and everyone was very rueful.

As he grew weaker, Eden was never able to deal adequately with the last great controversy of his life, caused by the publication in 1974 of Lord Bethell's book *The Last Secret: Forcible Repatriation to Russia, 1944–47*. Although David Carlton has written that 'there were of course lines of defence open to him',[117] Eden confined himself to the following private letter to Harold Caccia:

> In 1944/45 there were some difficult negotiations about prisoners. My chief concern was to get our men back from the camps in East Prussia and elsewhere as the Russian armies advanced. I raised this with Stalin in Moscow in 1944, he having spoken to me about Soviet 'volunteers' whom we had captured with the German army in France and now held in England . . . Our chief concern of course was to get our own prisoners back of which the greater part were probably in territories which the Russians had entered.[118]

Old age inevitably brought its partings. Bobbety Salisbury died on 23 February 1972 and Eden represented the Queen at his funeral at Hatfield. Emperor Haile Selassie of Ethiopia, deposed by a military uprising in 1974, died in captivity on 27 August 1975. Eden, who is commemorated to this day by a street named after him in Addis Ababa, composed a memorial tribute that was read by his nephew, Sir John Eden, at St George's Chapel, Windsor, on 14 October, as he was too ill to attend the service himself. 'From the hour of the invasion of his country to the hour of his death in captivity to his own people in 1975,' Eden wrote, 'his behaviour was unfailingly brave, calm, and dignified', words that are an apt description of Eden himself in the evening of his life.[119]

In the summer of 1976, Eden had a last meeting with Mountbatten at the time of the Garter Ceremony at Windsor. As was his custom, Eden was staying at Eton College with Harold Caccia, who had been Provost there since 1965. In January an article had appeared in the *Sunday Times* magazine. It was by Robert Lacey, who was preparing a book on the Queen to coincide with the Silver Jubilee in 1977.[120] In this article Lacey gave the impression that the Queen had disapproved of the Suez operation, but was unable to influence events because of her constitutional position.

The implication was that all would be revealed in the forthcoming book.

Robert Lacey had contacted Eden during his research and, despite the fact that he was not well, Eden had seen him and also answered various points by letter. The *Sunday Times* article led to a further correspondence. 'I must say to you categorically that the Queen never protested strongly or otherwise to me about Suez', Eden wrote on 22 March, 'nor did she ever indicate to me anger or humiliation. On the contrary.'[121] Lacey replied that he had been given the information by two persons very close to the Queen. Eden believed these to be the Duke of Edinburgh and Lord Mountbatten. He was determined to find out and scotch inaccuracies before they were published and became accepted as gospel. In this, he was concerned not only with his own reputation, but also with his wish to protect the Queen from charges that she had become involved in the political arena, irrespective of her opinions.

Eden, who knew the Queen's views, never made them public, as he felt this would be a breach of confidence between the Prime Minister and his sovereign. He did not see why somebody else should now go into print, especially if he had relied on the views of Mountbatten, who, in Eden's opinion, was 'ga-ga' and 'a congenital liar.'[122]*

At Eden's request, Mountbatten came down on 13 June from Windsor Castle, where he was staying, to see him at the Provost's Lodge. The appointment was fixed for 5 p.m., but Mountbatten was late, as his diary records:

> I lost my way going to the Provost's Lodge at Eton College and only arrived at 1715. Clarissa Avon and Lady Caccia were in the garden waiting for me and took me up to see Anthony in his bed upstairs. He looked very ill and rather sad.

As time was short, the substantive business of the meeting then began. Mountbatten's diary for the day says:

> He had particularly asked to see me to complain about a statement in an article in the *Sunday Times* magazine in which the author, a man called Lacey, had made a statement implying that people close to the Queen knew how much she disapproved of the combined operations against the Egyptians but that there was no constitutional means of her stopping it. He then showed me a letter from Lacey saying he had got this information from two very intimate friends of the Royal Family who were in a position to know. He assumed one might have been Philip but I pointed out he had been in the Antar[c]tic at the time; and the other might be me. I didn't attempt to deny it; I said that I had been asked

---

*Indeed, Eden had earlier refused to take part in the television series on Mountbatten's career because of the untruths the script required him to utter. Private information.

officially by Martin Charteris to see this man to help him and had answered all his questions. It was the author himself who had put the question, and I thought I had answered it sufficiently tactfully not to produce the particular statement that had appeared. I was sorry about this.

Anthony then told me that if, in fact, this statement was repeated in the book which he understood Lacey was writing he would have to take official action on this, and he hoped therefore that it would not appear in the book. I promised to talk to Martin Charteris and felt I could assure him that Martin could stop anything being put in the book that Anthony strongly objected to.[123]

The matter did not end there. An extended four-way correspondence then developed, involving Eden, Selwyn Lloyd, Home and Sir Martin Charteris, the Queen's private secretary, who acted as a go-between and arbiter.* 'On each of the situations in which I myself was concerned,' Selwyn Lloyd wrote bluntly to Lacey on 31 August 1976, 'you are inaccurate in detail according to my recollection.'[124]

Alec Home also corrected many points on political matters and country life on the royal estates. 'I enclose a copy of my latest exchange with Mr. Lacey,' he wrote to Martin Charteris on 2 September 1976, 'I somehow don't think I should like to be next to him on the moors!'[125] Although Eden did not survive to read Lacey's book, *Majesty*, the controversy was an unwelcome intrusion in the last months of his life. In his extensive correspondence with Sir Martin Charteris, he returned time and again to 'this tiresome business'. One of the last letters he ever wrote was to Charteris about Lacey's revised typescript. 'Lacey has not accepted the corrections of fact to which I had drawn his attention,' he commented with resignation.[126]

The importance of the Lacey book lay in its pioneering examination, with quasi-official blessing, of the role of the contemporary monarchy. The downside was the author's unwillingness to accept factual corrections from Eden, Selwyn Lloyd and others.† The former sycophancies, though not entirely ended by *Majesty*, were now seen as clearly belonging to an earlier, more deferential age. This new approach was totally alien to figures of Eden's generation, one of whose few revelations about the monarchy (and then in the privacy of his diary) was to comment that Queen Mary's experience and common sense would have well qualified her to be Foreign

---

*One of the aspects common to the Eden, Home and Lloyd papers is the section in all three collections devoted to correspondence with, and about, Lacey, often including copies of material in the other ones. The tone of the responses is by turns suspicious, outraged and wryly amused.
†I am grateful to Mr Robert Lacey for speaking to me about these matters.

Secretary. The idea that he should say whether the Queen was 'for' or 'against' Suez was inconceivable, and his comments to Lacey were impeccably constitutional, stating that the Queen did not disapprove of the operation, while not claiming that she was pro-Suez.[127]

Majesty left a clear impression of the Queen's lack of sympathy for Eden's policies. In the subsequent welter of books on the monarchy, two in the Lacey mould, published in 1996, are of particular note, also examining the monarchy through well-researched analysis, tacitly assisted by the Palace. *Elizabeth* by Sarah Bradford and *The Queen* by Ben Pimlott. But two decades after the Silver Jubilee the ground rules had changed. Sarah Bradford specifically quotes a close friend of the Queen as saying that her private view of the Suez operation was that it was 'idiotic'.[128] Ben Pimlott goes further, naming Lord Charteris (as Sir Martin Charteris had then become), as his source for Mountbatten telling the Queen that 'they are being absolutely lunatic', and his (Charteris's) own opinion that 'the Queen believed Eden was mad'.[129]

The net effect of Lacey, Bradford and Pimlott was thus conclusive to the interested general reader. The Queen was against Suez, even vehemently so, yet was unable constitutionally to do anything about it. Once established in the public psyche, such a story soon becomes an accepted truth.[130]

Sarah Bradford does not cite her source for the 'idiotic' comment, but two of the key authorities for Lacey and Pimlott (Mountbatten and Charteris) were not impartial witnesses, both being violently opposed to the Suez operation, at the time and subsequently. Both also shared a tendency to hyperbole. When Lord Charteris was interviewed by the *Spectator* magazine in 1994, he was quoted as saying that the Duchess of York, one of the Queen's daughters-in-law, was 'vulgar, vulgar, vulgar'. Subsequent comment in the Press suggested that the Palace felt he had, in old age, become something of a loose cannon himself. Reticence was never part of the Mountbatten character either, and in addition he had a love of intrigue. Gerald Templer once said to him, 'Dickie, you're so crooked that if you swallowed a nail you'd shit a corkscrew',[131] an insult that appealed to Mounbatten so much that he often repeated it as his own *bon mot*, substituting other names for his own as the occasion merited. When Suez came under the historical spotlight, both Mountbatten and Charteris – now old men – were keen to put down markers, establishing their position clearly on the 'right' side of the barricades.

When Eden had been in Jamaica during the latter part of the Suez crisis, the Cabinet Secretary Norman Brook had deliberately kept back some of the technical details of what was unfolding, lest Eden be tempted to intervene from afar. Now he gave Eden much comfort over the Lacey controversy by new insights he had himself privately acquired from contacts at the highest level.[132] Another acute observer of the political and social scene had already recorded his impressions of attitudes to Suez. 'Have a talk with Martin Charteris,' Harold Nicolson wrote on 13 November 1956 in a previously unpublished section of his diary. 'He thinks the Eden policy disastrous but confesses that "the Palace" thinks it wonderful.'[133]

'Idiotic', 'mad' and 'wonderful' are not epithets that ring true, if they reflect the considered response of an experienced and informed witness to a situation of ambiguity and great intricacy. When Eden was approached by Lacey for his version in early 1976, the whole tradition from which he sprang precluded him from making public the details of what had actually transpired between the monarch and himself at their Tuesday audiences, which during Suez were more extended than normal.

Until the records of the present Queen's reign are opened for the official biographer after her lifetime, the precise details of what she thought of Suez will remain largely a matter of speculation, and in a constitutional monarchy it is right that this should be the case. Even then, judging by the precedent of earlier reigns, it is unlikely that any hint of disagreement with her Prime Ministers would appear in the papers, for no minutes are taken of the Prime Minister's weekly audiences, which serve a therapeutic function on both sides. Prime Ministers can use these sessions to tell the monarch their concerns, and they would not do so if they knew that these concerns would eventually be available publicly. As a result, the version that has largely been accepted since the time of the Silver Jubilee is by no means the final word.

Eden's record might have had particular appeal to the Palace – his outstanding war service, his courage in the 1930s, the support and aid he gave Churchill during the war, and his considerable negotiating skills, particularly at the beginning of the Queen's reign, even the shared interest in painting. It is significant that the Queen and the Duke of Edinburgh subsequently accepted Eden's private hospitality, and kept in touch with him, and later with his widow. On the day of Eden's death, the Queen wrote privately to Clarissa, 'He will be remembered in history above all as an outstanding diplomat and as a man of courage and integrity.'[134] Even allowing for the courtesies attending bereavements, the chosen words are very revealing.

Eden spent much of his last three winters at Hobe Sound in Florida, where he and his wife were always welcome guests of the Averill Harrimans. By 1976 he was getting progressively weaker.'Ill health is gradually robbing him of his zest for life,' Clarissa wrote to Mrs Thatcher.[135]

There was to be one last visit to the Harrimans, where there would be sunshine and companionship. Although Eden and Averill Harriman had never been friends during their public careers, they were now two of the few who were left to talk of the old times, and this was of comfort and great interest for Eden.

It became clear that Eden had not long to live, after a Boston doctor came down and X-rays showed cancer of the liver. Alerted by Winston Churchill (Sir Winston's grandson and MP for Stretford), the Prime Minister, James Callaghan, made immediate arrangements for an RAF plane, which was bringing home personnel from the Washington Embassy, to be diverted to Miami to pick up Eden and bring him home to England, where he had expressed the wish to be at the end. Although some churlish spirits, not knowing the plane was going anyway, questioned both the expense and the necessity of help, Callaghan was in absolutely no doubt that it was the correct thing. It was the least his country could do.[136] Eden was flown back to England on 9 January 1977, the twentieth anniversary of his resignation as Prime Minister.

A statement was issued to the Press Association on 10 January. It said simply, 'Lord Avon's doctor has seen him this evening. There is no material change in his condition, which remains serious. No further bulletin will be issued unless there is a change.'[137]

After the RAF jet had landed at Lyneham, a police-escorted ambulance took the Edens back to Alvediston. A vast stack of letters awaited, from friends and colleagues, but also from members of the public. Many came from the North Country. All of them were answered by his wife.

Anthony Eden, 1st Earl of Avon, died, 'as he lived, with great dignity and courage',[138] just after 11 a.m. on 14 January 1977. Clarissa and his surviving son, Nicholas, were at his side. The first caller at Alvediston was his nephew, Sir John Eden, who arrived at 1 p.m. After spending some time with Clarissa and Nicholas, he spoke briefly to reporters at the gates of Alvediston Manor as he left. 'Lord Avon,' he said, 'was a man who had tremendous understanding, not just of international relations, but of human relationships. I think it is the latter aspect which particularly endeared him to people throughout this country and elsewhere.'[139]

Letters poured into Alvediston from all over the world, and from all sides of the political spectrum. Herbert Morrison's widow, actually a fervent Tory who thought Herbert had rather let the side down, wrote, 'You were both so kind to Herbert and myself at all times.'[140] One surprise was the existence of so many eponymous societies, previously unknown to the family, such as the Anthony Eden Women's Luncheon Club, Hall Green, Birmingham. William Strang, whose knowledge of Eden at the Foreign Office went back to pre-war League of Nations days, nevertheless stressed the primacy of Eden's role during the Second World War:

> In recollection, my mind returns again and again to the war years and to his unique relationship with the Prime Minister. As he said, they worked hand in hand. Herbert Morrison said that they were like father and son. The Prime Minister told him in 1940, 'we shall win this war together'. And so it was. Of course, they had differences, often because the Prime Minister had to have a care for his relationship with the President. And of course they fought. But in essentials they were at one. Their differences were argued out in the open, and again and again Anthony was able to curb the Prime Minister's waywardness and keep things on the right lines. This process was of inestimable value to us in the War.[141]

'You have been simply wonderful in looking after him during so many years when his health was so often bad,' wrote Rab Butler to Clarissa. 'When I spoke to Horace Evans in the drawing room of No 10 he said that the length of Anthony's life would depend largely on personal care and it was your care that brought him to a ripe age.'[142]

Many Conservatives with left-of-centre views on domestic policies – Rab Butler and Iain Macleod, for instance – are often accorded almost iconic status, especially by non-Conservatives. This never happened to Eden, who was associated more with foreign affairs, yet the thrust and drive of his Skeltonian vision was the equal of any in the post-war period of consensual reconstruction.

Harold Macmillan was one of many who predicted that history would be kind in the longer perspective. 'I hope you were pleased with what has been published. On the whole I thought most of the papers wrote intelligently as well as sympathetically,' he wrote to Eden's widow on 24 January. 'Anthony's reputation, of course, unlike that of many politicians will continue to grow as the years pass. Apart from his dedication to the public interests, his very remarkable grasp of the inherent problems that faced our country both before and since the war is indeed becoming apparent to those who had been his critics.'[143] Clarissa replied, 'Of the tributes I thought Ted [Heath] perceptive when he said that Anthony liked the people & the people liked him. He fought his last illness with doggedness & optimism – & we neither of us perhaps faced the fact that he was failing so fast.'[144]

In October 1968 Eden with his wife had chosen the site for his burial in the churchyard of St Mary's Church, Alvediston. 'It is 6 yards west of the nut tree that stands near the gate at the Eastern entrance to the graveyard.'[145] Like Edmund Burke, he preferred to sleep in the corner of a little country churchyard, rather than in the tomb of the Capulets.[146] There he was laid to rest in a quiet family service, conducted by the Vicar of Alvediston, the Revd John Williams, and the former Bishop of Sherborne, the Right Revd Victor Pike, on 17 January. Reynolds Stone, who had engraved the memorial stone for Winston Churchill in Westminster Abbey, executed the lettering ANTHONY EDEN EARL OF AVON 1897–1977 on the top of the gravestone, and round its four sides the outlines of his career:

MEMBER OF PARLIAMENT 1923–1957

SECRETARY OF STATE FOR FOREIGN AFFAIRS
1935–38   1940–45   1951–55

PRIME MINISTER 1955–57

KNIGHT OF THE GARTER   HOLDER OF THE MILITARY CROSS

In 1985 the ashes of Nicholas Avon were buried beside his father. Nicholas died in August that year, one of the early victims of AIDS, just as he was becoming established in his career as a minister in the Thatcher Government. The earldom became extinct.

The reaction of the Conservative Party did not reflect well on a certain homophobic tendency in its ranks. The Conservative 'house' newspaper, *Newsline*, failed to publish an obituary of Nicholas Avon, and he was airbrushed from party history, until *The Times* published an article (5 November 1985), 'Drawing the Line', on the mean-mindedness of his posthumous treatment. The Queen and the Queen Mother were represented at his memorial service at St Margaret's, Westminster, on 13 November 1985, when William Whitelaw, Lord President of the Council, read the lesson. Ironically, Whitelaw was one of those who had inadvertently spread the news of the nature of Nicholas Avon's fatal illness when he told a fellow MP in the House of Commons tea-room *sotto voce*. Unfortunately, Whitelaw's idea of a stage whisper never found favour with the Noise Abatement Society, and the news was round the green-eyed jungle of Westminster within hours, although many of those close to Nicholas Avon had already heard the facts from his colleague, Lord Trefgarne, who had visited him in hospital.

'He was a very private person, and extremely difficult to know,' wrote Sir Peter Hordern, who published an appreciation in *The Times*. 'He was a fine person, completely honourable, like his father, and shared his mother's taste for entertainment and jazz. I think he was most at home in the Territorial Army where he was highly respected.'[147]

Anthony Eden's death on 14 January 1977 was inevitably the occasion for tributes and assessments from across the political spectrum, both in Britain and abroad. Above all, he was recognised as an *international* figure. When he had retired from the Premiership in January 1957, Parliament had not been sitting and the eventual tributes two weeks later had been inevitably low-key. Hugh Gaitskell, surprisingly, was the only Parliamentarian who spoke.[148] In 1977, Parliament met on 17 January, the day of Eden's funeral at Alvediston. After tributes from the Prime Minister, James Callaghan, and the leader of the Opposition, Margaret Thatcher, Edward Heath spoke of what Eden had meant to him:

> For my generation at university, in the second half of the 1930s, Anthony Eden personified the struggle against tyranny in Europe. He had a deep and passionate belief in the maintenance of the rule of law. I do not believe it possible to understand any period of his life or any aspect of his career without recognising how deep that belief went.[149]

The House then adjourned, though not before a protest by Dennis Skinner on the grounds that Parliament had obligations to the electorate, who could not clock on and off at will, as the MPs were doing. Although such an adjournment was traditional, what Dennis Skinner and others did not know was that Michael Cocks, the Government Chief Whip, had calculated that the Government was two votes short of a majority for a crucial vote. The adjournment solved the short-term difficulty for an administration that two months later would be forced into a formal alliance with the Liberal Party to survive. Ironically, the indirect impact of Eden's death was to shore up temporarily an ailing Labour Government.[150]

The House of Lords met for the first time after Eden's death on 18 January. The principal tributes were paid by Selwyn Lloyd and Alec Home, the two senior figures of the political scene in the 1950s most closely associated with him. Harold Caccia also spoke, especially of his association with Eden in the 1930s. Fittingly, one of the most personal assessments came from the recently ennobled Robert Carr:

> His great concern was with thoughts of joint consultation, the sharing of information, of decision-taking, of partnership. He kept using the phrase 'a property-owning democracy'. Although that was largely thought of in terms of home ownership, in his mind the really important part of it was the ownership of responsibility, the sense of ownership of one's job, of proper dignity and satisfaction in one's work. That was what he meant to be the domestic theme of his Premiership.'[151]

Memorial services followed, at St George's Chapel, Windsor, where his Garter Banner was returned on 8 February, and at the parish church of St Mary's, Warwick, in the heart of his former constituency, on 13 February. Then on 15 February services were held at the Anglican Cathedral, Bermuda, and at Westminster Abbey, 'that temple of silence and reconciliation where the enmities of twenty generations lie buried'.[152] James Callaghan and all former Prime Ministers – Macmillan, Home, Wilson and Heath – attended.

Eden had arranged many of the details himself, choosing the Sentences used at Bobbety Salisbury's funeral, the Prayers from the Memorial Service for the murdered King Faisal II and his family in 1958, and the Blessing 'as written on Attlee's service paper.'[153] He specified that Spenser's lines 'Sleep after toil, port after stormy seas, Ease after war, death after life does greatly please' and the valediction from *Cymbeline* – 'Fear no more the heat of the sun' – should be printed in the service booklet.[154] The music included Cecil Spring-Rice's great patriotic hymn 'I vow to thee my country', and Lvov's Russian Hymn. The service ended with the band and buglers of the 1st Battalion the Royal Green Jackets playing the Regimental March of the King's Royal Rifle Corps.

When Nicholas Avon was finalising the details of these services with his stepmother, he wrote, echoing the wishes of Thomas Hardy's choirmaster, 'My father was old-fashioned and preferred everything the old way.'[155]

It was indeed the passing of a distinctive phase in British public life, of gentlemanly reserve and reticence, and of a straightforward, sincere sense of national allegiance. As Clarissa Avon wrote to the Queen Mother, 'He is the last of the old era to go. He would not have wished to stay much longer in the modern world, bravely though he has borne his illness for so long.'[156]

POSTLUDE

Either a principled prince among men, the unluckiest but most
handsome leader the Tory Party ever had, or a hysterical self-
serving prima donna, depending on one's point of view.

Alex Danchev and Daniel Todman[1]

There have been politicians more successful, or more subtle;
there have been none more tenacious or more tolerant.

C. V. Wedgwood on William the Silent[2]

St. Mary's Church, Alvediston

At Christmas 1950, Nicholas Eden gave his father a present of C. V. Wedgwood's biography of William the Silent. Eden was absorbed both by the style of the book and the example of the man it portrayed, writing revealingly in his diary:

> Thanks to Nicholas am reading Miss Wedgwood's *William the Silent*. Here was a man. I have never yet met a figure in history with whose outlook, character & politics I sympathise more whole heartedly. I should like to be just like him. Then his wretched domestic problems. He rose above all this yet this is one thing I cannot understand how he could have done. To have his 13 year old son, then his only son, virtually a hostage among those merciless Spaniards, whose cruelty has always been so unspeakable. I have ever disliked Spaniards, just for that cruelty. They are the antithesis of toleration, & for me to be civilised is to be tolerant.[3]

C. V. Wedgwood's elegant summation of William the Silent could have been of Eden himself:

> Few statesmen in any period, none in his own, cared so deeply for the ordinary comfort and the trivial happiness of the thousands of individuals who are 'the people'. He neither idealised nor overestimated them and he knew that they were often wrong, for what political education had they yet had? But he believed in them, not merely as a theoretical concept, but as individuals, as men. Therein lay the secret of the profound and enduring love between him and them.[4]

Eden had a similar sensitivity, which sprang in part from the paternalistic tradition of a particular kind of Englishness. 'To be civilised' was indeed 'to tolerate'. Clement Attlee had the same awareness of the feelings of others, though his concern took him in a different political direction from Eden, finding its first fulfilment in the East End of London and benevolent Christian Socialism. Eden's career demonstrated that such understanding care was not incompatible with Conservatism. But for both of them – Major Attlee and Captain Eden as they were initially known in Parliament – the military experience of their young days, with responsibility for men's lives, coloured many of their later actions and impulses. 'War promoted working together into something good and true and rare, the like of which was never to be found in civil life,' Eden wrote of the trenches. 'It was our compensation.'[5]

One night, when off duty, Eden went out alone into no-man's-land to bring back a poppy he had noticed blooming in the scarred earth. In one sense, the rest of Eden's life after the Great War was an anticlimax and a disappointment.

Much that Eden held in respect was in full retreat by the time of his death. He had always abhorred the shrill partisanship of Westminster, its sick hurry and divided aims. In the last years of his life, he heard from Selwyn Lloyd how the post of Speaker gave him an overview denied to other MPs, as from Speaker's House he had the first view of the next raucous demonstration coming over Westminster Bridge. Eden was a child of Empire, yet by the time of his death even this seemingly immutable institution had largely disappeared. 'We are a very rich and a very vulnerable Empire,' Neville Chamberlain had written in 1938, 'and there are plenty of poor adventurers not very far away who look on us with hungry eyes'.[6] The vulnerability was to prove more significant than the wealth. By 1997, the centenary of Eden's birth, Britain's handover of Hong Kong to China completed the process of disbandment.

Even the moderate Conservatism, of which he had been a principal advocate, had been eclipsed by the beginnings of the Thatcherite revolution. During Eden's eighty years the world changed for ever. His father had been born in the year that *David Copperfield* appeared; the son outlived the *Apollo* manned moon missions. It was not just the trenches that were 'another world'; he died in an alien world which had bypassed or trampled on so many of the things he held dear.

The battle over Eden's reputation began long before his death, and continues to this day. Many divergent views have held the field at differing times, for that is the nature of historical revisionism.

Alan Campbell Johnson, who published what he called 'an informal record of a premature experiment in international collaboration'[7] in 1938, just after Eden's resignation, placed the hopes of the younger generation in the speedy reassimilation of Eden into the highest ranks of Government. The successive volumes of Churchill's war memoirs in the 1940s reinforced this view of history.

The two interim lives by Dennis Bardens and Lewis Broad that appeared in 1955, as Eden assumed the Premiership, together with that by William Rees-Mogg in 1956, all pre-dated Suez, and were respectful accounts – the Rees-Mogg in particular showing that Eden's judgement in foreign affairs was unfailingly sound. The fact that this latter book is no longer listed by Rees-Mogg in his *Who's Who* entry suggests a degree of reservation about

Eden with Robert Menzies, during the Commonwealth
Prime Ministers' Conference, June 1956.

(*Left*) Archbishop Fisher
in Lambeth Palace Chapel.

(*Below*) Eden with John Foster Dulles at No 10
at the height of the Suez crisis in August 1956.

At Chequers.
(*Clockwise*) Patrick Buchan–Hepburn
with Eden. Beaverbrook with Eden.
Nicholas Eden with Sir William Hayter
and Rab Butler. Pandit Nehru and
Walter Monckton.

(*Clockwise*) Gaitskell with Bulganin. Norman Brook with General Templer. Air Chief Marshal Sir Dermot Boyle, Marshal of the RAF Sir William Dickson, First Sea Lord Mountbatten, Eden with his back to the camera. Jim Thomas with Harold Macmillan.

(*Right*) Winston at Chequers in 1956.

(*Right*) Sid Holland, the Prime Minister of New Zealand, welcomes Eden to his country in 1957, after Eden's post-Suez resignation and recuperative sea-voyage.

(*Above*) Anthony Eden and Selwyn Lloyd at Broadchalke, where they discussed the many issues raised by Suez. 30 May 1958.

(*Left*) Nicholas Eden. 'He was a fine person, completely honourable, like his father, and shared his mother's taste for entertainment and jazz.'

(*Left*) A smiling Queen Elizabeth in a Caribbean downpour. The private royal visit to Villa Nova, 15 February 1966.
(*Above*) Lord Avon at de Gaulle's funeral, November 1970, with, among others, a top-hatted Harold Macmillan, Harold Wilson, Edward Heath and the Prince of Wales.

(*Above*) An unexpected late friendship: with Roy Welensky at Alvediston.

(*Left*) Meeting Haile Selassie in Bermuda. Lord Avon wrote a special tribute for his memorial service in 1975.

With contrasting bruisers:
President Johnson at the
White House (*above*)
and Avon Priam (*right*).

'Fear no more the heat of the sun.' The Avons in the garden of the British Embassy in Paris.

what later unfolded. It was only after Eden had retired that the A. J. P. Taylor school of historians sharpened their pens.

Discounting Randolph Churchill's vitriolic 1959 polemic, *The Rise and Fall of Sir Anthony Eden* (inevitably the epitome of the 'hysterical self-serving prima donna' school of thought), the first account of Eden's whole career, published in 1976 shortly before his death, came in a sympathetic, balanced and accessible account by Sidney Aster. Considering that the volume was part of a series edited by A. J. P. Taylor, who provided a characteristically acerbic introduction, this was quite an achievement. Indeed, Robert Rhodes James considered it perhaps the most skilful of all the Eden biographies. But Aster's book did not have the field to itself for long. In 1981 David Carlton published his devastating critique of Eden – ten years in the making, less polemical than Randolph Churchill's, but more powerful for that – addressing all the major issues from the perspective of an experienced and expert commentator on international relations, and finding against Eden in virtually all the major watersheds of his career. But it was primarily a diplomatic account, rather than a political one, and was less concerned with the ebb and flow of parliamentary life. Nevertheless, it established the marker that all subsequent writers on Eden have had to address, and as a result Carlton's book has a serious claim to be considered the most influential of all Eden studies. Carlton returned to his theme in other works not primarily about Eden, such as *Churchill and the Soviet Union* (2000).

Carlton's book certainly weighed very heavily on the first biography to be based on Eden's private papers, by Robert Rhodes James, which appeared in late 1986. Substantially a reply to Carlton and the case for the defence, Rhodes James's biography countered the prevailing conventional judgements and consequently was ahead of its time, and not to everyone's taste. Few could deny, however, the understanding and responsiveness with which Rhodes James brought out both the sadnesses of Eden's life and his aesthetic sensibilities. Nevertheless, some critics felt that Rhodes James had paid too heavily for the help afforded him by the widow, the dilemma faced by many 'authorised' biographers. Robert Skidelsky concluded that Rhodes James's book would 'delight the middlebrow and confirm them in their judgment that all is for the best, or would be if we had decent and honourable chaps like Anthony Eden running the show today', a lesson he thought mislearned.[8]

Victor Rothwell's thoughtful study of 1992, eschewing the personal element, concentrated entirely on the political aspect, and remains the fairest short introduction to the core years from 1931 to 1957. David Dutton's *Anthony Eden: A Life and Reputation*, published in 1997 – not a conventional biography, but a series of linked essays dealing with major

599

aspects and themes of Eden's career – took into account the considerable international scholarship on Eden, much of it in specialist academic publications and journals, and is an indispensable bran-tub of treasures based on primary sources.[9]

Modern political bibliographies also contain countless references to articles, pamphlets and theses on all aspects of Eden's career. Essentially an extended thesis, A. R. Peters's book *Anthony Eden at the Foreign Office 1931–1938* (1986) is one of the most detailed and far-reaching accounts from primary sources of what increasingly appear as the key years. In any assessment of Eden's career, it remains one of the authoritative accounts. No less exhaustive is Elizabeth Barker's influential *Churchill and Eden at War* (1978). John Young's compendium of essays on *The Foreign Policy of Churchill's Peacetime Administration 1951–1955* (1988) completes an essential triptych. A more unsympathetic overall account can be found in Geoffrey McDermott's *The Eden Legacy and the Decline of British Diplomacy* (1969). Keith Kyle's magisterial account *Suez* (1991) is a source of the utmost importance, not least because of the objective way in which Kyle separates any personal feelings about the crisis from his analysis of its origins, course and consequences. The Avon Papers, Eden's gift to the nation, remain open to all *bona-fide* researchers at Birmingham University.

'Biography,' said Arthur Balfour, 'should be written by an acute enemy.'[10] Macaulay, for his part, warned how biographers and all 'who employ themselves in illustrating the lives ... of others' were 'peculiarly exposed to the ... disease of admiration'.[11] Over the years many have been ready to cast the first stone and not all have bludgeoned and flailed counter-productively like Randolph Churchill.

'A politician's character and position are measured in his day by party standards,' wrote Winston Churchill. 'When he is dead, all that he achieved in the name of party is at an end. The eulogies and censures of partisans are powerless to affect his ultimate reputation. The scales wherein he was weighed are broken. The years to come bring weights and measures of their own.'[12]

The Times shrewdly noted in its lengthy obituary of Eden that 'he was the last Prime Minister to believe Britain was a great power, and the first to confront a crisis which proved she was not'. And the paper accurately forecast that perspectives would change. 'The noise of his sudden and precipitous fall obscured for a time the high services he had long rendered to the nation and to the cause of world peace. But when the dust has settled they will stand out as clearly as before.'[13]

Unusually among twentieth-century Prime Ministers (Bonar Law and

Alec Douglas-Home are the only parallels), Anthony Eden's reputation
does not rest on his time in Downing Street. Along with Lloyd George,
Neville Chamberlain and Harold Macmillan, he is one of the four
twentieth-century Prime Ministers who never served as Leader of the
Opposition. Few Prime Ministers have been able to make a major impact
on the government machine without serving a full term. 'I am convinced
that it is essential to have a cumulative period of office of at least five
years,' Roy Jenkins has written, 'in order to rank as Prime Minister of
major impact.'[14] This stern judgement may be questioned over Balfour and
Heath, but there would be little doubt that it applies to Bonar Law, Alec
Home and Anthony Eden.[15]

Although he was not a Prime Minister of the front rank, Eden was a
figure who made a major impact on his party while leader, not least in his
underrated impact on its domestic political thinking, though, ironically, his
success in paving the way for a Social Democratic Britain was eventually
to have heavy electoral consequences for the Conservative Party. In addition, he was a Foreign Secretary whose three tenures of office coincided
with some of the most important events of the twentieth century. For those
who had grown up before the Second World War, he always remained an
unforgettable figure. 'Anthony was the last, for my generation, of those
who saved freedom for us all – who led and unified us in the dark days
from 1933 to the end', wrote one such on the day of Eden's death.[16] To
others, 'he was never primarily a political figure, but a fascinating human
being of the most diverse interests and talents'.[17]*

As Prime Minister, Eden was not an innovator, changing the institutions
of Government, like Thatcher; nor a reformer, bringing about a change of
direction in policy, like Attlee. He was not an egoist, who lived for the
adrenalin of office, like Lloyd George nor a balancer, like Alec Home.[18] As
Prime Minister, he defied pigeonholing. There was no continuity of theme
or approach in the relatively short time he was in Number 10. Among
twentieth-century Conservative leaders, only Sir Austen Chamberlain
(who was never Prime Minister) led the party for a shorter term, and of
those who did become Prime Minister, only Alec Douglas-Home led the
party for the same short time, to the very month.†

Another similarity between Eden and Home lies in the centrality of their
Foreign Secretaryships. Both failed to enhance their reputations by their

---

*Sir Anthony Nutting held the diametrically opposite view. He felt that Eden was not
interesting as a personality, only that the events in which he had been involved made him of
interest. The late Sir Anthony Nutting to the author, 4 November 1997.
†Lady Thatcher (15 years 9 months) and Sir Winston Churchill (14 years 9 months) head the
list. Sir Anthony Eden and Sir Alec Douglas-Home served for one year and nine months each,
though Eden was never Leader of the Opposition.

time in Downing Street. However, Lord Rosebery said that in politics it was the 'character breathing through the sentences that counts'.[19] Eden had character, and this was widely acknowledged at the time of his death.

Of the deaths of public figures, Nathaniel Hawthorne has written:

It is very singular how the effect of a man's death often seems to give people a truer idea of his character, whether for good or evil, than they have ever possessed while he was living and acting among them. Death is so genuine a fact that it excludes falsehood, or betrays its emptiness; it is a touchstone that proves the gold, and dishonours the baser metal.[20]

Eden was not dishonoured in death. Yet his life had a tragic dimension to it, which has not been diminished by the passage of time. 'No portrait can be true to life,' wrote Sir Austen Chamberlain, his first mentor, 'which has no shadows.'[21] There was something Shakespearean about the compass of Eden's career, both in its high spots and in its decline.

In letters to his wife in retirement, Churchill sometimes referred wryly to Eden and Clarissa as 'Anthony and Cleopatra,'[22] and of all the Shakespearean tragic heroes, it is Mark Antony whom Eden most resembles, of whom Agrippa said:

A rarer spirit never
Did steer humanity; but you, gods, will give us
Some faults to make us men.[23]

Eden's faults were pronounced. There were flaws of character and temperament. And yet he *was* 'a rare spirit' who stood out from the crowd.

His delayed inheritance was a cruel preparation for the highest office. Churchill, in a sense, made Eden's reputation with his response to the 1938 resignation; in the end, he did much to unmake it by unconscionable delay. 'I personally feel he is the greatest Englishman of this century & I think nothing can rob of him that,' Roy Welensky wrote of Churchill. 'But for just straight endearing qualities I would have preferred Anthony at any time.'[24] Anthony Nutting has written of Eden that 'he had for too long been the Golden Boy of the Tory Party, the glamorous Crown Prince awaiting the summons to mount the throne in place of the ageing Emperor.'[25]

Assessments of Eden have often relied on retrospective hindsight, the tendency to write the career backwards. If Suez was a mistake (first premiss), then the earlier crises were perhaps not successfully dealt with either (second premiss). The syllogistic inevitability of this approach has thus led Eden to be dubbed a less than staunch appeaser, wrong on Mussolini, and a less important social reformer than Rab Butler. These arguments do not stand up in the face of the evidence. The Italian archives show clearly how Mussolini and his cronies – 'gangsters' as Eden called them – were deeply concerned about Eden's continued influence on the course of British foreign policy before 1939. Eden, alone of the Cabinet in the 1930s, truly saw what Mussolini's intentions were, and the Italian archives show how relieved the Duce was when Eden resigned in February 1938. Even at the time, the Italians, as Count Grandi admits in his diaries, were apprehensive about the consequences for their nation of an Eden Premiership. His resignation was greeted with more relief in Rome than in Birmingham. Then, during the war, Eden understood Stalin far better than Churchill did, just as in the post-war years in Opposition he knew the vital importance of educating his party into 'One Nation' Conservatism. Even the Russians acknowledged Eden's foresightedness, discomfiting though this may have been for them. In 1961 Eden wrote to Edward Heath, 'I am told by an historian who has read the Russian documents that they treat me with more respect in their record than they do any other Western politician of the time!'[26]

Had the Anglo-French venture succeeded in 1956, there would almost certainly have been no Middle East war in 1967, and probably no war in 1973 also. British and French attitudes after 1957 would have been different, too. De Gaulle was disgusted by Britain 'running out' at the behest of the Americans, which influenced his attitude to Britain as a Trojan horse in the European Community. The French were one of the first to realise subsequently that America's interests were not those of Europe. Through his friendship with de Gaulle, Eden would almost certainly have taken that line too, had he remained in Downing Street, and there would have been none of Macmillan's abasement before the Americans.

In fact, looking at Eden's career up to the evening of 26 July 1956, when he received the news of Nasser's nationalisation of the Suez Canal Company, he was correct on all the major issues that he faced; 'on the money', as the Americans might have put it. It could be argued that before the war he had demonised Mussolini excessively, and only belatedly came to an understanding of Hitler's greater malevolent potential against common humanity. Similarly, he underestimated the threat the Soviets would pose after the war. But his one main regret, and lasting cause for self-reproach, about which he was quite frank, was that Hitler was not opposed after the occupation of the Rhineland in 1936. The Nyon Conference showed later what could be done by standing four-square. So inevitably, on that sultry July evening in 1956, for one of his generation the memory of Hitler and the Rhineland meant that the impulse was to say, 'Never again'. After all, it was merely how the Americans and the Labour Party had responded to the Persian oil crisis in 1951. As Andrew

Roberts has expressed it, with characteristic clarity in the face of received opinion:

> The hypocrisy of both the Americans and the Labour party over Suez is best illustrated by their reaction to the nationalisation of British oil interests by Dr Mussadeq of Iran in 1951. For all its later moralising about Third World self-determination the Labour government was perfectly ready to topple Mussadeq, but feared, as the Cabinet minutes put it, 'the attitude of the United States government'. Equally American politicians who had acquiesced in the CIA/MI6 coup that had removed Mossadeq in 1953, started mouthing banalities about the brotherhood of man when it came to the 1956 presidential election.

Nor was that all. Roberts continues:

> The most nauseating part of the liberal internationalist mantra, however, is their outraged sensibilities over Eden's collusion with Israel. Without secret diplomacy and alliances, let alone plans of attack, this country would not have won the Napoleonic wars, or staved off involvement in every European conflict since the Crimean war. For Labour politicians who hid the existence of the Chevaline nuclear deterrent from their Cabinet colleagues to denounce Eden for misleading parliament is grotesque. Without collusion the Israelis would not have destroyed one third of the Soviet-built Egyptian air force, which would otherwise have been directed against our servicemen.[27]

Talleyrand and Bismarck did not proclaim their diplomacy from the rooftops for all to hear. In any case, Suez was a sudden bright meteor that soon burned itself out. 'With perspective Suez may come to seem a relatively unimportant event in and of itself, more symbolic than seminal, more an effect than a cause of national decline,' David Carlton has acknowledged. 'For Suez had remarkably few consequences, favourable or otherwise.'[28]

The obloquy for Eden during and after Suez crossed party lines, but increasingly the events of 1956 seem a dramatic *cul-de-sac*, or a settling into place of the stones of history, not the beginning of a fresh landslide by ill-advised tampering with the loose and unstable boulders that marked the precarious nature of Britain's imperial legacy. Europhiles, remembering Messina, may argue they have a better case over which to excoriate Eden, but even there they would find many Europhobes rising in his defence.

During Suez, Eden had the misfortune to be surrounded by some irresolute colleagues (and, in Macmillan, one who was resolute in different directions), a divided Opposition, a lack of wartime controls and a climate of imperialistic guilt, skilfully appealed to by the liberal intelligentsia, notably David Astor's *Observer*, though some leading intellectuals such as Gilbert Murray and John Sparrow were never part of that grouping. Eden was covertly betrayed by those whom he thought he could trust, notably Macmillan and Butler from the Cabinet, Mountbatten among the Chiefs of Staff, and William Clark, his own press officer.

Rab Butler, who was at best equivocal about Eden during his lifetime, later mellowed in his assessment. Although it pained him to admit it, he did say in 1979, 'I think there was something of the statesman about him. He was a wonderful diplomatist.' But even then there was a Rabbism in the tail. 'He listened to all the Sirs at the Foreign Office, and no man could ever wear a grey suit better.'[29]

Lady Violet Bonham Carter, who was a close observer of Eden, both in his prime and later, recorded her feelings at the moment of Eden's downfall:

> I feel – who cldn't? – the tragic poignancy of Anthony's exit. Politics are his only interest. To be P.M. was his life's one aim. He waits – loyally but impatiently for W. to go ('those hungry eyes' as W. used to say to me). At last the cup is handed to him. He has a triumphant election. Then everything begins to go awry – but not catastrophically. Finally he himself accomplishes his own destruction by the suicidal blunder of Suez. (Was it health that drove him into this madness? And how far did that disaster contribute to the undermining of his health?) Now he faces a complete vacuum. Politics have always been his be-all & his end-all. He cares for nothing else. And he will have no chance of redeeming his reputation in the eyes of the present or of posterity. It is a Greek tragedy.[30]

On one thing Violet Bonham Carter was wrong: Eden did have a hinterland beyond politics and did know that there was a world elsewhere. He was a man who felt deeply about the welfare of his country, the betterment of the lot of his fellow countrymen, the beauty of artistic genius, the wisdom to be found in books, the Englishness at the heart of the constituency he served for over three decades, and the quietness of the Wiltshire valley where he spent the evening of his life.

In his commonplace book, Eden kept quotations and sayings that he felt particularly apt. One of these was by Lord Acton: 'Ideals in politics are never realised, but the pursuit of them determines history.' Eden pursued many goals and not all of them were by any means achieved, but nevertheless he was always motivated by a patriotism that was not narrow and isolationist, but outward-looking and inclusive. Even in reduced circumstances – circumstances that could never have been predicted at the time of his birth – Britain had a contribution, he felt, to make in the international context, particularly through the ties that bound the Commonwealth as a unique institution. When these ties held, he felt there was nothing that Britain could not achieve. Eden had every cause to be a pessimist, and there were low points when it seemed that nothing would come right. As Ulysses said in Eden's beloved *Troilus and Cressida*:

> O, let not virtue seek
> Remuneration for the thing it was;
> For beauty, wit,
> High birth, vigour of bone, desert in service,
> Love, friendship, charity, are subjects all
> To envious and calumniating time.[31]

Eden had high birth, vigour of bone and desert in service. 'He belonged in spirit to an earlier, a more generous and more cultured age than this of narrowness and authority,' C. V. Wedgwood wrote of William the Silent, adding, 'He is one of that small band of statesmen whose service to humanity is greater than their service to their time or their people.'[32] It is a judgement that applies equally well to the life and times of Anthony Eden, 1st Earl of Avon, whose character was shaped by his early experience of the sufferings of humanity, and who in later life was to do the state much service.

'Men's evil manners live in brass,' wrote Shakespeare, 'their virtues we write in water.'[33] So, for too long, it was to prove with Eden. Perhaps over-praised in his pre-war days, not least by the gilded pen of Winston Churchill, he was subject to disproportionate derogation during and after his time as the unluckiest of twentieth-century Prime Ministers, though Robert Skidelsky thought the real trouble was the other way round. 'Eden's problem was not that he was denied luck at crucial moments,' he wrote, 'but that for most of his life he had too much political good luck for his own good.'[34] If so, that is one form of unluckiness.

Since Eden's death in 1977 his reputation has been revalued. Ironically, this has been accompanied by a rehabilitation of the reputation of Neville Chamberlain, with whom his career was so closely bound. Churchill's reputation, too, has not been immune from revisionism. Many perceptions about the crucial years from 1937 to 1945, which lie at the heart of Eden's career, have been altered in recent years, and will no doubt continue to shift, for stasis is inimical to historical enquiry.

The last official to see Eden was Sir Peter Ramsbotham, the British Ambassador in Washington, who went to Hobe Sound in December 1976. There was Eden, gentle, gallant, courteous, with no bitterness, and exhibiting beautiful manners to those who were doing their best to relieve the suffering of his last days. Instinctively, all knew that they were in the presence of a great man. There was no element of self-pity or recrimination. He was at peace with himself and the world. 'I will always remember our parting, as he stood on the steps of the house, took off his hat and bowed towards my wife in farewell,' Ramsbotham recalled.[35]

'Life is a comedy to those who think,' wrote Eden in his diary on 8 September 1975, 'a tragedy to those who feel.'[36] For one who felt so deeply for the welfare of his country and his countrymen, from North Country days with his regiment at Duncombe Park, to the grim 1970s of his final decade when so many were hit by inflation and industrial unrest, the elements of personal and political tragedy proved an inescapable portion. In the end, however, such trials fortified his long-held trust and belief in the indomitable spirit of the British people in adversity, which during some of the darkest days in their history he had done so much to uphold and sustain.

Eden's Resignation Speech, House of Commons, 21 February 1938

I rise to ask the leave of the House to make a personal explanation. This is for me, both on personal and political grounds, a most painful occasion. No man would willingly sever the links which bind him with his colleagues and friends, still less when, as in my case, I am only too conscious to how great an extent those colleagues have encouraged and sustained me during the two years that I have held the responsible office from which I have just resigned. But, Sir, there are occasions when strong political convictions must override all other considerations. Of such occasions only the individual himself can be the judge; no man can be the keeper of another man's conscience. Therefore, I stand before the House today to give the House in a few brief sentences my reasons for having resigned the office of Foreign Secretary.

First let me make plain that the ultimate aim of us all, the objective of the foreign policy of this country, is, and must always be, the maintenance of peace. If, however, peace is to be enduring it must rest on foundations of frank reciprocity and mutual respect. If we accept this basis for our foreign policy it follows that we must be ready to negotiate with all countries, whatever their form of government, in order to promote international understanding, but we must also be watchful that in our conception of such negotiations, and in the method by which we seek to further them, we are in fact strengthening, not undermining, the foundations upon which international confidence rests. With that introduction I come to the immediate issue which unhappily divides me from my colleagues. It will be known to the House that certain exchanges of view have been taking place between the Italian Government and His Majesty's Government in respect to the opening of conversations between the two Governments. Indeed His Majesty's Government have been committed to the principle of such conversations ever since my right hon. Friend the Prime Minister himself exchanged letters with Signor Mussolini last summer. There is no dispute anywhere about that.

The immediate issue is as to whether official conversations should be opened in Rome now. It is my conviction that the attitude of the Italian Government to international problems in general, and to this country in particular, is not yet such as to justify this course. The ground has been in no respect prepared. Propaganda against this country by the Italian Government is rife throughout the world. I am myself pledged to this House not to open conversations until this hostile propaganda ceases.

I do not want to stress the personal position, which is relatively unimportant, but I must mention in passing the difficult position in which I must have been placed, had I to announce to the House in existing conditions the opening of such conversations. Moreover, little progress, in fact, though much in promise, has yet been made with the solution of the Spanish problem. Let me make it plain. I do not suggest and I would not advocate that the Government should refuse conversations with the Italian Government, or indeed with any other Government which shows any disposition to conversations with us for the betterment of international understandings, yet we must be convinced that the conditions in which these conversations take place are such as to make for the likelihood, if not for the certainty, of their success. I contend that these conditions do not exist today.

I am compelled for a few moments, if the House will allow me, to review the past with this situation as the background. While I was privileged to be Foreign Secretary I was responsible for several attempts in the past eighteen months to better our relations with Italy. They have all failed in the main, though not wholly, because of the Spanish problem. I think it likely that the House may wonder why I at this hour place so much emphasis on performance as opposed to promise, and even why I speak so much of the Spanish problem. It is only because it happens to be in this instance an example. We cannot consider this problem except in relation to the international situation as a whole. In January of last year, after difficult negotiations, we signed the Anglo-Italian Agreement, but within a very few days, indeed almost simultaneously, the first considerable consignment of Italian troops left for Spain. It may be held that this was not considered a breach of the letter of our understanding, but no one, I think, surely will contend that it did not run counter to its spirit. That same agreement contained a clause – a specific clause – dealing with the cessation of propaganda, yet propaganda was scarcely dimmed for an instant.

Again last summer my right hon. Friend the Prime Minister and Signor Mussolini exchanged letters, and after that in a few days the relations between our two countries took a marked turn for the better. Of that there can be no doubt. Then what happened? Then ensued the incidents in the Mediterranean[1] with which the House is familiar and the glorification by the Head of the Italian Government of the victories of Italian forces in Spain. My submission is that we cannot risk a further repetition of these experiences.

Recent months, recent weeks, recent days have seen the successive violation of international agreements and attempts to secure political decisions by forcible means. We are in the presence of the progressive deterioration of respect for international obligations. It is quite impossible to judge these things in a vacuum. In the light – my judgement may well be wrong – of the present international situation, this is a moment for this country to stand firm, not to plunge into negotiations unprepared, with the full knowledge that the chief obstacle to their success has not been resolved.

The programme which I have outlined seems to me a not unreasonable programme. Indeed, if the desire of the two parties be to reach agreement on all subjects outstanding between them, including Spain, I am quite confident that it is the best method to pursue. It is the traditional method of diplomacy to prepare for conversations before they are formally opened. It is seldom right to depart from that traditional method, which has been tested by time and experience. It is certainly never right to do so because one party to the negotiations intimates that it is now or never. Agreements that are worthwhile are never made on the basis of a threat. Nor in the past has this country been willing to negotiate in such conditions. I repeat that if our objective is to promote a Mediterranean agreement, to promote lasting appeasement, then the method which I have described is not only the best, but the only possible, and the only one consonant with our position in the world.

I may be told that by insisting that positive progress must be made with the Spanish question before formal conversations are opened between His Majesty's Government and the Italian Government in Rome, I am asking one party to the negotiations to yield in advance certain advantages that that party now enjoys. I shall not for one moment seek to argue whether those advantages, if indeed they be advantages, are legitimate ones. But it has never entered into my conception to suggest that the Italian forces should be withdrawn from Spain alone, but only that the Italian Government should agree and carry out with others a fair scheme for the proportionate withdrawal of all foreigners from Spain.

I am conscious – that is, of course, why I stand here – that my right hon. Friend the Prime Minister and my colleagues take another view. They believe in their policy, and they believe in their method, and they may be right. But, if they are right, their chances of success will certainly be enhanced if their policy is pursued by another Foreign Secretary, one who has complete conviction in the methods which he is being asked to employ. It may even be that my resignation will facilitate the course of these negotiations. If so, nobody will be more pleased than I.

I have spoken to the House of the immediate difference that has divided me from my colleagues, but I should not be frank with the House if I were to pretend that is an isolated issue as between my right hon. Friend the Prime Minister and myself. It is not. Within the last few weeks upon one most important decision of foreign policy which did not concern Italy at all, the difference was fundamental. My right hon. Friend is, I know, conscious of this. Moreover, it has recently become clear to me, and I think to him, that there is between us a real difference of outlook and method. It may be argued, perhaps I shall be told, that this is not a difference of fundamental principles. Well, in the sense that the object of all foreign policy is the maintenance of peace, that is of course perfectly true. But in international affairs can anyone define where outlook and methods end and principles begin? If the Government of this country is to speak with undivided voice in international affairs, it is essential that the Prime Minister and the Foreign Secretary should have a similar outlook and wish to pursue similar methods.

The more intense the interest which each one of them takes in the conduct of international affairs, the more imperative does this unity become. My right hon. Friend has strong views on foreign policy, and I respect him for it; and I have strong views, too. Since we are, as I know, both of us conscious that those views have resulted in a divergence, not of aim, but of outlook and of approach, it is clearly in the national interest that unity should be restored at the earliest possible moment.

Of late the conviction has steadily grown upon me that there has been too keen a desire on our part to make terms with others, rather than that others should make terms with us. This never was the attitude of this country in the past. It should not, in the interests of peace, be our attitude today. The events of the last few days, which have dealt with one particular issue, have merely brought to a head other and more far-reaching differences, not if you will, in objectives, but in outlook and approach. I do not believe that we can make progress in European appeasement, more particularly in the light of the events of the past few days – and those events must surely be present in all our minds – if we allow the impression to gain currency abroad that we yield to constant pressure. I am certain in my own mind that progress depends above all on the temper of the nation, and that temper must find expression in a firm spirit. That spirit, I am confident, is there. Not to give voice to it is, I believe, fair neither to this country nor to the world.[2]

Eden's Speech on the Property-Owning Democracy, Conservative Party Conference, Blackpool, 3 October 1946

Eden's speech was made in reply to a resolution moved by Aubrey Jones, candidate at the Heywood and Radcliffe by-election, on the difference between the Conservative and Socialist views on domestic affairs.

A good service has been done to the Conference and to the party by Mr Aubrey Jones and others in tabling these Resolutions. Their point of view is not identical but their purpose is the same. They seek to give expression to a way of life for the British people under which industry may prosper and men may be free. I have noticed that much abuse has been showered upon our party previous to this Conference. Mr Clement Davies [Liberal leader] accuses us of being too amorous. He indignantly repels our alleged advances. I suspect his political chastity which I note is only equalled by its political futility. And then there is the Attorney-General [Sir Hartley Shawcross]. I never know whether he is coming or going.[1] One day it is abuse, the next day it is apology. It is immaterial to us under which threat we live today. Our concern at this Conference is with ourselves. We are not supplicants to anyone. We seek to state our faith and by that faith we would be judged.

Until a few months ago the Socialist had one advantage in any discussion of domestic policies with his Liberal or Conservative rivals. He had a sovereign remedy which he was always ready to put forward, nationalisation. And as that experiment had never been tried in a productive industry in this country, the Socialist was likely to receive that benefit of the doubt which a man with a heavy cold will often extend to a new remedy, even though he knows in his heart that there is no escape from working the wretched thing through. But now all this is changed or changing. We are moving from the realms of advocacy to those of practical experiment. The nationalisation of the coal mines is already law, and other industries are under sentence. Experience up to date is not heartening for the nationalisers. Progress in the coal-mining industry is not encouraging. The approach of the appointed day has brought no upward surge in output. We may be sure that, as the evidence of failure accumulates, the search among the more intelligent and less bigoted voters for constructive alternatives will grow. It is in this sphere that we have an essential job of work to do.

Long experience has taught us that to offer to the people any single panacea as the Socialists offer nationalisation would be merely to delude ourselves and them. Life is not as simple as that. For the manifold and diverse problems that face us, manifold and diverse solutions must of necessity be required. But this I believe we can say, that there is one single principle that will unite all the solutions that we shall seek and propound. There is one principle underlying our approach to all these problems, a principle on which we stand in fundamental opposition to Socialism. The objective of Socialism is State ownership of all the means of production, distribution and exchange. Our objective is a nation-wide property-owning democracy. These objectives are fundamentally opposed. Whereas the Socialist purpose is the concentration of ownership in the hands of the State, ours is the distribution of ownership over the widest practicable number of individuals.

Both parties believe in a form of capitalism; but, whereas our opponents believe in State capitalism, we believe in the widest measure of individual capitalism. I believe this to be a fundamental principle of political philosophy. Man should be master of his environment and not its slave. That is what freedom means. It is precisely in the conception of ownership that man achieves mastery over his environment. Upon the institution of property depends the fulfilment of individual personality and the maintenance of individual liberty.

In a Socialist State, where ownership is the monopoly of the Government, where everyone must rely on the State for his job, his roof, his livelihood, individual responsibility and individual liberty must wither and die. And so it is that we of the Conservative Party must maintain that the ownership of property is not a crime or a sin, but a reward, a right and a responsibility that must be shared as equitably as possible among all our citizens.

We believe, for example, that it is desirable to elaborate schemes whereby the private citizen and the returned soldier should be in a position not only to rent a house but to own one. We believe that the tenant farmer should be assisted and encouraged to become an owner-occupier. We would welcome schemes designed to enable the workers in industry to participate in its development and in the ownership of industry to a greater degree than they do at present.

How is this wider distribution of ownership to be achieved? There is one way in which it certainly cannot be achieved, and that is by mere redistribution of existing income. That field has already been pretty thoroughly ploughed over. The amount left, after deduction of tax, in the hands of all those earning £2,000 a year and over is equal to about one-fortieth part of the total gross national income. Therefore, 'soaking the rich' is not going to benefit anybody. On the contrary, it may well be that we are reaching a state where excessive taxation of any section of the community will lead only to a reduction in the total amount of wealth produced. Incentive is necessary at all levels.

The fundamental condition for achieving a wider distribution of ownership is surely a great increase in the production of wealth in the country and in particular in the productivity of industry. The saving by an individual that leads to ownership can be achieved only where there is a sufficient margin of income over the requirements of day-to-day consumption. Recent developments in scientific methods of production and in the technique of industrial organisation hold out possibilities of a very substantial increase in the rate of growth of our national income. But this will be achieved only by a united national effort. It does no service to this country to dwell as Socialists do, on the antagonisms between capital and labour, between individual enterprise and the function of Government. Rather we should concentrate on the essential unity of purpose between them that does exist and the harmony of operation that can be achieved.

It is becoming almost a commonplace to talk of Government, capital and labour as partners in industry. It is essential that we should make this conception a reality. It is no good Ministers appealing for a Dunkirk spirit in industry during the week and beating up the leaders of industry every week-end. I hope to have an opportunity to deal more fully with this aspect of our policy at Liverpool tomorrow night.

Our first concern then is with the national income. Our next is with the individual income. A national production drive will require extra effort from every citizen. The individual must therefore be satisfied that his increased efforts will bring him a commensurate reward and that a fair proportion of the money he receives will remain his to spend or save. It must not be snatched away by a rapacious Chancellor or drained away by the burdens of ill health or unemployment. The feeling sedulously fostered for years past by Left Wing propaganda that increased effort brings no comparable reward to the worker is responsible for many of the difficulties that are facing us in industrial relations today. This myth must be dispelled.

The relation of individual effort to real earnings must be made clear. Essentially these are problems for industry itself, to be worked out through the traditional methods of voluntary negotiation. But this is not a matter that can be ignored by Government. It is for them to give the inspiration. At the same time I think we should do well to study the various schemes for co-partnership in industry, for employee participation in profits and so on, which have been attempted and many of which are at present in operation in this country.

There are many difficulties and possibly dangers inherent in some of these plans, but there are also, to my mind, considerable possibilities that we must explore. Then in finance we should do well to recall Mr Gladstone's injunction to allow money to fructify in the pockets of the people. This is the right policy for a free democracy, right so long as we can ensure that money fructifies in the pockets of all the people and that its distribution is allied as closely as possible to ability and effort. But it cannot be reconciled with excessive levels of taxation.

Finally there are the personal sufferings of unemployment and ill health which have so often led to the loss of hard-won savings. All parties hope that it will be possible in future to abolish mass unemployment. The Coalition Government produced a scheme for this purpose embodied in the White Paper of 1944. I believe that the methods set out in that Paper afford the best prospect we have so far known of countering the tragic effects of cyclical unemployment.

Similarly, the great schemes of National Insurance hammered out by the Coalition, which came as the culmination of the long development of contributory insurance in this country, provide every citizen with an income, as of right, to tide him over times of difficulty and interrupted earning. In the years to come, if we develop the comprehensive medical service, to which principle we as a party have given our support, if we can avoid mass unemployment, if we can carry out these great schemes of national insurance, we shall have swept away many of the barriers to widespread saving and property owning which formerly existed.

There is to my mind no doubt that the present moment is one of the utmost significance for the future of the Conservative Party. The world in which we live has changed in the past few years to a degree which we cannot perhaps yet fully realise. The changes that are coming may be even greater and more radical. Now is the time to take stock and to readjust ourselves to the present and to the future so far as it can be foreseen.

The defeat that we sustained last year, grievous as it was, is in this respect a blessing, because it gives us an opportunity to redefine our faith and our political objectives, and to prepare ourselves for the long and crucial struggles of the succeeding years. We must not live in the past. As we walk forward into the age of atomic power and of increasingly rapid scientific development we must be prepared to adjust our ideas to the developing needs of the nation. Objectively, open-mindedly, we must draw guidance from the lessons of the past. That is one of the peculiar virtues of our Conservative Party. It was never more necessary than it is today.

There can be no doubt that we as a people have the power to achieve new standards of material prosperity that would have seemed unattainable barely a few years ago. By the full application of modern scientific methods of production and organisation, developed not as a brake on, but in partnership with, the individual drive and initiative which has characterised our free-enterprise system in the past, we can produce far more of all the things that are necessary and desirable for human existence. But, as this process develops, for develop it inevitably will, there is an increasing danger that we may find ourselves enmeshed in the cogs of our own economic machine. We may find that in achieving greater material prosperity we have lost far more in matters of the spirit. You cannot, to my mind, make a clear-cut division between a man's working life and his leisure time. If he is a slave at his work, he cannot be a free man away from it. We must have regard for the whole man. That is why I believe that the development of State Socialism will be fatal to individual liberty and responsibility.

But let us not, on the other hand, forget that the development of large-scale economic processes, of vast industrial units, will inevitably have just that effect, unless we take positive action to avoid it.

It is essential that the worker in industry should have the status of an individual and not of a mere cog in a soulless machine. To substitute the State for the private employer as boss won't give the worker that status. He will never have it under Socialism. Nor will he achieve it in the economy of the twentieth century under a system of free enterprise unless we are prepared to foster and encourage schemes for the distribution of capital ownership over a wide area, and for giving men and women a closer interest and share in the purpose and operation of the industry that employs them.

We cannot all be our own masters, doctors, lawyers, craftsmen, small-holders, shopkeepers. There has always been an important place in the economy of this country for those whom it is present-day jargon to describe as self-employed. May they continue to increase in numbers and to maintain their essential independence.

But let us not forget that in modern times the great majority of our people are employed either as wage or salary earners. Freedom for them in their employment cannot be the same as it is for the barrister or the costermonger, who is his own master, but it can be none the less real. The key to it, I believe, is knowledge. We must not be content that the work people in our industries should be mere units of labour. We must regard them as individuals who have a right to share in the knowledge of the common purpose of the industry in which they are working. If capital and labour are to be partners, they must be full partners, and labour is entitled to expect full information as to the achievements and the purposes of industry and the distribution of its fruits. Nothing less than this matches up to the needs of human personality.

I have been talking in broad general terms, but in the time at my disposal it has been impossible to do otherwise. It has been my purpose to describe what is the fundamental difference between the Conservative and the Socialist approach to the problems of this country, present and future.

We base ourselves upon the individual, upon the need to develop the individual personality. We recognise that the individual can develop only through membership of a living, united community. But unity is not mere uniformity; it can be created only out of diversity, only from harmonising the desires, the aspirations and the efforts of the human beings who make a nation. Socialism says to a man: 'You are a unit in the State. Work hard for the State, as the State thinks best, and the State will provide you with what it thinks you should have.'

We say: 'You are an individual. Choose your own way in life and seek to develop to the full your own talents. If you do this, and if you are prepared to accept the obligations that are essential to life in an ordered community, then we regard it as the duty of Government to see that out of the fruits of your labour you can build a life of your own, for yourself and your family, and at the same time feel the satisfaction of sharing in the common purpose of a free society.'

The Protocol of Sèvres, 24 October 1956

PROTOCOLE (original French version)

Les résultats des conversations qui se sont déroulées à SEVRES du 22 au 24 Octobre 1956 entre les représentants des Gouvernements du Royaume-Uni, de l'Etat-d'Israël et de la France sont les suivants:

1 – Les Forces Israéliennes lancent le 23 Oct 1956[1] dans la soirée une opération d'envergure contre les Forces Egyptiennes en vue d'atteindre le lendemain la Zone du Canal.

2 – Les Gouvernements Britannique et Français constatant ces évènements adressent respectivement et simultanément dans la journée du 30 Oct 1956[2] au Gouvernment Egyptien et Israëlien les deux appels répondant aux lignes directrice suivantes:

A/ – *Au Gouvernement Egyptien*

a) – arrêter toute action de guerre.
b) – retirer toutes ses troupes à la distance de 10 milles du Canal.
c) – accepter l'occupation temporaire des positions clés sur le Canal par les Forces Anglo-Françaises pour garantir la liberté du transit sur le Canal par les navires de toutes Nations jusqu'à un règlement définitif.

[End of page 1. Initialled by David Ben-Gurion, Christian Pineau and Patrick Dean – D B-G, P, PD]

B/ – *Au Gouvernement Israëlien*
a) – arrêter toute action de guerre.
b) – retirer toutes ses troupes à la distance de 10 milles à l'Est du Canal.

Par ailleurs le Gouvernement Israëlien sera informé de ce que les Gouvernements Français et Britannique ont demandés au Gouvernement Egyptien d'accepter l'occupation temporaire des positions clés sur le Canal par les Forces Anglo-Françaises.

Il est entendu que si l'un des deux Gouvernements refusait, on ne donnait pas son accord, dans un délai de 12 H. Les Forces Anglo-

Françaises interviendraient avec les moyens nécessaires pour que leurs demandes soient acceptées.

C/ – Les Représentants des Trois Gouvernements sont d'accord pour que le Gouvernement Israëlien ne soit pas tenu d'accepter les clauses de l'appel qui lui est adressé, dans le cas ou le Gouvernement Egyptien n'accepterait pas celles de l'appel qui lui est adressé d'autre part.

[End of page 2. Initialled as at end of page 1.]

3 – Dans le cas ou le Gouvernement EGYPTIEN n'aurait pas dans les délais fixés donné son accord aux clauses de l'appel qui lui a été adressé)[3] les Forces Anglo-Françaises déclencheront le 31 Octobre[4] dans les premières heures de la matinée les opérations militaires contre les Forces Egyptiennes.

4 – Le Gouvernement Israëlien enverra des Forces afin d'occuper la côte OUEST du Golfe d'AKABA et le groupe des Îles TIRANE et SANAFIR pour assurer la liberté de navigation dans le golfe d'AKABA.

5 – Israël s'engage à ne pas attaquer la JORDANIE pendant la période des opérations contre l'EGYPTE.

Mais, au cas ou dans le même période la JORDANIE attaquerait Israël, le Gouvernement Britannique s'engage à ne pas venir en aide à la JORDANIE.

6 – Les dispositions du présent PROTOCOLE doivent demeurir rigoureusement secrètes.

7 – Elles entreront en vigueur après l'accord des Trois Gouvernements.

[Signed] *Christian Pineau   D Ben-Gurion*
        Patrick Dean

British Ambassadors to the Major Powers, 1935–57

(Titles as during terms of office)

France

Apr. 1934	Sir George Clerk
Apr. 1937	Sir Eric Phipps
Nov. 1939	Sir Ronald Campbell (Mission withdrawn June 1940)
Oct. 1944	Duff Cooper
Jan. 1948	Sir Oliver Harvey
Apr. 1954	Sir Gladwyn Jebb (until April 1960)

Germany

Aug. 1933	Sir Eric Phipps
Apr. 1937	Sir Nevile Henderson (Mission withdrawn September 1939) (1945–9 Military Governors)
Mar. 1949–Sep. 1953	British High Commissioners:
Mar. 1949	Sir Brian Robertson
Jun. 1950	Sir Ivone Kirkpatrick
Sep. 1953	Sir Frederick Hoyer Millar
	Ambassador to West Germany:
May 1955	Sir Frederick Hoyer Millar (until February 1957)

Italy

Oct. 1933	Sir Eric Drummond (Earl of Perth from 1937)
May 1939	Sir Percy Loraine (Mission withdrawn June 1940)
Apr. 1944	Sir Noel Charles (1944 High Commissioner, 1945 Representative of HM Government)
Oct. 1947	Sir Victor Mallet
Nov. 1953	Sir Ashley Clarke (until September 1962)

Russia

Oct. 1933	Viscount Chilston
Jan. 1939	Sir William Seeds
Jun. 1940	Sir Stafford Cripps

Feb. 1942	Sir Archibald Clark Kerr (Lord Inverchapel from 1946)
May 1946	Sir Maurice Peterson
Jun. 1949	Sir David Kelly
Oct. 1951	Sir Alvary Gascoigne
Oct. 1953	Sir William Hayter (until February 1957)

United States of America

Mar. 1930	Sir Ronald Lindsay
Aug. 1939	Marquess of Lothian
Jan. 1941	Viscount Halifax (Earl Halifax from May 1944)
May 1946	Lord Inverchapel
May 1948	Sir Oliver Franks
Dec. 1952	Sir Roger Makins
Nov. 1956	Sir Harold Caccia (until October 1961)

United Nations

Feb. 1946	Sir Alexander Cadogan
Jun. 1950	Sir Gladwyn Jebb
Mar. 1954	Sir Pierson Dixon (until September 1960)

Select Bibliography

Private Papers
1. *Avon Papers*
The Avon Papers are housed in the Special Collections in the Heslop Room at Birmingham University Library. The originals of the Avon Foreign Office Papers (FO 954) are also held at Birmingham.

2. *Other private papers*
Royal Archives, Windsor Castle (by gracious permission of Her Majesty The Queen):
King George V and Queen Mary papers
King George VI papers
Earl and Countess of Athlone papers

Earl Alexander of Tunis (Public Record Office)
Lord Allan of Kilmahew papers (courtesy of Lady Allan of Kilmahew)
Earl Attlee papers (Bodleian Library, Oxford, and Churchill College, Cambridge)
The Countess of Avon papers (courtesy of the Countess of Avon)
Earl Baldwin papers (Cambridge University Library)
Lord Beaverbrook papers (House of Lords Record Office)
Bishop George Bell papers (Lambeth Palace Library)
Ernest Bevin papers (Churchill College, Cambridge)
Lady Violet Bonham Carter papers (Bodleian Library, Oxford)
Viscount Boyd of Merton papers (Bodleian Library, Oxford)
Lord Butler of Saffron Walden papers (Trinity College, Cambridge)
Lord Caccia papers (Eton College, Windsor)
Sir Alexander Cadogan papers (Churchill College, Cambridge)
Viscount Caldecote papers (Churchill College, Cambridge)
Lord Robert Cecil papers (Hatfield House, Hatfield, courtesy of the Marquess of Salisbury))
Sir Austen Chamberlain papers (Birmingham University Library)
Neville Chamberlain papers (Birmingham University Library)
Viscount Chandos papers (Churchill College, Cambridge)
Chartwell papers (Churchill College, Cambridge)
Viscount Cherwell papers (Nuffield College, Oxford)

Sir Winston Churchill papers (Churchill College, Cambridge)
Viscount Cilcennin papers (Carmarthenshire Record Office)
William Clark papers (Bodleian Library, Oxford)
Canon John Collins papers (Lambeth Palace Library)
Sir John Colville papers (Churchill College, Cambridge)
Sir Stafford Cripps papers (Nuffield College, Oxford)
Viscount Crookshank papers (Bodleian Library, Oxford)
Lord Dalton papers (Nuffield College, Oxford)
Viscount Davidson papers (House of Lords Record Office)
Sir Patrick Dean papers (courtesy of the late Sir Patrick Dean)
Sir Pierson Dixon papers (courtesy of Mr Piers Dixon)
Sir Douglas Dodds-Parker (Magdalen College, Oxford, courtesy of Sir Douglas Dodds-Parker)
Sir Thomas Dugdale papers (courtesy of Lord Crathorne)
Lord Duncan-Sandys papers (Churchill College, Cambridge)
Dwight D. Eisenhower papers (Eisenhower Presidential Library, Abilene, Kansas)
Baroness Elliot of Harwood papers (in private possession)
Lady Emmett papers (Bodleian Library, Oxford)
Lord Fisher of Lambeth papers (Lambeth Palace Library)
Lord Gladwyn papers (Churchill College, Cambridge)
Lord Gordon-Walker papers (Churchill College, Cambridge)
Sir William Gorell Barnes papers (Churchill College, Cambridge)
Lord Hailes papers (Churchill College, Cambridge)
Sir William Haley papers (Churchill College, Cambridge)
Lord Halifax papers (Borthwick Institute, York)
Lord Hankey papers (Churchill College, Cambridge)
Lord Home of the Hirsel papers (courtesy of the 15th Earl of Home)
Lord Hore-Belisha papers (Churchill College, Cambridge)
Viscount Inskip papers (Churchill College, Cambridge)
Lord Killearn papers (Middle East Centre, St Antony's College, Oxford)
Earl of Kilmuir papers (Churchill College, Cambridge)
Lord Lloyd papers (Churchill College, Cambridge)
Earl Lloyd-George of Dwyfor papers (House of Lords Record Office)
Sir Donald Logan papers (courtesy of Sir Donald Logan)
Hugh Lunghi papers (courtesy of Mr Hugh Lunghi)
Ramsay MacDonald papers (Public Record Office, Kew)
Arthur Mann papers (Bodleian Library, Oxford)
Viscount Margesson papers (Churchill College, Cambridge)
René Massigli papers (Quai d'Orsay, Paris)
Guy Mollet papers (Guy Mollet Archives, Paris)
Viscount Monckton of Brenchley papers (Bodleian Library, Oxford)

Lord Morrison of Lambeth papers (Nuffield College, Oxford)
Sir Charles Mott-Radclyffe papers (Middle East Centre, St Antony's College, Oxford)
Earl Mountbatten of Burma papers (University of Southampton)
Lord Normanbrook papers (Bodleian Library, Oxford)
Viscount Norwich papers (Churchill College, Cambridge)
Sir Eric Phipps papers (Churchill College, Cambridge)
Antoine Pinay papers (Quai d'Orsay, Paris)
Christian Pineau papers (Quai d'Orsay, Paris)
Lord Reading papers (India Office Library, London)
Sir Patrick Reilly papers (courtesy of the late Sir Patrick Reilly)
Lord Reith diaries (unpublished material, BBC Written Archives, Caversham)
Kenneth Rose papers (courtesy of Mr Kenneth Rose)
Sir Anthony Rumbold papers (Bodleian Library, Oxford)
Sir Horace Rumbold papers (Bodleian Library, Oxford)
Lord Salisbury papers (Hatfield House, Hatfield, courtesy of the Marquess of Salisbury)
Lord Selwyn-Lloyd papers (Churchill College, Cambridge)
Lord Sherfield papers (courtesy of the late Lord Sherfield)
Viscount Simon papers (Bodleian Library, Oxford)
Lord Soames papers (Churchill College, Cambridge, courtesy of Lady Soames)
Major-General Sir Louis Spears papers (Middle East Centre, St Antony's College, Oxford)
Baroness Spencer-Churchill papers (Churchill College, Cambridge, courtesy of Lady Soames)
Lord Stockton papers (Bodleian Library, Oxford)
Bishop Robert Stopford papers (Lambeth Palace Library)
Lord Strang papers (Churchill College, Cambridge)
Earl of Swinton papers (Churchill College, Cambridge)
Viscount Templewood papers (Cambridge University Library)
Viscount Thurso papers (Churchill College, Cambridge)
Lord Vansittart papers (Churchill College, Cambridge)
Lord Willoughby de Broke papers (House of Lords Record Office)
Sir Horace Wilson papers (Public Record Office, Kew)
Earl of Woolton papers (Bodleian Library, Oxford)

3 *Oral history transcripts* (John F. Kennedy Library, Boston)
Chester Cooper
Sir Alec Douglas-Home (later Lord Home of the Hirsel)
Lord Gore-Booth

Averell Harriman
Sir Patrick Reilly
Dean Rusk
Sir Humphrey (later Lord) Trevelyan
Sir Michael Wright

Public and Institutional Records
1. *State Papers* (Public Record Office, Kew)
Individual files are listed in the notes.
Documenti diplomatici italiani, 8th Series, Rome.
Documents Diplomatiques Français 1932–1939, 1st and 2nd Series, Paris, 1973.
Documents on British Foreign Policy, 1919–1939, Series 1, Series 2, Series 3, edited by E. L. Woodward, W. N. Medlicott, and Douglas Dakin, M. E. Lambert, Rohan Butler, J. P. T. Bury, Gillian Bennett and Keith A. Hamilton, HMSO, 1946–1997.
Documents on British Policy Overseas, Series 1, Vol. 1, edited by Rohan Butler and M. E. Pelly, HMSO, 1984.
Documents on British Policy Overseas, Series 1, Vols 1 and 2, edited by Roger Bullen and M. E. Pelly, HMSO, 1985 and 1986.
Documents on German Foreign Policy 1918–1945, Series C and Series D, HMSO, edited by Margaret Lambert *et al.*, 1949–1983.
Memorandum on relations between the United Kingdom, the United States and France in the months following Egyptian nationalisation of the Suez Canal Company in 1956, PRO. FO 800/728.
Proposals for the Reform of the Foreign Service (Cmd 6420), January 1943.

2. *Other records*
Archives du Ministère des Affaires étrangères, Quai d'Orsay, Paris.
BBC Written Archives (Caversham Park, Reading).
Christ Church College, Oxford.
Eton College.
Foreign Relations of the United States, Vol. XVI: The Suez Crisis, 26 July–31 December 1956, edited by Nina J. Noring, Department of State, Washington, DC, 1990.
Keesing's Contemporary Archives, 1945–1977.
Mass Observation files (Sussex University).
News International plc, Archives (*The Times* Archives and Record Office, London).
Oxford University Calendar, 1919–1923 (Clarendon Press, Oxford).
Sandroyd School, Tollard Royal (formerly at Cobham).

Warwick and Leamington Conservative Association Records (Salisbury Hall, Leamington Spa).
Warwick and Leamington Conservative Association Minute Books (Warwick County Record Office, Warwick).
Who's Who 1924–1977 (A. & C. Black).
Who Was Who 1897–1980 (A. & C. Black).

3. *Published official and party documents*
Annual Register.
Conservative Party Archives (Bodleian Library, Oxford).
Proposals for the Reform of the Foreign Service (1943), Cmd. 6420.
Report of the Crimea Conference (11 February 1945), Cmd. 6598.
Report on Social Insurance & Allied Services (December 1942), Cmd. 6404.

The Press and Periodical Literature
1. *National and foreign*
Daily Express, Daily Graphic, Daily Herald, Daily Mail, Daily Mirror, Daily Record, Daily Telegraph, Daily Worker, Evening Dispatch, Evening News, Evening Standard, Financial Times, Glasgow Herald, Guardian, Independent, Manchester Guardian, Morning Post, Morning Star, New York Herald Tribune, New York Times, News Chronicle, News of the World, Observer, People, The Scotsman, Sunday Chronicle, Sunday Express, Sunday Telegraph, Sunday Times, The Times.

2. *Local and regional*
Belfast Telegraph, Birmingham Daily Mail, Birmingham Post, Coventry Herald, Durham County Advertiser, Labour Chronicle, Leamington Chronicle, Leamington Spa Courier and Warwickshire Standard, Midland Daily Telegraph, North Eastern Gazette, The Salisbury Journal, Stratford-on-Avon Herald, Warwick Advertiser, Western Daily Press, Yorkshire Post.

3. *Journals and periodicals*
Apollo, Church Times, Contemporary British History, Contemporary Record, Crossbow, Economic History Review, The Economist, English Historical Review, Eton College Chronicle, Foreign Affairs: An American Quarterly Review, Historical Journal, History Today, Illustrated London News, Intelligence and National Security, International Affairs, The International History Review, Journal of Politics, Life, Listener, London School of Economics Quarterly, Middle Eastern Affairs, New Statesman & Nation, Newsweek, Paris Match, Punch, The Sandroydian, Spectator, Tatler, Times Literary Supplement, Twentieth Century British History.

Published Works by Lord Avon

1. *Books*

Places in the Sun, John Murray, 1926.

Foreign Affairs, Faber & Faber, 1939.

Freedom and Order: Selected Speeches, 1939–1946, Faber & Faber, 1947.

Days for Decision: Selected Speeches, 1946–1949, Faber & Faber, 1949.

The Eden Memoirs: Full Circle, Cassell, 1960.

The Eden Memoirs: Facing the Dictators, Cassell, 1962.

The Eden Memoirs: The Reckoning, Cassell, 1965.

Towards Peace in Indo-China, Royal Institute of International Affairs, Oxford University Press, 1966.

Another World: 1897–1917, Allen Lane, 1976.

2. *Other published works*

'Conservative Policies and Objectives', Conservative Central Office, 1946.

'Britain in World Strategy', *Foreign Affairs*, 29, 1950–1.

'The Slender Margin of Safety', *Foreign Affairs*, 39, 1960–1.

Secondary Sources

1. *Published works*

(All books are published in London, unless otherwise indicated)

Dean Acheson, *Present at the Creation: My Years in the State Department*, Hamish Hamilton, 1970.

R. J. Q. Adams, *British Politics and Foreign Policy in the Age of Appeasement, 1935–1939*, Macmillan, 1993.

Paul Addison, *The Road to 1945*, Jonathan Cape, 1975.

____, *Churchill on the Home Front 1900–1955*, Pimlico edition, 1993.

Jonathan Aitken, *Nixon: A Life*, Weidenfeld & Nicolson, 1993.

Stephen Ambrose, *Eisenhower The President, Volume 2, 1952–1969*, Allen & Unwin, 1984.

Julian Amery, *Approach March*, Hutchinson, 1973.

Leo Amery, *My Political Life: Volume Two War and Peace 1914–1929*, Hutchinson, 1953.

____, *My Political Life: Volume Three The Unforgiving Years 1929–1940*, Hutchinson, 1955.

Mark Amory (ed.), *The Letters of Ann Fleming*, Collins Harvill, 1985.

Noel Annan, *Our Age: Portrait of a Generation*, Weidenfeld & Nicolson, 1990.

Sidney Aster, *Anthony Eden*, Weidenfeld & Nicolson, 1976.

David Attenborough, *Life on Air: Memoirs of a Broadcaster*, BBC Books, 2002

Walter Bagehot, *The English Constitution*, Fontana paperback, 1963.

Stuart Ball (ed.), *Parliament and Politics in the Age of Baldwin and MacDonald: The Headlam Diaries 1923–1935*, The Historians' Press, 1992.

____, *Parliament and Politics in the Age of Churchill and Attlee: The Headlam Diaries 1935–1951*, Royal Historical Society, Cambridge University Press, Cambridge, 1999.

James Barber, *The Prime Minister since 1945*, Blackwell, Oxford, 1991.

Dennis Bardens, *Portrait of a Statesman: The personal life-story of Sir Anthony Eden*, Frederick Muller, 1955.

A. J. Barker, *Suez: The Seven-Day War*, Faber & Faber, 1964.

Elizabeth Barker, *Churchill and Eden at War*, Macmillan, 1978.

John Barnes and David Nicholson (eds), *The Leo Amery Diaries: Volume One 1896–1929*, Hutchinson, 1980.

____, *The Empire at Bay: the Leo Amery Diaries 1929–1945*, Hutchinson, 1988.

Correlli Barnett, *The Verdict of Peace: Britain between Her Yesterday and the Future*, Macmillan, 2001.

C. J. Bartlett, *A Political History of Anglo-American Relations since 1945*, Longmans, 1992.

Michael Bar-Zohar, *The Armed Prophet: A Biography of Ben Gurion*, Arthur Barker, 1967.

Reginald Bassett, *Democracy and Foreign Policy: A Case History. The Sino-Japanese Dispute 1931–1933*, Longmans, Green & Co., 1952.

____, *Nineteen Thirty-One: Political Crisis*, Macmillan, 1958.

Sally Beauman, *The Royal Shakespeare Company: A History of Ten Decades*, Oxford University Press, Oxford, 1982.

Lord Beaverbrook, *Men and Power 1917–1918*, Hutchinson, 1956.

David Ben Gurion, *Israel: Years of Challenge*, Anthony Blond, 1964.

Tony Benn, *Years of Hope: Diaries, Papers and Letters 1940–1962*, Hutchinson, 1994.

____, *Out of the Wilderness: Diaries 1963–1967*, Hutchinson, 1987.

____, *Office without Power: Diaries 1968–1972*, Hutchinson, 1988.

____, *Against the Tide: Diaries 1973–1976*, Hutchinson, 1989.

____, *Conflicts of Interest: Diaries 1977–1980*, Hutchinson, 1990.

Alan Bennett, *Forty Years On*, Faber & Faber, 1969.

John Biggs-Davison, *George Wyndham: A Study in Toryism*, Hodder & Stoughton, 1951.

George Bilainkin, *Maisky: Ten Years Ambassador*, George Allen & Unwin, 1944.

Earl of Birkenhead, *The Prof in Two Worlds: The official life of Professor F. A. Lindeman, Viscount Cherwell*, Collins, 1961.

____, *The Life of Lord Halifax*, Hamish Hamilton, 1965.

____, *Walter Monckton: The Life of Viscount Monckton of Brenchley*, Weidenfeld & Nicolson, 1969.

Robert Blake, *The Unknown Prime Minister: The Life and Times of Andrew Bonar Law*, Eyre & Spottiswoode, 1955.

____, *Disraeli*, Methuen paperback, 1969.

____, *The Conservative Party from Peel to Thatcher*, Methuen, 1985.

____, *The Decline of Power 1915–1964*, Granada, 1985.

Robert Blake and Wm. Roger Louis (eds), *Churchill*, Oxford University Press, Oxford, 1993.

Robert Blake and C.S. Nicholls (eds), *The Dictionary of National Biography 1971–1980*, Oxford University Press, Oxford, 1986.

____, *The Dictionary of National Biography 1981–1985*, Oxford University Press, Oxford, 1990.

Margaret Blanche, *The Countess of Warwick*, Cassell, 1967.

Vernon Bogdanor, *The Monarchy and the Constitution*, Clarendon Press, Oxford, 1995.

Vernon Bogdanor and Robert Skidelsky (eds), *The Age of Affluence*, Macmillan, 1970.

Lord Boothby, *My Yesterday, Your Tomorrow*, Hutchinson, 1962.

____, *Recollections of a Rebel*, Hutchinson, 1978.

R. J. B. Bosworth, *Mussolini*, Arnold, 2002.

Claude Bouchinet-Serreules, *Nous Étions Faits Pour Être Libres*, Bernard Grasset, Paris, 2000.

Tom Bower, *The Perfect English Spy: Sir Dick White and the Secret War 1935–1990*, Heinemann, 1995.

Francis Boyd, *Richard Austen Butler*, Rockcliff, 1956.

John Boyd-Carpenter, *Way of Life: The Memoirs of John Boyd-Carpenter*, Sidgwick & Jackson, 1980.

Lord Boyd Orr, *As I Recall*, MacGibbon & Kee, 1966.

Russell Braddon, *Suez: Splitting of a Nation*, Collins, 1973.

Sarah Bradford, *Elizabeth: A Biography of Her Majesty the Queen*, Heinemann, 1996.

Henry Brandon, *Special Relationships: a foreign correspondent's memoirs from Roosevelt to Reagan*, Macmillan, 1989.

Richard Breitman, *Official Secrets: What the Nazis Planned, What the British and Americans Knew*, Hill and Wang, New York, 1999.

Piers Brendon, *The Dark Valley: A Panorama of the 1930s*, Jonathan Cape, 2000.

Asa Briggs, *The History of Broadcasting in the United Kingdom Volume 5: Competition 1955–1974*, Oxford University Press, Oxford, 1995.

Douglas Brinkley, *Dean Acheson: The Cold War Years 1953–1971*, Yale University Press, New Haven, 1992.

Sam Brittan, *Steering the Economy*, Penguin Books, Harmondsworth, revised edition, 1971.

Merry and Serge Bromberger, *Secrets of Suez*, Pan Books and Sidgwick & Jackson, 1957.

George Brown, *In My Way*, Gollancz, 1971.

Richard Buckle (ed.), *Self Portrait with Friends: The Selected Diaries of Cecil Beaton 1926–1974*, Weidenfeld & Nicolson, 1979.

Alan Bullock, *Ernest Bevin, Foreign Secretary 1945–1951*, Heinemann, 1983.

____, *Ernest Bevin: A Biography*, Politico's, 2002.

Ivor Bulmer-Thomas, *The Growth of the British Party System: Volume 2, 1924–1966*, John Baker, 1967.

Simon Burgess, *Stafford Cripps: A Political Life*, Gollancz, 1999.

Trevor Burridge, *Clement Attlee: A Political Biography*, Jonathan Cape, 1985.

David Butler, *The British General Election of 1951*, Macmillan, 1952.

____, *The British General Election of 1955*, Macmillan, 1955.

David Butler and Anne Sloman, *British Political Facts 1900–1975*, Macmillan, 1975.

Lord Butler, *The Art of the Possible*, Penguin Books, Harmondsworth, revised edition, 1973.

____, *The Art of Memory: Friends in Perspective*, Hodder, 1982.

Mollie Butler, *August and Rab: A Memoir*, Weidenfeld & Nicolson, 1987.

Ronald Butt, *The Power of Parliament*, Constable, 2nd edition, 1969.

L. S. R. Byrne and E. L. Churchill, *Changing Eton*, Jonathan Cape, 1937.

James Cable, *The Geneva Conference of 1954 on Indochina*, Macmillan, revised edition, 2000.

James Callaghan, *Time and Chance*, Collins, 1987.

John Campbell, *Nye Bevan and the Mirage of British Socialism*, Weidenfeld & Nicolson, 1987.

____, *Edward Heath: A Biography*, Jonathan Cape, 1993.

Alan Campbell Johnson, *Anthony Eden: A Biography*, Robert Hale, 1938.

David Cannadine, *The Decline and Fall of the British Aristocracy*, Yale University Press, 1990.

Tim Card, *Eton Renewed: A History from 1860 to the Present Day*, John Murray, 1994.

David Carlton, *Anthony Eden: A Biography*, Allen Lane, 1981.

____, *Churchill and the Soviet Union*, Manchester University Press, Manchester, 2000.

Edward Carpenter, *Archbishop Fisher: His Life and Times*, The Canterbury Press, Norwich, 1991.

Lord Carrington, *Reflect on Things Past: The Memoirs of Lord Carrington*, Collins, 1988.

Michael Carver, *Out of Step: The Memoirs of Field Marshal Lord Carver*, Hutchinson, 1989.

Lord Casey, *Australian Foreign Minister: The Diaries of R. G. Casey 1951–1960*, Collins, 1962.

____, *The Future of the Commonwealth*, Frederick Muller, 1963.

Cato (Michael Foot, Peter Howard and Frank Owen), *Guilty Men*, Gollancz, 1940.

Sir Austen Chamberlain, *Down the Years*, Cassell, 1935.

Lord Chandos, *The Memoirs of Lord Chandos*, The Bodley Head, 1962.

John Charmley, *Duff Cooper: The Authorized Biography*, Weidenfeld & Nicolson, 1986.

____, *Lord Lloyd and the Decline of the British Empire*, Weidenfeld & Nicolson, 1987.

____, *Chamberlain and the Lost Peace*, John Curtis, Hodder & Stoughton, 1989.

____, *Churchill's Grand Alliance: The Anglo-American Special Relationship 1940–1957*, John Curtis, Hodder & Stoughton, 1995.

Jean Chauvel, *Commentaire Vol III–De Berne à Paris (1952–1962)*, Fayard, Paris, 1973.

Arthur Christiansen, *Headlines All My Life*, Heinemann, 1961.

Randolph S. Churchill, *The Rise and Fall of Sir Anthony Eden*, MacGibbon & Kee, 1959.

____, *Lord Derby: King of Lancashire*, Heinemann, 1959.

Winston S. Churchill, *Thoughts and Adventures*, Butterworth, 1932.

____, *The Second World War*, 6 volumes, Cassell, 1948–54.

Winston S. Churchill [Jr], *His Father's Son: The life of Randolph Churchill*, Weidenfeld & Nicolson, 1996.

Count Ciano, *Ciano's Diary 1939–1943*, Heinemann, 1947.

____, *Ciano's Diary 1937–1938*, Methuen, 1952.

Alan Clark (ed.), *A Good Innings: the Private Papers of Viscount Lee of Fareham*, John Murray, 1974.

William Clark, *From Three Worlds: Memoirs*, Sidgwick & Jackson, 1986.

Peter Clarke, *A Question of Leadership: Gladstone to Thatcher*, Hamish Hamilton, 1991.

____, *The Cripps Version: The Life of Sir Stafford Cripps 1889–1952*, Allen Lane, The Penguin Press, 2002.

Michael Cockerell, *Live from Number 10: The Inside Story of Prime Ministers and Television*, Faber & Faber, 1988.

Richard Cockett, *Twilight of Truth: Chamberlain, Appeasement and the Manipulation of the Press*, Weidenfeld & Nicolson, 1989.

John Colville, *Footprints in Time*, Collins, 1976.

____, *The Churchillians*, Weidenfeld & Nicolson, 1981.

____, *The Fringes of Power: Downing Street Diaries 1939–1955*, Hodder & Stoughton, 1985.

____, *Those Lambtons! A Most Unusual Family*, Hodder & Stoughton, 1988.

Ian Colvin, *Vansittart in Office*, Gollancz, 1965.

Henry Colyton, *Occasion, Chance and Change: A Memoir 1902–1946*, Michael Russell, Norwich, 1993.

Chris Cook, *Sources in British Political History 1900–1951, 5 volumes*, Macmillan, 1975.

Chris Cook and John Ramsden (eds), *By-Elections in British Politics*, Macmillan, 1973.

Chris Cook, Jane Leonard and Peter Leese, *The Longman Guide to Sources in Contemporary British History: Volume 2 Individuals*, Longman, 1994.

Duff Cooper, *Old Men Forget*, Hart-Davis, 1953.

Colin Coote, *A Companion of Honour: The Story of Walter Elliot*, Collins, 1965.

Patrick Cosgrave, *R. A. Butler: An English Life*, Quartet, 1981.

Maurice Cowling, *The Impact of Labour 1920–1924*, Cambridge University Press, Cambridge, 1971.

____, *The Impact of Hitler: British politics and British policy 1933–1940*, Cambridge University Press, Cambridge, 1975.

Percy Cradock, *Know Your Enemy: How the Joint Intelligence Committee saw the World*, John Murray, 2002.

W. Craig and F. Loewenheim, *The Diplomats 1939–1979*, Princeton University Press, Princeton, 1994.

Arthur Christiansen, *Headlines all my Life*, Heinemann, 1961.

Anthony Crosland, *The Future of Socialism*, Jonathan Cape, 1980.

Colin Cross, *Philip Snowden*, Barrie and Rockcliff, 1966.

J. A. Cross, *Sir Samuel Hoare: A Political Biography*, Jonathan Cape, 1977.

____, *Lord Swinton*, Oxford University Press, Oxford, 1982.

Richard Crossman, *The Backbench Diaries of Richard Crossman* (edited by Janet Morgan), Hamish Hamilton and Jonathan Cape, 1981.

N. J. Crowson (ed.), *Fleet Street, Press Barons and Politics: The Journals of Collin Brooks 1932–1940*, Royal Historical Society, Cambridge University Press, Cambridge, 1998.

Lord Curzon, *Persia and the Persian Question*, 2 volumes, 1892, reprinted by Frank Cass, 1966.

Tam Dalyell, *Dick Crossman: A Portrait*, Weidenfeld & Nicolson, 1989.

Alex Danchev and Daniel Todman (eds), *Field Marshal Lord Alanbrooke: War Diaries 1939–1945*, Weidenfeld & Nicolson, 2001.

Danny Danziger (ed.), *Eton Voices*, Viking, 1982.

Russell Davies and Liz Ottaway, *Vicky*, Secker & Warburg, 1987.

Robin Day, *Grand Inquisitor*, Weidenfeld & Nicolson, 1989.

____, *But With Respect: Memorable TV Interviews*, Orion paperback, 1994.

Gerard J. De Groot, *Liberal Crusader: The Life of Sir Archibald Sinclair*, Hurst & Company, 1993.

John Dickie, *The Uncommon Commoner: A Study of Sir Alec Douglas-Home*, Pall Mall Press, 1964.

____, *Inside the Foreign Office*, Chapmans, 1992.

____, *'Special No More': Anglo-American Relations – Rhetoric and Reality*, Weidenfeld & Nicolson, 1994.

David Dilks, *Neville Chamberlain Volume One: Pioneering and Reform, 1869–1929*, Cambridge University Press, Cambridge, 1984.

David Dilks (ed.), *The Diary of Sir Alexander Cadogan 1938–1943*, Cassell, 1971.

Piers Dixon, *Double Diploma: The Life of Sir Pierson Dixon*, Hutchinson, 1968.

Sir Douglas Dodds-Parker, *Political Eunuch*, Springwood Books, 1986.

Frances Donaldson, *Edward VIII*, Weidenfeld & Nicolson, 1974.

Bernard Donoughue and G. W. Jones, *Herbert Morrison: Portrait of a Politician*, Weidenfeld & Nicolson, 1973.

Charles Douglas-Home, *Evelyn Baring: The Last Proconsul*, Collins, 1978.

David Dutton, *Austen Chamberlain: Gentleman in Politics*, Ross Anderson Publications, Bolton, 1985.

____, *Simon: A Political Biography of Sir John Simon*, Aurum Press, 1992.

____, *Anthony Eden: A Life and Reputation*, Arnold, 1997.

____, *Neville Chamberlain*, Arnold, 2001.

James Eayrs, *The Commonwealth and Suez*, Oxford University Press, Oxford, 1964.

Robert Allan Eden, *Some Historical Notes on the Eden Family*, Blades, East & Blades, 1907.

Max Egremont, *The Cousins: The friendship, opinions and activities of Wilfrid Scawen Blunt and George Wyndham*, Collins, 1977.

Dwight D. Eisenhower, *The White House Years: Mandate for Change 1953–1956*, Heinemann, 1956.

____, *Balfour: A Life of Arthur James Balfour*, Collins, 1980.

D. H. Elletson, *Chequers and the Prime Ministers*, Robert Hale, 1970.

J. T. Emmerson, *The Rhineland Crisis 7 March 1936: A study in multilateral diplomacy*, Maurice Temple Smith, 1977.

Leon D. Epstein, *British Politics in the Suez Crisis*, Pall Mall Press, 1964.

John Erickson (ed.), *Main Front: Soviet Leaders Look Back on World War II*, Brassey's Defence Publishers, 1987.

Mahmoud Fawzi, *Suez 1956: An Egyptian Perspective*, Shourouk International, 1988.

Keith Feiling, *The Life of Neville Chamberlain*, Macmillan, 1946.

Robert H. Ferrell (ed.), *Dear Bess: the Letters of Harry to Bess Truman 1910–1959*, W. W. Norton, New York, 1983.

Herman Finer, *Dulles over Suez*, Heinemann, 1964.

Nigel Fisher, *Iain Macleod*, Deutsch, 1973.

____, *The Tory Leaders: Their Struggle for Power*, Weidenfeld & Nicolson, 1977.

____, *Harold Macmillan*, Weidenfeld & Nicolson, 1982.

Hugh Foot, *A Start in Freedom*, Hodder & Stoughton, 1964.

Joseph Frankel, *The Making of Foreign Policy*, Oxford University Press, Oxford, 1963.

____, *British Foreign Policy 1945–1973*, Oxford University Press, Oxford, 1975.

Douglas Arnold Franklin, *Aspirations for Greatness: John Foster Dulles, Anthony Eden and the Conduct of Anglo-American Diplomacy, 1951–1956*, UMI, University of Kentucky, Kentucky, 1995.

Steven Z. Freiberger, *Dawn Over Suez: The Rise of American Power in the Middle East 1953–1957*, Ivan R. Dee, Chicago, 1992.

J. K. Galbraith, *The Affluent Society*, Penguin Books, Harmondsworth, 1965.

Joe Garner, *The Commonwealth Office 1925–1968*, Heinemann, 1978.

Martin Gilbert, *The Roots of Appeasement*, Weidenfeld & Nicolson, 1966.

____, *Winston S. Churchill: Volume V 1922–1939*, Heinemann, 1976.

____, *Finest Hour: Winston S. Churchill 1939–1941*, Heinemann, 1983.

____, *Road to Victory: Winston S. Churchill 1941–1945*, Heinemann, 1986.

____, *Never Despair: Winston S. Churchill 1945–1965*, Heinemann, 1988.

____, *A History of the Twentieth Century: Volume Two 1933–1951*, HarperCollins, 1998.

Martin Gilbert (ed.), *Winston S. Churchill Companion Volume V: Part 2 The Wilderness Years 1929–1935*, Heinemann, 1981.

____, *Ibid., Part 3 The Coming of War 1936–1939*, Heinemann, 1982.

Donald Gillies, *Radical Diplomat: The Life of Archibald Clark Kerr, Lord Inverchapel, 1882–1951*, I. B. Tauris, 1999.

Cynthia Gladwyn, *The Paris Embassy*, Collins, 1976.

Lord Gladwyn, *The Memoirs of Lord Gladwyn*, Weidenfeld & Nicolson, 1972.

Grace Wyndham Goldie, *Facing the Nation: Television and Politics 1936–1976*, Bodley Head, 1977.

Philip Goodhart, *The 1922: The Story of the Conservative Backbenchers' Parliamentary Committee*, Macmillan, 1973.

Patrick Gordon Walker, *The Cabinet*, Jonathan Cape, 1972.

Paul Gore-Booth, *With Great Truth and Respect*, Constable, 1974.

A. Gorst, L. Johnson and W. S. Lucas, *Post War Britain 1945–1964: Themes and Perspectives*, Pinter, 1989.

Denis Greenhill, *More By Accident*, Wilton 65, York, 1992.

Richard Griffiths, *Fellow Travellers of the Right: British Enthusiasts for Nazi Germany 1933–1939*, Constable, 1980.

John Grigg, *1943: The Victory That Never Was*, Penguin Books, Harmondsworth, revised edition, 1999.

Andrei Gromyko, *Memoirs*, Hutchinson, 1989.

G. Hagglof, *Diplomat: Memoirs of a Swedish Envoy in London, Paris, Berlin, Moscow and Washington*, Bodley Head, 1972.

Lord Hailsham, *The Door Wherein I went*, Collins, 1975.

____, *A Sparrow's Flight: Memoirs*, Collins, 1990.

Kenneth Harris, *Attlee*, Weidenfeld & Nicolson, 1982.

Ralph Harris, *Politics without Prejudice: A Political Appreciation of the Rt. Hon. Richard Austen Butler*, Staples Press, 1956.

Rupert Hart-Davis (ed.), *The Lyttelton Hart-Davis Letters: The Correspondence of George Lyttelton and Rupert Hart-Davis, Volumes One and Two 1955–1957*, John Murray paperback, 1985.

John Harvey (ed.), *The Diplomatic Diaries of Oliver Harvey 1937–1940*, Collins, 1970.

____, *The War Diaries of Oliver Harvey 1941–1945*, Collins, 1978.

Jonathan Haslam, *The Soviet Union and the Struggle for Collective Security in Europe 1933–1939*, Macmillan, 1984.

Sir William Hayter, *A Double Life*, Hamish Hamilton, 1974.

Sir Edward Heath, *The Course of My Life: The Autobiography of Sir Edward Heath*, Hodder & Stoughton, 1998.

Simon Heffer, *Like the Roman: The Life of Enoch Powell*, Weidenfeld & Nicolson, 1998.

Mohamed H. Heikal, *Nasser: The Cairo Documents*, New English Library, 1972.

____, *Cutting the Lion's Tail: Suez through Egyptian Eyes*, André Deutsch, 1986.

Sir Nevile Henderson, *Failure of a Mission*, Hodder & Stoughton, 1940.

Sir Nicholas Henderson, *The Private Office Revisited*, Profile Books, 2001.

____, *Mandarin: The Diaries of Nicholas Henderson*, Weidenfeld & Nicolson, 1994.

Peter Hennessy, *Whitehall*, Secker & Warburg, 1989.

____, *Never Again: Britain 1945–1951*, Jonathan Cape, 1992.

____, *Muddling Through: Power, Politics and the Quality of Government in Postwar Britain*, Gollancz, 1996.

____, *The Prime Minister: The Office and Its Holders Since 1945*, Allen Lane, The Penguin Press, 2000.

____, *The Secret State: Whitehall and the Cold War*, Allen Lane, The Penguin Press, 2002.

Peter Hennessy and Anthony Seldon (eds), *Ruling Performance: British Governments from Attlee to Thatcher*, Blackwell, Oxford, 1987.

The History of The Times Volume IV, Pt II 1921–1948, The Times, 1952.

Sir Samuel Hoare, Viscount Templewood, *Nine Troubled Years*, Collins, 1954.

J. D. Hoffman, *The Conservative Party in Opposition, 1945–1951*, MacGibbon & Kee, 1964.

Lord Home, *The Way the Wind Blows: An Autobiography*, Collins, 1976.

Alistair Horne, *Macmillan 1894–1956: Volume 1 of the Official Biography*, Macmillan, 1988.

____, *Macmillan 1957–1986: Volume 2 of the Official Biography*, Macmillan, 1989.

Anthony Howard, *R. A. B.: The Life of R. A. Butler*, Jonathan Cape, 1985.

____, *Crossman: The Pursuit of Power*, Jonathan Cape, 1990.

Anthony Howard (ed.), *The Crossman Diaries*, Magnum paperback condensed version, 1979.

T. E. B. Howarth, *Prospect and Reality: Great Britain 1945–1955*, Collins, 1985.

Geoffrey Howe, *Conflict of Loyalty*, Macmillan, 1994.

Cordell Hull, *The Memoirs of Cordell Hull: Two Volumes*, Hodder & Stoughton, 1948.

George Hutchinson, *The Last Edwardian at No. 10*, Grafton Books, 1980.

F. A. Iremonger, *William Temple: Archbishop of Canterbury*, Oxford University Press, Oxford, 1948.

Lord Ismay, *The Memoirs of General the Lord Ismay*, Heinemann, 1960.

Douglas Jay, *The Socialist Case*, Faber & Faber, 1937.

____, *Change and Fortune: A Political Record*, Hutchinson, 1980.

Miles Jebb (ed.), *The Diaries of Cynthia Gladwyn*, Constable, 1995.

Roy Jenkins, *Asquith*, Collins, 1964.

____, *Nine Men of Power*, Hamish Hamilton, 1974.

____, *Truman*, Collins, 1986.

____, *Baldwin*, Collins, 1987.

____, *Gallery of 20th Century Portraits*, David & Charles, Newton Abbot, 1988.

____, *A Life at the Centre*, Macmillan, 1991.

____, *Portraits and Miniatures*, Macmillan, 1993.

____, *The Chancellors*, Macmillan, 1998.

____, *Churchill*, Macmillan, 2001.

Thomas Jones, *Whitehall Diary Volume II 1926–1930*, Oxford University Press, Oxford, 1971.

____, *A Diary with Letters 1931–1950*, Oxford University Press, Oxford, 1954.

Denis Judd, *Lord Reading: Rufus Isaacs, First Marquess of Reading, Lord Chief Justice & Viceroy of India, 1860–1935*, Weidenfeld & Nicolson, 1982.

David M. Kennedy, *Freedom from Fear: The American People in Depression and War, 1929–1945*, Oxford University Press, New York, 1999.

François Kersaudy, *Churchill and de Gaulle*, Fontana paperback edition, 1981.

____, *Churchill: Le Pouvoir de l'Imagination*, Éditions Tallandier, Paris, 2000.

J. M. Keynes, *The Economic Consequences of the Peace*, Macmillan paperback, 1984.

Earl of Kilmuir, *Political Adventure, The Memoirs of the Earl of Kilmuir*, Weidenfeld & Nicolson, 1964.

Cole C. Kingseed, *Eisenhower and the Suez Crisis of 1956*, Louisiana State University Press, Baton Rouge, Louisiana, 1995.

Sir Ivone Kirkpatrick, *The Inner Circle: Memoirs of Ivone Kirkpatrick*, Macmillan, 1959.

Henry Kissinger, *Diplomacy*, Simon & Schuster, New York, 1994.

Diana B. Kunz, *The Economic Diplomacy of the Suez Crisis*, University of North Carolina Press, 1991, Chapel Hill and London.

Keith Kyle, *Suez*, Weidenfeld & Nicolson, 1991.

____, *Suez: Britain's End of Empire in the Middle East*, I. B. Tauris, 2003.

David Kynaston, *The City of London Volume IV: A Club No More 1945–2000*, Chatto & Windus, 2001.

Jean Lacouture, *Pierre Mendès-France*, Holmes & Meier, New York, 1984.

Richard Lamb, *The Failure of the Eden Government*, Sidgwick & Jackson, 1987.

____, *The Drift to War 1922–1939*, W. H. Allen, 1989.

____, *Churchill as War Leader: Right or Wrong?*, Bloomsbury, 1991.

____, *The Macmillan Years 1957–1963: The Emerging Truth*, John Murray, 1995.

____, *Mussolini and the British*, John Murray, 1997.

Brian Lapping, *End of Empire*, Grafton Books, Paladin paperback, 1989.

Zig Layton-Henry (ed.), *Conservative Party Politics*, Macmillan, 1980.

Ronald Lewin, *Ultra Goes to War: The Secret Story*, Arrow Books, 1980.

Selwyn Lloyd, *Suez 1956: A Personal Account*, Jonathan Cape, 1978.

Lord Longford, *A History of the House of Lords*, Collins, 1988.

Wm R. Louis and H. Bull, *The Special Relationship: Anglo-American Relations since 1945*, Clarendon Press, Oxford, 1986.

Wm Roger Louis and Roger Owen (eds), *Suez 1956: The Crisis and its Consequences*, Clarendon Press paperback, Oxford, 1991.

Richard Lovell, *Churchill's Doctor: A Biography of Lord Moran*, Royal Society of Medicine Services Ltd, 1992.

W. Scott Lucas, *Divided We Stand: Britain, the US and the Suez Crisis*, Hodder & Stoughton paperback, 1996.

Andrew Lycett, *Ian Fleming*, Weidenfeld & Nicolson, 1992.

Charles Lysaght, *Brendan Bracken*, Allen Lane, 1979.

Oliver Lyttelton, Viscount Chandos, *The Memoirs of Lord Chandos*, Bodley Head, 1962.

R. B. McCallum and Alison Readman, *The British General Election of 1945*, Oxford University Press, Oxford, 1947.

Martin McCauley (ed.), *Communist Power in Europe 1944–1949*, Macmillan, 1977.

Geoffrey McDermott, *The Eden Legacy and the Decline of British Diplomacy*, Leslie Frewin, 1969.

Iverach McDonald, *A Man of the Times*, Hamish Hamilton, 1976.

Lyn Macdonald, *Somme*, Michael Joseph, 1983.

Malcolm MacDonald, *Titans and Others*, Collins, 1972.

Frank McDonough, *Neville Chamberlain, Appeasement and the British Road to War*, Manchester University Press, Manchester, 1998.

Donald MacDougall, *Don and Mandarin: Memoirs of an Economist*, John Murray, 1987.

Norman McGowan, *My Years with Churchill*, Souvenir Press, 1958.

Denis Mack Smith, *Mussolini*, Granada, 1983.

J. W. Mackail and Guy Wyndham, *Life and Letters of George Wyndham: Volume 1*, Hutchinson, 1925.

Robert McKenzie, *British Political Parties*, Heinemann, 1967.

John P. Mackintosh, *The British Cabinet*, 3rd edition, Stevens & Sons, 1977.

John P. Mackintosh (ed.), *British Prime Ministers of the Twentieth Century, Volume 2: Churchill to Callaghan*, Weidenfeld & Nicolson, 1978.

Fitzroy Maclean, *Eastern Approaches*, Jonathan Cape, 1949.

Iain Macleod, *Neville Chamberlain*, Muller, 1961.

David S. McLellan, *Dean Acheson: The State Department Years*, Dodd, Mead & Company, New York, 1976.

Harold Macmillan, *Winds of Change 1914–1939*, Macmillan, 1966.

____, *The Blast of War 1939–1945*, Macmillan, 1967.

____, *Tides of Fortune 1945–1955*, Macmillan, 1969.

____, *Riding the Storm 1956–1959*, Macmillan, 1971.

____, *Pointing the Way 1959–1961*, Macmillan, 1972.

____, *At the End of the Day 1961–1963*, Macmillan, 1973.

____, *War Diaries: Politics and War in the Mediterranean January 1943–May 1945*, Macmillan, 1984.

Ivan Maisky, *Memoirs of a Soviet Ambassador: The War 1939–1943*, Hutchinson, 1967.

Robert Mallett, *The Italian Navy and Fascist Expansionism 1935–1940*, Frank Cass, 1998.

Nicholas Mansergh, *The Commonwealth Experience*, Weidenfeld & Nicolson, 1969.

Nicholas Mansergh (ed.), *India: The Transfer of Power, Volume III, 21 September 1942–12 June 1943*, H.M.S.O., 1971.

James Margach, *The Abuse of Power*, W. H. Allen, 1978.

David Marquand, *Ramsay MacDonald*, Jonathan Cape, 1977.

Reginald Maudling, *Memoirs*, Sidgwick & Jackson, 1978.

Robert Menzies, *Afternoon Light: Some Memories of Men and Events*, Cassell, 1967.

Keith Middlemass, *Power, Competition and the State, Volume One: Britain in Search of Balance, 1940–1961*, Macmillan, 1986.

Keith Middlemass and John Barnes, *Baldwin: A Biography*, Weidenfeld & Nicolson, 1969.

T.B. Millar (ed.), *Australian Foreign Minister: The Diaries of R. G. Casey 1951–1960*, Collins, 1972.

Walter Millis (ed.), *The Forrestal Diaries*, Cassell, 1952.

Alan S. Milward, *The United Kingdom and the European Community, Volume 1: The Rise and Fall of a National Strategy 1945–1963*, Frank Cass, 2002.

Adrian Mitchell, *Heart on the Left: Poems 1953–1984*, Bloodaxe Books, Newcastle-upon-Tyne, 1997.

D.E. Moggridge, *Maynard Keynes: An Economist's Biography*, Routledge, 1992.

Anthony Moncrieff (ed.), *Suez: Ten Years Later*, BBC Publications, 1967.

Anthony Montague Browne, *Long Sunset: Memoirs of Winston Churchill's Last Private Secretary*, Cassell, 1995.

Geoffrey Moorhouse, *The Diplomats: The Foreign Office Today*, Jonathan Cape, 1977.

639

Lord Moran, *Winston Churchill: The Struggle for Survival 1940–1965*, Sphere Books paperback, 1968.

Austen Morgan, *Harold Wilson*, Pluto Press, 1992.

Janet Morgan (ed.), *The Backbench Diaries of Richard Crossman*, Hamish Hamilton and Jonathan Cape, 1981.

Kenneth and Jane Morgan, *Portrait of a Progressive: The Political Career of Christopher, Viscount Addison*, Clarendon Press, Oxford, 1980.

Kenneth O. Morgan, *Labour in Power 1945–1951*, Clarendon Press, Oxford, 1984.

____, *The People's Peace: British History 1945–1989*, Oxford University Press, Oxford, 1990.

____, *Callaghan: A Life*, Oxford University Press, Oxford, 1997.

James Morris, *Heaven's Command: An Imperial Progress*, Penguin Books, Harmondsworth, 1979.

____, *Farewell the Trumpets: An Imperial Retreat*, Penguin Books, Harmondsworth, 1979.

Charlotte Mosley (ed.), *The Letters of Nancy Mitford and Evelyn Waugh*, Hodder & Stoughton, 1996.

Charles Mott-Radclyffe, *Foreign Body in the Eye: A Memoir of the Foreign Service Old and New*, Leo Cooper, 1955.

C. L. Mowat, *Britain between the Wars 1918–1940*, Methuen paperback, 1968.

Philip Murphy, *Alan Lennox-Boyd: a biography*, I. B. Tauris, 1999.

Robert Murphy, *Diplomat among Warriors*, Collins, 1964.

Ian Nairn and Nikolaus Pevsner, *The Buildings of England: Sussex*, Penguin Books, Harmondsworth, 1985 edition.

H. G. Nicholas, *The British General Election of 1950*, Macmillan, 1951.

Harold Nicolson, *King George V: His Life and Reign*, Constable, 1952.

____, *Diaries and Letters: 1930–1962*, edited by Nigel Nicolson, 3 volumes, Collins, 1966, 1967, 1968.

Nigel Nicolson, *People and Parliament*, Weidenfeld & Nicolson, 1958.

Nigel Nicolson (ed.), *Vita and Harold: The letters of Vita Sackville-West and Harold Nicolson, 1910–1962*, Weidenfeld & Nicolson, 1992.

F. S. Northedge, *The Troubled Giant: Britain among the Great Powers, 1916–1939*, George Bell and Sons, 1966.

John Nott, *Here Today, Gone Tomorrow: Recollections of an Errant Politician*, Politico's, 2002.

Anthony Nutting, *No End of a Lesson: The Story of Suez*, Constable, 1967.

____, *Nasser*, Constable, 1972.

F. S. Oliver, *The Endless Adventure*, Macmillan, 1935.

George Orwell, *Homage to Catalonia*, Secker & Warburg, 1938.

R. A. C. Parker, *Chamberlain and Appeasement: British Policy and the Coming of the Second World War*, Macmillan, 1993.

____, *Churchill and Appeasement*, Macmillan, 2000.

Anthony Parsons, *From Cold War to Hot Peace: UN Interventions 1947–1995*, Michael Joseph, 1995.

Peter Paterson, *Tired and Emotional: The Life of Lord George-Brown*, Chatto & Windus, 1993.

Drew Pearson, *Diaries 1949–1959*, edited by Tyler Abell, Jonathan Cape, 1974.

Jonathan Pearson, *Sir Anthony Eden and the Suez Crisis: Reluctant Gamble*, Palgrave Macmillan, Basingstoke, 2003.

Henry Pelling, *Winston Churchill*, Macmillan, 1974.

____, *Churchill's Peacetime Ministry, 1951–1955*, Macmillan Press, Basingstoke, 1997.

A. D. Peters, *Anthony Eden at the Foreign Office 1931–1938*, Gower Publishing, Aldershot, 1986.

Sir Charles Petrie, *The Chamberlain Tradition*, Lovat Dixon, 1938.

____, *The Life and Letters of the Rt. Hon. Sir J. Austen Chamberlain, 2 volumes*, Cassell, 1939–40.

Ben Pimlott, *Hugh Dalton*, Jonathan Cape, 1986.

____, *Harold Wilson*, HarperCollins, 1992.

____, *The Queen: A Biography of Elizabeth II*, HarperCollins, 1996.

Ben Pimlott (ed.), *The Second World War Diary of Hugh Dalton 1940–45*, Jonathan Cape,1986.

____, *The Political Diary of Hugh Dalton 1918–40, 1945–60*, Jonathan Cape, 1986.

Chapman Pincher, *Their Trade is Treachery*, Sidgwick & Jackson, 1981.

Edwin Plowden, *An Industrialist in the Treasury: The Post-War Years*, André Deutsch, 1989.

Clive Ponting, *Churchill*, Sinclair-Stevenson, 1994.

James Pope-Hennessy, *Queen Mary 1867–1953*, George Allen & Unwin, 1959.

Mark Pottle and Mark Bonham Carter (eds), *Lantern Slides: The Diaries and Letters of Violet Bonham Carter 1904–1914*, Weidenfeld & Nicolson, 1996.

Mark Pottle (ed.), *Champion Redoubtable: The Diaries and Letters of Violet Bonham Carter 1914–1945*, Weidenfeld & Nicolson, 1998.

____, *Daring to Hope: The Diaries and Letters of Violet Bonham Carter 1946–1969*, Weidenfeld & Nicolson, 2000.

Enoch Powell, *Joseph Chamberlain*, Thames and Hudson, 1977.

J. B. Priestley, *English Journey*, Penguin Books paperback, Harmondsworth, 1977.

John Ramsden, *A History of the Conservative Party: The Age of Churchill & Eden, 1940–1957*, Longman, 1995.

Robert F. Randle, *Geneva 1954: The Settlement of the Indochinese War*, Princeton University Press, Princeton, New Jersey, 1969.

William Rees-Mogg, *Sir Anthony Eden*, Rockcliff, 1956.

John Redcliffe-Maud, *Experiences of an Optimist, The Memoirs of John Redcliffe-Maud*, Hamish Hamilton, 1981.

David Reynolds, *Britannia Overruled: British Policy and World Power in the 20th Century*, Longman, 1991.

Robert Rhodes James, *Churchill: A Study in Failure*, Weidenfeld & Nicolson, 1970.

____, *Anthony Eden*, Weidenfeld & Nicolson, 1986.

____, *Bob Boothby: A Portrait*, John Curtis, Hodder & Stoughton, 1991.

____, *A Spirit Undaunted: The Political Role of George VI*, Little Brown, 1998.

Robert Rhodes James (ed.), *Chips: The Diaries of Sir Henry Channon*, Weidenfeld & Nicolson, 1967.

____ (ed.), *Memoirs of a Conservative: J. C. C. Davidson's Memoirs and Papers, 1910–1937*, Weidenfeld & Nicolson, 1969.

Peter Riddell, *Honest Opportunism: The Rise of the Career Politician*, Hamish Hamilton, 1993.

Andrew Roberts, *The Holy Fox: A Biography of Lord Halifax*, Weidenfeld & Nicolson, 1991.

____, *Eminent Churchillians*, Weidenfeld & Nicolson, 1994.

Frank Roberts, *Dealing with Dictators: The Destruction and Revival of Europe 1930–1970*, Weidenfeld & Nicolson, 1991.

Kenneth Rose, *Superior Person: A Portrait of Curzon and His Circle in late Victorian Britain*, Weidenfeld & Nicolson, 1969.

____, *The Later Cecils*, Weidenfeld & Nicolson, 1975.

____, *King George V*, Weidenfeld & Nicolson, 1983.

____, *Kings, Queens & Courtiers: Intimate Portraits of the Royal House of Windsor from its foundation to the present day*, Weidenfeld & Nicolson, 1985.

Stephen Roskill, *Hankey: Man of Secrets, Volume II 1919–1931*, Collins, 1972.

____, *Hankey: Man of Secrets, Volume III 1931–1963*, Collins, 1974.

G. Ross (ed.), *The Foreign Office and the Kremlin: British Documents on Anglo-Soviet Relations 1941–1945*, Cambridge University Press, Cambridge, 1984.

Sir John Rothenstein, *Summer's Lease: Autobiography 1901–1938*, Hamish Hamilton, 1965.

Victor Rothwell, *Anthony Eden: A Political Biography 1931–1957*,

Manchester University Press, Manchester, 1992.

Anthony Sampson, *The Anatomy of Britain*, Hodder & Stoughton, 1962.

___, *Macmillan: A Study in Ambiguity*, Allen Lane, 1967.

A. O. Sarkissian (ed.), *Studies in Diplomatic History and Historiography*, Longmans Green, 1961.

Thomas J. Schoenbaum, *Waging Peace and War: Dean Rusk in the Truman, Kennedy & Johnson Years*, Simon & Schuster, New York, 1988.

Robert C. Self (ed.), *The Austen Chamberlain Diary Letters: The correspondence of Sir Austen Chamberlain with his sisters Hilda and Ida, 1916–1937*, Cambridge University Press for the Royal Historical Association, 1995.

Anthony Seldon, *Churchill's Indian Summer: The Conservative Government 1951–1955*, Hodder & Stoughton, 1981.

Anthony Seldon and Stuart Ball (eds), *Conservative Century: The Conservative Party since 1900*, Oxford University Press, Oxford, 1994.

Tony Shaw, *Eden, Suez and the Mass Media: Propaganda and Persuasion during the Suez Crisis*, I. B. Tauris, 1996.

Hartley Shawcross, *Life Sentence*, Constable, 1995.

Robert Shepherd, *A Class Divided: Appeasement and the Road to Munich 1938*, Macmillan, 1988.

___, *The Power Brokers: The Tory Party and Its Leaders*, Hutchinson, 1991.

___, *Iain Macleod*, Hutchinson, 1994.

Avi Shlaim, *The Iron Wall: Israel and the Arab World*, Penguin Books, 2001.

Avi Shlaim, Peter Jones and Keith Sainsbury, *British Foreign Secretaries since 1945*, David & Charles, Newton Abbot, 1977.

Evelyn Shuckburgh, *Descent to Suez: Diaries 1951–1956*, edited by John Charmley, Weidenfeld & Nicolson, 1986.

Viscount Simon, *Retrospect: The Memoirs of the Rt. Hon. Viscount Simon*, Hutchinson, 1952.

Michael Sissons and Philip French (eds), *Age of Austerity: 1945–1951*, Penguin Books, Harmondsworth, 1964.

Noel Skelton, *Constructive Conservatism*, Blackwood, Edinburgh, 1924.

Robert Skidelsky, *Oswald Mosley*, Macmillan, 1975.

___, *Interests and Obsessions: Historical Essays*, Macmillan, 1993.

Arnold Smith, *Stitches in Time: The Commonwealth in World Politics*, André Deutsch, 1981.

Gaddis Smith, *Dean Acheson*, Cooper Square Publishers, New York, 1972.

Mary Soames, *Clementine Churchill*, Cassell, 1979.

Mary Soames (ed.), *Speaking for Themselves: The personal letters of Winston and Clementine Churchill*, Doubleday, 1998.

Meier Sompolinsky, *Britain and the Holocaust: The Failure of Anglo-Jewish Leadership?*, Sussex Academic Press, Brighton, 1999.

Gerald Sparrow, *RAB: Study of a Statesman*, Odhams, 1965.

Tom Stannage, *Baldwin Thwarts the Opposition: The British General Election of 1935*, Croom Helm, 1980.

David Steel, *Against Goliath: David Steel's Story*, Weidenfeld & Nicolson, 1989.

Michael Stenton, *Radio London and Resistance in Occupied Europe: British Political Warfare 1939–1943*, Oxford University Press, Oxford, 2000.

Michael Stewart, *Life and Labour: An Autobiography*, Sidgwick & Jackson, 1980.

Henry L. Stimson, *The Far Eastern Crisis: Recollections and Observations*, Harper & Brothers, New York, 1936.

Henry L. Stimson and McGeorge Bundy, *On Active Service in Peace and War*, Harper & Brothers, New York, 1948.

James Stuart, *Within the Fringe*, Bodley Head, 1967.

C. L. Sulzberger, *The Last of the Giants*, Weidenfeld & Nicolson, 1970.

Earl of Swinton, *Sixty Years of Power*, Hutchinson, 1966.

A. J. P. Taylor, *The Origins of the Second World War*, Penguin Books, Harmondsworth, 1964.

____, *English History 1914–1945*, Oxford University Press, Oxford, 1965.

____, *Beaverbrook*, Penguin Books, Harmondsworth, 1974.

Major-General A. C. Temperley, *The Whispering Gallery of Europe*, Collins, 1938.

Hugh Thomas, *The Suez Affair*, Weidenfeld & Nicolson, 1967.

Alan Thompson, *The Day Before Yesterday*, Sidgwick & Jackson, 1971.

Neville Thompson, *The Anti-Appeasers: Conservative Opposition to Appeasement in the 1930s*, Clarendon Press, Oxford, 1971.

Christopher Thorne, *The Limits of Foreign Policy: The West, the League, and the Far Eastern Crisis of 1931–1933*, Hamish Hamilton, 1972.

____, *Allies of a Kind: The United States, Britain, and the War against Japan, 1941–1945*, Hamish Hamilton, 1978.

Andrew Thorpe, *The British General Election of 1931*, Clarendon Press, Oxford, 1991.

D. R. Thorpe, *The Uncrowned Prime Ministers: a study of Sir Austen Chamberlain, Lord Curzon and Lord Butler*, Darkhorse Publishing, 1980.

____, *Selwyn Lloyd*, Jonathan Cape, 1989.

____, *Alec Douglas-Home*, Sinclair-Stevenson, 1996.

Viscount Tonypandy, *George Thomas, Mr Speaker: The Memoirs of Viscount Tonypandy*, Century Publishing, 1985.

Mario Toscano, *Designs in Diplomacy: Pages from European Diplomatic History in the 20th Century* (translated and edited by George A. Carbone), John Hopkins Press, Baltimore and London, 1970.

Michael Tracey, *A Variety of Lives: A Biography of Sir Hugh Greene*, Bodley Head, 1983.

Ronald Tree, *When the Moon was High: Memoirs of Peace and War 1897–1942*, Macmillan, 1975.

Humphrey Trevelyan, *The Middle East in Revolution*, Macmillan, 1970.

____, *Worlds Apart: China 1953–5, Soviet Union 1962–5*, Macmillan, 1971.

Selwyn Ilan Troën and Moshe Shemesh, *The Suez-Sinai Crisis 1956: Retrospective and Reappraisal*, Frank Cass, 1989.

John Turner, *Macmillan*, Longman, 1994.

Arthur H. Vandenberg, Jr (ed.), *The Private Papers of Senator Arthur Vandenberg*, Gollancz, 1953.

Lord Vansittart, *The Mist Procession*, Hutchinson, 1958.

Peter Vansittart, *In the Fifties*, John Murray, 1995.

Herbert van Thal (ed.), *The Prime Ministers: Volume Two, From Lord John Russell to Edward Heath*, George Allen & Unwin, 1975.

Dennis Walters, *Not Always with the Pack*, Constable, 1989.

Gerald Warner, *The Scottish Tory Party: A History*, Weidenfeld & Nicolson, 1988.

Alan Watkins, *A Conservative Coup: The Fall of Margaret Thatcher*, Duckworth, second edition, 1992.

Harold Watkinson, *Turning Points: A Record of our Times*, Michael Russell, Salisbury, 1986.

D. C. Watt, *Succeeding John Bull*, Cambridge University Press, Cambridge, 1984.

Evelyn Waugh, *Scoop*, Penguin Books, Harmondsworth, 1963 edition.

Sir Roy Welensky, *Welensky's 4000 Days: The Life and Death of the Federation of Rhodesia and Nyasaland*, Collins, 1964.

Sumner Welles, *Time for Decision*, Hamish Hamilton, 1944.

____, *Seven Decisions That Shaped History*, Harper and Brothers, New York, 1951.

Nigel West, *Molehunt: The full story of the Soviet Spy in MI5*, Weidenfeld & Nicolson, 1987.

John W. Wheeler-Bennett, *King George VI: His Life and Reign*, Macmillan, 1958.

____, *Munich: Prologue to Tragedy*, Macmillan, 1963 edition.

William Whitelaw, *The Whitelaw Memoirs*, Aurum Press, 1989.

L. G. Wickham Legg and E. T. Williams (eds), *The Dictionary of National Biography 1941–1950*, Oxford University Press, Oxford, 1959.

Charles Williams, *The Last Great Frenchman*, Little, Brown & Company, 1993.

____, *Adenauer: The Father of the New Germany*, Little, Brown and Company, 2000.

E. T. Williams and Helen H. Palmer (eds), *The Dictionary of National Biography 1951–1960*, Clarendon Press, Oxford, 1971.

E. T. Williams and C. S. Nicholls (eds), *The Dictionary of National Biography 1961–1970*, Clarendon Press, Oxford, 1981.

Francis Williams, *A Pattern of Rulers*, Longmans, 1965.

Philip Williams, *Hugh Gaitskell: A Political Biography*, Jonathan Cape, 1979.

Philip Williams (ed.), *The Diary of Hugh Gaitskell 1945–1956*, Jonathan Cape, 1983.

Raymond Williams, *Culture and Society 1780–1950*, Penguin Books, Harmondsworth, 1961.

Philip Williamson, *Stanley Baldwin: Conservative leadership and national values*, Cambridge University Press, Cambridge, 1999.

Roger Wilmut (ed.), *The Complete Beyond the Fringe*, Methuen, 1987.

Harold Wilson, *Memoirs: The Making of a Prime Minister 1916–1964*, Weidenfeld & Nicolson/Michael Joseph, 1986.

John Wilson, *CB: A Life of Sir Henry Campbell-Bannerman*, Constable, 1973.

Windsor, HRH The Duke of, *A King's Story: The Memoirs of H.R.H. The Duke of Windsor*, Pan Books paperback, 1957.

John Winton, *Cunningham: The Greatest Admiral since Nelson*, John Murray, 1998.

J. R. T. Wood (ed.), *The Welensky Papers: A History of the Federation of Rhodesia and Nyasaland*, Graham Publishing, Durban, 1983.

C. M. Woodhouse, *British Foreign Policy since the Second World War*, Hutchinson, 1961.

____, *Something Ventured*, Granada, 1982.

Lord Woolton, *The Memoirs of the Rt. Hon. the Earl of Woolton*, Cassell, 1959.

Peter Wright, *Spycatcher: The Candid Autobiography of a Senior Intelligence Officer*, Viking, New York, 1987.

M. E. Yapp (ed.), *Politics and Diplomacy in Egypt: The Diaries of Sir Miles Lampson 1935–1937*, Oxford University Press, Oxford, 1997.

Hugo Young, *This Blessed Plot: Britain and Europe from Churchill to Blair*, Macmillan, 1998.

John W. Young (ed.), *The Foreign Policy of Churchill's Peacetime*

Administration 1951–1955, Leicester University Press, Leicester, 1988.

Kenneth Young, *Rhodesia and Independence: A Study in British Colonial Policy*, Dent, revised edition, 1969.

____, *Sir Alec Douglas-Home*, Dent, 1970.

Kenneth Young (ed.), *The Diaries of Sir Robert Bruce Lockhart: Volume One 1915–1938; Volume Two 1939–1965*, Macmillan, 1973 and 1980.

Michael Young, *The Rise of the Meritocracy*, Penguin Books, Harmondsworth, 1961.

Philip Ziegler, *Melbourne: A Biography of William Lamb 2nd Viscount Melbourne*, Collins, 1976.

____, *Mountbatten: the official biography*, Collins, 1985.

____, *Wilson: the Authorised Life*, Weidenfeld & Nicolson, 1993.

Solly Zuckerman, *Monkeys, Men and Missiles: An Autobiography 1946–1988*, Collins, 1988.

2. *Articles, essays, lectures and pamphlets*

R. K. Alderman and Martin J. Smith, 'Can British Prime Ministers be given the push by their Parties?', *Parliamentary Affairs*, July 1990.

R. J. Aldrich, 'Intelligence, Anglo-American Relations and the Suez Crisis, 1956', *Intelligence and National Security*, Vol. 9, No. 3 (July 1994).

Winthrop Aldrich, 'The Suez Crisis: A Footnote to History', *Foreign Affairs*, January 1967.

Lord Avon, 'The Man of Munich', *Times Literary Supplement*, 1 December 1961.

Peter Beck, 'Politicians versus Historians: Lord Avon's "Appeasement Battle" against "Lamentably Appeasement-Minded" Historians', *Twentieth Century British History*, Vol. 9, No. 3, 1998.

John W. Braasch, M.D., *Anthony Eden's Biliary Tract Saga*, Lahey Clinic, Massachusetts, 2002.

R. A. Butler, *Fundamental Issues*, Conservative Political Centre, 1946.

Christopher Coker, *Who Only England Know: Conservatives and Foreign Policy*, Institute for European Defence & Strategic Studies, 1990.

David Day, 'Churchill and his War Rivals', *History Today*, April 1991.

Sir Patrick Dean, 'Memorandum by Sir Patrick Dean–1986', Patrick Dean papers.

Professor David Dilks, 'The Office of Prime Minister in Twentieth-Century Britain', 18 November 1992, Hull University Press, 1993.

____, 'From Trustee to Partner: The British Government & Empire in the 1950s', six lectures to mark the tenure of the Colonial Office by Alan Lennox-Boyd, 1st Viscount Boyd of Merton, Rhodes House, Oxford, 1993.

_____, 'Communications, The Commonwealth and the Future', 10 May 1994, Hull University Press, 1994.

_____, 'de Gaulle and the British', 22 June 1994, Paris, privately printed.

_____, 'The Conference at Potsdam, 1945', Hull University Press, 1995.

_____, 'Britain, the Commonwealth and the Wider World, 1939–45', lecture at the Conference on 'The Role of the Commonwealth in the Second World War', St Antony's College, Oxford, 8 April 1998.

_____, 'We must Hope for the Best and Prepare for the Worst': The Prime Minister, the Cabinet and Hitler's Germany, 1937–1939', *Proceedings of the British Academy*, Vol. LXIII, 1987.

David Dutton, 'Living with Collusion: Anthony Eden and the Later History of the Suez Crisis', *Contemporary Record*, Vol. 5, No. 2 (Autumn 1991).

Sir Michael Fraser, 'The Conservative Research Department & Conservative Recovery after 1945', privately circulated, August 1961.

Sir Nicholas Henderson, 'Hitler and the Rhineland, 1936: A Decisive Turning-Point', *History Today*, Vol. 42, October 1992.

Professor Peter Hennessy, 'Searching for the "Great Ghost": The Palace, the Premiership, The Cabinet and the Constitution in the Post-war Period', Queen Mary and Westfield College, 1 February 1994.

Professor Peter Hennessy and Mark Laity, 'Suez – What the Papers say', *Contemporary Record*, Vol. 1, No. 1 (Spring 1987).

Roy Jenkins, 'Anthony Eden in the Thirties', *Daily Telegraph*, 19 November 1962.

Saul Kelly, 'A very considerable and largely unsung success: Sir Roger Makins' Washington Embassy, 1953–1956', *Anglo-American Relations in the Twentieth Century* (edited by Jonathan Hollowell), Macmillan, 2000.

Saul Kelly and Anthony Gorst (eds), 'Whitehall and the Suez Crisis', *Contemporary British History* (Special Issue), Vol. 13, No. 2, Frank Cass Publishers, Ilford, 1999.

Keith Kyle, 'Suez Revisited', Lecture to the Thackeray Society, Reform Club, 30 March 2000.

Diana Kunz, 'Did Macmillan Lie over Suez?', *The Spectator*, 3 November 1990.

Sir Donald Logan, 'Suez: Meetings at Sèvres 22–25 October 1956. Narrative,' Donald Logan papers.

_____, 'Comments' (Memorandum on the Suez Section of Richard Lamb's *The Failure of the Eden Government*, Sidgwick & Jackson, 1987), Donald Logan papers.

William Roger Louis, 'Harold Macmillan and the Middle East Crisis of 1958', *Proceedings of the British Academy*, 94, 207–28, London (1996).

W. Scott Lucas, 'Suez, the Americans and the Overthrow of Anthony Eden', *London School of Economics Quarterly*, pp. 254–77, September 1987.

Hugh Lunghi, 'Yalta – Forty Years On', privately printed, 1985.

Ben Macintyre, 'Eden's secret American beauty', *The Times*, 3 June 2000.

Robert Mallett, 'Fascist Foreign Policy and Official Italian Views of Anthony Eden in the 1930s', *The Historical Journal*, 43, 1 (2000).

Geoffrey Marston, 'Armed intervention in the 1956 Suez Canal crisis: the legal advice tendered to the British Government', *The International and Comparative Law Quarterly*, Vol. 37 (1988).

William C. Mills, 'The Chamberlain-Grandi Conversations of July–August 1937 and the Appeasement of Italy', *The International History Review*, Vol. XIX, No. 3, August 1997.

Sir Anthony Nutting, 'Another Eden', *The Spectator*, 1 May 1976.

R. A. C. Parker, 'Great Britain, France and the Ethiopian Crisis 1935–1936', *English Historical Review*, Vol. 89, 1974.

Christopher Patten, 'R. A. Butler – What We Missed', Inaugural R. A. Butler Lecture, Coningsby Club, 25 May 1994.

Ben Pimlott, 'E. D. C., W. E. U., and Mr Eden', privately printed, July 1969.

Andrew Roberts, 'Betrayal of the brave at Suez', *Sunday Times*, 20 October 1996.

N. Rose, 'The Resignation of Sir Anthony Eden', *Historical Journal*, 25, pp. 911–31, 1982.

Avi Shlaim, 'The Protocol of Sèvres, 1956: anatomy of a war plot', *International Affairs*, Vol. 73, No. 3, 1997.

Noel Skelton, 'The Conservative Task: A Property-Owning Democracy', *Yorkshire Post*, 23 January 1930.

Denys Sutton, 'A Statesman's Collection', *Apollo*, June 1969.

Laurence Thompson, 'Man in the Red', five articles on R. A. Butler, *News Chronicle*, September 1955.

'Under the Umbrella' (centenary tribute to Neville Chamberlain), *The Spectator*, 27 March 1969.

Geoffrey Warner, '"Collusion" and the Suez Crisis of 1956', *International Affairs*, Vol. 55, 1979.

H. J. Yasamee, 'Anthony Eden and Europe, November 1951', Foreign Office Historical Branch, Occasional Paper, 1987.

3. Unpublished theses, etc.
Matthew Cotton, 'Eden, Suez and the Lessons of the 1930s', M.Phil. thesis, Bodleian Library, Oxford 1999.

Sir Knox Cunningham, 'One Man Dog: the Memoirs of Harold

Macmillan's Private Secretary', in the possession of the Drapers' Company.

Sylvia Goodfellow, 'R. A. Butler and the Conservative Party Committee on Post-War Problems', private memorandum.

Robert L. Johnston, 'The Premiership of Sir Anthony Eden: A Study of the Man and the Office', Ph.D. thesis, University of California, 1962.

Dr. Susan Onslow, 'Conservative Backbench Debate and its influence on British Foreign Policy 1948–1956', Ph.D. thesis, University of London/London School of Economics, 1995.

M. T. Thornhill, 'Britain and the Egyptian Question, 1950–54', Ph.D. thesis, Bodleian Library, Oxford, 1995.

Broadcast Programmes

1. *Radio*

Transcripts in the BBC Written Archives, Caversham:

'A Canal Too Far', presented by Peter Hennessy, BBC Radio 4, 31 January 1986.

'Assignment: Suez – The Propaganda War', BBC World Service, 31 October 1996.

'The Dictator's Foe', BBC Radio 4, obituary tribute to Lord Avon, 14 January 1977.

'Into the Darkness', BBC Radio 5, 21 July 1994.

'The Makers of Modern Politics. 3: Rab Butler – Artist of the Possible' by Anthony Howard. BBC Radio 4, 27 April 1995.

'Nasser's Eden' by Howard Brenton, BBC Radio 4, 30 October 1998.

'Neither War nor Peace at 10 Downing Street', BBC Radio 4, 1997.

'The Propaganda of Truth', BBC Radio 4, Autumn 1994.

'Suez: Ten Years After', BBC Radio 4, July 1966.

2. *Television*

'Anthony Eden: A Rather English Statesman', 3BMTV for BBC2 'Reputations', 6 June 2000.

'At the End of the Day', Harold Macmillan/Robert McKenzie interview, BBC TV, 1973.

'The Day Before Yesterday', Thames Television, 1971.

'End of Empire', Granada Television, 1985.

'God Bless You, Mr Chamberlain' by Robert Harris, BBC Television, 23 September 1988.

'The Life and Times of Lord Mountbatten', twelve-part ITV television series, 1969.

'Reputations: R. A. Butler' by Anthony Howard, BBC Television, 13 July 1983.

'The Suez Crisis', BBC1, 22 October 1996.

'Suez: A personal view by historian Andrew Roberts', BBC2, 23 October 1996.

'Television and Number 10', BBC Television, 1988.

'The Twentieth Century Remembered', interviews with Professor David Dilks, BBC Television, 13 July, 22 July, 29 July and 5 August, 1982.

'Westminster's Secret Service', a report by Michael Cockerell on the world of the Government Whips, BBC Television, 21 May 1995.

3. *Video material*

British Pathé News, 'A Year to Remember: 1945–1957', British Pathé News Ltd.

Gramophone Recordings

'British Prime Ministers: 1924–1964', BBC Records, REB 39M, 1969.

Acknowledgments

Material from the Royal Archives is published by gracious permission of Her Majesty Queen Elizabeth II.

Crown Copyright material in the Public Record Office and other archives is reproduced by permission of the Controller of Her Majesty's Stationery Office.

Material from the Avon Papers, Birmingham University Library, is reproduced by permission of The Countess of Avon and the Avon Trustees. Extracts from the papers and correspondence of the Countess of Avon are reproduced by permission of the Countess of Avon.

The author and publishers are also grateful to the following for permission to reproduce copyright material:
The Hon. Leo Amery for extracts from the diaries of Leo S. Amery; the Earl Attlee for extracts from the private letters of the 1st Earl Attlee; the Syndics of Cambridge University Library for extracts from the papers of Earl Baldwin of Bewdley; the Clerk of the Records, House of Lords Record Office, acting on behalf of the Beaverbrook Trust, for extracts from the papers of Lord Beaverbrook, and for an extract from a letter by A. J. Sylvester in the Earl Lloyd George of Dwyfor Papers; John Murray (Publishers) Ltd for extracts from John Betjeman's *Margate 1940* and *On the Death of King George V*; Dr. Judith Bogdanor for her memorandum on Eden's paternity; the Bodleian Library, Oxford, for access to Eden material in the Viscount Boyd of Merton papers; John W. Braasch M.D. for an extract from 'Anthony Eden's Biliary Tract Saga'; the Royal Historical Society for extracts from the diaries of Collin Brooks and Sir Cuthbert Headlam; lines from a poem by Gerald Bullett are reproduced by permission of PFD on behalf of the estate of Gerald Bullett; Lady Butler of Saffron Walden for extracts from letters by Lord Butler of Saffron Walden; the Master and Fellows of Trinity College for extracts from the Lord Butler of Saffron Walden papers; the Hon. Clarissa Pryce-Jones on behalf of the Caccia family for extracts from the papers of Lord Caccia; the Master and Fellows of Churchill College, Cambridge, for extracts from the diaries and papers of Sir Alexander Cadogan; Lord Carr of Hadley for extracts from letters by him; the University of Birmingham for extracts from the papers of Sir Austen Chamberlain and Neville Chamberlain; the Rt Hon. The Lord Kelvedon for extracts from the diaries of Sir Henry Channon;

extracts from the Archives of Christ Church Church are by kind permission of the Governing Body of Christ Church, Oxford; the Sir Winston Churchill Archive Trust for material from the Churchill papers (CHAR and CHUR), and the Master, Fellows and Scholars of Churchill College as custodians of the collection; the Master and Fellows of Churchill College, Cambridge, for letters by Baroness Spencer-Churchill in the Clementine Spencer Churchill collection (CSCT); extracts from private letters by Sir Winston Churchill and from a letter by Randolph Churchill are reproduced with permission of Curtis Brown Ltd, London on behalf of Winston S. Churchill, Copyright Winston S. Churchill; the Carmarthenshire Archives Services for extracts from the papers of Viscount Cilcennin (J. P. L. Thomas); Lord Hemingford and the Bodleian Library, Oxford for extracts from the diaries and papers of the William Clark; Lady Margaret Colville for a letter by Sir John Colville; Viscount Norwich for an extract from a letter by Alfred Duff Cooper; the Bodleian Library as custodians for extracts from the Viscount Crookshank papers; Professor David Dilks for extracts from his writings and editorial material in the Cadogan diaries; the London School of Economics for extracts from the Dalton Papers, British Library of Political and Economic Science; Mr Piers Dixon for extracts from the diaries and papers of Sir Pierson Dixon; Sir Douglas Dodds-Parker for extracts from his papers and a letter; the Dwight D. Eisenhower Library, Abilene, for extracts from the John Foster Dulles Oral Archive; Lord Eden of Winton for extracts from letters by Sir Timothy Eden; John S. D. Eisenhower and the Dwight D. Eisenhower Library, Abilene, for extracts from the papers and letters of President Dwight D. Eisenhower; the Provost and Fellows of Eton College for material from the Eton College Archives; Lambeth Palace Library for extracts from the papers of Archbishop Lord Fisher of Lambeth; Sir Philip Goodhart for a letter by the late Professor Arthur Goodhart; Mr Donald Haley for access to, and use of extracts from, the Sir William Haley Archive, and the Master, Fellows and Scholars of Churchill College, Cambridge as custodians of the collection; the Borthwick Institute of Historical Research, University of York for extracts from the papers of the Earl of Halifax; Curtis Brown on behalf of Peter Hall for a letter by him, Copyright © Peter Hall 1966; the Lord Hankey for letters by the 1st Lord Hankey; Lord Harvey of Tasburgh, the Hon. Mrs. John Harvey and Mr Robert Harvey for extracts from the diaries of Sir Oliver Harvey; the Earl of Home for extracts from the papers of Lord Home of the Hirsel and from the diary of Lady Home of the Hirsel; Sir Peter Hordern for a letter by him; the late the Rt. Hon. Lord Jenkins of Hillhead for an extract from his writings; the Middle East Centre, St. Antony's College, Oxford for extracts from the papers of Lord Killearn; Lady Miranda Cormack for an extract from the diaries of the Earl of Kilmuir, and the Master, Fellows and Scholars of Churchill College, Cambridge as custodians of the collection; Dr. John Charmley for an extract from a letter of Lord Lloyd of Dolobran; the Trustees of the Selwyn Lloyd estate for extracts from the Selwyn Lloyd papers, and the Master, Fellows and Scholars of Churchill College, Cambridge as custodians of the collection, at Churchill College, Cambridge; Mr Hugh Lunghi for extracts from his diaries and papers; Deirde Grieve for an extract from an unpublished poem by Hugh MacDiarmid; Mr Philip Mallett for a letter by the late Sir Victor Mallett; Mr Peter Wright and the Bodleian Library, Oxford for an extract from a letter by Arthur Mann; Lord Moran for extracts from the diaries of the 1st Baron Moran; the Rt. Hon. Peter Mandelson for a letter by Baroness Morrison of Lambeth; the Middle East Centre, St. Antony's College, Oxford for an extract from the papers of Sir Charles Mott-Radclyffe; the Trustees of the Broadlands Archives for extracts from the diaries and Suez file of Earl Mountbatten of Burma; Nigel Nicolson for extracts from the letters of Sir Harold Nicolson, and from the typescript diaries of Sir Harold Nicolson at Balliol College, Oxford; the Bodleian Library, Oxford as custodians for extracts from the Lord Normanbrook papers; Professor Ben Pimlott for extracts from his privately printed paper, 'E.D.C., W.E.U., and Mr Eden'; the Hon. Sir Peter Ramsbotham for use of copyright material; the late Sir Patrick Reilly for material from a private memorandum on Eden's career; Mr Andrew Roberts for extracts from his writings; Kenneth Rose for material from his papers; the Governors of the Royal Shakespeare Company, Stratford-upon-Avon for extracts from Governors' Minutes; the Marquess of Salisbury for extracts from the papers of Viscount Cecil of Chelwood and the 5th Marquess of Salisbury; Mr John Simon and the Bodleian Library, Oxford for an extract from the diary of Viscount Simon; the Trustees of the Harold Macmillan Book Trust for extracts from the diaries, letter and papers of the 1st Earl of Stockton, and the Bodleian Library, Oxford as custodians of the material; Lord Strang for a letter by the 1st Baron Strang; the Syndics of Cambridge University Library for extracts from the papers of Viscount Templewood; and Rhodes House Library for extracts from the papers of Sir Roy Welensky.

NOTES

AUTHOR'S PREFACE

1 Robert Rhodes James, *Anthony Eden*, Weidenfeld & Nicolson, 1986, p.xiv.
2 Merry and Serge Bromberger, *Secrets of Suez*, Pan Books, 1957, p.160.
3 Peter Hennessy, *The Prime Minister: The Office and Its Holders Since 1945*, Allen Lane, 2000, p.532.
4 See Edward Kean, 'Premiers' pecking order unsettled', *Daily Telegraph*, 31 December 1999.
5 Lord Home, *The Way the Wind Blows*, Collins, 1976, p.97.
6 Eden note of 11 January 1957, recording details of his farewell audience at Sandringham four days earlier. Avon Papers, Birmingham University Library. AP 20/33/12A.
7 Anthony Eden to Dame Ivy Chamberlain, 17 March 1937. Austen Chamberlain Papers, Birmingham University Library. AC 59/85.
8 Or quartet, if one includes with Grey, Eden and Bevin, as Roy Jenkins does, Lord Lansdowne, 'because he was the architect of the Anglo-French Entente of 1903 and therefore set the course of British foreign and defence policy for the next 37 years.' Roy Jenkins, *Nine Men of Power*, Hamish Hamilton, 1974, p.64.

PRELUDE

1 AP 7/25/19.
2 AP 22/18/4.
3 Thomas Hardy, *The Dynasts*, II.v.
4 Anthony Nutting, *No End of a Lesson*, Constable, 1967.

5 Anthony Eden to Lady Eden, 21 October 1915. AP 22/1/183.
6 Anthony Eden to Lady Eden, after the death of his colonel, 18 September 1916. AP 22/1/252.
7 Broadcast of 11 September 1939. Reprinted in Anthony Eden, *Freedom and Order: selected speeches 1939–1946*, Faber & Faber, 1947, p.44.
8 The second Nicholas Eden's life was also to end prematurely. He died in 1985 at the age of fifty-four. (See Chapter 20.)
9 Simon Eden to Anthony Eden, 6 June 1945. AP 22/7/17.
10 Anthony Eden to Lady Eden, 3 April 1922. AP 22/1/312.
11 *Daily Mail*, 23 June 1897.
12 *The Times*, 23 June 1897.
13 Balfour papers, Whittingehame 281. Cited in Max Egremont, *Balfour: A Life of James Arthur Balfour*, Collins, 1980, p.179.
14 Sir Peter Tapsell to the author, 27 January 1999. Peter Tapsell was Eden's personal assistant throughout the 1955 General Election.
15 Live broadcast, 10 Downing Street, 3 November 1956.
16 Peter Hennessy, *The Prime Minister: The Office and Its Holders since 1945*, Allen Lane, The Penguin Press, 2000, p.247.
17 'We are in an armed conflict,' said Eden in the House of Commons on 1 November 1956. 'There has been no declaration of war.' Hansard, 1 November 1956, col. 1641.
18 Anthony Eden diary, 5 August 1914. AP 20/1/2.
19 Sir Douglas Dodds-Parker to the Countess of Avon, 14 January 1977. AP 34/21/1.
20 Anthony Eden, *Another World*

1897–1917, Allen Lane, 1976, p.11. Windlestone Hall became a residential school for pupils with special needs, and, sadly, went into a further spiral of decline. In September 1998 it was summarily closed after a police inquiry into allegations of cruelty and physical abuse.

21 Anthony Eden to Lady Eden, 28 April 1915. AP 22/1/170.

22 Anthony Eden to Lady Eden, 17 June 1915. AP 22/1/175.

23 Cited in C. L. Mowat, *Britain between the Wars*, Methuen paperback, 1968, p.1.

24 At Versailles, Lloyd George was arguably the dominating figure among the 'Big Four', where the other Great Powers were represented by Clemenceau (France), Wilson (United States of America) and Orlando (Italy), who was very much the minor figure. At Potsdam, twenty-six years later, Stalin (Russia) and Truman (United States) wielded the real power. Churchill's position – and, after the General Election, Attlee's – was more akin to that of Orlando at Versailles and, as any visitor to Potsdam can see, the British were even accommodated in an annexe to the main residences.

25 Eden speech, 7 May 1945. Reprinted in Anthony Eden, *Freedom and Order: selected speeches 1939–1946*, Faber & Faber, 1947, p.342.

26 Lord Avon, *Facing the Dictators*, Cassell, 1962, p.4.

27 Cited by Sidney Aster, *Anthony Eden*, Weidenfeld & Nicolson, 1976, p.1.

28 Eden was Foreign Secretary for more than ten years in five separate administrations, a span surpassed in the twentieth century only by Sir Edward Grey. In the Baldwin and Chamberlain Governments, Eden was Foreign Secretary from 22 December 1935 until 20 February 1938; in Churchill's wartime National Government from 22 December 1940 until 23 May 1945; in Churchill's Caretaker Government from 23 May 1945 until 27 July 1945; and in Churchill's peacetime Government from 28 October 1951 until 6 April 1955 – a total of ten years, two months and ten days.

CHAPTER I
The Way They Lived Then

1 Private notes by Anthony Eden. Countess of Avon papers.

2 Anthony Eden, *Another World 1897–1917*, Allen Lane, 1976, p.13.

3 Stockton papers, FCD 8 File 002. File on the 1963 Conservative leadership struggle.

4 A detailed account of Eden's ancestors can be found in Robert Allan Eden, *Some Historical Notes on the Eden Family*, Blades, East & Blades, 1907, p.12.

5 Charles Wolfe, *The Burial of Sir John Moore at Corunna*, ii. *Newry Telegraph*, 1817.

6 Unpublished memoir of Lady (Sybil) Eden. AP 22/14/22.

7 AP 22/14/12.

8 Robert Allan Eden, op. cit., p.7.

9 SELO 184 (3). Selwyn Lloyd papers, Churchill College, Cambridge. Such private comments were far from unusual with Macmillan, and the divergence in their attitudes, not only on this matter, was to be an underlying theme in Eden's life.

10 Countess of Avon to the author, 22 January 2002.

11 In 1984, with the Mortuary Chapel in a state of advanced disrepair, the remains of all the Edens at Windlestone were reburied in West Auckland, the family's homestead in the sixteenth century.

12 AP 22/14/12.

13 Although this was recorded at one stage in *Burke's Peerage*, Sir William regretted the move, for the name lapsed and later editions of *Burke* correctly gave Eden once more as the family name. Kenneth Rose papers.

14 Timothy Eden, *The Tribulations of a Baronet*, Macmillan, 1933, p.44.

15 Ibid., p.14.

16 Anthony Eden, op. cit., p.14.
17 Timothy Eden, op. cit., pp.173, 179.
18 See Chapter 11 for the account of Simon Eden's death and the news reaching the Potsdam Conference.
19 Lord Moran, *Winston Churchill: The Struggle for Survival 1940–1965*, Sphere Books paperback, 1968, p.744.
20 *Vide* Robert Rhodes James, *Anthony Eden*, Weidenfeld & Nicolson, 1986, pp.14–18.
21 John Biggs-Davison, *George Wyndham: A Study in Toryism*, Hodder & Stoughton, 1951, p.235.
22 Max Egremont, *Balfour: A Life of Arthur James Balfour*, Collins, 1980, p.110.
23 The bust is no longer at the Musée Rodin ('Pas ici,' I was told when visiting the museum in Paris in November 2000), though illustrations appear in various guide books there.
24 Miles Jebb (ed.), *The Diaries of Cynthia Gladwyn*, Constable, 1995, p.258.
25 George Wyndham (ed.), *The Poems of Shakespeare edited with an introduction and notes by George Wyndham*, Methuen & Co., 1898.
26 J. W. Mackail and Guy Wyndham, *The Life and Letters of George Wyndham: Volume 1*, Hutchinson, 1925, pp.267–8
27 George Wyndham to Madeline Wyndham, 15 August 1896. Ibid., p.297.
28 I am grateful to Dr Judith Bogdanor of the Jericho Health Centre, Oxford, for the following conclusions:
Scenarios concerning Eden's conception
For conception to have occurred on or just before 14.8.1896, his expected date of delivery would have been 8.5.1897. (Full-term pregnancy is thirty-eight weeks from *conception* to delivery, but is often calculated as forty weeks from the first day of the last menstrual period.) He was a large baby and therefore could *possibly* have been 2–3 weeks overdue.

38 + 3 = 41 weeks.
41 weeks from the latest possible date of conception by Wyndham 14.8.1896 = 29.5.1897.
I do not think it is at all possible that he was five weeks overdue, as the stillbirth rates rise sharply for post-mature babies. Assuming he was born at full term on 12.6.1897, his conception would have occurred around 19/20.9.1896. He is *very unlikely* to have been conceived *later than* 16.10.1896 as his weight of 8–9 lb is unlikely to have been achieved by a baby born more than four weeks prematurely.
For Eden to have been conceived by Wyndham on or after 1.12.1896, his full-term due date would have been 23.8.1897, and on 12.6.1897 he would have been only twenty-nine weeks *in utero* and could not have been born weighing 8–9 lb, at that extreme prematurity. Premature babies in that era were unlikely to survive and would not have been that heavy.
Given these dates, I would think that George Wyndham could not have been Eden's father.
29 AP 22/19/1.
30 Anthony Eden to Lady Eden, 15 June 1913. AP 22/1/122.
31 Anthony Eden, diary, 23 March 1932. AP 20/1/12.
32 AP 22/14/12.
33 Handwritten note of 14 December 1943. FO 371/37554/49.
34 Violet Asquith diary, 24 October 1905. Quoted in *Lantern Slides: The Diaries and Letters of Violet Bonham Carter 1904–1914*, edited by Mark Bonham Carter and Mark Pottle, Weidenfeld & Nicolson 1996, p.78. Easton Grey, the home of Margot Asquith's sister, Lucy Graham Smith, was a late eighteenth-century manor house on the Avon four miles west of Malmesbury.
35 AP 7/25/19.
36 Anthony Eden, op. cit., p.16.
37 See Chapter 3 for Eden's letter to his sister.
38 Anthony Eden diary, 19 January

1913 (when Eden was fifteen). A later pencilled note on the original diary entry is in his later hand. AP 20/1/24.

39 Austin Caverhill, *Rushmore – Then and Now*, privately printed by Sandroyd School, 1988, p.37. It was Eden's warnings over the rise of the dictators, and the dismay over the Munich Agreement in September 1938, that led the then Headmaster, Mr H. ff Ozanne, to seek at once that autumn new premises in the West Country. Ozanne negotiated a lease of Rushmore House, Tollard Royal, the home of General Pitt-Rivers, in March 1939, and moved the school there in the autumn of that year, to the site it still occupies, a few miles south of Alvediston, the village of Eden's last home and burial place. A large photograph of the 1st Earl of Avon ('O.S.') hangs today over the chimneypiece in the library. Reed's School occupies the original site of Sandroyd in Cobham.

40 *The Sandroydian*, January 1911.

41 *Ibid*., August 1907. This was a source of continued embarrassment for most of Eden's time at Sandroyd. Ironically, swimming was to be one of his principal recreations in adulthood. On honeymoon with his second wife in August 1952 he abruptly changed hotels on arrival, as the original hotel had no swimming pool.

42 Anthony Eden to Lady Eden, 24 October 1909. AP 22/1/86.

43 Anthony Eden to Lady Eden, 13 November 1909. AP 22/1/90.

44 AP 22/14/12.

45 Anthony Eden, op. cit., p.35.

46 Lady Eden to Anthony Eden, 11 June 1908. AP 22/1/67.

47 AP 22/14/12. Warwick and Leamington Conservative Association Records, Leamington.

48 Anthony Eden, *Facing the Dictators*, Cassell, 1962, p.3.

49 Anthony Eden to Lady Eden, 3 April 1910. AP 22/1/96. The book he was reading was D. W. Lusk, *Politics and Politicians: a succinct history of*

the politics of Illinois from 1856–1884, Springfield, Illinois, 1884, an esoteric choice for a twelve-year-old.

50 *The Sandroydian*, January 1911.

51 'In spite of his size and strength he was extraordinarily supple, and it was the india-rubber-like quality of his muscles that won him the soubriquet of "Jelly".' *Eton College Chronicle*, July 1943.

52 George Lyttelton to Rupert Hart-Davis, 15 February 1956. *The Lyttelton Hart-Davis Letters: Correspondence of George Lyttelton and Rupert Hart-Davis, Volumes One and Two 1955–1957*, edited by Sir Rupert Hart-Davis, John Murray paperback, 1985, p.82.

53 A legendary victory over Harrow at Lord's, achieved largely through the exploits of the Eton Captain, R. St L. Fowler. Walter Monckton, Eden's Defence Secretary during Suez, was in the Harrow side.

54 Robert Rhodes James, *Victor Cazalet; A Portrait*, Hamish Hamilton, 1976, p.10.

55 George Lyttelton to Rupert Hart-Davis, 22 February 1961, op. cit., *Volumes Five and Six 1960–1962*, 1987, p.216.

56 AP 22/15/114.

57 E. L. Churchill's House Debating Society records, 1904–18. Eton College Library.

58 E. L. Churchill to Lady Eden, July 1912. AP 22/15/57.'

59 Ernest C. Churchill to Lady Eden, July 1913. AP 22/15/73.

60 Anthony Eden diary 1914. AP 20/1/2.

61 *E. L. Churchill's House Book 1904–1923*. Eton College Library.

62 Tim Card, *Eton Renewed*, John Murray, 1994, p.142.

63 As Lyttelton had previously been Master (Headmaster) of Haileybury, he was Headmaster to three future Prime Ministers – Clement Attlee, Harold Macmillan and Anthony Eden.

64 E. L. Churchill to Lady Eden, 21 June 1915. AP 22/114/15.

65 AP 7/25/43.

66 In a wartime conversation with the American Secretary of the Navy, James V. Forrestal (1892–1949). Walter Millis (ed.), *The Forrestal Diaries*, Cassell, 1952, pp.63–64.

CHAPTER 2

In the Ranks of Death

1 Anthony Eden diary, 5 February 1913 and 1 January 1914. AP 20/1/1.
2 Early manuscript draft of *Another World*. AP 7/25/19.
3 Anthony Eden diary. 20 October 1914. AP 20/1/2.
4 Anthony Eden to Lady Eden, 20 and 23 October 1914. AP 22/1/142–3. Before Agincourt, Henry V tells his troops:
　I would not lose so great an honour As one man more, methinks, would share from me.
　　　　Henry V, IV.iii. 31–2.
5 Lady Eden to Anthony Eden, 25 November 1914. AP 22/1/153.
6 Anthony Eden diary, 5 August 1914. AP 20/1/2.
7 Anthony Eden diary, 27 October 1913. AP 20/1/1.
8 Anthony Eden to Lady Eden, 9 May 1915. AP 22/1/171.
9 Roy Jenkins, *Asquith*, Collins, 1964, p.343.
10 Part of the royalties from *Another World* were paid to the Rifleman's Aid Society from 1976.
11 As in a postcard message to Lady Eden on 27 January 1916. AP 22/1/229.
12 Present-day visitors to Duncombe Park learn of Eden's involvement through a promotional video.
13 Lyn Macdonald, *Somme*, Michael Joseph, 1983, p.273.
14 Anthony Eden to Lady Eden, 1 November 1914. AP 22/1/145. Eden and Tillett were later to be colleagues in the 1929–31 Parliament, when Tillett was MP for North Salford.
15 Anthony Eden, *Another World 1897–1917*, Allen Lane, 1976, p.67.

16 Anthony Eden to Lady Eden, 10 December 1915. AP 22/1/196.
17 Anthony Eden to Lady Eden, 31 December 1915. AP 22/1/201.
18 Anthony Eden to Lady Eden, 6 January 1916. AP 22/1/220.
19 Nicholas Eden to Lady Eden, 16 December 1916. AP 22/14/12.
20 Nicholas Eden to Lady Brooke, 6 May 1916. AP 22/5/15.
21 Anthony Eden to Lady Eden, 17 March 1916. AP 22/1/243.
22 Lyn Macdonald, op. cit., p.273.
23 Anthony Eden, op. cit., p.76.
24 AP 7/25/19.
25 *Song of Solomon*, 8.vii. AP 22/6/12.
26 Alan Clark (ed.), *A Good Innings: the Private Papers of Viscount Lee of Fareham*, John Murray, 1974, p.154.
27 Margot Asquith diary, cited in Randolph S. Churchill, *Lord Derby: King of Lancashire*, Heinemann, 1959, p.213.
28 Anthony Eden to Lady Brooke, 6 June 1916. AP 22/2/32.
29 Anthony Eden, op. cit., p.91.
30 Warwick and Leamington Conservative Association Records, and AP 7/25/43.
31 Anthony Eden to Lady Eden, 30 August 1916. AP 22/1/250. Romania had entered the war against Germany on 27 August 1916.
32 Anthony Eden to Lady Brooke, 16 September 1916. AP 22/2/41.
33 Anthony Eden to Lady Brooke, 11 October 1916. AP 22/2/45.
34 Anthony Eden to Lady Brooke, 9 November 1916. AP 22/2/47.
35 Anthony Eden to Lady Brooke, 24 December 1916. AP 22/2/50.
36 Lt-Col. Talbot Jarvis to Lady Eden, 16 June 1917. AP 22/1/254.
37 Anthony Eden to the Public Record Office, 20 December 1971. AP 26/611/18.
38 Anthony Eden to Lady Brooke, 8 June 1917. AP 22/5/56.
39 Anthony Eden to Lady Brooke, 23 December 1917. AP 22/2/68. A reference to Lloyd George's speech in the House of Commons on the proposed Supreme War Council at

Versailles which the military feared would reduce the authority of the General Staff.

40 Anthony Eden to Lady Brooke, 14 April 1918. AP 22/2/76.

41 The jury is still out on whether Maurice was right.

42 Anthony Eden, *Facing the Dictators*, Cassell, 1962, p.139.

43 Anthony Eden to Lady Brooke, 15 November 1918. AP 20/2/93.

44 Before the Election, Lloyd George had sent a letter of endorsement to those candidates officially included in his coalition. As endorsements for Liberals depended largely on voting records from the Maurice Debate, the Asquithian Liberals were excluded. Asquith derisively dubbed the letter 'the Coupon', which became the collective name for Lloyd George's temporary coalition of Unionists (under Bonar Law), Coalition Liberals and eighteen Labour candidates not with the official Labour campaign.

45 Pencilled note on p.138 of Eden's copy of Hitler's *Mein Kampf*. Copy in the possession of the Countess of Avon.

46 Anthony Eden to Lady Eden, 25 May 1919. AP 22/1/288.

47 Pierre Corneille, *Le Cid*, IV.iv. 1377–8.

CHAPTER 3

Oxford and Political Apprenticeship

1 Anthony Eden to Lady Brooke, 30 October and 21 July 1917. AP 22/2/64 and AP 22/2/58.

2 Cited by Lord Beaverbrook, *Men and Power 1917–1918*, Hutchinson, 1956, caption to illustration opposite p.324.

3 C. L. Mowat, *Britain Between the Wars 1918–1940*, Methuen, revised paperback, 1968, p.27.

4 Maurice Cowling in *The Impact of Labour 1920–1924*, Cambridge University Press, Cambridge, 1971, p.1, identifies Spen Valley as the beginning of modern British politics.

5 Anthony Eden to Lady Eden, 14 March 1919. AP 22/1/273.

6 Speech at the San Francisco Conference, 26 April 1945.

7 Anthony Eden to Lady Warwick, 22 January 1919. AP 22/2/4.

8 Anthony Eden to Lady Warwick, 23 February 1919. AP 22/2/7.

9 Unpublished memoir of Lady Eden, AP 22/14/22.

10 Lady Eden to Dr Thomas Banks Strong, 24 July 1919. Archives of Christ Church, Oxford.

11 Harold Macmillan, *War Diaries: Politics and War in the Mediterranean January 1943–May 1945*, Macmillan, 1984, entry for 4 June 1943, p.110.

12 The hierarchy of the Oxford colleges was not subsumed in tacit politenesses. Before the war when Raymond Asquith, the Prime Minister's son, told his scout at Balliol that he would be away at Cambridge for the week, the scout replied, 'Cambridge, sir? Isn't that rather in the Keble line?' Private information.

13 The name of Eden's eldest son, Simon, can be seen on the memorial to the dead of the Second World War in the west porch.

14 Edward Fitzgerald's poem was *The Rubáiyát of Omar Khayyám*. AP 22/24/27.

15 Sir Timothy Eden to J. C. Masterman, 10 May 1921. Archives of Christ Church, Oxford.

16 The Earl of Avon to Geoffrey Huskinson, 5 November 1974. AP 7/25/38A.

17 AP 4/1/1.

18 In *Reputations: Anthony Eden – A Rather English Statesman*, 3BM Television for BBC 2, 6 June 2000.

19 AP 22/17/1.

20 AP 22/17/3.

21 AP 22/17/3.

22 Sir John Rothenstein, *Summer's Lease: Autobiography 1901–1938*, Hamish Hamilton, 1965, pp.89–90. The quarrel was over Whistler's portrait of Lady Eden, a matter eventually resolved in Sir William's

favour in the courts.

23 Henry Channon diary, 21 February 1935, op. cit., p.26.

24 Anthony Eden to Lady Eden, 12 April 1922. AP 22/1/331.

25 Private information.

26 Anthony Eden diary, 12 March, 18 March, 30 January and 24 March 1923. AP 20/1/3.

27 Anthony Eden, *Facing the Dictators*, Cassell, 1962, p.4.

28 Robert Bruce-Lockhart diary, 18 April 1939. *The Diaries of Sir Robert Bruce-Lockhart: Volume Two 1939-1965*, edited by Kenneth Young, Macmillan, 1980, p.40.

29 Certificate of 24 March 1923. AP 22/24/27.

30 Anthony Eden to the Dean of Christ Church, 24 October 1930. Archives of Christ Church, Oxford. DP xx.c. I (Eden).

31 Archives of Christ Church, Oxford. The embarrassment felt by the college retrospectively over its treatment of the House's twelfth Prime Minister can be seen by the fact that when Lewis Broad started work on his biography of Eden (*Sir Anthony Eden: The Chronicles of a Career*, Hutchinson, 1955), although Christ Church records were made available to him, it was felt best not to divulge details of the unedifying squabble about the alleged non-payment of battels.

32 The figures usually quoted are 187 to 87, but ballot papers in the Austen Chamberlain papers show this to be inaccurate. With three abstentions, the total attending was 274. Austen Chamberlain papers, University Library, Birmingham. AC 33/2/88

33 Stuart Ball (ed.), in the introduction to *Parliament and Politics in the Age of Baldwin and Macdonald: The Headlam Diaries 1923-1935*, The Historians' Press, 1992, p.9.

34 Anthony Eden, op. cit., p.36.

35 Ibid., p.100. The grandee who put up the money was George Stobart (1873-1943), High Sheriff of County Durham. Entry for 29 September 1926.

36 Ibid., p.42. Entry for 29 August 1924.

37 Anthony Eden to Lady Eden, 3 April 1922. AP 22/1/328.

38 C. L. Mowat, op. cit., pp.168-9.

39 Cabinet minutes, 31 January 1919. CAB 23/9.

40 Anthony Eden to Lady Eden, 22 March 1914. AP 22/1/37.

41 Private information.

42 Hansard, House of Lords, 18 January 1977.

43 Anthony Eden diary, 21 May 1923. AP 20/1/3.

44 A remark made to the lobby correspondent of the *Yorkshire Post* on the steps of the Carlton Club before the fateful meeting on 19 October 1922.

45 *Vide* D.R. Thorpe, *The Uncrowned Prime Ministers*, Darkhorse Publishing, 1980, pp.146-50, for a full account of the circumstances of George V's decision.

46 *Yorkshire Post*, 2 December 1936.

47 The late Sir Martyn Beckett to the author, 5 June 1998. Sir Rupert Hart-Davis died on 8 December 1999. The obituaries in *The Times*, *Daily Telegraph* and *Independent* drew attention to his disputed paternity, but did not identify the father, whom the mother in an unguarded moment said could have been one of four suitors. Private information.

48 Anthony Eden diary, 9 July, 28 July, 31 July 1923, 1 August, 7 September 1923. AP 20/1/3.

49 The late Sir Martyn Beckett to the author, 5 June 1998.

50 Anthony Eden diary, 22 October 1923. AP 20/1/3.

51 The Leicester East by-election in 1922 followed the appointment of the Attorney-General, Sir Gordon Hewart, to the post of Lord Chief Justice. He was succeeded as Attorney-General by Eden's predecessor as MP at Warwick and Leamington.

52 Sidney Aster mistakenly identifies Eden's patron as the 20th Lord Willoughby de Broke (1896-1986), the 19th Baron's only son, who did

not inherit the title until 16 December 1923. This error is compounded by Robert Rhodes James, who also states that Eden's patron was the twenty-seven-year old 20th Baron Willoughby de Broke, adding that he favoured Eden's candidature because they were both youthful holders of the Military Cross. Sidney Aster, *Anthony Eden*, Weidenfeld & Nicolson, 1976, p.11, and Robert Rhodes James, *Anthony Eden*, Weidenfeld & Nicolson, 1986, p.72 and index, p.664. Lewis Broad correctly refers to 'the late Lord Willoughby de Broke' in *Sir Anthony Eden: The Chronicles of a Career*, Hutchinson, 1955, p.24.

53 Warwick and Leamington Conservative Association Minute Book, 1923. Warwick County Record Office, Warwick. File CR 1392.

54 Margaret Blanche,*The Countess of Warwick*, Cassell, 1967, p.275.

55 Anthony Eden diary, 5 November 1923. AP 20/1/3.

56 Bonar Law served as Prime Minister for the shortest time that century, 23 October 1922–20 May 1923. After Sir Alec Douglas-Home, 18 October 1963–16 October 1964, Eden served for the next shortest duration, 6 April 1955–9 January 1957.

57 John Barnes and David Nicholson (eds), *The Empire at Bay: the Leo Amery Diaries, 1929–1945*, Hutchinson, 1988, pp.638 and 696.

58 In the 1922 General Election campaign Bonar Law promised that 'this Parliament will not make any fundamental change in the fiscal system of the country' (i.e. Free Trade). In a speech at Plymouth on 25 October 1923, Baldwin – Bonar Law's successor as Prime Minister – said the only way of fighting unemployment was 'by protecting the home market'. As Baldwin also said that he was bound by Bonar Law's Free Trade pledge of 1922, an Election was thus inevitable in the near future. It came sooner than many Conservatives thought, or

indeed wanted.

59 See Chapter 12 for a description of the build-up to the 1950 election, when the constituency was subdivided.

60 Kenneth Rose, *King George V*, Weidenfeld & Nicolson, 1983, p.326.

CHAPTER 4
From Warwick to Geneva

1 John Barnes and David Nicholson (eds), *The Leo Amery Diaries: Volume One 1896–1929*, Hutchinson, 1980, p.361.
2 Austen Chamberlain papers. AC 5/1/336.
3 AP 20/1/4.
4 Anthony Eden diary, 31 December 1923. AP 20/1/3.
5 Anthony Eden diary, 28 October 1923. AP 20/1/3.
6 Anthony Eden diary, 7 January 1924. AP 20/1/4.
7 Anthony Eden diary, 11 February 1924. AP 20/1/4.
8 *London Labour Chronicle*, December 1923.
9 Leo Amery diary, 8 December 1923, op. cit., p.361.
10 Quoted in J. M. Keynes, *The Economic Consequences of the Peace*, Macmillan paperback, 1984, p.91.
11 Leo Amery diary, 19 September 1924, op. cit., p.386. Roger Lumley, 11th Earl of Scarborough (1896–1969), MP for Hull East, was a close friend of Eden, his predecessor as PPS to the Foreign Secretary, Sir Austen Chamberlain, and godfather to the Edens' second son, Nicholas, from 1930.
12 Winston S. Churchill, *Thoughts and Adventures*, Butterworth, 1932, p.213.
13 *Vide* M. Swenarton and S. Taylor, 'The Scale and Nature of the Growth of Owner-Occupation in Britain between the Wars', *Economic History Review*, 2, 38 (1985).

14 The house, 8 Lord North Street, was sold in February 2001 for £2.3 million, the agents stating that this was 'a good price as the house needs a lot of money spent on it'. *The Times*, 20 February 2001.

15 Anthony Eden diary, 24 January 1924 and 14 March 1925. AP 20/1/4 and AP 20/1/5.

16 Anthony Eden, *Facing the Dictators*, Cassell, 1962, p.5.

17 Anthony Eden diary, 19 February 1924. AP 20/1/4.

18 Speech at the Labour Party Conference, 3 October 1957.

19 Hansard, 19 February 1924.

20 Hansard, 10 November 1932.

21 Thomas Hardy, *The Trumpet Major*, Smith Elder, 1880, Chapter XXIII, 'Military Preparations on an Extended Scale'.

22 Anthony Eden diary, 20 May 1924. AP 20/1/4.

23 Anthony Eden diary, 7 March 1924. AP 20/1/4.

24 Anthony Eden diary, 5 April 1924. AP 20/1/4.

25 Hansard, 1 April 1924.

26 Anthony Eden diary, 7 April 1924. AP 20/1/4.

27 Anthony Eden diary, 21 April, 22 April and 23 April 1924. AP 20/1/4. The first volume of his memoirs (1960) was called *Full Circle*, from Edmund's speech in *King Lear*, V. iii. 173–4.

28 Anthony Eden diary, 25 April 1924. AP 20/1/4. In this, Beatrice Eden prefigured Harold Wilson's wife, Mary, who would always have preferred life as an Oxford don's wife.

29 Anthony Eden diary, 29 April 1924. AP 20/1/4. The Liberal Chancellor of the Exchequer, Reginald McKenna, had imposed duties on a wide variety of imports in the 1915 Budget.

30 Anthony Eden diary, 3 June and 4 June 1924. AP 20/1/4.

31 Earl of Avon speech, Stratford-upon-Avon, 23 April 1964. The speech that Eden so admired begins with the celebrated line 'Time hath, my lord, a wallet at his back'. *Troilus and Cressida*, III.iii.146–91.

32 Anthony Eden diary, 9 August 1924. AP 20/1/4.

33 Anthony Eden diary, 4 May 1924. AP 20/1/4. Archbishop Lang speech, 13 December 1936. Lang's strictures led to the wide circulation of the following lines:
My Lord Archbishop, what a scold you are!
And when your man is down how bold you are!
Of charity how oddly scant you are!
And auld Lang Swine, how full of Cantuar!

34 Stephen Roskill, *Hankey Man of Secrets: Volume II 1919–1931*, Collins, 1972, p.376.

35 Anthony Eden diary, 6 October 1924. AP 20/1/4.

36 The other was on 28 March 1979, when the Labour Government of James Callaghan was defeated by 311 votes to 310, paving the way for a Conservative victory at the subsequent General Election. Eden faced two such confidence votes over Suez – on 1 November 1956 and 6 December 1956 – but the Government won both.

37 Anthony Eden diary, 8 October 1924. AP 20/1/4.

38 Anthony Eden diary, 29 October 1924. AP 20/1/4.

39 Anthony Eden diary, 30 October 1924. AP 20/1/4.

40 Anthony Eden, 8 November 1924. AP 20/1/4.

41 Arthur Mann to Anthony Eden, 21 June 1945. AP 20/42/87.

42 Anthony Eden diary, 12 November and 13 November 1924. AP 20/1/4.

43 The other three were Neville Chamberlain, Harold Macmillan and John Major.

44 Alan Campbell Johnson, *Anthony Eden*, Robert Hale, 1938, p.79.

45 Anthony Eden diary, 11 January 1925. AP 20/1/5.

46 Anthony Eden diary, 17 February 1925. AP 20/1/5.

47 The days of renowned parliamentary poets, such as Andrew Marvell, were long gone. Clement Attlee dabbled

in amateur versifying, but when one of his ministers, John Strachey, sought permission to publish his verse, the request was refused on the grounds that 'the lines don't scan'. Kenneth Harris, *Attlee*, Weidenfeld & Nicolson, 1982, p.409.

48 Much material on Skelton is contained in the Baroness Elliot of Harwood papers.

49 Noel Skelton, *Constructive Conservatism*, Blackwood, Edinburgh, 1924, p17.

50 Noel Skelton, 'The Conservative Task: A Property-Owning Democracy', *Yorkshire Post*, 23 January 1930.

51 Earl of Avon to Sir Alec Douglas-Home, 28 September 1964. AP23/27/35.

52 Anthony Eden diary, 28 April 1925. AP 20/1/5.

53 Anthony Eden diary, 17 August 1925. AP 20/1/5.

54 Anthony Eden diary, 21 and 22 November 1925. AP 20/1/5.

55 Anthony Eden diary, 30 November 1925. AP 20/1/5.

56 Sir Philip Cunliffe-Lister (1884–1973) was known by several different names. Born Philip Lloyd-Greame, he assumed the name Cunliffe-Lister in 1924, when his wife inherited the Masham estate in Yorkshire, before becoming Viscount Swinton in 1935. His Cabinet career ended in April 1955 when Eden did not reappoint him Commonwealth Secretary. As the first Earl of Swinton (from 1955) he was active in the Lords, and his home, as Swinton Conservative College, became an important nursery for aspiring politicians. An American academic once betrayed his unfamiliarity with English customs, when he described a pre-war meeting, at which he claimed the three participants were Philip Lloyd-Greame, Philip Cunliffe-Lister and Viscount Swinton.

57 Anthony Eden, *Places in the Sun*, John Murray, 1926, p.vii.

58 Anthony Eden diary, 7 December 1925. AP 20/1/5.

59 Anthony Eden diary, 17 December 1925. AP 20/1/5.

60 Anthony Eden diary, 8 December 1925. AP 20/1/5.

61 Hansard, 21 December 1925.

62 Beaverbrook's attitude to Eden mellowed the moment he became Prime Minister, a process engineered by Brendan Bracken, and he later became a generous friend to Eden in his retirement. *Vide* A. J. P. Taylor, *Beaverbrook*, Penguin paperback edition, 1974, p.813.

63 Anthony Eden diary, 21 December 1925. AP 20/1/5.

64 Anthony Eden diary, 17 December 1925. AP 20/1/5.

65 Anthony Eden diary, 31 December 1925. AP 20/1/5.

66 Sir Austen Chamberlain to Viscount d'Abernon (the British Ambassador in Berlin), 23 April 1926. AC 53/222

67 A remark Baldwin made to Dr Thomas Jones, Deputy Secretary of the Cabinet. Leo Amery, *My Political Life: Volume Two War and Peace 1914–1929*, Hutchinson, 1953, p.280. 'The Goat' was Lloyd George's nickname, as it had been for one of his predecessors as Chancellor of the Exchequer, the prim-bearded Sir Stafford Northcote, but not for the same reason.

68 Hansard, 23 March 1926.

69 Anthony Eden diary, 1 May 1926. AP 20/1/6.

70 Anthony Eden diary, 4 May 1926. AP 20/1/6.

71 C. L. Mowat, *Britain between the Wars 1918–1940*, Methuen paperback, 1968, p.329.

72 Anthony Eden diary, 13 May 1926. AP 20/1/6.

73 Anthony Eden diary, 14 July 1925. AP 20/1/5.

74 William Hague is the only other Conservative leader not to have succeeded to the Premiership in the twentieth century.

75 A remark attributed to both Winston Churchill and F. E. Smith.

76 Reminiscences of 1926. AP 33/1/91.

77 Ivy Chamberlain had been awarded the DBE after Locarno in recognition of her contribution.

78 Benito Mussolini to Sir Robert Graham, British Ambassador in Italy, 20 December 1925. FO 371/11561.

79 Bonar Law to the legendary Downing Street secretary, Miss Edith Watson. Robert Blake, *The Unknown Prime Minister: The Life and Times of Andrew Bonar Law 1858–1923*, Eyre & Spottiswoode, 1955, p.486.

80 Austen Chamberlain to Lord Salisbury (the Lord Privy Seal), 1 November 1927. AC 54/444.

81 Anthony Eden diary, 8 June 1927. AP 20/1/7.

82 Anthony Eden diary, 7 December 1926. AC 20/1/6.

83 Anthony Eden, *Facing the Dictators*, p.9.

84 Sir Austen Chamberlain, *Down the Years*, Cassell, 1935, p.183.

85 Anthony Eden diary, 2 September 1928. AP 20/1/8.

86 Anthony Eden diary, 15 October 1928. AP 20/1/8.

87 Anthony Eden diary, 18 October 1928. AP 20/1/8.

88 Speech by David Lloyd George in the Free Trade Hall, Manchester, 12 April 1929.

89 Anthony Eden diary, 24 May and 26 May 1929. AC 20/1/9.

90 Anthony Eden diary, 30 May 1929. AC 20/1/9.

91 Leo Amery diary, 3 June 1929, op. cit., p.597.

CHAPTER 5
'A Potential Foreign Secretary'

1 Quoted in Mary Soames (ed.), *Speaking for Themselves: The Personal Letters of Winston & Clementine Churchill*, Doubleday, 1998, p.332.

2 The 1930s may have had a bad press from posterity, but for historians they have been a subject of continuing fascination. *Vide* Piers Brendon, *The Dark Valley: A Panorama of the 1930s*, Jonathan Cape, 2000, for a modern assessment.

3 C. C. Mowat, *Britain between the Wars 1918–1940*, Methuen paperback edition, 1968, p. 480.

4 Speech by Stanley Baldwin at the Queen's Hall, London, 18 March 1931.

5 Anthony Eden diary, 29 March 1931. AP 20/1/11.

6 Anthony Eden diary, 12 March 1931. AP 20/1/11.

7 Anthony Eden letter to *The Times*, 6 October 1930.

8 Hansard, 16 April 1930.

9 Anthony Eden, *Facing the Dictators*, Cassell, 1962, p.12.

10 Hansard, 3 July 1929.

11 Denis Mack Smith, *Mussolini*, Granada Publishing, 1983, p.201.

12 Hansard, 5 July 1929.

13 Anthony Eden, op. cit., p.153.

14 Anthony Eden, op. cit., p.12.

15 Hansard, 29 June 1931.

16 Hugh Dalton diary, 23 December 1929. Ben Pimlott (ed.), *The Political Diary of Hugh Dalton 1918–1940, 1945–1960*, Jonathan Cape, 1986, p.83.

17 Hansard, 23 December 1929.

18 At a lunch with Eden. Anthony Eden diary, 13 April 1930. AP 20/1/10.

19 Anthony Eden to Stanley Baldwin, 1 May 1933. AP 14/1/144.

20 Anthony Eden to Winston Churchill, 14 September 1937. Churchill papers, 2/302. Churchill College, Cambridge.

21 Eden referred to Mussolini as a 'complete gangster' on several occasions. This quotation comes from a letter to Neville Chamberlain on 9 January 1938. FO 954/6A.

22 Colin Cross, *Philip Snowden*, Barrie & Rockcliff, 1966, p.248.

23 Hansard, 16 April 1930.

24 Anthony Eden diary, 3 October 1930. AP 20/1/10.

25 Anthony Eden diary, 10 May 1930. AP 20/1/10.

26 Dilke never recovered from his involvement in the Crawford divorce case in 1886, and Parnell's career was ruined when he was cited as co-respondent in the O'Shea divorce case in November 1890.

27 Private information.

28 Henry Channon diary, 26 January 1953. Robert Rhodes James (ed.), *Chips: The Diaries of Sir Henry Channon*, Weidenfeld & Nicolson, 1967, p.471.

29 Graham C. Greene to the author, 26 March 2001. In fact, the BBC's Chairman was more concerned about whether Greene was a Catholic. Michael Tracey, *A Variety of Lives: A Biography of Sir Hugh Greene*, Bodley Head, 1983, p.180.

30 Hansard, 3 November 1930.

31 Anthony Eden diary, 31 December 1930. AP 20/1/10.

32 Anthony Eden diary, 17 January 1931. AP 20/1/11.

33 Anthony Eden diary, 4 March 1931. AP 20/1/11.

34 Anthony Eden diary, 5 March 1931. AP 20/1/11.

35 Roy Jenkins, 'Anthony Eden in the Thirties', *Daily Telegraph*, 19 November 1962.

36 Hansard, 29 June 1931.

37 Anthony Eden diary, 19 May 1931. AP 20/1/11.

38 Anthony Eden diary, 18 June 1931. AP 20/1/11.

39 On 3 September 1931 Eden became Under-Secretary at the Foreign Office; Walter Elliot, Financial Secretary to the Treasury; Oliver Stanley, Under-Secretary at the Home Office; and Noel Skelton, Under-Secretary at the Scottish Office.

40 Robert Blake, *The Unknown Prime Minister: The Life and Times of Andrew Bonar Law 1858–1923*, Eyre & Spottiswoode, 1955, p.340.

41 Colin Coote, *A Companion of Honour: The Story of Walter Elliot*, Collins, 1965, p.124.

42 Anthony Eden diary, 27 August and 28 August 1931. AP 20/1/11.

43 Lord Reading shares with Lord Halifax the distinction of holding an unusual triptych of offices, though in Halifax's case the sequence was Delhi, London and Washington, while in Reading's case it was Washington, Delhi and London. Eden became Foreign Secretary on 22 December 1935; Reading died on 29 December 1935.

44 Hansard, 10 September 1931.

45 Anthony Eden diary, 1 July 1931. AP 20/1/11.

46 Anthony Eden diary, 1 September 1931. AP 20/1/11.

47 Anthony Eden to the Marquess of Reading, undated letter of 1934, Eur F 118/18/6. Reading papers, India Office Library, London.

48 David Dutton, *Simon: A political biography of Sir John Simon*, Aurum, 1992, p.337.

49 Aristide Briand's career had gone into sharp decline after his infamous golf match against Lloyd George. On 9 January 1922, Briand who had never played golf before, accepted Lloyd George's challenge to a match after a somewhat bibulous luncheon at Cannes Golf Club. Photographs of Briand's undignified efforts appeared in the French Press the next day, with critical comment, and led to his resignation. But Simon, a future Captain of the Royal and Ancient, used golf assiduously for social networking and was actually offered the Chairmanship of the Indian Commission while golfing at Tadmarton Heath, near his Manor House at Fritwell in Oxfordshire. The lych-gate at St Olave's Church, Fritwell, contains a memorial to Simon.

50 Anthony Eden to Beatrice Eden, 20 May 1933. AP 22/6/168.

51 Henry Colyton, *Occasion, Chance and Change: A Memoir 1902–1946*, Michael Russell, Norwich, 1993, p.91. Yet in his memoirs Simon claimed of these years, 'I never worked harder.' Viscount Simon, *Retrospect: The Memoirs of the Rt Hon. Viscount Simon*, Hutchinson, 1952, p.177.

52 Anthony Eden to Sir Robert Vansittart, 4 August 1937. AP 13/1/58D.

53 Anthony Eden diary, 16 November 1936. AP 20/1/16.

54 Hugh Dalton diary, 12 April 1938. Ben Pimlott (editor), op. cit., p.231.

55 Anthony Eden, op. cit., p.242.

56 David Dilks (editor), *The Diaries of Sir Alexander Cadogan, 1938–1945*, Cassell, 1971, p.345.

57 The late Lord Colyton to the author, 31 October 1995, a few days before his death, which was prematurely reported in the *Daily Telegraph*. Sadly, reports of his death, unlike Mark Twain's, did not long prove an exaggeration, when the *Daily Telegraph* published an apology and a second, revised obituary.

58 Kenneth Rose, *The Later Cecils*, Weidenfeld & Nicolson, 1975, p.130. Lord Robert Cecil's brother, Lord Hugh Cecil, was more conventional in such matters, as Provost of Eton in the 1930s. A new beak, invited to dine in the Provost's Lodge, asked if he should dress for dinner. 'No,' replied the Provost, 'black tie will be fine.' The late Oliver van Oss to the author in 1966.

59 D. R. Thorpe, *Selwyn Lloyd*, Jonathan Cape, 1989, p.418.

60 The late Lord Colyton to the author, 31 October 1995.

61 Anthony Eden diary, 22 December 1931. AP 20/1/11.

62 Quoted in David Dutton, op. cit, p.166, f-n. 29.

63 Anthony Eden diary, 26 July 1932. AP 20/1/12. Important moments in Eden's career recurred with uncanny frequency on 26 July. It was the day of the Conservative defeat in the General Election in 1945; the day Nasser nationalised the Suez Canal in 1956; and the day Eden entered the Lords as the Earl of Avon in 1961.

64 Major-General A. C. Temperley, *The Whispering Gallery of Europe*, Collins, 1938, p.175. After one press conference, Eden was described by a French journalist as 'ce jeune homme terrible qui aime tellement la paix'. Henry Colyton, op. cit., p.86.

65 David Dilks (ed.), op. cit., p.7.

66 F. A. Iremonger, *William Temple: Archbishop of Canterbury*, Oxford University Press, Oxford, 1948, pp.376 and 441.

67 Anthony Eden diary, 18 February 1932. AP 20/1/12.

68 Henry L. Stimson and McGeorge Bundy, *On Active Service in Peace and War*, Harper & Brothers, New York, 1948.

69 Hansard, 29 February 1932.

70 See Reginald Bassett, *Democracy and Foreign Policy: A Case History. The Sino-Japanese Dispute 1931–1933*, Longmans, Green and Co., 1952, and Christopher Thorne, *The Limits of Foreign Policy: The West, the League and the Far Eastern Crisis of 1931–1933*, Hamish Hamilton, 1972.

71 A. J. P. Taylor, *The Origins of the Second World War*, Penguin Books, Harmondsworth, 1964 p.92.

72 Quoted in Christopher Thorne, *Allies of a Kind: The United States, Britain and the War against Japan, 1941–1945*, Hamish Hamilton, 1978, p.30.

73 Anthony Eden diary, 30 September 1932. AP 20/1/12.

74 Lord Vansittart, *The Mist Procession*, Hutchinson, 1958, p.486.

75 Anthony Eden diary, 14 April 1932. AP 20/1/12.

76 *Henry VI Part Three*, IV.viii. 9.

77 A full account of the occasion can be found in Sally Beauman, *The Royal Shakespeare Company: A History of Ten Decades*, Oxford University Press, Oxford, 1982, pp.110–22.

78 Anthony Eden diary, 7 July and 16 August 1932. AP 20/1/12.

79 Anthony Eden diary, 7 January 1933. AP 20/1/13.

80 Cordell Hull, *The Memoirs of Cordell Hull: Volume Two*, Hodder & Stoughton, 1948, p.1474.

81 Evelyn Waugh, *Scoop*, Penguin Books, Harmondsworth, 1963 edition, p.14.

82 Anthony Eden to Beatrice Eden, 15 February 1933. AP 22/6/163.

83 Ministerial Committee on the 1932
Disarmament Conference. D.C. (M)
(32) minutes, MDP 1/591. 2 March
1933. PRO. CAB 21/379.
84 *News Chronicle*, 4 April 1933.
85 David Marquand, *Ramsay
MacDonald*, Jonathan Cape, 1977,
p.754.
86 Cuthbert Headlam diary, 23 March
1933. Stuart Ball (ed.), *Parliament
and Politics in the Age of Baldwin
and MacDonald: The Headlam
Diaries 1923–1935*, The Historians'
Press, 1992, p.264.
87 Sir Austen Chamberlain to Hilda
Chamberlain, 26 March 1933. AC
5/1/612.
88 Sir Austen Chamberlain to Hilda
Chamberlain, 3 July 1933. AC
5/1/624.
89 Anthony Eden to Sir John Simon, 1
May 1933. Simon papers, box 76,
fol. 120–3.
90 Anthony Eden diary, 14 October
1933. AP 20/1/13.
91 AP 3/1/1.
92 Hansard. 7 November 1933.
93 Anthony Eden diary, 19 December
1933. AP 20/1/13.
94 Henry Channon diary, 18 January
1934. Robert Rhodes James (ed.),
op. cit., p.22.
95 J. A. Barlow to Sir Clive Wigram, 20
December 1933. Royal Archives.
RA. PS/GV/K. 2339/19.
96 Cuthbert Headlam diary, 3 January
1934. Stuart Ball (ed.), op. cit.,
p.289.
97 F. H. Mitchell to Anthony Eden., 30
December 1933. AP 3/1/1.
98 Anthony Eden diary, 6 January
1934. AP 20/1/14.
99 Harold Nicolson, *King George the
Fifth: His Life and Reign*, Constable,
1952, f-n. pp.518–19.
100 Anthony Eden diary, 6 January
1934. AP 20/1/14.
101 Simon Burgess, *Stafford Cripps: A
Political Life*, Gollancz, 1999, p.88.
102 Anthony Eden diary, 7 January
1934. AP 20/1/14.
103 *Hamlet*, II.ii.130.
104 Hansard (House of Lords), 7 March
1961.
105 See Chapter 16.
106 Butler and Macmillan were the only
serious candidates to succeed Eden,
though the *Daily Worker* of 10
January 1957 tipped Selwyn Lloyd.
See Chapter 18.
107 Notice of J. P. L. Thomas, Viscount
Cilcennin, by Kenneth Rose.
*Dictionary of National Biography
1951–1960*, Oxford University
Press, Oxford, 1971, p.967.
108 See, in particular, Chapter 12.
109 Hansard, 6 February 1934.
110 Lord Cranborne, 'Memorandum on
Tour of European Capitals with Mr
Anthony Eden, February 1934.'
Salisbury papers, Hatfield House.
111 Cynthia Gladwyn, *The Paris
Embassy*, Collins, 1976, pp.207–8.
112 Anthony Eden diary, 17 February
1934. AP 20/1/14.
113 Anthony Eden, op. cit., p.108. On
Barthou's death, Eden reflected on
the times they had together. Despite
everything, he counted him a friend.
His favourite memory was when a
delegate had said to Barthou at
Geneva, 'Permettez-moi de vous
présenter ma femme. Elle est pure
espagnole.' To which Barthou had
replied, 'Oh ça me n'interesse pas.
Moi je préfère les espagnoles
impures.' Anthony Eden diary, 9
October 1934. AP 20/1/14.
114 Anthony Eden to Sir John Simon, 18
February 1934. PRO. FO 800/289.
115 Anthony Eden diary, 9 October
1934. AP 20/1/14.
116 Lord Cranborne Memorandum.
117 A list of the British Ambassadors to
the major powers from 1935 to
1957 is included as Appendix IV.
118 Anthony Eden diary, 20 February
1934. AP 20/1/14.
119 Lord Cranborne Memorandum.
120 Anthony Eden diary, 21 February
1934. AP 20/1/14.
121 *News Chronicle*, 21 September
1936.
122 Quoted in Philip Ziegler, *King
Edward VIII: The Official
Biography*, Collins, 1990, p.391.
123 Anthony Eden to Stanley Baldwin,
21 February 1934. Baldwin papers,
Cambridge University Library, vol.
122, ff.31–3.

124 Anthony Eden diary, 22 February 1934. AP 20/1/14.
125 Anthony Eden diary, 24 February 1934. AP 20/1/14.
126 Lord Cranborne Memorandum.
127 *Observer*, 25 February 1934.
128 Ian Colvin, *Vansittart in Office*, Gollancz, 1965, p.170.
129 Robert Mallett, 'Fascist Foreign Policy and Official Italian Views of Anthony Eden in the 1930s', *The Historical Journal*, 43, 1 (2000), pp.157–87.
130 Anthony Eden diary, 26 February 1934. AP 20/1/14.
131 Lord Cranborne Memorandum.
132 Quoted in Piers Brendon, op cit., p.271.
133 Lord Cranborne Memorandum.
134 Günter Grass's play *The Plebeians Rehearse the Uprising* traces the connection between the civil disturbances in Berlin in 1953 and Bertolt Brecht's adaptation of *Coriolanus*.
135 Anthony Eden, op. cit., p.82.
136 Lord Cranborne Memorandum.
137 See Mario Toscano, 'Eden's Mission to Rome on the Eve of the Italo-Ethiopian Conflict.' A. O. Sarkissian (ed.), *Studies in Diplomatic History and Historiography*, Longmans, Green, 1961.
138 Hansard, 14 March 1934. At the East Fulham by-election on 25 October 1933, eleven days after Germany had left the League of Nations, a Conservative majority of 14,521 was turned into a Labour one of 4,840, a swing of 29.1 per cent. The result was interpreted as a vote against rearmament, which was strongly advocated by the Conservative candidate W. J. Waldron, and for pacifism. Together with the vote (by 275 votes to 153) at the Oxford Union on 3 February 1933 that 'this House will in no circumstances fight for its King and Country', East Fulham has entered the mythology of the appeasement era. See Martin Ceadel, 'Interpreting East Fulham,' in Chris Cook and John Ramsden (eds), *By-Elections in British Politics*, Macmillan, 1973.
139 Hansard, 30 July 1934.
140 Anthony Eden diary, 23 May 1934. AP 20/1/14.
141 Speech at Kenilworth, 28 June 1934. Records of Warwick and Leamington Conservative Association.
142 Anthony Eden diary, 3 August 1934. AP 20/1/14.
143 Anthony Eden to Sir John Simon, 19 September 1934. Simon papers, Bodleian Library, Oxford, box 79, fol.78.
144 Anthony Eden diary, 9 October 1934. AP 20/1/14.
145 Anthony Eden, op. cit., pp.111–12.
146 Major-General A. C. Temperley, op. cit., pp.299, 296, 330. See Chapter 6 for the Abyssinian crisis.
147 Anthony Eden diary, 7 December 1934. AP 20/1/14.
148 Anthony Eden diary, 2 November 1934.
149 Anthony Eden, op. cit., p.122.
150 Anthony Eden diary, 7 November 1934. AP 20/1/14.
151 Major-General A.C. Temperley, op. cit., p.248.
152 Anthony Eden diary, 8 November 1934. AP 20/1/14.
153 Henry J. Stimson, *The Far Eastern Crisis: Recollections and Observations*, Harper & Brothers, New York, 1936, p.233.
154 Anthony Eden to Alec Cadogan, 15 March 1935. AP 14/1/405B.
155 Anthony Eden diary, 2 March 1935. AP 20/1/15.
156 *The Times*, 9 January 1935.

CHAPTER 6

Burdens of Office

1 Harold Nicolson papers, Balliol College, Oxford.
2 Sir Samuel Hoare, Viscount Templewood, *Nine Troubled Years*, Collins, 1954, pp.107–8.
3 Hansard, 14 December 1950.
4 Anthony Eden, *Facing the Dictators*, p.124.
5 Anthony Eden diary, 23 March 1935. AP 20/1/15.

6 Anthony Eden diary, 24 March
1935. AP 20/1/15.
7 Lord Cranborne, 'Diary of a Visit to
Berlin, Moscow, Warsaw & Prague
with Anthony Eden, March–April
1935'. Salisbury papers, Hatfield
House.
8 Anthony Eden diary, 25 March
1934. AP 20/1/15.
9 *DGFP*, Series C, vol. III, p.1061.
10 Anthony Eden diary, 26 March
1934. AP 20/1/15.
11 Quoted in Keith Middlemass and
John Barnes, *Baldwin: A Biography*,
Weidenfeld & Nicolson, 1969,
p.799.
12 *Hamlet*, IV.iv. 18–19.
13 Anthony Eden, op. cit., p.142. Full
documentation of the Moscow,
Warsaw and Prague visits can be
found in *DBFP*, Second Series, vol.
XII.
14 George Bilainkin, *Maisky: The Ten
Years Ambassador*, George Allen &
Unwin, 1944, p.136.
15 Lord Cranborne Memorandum.
16 Anthony Eden, op. cit., p.162.
17 Anthony Eden diary, 24 April 1935.
AP 20/1/15.
18 Professor Edward Ullendorff to the
author, 5 November 1997. The name
remains to the present day, as does
another in his honour in Corinth.
19 Anthony Eden, op. cit., p.159.
20 Anthony Eden, op. cit., p.162.
21 *DBFP*, Second Series, vol. XII, p.
804.
22 Anthony Eden, op. cit., p.170.
23 PRO. CAB 23/81. CC 20 (35) 1, 8
April 1935.
24 PRO. CAB 23/81. CC 20 (35) 1, 8
April 1935.
25 In answer to a question from
Alexander Werth, diplomatic
correspondent of the *Manchester
Guardian*. Richard Lamb, *Mussolini
and the British*, John Murray, 1997,
p.120.
26 Thomas Jones to Dr. Abraham
Flexner, 25 April 1936, Thomas
Jones, *A Diary with Letters,
1931–1950*, Oxford University
Press, Oxford, 1954, p.187.
27 Anthony Eden diary, 11 May 1935.
AP 20/1/15.

28 Sir Philip Sassoon to Anthony Eden,
April 1935. AP 14/1/206C.
29 Anthony Eden, op. cit., p.189.
30 Baron Pompeo Aloisi to Benito
Mussolini, 26 May 1935. Quoted in
Robert Mallet, 'Fascist Foreign
Policy and Official Italian Views of
Anthony Eden in the 1930s',
Historical Journal, 43, 1 (2000),
p.164.
31 *DBFP*, Second Series, vol. XIV,
p.291.
32 Harold Nicolson diary, 26 May
1935. Harold Nicolson papers,
Balliol College, Oxford.
33 *DBFP*, Second Series, vol. XIV,
p.292.
34 Anthony Eden, op. cit., p.214.
35 Earl of Avon to René Massigli, 4
July 1964. Massigli papers. Quai
d'Orsay, Paris.
36 'Conversations at Cliveden', Thomas
Jones to Lady Grigg,1 June 1936,
op. cit., p.150.
37 C. L. Mowat, *Britain between the
Wars*, Methuen paperback, 1968,
p.460.
38 Kenneth Rose, *King George V*,
Weidenfeld & Nicolson, 1983, p.xii.
39 Neville Chamberlain to Hilda
Chamberlain. NC 18/1/934. Despite
such unpopularity, Simon
nevertheless proved one of the great
survivors of twentieth-century
politics, the first of only three men
(the other two were Rab Butler and
James Callaghan) to hold the three
great offices of state, and uniquely,
in addition, the Lord
Chancellorship.
40 Anthony Eden diary, 29 September
1931. AP 20/1/11.
41 Quoted in Piers Brendon, *The Dark
Valley: A Panorama of the 1930s*,
Jonathan Cape, 2000, p.270.
42 Twenty years later, when Eden
formed his first Cabinet, he found
that these things were easier said
than done. His own administration
in April 1955 also had an inherited
air, and, like Baldwin, he was to
change his Foreign Secretary before
Christmas. See Chapter 16.
43 Thomas Jones, op. cit., p.147.
44 PRO. CAB 23/83.

45 *The Spectator*, 18 October 1935.

46 Robert Mallett, *The Italian Navy and Fascist Expansionism, 1935–1940*, Frank Cass, 1998, p.2.

47 *Vide* David Carlton, *Anthony Eden: A Biography*, Allen & Unwin paperback, 1986, p.65.

48 A. J. P. Taylor, *English History 1914–1945*, Oxford University Press, Oxford, 1965, p.627.

49 See in particular A. J. P. Taylor, op. cit., pp.420–1.

50 Richard Lamb, *Mussolini and the British*, John Murray, 1997, p.152.

51 Anthony Eden, op. cit., p.324.

52 Martin Gilbert, *Winston S. Churchill Volume V 1922–1939*, Heinemann, 1976, p.903.

53 Oliver Harvey diary, 8 November 1941. John Harvey (ed.), *The War Diaries of Oliver Harvey 1941–1945*, Collins, 1978, p.61.

54 Anthony Eden, op. cit., p.237.

55 This was first disclosed by the Italian historian Renzo De Felice in 1974.

56 Leopold von Hoesch Memorandum, 2 July 1935. *DGFP*, Series C, vol. IV, p.393.

57 Anthony Eden telegram, 25 June 1935. *DBFP*, Second Series, vol. XIV, p.334.

58 PRO. Minute J 844/1/1 of 27 November 1935. FO 800/307.

59 Mario Toscano, 'Eden's Mission to Rome on the Eve of the Italo-Ethiopian Conflict', A.O. Sarkissian (ed.), *Studies in Diplomatic History and Historiography*, Longmans, Green, 1961, pp.141–2.

60 Mario Toscano, op. cit., p.126.

61 Anthony Eden, op. cit., p.225.

62 Count Grandi to Benito Mussolini, 2 July 1935. *Documenti diplomatici italiani*, 8th Series, number 1, document 475. (Translation by Dr Robert Mallett.)

63 PRO. Minutes of meeting on 22 July 1935. CAB 23/82.

64 Sir Robert Vansittart to Anthony Eden, 19 September 1935. AP 20/4/1.

65 Count Grandi to Benito Mussolini, 13 October 1935. Archivio Storico del Ministero degli Affari Esteri, busta 927, fascicolo 1. I am grateful to Dr Robert Mallett for translation of this document.

66 PRO. Sir Samuel Hoare to Anthony Eden, 16 October 1935. FO 800/295.

67 This was the first of Eden's five 'freedoms', the others being in Athens (1944), Durham (1945), Warwick (1947) and Perth (1956).

68 Attlee was still Labour leader twenty years later when Eden was Prime Minister. Of the five General Elections he fought as leader, Labour lost three, and on the two occasions Attlee chose the date for dissolution (February 1950 and October 1951) he did so injudiciously. Attlee's one glittering triumph at the polls in July 1945 has disguised the fact that his electoral record was not in fact outstanding, certainly compared to other Labour leaders such as Harold Wilson and Tony Blair. But the one contest where no blame could be attached to him for Labour's defeat was in the special circumstances of 1935.

69 Tom Stannage, *Baldwin Thwarts the Opposition: The British General Election of 1935*, Croom Helm, 1980, p.245.

70 AP 20/4/12.

71 Sir Samuel Hoare to Stanley Baldwin, 8 December 1935. AP 20/4/12B.

72 Robert Rhodes James, *Memoirs of a Conservative: J.C.C. Davidson's Memoirs and Papers, 1910–1937*, Weidenfeld & Nicolson, 1969, p.409.

73 Anthony Eden telegram, 12 December 1935. *DBFP*, Second Series, vol. XV, p.464.

74 PRO. Cabinet Minutes, 18 December 1935. CAB 28/90B.

75 *Julius Caesar*, II.i. 171–3.

76 Hansard, 19 December 1935.

77 Anthony Eden to Winston Churchill, 19 March 1948. Churchill papers. CHUR 4/144A.

78 The fullest account of the crisis can be read in J. A. Cross, *Sir Samuel Hoare: A Political Biography*, Jonathan Cape, 1977, pp.225–65.

79 R. A. C. Parker, 'Great Britain,

France and the Ethiopian Crisis 1935–1936', *English Historical Review*, vol. 89, 1974, p.324.

80 Accounts of Eden's appointment to the post of Foreign Secretary are in Anthony Eden, op. cit., pp.315–17, and John Barnes and Keith Middlemass, op.cit., pp.896–7.

81 Anthony Eden diary, 23 December 1935. AP 20/1/15.

82 Anthony Eden, op. cit., p.317.

83 Winston Churchill to Clementine Churchill, 26 December 1935. *Speaking for Themselves: The Personal Letters of Winston and Clementine Churchill*, edited by their daughter Mary Soames, Doubleday,1998, p.402.

84 Sir Eric Drummond to Anthony Eden, 27 December 1935. *DBFP*, Second Series, vol. XV, p.529.

85 M. Corbin to Pierre Laval, 23 December 1935. M. François-Ponnet to Pierre Laval, 24 December 1935. *Documents Diplomatiques Français 1932–1939*, 1st Series, vol. XIII, Paris 1973, pp.691, 707.

86 Ulrich von Hassell Memorandum, 19 December 1935. *DGFP*, Series C, vol. IV, p.929.

87 Dokumenty Vneshnei Politiki SSSR, doc. 447, quoted in Jonathan Haslam, *The Soviet Union and the Struggle for Collective Security in Europe 1933–1939*, Macmillan, 1984, pp.74–5.

88 Sir Isaac A. Isaacs despatch of 24 December 1935. RA GEO V. P. 284/404, This (slightly inaccurate) quotation from *Henry IV Part One*, II.ii. 9–10, was to be cited (correctly) by Neville Chamberlain on 29 September at Heston Airport before he flew to meet Hitler at Munich.

89 Lord Lloyd to Lady Lloyd, 24 May 1936. Lloyd papers, Churchill College, Cambridge. GLLD 4.

90 Collin Brooks diary, 22 December 1935 and 21 February 1938. *Fleet Street, Press Barons and Politics: The Journals of Collin Brooks, 1932–1940* (edited by N. J. Crowson), Cambridge University Press, Cambridge, for the Royal Historical Society, 1998, p.148 and

pp.196–7.

91 Cuthbert Headlam diary, 22 December 1935. *Parliament and Politics in the Age of Churchill and Attlee; The Headlam Diaries 1935–1951* (edited by Stuart Ball), Cambridge University Press, Cambridge, for the Royal Historical Society, 1999, p.81.

92 Anthony Eden diary, 24 December 1935. AP 20/1/15.

93 PRO. DO 114/68.

94 Anthony Eden diary, 24 December 1935. AP 20/1/15.

95 Anthony Eden diary, 6 September 1942. AP 20/1/22.

96 'Impression of a fortnight with the Edens in the South of France. By Harold Caccia. Written 27 & 28 Feb 1937.' Lord Caccia papers (Eton College Library).

97 Thomas Jones diary, 27 July 1936. Thomas Jones, op. cit., p.231.

98 Lord Home, *The Way the Wind Blows*, Collins, 1976, p.29.

99 Anthony Eden diary, 20 May 1936. AP 20/1/16.

100 *Vide* 'Proposals for the Reform of the Foreign Service' (Cmd 6420), 1943. The impact of the subsequent reforms in the late 1940s is discussed in Chapter 10.

101 PRO. CAB 158/30.

102 FO 371/19879.

103 John Betjeman, 'On the Death of King George V'.

104 Kenneth Rose, op. cit., p.404.

105 Private information. See also Frances Donaldson, *Edward VIII*, Weidenfeld & Nicolson, 1974, p.192.

106 PRO. CC 3 (36) 4. CAB 23/83.

107 PRO. Cabinet Meeting, 29 January 1936. CAB 23/83.

108 Anthony Eden, 'Memorandum on Policy towards Germany', 11 February, 1936. C 997/4/18.

109 Hansard, 25 February 1936.

110 Sir Nicholas Henderson, 'Hitler and the Rhineland, 1936: A Decisive Turning Point', *History Today*, Volume 42, October 1992, p.18. Nicholas Henderson was Eden's private secretary, 1944–5.

111 Cabinet minutes, 11 March 1936.

PRO. CAB 23/83.

112 Anthony Eden to Sir George Clerk, 14 March 1936, *DBFP*, 2nd Series, vol. 16, no. 91.

113 Anthony Eden, op. cit., pp.346–7.

114 Leo Amery diary, 7 March 1936. John Barnes and David Nicholson (eds), op. cit., p.410.

115 Neville Chamberlain to Ida Chamberlain, 28 March 1936. Neville Chamberlain papers, Birmingham University Library. NC 18/1.

116 Earl of Avon to Sir Robert (Robin) Hankey, 6 December 1961. AP 23/35/19A.

117 Quoted by Sir Nicholas Henderson, op. cit., p.19.

118 Sir Alexander Cadogan diary, 1 December 1941. Cadogan Papers, Churchill College, Cambridge. ACAD 1/10.

119 A comprehensive account of the on-going historical debate over Chamberlain's reputation can be found in David Dutton, *Neville Chamberlain*, Arnold, 2001, *passim*.

120 Anthony Eden diary, 27 April 1936. AP 20/1/16.

121 Anthony Eden Memorandum, 'On the present position of negotiations for an Anglo-Egyptian Treaty', 25 April 1936. J 3548/2/16. *DBFP*, Second Series, vol. XVI, p.357. See Chapter 12 for details of the renegotiation of this Treaty in 1954.

122 Memorandum by Mr Somers-Cocks on the Anglo-Egyptian Treaty of 26 August 1936. *DBFP*, Second Series, vol. XVI, p.808.

123 Anthony Eden to Stanley Baldwin, 20 August 1936. FO 954/Vol. 27, fol. 22.

124 Archibald Clark Kerr to Anthony Eden, 18 August 1936. Anthony Eden to Sir John Wardlaw Milne, 20 August 1936. Foreign Office Papers of Anthony Eden, Birmingham University Library. FO 954/vol. 5, fol. 16. Sir John Wardlaw Milne's footnote in history came with his suggestion in a Censure Debate in the House of Commons on 1 July 1942 that the Duke of Gloucester should be appointed Commander-in-Chief of the British Army.

125 Anthony Eden diary, 5 June 1936. AP 20/1/16.

126 Thomas Jones to Lady Grigg, 3 May 1936. Thomas Jones, op. cit., p.193.

127 Andrew Roberts, *The Holy Fox: A Biography of Lord Halifax*, Weidenfeld & Nicolson, 1991, p.55.

128 Anthony Eden, op. cit., p.381.

129 Roy Jenkins, quoted in 'Léon Blum', *Nine Men of Power*, Hamish Hamilton, 1974, p.49.

130 FO 954/vol. 27, fol. 19.

131 Hansard, 29 October 1936.

132 *DGFP 1918–1945*, Series C, vol. V, Document 533. Mario Toscano, *Designs in Diplomacy: Pages from European Diplomatic History in the 20th Century*, translated and edited by George A. Carbone, John Hopkins Press, Baltimore and London, 1970, pp. 410–11.

133 Count Ciano, *Ciano's Diary 1937–1938*, Methuen, 1952, p.27.

134 David Carlton, *Anthony Eden: A Biography*, Allen Lane, 1981, p.97.

135 The others were a DCL from Durham University in 1937 and an Honorary Degree at Columbia University in 1952.

136 Philip Ziegler, *Wilson: The Authorised Life*, Weidenfeld & Nicolson, 1993, p.21.

137 Anthony Eden diary, 5 December 1936. AP 20/1/16.

138 Leo Amery diary, 7 December 1936. John Barnes and David Nicholson, op. cit., p.432.

139 Queen Mary to the Duke of Windsor, 5 July 1938. Quoted James Pope-Hennessy, *Queen Mary 1867–1953*, George Allen & Unwin, 1959, p.575.

140 Anthony Eden diary, 17 December 1936. AP 20/1/16.

141 The Duke of Windsor, *A King's Story: The Memoirs of H.R.H. The Duke of Windsor*, Pan Books paperback, 1957, p.296.

142 Private information.

143 Sir Robert Vansittart to Sir Alexander Hardinge, 4 May 1937. FO 954/vol. 33, fol. 6.

144 Memorandum on the Duke of Windsor's visit to Hitler. FO

954/vol. 33, fol. 131

145 Anthony Eden to Stanley Baldwin, 27 December 1936. Earl Baldwin papers, Cambridge University Library, vol. 124, ff. 55–7.

146 Sir Antony Acland, Permanent Under-Secretary and Head of the Diplomatic Service, became Ambassador in Washington in 1986, but special circumstances obtained. It remained an unusual career move.

147 Anthony Eden diary, 21 December 1936. AP 20/1/16.

148 Sir Nevile Henderson, *Failure of a Mission*, Hodder & Stoughton, 1940, p.1.

149 Donald Gillies, *Radical Diplomat: The Life of Archibald Clark Kerr, Lord Inverchapel, 1882–1951*, I. B. Tauris, 1999, p.81.

150 Anthony Eden Memorandum on Spain, 8 January 1937. W 1612/1/41.

151 Anthony Eden to Sir Eric Drummond, 24 February 1937. Telegram R 1295/135/22.

152 Anthony Eden to Lord Wigram, 5 March 1937. RA PS/GVI/C/033/08.

153 Anthony Eden to Dame Ivy Chamberlain, 17 March 1937. Austen Chamberlain papers, Birmingham University Library. AC 59/85.

154 Anthony Eden diary, 9 June 1936. AP 20/1/16.

155 A. J. Sylvester to David Lloyd George, 21 May 1935. Earl Lloyd-George papers, House of Lords Record Office. LG/G/22/1/10.

156 David Margesson Memorandum for the Prime Minister, 17 March 1938. Neville Chamberlain papers, Birmingham University Library. NC 7/11/31/188.

157 Anthony Eden, op. cit., p.319.

158 Oliver Harvey diary, 26 March 1937. Oliver Harvey, op. cit., p.34.

CHAPTER 7

The Path to Resignation

1 NC 18/1/1073.

2 AP 20/1/18.

3 Commander Thomas Woodrooffe broadcast, BBC, 20 May 1936.

4 Sir Cuthbert Headlam diary, 7 March 1937. Stuart Ball (ed.), *Parliament and Politics in the Age of Churchill and Attlee: The Headlam Diaries 1935–1951*, Cambridge University Press, Cambridge, for the Royal Historical Society, 1999, p.108.

5 Neville Chamberlain to Ida Chamberlain, 8 August 1937. NC 18/1/1015.

6 PRO. CAB 127/158.

7 Anthony Eden diary, 15 October 1941. AP 20/1/21.

8 Francis Williams, *A Pattern of Rulers*, Longmans, 1965, p.135.

9 Neville Chamberlain to Hilda Chamberlain, 1 August 1937. NC 18/1/1014.

10 Account of 1937–8, Viscount Cilcennin papers, Carmarthen Record Office. Ms. cilc. coll 50.

11 PRO. FO 371/3201.

12 David M. Kennedy, *Freedom from Fear: The American People in Depression and War, 1929–1945*, Oxford University Press, New York, 1999, p.405.

13 Anthony Eden to Sir Ronald Lindsay, 10 March 1937. PRO. FO 371/20651.

14 AP 14/1/666B.

15 Quoted in Denis Mack Smith, *Mussolini*, Granada Publishing, 1983, p.263

16 PRO. CAB 23/88.

17 Anthony Eden diary, 15 March 1937. AP 20/1/17. This was the first mention in Eden's diary of Ernest Bevin, with whom he was to work closely during the Second World War, and whom he admired greatly.

18 Sir Nevile Henderson to Anthony Eden, 15 July 1937. FO 954/10A, fol. 37/29.

19 Sir Maurice Hankey to Robin Hankey, 8 June 1937. Stephen Roskill, *Hankey Man of Secrets: Volume III – 1963*, Collins, 1974, pp.280–1.

20 Sir Maurice Hankey to Robin Hankey, 7 March and 21 November 1937, op. cit., pp.277, 265.

21 Neville Chamberlain to Benito Mussolini, 27 July 1937. PRO. PREM 1/276.
22 Neville Chamberlain diary, 19 February 1938. NC 2/24A.
23 Anthony Eden to Lord Halifax, 11 August 1937. PRO. FO 800/309.
24 PRO. CAB 23/89.
25 Anthony Eden to Lord Wigram, 5 March 1937. RA PS GVI C/033/08.
26 Anthony Eden to Winston Churchill, 14 September 1937. Churchill papers, Churchill College, Cambridge, CHAR 2/302.
27 Andrew Roberts, *The Holy Fox: A Biography of Lord Halifax*, Weidenfeld & Nicolson, 1991, p.65.
28 Sir Nevile Henderson, *Failure of a Mission*, Hodder & Stoughton, 1940, p.85.
29 Oliver Harvey diary, 7 November 1937. John Harvey (ed.), *The Diplomatic Diaries of Oliver Harvey 1937–1940*, Collins, 1970, p.57.
30 Anthony Eden to Neville Chamberlain, 3 November 1937. PRO. PREM 1/210.
31 Andrew Roberts, op. cit., p.63.
32 Oliver Harvey diary, 8 November 1937, op. cit., p.58. Anthony Eden, *Facing the Dictators*, Cassell, 1962, pp.512–3.
33 Oliver Harvey diary, 3 November 1937, op. cit., p.56.
34 The story was first revealed by the Earl of Birkenhead in *Halifax: The Life of Lord Halifax*, Hamish Hamilton, 1965, p.368.
35 Anthony Eden, op. cit., p.515.
36 President Roosevelt speech, Chicago, 5 October 1937. David M. Kennedy, op. cit., p.405.
37 Oliver Harvey diary, 2 October 1937, op. cit., p.49.
38 *Hansard*, 1 November 1937.
39 Neville Chamberlain to Hilda Chamberlain, 17 December 1937. NC 18/1/1032.
40 William C. Mills, 'The Chamberlain-Grandi Conversations of July–August 1937 and the Appeasement of Italy', *The International History Review*, vol. XIX, no. 3: August 1997, p.619.
41 Neville Chamberlain to Hilda Chamberlain, 24 October 1937. NC 18/1/1025.
42 Sir Robert Vansittart to Anthony Eden, 9 December 1937. AP 20/5/32.
43 Ian Colvin, *Vansittart in Office*, Gollancz, 1965, p.172.
44 Sir Horace Rumbold to Anthony Rumbold, 10 January 1938. Sir Anthony Rumbold papers, Bodleian Library Oxford. AR Box 5.
45 Anthony Eden to HM King George VI, 31 December 1937. FO 954/vol. 5, ff. 35–8.
46 Anthony Eden to Neville Chamberlain, 31 December 1937. PRO. FO 954/7.
47 Anthony Eden diary, 5 January 1938. AP 20/1/18.
48 Anthony Eden to Neville Chamberlain, 9 January 1938. Neville Chamberlain to Anthony Eden, 13 January 1938. FO 954/vol. 6, ff. 286 and 289.
49 Anthony Eden to Neville Chamberlain, 17 January 1938. AP 20/6/8.
50 Anthony Eden diary, 14 January 1938. AP 20/1/18.
51 Account of Anthony Eden's resignation. Viscount Cilcennin papers, Carmarthen Record Office. Ms. cilc. coll. 61.
52 Sumner Welles, *Seven Decisions That Shaped History*, Harper and Brothers, New York, 1951, p.27.
53 Account of Anthony Eden's resignation, Viscount Cilcennin, op. cit.
54 Anthony Eden diary, 15 January 1938. AP 20/1/18.
55 Anthony Eden diary, 16 January 1938. AP 20/1/18.
56 Anthony Eden diary, 17 January 1938. AP 20/1/18.
57 Account of Anthony Eden's resignation, Viscount Cilcennin, op. cit.
58 Anthony Eden, op. cit., p.560.
59 Oliver Harvey diary, 20 January 1938, op. cit., p.76.
60 Oliver Harvey diary, 21 January 1938, op. cit., p.77.
61 Anthony Eden to Neville Chamberlain, 8 February 1938.

Neville Chamberlain to Anthony
Eden, 8 February 1938. PRO.
PREM 1/126.
62 Oliver Harvey diary, 13 February
1938, op. cit., p.89.
63 Oliver Harvey diary, 17 February
1938, op. cit., p.92.
64 Quoted in R.A.C. Parker,
*Chamberlain and Appeasement:
British Policy and the Coming of the
Second World War*, Macmillan,
1993, p.121.
65 Oliver Harvey diary, 18 February
1938, op. cit., p.93.
66 Lord Halifax, 'A Record of Events
connected with Anthony Eden's
resignation February 19–20th 1938',
Halifax papers, the Borthwick
Institute of Historical Research,
York. File A4 410 4 11.
Interestingly, there is also a duplicate
copy of this memorandum and
related correspondence in the
Templewood Papers (Sir Samuel
Hoare), Cambridge University
Library, Box X, File 3.
67 Anthony Eden diary, 20 February
1938. AP 20/1/18.
68 Anthony Eden, op. cit., p.592.
69 AP 20/6/31.
70 Anthony Eden to Neville
Chamberlain, 20 February 1938.
PRO. PREM 5/158.
71 Account of Anthony Eden's
resignation. Viscount Cilcennin op.
cit.
72 Lord Halifax Memorandum, op. cit.
73 Sir Horace Rumbold to Anthony
Rumbold, 2 March 1938. Anthony
Rumbold papers, loc. cit. AR Box 5.
74 John Redcliffe-Maud, *Experiences of
an Optimist: The Memoirs of John
Redcliffe-Maud*, Hamish Hamilton,
1981, p.28.
75 Sir Alexander Hardinge
Memorandum on the Resignation of
the Foreign Secretary, 20 February
1938. RA PS GVI C 063/02. When
Hankey heard of the King's concern,
he streamlined processes to ensure
that such a thing never happened
again.The range of papers taken by
the Royal Household had increased
since the days of the General Strike.
When the Prime Minister's then

Private Secretary had warned Clive
Wigram, King George V's Assistant
Private Secretary, not to be alarmed
when the *Daily Mail* failed to
appear, he was told, 'We don't take
the *Daily Mail* or the *Daily Express*.'
Thomas Jones, *Whitehall Diary,
Volume II 1926–1930*, Oxford
University Press, Oxford, 1971,
p.33.
76 Lord Cudlipp obituary. *The Times*,
18 May 1998.
77 Quoted in Martin Gilbert, *Winston
S. Churchill: Volume V 1922–1939*,
Heinemann,1976, p.903.
78 Sir Horace Rumbold to Anthony
Eden, 22 February 1938. Quoted in
Anthony Eden, op. cit., p.603.
79 Anthony Eden to Lord Halifax, 5
March 1938. Halifax Memorandum,
op. cit.

CHAPTER 8
A New and Sharper Sword

1 Hugh MacDiarmid, 'When the
Gangs come to London: On the
Recent Thanksgiving for "Peace",'
Times Literary Supplement, 17
March 2000, p.15. The poem lay
undiscovered for over sixty years.
2 *New York Herald Tribune*, 19
December 1938.
3 When Churchill was drafting *The
Gathering Storm*, the first volume of
his war memoirs, in August 1947,
Eden reminded him that not all the
Press was behind appeasement.
Anthony Eden Memorandum on
Churchill's Draft Memoirs, August
1947. AP 19/4/4.
4 *The Times*, 26 February 1938.
Halifax's father, Eden's mother and
Sir Edward Grey were grandchildren
of three Grey brothers, the eldest of
whom was Prime Minister at the
time of the Great Reform Bill in
1832.
5 M. François-Poncet to M. Delbos,
20 February 1938. M. Corbin to M.
Paul-Boncour, 19 March 1938.
*Documents Diplomatiques Français
1932–1939*, 2nd Series, vol. VIII,
Paris, 1973. Document 216, p.434

and Document 512, pp.935–6.

6 Frank McDonough, *Neville Chamberlain, Appeasement and the British Road to War*, Manchester University Press, Manchester, 1998, p.127.

7 Sir Gervase Beckett had died on 24 August 1937. Beatrice Eden was to be buried at Kirkdale in 1957 after her premature death from cancer.

8 See Appendix I.

9 Robert Skidelsky, *Oswald Mosley*, Macmillan, 1975, p.216.

10 Hansard, 21 February 1938. Ironically, this latter passage was to be repeated by Sir Anthony Nutting, when he resigned from Eden's Government over Suez in November 1956. D. R. Thorpe, 'Sir Anthony Nutting', Obituary, *Independent*, 3 March 1999.

11 Hansard, 21 February 1938.

12 Harold Nicolson diary, 21 February 1938. Harold Nicolson papers, Balliol College, Oxford.

13 Harold Nicolson to Vita Sackville-West, 2 March 1938. Quoted in Martin Gilbert (ed.), *Winston S. Churchill, Companion Volume V, Part 3: The Coming of War 1936–1939*, Heinemann, 1982, p.922. Malcolm MacDonald's star had risen as his father's had declined. His career was of great significance for Eden over Indo-China and India in the 1950s.

14 Hansard, 21 February 1938.

15 Sir Henry Channon diary, 24 February 1938. Robert Rhodes James (ed.), *Chips: The Diaries of Sir Henry Channon*, Weidenfeld & Nicolson, 1967, pp.146–7.

16 Neville Chamberlain to Anthony Eden, 26 February 1938. AP 20/6/10.

17 Sir Geoffrey Howe's resignation speech in the House of Commons on 13 November 1990 triggered the events that led to the fall of Mrs Thatcher as Prime Minister fifteen days later.

18 Winston Churchill to Anthony Eden, 21 February 1938. AP 8/2/44.

19 See Richard Cockett, *Twilight of Truth: Chamberlain, Appeasement and the Manipulation of the Press*, Weidenfeld & Nicolson, 1989, *passim*, for a comprehensive account of this process.

20 *Hansard*, 22 February 1938.

21 Count Ciano diary, 20 February 1938. *Ciano's Diary 1937–1938*, Methuen, 1952, pp.77–8.

22 Sir Nevile Henderson to Lord Halifax, 27 February 1938. PRO. FO 800/313.

23 Anthony Eden to Viscount Cranborne, 2 March 1938. Salisbury papers, Hatfield House. Box J3.

24 Anthony Eden to Viscount Cranborne, 21 June 1938. Salisbury papers, Hatfield House. Box J3.

25 Anthony Eden to Winston Churchill, 22 April 1938. AP 20/6/12A.

26 Hugh Dalton diary, 8 April 1938. Ben Pimlott (ed.), *The Political Diary of Hugh Dalton 1918–40, 1945–60*, Jonathan Cape, 1986, p.227.

27 Harry Crookshank diary, 19 July 1938. Viscount Crookshank papers, Bodleian Library, Oxford, Mss Eng Hist d 359.

28 Walter Runciman, later 2nd Viscount Runciman (1900–89), and a past Chairman of the North of England Shipowners' Association.

29 Anthony Eden to Stanley Baldwin, 19 August 1938. Baldwin papers, Cambridge University Library. vol. 174.

30 See Chapter 12.

31 J. B. Priestley, *English Journey*, Penguin Books paperback, Harmondsworth, 1977, p.302.

32 John Betjeman, 'Margate', 1940.

33 AP 7/13/26.

34 *The Times*, 12 September 1938.

35 Anthony Eden diary, 24 September 1938. AP 20/118.

36 Duff Cooper, *Old Men Forget*, Rupert Hart-Davis, 1953, p.235.

37 Harold Nicolson diary, 28 September 1938. Nicolson papers, Balliol College, Oxford. Sir Walter Liddall (1884–1963) was the National Conservative MP for Lincoln City. Sir Henry Channon diary, 28 September 1938, op. cit., p.171. Sir John Simon diary, 28

September 1938. Simon papers, Bodleian Library, Oxford. MSS Simon 10.

38 Leo Amery diary, 30 September 1938. John Barnes and David Nicholson (eds), *The Empire at Bay: The Leo Amery Diaries 1929–1945*, Hutchinson, 1988, pp.522–3.

39 See Chapters 13 and 14.

40 G. Hagglof, *Diplomat: Memoirs of a Swedish Envoy in London, Paris, Berlin, Moscow and Washington*, Bodley Head, 1972, p.79.

41 Anthony Eden, *The Reckoning*, Cassell, 1965, p.33.

42 Anthony Eden to Winston Churchill, 28 April 1942. AP 20/9/75. Anthony Eden diary, 8 October 1941. AP 20/1/21.

43 Sir Alexander Cadogan diary, 1 October 1938. David Dilks (ed.), Cadogan papers, Churchill College, Cambridge. ACAD 1/7.

44 Private information.

45 Lady Violet Bonham Carter diary, 14 May 1957. Mark Pottle (ed.), *Champion Redoubtable: The Diaries and Letters of Violet Bonham Carter 1914–1945*, Weidenfeld & Nicolson, 1988, p.191.

46 Hugh MacDiarmid, 'When the Gangs Come to London: On the Recent Thanksgiving "Peace",' *Times Literary Supplement* 17 March 2000. This poem lay undiscovered for more than sixty years.

47 David Dutton, *Neville Chamberlain*, Arnold, 2001, p.55.

48 Hansard, 5 October 1938.

49 Hansard, 3 October 1938.

50 Oliver Harvey diary, 11 October 1938, op. cit., p.212.

51 Anthony Eden, op. cit., p.39.

52 Harold Nicolson to Vita Sackville-West, 11 November 1938. Nicolson papers, Balliol College, Oxford.

53 Anthony Eden diary, 11 October 1938. AP 20/1/18.

54 Manuscript note on Munich. Countess of Avon papers.

55 *New York Herald Tribune*, 19 December 1938. Stanley Baldwin kept a copy of this cutting in his papers.

56 AP 20/7/1A.

57 Sir Victor Mallett to the Earl of Halifax, 15 December 1938. Copy in AP 20/6/27.

58 Anthony Eden to Earl Baldwin of Bewdley, 19 December 1938. Baldwin papers, Cambridge University Library, vol. 124, fol. 155.

59 Thomas Jones diary, 24 October 1937. Thomas Jones, *A Diary with Letters 1931–1950*, Oxford University Press, Oxford, 1954, pp.369–70.

60 Richard Griffiths, *Fellow Travellers of the Right: British Enthusiasts for Nazi Germany 1933–1939*, Constable, 1980, pp.285–6.

61 J. P. L. Thomas to Viscount Cranborne, 8 March 1939. Salisbury papers, Hatfield House, Box J3.

62 Anthony Eden, op. cit., p.48.

63 Anthony Eden, op. cit., p.60.

64 *The Tatler*, 6 September 1939.

65 Anthony Eden, op. cit., p.62.

66 Anthony Eden to Viscount Cranborne, 3 September 1939. Salisbury papers, Hatfield House, Box J3.

CHAPTER 9

Uphill All the Way

1 AP 20/1/20.

2 AP 20/1/21.

3 FO 954/vol. 27 (Spain), fol. 102. Original copy in Avon Papers, Birmingham University Library.

4 From Lord Avon statement, 17 June 1966, on the publication of Lord Moran's *Winston Churchill: The Struggle for Survival, 1940–1965*. AP 19/2/141B.

5 Dominions Office files, AP 20/7/51A.

6 Edward Cavendish, 10th Duke of Devonshire (1895–1950). The close social world at the Foreign and Dominions Offices at the beginning of the war is reflected not only in the links between Halifax and Eden (who were related by both blood and marriage) but also by those

between Devonshire and Cranborne (Dominions Secretary from October 1940), who were brothers-in-law and Eton contemporaries of Eden. Cranborne's wife was the daughter of Lord Richard Frederick Cavendish, Devonshire's uncle. In addition, Harold Macmillan's wife was the former Lady Dorothy Cavendish.

7 Norman Archer note on Dominions Office in 1939–40, 29 May 1962. AP 27/1/62E.

8 Anthony Eden, *The Reckoning*, Cassell, 1965, p.69.

9 John Loader Maffey, first Baron Rugby (1877–1969). One of his grandsons was the Conservative M.P. Jonathan Aitken, sometime Financial Secretary to the Treasury.

10 Anthony Eden broadcast to the USA, 10 September 1939. AP 20/7/25.

11 AP 20/7/64A.

12 Norman Archer note.

13 Speech at the Philharmonic Hall, Liverpool, 29 February 1940. Anthony Eden, *Freedom and Order: Selected Speeches 1939-1946*, Faber & Faber, 1947, p.62.

14 Winston Churchill to Major-General Hastings Ismay, 15 February 1941. PRO. PREM 3/306.

15 Anthony Eden, *The Reckoning*, op. cit., p.133.

16 Anthony Eden, ibid., p.87.

17 Sir Miles Lampson to Sir Horace Wilson, 17 February 1940. AP 20/8/291A.

18 Harold Nicolson diary, 27 June 1939. Nicolson papers, Balliol College, Oxford.

19 Leo Amery diary, 27 September and 4 October 1939. John Barnes and David Nicholson (eds), *The Empire at Bay: The Leo Amery Diaries 1929–1945*, Hutchinson, 1988, p.573.

20 Anthony Eden diary, 4 October 1939. AP 20/1/19.

21 Anthony Eden to Earl Baldwin, 7 September 1939. Baldwin papers, Cambridge University Library, vol. 174, fol. 122.

22 Charles Mott-Radclyffe, *Foreign Body in the Eye: A Memoir of the*

Foreign Service Old and New, Leo Cooper, 1975, p.117.

23 Oliver Harvey diary, 24 December 1939. John Harvey (ed.), *The Diplomatic Diaries of Oliver Harvey 1937–1940*, Collins, 1970, p.332.

24 Selwyn Lloyd papers, Churchill College, Cambridge. SELO 108 (6).

25 Leslie Hore-Belisha diary, 5 January 1940. Hore-Belisha papers, Churchill College, Cambridge. HOBE 1/7.

26 J. P. L. Thomas to Earl Baldwin, 7 January 1940. Baldwin papers, Cambridge University Library, vol. 174, ff. 266–8. 'Lying fairly pretty' is a startling replication of Harvey's unusual phrase and suggests that the two had been talking together about Eden's prospects.

27 Oliver Harvey diary, 27 March 1940, op. cit., p.343.

28 PRO. CAB 99/1.

29 See Professor David Dilks, 'Britain, the Commonwealth and the Wider World', paper presented to the conference on 'The Role of the Commonwealth in the Second World War', St. Antony's College, Oxford, 8 April 1998.

30 Anthony Eden despatch, 11 December 1943. PRO. FO 371/50373.

31 Meeting of Dominion Prime Ministers, 1 May 1944. PRO. PREM 4/42/5.

32 Anthony Eden diary, 9 May 1940. AP 20/1/20.

33 Diary note of conversation with Churchill on 29 July 1940 when the Prime Minister was considering Government reconstruction following Neville Chamberlain's worsening health. AP 20 20/1/20.

34 Anthony Eden to Winston Churchill, 3 June 1940. AP 20/8/9.

35 Hansard, 13 May 1940.

36 Hansard, 21 May 1940.

37 Winston Churchill to Anthony Eden, 26 June 1940. AP 20/8/26. Alfred Duff Cooper to Winston Churchill, with copy to Anthony Eden, 3 July 1940. AP 20/8/43B.

38 The original minutes are preserved in the Avon Papers at Birmingham

University and were the primary source material for Eden's record of the war in his memoirs.

39 Winston Churchill to Anthony Eden, 17 May 1940. AP 20/8/2. Anthony Eden to Winston Churchill, 23 June 1940. AP 20/8/24A.

40 Anthony Eden to Winston Churchill, 12 June 1940. AP 20/8/15.

41 See Mary Soames, *Clementine Churchill*, Cassell, 1979, pp.382–3.

42 Anthony Eden diary, 14 August and 21 August 1940. AP 20/1/20.

43 Anthony Eden diary, 5 August 1940. AP 20/1/20.

44 Eden diary, 15 June 1941. AP 20/1/21.

45 Winston Churchill to Anthony Eden, 27 August 1941. PRO. PREM 3 120.5. Anthony Eden to Winston Churchill, 1 September 1941. PRO. FO 371/285545.

46 Anthony Eden diary, 8 September, 21 September, 24 September and 30 September 1940. AP 20/1/20.

47 Cited in Bernard Donoughue and G. W. Jones, *Herbert Morrison: Portrait of a Politician*, Weidenfeld & Nicolson, 1973, p.281.

48 AP 20/1/20.

49 AP 20/1/21.

50 Neville Chamberlain to Anthony Eden, 11 October 1940. AP 20/8/314.

51 Hansard, 12 November 1940.

52 Professor David Dilks, a great admirer of Eden, who worked with him on his memoirs, was nevertheless to write also a definitive and approbative biography of Chamberlain's career up to 1929, with the second volume eagerly awaited.

53 Hansard, 12 November 1940.

54 Anthony Eden diary, 21 September and 22 September 1940. AP 20/1/20. Ibid. 25 April 1941. AP 20/1/21.

55 John Winton, *Cunningham: The Greatest Admiral since Nelson*, John Murray, 1998, p.109.

56 Sir Miles Lampson (Lord Killearn) diary, 20 October 1940. Middle East Centre, St Antony's College, Oxford.

57 Henry Channon diary, 12 December 1940. Robert Rhodes James (ed.), *Chips: The Diaries of Sir Henry Channon*, Weidenfeld & Nicolson, 1967, p.279.

58 Leo Amery diary, 12 December 1940, op. cit., p.668.

59 Anthony Eden diary, 16 December 1940. AP 20/1/20A.

60 Anthony Eden diary, 17 December, 19 December and 20 December 1940. AP 20/1/20.

61 Sir Alexander Cadogan diary, 6 January 1941.

62 Oliver Harvey diary, 22 December 1940. John Harvey (ed.), *The War Diaries of Oliver Harvey*, Collins, 1978, p.10.

63 Oliver Harvey diary, 25 June 1941, op. cit., p.15.

64 Hugh Dalton diary, 10 May 1941. Ben Pimlott (ed.), *The Second World War Diary of Hugh Dalton 1940–1945*, Jonathan Cape, 1986, p.200. Ponsonby was Chairman of the Council of the Royal Empire Society from 1954 to 1957. Eden created him a Baronet in 1956.

65 Sir Cuthbert Headlam diary, 22 September 1943. Stuart Ball (ed.), *Parliament and Politics in the Age of Churchill and Attlee:The Headlam Diaries 1935–1951*, Cambridge University Press, Cambridge, for the Royal Historical Society, 1999, p.384.

66 R. A. Butler diary, 22 December 1940. Lord Butler of Saffron Walden papers, Trinity College, Cambridge. File G13.

67 Anthony Eden diary, 2 January 1941. AP 20/1/21.

68 Oliver Harvey diary, 24 September 1943, op. cit., p.300.

69 See Chapter 10.

70 Sir Alexander Cadogan diary, 9 June 1945. Cadogan Papers, Churchill College, Cambridge. ACAD 1/15. 'With characteristic precision,' David Dilks has written, 'he kept a record accurate to the nearest mile.' David Dilks (ed.), *The Diaries of Sir Alexander Cadogan, 1938–1945*, Cassell, 1971, p.751 and f-n. In the 1950s, John Foster Dulles, the

United States Secretary of State, exceeded even these totals, which led some to quip that he had an infinite capacity for taking planes.

71 Anthony Eden diary, 4 January 1941. AP 20/1/21.

72 Sir Miles Lampson diary, 1 January 1941, op. cit.

73 Anthony Eden to Winston Churchill, 6 January 1941. PRO. FO 371/29776.

74 Sir Pierson Dixon (1904–65) was to become Eden's Principal Private Secretary in 1943 and one of the most important figures in his professional life. His association with Eden was bounded by two crises – the Balkan mission in 1941 and the Suez crisis in 1956, when Dixon was the United Kingdom's Permanent Representative at the United Nations.

75 See Charles Mott-Radclyffe, op. cit., p.68.

76 Randolph Churchill to Winston Churchill, 6 April 1941. CHAR 1/362/12–15. Chartwell papers, Churchill College, Cambridge.

77 Cited in Randolph S. Churchill, The Rise and Fall of Sir Anthony Eden, MacGibbon & Kee, 1959, p.179.

78 Anthony Eden to Winston Churchill, 28 February 1941. PRO. PREM 3/206/3.

79 Sir Stafford Cripps diary, 8 March 1941. Peter Clarke, The Cripps Version: The Life of Sir Stafford Cripps 1889–1952, Allen Lane, The Penguin Press, 2002, p.213.

80 Ibid., p.213.

81 Anthony Eden to Winston Churchill, 28 March 1941. PRO. FO 371/29782.

82 General Sir Alan Brooke diary, 4 April 1941. Alex Danchev and Daniel Todman (eds), Field Marshal Lord Alanbrooke War Diaries 1939–1945, Weidenfeld & Nicolson, 2001, p.150.

83 The failure of the Dieppe Raid on 19 August 1942 was widely blamed on Mountbatten.

84 Sir Miles Lampson diary, 10 March 1941, op. cit.

85 Sir Miles Lampson diary, 24 March 1941, op. cit.

86 Hugh Dalton diary, 28 April 1941, op. cit., p. 190.

87 Ibid.

88 Hugh Dalton diary, 6 May 1941, op. cit., p.198.

89 Pierson Dixon diary, 8 April 1941. Piers Dixon, Double Diploma: The Life of Sir Pierson Dixon, Hutchinson, 1968, p.86. Eden was to meet Anthony Quayle a great deal after the war at the Shakespeare Memorial Theatre in Stratford and they became good friends. Eden much admired his performance as Hector in Troilus and Cressida.

90 Hugh Gaitskell diary, 5 September 1956. Philip M. Williams (ed.), The Diary of Hugh Gaitskell 1945–1956, Jonathan Cape, 1983, p.596.

91 Winston Churchill to Lieutenant-General Sir Archibald Wavell, 10 January 1941. PRO. CAB 105/1.

92 See Chapters 17 and 18.

93 PRO. CAB 65/21.

94 Sir Miles Lampson diary, 6 March 1941, op. cit.

95 Anthony Eden diary, 27 May 1941. AP 20/1/21.

96 A memorial book listing the 1,397 crew lost is in the village church at Boldre in Hampshire, where the pages are still turned daily.

97 Anthony Eden, op. cit., p.256.

98 Anthony Eden to Viscount Simon, 28 May 1941. Simon papers, Bodleian Library, Oxford. Box 88, ff. 39–43.

99 Ian Nairn and Nikolaus Pevsner, The Buildings of England: Sussex, Penguin Books, Harmondsworth, 1988 edition, p195. Binderton House is now converted into flats.

100 See Chapter 10.

101 Anthony Eden diary, 5 September and 10 October 1941. AP 20/1/21.

102 AP 11. Tory Party Material File.

103 Anthony Eden diary, 25 September and 26 September 1941. AP 20/1/21.

CHAPTER 10

Alliances and Conferences

1 Anthony Eden, *The Reckoning*, Cassell, 1965, p.403.
2 PRO. CAB 81/103.
3 Sir Miles Lampson diary, 22 June 1941, op. cit.
4 Winston Churchill to Anthony Eden, 23 February 1941. PRO. PREM 3/396/16.
5 Minute of meeting on 13 June 1941. PRO. FO 418/87.
6 PRO. CAB 122/100.
7 Oliver Harvey diary, 31 August 1941. John Harvey (ed.), *The War Diaries of Oliver Harvey*, Collins, 1978, p.39.
8 Harold Nicolson to Vita Sackville-West, 22 October 1941. Nigel Nicolson (ed.), *Vita and Harold: The letters of Vita Sackville-West and Harold Nicolson 1910–1962*, Weidenfeld & Nicolson, 1992, p.342.
9 *The Times*, 9 March 2002.
10 The late Sir Frank Roberts to the author, 1 July 1992.
11 It was from this same office that Sir Austen Chamberlain, as 1st Lord of the Admiralty, had heard news of the Invergordon 'Mutiny' during the financial crisis of 1931.
12 A similar episode occurred as D-Day approached in June 1944, when Churchill's determination to cross the Channel on the day of the invasion was averted only by the personal intervention of King George VI.
13 Oliver Harvey diary, 8 December 1941, op. cit., p.70.
14 The late Sir Frank Roberts to the author, 1 July 1992.
15 Ivan Maisky, *Memoirs of a Soviet Ambassador: The War 1939–1943*, Hutchinson, 1967, p.227.
16 Oliver Harvey diary, 31 August 1941, op. cit.
17 Cited in Winston S. Churchill, *The Second World War*, Volume III, Cassell, 1950, p.607.
18 PRO. CAB 66/19.
19 Sir Alan Brooke diary, 4 December 1941. Alex Danchev and Daniel Todman (eds), *Field Marshal Lord Alanbrooke: War Diaries 1939–1945*, Weidenfeld & Nicolson, 2001, p.207.
20 PRO. FO 371/32898/N1162 and WO 178/90.
21 Record of 18 December 1941. PRO. FO 371/32874/N109.
22 Sir Roger Bannister, prospective biographer of Nye, to the author, 10 April 2000.
23 Anthony Eden, op. cit., p.291.
24 Eden's summary of his talks with Stalin. PRO. PREM 394/3.
25 The late Sir Frank Roberts to the author, 1 July 1992.
26 Anthony Eden to Sir Alexander Hardinge, 27 May 1942. RA PS GVI C 150 05.
27 John Erickson (ed.), *Main Front: Soviet Leaders Look Back on World War II*, chapter by Marshal of the Soviet Union Georgi Zhukov, Brassey's Defence Publishers, 1987, p.41.
28 Anthony Eden to King George VI, 31 December 1941. RA PS GVI C 150 03.
29 Anthony Eden to the Earl of Halifax, 22 January 1942. FO 954/29/1000818.
30 David Day, 'Churchill and his War Rivals', *History Today*, April 1991, p.16.
31 Ibid., p. 20.
32 Anthony Eden to Baron Cecil of Essendon, 3 April 1942. Salisbury papers, Hatfield House. Box J3. Cecil succeeded his father as the 4th Marquess of Salisbury in 1947.
33 Speech of 4 January 1942. Anthony Eden, *Freedom and Order: Selected Speeches 1939–1946*, Faber and Faber, 1947, p.144.
34 John Grigg, *1943: The Victory That Never Was*, Penguin Books, Harmondsworth, revised edition, 1999, p.35.
35 Sir Winston Churchill to King George VI, 16 June 1942. RA PS GVI C 069/17. Of the second letter, one person close to Anderson said, 'It's a good job that Ava [Sir John Anderson's second wife] never knew about this letter, or she would

probably have had Winston and
Anthony poisoned.' (Private
information.) After the death of
Ava's first husband, Ralph Wigram,
on New Year's Eve 1937, Churchill
wrote, 'Poor Ava is all adrift now
. . . He was her contact with g[reat]
affairs.' Quoted in Martin Gilbert,
*Winston S. Churchill Volume V
1922–1939*, Heinemann, 1976,
pp.833–4.

36 Peter Clarke, *The Cripps Version:
The Life of Sir Stafford Cripps
1889–1952*, Allen Lane, The
Penguin Press, 2002, p.363.

37 John Spencer Churchill
(1880–1947). In August 1952, Eden
was to marry Jack Churchill's
daughter, Clarissa.

38 Anthony Eden diary, 2 July 1942.
AP 20/1/22.

39 Anthony Eden diary, 12 March
1942. AP 20/1/22.

40 Anthony Eden, op. cit., p.317.

41 PRO. CAB 65/43.

42 Speech to the West Essex
Conservative Association, 23
February 1931.

43 Anthony Eden to Winston Churchill,
20 January 1942. PRO. FO
371/31873.

44 Winston Churchill to Anthony Eden,
28 February 1943. PRO. FO
371/36013.

45 Anthony Eden diary, 11 May 1942.
AP 20/1/22.

46 Mary Soames, *Clementine Churchill*,
Cassell, 1979, pp.230–1.

47 Anthony Eden diary, 28 November
1942. AP 20/1/22.

48 Private information.

49 Anthony Eden diary, 6 October
1942. AP 20/1/22.

50 Anthony Eden diary, 12 February
1943. AP 20/1/23.

51 Sir Timothy Eden to Anthony Eden,
15 February 1943. AP 22/4/45.

52 Anthony Eden diary, 5 August 1942.
AP 20/1/22.

53 Anthony Eden diary, 7 August, 9
August and 14 August 1942. AP
20/1/22. The Lady Chetwynd to
whom Eden objected was not a
blood relative, but the daughter-in-
law of the Hon. Mary Eden, third

daughter of the 4th Baron Auckland
and wife of the 8th Viscount
Chetwynd.

54 Anthony Eden diary, 6 September
1942. AP 20/1/22.

55 Speech at the Lord Mayor's
Mansion House Luncheon, 10
November 1942.

56 Brendan Bracken to Anthony Eden,
13 November 1942. PRO. FO
954/8.

57 Oliver Harvey diary, 14 November
1942, op. cit., p.182.

58 Anthony Eden to Winston Churchill,
26 November 1942. Anthony Eden,
op. cit., p.354.

59 Anthony Eden diary, 24 December
1942. AP 20/1/22.

60 *Vide* Richard Breitman, *Official
Secrets: What the Nazis Planned,
What the British and Americans
Knew*, Hill and Wang, New York,
1999.

61 Anthony Eden diary, 17 December
1942. AP 20/1/22.

62 Oliver Harvey diary, 15 October
1942, op. cit., p.168.

63 The Four Power Plan. PRO. PREM
4/110/7.

64 *Proposals for the Reform of the
Foreign Service*, Cmd 6420, January
1943.

65 The late Sir Frank Roberts (Bevin's
private secretary 1947–9), to the
author, 1 July 1992.

66 Ibid.

67 Anthony Eden diary, 4 February
1943. AP 20/1/23.

68 Speech at Merthyr Tydfil, 29 March
1942.

69 Oliver Harvey diary, 13 March
1943, op. cit., p 229.

70 Anthony Eden, op. cit., p.376.

71 Earl of Halifax, Report on Visit of
Secretary of State to Washington,
30 March 1943. PRO. PREM
3/476/9.

72 The Earl of Athlone to Queen Mary,
6 April 1943. RA GV/CC 53/1132.

73 Oliver Harvey diary, 3 April 1943,
op. cit., p.243.

74 Sir Alexander Cadogan diary,
editorial material alongside entry of
15 April 1943. David Dilks (ed.),
The Diaries of Sir Alexander

Cadogan 1938–1945, Cassell, 1971, p.521.

75 Noel Newsome diary, 7 May 1943, cited in Michael Stenton, *Radio London and Resistance in Occupied Europe: British Political Warfare 1939–1943*, Oxford University Press, Oxford, 2000, p.305. Michael Stenton, ibid., p.311.

76 Oliver Harvey diary, 16 April 1943, op. cit., p.245.

77 Leo Amery diary, 15 February 1943. John Barnes and David Nicholson (eds), *The Empire at Bay: The Leo Amery Diaries 1929–1945*, Hutchinson, 1988, p.873.

78 Oliver Harvey diary, 21 April 1943, op. cit., p.246.

79 King George VI to Winston Churchill, 28 April 1943. RA PS GVI C 069/30.

80 Leo Amery to Anthony Eden, 9 May 1943. AP 20/10/653.

81 Oliver Harvey diary, 18 May 1943, op. cit., p.257.

82 Sir Henry Channon diary, 27 May 1943. Robert Rhodes James (ed.), *Chips: The Diaries of Sir Henry Channon*, Weidenfeld & Nicolson, 1967, p.360.

83 Field Marshall Sir Archibald Wavell to Anthony Eden, 17 June 1943. AP 20/10/658.

84 Anthony Eden diary, 10 June 1943. AP 20/1/23.

85 Leo Amery diary, 9 September 1942, op. cit., p.832.

86 Harold Macmillan diary, 4 June 1943. *War Diaries: Politics and War in the Mediterranean, January 1943–May 1945*, Macmillan, 1984, p.110.

87 Anthony Eden to Winston Churchill, 12 July 1954. FO 954/25B.

88 Anthony Eden to Winston Churchill, 13 July 1943. FO 954/8/43/128A.

89 Anthony Eden diary, 25 July 1943. AP 20/1/23.

90 Anthony Eden diary, 20 August 1943. AP 20/1/23.

91 Anthony Eden, op. cit., p.403.

92 Hartley Shawcross, *Life Sentence*, Constable, 1995, p.87.

93 Lord Ismay, *The Memoirs of General the Lord Ismay*, Heinemann, 1960, p. 327.

94 Anthony Eden to Winston Churchill, 2 November 1943. PM Telegram T. 1829/3. Churchill papers, Churchill College, Cambridge. CHAR 20/123–33.

95 Anthony Eden diary, 25 November 1943. AP 20/1/23.

96 Sir Miles Lampson diary, 27 November 1943. Middle East Centre, St Antony's College, Oxford.

97 Anthony Eden Miscellaneous Notebooks. AP 7/26/32.

98 Hugh Lunghi to the author, 1 July 2000.

99 Private information.

100 G. M. Wilson to Sir Archibald Clark Kerr, 15 May 1944, loc. cit.

101 Hugh Lunghi diary, 30 November 1943.

102 Hugh Lunghi to the author, 1 July 2000.

103 Anthony Eden diary, 25 April 1943. AP 20/1/23.

104 Winston Churchill to Lady Violet Bonham Carter, 1 August 1944, loc. cit.

105 Sir Alexander Cadogan to the Earl of Halifax, 9 December 1940, cited in David Dilks (ed.), op. cit., p.586.

106 Anthony Eden diary, 28 November 1943. AP 20/1/23.

107 Sir Owen O'Malley to Anthony Eden, 22 January 1944. FO 954/20A.

108 Lord Robert Cecil papers, Hatfield House. Note of meeting on 13 January 1944. CHE71/151.

109 Eden diary, 19 January 1944. AP 20/1/24.

110 Eden diary, 11 March 1944. Ibid.

111 Anthony Eden to Winston Churchill, 17 December 1942. AP 20/9/308.

112 Anthony Eden diary, 10 June 1943. AP 20/1/23.

113 Eden diary, 18 January 1944. AP 20/1/24.

114 Eden diary, 21 January 1944. Ibid.

115 Eden diary, 24 January 1944. Ibid.

116 Anthony Eden diary, 6 June, 9 June and 16 June 1944. AP 20/1/24.

117 Between 13 and 30 June 1944 2,452 bombs were launched against the southern part of England; 121 people were killed at the morning

service in the Guards' Chapel, including 63 soldiers.

118 Eden diary, 18 June 1944. AP 20/1/24.

119 1st Baron Moyne (1880-1944) was the Deputy Minister of State in Cairo from 1942 to 1944.

120 Harold Macmillan diary, op. cit., entry for 21 June 1944, p.471.

121 C. M. Woodhouse, *Something Ventured*, Granada, 1982, p.86.

122 *King John*, V.vii.112-13.

123 Anthony Eden diary, 4 August 1944. AP 20/1/24. By Eden's second marriage in August 1952, Churchill became step-great-uncle to Nicholas.

124 AP 7/25/19.

125 Meier Sompolinsky, *Britain and the Holocaust: The Failure of Anglo-Jewish Leadership?*, Sussex Academic Press, Brighton, 1999, p.2.

126 Oliver Harvey diary, 30 November 1942, op. cit., p.194.

127 Meier Sompolinsky, op. cit., p.208.

128 *Vide* Alistair Horne, *Macmillan 1894-1956: Volume 1 of the Official Biography*, Macmillan, 1988, pp.252-78.

129 Lord Moran diary, 9 October 1944. Lord Moran, *Winston Churchill: The Struggle for Survival 1940-1945*, Sphere paperback, 1968, p.215.

130 Anthony Eden to British Ambassadors, 30 March and 10 November 1944; Anthony Eden to Gordon Vereker, 15 November 1944. PRO. FO 505/497.

131 *Daily Telegraph*, 21 July 1999.

132 Professor William D. Rubinstein, letter to *The Times*, 27 July 1999.

133 Anthony Eden to Winston Churchill, 29 November 1944. PRO. PM Minute 44/732.

134 Anthony Eden diary, 17 November 1944. AP 20/1/24.

135 Anthony Eden diary, 21 December 1944. AP 20/1/24.

136 Alistair Horne, op. cit., p.238.

137 Anthony Eden, op. cit., p.503.

138 Winston Churchill to Anthony Eden 31 December 1944, loc. cit.

CHAPTER 11

Avoiding Versailles

1 AP 20/1/25.

2 Simon Eden to Anthony Eden, May 1945. AP 22/7/17.

3 Winston Churchill to King George VI, 28 January 1945. Chartwell papers, Churchill College, Cambridge. CHAR 20/193A/77.

4 Anthony Eden diary, 17 July 1945. AP 20/1/25

5 Anthony Eden diary, 12 January 1945. AP 20/1/25.

6 Anthony Eden to Winston Churchill, 16 January 1945. PRO. PREM 3/185/4.

7 Winston Churchill to Anthony Eden, 25 January 1945. PRO. PREM 3/185/4.

8 Anthony Eden diary, 4 January 1945. AP 20/1/25.

9 Private note in Eden's library, in the possession of the Countess of Avon.

10 Hugh Lunghi to the author, 1 July 2000.

11 Sir Alexander Cadogan diary, 11 February 1945. David Dilks (ed.), *The Diaries of Sir Alexander Cadogan 1938-1945*, Cadogan papers, Churchill College, Cambridge, ACAD 1/15.

12 John Colville, *The Fringes of Power: Downing Street Diaries 1939-1955*, Hodder & Stoughton, 1985, p.560.

13 War Cabinet Minutes, 19 and 21 February 1945. PRO. CAB 65/51.

14 PRO. FO 371/47850.

15 Sir Henry Channon diary, 10 January 1946. Robert Rhodes James (ed.), *Chips: The Diaries of Sir Henry Channon*, Weidenfeld & Nicolson, 1967, p.414.

16 Anthony Eden to Winston Churchill, 20 March 1945. Winston Churchill to Anthony Eden, 25 March 1945. PRO. FO 954/494.

17 The Countess of Athlone to Queen Mary, 16 April 1945. RA GV/CC 53/1381.

18 Harry S. Truman to Bess Truman, 27 July 1945. Robert H. Ferrell (ed.), *Dear Bess: The Letters of Harry to Bess Truman 1910-1959*,

W. W. Norton, New York, 1983, p.522.

19 Anthony Eden minute, 15 April 1945. PRO. PREM 3/356/6.

20 Donald Gillies, *Radical Diplomat: The Life of Archibald Clark Kerr, Lord Inverchapel, 1882–1951*, I.B. Tauris, 1999, p.169.

21 Anthony Eden to Winston Churchill, 8 May 1945. AP 20/218/36.

22 See Chapter 18.

23 Arthur Vandenberg diary, 13 May–17 April 1945. Arthur J. Vandenberg, Jr, *The Private Papers of Senator Arthur Vandenberg*, Victor Gollancz, 1953, pp.191, 170.

24 Clement Attlee to Winston Churchill, 28 April 1945. Minute T 670/5. AP 20/216.

25 Anthony Eden to Winston Churchill, 9 May 1945. AP 20/218/63. It was five years to the day since the crucial meeting between Chamberlain, Halifax and Churchill that was to bring Churchill to power in the aftermath of the Norway Debate.

26 Anthony Eden to Winston Churchill, 14 May 1945. AP 20/219/44.

27 Martin Gilbert, *Never Despair: Winston S. Churchill 1945–1965*, Heinemann, 1988, f-n. p.27.

28 Lord Cecil of Essendon to Sir Alan Lascelles, 14 July 1945, RA PS GVI C 250/4.

29 Drew Pearson, *Drew Pearson Diaries 1949–1959*, edited by Tyler Abell, Jonathan Cape, 1974, p.413.

30 Anthony Eden diary, 15 June 1945. AP 20/1/25.

31 Peter Wright, *Spycatcher: The Candid Autobiography of a Senior Intelligence Officer*, Viking, New York, 1987, p.373.

32 Private information.

33 Lady Eden to Anthony Eden, 10 June 1945. AP 22/1/362.

34 Simon Eden to Anthony Eden, undated letter June 1945, and 6 June 1945. AP22/7/17–18.

35 Martin Gilbert, op. cit., p.32

36 Anthony Eden, *Freedom and Order: Selected Speeches 1939–1946*, Faber & Faber, 1947, p.355.

37 Private Memorandum on Anthony Eden's career by Sir Patrick Reilly,

sent to the author, 16 May 1997.

38 Anthony Eden diary, 27 June 1945. AP 20/1/25. Air Chief Marshal Sir Keith Park (1892–1975) was the Allied Air Commander in South-East Asia from February 1945. In subsequent correspondence Eden found that Park lived near him in Itchenor, where he kept a cottage as a base for sailing. One of Park's two sons was also killed on active service.

39 Anthony Eden diary, 28 June 1945. AP 20/42/28.

40 Anthony Eden to J. P. L. Thomas, 28 June 1945. Cilcennin papers, Cilc. coll., box 1, letter 9. Carmarthenshire Record Office.

41 Sir Robert Bruce Lockhart diary, 4 July 1945. Kenneth Young (ed.), *The Diaries of Sir Robert Bruce-Lockhart: Volume II, 1939–1965*, Macmillan, 1980, p.462.

42 Anthony Eden diary, 5 July 1945. AP 20/1/25.

43 Anthony Eden diary, 6 July 1945. AP 20/1/25.

44 Anthony Eden diary, 14 July 1945. AP 20/1/25.

45 Anthony Eden diary, 20 July 1945. AP 20/1/25. Marshal of the Royal Air Force Sir Charles ('Peter') Portal, later Viscount Portal of Hungerford (1893–1971), shared with Eden (and Simon) a Christ Church education, and later both were to be Knights of the Garter.

46 Richard Lovell, *Churchill's Doctor: A Biography of Lord Moran*, Royal Society of Medicine Services, 1992, p.270.

47 AP 22/7/71. Sheila Smith lived on the Woodstock Road in north Oxford. For nearly four years the author passed the house on a regular basis, whilst travelling to the libraries of Oxford. Memories of Simon, and the central tragedy of Eden's life, always seemed very close.

48 AP 22/7/37.

49 Quoted by David Dilks, *The Conference at Potsdam, 1945*, University of Hull Press, 1995, p.14.

50 Anthony Eden to Winston Churchill, 10 July 1945. PRO. FO 800/416/63.
51 Lord Dunglass to Anthony Eden, 11 July 1945. PRO. FO Telegram N 896/6/55.
52 Anthony Eden to Winston Churchill, 13 July 1945, and to Pierson Dixon, 13 July 1945. FO 954/19/45/18 and Tel U 605/51/70.
53 PRO. FO 934/2/8.
54 Anthony Eden to Winston Churchill, 17 July 1945. PRO. FO 934/1/5(2).
55 Record of 3rd Plenary Session, 19 July 1945. PRO. U 6197/3628/70.
56 Anthony Eden to Clement Attlee, 23 July 1945. FO 954/22/45/60.
57 Anthony Eden note on 26 July 1945. Miscellaneous notebooks. AP 7/26/32.
58 Anthony Eden diary, 27 July 1945. AP 20/1/25.
59 PRO. FO 934/5/48 (5).
60 Anthony Eden to Sir Alexander Cadogan, 4 August 1945. Cadogan papers, Churchill College, Cambridge. CAD 4/2.
61 Sir Alan Lascelles record of Dissolution Honours, July 1945. RA PS GVI C 254/002.
62 Harry S. Truman to Bess Truman, 27 July 1945. Robert H. Ferrell (ed.), op. cit., p.522.
63 PRO. FO 800/417/64.
64 Clement Attlee to Anthony Eden, 1 August 1945. PRO. PREM 3/430/14.
65 Anthony Eden to Clement Attlee, undated letter of August 1945. Attlee papers, Bodleian Library, Oxford. MS Attlee, dep 18, ff. 102–3.
66 Mary Soames, *Clementine Churchill*, Cassell, 1979, p.386.
67 Earl Attlee to the Earl of Avon, 5 July 1963. Loc. cit.
68 Robert Blake, *The Conservative Party from Peel to Churchill*, Eyre & Spottiswoode, 1970, p.266.
69 Private note in Eden's library, in the possession of the Countess of Avon.
70 Anthony Eden diary, 1 August 1945. AP 20/1/25.

INTERLUDE
Peacocks and Lilies

1 Anthony Eden to Lady Eden, 11 August 1921. AP 22/1/310.
2 Anthony Eden, *Another World 1897–1917*, Allen Lane, 1976. p.14.
3 Anthony Eden diary, 16 January 1926. AP 20/1/6. Without knowing of this diary entry, the Countess of Avon expressed similar views to the author about the 1998 Sargent exhibition at the Tate Gallery, and in the case of the room devoted to watercolours of Venice, identical ones.
4 Archives of Christ Church, Oxford.
5 The Countess of Avon to the author, 6 July 1999.
6 Denys Sutton, 'A Statesman's Collection', *Apollo*, June 1969, pp.480–7, which also has an inventory of Eden's purchases, and illustrated material.
7 Literary jottings, 24 January 1923. AP 22/15/128.
8 Anthony Eden diary, 26 December 1933. AP 20/1/13.
9 'Time hath, my lord, a wallet at his back . . . And drave great Mars to faction.' *Troilus and Cressida*, III.iii. 145–90.
10 Anthony Eden diary, 9 August 1941. AP 20/1/21. Nicholas was ten at the time.
11 Anthony Eden diary, 15 July 1941. AP 20/1/21.
12 Anthony Eden diary, 12 August 1942. AP 20/1/22.
13 Private note in Eden's library, in the possession of the Countess of Avon.
14 'Mourir pour le pays n'est pas un triste sort; C'est s'immortaliser par une belle mort.' *Le Cid*, IV.iv. 1377–8.
15 Sir Anthony Eden to Lord Salisbury, 22 July. Salisbury papers, Hatfield House. File B, 1956–60.
16 Rupert Hart-Davis (ed.), *The Lyttelton Hart-Davis Letters: Volumes One and Two 1955–1957*, John Murray paperback, 1985, p.61.

CHAPTER 12

Towards the Property-Owning Democracy

1 Ben Pimlott (ed.), *The Political Diary of Hugh Dalton 1918–1940, 1945–1960*, Jonathan Cape, 1986, p.365.

2 AP 20/14/34.

3 Countess of Avon Papers.

4 Kenneth O. Morgan, *Labour in Power 1945–1951*, Clarendon Press, Oxford, 1984, p.104.

5 Mark Pottle (ed.), *Daring to Hope: The Diaries and Letters of Violet Bonham Carter 1946–1969*, Weidenfeld & Nicholson, 2000, p.166.

6 Sir Peter Tapsell to the author, 27 January 1999. I am grateful to other friends of Eden, who prefer not to be named, for their help with this section.

7 Alistair Forbes, 'Miscast for the lead', *The Spectator*, 14/21 December 1996. Lady Caroline Paget married Sir Michael Duff on 14 July 1949. They had an adopted son, but Eden was not the father. The Marquess of Anglesey to the author, 12 September 2001. This is confirmed by other private evidence.

8 Private information.

9 Violet Bonham Carter diary, 11 October 1943. Mark Pottle (ed.), *Champion Redoubtable: The Diaries and Letters of Violet Bonham Carter 1914–1945*, Weidenfeld & Nicolson, 1998, p.281.

10 Private information.

11 Beatrice Eden to Anthony Eden, 10 June 1947. AP 22/6/144.

12 Trygve Lie (1896–68), a Norwegian lawyer, was elected as the first UN Secretary-General in January 1946.

13 Anthony Eden to Lord Cecil of Essendon, 3 January 1946. Salisbury papers, Hatfield House, box J3.

14 Anthony Eden to Lord Cecil of Essendon, 15 March 1946. Ibid.

15 Anthony Eden to Lord Cecil of Essendon, 12 May 1946. Ibid.

16 One of the reasons Eden appointed Robert Carr as his Parliamentary Private Secretary in November 1951 was that he believed Carr was one of the few younger MPs who understood, or was even interested in, industrial policy.

17 Anthony Eden to Lord Cecil of Essendon, 7 August 1946. Salisbury papers, Hatfield House, box J3.

18 Anthony Eden to Lord Cecil of Essendon, 27 August 1946. Ibid.

19 D. R. Thorpe, 'Sir Anthony Nutting', Obituary, *Independent*, 3 March 1999.

20 Selwyn Lloyd, *Suez 1956: A Personal Account*, Jonathan Cape, 1978, p.4.

21 The Earl of Avon to Selwyn Lloyd, 13 October 1962. Selwyn Lloyd papers, Churchill College, Cambridge. SELO 222 (4).

22 Reprinted in Anthony Eden, *Conservative Policies and Objectives*, Conservative Central Office, 1946, p.4.

23 Printed as Appendix II.

24 Speech of 3 October 1946. Anthony Eden, *Freedom and Order: Selected Speeches 1939–1946*, Faber & Faber, 1947, p.420.

25 *Antony and Cleopatra*, I.iii. 35–6.

26 Earl Beatty subsequently married again (for the third time). In 1974 his widow married John (later Sir John) Nutting, son of Sir Anthony Nutting, Minister of State at the Foreign Office at the time of Suez. Dorothy Beatty also remarried and now lives in America.

27 Private information.

28 For a detailed account of this period, see J. D. Hoffman, *The Conservative Party in Opposition 1945–1951*, MacGibbon & Kee, 1964.

29 *Vide* 'Mr Eden on the Charter', *The Times*, 19 May 1947.

30 Sir Cuthbert Headlam diary, 4 October 1947, loc. cit.

31 Sir Cuthbert Headlam diary, 1 August and 2 August 1947. Op. cit., pp.515–16.

32 Warwick and Leamington Conservative Association Minute Book, 1948. Warwick County Record Office, Warwick. File CR 1392.

33 Violet Bonham Carter diary, 30

April 1948. *Daring to Hope,* op. cit., pp.48–9.

34 Violet Bonham Carter diary, 8 May 1948. Ibid., p 50.

35 As in his speech on 7 May 1948 at The Hague Conference of the United Europe Movement.

36 Max Beloff, 'Churchill and Europe', in Robert Blake and William Roger Louis, *Churchill,* Oxford University Press, Oxford, 1993, p.454.

37 Anthony Eden to the Marquess of Salisbury, 21 March 1948. Salisbury papers, Hatfield House, box J3.

38 Anthony Eden to Sir Alan Lascelles, 29 March 1948. RA PS GVI PS 06670.

39 Anthony Eden to Sir Alan Lascelles, 18 January 1946. RA PS GVI C 063/12.

40 Hansard, 19 June 1947.

41 Sir Cuthbert Headlam diary, 9 July 1948. Stuart Ball (ed.), op. cit., pp.561–2.

42 1949 was the last Conservative Conference to be held in London.

43 Private information.

44 A phrase used by Douglas Jay, Economic Secretary to the Treasury, in 1947.

45 Warwick and Leamington Conservative Association Records, Salisbury Hall, Leamington. Eden had in fact first been elected on 6 December 1923, but a summer celebration was felt to be more appropriate.

46 Private information. Eden was never tempted down that particular route. Selwyn Lloyd's marriage to his Westminster secretary did not last long.

47 John Devine to the author, 12 August 1999.

48 *Birmingham Post,* 21 January 1950.

49 Kenneth Rose papers.

50 Alec Home could never recall being asked to give a surgery of any kind in his Lanark constituency. Lord Home to the author, 9 August 1991.

51 Nigel Spearing (Labour MP for Acton 1970–4, Newham 1974–97) to the author, 20 January 1998.

52 I am grateful to Mr John Devine for showing me a copy of this letter. The number of votes omitted was 1,915, of which 1,027 were for Eden and 888 for Bithell.

53 Anthony Eden to the Marquess of Salisbury, 3 March 1950. Salisbury papers, Hatfield House, box J3.

54 Memorandum by Sir Alan Lascelles on the political crisis, 21 April 1950. RA PS GVI C 320/02.

55 Robert Carr (later Lord Carr of Hadley) became Home Secretary during the Heath Government and was acting Conservative leader after Heath's resignation on 4 February 1975, before the internal party election produced Mrs Thatcher as the new leader a week later.

56 Hansard, 5 July 1950.

57 Hansard, 1 May 1951.

58 Anthony Eden to Nicholas Eden, 30 January 1951. AP 22/9/81.

59 Anthony Eden to Nicholas Eden, 17 February 1951. AP 22/9/84. 'The Great Debate', as Tories dubbed it, took place on 15 February. To their discomfiture, the Government won by twenty-five votes, six Liberals voting with the Government.

60 Anthony Eden to Sir Alan Lascelles, 17 February 1951. RA PS GVI PS 09971/008.

61 John Devine to the author, 12 August 1999.

62 Anthony Eden to Nicholas Eden, 25 February 1951. AP 22/9/85.

63 Anthony Eden to Nicholas Eden, 15 July 1951. AP 22/9/100.

64 Anthony Eden to Nicholas Eden, 25 February 1951. AP 22/9/85. Eden gave his son strict instructions to keep this story to himself and not leave the letter lying about where it could be seen.

65 Anthony Eden to Nicholas Eden, 25 February 1951. AP 22/9/85.

66 Anthony Eden to Nicholas Eden, 3 March 1951. AP 22/9/86.

67 Anthony Eden to Nicholas Eden, 9 April 1951. AP 22/9/94.

68 Anthony Eden to Nicholas Eden, 11 March 1951. AP 22/9/87.

69 Anthony Eden to Nicholas Eden, 21 March 1951. AP 22/9/89.

70 John Devine to the author, 12 August 1999.

71 Anthony Eden to Nicholas Eden, 16 April 1951. AP 22/9/95.
72 John Devine to the author, 12 August 1999.
73 John Ramsden, op. cit., p.228.
74 Churchill launched a successful libel case against the *Daily Mirror* over these claims.
75 Evelyn Shuckburgh, *Descent to Suez: Diaries: 1951–56*, Weidenfeld & Nicolson, 1986, p.13.

CHAPTER 13

Coming Home

1 John Colville, *The Fringes of Power: Downing Street Diaries 1939-1955*, Hodder & Stoughton, 1985, p.651.
2 R. A. Butler, *The Art of the Possible: The Memoirs of Lord Butler*, Penguin Books, Harmondsworth, 1973, p.175.
3 Dean Acheson, *Present at the Creation: My Years in the State Department*, Hamish Hamilton, 1970, p.511.
4 David S. McLellan, *Dean Acheson: The State Department Years*, Dodd, Mead & Company, New York, 1976, p.390.
5 The late Sir Patrick Reilly to the author, 20 November 1998.
6 Anthony Eden diary, 2 November 1950. AP 20/1/27.
7 PRO. 'British Overseas Obligations', 18 June 1952. CAB 129/53. C (52) 202.
8 PRO. 3 October 1952. CAB 129/55.
9 Private information from several sources.
10 *The Spectator*, 23 June 1952.
11 Private information.
12 Viscount Crookshank diary, 16 June 1952. Crookshank papers, Bodleian Library, Oxford.
13 Private information.
14 Lord Carr of Hadley to the author, 30 January 1997.
15 Jo Grimond, *Memoirs*, Heinemann, 1979, p.193.
16 The late Lord Amery of Lustleigh to the author, 30 January 1996.
17 Richard Crossman diary, 6 November 1951. Janet Morgan (ed.), *The Backbench Diaries of Richard Crossman*, Hamish Hamilton and Jonathan Cape, 1981, p.32.
18 The late Sir Frank Roberts to the author, 1 July 1992.
19 Anthony Eden Memorandum to the British delegation at Strasbourg, 6 December 1951. PRO. Telegram no. 75, WU 10726/85.
20 PRO. PREM 11/153. PM Minute 51/148.
21 Hansard, 5 February 1952.
22 Dean Acheson, op. cit., p.600.
23 Speech at Columbia University, 11 January 1952.
24 Hansard, 26 June 1950.
25 Earl of Avon to Robert Carr, 2 July 1969. AP 23/16/50A.
26 PRO. CAB 129/52.
27 Churchill's letter to Mrs Charles Moss, a document of considerable historical importance, was released to the Press by Anthony Montague Browne in July 1962 when Viscount Montgomery had declared, after visiting Churchill in the Middlesex Hospital, that Churchill was against Britain joining the Common Market. See Anthony Montague Browne, *Long Sunset: Memoirs of Winston Churchill's Last Private Secretary*, Cassell, 1995, pp.273–4.
28 Gaddis Smith, *Dean Acheson*, Cooper Square Publishers, New York, 1972, p.297.
29 Private information.
30 Hansard, 5 February 1952.
31 Dean Acheson, op. cit., p.566.
32 *Henry V*, IV.i. 256–7. Warwick and Leamington Conservative Association Records.
33 Dean Acheson, op. cit., p 611.
34 Private information.
35 Memorandum by Anthony Eden, 15 February 1952. PRO. CAB 129/49.
36 Anthony Eden to Winston Churchill, 1 December 1951. PRO. FO 371/96464.
37 Alan S. Milward, *The United Kingdom and the European Community Volume 1: The Rise and Fall of a National Strategy 1945–1963*, Frank Cass, 2002, p.96.

38 Anthony Eden to Winston Churchill, 17 March 1952. PRO. PREM 11/153.

39 Anthony Eden to Winston Churchill, 23 February 1952, PRO. PREM 11/138.

40 Anthony Eden diary, 29 February 1952. AP 20/1/28.

41 David Kynaston, *The City of London, Volume IV: A Club No More 1945–2000*, Chatto & Windus, 2001, p.49.

42 Edwin Plowden, *An Industrialist in the Treasury: The Post-War Years*, André Deutsch, 1989, p.156.

43 Private information. Also it was clear from the author's conversations with the late Lord Butler of Saffron Walden on 20 November 1975 that this was the case.

44 Hugh Gaitskell diary, 9 November 1954. Philip M. Williams (ed.), *The Diary of Hugh Gaitskell 1945–1956*, Jonathan Cape, 1983, p.316.

45 Anthony Eden to Sir Winston Churchill, 29 October 1953. AP 20/16/73.

46 Acheson revealed these details at a seminar at Princeton University on 13 December 1953 after his term as Secretary of State.

47 'A Clash of Personalities: Eden vs Acheson', *Newsweek*, 14 April 1952.

48 Dean Acheson, op. cit., p.662.

49 Anthony Eden to Nicholas Eden, 27 July 1952. AP 22/9/126.

50 Clarissa Churchill to Mrs Winston Churchill, undated letter of July 1952. Lady Spencer-Churchill papers, Churchill College, Cambridge. CSCT 3/89.

51 A special licence was necessary, which cost £3 6s. 9d., and the ceremony was conducted by Superintendent James Holiday.

52 *Manchester Guardian*, 15 August 1952.

53 The Archbishop of Canterbury to Mr Peter Winckworth, 8 October 1952. Archbishop Fisher papers, Lambeth Palace, vol. 99, fol. 299.

54 J. P. L. Thomas to Anthony Eden, 26 August 1952. AP 14/3/177.

55 Winston S. Churchill, *His Father's Son: The Life of Randolph Churchill*, Weidenfeld & Nicolson, 1996, p.336.

56 Private information.

57 Mr and Mrs Anthony Eden to Mr and Mrs Winston Churchill, 14 August 1952. Chartwell papers, Churchill College, Cambridge. CHAR 2/216.

58 Sir Ivo Mallett to Anthony Eden, 26 September 1952. PRO. FO 371/102181.

59 Dean Acheson to Anthony Eden, 1 November 1954. AP 14/3/506A.

60 Anthony Eden to Mrs Eden, 18 September 1952. AP 20/45/23.

61 Evelyn Shuckburgh diary, 3 November 1952. Evelyn Shuckburgh, *Descent to Suez: Diaries 1951–1956*, Weidenfeld & Nicolson, 1986, p.47.

62 Anthony Eden to Mrs Eden, 24 September 1952. AP 20/45/24.

63 Evelyn Shuckburgh diary, 11 November 1952. Evelyn Shuckburgh, op. cit., p.50.

64 Dwight D. Eisenhower, *The White House Years: Mandate for Change 1953–1956*, Heinemann, 1963, p.142.

65 Anthony Seldon, *Churchill's Indian Summer: The Conservative Government 1951–55*, Hodder & Stoughton, 1981, pp.389–90.

66 Dwight D. Eisenhower diary, 6 January 1953. Eisenhower Library, Abilene, Kansas. International Series, file DDE.

67 John Colville diary, 24 July and 6 January 1953. John Colville, op. cit., pp.672, 660.

68 General Kenneth Anderson of the second Army.

69 Private information.

70 Private information

71 Evelyn Shuckburgh diary, 29 January 1953. Evelyn Shuckburgh, op. cit., p.75.

72 Anthony Eden diary, 4 March 1953. AP 20/1/29.

73 Anthony Eden diary, 24 January 1953. AP 20/1/29.

74 Anthony Eden diary, 2 April and 4 April 1953. AP 20/1/29. Baron (Horace) Evans (1903–63) was physician to Queen Mary, King George VI and Queen Elizabeth II. John Basil Hume (1893–1974) was general consulting surgeon at St Bartholomew's Hospital, a northerner, educated at Bootham School, York, with distinguished medical service during the war. He was one of the most respected surgeons of his generation.

75 Ann Fleming to Lady Diana Cooper, 2 May 1953. Mark Amory (ed.), *The Letters of Ann Fleming*, Collins Harvill, 1985, p.128.

76 This account is drawn from private information from several sources.

77 Details in AP 20/16/117.

78 Hansard, 11 May 1953.

79 Anthony Eden diary, 27 November 1954. AP 20/1/30. The enduring strength of Eden's feeling can be seen from the fact that this diary entry was written eighteen months after the event.

80 Anthony Eden to Queen Elizabeth II, undated letter during Coronation week, June 1953. AP 14/3/273.

81 D. R. Thorpe, op. cit., p.171.

82 The late Lord Sherfield to the author, 13 February 1996.

83 Note of 13 June 1953 in the Salisbury papers, Hatfield House, box J3.

84 *Vide* D. R. Thorpe, op. cit., ch. 6 *passim*.

85 AP 20/16/119A. Anthony Eden to Evelyn Shuckburgh, 22 June 1953. AP 20/16/119B.

86 Beveridge Broadcasting Committee, paper no. 317. PRO. HO 254/9.

87 John Colville to Mrs Eden, 26 June 1953. AP 20/16/123.

88 R. A. Butler to Anthony Eden, 27 June 1953. AP 20/16/124.

89 Anthony Eden to John Colville, 1 July 1953. R. A. Colville Papers. I am grateful to Lady de Bellaigue, Registrar at the Royal Library, for discovering this manuscript letter in a 1950s' file in the Royal Archives at Windsor. The original has since been placed with the Colville Papers at Churchill College, Cambridge (CLVL).

90 J. P. L. Thomas to Anthony Eden, 29 June 1953. AP 20/16/125.

91 Lord Moran diary, 26 June 1953. Lord Moran, *Winston Churchill: The Struggle for Survival 1940–1965*, Sphere paperback, 1968, p.437.

92 Evelyn Shuckburgh to Anthony Eden, 23 July 1953. AP 20/16/140.

93 The Marquess of Salisbury to Anthony Eden, 14 August 1953. AP 20/16/142.

94 Violet Bonham Carter diary, 6 August 1953. Mark Pottle (ed.), op. cit., p.129.

95 Robert Carr to Anthony Eden, 29 August 1953. AP 20/16/143.

96 Anthony Eden diary, 2 September 1953 (a retrospective entry). AP 20/1/29A.

97 Anthony Eden to Lord Salisbury, 31 August 1953. Salisbury papers, Hatfield House, box J3.

98 D. R. Thorpe, op. cit., p.176.

99 Robert Carr to Anthony Eden, 20 September 1953. AP 20/16/150.

100 Evelyn Shuckburgh to Anthony Eden, 22 September 1953. AP 20/10/152.

101 The late Lord Butler of Saffron Walden to the author, 20 November 1975.

102 Private information.

103 Evelyn Shuckburgh diary, 26 February 1953. Evelyn Shuckburgh, op. cit., p.78.

CHAPTER 14

Waging Peace

1 Anthony Eden diary, 1 October 1953. AP 20/1/29A.

2 Anthony Eden diary, 1 October 1953. AP 20/1/29A.

3 Edward Heath, *The Course of My Life: My Autobiography*, Hodder & Stoughton, 1998, p.601.

4 Minute of 29 December 1953. PRO. FO 371/111690/1051/3.

5 Anthony Eden, *Full Circle*, Cassell, 1960, p.49.

6 Iverach McDonald to the author, 7 November 1997.
7 Private information.
8 Private information.
9 Anthony Eden to Clarissa Eden, 2 December 1953. AP 20/45/31.
10 James Cable, *The Geneva Conference of 1954 on Indochina*, Macmillan, revised edition, 2000, p.37.
11 PRO. CAB 128/26.
12 Selwyn Lloyd diary, 5 January 1954. Selwyn Lloyd papers, Churchill College, Cambridge. SELO 278 (3).
13 Anthony Eden to Clarissa Eden, 25 January 1954. AP 20/45/37.
14 Report by Sir Frank Roberts, Deputy-Under Secretary, for Sir Ivone Kirkpatrick, 29 January 1954. AP 20/17/155.
15 Anthony Eden to Sir Winston Churchill, 14 February 1954. PRO. PREM 11/665.
16 Anthony Eden to Clarissa Eden, 28 January 1954. AP 25/1/40.
17 Robert Carr to Anthony Eden, 7 February 1954. AP 20/17/163.
18 J. P. L. Thomas to Anthony Eden, 30 January 1954. AP 20/17/156.
19 Cabinet Minutes of 22 February 1954. PRO. CAB 128/27.
20 AP 20/54/7.
21 *Daily Mirror*, 1 April 1954. *New York Times*, 31 March 1954.
22 Sir Anthony Montague Browne to the author, 5 August 1998.
23 Evelyn Shuckburgh diary, 5 April and 31 March 1954. Evelyn Shuckburgh, *Descent to Suez: Diaries 1951–1956*, Weidenfeld & Nicolson, 1986, pp.160, 157.
24 The opinion of several figures to the author.
25 Anthony Eden to Lord Salisbury, 21 August 1954. AP 20/17/177.
26 James Cable, op. cit., p.3. I am grateful to the late Sir James Cable for discussing the issues of Geneva with me.
27 PRO. CAB 129/67.
28 *Foreign Relations of the United States (FRUS)*, vol. XIII, Part One, p.1187.
29 Cabinet meeting, 7 April 1954. PRO. CAB 129/65.
30 Anthony Eden to Sir Roger Makins, 17 April 1954. PRO. FO 371/112053.
31 Cabinet meeting, 11 January 1954. PRO. CAB 129/65.
32 Quoted in James Cable, op. cit., p.66.
33 In 1955 Lord Home's wife, Elizabeth, was only allowed to accompany her husband on the second, inward half of his Commonwealth tour.
34 Evidence from members of the British team.
35 Eden was very critical of the Radford Plan in his comments in the Wheeler-Bennett copy of Robert Randle's book.
36 PRO. FO 371/112057.
37 *The Times*, 17 May 1954.
38 Mrs Patricia Roberts, a secretary at the Conference, to the author, 22 June 2000.
39 Anthony Eden Memorandum, 2 May 1954. PRO. FO 371/112058.
40 Anthony Eden diary, 3 May 1954. AP 20/1/30.
41 PRO. FO 371/112061.
42 Private information.
43 Anthony Eden diary, 27 May 1954. AP 20/1/30.
44 Anthony Eden to Clarissa Eden, 2 June 1954. AP 20/45/51.
45 PRO. FO 371/112073.
46 Jean Chauvel, *Commentaire Vol. III – De Berne à Paris (1952–1962)*, Fayard, Paris, 1973, p.57.
47 Lord Moran diary, 28 April 1953. Lord Moran, *Winston Churchill: The Struggle for Survival 1940–1965*, Sphere Books, 1968 edition, p.428.
48 Jean Lacouture, *Pierre Mendès-France*, Holmes & Meier, New York, 1984, p.231.
49 Anthony Eden to Lord Salisbury, 17 July 1954. Salisbury papers, Hatfield House, box J3.
50 See in particular David Carlton, *Anthony Eden: A Biography*, Allen & Unwin, paperback edition, 1986, pp.347–56.
51 On receiving the Aspen Award, 1964.
52 James Cable, op. cit., p.3.

53 Robert F. Randle, *Geneva 1954: The Settlement of the Indochinese War*, Princeton University Press, Princeton, New Jersey, 1969, p.568. Eden highlighted this paragraph in the Wheeler-Bennett copy.

54 Anthony Eden diary, 14 and 15 September 1954. AP 20/1/30.

55 Anthony Eden, op. cit., p.188.

56 A phrase Churchill used to Eisenhower on more than one occasion.

57 Anthony Eden diary, 27 November 1954. AP 20/1/30.

58 Sir Ivone Kirkpatrick, *The Inner Circle: Memoirs of Ivone Kirkpatrick*, Macmillan, 1959, p.242.

59 Charles Williams, *Adenauer: The Father of the New Germany*, Little, Brown and Company, 2000, p.419.

60 Ben Pimlott, 'E.D.C., W.E.U. and Mr Eden', privately printed paper, July 1969. The paper was prepared at Eden's request by Ben Pimlott.

61 The late Sir Frank Roberts to the author, 1 July 1992. See also Frank Roberts, *Dealing with Dictators: The Destruction and Revival of Europe 1930–1970*, Weidenfeld & Nicolson, 1991, pp.169–72.

62 Kenneth Rose, *King George V*, Weidenfeld & Nicolson, 1983, p.237.

63 Anthony Eden to Clarissa Eden, 26 June 1954. AP 20/45/54.

CHAPTER 15

Waiting for Winston

1 AP 20/17/180.

2 Oliver Goldsmith, *The Deserted Village*, line 97.

3 Because of the peculiarities of the British electoral system, a plurality of votes did not on this occasion bring the largest number of seats. The reverse situation (to the Conservatives' disadvantage) obtained in the February 1974 General Election.

4 Anthony Seldon, *Churchill's Indian Summer: The Conservative Government 1951–1955*, Hodder & Stoughton, 1981, p.51.

5 Clive Ponting, *Churchill*, Sinclair-Stevenson, 1994, p.781.

6 Anthony Eden diary, 27 August 1954. AP 20/1/30.

7 Harold Macmillan to Anthony Eden, 9 September 1954. AP 20/17/192.

8 J.P.L. Thomas wrote 'This is intolerable' J.P.L. Thomas to Anthony Eden, 30 August 1954. AP 20/17/180.

9 Dr John Lloyd had died on 17 August 1954 in his ninetieth year.

10 Sir Winston Churchill to Anthony Eden, 24 August 1954. AP 20/17/179.

11 Private information.

12 Sir Winston Churchill to Anthony Eden, 11 December 1953. AP 20/16/21.

13 D. R. Thorpe, *Selwyn Lloyd*, Jonathan Cape, 1989, p. 211.

14 Selwyn Lloyd Memorandum. Selwyn Lloyd papers, Churchill College, Cambridge. SELO 313 (1).

15 These circumstances contributed to a most unusual pattern. When Eden entered Number 10 Downing Street on 6 April 1955, he seemed better qualified by past experience for the post than virtually all of his twentieth-century predecessors; yet when he left office, with hindsight it could be seen that he was a Prime Minister whose career had already peaked. On becoming Prime Minister, Eden had occupied a 'great office' of state for twelve years, experience way beyond any of his ten twentieth-century predecessors, of whom Asquith and Churchill had both been Home Secretary and Chancellor of the Exchequer for a total of six years, while Bonar Law, Baldwin and Neville Chamberlain had been at the Treasury for three years, seven months and seven years respectively.

16 Anthony Eden diary, 27 August 1954. AP 20/1/30.

17 Anthony Eden to Lord Salisbury, 26 August 1954. Salisbury papers, Hatfield House, box J3.

18 *The Spectator*, 17 September, 1954.

19 Anthony Eden to Lord Salisbury, 4 September 1954. Salisbury papers, Hatfield House, Box J3.

20 Letter to Archbishop Fisher, 9 June 1955. Fisher papers, Lambeth Palace, vol.155, fol. 258.

21 Robert Carr to Anthony Eden, 7 February 1954. AP 20/17/176.

22 Charles Mott-Radclyffe, Memorandum on the Canal Zone Base, 4 May 1954. Mott-Radclyffe papers. Middle East Centre, St Antony's College, Oxford, file DT 107.83.

23 Speech at the Mansion House, 10 November 1942.

24 For an account of these differences see John Colville, *The Fringes of Power: Downing Street Diaries 1939–1955*, Hodder & Stoughton, 1985, pp. 694–700.

25 Anthony Eden diary, 21 December 1954. AP 20/1/30.

26 Private information from several sources.

27 Evidence of a Cabinet Minister at the time.

28 Sir Anthony Eden diary, 17 December 1954. AP 20/1/30.

29 Sir Anthony Eden diary, 6 January 1955. AP 20/1/31.

30 Sir Anthony Eden diary, 1 February 1955. AP 20/1/31.

31 The late Lord Amery of Lustleigh to the author, 30 January 1996.

32 The late Sir Anthony Nutting to the author, 4 November 1997. See also Anthony Nutting, *Nasser*, Constable, 1972, p.75.

33 Mohammed H. Heikal, *Cutting the Lion's Tail: Suez Through Egyptian Eyes*, André Deutsch, 1986, p.64.

34 Ibid., p. 65.

35 PRO. FO 371/113609.

36 Private information.

37 *Vide* Roy Jenkins, *Churchill*, Macmillan, 2001, p.183.

38 Private information.

39 Harold Macmillan diary, 14 March 1955. Stockton papers, Bodleian Library, Oxford. MS Macmillan dep. d. 20.

40 Sir Anthony Eden to Lord Salisbury, 29 March 1955. Salisbury papers, Hatfield House, box J3.

41 Clarissa Eden to Randolph Churchill, two letters of 5 April 1955. Randolph Churchill to Clarissa Eden, 5 April 1955. Quoted in Winston S. Churchill, *His Father's Son: The Life of Randolph Churchill*, Weidenfeld & Nicolson, 1996, pp.332–3.

42 PRO. CAB 128/28.

43 Private information.

44 John Colville, *The Churchillians*, Weidenfeld & Nicolson, 1981, p.171.

45 Paul Addison, *Churchill on the Home Front 1900–1955*, Pimlico paperback, 1993, pp. 419–20.

46 The BBC had started broadcasting *Listen with Mother* in 1950. It was an essential memory of so many families during that decade.

47 Harold Macmillan to the author, Birch Grove House, 23 April 1975.

48 Harold Macmillan diary, 17 July 1952. Stockton papers, Bodleian Library, Oxford. MS Macmillan dep. d. 11.

CHAPTER 16

'A Pretty Tough Assignment'

1 Reported in Richard Crossman's diary, 7 April 1955. Janet Morgan (ed.), *The Backbench Diaries of Richard Crossman*, Hamish Hamilton and Jonathan Cape, 1981, p.416.

2 Harold Macmillan diary, 6 April 1995. Macmillan papers, Bodleian Library, Oxford. MSS Macmillan dep. d. 20.

3 J. A. Cross, *Lord Swinton*, Oxford University Press, Oxford, 1982, p.284.

4 Hugh Dalton diary, 1 April 1955. Ben Pimlott (ed.), *The Political Diary of Hugh Dalton 1918–40, 1945–60*, Jonathan Cape, 1986, p.658.

5 *The Spectator*, 8 April 1955. I am grateful to Lord Gilmour of Craigmillar for making available a complete run of *The Spectator* for Eden's time as Prime Minister.

6 Private information.
7 Harold Macmillan diary, 6 April 1955, loc. cit.
8 Lord Carr of Hadley to the author, 20 May 1997.
9 Anthony Eden, *Full Circle*, 1960, pp.273–4.
10 Lord Salisbury to Sir Anthony Eden, 13 April 1955. Salisbury papers, Hatfield House, box J3.
11 Memorandum by the Earl of Avon, 4 September 1969. AP 23/27/42A. The views expressed in this memorandum were not held by everyone. The Revd V. H. H. Green asked the author about his biographical subjects at High Table at Lincoln College, Oxford, in 1995. On being told the most recent were Selwyn Lloyd, Alec Douglas-Home and (prospectively) Anthony Eden, he replied, 'Good heavens, you do choose some second-rate people'! The legendary Downing Street secretary, Miss Edith Watson, had predicted in 1939 that Home (then Lord Dunglass, and Neville Chamberlain's PPS) would one day be Prime Minister.
12 Oliver Harvey diary, 15 October 1937. John Harvey (ed.), *The Diplomatic Diaries of Oliver Harvey 1937–1940*, Collins, 1970, p.51. J. A. Cross's biography, op. cit., shows clearly Swinton's skills as an administrator, but Harvey's view of Swinton's political skills is not entirely untrue, even if unkind.
13 Sir Anthony Eden to Sir Winston Churchill, 8 April 1955. PRO. PREM 11/864.
14 Private information.
15 John Devine to the author, 12 August 1999.
16 Hugh Dalton diary, 26 May 1955, op. cit., p.671.
17 Dr David Butler to the author, 25 January 1995.
18 Harold Macmillan diary, 5 May 1955, loc. cit.
19 Sir Alec Douglas-Home's non-ticketed political meeting during the 1964 General Election campaign at the Bull Ring in Birmingham, where Eden had had a great success in May 1955, was an anachronistic miscalculation by Geoffrey Lloyd, MP for Sutton Coldfield, which did the Conservative Party campaign irreparable damage. *Vide* D. R. Thorpe, *Alec Douglas-Home*, Sinclair-Stevenson, 1996, p.368.
20 David Butler, *The British General Election of 1955*, Macmillan, 1955, p.61.
21 Mark Amory (ed.), *The Letters of Ann Fleming*, Collins Harvill, 1985, p. 183.
22 Sir Anthony Eden diary, 26 May 1955. AP 20/1/31.
23 Sir Anthony Eden diary, 27 May 1955. AP 20/1/31.
24 PRO. CAB 134/1273.
25 Anthony Eden, op. cit., p. 279.
26 Peter Hennessy, *Whitehall*, Secker & Warburg, 1989, p.138.
27 In conversation with Lord Moran. Lord Moran diary, 3 August 1959. Lord Moran, *Winston S. Churchill: The Struggle for Survival 1940–1965*, Sphere paperback, 1968, p.796.
28 Lady Allan to the author, 29 April 1997.
29 William Clark diary, 20 September 1955. MS William Clark 160. Bodleian Library, Oxford.
30 William Clark diary, 15–16 October 1955, loc. cit.
31 The late Lord Home of the Hirsel to the author, 6 August 1992.
32 Harold Nicolson diary, 1 December 1955. Harold Nicolson papers, Balliol College, Oxford.
33 Private information.
34 Private information.
35 As on 1 June 1959, when the Russians thought Selwyn Lloyd was about to be sacked as Foreign Secretary because of an article in *The Times*.
36 Sir William Haley diary, 4 July 1955. Haley Papers, Churchill College, Cambridge, file HALY 13/9.
37 Harold Macmillan diary, 19 July and 22 July 1955. Macmillan papers, Bodleian Library, Oxford. MSS. Macmillan dep. d. 21.

38 At a Press conference on 24 July 1955.

39 Sir Anthony Eden diary, 4 August 1955. AP 20/1/31.

40 PRO. FO 800/437.

41 Sir William Haley diary, 29 September 1955, loc. cit.

42 Sir Anthony Eden diary, 31 December 1955. AP 20/1/31.

43 Sir Anthony Eden diary, 15 October 1955. AP 20/1/311.

44 Sir Anthony Eden diary, 1 October 1955. AP 20/1/31.

45 Harold Macmillan diary, 31 October 1955. Stockton papers, Bodleian Library, Oxford. MSS. Macmillan dep. d. 24.

46 Sir William Haley diary, 29 September 1955, loc. cit.

47 Sir Anthony Eden to Lord Salisbury, 18 September 1955. Salisbury papers, Hatfield House, box J3.

48 Sir Anthony Eden diary, 24 August 1955. AP 20/1/31.

49 Sir Anthony Eden to R. A. Butler, 3 September 1955. AP 20/20/69.

50 Sir Anthony Eden diary, 26 August 1955. AP 20/1/31.

51 Hansard, 26 October 1955.

52 29 May 1956. PRO. PREM 11/414.

53 A point made to the author by six Prime Ministers over the years.

54 Peter Hennessy, *The Prime Minister: The Office and Its Holders since 1945*, Allen Lane, The Penguin Press, 2000, p.213.

55 As Eden was to find in retirement, when he missed his 'slot' with Alec Douglas-Home in April 1964 and had to leave without seeing the Prime Minister. D. R. Thorpe, *Alec Douglas-Home*, Sinclair-Stevenson, 1996, p.325.

56 Private information.

57 Evidence of one who was present on 27 July 1956.

58 Evelyn Shuckburgh, *Descent to Suez: Diaries 1951–1956*, Weidenfeld & Nicolson, 1986, p.18.

59 Cited in Hugo Young, *This Blessed Plot: Britain and Europe from Churchill to Blair*, Macmillan, 1998, p.83. Foreign Office responses to Messina are in FO 371/116038-40 (PRO).

60 PRO. FO 371/115999.

61 Sir Ashley Clarke to John Coulson, 11 June 1955. PRO. FO 371/116040.

62 Jean Monnet in conversation with Cecil M. Weir, UK delegate to the Coal and Steel Community in Luxembourg, 3 June 1955. PRO. FO 371/116038.

63 PRO. PREM 11/1333.

64 Sir Roger Makins to Sir Harold Caccia, 23 December 1955. PRO. FO 371/115999.

65 Ben Pimlott, 'E.D.C., W.E.U. and Mr Eden', privately printed paper, July 1969.

66 Hansard, 26 November 1956.

67 PRO. CAB 129/77.

68 In the run-up to the 1997 General Election, Charles Falconer was reportedly unable to secure nomination for a winnable Labour seat, as his four children were at private schools. He was ennobled so that he could become a member of the Blair Government.

69 Technical College Development Plan, November 1955. PRO. ED 46/1000.

70 Cmd. 9703.

71 Richard Lamb, *The Failure of the Eden Government*, Sidgwick & Jackson, 1987, p.32.

72 AP 7/26/1.

73 Harry Crookshank diary, 16 December 1955. Crookshank papers, Bodleian Library, Oxford. MS Eng Hist d. 361.

74 Sir Anthony Eden to Harold Macmillan, 7 December 1955. Macmillan papers, Bodleian Library, Oxford. MSS. Macmillan dep. d. 24.

75 Sir Anthony Eden diary, 16 October 1955. AP 20/1/31.

76 Selwyn Lloyd papers, Churchill College, Cambridge. SELO 180 (4).

77 Ibid.

78 Earl of Birkenhead, *Walter Monckton: The Life of Viscount Monckton of Brenchley*, Weidenfeld & Nicolson, 1969, p.305.

79 Sir John Smyth was a Parliamentary Secretary at the Ministry of Pensions. The Victoria Cross was instituted in 1856 during the

Crimean War for acts of
conspicuous bravery.
80 Private information.
81 Sir Anthony Eden diary, 6 February
1955. AP 20/1/31.
82 Private information.
83 Baroness Martine de Courcel to the
author, 6 November 2000.
84 *Daily Telegraph*, 3 January 1956.
85 The late Sir Anthony Nutting to the
author, 4 November 1997.
86 'Begging' the Prime Minister to deny
his resignation is a strange tactic,
and some felt Clark had a hidden
agenda (private information); for
Eden to agree, even 'reluctantly',
was a compromising response, not
fully thought through, which
inevitably rebounded. Churchill
always told his wife, during fraught
moments at Chartwell, that servants
were there to save worry, not create
it; Press Secretaries come into that
category too, and by this criterion
Clark failed the test.
87 Countess of Avon to the author, 12
February 2002.
88 Anthony Howard, *RAB: The Life of
R. A. Butler*, Jonathan Cape, 1987,
p.222.
89 *The Times*, 2 January 1956.
90 Sir William Haley diary, 8 January
1956, loc. cit.
91 Hugh Gaitskell, dictated diary note
of 9 January 1956. Philip M.
Williams (ed.), *The Diary of Hugh
Gaitskell 1945–1956*, Jonathan
Cape, 1983, p.411.

CHAPTER 17

The Sparks Fly Upwards

1 Anthony Eden, *Full Circle*, Cassell,
1960, p.338.
2 Sir Anthony Eden diary, 29
February 1956. AP 20/1/32.
3 D. R. Thorpe, *Selwyn Lloyd*,
Jonathan Cape, 1989, p.200.
4 Selwyn Lloyd to Sir Anthony Eden,
3 March 1956. PRO. PREM
11/1476.
5 Professor Edward Ullendorff to the
author, 5 November 1997.

6 Mohamed H. Heikal, *Nasser: The
Cairo Documents*, New English
Library, 1972, p.88.
7 Anthony Eden, op. cit., p.352.
Clarissa Eden diary, 7 March 1956.
Countess of Avon papers. Hugh
Gaitskell diary, 9 March 1956.
Philip M. Williams (ed.), *The Diary
of Hugh Gaitskell 1945–1956*,
Jonathan Cape, 1983, p.465.
Harold Macmillan diary, 8 October
1955. Macmillan papers, Bodleian
Library, Oxford. MSS. Macmillan
dep. d. 23.
8 Sir Anthony Eden to President
Dwight D. Eisenhower, 5 March
1956. PRO. FO 371/121540.
9 Quoted in Alan Thompson, *The Day
Before Yesterday*, Sidgwick &
Jackson, 1971, p.125.
10 At the late-night meetings on Cyprus
in the first week of March, Eden
appeared to one official tired, tetchy,
under strain and peremptory, a
mood not improved by the demands
of the debate on Glubb Pasha's
dismissal. Glubb had recently
lunched with the Edens at Chequers,
when he was notably depressed.
(Countess of Avon to the author, 12
February 2002.) Yet in the days
following Nasser's nationalisation of
the Suez Canal Company on 26 July,
when Eden was focusing almost
exclusively on this one major issue,
the same official found Eden a
changed man: calm, self-possessed,
exuding quiet confidence and in
complete mastery of the military,
civil and colonial details of his brief.
(Paul Odgers to the author, 20
November 1997.)
11 John Ramsden, *A History of the
Conservative Party: The Age of
Churchill & Eden 1940–1957*,
Longman, 1995, pp.295–6.
12 Cilcennin was ready to go in May,
when suddenly the Commander
Crabb affair blew up, over the
disappearance of the frogman
inspecting the Russian cruiser that
had brought Bulganin and
Khrushchev to England for an
official visit. Departure then would
inevitably appear as a dismissal,

something the First Sea Lord, Mountbatten, warned would 'grieve the Navy very much'. (Record of Lord Mountbatten's meeting with Walter Monckton, 24 February 1956. Quoted in Philip Ziegler, *Mountbatten: The Official Biography*, Collins, 1985, p.536). So Cilcennin stayed on for a further spell, much to the chagrin of Lord Hailsham, First Lord-in-waiting, who now found himself in limbo between his career at the Bar and the Admiralty. (Lord Hailsham, *A Sparrow's Flight: Memoirs*, Collins, 1990, p.282). Then came President Nasser's nationalisation of the Canal Company on 26 July, so Cilcennin's departure was delayed yet again, and it was not until 2 September that Hailsham finally succeeded him.

13 Lord Salisbury to Sir Anthony Eden, 9 April 1956. Salisbury papers, Hatfield House, file B 1956–60.

14 On 29 March 1957, Salisbury did finally resign, ostensibly over the release of Archbishop Makarios from detention, although the real reason was deeper disillusionment with Macmillan's policy drift. Home was not asked this time to persuade Salisbury to think again, but was appointed to replace him as Lord President. Not a dog barked, and arguably the Salisbury influence was never the same again.

15 Private information. *Vide* John Turner, *Macmillan*, Longman, 1994, p.109.

16 *Hansard*, 17 April 1956.

17 Lord Beaverbrook to Brendan Bracken, 23 January 1956. Beaverbrook papers, House of Lords Record Office, file BBK C58.

18 Private information.

19 Roger Wilmut (ed.), *The Complete Beyond the Fringe*, Methuen, 1987, p.54.

20 Many mysteries still surround this episode. I am grateful to the late Sir Patrick Reilly for guiding me through some of its intricacies.

21 The comment to the author of one who was present.

22 Percy Cradock, *Know Your Enemy: How the Joint Intelligence Committee Saw the World*, John Murray, 2002, p.266.

23 *Hansard*, 4 May 1956.

24 *Much Ado About Nothing*, III.v.18.

25 Sir Waldron Smithers to Anthony Eden, 7 January 1953. AP 11/10/85C. 'Please draft thanks!!' Eden minuted on the letter.

26 Sir Anthony Eden to Selwyn Lloyd, 4 May 1956. AP 20/21/93. 'The Voice of the Arabs' (mistakenly called 'The Voice of Egypt' by Eden) had been founded by Neguib in 1953. After air attacks on 2 November, Radio Cairo went off the air, and 'The Voice of Britain', operating from the Near East Broadcasting Station in Cyprus took over its wavelength. But the Egyptian propaganda had already achieved its aim.

27 *Hansard*, 15 May 1956.

28 Anthony Eden to Dwight D. Eisenhower, 1 April 1953. AP 20/16/26A.

29 Quoted in Anthony Nutting, *Nasser*, Constable, 1972, p.144.

30 PRO. CAB 158/25. JIC (56) 80.

31 Private information.

32 Article I, Convention of Constantinople, 1888.

33 Keith Kyle, 'Suez Revisited'. Lecture to the Thackeray Society of the Reform Club, 30 March 2000.

34 Hugh Gaitskell diary, 26 July 1956. Philip M. Williams (ed.), op. cit., p.553.

35 Ibid., pp.455, 557.

36 William Clark diary, 26 July 1956. William Clark papers, Bodleian Library, Oxford. MS William Clark 160.

37 Uncatalogued Home papers, The Hirsel, Coldstream.

38 Henrik Ibsen, *The Master Builder*, Act One.

39 See below.

40 Sir Anthony Eden to Lord Caccia, 31 January 1960. Caccia papers (in the possession of the Caccia family, Builth Wells).

41 Viscount Kilmuir diary, 26 July

1956. Kilmuir papers, Churchill College, Cambridge. KLMR 1/5.

42 Cabinet Minutes, 27 July 1956. PRO. CAB 128/30.

43 Professor Arthur Goodhart letter to *The Times*, 11 August 1956.

44 *The Life and Times of Lord Mountbatten*, twelve-part ITV series, 1969.

45 Hansard, 6 May 1936.

46 William Clark papers, Bodleian Library, Oxford. Clark MS. Eng. 4814.

47 Kenneth Rose papers. Kenneth Rose contributed the notice of Cilcennin's life to the *Dictionary of National Biography*.

48 *Daily Mirror*, 27 July 1956 and 30 July 1956.

49 Cabinet Minutes, 27 July 1956, loc. cit.

50 See Anthony Howard, *RAB: The Life of R. A. Butler*, Jonathan Cape, 1987, p.231.

51 J. P. Mackintosh, *The British Cabinet*, 3rd edition, Stevens & Sons, 1977, p.24.

52 Sir Anthony Eden to President Dwight D. Eisenhower, 27 July 1956. PRO. PREM 11/1177.

53 Quoted in Keith Kyle, *Suez*, Weidenfeld & Nicholson, 1991, p.386.

54 Quoted in Martin Gilbert, *'Never Despair': Winston S. Churchill 1945–1965*, Heinemann, 1988, p.1222.

55 Lord Moran diary, 1 August 1956. Lord Moran, *Winston Churchill: The Struggle for Survival, 1940–1965*, Sphere Books, paperback, 1968, p.735.

56 Hansard, 2 August 1956.

57 Quoted in Kenneth Harris, *Attlee*, Weidenfeld & Nicolson, 1982, p.547.

58 Hansard, 2 August 1956.

59 Count Grandi to Benito Mussolini, 2 July 1935. *Documenti diplomatici italiani*, 8th series, no. 1, document 475.

60 Sir Ralph Stevenson to Harold Macmillan, 10 May 1955. PRO. FO 371/115868.

61 Quoted in Jan Morris, *Heaven's Command: An Imperial Progress*, Penguin Books, Harmondsworth, paperback, 1979, f-n., p.492.

CHAPTER 18
Into the Maze

1 PRO. 'Suez Canal'. CAB 129/54. C (52).

2 Cited in Simon Heffer, *Like the Roman: The Life of Enoch Powell*, Weidenfeld & Nicolson, 1998, pp.122–3.

3 R. A. C. Parker, *Chamberlain and Appeasement: British Policy and the Coming of the Second World War*, Macmillan, 1993, p.1.

4 Memorandum of 20 March 1945. PRO. CAB 66/63. JIC Basic Planning Assumption, 8 April 1948. PRO. CAB 158/3.

5 Sir Norman Brook to Sir Anthony Eden, 21 April 1955. PRO. DEFE 13/45.

6 Sidney Aster, *Anthony Eden*, Weidenfeld & Nicolson, 1976, p.165.

7 Minute by R. J. Bowker, Assistant Under-Secretary for Middle Eastern Affairs, 10 January 1951. PRO. FO 371/912219.

8 Minute of 31 July 1956. PRO. DEFE 4/89. COS (56) 75th Meeting.

9 *The Times*, 27 July 1956. Iverach McDonald wrote this leader in the absence on holiday of the Editor, Sir William Haley. Iverach McDonald to the author, 7 November 1977. For the paper's reaction to Suez, see also Iverach McDonald, *The History of 'The Times': Volume V Struggles in War and Peace 1939–1966*, Times Books, 1986.

10 *Daily Herald*, 28 July 1956. *News Chronicle*, 28 July 1956.

11 PRO. FO 371/115874.

12 *Vide* John Nott, *Here Today, Gone Tomorrow: Recollections of an Errant Politician*, Politico's, 2002.

13 Tony Shaw, *Eden, Suez and the Mass Media: Propaganda and Persuasion during the Suez Crisis*, I. B. Tauris, 1996, p.192.

14 Iverach McDonald, op. cit., p.26.
15 A *bon mot* that was in circulation before Suez, but now repeated.
16 Sir Nicholas Henderson to the author, 13 October 2001.
17 Memorandum by Sir Anthony Eden, 15 June 1956. PRO. CAB 134/1315, PR (56) 11.
18 Anthony Eden, 'Britain and the Middle East', *Sunday Chronicle*, 8 February 1948. AP 7/14/75.
19 Cabinet du Ministre: Pineau 1956–8 (Afrique, Levant, Egypte – Suez). Archives, Ministère des Affaires étrangères, Quai d'Orsay, Paris.
20 William Clark diary, 29 July 1956. William Clark papers, Bodleian Library, Oxford. MS William Clark 160.
21 *Observer*, 24 May 1925.
22 Words overheard by one present in Downing Street. As in the previous chapter, and in the next, to avoid repetition, 'Private information', which is so profuse, will not normally be specified for material in that category.
23 Broadlands Archives, Southampton University. Suez File N 106. The use of military terminology for timings was characteristic of Mountbatten.
24 Keith Kyle, *Suez*, Weidenfeld & Nicolson, 1991, p.467.
25 Ibid., p.350.
26 Brigadier Darling to General Stockwell, 8 November 1956. PRO. WO 288/1. See also, 'General Sir Kenneth Darling', Obituary, *The Times*, 4 November 1998.
27 *Vide* Anthony Gorst, 'A Modern Major General': General Sir Gerald Templer, Chief of the Imperial General Staff', *Contemporary British History, Volume 13, Summer 1991, Number 2*, pp.29–45, for a detailed account of Templer's contribution.
28 *The Life and Times of Lord Mountbatten*, twelve-part ITV television series, 1969.
29 William Clark, *From Three Worlds: Memoirs*, Sidgwick & Jackson, 1986, p.160.
30 PRO. FO 371/119154.
31 Evelyn Shuckburgh diary, 24 September 1956. Evelyn Shuckburgh, *Descent to Suez: Diaries 1951–56*, Weidenfeld & Nicolson, 1986, p.360.
32 David Carlton, *Anthony Eden: A Biography*, Unwin paperback, 1986, p.472.
33 Hugh Thomas, *The Suez Affair*, Weidenfeld & Nicolson, revised paperback, 1986, p.115. Eden's detailed analysis of the errors of fact in the book are in AP 4/3/25. One important error he missed comes on p.122, even in the revised 1986 edition, where Thomas writes of the British duo at the first Sèvres meeting on 22 October, 'There is no reason now to doubt that this was Lloyd and the official Patrick Dean.' There is every reason to doubt it. Lloyd was in fact accompanied by his assistant private secretary, Donald Logan. Dean attended the second meeting on 24 October with Logan.
34 Keith Kyle in his magisterial account of Suez follows the Thomas line, saying that Caccia's 'slow way by sea' was 'an arrangement that did not strike the Americans as, and indeed was not, accidental'. Keith Kyle, *Suez*, Weidenfeld & Nicolson, 1991, p.345. With considerable irony in the light of Hugh Thomas's later political odyssey, Selwyn Lloyd wrote to Thomas in February 1967, 'I am bound to say that there is still a great deal in your narrative and your conclusion with which I profoundly disagree. Nevertheless I believe that you have tried to be fair and to discount your own prejudices – as you are a dangerous leftist, so I am told, that is saying a great deal!!' Selwyn Lloyd papers, Churchill College, Cambridge. SELO 237 (3).
35 Yet within two months, Caccia was able to report to Macmillan, by then Prime Minister, 'Personally, I have had nothing but friendliness from the various members of the Administration and by now, for most of them, any old scores against us are as good as forgotten.' Sir Harold Caccia to Harold Macmillan, 28 February 1957. Lord

Caccia papers, Eton College Library.

36 At an early stage in the research for the present biography, the Caccia family made Caccia's papers, a virgin archive, available to the author. In any quest for evidence there are always special moments. Opening boxes in Builth Wells, from which tumbled handwritten letters from Queen Victoria, as well as Caccia's diaries and letters of his time with Eden, was one such.

37 D. R. Thorpe, *Selwyn Lloyd*, Jonathan Cape, 1989, p.196.

38 'Notes on 1956'. William Clark papers, loc. cit. Ms. Eng. 4814.

39 Arthur Christiansen, *Headlines All My Life*, Heinemann, 1964, p.283.

40 Iverach McDonald, *A Man of the Times*, Hamish Hamilton, 1976, p.148.

41 Broadcast of 8 August 1956. BBC Records, Caversham.

42 Harold Nicolson diary, 8 August 1956. Nicolson papers, Balliol College, Oxford.

43 Quoted in Michael Cockerell, *Live from Number 10: The Inside Story of Prime Ministers and Television*, Faber & Faber, 1988, p.45.

44 Details from papers seen on a confidential basis.

45 Sir Anthony Eden to Sir Alexander Cadogan, 16 August 1956. Cadogan papers, Churchill College, Cambridge. ACAD 4/5.

46 Speech at the opening of the Gateshead Conservative Association Headquarters, 20 November 1956. During those frenetic months she once heard John Foster Dulles say to a fellow guest at the Prime Minister's table, 'I bet you five pounds I can tell you exactly what every course is going to be.' The lost bet was a tribute to Clarissa's steadiness and quiet powers of organisation, one of the supportive ways in which she presided in Downing Street during the great post-war crisis that was to be the central drama of her husband's Premiership.

47 Lady Gladwyn diary, 14 November 1956. Miles Jebb (ed.), *The Diaries*

of Cynthia Gladwyn, Constable, 1995, p.191.

48 Sir Henry Marten (1872–1948), Provost of Eton and tutor to Princess Elizabeth. 'Such a mistake to have that lesson,' Lord Hugh Cecil said after Marten's funeral in Eton College Chapel. 'There is nothing Marten would less like to see than "a new heaven and a new earth".' Kenneth Rose, *The Later Cecils*, Weidenfeld & Nicolson, 1975, p.290.

49 '1956 The Queen'. PRO. PREM 11/1163.

50 PRO. FO 371/121748.

51 James Eayrs, *The Commonwealth and Suez*, Oxford University Press, Oxford, 1964, pp.15–16.

52 The late Lord Home of the Hirsel to the author, 6 August 1992.

53 AP 23/27/26.

54 D. R. Thorpe, *Alec Douglas-Home*, Sinclair-Stevenson, 1996, p.176.

55 Gallup Poll findings, November 1956.

56 Hansard, 30 July 1956.

57 Robert Murphy, *Diplomat Among Warriors*, Collins, 1964, p. 379.

58 PRO. PREM 11/1098.

59 John Foster Dulles to President Dwight D. Eisenhower, 19 August 1956. *Foreign Relations of the United States (FRUS), 1955–1957, Volume XVI Suez Crisis, July 26–December 31, 1956*, United States Government Printing Office, Washington, 1990, Telegram 684A.86/8-1956.

60 Hansard, 2 August 1956.

61 Sir Anthony Eden to President Dwight D. Eisenhower, 5 August 1956. PRO. PREM 11/1098.

62 David Ben-Gurion diary, 3 August 1956. Quoted in Selwyn Ilan Troën & Moshe Shemesh (eds), *The Suez-Sinai Crisis 1956: Retrospective and Reappraisal*, Frank Cass, 1990, p.292.

63 William Clark diary, 22 August 1956, loc. cit. MS William Clark 160.

64 Memorandum of a conversation between Dulles and Harold Macmillan, 21 August 1956. Dulles

papers, General Memoranda of Conversations, Eisenhower Library, Abilene, Kansas.

65 Martin Gilbert, *Never Despair: Winston S. Churchill 1945–1965*, Heinemann, 1988, p.1203.

66 Sir Anthony Eden diary, 14 August 1956. AP 20/1/32.

67 Harold Macmillan to the author, 23 April 1975.

68 Non-attributable private interview.

69 Sir Anthony Eden diary, 15 August 1956. Ibid.

70 Sir Anthony Eden to Sir Winston Churchill, 17 August 1956. Chartwell papers, Churchill College, Cambridge. CHAR 2/216.

71 Quoted in Robert Menzies, *Afternoon light: some memories of men and events*, Cassell, 1967, p.165.

72 Sir Robert Menzies to Sir Anthony Eden, 9 September 1956. AP 23/51/1.

73 Selwyn Lloyd, *Suez 1956: A Personal Account*, Jonathan Cape, 1978, p.34.

74 Lord Salisbury to Sir Anthony Eden, 24 August 1956. PRO. PREM 11/1102.

75 The Earl of Home to Sir Anthony Eden, 22 and 25 August 1956. PRO. PREM 11/1152.

76 Lady Eden diary, 27 August 1956. Countess of Avon papers.

77 'A Canal Too Far', BBC Radio 3, 31 January 1987.

78 Sir Anthony Eden to Sir Winston Churchill, 17 September 1956. Chartwell papers, loc. cit. CHAR 2/216.

79 Sir William Haley diary, 28 August 1956. Haley papers, Churchill College, Cambridge. HALY 13/9.

80 President Dwight D. Eisenhower to Sir Anthony Eden, 3 September 1956. PRO. PREM 11/1100.

81 Selwyn Lloyd papers, loc. cit. SELO 237 (3).

82 Harold Macmillan to Sir Anthony Eden, 26 September 1956. PRO. PREM 11/1102.

83 President Dwight D. Eisenhower to Sir Anthony Eden, 8 September 1956. PRO. FO 800/726T. 1839.

84 Sir Gladwyn Jebb to Selwyn Lloyd, 17 October 1956. Sir Anthony Eden to Selwyn Lloyd, 19 October 1956. PRO. PREM 11/1126.

85 Sir Gladwyn Jebb to Sir Ivone Kirkpatrick, 25 October 1956. Lord Gladwyn papers, Churchill College, Cambridge. GLAD 1/4/3A. When the author interviewed Lord Gladwyn in 1986 for his biography of Selwyn Lloyd, Lord Gladwyn said that he would 'look out some papers'. A few days later, a large package containing the original draft of the above letter, arrived at the author's home address by ordinary unregistered post. When Lord Gladwyn saw this letter again after thirty years, he felt it better not to publish it in his own lifetime. Fortunately, this primary material is now safely housed and catalogued at Churchill College.

86 Quoted in Keith Kyle, op. cit., p.273.

87 Sir Anthony Eden to Selwyn Lloyd, 5 and 8 October 1956. PRO. FO 800/725.

88 PRO. FO 371/121780.

89 AP 20/49/42A.

90 Anthony Eden, *Full Circle*, Cassell, 1960, p.508.

91 Sir Anthony Eden to Selwyn Lloyd, 14 October 1956. PRO. PREM 11/1102.

92 The late Sir Anthony Nutting to the author, 4 November 1997.

93 Anthony Nutting, *No End of a Lesson: The Story of Suez*, Constable, 1967, p.98.

94 PRO. FO 800/725.

95 Selwyn Lloyd papers, loc. cit. SELO 129 (1).

96 The fullest accounts are in Avi Shlaim, 'The Protocol of Sèvres, 1956: anatomy of a war plot', *International Affairs*, vol. 73, 1997, pp.509–30, and Keith Kyle, op. cit., pp.314–31. The three British participants have all left their accounts. See Selwyn Lloyd, op. cit, pp.180–7. See also Donald Logan, 'Suez: meetings at Sèvres, 22–25 October 1956', which was published in the *Financial Times* on 8

November 1986. There are copies in the Selwyn Lloyd papers, loc. cit., SELO 202 (6); the Public Record Office; and the Bodleian Library, Oxford. 'Comments' by Donald Logan on *The Failure of the Eden Government by Richard Lamb*, which gives further details, is in the Selwyn Lloyd papers, SELO 30. 'Memorandum by Sir Patrick Dean – 1986' is in private circulation. Details in this account are taken from all these documents.

97 Professor Avi Shlaim to the author, 13 October 1997.

98 Selwyn Lloyd to Christian Pineau, 23 October 1956. Original copy in Guy Mollet Archives, Paris.

99 Christian Pineau, *1956 Suez*, Éditions Robert Laffont, Paris, 1976, p.150.

100 Cabinet Minutes, 24 October 1956. PRO. CAB 128/30.

101 Cabinet Minutes, 25 October 1956. PRO. CAB 128/30.

102 Sir Anthony Eden to Guy Mollet, 25 and 28 October 1956. Original copies in Guy Mollet Archives, Paris.

103 Anthony Montague Browne, *Long Sunset: Memoirs of Winston Churchill's Last Private Secretary*, Cassell, 1995, pp.210–11. Sir Anthony Montague Browne to the author, 5 August 1998.

104 Sir William Haley diary, 30 October 1956, loc. cit. HALY 13/9.

105 Sir Anthony Eden to President Dwight D. Eisenhower, 30 October 1956. PRO. PREM 11/1105.

106 Anthony Eden, op. cit., p.527.

107 Correlli Barnett, *The Verdict of Peace: Britain Between Her Yesterday and the Future*, Macmillan, 2001, p.491.

108 The late Sir John Coulson to the author, 1986.

109 William Clark diary, 30 and 31 October 1956, loc. cit. MS William Clark 160.

110 Anthony Eden, op. cit., pp.521–2.

111 Countess of Home diary, 31 October 1956, loc. cit.

CHAPTER 19
Last Months in Office

1 Neville Chamberlain papers, Birmingham University Library. NC 18/1/1032.

2 J. T. Emmerson, *The Rhineland Crisis 7 March 1936: A study in multilateral diplomacy*, Maurice Temple Smith, 1977, p.247.

3 William Clark diary, 1 November 1956. MS. William Clark 160. Bodleian Library, Oxford. William Clark was normally very critical of Eden's bursts of temper. Although parts of Clark's diary have to be taken with a pinch of salt, this unsolicited comment is corroborated by others.

4 *Sunday Telegraph*, 6 October 1996.

5 Selwyn Lloyd, *Suez 1956: A Personal Account*, Jonathan Cape, 1978, p.237.

6 PRO. PREM 11/1105.

7 *Scotsman*, 1 November 1956.

8 Iverach McDonald to the author, 7 November 1997.

9 Hansard, 1 November 1956.

10 Private information.

11 Philip M. Williams, *Hugh Gaitskell: A Political Biography*, Jonathan Cape, 1979, p.439.

12 The author witnessed its burning as a thirteen-year-old pupil at Fettes.

13 Hansard, 31 October and 13 November 1956.

14 Hansard, 1 November and 13 November 1956.

15 The Countess of Avon to the author, 12 February 2002.

16 William Roger Louis, 'Harold Macmillan and the Middle East Crisis of 1958', *Proceedings of the British Academy*, 94, 207–28 (1996).

17 See Chapter 20.

18 Selwyn Lloyd papers, Churchill College, Cambridge. SELO 129 (2). PRO. CAB 134/1216.

19 Archbishop Fisher to Lord Hailsham, 6 November 1956. Lord Fisher of Lambeth papers, Lambeth Palace Library, vol. 171, fol. 284.

20 Sir Anthony Eden to the Archbishop of Canterbury, 10 November 1956.

Lord Fisher of Lambeth papers, loc. cit., vol. 171, fol. 287.

21 Quoted in Herman Finer, *Dulles Over Suez*, Heinemann, 1964, p.397.

22 Richard M. Nixon to Julian Amery, 21 January 1987. Quoted in Jonathan Aitken, *Nixon: A Life*, Weidenfeld & Nicolson, 1993, p.244.

23 Sir William Haley to Lady Violet Bonham Carter, 10 December 1956. Bonham Carter Mss, Bodleian Library, Oxford.

24 Peter Hennessy, *The Prime Minister: The Office and its Holders since 1945*, Allen Lane, The Penguin Press, 2000, p.247.

25 BBC Records, Caversham.

26 Tony Shaw, 'Cadogan's Last Fling: Sir Alexander Cadogan, Chairman of the Board of Governors of the BBC', *Contemporary British History*, vol. 13, Summer 1999, no. 2, Special Issue: Whitehall and the Suez Crisis, p.140. Cadogan papers, Churchill College, Cambridge. ACAD 1/27.

27 Keith Kyle, *Suez*, Weidenfeld & Nicolson, 1991, pp.433–4.

28 John Devine to the author, 12 August 1999.

29 Ministry of Defence records. Lord Duncan-Sandys papers, Churchill College, Cambridge. DSND 6/29.

30 Countess of Home diary, 4 November 1956. Home papers, The Hirsel, Coldstream.

31 *News Chronicle*, 5 November 1956.

32 Hansard, 16 May 1957.

33 The Countess of Avon to the author, 12 February 2002.

34 Guy Mollet papers, Archives Guy Mollet, Paris.

35 Lady Eden diary, 4 November 1956. Countess of Avon papers.

36 January 1957 diary summary. AP 20/2/5.

37 Quoted in W. Scott Lucas, *Divided We Stand: Britain, the US and the Suez Crisis*, Hodder & Stoughton paperback, 1996, p.290.

38 Sir Pierson Dixon diary, 6 November 1956 (in possession of Mr Piers Dixon).

39 Piers Dixon, *Double Diploma: The Life of Sir Pierson Dixon, Don and Diplomat*, Hutchinson, 1968, p.272.

40 Sir Anthony Eden to President Dwight D. Eisenhower, 5 November 1956. PRO. PREM. 11/1177.

41 *Foreign Relations of the United States (FRUS): Volume XVI, Suez Crisis July 26–December 31 1956*, United States Government Printing Office, Washington, 1990, pp.1025–7.

42 Sir Harold Caccia to Selwyn Lloyd, 8 November 1956. PRO. T 236/4189.

43 PRO. PREM 11/1090.

44 The late Sir Anthony Nutting to the author, 4 November 1997.

45 William Clark diary, 3 November 1956, loc. cit. This entry reveals details of the scheme to impugn Nutting's motives. In 1987 Sir Anthony Nutting, having taken counsel's advice over Robert Rhodes James's biography of Eden, placed a notice in *The Times* 'for the Historical Record' denying that there were 'documents which, if revealed, would have done him great harm'. See Robert Rhodes James, *Anthony Eden*, Weidenfeld & Nicolson, 1986, p.615.

46 Ann Lane, 'The Past as Matrix: Sir Ivone Kirkpatrick, Permanent Under-Secretary for Foreign Affairs', *Contemporary British History*, op. cit., pp.214–15.

47 Countess of Home diary, 9 November 1956, loc. cit.

48 Sir Robert Rhodes James to the author, 2 March 1999.

49 Patrick Gordon Walker diary, 23 December 1956. Lord Gordon-Walker papers, Churchill College, Cambridge. File GNWR 1/13, which contains much interesting material on the Labour Party's response to the Suez crisis.

50 Nigel Nicolson, *People and Parliament*, Weidenfeld & Nicolson, 1958, p. 133.

51 Sir Anthony Eden to Guy Mollet, 12 November 1956. Guy Mollet papers, loc. cit. Dossier 4, no. 10, November 1956.

52 Resignation speech in the House of Commons, Hansard, 21 February 1938. The full text is in Appendix I.

53 Anthony Nutting, *No End of a Lesson*, Constable 1967, p.123. Despite Eden saying that he hoped 'we shall see something of each other in the future', it was not to be, to Nutting's lasting regret. Sir John Nutting to the author, 16 January 2000.

54 The late Sir Robert Rhodes James to the author, 27 February 1999.

55 Sir John Nutting to the author, 16 January 2000.

56 Iverach McDonald to the author, 7 November 1997. Information from a confidential source who was present in the old Home Office building as the dignitaries gathered for the wreath-laying.

57 Sir Anthony Eden diary, 21 August 1956. AP 20/1/32.

58 *Daily Mirror*, 1 December 1956. Competitors had to write a 500-word essay on 'What the British Government should now do to regain our alliance with America, improve relations within the Commonwealth, and restore a sense of unity in our own country'.

59 Mark Amory (ed.), *The Letters of Ann Fleming*, Collins Harvill, 1985, p.188.

60 Andrew Lycett, *Ian Fleming*, Weidenfeld & Nicolson, 1995, p.303. George VI's tour to South Africa during the dreadful British winter of 1947 led to much royal soul-searching. James Callaghan's 'beach-hut' summit with President Carter at Guadeloupe in 1979, while Britain was in the last throes of the 'winter of discontent', did not, and this had a damaging political effect.

61 *Newsweek*, 10 December 1956.

62 Andrew Lycett, op. cit., p.305.

63 Clarissa Eden to Ann Fleming. Ibid., p.305.

64 Ann Fleming to Cecil Beaton, 15 January 1957. Mark Amory, op. cit., p.190.

65 Ibid., f-n. p.192.

66 D. R. Thorpe, *The Uncrowned Prime Ministers*, Darkhorse Publishing, 1980, p.xiii.

67 W. Scott Lucas, op. cit., pp.311, 312.

68 *The Spectator*, 7 December 1956.

69 D. R. Thorpe, *Alec Douglas-Home*, Sinclair-Stevenson, 1996, pp.267-8 and pp.298-9.

70 Memorandum of a conversation, Secretary Dulles' Room, Walter Reed Hospital, Washington, 7 November 1956, 11.10 a.m. *FRUS*, op. cit., p.1049.

71 Russell Braddon, *Suez: Splitting of a Nation*, Collins, 1973, p.11. George Humphrey has been confused by some commentators with Hubert Humphrey, a later US Democratic Presidential candidate, notably by Richard Lamb in *The Failure of the Eden Government*, p.287 and onwards.

72 Selwyn Lloyd, *Suez 1956: A Personal Account*, Jonathan Cape, 1978, p.219.

73 *FRUS*, op. cit., pp.1150-2.

74 Ibid., op. cit., pp.1150-2.

75 Ibid., op. cit., p. 1163.

76 Record of Aldrich-Hoover phone conversations, 19 November 1956. Ibid.

77 Winthrop Aldrich, Telegram 2814 to the Department of State, 19 November 1956. Ibid., p.1163.

78 Cole C. Kingseed, *Eisenhower and the Suez Crisis of 1956*, Louisiana State University Press, Baton Rouge, 1995, p.140.

79 Selwyn Lloyd, op. cit., p.206.

80 *FRUS*, op. cit., p.1171.

81 Ibid., p.1175.

82 Ibid. Eisenhower papers, Eisenhower Library, Abilene, Kansas. Ann Whitman diaries, Box 19, November 1956.

83 Brendan Bracken to Lord Beaverbrook, 7 December 1956. Beaverbrook papers, House of Lords Record Office. File BK C/17.

84 Steven Z. Freiberger, *Dawn over Suez: The Rise of American Power in the Middle East, 1953–1957*, Ivan R. Dee, Chicago, 1992, f-n., p.266.

85 Harold Nicolson diary, 5 December 1956. Balliol College, Oxford.

86 Lord Butler of Saffron Walden papers, Trinity College, Cambridge, Box G 46/8, ff. iv–v.

87 Lord Fisher of Lambeth papers, loc. cit., vol. 171, ff. 341.–5.

88 Private information.

89 Violet Bonham Carter diary, 1 April 1955. Mark Pottle (ed.), *Daring to Hope: The Diaries and Letters of Violet Bonham Carter 1945–1969*, Weidenfeld & Nicolson, 2000, p.147.

90 General Sir Charles Keightley Memorandum, 12 November 1957. PRO. AIR 8/1940.

91 Introduction to J. T. Emmerson, op. cit., pp.12–13.

92 Sir Anthony Eden to Robert Allan, 4 May 1957. Lord Allan of Kilmahew papers (courtesy of Lady Allan).

93 Quoted in Percy Cradock, *Know Your Enemy: How the Joint Intelligence Committee Saw the World*, John Murray, 2002, p.132.

94 The Earl of Avon to Lord Beaverbrook, 13 April 1964. Beaverbrook papers, House of Lords Record Office, file BK C/18.

95 Lady Eden diary, 14 December 1956, loc. cit.

96 Lady Gladwyn diary, 9 January 1957. Miles Jebb (ed.), *The Diaries of Cynthia Gladwyn*, Constable, 1995, p.198.

97 Confirmed to the author by the Countess of Avon. *Vide* Kenneth Rose, 'Did Eden live on stimulants?', Albany column, *Sunday Telegraph*, 6 October 1996.

98 R. A. Butler to Sir Anthony Eden, 12 December 1956. AP 20/25/252.

99 Brendan Bracken to Lord Beaverbrook, 23 January 1957. Beaverbrook papers, loc. cit., file BK C/17.

100 Richard Crossman diary, 18 December 1956. Janet Morgan (ed.), *The Backbench Diaries of Richard Crossman*, Hamish Hamilton and Jonathan Cape, 1981, p.555.

101 Hansard, 20 December 1956.

102 Nigel Nicolson notes on 1922 Committee meeting, 18 December 1956. Harold Nicolson diary, loc. cit.

103 Earl of Kilmuir, *Political Adventure: The Memoirs of the Earl of Kilmuir*, Weidenfeld & Nicolson, 1964, p.284.

104 Sir Douglas Dodds-Parker papers, Magdalen College, Oxford. File MC. P2/9/IMS/1.

105 PRO. T 172/2152.

106 PRO. CAB 129/84.

107 Sir Anthony Eden diary, 3 January 1957. AP 20/2/5.

108 Sir Anthony Eden to Lord Salisbury, 9 January 1957. Salisbury papers, Hatfield House, file B: 1956–60.

109 '1957': Manuscript Memorandum by the 5th Marquess of Salisbury. Salisbury Papers, loc. cit. File B: 1956–60.

110 Sir Anthony Eden to Sir Winston Churchill, 9 January 1957. Chartwell papers, Churchill College, Cambridge. 2/216.

111 Sir Douglas Dodds-Parker papers, loc. cit. File MC P2/9/IMS/1.

112 Harold Macmillan, *Riding the Storm, 1955–1959*, Macmillan, 1971, p.184.

113 Robert Blake, Notice of Sir Anthony Eden's life, *Dictionary of National Biography 1971–1980*, edited by Robert Blake and C. S. Nicholls, Oxford University Press, Oxford, 1980, p.271.

114 Note on resignation audience. AP 20/33/12A.

115 The Earl of Avon to Sir Michael Adeane, 27 November 1970. AP 23/2/20A.

116 Vernon Bogdanor, *The Monarchy and the Constitution*, Clarendon Press, Oxford, 1995, f-n., p.94.

117 See Chapter 20 for the account of Avon's meeting with Lord Mountbatten on 13 June 1976.

118 Anthony Howard, *RAB: The Life of R.A. Butler*, Jonathan Cape, 1987, f-n. p.248.

119 Lady Eden to R. A. Butler, 10 January 1957. Quoted by Lord Butler in *The Art of the Possible: The Memoirs of Lord Butler*, revised paperback, Penguin Books, Harmondsworth, 1973, p.197.

120 Sir Anthony Eden to Eric Claridge, 10 January 1957. Warwick and

Leamington Conservative
Association records, Salisbury Hall,
Leamington.
121 *Leamington Spa Courier and
Warwickshire Standard*, 21
February 1957.
122 Max Beloff, 'The Crisis and its
Consequences for the Conservative
Party' in William Roger Louis and
Roger Owen, *Suez 1956: The Crisis
and Its Consequences*, Clarendon
Press, Oxford, 1991, p.404.
123 Anthony Eden, 'Thoughts',
December 1956. PRO. PREM
11/1138.
124 Lord Beaverbrook to Sir Anthony
Eden, 23 January 1957.
Beaverbrook papers, loc. cit. File
BBK C/59.
125 Alan Thompson, *The Day Before
Yesterday*, Granada Publishing
Limited, 1971, p.145.

CHAPTER 20

'The Past Gone, Seize Today'

1 Quoted in Roy Jenkins, *The
Chancellors*, Macmillan, 1998,
p.187.
2 The agreement was signed on 10
December 1957. AP 7/21/1. Eden
continued to be well advised
financially as to tax liabilities and
his will was eventually to be proved
for £82,670.
3 Sir Anthony Eden to Lord Salisbury,
21 January, 5 April and 27 July
1957. Salisbury papers, Hatfield
House. File B: 1956–60.
4 Queen Elizabeth II to Sir Anthony
Eden, 11 October 1957. AP 30/A/5a.
5 Queen Elizabeth II to Sir Anthony
Eden, 16 January 1958. AP 30/A/6a.
6 Sir Anthony Eden to Selwyn Lloyd,
27 January 1957. Selwyn Lloyd
papers, Churchill College,
Cambridge. SELO 88 (3).
7 John Prescott to the author, 21
January 1997.
8 Lady Eden to Lord Beaverbrook, 22
May 1957. Beaverbrook papers,
House of Lords Record Office. File
BBK C17.

9 A. J. P. Taylor, *Beaverbrook*,
Penguin paperback, Penguin Books,
Harmondsworth, 1972, p.813.
10 Villa Nova visitors' book, Countess
of Avon papers. The house was
converted into a country-house hotel
in 2001.
11 The Earl of Avon to Harold
Macmillan, 14 July 1965. AP
23/48/56B.
12 Sir Pierson Dixon, 'Discussion with
Sir Anthony Eden at Government
House, Ottawa, 25–6 May 1957.'
Sir Pierson Dixon papers, courtesy
of Mr Piers Dixon.
13 Sir Pierson Dixon, 'Notes on talk
with Sir Anthony Eden, 17 April
1958 at Donnington Grove,
Newbury, Berks.' Sir Pierson Dixon
papers, courtesy of Mr Piers Dixon.
14 Sir Anthony Eden to Francis
Mathew, 21 July 1958. AP 7/21/19.
15 Sir Anthony Eden to Sir Winston
Churchill, 17 June 1959. AP
19/2/19.
16 See Keith Kyle, *Suez*, Weidenfeld &
Nicolson, 1991, pp.516–18, for a
chronology of the suspicions about
collusion and the watershed
moment of the publication of
Nutting's book.
17 A. J. P. Taylor, *English History
1914–1945*, Clarendon Press,
Oxford, 1965, pp. 627, 639.
18 Earl Attlee to the Earl of Avon, 30
March 1965. AP 27/1/80G.
19 David Carlton, *Anthony Eden: A
Biography*, Allen & Unwin
paperback 1986, p.469.
20 Evelyn Waugh to Nancy Mitford,
13 January 1960. Charlotte Mosley
(ed.), *The Letters of Nancy Mitford
and Evelyn Waugh*, Hodder &
Stoughton, 1996, p.419.
21 John Devine to the author, 12
August 1999.
22 AP 7/18/30A.
23 John W. Braasch, MD, 'Anthony
Eden's Biliary Tract Saga', Lahey
Clinic, Massachusetts, privately
printed, 2002.
24 AP 39/3 and AP 391/1.
25 Earl of Avon to M. René Massigli,
4 July 1964. Massigli papers, Quai
d'Orsay, Paris.

26 Earl of Avon to A. J. Barker, 14 April 1964. AP 27/1/112G.
27 Sir Roy Welensky to the Earl of Avon, 7 August 1967. Welensky papers, Rhodes House, Oxford. File 730/2.
28 Alistair Kingston to the author, 1 June 1997.
29 D. R. Thorpe, *Alec Douglas-Home*, Sinclair-Stevenson, 1996, p.413.
30 Anthony Montague Browne, *Long Sunset: Memoirs of Winston Churchill's Last Private Secretary*, Cassell, 1995, p.288.
31 Sir Anthony Eden to Sir Winston Churchill, 2 January 1958. AP 19/2/6.
32 Tam Dalyell to the author, 21 January 1997.
33 D. R. Thorpe, *Selwyn Lloyd*, Jonathan Cape, 1989, pp.260–1.
34 Lord Thomas of Swynnerton to the author, 1986.
35 Though Antony Head – successively War Secretary and Defence Secretary during the crisis, and renowned for his earthy metaphors – recollecting Suez in the tranquillity of retirement, was prone to say that the problem was that there was too much foreplay and not enough orgasm. (Private information, with adjectives omitted.)
36 Selwyn Lloyd papers, loc. cit. SELO 237 (3).
37 Earl of Avon memorandum on Suez, 9 September 1968. Countess of Avon papers. The part played by Mountbatten in falsely disseminating the Queen's supposed views is outlined below.
38 Earl of Avon to Lord Beaverbrook, 10 October 1963. Beaverbrook papers, loc. cit. File BBK C 18.
39 Harold Wilson to Sir Burke Trend, 10 April 1967. Sir Burke Trend to Harold Wilson, 12 April 1967. Sir Burke Trend note of meeting on 18 April 1967. Sir Burke Trend to Harold Wilson, 27 June 1967. PRO. PREM 13/1556.
40 Lord Normanbrook to Freddie Bishop, 12 June 1967. Lord Normanbrook papers. Bodleian Library, Oxford. Ms. Eng Lett c.

274. Box 2, fol. 300.
41 See D. R. Thorpe, 'Sir Anthony Nutting', Obituary, *Independent*, 3 March 1999.
42 Selwyn Lloyd papers, loc. cit. SELO 237 (3).
43 Douglas Jay, *Change and Fortune: A Political Record*, Hutchinson, 1980, p.261.
44 Robert Blake, Eden chapter, in J. P. Mackintosh (ed.), *British Prime Ministers in the Twentieth Century, Volume 2: Churchill to Callaghan*, Weidenfeld & Nicolson, 1978, pp.112–3.
45 Sir Anthony Eden to Lord Salisbury, 14 December 1959, loc. cit. File B: 1956–60.
46 Sir Anthony Eden to Sir Harold Caccia, 31 January 1960. Sir Harold Caccia to Sir Anthony Eden, 9 February 1960. Caccia papers, Eton College Library.
47 From Adrian Mitchell, *Heart on the Left: Poems 1953–1984*, Bloodaxe Books, Newcastle-upon-Tyne, 1997.
48 I am grateful to Professor Stanley Wells, Deputy Chairman of the Royal Shakespeare Company, and Lady Anderson, Governor, for their help over this section.
49 While Chancellor of the Exchequer, Chamberlain had conducted an erudite correspondence with John Dover Wilson in the autumn of 1935 on the issues raised by Dover Wilson's newly published book, *What Happens in Hamlet*.
50 The Earl of Avon to Sir Fordham Flower, 4 August 1965. AP 26/68/87.
51 Robert Rhodes James was to end his biography of Eden by quoting the lines in *King Lear* from which the words are taken.
52 *Troilus and Cressida*, I.iii.109–10.
53 *Vide* D. R. Thorpe, *Alec Douglas-Home*, loc. cit., pp.395–7.
54 Royal Shakespeare Company Governors' Minutes after Eden had chaired his last meeting as President at the Waldorf Hotel, London, on 14 July 1966. AP 26/68/41.

55 Minute recording Eden's re-election as Governor at the age of seventy, 3 July 1967. AP 26/68/96.

56 Sir Anthony Eden to E. R. Bosley, 7 November 1958. AP 26/68/1.

57 The production of *The Public Bath* in 1964, in which Glenda Jackson appeared as both Jacqueline Kennedy and Christine Keeler, was ahead of the time in its use of nudity.

58 The Countess of Avon to the author, 26 September 2000.

59 AP 26/68/38.

60 The Earl of Avon to Harold Macmillan, 11 October 1962. PRO. PREM 11/3784. Maudling had become Chancellor of the Exchequer after the Night of the Long Knives in July 1962. It is a sign of Eden's distancing from the contemporary House of Commons that he should refer to Maudling as 'Reg', when he was then universally known by his contemporaries as 'Reggie'.

61 Sally Beauman, *The Royal Shakespeare Company: A History of Ten Decades*, Oxford University Press, Oxford, 1982, pp. 264–5. The book is an essential source on the Stratford theatre and its company.

62 The Earl of Avon to Mrs Milne, 29 August 1963. AP 26/68/86.

63 Sir Denys Lowson and others to the Earl of Avon, 25 September 1964. AP 26/68/37.

64 The full title of the play was *The Persecution and Assassination of Marat as Performed by the inmates of the Asylum of Charenton under the Direction of the Marquis de Sade.*

65 Olga Ironside Wood to the Earl of Avon, 28 September 1964. AP 26/68/47.

66 The Earl of Avon to Olga Ironside Wood, 7 October 1964. AP 26/68/48.

67 Peter Hall to the Earl of Avon, 17 August 1966. AP 26/68/80.

68 Earl of Avon to Sir Fordham Flower, 4 August 1965. AP 26/68/87.

69 To the immense benefit of researchers, who can cross-reference material relating to Eden and the Chamberlain half-brothers within minutes.

70 These could form one of the great multi-volumed collections of letters of twentieth-century political life. Space permits only the smallest selection in the present volume.

71 Sir Anthony Eden to Sir Winston Churchill, 29 April 1958. AP 19/2/8A.

72 Sir Anthony Eden to M. Guy Mollet, 10 March 1958. Guy Mollet Archives, L'Office Universitaire de la Recherche Socialiste, Paris.

73 Sir Anthony Eden to Harold Macmillan, 2 October 1957. AP 23/48/9A.

74 Sir Anthony Eden to Lord Hailes, 5 October and 20 October 1959. Hailes papers, Churchill College, Cambridge. HAIS 4/11.

75 Sir Anthony Eden to Alan Lennox-Boyd, 21 October 1959. Viscount Boyd of Merton papers, Bodleian Library, Oxford. Mss Eng. c.3397. f. 86.

76 Rather like the saga surrounding the J. L. Garvin life of Joseph Chamberlain, eventually completed by Julian Amery, this project was to undergo many a metamorphosis. As a founding Fellow of St Antony's College, Oxford, Jack Wheeler-Bennett engaged a young colleague, A. J. ('Tony') Nicholls, to help him in the task. It was tacitly understood that if Wheeler-Bennett's health proved unequal to the task, Nicholls would take over, rather in the manner that Martin Gilbert eventually succeeded Randolph Churchill as Sir Winston Churchill's official biographer, and a formal agreement to this effect was undertaken on 13 November 1973. (AP 23/37/40.) However, when Wheeler-Bennett died in December 1975, Nicholls had a change of heart and the following April honourably asked to be released from the undertaking, the hurdle being Suez, for which he had no political sympathy. (A. J. Nicholls to the author in various conversations,

when the author was a visiting Fellow at St Antony's College, 1997–8.) Martin Gilbert was then invited to undertake the task, but the scale of the Churchill research meant that not even preliminary work could be undertaken on Eden for many years. The mantle finally fell on Sir Robert Rhodes James, Conservative MP for Cambridge and the accomplished biographer (among other subjects) of Lord Randolph Churchill (Lady Avon's grandfather), Lord Rosebery and Prince Albert. The book appeared in 1986, the thirtieth anniversary of Suez. Five years later, as perspectives changed, the Countess of Avon invited the present author to undertake another life, what one newspaper dubbed 'this other Eden'. ('Mandrake', *Sunday Telegraph*, 8 August 1993.)

77 Sir Anthony Eden to Lord Salisbury, 29 May 1960. Salisbury papers, loc. cit. File B. 1956–60.

78 Sir Anthony Eden to Harold Macmillan, 29 May 1961. AP 23/48/35.

79 Lady Eden to Lord Beaverbrook, 5 May 1961. Beaverbrook papers, loc. cit. BBK C18.

80 The Earl of Avon to Stanley Morrison, 17 August 1961. AP 24/52/7.

81 Earl of Avon to the Marquess of Salisbury, 17 August 1961 and, as Sir Anthony Eden, 2 February 1961. AP 23/60/68 and Salisbury papers, loc. cit. File C: 1961–64.

82 Sir Norman Brook note on meeting with the Earl of Avon, 18 October 1961. PRO. PREM 11/3228.

83 Earl of Avon to Lord Ismay, 26 September 1961. AP 23/41/2A.

84 Earl of Avon to Arthur Mann, 5 April 1963. AP 24/47/59A.

85 Philip de Zulueta note of 28 May 1962. PRO. PREM 11/4233.

86 The Earl of Avon to Sir Winston Churchill, 1 September 1961. AP 19/2/41.

87 Lord Beaverbrook to the Earl of Avon, 7 March 1962. Beaverbrook papers, loc. cit. File BBK C18.

88 Lord Avon, 'The Man of Munich', *Times Literary Supplement*, 1 December 1961.

89 Selwyn Lloyd Memorandum on the events of July and August 1962. Selwyn Lloyd papers, loc. cit. SELO 88(3).

90 The Earl of Avon to Harold Macmillan, 22 September 1967. AP 23/48/83.

91 Earl of Avon to Lord Beaverbrook, 26 September 1962. Beaverbrook papers, loc. cit. File BBK C18.

92 Canvass of active Conservative peers by Earl St Aldwyn, October 1963. PRO. PREM 11/5008.

93 Earl of Avon to Lord Beaverbrook, 21 July 1963. Beaverbrook papers, loc. cit. File BBK C18.

94 Earl of Avon to Lord Lambton, 18 April 1964. AP 23/43/53A.

95 President Dwight. D. Eisenhower to the Earl of Avon, 23 June 1964. AP 23/29/22D.

96 Quoted by Lord Deedes in the *Daily Telegraph*, 22 September 1997.

97 Earl of Avon to Sir Alec Douglas-Home, 28 September 1964. AP 23/27/35.

98 Hansard, 25 January 1965. AP 19/2/101.

99 Richard Crossman diary, 30 January 1965. Anthony Howard (ed.), *The Crossman Diaries*, Magnum paperback condensed version, 1979, p.71. The other pall-bearers were Lord Alexander, Lord Bridges, Lord Ismay, Harold Macmillan, Sir Robert Menzies, Lord Mountbatten, Lord Normanbrook, Lord Portal (who had personally brought Eden news at Potsdam of the death of Simon Eden), and Lord Templer, a quintessential cross-section of the old Establishment.

100 Earl of Avon to Lady Churchill, 7 February 1965. AP 19/3/6.

101 The most important exception – to Avon's mind – being, not Sir Anthony Nutting, but Sir Evelyn Shuckburgh, even though he did not live to see the publication of the Shuckburgh diaries.

102 Richard Lovell, *Churchill's Doctor: A Biography of Lord Moran*, Royal

Society of Medicine Services, 1992, p.381.

103 Earl of Avon to Hamilton F. Armstrong, editor of *Foreign Affairs*, an American quarterly review, 10 June 1965. AP 27/1/69.

104 Earl of Avon to Edward Heath, 14 May 1966. AP 23/38/15A.

105 Quoted in Simon Heffer, op. cit., pp.255, 199.

106 Earl of Avon to Lord Lambton, 16 June 1970. AP 23/43/162B.

107 Earl of Avon to Edward Heath, 18 June 1970. AP 23/38/36.

108 Earl of Avon to Dean Acheson, 22 June 1970. AP 23/1/52.

109 Richard Buckle (ed.), *Self Portrait with Friends: The Selected Diaries of Cecil Beaton, 1926–1974*, Weidenfeld & Nicolson, 1979, p.384.

110 Quoted by the Earl of Avon in a letter to Lord Caccia, 28 June 1972. AP 23/14/55A.

111 Earl of Avon to Guy Mollet, 15 October 1968. Guy Mollet papers, loc. cit.

112 Earl of Avon to Lord Salisbury, 26 January 1969. Salisbury papers, loc. cit. File D: 1965–72.

113 Hansard, 26 August 1968.

114 D. R. Thorpe, 'Richard Lamb', Obituary, *Independent*, 6 January 2000. In his later career as a political historian, Lamb was to publish *The Failure of the Eden Government* (1987) with a somewhat apologetic foreword, because of his earlier association with Eden.

115 The Earl of Avon to Sir Roy Welensky, 2 October 1970. Sir Roy Welensky note. Welensky papers, loc. cit. File 730/2 and File 760/4.

116 Ann Fleming to Evelyn Waugh, 7 November 1960. Mark Amory (ed.), *The Letters of Ann Fleming*, Collins Harvill, 1985, p.274.

117 David Carlton, op. cit., p.473.

118 Earl of Avon to Lord Caccia, 24 April 1974. AP 23/14/58.

119 'Emperor Haile Selassie I: Memorial Tribute by The Earl of Avon'. Copy by courtesy of Professor Edward Ullendorff.

120 Robert Lacey, *Majesty: Elizabeth II and the House of Windsor*, Hutchinson, 1977.

121 Earl of Avon to Robert Lacey, 22 March 1976. AP 123/18/25.

122 AP 20/2/5.

123 Earl Mountbatten of Burma Tour Diary, 13 June 1976. Tour Diaries. Broadlands Archives, University of Southampton.

124 Lord Selwyn-Lloyd to Robert Lacey, 31 August 1976. Selwyn Lloyd papers, loc. cit. SELO 125 (3).

125 Lord Home to Sir Martin Charteris, 2 September 1976. Lord Home papers. The Hirsel, Coldstream.

126 The Earl of Avon to Sir Martin Charteris, 9 August and 13 December 1976. AP 23/18/19 and AP 23/18/24.

127 Robert Lacey, op. cit., p.238.

128 Sarah Bradford, *Elizabeth: A Biography of Her Majesty the Queen*, Heinemann, 1996, p.234.

129 Ben Pimlott, *The Queen: A Biography of Elizabeth II*, HarperCollins, 1996, pp.254, 255.

130 On 20 July 1986 the *Sunday Times* was instrumental in establishing the received opinion that the Queen found Margaret Thatcher's policies 'uncaring, confrontational and socially divisive'.

131 Philip Ziegler, *Mountbatten: The Official Biography*, Collins, 1985, p.528.

132 AP 33/7/ii.

133 Harold Nicolson diary, 13 November 1956. Nicolson papers, Balliol College, Oxford.

134 *The Times*, 15 January 1977.

135 The Countess of Avon to Mrs Margaret Thatcher, 1 September 1976. AP 23/62/1A.

136 Lord Callaghan of Cardiff to the author, 29 October 1992.

137 AP 34/1.

138 The Countess of Avon to Queen Elizabeth II, 16 January 1977. AP 34/20/1.

139 *The Salisbury Journal*, 20 January 1977.

140 Lady Morrison of Lambeth to the Countess of Avon, 20 January 1977. AP 34/4/20/1.

141 Lord Strang to the Countess of Avon, 19 January 1977. Ibid.

142 Lord Butler of Saffron Walden to the Countess of Avon, 17 February 1977. AP 34/6/1.

143 Harold Macmillan to the Countess of Avon , 24 January 1977. Ibid.

144 The Countess of Avon to Harold Macmillan, 9 February 1977. Stockton papers, now in the Bodleian Library, Oxford, but seen by the author at Birch Grove House, uncatalogued.

145 Lord Avon note of 3 October 1968. AP 34.

146 Edmund Burke, letter to Matthew Smith, 1750.

147 Sir Peter Hordern to the author, 1 June 1998.

148 See Hansard, House of Commons Debates, vol. 563, 22 January 1957, cols 36–38.

149 Hansard, House of Commons Parliamentary Debates, vol. 924, 17 January 1977, col. 43.

150 Lord Wakeham to the author, 6 June 1997.

151 Hansard, House of Lords Parliamentary Debates, Vol. 379, 18 January 1977, col. 21.

152 Lord Macaulay, *Warren Hastings*, essay, reprinted October 1941.

153 Lord Avon, Notes for Memorial Service. Countess of Avon papers.

154 Spenser, *Faerie Queen*, Book I, Canto ix. *Cymbeline*, IV.ii.

155 The 2nd Earl of Avon to the Revd Canon Julian Rudd, 24 January 1977. AP 34. Unlike Lord Avon, Thomas Hardy's choirmaster was denied his wishes. 'That old-fashioned way Requires a fine day, And it seems to me It had better not be.' Thomas Hardy, *The Choirmaster's Burial*.

156 The Countess of Avon to Queen Elizabeth, January 1977. AP 34/20/1.

POSTLUDE

1 Biographical note in the introduction to the Alanbrooke diaries, Alex Danchev and Daniel Todman (eds), *War Diaries 1939–1945: Field Marshal Lord Alanbrooke*, Weidenfeld & Nicolson, 2001, p.xlvi.

2 C. V. Wedgwood, *William the Silent*, Jonathan Cape, 1944, p.253.

3 Anthony Eden diary, 19 January 1951. AP 20/1/27.

4 C. V. Wedgwood, op. cit., p.253.

5 Anthony Eden, *Another World: 1897–1917*, Allen Lane, 1976, p.148.

6 Neville Chamberlain to Mrs Morton Prince, 16 January 1938. Quoted in Keith Feiling, *The Life of Neville Chamberlain*, Macmillan, 1946, p.323.

7 Alan Campbell Johnson, *Anthony Eden: A Biography*, Robert Hale, 1938, p.10.

8 Robert Skidelsky, 'Anthony Eden', in *Interests and Obsessions: Historical Essays*, Macmillan, 1993, p.336.

9 In 2001 Dr Dutton was to publish arguably the best single-volume account of Neville Chamberlain's career, demonstrating clearly that it was possible to admire the two great pre-war adversaries simultaneously.

10 *Observer*, 30 January 1927.

11 Lord Macaulay, *William Pitt, Earl of Chatham*, essay of January 1834.

12 Winston S. Churchill, *Lord Randolph Churchill: Volume 2*, Macmillan, 1906, p.488.

13 *The Times*, 15 January 1977.

14 Roy Jenkins, *Portraits and Miniatures*, Macmillan, 1993, p.124.

15 Balfour and Heath, the only bachelor Prime Ministers of the century, each lost three General Elections, before losing the leadership of the Conservative Party in the wake of the third defeat.

16 Sir Douglas Dodds-Parker to the Countess of Avon, 14 January 1977. AP 34/4/20/1.

17 Ursula Branston to the Countess of Avon, 14 January 1977. Ibid.

18 Professor Philip Norton has identified these four categories of

Prime Minister. Lord Norton of Louth to the author, 28 November 1990.

19 Cited by Jonathan Aitken in his notice of Selwyn Lloyd, *Dictionary of National Biography 1971–1980*, Oxford University Press, Oxford, 1986, p.514.

20 Nathaniel Hawthorne, *The House of the Seven Gables*, Chapter 21.

21 Sir Austen Chamberlain, *Down the Years*, Cassell, 1935, p.191.

22 As in the letter of 10 August 1955, *Speaking for Themselves: The personal letters of Winston and Clementine Churchill*, edited by Mary Soames, Doubleday, 1998, p.595.

23 *Antony and Cleopatra*, V.i. 31–2.

24 Sir Roy Welensky to Sir Archibald James, 16 December 1963. Welensky papers, Rhodes House, Oxford. File 627/7.

25 Anthony Nutting, 'Sir Anthony Eden', in *The Prime Ministers: Volume the Second From Lord John Russell to Edward Heath*, George Allen & Unwin, 1975, p.341.

26 Sir Anthony Eden to Edward Heath, 8 May 1961. AP 23/38/6A. A point confirmed more recently to the author by Dr. Jonathan Haslam.

27 Andrew Roberts, 'Betrayal of the brave at Suez', *Sunday Times*, 20 October 1996.

28 David Carlton, *Anthony Eden: A Biography*, Allen & Unwin paperback, 1986, p.478.

29 Lord Butler of Saffron Walden to Kenneth Rose, 27 May 1979. Kenneth Rose papers.

30 Violet Bonham Carter diary, 10 January 1957. Mark Pottle (ed.), *Daring to Hope: The Diaries and Letters of Violet Bonham Carter 1945–1969*, Weidenfeld & Nicolson, 2000, p.184.

31 *Troilus and Cressida*, III.iii. 170–5.
32 C. V. Wedgwood, op. cit., p.253.
33 *Henry VIII*, IV.ii. 45–6.
34 Robert Skidelsky, op. cit., p.335.
35 Sir Peter Ramsbotham to the author, 24 June 1997.
36 Earl of Avon diary, 8 September 1975. AP 20/2/20.

APPENDIX I

Eden's Resignation Speech

1 Submarine attacks.
2 Hansard Parliamentary Debates: 332, H.C. DEB (Fifth Series).

APPENDIX II

Eden's Speech on the Property-Owning Democracy

1 Churchill later dubbed him 'Sir Shortly Floor-Cross'.

APPENDIX III

The Protocol of Sèvres

1 This inked-in date is the one on the original, one day prior to the drawing up of the Protocol, and is a sign of the haste with which the document was drawn up. The actual date on which the attack took place was 29 October, which is the date given in Christian Pineau's summary of the seven main points of the Protocol, in Christian Pineau, *1956 Suez*, Éditions Robert Laffont, Paris, 1976 paperback.

2 Date added by hand.
3 The single closed bracket was added by hand.
4 Date added by hand.

INDEX

The following abbreviations are used:

AC	Sir Austen Chamberlain
AE	Sir Anthony Eden
BBC	British Broadcasting Corporation
BEF	British Expeditionary Force
C of E	Chancellor of the Exchequer
CIGS	Chief of the Imperial General Staff
FDR	Franklin Delano Roosevelt
f-n	footnote
FO	Foreign Office
FS	Foreign Secretary
H of C	House of Commons
HM	His/Her Majesty (in royal context)/ Harold Macmillan (otherwise)
HMG	His/Her Majesty's Government
HRH	His/Her Royal Highness
JIC	Joint Intelligence Committee
KRRC	King's Royal Rifle Corps
LG	Lloyd George
MC	Military Cross
MP	Member of Parliament
NC	Neville Chamberlain
PM	Prime Minister
POW	Prisoner of War
PPS	Parliamentary Private Secretary
PUS	Permanent Under Secretary
RAB	R.A. Butler
RAF	Royal Air Force
SB	Stanley Baldwin
SCUA	Suez Canal Users' Association
TGWU	Transport and General Workers' Union
WEU	Western European Union
WSC	Sir Winston Churchill
UN	United Nations
US	United States

past, 381; wishes WSC would retire, 382; AE visits, 467; AE keeps informed, 466, 474; & Suez, 502–504, 507, 508, 520, 529; & AE's telephone calls to during, 529–530; & US Presidential Election, 536–538; writes to AE on Suez, 579–580

El Alamein, Battle of, 272, 278

Elizabeth, HM Queen, consort of HM King George VI (*later* Queen Elizabeth the Queen Mother), 183, 347, 444, 592, 594; AE first meets, 125; changing views of towards AE, 183; visits AE's constituency, 359; advises never to accept present that eats, 470

Elizabeth II, HM Queen, 13, 371, 375, 389, 394, 415, 433, 447–448, 479, 484, 500–501, 548, 554, 592; AE first meets as Princess Elizabeth, 125; coronation of, 384, 417; Silver Jubilee, 6; AE visits at Balmoral, 9; at WSC retirement dinner, 429; & Suez, 585–589; & AE's Earldom, 575; accepts the Avon's private hospitality, 584; writes to Countess of Avon on AE's death, 589

Elliot, Walter, 81, 98, 154, 197, 210, 206

Ellis, Ruth, 454

Empire Air Training Scheme, 276, 282–283; & Simon Eden, 276, 282–283

Empire Day (24 May), AE's respect for, 6

Encounter, 567

Epping, constituency of, 69; WSC candidate for, 69, and MP for, 78

Erne, 5th Earl of, 249

Erne, Davina Countess of, 249, 294–295; & relationship with AE, 249; marries Monty Woodhouse, 294–295; joint memorial service for at New College, Oxford, f-n. 295

Erroll, Frederick (*later* 1st Baron Erroll of Hale), 341

'Essex man', f-n 543

Ethiopia (see also Abyssinia), Italian invasion of, 115

Eton College, Windsor, 23, 25–28, 30, 31, 45, 49, 53, 172, 181, 220, 345,

407, 456, 585–586; losses in Great War, 27

Eton Society ('Pop'), 25; & Curzon, 25; AE's failure to be elected to, 25

European Defence Community (EDC), 226, 300, 362, 368, 369, 371, 395, 397–398, 399, 413, 414, 420

European Economic Community (EEC), 369

Evans, Dame Edith, 570

Evans, Sir Horace (*later* Baron Evans), 384–385, 389, 392, 544

Evening Standard, 500

Eyres-Monsell, Sir Bolton (*later* 1st Viscount Monsell), 114; as Conservative Chief Whip, 86

Fabritius, Carel, 16

Fairbanks, Douglas Jr, 245

Fairfax family, 14

Faisal II, King of Iraq, 475, 594

Falklands War (1982), 28, 482, 491, 526

Farouk I, King of Egypt, 370, 489; AE meets, 239

Faure, Edgar, 445

Fawkes, Guy, 523

Fawzi, Dr Mahmoud, 491, 503, 511, 512, 514

Festing, General Sir Francis, 424

Fettes College, effigy of Gaitskell burnt at on Guy Fawkes night (1956), 523

Feversham, Col. Charles, Earl of, 42, 170; AE's description of, 33; AE's tribute to, 36–37; helps AE to commission in KRRC, 32; death of 3, 34, 37, 38

Feversham, Countess of, 'Queenie', (*formerly* Marjorie Greville, *later* Lady Beckett), 32, 59, 60, 64

Fielding, Henry, 179

Finer, Herman, 579

Fisher, Dr. Geoffrey Francis (*later* Baron Fisher of Lambeth), Archbishop of Canterbury, 378, 423, 446, 523, 524, 525, 536; considers AE's divorce 'an ecclesiastical stigma of departure from a true understanding', 378; & AE's marriage to Clarissa Churchill, 378; & corporal punishment at Repton, f-n